Practical Boat Buying

3rd edition

by the editors of

Practical Sailor

Belvoir Publications, Inc.

75 Holly Hill Lane
Greenwich, CT 06830

Library of Congress Cataloging in Publication Data

Practical Sailor

    Practical Boat Buying, 3rd edition

    1. Boating, sailboat evaluation
    1. Title

© 1994 Belvoir Publications, Inc.
ISBN-1-879620-20-0

Contents

Introduction

"Is this the right boat for me?"

That's a question that every boat owner asked at some point before the purchase. It's an important question, and the key to answering it lies in having some inside information about the boat before the check is signed. Where are its weak points? What should the buyer be looking for? How do other owners feel about the boat? Most importantly, is the price fair?

Practical Boat Buying answers those questions, and more, for over 110 sailboats ranging from 20-foot daysailers to half-million-dollar world cruisers, from classics dating back to the earliest days of fiberglass sailboats (some of which are real bargains) to the latest high-tech yachts.

These pages represent more than twelve years of evaluation and experience on the part of the editors of *The Practical Sailor*, boat owners and avid sailors themselves. Each of the reviews is a detailed look at the boat, its history, construction details, handling characteristics, and livability, from authors that are intimately familiar not only with how boats are made, but what it's like to own one.

In addition to their own expertise, the editors have drawn on the knowledge of those who know more than anyone about the boats: the owners, themselves. Many of the boat reviews in these pages include comments and opinions from those who've lived with the vessel.

Finally, each review includes pricing information for the boat, and in the case of older boats a price history that helps judge how well a given boat holds its value.

This third edition of *Practical Boat Buying* closes with greatly expanded appendices that cover a variety of topics ranging from maintenance to outfitting.

Though this is the largest single collection of sailboat reviews we've ever published, we can't hope to cover the entire spectrum of boats. With literally hundreds of different designs available to the buyer interested in a used yacht, it's impractical to cover every model ever made. We're confident, however, that you'll find here several that meet your needs and desires in a sailboat, no matter what they may be.

Even if the specific boat you're looking for is not included here, you can learn a great deal about the industry, the builders, and good and bad construction practices by reading the reviews of similar vessels.

We can't answer that all-important "is she right?" question for you, but we can give you the insight and information you need to answer it for yourself. Good luck, and good sailing.

Andrew Douglas
Editor, Belvoir Books
Greenwich CT 1994

Cal 20

This diminutive three-decade-old Bill Lapworth racer-cruiser is a bargain by any standard.

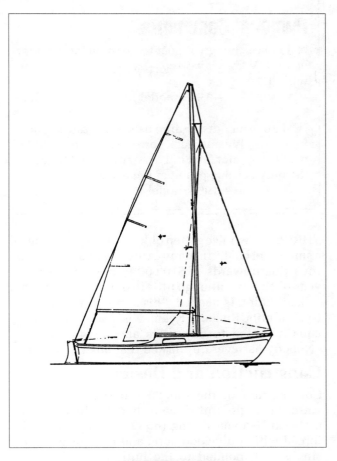

The venerable Cal 20 is experiencing a resurgence as both a one-design racer and small family daysailer/cruiser over 30 years after it was designed in 1961 by C. William Lapworth for Jensen Marine of Costa Mesa, California. The boat's appeal, now, is the same as when it first hit the market—economy (you can still get one for under $3,000), performance, ease of handling and surprising seaworthiness in a 20-footer.

The Boat and the Builder

Lapworth's connection to Jensen Marine extends back to the mid-1950s when he designed the Cal 24, first as a centerboarder, later available in a fin keel version. After moderate success of the 24, described in early Jensen literature as "a racing bomb," builder Jack Jensen asked Lapworth to design a larger model in the 30-foot range. But tooling took longer than expected, Lapworth said, and in the meantime he designed, and Jensen began producing, the Cal (originally California) 20.

Lapworth, working with Jensen, designed the 20 "primarily as an entry level boat for people who'd been sailing small boats—Lightnings, open-deck dinghies." Although the 20 was intended to be a small cruiser, Lapworth says boats at the time were expected to perform double-duty as racers, so he included a Star Class-style bulbed keel.

The result was a happy blend of performance and amiability, and the Cal immediately caught on with the small-boat public. Racers quickly took notice of the new midget racer when hull #3, alone among a bigger-boat fleet in a San Francisco Bay race, was able to keep its spinnaker flying after everyone else had shortened sail.

All told, 1,960 Cal 20s were made between 1961 and 1974, "and there could have been a lot more,"

Specifications

LOA	20' 0"
LWL	18' 0"
Beam	7' 0"
Draft	3' 4"
Displacement	1,950 lbs.
Ballast	900 lbs.
Sail area	196 sq. ft.

Lapworth says today. "It would have been a great boat for a club racer all over the country." All the 20s were built by Jensen, which discontinued the model before the Cal line was sold to O'Day (later Bangor Punta).

Cal 20 racing fleets have reappeared in the last few years, primarily in California, where there are "at least 100 in the harbor at Alamitos Bay, 30 miles from Mecca (Costa Mesa)," according to Richard Ryan of Long Beach, who has been racing his Cal since 1968. There also are large fleets in San Pedro, San Francisco, Hawaii and in the Great Lakes, said Gurden Hutchins, former class secretary. "Almost none of the Cals have fallen into disuse."

Mike George of San Pedro, who refurbishes Cals, said the new Cal 20 racers include "a lot of IOR and

Owners' Comments

"Old class, but great boat to learn on after centerboards. Very seaworthy—have done blue water with it."

—1968 model in Washington State

"Cal 20 is an outstanding used boat value. Check for rot in plywood deck core and delamination of headliner—not fatal but a nasty repair job. This is the only serious problem I'm aware of."

—1966 model in St. Clair, Michigan

"It sails like a dinghy, but has a full cabin. The beauty of a Cal 20 is that it actually fits a six-foot person."

—1968 model in Southern California

"The boat's cosmetics are suffering slightly because of its age. In general, they are amazingly durable and maintainable. They also perform very well."

—1962 model in Southern California

PHRF guys, who've gotten older and were looking for a small keel boat." In many cases, the new owners are investing upwards of $10,000 to upgrade their 20-year-old boats, although little in the way of structural rehabilitation is needed. "It's a mild form of insanity," admits Richard Ryan, who says the boat is equally suited to daysailers and coastal cruisers. "Nobody has ever duplicated that boat," he said.

Construction and Design

Construction of the Cal 20 hull was straightforward—a single unit of hand laid laminate of mat, cloth and woven roving (no core); the deck, reinforced with a plywood core, and cockpit pan are a single unit, bonded to the hull with an external double-flange "hat joint," pop riveted, glued and the seam glassed over with two layers of mat and cloth. Some of the older boats have experienced minor delamination of the deck core, especially around the winches where water has seeped in. Because the wood is clear-glassed inside, the problem is easily detected, according to Mike George.

At more than 1,000 pounds, the hull is fairly solid for a 20-footer, and the hand laid construction apparently accounts for the Cal's relatively blister-free history.

In designing the 20, Lapworth tried to avoid creating a scaled-down version of a larger boat. To avoid an ungainly cabin top, the designer instead gave the boat a raised foredeck, which provides extra room below and makes for easier maneuvering on deck. "I wanted to make the boat people-sized," he said.

The eight-foot, self-bailing cockpit is roomy enough to seat four comfortably. There's only a single locker on the starboard side leading below to what one owner calls the "dungeon" area of the Cal; a second locker on the port side would be a big help. Some Cal passengers complain about the lack of a comfortable backrest, the coamings being too low to provide support. On our own Cal 20 (*Eclipse*, hull #1473), the addition of stainless side railings solved the comfort problem.

A motor well at the rear of the cockpit floor creates the usual open-well problems, including some surging during a following sea. There are lower and upper hatches to seal off the well, which also serves as the drain, but some non-racers have simply glassed over the bottom and mounted the standard 6-hp. outboard on the transom. (A very few 20s were built without the well at Jensen's New Jersey plant toward the end of production.)

Rig

The standard rig is a fractional 26' 3" anodized aluminum spar designed by Lapworth for Jensen. Hulls from #51 to #340 were equipped with a similar mast, a Sparcraft S104, before the company reverted to the original design. In any form, "It's a good extrusion for the boat," said Steve Seal, who stocks parts for the Cal 20 at his Alameda workshop.

Standing rigging is 1/8" for the headstay, uppers and lowers and 3/32" for the backstay and jumpers. Jensen's "Hawaii rig" goes up a size for all stays, although Seal says it isn't necessary under normal sailing conditions, except for the backstay, which he recommended be upgraded to 1/8".

The weakest parts of the Cal rig, Seal said, are the original spreader brackets, which can crack. He supplies a heavy duty version which he says solves the problem. Older boats that have been sailed hard may also experience load problems with the headstay and after lowers, which are fitted to chainplates on the deck. The usual solution is to attach the headstay to a tang or straps fastened directly to the hull at the bow, and to support the aft lowers from belowdecks with beefed-up chainplates.

Class rules prohibit travelers, which place the mainsheet cam cleat in an awkward position behind the tiller. Some racers have resolved the situation by installing a "barney post" at mid-cockpit; for non-racers, the addition of a traveler makes the most sense. Whether racing or daysailing, the running rigging can be arranged so that it's easily handled from the cockpit. The absence of a cabin top enables jib sheets to be led across the deck to the windward winch for weather sheeting, allowing crew to remain on the high side.

Performance Under Sail

With 1,000 pounds in the hull and 900 or so (the keels, cast in Mexico, tend to vary in weight and shape) down low in the cast iron bulb keel, the Cal 20 is relatively stiff for a small boat. Owners love to boast about heavy air performance and we have to admit to keeping up full sail (downwind) in 30 knots on occasion.

The Cal goes well to windward with minimal heel, which makes it an excellent boat for beginners or families. Freeboard is high enough to keep the ride dry, except for occasional spray as the blunt bow bangs into waves.

Some owners, especially racers, have improved pointing and tracking by fairing out the fin portion of the keel, creating essentially NACA-type foils. The Cal class now limits keel thickness to no more than 1 1/2 inches at the broadest part of the fin. The iron bulb tends to pit and requires occasional sanding. (Adding a layer of rust preventative before painting slows the process.) Aside from some bow pounding in seas, the only complaint (of some owners) is a bit too much weather helm as the wind pipes up. Keep-

ing up the genoa (almost a working jib for this undercanvassed boat) reduces any excessive helm. For easier singlehanding, the genoa on *Eclipse* is sheeted through a block about halfway down the cockpit, then back to the decktop winch. Pronounced weather or lee helm may also be caused by a mishshapen or mis-aligned keel—both correctable.

With a PHRF rating ranging anywhere from 261 to 288 (a J/22, by contrast is 174 to 186, and Catalina's Capri 22 is 180 to 210), the 20 is no rocket. But when the wind picks up, the Cal, steadied by its bulb keel, still will carry full main and jib while others are forced to reef down. One owner referred to the 20 as the "forerunner" to the J/24—a not inaccurate description, Lapworth said, except the Cal can be raced with just two or three crew members.

The Cal's seaworthiness is legendary—at least among Cal owners. Kun Poi Chin recounted his solo trip from San Francisco to Hawaii in 1980 in *Cruising World*. Earlier, George Cadwalader and crew Duncan Spencer safely sailed a 20 from Newport, R.I. to Crookhaven, Ireland. Despite its dinghy-like characteristics, the boat remains one that can safely be used

The interior is not large—it's a pocket cruiser—but is adequate for weekending. The flush deck certainly helps open up space.

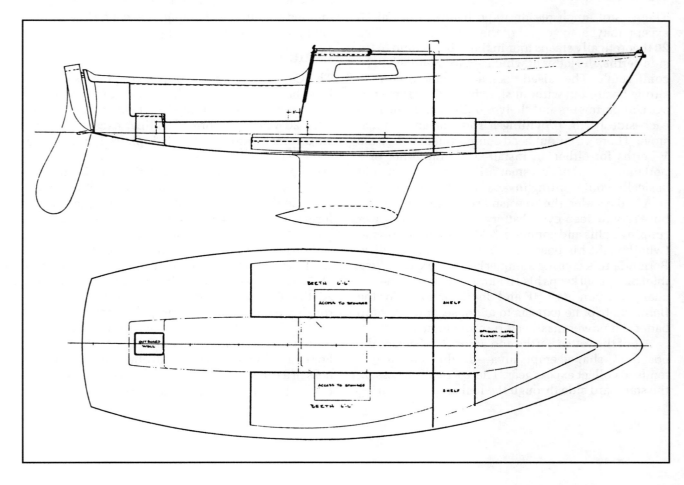

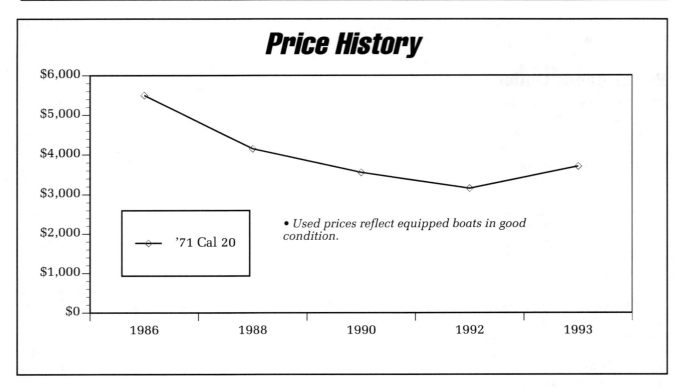

Price History

Used prices reflect equipped boats in good condition.

'71 Cal 20

for coastal cruising. Offshore, one would want to reduce the volume of the cockpit and footwell.

Belowdecks

There's not much reason to go below on a Cal 20 except, maybe, to get out of the sun or to sleep. The 20 theoretically sleeps four in the V-berths and 6' 10" side berths, the latter of which are long enough to be comfortable. The raised deck arrangement permits sitting headroom without slouching. There are storage compartments and shelves built in at the head of each side berth, providing a spot for an optional stove. There's a cutout head compartment before the V-berths for either an installed marine toilet or a portable one. There's a smattering of wood trim, but basically you're sitting in a painted fiberglass shell.

As a daysailer, the 20 wasn't set up for electricity, but a 12-volt deep-cycle battery is sufficient to power running lights and compass. A Massachusetts owner (who bought his boat last year and plans a sail to Bermuda this coming summer) said a six-watt flexible solar panel keeps his 100-amp battery adequately charged to run his VHF and depthsounder. For the Bermuda trip, he expects to add a second 100-amp battery to power masthead running lights.

Aft of the settee berths and across the back of the boat is a U-shaped empty area—the dungeon, which tends to collect excess gear. There's ready access on the starboard side through the locker, but venturing into the port region is akin to spelunking. For handier storage, *Eclipse* has been fitted with a portable locker just inside the companionway entrance, which serves as a step as well as a seat. Between the locker and a molded-in bulkhead along the centerline is just enough room for a battery box.

Conclusions

The Cal 20 was designed as a simple-to-sail entry level boat, without frills but with attention to solid construction. Structurally, the boats remain sound after 20 years or more of sailing, except for some stress cracks around the chainplates and some instances of deck core delamination. Anyone considering purchasing a 20 should also check the eight keel bolts, another potential deterioration point. Fred Cook, vice president at Schaeffer Marine and former engineer for Jensen, suggests removing the bolts one at a time and checking for corrosion.

You can buy an uncared-for boat for about $2,000, while upgraded versions will carry an asking price of $5,000 or more—a good value for the versatile sailer. All the 20s, from the earliest to the last off the line, are roughly equal in quality and performance.

For racers, the 20 represents an affordable one-design that will be closely matched to its brethren. For recreational sailors, the 20 offers the responsiveness of a dinghy—they're fun to sail—with the security and stability of a far bigger boat. • **PS**

Catalina 22

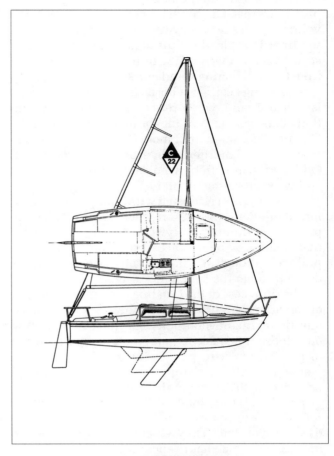

For those to whom price is all-important, the Catalina 22 is appealing—but it's lacking in performance.

In its 10th anniversary issue in 1980, *Sail* magazine named the Catalina 22 the boat that had represented the "breakthrough" in "trailer/cruisers" in those 10 years. We might quibble with its selection over more out-and-out trailerable boats such as the Ventures, but there is no denying the popularity of the Catalina: more than 10,000 have been built and sales continue to be strong.

For many buyers the Catalina 22 is their first "big" boat and an introduction to the Catalina line. Many remain with Catalina and buy up within that line.

Catalina is the largest boatbuilder in the world in dollar volume and the firm is one of the lasting success stories in the industry. It foregoes national advertising in favor of local dealer-sponsored ads, and has remained a privately owned (in fact, one man—Frank Butler) company while the trend has been toward conglomerate-owned boatbuilding.

Simply stated, Catalina builds boats to a price—a low price—making the most of volume buying of materials and hardware, long-lived models, a high degree of standardization, and all the cost savings of high volume production. The Catalina 22 was the first boat built by Catalina.

The 22 is a dated boat. A lot has happened in boat design and construction since she was introduced. Not all that has happened has been good, but many of the boats on the market with which the Catalina 22 competes for sales perform better and have accommodations more comfortable than the venerable Catalina. Yet it is to Catalina's credit that the 22 continues to sell and continues to be many sailors' first boat.

Construction

It's hard to argue with the construction of a boat after 10,000 have been built, but we do. The *PS* evaluation

Specifications

LOA	21' 6"
LWL	19' 4"
Beam	7' 8"
Draft	3' 6" (fixed), 2' (swing keel)
Displacement	2,490/2,250 lbs.
Ballast	800/550 lbs.
Sail area	212 sq. ft.

of the Catalina 30 notes that the hull-to-deck joint—a plywood reinforced hull flange joined to the deck with a rigid polyester "slurry" and self-tapping fasteners—is not our idea of acceptable construction. The same type of joint is used on the 22 although we are less concerned because obviously the structure is for a much smaller boat which, unlike the 30, is not marketed for offshore sailing.

Catalina Yachts is proud of the contention that the Catalina 22 has remained essentially unchanged from the day it was introduced in 1969. Only the pivot for the swing keel version was changed about boat #250 and then, according to a Catalina statement, it was done for production purposes. Later a pop-top option was added and now 90% of the boats sold have this feature.

Catalina takes credit for pioneering the one-piece hull liner that has become standard in most high volume small boats. However, it should be noted that the liner is basically a cosmetic component, not a structural member, and the hull must get its strength from the hull laminate and bulkhead reinforcement.

The swing keel, also chosen by 90% of the buyers, is cast iron and, when retracted, remains substantially exposed (accounting for more than half of the 2' draft of the shoal draft model). It is a rough 550 lb iron casting of indifferent hydrodynamic efficiency. Oddly its configuration hoisted encourages ropes and weeds hanging up on its forward edge.

The swing keel is hoisted with a simple reel winch located under a vestigal bridgedeck with its handle protruding through a plywood facing. We'd guess that Catalina owners soon become conditioned to its presence, though it can trip those stepping up or down through the companionway.

The drop keel of the Catalina evoked a number of observations from owners in the *PS* boat owners' questionnaire. Several note that the keel mounting bolts loosen and leak in time. Another reports he had to replace his wire pennant twice. Replacing the pennant requires hoisting the boat high enough to have access to the top of the keel.

As with all Catalina-built boats, decor is a major selling point. The line, including the 22, is attractively appointed. They create a highly favorable impression which has to encourage sales, especially for first time boat buyers.

In fact, the Catalina 22 outside and inside is one of the most visually appealing small boats we have seen. It has enough trim and finish to look pretty. Similarly, her hull and rig, although dated, are well proportioned. It is about her performance and livability that we have the most serious qualms.

Performance

By any objective standard the Catalina 22 is hardly a sprightly performing small boat. There have been too many compromises to performance: trailerability, shoal draft, cockpit space, low cost, and interior accommodations, as well as giving her a placid disposition for novice sailors. The boat needs a genoa jib, a smoother, and more efficient swing or fin keel shape and some hardware of even the most modest go-fast variety. Even then the prognosis is that she will remain a rather tubby boat in an age when much of the fun of boats is in their responsiveness, if not speed.

With almost all the Catalinas having been built with the swing keel, the appeal has been her shallow draft for trailering. Yet even with 2' of draft with the keel hoisted, the boat has too much draft for beaching. Given the tradeoff in performance, the difficulty of maintenance, and loss of stability, one hopes that indeed buyers of the swing keel 22 have made good use of it for trailering.

The deck of the Catalina 22 is a decidedly unhandy working platform. The sidedecks are narrow and obstructed by jib sheets and blocks. The three shrouds per side effectively block access to the foredeck, and complicate headsail trim and passage of the jib across in tacking. In fact, so difficult is it to go forward on the 22 we recommend getting rid of the

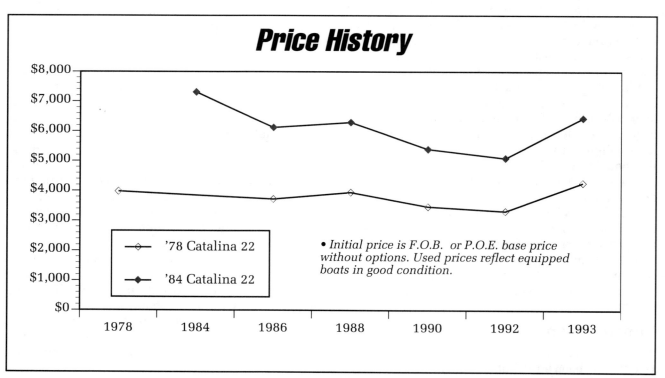

Price History

Legend:
- ◇— '78 Catalina 22
- ◆— '84 Catalina 22

• *Initial price is F.O.B. or P.O.E. base price without options. Used prices reflect equipped boats in good condition.*

lifelines. They are already too low to offer anything but token protection and they anchor near the base of the bow pulpit where they give no protection. Instead, handrails should be installed on the cabin top.

Livability

Ironically for a boat as popular as the Catalina, the boat incorporates the most incredible amount of wasted space we have ever seen in a sailboat large or small. In a size where stowage is at such a premium, there is a cavernous unusable space. The entire area under the cockpit and most of the area under the port cockpit seat (except where the gas tank sits) is all but inaccessible. The loss of this space limits stowage to scuttles under the berth bases.

The convertible dinette which seats only two with elbow room is a vestige of the 22's design era and the vee berths forward form that singularly noisome combination of bathroom and bedroom away from which human beings evolved about the time they moved out of caves.

The result is that the Catalina 22 has but one berth suitable for sleeping, the settee on the starboard side, and even that berth is shared with the optional galley facility that in use takes up about half the berth area. The Catalina 22s now have a pop-top as standard; most of the cabin top lifts 10" on four pipe supports. Most owners we have heard from seem to like the system, particularly those in warmer areas. Headroom at anchor is pleasant but we'd rather see room for stowage, sleeping, etc. as well.

One definitely unappealing and even unsafe item is the stowage for the remote gas tank for a transom-mounted outboard auxiliary. The tank sits on a molded shelf (part of the hull liner) in a seat locker at the after end of the cockpit. This puts the gasoline inside the boat including the cabin. The locker is vented but it should also be isolated. Spilled fuel can make its way unimpeded to the inaccessible low point under the cockpit. Moreover, there is no way to strap the tank securely nor a way to route the hose without pinching.

There's a strange and stubborn attitude at Catalina Yachts in reaction to any criticism of its boats, a righteousness that is exemplified by the notion that if one has sold several thousand of them, then nothing is wrong with them. Well, there *are* things wrong, and the gasoline stowage in the cockpit locker of the 22 footer is one egregious example.

One of the Catalina's better features is her cockpit. It is long (7') and comfortable, a place where the crew can sit with support for their backs, a place to brace their feet, and with room to avoid the tiller. It is unobstructed by the mainsheet that trims to a rod traveler on the stern.

Conclusions

Many boat buyers shop for a boat of this type with price foremost in mind. They probably will get no farther than their local Catalina dealer, where they can get a boat that is the same size and similarly equipped as boats costing far more. It's apt to be a boat identical to many of those sailing on the same waters. Better still, they are more than likely to have sailing friends who not only have (or had) a Catalina but belong to one of the most widespread and active owners' class associations in the sport. The whole package has a powerful appeal superbly orchestrated by the Catalina organization.

For performance, accommodations and even construction they might do better at a higher price, but the prospective buyer of the Catalina is likely to be unsure of what to look for. Understandably they turn to the 22.

At a weight of about 2,500 lbs. loaded for the road plus a trailer, the Catalina 22 has marginal trailerability behind the modern small car. For this reason *PS* urges buyers to consider carefully before purchasing a trailer with the boat. Unless and until they are convinced they will trailer the boat enough to make a trailer's purchase worthwhile, it could be a waste of money. One Catalina salesman we overheard talking with a client gave this advice and spelled out the reasons. High marks to that chap. Later he ruefully admitted to us that many buyers ignore his suggestion.

For the "sailaway package" price, the buyer gets some features he might not opt for if he had a choice (e.g. the pop-top, Mercury outboard, and lifelines and stanchions). However, Catalina Yachts, like Hunter Marine, has learned the advantages of packaged boats with bottom line pricing that is still lower than competitors' so called base boat prices. And boat buyers get what they need (and probably want) without having to know what they need or want.

Other than price, *PS* sees little to recommend the Catalina 22 over many other boats of the same size on the market. **• PS**

O'Day 22

A nice cockpit, a touch of privacy and good looks, but performance is not a strong suit here.

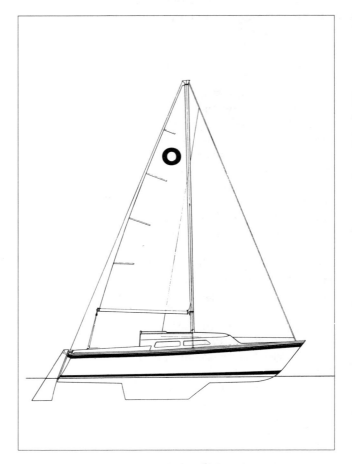

O'Day Boats was around a long time by fiberglass boatbuilding standards—about 30 years. Originally O'Day was a leader in small boats typified by the Fox-designed Day Sailer.

By the early '70s O'Day had moved into the trailerable cruising boat market. In the meantime the firm was acquired by Bangor Punta along with such other major boat builders as Cal and Ranger Yachts. In later years, with the decline in volume sales of small boats, O'Day had problems. To help alleviate these, O'Day produced larger and larger boats, first a 30, then a 32, and more recently a 34 and a 37.

All the cruising size boats in the O'Day line were designed by C. Raymond Hunt Associates in one of the most enduring designer-builder relationships in the industry (rivaled, in fact, only by Bill Lapworth's tenure as Cal's house designer and Bruce King's with Ericson Yachts). The result of the relationship is a family resemblance in the O'Day line that is more than superficial. What proves popular in one boat is apt to be adopted in subsequent kin. Therefore, any study of the O'Day offerings over the years reflects a process of evolution.

When it was introduced, the O'Day 22 was touted as a competitive contender on the race course, a contrasting companion to the rather hazy 23-footer which it would soon phase out. The 22 had a masthead rig, a stylish rake to the transom, shallow (23") draft with a short stub keel and no centerboard, light weight (advertised 1,800 lbs) for trailering, and a price under $3,000.

Later, the 22 acquired a fractional rig, a centerboard, 300 advertised pounds and a price tag almost $7,000 higher.

Construction

O'Day once set a standard for small boat construction

Specifications

LOA	21' 8"
LWL	18' 11"
Beam	7' 2"
Draft	1' 3"/4' 3" (board up/down)
Displacement	2,183 lbs.
Ballast	800 lbs.
Sail area	198 sq. ft.

and styling. That was before on and off labor problems in its plant, management changes under Bangor Punta, the decline in sales of boats in its size range, and increasingly fierce competition for buyers who became more cost than quality conscious. The later O'Day 22s were, frankly, a mixed bag of quality and shabbiness.

The spars, rigging, and hardware are as high quality as we have seen in comparable boats. Our only reservation is with the stamped stainless steel hinged mast step that we know from personal experience requires a steady hand and boat when raising or lowering a mast.

We also think that a mainsheet which terminates in a cam action cleat 16" up the single backstay may be economical and simple but it is neither efficient

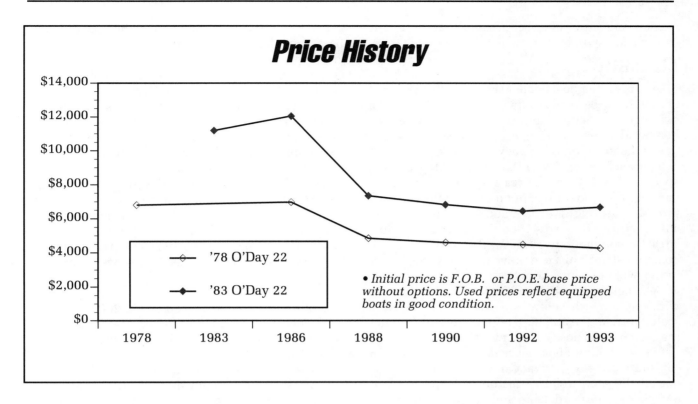

Price History

| | '78 O'Day 22 |
| | '83 O'Day 22 |

• *Initial price is F.O.B. or P.O.E. base price without options. Used prices reflect equipped boats in good condition.*

nor handy, again a reflection of scrimping to keep price low.

The quality of O'Day fiberglass laminates was historically high but there have been reader reports of gelcoat voids and there is consistent evidence of printthrough (pattern of laminate in gelcoat). Exterior styling and proportions are superb, an opinion iterated by owners who have returned the *PS* Boat Owners' Questionnaires. The O'Day 22, despite her age, is still not outdated.

On a boat of this size and price, a minimum of exterior trim is understandable. What is less understandable is the poor quality of the interior finish and decor. Belowdecks the O'Day 22 epitomizes the pejorative label *Clorox bottle*, used to describe fiberglass boats. Sloppily fitted bits of teak trim are matched against teak-printed Formica, at best a tacky combination. Cabinetry, such as there is, is flimsy, and in general the whole impression is of lackluster attention to details.

Performance

Without a centerboard the O'Day 22 simply did not have the performance to go with her racy image. Even with the centerboard she is hardly a ball of fire under sail. She does not point well; tacking through 100 degrees is not uncommon and she is tender, with a disconcerting desire to round up when a puff hits. In light air, with her 3/4 fore triangle and working jib she is undercanvassed and sluggish. In such conditions a genoa with substantial overlap is essential.

Since changing jibs is at best a dicey exercise on a 22 footer, the first step in reducing sail is to reef the mainsail. Jiffy reefing is standard and owners of the O'Day should have a system in good working order and know how to use it. Owners of the boat in waters where squalls are a threat may also want to consider roller furling for the larger jib, trading off the loss of performance and added cost for such a rig for the convenience and, in the case of this boat, the safety.

The O'Day is most hurt in light air downwind and most owners will want either an 8'-or-so whisker pole for winging the jib, or a spinnaker. It is a fun boat on which to learn spinnaker handling. With her fractional rig the spinnaker is relatively small and yet the boat is big enough to provide a foredeck platform for setting the sail.

The trouble is that the O'Day 22 scrimps on the hardware needed for ease of handling with or without a spinnaker. The two #10 Barient sheet winches are, in our opinion, inadequate for anything larger than a working jib and we suggest replacing them with optional #16s. Similarly, the working jib sheets lead to fixed blocks whereas lengths of track with adjustable blocks (fitted to some boats as an option) are far better for optimizing sail trim.

The O'Day did not come with halyard winches as standard. It is a large boat for setting and reefing sails with hand tension alone. Most owners will want at least one small winch (#10) on the cabin roof, with the jib and main halyards led aft through jam cleats or stoppers to the winch.

The fairing of the O'Day 22 underwater is better than average, helped by the fact that the lead ballast is encapsulated in the fiberglass hull molding. The centerboard will, however, be difficult to maintain.

Livability

Like many other boats of her size on the market, the O'Day 22 is basically a daysailer with incidental overnight accommodations, notwithstanding that her builder (or its ad agency) made much of its questionable comfort, privacy, and space.

The cockpit of the O'Day is almost perfect: a spacious 6-1/2' long, the seats are spaced to allow bracing of feet on the one opposite, and the coaming provides a feeling of security and serves as a comfortable arm rest. It is also self-bailing although the low sill at the companionway means that the lower hatch board must be in place to prevent water going below in the event of a knockdown.

Seat locker space is excellent for a boat of this size with quarterberth below and we like the separate sealed well for the outboard remote gas tank (but not the fact that the hose can be pinched in use).

O'Day literature boasts berths for two couples in "absolute privacy." Privacy in a 22 footer has to be one of the more relative features. A sliding door encloses the forward cabin and another, the head.

The layout of the O'Day 22 is a noteworthy example of the tradeoff between an enclosed head and berth space. It does indeed have a head area that can be enclosed, a rare feature indeed on a boat of this size. With a conventional marine toilet and through-hull discharge where permitted, this would be a most serviceable facility.

The tradeoff is a pair of terrible vee berths forward. Coming to a point at the forward end, there is simply not enough room for two adults on even the most intimate terms. They are thus suitable only for a pair of small children who do not suffer from sibling rivalry.

By contrast the two settee berths in the main cabin are a bit narrow but a fit place for two adults to sleep. In contrast to the dinette layout of other boats, we think the more traditional layout of the O'Day would be the choice for most owners, especially those cruising with children. However, the settees are not comfortable to sit on, lacking as they do backrests.

The initial version of the O'Day had the then fashionable dinette arrangement but this was quickly replaced by a pair of opposing settees. We doubt if many owners would bother setting up the portable cabin table between the berths, as it prevents the fore and aft passage through the cabin.

The galley with its small sink and space for a two-burner stove is rudimentary but adequate for a boat of this size, Inadequate is the bin/hanging locker opposite the head. Its usefulness escapes us. Enclosed, it could have been better used space. But then the O'Day 22 desperately needs stowage space.

Conclusions

At a minimum trailering weight of 2,200 lbs. (more realistically 2,500 plus the trailer), the O'Day 22 is above the maximum for trailering without a heavy car and special gear.

If she isn't going to be trailered and launched off a ramp, the 2' minimum draft is an unwarranted sacrifice of performance and stability. We would look for a fin keel boat unless shoal draft is the highest priority.

On the other hand, with some additional sails and hardware the O'Day 22 should appeal to the sailor who wants a minimum size (and therefore price) boat primarily for daysailing and occasional weekend cruising (maximum one couple plus two young children).

Clearly the O'Day 22 is a minimum boat built tightly to a price. She is attractively styled. As she is apt to be a first boat, resale is important. O'Day boats have enjoyed good value on the used boat market.

For about $6,000 for a ten-year-old model, you get a sleek looking small boat with a good cockpit, a modicum of privacy and two good berths. You also get a schlocky decor and a slow boat.   • **PS**

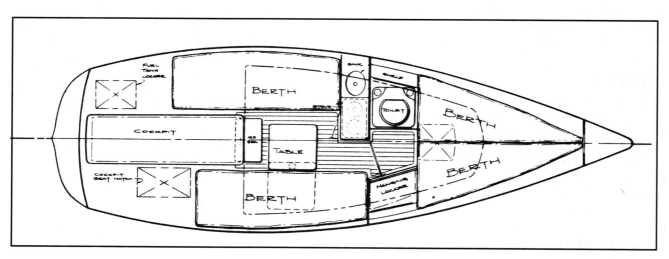

Sea Sprite

One of the oldest fiberglass boats, this traditional overnighter is long on looks, short on space.

The Sea Sprite 23 is a trim but rugged daysailer-overnighter from naval architect Carl A. Alberg that enjoyed a 25-year production run under several different Rhode Island builders, most notably Clarke Ryder. It's a typical Alberg design—narrow beam, full keel and conservative ballast-to-displacement ratio and graceful lines. This is a boat that still turns heads when it sails into a harbor.

History

The origins of the Sea Sprite 23 go back to 1958 when the small American Boat Building company of East Greenwich, Rhode Island, wanted to expand its product line, consisting at the time of the Block Island 40. Carl Alberg, then in the U.S. Coast Guard, came up with a 22 1/2-foot, full-keel design. (We're not sure what Alberg's duties were in the Coast Guard, but they apparently left plenty of free time; besides the Sea Sprite, Alberg also drew the Pearson Triton and Bristol 27 while in the service.) The Sprite, incidentally, was first marketed as a 22; a later builder accentuated the positive and it became the 23.

American Boat Building employee Tom Potter remembers being asked to test sail the new design. "We were terribly impressed by the boat, the way it performed." It was, Potter said, typical of most of the boats Alberg would design over the years—"sensible boats you could take to sea."

When American Boat Building dissolved during the early 1960s, production of the Sea Sprite was taken over by the nearby Wickford Shipyard, which built it for several years, after which the molds passed briefly to Sailstar, another small Rhode Island company, then to Clint Pearson, who was starting up his own Bristol Boat Company across Narragansett Bay.

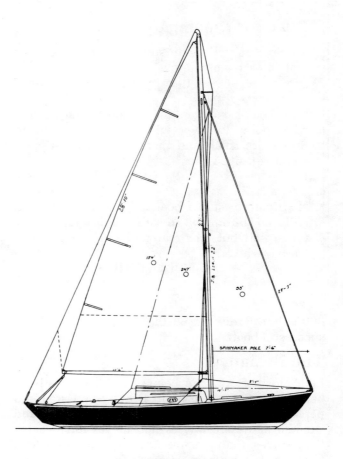

Specifications

LOA	22' 6"
LWL	16' 3"
Beam	7' 0"
Draft	3' 0"
Displacement	3,350 lbs.
Ballast	1,400 lbs.
Sail area	247 sq. ft.

Earlier, cousins Clint and Everett Pearson had obtained the rights to the Triton, which American Boat Building for some reason had not wanted. But when Bristol employee Paul Coble designed the Corsair 24, the rights to the Sea Sprite were sold to another Bristol builder, Clarke E. Ryder. This was about 1974, and Ryder continued to build the 23 until 1985 when his company folded.

Ryder built new molds for the boat, encapsulating the heretofore external lead keel and creating a self-bailing cockpit. Except for a few other minor changes and the introduction of hull colors besides white—bright red, blue and green—the Sea Sprite 23 built by Ryder (he began with hull #525) was fundamentally the same as the first off the line at American Boat Building. All told, the model reached a run of nearly

Owners' Comments

"Basically a well-made, sturdy, salty-looking boat that is reasonably quick."
—1981 model in Massachusetts

"The boat is excellent for daysailing but it is not comfortable for overnight or weekend cruises. Bunks are small and there is no back support when you sit inside."
—1974 model in Virginia

"Particularly stable boat for getting wife (and) children introduced to sailing. Very responsive under sail but also extremely forgiving to the learner who errs."
—1977 model in Rhode Island

"The electrical system was inadequate and I have replaced it with an eight-circuit panel."
—1981 model in Wisconsin

"Very capable on all headings."
—1970 model in Vermont

"Stay away from early models. They have not aged well, with significant mast step and chainplate problems. Later models (after 1969) have fared much better."
—1971 model in Rhode Island

"Interior (space) sacrificed for appearance of lines and seaworthiness."
—1974 model in New York

800 before Ryder closed the doors on this highly successful boat.

The Design

Like most of Alberg's boats, the 23 is relatively narrow of beam (7' 0") and heavily ballasted—43 percent of its weight is in the full keel. Freeboard and superstructure are low, which makes for pleasing lines but less than spacious accommodations below. In short, this is a boat designed for sailing and not lounging around belowdecks.

With a waterline length of just 16' 3", the boat rated well (16.6) under the old Cruising Club of America (CCA) rules. It is intended to heel 30 degrees or so when underway (some regard this as initial tenderness), adding waterline length and increasing hull speed. The heeling angle plus the low freeboard—the rail gets close to the water—can bring an occasional dousing for the crew in a chop. But the boat is inherently stable, and the gentle sheer and distinctive overhangs add to its seagoing profile. The 23 draws only three feet, virtually shoal draft and less than many smaller boats.

Under the more modern PHRF rating system, which is a performance-based handicap system rather than a measurment rule, the Sprite has an average rating of about 270 seconds per mile—hardly a rule-beater, but reasonably fast for a full-keeled 23-footer. (One owner crowed about beating those "tubby" Cape Dorys—in all likelihood a competing Alberg design.)

The Sprite carries a modest 247 square feet of sail under main and working jib. (The newer O'Day 23, by contrast, is lighter by almost 300 pounds and has 246 square feet.) Early in its career, the Sea Sprite also came in a daysailer model, with an eight-foot cockpit instead of the standard six, and with two

berths below instead of four, and no galley or icebox. Apparently few were made, which is understandable because the standard model has ample cockpit space and little enough room below.

Construction

The hull, deck and cabinhouse of the Ryder-built boats are solid, hand-laid fiberglass for a tight, sound body. One owner called the boat "overbuilt." The hull/deck joint is a typical inward flange sealed with 3M 5200 and fastened with machine screws.

Most fiberglass boats older than 10 to 15 years show deterioration of the gelcoat and require painting. This will be true of many used Sea Sprites, too. None of the owners who responded to our survey reported gelcoat blistering, however. Some of the earlier models seemed to experience slight leaks around the mast step or chainplates; several of the Ryder boats apparently had leaking from the pulpit stanchions. Otherwise, the interiors are reported to be dry. Overall, the Sea Sprites seem to be structurally sound with no major repairs called for and few, if any, cosmetic problems. A 1983 model we sailed looked almost new.

The Sea Sprite was built as a top-of-the-line "sailing yacht," as company literature described it. The quality shows in the non-skid surfaces on the deck and deckhouse, the standard bronze hardware, including opening portlights, and in the generous use of wood—mahogany coamings and backrest and teak grabrails above, and lots of teak trim below. Ryder introduced a full interior liner (previous models were painted fiberglass), and the judicious use of holly and teak helps offset the shiny white surfaces. We don't know whether the Sea Sprite's teak cockpit grids were standard on all models, but they are a nice touch.

The boats, at least the Ryder version, carry a 30-foot fractionally rigged mast by Hall Spars. The mast is deck-stepped and halyards are led internally. The small deckhouse makes for a roomy foredeck, which is reached via comfortably wide walkways.

Performance

Several of our readers say the Sea Sprite exhibits fairly sluggish light-air performance, which is a common complaint among smaller full-keel boats. Others have found that raising a 130- or 150-percent genoa in winds under 10 knots makes a definite improvement.

Performance improves noticeably as the wind pipes up and the boat digs in. Although the rail is near the water, the boat, once in its sailing mode, seems very stable and the steering nicely balanced with just a hint of weather helm. The low freeboard enhances the feeling of being on the water which, for a small-boat enthusiast at least, is worth the occasional spray in a head sea. And while the keel-hung rudder doesn't respond as rapidly as a spade would, the 23 tacks smartly enough. One owner, who now sails a J/Boat, remembered his Sea Sprite's tacking ability as "not unreasonably slow."

This is a small boat that handles well when the going gets rough and goes readily offshore—no worries about early reefing here. One owner we know said he "never thought twice" about sailing his Sea Sprite to Block Island or Cuttyhunk. In fact, Ryder used to tout a transatlantic trip—60 days from Wickford, Rhode Island to Falmouth, England—made in 1974 by a 21-year-old singlehander as evidence of the boat's ocean-going qualities. (The only damage—to the skipper—occurred when he tripped on the dock in England and broke his ankle.)

Moving under power, however, is another matter. A 4-hp outboard, which is located in a well aft of the tiller, will get the boat to hull speed; anything smaller is a strain, more than 6 hp and you may experience control problems. The outboard well is the usual nuisance and several readers surveyed either had banished the motor below or would like to. The best that can be said for the well is that it preserves the lines of the boat. Outboard performance is inversely proportionate to wind and waves. Having once fought a losing battle against gusting winds, tide and current, with ground speed reduced to about zero, we can attest to the Sea Sprite's poor performance under power in these conditions. If only the channel had been wide enough to hoist the sails....

Ryder for a time offered an optional Yanmar Model 1 GM diesel. This would no doubt eliminate many of the headaches associated with the outboard motor and well, but the weight and expense of an inboard seems difficult to justify. None of the readers responding to our questionnaire own inboard models.

Interior

Down below, the cabin is light and reasonably airy with two opening ports and a smoked hatch. Despite some complaints about the lack of room (even Clarke Ryder says the interior is best suited for stowing stuff) we found there was satisfactory sitting headroom if you are under six feet. The 6' 0" V-berths are

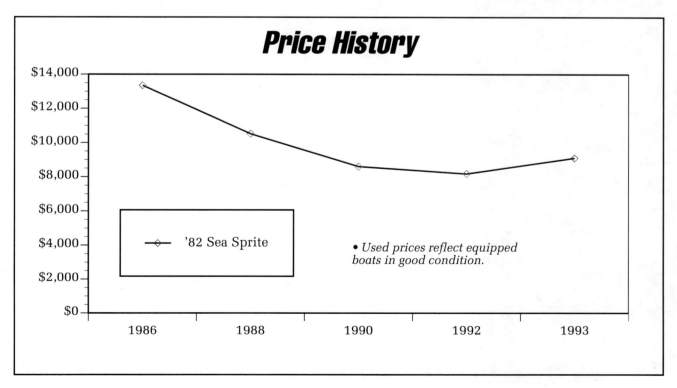

• *Used prices reflect equipped boats in good condition.*

too short and have minimal clearance; the 6' 3" settee berths in the main cabin disappear quickly under the cockpit seats. This is an interior that is definitely not for the claustrophobic, but at least you won't need lee cloths. The marine head (many owners have replaced it with a portable head) is located in a wedge at the foot of the V-berths where its virtual inaccessibility makes the privacy issue moot. To be fair, this is typical of the arrangements on most boats of this size.

To starboard, between the forward and main berths, is the "galley," consisting of a sink and some stowage. To port, there's an insulated icebox and more dry storage. The sink, fed by a 10-gallon fiberglass water tank under the starboard berth, drains via a through-hull. The icebox drains into the bilge. There's more stowage, under bunks and here and there, but it's basically covered openings to the bilge. On deck, there's good storage space in a port locker and a fuel locker to starboard that's sized for a three-gallon tank.

Conclusions

The Sea Sprite 23 isn't for everyone. A lack of space and accommodations relegates it to the daysailer/occasional overnighter category. Although it lacks cruising luxuries, it is an exceptional daysailer—seaworthy and strongly built, and with a sailing range that belies its small size. Its stability and ease of handling make it a good choice for the older sailor who doesn't need a big boat anymore, or for a small family primarily interested in day sailing.

We saw several Sea Sprites listed for sale this past fall (1991) in the $6,500 range—a good price for a well-built boat that's going to be around for a while. Older Sprites originally sold for $5,000 (minus sails) with the later Ryder models going for about $11,000.

The Sprites can be said to have held their value well while still representing a bargain relative to what you get. As Clarke Ryder says, "They sail like a charm and they're pretty. People who have them love them."   • **PS**

Tanzer 22

A peppy little boat that sails well but suffers badly from mediocre accommodations.

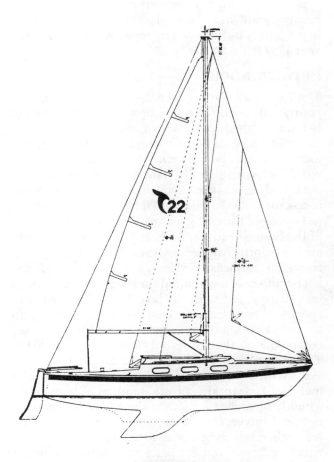

Like the O'Day 22 and the Catalina 22, the Tanzer 22 was a longtime member in her builder's line of boats. Designed by Johann Tanzer, the Tanzer 22 was originally built exclusively in Canada but later was built also in North Carolina and Washington, which gave the boat widespread geographical distribution as well as saving on duty for US buyers.

Dating from 1970, the 22 was a staple in the Tanzer line. Helping that growth was a strong Tanzer 22 Class Association that boasts several hundred members in the US and Canada. The association sponsors both racing and cruising. Such an organization has much to recommend it, both to the builder in his marketing efforts and to owners for the camaraderie and the ready resale market it affords, Best of all, for both sides there is a source of feedback on weaknesses, changes, and policies. Especially in areas where the organization is strong, Tanzer 22s have appreciated in value.

One drawback to promotion as a one-design boat is that the design has to remain essentially static to protect older boats. Even desirable changes may not be possible. This means that the initial design has to be successful. It is to Tanzer's credit that despite the age of the 22's design, the boat remains a popular product, albeit a bit out of date for today's styling.

Construction

The Tanzer 22 seems to be well built, perhaps better than the average small boat. There is no evidence of flexing or gelcoat crazing, two common symptoms of the under-built or poorly engineered hull and deck structure. The hull-to-deck joint is a combination of semi-rigid adhesive and 3/16" machine screws on 6" centers holding together an exterior flange, a construction method *PS* approves in a boat of this size.

Specifications

LOA	22' 6"
LWL	19' 9"
Beam	7' 10"
Draft	2' 0" (keel/cb), 3' 5" (fixed)
Displacement	3,100/2,900 lbs.
Ballast	1,500/1,250 lbs.
Sail area	227 sq. ft.

The resulting flange is one which would be difficult to repair in event of damage. However, it is covered with a vinyl molding that does afford better than average protection.

As is typical of boats of this size, the interior is a molded fiberglass head liner and hull liner. The hull liner incorporates all the basic components of the layout—berths, cabinets, cabin, sole, etc. In a small boat it is a most practical interior. The disadvantage is the difficulty of attaching add-on deck hardware and repairing damage to the hull laminate behind it.

Certain details of the Tanzer 22 are bothersome. For instance, the rudder is a two-part molded piece with a flange around the edge. While strong, it is needlessly crude in this day of well faired rudders. For another instance, a foredeck well which is now standard (and a good feature on a small boat) carries a solid, heavy fiberglass cover, loose and held in place only by flimsy wood toggles. However, these are correctable details.

Performance

The Tanzer 22, particularly the full keel version, is a peppy little boat, among the best performing boats of her size, weight, price and purpose. She rates and sails with boats 2' longer, years more modern, and touted for their performance. What she might do to windward with an up-to-date keel shape rather than the less efficient swept back fin makes for interesting conjecture. The same goes for her rudder shape.

Fairing of the cast iron keel is only adequate and of the flanged rudder, poor. If performance in light air is a priority, owners will want to work at getting smoother surfaces. Performance upwind with the keel-centerboard combination shoal draft version is less snappy, but with the board raised, downwind speed—already the envy of sailors on other boats up to about 26'—should be even better. This point may be a moot one, though, as only a small fraction of the Tanzers sold are the shoal draft model.

As with most boats of her size on the market, the mainsail and working jib are standard. A larger jib is a highly desirable option. As sheet winches were all optional, buyers should look for the larger two-speed ones when selecting a boat. Similarly with the spinnaker and gear: opt for pairs of coaming-mounted winches. We also recommend the cockpit-led halyards. Tanzer 22 owners responding to the *PS* owners' questionnaire also mention jiffy reefing, trav-

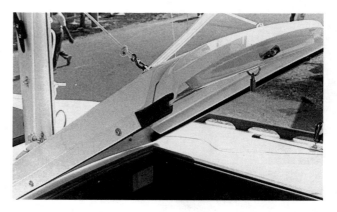

A lack of headroom is alleviated somewhat by a pop-top hatch. These tend to leak, however.

eler, Cunningham and vang as highly desirable options, again a reflection of their interest in sail handling and performance.

However, while the Tanzer 22 is a relatively smart performer and with add-on gear can be made more so, do not mistake her potential for that of the hot dinghy types such as the J/24 and its ilk.

Livability

In keeping with our belief that the cockpit is the most critical area for comfort in a boat of this size, we have reservations about the cockpit of the Tanzer 22. It is large, wider than average, which is a virtue and a fault, On the one hand, there is plenty of space to stretch out; six adults can sit down inside the coamings that offer both protection and support. The distance between the seats allows for bracing with

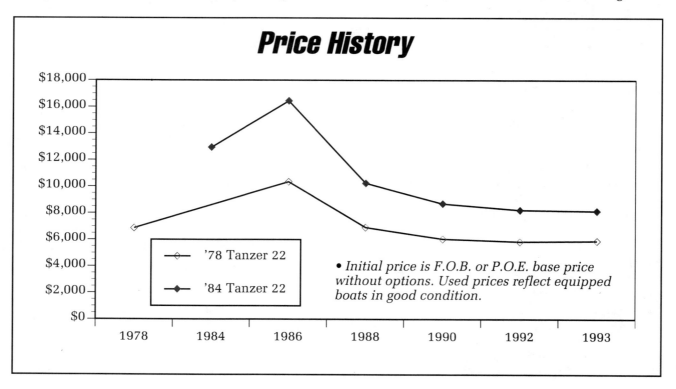

Price History

'78 Tanzer 22
'84 Tanzer 22

• *Initial price is F.O.B. or P.O.E. base price without options. Used prices reflect equipped boats in good condition.*

the feet and the short tiller leaves most of the cockpit free of its swing.

On the negative side, though, this width coupled with the 22's low freeboard invites water aboard in the event of a severe knockdown. And it is a big cockpit which can hold much water.

Those sitting on the leeward side in a breeze are going to be on intimate terms with the water, although the raised deck does afford protection not found on boats with trunk cabin configurations. There is no bridgedeck, merely a low (too low) sill in the companionway.

Unfortunately the cockpit is complicated by the mainsheet that is fixed to the center of the cockpit floor just forward of the tiller. It is handy to the helmsman and safer than a sheet with traveler mounted on a bridgedeck at the forward end of the cockpit, but it does effectively divide the cockpit and reduce its spaciousness. A traveler was optional equipment but does nothing to alleviate the fault with location.

Do not be put off by the fact that the cabin house extends to the sheer, a rather old fashioned feature. While it does make going forward a bit more awkward, the deck space it provides is welcome. Best of all is the interior space that is obtained in a boat that, with her low sheer, would otherwise be hopelessly cramped below.

The Tanzer 22, like the Catalina 22, is a victim of the time when she was designed. In the late 1960s the boat buying public became infatuated with dinettes. Boat builders obliged. The fad expired when owners tried to eat at the table and sleep on the so-called double berth converted from the dinette. In the five-year interval a lot of boats were built with that feature, including the Tanzer 22.

The dinette leaves the Tanzer 22 with but one proper berth, a good quarterberth, plus a pair of vee berths forward. The vee berths suffer from vee-berth syndrome—stacked feet. This, coupled with the portable head located under them gives the Tanzer 22 one of the less appealing layouts we have seen.

As if this were not enough, the icebox (standard) more properly belongs on a powerboat than a sailboat. It is one of those infernal built-in front-opening types: open the door with the boat heeled on starboard tack and be buried by the contents. Moreover, front-opening boxes such as this lose their cold with every opening (or what is left of the cold; insulation is only 1" of styrofoam).

In an attempt to provide some sunny weather headroom, Tanzer also offered a "convertible hatch" whereby the sliding companionway hatch assembly is hinged and can be raised to boom height. It was a $400 option that can also be retrofitted by owners on older 22s. 90% of the 22s came fitted with the device. As with the pop-top option on other boats, we've found it a bit impractical.

Conclusions

In sum, the Tanzer 22 is a moderately well built boat with mediocre accommodations and better than average performance. Buyers into fleets of Tanzer 22s will benefit from an active family racing and cruising program. As with almost all boats of this size, we think the deep keel version is better than the shoal draft version as the boat is apt to be too much for most sailors to trailer.

The deck and the cockpit of the Tanzer should appeal to a family sailor looking for daysailing room. The interior will have much less appeal and we recommend any prospective buyers do some shopping around to see what layouts are most suitable for the type of sailing they plan to do before settling on this boat.　　　　　　　　• PS

The interior is a good example of what happens when a builder tries to cram too much into a small hull.

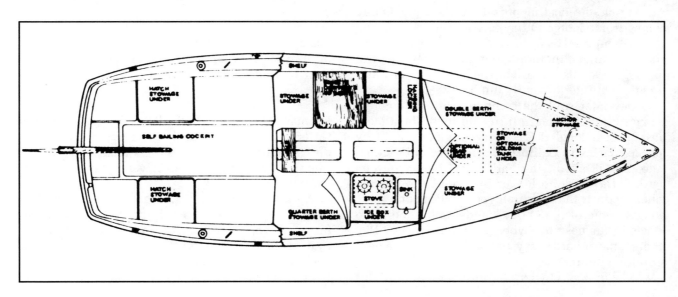

O'Day 23

Is this the ideal trailer sailer? No, but this "camp cruiser" does manage to come close.

The boom in sailing broke the sound barrier during the 1970s. It was gaining altitude during the 1960s, with the development of cost-efficient fiberglass tooling and layup methods. The 1980s saw the industry in decline. But back in the heyday of the hippies, Mr. Natural and the various manifestations of the back-to-earth movement, sailing was "green," environmentally and politically correct. OPEC oil embargo? Who cares!

Trailer sailers helped lead the way for many large production boatbuilders. Among the early names of car towable cruisers were Venture, Catalina, Balboa, Aquarius, Paceship and O'Day. The O'Day 20, 22, 23 and 25 gave the company a complete line of trailer sailers. To our way of thinking, the 23 was perhaps the best of the lot, at least in terms of interior space, performance and trailerability.

History

At the risk of repeating ourselves, the name O'Day comes from George O'Day, a gold medalist in the 1960 Olympics. His forthcoming line of small fiberglass daysailers, including the immensely successful O'Day Day Sailer, established the company as a premiere builder of family fun boats.

O'Day later sold the company to conglomerate Bangor Punta, which in turn sold its sailboat business to Lear Siegler. Cal boats, originally built by Jensen Marine in California, also were built alongside the O'Days at the Fall River, Massachusetts yard. O'Days are no longer in production, having fallen victim to the bankruptcy courts. Pearson Yachts bought some of the O'Day molds, but it too is no longer in business. Just where the molds to the O'Day 23 are today is hard to say, probably stacked in a field sprouting poppies.

We have Boat Owner Questionnaires on file for

Specifications

LOA	22' 9"
LWL	19' 6"
Beam	7' 11"
Draft	2' 3"/5' 4" (board up/down)
Displacement	3,085 lbs.
Ballast	1,200 lbs.
Sail area	246 sq. ft.

boats ranging from hull #1, built in 1972, to boats built in 1985. We're not sure how many O'Day 23s were built all told, but it must be several thousand.

The Design

For many years, the principal designer for O'Day was C. Raymond Hunt Associates of Boston. The firm designed all of the trailer sailers mentioned above. The chief designer in recent years has been John Deknatel.

All except the O'Day 22 are keel-centerboarders (the 22 has a fixed, shoal draft keel). This feature helps set the O'Day 23 apart from many of the other trailer sailers built in the 1970s. Most had fixed stub keels, like the 22, or more commonly, swing keels in which the entire ballast—say, 550 pounds—was

Owners' Comments

"A good weekender for very sheltered waters. In winds over 20 knots, I question her seaworthiness and strength of fittings."

—1982 model in New York

"We have noticed in rough weather, when a wave would slam against the underside, that the hull would flex and the boat vibrate, due to lack of lateral support of the fiberglass."

—1982 model in Ontario, Canada

"Good starter boat. Overall quality very good. Interior accomodations only okay for occasional overniter. Boat is fine for protected and semi-protected areas. Regular trailer sailing would be a nuisance."

—1981 model in Massachusetts

"Basically good boat. Excellent value. Good looking. Quite fast when trimmed right. Very stiff, easy to sail. Beats most 25-26-footers. Roomy interior. High-utility, large stowage areas under all bunks and seats. Pop top is great. Gives immediate ventilation and 6' 4" headroom."

—1973 model in Indiana

"Very happy with boat except holding a course when wind gets stiff. This boat has lots of room due to galley and sink being in drawer slides under cockpit."

—1978 model in Washington

"Deck and cockpit gelcoat is too thin and has air pockets under it resulting in little holes appearing in gelcoat."

—1973 model in Maryland

---

retracted and lowered by means of a simple ratchet winch. This placed a lot of load on the pivot pin. The keel's trunk also is an intrusion in the living area of the cabin. And there was seldom a guaranteed method of preventing the keel from retracting during a knockdown.

A keel-centerboard arrangement places most of the ballast in the stub keel, where it is firmly joined to the hull. The centerboard gives better upwind performance than the shoal draft stub keel, and if weighted 150 pounds or so, also provides some additional righting moment. The main disadvantage of the keel-centerboard configuration is a somewhat greater fixed draft than the swing keel, which makes launching and loading from a trailer more difficult.

At 3,085 pounds dry, the O'Day 23 is not an easily trailered boat. Though people do dry sail such boats, our own experience suggests limiting trailering to twice a season—to and from marina—and once or twice to some more exotic crusing ground for summer vacations. It's simply too much work to manhandle a 1-1/2-ton boat every weekend. Besides, the boat will inevitably suffer more wear and tear on the road than in the water. As one reader put it, "Once it is in water, good, once it is on road, good. In between, it can be *hell!*"

The O'Day 23 has a generous 1,200 pounds of ballast, which makes her reasonably stiff. Readers' responses appear divided on the issue of stability. One comments that "She seems stiff compared to other boats," while another says, "Boat appears to be tender, at least initially." Most recommend reefing early, before the wind reaches 20 knots—that's good advice for most boats up to 35 feet! It must be remembered that this is a 23-foot centerboarder.

Good looks do much to recommend this boat. The lines are not disrupted by attempts to maximize interior volume or distinguish her from other designs. The sheer is relatively flat, there is good rake to the bow, and the cabin has been kept in proportion to the length and height of the topsides.

Molded fiberglass coamings provide some back support. The outboard rudder, while a trademark of smaller boats, is simple and easy to maintain and repair. The cockpit is self-bailing.

Like most trailer sailers, the rig isn't terribly large. Still, its 246 square feet of sail area compares favorably with other similarly sized boats. The Paceship 23, for example, has 223 sq. ft., the Tanzer 22 230 sq. ft. and the fixed keel Ranger 23 263 sq. ft..

Construction

There is nothing exotic about most boats built in the 1970s, and the O'Day line is no exception. The hull of the O'Day 23 is solid fiberglass. Balsa core is used in the deck. The hull-to-deck joint, according to an early brochure, is "lapped, sealed, mechanically fastened, and covered with a two-piece vinyl gunwale guard." Ballast is internally capsulated lead; the centerboard is "lightly weighted."

The rudder is foam-cored, which one reader said delaminated after three years. Other complaints include gelcoat voids, the liner squeaking against the main bulkhead, deck leaks, weak foredeck, and so on. Most readers, however, felt the boat is reasonably well constructed.

A fiberglass liner was used to hide the overhead and a fiberglass pan used to form the cabin sole and furniture foundations. We're not fond of such moldings, as they tend to sweat, amplify sound and make it difficult to access all parts of the hull. But this is what you get in a mass produced boat—in the 1970s and today. If you want a fiberglass boat with an all-wood interior, you must either buy a very old boat or a custom one.

If you're looking for a trailer sailer, you probably won't have a choice. Our only suggestion, for safety's sake, is to investigate all of the bins and stowage compartments to make sure all through-hull fittings and vulnerable sections of the hull are accessible. It isn't too difficult to cut out additional inspection ports with a sabre saw.

The hardware and equipment is generally of good quality: Barient winches, Whale Gusher bilge pump, and Scotchgard-treated fabrics. Tabernacles were standard for raising and lowering the mast. Also standard in 1981 were genoa tracks and lead blocks, topping lift, jiffy reefing, bow pulpit, stanchions and lifelines, foredeck anchor locker, icebox and mooring cleats. Don't laugh. In the 1970s it wasn't uncommon to find such basic items as optional extras. In fact, much of the above-mentioned equipment was extra on the O'Day 23 in 1979—lifelines and stanchions $240, toilet $115, four-inch cowl vent $43, winch handle $34 and an outhaul $18!

Performance

Reader responses regarding sailing performance again varied widely, perhaps reflecting the fact that this is, for many, an entry-level boat. Such persons' previous sailing experience is likely to range from little to none. Ratings for upwind speed ranged from below average to outstanding. "The boat seems to point significantly higher than others," said one reader. "We beat a Hughes 26," wrote another. "They had a genoa and we only had a working jib."

About a quarter of the owners weren't so enchanted. Whereas one reader said it has "Poor performance in light air," another said, "It is very fast in light air."

Ratings of downwind performance were equally fluky. Most owners, however, don't own spinnakers, and not all even own genoas. For them, downwind performance is bound to suffer.

Overall, our impression is that the boat sails fairly well. On our one outing on the Detroit River in Michigan, we felt she was nimble and certainly no sluggard. A genoa is bound to help, especially since the O'Day 23 weighs more than most trailer sailers of this length.

Auxiliary power is furnished by an outboard. Owners report good performance from a Johnson 6- and 9.5-hp., Honda 7.5-hp. and 10-hp., even a Volvo 9-hp. One owner said that since his boat "moves in a whisper of wind," he doesn't carry an outboard!

A tank locker is provided under the starboard seat, convenient to the transom motor mount.

With an outboard the skipper may turn the motor at the same time as the tiller to reduce the turning radius and to direct the boat straight and true while backing down. Performance under power isn't really an issue with a trailer sailer.

Interior

The layout is very straightforward and likable: 6' 3" V-berths forward, head compartment with sink and

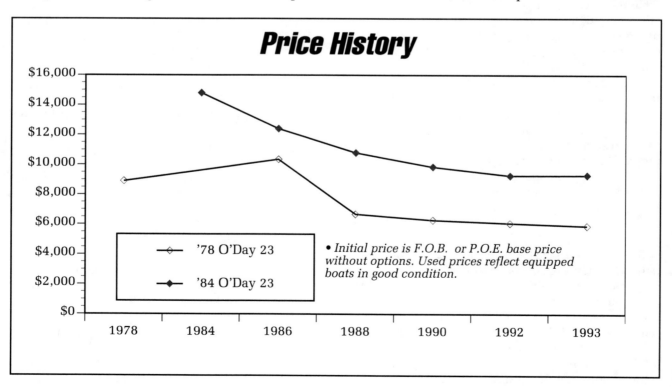

Price History

• Initial price is F.O.B. or P.O.E. base price without options. Used prices reflect equipped boats in good condition.

hanging locker amidships forward of the main bulkhead (yes, there is a privacy door), 6' 7" settee/berths in the main cabin with fold-out table, and small galley aft. Molded galley units port and starboard, containing the stove and sink, slide out from under the cockpit seats.

Headroom is sitting, though a pop top was offered for a while. These permit one to stand up in a small boat, but do tend to leak.

Most owners seem satisfied with the livability of the O'Day 23's accomodation plan. Of course there are the expected complaints about headroom, the small galley and berth width. These remarks were perhaps best summed up by the owner who wrote, "They pack a lot in, but it's still a 23-footer."

Conclusion

The O'Day seems to us to be one of the better trailer sailers of the 1970s. It's styling is up-to-date, as is the design, and construction and performance are as good or better than most others.

Its shortcomings are for the most part a product of its production line assembly, and its classification as a trailer sailer, which is responsible for keeping the rig short, weight low and the keel-centerboard less than perfect. Complaints about flexing hull and deck sections could be corrected by reinforcing these areas. Such problems shouldn't pose a safety risk unless you were planning a blue-water passage, which you shouldn't be doing anyway. • **PS**

Hunter 23.5

This family cruiser is innovative and has lots of room. In gusty winds, however, it is quick to stall.

H unter Marine Corp. is noted for its slick, innovative and low-cost mass production sailers. The Hunter 23.5, new in 1992, fits the bill in all respects.

The 23.5 was designed as a trailerable family cruiser for entry-level sailors. Like most Hunters, the boat offers lots of space in the cockpit and down below, and comes with the famous Cruise Pac, which provides just about anything a customer needs, including sails, motor, trailer, lifelines, anchor, life jackets, flares and a copy of *Chapman's Piloting, Seamanship and Small Boat Handling.* It's this type of marketing (plus price: the 1992 price was $13,500) that has helped make Hunter one of the most successful sailboat producers in the U.S.

No one has ever faulted the Alachua, Florida, builder for offering anything but fresh, well-thought-out designs. The most striking feature of the 23.5 is its water ballast system, new to Hunter. The system permits an operator to remove 1,000 pounds of ballast from the trailering weight. A retractable centerboard, kick-up rudder and mast that's fairly easy to step and unstep further enhances trailerability. All told, boat, motor and trailer weigh a combined 2,450 pounds. This model also contains enough foam to provide positive flotation.

While Hunter has enjoyed considerable success with the buying public, it has also suffered from a negative image problem. Earlier *PS* reviews have criticized Hunter products for a lack of quality control—various systems kinks, lightweight hulls, poor finish work and general absence of blue-water seaworthiness. On the other hand, Hunter owners, while acknowledging a prevailing lack of respect, frequently defend their choice. In the realm of objective data, Coast Guard complaint and recall statistics reveal that Hunter has a better than average record when it

Specifications

LOA	23' 5"
LWL	21' 5"
Beam	8' 4"
Draft (board up/down)	1' 6"/5' 6"
Displacement	2,000 lbs.
Water Ballast	1,000 lbs.
Sail area	236 sq. ft.

comes to hull blistering. (Hunter offers five-year bottom blister warranty protection for the 23.5.) Clearly, the company is doing something right. The model we inspected (hull #8) showed, with very few exceptions, careful attention to detail and finish work in even the least accessible places—more than you'd expect on a $13,500 boat. But it is also a boat with some inherent contradictions, in our opinion.

The Boat

The 23.5 is a highly engineered product with lots of thoughtful features. Hunter, unlike some builders, constructs a mock-up, followed by a prototype that is extensively tested before final design decisions are made. The hull form is modern looking, almost powerboaty in appearance from some angles. Continuing a tendency evident in recent Hunters, the design team has given the 23.5 a relatively full hull, and raised the freeboard to reduce the cabin height, as well as add room below and keep those up top dry in a chop. Because the cabin extends to the rail (no side decks), you must climb over the cabin top to get to the foredeck.

The rig (a B&R design) consists of a 28-foot Z. Spar mast, fractionally rigged with swept-back spreaders that eliminate the need for a backstay (and make unstepping/stepping, hence trailering, simpler); for the most part, the uppers are aft of the "after" lowers—until deck level—creating a triangular support system. Main and jib halyards are internal and led back to the cockpit. Power comes from a fully battened mainsail and 110-percent jib (UK Sailmakers—Hong Kong) with a total of 236 square feet. For steering, the traditional wooden tiller has been replaced with a brushed aluminum tube that arches over the walk-through transom (swim ladder comes standard). The aluminum, said chief designer Rob Mazza, weathers better and is easier to arch in order to keep the rudder low and the tiller sufficiently high. Many helmsmen will use the standard Ronstan X-10 tiller extension.

The water ballast/keel system constitutes the key feature of the 23.5. The water ballast—125 gallons, or 1,000 pounds—takes about two minutes to bring on board. The system is activated by flipping up a lid at the base of the companionway, opening a vent and turning a T-valve; the valve in turn drops a circular stainless steel plate aft of the keel, exposing four holes in the hull. (The plate can then be closed flush.) And while you can't jettison the water downwind, you can swing up the centerboard to reduce draft to 18 inches. The 4-foot centerboard, controlled by the outboard line to the cockpit, moves easily up and down via a cascade block and tackle arrangement.

The apparent thinking of Hunter engineers was to provide a simple, one-step water ballast system that keeps draft shallow while lowering the center of gravity for added stability and righting moment. The ballast—about 16 cubic feet in volume—lies immediately below the waterline. When the water is added, the boat sinks several inches. Nevertheless, while the water adds 1,000 pounds to the overall displacement, its location does not seem to provide sufficient righting moment for windward work in gusty conditions. On racing boats, water ballast is carried above the waterline and outboard under the settees, which of course provides more righting moment. But this water must be pumped into the chambers and drained before tacking—too complicated for Hunter's purposes.

Construction of the boat is fairly straightforward, with balsa in the hull and plywood in the deck. The plywood core has the potential to encourage water migration should a deck leak occur at some point. The deck/hull joint, with a roll similar to a Hobie 18—a "modified shoebox," one Hunter engineer described it—is bonded with glass and further fastened by flathead screws through the rubrail. Stanchions, fastened to aluminum backing plates that are glassed in, are sturdy. Though not a heavily-built boat, the 23 looks solid enough; in the absence of a graceful hull form—no sheer here—Hunter provides some added dash with a smoked forward-facing window and a green and purple hull swoosh graphic, which apparently has drawn strong reaction, pro and con (We liked it). Oddly, there is no waterline or boot scribed in the hull. Perhaps Hunter anticipates owners drysailing the 23.5, but the absence of a waterline mark will make bottom painting a difficult chore the first time.

Performance

We test sailed the 23.5 off Newport, Rhode Island. In light-air conditions, the shallow-body, lightweight boat (displacement 3,000 pounds with the water ballast) moved up to speed quickly. The boat pointed high and the few light puffs we experienced produced no noticeable helm. We did have some problem finding a definitive groove, especially after tacking. The boat glided through the water easily on a reach and downwind, with the board up, sped along as much as a 23-footer can (Mazza said it will surf under the right conditions). We moved relatively faster, in fact, than a Nonsuch 27 on the same tack.

In stronger 15-20 knot winds, it is a whole different experience. With a single reef in the mainsail, the boat consistently rounds up and stalls. In addition to the boat's higher vertical center of gravity, this tendency may also be due to the very high-aspect ratio centerboard, which is generally associated with quick stall characteristics.

Complicating matters is the way the rig and sheeting are set up. With no backstay (or topping lift) and no traveler, and with the main sheeted down and far forward near the companionway, the main and sheet are highly stressed. And because the cam cleat for the mainsheet is down near the cockpit sole, it's difficult to reach—especially in heavy air on a beat, when the helmsman and everyone else is out on the rail. The rounding up and stalling require constant spilling of the main. This may be okay (if tiring) for the experienced sailor, but a bit strenuous and nerve-wracking for the beginner at whom this boat is marketed.

Instead of a single reef, one solution might be to take a second reef in the main in anything approaching 15 knots, but that's not much of a solution. With 236 square feet of sail—128 in the main, 108 in the foretriangle—for a sail area-displacement ratio of 18.9, the boat should not be overpowered. (The O'Day 23, of about the same displacement, but with

200 more pounds of ballast, carries 246 square feet) Another solution, although it breaks up the cockpit, might be a barney post where there's already a slot for the cockpit table, a system that worked well enough in the Alerion-Express. A traveler would be even better, though obviously Hunter wanted to keep the cockpit clear of obstructions as well as avoid the added cost.

Accommodations

You get a lot for your money with this Hunter model. One thing you get a lot of is interior space or, as company literature describes it, "a 25-foot boat in a 23.5 hull." The main cabin is sizable and has more headroom than we've seen on a 23-footer. A pop-top hatch allows those down below to stand up in the center of the cabin. An optional canvas camper top ($300) provides protection from the elements. Pop-tops are notoriously leaky, and we can't vouch for this one's water tightness; however, Hunter has provided drains all around.

The smoked pop-top, plus three ports per side in the main cabin (two small circles, one longer swoosh-style forward) and the forward-facing window provide plenty of light. Hunter has made no attempt to yacht-up the interior: What you get is a basic cream-colored liner, offset on a portion of the topsides by a close-weave grayish fabric someone called "monkey fur." Despite the plainness, we liked the clean look of the interior.

Aft to port in the main cabin you get a galley station with a one-burner alcohol stove, sink, and fold-out table with storage below. You won't be whipping up any *Cruising World*-style feasts in this galley, but it's nice to be able to heat up some coffee or a cup of soup. Forward of the galley is a small settee/berth, sized right for a child, with storage beneath and a cutout for a portable ice chest. Opposite is a somewhat longer settee/berth of less than six feet, with more storage and a battery compartment below. On the centerline is a slot for a small table that also can be set up in the cockpit.

There are a number of helpful additions: an automatic bilge pump, access plates underneath the cockpit winches. The portable toilet is located to starboard behind a half-bulkhead and privacy cur-

The interior is roomy for a boat of this size, though the berths are a bit on the cramped side. Extra headroom is afforded by a pop-top hatch which can be fitted with an optional canvas camper top.

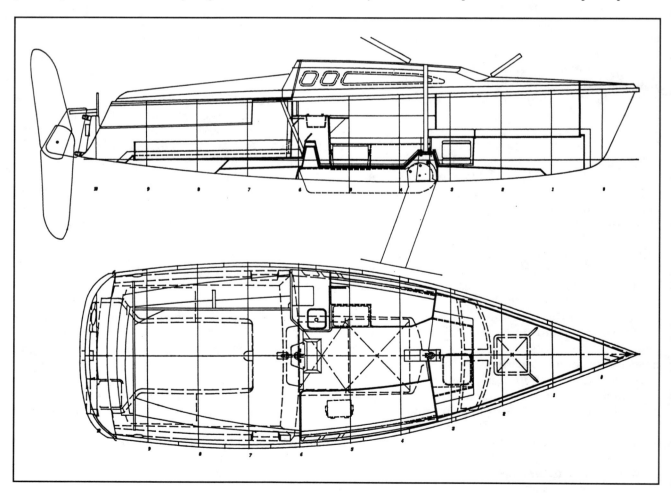

tain, and under the V-berth. Aside from the standard V-berth in the bow, which seems a bit cramped, there's a double berth (plus stowage) aft of the main cabin, under the cockpit and seats (not for the claustrophobic). It was back here in the bowels of the boat that we spotted the only untrimmed fiberglass.

On deck, there's an equally roomy cockpit—7' 9" long and 6' 2" from coaming to coaming. The relatively wide beam makes the addition of a ridge along the centerline for use as a footrest a welcome touch. Foam padding on the seatbacks is another. A lazaret on either side provides on-deck stowage. There's a #8 Barient winch on either side of the cabin top, each with an attendant cleat. Lines are meant to be kept in the no-name stoppers to starboard. Because of the profusion of lines led back on the starboard side, we'd prefer an extra cleat and winch.

Nonskid is molded in. The foredeck holds an anchor locker, which also contains a padeye for the stepping/unstepping operation. Skipping the details of this procedure—which involves use of a gin pole, the main and jib halyards and a bridle that controls lateral movement—we'd say that Hunter has devised as easy a way to drop a mast as is possible. Once

down, the forward end rests in a U-shaped bend in the bow pulpit, the aft end on a roller-topped pole fitted at the transom.

Conclusions

In its attempt to create a simply operated, easily trailered, entry-level boat at a good price, Hunter has come up with some clever compromises. But they are compromises just the same. The 23.5 sails well on all points in light air; it does well off the wind in heavier air. Windward work over 15 knots in this boat is poor in our estimation. We'd strongly recommend that potential customers thoroughly test sail the boat in a variety of wind conditions, experimenting with one or two reefs, to be certain it's something they're able—and willing—to handle.

The Hunter 23.5 is clearly striking a chord with some buyers, and assuming many are entry-level sailors, we think it's great that this boat is attracting newcomers to the sport. The design represents a clever way of managing the trailering problem (i.e., weight and draft). At the same time, we can't help but wonder if its behavior in gusty winds is worth the convenience of dumping ballast on the launch ramp. **• PS**

The Flicka

High-priced and truly unique, the Flicka has come close to reaching cult status.

The Pacific Seacraft Flicka has perhaps received more "press" in the last few years than any other sailboat, certainly more than any production boat her "size." Publicity does not necessarily make a boat good but it sure does create interest.

The Flicka is unique. There are no other production boats like her and only a few, such as the Falmouth Cutter and the Stone Horse, that offer the Flicka's combination of traditional (or quasi-traditional) styling and heavy displacement in a small cruising yacht.

As the number of Flickas built by Pacific Seacraft passed 300 plus an indeterminate number built by amateurs early in its history, the boat seems to have become almost a cult object. High priced, distinctive, relatively rare but with wide geographical distribution and easily recognized, the Flicka invariably attracts attention and seems to stimulate extraordinary pride of ownership, The owners we talked to in preparing this evaluation all seem to be articulate, savvy, and involved. Moreover, they all show an uncommon fondness for their boats.

The Flicka was designed by Bruce Bingham, who was known as an illustrator, especially for his popular Sailor's Sketchbook in *Sail*. Originally the Flicka was intended for amateur construction, the plans available from Bingham. She was designed to be a cruising boat within both the means and the level of skill of the builder who would start from scratch. Later the plans were picked up by a builder who produced the boat in kit form, a short lived operation, as was another attempt to produce the boat in ferro-cement.

Pacific Seacraft acquired the molds in 1978 and, with only minor changes, the boat as built by Seacraft remained the same until 1983, when a new deck

Specifications

LOA	23' 7"
LWL	18' 2"
Beam	8' 0"
Draft	3' 3"
Displacement	5,500 lbs.
Ballast	4,750 lbs.
Sail area, sq. ft.	250 sloop, 288 gaff

mold was tooled to replace the worn-out original. A number of the modifications made early in 1983 are described throughout this evaluation.

Seacraft is a modest sized builder which has specialized in heavier displacement boats. The first boat in the Seacraft line was a 25-footer, followed by the 31' Mariah, the Flicka, the Orion 27, and most recently the Crealock 37.

Seacraft has 22 dealers nationwide but concentrated on the coasts. Apparently the firm was able to survive the hard times that have befallen some if its brethren, giving credence to the axiom that to succeed a boatbuilder should produce an expensive boat to quality standards that appeals to a limited number of enthusiastic buyers.

The hull of the Flicka is "traditional" with slack

An airy cabin with 5' 11" headroom over its full length is a distinctive feature of the Flicka. It's still only a 20-footer, though—this photo was taken from the companionway sill.

bilges, a full keel, a sweeping shear accented with cove stripe and scrollwork, and bowsprit over a bobbed stem profile. In all, the Flicka is not an actual replica, but she does fulfill most sailors' idea of what a pocket-sized classic boat should look like whether or not they are turned on to that idea.

The new price of the Flicka in the early '80s ranged from about $13,000 for a basic kit for amateur completion to $36,000 for a "deluxe" version, with $25,000 a realistic figure for a well-appointed standard model. This was a high tab for a boat barely 18' long on the waterline, 20' on deck (LOD), and less than 24' overall with appendages. With that high priced package you got a roomy, heavy and well built boat that appealed to many sailors' dreams if not to their pocketbooks.

Construction

The Flicka *looks* well built even to an untrained eye. And to the trained eye that impression is not deceiving. This is a boat that should be fully capable of making offshore passages. The basic question any buyer must ask is whether he is willing to pay (in money and performance) for this capability for the far less rigorous cruising on Lake Mead or Chesapeake Bay, to Catalina Island, or up and down the New England coast.

The hull of the Flicka is a solid fiberglass laminate to a layup schedule adequate for most 30-footers of moderate displacement.

The deck has a plywood core rather than the balsa core common in production boats. In a boat of this displacement-length ratio the heavier plywood re-

duces stability but probably only marginally. Its virtue is that installation of add-on deck hardware is easier.

The hull-to-deck joint is done in a manner *PS* strongly advocates: the hull has an inward flange on which the deck molding fits, bonded with a semi-rigid polyurethane adhesive/sealant and through bolted with 1/4" stainless steel bolts on 4" centers. These bolts also secure the standard aluminum rail extrusion; on boats with the optional teak caprail in lieu of the aluminum, the bolts pass through the fiberglass, and the caprail is then fastened with self-tapping screws. As the rail sits atop a 1/2" riser, water cannot puddle at the joint. We have heard no reports of any hull-to-deck joint failure in a production Flicka.

The interior of the boat uses a molded hull liner that is tab bonded to the hull. Given the ruggedness of the hull laminate, we doubt if this stiffening adds much to the hull itself, but it does make the relatively thin laminate of the liner feel solid under foot.

One of the more serious questions we have about the engineering of the Flicka is the under-deck mast support. Reflecting the quest for a completely open interior, the design incorporates a fiberglass/wood composite beam under the cabin house roof which transfers the mast stresses through the house sides to the underdeck bulkheads. Apparently these bulkheads are not bonded to the hull itself, only to the liner.

The builder defends this construction, claiming that it will support over 8,000 lbs (more than the Flicka's displacement). In addition, beginning in 1983, a turned oak handhold post was added between the mast support beam and cabin sole, which further increases the strength of the mast support system.

Cabinetry, detailing, and finish are top quality for a production boat. However, keep in mind that the basic interior component is a fiberglass molding. Functionally the ease of keeping a molded liner clean has much to recommend it; aesthetically the sterility of the gelcoat may offend some tastes.

A few other specific construction details deserve note:

• The hardware on the Flicka is generally excellent, whether it is the standard or the optional cast bronze package, provided your taste allows for a mixture of traditional and modern. Since weight has not been a factor, most of the fittings are rugged, even massive. All through hull fittings are fitted with seacocks. Particularly impressive is the tabernacle mast step, a contrast with the flimsy sheet steel versions on cheaper boats. A notable exception to this endorsement are a pair of inadequate forward chocks.

• The scribed "planking seams" in the fiberglass topsides as well as the scrollwork are especially well done. However, any owner of a wood boat who has spent untold hours fairing topsides to get rid of real seams has to wonder at anyone's purposely delineating phony seams in fiberglass.

• There is a removable section of cockpit sole over the engine compartment that gives superb access for servicing the engine and permits its installation or removal without tearing up the interior. It is a feature many boats with under-cockpit engines should envy given the chronic inaccessibility of such installations. Access to the Flicka's engine from the cabin is no better than that on most boats even for routinely checking the oil level.

• External chainplates eliminate a common source of through-deck leaks but at the expense of exposing the chainplates to damage.

• There is good access to the underside of the deck and coaming for installation of deck hardware. The headliner in the cabin is zippered vinyl.

• Anyone with a modern boat with its vestigal bilge sump has to appreciate the Flicka's deep sump in the after end of the keel.

• The ballast (1,750 lbs of lead) is encapsulated in the molded hull, risking more structural damage in a hard grounding than exposed ballast but eliminating possible leaking around keel bolts.

Handling Under Sail

In an era that has brought sailors such hot little boats as the Moors 24, the Santa Cruz 27, and the J/24, any talk about the performance of a boat with three times their displacement-length ratio has to be in purely relative terms. In drifting conditions the Flicka simply has too much weight and too much wetted surface area to accelerate. Add some choppiness to the sea and she seems to take forever to get under way.

When the wind gets up to 10 knots or so, the Flicka begins to perk up, but then only if sea conditions remain moderate. With the wind rising above 10 or 12 knots the Flicka becomes an increasingly able sailer.

However, she is initially a very tender boat and is quick to assume a 15 degree angle of heel, in contrast to most lighter, shallower, flatter boats that carry less sail but accelerate out from under a puff before they heel.

For those who were wondering how it's possible to cram an enclosed head, full galley and berths into a 20-foot hull, here it is. The alternate interior extends the setee into the space occupied by the head.

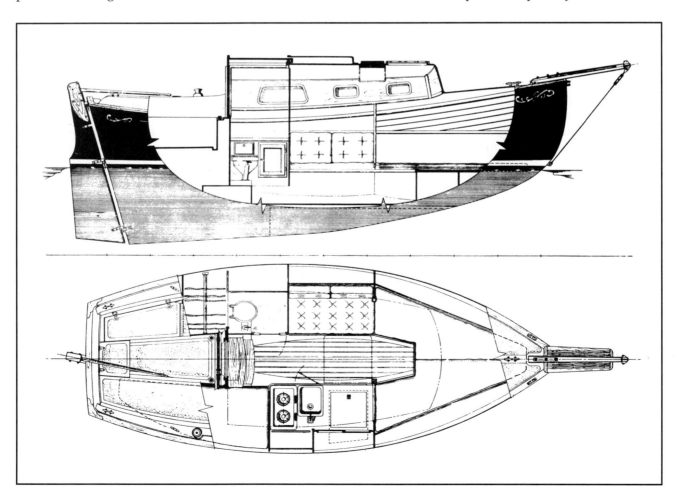

In winds over 15 knots the Flicka feels like much more boat than her short length would suggest. As she heels her stability increases reassuringly. Her movement through the water is firmer and she tracks remarkably well, a long lost virtue in an age of boats with fin keels and spade rudders, Owners unanimously applaud her ability to sail herself for long stretches even when they change her trim by going forward or below.

PS suggests those looking at—and reading about—the Flicka discount tales of fast passages. While it is certainly true that the boat is capable of good speed under optimum conditions, she is not a boat that should generate unduly optimistic expectations. In short, there may be a lot of reasons to own a Flicka, but speed is not one of them.

One mitigating factor is that performance consists not only of speed but also ease of handling, stability, steadiness, and even comfort. In this respect, the Flicka may not go fast but she should be pleasant enough to sail that getting there fast may not be important.

The Flicka comes with two alternative rigs, the standard masthead marconi sloop and the optional gaff-rigged cutter. Most of the boats have been sold as sloops. The gaff cutter is a more "shippy" looking rig, but for good reasons most modern sailors will forego a gaff mainsail.

If you regularly sail in windy or squally conditions, you might want to consider a staysail for the sloop rig. However, for a 20' boat an inventory of mainsail fitted with slab reefing, a working jib, and a genoa with 130% to 150% overlap should be adequate. For added performance the next sail to consider is a spinnaker and, if offshore passages are contemplated, a storm jib.

Handling Under Power

Any observations about handling under power raise the question of inboard versus outboard power. In fact, this may be the most crucial issue a potential Flicka owner faces. In making the decision, start with an observation: at a cruising displacement of over 5,000 lbs, the Flicka is at the upper limit for outboard auxiliary power. Then move to a second observation: small one-cylinder diesel engines such as the Yanmar and BMW fit readily into the Flicka, albeit at the expense of some valuable space under the cockpit sole.

Without going into all the pros and cons of one type of power versus another, we suggest installation of a diesel inboard either as original equipment or as soon after purchase as feasible. The Flicka is a boat that seems to beg for inboard power (most small boats do not); she has the space, and weight is not critical. Moreover, cost should not be critical either. Inboard power adds about 10% to the cost of the boat with outboard power, a small percentage of an expensive package. Much of the additional cost is apt to be recoverable at resale whereas the depreciation on an outboard in five years virtually amounts to its original value.

Deck Layout

Any discussion of the livability of the Flicka should be prefaced by a reminder that above decks this is a

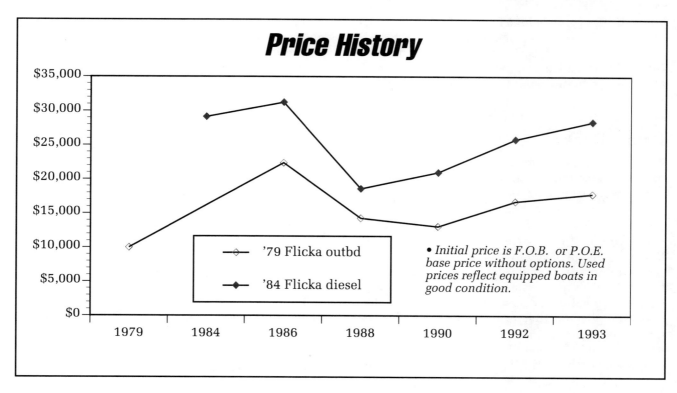

Price History

* Initial price is F.O.B. or P.O.E. base price without options. Used prices reflect equipped boats in good condition.

Legend: ◇ '79 Flicka outbd — ◆ '84 Flicka diesel

crowded, cluttered 20 footer and below decks this is a boat with the space of a 26 footer. The Flicka is a boat with enough space below for one couple to live aboard and yet small enough topside for them to handle easily.

Nowhere is the small size of the Flicka more apparent than on deck and in her cockpit. The short cockpit (a seat length of barely over 5', too short to stretch out for a nap), a high cabin house, sidedecks too narrow to walk on to windward with the boat heeled and always obstructed by shrouds, the awkwardness of a bowsprit, and lifelines that interfere with jib sheet winching are all indicative of the crowded deck plan.

The stern pulpit is an attractive option. However, it makes manual control of a transom-mounted outboard difficult. The pulpit incorporates the mainsheet traveler although the lead for close sheeting is poor. In 1983 an optional roller bearing traveler arrangement which spans the bridge was offered, and it provides a much better lead for close sheeting, at the expense of a certain amount of living space in the cockpit.

For outboard powered Flickas there is a lidded box that permits stowage of the fuel tank at the after end of the cockpit, a sensible and safe feature. For those owners who want propane and have inboard power, this same space fitted with a sealed box and through-transom vents would make a suitable place for gas bottles.

At the other end of the cockpit, the lack of a bridgedeck or high sill is, in our opinion, decidedly unseamanlike. The Flicka should have at least semi-permanent means of keeping water in a flooded cockpit from going below. One of the 1983 changes was the addition of a bridgedeck.

If we owned a Flicka we would run all halyards (plus a jib downhaul) aft to the cockpit on the cabin top. We would not rig a fixed staysail stay, and we would certainly not use a clubfooted staysail. The boom should have a permanent vang.

Below Decks

The builder has made every effort to keep the interior of the Flicka open and unobstructed from the companionway to the chain locker, a noble endeavor that gives an impression of spaciousness rivaling that of 30 footers. Headroom is 5' 11" for the length of the cabin (find that in another boat-shaped 20 footer!). Better yet, height is retained over the galley counter, the settee berth, and the after section of the vee berths. Flicka's high topsides permit outboard bookshelves and galley lockers, stowage under the deck over the vee berths, and headroom over the quarterberth.

Two notable features of the interior are conspicuous as soon as the initial impression wears off. There is no enclosed head in pre-1983 models, and there is no sleeping privacy. How important these factors are is purely a matter of individual taste and priorities. For a cruising couple a four-berth layout is a waste of space. The manufacturer, taking this into account, made space for the enclosed head offered in 1983 by shortening the starboard settee berth from 6' 5" down to 4' 2".

Incidentally, this observation about berths is not meant to imply any special deficiency in the Flicka. It is true of too many boats on the market. They are built for a boat buying public that seems to think the number of berths is almost as important as whether the boat will float.

The absence of an enclosed head in a small yacht of the proportions of a Flicka requires a conscious decision from any potential owner. The small space between the vee berths is designed to hold a self-contained head. A "privacy curtain" that slides across the cabin gives a modicum of respectability. Of course, its use is discouraged when anyone is sleeping forward. One owner solves this by lugging the head to the after end of the cockpit at night and encloses the cockpit with a tent, thus creating a privy or outhouse that boasts perfect ventilation. We hesitate to suggest his lugging it another few inches aft.

Less enterprising owners could consider installing a conventional marine toilet plus a holding tank under the vee berths. If sailing is done in waters where a through-hull fitting and diverter valve are permitted, then such a system is far more worthwhile than any self-contained system. Such a unit should make sharing your bed with the head as palatable as it will ever be.

Frankly, the lack of an enclosed head in a boat that otherwise can boast of being a miniature yacht is the most serious drawback to her interior, surplus berths notwithstanding.

Virtually every owner we talked with has added stowage space one way or another. Some have done it by removing the fiberglass bins that fit into the scuttles under the berths, others enlarge the shelves behind the settee berth and over the forward berths and others cut openings through the liner to give access to unused space.

Other modifications owners report having done include fitting the boat with a gimballed stove, adding fresh water tankage (20 gals standard), installing a third battery and/or moving them forward to help overcome a tendency for the Flicka to trim down by her stern, and fitting the cockpit with a companionway dodger.

One feature that does not seem to need any improvement is ventilation. The Flicka has an uncommonly airy interior, although we would add an opening port in the cockpit seat riser for the quarterberth. Her vertical after bulkhead means that a hatchboard can be left out for air without rain getting into the cabin.

Anyone considering the Flicka should ask Pacific Seacraft for a copy of the articles written by Bruce Bingham and Katy Burke on the changes they made to their *Sabrina* while living aboard and cruising extensively for more than two years

Conclusions

Buyers put off by the price of the Flicka should consider the fact that this is a 20' boat with the weight and space of a 26- to 28-footer of more modern proportions. That still may not put her high all-up price tag in crystal clear perspective. It shouldn't. The Flicka is still an extremely expensive boat. She still has a waterline length of merely 15', true accommodations for two, a too cozy cockpit, and a lot of sail area and rigging not found on more conventional contemporary boats. Nor does she have the performance to rival more modern designs. (One owner reports a PHRF rating for his Flicka of about 300 seconds per mile, a figure that drops her off the handicap scale of most base rating lists we've seen.)

At the same time the Flicka is a quality package that should take a singlehander or couple anywhere they might wish to sail her. There are not many production boats anywhere near her size and price that can make that claim.

The faults with the Flicka have to be weighed against her virtues as is the case with choosing any boat. Fortunately, though, her faults are the type that can be readily seen; they are not the invisible ones of structure, handling, or engineering so typical of other production boats. Similarly her virtues are traditional and time tested, She is built by a firm to whom the owners give high marks for interest and cooperation and the Flickas on the used boat market have maintained their value better than the average production boat. At the bottom line is a boat with much to recommend her. • **PS**

Com-Pac 23

She may be heavier and slower than some, but this miniature yacht has a strong following.

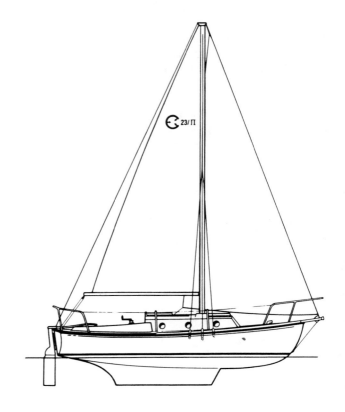

The Com-Pac 23 bucks all trends in modern pocket cruiser design. It's heavy. It's slow compared to modern, lighter, small boats. It's barely trailerable. And it's old-fashioned looking. So how has the Hutchins Company managed to sell hundreds of them?

The simple answer is owner loyalty. Like the followers of a backwoods preacher, Com-Pac owners have unquestionable faith in their boats. They "believe!" And if our boat owner surveys are any indication, every one of those owners is itching to spread the gospel.

It's a phenomenon we've seen in a number of traditional boat lines, like the Cape Dory. The builder designs a line of boats to a common theme or general appearance. In this case the motif is that of the miniature yacht. Then the builder constructs and prices the boats to a level that avoids the dreaded label of "economy" or "entry level."

Finally, after he's hooked a sailor who thinks his boat is "neat," he reinforces the image by lavishing the sailor with customer service. If all goes according to plan, that sailor becomes a "believer," who then buys successively larger models from the builder's line. The buyer is happy; the builder is happy, too.

Hutchins Company is a partnership between businessman Les Hutchins and boatbuilder Buc Thomas. The company was formed in 1974 to produce the Com-Pac 16. The 16 was inspired by the success of the Newport 16 and the Lapworth 16, and was designed for the Florida market. It was stable, sedate, had shoal draft and a big cockpit. While aimed at the elderly retiree, the Com-Pac 16 also became popular with young families.

Buc Thomas says the 16 became a "cult boat," with whole sailing clubs formed around the design. The 16's low freeboard, sweeping sheer, and boxy

Specifications

LOA	23' 11"
LWL	20' 2"
Beam	7' 10"
Draft	2' 3"
Displacement	3,000 lbs.
Ballast	1,340 lbs.
Sail area	250 sq. ft.

cabin became the Com-Pac "look." Says Thomas, "If you gave a kid a pencil and a piece of paper and asked him to draw a boat, he'd probably draw the Com-Pac 16." At the peak of the 16's production, Hutchins was shipping as many as 44 boats a month. All told, between 2,500 and 3,000 have been built.

In 1981, Hutchins decided to capitalize on those young families that had outgrown the Com-Pac 16. The 23 was introduced, followed by the 19, 27, and 14. A 33-footer was introduced in 1990. The 19 and the 27 are Bob Johnson designs (of Island Packet fame); all others are Clark Mills designs (of Windmill and Optimist Dinghy fame).

A new Com-Pac 23 retails in the mid-teens. That includes a set of working sails, but no outboard, trailer, or shipping. All-up the boat could easily top

$20,000. That still puts her price substantially above that of the economy trailer sailer of her size.

Hutchins breaks the price into four approximately equal categories: 1/4 for materials, 1/4 for labor, 1/4 for marketing and 1/4 for profit and overhead.

While a builder like MacGregor will save money on its trailer sailers by making every part of the boat "in house", Hutchins "farms out" much of its production. The hulls and decks are molded by an independent fiberglass shop. The spars are done by one fabricator, the rigging by another. Hutchins does make trailers for their smaller models, but the Com-Pac 23 uses a trailer from Magic Tilt.

Only the final assembly is done at the Hutchins plant. If it were not for the proliferation of boatbuilders in the Clearwater area, this extensive use of subcontractors could add substantially to the cost to the boat. Luckily, there are enough builders sharing subcontractors in the area to keep the price reasonable.

The Com-Pac 23 has undergone two design revisions. The original boat is now called the MK I. On the MK II version a bowsprit was added to balance the helm. The current version—the MK III—has a new deck mold with a more attractive cockpit coaming and halyards led aft.

Construction

Readers say they feel "safe" in their Com-Pac 23s, that the boat can take any kind of weather you can throw at it. Understand that most Com-Pac 23s are sailed on smaller lakes and other protected bodies of water. The boat is not poorly built, as are some of her cheaper competitors, but we would not call her overbuilt, either.

The hull is molded of solid fiberglass. The glass is a mixture of mat, roving, and bi-axial and tri-axial cloth. Instead of a molded interior pan, Hutchins uses a pieced-in interior of plywood. If done properly, a pieced-in interior can give the hull more rigidity, because each piece can be filleted and taped with fiberglass along the entire length of each joint. Molded pans are usually set in putty and only "spot" taped. Unfortunately, Hutchins doesn't take advantage of the structural opportunities of a pieced-in interior. The plywood is only taped on one side, and the taping is average at best, with no fillet.

The shroud tangs are bolted directly to the hull. The main interior bulkhead is cut away radically to make the interior more open. This leaves a bulkhead in two halves, without support directly under the deck-stepped mast. The bulkhead is only attached to the deck with several #10 screws, and is not taped to the hull for much of its length.

The deck is delivered to Hutchins in solid fiberglass. Hutchins then trowels a microballoon-type putty of silica beads onto horizontal deck surfaces.

This acts as a core to stiffen the deck. To finish exposed portions of the cabin overhead, an interior mold is sprayed with white gelcoat and pressed into the wet putty. The result is clean and attractive, scored to resemble a planked cabin overhead.

Because the core is a solid, non-compressible putty, simple washers with acorn nuts can be used to mount most deck hardware. The stanchion bases have backing plates.

The hull-to-deck joint is an outward turned flange, glued together with 3M 5200 and through-bolted. At one time Hutchins used pop rivets instead of bolts, because 5200 alone will provide a bond of adequate strength. Pop rivets made the customers uncomfortable, says Buc Thomas, so they switched to bolts. The exterior of the hull-to-deck flange is covered with a rubrail. The interior is made waterproof with a fillet of caulking.

The long, shallow, shoal draft keel uses internal ballast. Of an overall displacement of 3,000 pounds, 1,340 pounds are ballast. Approximately 50% of the ballast is in the form of lead pigs placed into the keel sump. The remainder is concrete poured over the lead to keep it in place.

All Com-Pacs are molded with the same gelcoat color scheme. Both hull and deck are white. The hulls also have a wide brown sheer stripe under the gunwale. This makes the sheer more attractive, but being brown, the gelcoat tends to get hot in sunlight and show more "print-through" with age. The nonskid on the deck is finished off in a pleasing, non-eye-straining, light brown color.

Fifteen percent of the reader surveys on the Com-Pac 23 report bottom blistering. Hutchins offers only a one-year warranty on blistering, which we consider inadequate, as blistering often takes several years to appear.

Rig

To some, the rig of the Com-Pac 23 may seem as traditional as the appearance of the boat; to us the rig seems rudimentary. The mast is untapered. The halyards are rope and led externally.

The spreaders are simple tubes in external sockets. This type of spreader arrangement would be asking for trouble on a more bendy mast. Fortunately, the boat is equipped with fore and aft lower shrouds. These two shrouds can be tuned to prevent the mast from bending.

All rigging is of adequate size—5/32" wire. All terminals are swaged. Open bodied turnbuckles are used. The mast is deck-stepped in a stainless steel tabernacle.

The boat is equipped with hardware that, if anything, is undersized—all too typical on trailer sailers and pocket cruisers. There is no boom vang or mainsheet traveler.

Most deck fittings are bedded with 5200, a polyurethane adhesive. A polysulfide sealant would be preferable, because it would be much easier to remove and replace the hardware with fittings of better quality. The hatches are properly bedded with silicone sealant.

Handling Under Sail

The Com-Pac 23 isn't fast, but she isn't a dog, either. With a PHRF rating of about 260, she is about 10 seconds a mile faster than a Catalina 22 and about 20 seconds a mile faster than an O'Day 22.

Com-Pac 23 owners say that the boat is at her best in moderate to heavy air, and is slowest compared to other boats when sailing downwind and in light air. One owner called her performance in those conditions "painfully slow;;" but most were pleased with her overall performance.

The shrouds, being mounted on the rail, dictate a wide sheeting angle. To reduce chafe of the headsail against the bow pulpit, the clew has to be cut high. Both of these contribute to the boat's lackluster upwind performance.

A 150% genoa would help light air speed, as would a spinnaker downwind. However, 85% of the Com-Pac 23s in our reader survey are only used for daysailing. Since there is no pressing need to cover a lot of ground on a daysail, the extra canvas is of questionable importance.

Owners of MK I Com-Pac 23s complain of excessive weather helm. The builder advises MK I owners to alter the kick-up rudder so that the rudder blade angles forward of vertical. This won't make the boat any faster—the helm will still need to be pulled off centerline in a strong breeze—but it will ease the load on the tiller. A bowsprit was added to the MK II version to balance the sailplan.

Owners also report that the Com-Pac 23 is initially tender, but then develops adequate stability with the crew sitting comfortably in the cockpit. The designer of the Com-Pac 23 gave her a long, shallow keel—about 8' long to be exact. He scaled the width of the keel to the length, so although it is a nice airfoil, it is at least a foot wide at its maximum thickness.

The boat might be a bit faster with a thinner keel and a higher lead-to-concrete ratio. The keel sump molding is quite fair, much better than the external iron or lead keel found on the typical economy boat of this size.

By contrast, the kick-up rudder of the Com-Pac 23 is a crude 3/8" aluminum plate, with square, unfinished edges. The rudder head is cast aluminum. The fit of the tiller, rudder and pintles is snug.

Owners say the boat needs either a boom vang or a mainsheet traveler to control twist in the mainsail and make sailing in a strong breeze easier.

A boom vang is much simpler to rig than a traveler, and can do the work of a traveler if tensioned properly when sailing upwind. The concept of using a vang for leech tension upwind is foreign to most sailors, but it does work, assuming the gooseneck can withstand the additional load.

Handling Under Power/Trailering

It's difficult to decide if the Com-Pac 23 is a trailer

A bowsprit was added to the Com-Pac 23 Mk II, which cured the weather helm of the Mk I version, and provided anchor storage normally found only on larger boats.

sailer or a pocket cruiser. At 3,000 pounds she is not easily trailered. You need a full-size truck or a large, eight-cylinder car to pull her. A Magic Tilt, double-axle galvanized trailer is available as a $2,400 option. Equipped with surge brakes and keel guides, it is designed as a float-off trailer. There is no lifting eye in the cabin sole; to launch her with a crane will take slings and a spreader frame.

The Com-Pac 23 could be trailered on a single-axle trailer, provided the trips were only of a few hours duration. A single axle makes the trailer easier to hand-maneuver in a parking lot. However, a double axle gives you a safer, steadier ride on long trips.

With her displacement and 2' 3" draft, you may need to fabricate a tongue extension to get her to float off the trailer at many launching ramps. We're not sure why her rudder is designed with a kick-up feature, because it doesn't extend below the keel when fully down.

For many owners the Com-Pac 23 is a pocket cruiser, not a trailer sailer. With her weight and fixed keel she is more seaworthy than many trailer sailers. Her ground tackle is stored on a bowsprit roller and in a chain locker in the forepeak. That really isn't necessary on a boat this small, but it's a nice feature nonetheless.

The outboard of choice for many of our readers with Com-Pac 23s is the Honda 7.5. There are two large cockpit lockers, each of which could easily hold the outboard for storage. There is open storage for a gasoline tank under the tiller; it includes a drip pan which drains overboard.

The boat is equipped with an Eez-In, fold-up outboard bracket. The afterdeck is only 6" wide, so it is just a short reach to the outboard controls. The mainsheet is a bridled purchase on the stern, which may chafe against the outboard when the motor is raised and kicked up.

On Deck

The cockpit of the Com-Pac 23 is 7' long. The tiller is long enough for easy steering, but not so long as to intrude on cockpit space. The seatbacks are high, but not angled outboard enough to be really comfortable.

Being part of the seatbacks, the cockpit coaming is also high. The height is needed to keep the cockpit dry, as the attractive sheer has left the Com-Pac 23 with relatively low freeboard. On the Mk III version the horizontal surface of the coaming has been angled downward. This makes the coaming more eye-pleasing, and allows the builder to mount the winches without angled base pads.

The jibsheet winches are single-speed Lewmar #6s. They would have to be upgraded if you added a 150% genoa. The jib sheets to Ronstan tracks and cars, the mainsail to a Ronstan swivel cleat on the stern. These fittings are somewhat undersize. Several owners report that they have replaced the mainsheet cleat with a Harken swivel base. This provides a constant cleating angle so you can trim and release the sheet without contortions.

A bilge pump is mounted in the cockpit, and pumps directly overboard. Should the pump clog or fail, there is no access to the sump through the cabin sole. Luckily, the sump is relatively deep for a boat of this size.

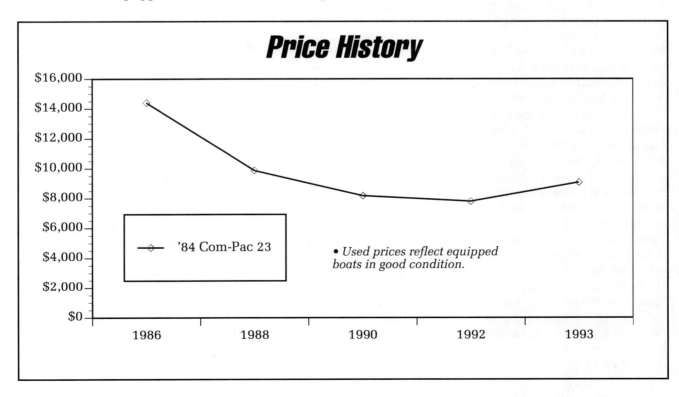

Price History

- Used prices reflect equipped boats in good condition.

Legend: ◇ '84 Com-Pac 23

The standard boat is equipped with a pulpit, pushpit, stanchions, and single lifelines. There have been a few owner complaints about stanchion bases breaking on older boats. Now the bases are reinforced with extra strapping above the base socket.

The cockpit has two large storage lockers. The locker hatches are fitted with good scuppers, so they shouldn't leak. However, the lockers are not sealed off from the rest of the boat, and the hatches have no hasps to lock them shut. Should the boat broach or capsize, the hatch could open and let water below, risking a sinking. Smaller Com-Pac models have built-in flotation; the 23 does not.

There is adequate deck space to walk forward without stepping on the cabin top. The cabin house is fitted with two sets of handrails.

The non-skid deck surface is adequate, but on the MK III the non-skid has been removed from the area around the cockpit coaming. The builder said this was done to satisfy their liability insurance. Apparently the insurance company thought that having non-skid in that area was inviting people to step where they shouldn't. Sounds dumb to us.

Belowdecks

We suspect that the interior is the Com-Pac 23's selling point. It is nothing like that of most boats its size. When you first go belowdecks, you think you've just stepped aboard a much larger boat, only everything is in miniature.

The interior is dark. All of the interior joinerwork is teak-faced plywood; there is no molded fiberglass interior. The sides of the cabin house are also finished in teak veneer. Only on close inspection do you notice that the joinerwork is average in quality.

There are several nice touches. The cabin overhead is finished with a molded white gelcoat, scored to resemble planking. The cabin sole is teak and holly. The hull sides are covered with white plastic, with teak battens fastened over the plastic.

Ventilation is very good. The six bronze opening ports can be fitted with screens. There is a Bomar forward hatch that can be set open at various angles—much nicer than the molded hatches found on the cheaper trailer sailers. Finally, there is a cowl vent over the foot of the V-berth.

The main bulkhead is cut away under the mast and under the sides of the cabin house. This provides some privacy without closing off the forward berth. It also offers support for the deck-stepped mast, while avoiding a compression post that would obstruct passage to the forward berth. A single cabin light is mounted on the bulkhead.

There is sitting headroom belowdecks for a 7-footer, but no standing headroom. The V-berth is 6' long and over 3' wide at the foot. The cushions are too thin for real comfort.

The quarterberths are narrow, because there are shelves and lockers outboard of the berths. This is a feature typically seen on a larger boat, but on the Com-Pac 23 it just serves to cramp the interior. It also means there are no padded seatbacks, so sitting belowdecks is uncomfortable.

There is a space for a portable head under the V-berth. We wouldn't want to sleep over one of those things, no matter how good the ventilation.

Under the lifting companionway step is storage for dinnerware, a 32-quart portable ice chest (not included) and the cabin table. Behind the ice chest there is a box for items not often needed.

The table is a simple, sturdy design. It is notched to drop in between the two halves of the main bulkhead. The leg is a single post that inserts into a socket on the table underside. There are no hinges to break. A child can set it up, and it doesn't wobble when assembled. Seating space at the small table is for two.

The galley is modeled after that used by the Catalina 22. The stove slides on tracks to store above the foot of the port quarterberth; the sink slides to store above the starboard quarterberth. An Origo 2000, fueled by alcohol, is the standard stove.

Several owners commented that the sink is so small it is practically useless. It trails hoses to a 13.5 gallon water tank, which has a deck fill. The sink drains into the bilge. If you're going to have a tank that big, you should also have a sink big enough to wash dishes and drain overboard.

There are many shelves and compartments, in fitting with the miniaturized big boat motif. Unfortunately, that doesn't leave any lockers, save the cockpit lockers, to store gear of substantial size.

Conclusions

The Com-Pac 23 is a good little boat. It has the lines and interior flavor of a much larger boat. Is she a trailer sailer or a pocket cruiser? We guess her owners think of her as a miniature yacht.

We can think of a lot of boats her size which are faster. We can think of boats which are better built. There are boats which are more trailerable, and there are boats which are less expensive. In short, there are a lot of boats out there that might be more practical for many sailors.

But we can't think of any boat her size with such an attractive traditional appearance or an interior that lets you pretend that you're going yachting instead of sailing. We admit that, being a miniaturized version of a larger boat, the interior is somewhat cramped. But who cares? If you want to impress your friends without taking a second mortgage on your house, we can think of no better way than with a Com-Pac 23. And who knows, your friend might become a "believer," too. **• PS**

Quickstep 24

This Ted Brewer design with the cutaway full keel might be the pocket cruiser you're looking for.

For a little boat that's been in serious production less than 10 years, the Quickstep 24 has a lot of history. It would be hard to guess from the Quickstep's classic lines that when Ted Brewer designed this daysailer/pocket cruiser in the late 70s, it was intended to be built as a production aluminum-hulled boat. That scheme didn't work (the aluminum plates would have required welding), so the design rights were sold to ocean racer Bill Stannard, who wanted a sturdy fiberglass coastal cruiser capable of making passages to Block Island and Nantucket.

Stannard, in turn, sold his rights in 1984, after just 23 boats had been made, to Gary Lannigan, who was marketing director at the time for C.E. Ryder in Bristol, Rhode Island, where the Quickstep hulls were being molded (and where Sea Sprite was built at the same time).

Though the designer might argue, the popular conception of a Brewer boat is a moderately conservative, traditional-looking craft with (almost) a full keel. The Quickstep fits this image, with an attractive, in this case, rounded stern and a full keel that features what fellow designer Bob Perry calls the "Brewer bite"—cutaways in the forefoot and just before the rudder. Brewer said his intention was to create something between a full keel and a fin keel/spade rudder, reducing wetted surface and enhancing turning ability.

The Quickstep is an unpretentious but extremely well put together little boat that's worth a second glance—if you're not captivated at first sight. One former owner (who moved up to a 35' Dickerson to live aboard) recalled it as a "very, very pretty boat" that often drew compliments.

The Lannigans estimate that Quickstep owners are split among small families who fit the boat,

Specifications

LOA	23' 11"
LWL	19' 0"
Beam	7' 11"
Draft	3' 4"
Displacement	4,000 lbs.
Ballast	1,900 lbs.
Sail area	259 sq. ft.

sailors who eventually will move up in size, and those who have owned larger boats but for some reason—age, difficulty in finding crew—are looking for something more manageable. Some use it primarily as a comfortable daysailer, others as a weekend, or week-long cruiser. Ted Brewer thinks it would make a good club or one-design racer. Annie Lannigan calls it a niche boat, but apparently it represents different niches for different folks.

Construction

The Quickstep has had a number of builders over the years, including C.E. Ryder, the Anchorage's Dyer Dinghy plant, where production eventually outstripped capacity, and Shannon Boat Co., where owner Walter Schulz modified the laminate, replac-

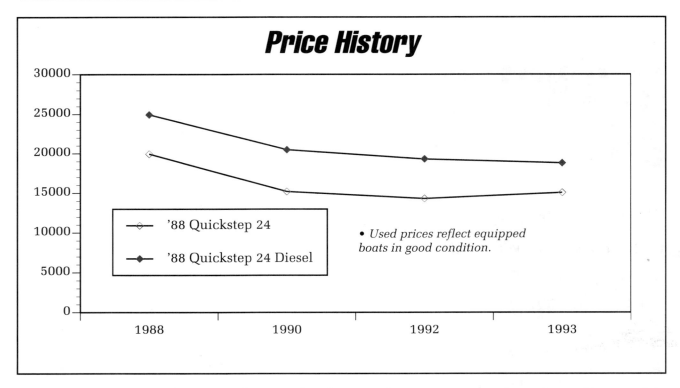

Price History

- '88 Quickstep 24
- '88 Quickstep 24 Diesel

• *Used prices reflect equipped boats in good condition.*

ing the woven roving with 1808 unidirectional and 1805 biaxial rovings. These are also used to beef up critical points, such as the stem and leading edge of the keel. A layer of vinylester resin, for blister protection, is added below the waterline (Quickstep reports no blistering problems with any of its hulls to date).

The isophthalic gelcoat has a thickness of 22 mils, about right for a cruising sailboat, Schulz said, but considerably thicker than that of many of today's production boats. This is especially important because most Quickstep buyers choose dark hulls where "print through" is more noticeable. (The standard hull is white.)

The deck is balsa-cored in the flat areas with molded-in nonskid; Shultz replaced the Coremat on the trunk sides with Tigercore. The hull-to-deck joint is a standard inboard flange, fastened with 3M 5200 sealant, #14 stainless steel screws on 8" centers and 1/4" stainless bolts on 8" centers. The keel is 1,900 pounds of cast lead, internally bonded, which gives the 24 a 47.5% ballast to displacement ratio.

Overall, the boat conveys the look and feel of solidity, secure but not overbuilt.

Rig

The standard rig for the 24 is a 27' 6" anodized aluminum DM 500 mast from Dwyer Aluminum Mast in Branford, Connecticut. The mast is deck-stepped in a hinged aluminum pulpit. The rigging is 3/16" wire for the headstay, backstay and uppers; the lower shrouds are 5/32" stainless. The deck hardware is adequately sized with Lewmar #8 jib sheet winches, up one size from the earliest models. (Lewmar also supplies the four opening ports and smoked forward hatch.) Jib sheet leads are well-positioned.

The Quickstep is set up for shorthanded sailing, with all running rigging leading back to the cockpit. Adding the optional Quick Reef and Quickshute (a flat-cut cross between a drifter and a cruising spinnaker) systems makes things even easier for singlehanding. The only inconvenience—and a slight one at that—is the mainsheet tackle arrangement which sheets to starboard rather than at the centerline. The reason, presumably, is to stay clear of the outboard, which is mounted in a well before the transom.

Performance Under Sail

Despite its 4,000 pounds of displacement, sturdy hull and full keel, the 24 is surprisingly agile and peppy—maybe it's the Brewer Bite. While no rocket, the Quickstep is PHRF-rated at 25 or more seconds faster per mile than the Sea Sprite 23, and also beats the Compac 23 and Cape Dory 25. In contrast, it's rated slightly slower than an Irwin 24, or a Catalina 25.

With 259 square feet of sail, well balanced between main and foretriangle, the boat is moderately powered with a smooth, easy helm. Sailmaker Steve Thurston, who supplies some sails (Hood does most for the 24), said the Quickstep performs best with a 130—135% jib, possibly 150% for lighter air grounds, such as Long Island Sound. The Lannigans recommend 110s for most of their customers.

The 24 tacks easily, with just a hint of pausing but no stalling enroute, and quickly regains speed. On a July day with light and variable winds (and one brief thunderhead), Quickstep hull #139, *Blue Moon* out of Bristol, sailed better than 5 knots to windward (with a single-reefed main and 110% roller-furled jib), and 6.2 knots on a beam reach in fairly flat waters in upper Narragansett Bay, according to the on-board knotmeter. As a fairly stiff boat, we'd expect—and owners confirm—the 24 to perform well in heavier air, too. The slowest point of sail, this day, was the dead run.

The Quickstep comes without power, but the builder recommends either a Yamaha 8-hp outboard or Yanmar 1 GM diesel. Unless you really prefer diesel or plan extended cruising, it doesn't seem necessary. *Blue Moon* moved along steadily, albeit in calm water, powered by a Mariner 9. The fuel locker to starboard is designed to hold a six-gallon gasoline tank. The only drawback is the drag created by an outboard and the open well, but it's doubtful that's more than a three-blade prop would cause, and Quickstep claims removing the motor improves speed by just 1/10 of a knot. The centerline position of the motor makes for easier handling than a transom-mounted outboard off to one side, and the arm can be swung in concert with the tiller for more emphasis during a turn.

On Deck

Topsides, Brewer has created extra elbow room (7' 4") in the cockpit by moving the house fairly far forward. There's easily room for four adults, without one being the odd person out. Schulz credits Brewer with drawing a freeboard that's as close to the action (just over 2') as a small boat should be (while minimizing windage and instability), but not so close that the crew get soaked. Teak coamings help keep the cockpit dry and add to a sense of security—especially, we imagine, for families with small children. Brewer has kept the cabin trunk to a reasonable height, so sightlines over the bow are clear.

The cockpit is clean and easy to move about in, and gaining the foredeck is a straightforward operation. Teak handrails on the cabin top and teak toerails all around make the trip easier. A stainless bow pulpit is standard. There's also a stainless stemhead fitting. Chainplates are stainless and the bow and stern cleats and chocks are Marinium.

The Quickstep is equipped with a Bosworth Guzzler 500 hand bilge pump, accessible through an aft port locker. Earlier Quicksteps provided a second cockpit locker in place of the port berth. *Blue Moon's* owner did the same thing as an option and it's an arrangement we liked even if it meant surrendering a quarter berth.

Belowdecks

Down below, Brewer once again did not overdo things, creating a pleasantly bright and open cabin without any pretension to standing headroom. There's just enough wood trim (the cabin sole is teak and holly) here and there to create a yachty feeling. The four ports, with screens, provide plenty of light.

The forward position of the cabin allows some extra headroom at the entrance to the V-berths where adults will want to sleep. The quarter berth is a tight squeeze—best left to children. All cushions are fabric covered and 4" thick. *Blue Moon's* throwback to the original three-berth arrangment creates a small, handy seat just inside the companionway. The owner also lined the cabin ceiling with ash, another option, which added to the warm feeling below.

Between the open cabin and the forward berths, to port and starboard respectively, are an icebox and a stainless galley sink with water from a 20-gallon tank, all standard. The sink discharges overboard, the ice chest into the bilge. Quickstep now offers to put a portable cooler positioned just inside the companionway—a good idea because the single step down is a bit of a stretch. This frees up space for extra storage at the head of the port berth. Or, you can use the room to install a small stove, an option that goes a long way to converting a day sailor to a cruiser. The Quickstep has a neat table, which can be set into a socket either belowdecks or up in the cockpit and stored away when not in use.

There's a hinged head compartment before the V-berths, just forward of the compression posts, for either a portable or installed marine toilet. The lack of privacy, not unusual on smaller boats, may be a deterrent. There is a forward anchor line locker and more storage aft, under the berths and sink, although the extra sail locker gained by the three-berth arrangement would be handy for stashing larger items.

Conclusions

The Quickstep 24 is a stable alternative to some of the lighter, shoal draft production boats in today's market (draft is just 3' 41/2"). It's a good-looking boat that handles as well as it looks. The Quickstep is fine as it comes standard from the factory but, as a semi-custom boat, can be individualized (higher toe rails, bronze hardware, etc.) without much ado. • **PS**

The J/24

The right boat at the right time, the J/24 has proven to be a wildly successful one-design racer.

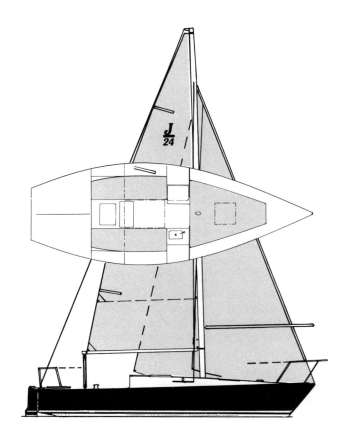

The J/24 is one of those boats that happened along at just the right time, with the right marketing to a ready market. Some may wonder whether the tale of her success would make a better textbook or a better storybook. Either way, much of the marine industry has studied her story, and then flattered her with the praise of emulation. However, no imitation or variation of the J/24 has yet to achieve her popularity.

Since her humble beginnings in 1976 in the garage of an amateur designer, thousands of boats have been sold from factories in Rhode Island, California, Australia, Japan, Italy, England, France, Brazil and Argentina. All of the builders are licensed by a company called J-Boats to build the J/24 to strict one-design tolerances. J-Boats is owned and run by two brothers—Bob and Rod Johnstone (the J in J-Boats). Bob is the marketing whiz and Rod is the designer. Conservative estimates put their total revenue from the J/24, after buying the boats from the builders and selling them to the dealers, at several million dollars. Not bad considering how it all began....

Ragtime was a 24' inspiration evolved by Rod Johnstone and his family in their garage as a two-year weekend project. Rod was a salesman for a marine publication, and an avid racer with a successful background in high-performance one designs. He had undertaken, but never completed, the Westlawn home-study course in naval architecture (although he has since been awarded an honorary degree so the school could use his name in its advertisements). *Ragtime* was launched in 1976, and was an instant winner, taking 17 firsts in 19 starts in eastern Connecticut. People began asking for their own boats.

At this time, brother Bob, also a respected racer, was working in the marketing department of AMF Alcort (Sunfish, Paceship, etc.). When Alcort de-

Specifications

LOA	24' 0"
LWL	19' 5"
Beam	8' 11"
Draft	4' 0"
Displacement	3,100 lbs.
Ballast	950 lbs.
Sail area	261 sq. ft.

clined to produce the J/24, Bob quit and formed J-Boats. Tillotson-Pearson, builder of the Etchells 22 and the Freedom line of boats, was more receptive and production began in 1977. The first J/24s were as fast as *Ragtime*, and dominated regattas like the 1977 MORC Internationals. Bob made sure that the favorable results were well publicized; more than 200 boats were sold that year, and nearly 1,000 the next.

It was a big hit for a number of reasons. She moved into a void, appealing to two groups of sailors who were ripe for her type of racing: those who had outgrown athletic small boats, yet still yearned for the competition of one-design racing, and those who wished to compete without the expense, hassles and uncertainties of handicap racing.

The J/24 is a one design's one design. Like the

Laser, Windsurfer, and Hobie Cat, she is proprietary-built under the supervision of one company. Unlike most proprietary one designs, sails are not provided by the J/24's builder. This was a particularly astute move by the Johnstones as it involved sailmakers in the class. Sailmakers comprise many of the big names in racing; by getting them in the regatta results, the Johnstones added instant credibility to the J/24's budding status as a "hot" class. By the midwinter championship in 1979, almost every boat in the top 15 finishers had a sailmaker on board.

The big advantage that proprietary one designs have over "independent" one designs (classes with competing builders) is the power of centralized, big-bucks promotion. J-Boats has organized and promoted regattas, and had a heavy hand in running the class association. J/24s got a lot of press, thanks to J-Boats. Full color, multi-page advertisements appeared monthly in the slick sailing magazines. Promotion has been primary; money is no object. J/24s have been donated for several high visibility USYRU championships. Big discounts have been given for fleet purchases (sometimes to effectively crush interest in competing one designs).

With the help of British enthusiasts, the Johnstones were able to make the J/24 an IYRU (International Yacht Racing Union) recognized class. More international lobbying got the J/24 into the Pan American Games.

There are some disadvantages to proprietary one designs. First, the class is in a real bind if the builder goes bankrupt. Likewise if the builder should ever abuse his power by ignoring class administration or changing construction of the boat to suit economic demands. Although a proprietary builder faces competition from other types of boats, there is no competition building *his* boat. This can inflate the price, especially when there are three substantial markups in the pricing structure (builder, J-Boats, and the dealer).

Construction

The J/24 has the distinct advantage of having been produced in great numbers and been subjected to the rigors of hard racing. It's safe to say that nearly everything that could have broken, has broken, and that the J/24 is now almost bulletproof. J-Boats has done a commendable job in correcting nearly all of the "bugs" in the J/24. However, if you are planning to purchase a boat several years old you should be watchful for some of the old bugs.

Boats built during the first two years of production had particular problems with leaking along the hull-to-deck joint, delamination of the main bulkhead, and the attachment of the keel to the hull. The hull-to-deck leak was due to failure of the silicone sealant in the joint.

The inward-turning hull flange is overlapped by the deck, which is bedded in sealant and through-bolted at close intervals through a teak toe rail. Now this joint is bedded with 3M 5200, a pliable strong adhesive, and leaks are infrequent. Fortunately, the internal side of the joint is exposed throughout the boat's interior, so recaulking is not difficult.

Harder to rectify is the problem of delamination of the main bulkhead. J/24s are raced hard, often with substantial rig tension. The chainplates pierce the deck and are bolted to the main bulkhead. The plywood bulkhead is tabbed with fiberglass to the hull and deck. The mast is stepped through the deck and sits on an aluminum beam, which is also tabbed to the main bulkhead. Rig tension pulls upward on the bulkhead while mast compression pushes downward on the beam, resulting in tremendous shearing forces on the bulkhead and its tabbing.

On some of the older J/24s, the plywood has delaminated, letting the mast "sink" 1/4 inch or more. Owners of these boats have either returned them to the factory for replacement of the bulkhead, or ground off the delamination and reglassed the bulkhead themselves. The builder now uses a better grade of plywood and installs screws to reinforce the bulkhead tabbing. As an added precaution, the boat owner may wish to bolt the mast-bearing beam to the bulkhead with an angle-iron.

The third problem with some of the older J/24s is the keel-to-hull attachment. The builder used to fill the keel sump with a vermiculite mixture of resin and plant fiber. The keel bolts were fastened through the vermiculite which, when saturated with water, is less rigid than solid laminations of fiberglass. After several years of sailing, or a hard grounding, the keel bolts would begin to work, and the keel would loosen enough to be able to be wobbled by hand with the boat suspended from a hoist. The first sign of this problem is the appearance of a crack along the keel stub. Tightening of the keel bolts, which are quality stainless steel, is a simple but temporary fix. What is needed is a backing plate for the bolts, bedded on top of the vermiculite.

There was a variety of other problems with early J/24s: The mast has three internal halyards; two jib halyards exit below the headstay with the spinnaker halyard above. On the older boats, a large square hole was cut in the mast to accommodate the sheaves, leaving an open, poorly supported space adjacent to the spinnaker sheave. This is sometimes the source of mast cracks; the fix is to weld a plate over it.

In January of 1980, the J/24 got much-improved companionway and forward hatches. The hatches on older boats were molded of thin fiberglass, and had a tendency to leak and fracture under the weight of heavy crew members. The new forward hatches are lexan, and the companionway hatch is now much heavier with a lower profile.

The J/24's rudder is heavy and strong. The builder claims you can hang a 900 pound keel from the rudder tip without breaking it. Although the J/24's rudder pintles appear more than adequate, after several years of use they have been known to develop corrosion cracks where the pintle is welded to its strap. In 1981, the builder began equipping J/24s with weldless pintles; the builder also offers the new system as a replacement for old boats.

The starboard chainplate bolts through both the bulkhead and the hull liner. The port chainplate bolts through only the bulkhead. After the first two years of production, the port bulkhead was reinforced with fiberglass in the chainplate area. On earlier boats, a backing plate should be added to prevent the chainplate bolts from elongating their holes.

The hull and deck of the J/24 are cored with balsa, which makes them stiff, light, quiet and relatively condensation-free. We have heard of occasional delaminations resulting from trailering with improperly adjusted poppets.

There's no real cabin house, and no ports on a J/24. Hence there's little headroom. The sliding hatch and forward hatch are translucent, and let in a fair amount of light.

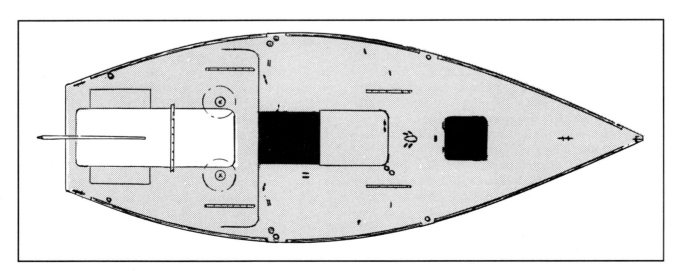

The Kenyon mast section is the same as that used on the Etchells 22, a bigger boat. It is more than adequate for any strength of wind.

The J/24 does not have positive flotation, and she has been known to capsize in severe conditions. This is usually not a problem as she floats on her side with the companionway well out of the water. However, should the leeward cockpit locker fall open, water can rush below, filling the cabin and causing her to sink. While fastening the lockers in heavy weather prevents the problem, the manufacturer began to seal off the lockers from the cabin with an additional bulkhead several years ago, as a safety measure.

Of the 2,500 J/24s sold in the US, nearly 2,000 of them have been built by Tillotson-Pearson in Rhode Island. The others were built by Performance Sailcraft in San Francisco, which is now defunct. New boats are now shipped cross country. Top west coast sailors tell us they favor the east coast built boats, claiming the keels and rudders on the west coast built boats are too thick to be competitive. The west coast keels are thick because they are covered with injection-molded gelcoat. Tillotson-Pearson fairs the keels with auto body putty.

Handling Under Sail

The J/24's PHRF rating ranges from 165 to 174, depending on the handicapper. She rates as fast as or faster than a C&C 30, Santana 30, or Pearson 30. One must remember that, because the J/24 has attracted competent owners, her PHRF rating is probably somewhat inflated. While the J/24 is an excellent training boat because she is so responsive, a begin-

ning racer may have an especially hard time making her perform to her PHRF rating.

Aside from her speed, the J/24's greatest asset is her maneuverability. With her stern hung rudder she can be turned in her own length, sculled out to a mooring in light air, and brought to a screeching halt by jamming the rudder over 90 degrees.

The J/24 has a narrow "groove;" it takes a lot of concentration to keep her going at top speed. She is sensitive to backstay trim, sheet tension, weight placement and lower shroud tension. The lower shrouds act like running backstays, because they are anchored aft of the mast. They must be loosened in light air to create some headstay sag, and then tightened in heavy air to straighten the mast, making backstay tension more effective in removing the sag.

Sheet tension is also critical. Top crews rarely cleat the genoa sheets, having one crewmember hold the tail while hiking from the rail. Some of the best sailors even lead the jib to the weather winch so the sail can be trimmed without sending crew weight to leeward.

The class rules allow you to race with a mainsail, a 150% genoa, a working jib and a single spinnaker. This makes sail selection simple and the inventory affordable (about $2,600 total). However, the one genoa must carry the boat all the way from a flat calm up to 20 knots or more. To be competitive in light air, the genoa must be full; yet to hold the boat level with this full genoa in a strong breeze, you need a lot of crew weight. Most of the top crews are now sailing with five people on board for a total crew weight of 800 to 900 pounds. The J/24 is a small boat, and the

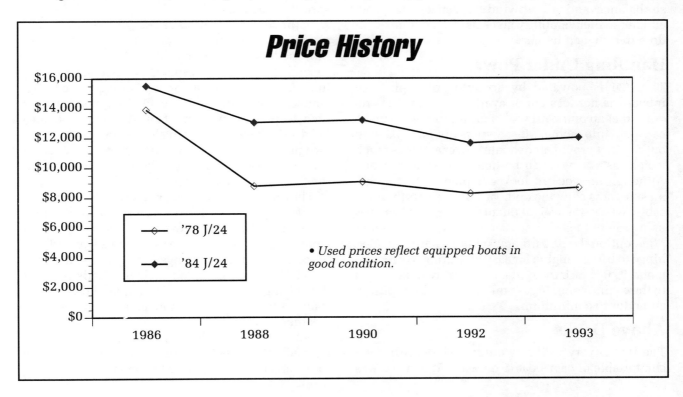

• Used prices reflect equipped boats in good condition.

additional fifth crew member really makes the boat cramped. Add to this the increasing trend of some skippers making the crew sit in the cabin on the leeward bunk in light air, and you have a boat which can be less than fun to crew on.

There are two worthwhile improvements that can help a J/24's performance. To decrease the boat's slight tendency toward a lee helm in light air, the mast should be cut to minimum length allowed in the class rules, and the headstay should be lengthened to the maximum allowed to give the mast more rake. The other improvement is fairing the keel to minimum dimensions. The keel is much thicker than is necessary for optimum performance. It comes relatively fair from the builder, but most owners will want to grind off the builder's auto-body filler and sharpen the trailing edge. On some of the older boats, the trailing edge is twice the minimum thickness. Some racers go so far as to spend $500-$1,000 to have the keel professionally faired.

While all indications are that the builder has excellent quality control, there have been complaints that some of the spars provided by Kenyon in the last two years have come with the wrong length shrouds, or widely differing bend characteristics. One top sailor said he would never buy a used J/24 without first making sure that he could make the mast to stand straight sideways with substantial shroud tension.

The J/24 is best suited for racing; there are many boats in her size range that are far more comfortable and practical for daysailing. However, the J/24 is a joy to sail under mainsail alone. Unlike most boats, she balances and sails upwind at a respectable speed, and her maneuverability gives her tremendous freedom in crowded harbors.

Handling Under Power

The J/24 is powered by an outboard engine; an inboard is not feasible or available. Class rules require that an outboard with a minimum of 3.5 hp be carried while racing. Most owners opt for a 3.5-4 hp outboard. It provides adequate power and is as much weight as you want to be hefting over a transom. Although the cockpit locker is plenty big enough, most owners stow the outboard under a berth in the cabin to keep the weight out of the stern. This makes using the outboard inconvenient. The factory-supplied optional outboard bracket has a spring-loaded hinge to lift the engine for easy mounting; we recommend it. Because the outboard is likely to be stored in the cabin, a remote gas tank will keep fuel spillage and odor to a minimum.

Above Decks

The J/24 is very well laid out, yet she is still not a comfortable or easy boat to crew on. When she was first launched, sailors said her layout could be no better, and she was copied by manufacturers of competing boats. However, after years of racing, sailors have discovered several things that could be improved.

Cockpit winches are located just forward of the mainsheet traveler, which spans the middle of the cockpit. Many sailors have moved the winches forward, so the crewmember tacking the genoa can face forward instead of aft during a tack.

The standard mainsheet cleat is attached to the traveler car so that, when you trim the sheet, you inadvertently pull the car to weather. Many sailors have solved this by mounting a fixed cleat with a swivel base at the center of the traveler bar.

On older boats the backstay was single-ended at the transom. Boats now come with a double-ended backstay led forward to the helmsman on each side of the cockpit. Foot blocks need to be mounted on the traveler to keep helmsmen from falling to leeward as the boat heels (you must steer from forward and well outboard of the traveler).

For those who plan to try cross-sheeting to the weather winch, leading the jib sheets through Harken ratchet blocks is advised. Most sailors will also want to mount barber haulers to pull the genoa sheet outboard in strong winds. Cam cleats for the barber haulers should be mounted on the companionway so they "self-cleat" when led to the weather winch.

Cabin-top winches for the halyards and spinnaker guys are optional and essential. Because the J/24 has single spinnaker sheets, most sailors mount "twings," which pull the guy down to the deck outboard of the shrouds when reaching.

In the search for a cleaner deck, it is now common to mount the spinnaker halyard cleat on the mast. Most sailors use only one jib halyard. Although a second jib halyard is optional, it is necessary only for long distance handicap racing. On short one design courses it is better to struggle along overpowered than to place crew weight on the bow to change headsails. Instruments are also unnecessary in one design racing. There are more than enough boats on a one design race course to judge your speed without the help of a speedometer.

The J/24 comes equipped with a Headfoil II grooved headstay system, which works very smoothly. Early boats came with Stern Twinstays, which have occasionally failed when the bearings freeze up with age. Some sailors have exchanged the grooved headstay system for cloth snaps on their headsails (you seldom change sails anyway). We applaud this idea, as it makes the sails all the more manageable in severe weather.

Although the flat decks are well suited for racing, the cockpit is less than comfortable for daysailing. There are no seat backs and the boom is dangerously low. Visibility with the deck-sweeping 150% genoa is terrible, and is often the cause of nightmarish collisions on crowded race courses. Lower life lines are optional and recommended for those who sail with children, but they interfere with fast tacks when racing.

The boom is rigged with a 4-to-1 vang, which is swiveled on the more recent J/24s to be adjustable from either rail on a windy spinnaker reach. The boom is also rigged with reef lines which exit through stoppers at the gooseneck.

Top sailors have discovered that the boat always sails better without a reef, which is a good thing, because the stoppers are both difficult to operate and have a history of slipping.

Below Decks

The interior is simple and functional. On most boats it is used for little more than sail storage. However, for a couple who enjoys roughing it, it could make for occasional weekend cruising. The first thing you notice when you go below is the lack of headroom. You can sit in comfort, but to move about you must crawl.

The interior is finished off in bare white gelcoat. Early boats had coarse, non-skid gelcoat on the overhead. While this may have been more attractive than smooth gelcoat, it really did a number on elbows and bald heads. It also tended to collect dirt and mildew. Earlier through-bolted deck fittings were capped with acorn nuts. Now the nuts lie flush with the overhead and induce far less pain when bumped.

A molded hull liner is used to form the two quarter berths, the cabin sole, and two lockers and a galley just aft of the main bulkhead. One locker is deep enough to serve as a wet locker for foul weather gear; the other is best used to store the rudiments of a meal. The galley consists of a sink with a hand pump. A small, two burner stove could be mounted in the small, removable "table" forward of the port quarter berth. The icebox, a large portable cooler made by Igloo, has a piece of teak glued to it and doubles as a companionway step. After a season or two of jumping on the ice chest, tack after tack, the lid disintegrates.

The forward V-berth, although divided by the mast, is still large and comfortable enough for a couple. The boat does not come equipped with a head. To avoid the extra drag of a through-hull fitting, portable heads are often used. We would rather use a cedar bucket—there simply isn't enough space in the cabin of a J/24 to cohabitate with a portable head. If you plan to seriously race, you won't want to load the boat's lockers with cruising equipment. If you do cruise, it will probably be out of a duffel bag.

J/24: How Trailerable?

The J/24 is not launchable from a boat ramp, unless the ramp is steep, paved or of hard sand, and you use a long extender between the tongue of the trailer and your trailer hitch. Her 3,100 pounds (fully loaded) require a big, 8-cylinder vehicle to tow her. She is easily launched from a 2-ton hoist which can attach to a strap on her keel bolts. However, the main hatch slides just far enough forward to allow the hoisting cable to clear it, so the hatch tends to get chewed by the cable.

The J/24 was originally designed to sail at a displacement of 2,800 pounds. The class minimum was later increased to 3,100. The original single axle trailer provide as a factory option was barely adequate for the intended, 2,800 pound boat, and totally inadequate for a fully loaded boat. Tales abound of blown tires and broken trailer welds. The factory now offers both a single and double axle trailer; we recommend the double axle.

If you want to seriously race a J/24, trailering is a necessity. Local fleets grow and shrink each year with the whims of their members, but national and regional regattas continue to attract many participants. Make no mistake, however; trailering is expensive. The owning and maintenance of a big car, the gas and tolls of trailering, and the housing of crew are not cheap.

Conclusions

The appeal of the J/24 is as a racer. If you plan to do anything else, she is not for you. Although the J/24 is relatively easy to sail, she is very difficult to sail well. To many people, she represents a chance to compete in the big leagues; by traveling to major regattas you can sail against some of the best sailors in the country. However, the big leagues are tough—if you like to race with a pick-up crew and a hangover you'd also better be satisfied with finishing last.

One appeal of the J/24 is that, unlike many big league boats, you can always come home and sail because the boat has so big a following. There are enough boats to race it one-design almost anywhere; and in a pinch, there is always handicap racing. As long as you don't want to travel, the boat is inexpensive to maintain.

Despite our effort to highlight every flaw that has appeared throughout the J/24's evolution, we'd like to emphasize that she is more hardy than most boats of her type. Few boats can take the punishment that a J/24 gets during a season of racing and come through with so few scars. No racing boat will appreciate; but the J/24 can keep her value.

The dream boat with the fairy tale success story has turned out, after all, to be a rugged winner in the real world. **• PS**

San Juan 24

A fast Quarter-Tonner that can still compete in PHRF, but numerous problems with quality deter us.

In the late 1960s and early 1970s, the Clark Boat Co. jumped on the trailer sailer bandwagon, and became a successful player in this decade-long market. Earlier, Bob and Carol Clark built Lightnings and Thistles, and later, with the business in the hands of their son Don, the company built boats as large as 34 feet. The last boats came out of the shop in 1986, the year the company went out of business.

While the San Juan 21 trailer sailer really established the Clark Boat Co., it was the more performance-oriented boats such as the San Juan 24 and 7.7 that gave it the reputation of a successful builder of faster, under-30-foot boats.

The Design

The San Juan 24 was designed by Canadian Bruce Kirby. Writing in the June 1977 issue of *Boating* magazine, Kirby said his directive from the Clarks was to produce a boat with eight-foot beam (for legal trailering), draw no more than four feet, and rate 18.0 under the IOR (International Offshore Rule) so it could qualify for Quarter Ton events. Because the San Juan 21 had developed a large class association, it also was hoped the 24 could be raced as a one-design. The Mark II version, introduced presumably in 1977, gave the boat a slightly longer waterline and higher (or more honest) displacement, as well as a few other minor changes.

Kirby wrote that the San Juan 24 was both a good racer and cruiser "...partly because my lack of familiarity with the IOR at the time the boat was designed (in the fall of 1971) kept me away from attempts at 'over optimization' through use of awkward bumps and hollows, and also steered me clear of the very low ballast ratios designers are using today to achieve minimum CGF (Center of Gravity Factor) under the IOR."

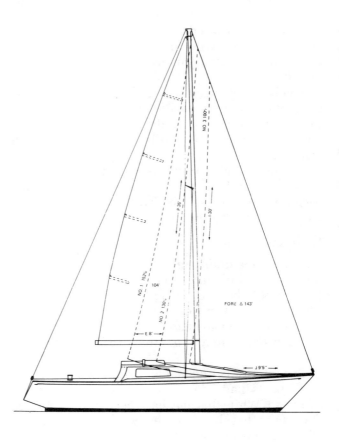

Specifications

LOA	24' 1"
LWL	19' 6"
Beam	8' 0"
Draft	4' 0"
Displacement	3,900 lbs.
Ballast	1,600 lbs.
Sail area	231 sq. ft.

He also noted his initial regret that he had to limit beam to eight feet (more beam would have allowed adding to sailing length), but said it turned out to be a good decision as the boat was enjoying good success. In hindsight, we wonder how many people want to trailer a 3,500-pound boat with a fixed, four-foot keel. Trailering boats has gone the way of the V-8 automobile engine. Sure, a percentage of racers are willing to make the investment in an expensive tow vehicle and trailer in order to compete in regattas around the country, but for most people, it's simply too much hassle.

Boats designed to the IOR were fated to near extinction as racers became more and more disenchanted with the funny bumps and how quickly a design became obsolete. The astounding success of

Owners' Comments

"Had to repair delaminations in the cockpit, deck, cabin roof and main bulkhead. Pulpit fittings are weak. Had blisters on hull. Got it recoated with epoxy."

—1974 model in Wyncote, PA

"Balances very well. Love the styling. Interior all you can expect on a 24-foot IOR type. Cockpit seats not comfortable. Layout is dated."

—1976 model in Columbia, SC

"It is tender up to 20 degrees, then very stiff. Excellent boat for light air areas. Good teaching boat. Sensitive to sail trim. Okay for short cruising. Excellent PHRF racer."

—1974 model in Sheboygan, WI

"It is basically a strong design, but needs major work to make it a competitive racer. It is fair for coastal cruising for one to three people. Cockpit drain and companionway design are not safe."

—1980 model in Phoenix, AZ

"In heavy air, boat performance falls off. Boat rolls going downwind."

—1976 model in Dallas, TX

---

the J/24 was due in part to the movement away from the IOR and toward one-design and PHRF (Performance Handicap Rating Formula) racing.

In fact, it's interesting to compare the specifications of the San Juan 24 and J/24. Rod Johnstone wasn't too worried about legal trailering limits when he gave the J/24 8' 11" of beam (people seem to trailer them home and to regattas anyway). Its waterline is longer and displacement, at 3,000 pounds, is significantly less. It is not surprising that the J/24 also is a faster boat; its PHRF rating of between 168 and 174 is quite a bit less than the San Juan 24's 210 to 216 rating.

Nevertheless, the San Juan 24 is a quick, responsive boat owing to its sharp entry, minimum wetted surface, shallow skeg and large rudder. Most owners says it handles sweetly. Still, the boat is not without its problems.

Performance

The most common complaint from readers completing our Boat Owner's Questionnaire is less-than-expected downwind performance. "Doesn't surf well," said one owner. "Unstable offwind with spinnaker," said another. "Must take caution with chute between 150 and 180 degrees," said a third. "She likes to roll."

Upwind is another story, with most owners agreeing that the San Juan 24's performance above a beam reach is above average. Many also noted that it performs well in light air.

The boat is for the most part well-balanced. "Very little weather helm; only a light touch on the tiller is required to maintain course," wrote one owner. "It's like having power steering," wrote another. On downwind headings, owner ratings are lower.

As might be expected of a relatively small fin keel racer, where crew weight on the rail is assumed, the boat's initial stability is poor. "Singlehanding in high winds does not work well," wrote an owner in Texas. "Tippy for size and weight; good ultimate stability," said a Nashville, Tennessee owner.

Most San Juan 24s use outboard engines for auxiliary power. Most owners use between six and 7.5 horsepower, which they say will push the boat at hull speed. A few boats were delivered with Atomic 4 inboards, but owners say the boat is too small for it. Bruce Kirby agrees.

Overall, the San Juan 24 performs very well, so long as you understand you're buying an ex-IOR racer and not a cruising boat, despite what the old advertisements say about dual-purpose.

Owners emphasize that the boat is not well suited to short-handed sailing, nor cruising in rough water and high winds. But then, neither is a J/24. If you get your kicks in PHRF racing, the San Juan 24 might be an economical boat to sail competitively.

Construction

Owners are quick to point out the boat's strengths and weaknesses in construction and materials. Most agree that the basic structure is strong. The solid fiberglass hull is about 7/16-inch thick on the bottom, and about 3/16-inch thick at the rail. Fabrics used are 1-1/2-ounce chopped strand and 22-ounce woven roving. The balsa-cored deck is joined to the hull with 10/24 stainless steel bolts on 6" centers.

Molded head liners and hull liners finish off much of the interior. The head liner does not cover the undersides of the side decks, so fittings are accessible. We're not as fond of hull liners to make up furniture foundations as they tend to be noisy, cold, and make modifications prohibitively difficult. But it's still the best way to deliver a decent product at an affordable price.

Despite having a basically sound hull and deck,

owners have numerous criticisms concerning other aspects of the boat's construction, including the lack of stern cleats, absence of bow chocks, no room in the bilge for a pump, weak pulpit fittings, deck delamination, undersized rigging, loose tolerances in the rudder post, poor traveler design, lightweight cockpit hatches, leaky hull/deck joint, bulkhead poorly bonded to deck, deck compression from rigging loads, etc.

While owner opinions vary widely as to overall construction quality, it is our definite impression that the San Juan 24 suffers in the details.

"Generally sloppy workmanship in all areas," said one owner. In checking out a used San Juan 24, we'd carefully check it for the above-mentioned problems.

Interior

As you can see from the layout drawing, the interior plan is straightforward with a V-berth forward, convertible dinette to port, galley and quarter berth to starboard. The dinette berth is 6' 10" long, but only 3 feet wide, so it hardly qualifies as a double. The quarter berth is 6' 5" long. Headroom is 5' 1".

A portable toilet may be fitted under the V-berth. Locating it here is a tough call on a 24-footer. Creating a private head shrinks the rest of the interior; but who's going to use the toilet at night with someone sleeping over it?

In the interest of saving weight, the galley sink is fed by a collapsible 5-gallon jug under the V-berth. Stowage is adequate, with a number of bins under the side decks and the galley. There's one drawer.

The main half-bulkhead in the first version of the San Juan 24 was removed in favor of a full privacy curtain in the Mk II version. A compression post carries the rigging loads.

Conclusion

The San Juan 24 is a good-looking boat that sails fast and handles like a sports car. But like a sports car, you wouldn't want to drive cross country, or even cross-state, in it. You'll feel every bump and the wheel requires constant attention. Clearly this is a racing boat, one that no longer can compete in the forum for which it was intended, the IOR. It also means you can probably pick one up cheap, but we would recommend it only if you're anxious to sail competitively in PHRF races.

As a cruiser or all-around family boat, the San Juan 24 seems to have many deficiencies. Not only is it skittish to handle, but the many small and not-so-small construction problems are daunting.

We'd be doubly certain to retain a good surveyor to check for major problems in a used boat such as deck delamination, deck compression, weak and broken fittings.

San Juan 24s have not held their value very well over the years, with ten-year-old boats going for only about half their new list price—and that didn't include sails, trailer, battery, pulpits and a lot of other necessary stuff.

We do not consider this good performance from an investment standpoint, but it's a moot point now. It seems that the San Juan 24's mediocre quality has caught up with it.   • **PS**

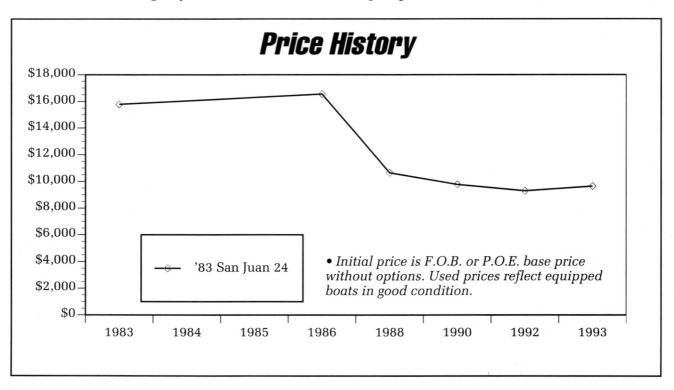

Price History

• *Initial price is F.O.B. or P.O.E. base price without options. Used prices reflect equipped boats in good condition.*

'83 San Juan 24

O'Day 25/ Montego 25

A pair of boats that are quite similar: both represent the transition from daysailer to small cruiser.

The O'Day 25 is really two boats; a fairly fast, stiff, deep keel boat, and a slower, tippier, keel-centerboarder which has made performance compromises in order to create a maximum size trailer sailer.

The Montego 25, on the other hand, despite its shoal and deep draft versions, is too deep, wide, and heavy for ordinary trailering. It is a transition yacht (a small cruiser, often trailerable, that tries to offer the performance and accommodations of a larger boat), by virtue of its size and accommodations.

The O'Day 25 is one of the most successful of all 25 footers. Thousands have been built, and they were cranked out at a steady pace by Bangor Punta's Fall River, Massachusetts plant until the model was discontinued in 1983. The O'Day 25 tries to be the all-purpose 25-footer, with short or tall rig, deep or shallow draft, outboard or inboard power.

In trying to build the 25-footer for everyone, O'Day made a number of compromises:

• The beam is limited to 8' for uncomplicated trailering.

• The shoal draft version lacks the stability to carry the tall rig the boat needs for really good performance.

• The boat is heavy enough to require a size of outboard for auxiliary power that is a big handful.

At the same time, the sheer volume of production of the O'Day 25 means it is a boat whose cost was kept to a minimum, a boat with an established market value and good resale potential almost everywhere, and a thoroughly debugged boat. All of these are important considerations for the buyer of a 25-footer, who may already be looking forward to owning a 27- or 28-footer a few years down the line.

In addition, the keel-centerboard version of the O'Day 25 does provide a maximum-size trailerable

Specifications - O'Day 25

LOA	24' 10"
LWL	21' 0"
Beam	8' 0"
Draft	2' 3" (cb), 4' 6" (keel)
Displacement, lbs.	4,007/3,962
Ballast, lbs.	1,825/1,775
Sail area, sq. ft.	270 (cb), 290 (keel)

cruiser with adequate accommodations for normal vacation-length coastal cruising. This assumes, of course, that you have a vehicle capable of towing 4,000+ lbs, and a heavy trailer—owners suggest a trailer with a capacity of 6,000 lbs. The O'Day 25 adds up to a big package for trailering.

By all indications it's a popular package. Almost 90% of the O'Day 25s sold were the trailerable keel-centerboard version.

Surprisingly, fewer than half the respondents to our owners' survey considered shoal draft or trailerability of primary importance in their decision to buy an O'Day 25. This may be a reflection of a common phenomenon: owners of maximum sized trailerables often find the hassle of trailering, launching, and rigging more than they care to go through for

Specifications - Montego 25

LOA .... 25' 3"
LWL .... 20' 6"
Beam .... 9' 1"
Draft .... 3' 6" (std), 4' 6" (deep)
Displacement .... 4,550 lbs.
Ballast .... 1,800 lbs.
Sail area .... 306 sq. ft. (100% jib)

a day or weekend of sailing. After a year or two of this the boat ends up in a slip or on a mooring.

With the Montego 25, the decision has already been made to move from a trailerable to a non-trailerable boat. Despite characteristics such as a shoal draft option and outboard power, the Montego 25 buyer has made the choice to move into a boat whose home for the sailing season is a marina, rather than the driveway at home.

The choice of shoal draft and outboard power for the Montego 25 are determined by the waters sailed and the depth of the buyer's pocket, rather than the need to keep weight and draft to a minimum for trailering.

Construction

The O'Day 25 and Montego 25 are generally similar in construction. Both are solid uncored hull layups with wood cored deck moldings. The Montego 25 uses plywood coring, the O'Day 25 uses balsa.

Both boats use what we consider to be "small boat" hull-to-deck joints. The O'Day 25 uses a simple coffee can or shoebox joint, fastened with self-tappers and adhesive compound. The Montego 25 uses an outward turning flange which is riveted and glassed over on the inside. Vinyl rubrails cover the hull-to-deck joints on both boats.

This is the maximum size boat suitable for external hull-to-deck joining. External joints are subject to damage in collisions or even in hard docking. Covering the external joint with a rubrail may give the impression that it's okay to use the joint as a bumper. It isn't.

Neither boat uses faired-in through hulls. A handy owner can resolve this lack in a couple of hours using epoxy and microballoons and a little elbow grease. Gelcoat quality of both boats is good.

Although both the Montego 25 and O'Day 25 come in shoal and deep draft versions, their approaches to the problem are quite different. Both the shoal and deep draft versions of the Montego 25 use external cast iron keels, bolted to a shallow keel stub. On the deep draft boat we examined, the keel had been faired to the stub using fiberglass cloth, which had begun to separate from the iron keel in several places after a season of use.

Any dings in an iron keel such as that of the Montego 25 should be ground to bright metal and coated with coal tar epoxy before applying bottom paint. Direct application of copper or tin bottom paint to an iron keel will create severe surface erosion if the boat is used in salt water.

The differing draft versions of the O'Day 25 are very different in character. To make the boat trailerable, the shoal draft O'Day 25 uses a long, shallow keel stub with inside lead ballast. A centerboard gives additional lateral plane for going to windward, but adds little to stability. Over the years, O'Day has gradually added several hundred pounds of inside ballast to the shoal draft 25 in order to improve stability, which has of course increased the weight for trailering.

In the deep draft O'Day 25, a deep glass stub keel replaces the long, shoal keel box of the centerboard boat. A high-aspect ratio fin keel is bolted to this stub keel, giving a substantial draft of 4' 6". The external keel casting is lead, but it took a little work to figure that out. Some at O'Day said the keel was iron, others insisted it was lead. The argument was settled by drilling into the keel casting. It is, we can report with confidence, lead.

It's a good thing that the keel is lead, because it needs a bit of fairing to improve efficiency. The trailing edge is blunt, and the keel casting is poorly faired to the fiberglass stub keel. Lead planes almost as easily as hard wood, so refairing the keel of the deep-draft O'Day 25 is a simple task. Of the dozen or so deep draft O'Day 25s we looked at, about half the owners had taken the time to fair the keels. It should be worth the effort in improved performance.

Some owners report trouble with the rudder of their O'Day 25. In the centerboard version the rudder is five inches deeper than the keel stub. This means that the first part of the boat to contact the bottom when you run aground is the rudder. If you're moving along at a fair clip, a grounding can tear the rudder off the stern of the boat. Construction of both boats is perfectly adequate for usage up to and including coastal cruising. We would not particularly want to take any boat of this size offshore, independent of the quality of construction.

Handling Under Sail

The fin keel, tall rig O'Day 25 and the deep draft Montego 25 have identical PHRF ratings of 219. The rating of the O'Day 25 changes significantly with different rig, keel, and engine combinations.

The outboard powered keel-centerboarder, for example, has a rating of 234—15 seconds per mile slower than the deep keel, tall rig boat. This difference reflects the vastly different character of the two versions of the same boat. The deep keel boat has a more efficient lateral plane and a lower center of gravity, giving much better performance than the keel-centerboard model. Owners report the keel-centerboard boat to be tippy, and the fin keel boat to be stiff.

In addition, the tall rig of the deep keel boat gives slightly greater sail area—enough to make the boat a competitive family racer. Unless very shoal draft and trailerability are essential, the deep keel, tall rig version of the O'Day 25 is the obvious choice. The extra stability, extra sail area, and underbody efficiency add up to a boat that behaves more like a big boat than a small boat.

Both the deep keel and shallow keel versions of the Montego 25 are good performers. If the depth of your sailing waters allows, we would choose the deep keel version for the greater stability and extra lateral plane.

The rigs of the O'Day 25 and the Montego 25 are almost identical Kenyon rigs, but halyards of the Montego 25 lead aft to winches, while O'Day's winches are mast mounted.

These are big boat rigs, with substantial mast sections, airfoil spreaders, and good-sized standing rigging. Booms are set up for jiffy reefing. Mast fittings, tangs, and chainplates are substantially heavier than would be found on boats only marginally smaller.

In other words, these boats have transcended the "toy boat" syndrome so often seen on boats in the 20' to 25' range, and have rigs strong enough for more than fair-weather sailing,

Handling Under Power

The 4,000 lb O'Day 25 and 4,500 lb Montego 25 are at the real outside limit for using outboard power. With high freeboard and no remote controls, starting and throttle operation are a bit of a nuisance, since the outboard must be mounted far down the transom to keep the prop in the water. Remote outboard controls are a must.

Most owners will use a 10 hp outboard on either boat. In a flat calm, it should easily be able to push the boat. However, once there is any wind or sea, the weight and windage of these boats mean that a 10 hp outboard is close to minimum power. Unfortunately, a larger outboard is heavier, more expensive, and stretches the capacity of most outboard brackets. In addition, the propeller of any outboard will have trouble staying in the water as the boat pitches.

The O'Day 25 has a molded-in outboard fuel tank holder in the port side of the cockpit. The Montego 25 has none, so right away you must figure out where you'll keep the gas tank.

There is a growing tendency to put small diesels in boats of this size. Both the Montego and the O'Day offered the Yanmar 1GM as optional auxiliary power. Inboard power adds over 100 lbs to the weight of the O'Day 25 compared to the outboard version.

For a boat that's already pushing the upper limit of easily trailerable weight, every pound hurts. However, inboard power greatly adds to either boat's function as a cruiser. If all your sailing is done on a lake—where strong winds and seas are not likely to be a problem—inboard power is probably an unnecessary expense. On the other hand, if you plan to do a considerable amount of cruising along the seacoast or in the Great Lakes, the convenience, range, and power of an inboard engine begins to make sense.

If we trailer-sailed on Lake Lanier, Georgia, for example, we might choose the centerboard O'Day 25 with outboard power. If we kept our O'Day 25 on a mooring in Newport, Rhode Island, and cruised to Block Island, Nantucket, and the Elizabeth Islands, we'd be more likely to choose the tall rig, deep keel O'Day 25 or the deep keel Montego 25 with inboard.

Deck Layout

Neither boat has a particularly complicated deck layout. Both have an anchor well forward, single lifelines, and a fairly large cockpit.

Because its shrouds are set well inboard, it's far easier to get to the foredeck of the Montego 25. The inboard shrouds should produce narrower sheeting angles and give better upwind performance.

Both boats have cockpit seats long enough to double as fair-weather berths. Both boats also have substantial bridgedecks, fitted with a mainsheet traveler. The mainsheet traveler on the O'Day 25, however, is merely a flat piece of track with a slider. Several O'Day 25 owners said they'd prefer a ball bearing traveler, such as that on the Montego 25. We would, too.

The tiller on both boats takes up a lot of the cockpit. In addition, the tiller fitting of the Montego 25 we examined had a fair amount of play in it. O'Day 25 owners report the same problem. This can frequently be remedied by the owner.

Belowdecks

The trade-off between a trailerable 25 footer and one not constrained in beam by the highway laws is readily apparent when comparing accommodations of the Montego 25 and the O'Day 25. The extra foot of beam of the Montego 25 gives the boat much greater interior volume than the O'Day 25.

O'Day had the fine art of mass production boatbuilding down pat. Nowhere is this better seen than in the interior of the O'Day 25. Much of the interior furniture is incorporated in the body pan. A fiberglass headliner finishes off the overhead. This saves a lot of time in building the boat, and keeps the cost down.

On the other hand, the Montego 25 also uses a molded body pan, but does not use a deck liner. instead, the inside of the cabin trunk is faced with teak veneer, and the overhead is finished with a vinyl liner. The cabin sole of the Montego 25 is teak ply, and the boat uses a solid teak companionway ladder and solid teak companionway drop boards.

By contrast, the O'Day 25 has a fiberglass cabin sole, and uses a molded box step and the top of the galley counter as a companionway ladder. In other words, finish detail of the Montego 25 is better than that of the O'Day 25, and you pay a price for the difference.

Interior accommodations of the two boats are remarkably similar, but the extra beam of the Montego 25 gives greater elbow room. Headroom of the Montego 25 is almost 6' under the main hatch. The O'Day 25 has 5' 6" headroom.

With V-berths forward, two main cabin settees, and a quarterberth, each boat sleeps five, although a slide-out settee in each brings nominal sleeping capacity to six. Do you really want to sleep six on a 25 footer? The zoo that the interior of either boat would be on a rainy morning when everyone was trying to get up and get dressed would probably be enough to turn the most sociable of sailors into a singlehander. Unfortunately, the "How many does she sleep?" syndrome is alive and well in both boats, at the expense of storage space and galley space.

Both boats are big enough to have a separate head compartment. Separate from the main cabin, that is. The head is really part of the forward cabin on both boats, a not unreasonable compromise in a five-berth 25 footer.

Small boat galleys rarely offer much except headaches for the cook, and neither of these boats is an exception. The O'Day 25's icebox is tiny—the auxiliary box in the cockpit is really a daytime beer cooler—and is almost cut in half by the centerboard pennant trunk. While the O'Day 25 has a deep sink,

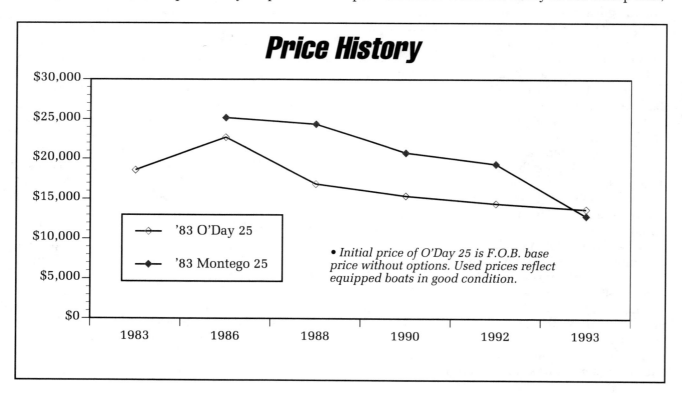

Price History

• Initial price of O'Day 25 is F.O.B. base price without options. Used prices reflect equipped boats in good condition.

— '83 O'Day 25
— '83 Montego 25

it is almost directly underneath the companionway. Coming below with the boat heeled on port tack you're likely to put your foot in the sink.

The Montego 25 has a larger icebox with an insulated lid. The insulation for the lid is styrofoam, however, and is exposed on the underside of the lid. It is likely to take a lot of abuse.

The Montego 25 has a slide-away two burner alcohol galley stove which stores over the quarterberth. It is slightly easier to use than the same stove on the O'Day 25, which must be removed from a storage compartment and set on the galley counter for use. Since cooking under way is barely practical on a boat of this size, the lack of gimballing for the stoves is not a serious shortcoming.

Both boats have a reasonable amount of storage, as long as you don't want to unpack your seabag. Under-settee storage bins, found on both boats, would be far more useful with drop-in molded plastic trays, which are better for keeping things dry. O'Day offered the plastic trays as an option in the 25.

Conclusions

Both the Montego 25 and the O'Day 25 are good examples of the transition yacht—boats for owners wishing to move up from trailer sailers to small cruisers. Both retain some small boat features — outboard power, shoal draft options—while having many of the basic components of larger boats. These big boat features include deep draft options, sturdy cruising-type rigs, inboard power options, enclosed heads, and permanent galleys.

The shoal draft version of the O'Day 25 is still trailerable, but it is at the outside limit of size and displacement. The compromises in performance to make the O'Day 25 trailerable—short rig, less stability, keel-centerboard configuration—make the trailerable version of the boat more of a "small boat" than a "big boat."

Equipped with an inboard engine and a deep keel, either boat will make a good coastal cruiser for a couple with two small children, Putting more people on the boat for anything but daysailing will be more like camping out than cruising. The deep keel, tall rig O'Day 25 represents just about the minimum investment you can make in an inboard-powered pocket cruiser. For the couple or small family moving up from a trailer-sailer such as the O'Day 22, Catalina 22, or MacGregor 22, either the Montego 25 or the O'Day 25 provides a true transition from the weekender to the true pocket cruiser, at a minimum investment. **• PS**

Morgan 24/25

She's fast and roomy, but plagued by centerboard problems that are tough to avoid.

Back in 1965, a St. Petersburg, Florida sailmaker named Charlie Morgan, who had been dabbling with custom racing yacht design and had come up with a remarkable string of winners, started producing a series of small- to medium-sized production boats. Introduced late that year, the Morgan 24 joined the Morgan 30, 34 and 38, becoming an instant success as a fast cruiser and club racer.

In 1968 the Morgan Yacht Corporation was bought by the conglomerate, Beatrice Foods, and by early 1969 the Morgan 24 had been renamed the Morgan 25, with some changes in specifications and options. For example, although the actual length overall remained at 24' 11-3/4", the advertised length moved from 24' 11" to 25' 0"; inboard diesel and gasoline engine options were offered in addition to outboard power; toerails switched from teak to molded fiberglass; and the transom outboard cutout was eliminated in favor of an optional outboard bracket.

Morgan Yachts was later resold to Thor Industries and most recently to Catalina Yachts. After about 1972 more changes were made. The hull-deck connection went from through-bolted to pop-riveted; rigging blocks were downsized; window frames were changed from silver anodized aluminum to black plastic; the water tank changed from stainless steel (Monel in the early boats) to galvanized. The last Morgan 25s were built in 1976. Over the years, between 400 and 500 were built.

Design

The Morgan 24/25's long waterline, very well balanced hull, relatively low wetted surface, large sailplan (for its vintage), and attention to small details like well-shaped foil blades and flush-faced through-hulls, provide good speed and close-winded sailing for the racer. At the same time, its shallow

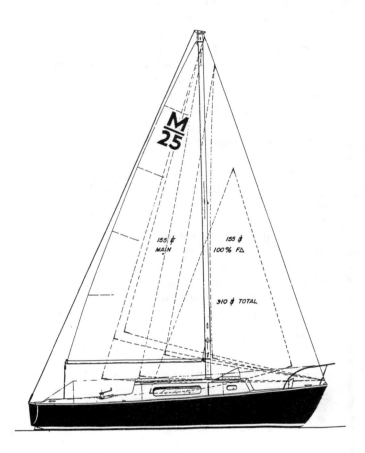

Specifications

LOA	24' 11"
LWL	21' 6"
Beam	8' 0"
Draft (board up/down)	2' 9"/6' 6"
Displacement	5,000 lbs.
Ballast	1,900 lbs.
Sail area	310 sq. ft.

draft (2' 9" board up) and relatively roomy layout below appeal to the cruising sailor.

The boat has firm bilges to help with form stability, and a reasonable 5,000 pounds of displacement. However, with ballast placed relatively high due to the shallowness of its keel, the Morgan 24/25 is a bit on the tender side in heavy air.

On Deck

The cockpit is eight feet long, but underway it comfortably seats just two on each side of a long (4-1/2') low tiller that extends within 22 inches of the companionway. In a race, the third and fourth crew, if any, have to move from cockpit to cabintop, due to crowding and because the boat tends to get stern-heavy with crew weight aft. Because of this, serious

Owners' Comments

"A well-built, good-sailing boat with more than average comfort and convenience below for several days of cruising. We have been in 30-40 knot winds with complete confidence and control. Highly recommended."

1967 boat in California

"The 24 is a 'best buy' in the 25-foot size range. A few other boats are faster, a few are built more solidly, a few have more room. But I haven't seen any that are faster and more solid and roomier. Just returned from a 1,000+ mile cruise up to Maine without incident."

1967 boat in Connecticut

racers tend to remove the outboard engine from the transom and stow it below, if rules permit.

The cockpit sole slopes aft to a single centerline scupper through the transom, and this works satisfactorily except for a puddle of water that gathers on the leeward side in rain, and except for the smallish scupper size (1-1/4" diameter), which some owners have enlarged for faster drainage.

The base M/24 was offered as a relatively bare cruising version, with small (#2) South Coast sheet winches, end-boom sheeting without a traveler, short genoa tracks along the toerails, and no spinnaker gear. An extra-cost optional "racing package" included spinnaker gear, #3 genoa winches, longer genoa track, six extra cleats, two extra genoa cars, boom vang, snatch blocks, and traveler. Other extras included stainless bow pulpit, lifelines and stanchions, interior and running lights, and compass. The factory-installed options were fairly expensive, with the result that many sailors bought the base version and added equipment themselves. That, plus the fact that M/24s were available at one point as kits, may account for the wide variation in quality, style, and placement of equipment.

Construction

As one owner puts it, only slightly mixing metaphors, "The Morgan is a Chevrolet, not a Hinckley." For the most part, owners mention defects in passing but on the whole are very satisfied. One says his forward V-berth bulkhead came loose and had to be refastened, but also reports that fiberglass work is generally neat and strong.

Most boats came off the line with faucet-type gate valves on the through-hulls; many owners report replacing them with more suitable barrel or ball valves.

On the older 24s with teak toerails, the deck is fastened to the hull along a wide L-shaped flange with 1/4-inch stainless bolts on 2-inch centers, with every other bolt passing through both teak and fiberglass—a very strong arrangement. But on the newer 25s, the teak rail was eliminated and the joint fastened with pop rivets, a weaker system that is more likely to leak.

Common problems on both 24s and 25s include leaky windows and crazed Plexiglas; a mast hinge that is virtually useless due to lack of provision for preventing side sway when lowering or raising the mast; dissatisfaction with the dated appearance of the simulated wood-grain mica bulkhead finish, which requires major effort to remove and replace; and centerboard difficulties.

The centerboard pennant arrangement is probably the weakest design detail on the boat. The board itself is a well-shaped, high-aspect ratio, solid fiberglass unit in a trunk beneath the cabin sole. The 1/8-inch stainless steel pennant wire attaches at one end of a groove molded into the top of the board, winds its way via a stainless steel piston through a stuffing box to a turning sheave forward, then through two more sheaves an to a small winch mounted on the cockpit wall. Several problems can arise due to this design. The lower portion of the pennant, being exposed to seawater, tends to corrode rapidly, and is impossible to inspect without complete disassembly. Hence frequent inspection, requiring a haul-out or scuba gear, is advised. In southern waters, some pennants have failed in less than a year. Additionally, several owners report trouble with cracking and leaking in the short stub of hose that bridges the stuffing box and trunk. And unless the owner adds stops at both its ends, the piston can part company with the stuffing box and possibly sink the boat.

Other centerboard-related problems: The turning sheave, under the sole forward of the trunk, is almost inaccessible; owners are well advised to cut an access hole and lubricate the sheave frequently to minimize corrosion. And on some boards, insufficient glass reinforcement around the pin can result in eventual cracking or breakage at the pin hole.

Interior

The 24s and 25s at various times were made with two

different interior arrangements: (1) a dinette model with a single sail locker to port, and (2) a two-quarterberth model with twin sail lockers. The dinette version has less space for sail stowage, and there is a considerable amount of wasted space under the starboard cockpit seat unless an access hole is cut in the plywood bulkhead aft of the quarterberth (which is often done). For cruising, however, the dinette model wins hands down, given the greater storage space in the galley and a hanging locker, better privacy inherent in the position of the offset head, and a sizable table for dining or laying out charts. Sitting at the dinette is uncomfortable for four people due to the deck overhanging the outboard seats. In all, most agree that the 24/25 is really a two-sleeper, two-eater vessel.

Still, the boat has practically all the interior conveniences one could want in a small cruiser, including galley, sink, ice chest, marine toilet in a private compartment, good sized berths, long self-bailing cockpit with at least one sail locker, and 5' 8" headroom.

The sixtyish interior aesthetics are not great and vary with model year. In 1965 the Morgan brochure says "mahogany interior trim" but by 1967 the standard interior was "bulkheads... paneled in wood-grained mica, with oiled American Walnut trim." Carpeted cabin sole was standard, with a teak sole optional.

A common complaint among owners is that there is no good place to store a portable gas tank. The usual place is in the cabin, aft of the companionway ladder, but that can be a source of annoying—and dangerous—fumes. A 6-gallon tank can be wedged between the cockpit seats, but limits footroom and movement around the cockpit, and the extra weight in the cockpit does nothing to help performance.

Other complaints include the fact that the icebox drain runs into the bilge, providing a source of potential odors; and that ventilation is only so-so. A cowl vent fitted on the foredeck, plus a mushroom vent over the forward hatch, are recommended additions.

Performance

The long, deep board helps the 24/25 to point high,

There were two interior layouts offered. This one has anchor and sail lockers, but the alternative (a dinette arrangement) has more overall interior room, with a long galley counter and hanging locker.

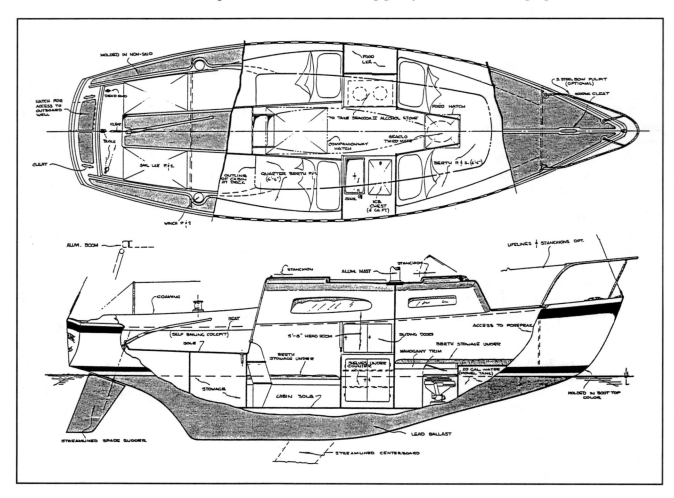

and its low wetted surface, especially with board up, gives extra speed on reaches and runs. The boat performs best in 5 to 15 knots of breeze, but can handle much higher winds when properly reefed, though several owners reported that the boat "could be a bit stiffer."

The 24/25 is unusually well balanced, and in ordinary weather can be made to self-steer on a beat or close reach with tiller lashed. However, in very heavy air carrying a chute, it has a marked tendency to broach.

A typical PHRF rating is 219, compared to a J/24 at 171 and a Cape Dory 25 at 261.

Conclusion

Pride of ownership seems particularly evident among owners of the early M/24s, who tend to turn up their noses at the later M/25 as a less sturdy and well-appointed boat. Over the years, both models, and particularly kit boats, are likely to have had major changes to equipment and rigging, some good, some bad. Consequently, prospective buyers should check to be sure any such modifications are appropriate, and should keep in mind that these boats are now 18 to 28 years old, so should be closely inspected for gear that can fail due to aging. Most such gear is repairable, but at a cost. Still, if you find one on which extensive work isn't necessary, it can be a real bargain as well as a real pleasure to own and use.

In 1972 the Morgan 25 had a base price of $7,495. Earlier models in reasonable condition can be had today for about $5,000, more depending on sail inventories end equipment. Inboard models of the 25 are higher yet, though we feel the outboard model is a better choice.

The Morgan 24/25 makes a wonderful small cruiser and club racer, and can be a solid value if you buy the right boat. Construction quality has varied over the years, and so has quality and quantity of equipment purchased by individual owners. Moreover, all 24s and 25s, even the good ones, are beginning to show their age. Buyers are advised to make a careful inspection to be sure they're not getting a boat with more problems than they care to handle. • **PS**

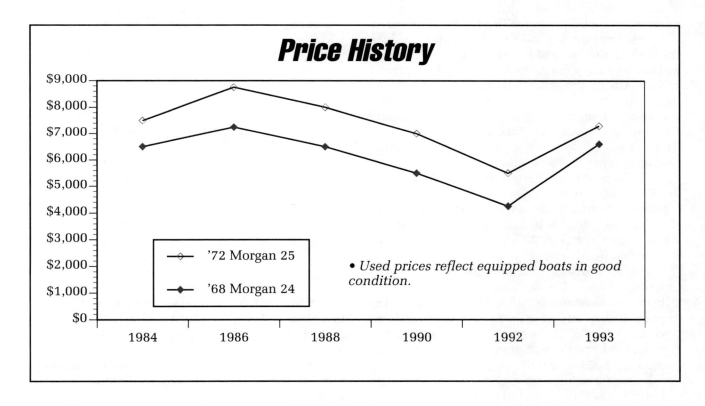

Price History

• *Used prices reflect equipped boats in good condition.*

Legend: '72 Morgan 25, '68 Morgan 24

Cape Dory 25 and 25D

These sisters are actually very different boats. One is a weekender/daysailer, the other, a true cruiser.

Cape Dory Yachts was, until its demise a couple of years ago, one of the more conservative firms in the boatbuilding industry. With the exception of a brief fling with modern cruiser-racers—the Intrepid series—the company's stock in trade since the late 1960s was traditional, full keel auxiliaries and sailboats, most from the design board of Carl Alberg, the octogenarian dean of American designers. It is ironic that a man who began his designing career drawing schooners and Universal Rule racing sloops in the office of John Alden should find his greatest popularity designing production fiberglass boats 60 years later.

Since he picked up the tooling for the well known 18' 6" Typhoon in 1969, Cape Dory owner Andrew Vavolotis showed an almost unswerving loyalty to the long keel with attached rudder, and to designs by Alberg. The Cape Dory 25 is one of the few designs not created by Alberg.

Credit for the basic design of the Cape Dory goes to George Stadel. The boat was originally built by Allied as the Greenwich 24. Vavolotis purchased the tooling during one of Allied's frequent business disasters, redesigned the boat to suit his own ideas, and put the Cape Dory 25 into production in 1973. Hundreds of 25s were built, and the boat has rightly been termed a modern classic.

In the fall of 1981, Cape Dory introduced a new 25 footer, the 25D. "D" is for diesel, but there's much more difference between the two boats than just the powerplant. Although a certain amount of confusion has existed about the two boats, the only thing that the 25 and the 25D have in common is overall length. The 25D was an entirely different boat: wider, heavier, deeper, with inboard engine, a dramatically different interior, and a new price tag 50% higher than that of the 25.

Specifications - 25

LOA	24' 10"
LWL	18' 0"
Beam	7' 3"
Draft	3' 0"
Displacement	4,000 lbs.
Ballast	1,700 lbs.
Sail area	264 sq. ft.

In a time when retrenchment was the watchword in the boatbuilding industry, Vavolotis had a cheshire cat grin on his face when he said, "We've found our niche in the industry."

For a number of years, that niche was narrow indeed. While racer-cruisers proliferated in the 1970's, while the fat fin-keeler with the high aspect ratio rig became the industry vogue, Cape Dory continued to espouse long keels with attached rudders, relatively narrow beam, attractive sheer lines, moderate freeboard, and substantial overhangs—"old fashioned" boats.

While there are a number of companies that offer a few traditional, heavy displacement boats, no other builder can claim a full line of ultraconservative designs. It might seem that Cape Dory created so

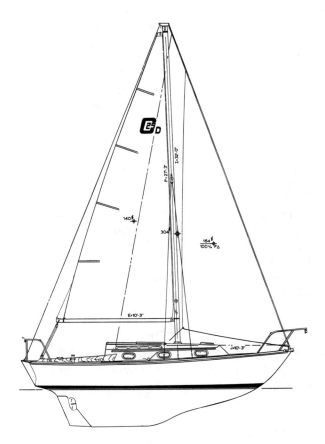

Specifications - 25D

LOA	25' 0"
LWL	19' 0"
Beam	8' 0"
Draft	3' 6"
Displacement	5,120 lbs.
Ballast	2,050 lbs.
Sail area	304 sq. ft.

many models that their prime competition was between boats in their own line, but apparently there was enough product differentiation to support several different models between 25' and 30'.

Cape Dory customer loyalty is tremendous. Probably more owners trade up through the line than change builders when the time comes to upgrade, The cynic might say that it's because no other builder caters exclusively to buyers of "traditional" boats. In fact, a large percentage of the product loyalty is generated by consistently good quality, high resale value.

Cape Dory boats are not for everyone, By any standard, both the 25 and the 25D are heavy displacement boats.

Interior volume of both boats is substantially less

than that of "modern" 25-footers due to their relatively narrow beam and short waterline. By way of comparison, the Ericson 25 is almost three feet longer on the waterline and over a foot wider than the Cape Dory 25D, with almost identical displacement, ballast, sail area, and price.

The Cape Dory 25 is really a daysailing and weekending boat. Although the boat has berths for 4, accommodations are cramped and creature comforts minimal.

The 25D is a very different concept. She is a miniature cruising yacht. Inevitably she will be compared to that star of an earlier generation of pocket cruisers, the Laurent Giles designed Vertue.

Construction

Construction of all boats in the Cape Dory line is similar. Hulls are moderately heavy solid glass layups of mat and roving. Ballast in all cases is a lead casting. The casting is carried in a hollow keel molding, with voids between the casting and the molded shell filled with polyester slurry. The casting is heavily glassed over on the inside of the hull. While the workmanship and materials used in these ballast installations are excellent, we prefer an external, bolted-on lead casting for its shock absorbing qualities.

Decks and cabin tops are cored with end grain balsa. This results in a firm, stiff surface with good sound-absorbing and insulation properties. Gelcoat quality of the 25 and 25D is excellent. Light roving printthrough is evident, but there are neither external hard spots nor evidence of distortion of the hull from the attachment of the deck.

Cape Dory uses a wide internal flange for attachment of the deck molding. The deck is joined to the hull using a semi-rigid polyester compound. This joint is incidentally reinforced by the screws which attach the toe rail, by the through bolts of the pulpits and lifeline stanchions, by the chainplate bolts, and by deck hardware bolts. Our belt and suspenders approach to construction would prefer through bolting of the joint at close intervals in addition to the chemical bond and random fastening.

Cape Dory's chainplate installations merit special comment. On the 25D, shrouds are attached to cast bronze lugs which rest on the deck over the hull/deck flange. Each of these lugs is bolted through the flange with two 3/8" diameter stainless steel machine screws. On the underside of the hull flange, a heavy aluminum plate is glassed in place using unidirectional roving, which also extends down the inside of the hull.

This is an immensely strong installation for a boat of 5,000 pounds displacement. The chainplates are less prone to leakage than conventional flat bar stock plates bolted to bulkheads.

The only disadvantage of this system is that it locates the chainplates at the outboard edge of the deck. This gives the shrouds a wide base for supporting the mast, but interferes with close sheeting of overlapping headsails.

All Cape Dory rudders are hung from the back of the keel. The primary advantages of this type of rudder are strength—a fairly important consideration for the cruising yacht—and relative invulnerability to damage.

The only real drawback to Cape Dory's rudder installation is that dropping the rudder for repair is fairly complex. The cast bronze gudgeon/heel fitting must be removed by grinding off the heads of its fastenings at the base of the keel. Then the rudder and stock are pulled out from below, necessitating either a deep hole under the boat or lifting the boat with a crane or Travelift while the rudder is being removed.

All deck hardware is through bolted using stainless steel bolts and aluminum backing plates. The forestay fittings on both the 25 and 25D are heavy bronze castings, as are cleats, winch islands, and portlights.

We have one reservation about Cape Dory's hardware installations. The mixture of bronze castings, stainless bolts, and aluminum backing plates strikes us as less than ideal. While the deck hardware is not immersed in an electrolyte, there is a difference in voltage potential between the aluminum backing plate and the manganese bronze casting. The type 304 austenitic stainless fastenings are relatively inert, but they do join very dissimilar metals, Below the waterline, Cape Dory uses silicon bronze fastenings in their bronze castings.

Cape Dory had its own hardware division—Spartan Marine Products—which produced a broad range of deck and hull hardware, as well as assembling all spars for Cape Dory. Spartan was founded in 1975 when it became increasingly difficult to get cast bronze hardware to complement Cape Dory's traditional designs.

We have previously been critical of Spartan for the poor finish quality of their products. While their castings were excellent, the hardware was only available in what is traditionally known as "burnished" finish—ground and tumble polished to remove roughness from the casting process, but not mirror finished. Later on Spartan offered most of their hardware in burnished, polished, or chrome finish. Polished hardware truly accents the classic yacht. In acknowledgment of that fact, Cape Dory made polished hardware standard on their flagship 36-footer.

Spartan seacocks are used on all through hull fittings below the water on the 25D, including head intake and discharge, cockpit scuppers, engine cooling water intake, and galley sink drain. Engine exhaust and bilge pump discharge exit through the transom, and have no provision for shutoff. On the 25, bronze ball valves are used in place of seacocks.

The 25D uses a full molded hull liner which incorporates all the major furniture components. Interior trim and systems are installed in the liner before it is fiberglassed into the hull. The liner itself is a heavy solid layup almost as thick as the hull. The only disadvantage to the full hull liner is limited access to the inner surface of the hull in the event of catastrophic damage. Bilge access in the 25D, for example, is only through a small trap in the main cabin sole. Repairs requiring access to the inside of the hull skin will require major surgery.

The general standard of workmanship in Cape Dory boats is very good, and both the 25 and 25D sustain this standard. The 25D, with its emphasis on fairly serious cruising, is a far more complex boat than the 25 in both systems and construction. The 25D is probably one of the strongest boats of her size on the market.

Handling Under Sail

While both the 25 and 25D are cruising boats, neither should be a dog under sail. Owners of the 25 report average speed compared to other boats that size.

Thanks to a ballast/displacement ratio of almost 43%, the 25 is a stiff boat despite her narrow beam and slack bilges. Stability is enhanced by a short, low aspect ratio rig. Owners report that a 150% genoa is a must to keep the 25 moving in light air.

The 25D may actually have better performance potential than the 25. The 25D's rig is substantially more modern in design, with a mast 4 1/2' taller than that of the 25, a J measurement over a foot longer, and a higher aspect ratio mainsail. The extra 6" of draft, 9" of beam, hard bilges, and 350 pounds of additional ballast should make her quite stiff.

The 25D came with a recessed inboard jib track as well as the rail-mounted genoa track common to both boats. Both have full width mainsheet travelers mounted at the aft end of the cockpit.

Cape Dory boats 30' and under came with factory-supplied sails built by several different lofts. OEM sails rarely come up to the quality of sails custom built for a particular boat sailed in a specific locale. Though the stock sails may be adequate while you're learning to sail the boat, they probably won't be when you become interested enough in good performance to appreciate the difference between a mediocre suit of sails and a really good suit. With either the 25 or 25D, the first sail you'll want to add to the boat is a 150% genoa, no matter where you sail, A lot of sail area can compensate for a lot of wetted surface when sailing in light air.

Both the 25 and 25D have deck-stepped masts. In the 25, most of the mast compression is carried by the main cabin bulkhead. In the 25D, an aluminum compression column directly under the mast transfers the rig compression to the keel. Cape Dory's support systems for deck-stepped masts are among the best we've seen.

The mast on the 25D was originally designed to step through to the keel. The sales department feared that a large mast tube in the main cabin might turn off potential buyers, so the mast tubes were shortened, and a complex, more expensive deck stepping arrangement was incorporated. This isn't the first time in the industry the sales department has overridden the engineering department, and it won't be the last.

The main boom of the 25 is equipped with roller reefing, a method of sail reduction that has, thankfully, just about vanished. It is almost impossible to get good sail shape going to weather with a roller reefed main, and you really haven't lived until you've tried to crank in half a dozen rolls in a rising gale offshore while the reefing gear binds and the sail luff grinds itself to shreds in the reefing gear. Jiffy reefing, which is standard on the 25D, is preferable to roller reefing in almost every way.

In performance, neither the 25 nor the 25D will be mistaken for a racer-cruiser. Nevertheless, the owner concerned about improving performance can make real improvements by fairing in through hull fittings, wet sanding the bottom paint, and buying higher-performance sails.

Handling Under Power

A major difference between the 25 and 25D is their mechanical propulsion systems. The Cape Dory 25 has an outboard well at the aft end of the cockpit, while the 25D has inboard diesel power.

The outboard engine installation of the 25 is less than 100% successful, according to owners responding to our survey. The cover to the engine compartment must be kept open to provide adequate air for the outboard engine when running under power. The engine well resonates loudly, making the 25 noisy under power.

The 25 will accommodate engines up to 15 horsepower, but the most commonly used engines are the Johnson and Evinrude 9.9 horsepower units, which provide more than adequate power for the boat.

The engine's location aft of the rudder means that there is no prop wash effect on the rudder to aid low speed maneuvering. Coupled with the 25's long keel, this means that the boat will be slower to respond under power than a modern fin keeler of similar displacement.

Handling the 25 in reverse is a problem, according to owners. A large percentage report in our survey that the boat "doesn't maneuver in reverse worth a damn."

The 25D has a conventional inboard engine installation, using a raw-water-cooled Yanmar 1QM 7 1/2 horsepower diesel. At 154 pounds, this is one of the lightest small diesels available. The 13 gallon fuel tank, mounted under the cockpit, should give the 25D over 50 hours of operating time under power, or a range of about 250 miles.

A two-bladed solid bronze prop is standard, tucked in an aperture at the aft end of the keel. The aperture extends into the rudder, which will cause some cross

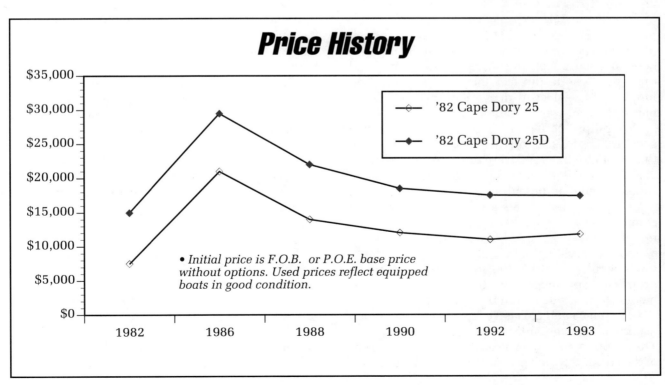

Price History

Legend:
- ◇ '82 Cape Dory 25
- ◆ '82 Cape Dory 25D

• Initial price is F.O.B. or P.O.E. base price without options. Used prices reflect equipped boats in good condition.

ventilation and slight loss of rudder efficiency under sail. The 2.62:1 reduction gear should allow the little engine to achieve full power in driving the 25D.

The engine installation is excellent, and meets ABYC standards for the installation of gasoline engines, as well as the far simpler standards for diesels. A lift-out plastic storage bin in the top of the engine box removes for routine service of belts and filters, as well as for checking oil. The compartment is not soundproofed.

More thorough access to the engine can be gained by removing the companionway ladder and unscrewing the plywood front panel of the engine box.

Deck Layout

The 25 and 25D share a simple, uncluttered deck layout, although the 25D has some features lacking in the 25. The 25D has a large foredeck anchor well capable of holding the normal working ground tackle for the boat. The 25D's stemhead casting incorporates an anchor roller. We would add a large eyebolt to the anchor well to secure the bitter end of the anchor rode.

While the 25 has a single centerline foredeck cleat, the 25D has twin cleats outboard of the well. Bowlines should be secured to the cleat on the opposite side from the bow chock to avoid blocking access to the well.

You can have any hull and deck color in a Cape Dory as long as it's Cape Dory off-white and tan. The white of the cabin house is a warm brownish white, and will not unduly reflect light on bright days. Tan nonskid areas avoid the desolate appearance of white on white found on some boats.

The 25 and 25D both have teak toerails and rubbing strake, teak cabintop handrails, and teak cockpit coamings. We strongly recommend that these be kept in good shape by the application of a teak dressing. Despite the fact that teak is reasonably forgiving of neglect, it does require some maintenance to avoid warping and checking.

Bow pulpit, stern pulpit, and single lifelines were standard on the 25D. A bow pulpit was standard on the 25, but lifelines and stern rail were optional. The 25D incorporates Aqua Signal international style running lights in the pulpits.

Cockpits of both boats are large and reasonably comfortable, although the coaming sides are vertical rather than being slanted at a good angle for really comfortable seating. Older models of the 25 had a low cockpit sill, with the lowest companionway drop board six inches above the cockpit sole. Newer models have a substantial bridgedeck.

Both the 25 and 25D have large cockpit scuppers leading to through hull fittings with shutoff valves. The scuppers are properly located at the forward end of the cockpit, which prevents flooding by the quarter wave.

There are large lockers under both cockpit seats on the 25. The 25D has a shallow locker to starboard over the quarterberth and a deep locker to port. Access to the stuffing box on the 25D is through the port locker.

The tiller on both boats takes up a lot of the cockpit whether sailing or at anchor. A few 25Ds have been delivered with pedestal steering, which seems a little presumptuous on a boat this size, but does free up the cockpit for seating.

With a good solid bridgedeck, big scuppers, and a companionway that is almost parallel sided, the 25D has a cockpit suited for offshore use, although its volume is at the upper limit for a small boat. The use of plywood drop boards is rather disappointing on a boat of this quality, A properly made solid board is as warpfree as plywood, and certainly looks better.

Belowdecks

The most obvious difference in the two boats is belowdecks. The 25 is a minimal short term cruiser for two adults and two children, while the 25D has a genuine cruising interior for a couple.

The 25 has what could best be described as stooping headroom. The forward cabin has a sharply tapered vee-berth that is too small for two normal size adults. Immediately aft is a cramped toilet compartment, divided from the vee-berths by a curtain and from the main cabin by folding doors.

The main cabin settees double as berths. Actually, they are berths doubling as settees, as there are no backrests for comfortable sitting. Because the galley sink hangs over the foot of the port settee, owners report that as a berth it is only comfortable for a fairly short person.

The galley consists of platforms port and starboard at the foot of the settees. The starboard platform can hold a two burner stove, which is optional, or can be used for navigating. The port counter contains the aforementioned sink. There is a small icebox under the companionway step.

Stepping from the 25 to the 25D is a confusing experience. On a marginally larger hull, Cape Dory has produced a boat with an interior that a couple could find comfortable for fairly extended cruising. Without substantially raising either freeboard or cabin trunk, the 25D has been provided honest headroom of about 5' 11".

One way this has been accomplished has been by dropping the cabin sole well into the bilge. Headroom is gained at the cost of cabin sole space. In this case, it's a fair tradeoff. The only real impingement into the headroom is the teak finishing piece for the overhead companionway hatch, which extends down a full two inches. Many people will find this a real headcracker.

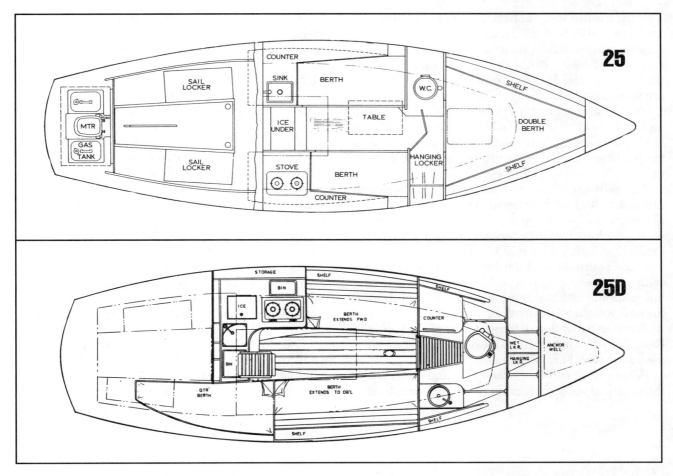

The interior of the 25D is unusual in that a forward cabin has been eliminated, and a huge head, which can be fitted with a shower, installed in the space that would otherwise be a cramped berth.

The head compartment has headroom of 5' 9", two hanging lockers, a small sink, and two solid towel rack/grab rails. Anyone who's spent any time in the head in rough weather will appreciate the grab rails.

Although there is little storage space in the head for sheets, towels, medicine, or other small items, there are two large blank bulkheads crying out for the handy boat owner to install cabinets or shelves.

The shower, if installed, drains directly into the bilge, an arrangement that leaves something to be desired, A Bomar hatch over the head provides good ventilation, as do the two opening ports in the head compartment.

Attractive is an overused word, but it is truly descriptive of the main cabin. The hull outboard of the settee is lined with ash, a welcome change from the teak used by most builders.

Main cabin settees extend through the head bulkhead into alcoves that form the dresser surfaces in the head. These alcoves are handy for storing bedding or other loose items under sail.

Cape Dory gets an A+ for main cabin settee comfort in the 25D. The settee backs are nicely padded,

The Cape Dory 25 displays a typical accomodation layout, with V-berths forward and a head between them and the main cabin. The 25D, on the other hand, eschews the extra berth space (of doubtful use on a 25' boat in any case) in favor of a large enclosed head and storage space, collectively taking up the forward third of the hull. Even so, there's a lot of wasted space in the head compartment that a resourceful owner could turn into useful storage.

properly angled, and the settee tops have been reduced to the proper width for comfortable seating. Thank God someone has discovered that most people don't sit bolt upright when they can avoid it. For sleeping, the backs fold up on hinges and latch out of the way.

The starboard settee extends, with a little maneuvering, to form a double, giving the 25D nominal accommodations for four adults. We doubt if two couples would really want to share one cabin on a 25 footer for any period of time.

A 20 gallon polyethylene water tank is mounted under the starboard quarterberth—undeniably the best berth in the boat, but one that is likely to be used more for storage than for sleeping if the boat is cruised by a couple, Ironically, this water capacity is four gallons less than that of the Cape Dory 25.

With a little imagination, the galley of the 25D could probably be made far more serviceable for the serious cruiser. There is little storage space for any quantity of food, although there is enough room under the bridgedeck and outboard of the stove to create much more.

The sink is tucked away under the bridgedeck, and truly is almost impossible to use. To reach the fresh water pump, being a contortionist would be a virtue. Washing dishes would be an acrobatic exercise.

The galley stove is a two burner recessed Kenyon alcohol model with integral tank, a type of stove about which we have grave reservations. Alcohol is a poor cooking fuel for a serious cruising boat, being expensive, bulky, and inefficient.

Cross ventilation of the main cabin is excellent, with four opening bronze ports. Cowl vents in dorade boxes should be fitted at the aft end of the main cabin for foul weather and offshore ventilation.

With the exception of the galley, the interior of the Cape Dory 25D is one of the most functional we have seen for a small cruising boat.

Putting the head in the forepeak and eliminating the cramped vee-berth are excellent ideas in a boat of this size. The lack of privacy in the head, a major complaint in small cruising boats, is a problem Cape Dory has solved in one bold stroke.

Conclusions

For two boats of similar size and type, the Cape Dory 25 and 25D are radically different from each other. The 25 is a daysailer and weekender, with cramped accommodations. The 25D has the potential to be a comfortable long-term cruiser for a couple, with a roomy interior whose only real flaw is a mediocre galley arrangement.

Construction of both boats is solid, and they are well finished, although not perfectly so. Finish detail on later boats is substantially better than on Cape Dory boats of the late '70s.

The 25D is tough enough to be a serious cruising boat, We would not be surprised to hear that someone sails one across the Atlantic, although ocean voyaging in so small a boat is not our personal cup of tea.

Cape Dory boats are for traditionalists. In a time when traditionalism and conservatism seem to be growing in popularity, the appeal of boats such as those produced by Cape Dory is assured.   • **PS**

Hunter 25

Be sure to check out those boats built between 1978 and 1981—owners think they're the best.

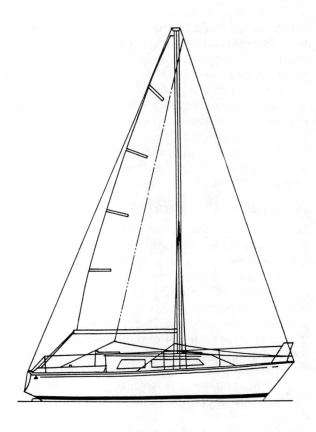

By the mid '80s, after only ten years in business, Hunter Marine had become one of the two leaders (with Catalina Yachts) in the volume of auxiliary-sized sailboats on the US market. And, like Catalina, the corporate philosophy at Hunter was to mass produce low priced boats with as few changes in tooling, hence design, as possible.

As a result, Hunter until 1978 had a line basically consisting of three boats: the Hunters 25, 27 and 30, added to thereafter by smaller (20' and 22') and larger (31, 34', 36', 37' and 54') while the original three remained in production. Only after nine years production was the 25 replaced in the line (with the 25.5) and, after 10 years, the 27 (by the 28.5).

The basic marketing program of Hunter has remained remarkably consistent since it produced its first boats in 1974. That policy has made price the single most important factor in selling its boats. With the cost savings from mass production and minimum changes in tooling, Hunter has sold by far the highest volume of the lowest priced boats of their size and type on the market for the last 10 years.

Hunter Yachts came into being amid the energy crunch in the early 1970s. Silverton, a large manufacturer of smaller powerboats, expanded to build "energy-conscious" sailboats. It started with three boats, two John Cherubini-designed performance cruisers, the Hunters 27 and 30, and a Robert Seidelmann/J. Cherubini-designed small (MORC) racer, the Hunter 25.

The original Hunter 25 was a racy boat with a wedge-shaped cabin trunk that limited interior space. That space was further restricted by a design parameter for trailering, an 8' beam.

From the outset Hunter has maintained a policy of selling its boats "fully equipped" so the original boats came with sails, dock lines and fenders, re-

Specifications

LOA	25' 0"
LWL	20' 2"
Beam	8' 0"
Draft	2' 11"/3' 11" (shoal/deep keel)
Displacement	4,400 lbs.
Ballast	1,800 lbs.
Sail area	256 sq. ft.

quired safety gear, etc. and no factory supplied options except a shoal draft keel (in the fall of 1978 this sales policy got a name, CruisePac). Price of the 25 in 1974 was quoted at less than $8,000 with the boats reportedly being offered to dealers at closer to $6,000 in order to encourage a high sales volume.

By 1975, the desired sales being apparently unattainable with a boat as performance-oriented as the 25, the boat was offered in a so-called "pop-top" version with a more box-like cabin trunk at a price just $150 above the $8,500 tag on the standard version. The hull, rig and interior layout remained essentially the same. The following year the original model was discontinued and a box cabin trunk model without a pop-top became the standard Hunter 25.

At the same time, in keeping with the cruising image and purpose, a Yanmar single-cylinder diesel engine became an option and much was made of the increased headroom (from 5' 2" to 5' 8"). Later still the transom was made more vertical (cockpit space having been at a premium and helping to cure the problem of mounting a outboard motor) and the headroom further increased.

In all over 2,000 25s were built, the exact number an oddly unavailable figure from Hunter Marine. Today they are probably the most universally recognized boat of their size and one of the most ubiquitous both in anchorages and on the used boat market, in brokers' listings and classified advertising.

A Look at the Boat

Looking critically at a boat with the sales success of the Hunter 25 invites contention, but it does have notable deficiencies as well as notable virtues. Its virtues start with price just as Hunter Marine intends they should. When low price is a chief priority, it buys a lot of boat in a Hunter 25. This axiom applies just as much to the used 25 as it did to the new. For the entry-level sailor or one moving up into a first boat suitable for cruising, the 25 offers good livability (space, berths, enclosed head, and cookable galley), at least average performance and stability, a functional decor and styling, easily maintained (or neglected) cosmetics, and adequate structural strength for semi-protected waters. And all of this is obtainable at a price that competes with typical prices for the smaller, more cramped 23 footers of similar vintage.

On a negative side, the 25 suffers from the original narrowish beam, an unfortunate parameter since the boat never proved practical for trailering. Worse still, the shoal draft version, otherwise a desirable feature in boats of this size and purpose, does not have top-notch performance or stability. The cockpit is short and cramped for daysailing with a crew of more than three or four, and the coaming is too low for back support.

In general the Hunter 25 performs adequately. Under PHRF a fin-keel 25 rates about 222 (shoal draft, 230 or so), letting it sail boat-for-boat with the Catalina 25 and the O'Day 25, two slightly higher priced but otherwise comparable boats in size and type. Windward performance is hurt by shrouds attached at the rail and by the heavy weather helm created as the 25 heels. The shoal version further suffers from excessive leeway.

Perhaps the most serious fault of the Hunter 25 (as well as a lot of other boats of her size) is the inadequacy of an outboard motor as auxiliary power. For a "transition cruiser" auxiliary power is a highly desirable feature. At 4500 pounds with considerable windage the 25 needs engine power unavailable with outboard motors of reasonable horsepower. Add to this problem the tendency of a transom-mounted engine to lift free of the water in pitching conditions as well as the awkwardness of operating engine controls from the end of a tiller in a tight cockpit and you have persuasive arguments in favor of inboard engines in boats of this size even at the considerable additional cost.

Since, with the exception of the short-lived Yanmar

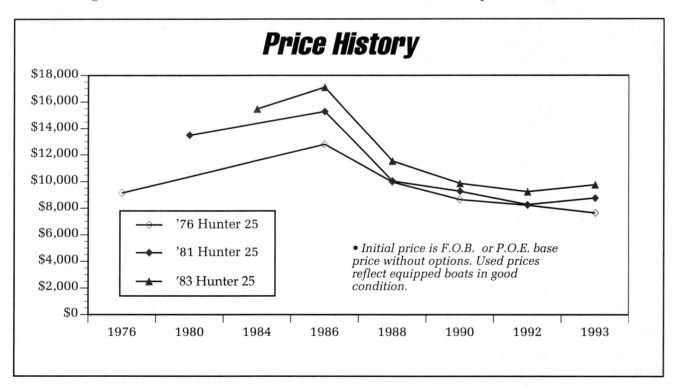

Price History

• Initial price is F.O.B. or P.O.E. base price without options. Used prices reflect equipped boats in good condition.

Legend:
- '76 Hunter 25
- '81 Hunter 25
- '83 Hunter 25

option and owner-retrofitted engines (usually Saildrives), Hunter 25s are not available with inboard power, they are probably not a good choice for a buyer wanting a small auxiliary cruising boat.

What To Look For

Anyone in the market for a lower priced boat has to be more aware of possible problems than those prepared to spend more. The reasons are two-fold. In the first place, quality in boats is to a large degree a function of price. Secondly, for the less expensive boat the cost of repairs or replacement becomes a greater proportion of the value of the boat. With this in mind, we suggest looking at the following:

• A number of owners report problems with gelcoat. Crazing, voids, and porosity (pinholes that trap dirt) are commonly cited faults, especially in the deck and cabinhouse. Also, Hunter used a stippled gelcoat non-skid deck surface that deteriorates over the years. This pattern can be restored but it is not an easy task for the average owner unfamiliar with working with gelcoat.

• About half of the Hunter owners (25s and 27s) whose *PS* Boat Owner's Questionnaires are in our files report at least "some" bottom blistering. Even if owner-refinished, the cost of ridding the boat of the pox could amount to 10% or more of the resale value of the boat and is unlikely to be more than tokenly recoverable in the sale price.

• Another oft-cited problem with the 25 is deck and cockpit-sole flexing. This flexing, while not a severe structural problem unless delamination has occured, is unnerving and offends our sense of what a boat *should* feel like underfoot. To check for delamination (separation of the outer fiberglass laminate from the core material) tap the whole deck *lightly* with a hard plastic object such as the handle of a screw driver. Voids produce a dull sound.

• Play in the rudder post seems common on the 25s. Of the three we specifically looked at, 1977-1980 vintage, all had a noticable degree of "slop" between the rudder post and the rudder tube. There is no simple or easy way to cure the ill that is more annoying than dangerous.

• Several readers report—and our findings support—the impression that 25 built between 1978 and 1981 are generally of at least a bit better quality than those built before or since. Note, however, there there can be no similar assurance that boats of that era were better maintained.

In our opinion the Hunter 25 does not recommend itself for any substantive restoration project except as it may help make the boat more enjoyable to own. With the number on the market, the basic functionality of the boat inside and out, and the low cost versus quality, expensive improvements do not produce commensurately higher value for the boat. At the same time, a polyurethane refinishing, bottom fairing (especially the iron keel), some dressing up of the decor (e.g., new berth upholstery), and a good choice of sails can do much to both the appearance and the pleasure of owning a 25.

One owner questionnaire voices the wonder of why Hunter-built boats tend to depreciate in contrast to other less popular boats. The reason is simple: the supply exceeds the demand. With the numbers built there are a lot on the used boat market. Many are also available because they were traded in on new boats, a source on the used boat market that tends to further depress selling price.

Conclusions

Frankly the Hunter 25 is best as a used boat when the most boat for the dollars is the overriding concern and, on a buyer's market, when a good deal presents itself. Yet even then there are roomier, faster, better finished, and more distinctive boats readily available at comparable prices. One example is the Catalina 25. More importantly we think buyers should think smaller if budget constraints are crucial because they will want better performance with outboard power or they should think inboard at 10-15% higher price if needing 25' and/or 4000+ pounds of boat.

If still otherwise sold on a Hunter 25, we would opt for a deep draft 25 for her performance and greater stability, and look for one that has had better-than-average maintenance to reduce the chances of serious problems. Whether valid or not, we'd also look for one built between 1978 and 1981—they have impressed owners as better boats. **• PS**

Ericson 25

Remarkably roomy for such a small boat, the 25 is well finished and offers enough performance for racing.

Just a few years ago, the prospective buyer of a 25' sailboat knew that some serious compromises awaited him. His 25-footer would probably have little more than sitting headroom, might have four shelves that could reasonably be called berths, and probably had a head stowed under the forward berth. The galley? With luck, a two-burner alcohol stove, maybe a sink, and a water tank holding ten gallons.

Auxiliary power? Usually a 6 hp outboard hanging off the stern or in a well in the lazarette.

With today's economy, more and more people who once might have considered a 30-footer are downscaling their size expectations to something more realistic, perhaps a 25- or 27-footer. While they may downgrade their expectations in terms of the length of their boats, they have not downgraded their expectations in terms of the size boat they want. This is not the contradiction it may seem. The fact is that there are a number of boats less than 27' in overall length that offer room and features akin to those offered in older 30' boats.

For better or worse, economic reality has forced many of us to downsize our boat expectations in much the way we downsized our automobile expectations.

Then came a new generation of small cruising auxiliaries. The modern 25' "family" sailboat has 6' headroom, berths for a family of five—if privacy isn't a high priority—enclosed head, and perhaps an inboard diesel engine. A regular miniature yacht.

The Ericson 25+ is a good example. The proof of the popularity of this concept shows in the numbers. Over 660 units were built in the first three years after the Ericson 25+ was introduced in late 1978.

Designer Bruce King had a long and successful relationship with Ericson Yachts, starting with the

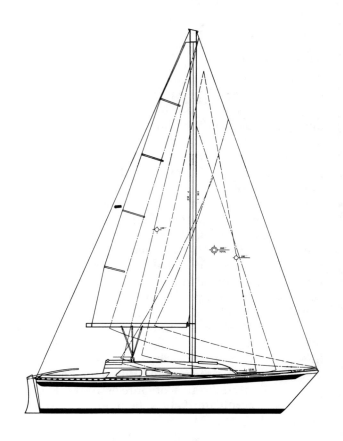

Specifications

LOA	25' 5"
LWL	21' 10"
Beam	9' 3"
Draft	4' 11" (std), 3' 11" (shoal)
Displacement	5,000 lbs.
Ballast	2,000 lbs.
Sail area	341 sq. ft.

Ericson 23, 30, 32, and 41 of the late 1960s. He has not been exclusively an Ericson "house" designer—witness the magnificent Herreshoff-inspired 90' ketch *Whitehawk* to his design—but the vast majority of Ericson boats came from his board.

Bruce King and Ericson found a formula not unlike that of Bill Shaw and Pearson: build a wide range of boats of similar type in two to three foot increments, develop customer loyalty, and watch the customers move up through the ranks. Keep the really popular models, such as the Pearson 35 or the Ericson 35, and bring out other models every few years to catch the latest trend. That formula worked whether you were on the East Coast or the West, and like Pearson, Ericson had the formula down pat.

With the exception of a few forays into the cruis-

The high-aspect-ratio 7/8 sloop rig indicates good light-air performance. To enhance windward ability, we recommend looking for a deep-draft boat, unless having shoal draft is a high priority.

ing market with the clipper-bowed Cruising 31 and the Cruising 38 (later to be called Independence), the Ericson formula produced a well finished cruiser-racer with good sailing characteristics. The Ericson 25+ was part of this successful formula.

Construction

The hull of the Ericson 25+ is a solid hand layup. A molded fiberglass body pan is glassed to the inside of the hull, functioning as the base for much of the interior furniture and adding a certain amount of rigidity to the hull. The deck, cockpit, and cabin trunk molding is balsa cored, with plywood replacing the balsa in high stress areas such as under the deck-stepped mast and where deck hardware is mounted.

Exterior glasswork is of good quality, with little roving printthrough, Gelcoat work is good.

The hull-to-deck joint depends on a secondary chemical bond. Both the hull and deck have an external molded flange. Glass-reinforced polyester resin is used as a bedding compound between these flanges. The inside of this joint is then lapped with four layers of fiberglass mat and cloth. This joint is covered on the outside by a plastic extrusion with a soft plastic insert which functions as a rub rail. We prefer a mechanically fastened hull-to-deck joint, because the strength of secondary chemical bonds is very difficult to evaluate.

The deck of the 25+ has a remarkably solid feel thanks to its cored construction. Neither the deck, cockpit, nor cabin top had any of the sponginess frequently associated with small boats.

Deck hardware of the 25+ is well mounted. Stanchions, pulpits, cleats, and winches have adequate aluminum bearing plates. The tiller head is a substantial chrome-plated bronze casting, The transom is plywood cored, greatly adding to its rigidity.

The mast of the 25+ is a black, deck-stepped extrusion. The stainless steel mast step looks surprisingly fragile. Because the mast is designed to be owner-stepped if desired, the forward lower half of the base of the mast is cut away to allow the mast to pivot forward for lowering. We doubt if there are many owners who will step their own masts. The design of the mast step to facilitate raising and lowering has greatly reduced the bearing surface of the heel of the mast.

In contrast to the mast step, the shroud chainplates are of surprisingly heavy construction. The 25+ utilizes Navtec chainplates, shroud terminals, and turnbuckles. Chainplates are strongly tied to the hull.

All through hull fittings below the waterline have Zytel valves, a reinforced plastic. Most have double-clamped hoses, but the icebox drain hose has a single clamp. Although modern plastics are strong, we suggest that you carefully inventory through hull fittings, as they are a major culprit in many sinkings of otherwise undamaged boats. Plastic valves may be immune to electrolysis, but they cannot be forgotten any more than bronze seacocks can be ignored.

Handling Under Sail

Despite the chubbiness of the 25+, owners report that

she is a fast boat under sail. There are a number of features that contribute to this speed, She has minimum wetted surface, despite a displacement that is average for her overall length, though fairly light for a waterline length of almost 22'.

The Ericson 25+, 28+, and 30+ all feature Bruce King's trademark, the "delta" fin keel. King states that this keel form has very low induced drag, and the 25's performance reinforces his belief. The optional shoal draft keel reduces draft a foot, reduces lateral plane, and no doubt reduces windward ability, Unless you are bound and determined to have a boat drawing under four feet, by all means get the deeper draft version.

The rig of the 25+ is a high aspect ratio 7/8 sloop rig. The mainsail hoist of 31.5' is unusual for a 25' boat. In light air, tall rigs are usually faster, and we would expect the boat's best point of sail to be upwind in light air. Since a great deal of the sailing in the world seems to be upwind in light air, this approach to the rig is a rational one.

With the addition of a backstay adjuster—easy because of the split backstay—it is possible to induce a reasonable amount of mast bend to control sail shape. A full width mainsheet traveler mounted on the cockpit bridgedeck greatly enhances mainsail control.

Shroud chainplates are set well inboard, allowing narrow headsail sheeting angles. The genoa track is also located inboard, almost against the cabin side.

There is no main boom topping lift, We think this is pretty indefensible on a cruising boat, and despite the additional windage, a topping lift is greatly to be desired on a racing boat. Without a topping lift, reefing becomes a real exercise in agility. Dropping the mainsail is greatly complicated, especially when cruising shorthanded. Should the main halyard break when sailing close hauled, the main boom could

brain anyone sitting on the leeward side of the cockpit.

Two-speed Barient headsail sheet winches were standard in later boats. There is room on the cockpit coamings both for the addition of secondary winches for spinnaker handling and the replacement of the standard winches with larger ones. A single halyard winch is mounted on the mast, There is no main halyard winch. We would choose the optional aft-leading halyards to facilitate shorthanded cruising.

The 25+ should sail with almost any other production cruiser-racer of her size. Her wide beam and deep draft should offset the additional heeling moment of the tall rig. Like all wide modern boats she should be sailed on her feet. Get the crew weight out on the weather rail in a breeze, and she should carry sail well.

Handling Under Power

There were probably more power options for the 25+ than any similar-sized boat on the market. They included: outboard power, OMC gas saildrive, Volvo diesel saildrive, and Yanmar diesel inboard.

The 25+ is small enough to be driven fairly well by a 10-hp outboard. There was about a $3,500 difference in equipping the boat with an outboard engine versus the diesel inboard. The choice depended largely on how the boat was to be used. Few boats of this size are used for long-distance cruising. For daysailing and racing, an outboard engine is more than adequate.

If extended coastal cruising is to be the boat's primary activity, then one of the inboard options

6' headroom in the main cabin, seating for six, and a large stand-up head distinguish the interior of the Ericson 25. This is offset somewhat by a rather small V-berth, but it's fine for children.

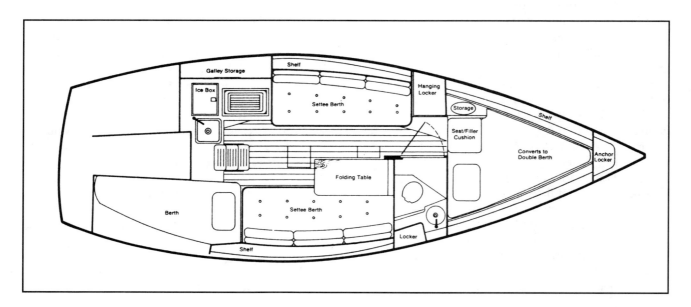

One of the design tricks used to gain all that headroom below is a sharply bowed cabinhouse roof.

should be considered. Frankly, we have little love for saildrive installations. If you really want an inboard engine, the Yanmar single cylinder inboard diesel is the real choice. No matter which engine is in the boat, it is equipped with a 20-gallon aluminum fuel tank.

With a one-cylinder diesel engine, given a four-knot cruising speed and fuel consumption of about 1/4 gallon per hour, the range under power is almost 350 miles—a truly astounding range for a 25' boat, That's probably more range under power than the average boat is likely to need for an entire season.

Deck Layout

With shroud chainplates set well inboard, and a reasonably narrow cabin trunk, working on the deck of the 25+ is fairly easy. There is adequate room between the shrouds and the lifelines to walk outboard of the shrouds with ease.

There is a small foredeck anchor well, adequate for the stowage of a single Danforth and rode. There are no bow chocks, but there are two cleats located forward at the outboard edge of the deck.

Molded-in nonskid of a color contrasting to the primary deck color was standard on the Ericson. This relieves eyestrain in bright sunlight and reduces the basically austere external appearance of the boat.

The cockpit of the 25+ is comfortable. Coamings are angled outward rather than being vertical, allowing a more natural sitting posture. As in most tiller-steered boats, the sweep of the tiller occupies a large percentage of the cockpit volume. In port, the tiller swings up and out of the way, providing uncrowded seating for up to six adults.

A single cockpit scupper 1—1/ 2" in diameter is recessed in a well at the back of the cockpit. The well allows water to drain on either tack. A stainless steel strainer over the scupper reduces its effective area by over 50%. Since the drain size is large enough to pass on through almost any debris that is likely to be found in the cockpit, we would remove the strainer for sailing. A single 1-1/2" diameter scupper has more cross sectional area than two 1" drains, and is less likely to clog.

There are two cockpit lockers. The starboard cockpit locker is a shallow pan suitable for storing small items such as winch handles and sail ties. At its after corner is a deeper bin which could make a handy icebox for cold drinks. The port locker is a large, deep affair which unfortunately suffers from the common failing of not being adequately separated from the

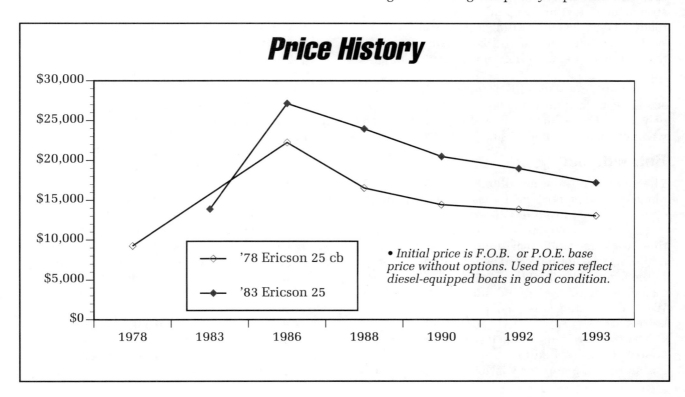

Price History

| | 1978 | 1983 | 1986 | 1988 | 1990 | 1992 | 1993 |

'78 Ericson 25 cb
'83 Ericson 25

• *Initial price is F.O.B. or P.O.E. base price without options. Used prices reflect diesel-equipped boats in good condition.*

under-cockpit area, A snap-in Dacron bag would convert this locker to reasonable sail stowage.

The companionway uses thick, well-made solid teak dropboards with proper step joints to prevent spray from working below, Unfortunately, the very strong taper to the companionway slides allows them to be removed by lifting less than an inch. For sailing in rough water, a positive means of securing these slides—a sliding bolt, for example—must be installed.

It is gratifying to see a real bridgedeck in a boat this size. Except for the strong taper to the companionway sides, this is one of the best designed cockpits we have seen in a small boat.

Belowdecks

The amount of interior volume in the 25+ is truly remarkable. The boat easily has the headroom and elbow room of most older 30-footers.

The forepeak contains the usual V-berth with a filler to form a nominal double. We truly mean nominal. Two normal-sized people simply do not fit in the forward berth of the Ericson 25+. Consider it a large single instead, or a double for two children. Water and holding tanks occupy the space under the berth.

The 25+ has a genuine enclosed, standup head, an almost unheard of luxury in a boat this size. The head has an opening port for ventilation. There are two

While the galley has some very good features, it's burdened with a Kenyon alcohol stove that can only be refilled when completely cold and an icebox that suffers both from exposed insulation and a poorly executed lid.

small lockers in the head, but both are largely occupied by plumbing hoses.

Opposite the head is a small hanging locker. This locker is fully lined with teak plywood, a nice finishing touch.

It is in the main cabin that the 25+ really shines. Headroom is an honest 6'. Two comfortable settee berths seat 6 in comfort, A fold-down drop-leaf table is big enough to serve 4, and is one of the sturdier tables of this type that we have seen.

The main cabin of the 25+ is well finished with a combination of off-white fiberglass and teak. This is a very successful decorating job, without so much teak as to turn the interior into a cave but with enough to give a well finished appearance. A ceiling of teak strips became standard later on in the production run, and the cabin trunk sides are veneered in teak. A teak and holly cabin sole came standard, with two access hatches to the bilge.

There is a real bilge, unusual in a boat of this size. The strainer for the cockpit-mounted Whale Gusher pump is accessible through a cabin sole hatch.

Under the settee on each side of the cabin there are

storage bins. These make use of molded polyethylene drop-in liners, a most practical solution which recognizes the reality that under-seat storage is rarely, if ever, completely dry. An optional extension to the starboard settee converts it to a double berth, but at the expense of easy access to the storage bins underneath.

The galley is surprisingly complete for a 25' boat. There is a well-insulated icebox of five cubic foot capacity. The insulation is exposed in the port cockpit locker, and will be vulnerable to damage from items stowed there. It could easily be sealed off with either plywood or fiberglass to protect it. The icebox lid is an uninsulated molding advertised as a removable serving tray. If it is used as a serving tray, then the icebox is uncovered, allowing the ice to melt. Whoever thought up that bright idea should go back to the drawing board or look around for some common sense.

For some reason, icebox lids are one of the poorest design features of most sailboats, It's quite remarkable on boats with otherwise thoughtful design and construction to see poor icebox design. Perhaps there is collusion between the Union of Icebox Designers and the Association of Manufacturers of Ice to maximize the consumption of ice aboard sailboats.

There are storage lockers both above and below the icebox-stove counter. The stove is a recessed Kenyon two-burner alcohol unit with a cutting block cover, These stoves have the fuel fill located between the two burners, and we feel they are a poor choice for use aboard a boat. The burners must be absolutely cool before the fuel tank is filled to eliminate the possibility of explosion or fire.

It is not necessary to step on the galley counter when coming down the companionway. This is a real plus. Footprints on the counters have never appealed to us.

A human-sized quarterberth is a welcome feature. With adequate headroom over, it eliminates the coffinlike aura of so many small-boat quarterberths, and is without a doubt the roomiest, most comfortable berth on the boat.

With an outboard engine, the room under the cockpit that would normally house an inboard is given over to storage. The tiny one-cylinder Yanmar diesel would easily shoehorn into the same space.

Without a doubt, the interior of the Ericson 25+ is a real accomplishment, It is well finished, generally well designed, and remarkably roomy for a boat of this overall length. There is some miniaturization of components, such as the galley sink, head sink, and hanging locker. Nonetheless, she's a big little boat, and would be truly comfortable for extended coastal cruising for a couple. That is something that can rarely be said for a 25' boat.

Conclusions

Ericson came very close to achieving their goals in the 25+. She is about as much boat as can be crammed into this overall length.

An interesting option is an E-Z Loader trailer. With a beam of over 9' and a weight of 5,000 pounds, the 25+ is no trailer sailer. It takes a large, powerful car or truck to tow a boat of this size, and the beam could present legal problems in some states. The trailer would be most useful for taking the boat home for winter storage, rather than frequent over-the-road transport.

Workmanship and finish detail are generally of good stock boat quality. Exposed joiner work is good. Fillet bonding varies from good to only fair, with glasswork generally good.

The Ericson 25+ is a good small cruiser for a young family, and offers enough sailing performance to be a reasonable choice for club racing.

Unlike many small cruiser-racers which concentrate on interior volume and forsake sailing ability, the 25+ really will sail. This means that the new sailor will not quickly outgrow her as he or she learns what makes a boat go fast. With good hardware such as Barient and Navtec and a fairly high degree of finish detail, it is easy to see why the boat fetches the prices it does.

For those used to less-expensive 25-footers, the cost will be a shock. It helps a little to think of her as a 28-footer with the stern cut off.

With an inboard diesel, a good light air rig, and lots of interior volume, she's a good little cruising boat for a couple. A maximum boat for minimum length, she's a modern solution to skyrocketing costs of sailing. At maximum price for her length when new, she's not an example of "more for less," but then, there's no free lunch in the sailboat market. That's for sure.　**• PS**

MacGregor 26

This water-ballasted trailer sailer is targeted right at the novice sailor; it's priced (and built) accordingly.

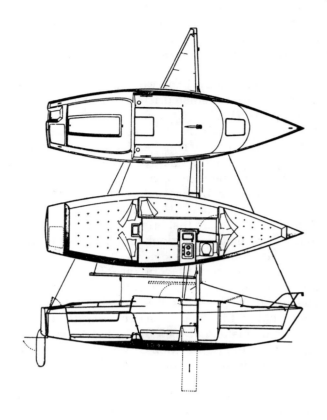

The MacGregor Yacht Corporation is a survivor. It stands as one of the few boatbuilders from the 1960s still in business and still making money. It also stands on a street in Costa Mesa, California that once housed now-defunct builders like Islander and Westsail.

MacGregor is, and always has been, a one-man show; in this case the man is Roger MacGregor. He founded the company in 1964 to prove the validity of his Stanford MBA thesis, the hypothesis of which was that boatbuilders would be more successful if they were more efficient. A "hobby" at first, with only 26 employees, MacGregor decided in 1967 to "really go at it."

Through the years, MacGregor has produced a number of boats, first under the Venture trademark, and for the last ten years, under the MacGregor name. The thrust of the line has always been aimed at the first time sailor; today Roger MacGregor has a better handle on that market than anyone else in the industry.

The first boat the company built was the Venture 21; it was discontinued in 1986, after 22 years in production. In the interim, a number of small boats were produced, like the Venture 22, 222, 23, 24, and 25. The only deviations from the trailerboat theme have been a 36' catamaran, and a 65' ULDB "sled," which is the only boat still in production other than the MacGregor 26.

Of the 25,000-odd boats built to date by MacGregor, 17,000 of them are MacGregor 25s. From this statistic, MacGregor learned that the trailerboat market prefers bigger boats, so he replaced the 25 in 1986 with the 26, a new, but similar design.

To get around the problem posed by smaller and smaller automobiles, they eliminated the 25's swing keel, which weighs 600 pounds. This leaves the 26

Specifications

LOA	25' 10"
LWL	23' 6"
Beam	7' 11"
Draft	1' 3"/5' 4" (board up/down)
Displacement	2,850 lbs. (tank full)
Ballast	1,200 lbs. (water)
Sail area	236 sq. ft.

weighing only 1,650 pounds (2,200 pounds with trailer), light enough for most mid-size cars. The lack of a keel also puts the boat lower to the road for less windage.

To provide stability lost by removing the keel, the MacGregor 26 was designed with a slight V to the bottom, which houses a water ballast compartment. The compartment holds an additional 1,200 pounds of water, to bring the total sailing weight up to 2,850 pounds.

Roger MacGregor says he knows why the boatbuilding industry has gone sour, and has found, in the MacGregor 26, the secret to success. He cites the common explanation that the market has dried up, that fewer people are interested in sailing at the introductory level because of the cost and complica-

tion. He has overcome those objections by making his boats very uncomplicated, writing lengthy instruction manuals in non-nautical terminology, and by having a dealer network that caters to the first time sailor.

One-half of MacGregor owners are beginning sailors, and the dealers know it. Most dealers go so far as to show the new owner how to rig and sail his boat, or arrange for sailing lessons, says MacGregor. Of the 40-odd *PS* boat owner evaluations returned on the MacGregor 25, not one reader had anything but kind words to say about his dealer. This is an exceptional record.

Another pitfall of modern boatbuilding that MacGregor has conquered is the prohibitive cost of compliance to environmental regulations. Because he owns his plant, Roger MacGregor says he can support the expense of compliance, while builders trying to get on their feet in rented property cannot.

MacGregor says many boatbuilders were closed after being purchased by conglomerates, because the conglomerates weren't willing to weather a sustained period of operating in the red. Roger MacGregor says he'll never sell his company; that's why he changed the name of his boats from Venture to MacGregor.

The biggest reason that builders fail, says MacGregor, is inefficiency. This is where MacGregor Yachts shines. The MacGregor 26 only has three options: cockpit cushions, bottom paint and surge brakes on the trailer.

The boat comes complete with trailer, sails, lifelines and pulpits, battery and lights. The only major item you have to buy is an outboard.

MacGregor takes pains to save money at every turn, right down to owning its own fleet of trucks. The dimensions of the MacGregor 26 were not determined by what would be seaworthy, or even what could be legally trailered: rather, the boat was laid out so that four of them would fit on the truck at a time.

Making the boat relatively complete accomplishes two things. First, it helps satisfy the most common owner complaint about the MacGregor 25—that the boats required too much additional equipment. Second, it simplifies the "tracking" of boats through production.

There is no need to keep track of which boat goes to which dealer while in production. If a dealer's sale falls through, he isn't stuck with an odd boat, because all boats are the same. Red tape and paperwork are drastically reduced.

Making all boats alike has allowed MacGregor to "jig" almost every step in production, saving a great deal of time. MacGregor says this saves about $800 per boat.

MacGregor also saves money by owning and maintaining a company fleet of trucks, complete with drivers and mechanics. The outside dimensions of the MacGregor 26 were determined by the space required to fit four of them, with trailers, on a company truck. Cost of shipping to the east coast is only $900.

MacGregor has individual shops to build trailers, spars and upholstery. While other builders usually farm out these tasks, MacGregor says they save money by doing them "in house."

Hull and Deck

The best way to describe the construction of the MacGregor 26 is "quick and dirty." The plant finishes four boats a day, five days a week. A hull is in the mold for only 13 hours.

There's a timetable to be met at each step of production. Production hangups aren't allowed. If the work gets a bit behind, the workers work a bit faster. Sloppiness is inevitable.

The construction flaws caused by this sloppiness are hidden from view, but the finish details are not. The MacGregor 26 will appear somewhat crude to the experienced sailor, but the "rough edges" may not be so apparent to the inexperienced sailor for whom she is intended.

This isn't to say that the buyer of a MacGregor 26 is getting a bad deal. On the contrary, the MacGregor 26 is a lot of boat for the money.

The MacGregor 26 hull is a solid fiberglass laminate, and a not particularly thick one: the laminate schedule calls for a total of 54 ounces of glass fiber per square yard (cloth and roving) below the waterline, and 30 ounces above the waterline—but remember that this is a lightweight boat.

MacGregor's immigrant work force lacks the skill needed to operate a chopper gun, or to trim the fiberglass to size by first rolling it onto the mold. To avoid mistakes—and improve efficiency— the fiberglass is cut to a table pattern, then folded and boxed, one box to each step of the lamination.

The flat areas of the deck are cored with plywood, which is pressed into wet fiberglass mat by laying dozens of weights on top of the wood. The overhead liner is installed onto the deck in the same manner.

To save time, the fastening holes for all of the deck fittings are made by dropping a single jig onto the deck and drilling the pattern of holes. Then the interior side of each hole is bored to 5/8" diameter, to countersink the nuts and washers. Finally, the nut is hidden by a plastic cap; this gives access to the fastenings should you want to replace deck hardware.

Small backing plates, made of scraps of fiberglass, are used on the bow cleats, but not on any other fittings. While the plywood core in the deck reduces the need for backing plates, the practice of countersinking the washers and nuts reduces the strength of the attachment. In addition, plywood is more likely than balsa core to absorb water and delaminate should the deck fittings leak or the lamination work be sloppy.

The hull-to-deck joint, fashioned by a deck flange overlapping the hull and hull liner, appears to be adequate. A rubrail is bolted through the joint with #10 bolts on 6" centers. Foam weatherstripping forms the bedding for the joint, but adds no strength. Final waterproofing is achieved by running a bead of 3M 5200 sealer/adhesive around the edge of the deck flange; 5200 is also used to bed deck fittings.

The hull liner is pressed into wet mat laid on the keelson. Then vertical surfaces of the liner, where accessible through holes cut in the liner for lockers, are glassed to the hull. To save time, no filleting is used; the tabbing of the liner is done with roving 8" wide. This is not a clean or particularly strong method, but it's adequate for the use for which the boat is designed.

The chainplates are bolted directly to the hull, at the outboard edge of the gunwale. The hull in the area of attachment is reinforced with an additional fiberglass at the rate of 150 ounces per square yard.

The cabin house extends to the edge of the deck, and there are no structural interior bulkheads save those formed by the hull liner. This design gives less support for loading from the rig than would be advisable when sailing in heavy seas.

MacGregor 25 owners complain of cockpit floor flexing and resultant gelcoat crazing. MacGregor says they have solved this problem on the 26 by adding extra fiberglass around the corners of the cockpit floor.

Rig

Our owner surveys did register complaints about the MacGregor 25's rig, which is virtually identical to that of the 26. Made by MacGregor, the mast is anodized but untapered.

The rigging is minimal, external and crude. The rig is fractional with swept-back upper and lower shrouds. The spreaders are tubes that swing freely on small, U-shaped brackets. If the spreaders were fixed they would add stiffness to the mast and safety in heavy air. With freely swinging spreaders the mast loses athwartships support when it bends excessively. Shroud tangs are external, but through-bolted. Halyards are external as well, and they cleat on the mast, not aft in the cockpit.

The shrouds terminate with Nico-pressed eyes, not swage fittings. While MacGregor says they've never had a failure, *PS* owner surveys contradict this contention. Plate adjusters are used instead of turnbuckles on the shrouds.

Daggerboard/Rudder

The MacGregor 26 has an unballasted daggerboard, housed in a trunk running from bilge to deck just aft of the mast. The trunk acts as a compression post for the deck-stepped mast. The trunk also bisects the water ballast tank, which is good and bad. If you were to fracture the trunk in a hard grounding, the ballast tank would leak, not the hull; but if the ballast tank leaks, you could lose the ballast required to keep the boat upright.

To solve this problem, MacGregor says, the daggerboards are designed to shear off in a hard grounding. Replacement boards are $125.

The innovative board and rudder are nicely shaped airfoils. Holes are drilled in them so they will fill with water when sailing. In the daggerboard, this is a good idea. It leaves it lightweight for trailering, yet allows it to have negative buoyancy so it won't float up when sailing.

In the rudder, however, it only makes the helm feel heavier and more sluggish. Rudder action is further aggravated by a sloppy pintle-to-gudgeon fit and play in the rudder head. The pintles, like all of the MacGregor 26's rigging, are underbuilt.

The daggerboard is short enough to be self-contained inside the trunk when trailering. This means that there isn't much board inside the trunk when it's lowered for sailing; this adds to the loads placed on the trunk. However, the ballast tank gives the trunk some extra support.

The fit between the board and trunk is not particularly tight; we expect you might hear it "thunk" as the boat rolls in waves.

Ballast Tank/Flotation

The most unique feature of the MacGregor 26 is her water ballast system.

Water ballast in sailboats is usually restricted to singlehanded offshore racers, where ballast tanks are mounted under the gunwale to add stability. Their system requires that the leeward tank be filled, and the weather tank emptied, before each tack.

MacGregor's system is different. Patterned after European trailer sailers, it uses a single ballast tank running the length of the bilge.

This configuration doesn't provide the leverage of a lead keel of similar weight, nor of a gunwale-mounted ballast tank, but it does make the boat self-righting. It takes 125 pounds to hold the tip of the MacGregor 26's mast in the water, says her builder, compared to only 75 pounds for the MacGregor 25.

The ballast tank can be opened and closed, and the water level inspected, from inside the cabin. The tank is closed by drawing a rubber-backed plate up into a recess in the keelson. The rubber must be kept clean of fouling or the tank could leak ballast when the boat heels.

The tank has a fiberglass baffle to keep the water from sloshing around when sailing. It takes about six minutes to fill or empty the tank when launching or hauling.

The MacGregor 26 has positive flotation when swamped, a commendable feature, especially in a lightweight, trailerable sailboat. The flotation is provided by blocks of styrofoam under the V-berth, aft berth, over the galley, and under the cockpit.

Styrofoam is preferable to sprayed-in urethane foam, because it's less likely to absorb water and doesn't expand when exposed to heat.

On the other hand, styrofoam blocks don't fill the compartments as completely as urethane foam, so some of the flotation space is wasted. For example, the styrofoam in the MacGregor 26 only fills one half of the space under the V-berth, yet the berth is closed off.

The waste is less serious than it might be, how-

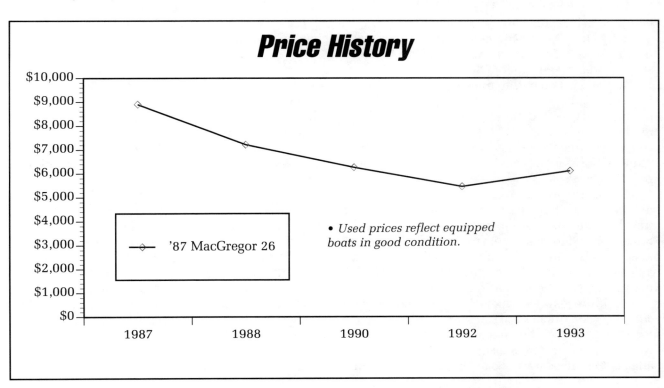

Used prices reflect equipped boats in good condition.

The deck molding is held in place by weights while the resin cures. The entire production process is set up to move as fast as possible, which means cutting corners everywhere.

ever, as the MacGregor 26 needs only 14 cubic feet of flotation because her water ballast is neutrally buoyant. The MacGregor 25 has 25 cubic feet of flotation.

Handling On the Water

The MacGregor 26 is not a performance boat. She is hampered by a rig which is too small for light air and too flimsy for heavy air. The standard boat comes equipped with a main and working jib from Gaastra, a quality Hong Kong sailmaker. The cloth weight is on the light side, but the workmanship and sail shape is above average for OEM sails.

Adding a genoa to the inventory would improve her reaching, but not her upwind performance. That's because the genoa has to sheet around her gunwale-mounted shrouds.

The working jib sheets inside the shrouds, which reduces the sheeting angle and allows the boat to point higher.

The MacGregor 26's rigging is too simple to make her handle well in a strong breeze. There is no traveler; the four-part mainsheet is fixed on the bridgedeck. There is no boom vang. The deck-stepped mast is light and bendy, but there are no backstay adjuster or turnbuckles on the shrouds to control mast bend. No tiller extension, either.

The jib leads are a fixed bullseye. Lewmar #6 single speed winches are standard. While adequate for the working jib, they are too small for a genoa. The cam cleats for the jib sheets are cheap and poorly angled. On the boat we looked at, the bedding com-

pound had gotten into and gummed up one of the cam cleats.

Halyards cleat on the mast, and reef lines and outhaul cleat on the end of the boom. The standard mainsail has two reefs. At least the MacGregor 26 is rigged for slab reefing; the 25 has roller reefing on the boom, which works poorly. The gooseneck and the reefing hook for the tack are lightly built.

The 1,200 pounds of water ballast sitting in the bilge is also a detriment to the performance of the MacGregor 26. Because the ballast runs for two-thirds of the length of the boat, she is heavy at the ends.

Combined with the sloppy rudder assembly, this makes her steer sluggishly and turn slowly. We also expect it will make her pitch more in a seaway. With the ballast in the bilge instead of hung from a keel, the boat is initially tender.

The outboard motor mounts directly on the transom, as it would on a dinghy. There is no external transom bracket. When tilted up, the head of the motor lies in a recess molded into the afterdeck. This doesn't make the outboard any more secure, but MacGregor says that it allows you to trailer with outboard attached because it doesn't hang far off the stern.

The MacGregor 26 has an afterdeck almost 3' long. This makes for a long reach to the motor controls. It's a good thing that the motor isn't mounted on an external bracket.

The afterdeck also houses a large lazarette that has more than enough space to stow the outboard and tank. The cockpit drains obstruct the lazarette, though, and are fabricated of unreinforced hose and fastened with single hose clamps. You'd have to be careful when stowing the motor.

Handling Off the Water

The boat comes equipped with a MacGregor-built trailer. Surge brakes are optional and recommended if you don't want to wear out your car brakes on lengthy road trips. The trailer is painted steel; a galvanized finish is not even offered, because California environmental laws make it cost-prohibitive, says MacGregor.

The trailer is made of steel channel with only a short section of the tongue made from steel box section tube. Channel can be kept from rusting because all surfaces are exposed and can be scraped and repainted. Box sections will eventually rust from the inside out.

MacGregor builds the trailers on a jig which rotates so all of the welds can be horizontally applied. The welding appears clean and completely encompasses the joints.

In preparation for painting the metal is only wire brushed. Although a zinc chromate primer is used, we suspect that the trailer will need to be repainted every other season if kept near salt water.

The MacGregor 26 sits low on her trailer because she has no external centerboard or swing keel. MacGregor 25 owners complain that a tongue extender is often needed to float their boat off the trailer. MacGregor says that the 26 will float off when the wheels are in only 2' 3" of water—9" less than the depth required for the 25. A jack stand would be useful, but the trailer does not come with one.

Because the mast is deck-stepped on a tabernacle, raising it simply requires that you walk it upright and attach the headstay. The swept-back shrouds only come taut when the mast is upright. To keep the mast from swaying sideways before the shrouds come taut, an extra set of in-line lower shrouds is rigged. To give you extra leverage when raising the mast, there is an optional "mast raising pole" which runs from the base of the mast to a tackle at the base of the headstay.

Belowdecks

For a trailer sailer, the MacGregor 26 is spacious belowdecks; but for your average 26-foot sailboat, she is cramped. The requirements for trailering require the boat be light, narrow and shallow. This doesn't leave a lot of interior volume.

The 26 is just big enough so that the daggerboard trunk is relatively unobtrusive, being used to form one side of the galley. The first thing you notice when going below is the huge, 9-square-foot mirror over the galley. MacGregor says the mirror adds the illusion of space. Even if the mirror were of better quality, so the reflection wasn't distorted, we'd still think it gaudy.

The galley is barely adequate, even for weekending. There's a molded sink with a collapsible 5-gallon water tank, removable for refilling. There's counter space, but no stove; mounting one would use up most of the counter. There's no table or icebox. There isn't even any space for a portable ice chest; it would have to live on top of a berth or in the middle of the cabin floor.

There is an enclosure for a head, but no head is provided. The enclosure is designed to fit a portable head.

The V-berth is very narrow at the foot. The settees are narrow, too, but they have seatback cushions and the port settee is 7' long. Under the cockpit is a queen size berth, a feature growing in popularity, even on boats this small.

There is plenty of sitting headroom, and a "pop top" for standing headroom. A dodger for the pop top is standard. The hatches are made by MacGregor and use weatherstripping for watertightness. We doubt that they would remain watertight with green water on deck.

The cabin house windows are bedded in silicone sealant with few mechanical fastenings.

The boat is equipped with a battery, running lights and two small cabin lights. Interior joinerwork is sparse and cheaply done. All pieces are cut by a pattern router to save time, and finished with imitation wood plastic veneer. The plastic peels off easily; we doubt it will stay on the facings of the joinerwork for very long.

There is almost no interior storage, save that inside the head compartment. There are small bins under the settees and aft berth, but much of that space is filled with flotation.

On Deck

To make space for the double berth under the cockpit, the cockpit floor had to be raised. This makes for cramped legroom and almost non-existent cockpit seatbacks.

MacGregor made an attempt to solve the seatback problem by installing stainless steel handrails along the cockpit coaming. The optional cockpit cushions package includes cushions for the seatbacks which attach to the handrails. This makes for comfortable sitting in calm conditions, but the cushions could be torn from their straps and washed overboard when water comes over the rail while sailing in a strong breeze.

The boat comes equipped with a bow pulpit and a set of stanchions and lifelines on each side of the cabin house. The lifelines are needed to go forward in safety because the cabin house extends all the way to the gunwale. The stanchion bases have extra bracing and seem adequately attached to the boat. The lifelines are run to the base rather than to the top of the bow pulpit. This makes for less wear and tear on the foot of the jib at the expense of a proper handhold to the bow.

Conclusions

At only about $10,000 new, the MacGregor 26 is a good deal. The water ballast makes her truly trailerable. For weekending on inland lakes she is an excellent choice. She's also a good choice for daysailing in protected waters if you cannot afford dock space or a mooring.

The boat has certain limitations, however. While she is simply rigged, that simplicity hampers her sailing ability and her seaworthiness. While there are no glaring structural flaws, the entire construction is just slipshod enough to make her unsuited to sailing where you might get caught in heavy weather.

We're sure that many passages have been made to places like Catalina Island in 20-25 knots of wind and healthy seas, but doing that on a regular basis in a MacGregor 26 is, in our opinion, asking for a pack of trouble.
• PS

S2 7.9

A fast boat targeted at a variety of sailors, the 7.9 makes a good racer, but not a cruiser.

After Leon Slikkers sold Slickcraft, his powerboat company, in the early 1970's, he built a sailboat factory the way a sailboat factory should be built. The result was S2 yachts and a factory quite in contrast to the normal dingy warehouse with blobbed polyester resin hardened on rough concrete floors.

Originally known for cruising designs, S2 Yachts opened their second decade in business by entering the high performance field, building first a trailerable racer/cruiser, the S2 7.9. The 7.9 stands for meters, which translates into American as 25' 11". The boat stayed in production up until S2 shut down its sailboat operations in 1986.

Designed by the Chicago-based naval architects Scott Graham and Eric Schlageter, the 7.9 was the first in a series of competitive production boats. The series was originally called "Grand Slam," but the company later dropped the designation. With over 400 built between the boat's introduction in 1982 and 1986, the 7.9 was relatively successful during a time when few boats in its size range were selling.

The 7.9 was a pricey boat for her size. Equipped with sail handling gear, four sails (main, jib, genoa, and spinnaker), outboard motor, speedo, and compass, her 1985 price was about $27,000. For comparison, a comparably equipped J/24 of the time would run you around $21,000, an Olson 25 about $22,000. Add an inboard engine, a trailer, and miscellaneous gear and you could easily have dropped $36,000 on the 7.9—a hefty tab for a 26' boat.

Construction

The hull and deck of the 7.9 are hand-laid fiberglass, cored with end-grain balsa. S2 bragged about its glasswork, and the company had a high reputation in the industry for both its gelcoat and its hand layup.

Specifications

LOA	25' 11"
LWL	21' 8"
Beam	9' 0"
Draft	1' 1"/5' 0" (board up/down)
Displacement	4,250 lbs.
Ballast	1,750 lbs.
Sail area	329 sq. ft.

Beginning somewhere around hull number 400, S2 switched from conventional polyester resin to a modified epoxy resin—AME 4000. The company claimed the epoxy resin is stronger, lighter, and less subject to blistering.

The hull is fair with no bumps or hard spots evident—probably the result of the company's practice of installing most of the interior before removing the hull from its mold. The gelcoat appears to be thicker than is usual in production boats—a good feature since minor scratches and dings can be "rubbed out" without penetrating to the laminate.

For their standard hull-to-deck joint, S2 used an inward turning flange onto which the deck molding is set—a desirable design, especially when bedded in flexible adhesive (such as 3M 5200) and through bolted at close intervals. However on the 7.9, rather than being through bolted, the deck is mechanically fastened to the hull only with screws through the slotted aluminum toerail, a detail that indicates the boat is not intended for heavy-duty offshore work.

The boat came with a one-design package of good quality deck hardware. All hardware is through bolted, with stainless backing plates on the lifeline stanchions but with only washers and nuts on all other hardware. This would seem to be problematic with the balsa core, but we have heard no reports of problems so far.

Although the company offered the boat in a fixed keel version, the vast majority of boats have a lead ballasted daggerboard.

The advantages of a daggerboard are, first, that it retracts to be flush with the bottom of the hull to make the boat trailer launchable, second, that you can float the boat in a mere 13" of water (though she will have no directional control with the board totally up—you'll need at least a foot of board showing for control under sail or power), and, third, with the board totally down, the boat has a 5' deep hydrodynamically efficient keel, a depth that would be extreme on a fixed-keel boat this size.

The disadvantage of the daggerboard will come in a hard grounding. Whereas a centerboard would kick out of the way, the board is likely to bash around a bit in its trunk. A nice detail by S2 is that the bottom opening of the trunk is surrounded by a strong weldment which will mitigate the potential damage to the hull from a grounding. Another potential disadvantage is that, on many boats, the daggerboard trunk messes up the interior, but the designers have done a good job on the 7.9, incorporating the daggerboard into a centerline bulkhead.

Nearly a third of the 1,750 pounds ballast is in the board, with the remaining two-thirds glassed to the interior of the hull. When the board is fully lowered, it fits snugly in a V-shaped crotch—a good design detail—but when it's raised out of the V using the three-part tackle and winch, it will bang about loosely in the daggerboard trunk. There is no way to pin the board down—an obvious potential problem in severe conditions.

The boat, however, has passed the MORC self-righting test with the daggerboard in the fully raised position. In the test, the mast-head is hove down to the water, the bagged mainsail and genoa are tied to the masthead, and the whole shebang released. This is not a test of ultimate stability, since other boats which passed the test have turtled and sunk, but it is reassuring. However, the design is clearly dependent mostly on its beamy hull form for righting and not on its ballast—another indication the boat is intended for close-to-shore sailing.

The transom-hung rudder—pivoted for trailering—is of foam-cored fiberglass (the foam gives it neutral bouyancy in water). We like the idea of a transom-hung rudder: it's accessible for inspection and service, it lessens the potential damage to the hull that can occur when a rudder smashes into something, and it gets the rudder farther away from the keel to give the tiller a more responsive feel.

The fractional rig—with mast and boom made by Offshore Spars—is dinghy-like, having swept-back spreaders which make the upper shrouds function as backstays. The actual backstay does virtually nothing to support the rig; instead, its primary function is to bend the mast to control mainsail performance. Although the mast is easily bendable, it's a surprisingly heavy section for a modern racing rig—it's also untapered. Everything is internal in the mast and boom, with all lines eventually coming back to the cockpit in typical modern racing style.

Upper and lower shrouds attach to inboard chainplates. The starboard chainplate is attached to a well bonded plywood bulkhead, but the port chainplate is longer, attached to the fiberglass structure which forms the front edge of the galley. Since there is a 2' "free span" of unsupported chainplate between the galley and deck, the chainplate in the highly-loaded rig works a lot, and one of the most common owner complaints about the boat is the leaking port chainplate that results.

A fiberglass floorpan makes up the berths, floor, and galley area. Instead of a ceiling, S2 uses carpeting for interior covering of the hull. One good detail about the carpeting is that Velcro will stick to it—you can hang anything anywhere—but we have to wonder how the carpet will stand up to salt accumulation. There is virtually no bilge, so water inside will turn everything soggy.

Generally, the boat is well constructed, with good detail work and hardware. While we believe that every "racer-cruiser" should be designed and built to handle extreme conditions offshore, the hull shape, the daggerboard design, and the hull-to-deck joint show us that S2 did not intend for this boat to be involved in those extremes.

Handling Under Power

The standard 7.9 is be outboard powered. The option was a BMW 7.5 hp one-lung diesel with the shockingly high price tag of $5400 new. When BMW got out of the marine business, S2 offered the boat with the 7.5 hp Yanmar.

The little diesel handles the boat well, though owners report that it will not punch through a heavy headsea. This is probably more the result of the folding Martec prop which comes as part of the inboard package rather than any lack of power in the engine.

The inboard installation is well done. The plywood stringers glassed to the hull support vibration-damping mounts for the engine. Standard installation includes a stainless steel eight gallon fuel tank, properly grounded, a heavy duty Purolator filter/water-separator, a waterlift muffler, and single-lever shift/throttle controls.

Both the fuel shut off and the fuel filter are difficult to get to—through an inspection port in the port quarterberth—but access to the engine is otherwise good, with hinged companionway steps opening out of the way so dipstick, decompression switch, engine controls, water pump are easy to get at. For more serious work on the engine, the quarterberth panels are removable for virtually total access. One good feature of the BMW is that it is the one engine we've ever seen that is actually easy to start by hand cranking. It made S2's one-battery installation workable. With the Yanmar, owners may want to look for a place to stow a second battery; offhand, there's no obviously good location.

As you might expect on a 4400 pound boat, the outboard is minimally adequate except for backing up and except in any wind or sea conditions.

We would normally recommend the inboard for the 7.9, but there is a problem—the underwater drag of the shaft, strut, and propeller—an important consideration for the racer.

Our conclusion is that the serious racer should probably look for the outboard model and just suffer the poor performance under power. If you will be primarily daysailing, weekending, and cruising, we recommend the inboard.

If you're planning a combination of racing and cruising, you'll just have to make a judgment which aspect you want to emphasize.

Handling Under Sail

The 7.9 is a proven performer under sail, being not only a fast boat for her size but also competitive in handicap racing under MORC and PHRF. Her PHRF rating of 168 says that she's about the same speed as the J/24, Merit 25, and similar current racing boats, and about the same speed as such older racer-cruisers as the Pearson 30, Cal 34, Catalina 30 tall rig, or Irwin 30.

With her narrow entry forward, a big fat rear end, and a fractional rig with most of the power in the mainsail, she will be better behaved than her high-performance cousins designed to the IOR rule. Owners report that her one bad habit is to wipe out in heavy puffs when beating.

Her dinghy-shaped hull means she'll have to be sailed flat for best performance, which in turn means lots of lard on the rail when the wind pipes up. Five people, the heavier the better, is *de rigueur* for heavy air racing.

For daysailing and cruising, she's got plenty of reefable sail area, and she should perform well with the four standard class sails: main, 155% genoa, 105% jib, and spinnaker.

Peak performance will take lots of tweaking and fiddling with the rig. This will be no problem for the high-performance dinghy sailor graduating to a cruising boat, but it will take a lot of learning about mastbend and sail shape for the newcomer. Nonetheless, even when not tuned to perfection, she should perform well enough to be a pleasant daysailer for the weekend hacker.

Deck Layout

The 7.9's inboard shrouds, wide decks, and big cockpit will make for pleasant moving about on deck. The nonskid is good—among the best we've seen in a production boat. It will remove skin from bare knuckles.

The boat will be sailed from the cockpit, and she's well laid out for sail handling. The primary winches are, if anything, oversize—a true rarity these days—and the secondary winches on the cabin top are adequate for halyard and spinnaker work. (Note, though, that the lead daggerboard is raised and lowered using the starboard secondary winch. One of our readers reports blowing up the winch; another says, "The #16 winch is inadequate for a woman or small man to handle the board.")

Like the J/24 and other performance boats, the helmsman and crew will sit on the deck rather than in the cockpit when racing. However, unlike the J/24, the 7.9 does have a true cockpit, and it's comfortable. The seat bottoms are slightly concave, the seat backs are nearly a foot high and contoured to support the small of the back, and seat-to-sole distance gives comfortable leg room. The mainsheet traveler is smack in the middle of the cockpit and will prove a shin ravager until you get used to it. But, the cockpit will comfortably daysail six and drink eight at dockside and is definitely a strong point for the boat.

There are two substantial cockpit lockers for stowage. Several owners report that the lockers leak—a nuisance in what appears to be an otherwise dry boat.

Belowdecks

As one owner puts it, "The interior does the best it can." With about 5' 4" headroom, the cabin will require stooping for most people. Still, we admire S2's restraint—they could have easily added 6" to the doghouse to get "standing" headroom. And to get a boat that would be as ugly as some of their early cruising models.

S2 was not suckered by the how-many-does-she-sleep syndrome for this model. Both quarterberths are long and wide, and the forward V-berth is truly sleepable with the boat dockside or at anchor. The only drawback to the arrangements is that the space between berth and side decks is so short that sitting upright will be uncomfortable for anyone over 6'.

The galley (or, more accurately, the galley area) is absolutely minimal, with a shallow sink and small icebox. There's a tiny counter area—either for counterspace or for a one-burner alcohol stove—but anyone wanting to weekend or cruise with more than PB&J's will have to revamp the galley.

The daggerboard trunk is well disguised, forming one wall of the head. The head itself is cramped, to say the least—you can sit on the Porta Potti, but your knees will stick out through the privacy curtain. Still, the head location is preferable to the all-too-common position under the V-berth.

Ventilation below is nonexistent. Opening ports were available as options. A small quarterberth opening port or a forepeak vent would be desirable.

Compared to a larger boat's "yacht" finish or even to a 25' cruising boat, the 7.9's interior will seem plain and functional.

On the other hand, it's luxurious compared to a J/24, J/27, Merit 25, or Evelyn 26. The boat can be weekended in comfort. If you can stand camping out, the boat can even be cruised.

Trailerability

With a 9' beam, the 7.9 is not legally trailerable in any state without special wide-load permits. Yet most of the boats have been sold with trailers, and the company boasts of its trailerability and easy launchability. How is this possible?

The consensus is that, with the daggerboard re-tracted, the boat sits so low on the trailer that it doesn't look that wide. A keelboat on a trailer—a Merit 25, for example—looks much bigger and a bored cop is more likely to stop and measure a keelboat than a 7.9. At any rate, 7.9s are trailered, and we know of none ever being ticketed or, for that matter, even questioned.

Conclusions

S2 did a good job of aiming the boat at a variety of sailors: racers, daysailors, and weekenders.

For racers interested in a one-design boat, the class is not strong outside the Great Lakes. But for the sailor into handicap racing, the boat seems a good possibility. It's definitely competitive in MORC and PHRF fleets. And unlike other high-performance boats its size—the Olson 25, J/24, Merit 25, Evelyn 26, or Capri 25—the 7.9 is a boat you could stand sleeping aboard or taking on a rainy overnight race.

For the sailor primarily interested in daysailing and weekending, the 7.9 will also be worth serious consideration. She is definitely on the pricey side for 26' boats, but her quality construction and equipment are what you get for the extra money. She may be a little on the high-performance side for the real novice, but her four-sail class package should be fairly easy to handle even for the newcomer.

We really could not recommend her as a cruiser. Well, maybe as a pocket cruiser. S2 clearly didn't intend her for cruising or offshore sailing; still, she's well made, a fast boat, and maybe if our seamanship were good enough...but no, if it's a fast cruiser we'd like at 25' to 26', we'll keep looking.　**• PS**

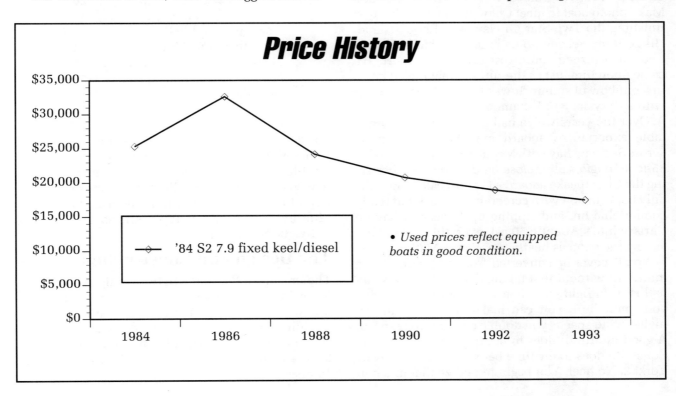

Price History

Legend: —◇— '84 S2 7.9 fixed keel/diesel

• Used prices reflect equipped boats in good condition.

Dragonfly 800

The Dragonfly is a speedy new Danish import that goes head-to-head with the popular F-27.

At the 1992 U.S. Sailboat Show in Annapolis, Maryland, there were more than a dozen multihulls on exhibit. How times have changed; just a few years before, bitter from lack of interest by the boating public, multihull builders and designers seemed to be saying, "If you ain't gonna buy me, then I ain't available...it ain't me you're looking for, babe!" Scorned, they pretty much kept to themselves.

But many multihullers persisted. And the record times of the big cats and tris in long-distance single- and double-handed events were too spectacular to go unnoticed. We'll never forget motoring out in a Mako photo boat to meet Chay Blyth and Rob James finishing the Two-Star off Newport, Rhode Island. His *Brittany Ferries GB* had made landfall off Cape Cod, then turned southwest toward Newport. We came upon him just as the sun set, making 20 knots in a rainbow of spume. It was hard to keep up, even with a Chrysler 318 V-8 under the saddle.

Over the years we've had a number of unforgettable experiences aboard multihulls—skimming across Saginaw Bay with Meade Gougeon aboard his 35-foot *Adagio,* sailing *close-hauled downwind;* cruising the Chesapeake aboard a Gemini catamaran, the only boat our son with cerebral palsy ever felt really comfortable on; and ripping up Buzzard's Bay on Chris White's Atlantic 50 cat, everything wire taut, slicing the chop as neatly as a Veg-A-Matic.

You'll never be converted from a monohull to a multihull without first taking a ride. What gets you is this: 1. In light air, when you would be motoring your monohull, you can make six knots, and in higher wind speeds you double or triple your speed. A good multihull does to ocean passages what the Concorde does to air time between Paris and New York. 2. No heel. You begin to realize that much of

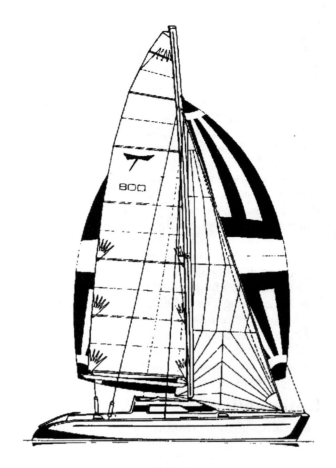

Specifications

LOA	26' 2"
LWL	24' 11"
Beam (max/folded)	19' 7"/9' 6"
Draft (board up/down)	1' 1"/4' 7"
Displacement	N/A
Weight	2,315 lbs.
Sail area	377 sq. ft.

the fatigue you've experienced in the past comes from sailing on your ear, every muscle tensed. 3. The multihull is a vast platform offering new freedom, new vistas, and, for the slightly misanthropic, new opportunities to get away from the rest of the crew. Multihulls have arrived, folks. And so has the Dragonfly 800 Swing Wing.

The Design and Construction

The Dragonfly 800 comes in two configurations, one for racing and one for what the company calls cruising, which is a misnomer only in that it implies a plodding demeanor, which is hardly the case. The essential difference is a taller mast and Kevlar sails for the racing model. Our test sail was aboard the "cruiser."

The designer of the Dragonfly is Borge Quorning, a Dane who also builds them. The first boat was launched in 1981; the 800 Swing Wing is a third generation model, introduced in 1989.

Construction is unidirectional fiberglass with Airex coring in the hull and deck. The glass work looks first-class with no ripples, clean edges, and many nice details such as a comfortable angle for the cockpit coaming/backrest. Most of the hardware is of good quality, including Frederiksen blocks and Andersen winches. An alleged bad batch of resin caused delamination of several rudders a couple of years ago, but, according to the importer, the problem has been rectified.

To retract its amas for berthing or trailering, the Dragonfly 800 incorporates a different method than the F-27, to which it is often compared. Whereas the F-27's crossbeams pull up and in, the Dragonfly's pivot aft. The advantage is that it's extremely easy to pull in an ama: Remove the aluminum strut between the hull and crossbeam, ease tension on the rig, loosen the netting and winch it in. The down side is that with both amas drawn in, the boat's beam is just over nine feet, which is wider than the legal road limit. For trailering, four bolts on each ama must be unscrewed and the ama removed. They stow upside down on the trailer. This isn't a big deal, but it does take a little longer than commissioning or decommissioning the F-27.

Clearly the rigging of the Dragonfly has been refined over the years as everything is very well thought out. All sail handling operations can be accomplished from the cockpit. For example, the drum of the roller furling gear is located below the deck (at the forward end of the anchor locker), and its control line is led aft to emerge underneath the traveler in the cockpit. Lines to haul the amas in and out emerge from seemingly nowhere on top of the cockpit coaming, right next to a winch. Very convenient. And a barberhauling system, led from the bow of each ama to blocks on the jib sheet, then to the aft end of each ama and into the cockpit, permit infinite and precise sheeting. The rotating mast also can be controlled from the cockpit. Most controls run through rope clutches on the coachroof.

Performance

We test sailed the Dragonfly 800 on Long Island Sound, on a chilly but sunny day in October. Winds were light—5 to 8 knots. Reaching we were able to sail at the speed of the wind, and nearly so upwind. We were reminded that in a monohull we'd probably be motoring.

Top speed, according to company literature, is about 25 knots, which would have to be one hell of an experience. Above 12 knots, we were told, you get a beautiful roostertail.

The boat tacks easily, pivoting about its centerboard. There is little if any helm, at least at slower speeds, and with the main and jib sheeted in for most points of sail, you feel like you're driving a go-cart in an empty mall parking lot—just aim and go.

Broad reaching we set the spinnaker, which on a multihull is easy because no pole is necessary. And with each clew sheeted to an ama, there is no fear of it wrapping the forestay.

An interesting characteristic of the Dragonfly is that when overpowered, the hull begins to lift and the rudder cavitates, causing the boat to round up. We're not sure we'd rely on this as our only clue to possible danger, but it's nice to know that the boat's natural inclination is to round up rather than flip.

The recommended outboard size is 6 hp., which will move the Dragonfly in flat water at 7.2 knots. It can be controlled from the cockpit, allowing you to turn both the motor and the tiller at the same time, in which case it will do donuts in its own length.

Interior

We've grown accustomed to the fact that small trimarans don't have the interior volume of a similar monohull. That said, we found the Dragonfly's accommodations cheerful and tastefully done.

The V-berths are quite long (about 7 feet), with a tinted skylight overhead. You can't sit up in bed, but there's ample leg room. A pull-down privacy blind separates the V-berths from the settees. An optional toilet may be installed under one cushion.

The settees in the main cabin have fold-out panels

underneath the cushions that secure against the centerboard trunk; the backrest cushions then fit over the panels and presto, you've got two 30-inch-wide bunks. Fitted over the centerboard trunk is a teak drop-leaf table. Aft is a small split galley with sink (17-gallon water tank) and single-burner Origo alcohol stove. We did note that the seacocks did not have flanges, which are recommended by ABYC.

With ash plywood overhead, designer lights, teak trim, and a nice view out the windows from a seated position, time spent belowdecks is pleasant and comfortable. Especially appreciated is the forward facing hatch, which allows a good deal of light and air into the cabin.

The cockpit can become an extension of the living space with the dodger and Bimini erected and zipped together. Both fold unobtrusively out of the way and are further illustrations of how everything on this boat fits together just so.

Conclusion

For us, buying a Dragonfly would be like buying a Porsche, a strong move that puts you back in touch with the road. Though company literature states that boats may be custom equipped at the factory for transoceanic passages, we would not attempt it. In fact, we like this boat better without confusing its purpose. To our mind it's a terrific daysailer and an adequate coastal cruiser.

Choosing between the Dragonfly 800 and F-27 is tough. With a 1993 base price of $49,500, the Dragonfly is about the same as an F-27, but includes many standard items that are optional on the F-27, such as sails and roller furling. It's also a foot shorter and does not have the F-27's aft cabin with extra berths. Frankly, we like the looks of the Dragonfly's open transom better, as well as the convenience it affords swimmers. On the other hand, the F-27's aft cabin gives some folks an added sense of security in the cockpit. Which you favor may depend on whether you need those extra berths. As far as main cabins go, we favor the Dragonfly's.

Our final impression of the Dragonfly 800 is that it's just plain fun to sail. We like it.   • **PS**

Compared to a same-length monohull, the Dragonfly cabin offers little space. However, that goes with the territory. What you get in exchange is sizzling performance.

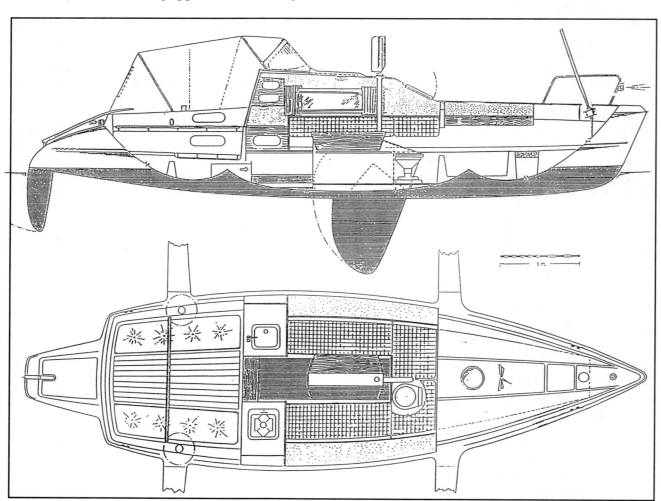

Catalina 270LE Beneteau 265

A head-to-head comparison of two new entry-level cruisers favors the Catalina on price and practicality

People who start in small boats and trade up often view 27 feet as some kind of milestone, and rightly so. At around 27 feet, an inboard engine and the possibility of standing headroom are enticing. Accommodations often become spacious enough for two couples or a family of four to live aboard for a couple of weeks without strain. And hull speed with appropriate sail and engine power typically permits average-weather runs of 35 to 40 miles in an 8-hour day—long enough legs to satisfy the wanderlust of most cruisers.

Two of the newest 27-foot cruising boat designs are from Beneteau and Catalina, both huge builders. Beneteau bills itself as the largest sailboat company in the world; Catalina lays claim to being the largest in the U.S. The new designs of both companies often set the tone for styling by other sailboat makers.

Checking out both boats at a mid-1993 show, we noticed that the base list price of the Beneteau First 285 with inboard ($38,050) was less than 10 percent above the base for the Catalina 270LE ($34,775). Their Euro-styled interior layouts were at least superficially similar as well, as were hull and sail plan dimensions. Which boat, we wondered, is the better buy, and for whom?

Design

Both the Beneteau and the Catalina utilize modern wide-body, fin-keel, spade-rudder configurations, relatively long waterlines, and moderate rigs with shrouds moved inboard to permit a narrower sheeting base. The Beneteau has a slightly shorter LOA but longer LWL (length waterline), and a nearly plumb bow. The 285's draft is mid-range (4' 2" vs. the Catalina's choice of 5' 0" deep fin or 3' 6" fin with wings).

Both test boats had inboards. Catalina does not offer

Specifications - Catalina 270LE

LOA	27' 0"
LWL	23' 9"
Beam	9' 3"
Draft (wing/fin)	3' 6"/5' 0"
Displacement	6,400 lbs.
Ballast	2,000 lbs.
Sail area	316 sq. ft.

an outboard option as it once did with its old 27. Catalina's chief engineer, Gerry Douglas, doesn't think it's suitable for a 27-footer, especially one weighing 6,400 pounds-and, he says, neither did most buyers of Catalina 27s over the last several years. (Among other problems, in a seaway an outboard prop tends to ventilate too much).

Still, Beneteau, with a 4,800-lb. boat, does offer an outboard version (base price $32,900 excluding engine, which is $5,150 below the inboard Beneteau price with engine) and recommends a 9.9-hp. outboard for those who wish to go this route. So far, few buyers have. Beyond the ventilating prop problem, the reason is mostly economic: By the time Beneteau buyers acquire the outboard engine and associated paraphernalia, the difference between inboard and

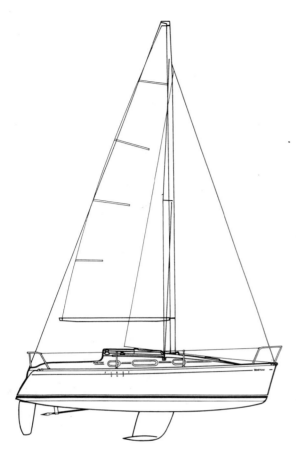

Specifications - Beneteau 265

LOA	26' 5"
LWL	24' 2"
Beam	9' 5"
Draft	4' 2"
Displacement	4,800 lbs.
Ballast	1,450 lbs.
Sail area	330 sq. ft.

outboard shrinks to around $3,500—and those who opt for the outboard miss the shore power option and electric hot water heater option which Beneteau throws in "free" with the inboard package.

The rigs of the two boats may appear quite similar at first glance, but upon close inspection a number of important differences emerge. The Beneteau features a seven-eighths rig with single spreaders, adjustable split backstay, mast stepped on deck with compression strut in the cabin, and shrouds tied into a force grid molded into the cabintop via a set of studs threaded into a patented configuration involving stemballs set into bronze plates. (We'd prefer a set of conventional—and more easily adjustable and replaceable—turnbuckles.) The mast is stepped on a hinge for lowering the spar at bridges, trailer ramps, or for maintenance, but Beneteau says use of the

hinge is not recommended without side-sway preventers—currently available as an option in Europe, but not in the U.S.

The Beneteau's genoa sheets lead to cars riding on C-shaped aluminum tracks, which double as handrails, on the cabintop. It's not easy to grab the tracks/rails, which require feeding your fingers through a narrow slot molded into the coachroof. We'd rather see separate handrails. We'd also prefer to see the Beneteau's cockpit-mounted mainsheet traveler track moved forward onto the cabintop (as the Catalina is configured), so crew moving from cockpit to cabin don't have to dodge the mainsheet and car. But, unfortunately, moving the track forward isn't feasible because of the long companionway bridge deck, which reaches forward beyond the boom's midpoint.

The Catalina's masthead rig, even with double spreaders (permitting use of a lighter spar than the Beneteau), is more conventional. Although the Catalina's mast is shorter and its mainsail is smaller, the foretriangle height is two feet longer than the Beneteau's, resulting in more total sail area when setting a big genoa. The Catalina's rig design strives for simplicity (no backstay bridle adjustment, no line-adjusted genoa car position as on the Beneteau), and ease of use. Helping to make sailing the Catalina a no-hassle experience is an impressive array of standard equipment not seen on the Beneteau: A double-ended mainsheet, adjustable either at a cam cleat on the traveler car or at a cabintop stopper, where a winch can be used; a pair of two-speed Lewmar self-tailing #30s (compared to Beneteau's single speed #16s); a standard 135-percent genoa on a good-quality Hood single-line furler (compared to Beneteau's standard 100-percent jib and furler hardware available only as an option); a total of five cabintop stoppers (vs. three for the Beneteau; Dutchman mainsail flaking system; and single-line reefing (though the Catalina test boat did not have single-line reefing rigged).

Other features on deck also favor the Catalina. Working aft from the bow: The welded pulpit, like the stanchions, is 1-inch stainless steel tubing (vs. the Beneteau's 7/8-inch), has two horizontal rails (vs. one for the Beneteau) and four legs (three for the Beneteau). There are twin anchor rollers at the stemhead (one on the Beneteau). Both boats have anchor lockers built into the forward deck, but the Beneteau's locker has a water tank fill cap in its bottom. This can make it extremely inconvenient to fill the tank when line and chain are piled over the cap. And the combination bow light is mounted directly behind and partly obscured by the center support of the pulpit.

Moving further aft, the Catalina's six stanchions are fitted with double lifelines and, being 24-3/4 inches off the deck, give a good measure of security. In contrast, the Beneteau has only four stanchions, less than 18 inches high, with single lifelines. The low lifelines are at "tripping height," and while the scale may be aesthetically pleasing, safety is compromised. If we were buying the Beneteau, we'd insist that she be retrofitted with taller stanchions.

The cockpits on both boats have comfortably high, canted coamings and angled seats. The Catalina's cockpit is noticeably roomier, due not only to the absence of a cockpit traveler, but also to the placement of the wheel way aft, with an athwartships helm seat 5 feet wide—big enough for three for cocktails at the mooring. On the Catalina, there's room for nine at the dock, as big a cockpit as could be desired in this size boat. And that doesn't include a pair of "observation seats" built into each corner of the pushpit.

In contrast, the Beneteau seats no more than seven at the dock, and that assumes that one passenger is seated atop the traveler and the tiller is swung up out of the way.

We have no objection to tillers—in fact we generally prefer them in this size boat—provided there's no noticeable drag in the rudder tube and that the forward end is a comfortable height over the sole. Unfortunately, the Beneteau failed both tests, even with the height adjustment screw at the rudder head in the extreme "down" position.

The Catalina's 32-inch stainless steel destroyer wheel on a pedestal is an Edson, a brand we associate with high quality and reliability. The size and placement is good for steering from either a sitting or standing position; brake and compass binnacle (4-inch Danforth Constellation) are standard; pedestal-mounted brackets for additional instruments such as depth sounder and speedo are extra.

The Beneteau's compass is optional, mounted along with any other optional instruments on the cabinhouse bulkhead, a better position for crew viewing but not as good for the helmsman.

Both boats have swim platforms and stainless swing-down swim ladders. The Catalina easily wins the Ladder Sweepstakes with a four-step, 24-inch wide ladder with flat plastic treads, compared to the Beneteau's three-step, 8-1/2-inch wide ladder with treads only 1-1/4-inch wide, made by flattening the stainless tubing a bit.

The Catalina's ladder swings up to form the center part of the pushpit, a clever and neat-looking design. The Beneteau ropes off the transom area with a length of lifeline and a pelican hook.

Both swim platforms are molded into "sugar-scoop" transoms, and both are elevated 9 inches off the water, with a bit of transom projecting below. The bottom of the Catalina's transom misses the water by a couple of inches, but the Beneteau's, with a short horizontal lip extending aft below the platform, is slightly immersed and thus attracts sea life, evident from the unsightly coating of saltwater slime on our test boat.

Construction

Both boats utilize external bolt-on lead keels, suitably thick fiberglass lay-up schedules, solid glass hulls and balsa-cored decks, and reasonably strong hull-deck connections. Both have highly engineered force grids molded into their hull liners, of particular note since the shrouds in both boats lead not to traditional chainplates but to intermediate tie rods, which in turn are joined to metal plates for the most

The Catalina's interior is brightened by the use of a two-layer Plexiglass skylight abaft the mast. The only real complaint we have is with the table, which has a troublesome lowering mechanism.

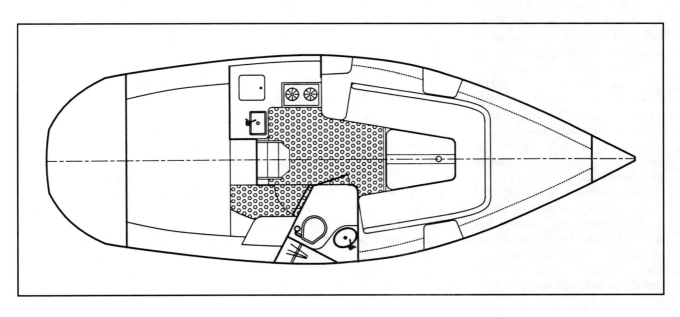

part hidden behind interior liners. On both boats we would prefer better inspection ports to view these crucial joints.

On both boats, the pulpits and stanchions are fastened to the deck with a single large threaded stud, projecting down through the deck and secured with a large washer and nut. Although this design is somewhat non-traditional, it seems solid enough. Still, we question what will happen to the deck when someone falls against a stanchion; four through-bolts and large backing plates to distribute the load would be better.

Even more dubious are the two parts of the backstay bridle on the Beneteau which are simply fastened to straps welded to the bases of the pushpit, rather than to their own chainplates. Because of the extra forces involved, we'd worry about stress cracks eventually appearing around these bases.

Deck hardware (blocks, tracks, hatches, ports) on the Catalina is mostly made by Garhauer, Nibo, and Beckson, all vendors noted for producing decent-quality but low-cost equipment. On the Beneteau, Harken, Spinlock, and Lewmar are predominant. As already mentioned, both boats use Lewmar winches. We judged all branded hardware on both boats to be of acceptable quality.

Performance

We did our testing on the Manatee River off the pier of Massey Yachts in Palmetto, Florida. (Massey sells both Catalina and Beneteau). The test Catalina was the wing-keel version; the Beneteau had the standard rig. (A tall rig is optional.)

Both boats seemed quite stiff, well balanced, and very responsive to the helm. Both could be spun in more or less their own length. The day we sailed the Beneteau, it was blowing 15 knots steadily and 20 in gusts, and the 265 heeled not more than 25 degrees close-hauled with full sail. This impressed us. So did the Catalina, which was at least as stable on a breezier day (wind 20-25, occasional gusts to 30) with full sail, only burying the rail once in a particularly vicious wind burst. In short, we wouldn't hesitate to sail either boat in gusty weather.

Though hard to judge in such strong, shifting winds, we think the Beneteau had the edge in sailing speed, as her statistics would indicate. Under power, however, her smaller engine and prop (single-cylinder, 9-hp., 26-CID Volvo, 15 x 12 optional folding prop) was definitely not as effective upwind as the Catalina's (three-cylinder, 18-hp, 37-CID Perkins, two-blade 13 x 10 prop). The Catalina's Perkins also was smoother and quieter, despite the fact that its engine box (two removable clam-shells back to back, of fiberglass-foam sandwich construction) had no added insulation, while the Beneteau's plywood box was lined with soft foam. Engine and shaft log access was very good on the Beneteau, superb on the Catalina.

At the moment, PHRF for the Beneteau is 168. The Catalina's is not yet determined, but we would anticipate it will come in around the 195-205 range.

Interior

The interior layouts on the two boats are quite similar: large double berth aft, galley to port next to the companionway, head opposite the galley, U-shaped dining area around a smallish table supported by the mast compression post, and V-berth forward.

These overall similarities make the differences between the designs more obvious. For example, on the Catalina the entrance to the double aft is via a solid teak door, whereas on the Beneteau it is through a sliding curtain.

All berths on both boats have comfortable 4-inch cushions. The aft berth on the Beneteau measures 60" x 77", and you sleep parallel to the keel; the Catalina is slightly narrower at 57 inches wide, is 74 inches to 86 inches long depending on which side you're on, and you sleep athwartships. We wouldn't be inclined to sleep two in either aft berth, since the inside party not only doesn't have much vertical roll-over room due to incursion of the cockpit sole, but also must crawl over the outside party to get up.

Neither the Catalina nor the Beneteau forward berths have these problems. On the Beneteau, you can lower the table and set up the berth without undue commotion; but setting up the Catalina berth involves a lot of fussy positioning of the raised forward seat and locking it in place with a pair of hard-to-reach latches. We'd like to see Catalina re-study the process to make set-up easier.

The forward berth on the Beneteau measures 19 inches at the front, 76 inches at the back, and is 88 inches long. On the Catalina it's 10 inches at the front, 68 inches at the back, and 75 inches long. Tall folks will appreciate the larger Beneteau berth.

The Beneteau has the edge on locker space, with three separate hanging lockers (including one open-air unit in the head), and a liquor cabinet under what a Beneteau brochure describes as a nav station. In reality, there's not enough space to unroll even a small chart on the work surface presented, which is effectively cut in two by a fiddle across its middle. Still, the "nav station" top gives the galley slave some countertop space—space sadly lacking in the galley where it should be. The Catalina also suffers from lack of sufficient galley top working space.

The use of maintenance-hungry exterior wood has been completely eliminated on the Catalina, and minimized on the Beneteau except for the companionway drop slides (King StarBoard plastic on the Catalina, nicely varnished cherry-veneer plywood on the Beneteau).

Below, both boats use some wood to visually warm up the otherwise mostly white interior. The surface is totally fiberglass on the Catalina, but on the Beneteau, soft white foam-backed vinyl lines the upper halves of the hull sides. If this vinyl is anything like the stuff used on boats 15 or 20 years ago, the foam backing can be expected to dry out and crumble to powder eventually.

Catalina's use of wood is sparing (varnished teak doors and trim, teak dining table, small patch of maple and teak sole forward), while Beneteau's is lavish (varnished cherry bulkheads and trim, full teak sole). The wood is set off on both boats by neatly made upholstery on berths and settees, on the Catalina by a combination of Ultrasuede-like material and light patterned cotton fabrics, on the Beneteau by a practical and soft dark green velvet.

The Beneteau interior gives an impression of good craftsmanship, above-average but not consummately executed, and a dark though pleasantly airy cabin. On the Catalina, the impression is of a more basic, but much lighter and equally airy boat. The Catalina's lightness is helped by a skylight of milk-white Plexiglas (two layers thick) abaft the mast, and more area in the main cabin ports. For ventilation, the Catalina has six opening ports plus a forward hatch, while the Beneteau has eight plus a forward hatch. Screens for the ports (but not for either the forward or main hatch) are standard on both the Catalina and the Beneteau. Neither boat has a roll-up sunshade over the forward hatch, which would be a nice touch.

The Bottom Line

To some extent, the choice between .. the Beneteau 265 and the Catalina 270 LE is a tradeoff between elegant French styling on the one hand, and no-nonsense American practicality on the other. (Of interest to "Buy America" advocates is the fact that both boats are built in the U.S., the Catalina in Woodland Hills, California, and the Beneteau in Marion, South Carolina.) <p2>The choice is also between the Beneteau's lighter hull with quicker acceleration, and the Catalina's equally maneuverable but heavier hull with greater load-carrying capacity and living space below.

All boats are compromises, and personal taste and prejudices do enter the picture. That said, we admit to a clear preference for the Catalina. We especially like the lightness and brightness of its interior, enhanced by numerous large ports and an overhead skylight. Most of all, we like the Catalina's greater value for the money—not just because the overall price is about 10 percent lower than a comparable Beneteau, but because of the better choice of standard items.

For example, note the differences between some of the Beneteau's items and the Catalina's: 9-hp. raw-water-cooled engine vs. 18-hp. freshwater-cooled; no engine tach or fuel gauge vs. both standard; 8.25-gallon fuel tank vs. 14 gallons; 16.25-gallon water tank vs. 26 gallons; holding tank 11.5 gallons vs. 18; single-speed #16 self-tailing Lewmars vs. two-speed #30 STs; a 1.6 gpm Shurno pressure water pump vs. a 2.8-gpm Shurno pump; a gimbaled two-burner non-pressure alcohol stove vs. a gimbaled two-burner LPG stove, and so on.

Now if Catalina would only install a good-size hanging locker, put in more working counter surface in the galley, make it easier to make up the forward berth....　　　　　　　　　　• **PS**

The Beneteau's interior is quite similar to the Catalina's. One big difference is the aft cabin berth, which is oriented fore-and-aft on the Beneteau, athwartships on the Catalina.

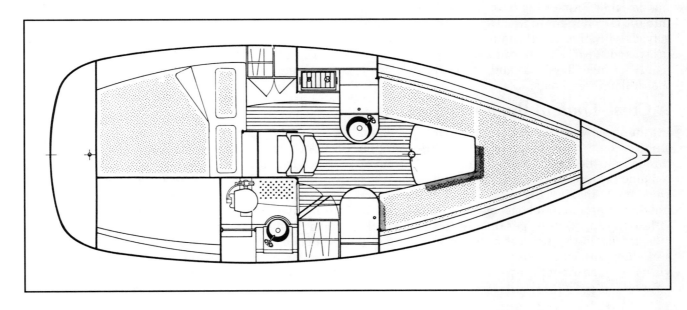

Ericson 27

With over 1,300 built, there should be plenty to choose from—but be sure to check out the later boats first.

In the sailboat industry Ericson Yachts was somewhat of the archetypal production boatbuilder: trendy, performance oriented, colorfully advertised, and, for the most part, successful. The Ericson line started in 1965 with the enduring 32 and 35, simple and stylized boats that sold mostly to West Coast buyers. The model line then grew, aimed largely at racing sailors, but with models successively introduced to fill in the line and keep Ericson buyers in that builder's boats, eventually reaching a high degree of acceptance throughout the country.

In the intervening years Ericson Yachts sold a lot of boats, and with them the firm developed a reputation for good quality and finish. The accolade is but partly deserved, at least in terms of other production builders such as Pearson Yachts and Cal Boats with whom Ericson can be compared.

The longtime designer of Ericson boats is California designer Bruce King with a brief Ericson foray into the racy designs of Ron Holland. When Ericson stayed with the contemporary style, the builder prospered. Two ersatz traditional designs, the Independence (nee Classic) 31 and 36 were busts as were the Holland race boats.

A Close Look at the Boat

In a number of ways the Ericson 27 can be considered an excellent representative of the Ericson line throughout the 1970s. Introduced in 1971, the 27 remained in production for nine years. In all, 1302 were built, making the 27 among the leaders in number of production boats built.

Initially the 27 was, per the fashion of the early '70s, marketed to a price as a stripped boat, simple and plain with an outboard engine as standard and virtually all gear but the essentials available only as options.

Specifications

LOA	26' 9"
LWL	20' 6"
Beam	9' 0"
Draft	3' 11"
Displacement	7,000 lbs.
Ballast	2,900 lbs.
Sail area	323 sq. ft.

Typically the 27 was sold with tiller steering and a conventional interior layout as a boat purportedly competitive under the then-young IOR but more popular with buyers looking for reasonable performance and comfort in a small cruising boat.

Auxiliary power was an outboard mounted in a cut-out on the centerline of the transom at the end of a longish straight cockpit. The interior decor was primarily mahogany plywood and boasted an enclosed head and reasonable headroom, two highly attractive features for early 1970s buyers finding many boats of comparable size more cramped.

In late 1974 Ericson began an upgrade of its entire line, changing to an interior teak finish, making much of the gear that had been optional standard, and appealing to a higher priced buyer. In that upgrade the 27 received a redesigned deck and cockpit with a ventilation hatch amidships, a T-shaped helmsman's station with pedestal steering aft. The transom cutout was eliminated and the mainsheet traveler moved from over the companionway to the cockpit.

At 27' and well over 6,000 pounds of displacement, the 27 begged for inboard auxiliary power, and in all about 80% of those built were delivered with an inboard. For most of that run the engine was the Atomic Four, although on occasion other engines such as the Bukh/Westerbeke Pilot 10 and Volvo MD6A were installed per buyers' desires. In the last year of production the standard engine was the Yanmar 8D diesel.

The Ericson 27, for all of her other possible virtues, does not boast much performance. Heavy (with inboard, a displacement to length ratio of 363), short rigged (sail area to displacement 14.1) and a bit squirrely in sloppy conditions with her spade rudder, the 27 has much to overcome. Under PHRF her rating is 225-230 putting her on a boat-for-boat basis with such smaller rivals as the O'Day 25, Catalina 25, and so-so performance boats as the Cape Dory 27 and Tartan 27. Ratings for 27s without inboard power are about the same, in part because of the similar displacement of the two versions (the outboard boats have 275 pounds of inside ballast to offset engine weight).

A handful of 27s were delivered with tall rigs, about 2' higher than standard, but the boat does not have the inherent stability to reap much benefit from the greater sail area.

As a cruiser the 27 is comfortable for a couple, cramped for more despite its five berths. The forward cabin is pointy, the quarterberth is a "cave," and the settee berths are a tad narrow. Ventilation is wretched, although better on later 27s with the midships hatch, and over the years many owners have retrofitted improvements.

Clearly the upgraded cockpit with wheel steering is also an improvement over the original. Ordinarily wheel steering in a 27-footer is a goodie, not a necessity. The Ericson 27 is an exception.

The 27 is not much fun to steer under power with wheel or tiller. The combination of the spade rudder and off center prop shaft keeps one's attention at the helm. With a tiller this means constant offsetting pressure. A wheel makes it easier although the infernal backstay prevents standing upright aft of the wheel. Worse still is that the 27 can develop considerable weather helm if pressed in a breeze. A number of owners report making rudder modifications (making the post vertical and/or increasing size) to improve handling.

What to Look For

There seems to be no question that the Ericson 27 was adequately built. Problems with even the earliest hulls are more apt to be cosmetic than structural, according to 27 owners.

The problems that do occur tend to be those typical of boats of similar vintage: leaky ports, gate valves in need of replacement, spar corrosion, etc. that a professional survey should turn up. Check the engine; a faulty exhaust fitting (replaced by Ericson

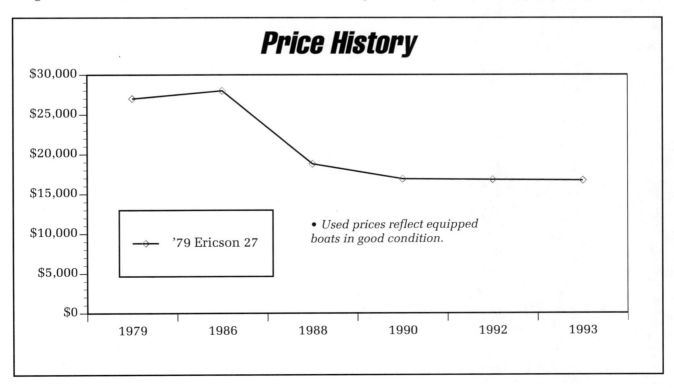

Price History

• *Used prices reflect equipped boats in good condition.*

Legend: ◇ '79 Ericson 27

on recall) resulted in water backing into some engines.

Buyers should give thought to which version of the 27 is most worth shopping for. We would look hardest for a post-1974 model, with its improved finish, redesigned cockpit, and more commonly found inboard auxiliary engine, paying particular attention to the condition of the engine.

Clearly the 27 can benefit from upgrading original equipment including winches, traveler, reefing gear, galley stove and icebox, increasing water tankage, etc. Retrofitting wheel steering is difficult and of dubious recoverable expense.

Generally condition, not age per se, is the most valid determinent of the value of a production boat over 6 to 8 years old. Not so with the Ericson 27. To our minds the improvements in the latter half of the production run—wheel steering (standard beginning with hull #754), the dressier and more heavily constructed interior, more standard equipment, etc.— are well worth what we find is the typical difference in selling prices between older and younger Ericson 27s.

Given the steady changes in the 27, especially the deck/cockpit redesign, there should be a much more notable difference in price, perhaps as much as several thousand dollars. Certainly it would behoove any prospective buyer to check the later 27s before committing to an earlier boat, unless the price of the older is much lower.

Conclusions

There seems no question that the Ericson 27 has some drawbacks that are crucial concerns to prospective buyers: sluggish performance, steering effort, too many berths, etc. Still, it can be a most attractive boat to buyers wanting reasonable cruising amenities in a moderate size boat for a modest price. The 27 is truly a small cruising boat with more to offer (at least in later models) than such boats of comparable vintage as the Catalina 27 or the Hunter 27, albeit typically at somewhat higher prices.

To the advantage of the potential buyer, there are a lot of 27s on the market from which to choose, more so in the West than the East. The key is to spend some time looking for the best deal in a later model with the desired features, especially inboard power and wheel steering. Then the conservative styling of the 27 and its basic ruggedness should work to preserve the boat's value, especially if the engine is maintained, the boat kept spiffy (and refinished when needed), and sails periodically replaced.   • **PS**

Catalina 27

The Catalina 27 is probably the most popular 27-footer ever built. Though cheaply made, owners love them.

Catalina Yachts is a strange company. The builder does no advertising—it's left up to the local dealers. The operation is owned and run by Frank Butler, who designs the boats, decides on who the dealers will be, sometimes answers his own phone, and for all we know sweeps up at the end of the day. He is probably one of the few people in the marine industry who has made money from building sailboats.

Catalina probably produces more pounds of sailboats every year than any other US builder, and has done so for a long time.

The Catalina 27 has been in production since 1971, and well over 6,000 of them have been built. This is undoubtedly the largest production run of any 27' sailboat in US history, and probably the biggest anywhere.

The flip side of the coin is that Catalinas are known as cheaply built boats, with lots of corners cut in places they shouldn't be cut. According to owners, Catalina dealers have what may be the worst track record in the business in providing warranty service. Yet the owners keep coming back for more, and they love their boats.

The Catalina factory, by contrast, has a pretty good record for solving customer complaints. It is quite common for Frank Butler himself to return owners' calls, making that owner a Catalina customer for life.

Because the Catalina 27 has been in production for so long, there have been numerous changes in the boats over the years. Most of these are small, but as a rule they have represented a steady stream of improvements. For this reason, more recent models are usually more desirable as used boats than earlier models.

At the same time, Catalina 27 owners seem to be inveterate tinkerers, constantly changing and im-

Specifications

LOA	26' 10"
LWL	21' 9"
Beam	8' 10"
Draft	3' 5"/4' 0" (shoal/std)
Displacement	7,300 lbs.
Ballast	3,150 lbs.

proving small details in the boat. It is not unusual to see an older Catalina 27 meticulously upgraded with many of the changes that are standard on newer models.

Sailing Performance

The variety of options that significantly affect the performance of the Catalina 27 means that you must carefully evaluate the individual boat when determining how she is likely to sail. Most Catalina 27s are the standard keel, standard rig model. About half of these have optional inboard engines, while the others have outboards mounted in an awkward cockpit well. The outboard-powered versions are slightly faster than the inboard boats, since they have less weight to drag through the water.

There is also a shoal keel model, and a tall rig

model. The shoal keel has a less-efficient foil, and is heavier than the deep keel to give the boat comparable stability.

The tall rig is favored in light air areas. Boats with the standard rig are generally equipped with 150% genoas to give them additional power in light air.

The standard keel, standard rig boat with inboard has a typical PHRF rating of 208. This puts the Catalina 27 at the fast end of the fleet of boats of its size and type, such as the Hunter 27, Ericson 27, and O'Day 27. Tall rig and outboard versions are slightly faster.

Because of the large number of Catalina 27s built, you are likely to find good racing for the boat in many areas all around the country, from southern California to the Great Lakes and Chesapeake Bay. A boat that is actively raced may have upgraded sail handling equipment—bigger winches, reinforced chainplates, better mainsheet traveler, more and better sails, etc. This could be a real plus in a used boat.

Because of the differences in rig, ballasting, keel, and engines, the various versions of the boat can't fairly race against each other as one-designs. The fastest version of the boat is the tall-rig, deep keel boat with outboard; the slowest, the short rig, shoal keel with inboard. You pays your money and takes your choice.

Engine

You can find everything from a beat-up 15-year-old outboard to a brand new diesel pushing the Catalina 27. Originally, you could have your choice of outboard or Atomic 4 gasoline inboard power. The Atomic 4 is twice as much power as the boat needs, but it was one of the most compact inboards made.

All the inboard engines are tucked away under the cockpit, and owners uniformly condemn the installation for its lack of access for service. On a scale of 1 to 5, with one being awful and five being great, the installation is typically rated one or less. Forewarned is forearmed.

At the same time, the outboard well doesn't win any points for accessibility either, and remote controls in the cockpit are a must for ease of operation. Getting the engine in and out of the well is a chore.

A 10 horse outboard is just about the right size for the boat, and should push her at hull speed in any conditions in which you would care to motor.

Inboard powerplants have been another story. In the late 1970s, a single-cylinder Petter diesel of about 6 hp was offered as an option. Owners report that the boat is grossly underpowered with this engine. In addition, parts are likely to be hard to find. We would definitely avoid the Petter diesel. Far more desirable is either the 11 or 14 horsepower Universal diesel offered in more recent models.

The Atomic 4 presents a dilemma. Though it has been discontinued, parts are readily available. On the other hand, access to the engine is so poor—oil changes require major contortions—that routine maintenance may have been neglected by the owner, shortening the engine's life. If service access is bad, we suspect that access to replace the engine would be abominable. Some owners report that service access has been improved by cutting holes in the bulkhead between the quarterberths and the engine.

Construction

The Catalina is the Volkswagen of the boat market. It's basic, but it will get you where you want to go. Originally, there were no backing plates on stanchions, rails, or deck hardware. This means that you're likely to find gelcoat cracks around these fittings on older boats. Many owners have chosen to upgrade this aspect of their boats, so you may find an older boat that has been conscientiously brought up to higher standards.

The through hull fittings on older boats are simply gate valves screwed onto pipe nipples glassed into the hull—a poor practice. Many owners have replaced these with proper seacock installations. Another problem with through hulls is the placement of the skin fitting for the icebox drain—it allows water to run back into the box when the boat is heeled.

"Minor" complaints from owners include gelcoat voids, deck delamination, leaking chainplates, leaking ports, and leaking hull-to-deck joints. Not all owners report these, of course, and the number of complaints may simply be a function of the huge number of Catalina 27s built.

Ironically, many of those with complaints love the boat, and say they would buy it again. While a number of Catalina buyers are first time boat owners, others buy the boat knowing the reputation for mediocre workmanship, but recognizing that they can get more boat for their dollar with Catalina than with almost any other boat built. They are willing to either accept the limitations, or do themselves the upgrading that they feel is required.

This results in a much higher level of satisfaction with the boat than you would expect with a low-priced product.

While some of the complaints about construction details are minor, others deserve immediate attention. In older boats, check the lower shroud U-bolt chainplates to see if they have been upgraded. A number of the original fittings have failed, causing the rig to go over the side.

Another rig weakness is the cast aluminum spreader sockets originally used on the mast. They should be replaced with the later stainless steel fabrications. Failures of the cast sockets have cost several rigs.

While the best location for a mainsheet traveler would be the forward end of the cockpit, there's no bridgedeck there for mounting it, so you're stuck with either the original location in the aft end of the cockpit, or the newer location over the companionway hatch. Unfortunately, there are several drawbacks to the latter spot: it wipes out the possibility of a companionway dodger, which would be a good idea due to the huge opening the hatch makes in the deck. Owners report that the forward location results in so much friction and additional sheet load that the mainsheet is hard to trim. In addition, the traveler in this position partially blocks off the main companionway opening.

Catalina hardware has never been much to write home about. Almost everything on the boat beyond the barest necessity is an option—and by "option" we mean, if you want it, you do it yourself. But of course if you like to fiddle with your boat, this can be seen as a plus.

There are few pieces of exterior trim: handrails on the cabin top, trim around the companionway. Trim takes time to put on, and teak costs money. Remember, this is a Volkswagen.

A big plus in later model boats is a seahood over the sliding companionway hatch. The old hatch design leaks badly if heavy spray or solid water comes aboard.

Later models also have a molded-in foredeck anchor well, a significant improvement.

The Catalina 27 has gradually gotten heavier over the years. The original displacement of the deep keel, outboard model was 5,650 pounds, with the shoal keel model about 500 pounds heavier. With the addition of a more sophisticated interior, inboard engine, fuel tanks, more interior trim, and many other improvements, displacement has crept up to about 6850 pounds for the deep keel versions, and 7,300 pounds for the shoal draft boat. This helps explain why a number of owners complain that the boat floats with her waterline submerged. It also means that if you want to race, you might want to consider an older, lighter model.

Interior

The Catalina 27 has more headroom than most 27-footers, and the huge companionway makes the interior seem exceptionally spacious when the hatch is open.

There have been two interiors: a traditional, aft galley layout, and a midships galley/dinette version. Although owners tend to prefer whichever layout they have, there is some consensus that the traditonal layout offers better storage and a more reasonable use of space. With the dinette made up into a double berth, that version has six berths—at least two more than you really want on a boat this size. On the aft galley model, the starboard settee makes up into a double, once again giving you six berths.

Unfortunately, not all the berths are very usable. Most owners report that the forward V-berths are too short and too narrow to be comfortable for two people, so try it out before deciding on the boat. The quarterberths are the only decent size berths on the boat.

Although there's a fair amount of storage space under the main cabin settees, it's hard to get to. A common owner modification is to add access doors to the settee faces, making it unnecessary to lift the seat cushions to get to the storage below.

A lot of owners consider the Catalina 27 a two-person boat, despite the number of berths. Six close friends on a boat this size could become bitter enemies on a rainy cruise that lasted a week or more, but that's a characteristic of 27-footers in general, not the Catalina 27 in particular.

Nominal headroom is 6' 1". This is on the centerline

There are two variations on the interior: the midships galley/dinette, shown here, and a more conventional aft galley layout. The consesus is that the aft galley layout has better storage and use of space.

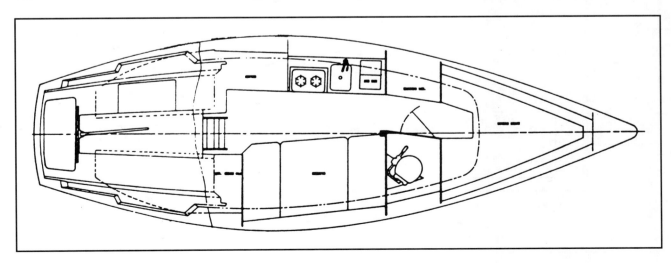

at the aft end of the main cabin. It's less everywhere else, but still more than you expect in a boat this size.

Originally, the boat's electrical panel was on the face of the port quarterberth—a poor location, vulnerable to spray through the companionway or water from the bilge. That rudimentary switch panel has been replaced on newer models with a good circuit breaker panel located in the starboard quarterberth— well-protected and reasonably accessible. We'd relocate the electrical panel on an older boat.

Icebox insulation on older boats is non-existent for all practical purposes. It's better on newer models, but it's still a far cry from a good icebox.

You are unlikely to find the Catalina 27 equipped with anything more sophisticated than a two-burner alcohol stove. As long as you don't do a lot of cooking this will be adequate, but longer cruises could turn into a grim test for the conscientious cook who wants to do much beyond heating up cans of stew or boiling water for coffee.

Ventilation of the interior ranges from poor to excellent, depending on either the age of the boat or the amount of upgrading done by the owners. In old boats, the forward cabin is stifling in hot weather. Newer boats have two aft-facing ventilation hatches over the head and passageway, as well as a hatch in the forward end of the cabin trunk. Unless added by owners, there is no provision for foul weather ventilation. Several cowl vents in dorade boxes would be a good addition for this boat.

All in all, the Catalina 27 has about as much interior room as it's possible to cram into a boat with a waterline of less than 22'. There is reasonable headroom without ungainly height of topsides— something a lot of small-boat designers have yet to accomplish.

Conclusions

Although there are smaller boats in the Catalina line, the 27 is a popular entry level daysailer and coastal cruiser. It's a good-looking boat, and it sails well.

There are many trade-offs inherent in buying an inexpensive boat, and the Catalina 27 is no exception. You won't find a lot of varnished teak or fancy systems in a Catalina 27. Unless upgraded by the owner, deck hardware and sail handling systems are likely to be rudimentary.

Because so many Catalina 27s have been built, there's usually a number of them on the market at any one time. Careful shopping should result in finding a vintage and level of equipment that match your taste and pocketbook.

Despite the fact that the Catalina 27 was designed and built as a coastal cruiser-racer, several have actually made circumnavigations. We don't recommend using the boat this way, but it goes to show that good preparation and seamanship may be more important than your boat when it comes to successful offshore voyaging.

There have been so many minor changes made to the Catalina 27 over the years that we doubt if anyone has kept up to date on all of them. Some of these upgrades are structurally important, such as the modification of the shroud attachments and the change in spreader fittings. Others, such as the foredeck anchor well, make the boat more useful.

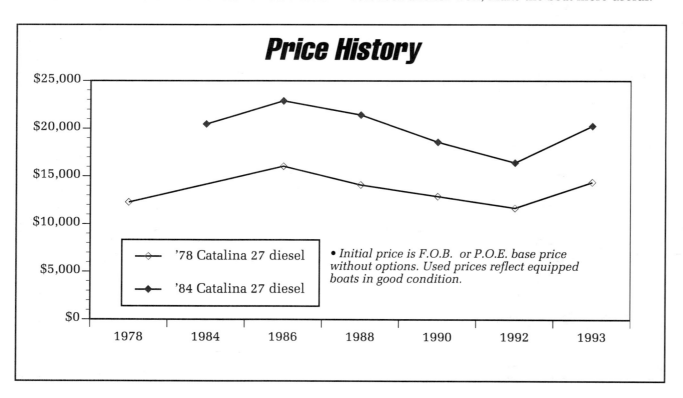

Price History

Legend:
—◇— '78 Catalina 27 diesel
—◆— '84 Catalina 27 diesel

• Initial price is F.O.B. or P.O.E. base price without options. Used prices reflect equipped boats in good condition.

If you get seriously interested in a Catalina 27, get a normal marine survey, and in addition, look for a knowledgeable Catalina 27 owner to go over the boat with you to point out specific potential problems. This may be one case in which the amateur surveyor has some advantages over the professional.

Don't buy a Catalina 27 thinking you're going to get Mercedes quality at a Volkswagen price. This is basic sailing transportation, an entry level boat. But if you recognize the boat for what it is, you probably won't be disappointed. Catalinas are always in demand, and they hold their value better than you would expect. Remember, however, that price will vary substantially with age, engine, and equipment. A new Catalina 27 costs several times the price of the original, 6,000 boats ago.

A lot of owners move up from the Catalina 27 to the Catalina 30. The boats are like peas in a pod in design, styling, and construction; anyone who is happy with the Catalina 27 is likely to be happy with the Catalina 30.

We're sure that fact is not lost on Frank Butler. He has a good record with the Catalina 27, and we suspect he's smiling all the way to the bank.• **PS**

Stiletto Catamaran

This so-called "coastal cruiser" (we don't think so) is far out on the fringe, but does offer some advantages.

Many sailors consider multihull sailing to be on the fringe of our sport. If that is true, then the Stiletto catamaran is dangling one hull off the edge. It's hard to mistake her appearance, with blazing topside graphics and aircraft-style, pop-top companionway hatches. It's also hard for the average sailor to appreciate the sophistication of the Stiletto's construction—epoxy-saturated fiberglass over a Nomex honeycomb core.

The 26' 10" Stiletto is anything but conventional. Multihulls larger than 20' can usually be classified into one of two genre. The largest group is that of the "cruising" multihull, characterized by beamy hulls, with a cabin house across the bridgedeck, stubby undercanvassed rigs, and monohull-like displacements. They often have mediocre performance, and are sometimes regarded with embarrassment by multihull enthusiasts.

The other genre of large multihulls is characterized by light displacement, powerful rigs and lean interiors. Custom ocean racing trimarans fall into this category, as do a very few production catamarans like the Stiletto.

The Stiletto's builder touted her trailerability, "scorching performance" and "cruising comforts." She is supposed to be the next step for the sailor weaned on small high-performance catamarans. In fact, three of the five owners we spoke to were former Hobie 16 sailors.

Almost anyone can understand why catamarans like the Hobie 16 are so popular—they offer breathtaking performance without making great demands on a sailor's expertise or pocketbook. To step up to a Stiletto is expensive, however. She was offered in three versions, along with a 30' version introduced in 1983. For $17,950 in 1982, the Standard Stiletto had a mainsail and all but stripped interior and no

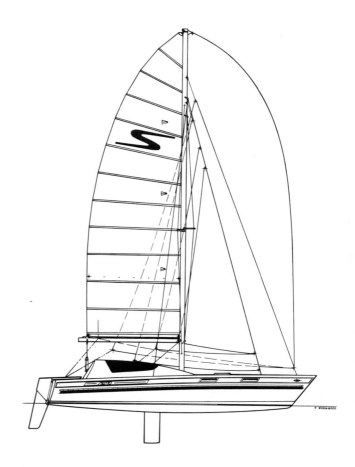

Specifications

LOA	26' 10"
LWL	24' 0"
Beam	13' 10"
Draft	9"/4' 0" (board up/down)
Displacement	1,100 lbs.
Ballast	N/A
Sail area	336 sq. ft.

options. The racing version, called the Championship Edition, came with a few options like deck hatches, rubrails and removable berths, plus extra racing sails, winches and a knotmeter; it cost $22,900. The cruising version, called the Special Edition, cost $24,900. That healthy chunk of cash bought the boat equipped with the options needed for pocket cruising, such as galley, head, berths, carpeted interior and running lights. Most Stilettos are Special Editions, followed by Standards and Championships.

Force Engineering (later Compodyne), a small, high-tech outfit in Florida, formed to build the Stiletto in 1978. Before he joined Force Engineering, co-owner/marketing director Larry Tibbe was an aircraft account salesman for Ciba-Geigy, a manufacturer of Nomex. Nomex coring is used in a variety of aircraft parts (for example, helicopter blades), as well as for the Stiletto's hulls. Force's survival strategy included the manufacture of several non-marine products out of Nomex, which helped them survive some bad times.

Construction

Very few boats are cored with Nomex honeycomb as are the Stiletto's hulls and bridgedeck. Sandwiching a core material between two layers of fiberglass laminate is not a new technique; many boatbuilders use cores of balsa wood, Airex foam or Klegecell foam. Core construction offers several advantages over single-skin construction. It is stiffer for a given weight, lighter for a given stiffness, makes the boat quieter and reduces condensation.

Honeycomb is rarely used for boatbuilding because the molding procedure is far more sophisticated (and expensive) than with balsa or foam cores. Honeycomb can be made of several materials. We question the use of paper or aluminum honeycomb in boats, because of their susceptibility to water damage should the outer laminate of the core be ruptured. The Stiletto's Nomex honeycomb core is made of nylon.

Force Engineering stated that a Nomex honeycomb-cored panel, for a given weight, is stronger, stiffer, less brittle and more puncture resistant than foam or wood cores. Nomex is also said to be impervious to water, so there would be no water migration between the honeycomb cells should the outer skin be ruptured.

These grandiose claims depend on a sophisticated and expensive molding procedure. Getting the honeycomb to bond to the fiberglass skins isn't easy. First, Force Engineering buys its fiberglass cloth preimpregnated with epoxy resin. Most boat builders use polyester resin, which is an inferior adhesive, and saturate the fiberglass after it has been laid into the mold—a messy and inexact procedure. Preimpregnated cloth, or "prepreg," has an exact resin-to-cloth ratio, which means that the builder always has the optimum strength-to-weight ratio. Most boat builders must err on the resin-rich side when saturating cloth, which increases weight but not strength.

To keep the prepreg cloth from curing before it is laid into the Stiletto mold, it must be shipped and stored in a refrigerator. To completely cure the prepreg after layup, the mold is placed in a modular oven and baked at 250 degrees for 90 minutes. At the same time, the fiberglass skins are vacuum-bagged to the honeycomb to ensure proper adhesion. Vacuum-bagging cored hulls is not a new technique, but for many builders it simply means laying a sheet of plastic into the mold and sucking the air out with a single pump (polypropylene line is often placed under the plastic to help distribute the vacuum). Force Engineering uses a blotter to absorb any excess resin and 16 spigots to distribute the vacuum, a more effective technique. When finished, each of the Stiletto's hulls weighs only 220 lbs. and is impressively strong and stiff.

The Stiletto's hull and bridgedeck may be state-of-the-art, but the rest of her rig, like her aluminum mast and crossbeams, is built with conventional (and relatively heavy) technology. All-up, the Stiletto weighs 1,100 to 1,570 lbs, depending on optional equipment.

We wonder whether building the Stiletto of Nomex is worth the extra trouble and expense, or if she is being used as a platform to prove the material's viability. Gelcoat cannot be used in the Stiletto's molding process. instead, each boat must be faired with putty and painted with polyurethane. Paint has the advantage that it will not chalk like gelcoat, but it is more susceptible to nicks, scrapes and peeling, especially if improperly applied.

The Stiletto's optional hull graphics are sticky-backed vinyl. Both the paint and the graphics were chipping on one five-year-old Stiletto we looked at.

The spars and the crossbeams are also painted with polyurethane. Although Force says it carefully sands and primes the spars, several of the masts we looked at had adhesion problems. The fittings were unbedded. The crossbeams were not anodized, and were only painted on the outside. Water can get inside the beams and accelerate corrosion.

The deck rests on an inward-turned hull flange, a common, safe design. But the deck is only epoxied to the hull without screws or bolts, inviting separation in the event of a catastrophic collision. Epoxy is undoubtedly stronger than polyester. However, we prefer mechanical fastenings in addition to a flexible adhesive like 3M 5200.

The Stiletto has a single daggerboard that is mounted on centerline through a slot in the bridgedeck. It is held snugly in place by a latticework of stainless steel tubes extending downward from the underside of the bridgedeck. This daggerboard frame is designed to collapse in the event of a hard grounding. There is no chance of the hull rupturing, as there would be with a daggerboard trunk built into the hull itself.

The Stiletto's single board is not as efficient as the dual boards found on other catamarans, and the board's support frame does tend to drag in the water while sailing. To keep water from squirting through the bridgedeck slot, the slot is covered by cloth gaskets. The gaskets occasionally jam.

The Stiletto has an airfoil daggerboard. Older models were made of wood, and chipped trailing edges were a common problem, The board is molded of fiberglass and more resistant to minor damage.

The Stiletto gets high marks for her rudders. They have strong aluminum heads and double lower pintles. To be beachable, a catamaran must have kick-up rudders; these kick-up systems often refuse to work when you need them most. However, the Stiletto's rudders worked smoothly and positively.

The Price of Performance

Multihulls are separated from the monohull mainstream by several things (in addition to the number of hulls). The first is performance. Multihulls, particularly catamarans, are lighter, more easily driven and hence far more exhilarating to sail than most monohulls. Yet even a novice can enjoy catamaran performance in most wind conditions because of the tremendous initial stability that a catamaran's beam offers.

The flip side of this hot performance is safety. Catamarans also have tremendous stability after they have capsized and turned turtle. All but the smallest catamarans are nearly impossible to right after they have gone completely upside down, especially if the mast is not airtight.

When reaching in strong winds, many catamarans have a nasty tendency to bury the leeward hull and pitchpole. Some cats can even be blown over backwards if a very strong puff catches the underside of the trampoline. Nearly all trimarans that are raced offshore have watertight hatches on the bottom of the main hull to allow escape if the boat flips over.

Another price of performance is comfort. Multihulls tend to be wet. When you're flying along at 20 knots, even a light spray can feel like a fire hose. It's harder to find a comfortable spot to relax in when you're sailing. The trampoline/bridgedeck separating the two hulls of a catamaran is usually flat—you sit on it, not in it. Moreover, the hulls of a thoroughbred multihull are narrow, so there is little space in which to put creature comforts. The wide-hulled, cabin-housed "cruising" catamarans are no more spritely than a monohull of similar displacement.

Multihulls are also less maneuverable than monohulls. They can be difficult to tack without getting into irons, and they have a much wider turning radius. Sailing in a crowded harbor takes greater care.

Trailerability

Force Engineering emphasized the Stiletto's trailerability. True, she is light enough to be pulled by a modern automobile of modest power. But all of the owners we talked to said they rarely, if ever, trail their boats. 80% of the boats were sold with trailers, but it appears that most are used only for winter storage.

Rigging and launching the Stiletto is not a simple chore, despite the fact that the builder claimed a man and woman can do it in only 45 minutes. Owners say it takes at least several men well over an hour to do the job. The Stiletto has a beam of 13' 10"; legal highway trailering width in most states is 8'. To solve this problem, both the Stiletto's crossbeams and the trailer collapse to legal width. The compression tube that spans the bows must be removed for trailering, as must the dolphin striker beneath the mast step, and the 125 lb bridgedeck.

To raise and lower the mast, the headstay is shackled to a short, pivoting gin pole mounted just aft of the trailer winch. The winch is used to pull the gin pole, which in turn provides leverage to hoist the heavy mast. Owners say that lifting the bridgedeck and manhandling the spar is next to impossible with just a man and woman. The Stiletto assembly manual points out, "...she never fails to draw a crowd, so help is usually available if you are shorthanded." As long as you have the muscle, this clever system does work.

Sailing

The Stiletto is a performance catamaran. In a breeze, owners report, she is as fast or faster than a Hobie 16, but a bit undercanvassed in light air, especially with her 106 square foot working jib. This is preferable to overcanvassing; a catamaran of the Stiletto's size cannot afford, for safety's sake, to be a bear in heavy air.

According to owners, the Stiletto does not have some of the bad heavy air habits of smaller catamarans. They say she is relatively dry to sail, does not hike up and "fly a hull" too easily, has no tendency to pitchpole, and does not get "light" as she comes off a big wave sailing upwind. Like most catamarans, the Stiletto has a fully battened mainsail. The advantage of these sails is that they can have a much larger roach, and because the battens dampen luffing, the sail will last much longer. However, this inability to luff can present a real safety problem in a sudden squall. It is prudent to reef when the wind reaches 20 knots. A smaller roached, short-battened cruising mainsail is available as an option for offshore cruising. The sails that came as standard equipment seem to be of better than average OEM quality.

Stiletto sailors told us that they sail very cautiously in a strong breeze, knowing the dangers of capsizing so large a multihull. Once capsized, a catamaran turns turtle (completely upside down) very quickly. A turtled multihull with a mast full of water is nearly impossible to right. The Stiletto's builder offers a self-righting kit as an option, but they have sold very few. The kit consists of a bulky foam float permanently mounted to the masthead, and a 17' righting pole stowed under the bridgedeck. The float is supposed to prevent the boat from turning turtle while the righting pole is extended outward and its three stays are rigged to the underside of the boat. Then two crew swim out to a ladder dangling from the end of the pole, climb up to right the boat, then quickly swim free before the ladder drags them 17' toward Davy Jones' Locker. It's no small wonder that the self-righting kit is not a popular option.

Force Engineering points out that the air cells of her honeycomb construction make her unsinkable in the event of a holing or capsize. However, they do not point out that once the hull is flooded, the boat cannot be sailed or motored home without inviting the flooded hull to submerge and pitchpole the boat. The Stiletto, like most high-performance catamarans, has a rotating mast. Owners say they have not had problems with the mast popping out of rotation while sailing upwind. The older masts have only athwartships diamond shrouds; the newer masts have an added third diamond extended forward to control fore-and-aft bend in a strong breeze. This three-diamond system is strongly welded together and a real plus for heavy weather sailing.

Deck Layout

The Stiletto has a solid bridgedeck stretched between the two hulls aft of the mast, and a polypropylene cloth trampoline forward of the mast. Those few sailors planning to venture offshore might want to remove the trampoline, lest it collect water in heavy seas. On Stilettos older than two years, the trampoline is laced with a series of hooks. On the newer boats the trampoline has bolt rope edges, and slides into tracks on the hull and crossbeams, a simpler and cleaner system.

The bridgedeck, which is where you spend most of your time, has no seats and is said by several owners to be uncomfortable. Because of this, the temptation when sailing is to sit on top of the flimsy companionway hatches. We feel that a "cruising" catamaran should have proper seats with angled seatbacks.

A wire stretched between the bows forward of the headstay acts as a traveler for the optional reacher/drifter. Most sailors opt for this sail before they buy a cruising spinnaker. Poleless cruising spinnakers are more effective on a catamaran than on a monohull because they can be tacked on the weather hull, away from the blanketing effect of the mainsail. A roller furling headsail with a Hood Seafurl system was an option. Headsail winches were standard on the Championship Edition, otherwise they were an extra-cost option. A main halyard winch, which owners recommend, was another.

The Stiletto has a ball-bearing mainsheet traveler, a worthy item rarely found on catamarans. But the mainsheet has only a 6-to-1 purchase, which owners say is insufficient in a breeze. The tiller extension passes behind the mainsheet and the tiller crossbar is adjustable so you can align the two rudders. The jibsheets are led to Harken ratchets to make trimming easier. The outboard engine bracket is hung off the aft compression beam.

Interior

Those of you who have peeked below on the Stiletto might ask, "What interior?" It's a valid question. The Standard Stiletto version is nothing but an empty

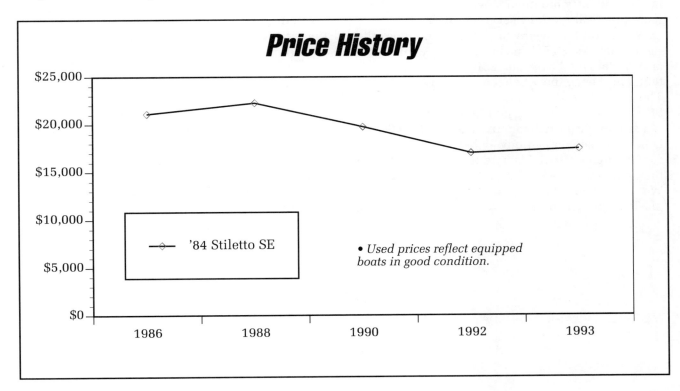

Price History

'84 Stiletto SE

• *Used prices reflect equipped boats in good condition.*

shell below. Depending on the care that was taken during the vacuum-bagging process, the interior hull surface can be smooth or quite rippled. Either way, the Nomex gives the boat a long-lasting smell similar to mouse droppings (we could still smell it on a five year old boat).

The popular Special Edition was described by the builder as a "luxury coastal cruiser"; though it cost nearly $25,000 new, we would be more comfortable on a Catalina 22. The Special Edition's interior is completely covered—ceilings, overhead and sole—with Aqua Tuft marine carpeting. Owners say it is durable and does not mildew, but we feel carpet belongs in a house, not a boat.

The Stiletto has the narrow hulls of a fast catamaran, which means that her berths are only 31" wide. The Special Edition has 14' of built-in berth forward of the companionway in each hull. For two people to sleep easily in a berth, they have to lie end-to-end. Crawling toward the bow to get to the forward berth is like crawling down a narrowing tunnel—it gave us claustrophobia. If a normal-sized couple really wanted a good night's sleep, they would have to bed down in separate hulls. There is some stowage area under the berths, but access to it is just plain difficult.

The Special Edition has a self-contained head under one berth. A pump-out head was not an option. The Special Edition also has a small galley built of "marble finish" plastic laminate over plywood; we think that even the most "with it" cat sailor would consider it gaudy. The galley has a sink with a hand pump and a two-gallon water tank. There is no permanently mounted stove; a portable stove is more practical for the weekend cruiser.

An option that we recommend is the mosquito-tight bridgedeck tent. The bridgedeck cushions that are standard on the Special Edition should make the tent, and hence the whole boat, somewhat livable. The Special Edition is also the only version of the Stiletto that has running and interior lights.

Perhaps the most distinctive feature of the Stiletto is her conical companionway hatches ("canopies," as in jet fighter-like). It's hard to be impartial about their appearance—you either like 'em or you don't. We don't. The canopies are formed of dark, bendy plastic. They open vertically like a pop-top hatch,

and swing on flimsy aluminum tubes that are not well secured to their mounts.

Owners say the canopies are watertight, but the rubber gaskets in which they sit were rotting badly on the older boats we saw. For that matter, the rubber gaskets on the bridgedeck were rotting, too. Trying to sleep in the Stiletto's hulls could be very stuffy on a rainy night. Because the canopies rock forward as they "pop-up," it's hard to leave them open a crack like a conventional hatch, and there are no companionway boards.

Conclusions

There is probably no production hull built in the US with a better strength-to-weight ratio than the Stiletto catamaran. Her Nomex honeycomb fabrication is truly impressive. But is it necessary? Just as some builders "overkill" with heavy solid laminates, we feel that Force Engineering overkilled in the other direction. Conventional coring probably could have created an adequately strong and light boat that would have provided just as much sailing fun for less money.

The next question is, "What do you do with her?" The Stiletto seems to appeal to the catamaran sailor hooked on high performance, but who wants a boat in which he can "go someplace." The Stiletto is quick, but she won't get someplace any faster than a small catamaran. She may be dryer, but she still lacks comfortable seating and sleeping. When you get to where you are going you have very little comfort for the money you've spent on the boat. And when you get home, you have a considerable chore ahead of you if you plan to load her onto a trailer.

All the owners we talked to said they love the way the boat sails and have no complaints about her construction. Yet we still don't feel the Stiletto is practical. There are other, less expensive options for the multihull sailor who wants to weekend cruise. Any catamaran can be rigged with a tent on the trampoline/bridgedeck. Inflatable air mattresses stow easily and make fine temporary berths. And some catamarans, such as the much-less-expensive P-Cat 2/18, have the dry stowage in their hulls to carry camping supplies. Small catamarans are ultimately safer, because they can be righted from a capsize, and they are infinitely easier to trailer. • **PS**

Tartan 27

Though there are limitations to the Tartan 27, in many ways she is typical of the best of used boats.

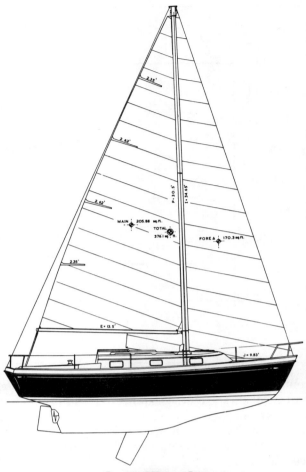

Any article on the Tartan 27 has to approach being a historical treatise since this is a truly venerable craft by any standard, ancient or modern. The origins of Tartan Marine rest in Douglass & MacLeod Plastics, and in Charles Britton.

In the spring of 1971, Britton (who had been building the Tartan line at Douglass & MacLeod formed Tartan Marine, a boatbuilding firm that has a long-standing reputation for producing quality boats that remain in production far longer than the average for stock fiberglass craft. The Tartans 27, 30, 34, and 37 have been available for more years than most boatbuilders with competing products have been in business. In short, Tartan has had a successful sales record that has been the envy of the industry.

A Close Look at the Boat

The Tartan 27 went into production in 1961 with fiberglass boatbuilding in its toddler stage; production ceased in 1980, after 19 years interrupted only by a fire in 1972 that resulted in no 27s being built that year. The greatest number of 27s built in one year is 85; the year was 1964. In all, 712 Tartan 27s were built, including a dozen boats under license in California. Remarkably few significant changes were made to the boat until near the end of the long production run, after hull #650. Those that are noteworthy are as follows:

• **1966** External keel encapsulated and ballast increased by 350 pounds
• **1973** Deck redesigned with a longer cockpit and a bridgedeck plus some changes to the interior decor.
• **1977** Sheerline raised 4" and deck again redesigned, eliminating the rather boxy looking doghouse; interior given a more traditional layout. About 65 boats were built to this configuation before production ended in 1979.

Specifications

LOA	27' 0"
LWL	21' 5"
Beam	8' 7"
Draft	3' 2"/6' 4" (board up/down)
Displacement	7,400 lbs.
Ballast	2,400 lbs.
Sail area	376 sq. ft.

The Tartan 27 was designed by Sparkman & Stephens as a small and relatively narrow edition of the then popular hull form—a combination of keel and centerboard, moderately heavy displacement, and short overhangs topped with a low aspect masthead rig. In all, the 27 is what aficionados regard as a superb example of a small yacht of traditional proportions.

At the same time the boat is well constructed and finished and has at least adequate performance for a centerboard boat of her size, hull shape, and weight (average PHRF base rating, 235), sailing equal to such full keel counterparts as the Cape Dory 27 and the Triton. The 27 has a reputation as a well balanced boat capable of sailing with the helm unattended in moderate conditions, an advantage afforded by the

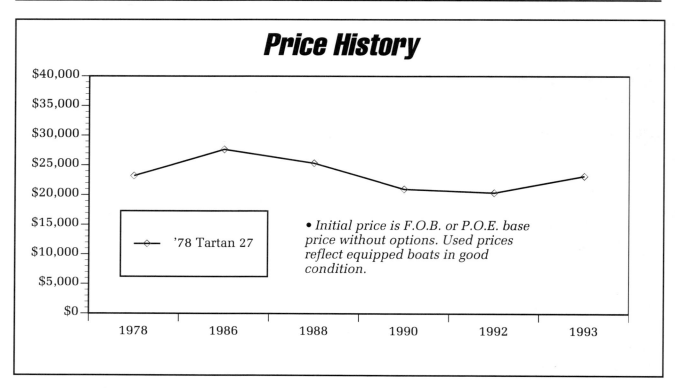

Price History

$40,000
$35,000
$30,000
$25,000
$20,000
$15,000
$10,000
$5,000
$0

1978   1986   1988   1990   1992   1993

◇— '78 Tartan 27

• *Initial price is F.O.B. or P.O.E. base price without options. Used prices reflect equipped boats in good condition.*

centerboard, short rig, and narrow beam. Like other narrow boats she tends be quick to heel initially but stiffens at an angle of 20 degrees or so. She should be sailed "on her feet," however, for optimum windward performance. Overpowered, she carries a heavy weather helm.

The 27 had two standard engine installations: until about 1975 the Atomic 4 was offered, and thereafter both the Atomic 4 and the Farymann one cylinder 12 hp diesel. About 85% of the 27s were fitted with the Atomic 4. Owners report the 27 comfortably overpowered with the Atomic 4, a bit underpowered with the Farymann. As with any long keel boat with the propeller in an aperture, backing down is an adventure.

The masthead rig of the 27 uses a large mainsail and modest sized foretriangle. Performance calls for overlapping headsails (as big as 176% LP for racing). A small number of 27s, for what we assume was quaintness rather than any practical reason, were rigged as yawls with handkerchief-sized mizzens on a mast stepped into the lazarette.

The original interior layout had a dinette, midships galley, cockpit-opening icebox, quarterberth, and small head—a cramped interior by "modern" standards. Later 27s had a more traditional layout with settee berths, an aft galley, no quarterberth, a chart table, and a larger athwartships head. The result is still cramped but with better use of space, especially with elimination of the dinette.

From all reports, the basic construction of the Tartan 27 has proven superb with few exceptions. The outward turned hull-to-deck flange is not one *PS*

recommends, being more subject to difficult-to-repair damage than the common inward flange. Breakage of the teak rubrail is a problem frequently mentioned by owners. At the same time the outward flange does help keep the deck and cockpit drier; complaints about leaking through this joint are notable for their absence.

Apparently many 27s were built with wood supports under the mast step. Several owners report eventual rotting of this wood with the subsequent collapse of the step, the result of water leaking around the mast partner. Similarly, several cite water damage to other wood structures such as bulkheads in way of the mast. Solution: stop the leaks, provide drainage and replace the wood at the first sign of deterioration.

Otherwise the most often mentioned problem is delamination of the balsa-cored deck, especially in the way of the chainplates that, improperly bedded or not checked periodically, let water seep in. This is a serious problem, hard to recify, but by no means unusual for older fiberglass boats.

Tartan 27 owners, at least the ones we have heard from, are a resourceful group. Many mention improvements they have made to their boats and amenities they have fitted. Add to this the remarkably useful *Tartan 27 Handbook* that the Chesapeake Bay class association put together and prospective owners have ample suggestions to work with.

What to Look For

We have already mentioned a couple of crucial items to check prior to purchasing a 27: the mast step and the possibility of deck delamination. Others that owners report are as follows:

• During the production history a variety of fuel tanks found their way into boats. Some have developed leaks; since the majority of 27s use gasoline, a leaking fuel tank is serious.

• The Atomic 4 engine for seeming eons has been as reliable a piece of marine machinery as has been devised by the hand of man. Engines 20+ years old are still performing in exemplary fashion. But they need care and attention; check for loss of compression, oil and water leaks, electrical corrosion, and cracked mounts in particular. The Farymann diesel is reliable but parts are expensive and vibration can loosen mounts, couplings, hose connections, etc.

• The centerboard pennant can wear through the tubing from the turning block to the trunk, both weakening the cable and eventually causing a leak.

• Most of the centerboards in the 27 are fiberglass-encapsulated steel plate (the first dozen boats had bronze). In time the board at the pivot can wear away, dropping the centerboard and letting it hang solely on its pennant (which, if weak, can break and lose the board). Check carefully for such wear.

• The rudder post has no bearing between it and the tube through which it runs. Eventually the wear between the post and tube produces sloppiness and noise. The best answer we have seen is to install an external bearing or collar at the upper end of the tube.

• In the words of the *Tartan 27 Handbook,* "Perhaps the weakest point on the Tartan 27 is the tiller head fitting." Both wear and cracking occur, neither particularly difficult to detect or remedy, but best to be forewarned.

Few boats the size of the Tartan 27 better lend themselves to substantial refurbishing. Owners detail complete restoration of interiors, repowering, the addition of amenties such as gas stoves, pressure water systems and the like, refinishing decks and topsides with polyurethane (many were built with colored gelcoat topsides that have become badly chalked), and a passel of other such improvements.

Components such as fiberglass hatches, rudders and centerboards are still available from the builder.

Conclusions

In many ways and for a variety of reasons a boat like the Tartan 27 is typical of the best offerings on the used boat market. The boat is fundamentally sound and reasonably available in a range of prices. Its inherent quality makes maintenance and upgrading practical. Strong owner associations and builder support are an invaluable resource rare among boats of this vintage. Besides, the 27 is a centerboarder that sails well, looks handsome, and stays together.

For this appeal the price is apt to be high, although boats in basically sound but cosmetically disasterous condition are available at prices that make refurbishing practical. The same can be said for relatively few smaller boats more than 15 years old. In our opinion the Tartan 27 should be a most attractive consideration for the buyer looking for quality on a modest budget, if willing to put effort into increasing the comfort, performance, and appearance of his boat rather than investing in it up front.

At the same time the 27 has its limitations: a cramped interior, "age spots" such as scruffy gelcoat, possible deck delamination, centerboard wear, gas engines getting on in years, and, in an age of sailing performance, so-so speed.

Virtues and flaws balanced, however, the Tartan 27 strikes us as having most of what we would look for in an older small cruising boat from the standpoint of ruggedness, appearance, function, and equity. They may seem costly but we suspect that even Tartan 27s built in the 1960s will be around far longer than a lot of cheaper boats 10 or 15 years younger. And we like the last version of the 27, the one with the higher topsides, lower cabin profile, and, to our mind, more comfortable interior layout. These are classic used boats of their type.   • **PS**

Shown here is the later—and in our opinion, more comfortable—interior layout.

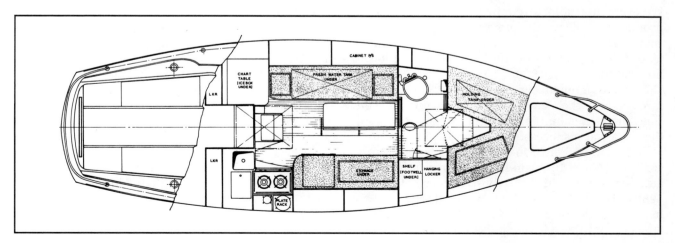

Albin Vega

A lightweight 27-footer that's designed for offshore. Suited to an average couple, it's a good value.

L ike a lot of people, our first recollection of the Albin Vega was an advertisement in the sailing magazines. In the early 1970s, a time when California production coastal cruisers dominated the American market, this little Swedish import was hyped as a serious offshore cruiser. Our reaction was, "What has this boat got that the others don't?"

The ad photo showed the Vega backlit by a late afternoon sun, sailing out to sea. The copy touted it as a "…four berth diesel cruiser built of reinforced fiberglass…" that "…sails in her own class and holds the record for the fastest Atlantic crossing." Other noteworthy gear mentioned was the single lever, variable pitch prop, dodger and stainless steel sink with fresh and sea water foot pumps. One surmised from the above that the Vega was light, fast, seaworthy and cruisable. Seventeen years later, it's easier to put the Vega in perspective. The boat comes close to its billing, but it's not without its flaws.

Specifications

LOA	27' 1"
LWL	23' 0"
Beam	8' 0"
Draft	3' 10"
Displacement	5,070 lbs.
Ballast	2,017 lbs.
Sail area	341 sq. ft.

Design and Construction

We were not able to confirm the exact dates of production, but we do know that the boat was designed in 1966. Responses to our Boat Owner's Questionnaire range from hull #249, built in 1968, to hull #3361 built in 1979.

Sailed as a one-design in Europe, the Vega made inroads into the American sailing scene as well. They are still commonly sighted. By any standard, the Vega was a successful design.

Designed by Per Brohall, the Vega has a narrow, easily driven hull. Beam is just eight feet, a foot or more narrower than similarly sized boats of the late 1980s. The hull is shallow, with a large cutaway forward of the so-called "full keel." The rudder is attached but there is no aperture for the propeller.

The shaft exits the deadwood just above the rudder, under the counter. More on this later.

In profile, the sheer is reversed. This gives the boat an odd look, though certainly not an unpleasant one. Reverse sheer is used mainly on smaller boats to increase interior space. Also, the tumblehome of the topsides (the middle of the hull above the waterline is wider than at the toerail) causes the hull, rather than the stronger hull-deck joint and rail, to take the brunt of bumpings with pilings.

A teak rubrail could be through-bolted along the most exposed area, which would protect a new paint job but which might be difficult to make aesthetically pleasing. A rubrail should follow, to some extent, the line of the sheer, and on a boat with reverse sheer, this would produce a very strange

Owners' Comments

"Must be reefed at 12 to 14 knots of wind, but still handles well. Somewhat underpowered with Volvo Penta MD6 of 10 hp. Get a good mechanic for diesel and reversing mechanism."
—1973 model in Rhode Island

"In the 10K price range, the Albin Vega makes offshore cruising relatively affordable."
—1973 model in North Carolina

"Stern shaft bearing is metric and an oddball size. Everything else is also metric. Find someone who sells metric bronze machine screws and become his best friend."
—Hull #77 in Southern California

"The chainplates are nothing more than inverted stainless steel U-bolts fastened into the hull-to-deck joint with a piece of aluminum channel as a backing plate. This may seem weak, but in older boats one will not see stress cracks so this may be strong enough. The mast support structure can be aggravated by over tightened rigging."
—1971 model in Virginia

"I hit the top of a large mountain at about four knots. Stopped the poor lady in her tracks, but only cosmetic damage to the keel."
—1977 model in Texas

"Excellent boat for two people to coastal cruise. Parts for feathering prop, stuffing box, etc. can be hard to get and are expensive."
—1979 model in Massachusetts

looking rubrail! Some experimentation on paper would be wise.

The hull and deck are built of fiberglass—chopped strand mat and woven roving bonded with polyester resin—with coring in the deck and coachroof. Company literature asserted that the hulls are 3/8" thick at the toerail, increasing to 1" at the base of the keel. There is ample evidence, however, that some panels, such as the cabin sides, are too thin. On one boat we sailed, they oilcanned easily by pressing the hands against them. Also, the deck did not feel as solid as the advertisements would have us believe—perhaps we were witnessing deck delamination.

Excessive gel coat cracking is the only obvious result, but it is not comforting to feel a panel give. The boat has proven itself offshore, but this does not necessarily mean the structure is well-engineered. One reader wrote: "Hull suspiciously thin. The Vega is ocean rated (but) my only question is how much can it take."

John Neal, who sailed 14,000 miles throughout the South Pacific on a Vega in the mid-1970s and wrote about his adventures in a book titled *Log of the Mahina*, called the Vega sound, noting that his had survived collisions with coral heads.

Neal, however, also mentioned a problem we noticed, that of deck compression from the deck-stepped mast. Toward the end of his cruise, the main load-bearing bulkhead was actually warping. He wrote: "Upon close inspection, I found that one of the two supports on the main bulkhead had sheared its glue bond, breaking a three-eighths-inch stainless steel bolt, and had been forced through the fiberglass cabin sole. Also, the main port bulkhead had started to warp seriously at the top."

This problem, fortunately, is less common than it was in early fiberglass boats. So often we hear that older fiberglass boats were built much more strongly that today's. Well, it ain't necessarily so. The buyer of a Vega wishing to sail it hard should give some thought to solving this problem. Gluing and screwing plywood to the bulkhead for double thickness would help, as would replacing the overhead beams with larger ones. Of equal importance is transmitting the load from the sole to the hull. This would mean fiberglassing a support between the sole and hull—not an easy job, but a necessary one. Care should be taken not to create hard spots in the hull. The procedure for fitting bulkheads is covered in many books and involves cutting foam wedges to fit between the wood and hull, the joint amply covered with successively larger widths of fiberglass tape.

The hull-to-deck joint is an internal flange with pliant caulking ("2 pack rubber"), fastened through with 5/16" stainless steel bolts every five inches. None of our readers have reported leaking.

Some owners noted the weakness of the rudder. Neal lost his while hove to. After making repairs, he then hove to with slack in the tiller lashings, which worked.

Performance Under Sail

The Vega is a fine little sailer whose greatest virtue is manageability in a wide range of conditions. Nearly all owners remark how well the boat is balanced. We, too, noticed this trait immediately, admiring the light helm and good tracking.

Light air performance is criticized by numerous owners. When the wind blows over about 15 knots, they say, the boat really comes alive. We did not think the boat we sailed suffered terribly in lower wind speeds, but compared to a more contemporary coastal design with fin keel and larger rig, the Vega would undoubtedly come up short. This is an acceptable compromise for an offshore boat. Many owners say they can keep sailing when others are heading in, adding that the boat remains dry even in rough conditions.

As one would expect from her round bilges and relatively shallow keel, the Vega is initially a mite tender, heeling easily to about 15 degrees. Thereafter, with her shoulder buried, she becomes quite stiff. Again, this is not an undesirable trait for an offshore cruiser.

All in all, the Vega is a pleasure to steer. Unlike modern boats with spade rudders, that tend to stall when overcanvassed, the Vega remains under control at all times. We find that a most comforting characteristic—indeed, a prerequisite for safe, comfortable cruising.

Performance Under Power

The early Vegas were equipped with Albin 022 13 hp or Volvo MB10A 15 hp gas engines, later replaced with Volvo diesels, including the 10 hp MD6A and 13 hp MD7A. Some early Vegas did not have trans-

missions, using the Combi variable pitch prop instead. An owner of a 1976 model wrote that by the time Albin built his boat, a transmission had been added. The variable pitch prop was retained, using a single lever control without clutch. "This is an interesting piece of engineering," he wrote, "but hell to repair."

The variable pitch system is far superior to conventional propellers in terms of efficiency. However, it does have drawbacks, principally the grease seals that may leak. A number of readers wrote that parts for the Combi unit, as well as mechanics familiar with it, are hard to find.

Most owners report forward power as good, most saying she'll cruise at six knots. A few owners of the 10-hp diesel said the boat was slightly underpowered, which probably explains why later boats were fitted with the 13-hp model.

Reverse is another story. The value of the variable pitch Combi drive with 1.42:1 reduction gear, which provides greater power backing down, is mitigated

While its eight-foot beam is narrow by today's standards, the Vega has an easily driven hull form with four good berths, semi-private head and split galley. It also can be trailered.

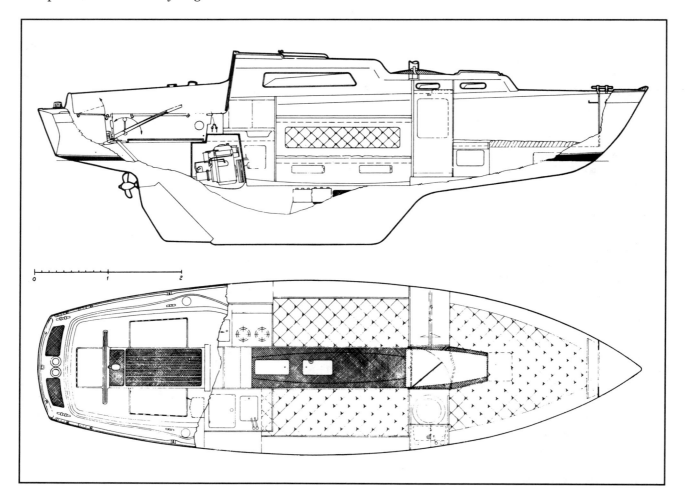

by the fact that the propeller is situated aft of the rudder. This makes the boat a devil to steer in reverse. Almost every owner reported difficulty with the boat in reverse, noting that manuevering in tight quarters requires extra vigilance.

On the plus side, the Volvo engines rate high in reliability. Accessibility is better than average. The real problems with the power train lie in maintaining the Combi drive, which is an asset if working properly and a liability if allowed to deteriorate.

The Interior

The Vega is not a large 27-footer by today's standards, yet its layout is quite serviceable for a couple despite the fact that headroom is just 5' 10" (actually 5' 7" in the boat we measured) in the main cabin. As the British designer Uffa Fox once said, "If you want to stand up, go on deck."

The straightforward layout includes V-berths forward (6' 0" starboard, 6' 6" port), a partially enclosed head compartment forward of the main bulkhead, 6' 1" and 6' 6" settees in the main cabin, and a galley split port and starboard by the companionway. There is ample stowage behind the seatbacks, under the settees and in various galley bins.

The dinette table removes for stowing, or for mounting in the cockpit; the two legs set in sockets sunk into the cabin sole and cockpit floor.

The main shortcoming of the plan is that the toilet is open to the V-berths, which is why this boat is best suited to a couple or small family, or at the least those of intimate relations!

Woodwork is hand-rubbed mahogany, which is quite attractive if maintained properly. The overhead has a fiberglass liner but the cabin and hull sides do not; the latter are covered with a foam-backed perforated vinyl. The cabin sole is fiberglass, which transmits cold and noise—best to cover with a moisture-resistant carpet.

All windows are fixed, which is typical of boats built in far northern climates. The rubber gaskets are a bit of a worry, as the material can degrade over time, permitting leaks.

An innovative ventilation system helps keep the interior dry and mildew at bay. Air is introduced through a ventilator in the forward cabin and exhausted via the mast and a cockpit ventilator.

Conclusion

The Albin Vega is an interesting boat, one that in many respects was ahead of its time. Except for the limitations mentioned, construction was essentially sound. The design is superb. We like the variable pitch propeller despite the extra maintenance required. Placing it in an aperture in front of the rudder would help performance in reverse a great deal, but this would have required a deeper hull form and thereby change the entire concept of the boat. Considering that sailboats spend very little time going backwards, we think Brohall made a good decision.

The base price of the Vega in 1977 was about $21,000, with a good list of standard gear. That boat today sells for about $16,000. Depending on condition, you could buy one for less. Any way you cut it, the Vega represents a good value—an ocean-going vessel for minimal investment. **• PS**

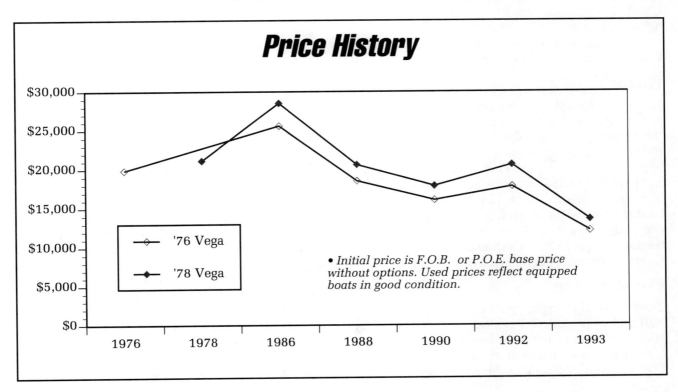

Price History

• Initial price is F.O.B. or P.O.E. base price without options. Used prices reflect equipped boats in good condition.

Legend:
- ◇ '76 Vega
- ◆ '78 Vega

The F-27

This unusual and innovative trimaran is not only fast, she can even fold up while still afloat.

Y ou can count the number of successful builders of production fiberglass cruising multihulls on the fingers of one hand. In the U.S., Tony Smith of Mayo, Maryland, who builds the 30' Gemini catamaran, is certainly a pioneer, having developed the ill-fated 26' Telstar trimaran many years ago (the molds were destroyed in a fire). Condor Ltd. and the Outrigger Boat Co. have made some inroads into the market and have helped in the grudging conversion of American sailors to multihulls.

A number of European builders, most notably the British builder Prout and more recently Prestige and Ohlala from France, import to the U.S. a handful of boats each year.

None, however, has made a splash as big as Ian Farrier's F-27 trailerable tri, first launched in 1985.

History

Farrier is a New Zealander who moved to Australia after college and began building small racing/cruising trimarans. His 19' Tramp was Australia's 1981 Boat of the Year. In 1984 he moved to California to begin work on the F-27 and to patent the folding mechanism that makes trailering possible.

When *PS* readers who own F-27s began writing to us about their boats, we took note. "Look at the F-27," they said, "it's something special." A number of them sent in our Owner's Questionnaire with raves about speed, construction and company service.

Construction

The F-27 is all fiberglass with a PVC foam core in the hull and deck. An NPG gelcoat is used, backed by AME 4000 (acrylic modified epoxy) resin. In areas of high stress, double bias fabrics, Kevlar, and carbon fiber are used. Vacuum bagging techniques are em

Specifications

LOA	27' 1"
LWL	26' 3"
Beam	19' 1"/8' 5" (folded)
Draft	4' 11"/1' 2" (board down/up)
Weight	2,600 lbs.
Ballast	N/A
Sail area	446 sq. ft.

ployed to ensure constant and uniform pressure on both sides of any laminate. Excess air and resin is bled off to achieve the desired, calculated weight. Light weight is essential to good multihull performance.

Unlike a monohull, which is built from basically two molds (hull and deck), the F-27 requires 52. Besides the main hull there are the two amas and four akas (cross beams), not to mention all the smaller moldings for the pop top, outboard well, hatches, and sinks. The F-27 possesses a definite "assembled" look rather than being a homogenous whole. As your eye surveys the numerous attachment points—hull/deck joints, akas to amas, etc.—there seem to be numerous potential weak spots. The builder, however, claims there have been no failures, and we have

Folding of the F-27 can be handled by one person and involves removing a total of eight bolts, two for each pivot point. Note the outboard sticking out of its well on the port quarter.

not had reports of any. This is no doubt due to the use of quality high-tech materials and extremely careful engineering. After all, the F-27 represents nearly two decades of refinement on the original concept, not unlike the last generation of Volkswagen Beetles.

Of particular interest are the folding akas. A company brochure explains: "The beams are bolted down into molded recesses with two bolts each, the bolts being anchored into specially reinforced internal bulkheads. Once bolted the beams are strong enough on their own for all loadings. However, add the lower struts (part of the folding mechanism) and these become the primary structural members, actually relieving all bending stresses from the inner ends of the beams. Sailing is then quite possible without any bolts in beams at all! The beam bolts thus act as a backup system in the unlikely event of a folding strut failure. But should this occur the beams simply take over all loadings making the inboard structure completely safe. The actual folding struts are precision engineered from solid high strength aluminum, with nylon bush inserts being used at the pivot points with stainless steel pivot bolts."

The akas can be folded underway while motoring, heading for the slip or launch ramp. Total beam with both amas folded in is 8' 5". Therein lies its appeal to Southern California sailors, who find slip space expensive if not unavailable. Also, it makes cruising Baja and the Sea of Cortez a practical adventure. Baja is the only really good cruising ground in that area, but too far to reach under sail for short term vacations. The trailering feature will be less appealing to sailors elsewhere, except that the ability to store the boat in the backyard saves yard fees and makes maintenance a far easier chore.

The centerboard and rudders are foam-cored fiberglass with carbon fiber added for strengthening. Unlike most builders, Corsair publishes its lamina-tion schedule for all parts; indeed, the documentation and control evidenced at Corsair is rather extraordinary in the sailing industry.

Much of the hardware is made by Harken, including the mainsheet traveler, blocks and cleats. One reader wrote, "As the boat is well rigged, you will not need to replace any of the rigging such as winches, etc. Everything is both top quality and over-engineered." The boat we sailed was equipped with Lewmar #30 jib sheet winches, #24 self-tailing genoa and halyard winches; the linestoppers were made by Antal.

Performance

The F-27 is a fast boat. Obviously, speed was a priority of the design. The rig is tall and no attempt was made to provide standing headroom in the cabin, which would have added windage and weight. Already it has achieved some success racing, though it can't be compared to monohulls and there are only a few other multihulls in its range (compare to the Newick-designed Somersault 26, Firefly 26, Dragonfly 25 and Stiletto 27). Unfortunately, we are unaware of any head-to-head competition between these boats.

We sailed Tony Cabot's new F-27 from his mooring in Squantum, Massachusetts, under mainsail and working jib. The fully battened main can be reefed on the roller boom, though there wasn't enough wind for us to see how the sail would set.

As we tacked out of Quincy Bay and into Boston Harbor, the wind was light (usually the case in test sails!). The boat moved effortlessly and heeled little (even in heavy weather, trimarans shouldn't heel more than 12° to 15°). The helm was very well balanced, requiring just fingertip control (one reader said he had tuned the rig to add a little weather helm).

Approaching a fleet of racing monohulls at the harbor entrance, the 30- and 40-footers were making just a knot or so and appeared virtually dead in the water. We, on the other hand, slipped past at five knots in about as much wind, and we confess to feeling quite smug. With the board down, we also were able to point fairly high with the apparent wind between 35° and 40°, though of course multihulls are more comfortable and efficient cracked off, especially in a sea. With the F-27, this is due in part to its relatively flat, planing bottom.

In normal conditions, the F-27 can be expected to make seven to eight knots to windward. On a spinnaker reach in winds over 20 knots, speeds faster than 20 knots are possible. Cabot told me that he'd tried his darnedest to tip the boat over, but couldn't do it (we assume he meant that the boat was not easily overpowered).

Though the F-27 is not as large a boat, with as much righting moment, as many sailors would prefer, it has made safe transoceanic passages, including California to Hawaii and New England to Europe.

Through-bolting the pop top is one safety measure you'd want to take for such a passage.

Interior

F-27 owners are somewhat apologetic about the livability of the interior, mostly because there isn't standing headroom except under the pop top, which covers the immediate galley area forward of the companionway. An optional screen/curtain encloses the sides for protection against mosquitos, gnats and other pests.

"The lack of interior space," one reader wrote, "is a drawback compared to a monohull."

The overall layout is clever but a bit cramped. The forward V-berth is suitable for but one medium-height person because the bow is too narrow for four feet. A head and sink are also located in this cabin, separated from the saloon by a partial bulkhead.

The main cabin has opposing settees with a convertible table hung on the daggerboard trunk. An optional insert unites the settees into one large berth. There is stowage outboard. The galley is aft with sink

Belowdecks there's not a great deal of room. The V-berth forward is too narrow for two people, and there's no standing headroom. Still, the accommodations are decent.

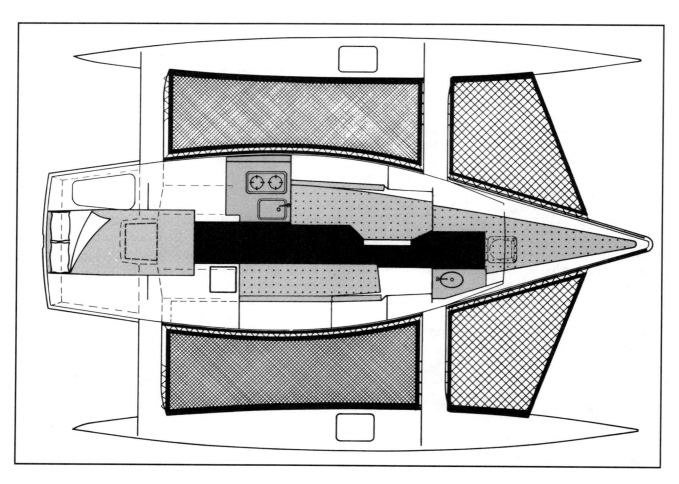

and flush mount stove top. The furniture foundations are fiberglass and are glassed to the hull. The access boards in the cabin sole are unvarnished teak-faced plywood. The single 12-volt battery is located in a starboard compartment between the settee and bulkhead, and there is a six-circuit electrical panel on the outside. Wiring is run through a molding behind the settees. The aft cabin sleeps two and has two windows in the transom, one vent and one lighting fixture. Kids will love it.

One difficulty monohull sailors have making the mental switch to multihulls is the comparative lightness or flimsiness of furnishings—no heavy teak cabinetry, no ash ceilings, in fact, not much wood at all unless it's veneer. Rather, it is customary to find extensive use of fabrics on the overhead and hull liners, and that is the case in the F-27. The attractiveness of such an interior depends largely on choice of fabrics (color, pattern, texture), and Corsair has done a decent job of it. Fiberglass molding edges are covered with a vinyl molding, which looks rather cheap but does the job. Again, saving weight is paramount.

The F-27 is definitely not a liveaboard boat, but is highly functional for short cruises. One reader said, "This has proven to be a very safe boat which both my wife and four-year-old son enjoy racing as well as cruising. The interior is small but is very livable for two weeks. We haven't tried staying on the boat longer than that."

Deck

The cockpit is small, as it should be for a boat touted as having offshore capabilities. It seats four with reasonable comfort. In good weather, crew can sit forward on the cabin trunk or on the netting between the main hull and amas. Moving about requires some care as the footing changes between the rigid structures and netting, and because all sail controls are led aft to the cockpit, there are winches, lines and linestoppers to trip on.

The nonskid is molded in and effective, though it looks hard to clean; we were not surprised to hear from readers confirming our suspicion.

Handling the tiller is easy, whether sitting athwartships or resting your back against the aft cabin bulkhead. Spray is deflected quite well by the tremendous flare in the topsides of the main hull. The lifeline stanchions give some security when seated, but are too low to do any good standing.

The rudder kicks up and lowers easily with dual control lines, as does the centerboard. Again, both can be managed from the cockpit.

The outboard motor sits in a well on the port quarter, and lifts by means of a block and tackle arrangement to clear the prop for sailing. Eliminating this source of drag under sail is a great bonus of small boats.

Conclusion

The F-27 is, in our opinion, an exceptional boat that offers decent accommodations and unparalleled performance for the standard price of $43,800 new. Options to consider are the toilet, solar panel, cabin table, sails, outboard (8-hp recommended), trailer, electronics and spinnaker.   • **PS**

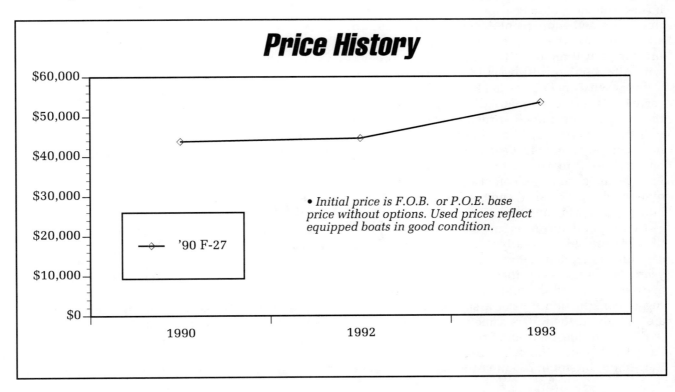

Price History

- *Initial price is F.O.B. or P.O.E. base price without options. Used prices reflect equipped boats in good condition.*

'90 F-27

Bristol 27

This solid '60s cruiser comes in several layouts and is a good value, but is short on space and features.

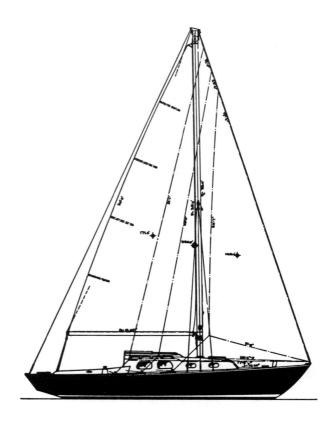

The Bristol 27 is a product of an early collaboration between Clint Pearson of Bristol, Rhode Island, and designer Carl Alberg. The stamp of both men is clearly evident in this solid-as-a-rock traditionally styled small cruiser.

The Boat and the Builder

Pearson, with his cousin Everett Pearson, was a founder of the original Pearson Yachts in 1955 and a pioneer in the mass production of fiberglass yachts. The boat that brought the company to prominence was the 28-foot Triton, drawn by Alberg, who at the time was still in the U.S. Coast Guard and designing boats on the side. Clint Pearson recalled recently that the Triton and subsequent Alberg designs were so successful that the firm found it cheaper to hire a full-time naval architect (Bill Shaw) than to work with Alberg on a royalty basis. (Alberg died in 1983.)

But when Clint Pearson left Pearson Yachts in the early 1960s, after Grumman Allied Industries bought the company, he quickly turned to Alberg for help with his new line of semi-custom boats. "The Triton had been very popular," Pearson said, "and Carl had been a nice guy to work with." Alberg drew the lines for a 27-footer to complement Bristol Yachts' only other model, a 19-footer, and the first Bristol 27 was built in the spring of 1965.

At this point, no one is sure exactly how many of the 27s were built. An early Bristol Yachts brochure says that more than 300 were sold in the first three years. The best guess is that 400 or more were built between 1965 and the mid-1970s. Because of their rugged construction, it's safe to say that most of them are still plying the waters somewhere today.

Except for the 1970s-era Bristol 24, designed by Paul Coble, and the 27.7, designed by Halsey Herreshoff, Bristol in recent years has concentrated

Specifications

LOA	27' 2"
LWL	19' 9"
Beam	8' 0"
Draft	4' 0"
Displacement	6,600 lbs.
Ballast	2,575 lbs.
Sail area	340 sq. ft.

on much larger boats. The company, although much reduced in workforce, was still operating in the fall of 1991, concentrating on the 47.7 and a 35.5, both Ted Hood designs.

The Design

The Bristol 27 is a product of its era and of the traditional bent of Alberg's thinking—that is, a combination cruiser and club racer. At 6,600 pounds displacement with 2,575 pounds of internal lead ballast in its full keel, the boat is fairly heavy by contemporary standards. Fast enough on its own merits, it has an average PHRF rating of 234. By comparison, the lighter Catalina 27 with fin keel and spade rudder has a PHRF rating of about 210, and the Cal 27, also with a divided underbody, a rating of 192

Owners' Comments

"I think this is one of the most overlooked, unappreciated yachts in existence."
—1966 model in Georgia

"It won't win races, but it will take care of you in all weather."
—1974 model in New Jersey

"Poor windward performance seems to be the only fault of this older design."
—1970 model in Massachusetts

"It's so trustworthy and so well-behaved. The real secret is shortening sail quickly. Other than that, no problem."
—1974 model in Rhode Island

"Excellent boat for a family wanting a good weekend boat and for anyone getting into cruising for the first time—easy to operate, easy to move about on."
—1966 model in Illinois

"I have been offshore in full gale force winds, 45-plus knots for several days, and the boat fared a lot better than I did. I never felt like the boat was in trouble or having problems."
—1966 model in California

"A satisfactory dining table (standard model) for cabin and/or cockpit seems very elusive. Should have been engineered by builder."
—1966 model in New Jersey

to 200. Clearly, the Bristol was designed to be seaworthy rather than swift.

With its narrow beam (just eight feet), fair sheer line and generous overhangs, the 27 is pleasing to the eye. Unfortunately, the exaggerated stepped cabin top, which towers over the deck, is out of proportion to the height of the topsides. (A dodger helps camouflage its ungainly appearance.) The boat has a short waterline of only 19' 9", which is typical of boats designed under the old Cruising Club of America racing rule. The idea was to save rating with a short waterline; once heeled, however, part of the long overhangs become immersed and effective sailing length increases by several feet. Thus, it's displacement/length ratio of 382 is deceiving. Assuming a sailing length of 22 feet, the number drops to 276. Still, these are good numbers for a traditional cruising sailboat.

The keel, though full, has a gently curving forefoot to aid in maneuvering. The lead ballast is encapsulated inside the keel and the rudder is hung on the trailing edge, where it is well protected from grounding.

The 27 was produced in three models: the Weekender, which features an eight-foot cockpit, but less room below, and two versions of the standard cruising model, with a 6' 2" cockpit. One has opposing settees in the main cabin and a split galley aft; the other has the galley to starboard and a convertible dinette to port. The dinette model, with the galley and a table to port, proved the most popular, despite the loss of the starboard sea berth. The table was no doubt part of its appeal, and the galley is easier to work at, though the sink is a bit far off the centerline and may not drain when the boat is heeled far over.

Some owners of the settee version complained that no provision had been made for a table.

Some of the earliest models featured a bridgedeck, which added to the seamanlike appearance, but was later dropped in favor of a low sill. The bridgedeck is safer, but the sill is easier to step over when going below.

Construction

The Bristol 27, like most Bristol yachts, was built like a brick lighthouse. The hull is solid hand-laid fiberglass, "largely woven roving," according to company literature. "We probably overdid it on the fiberglass work" because of the relative unfamiliarity of the new material, said Eddie Medeiros, a longtime Bristol Yachts employee who is now vice president for operations. He estimates the hull is 1/2-inch thick below the waterline and 3/8-inch thick above.

The deck, deckhouse and cockpit are integrally molded; the hull-deck joint is through-bolted and caulked. In reviewing *Practical Sailor* survey responses on the 27, we found a number of owners who complained of hull-deck leaking. Deck and walkways are coated with Dexoleum, a non-skid coating that, on the boat we sailed, is beginning to show wear. There's a teak cap rail and teak grab rails (as well as teak hand rails in the companionway and main cabin).

The masthead rig is a 31' 9" anodized aluminum extrusion of Bristol's design, with a 12-foot boom equipped with a spring-type roller reefing gooseneck. Shrouds are 7/32-inch stainless steel wire and the 7/16-inch turnbuckles are chrome-plated Monel. Hardware and equipment are of good quality—Lewmar #8 winches, for example. (The molded-in winch supports on the 27 we looked at were beginning to show some crazing.) Pulpits and lifelines were standard equipment.

Early models had an outboard well, but most of the boats we've seen are inboard-powered, either with an Atomic 4 or the optional Westerbeke Pilot 10 diesel. The inboards add some weight (as reflected in the PHRF rating) but greatly enhance performance under power, according to owners. Many owners of outboard models said there was insufficient power to make good progress motoring to windward, and that the prop is prone to cavitation when hobbyhorsing in a following sea or motoring to windward in a chop. These factors, plus the difficulty in raising the outboard (drag and corrosion problems) and the tendency of the well to flood prompt us to strongly recommend the inboard model.

Performance

A number of owners who responded to our survey, and some we talked to, complained that the boat was initially very tender. One owner said he added 500 pounds of ballast. Some said they routinely reefed the mainsail in any wind over about 12 knots to keep the boat under control and the helm balanced. Others, including the owner of hull #156, the *Nancy Jane* out of Newport, indicated no problems with excessive heeling or tenderness. We decided to find out for ourselves on a late summer day that began with small craft advisories and settled into a steady 15-mph northwesterly punctuated by occasional puffs.

Under a full main and a working jib, the boat experienced no difficulty. It *does* heel over—then digs in and stays there. "It hangs tough," is Clint Pearson's expression. This initial tenderness—almost too strong a term for the 15 or 20 degrees of heel—belies its ultimate stability. We've heard of few knockdowns of Bristol 27s, even among those who routinely go offshore.

Gusts caused the boat to dig in a bit further and to round up slightly on its own; the stronger the wind, the higher it pointed. Except for a hint of weather helm caused by the relatively large main and small foretriangle—no problem for an afternoon sail but potentially tiring on a longer passage—the boat handled easily on all points of sail. The sensation of excessive helm is easily solved by a reef in the main or the use of a larger jib; with a 150-percent genoa, the owner of our test boat said the Bristol 27 balances perfectly. Despite the boat's bulk and the extra windage created by the stepped cabin, the boat is nimble, tacking neatly and jibing with hardly a jar. The overall feeling is one of solidity, not stodginess.

Belowdecks

Down below, the traditional styling (one owner re-

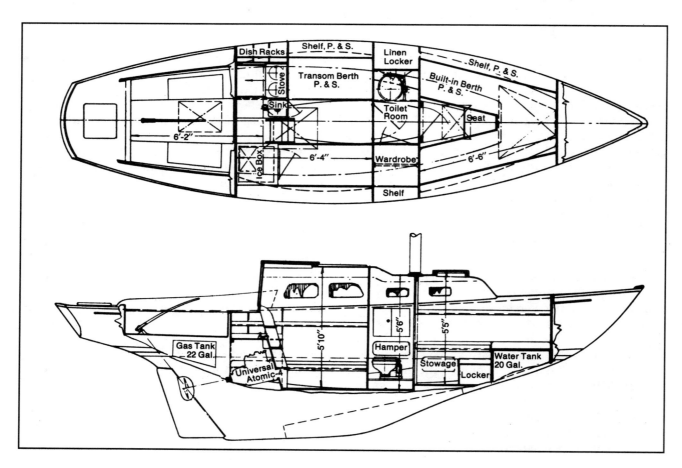

ferred to it as "old-fashioned") continues, with less room than you'd expect to find on a newer, beamier 27-footer. Here one can be grateful for the raised cabin top that provides plenty of standing headroom in the main cabin. There's a fiberglass liner that hides the overhead, but just enough Philippine mahogany in the trim and bulkheads for warmth. The one sour note is some jarring 60s-style coloring—mustard or pea-green—for the laminated plastic veneers. Four fixed ports in the main cabin, four smaller ports in the head and forward cabin (one opening in each), and a translucent forward hatch provide lots of light. Some owners we know have added a Dorade vent farther forward, over the chain locker, for extra ventilation.

The dinette model has a swiveling table to port that can be removed to convert the settee to a double berth. A compact galley lines the starboard side of the main cabin. The galley includes an ice box, a sink and a two-burner alcohol stove. Several owners said they have replaced the original pressurized version with the safer Swedish-made Origo, which fits the space exactly. The alternative cruising model has a second transom berth in place of the galley, with the galley components installed along the aft bulkhead on either side of the companionway. (The dinette model has a starboard quarter berth aft of the galley.) There is ample storage space, including a hanging locker.

Inboard engine access is simple—either open a hatch below the companionway or remove the steps completely. The cruising models have an enclosed head forward of the port berth, with 5' 10" of head-room, and two 6' 6" forward berths (the rare weekender model has 6' 7" V-berths). On deck, there are several storage options—port and starboard lockers and a roomy lazarette aft of the tiller. The interior might be a bit snug, but Bristol Yachts managed to fit in the basics. It's definitely a Plain Jane below, but this is one area where owners can easily customize to suit their taste.

Conclusions

If you are looking for seaworthiness and stability in a small cruiser, and if you don't mind a traditional interior that foregoes some of the elbow space of a beamier boat, the Bristol 27 is worth considering. Given its structural soundness—these boats will be around for some time—and given its modest price in today's soft market, we'd rate it an exceptional value for a used boat. Keep in mind, however, that it's a small cruiser—roomy enough for a couple, and possibly a child or two, but slightly cramped down below and in the cockpit for four adults.

Bristol Yachts is still in business, but barely. The headquarters have been moved to the family-owned boat yard (Poppasquash Rd., Bristol, RI 02809) and only a few boats are under construction. Don't expect much help on matters relating to older boats, especially since many owners said the company was poor in its customer relations once the sale was completed.

The Bristol 27 sold originally for a base price of about $13,000, increasing to $18,400 by 1976, and held its value well until the most recent drastic falloff in used boat prices.   • **PS**

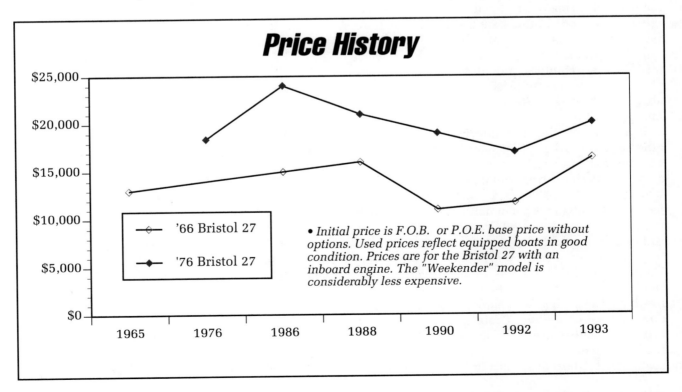

Price History

• *Initial price is F.O.B. or P.O.E. base price without options. Used prices reflect equipped boats in good condition. Prices are for the Bristol 27 with an inboard engine. The "Weekender" model is considerably less expensive.*

Legend:
'66 Bristol 27
'76 Bristol 27

Hunter 27

The Hunter 27 is a boat built to a price—a low price—and it shows; but it may represent a good value.

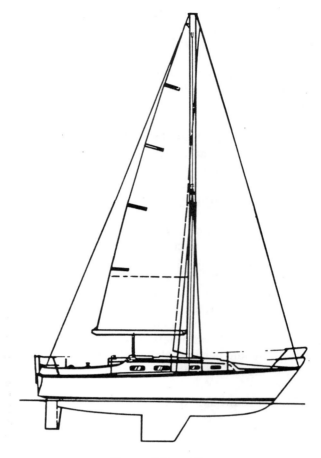

Specifications

LOA	27' 2"
LWL	22' 0"
Beam	9' 3"
Draft	3' 3" (shoal), 4' 3" (deep)
Displacement	7,000 lbs.
Ballast	3,200 (shoal) 3,000 (deep)
Sail area	360 sq. ft.

The Hunter 27 is the smallest boat in the Hunter line, which runs up to 43' in length. The Hunter 27 is a popular boat with first-time sailboat buyers, and with small-boat sailors purchasing their first auxiliary cruising boat. Since the boat was introduced in 1975, thousands have been built.

Like other boats with a reasonably long production run, the Hunter 27 has gone through minor changes since its introduction. Wheel steering is now standard. The boat utilizes a split backstay to allow a stern boarding ladder and to prevent the helmsman from hitting his head on a centerline backstay. All the ports open for ventilation, The mainsheet lead has been altered, and there have been other minor modifications, such as a switch to European-style pulpits and running lights.

Judging from the response of Hunter owners we've talked to, all Hunters, including the 27, are purchased for one reason: price. The Hunter 27 is just about the cheapest diesel-powered 27' cruising boat money can buy.

In their advertising literature, Hunter stresses that efficiency in construction, standardization of components, and low overhead keep their prices low, To some extent, this is true, and it is neither new, nor is it anything to be ashamed of. The Herreshoff Manufacturing Company, known neither for cheap boats nor low quality, pioneered in component standardization and assembly-line construction.

By eliminating factory-installed options, every Hunter 27 can be built the same. No going to the stockroom for an optional item. No time-consuming reading of each boat's specifications as it moves down the assembly line. There are trade-offs, however. An inability to custom-tailor a boat. A lack of flexibility in deck layout. The Hunter 27 owner must customize his boat at the dealer level, or do it himself. This appeals to dealers, who often make as much on the installation of options as they do on commissions.

The Hunter 27 is a bit high-sided and sterile looking. High freeboard and a high cabin trunk are almost necessary in a 27, boat that claims over 6' of headroom. The sterility comes from the Hunter bone white on bone white color scheme, and paucity of external teak trim. Exterior teak is to the fiberglass boatbuilding industry what chrome is to Detroit. There are no hull and deck color options.

Construction

Construction of the Hunter 27 is solid glass layup, with plywood reinforcement in high-stress areas such as winch mountings and locker tops. Gelcoat

Owners feel the cockpit is small, but wheel steering really helps. Provision for emergency steering is excellent—note the tiller socket behind the wheel.

and finish quality of the hull molding are good. No roving printthrough is evident, and the hull is quite fair—more than can be said for many more expensive boats.

The hull-to-deck joint of the Hunter 27 is simple and strong. The hull molding has an internal flange molded at right angles to the hull at deck level. This flange is heavily coated with adhesive bedding, the deck molding is laid over the flange, and the joint covered with a slotted aluminum toerail which is through-bolted with stainless steel bolts at 6-inch intervals. This is an obvious and very satisfactory answer to the hull-to-deck joint problem. The flaying surfaces of the joint appear to match well, and the adhesive compound has squeezed out along the joint where it can be inspected.

Across the transom, the joint is less satisfactory. The gelcoat and putty with which the joint is faired at the stern was sloppy on every Hunter 27 we examined.

The keel of the Hunter 27 is a narrow, high aspect lead fin weighing 3,000 lbs. The shoal draft version has a much shallower lead fin weighing 3,200 lbs. The additional weight of the shoal keel is to make up for the shift in the vertical center of gravity of the boat that would occur if a shoal keel of the same weight as the deep fin were to be used.

The keel-to-hull joint has caused problems in some Hunter 27s. The narrowness of the lead keel at the point of attachment to the hull results in considerable leverage on the hull when the boat heels. Several Hunter 27 owners who returned *The Practical Sailor* boat owner evaluations report oilcanning of the hull, leaking keelbolts, or vertical misalignment of the hull and keel. We have observed this vertical misalignment in the Hunter 25, but we have not seen it specifically in the 27.

The chainplates of the Hunter 27 consist of stainless steel U-bolts fastened through the anodized aluminum toerail. No backing plates are used with these. The chainplates are likely to carry any load to which they will normally be subjected. However, a simple U-bolt, no matter how heavy, is a poor choice for a primary chainplate unless the arc of the U-bolt is radiused to the diameter of the clevis pin which goes through it, and unless the strain on the bolt lines up with its vertical axis, U-bolt chainplates of the correct configuration are used in some European boats, notably the Nicholson and Bowman lines. Both of these lines of boats carry Lloyd's Bureau of Shipping classification certificates. We strongly suggest that Hunter 27 owners consider installing aluminum or stainless steel backing plates under their U-bolt chainplates, and check them periodically to be sure that the nuts are tight. With only two nuts on each shroud anchorage, this check is extremely important.

The rig is a modern, high aspect ratio masthead sloop. The mast is a deck-stepped, white Kenyon spar, supported by a wood compression column attached to the main bulkhead. We have seen no sign of compression stress in the Hunter 27 mast step. Hunter uses gate valves on underwater skin fittings. We prefer seacocks. We also prefer some kind of shutoff valve on any skin fitting remotely near the waterline. Few builders provide them. Hunter is no exception.

Handling Under Sail

The Hunter 27 comes with a mainsail and 110% genoa. The total sail area with this configuration is 360 square feet, an average amount for a modern 7,000 lb boat. A larger genoa will be required for sailing in light-air areas.

Despite a ballast/displacement ratio of almost 43%, owners do not consider the Hunter 27 a stiff boat under sail. They also consider the boat's performance under sail only fair to good. There are several reasons for the boat's mediocre sailing qualities.

First of all, the boat comes factory-equipped with sails. This means cheaper sails, for they are bought in quantity by the builder. It also, almost inevitably, means sails that are not designed for specific local conditions. Average sails make for average performance.

There is no provision for headsail sheeting angle adjustment. Without a genoa track, all headsails must sheet to the slotted toerail. On a wide 27-footer

with this arrangement, the headsail slot will rarely be the proper width for good windward performance. With a small headsail, the lead will almost always be too far outboard.

There is also no traveler for the main sheet. This limits the creation of the proper angle of attack of the mainsail, and complicates draft control.

A relatively fat boat such as the Hunter 27 rapidly acquires weather helm as the boat heels. This is due in part to the asymmetry of the boat's submerged sections. The judicious use of sail controls such as travelers, vangs, and flattening reefs greatly enhances the ability to keep the boat sailing on her feet, which will help reduce weather helm. Hunter 27 owners complain that the boat suffers from extreme weather helm.

Chainplates set at the outboard edge of the deck also compromise windward performance. This arrangement makes it almost impossible to close the slot effectively with a large headsail.

If the Hunter 27 were equipped with well-made sails, inboard chainplates, inboard and outboard headsail tracks, a good vang, and a mainsheet traveler, we suspect that there would be a substantial improvement in the boat's windward ability. There would also be a marked difference in price. Should you desire to make these changes, the parts would probably cost upwards of $1,500. Then the problems begin. How do you attach the chainplates? Will the deck take the vertical loading that will be on the track? Can the boom handle heavy vang loads? We are not talking about turning the Hunter 27 into a hot racer. We are only talking about improving the performance of the boat to a reasonable level for cruising.

Good ventilation, storage and headroom mark the interior of the Hunter 27. Seating room on the settees was compromised to make more room for the galley and quarterberth, a fair tradeoff.

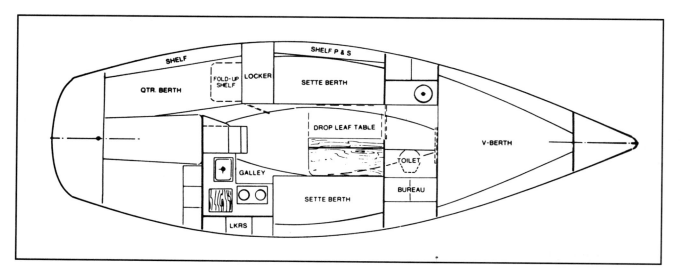

Windward performance, then, is one of the trade-offs made for low price. Only the prospective purchaser, after considering how the boat is to be used, can decide how much that is worth.

Since the shoal-draft Hunter 27 is more heavily ballasted than the deep-draft version, its stability is likely to be similar. However, the deep, high aspect ratio fin is likely to be more efficient.

Handling Under Power

With only eight horsepower to push around a 7,000 lb, high-sided boat, do not expect a Hunter 27 to be a sprightly performer under power.

In 1979, the power plant of the Hunter 27 was changed from the eight horsepower Renault diesel. The Renault diesels were relatively untried in the US marine market. The early Yanmar engines, though noisy and noted for their vibration, are also known for their reliability.

At least one owner we talked to was, to put it mildly, disappointed with the Renault installation. Although the engine runs well, the attachment of the shifting mechanism to the transmission lever has the disconcerting habit of vibrating itself loose. When docking, the results of this shortcoming could be less than amusing to both the boat owner and his insurance company.

Owners of Renault-powered Hunter 27s should definitely be aware of this potential problem.

Another owner reported leaking strut bolts and shaft wear due to improper shaft alignment, All engine installations should be realigned after the boat is launched for the first time. This should be a routine part of commissioning, but it rarely is. A given used Hunter 27 may not have had it done.

Engine access is good, behind the removable companionway ladder. There is partial soundproofing in the engine enclosure, but not enough to shield the interior from a substantial amount of noise.

Fuel capacity is 12.5 gallons, in an aluminum tank located in the starboard cockpit locker. The tank is held in place by a stainless steel strap, There is no grounding jumper between the fuel fill and the tank. This is in violation of the standards for fuel tank installation of the American Boat and Yacht Council, which sets minimum standards used in the industry.

Owners consider the boat underpowered with either the Renault or Yanmar engines. They consider the boat's performance under power only fair to good.

Deck Layout

Because the Hunter 27's decks are relatively free of sail control hardware, there are relatively few toe stubbers. Even the grayest cloud has a silver lining.

New Hunter 27s have international style running lights mounted on the bow and stern pulpits. These are far superior to the in-hull running lights on older Hunters, and better than those used on many more expensive boats. New boats also have a good-sized foredeck anchor well, incorporating a well-designed latch and a heavy stainless steel eye for the attachment of the bitter end of the anchor rode. The well has a large scupper which drains through the stem.

Although owners consider the cockpit of the Hunter 27 small, we find it comfortable for five, and

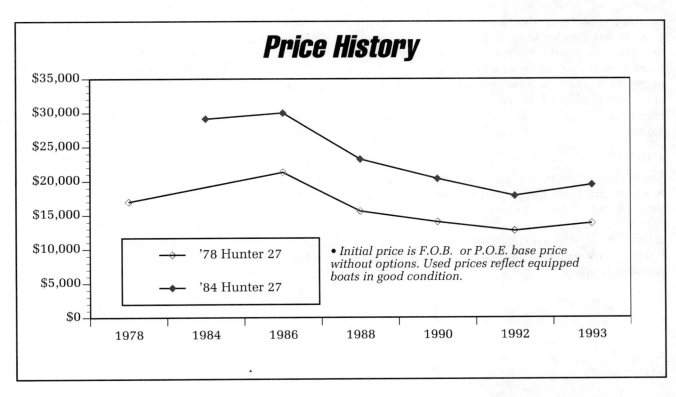

Price History

• Initial price is F.O.B. or P.O.E. base price without options. Used prices reflect equipped boats in good condition.

Legend:
- '78 Hunter 27
- '84 Hunter 27

certainly large enough for a 27' boat. Wheel steering has definitely made the cockpit seem bigger. With five people in the cockpit, the stern of the boat begins to squat. A bigger cockpit would only encourage sailing with more people, causing the boat to squat even more.

Late models have Yacht Specialties pedestal steering. There is good provision for an emergency tiller, which is supplied with the boat.

Access to the steering gear is excellent, through the lazarette locker. Unfortunately, because the steering gear, scupper hoses, and exhaust hose go through this locker, it cannot be used for storage. To do so would be to risk damage to vital parts of the ship's systems.

There is a large locker under the starboard cockpit seat. Unfortunately, because the fuel tank is located in this locker, nothing can really be stowed there without risking damage to the fuel system. Wet lines or sails stored in the locker would drip on the aluminum tank, inviting corrosion. Shelves installed in both these lockers would make them more useful.

To raise the cockpit sill above the level of the lowest cockpit coaming, the lower dropboard must be left in place, This complicates access below when underway, but having the companionway blocked up to deck level is essential for sailing in unsheltered waters or heavy weather.

The cockpit bulkhead slopes forward. This means that a dodger must be installed if one wishes to ventilate the cabin in rain or heavy weather.

The high cockpit coamings provide good backrests for those sitting in the cockpit. They should also help keep the cockpit dry. These coamings have molded-in sheet winch islands. The owner wishing to upgrade to winches larger than the standard Lewmar 7s will discover that the islands are too small for a much larger winch. For the owner who wishes to use a large genoa, this could be a real problem. Despite these shortcomings, the T-shaped cockpit is reasonably comfortable, and is one of the boat's better design features.

Interior

The Hunter 27 is a roomy boat. Headroom is just over 6' under the main hatch, and almost 5' 10" at the forward end of the main cabin.

The forepeak contains a double berth. Aft of that cabin is a full-width head. Newer Hunter 27s have a holding tank system. Older boats are likely to have portable heads.

The main cabin has settee berths port and starboard. These settees extend under the forward bulkhead. While this arrangement reduces seating area, it also allows more room for the galley and quarterberth. It's a reasonable trade-off.

To port, at the aft end of the cabin, there is a quarterberth. A folding chart table is located over the forward end of the quarterberth. To starboard is the galley, with sink, two-burner alcohol stove, and icebox.

With eight opening ports, two opening hatches, and the companionway, ventilation in newer Hunter 27s is excellent at anchor in good weather. Older models have fewer opening ports. As with many boats, there is no provision for ventilation in heavy weather.

With a molded glass headliner, teak-finished bulkheads, solid teak trim, and teak cabin sole, the cabin has a finished appearance. There is good storage for a boat of this size for short-term cruising. Joinerwork is of fair stock boat quality.

Conclusions

A new Hunter 27 in the '80s was about the least expensive boat in its class—far cheaper than many other boats of this size. The boat also comes standard with items that are optional on other boats, such as wheel steering, life jackets, anchor, and fire extinguishers.

However, it is not realistic to expect a boat that is 15% cheaper than another boat of the same size and type to be equivalent in quality. There is just so much that efficiency, standardization, and bulk buying can do toward reducing the price of a boat. Inevitably, the price of a boat is a function the time, materials, and incidental costs that go into it. There is no magic way to reduce the cost of building a boat.

The Hunter 27 graphically demonstrates how costs can be reduced. A great deal of time is saved in construction by hurrying finish work, by using staples instead of screws, by eliminating the necessity to customize each boat.

Hunter owners are the first to admit the influence that the low price of the boat had on their boat-buying decision. Many are happy with their boats, some are defensive about them, and others are really unhappy with them. For the relatively unsophisticated sailboat buyer—the new sailor, the powerboat convert—the Hunter 27 may represent a good value. As his experience grows, we expect he will be willing to pay more, in order to get more. • **PS**

Lancer 28

This maximum-size trailer sailer shows the compromises needed to haul a boat on the road.

Lancer Yachts was an offshoot of the remarkably complex and inbred family tree known as California boatbuilding. Lancer principals Dick Valdes and Maury Threinen founded Columbia Yachts back in the late 1950s, built boats under contract for Islander, sold Columbia to Whittaker, and got back into the sailboat business in 1974 by forming Lancer Yachts.

The names that passed through this Columbia connection read like a who's who of fiberglass boatbuilding. Designer Bruce King was a draftsman for Columbia. Ericson founder Kurt Densmore was a Columbia plant manager, and Frank Butler—owner of Catalina Yachts, probably the biggest sailboat builder in the country—ran the Coronado division of Columbia.

It's no wonder that many California-built boats from the 1970s bear a strong family resemblance: they're practically first cousins.

Lancer Yachts built a rather astonishing variety of boats before going out of business in 1986. None of the Lancers can be considered a classic. Rather, the boats were a mirror of their times, and this constant change may have been what finally did in the company.

In 1983 alone, Lancer offered 13 different boats ranging in size from a 25' trailer sailer to a 65' motorsailer. The sheer variety of models reduces efficiency in production, and to stay competitive in price, you must shave profit margins closer and closer.

Perhaps the most interesting boats ever produced by Lancer were those in a series of high-performance motorsailers built in the mid-1980s. These boats ranged from the 25' Powersailer up to the 65' Motorsailer, and were characterized by huge engines relative to their displacements in an attempt to get

Specifications

LOA	27' 8"
LWL	23' 11"
Beam	8' 0"
Draft	2' 10"
Displacement	4,900 lbs.
Ballast	2,200 lbs.

both powerboat and sailboat performance out of the same hull. The Powersailer 27, for example, was designed for outboards of up to 200 hp. The 44' high-performance motorsailer had engine options up to twin 200 hp turbocharged diesels.

The idea was to capture a crossover market which really wanted a powerboat, but felt that sailboats were the way to go due to real or imagined fuel shortages.

Needless to say, these boats had a somewhat limited appeal, and the return of cheap oil spelled their doom.

By comparison, the Lancer 28, built from 1977 to 1985, seems a rather tame and ordinary boat.

Part of the variety in the Lancer line stems from the use of a number of different designers. Most builders use a single designer or design team. Lancer

Owners' Comments

"If you insist, as we did, on the largest possible trailerable boat, this is probably about as well as you're going to do. Be advised, however, that the shoal keel is very inefficient when going to windward, although it's quite satisfactory on other points of sail. The boat will point quite high, but makes excessive leeway when heeled."

—1979 model in Georgia

"The first reason I bought the boat was trailerability. Then came construction, styling and livability. I'd like to be able to sail to windward better, but off the wind, I can blow the socks off other boats. My only complaint about the interior is that if a person is working in the galley, it's difficult for someone else to get by."

—1979 model in Michigan

"I bought the boat for its cost, size and trailerability. We've had boat pox at the waterline, some stress cracks on deck, and water leakage in, around and through the toerail. The shoal-draft keel creates problems in pointing and speed upwind, but it is a stiff boat, good for family cruising. I've had some overheating problems with the Renault diesel. The engine might be undersized."

—1979 model in Ohio

"The shoal keel makes her tender, but the boat stiffens up at a fairly steep angle. There are absolutely no handholds below. The non-zippered full headliner makes it very difficult to install anything on deck.

"The mast is stepped on deck, with no compression post. Our deck collapsed partially under the strain. We added a compression post and knees, but the deck is still concave in the step area.

"We've had some leaking through the toerail and chainplates during rail-down sailing, which is most of the time here. There are major leaks around the main hatch during wind-driven rainstorms.

"The boat seems to be built for the lighter winds around LA. We are usually reefed here, but as long as the boat is not overpowered she makes a great daysailer. Surfing is really great in this light hull.

"The light weight and shoal draft make her a little squirrely; the helmsman almost never can relax. For cruising this can get tiring."

—1980 model in Hawaii

"The boat is not made for heavy seas. It is very tender.

"It has been a better boat than I thought it would be. We have modified the interior and fitted a dodger for cruising, and we enjoy the boat a lot, staying in San Francisco Bay and the Delta. We used the boat 150 days last year, 10% for daysailing, 90% for coastal cruising."

—1982 model in California

"We had the factory retrofit the boat with a two-cylinder Yanmar diesel a year after we bought the boat. With a three-bladed prop this is 500% better than an outboard on a bracket.

"This boat is not meant to be an offshore cruiser, and is probably perfect for our use as a large daysailer and occasional overnighter.

"The shallow draft and narrow beam seem to contribute to initial instability, but she stiffens up the further she heels.

"The boat sleeps my wife, myself and our seven kids all inside the cabin at once, but it is more comfortable with only three or four of the kids."

—1982 model in Colorado

was building designs by Bill Lee, C&C, Bruce Farr, and Shad Turner—all at the same time.

Turner designed both the 25 and 28, the smallest Lancers from 1977 to 1983. Both are shoal-draft fixed-keel trailerables. The 25 and 28 are attractive boats with short ends, flattish sheer, and Swan-type bubble deckhouses.

When the Lancer 28 entered production in 1977, trailer sailers were a hot item. And the more you could cram into a boat that could be towed behind your car, the better the consumer liked it.

Sailing Performance

In a lot of ways, the Lancer 28 is a good study in the compromises that are inherent in creating a relatively big boat that can be lugged around from place to place on a trailer. Sailing performance is one of those compromises.

Small boats get stability either from wide beam or deep, heavy keels. The Lancer 28 has neither.

To keep weight to a level that can be towed behind a car, trailerables such as the Lancer 28 tend to be lighter in weight and more lightly ballasted than boats of the same size designed to be kept in the water rather than taken home at the end of the day. The Lancer 28's 44% ballast/displacement ratio may sound high, but the actual amount of ballast—2200 pounds—is fairly low for a 28' boat. By way of comparison, the Ranger 28, at about the same displacement, has 600 pounds more ballast.

It's not just the weight of ballast that counts, it's the location. Because of the Lancer 28's shoal draft—less than 3'—the ballast cannot be located very far down. A fin keel 28-footer of the same displacement would draw 4' or more, and have a correspondingly lower center of gravity.

What this means is that the Lancer 28 is tippy. Most owners in our survey consider the boat about average in stability, but in our experience, an "average" rating usually means a fairly tender boat.

The narrow 8' beam doesn't help stability, either. In many states 8' is as wide as you can go without special trailering permits, so you find an awful lot of trailer sailers 8' wide, no matter what their length.

The fixed keel of the Lancer 28 is a poor shape for windward performance. The keel is a hollow fiberglass box, with the cabin sole dropped down inside it. The keel is much wider than it should be for good performance, and its long, shallow shape does little as an efficient foil.

This is a boat that must be sailed upright. When the boat heels over, there is little to stop it from moving sideways. A centerboard would probably make a dramatic improvement in windward performance, but it was not an option.

Off the wind, performance is substantially better. Owners rate it average to above average in reaching and downwind performance.

The boat was built with both fractional and masthead rigs, with the fractional rig stepped further forward. The fractional boat should be better balanced, and is faster.

The Lancer 28 is no speed demon, with an average PHRF rating of 258 for the masthead version. The fractional rig is about 10 seconds per mile faster. By way of comparison, the Hunter 27 rates about 216, the Ericson 27 about 220, the Ranger 28 about 186, the Catalina 27 about 204. Any of these boats will chew up and spit out the Lancer 28.

You don't buy this boat for speed. It's a noncompetitive daysailer and weekend trailer cruiser.

Engine

Most Lancers under 30' were powered by outboards, although inboard engines were frequently options. An inboard engine in the Lancer 28 adds several hundred pounds of weight to a boat that is already near the upper limit for trailering.

While most Lancer 28s have outboards, a number of different inboard engine configurations and models were used over the course of production, including Petter, Renault and Yanmar diesels; a 10 hp gas inboard; and an OMC saildrive.

If the boat is really to be trailered, an outboard engine is preferable. An outboard can be flushed with fresh water after every cruise in salt water. The outboard and its fuel tank will come in at less than half the weight of any of the inboards. When the time comes to replace the engine, an outboard will cost about half what an inboard will cost, and you don't have to worry about whether or not it will fit in the boat.

The outboard well in the stern of the Lancer 28 is pretty good. The engine stays in the water even in rough conditions, and the weight isn't cantilevered out over the stern to add to pitching moment.

We'd be wary of purchasing a boat with a saildrive that has been used in salt water. A lot of owners are less than faithful about flushing out saildrives after each use, yet the innards are as vulnerable to corrosion as an outboard.

Likewise, parts for small diesel inboards are disproportionately expensive, and may be hard to find for any of the engines used in the boat except the Yanmar.

The inboard engine is tucked in a box under the companionway ladder, and owners rate the installation about average for accessibility.

A 10-horse outboard will move this boat along just

In order to gain some interior headroom, the designer dropped the cabin sole a foot down into the keel. This resulted in a fat keel and a narrow cabin sole, lending the feeling that you're standing in a hole.

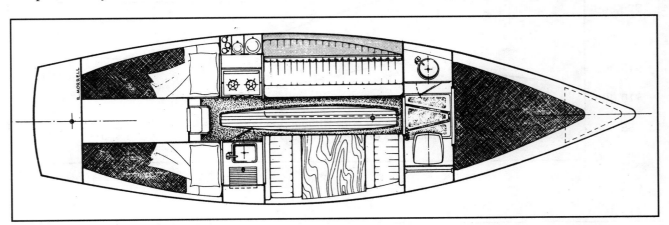

fine, even in a chop. Take good care of it—flushing with fresh water after use in salt water—and an outboard will easily last for seven or eight years. Neglect it, and your first season may be its last.

Construction

To keep weight down for trailering, construction of the Lancer 28 is fairly light. To keep price down, finish detail is not particularly refined.

In its description of their fleet, Lancer described the 28 as bringing "real ocean-going capability to trailer boating." We think you'd have to use a lot of imagination to consider this a boat for serious sailing in the ocean: the design and construction are those of a coastal cruiser and daysailer.

With the masthead rig, a compression column in the middle of the main cabin is required for underdeck support; the fractional rig utilizes the forward bulkhead. Check for compression and stress cracks around either mast step.

The companionway dropboards are light plywood, and the companionway opening has so much taper that the boards can be removed by lifting them only a few inches. This may be convenient and give a lot of ventilation below, but it also means that the dropboards could fall out in a severe knockdown. The sliding companionway hatch is also wide, and not well sealed against boarding waves.

Several owners in our survey comment that the mast tabernacle is not strong enough, and that there is a lot of friction in the system when raising and lowering the mast.

The rig is quite tall—about 31' above the top of the cabin with the masthead rig, and the fractional rig is taller still—so a lot of care is required in stepping and unstepping the mast. That's one trade-off with a maximum-size trailerable boat: you're getting at the limit for easy rigging and unrigging without a fairly sophisticated tabernacle, which the boat doesn't have.

Owner complaints about structural flaws include leaking hull-to-deck joints and leaking ports. Finding deck leaks is complicated by the vinyl headliner. Water may find its way along a circuitous route before it deposits itself on your head, and leaks may be next to impossible to trace. Look carefully for signs of drips and discoloration on the vinyl, particularly around every joint in the liner.

In general, there are numerous reports of deck leaks in our surveys. This is fairly common in relatively inexpensive mass-produced boats such as the Lancer 28, but it is a problem that can make your life miserable when cruising.

Although bottom blistering is usually less of a problem with trailerable boats than with boats kept in the water, several owners report blistering or other types of gelcoat flaws, such as crazing or stress cracks.

Interior

The Lancer 28 was designed in a time when it was fashionable to jam the maximum number of berths in the shortest possible overall boat length. It is true that there are six berths in the original version of this boat. It is also true that headroom at the aft end of the main cabin is 6' 2". However, just as the rooms in tract

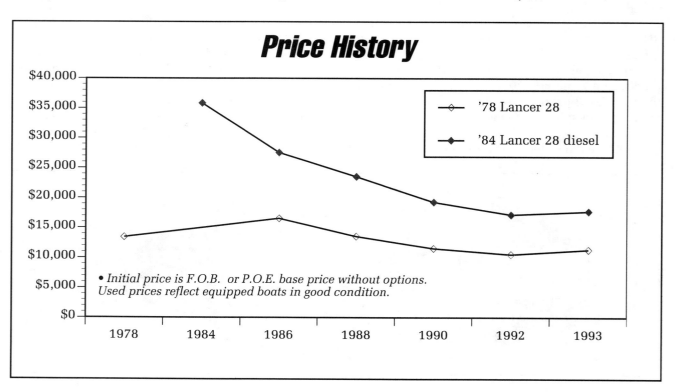

Price History

Legend:
- ◇— '78 Lancer 28
- ◆— '84 Lancer 28 diesel

• *Initial price is F.O.B. or P.O.E. base price without options. Used prices reflect equipped boats in good condition.*

houses look a lot smaller in the flesh than they look in those wonderful wide-angle architectural photographs, the reality of the interior of the Lancer 28 is a little different from the promise.

Main cabin headroom comes from dropping the cabin sole 1' into the keel stub. What this means is that you have a very long, narrow section of cabin sole over which there is reasonable headroom. But the effect is a little strange: you feel like you're standing in a hole.

Frankly, this dropped cabin sole is a pretty mediocre idea. In the galley, where you could use the headroom, it's not even easy to turn around because the dropped sole is so narrow. You'd be better off sitting on a little folding stool.

Without the dropped sole, headroom would be 5' 2" or so. You would have trouble selling that amount of headroom in a 28-footer, even a trailerable boat.

Forward, there is a narrow double berth with a storage locker below. In 1979, the forepeak berth was replaced in the Mark V version with a sail storage area. There is no provision for ventilation in this space. The bubble-type deckhouse fairs into the foredeck over the forward cabin, so there is reasonable sitting headroom over the berth. Actually, "cabin" is a misnomer: it is really just a berth, separated from the head by a bulkhead.

Just aft of the forward berth, a narrow head compartment spans the width of the boat. It gives you as much privacy as you can get in a trailer boat—which isn't that much—and has a hatch overhead for ventilation. Some of these boats are equipped with self-contained toilets, while others have more conventional overboard-discharge toilets. Your sailing waters will dictate which arrangement you need.

There are two berths in the main cabin, On the port side is a conventional settee berth. On the starboard side, the dinette table drops to form a fairly wide berth, but don't let anyone try to tell you it's a double.

Dinettes don't really work on narrow boats. You feel like you're sitting in a narrow booth at the corner drugstore, which is fine if you happen to be a teenager—but not if you're an adult. In this case, it's a really tight squeeze for four people to fit into the dinette. On the other hand, it's great seating for two.

Over the years, Lancer has actually done some pretty inventive things with interiors. Their boats had a California/European crossbred look that was always the talk of boatshow crowds, with wild colors and fabrics.

But the interior of the Lancer 28 is basically Neo-Padded Cell. Almost every surface is covered with either carpeting, upholstery, or padded vinyl.

Lancer isn't the only builder guilty of this. Early Swans such as the Swan 43 were similarly padded.

It may seem like a good idea—if you get thrown against it you won't get hurt—but we've never cared for the look of padding. Owning a boat is precariously close to insanity in any case: reminders of that when belowdecks are not particularly welcome.

The galley occupies both sides of the aft end of the main cabin, with a two-burner stove and lockers to port, and a sink, icebox and lockers to starboard. It's quite workable.

Aft, there are quarterberths under both sides of the cockpit. They are very narrow at the foot. Your head and shoulders, however, are not stuffed under the cockpit, so the berths are not claustrophobic, although they are likely to be pretty hot in warm weather.

It's not realistic to expect a lot of interior room in a hull as narrow as the Lancer 28. But the boat has a relatively long waterline, and the low-profile cabin trunk is also quite long, increasing the feeling of space.

Conclusions

The Lancer 28 is a maximum-size trailerable boat. The weight of about 5000 pounds will require a serious pulling vehicle if anything other than a once-yearly trip to and from the launching ramp is planned.

Despite the six berths in the boat, we wouldn't recommend it for four adults for anything longer than a weekend. For a young family with several children, the Lancer 28 could be seen as a floating camper.

The performance compromises that are a result of the shoal keel, high center of gravity and narrow beam have to be weighed against the fact that you can put the boat behind a big car or truck and take off for cruising areas that you might otherwise never reach with a 28' boat.

If you really aren't going to trailer the boat, there are a lot of other boats around 28' long that will give you better performance and better accommodations. The extra foot or so of beam and ton of displacement that you would get in most non-trailerable 28-footers translates into a lot more usable volume, and in most cases, better performance. At the same time, a Lancer 28 costs less than most 28-footers.

Keeping a boat in a marina or on a mooring can be an expensive proposition. You can greatly reduce your sailing costs by owning a trailerable boat. The problem is that a trailerable as big as the Lancer 28 is a bit of a handful to tow, launch, and rig. You're not going to hitch it up to the family station wagon after a day at the office and launch it for an evening cruise.

If you need a trailerable boat that can accommodate two adults and several children for relatively short-term cruising, the Lancer 28 makes sense. But don't expect to get six berths, "full headroom," shoal draft, and trailerability in a 28' boat without some fairly substantial compromises. **• PS**

Newport 28 and 28 II

While there were questions about quality, the 28 is a good entry-level cruiser-racer for those on a budget.

The Newport 28 was one of the longer-lived small production cruising boats, having been in production from 1974 through 1987. Almost 1,000 of the C&C-designed boats were built by Capital Yachts of Harbor City, California.

There is a strong family resemblance between the Newport 28 and other C&C designs of the same period. In addition to the Newport 28, Capital built the Newport 41, another mid-1970s C&C design. The styling of both boats is characterized by the sweeping attractive sheerlines for which C&C is justifiably known.

As with any boat whose production run spanned more than a decade, many changes were made in the Newport 28, both outside and inside, over the years. The original scimitar-shaped keel and rudder gave way to more modern high aspect ratio appendages with 1983 models, increasing draft from 4' 6" to 5' 2". A shoal draft version drawing 4' was optional, but less popular than the deep-keel boat. Versions with the modern keel are designated Newport 28-II.

Specifications

LOA	28' 0"
LWL	23' 6"
Beam	9' 6"
Draft	5' 3"
Displacement	7,000 lbs.
Ballast	2,900 lbs.
Sail area	395 sq. ft.

Sailing Performance

The Newport 28 has a tall, high aspect ratio masthead rig. The newer deep keel models are about six seconds per mile faster than the original version of the boat, which typically sails with a PHRF rating of 192. This is comparable to other cruiser-racers of the same size.

Despite a fairly high ballast/displacement ratio, owners report that the boat is tender. This is due in part to the fairly round midship section, and in part to the fact that few 28' boats are really very stiff.

Racing in Newport 28s is quite keen in some areas, particularly on the West Coast, where there are large fleets that race both as one-designs and under PHRF. The boat is a competitive PHRF racer, and enough boats have been rated so that its handicap appears fair. This means you are likely to get a rating based on the boat's performance, not on your own sailing ability.

Most owners report that the boat is very well balanced. This is typical of C&C designs, which usually have fairly small mainsails. With a large foretriangle and a small mainsail, it may be necessary to rake the mast aft slightly to give the boat a little weather helm. It's far easier to add weather helm than to reduce it.

Construction

Make no mistake about it, the Newport 28 is a boat built to a price. A common complaint by owners is mediocre fitting of woodwork, leaking hull-to-deck

Owners' Comments

"A family of five can cruise in comfort for two weeks. It is also small enough to be handled alone or with my wife. A good boat for a growing family."

—1976 boat in Washington

"Lack of storage space is the only inconvenience of this boat. They have put storage in just about every conceivable place, but room is limited on a 28' boat."

—1986 model on the Texas Gulf coast

"Once one understands that Capital Yachts built boats to a price, one understands a few of the lapses. Through hulls are fitted with cheap plastic gate valves. I generally knew what I was buying and so live with it or plan to fix it, one of these days.

—1980 boat in San Diego

"Would not buy one without a careful survey."

—1977 boat in San Francisco area

"The Newport 28 is a good boat for the money . A good value, not a cheap boat. Certainly with an economically-priced boat there are no extras."

—1983 boat in New York

"Would I buy another one? Probably not. Life is too short to do everything I've done to the boat twice. Also, I now have her the way I want her."

—1978 boat in San Francisco area

joint, cockpit drains that are too small, plastic valves on through hull fittings, inadequate backing plates for hardware—in short, the entire litany of problems associated with boats built to be low in price.

One owner who races his boat hard noticed a large crack in the hull molding aft of the primary sheet winches, and discovered that he could see daylight through it. Apparently, the hull had been cracked in removing it from the mold, and the cracked patched over with auto body filler. This was on a new boat. The factory made good on that one.

Why would so many people buy a boat that apparently has a history of minor construction flaws and mediocre quality control?

The answer, according to owners, is that the basic styling, accommodations, and performance are better than other boats of the same size and type, making up for other shortcomings. When you buy a Chevrolet you know in advance that it isn't going to be built like a Mercedes.

Interior

The interior is one factor that many owners report is a major influence in their decision to buy a Newport 28. With a waterline length of 23' 6", there's a lot of interior for a 28' boat.

Despite the fairly low freeboard and pronounced concave sheer, there is just over 6' of headroom on centerline over the main cabin. The pronounced camber of the main cabintop keeps the deckhouse profile low, but at the expense of headroom, which diminishes very quickly away from the centerline. Fortunately, on a boat this small you're almost always walking near the centerline.

There have been three basic interior arrangements over the years: galley along the starboard side of the main cabin, galley aft on the port side, and galley aft on the starboard side. On later models, only the two aft galley configurations were available. The galley aft on starboard side is the only layout that offers a stove with oven, due to the setup of the main cabin settees.

Unfortunately, this galley arangement required cutting away the starboard main bulkhead beneath the chainplates to make the starboard settee long enough for sleeping, which in our opinion is a structural compromise.

Since there are four other berths in the boat—two forward, the port settee, and a quarterberth—using the starboard settee as a berth isn't necessary with anything less than a full crew. For family cruising, it is likely that at least one member of the crew would be short enough to use the starboard settee even without the foot extension.

Engine

Originally, the boat was equipped with the Atomic Four gasoline inboard, a standard engine in most auxiliaries until the proliferation of diesel power in the early 1980s. Diesel power was optional until the introduction of the 28-II model.

Some boats have Yanmar diesels, others Universal. It took the builder a while to decide which diesel engine to use, as owners report engines ranging in horsepower from 11 to 18. To most owners, there appears to be little difference in performance between diesel engines of various sizes. All of the Universal diesels should be adequate for the boat, and the Atomic Four is far more power than she needs.

Obviously, the diesel engine is a big plus when shopping for a used boat. Retrofitting a diesel on a gas-powered boat of this size is usually more expense than can be justified unless you're planning to keep the boat for a long time.

Access to the engine for service varies from awful to good, depending on the model year. Fortunately, newer models have better access from the interior as well as a flush hatch in the cockpit sole directly over the engine.

Buying A Used Boat

Because so many owner complaints center on fairly mediocre construction detailing, a used boat should be carefully surveyed before purchase. Particular attention should be paid to structural details of the hull-to-deck joint, attachment of bulkheads, and mounting of deck hardware.

Obviously, a later model boat with a diesel engine is more desirable than an older boat with a gas engine. We would also consider the 28-II version with updated keel and rudder to be more desirable than the earlier design.

Because of the large number of Newport 28s built, at any given time there are a number of boats on the market. This means you should be able to find the combination of ingredients you're looking for for in age, power plant, keel, and interior layouts—especially if you're shopping on the West Coast.

It would be a good idea to look at all three interior arrangments before making a decision, although if you opt for a newer boat your choice will be between the two aft galley interiors.

Some of the boats have been seriously upgraded by owners, including such things as larger cockpit drains and higher quality hull hardware.

We would be wary about any boat that showed a lot of inexpert do-it-yourself characterisitics, such as caulking along the hull-to-deck joint, around the ports, or around the chainplates.

Although a tiller is standard, a fair number of boats have been equipped with wheel steering, either as an original option or as a retrofit.

The steering pedestal takes up far less room than the tiller, but it does require that the helmsman sit all the way in the back of the boat. While this arrangement keeps the cockpit less crowded for racing, it also puts all the helmsman's weight at the aft end of the boat—not a good place for it.

In addition, the helmsman on a wheel-steered boat cannot reach either the mainsheet or the jib sheets, a serious shortcoming. He furthermore has trouble hiding from rain and spray under a companionway dodger.

Life for the helmsman on a wheel-steered Newport 28 will be a lonely one. Wheel steering, being hardly necessary on a boat this size, is hardly desirable on the Newport 28.

Conclusion

The Newport 28 is a good entry-level cruiser-racer for someone wanting a reasonable combination of accommodations and performance, as long as you're not too persnickety about details. It would be a reasonable compromise for someone who likes more traditional appearance in a modern boat, but doesn't have the money to spend for a higher-quality boat of the same size and type, such as a Sabre 28. • **PS**

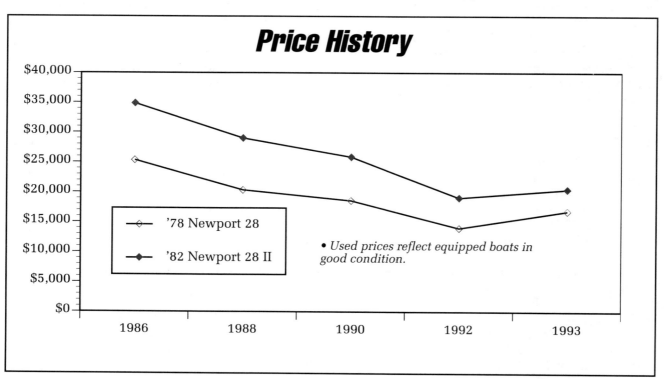

Price History

'78 Newport 28
'82 Newport 28 II

• *Used prices reflect equipped boats in good condition.*

S2 8.5 Meter

The 8.5 is good for cruising the coasts in comfort and style—as long as you like the modern look.

When Leon Slikkers founded S2 Yachts in 1973, much of the attention to detail that had previously characterized Slickcraft powerboats—Slikkers' earlier boatbuilding venture—traveled with him to the new boatbuilding company. In the 13 years S2 sailboats were in production (S2 still makes powerboats), the company produced a variety of modern cruising designs from the board of Arthur Edmunds, all characterized by longish fin keels, freestanding spade rudders, straight sheerlines, and a staggering variety of draft options and cockpit locations.

In the early '80s, S2 reached more for the performance market with the Grand Slam series of small boats, and the 10.3 "offshore racer-cruiser." These higher performance boats were designed by Scott Graham and Eric Schlageter, well known for their MORC and smaller IOR designs.

The S2 8.5 is a 28-footer cast in the company's traditional mold. Her hull dimensions, sail area, displacement, and general design characteristics put her square in the middle of the modern 28-footers such as the Tanzer 8.5, Newport 28, O'Day 28, and the Pearson 28.

The boat's styling is conventionally modern. She has a fairly straight sheer, fairly high freeboard, and low, raked cabin trunk with dark tinted flush ports.

Production of the 8.5 ran from 1981 to 1983. The boat was replaced by the similar S2 8.6, which continued until S2 stopped making sailboats in 1986.

Construction

The hull of the S2 8.5 is a solid hand layup. Glasswork is excellent, and is noted by owners as one of the main considerations in buying the boat. Gelcoat quality is excellent.

Slight roving printthrough is evident, but it is not

Specifications

LOA	28' 0"
LWL	22' 6"
Beam	9' 6"
Draft	4' 6" (deep keel), 3' 11" (shoal)
Displacement	7,600 lbs.
Ballast	3,000 lbs.
Sail area	400 sq. ft.

objectionable. Minor hard spots are visible in the topsides, probably caused by the attachment of interior furniture and bulkheads.

The deck molding is cored with end grain balsa, giving a solid feel underfoot as well as providing reasonable insulating properties.

S2's hull-to-deck joint is the basic type that we would like to see adopted throughout the industry. The hull molding has an inward-turning flange, onto which the deck molding is dropped. The joint is bedded in flexible sealant, and through bolted on six inch intervals by bolts passing through the full length slotted aluminum toerail. The joint is also through bolted across the stem.

All deck hardware is properly through bolted, although pulpits, cleats, and winches merely use nuts and washers on the underside of the deck, rather than the aluminum or stainless steel backing plates we prefer.

Another feature of the hull-to-deck joint is a heavy, semi-rigid vinyl rubrail at the sheerline, quite aptly termed a "crash rubrail" by S2. This will go a long way toward absorbing the shock of the inevitable encounters with docks and the other hard objects that seem to be attracted to the topsides of the typical sailboat. Although this rail is black when the boat is new, it had dulled to a chalky gray on older S2's we examined.

The builder advertises "bronze seacocks on all through hull fittings." These are not traditional tapered plug seacocks, but are ball valves mounted directly to through hull fittings. A proper seacock—whether it uses a ball valve or a tapered plug—has a heavy flange to allow through bolting to the hull. This is an important safety feature. Should a valve seize, it may become necessary to apply a great deal of leverage to the handle in order to open or close the valve. The deeply threaded through hull stem can easily break under these conditions, and more than one boat has been lost in this manner.

We also suggest that seacocks be installed on the cockpit drain scuppers and the bilge pump outlet, both of which may be under water while the boat is sailing. Light air performance would benefit by the fairing in of the through hull fittings, particularly the head intake and discharge, both of which are far enough forward to have a significant effect on water flow past the hull.

Ballast is a 3,000 pound lead casting, epoxied inside a hollow keel shell. We prefer an external lead casting bolted to the hull for its shock-absorbing qualities and ease of repair. This preference was reinforced recently when we examined an old Bristol 27 just sold by a friend. The surveyor noticed dampness near the bottom of the leading edge of the keel, which showed slight external damage. Probing the loose putty revealed some abrasion of the glass keel molding. In order to sell the boat, it was necessary to grind away a large portion of the glass at the front of the keel, dry out the ballast, and reglass the lead—a job that took several days of work and cost our friend a fair chunk of money.

Much of the boat's interior structure is plywood, glassed to the hull. Fillet bonding is neat and workmanlike with no rough edges to be found.

Chainplates are conventional stainless steel flat bar, bolted to bulkheads and plywood gussets in the main cabin. These are properly backed with stainless steel pads. Due to the fact that the hull is lined throughout with a carpet-like synthetic material, it is not possible to examine the bonding of the chainplate knees to the hull. The stemhead fitting is a stainless steel weldment, through bolted to the deck and hull

and reinforced inside the hull with a stainless steel gusset to prevent deflection of the deck from the pull aft of the headstay. We'd like to see a metal backup pad behind this fitting rather than the washers which are used.

General construction is thoughtful and well executed, with excellent glasswork, a strong and simple hull-to-deck joint, and reasonably installed hardware and fittings.

Handling Under Power

Although some early models of the 8.5 used a seven horsepower BMW diesel, the 1982 version employs an eight horsepower Yanmar. These small Yanmars are quite impressive, light in weight and far smoother than the company's older rockcrushers.

Because of the high freeboard and considerable windage of the 8.5, the standard engine is the absolute minimum power plant for the boat. Recognizing this fact, the company offered a 15 horsepower, two-cylinder Yanmar as an option. For another 75 pounds and $1,150, we would want this option on the boat if the ability to get places under power is a real consideration.

The extra fuel consumption of the larger engine will scarcely be noticed. The 18 gallon aluminum fuel tank will probably give a range under power of over 250 miles—more than adequate for a 28 foot cruising boat.

The fuel tank is located under the cockpit and is securely mounted and properly grounded. There is an easily reached fuel shut off between the engine and tank. Unfortunately, the fuel fill is located in the cockpit sole. Spilled diesel oil turns even the best fiberglass nonskid into an ice skating rink. Fuel fills should be located on deck, where spills can be efficiently washed away.

Engine access is via a large removable panel on the inboard face of the quarterberth. This panel lacks any kind of handhold to make it easily removable, which will discourage regular checking of the engine oil. The top companionway step also removes for access, but it's a long reach to the dipstick.

There is no oil pan under the engine. It will be necessary to be very careful when changing oil to keep the bilge clean. We have yet to see anyone change oil and filters on a boat engine without spilling something.

With the quarterberth panel removed, access for routine service is excellent. The quarterberth has remarkable headroom over, so that the mechanic will not feel like a trapped spelunker after a half hour of work. Engine removal will require some joinerwork disassembly.

Handling Under Sail

The S2 8.5 is no slug under sail. Her PHRF rating of

174 to 180 compares very favorably to other boats of her size and type. The Sabre 28, for example, has a rating of 198. The Pearson 28 about 195, and the O'Day 28 about 198.

Part of this is no doubt due to the fact that the standard sails on the boat come from the North loft. While North's OEM sails may not be the vertical cut Mylar-Kevlar wonders that adorn custom boats, they're a lot better than most.

S2 now uses Hall spars. The simple masthead rig is extremely clean, with airfoil spreaders and internal tangs. The boom features an internal outhaul and provision for two internally-led reefing lines, with cam cleats at the forward end of the boom.

The deck-stepped mast is mounted in a stainless steel deck plate incorporating plenty of holes for the attachment of blocks. Halyards and Cunningham lead aft along the cabin house top to a pair of Lewmar #8 winches. Lewmar #16s are optional, but hardly necessary.

The main is controlled by a six-part Harken rig mounted on the end of the boom, and a Kenyon traveler mounted on the aft cockpit coaming. This will work fine with the tiller-steered version of the boat. With wheel steering, the mainsheet is likely to be a nuisance to the helmsman.

Because of the end-of-boom sheeting, a boom vang will be essential for full mainsail control. Ironically, the boat's drawings show almost mid-boom sheeting, with the traveler mounted on the bridgedeck at the forward end of the cockpit. This is probably a better arrangement, although it heavily loads the center of the boom and requires more sheeting force.

Despite the fact that the shrouds are set well in from the rail, the boat lacks inboard headsail tracks. Rather, you are limited to snatch blocks shackled to the toerail track. A six-foot piece of track set inboard of the rail would be a useful addition.

Standard headsail sheet winches are two-speed Lewmar #30s. Options include both larger winches and self-tailers, both of which are worth considering for either racing or cruising. The cockpit coamings are wide enough for mounting larger primaries and secondaries.

The high-quality rig and sails add to the price of the S2, but they are additions well worth the cost.

Deck Layout

The deck layout of the 8.5 is clean and functional, with no toe stubbers to catch you unawares. There are two foredeck mooring cleats, but no bow chocks. The necessity to lead an anchor line well off the boat's centerline, coupled with high freeboard forward, is likely to result in a boat which sails around on her anchor or mooring. The 8.5 has a pair of wide stainless steel chafing strips at the bow which will greatly protect the deck from the chafe of the anchor line.

The 8.5's foredeck anchor well is one of the best we've seen. It is shallow—just deep enough to hold an anchor and adequate rode. There are double scuppers, which offer less likelihood of clogging. The lid is held on by a full-length piano hinge, and there is a positive latch.

The shallow locker well above the waterline means that water is less likely to enter through the scuppers, which can be a real problem with a deep anchor well. When the bow pitches into waves, a deep anchor well can fill with water, and if the scuppers clog with debris, you can find yourself sailing around with several hundred pounds of extra weight in the worst possible position. There is no provision for securing the bitter end of the anchor rode, but a big galvanized

Owners of 8.5s have little but praise for the interior of the boat. The cabin has a wide feeling, created by pushing everything outboard. The "chart area" on the plan is a myth, as far as we can tell.

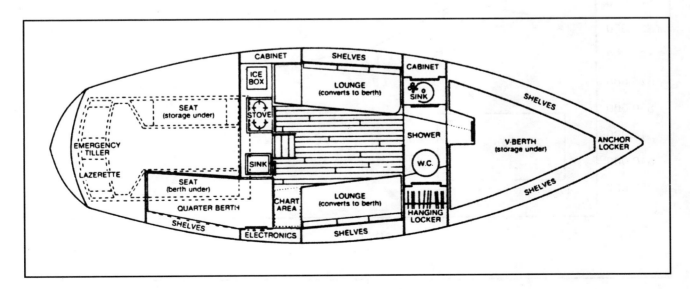

eyebolt installed in the well by the owner will solve that one.

The running lights leave something to be desired. Their location at deck level just aft of the stem makes them vulnerable to damage when handling ground tackle. We much prefer an international style bicolor mounted on the pulpit, another two feet off the water: easier to see, and out of the way. Wiring for the running lights is exposed in the anchor well, and should be secured out of the way.

A recessed teak handrail runs the full length of the cabin trunk, serving the dual function of heavy weather handhold and cabin trim piece. Its shape makes it far easier to oil or varnish than the conventional round handrail, although the wide, flat section seems somewhat awkward after years of grabbing round rails.

The 8.5's cockpit is the maximum size we'd want to see on a boat of this size. The T-shape is designed to accommodate the optional wheel steerer, yielding a somewhat odd layout for the tiller-steered version. A bench seat spans the aft end of the cockpit. Although this makes good seating in port, we doubt that you'd want anyone sitting there under sail: too much weight in the end of the boat. It does make a natural helmsman's seat for wheel steering.

The engine controls and instrument panel are also located at the aft end of the cockpit, and are basically inaccessible to the helmsman of a tiller-steered version.

There are two lifting lids in the aft cockpit bench, giving access to a cavernous space under the cockpit. To be useful, dacron bags should be fitted to the inside of these lockers. Then, they'll be handy stowage for spare sheets and blocks.

There are comfortable contoured seats along each side of the cockpit, with a huge locker under the port seat. Although plywood pen boards somewhat separate this locker from the engine space under the cockpit, it would be far too easy for deeply piled junk to get knocked over the board and into the engine. This locker should be partitioned into smaller spaces unless it is to be used exclusively as a sail locker.

The battery boxes, fitted at the forward end of the locker, could benefit from plywood or fiberglass lids to keep battery acid off gear which might find its way onto the batteries. The box is designed to take two batteries—one battery is standard—stored in plastic containers. A single lid covering the whole box would be more efficient.

The huge cockpit will accommodate up to six for sailing, and eight for in-port partying. The cockpit seat bottoms are contoured, and the cockpit coamings slope outboard for more comfortable seating. However, the seats are both too narrow and too short for sleeping,

The forward end of the cockpit is protected by a narrow bridgedeck. However, the cockpit coatings extend a full foot above the level of the bridgedeck, To block the companionway to the level of the top of the coamings will require leaving two of the three drop boards in place when sailing.

Although there is moderate taper to the sides of the companionway, making it easier to remove the drop boards, it is still necessary to lift each board about five inches before it can be removed. This is far

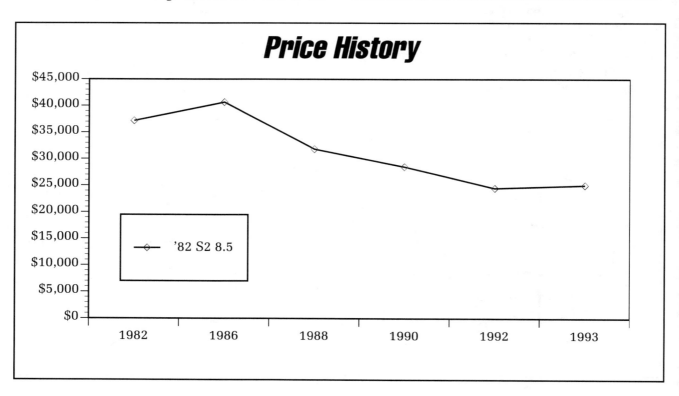

Price History

Legend: '82 S2 8.5

safer than many tapered companionways, where boards practically fall out if you look at them wrong. The companionway slide is one of the best we've seen. It's a contoured piece of acrylic fitted with a convenient grabrail. It slides easily in extruded aluminum channels, and is fitted with a fiberglass storm hood. As on many boats, the aft cabin bulkhead slopes forward, rendering it impossible to leave the drop boards out for ventilation when it rains.

Belowdecks

Owners consistently praise the interior design and finishing of S2 sailboats. From looking at the 8.5, it's pretty easy to see why.

There are no exposed interior fiberglass surfaces except the head floor pan molding. The hull and cabin overhead are lined with a carpet-like synthetic fabric. While this will undoubtedly cut down on condensation, we at first wondered how this fabric would hold up over time. Inevitably, the hull liner and even the overhead will get wet. In freshwater areas, this is no problem. The water will eventually evaporate. In salt water, however, wet fabric never seems to dry. Salt draws moisture like a magnet draws steel. Since first seeing this boat, however, we've had good experiences with the fabric. Be sure, however, to get a good wet-or-dry vacuum to keep it clean.

Interior layout is fairly conventional, with V-berths forward, and immediately aft, a full width head. The head can be closed off from both the forward cabin and the main cabin with solid doors—a real luxury in a boat this size. There is a large hanging locker in the head, and reasonable storage space for toilet articles.

The word for the main cabin is "wide," with the settees pushed as far outboard as they can go. Decor is a little heavy on the teak for our taste, but it is one of the better coordinated interiors we have seen. S2 had a good interior decorator.

A fold-down dining table seats four. When folded against the bulkhead, it is held in place by a single latch, which makes us nervous.

Neither settee is full length. The foot of the port settee runs under the galley counter, making it long enough for sleeping, although your feet may feel a little claustrophobic in the tiny footwell.

The starboard settee is an unusual configuration. The aftermost 12" of the settee folds up to form an arm rest, leaving a gap between the end of the settee and the head of the quarterberth.

Inexplicably, this gap is referred to on the accommodation plan as a "charting area," although there is neither a standard nor an optional chart table. It's sort of like the designer ran out of energy before completing the interior design.

Over the non-existent "charting area" is the best electrical panel we've seen on a 28 foot boat. The panel has a locking battery switch, battery test meter, and a panel with room for 14 circuit breakers, although only half are installed on the standard boat. The space is welcome, since with the proliferation of marine electronics most electrical panels are woefully inadequate.

Most quarterberths tend to induce claustrophobia. That of the 8.5 is more likely to exacerbate any tendencies you might have to agoraphobia. At last, a quarterberth which will not give you a concussion when you sit bolt upright in the middle of the night after your neighbor drags down on you in a wind shift.

The standard main cabin sole is carpet-covered fiberglass. For an additional $325, teak and holly was available for the traditionalist. We'd want it.

Unfortunately there is no access to the bilge in the main cabin. None. This is inexcusable, and could be dangerous. A few hours with a saber saw should solve this rather basic problem.

The galley is workable and accessible, with no awkward posturing required to do the dishes. The sink gets an A+. It is a full nine inches deep, is large enough to take a frying pan, and mounted close to the centerline.

In contrast, the icebox gets a C-. It is larger than normal on a boat of this size, but it drains to the bilge, has a poorly insulated top, and a tiny, uninsulated hatch without a trace of a gasket. Boo.

Because of limited counter space, the two burner Kenyon alcohol stove is mounted athwartships, rather than fore and aft. This means that the stove cannot be gimballed, and that it is necessary to reach across the inboard burner to reach the outboard one. Given the fact that countertop gimballed stoves are usually dangerous, the lack of gimballing doesn't bother us much. What does bother us is that if you want to upgrade the stove to something more functional, the limited space allocated will stretch your ingenuity.

A fold down table at the end of the galley counter gives additional counter space, but it must be left up in order to use the port settee for sleeping.

Roominess, excellent execution, and good color coordination are trademarks of the interiors of all S2s, and the 8.5 fits well into this enviable tradition.

Conclusions

The S2 8.5 is a good boat for cruising the Great Lakes or any coast in comfort and a certain amount of style. Her appearance may be a little modern for traditionalists, with her straight sheer and European-style cabin windows.

Pricey? Yes, but when you look at the things that go into the boat—the rig, good sails, and a comfortable, well finished interior—the price may seem a bit less painful. You still pay for what you get. • **PS**

Alerion-Express

The Alerion-Express is an updated, fiberglass version of a Narragansett Bay classic daysailer.

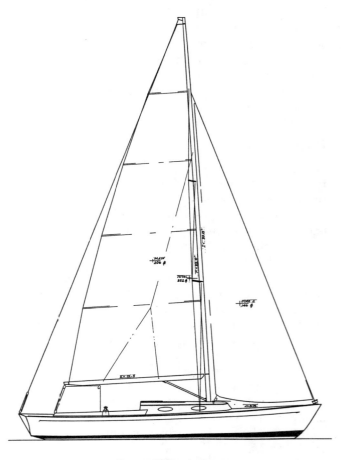

Specifications

LOA	28' 3"
LWL	22' 10"
Beam	8' 2"
Draft	4' 6"
Displacement	4,400 lbs.
Ballast	2,000 lbs.
Sail area	352 sq. ft.

The first Alerion was the 26-foot mahogany-planked daysailer Nathaniel Herreshoff built for himself around 1912, and which now reposes at Mystic Seaport in Connecticut. Many years later, in the 1970s, his grandson Halsey Herreshoff built a 25-foot version, a one-off that made its way to Florida where it was admired—and bought—by Alfred Sanford, father of Nantucket builders Alfie and Edward.

The Sanfords liked the boat so much they sought out the plans (Nathaniel's, not Halsey's) and began building a cold-molded carvel-planked 26-footer. The boat was faithful to the original, but half a foot beamier (for the inclusion of a modest interior), a bit shorter on the waterline, and with a small cutaway in the aft section of the keel. Like the original, the newer Alerion pointed high and was fast in light air, but was still capable of handling heavy weather. Halsey, meanwhile, produced about a dozen of his 25-foot models, in fiberglass, which reputedly were also good sailers.

The Sanford Boat Co. launched its first Alerion in 1978 and eventually built 20, raising the price over the years from $21,000 to $44,000. Edward Sanford says there are still several around, and owners have included such notables as America's Cup winner Bill Koch and singer Jimmy Buffet.

But a wooden boat, even a sweet sailing one like the Alerion, is not for everyone, so in the late 1980s Ralph Schacter, a sailor from Southport, Connecticut, commissioned West Coast naval architect Carl Schumacher, designer of the Express 27, to draw a boat that combined traditional appearance with modern materials and contemporary "go-fast" thinking. The result brought so many comments and inquiries that Schacter joined with Holby Marine of Bristol, Rhode Island, to build the boat on a produc-

tion basis. Holby built seven of the Alerion-Expresses in 1990, then sold the molds to Tillotson-Pearson Industries the following spring. By late 1992, some 25 had been built.

Design

Schumacher, a member of the California-Santa Cruz-ULDB school of design, might seem an odd choice to update a traditional design. But Schumacher's Alerion-Express is a happy hybrid (if such is possible) of the traditional and the contemporary, even if it's truly an Alerion in name only. "This is a modern yacht, not a warmed-over re-creation," Schumacher states in company promotional material.

Above the waterline, the new boat is, if anything,

The Alerion-Express is a very pretty boat, with low freeboard and graceful sheer.

more "classic" than its namesake, with increased overhangs and a fine rake to the bow (Herreshoff's original 26-footer had a relatively long 22-foot waterline, making it slightly stubby in appearance). the nine-foot-long cockpit is the same as the original, but Herreshoff's 7' 7" beam has been increased to 8' 2" with three berths (four in the latest design) added below.

In place of the old bunter rig is a Hall Spars aluminum extrusion, fractionally rigged mast (the same section as on the J/27), fully battened mainsail and small, self-tacking jib.

But it's below the surface that Schumacher's mark is evident. Herreshoff's short keel (2-1/2 feet) and centerboard combination (5-1/2-foot draw with the board down) has been replaced with a racer-type elliptical keel and equally modern spade rudder on a basically flat bottom. the design, coupled with lightweight foam core laminate construction (instead of Nat's mahogany-on-oak), makes for a low-resistance boat that's swift, especially off the wind.

Construction

Tillotson-Pearson has gained a reputation for high-quality construction, and the craftsmanship on the Alerion-Express maintains that standard. This is a good-looking, well put together boat, with no rough edges and no sign (to our eye) of slipshod technique. With a base price of $33,000 in 1992, this level of quality should be expected.

Hull and deck are vacuum-bagged end-grain balsa covered with uni- and bi-directional glass (of Tillotson's own formula) and a layer of vinylester resin to deter osmotic blistering. Construction techniques have reduced the weight several hundred pounds from the Holby model, according to chief

engineer Phil Mosher. Like all TPI boats, this one comes with a limited 10-year warranty against blistering. The hull and deck are through-bolted and bonded with 3M 5200.

This is an attractive boat: the hull is white with an inlaid 1/4-inch gold stripe; the deck is gray nonskid. An afterdeck adds to the traditional appearance. There's enough wood to catch the eye—a teak toerail, teak handrails and teak and Thiokol sole the length of the cockpit. Exterior teak comes sanded and oiled. There are four fixed Bomar ports on the cabin house, and a smoked Lewmar deck hatch. All fittings are quality, from the Lewmar winches to the Harken fairleads and jib track.

The Hall spar is keel-stepped, and TPI had reinforced the area over the external lead keel with a solid fiberglass transverse floor. The rudder stock is carbon fiber with Rulon bearings; the prop shaft has been changed from Holby's stainless steel to carbon fiber composite.

Performance

Schumacher designed the Alerion-Express to be a quick, lively sailer in keeping with the spirit, if not the form, of the Herreshoff original. TPI intends the boat for the experienced sailor, rather than the novice, who expects good performance but with a minimum of fuss and few if any crew. "Everyone who has bought the boat has had larger boats," Mosher said.

With its light weight, shallow bottom and low-drag keel and rudder, we expected the boat to be nimble, and it was. In 12 to 14 knots on Narragansett Bay, the boat quickly accelerated to hull speed under its big, fully battened main and 100-percent jib. With a total of 352 square feet of sail (206 in the main, 146 in the jib), the Alerion-Express is not overcanvassed, but carries plenty of sail for its weight (for a sail area/displacement ratio of 20.97, which is quite high). The boat has a PHRF rating of 141, slower than the J/

27 (120s), but considerably faster than similarly-sized cruiser-racers, including the C&C 29 and Beneteau 29, both with ratings in the 170s.

The tiller is very light, with just a touch of weather helm. the Alerion-Express tacked through 80 degrees easily and rapidly, with no searching for the groove on the new tack.

Because they feel there is insufficient form stability in the hull, engineers at TPI are contemplating adding a lead bulb to a glass fin to increase righting moment and, perhaps, performance to weather. The trade-off would be an increase in draft from 4' 6" to about 5'6".

"The Alerion has a lot of initial tenderness," Mosher said, adding that it is "not tender at all under sail." The 2,000 pounds of ballast gives it a ballast/displacement ratio of 45 percent. The displacement/length ratio is a moderately light 168.

Our experience in moderate, steady wind was that the boat did tend to heel initially, to about 17 degrees, but then established itself and stayed there. The degree of heel was not unpleasant at all, although from a marketing standpoint it might prove a deterrent to the "mom and pop" sailor, or a family with young members (we imagine the boat would appeal to some well-heeled first-boat buyers as well). But for the experienced sailor moving down in size, the boat will be a delight to sail.

The swept-back, double-spreader rig (37' 5" above the deck) has continuous rigging for easy adjustment. In addition to the upper shrouds, there are single lowers and intermediates. The backstay is adjustable as well via a line led under the afterdeck to the after edge of the cockpit. Former racers will appreciate being able to bend the spar to optimize performance.

Current models have the mainsheet fitted to a barney post (which doubles as a pedestal for a nice teak cockpit table). This may be a concession to the racing-minded sailor, but we found the post an obstruction, especially during tacks, that defeated the roominess of the cockpit. Future models will offer end-boom sheeting through the traveler as an option.

The whole setup—fully battened main fitted with lazy jacks, self-tacking jib and all lines led aft through

In keeping with the boat's intended purpose, accommodations below deck are simple and Spartan. There's much more living space in the cockpit.

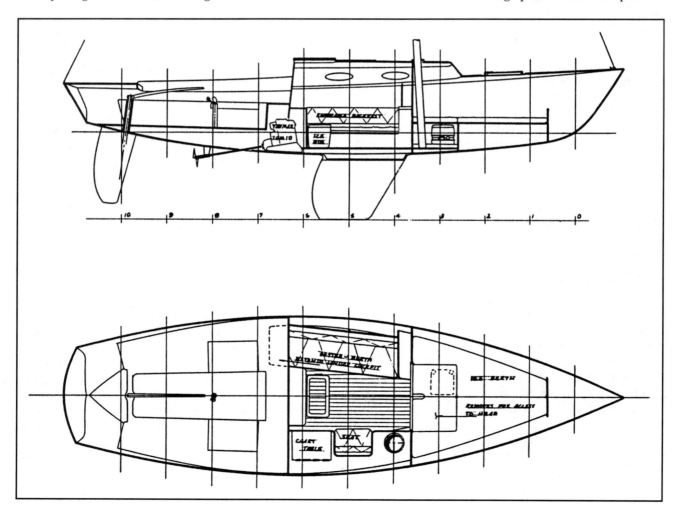

rope clutches—is intended to concentrate operations in the cockpit and generally make life easier, especially for the singlehander. Our particular main proved difficult to raise (even cranking the #7 winch) and lower; maybe it was sticky sail slides. The Shore sail was fitted with special load-bearing slides at the battens to make hoisting easier, but we still had problems. On the other hand, one Alerion-Express owner said he routinely raises his UK Sailmakers main by hand.

The Alerion-Express comes with a Hall Quik Vang for easier adjustment. Generally, the fully battened main requires some careful trimming of the boom, backstay and at the batten adjustments at the luff. The self-tacking jib is sheeted to a car on a custom Harken track. Because the track is short, sailing wing-on-wing requires use of a pole. Fortunately, there's a grooved storage area outboard of each cockpit seat, making storage of the poles and other gear easy and convenient. Harken roller furling for the 100-percent jib comes standard.

The Alerion-Express, like its early namesake, is a vaunted light-air performer. Mosher said it will reach hull speed in five knots of wind, a claim we find credible. one owner we spoke to said his boat points high, reaches beautifully and is only a bit cranky dead downwind. Initial tenderness or no, Mosher said he's been out in 30 knots with no difficulty—"It doesn't fall on its ear."

Accommodations

Because of the nine-foot cockpit and shallow hull, there's not a lot of room down below, but enough to qualify the Alerion-Express as an overnighter and occasional weekender. The hull and bulkheads are an airy white, set off by wood trim and a teak and holly sole. The interior plan is simple, with a V-berth in the bow. Unfortunately, the portable head is located beneath it. The current plan has a settee berth to port in the main cabin with a small seat between two storage compartments on the starboard side. The arrangement doesn't make a lot of sense, so TPI plans to replace the seat/storage area with a starboard settee.

A 38-gallon ice box inside the companionway does double duty as a step down. Behind the cooler, access to the engine compartment is easily achieved by removing either a front or top panel. The engine of choice, which cost an extra $5,300 in late 1992, is a 9-hp. Yanmar diesel, noisy in the extreme at low revs, but which moves the boat well.

Ample natural lighting flows through the four elliptical ports and the smoked 19" x 19" hatch forward; we can't be sure, but we suspect the three small interior lights make for dim lighting—fine for relaxing, possibly hard on the eyes for reading. A 12-volt DC system runs off an 80 amp-hour marine battery, controlled by a Bass electrical panel with six circuit breakers. There's a standard Guest battery switch.

The interior is a bit cramped for headroom, a problem TPI hopes to improve somewhat by converting the hatch to a double-slider. The house designers are also contemplating widening the companionway by nine inches. Cockpit hatches to port and starboard provide access to the aft regions below; there's further storage under the afterdeck.

Life on the Alerion-Express is meant to be lived in the cockpit, which is deep, comfortable and dry—except for occasional spray to remind forward passengers they're under sail. The seats are wide and comfortable, especially with the addition of cockpit cushions, but if anything the cockpit is a little too wide forward. That's fine when the boat sails flat, but heeling makes it necessary for a shorter person (say, under 5' 9") to scrunch down uncomfortably to brace their feet against the opposite side. On a long beat this could cause lower back fatigue.

Under the afterdeck is a teak rail with handy cup holders. A manual Whale bilge pump on the port side empties, unfortunately, via a ribbed plastic hose at the stern—a jarring touch in an otherwise genteel appearance. Cockpit drains consist of two Elvstrom-type openings at the rear of the cockpit, as on a J/24. They can be fastened shut, which is just as well because the leeward side tends to admit, rather than expel, water. Finally, one owner complained mildly about the need for stern chocks.

Minor criticism aside, the boat, inside and out, is functional and reasonably comfortable. the optional teak table that sits on the barney post is an inviting call to stay topsides. Removal of the post, however, which we'd prefer, means end-boom sheeting, which performance sailors probably won't like. It also raises the question of where and how to set up a table for the brie and chardonnay.

Conclusion

At a base price, in 1992, of $33,000, plus another $8,500 or so for sails and diesel, the Alerion-Express is a costly little daysailer/overnighter. What you get for your money is a well-built, lively 28-footer that sails as well as it looks. On the other hand, a Beneteau First 285 has a base price of about $46,000 and a Tartan Piper 28 about $60,000; but then, of course, they have substantially more accommodations.

It's still too soon for the Alerion-Express to have developed a resale market (no historical price data is avalable as yet), but the boat's traditional good looks and solid construction should help maintain its value well—especially if it catches on with that niche of the market that is looking for an easily maintained/sailed boat that provides some fun out on the water. **• PS**

Sabre 28

The Sabre 28 is an above-average coastal cruiser that should appeal to a couple or small family.

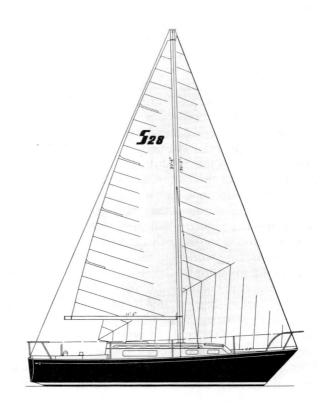

The Sabre 28 was the smallest boat in the line produced by Sabre Yachts of South Casco, Maine for much of the company's history. The production run of the 28 lasted 14 years, from 1972 to 1986.

The Sabre 28 was the only model produced by the company until 1977, when the Sabre 34 entered production. In 1979 the gap between the Sabre 28 and the 34 was filled with a 30-footer of a design very similar to that of her two sisters. In 1982, the Sabre 38 was introduced, and features both a standard and an aft-cabin layout. A 32 was added in 1984, a 36 in 1985, and a 42-footer in 1987. Along the way, the 28 acquired a ketch-rig option. The 28 was dropped at the same time the 42 was introduced.

All boats in the Sabre line are of the modern cruiser-racer type, with fin keel and skeg-hung spade rudder. With a 1981 base price of about $37,000, and an average delivered price in southern New England of about $40,000 without sails or electronics, the Sabre 28 was a relatively expensive 28' boat.

Despite a fairly high initial cost, the Sabre 28 has proved to be a good investment for her owners. One owner responding to *The Practical Sailor's* boatowners' survey reported that he paid $14,900 for his boat in 1973. That same boat in 1981 was worth about $24,000. A Sabre 28 purchased in 1976 cost $22,000, and was worth about $29,000 in 1981. The collapse of market values in the '90s is evident in the latest figures, however: a 1986 Sabre 28, which cost $48,900 new, is now worth only about $34,000. This is typical of recent trends, and does not reflect on the Sabre 28—indeed, it's held more of its value than many boats.

Owners report that the primary motivation for purchasing the boat can be summed up in one word: quality. Sabre is quite conscious of their image as

Specifications

LOA	28' 5"
LWL	22' 10"
Beam	9' 2"
Draft	4' 8" (std), 3' 10" (shoal)
Displacement	7,900 lbs.
Ballast	3,100 lbs.
Sail area	403 sq. ft.

producing a high-quality boat. The boat attracts buyers willing to pay a little more than average for a boat that is better than average.

As with all boats that have been in production for a number of years, the design of the Sabre 28 has evolved and improved over the years. In particular, a number of minor changes were made in August, 1982, some of which are noted below. Therefore, the price of a used Sabre 28 may be a function of whether it has some of the more desirable features.

The Sabre 28 is conventionally modern in appearance. She has a modest concave sheer, straight raked stern, and short after overhang.

Construction

The hull of the Sabre 28 is a slightly heavier-than-

average hand layup of mat and roving. Some roving printthrough is evident, but there are no visible hard spots in the hull. Gelcoat quality is excellent.

There are optional hull and deck colors besides the stock white on white. On an early Sabre 28 we examined, the red gelcoat had faded to a dull pink, and the boat was past due for painting. In general red hulls are more susceptible to fading.

The deck of the Sabre 28 is balsa-cored for stiffness, with plywood inserts at stress areas such as winch mountings. The hull-to-deck joint uses a fairly standard internal hull flange, butyl-bedded and through bolted on 6" centers with stainless steel bolts. These bolts also serve to attach a vinyl rubrail and the teak toerail. The hull-to-deck joint is through bolted across the transom.

All deck hardware, including stanchions, pulpits, and cleats, is through bolted and backed with thick aluminum plates which serve to distribute load. The stem fitting is a well-finished aluminum casting.

Skin fittings are recessed flush with the hull surface. All underwater through hull openings are fitted with bronze Spartan seacocks. Spartan seacocks have a short, lipped hose tailpiece rather than the more typical long straight tailpiece of other seacocks. This short tailpiece precludes double clamping of hoses. This single hose clamp on below-water fit-

tings is fine as long as the hose clamps are kept tight. We recommend that they be checked at regular intervals.

In general, construction details are among the best that we've seen on a production sailboat. All fillet bonding is absolutely neat. There are no rough fiberglass areas anywhere. All exposed interior fiberglass surfaces, such as bilges and the inside of lockers, are gelcoated or painted.

Although tiller steering is standard, about 90% of the boats were delivered with Edson pedestal wheel steerers equipped with Ritchie compasses. The wheel steering option has proven so popular that in 1976 the cockpit of the Sabre 28 was redesigned to accommodate the wheel without interfering with the seating arrangement. Access to the rudder stock for emergency steering is via a plastic plate in the cockpit sole. An emergency tiller is provided with wheel-steered boats.

The mast of the Sabre 25 is a straight section Awlgripped aluminum extrusion built by Rig-Rite. Internal halyards, internal clew outhaul, topping lift, and two-point jiffy reefing are standard, as is a transom-mounted ball-bearing mainsheet traveler. The mast is deck-stepped in an aluminum casting. In new boats, this mast step has been redesigned to incorporate attachment points for blocks, facilitating the leading of halyards aft to the cockpit. Halyard winches mounted on the cabin top are another popular option.

Mast compression is transferred to the hull structure by a teak compression column incorporated in the main bulkhead. Shroud chainplates are heavily through-bolted to the main bulkhead, which is solidly glassed to the hull.

Originally, the Sabre 28 was rigged with single upper and lower shrouds. In 1975 forward lower shrouds were added to reduce mast pumping under sail and vibration at the mooring. Mast vibration in high winds, even at anchor, is a common problem with deck-stepped masts. Not all older Sabre 28s have been retrofitted with the additional set of lower shrouds. If purchase of a pre-1975 model is contemplated, be sure to ascertain that the forward lower shrouds have been installed.

The ballast keel is an external lead casting, well faired to the hull. Keelbolts are accessible in the bilge for periodic tightening.

Construction of the Sabre 28 is strong without being overly heavy. There is no evidence of hurrying to finish the job anywhere in the boat.

Handling Under Sail

With optional wheel steering, optional cockpit-led halyards, and optional self-tailing headsail sheet winches, the Sabre 28 can easily be handled by one or two people. The mainsheet is within easy reach of the helmsman. Unfortunately, his head is also within easy reach of the mainsheet when jibing, except on newer boats; the mainsheet was relocated to the cabin top in 1982.

With main chainplates set well inboard, the headsail sheeting base of the boat is quite narrow, particularly if the boat is equipped with the optional inboard genoa track in addition to the standard toerail-mounted genoa track, The sheeting base is, for example, almost a foot narrower than that of the Hunter 27. This allows the Sabre 28 to be reasonably close-winded. With her relatively small wetted surface and a big genoa, she will be fast in light air.

Unless the water in your cruising area is spread very thin, we suggest you look for the standard keel version rather than the shoal keel. The shoal keel presents a less efficient lateral plane for windward work.

Some attention will have to be paid to the size of headsail used. Owners report that, although the Sabre 28 more than holds her own with other boats of her size and type, she is not a particularly stiff boat. Owners consider her performance well above average, although her PHRF rating suggests only average performance compared to similar cruiser-racers. Due to the off-center solid prop, the boat may be faster on one tack than the other, and owners who intend to race the Sabre 28 should experiment to see if this is the case.

Handling Under Power

Several different engines were used in the Sabre 28. Until 1975 all were equipped with the Atomic Four gasoline engine. In 1975 a 10 horsepower Volvo diesel was offered as an option. In 1978, both these engines were dropped, and the Volvo MD7A diesel became standard. The MD7A is a two cylinder engine rated at 13 horsepower. In 1981 it was replaced by the Westerbeke 13.

The propeller shaft on the right hand turning Atomic Four is offset to port. On the left hand turning Volvos, it is offset to starboard. On the earliest Sabre 28s the shaft was on centerline. This change in engines from right hand to left hand rotation means that replacement of engines in off-center located Atomic Four powered boats will be limited to either the Atomic Four gas engine or some other right hand

---

The standard interior can sleep six, which we feel is too many people for a 28-foot boat. Some older models have an alternate four-berth interior, which is more suitable.

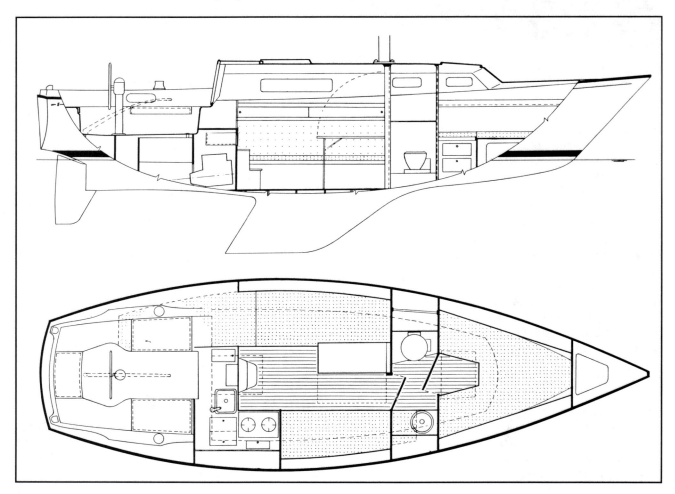

turning engine. Otherwise there will be considerable compromise in handling characteristics under power.

Owners report that engine access on early Atomic Four equipped models is poor. In current Volvo-powered models, access for routine service is good. Some joinerwork disassembly—planned in, fortunately—is required for engine removal, Routine service is via doors and panels.

There is no oil sump under the engine. Access to the stuffing box, needed annually for repacking and adjustment, is poor. Engine instruments—a full bank, with no idiot lights—are mounted in the bridgedeck, with engine starting and stopping controls under the helmsman's seat. While this may seem awkward at first, it does protect the always-vulnerable ignition switch from water. This is an unusual, but reasonable arrangement.

Owners consider the boat's handling under power to be good. With her fin keel and spade rudder, she will turn in a tight circle. Owners report that any of the engines will drive the boat at or near "hull speed" under most conditions,

Deck Layout

In 1976, a foredeck anchor well was added to the Sabre 28. The well is large enough to hold adequate primary ground tackle for the boat. It has provision for securing the bitter end of the anchor rode in boats built since 1982. We would add an eyebolt or U-bolt to the well for this purpose if it is not already there.

The water tank vent is located in the anchor well. This is a rational location for an item whose position is commonly an afterthought. Frequently, tank vents are located in the topsides, just below the sheer, This can cause backsiphoning of salt water into fuel or freshwater tanks. We saw this occur on several boats—not Sabres—in the 1979 Marion-Bermuda race, which featured four days of slogging to windward in heavy air.

The Sabre 28 is one of the few boats we have seen that uses Skene bow chocks. Skene chocks effectively hold the anchor rode or mooring lines in the chocks, even if the boat sails around on her anchor. This is an important consideration in many modern boats, for the Sabre 28, like many modern sloops of moderate displacement, probably sails almost as many miles while anchored or moored as when underway.

Heavy teak handrails and a very effective molded-in nonskid surface facilitate movement on deck in a seaway. The side decks are of necessity narrow due to the wide cabin trunk.

The cockpit of the Sabre 28 is large and comfortable. It is as large a cockpit as we would consider safe for offshore sailing on a 28' boat. With wheel steering the cockpit easily seats five.

Cockpit lockers deserve special comment. There are two molded-in recesses in the winch islands, handy for winch handles, sail stops, and other small items. There is a shallow lift-top locker under the port cockpit seat, a deeper locker under the helmsman's seat, and a deep locker under the starboard seat.

The deep starboard locker is bulkheaded off from the bowels of the boat so that sails, fenders, and lines will not migrate to the depths of the bilge. This locker

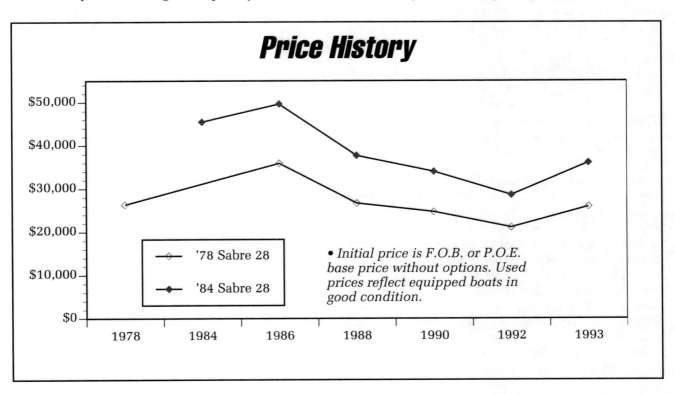

Price History

Legend:
- —◇— '78 Sabre 28
- —◆— '84 Sabre 28

• Initial price is F.O.B. or P.O.E. base price without options. Used prices reflect equipped boats in good condition.

contains built-in holders for the companionway drop boards and emergency tiller, as well as a shelf arranged for line stowage. Although the lid to this locker is a little small for the easy removal of sails, it is one of the best designed cockpit lockers we have seen.

By comparison, the companionway is a bit of a disappointment. Although it is suitably narrow and has a good bridgedeck, the opening is sharply tapered, allowing removal of the drop boards by lifting them only about an inch.

The drop boards themselves are 1/2" teak-faced plywood in early boats, solid teak in post-1982 models. The exposed edge grain of the plywood core will soon turn gray unless the boards are well varnished. Eventually they may delaminate. We believe that plywood should not be used where it will be subject to weathering. Frankly, the boards look a little cheap on a boat of this quality.

Newer boats have a transparent smoked plexiglass companionway hatch top. Older boats have fiberglass hatches. The plexiglass hatch allows a good deal of light below.

At night, when tied to the dock, it also allows people on the dock to stare into the main cabin. An often forgotten corollary to transparent hatches is that if they allow light below during the day, they allow it out at night. The glare of a white light belowdecks can wipe out the helmsman's night vision. Not a common problem, admittedly, but a real one nonetheless.

Belowdecks

The first impression of the Sabre 28 belowdecks is that she is roomy, neat, and well-finished. Headroom is 6' under the main hatch, and an honest 5' 11" in the main cabin.

The forward cabin contains V-berths with a filler to form a double. The 30-gallon molded polyethylene water tank is located under the forward berths. There is a drawer and a bin under each berth.

With the forward hatch open, it is possible to stand and dress comfortably with the berth filler removed.

The head is full width and closes off from both the forward cabin and main cabin by doors. The Sabre 28 came standard with a 22-gallon holding tank. A Y-valve diverter was optional.

Despite a lot of teak bulkheads and trim, the main cabin is bright and attractive. There are substantial grab rails overhead. The port settee extends to form a double berth. With all berths filled, the Sabre 28 sleeps six. Frankly, six people on a 28' boat is too many, even for a weekend. We would prefer an alternate four-berth interior arrangement that provides a larger galley. Some older Sabre 28s are equipped with such a layout.

A bulkhead-mounted fold-down cabin table seats four comfortably. It is secured in the folded position by a screw-type hatch dog, a good idea, since a rattling table can drive you to distraction.

At the after end of the main cabin, the galley is located to starboard, with a quarterberth to port. Galley storage is good, with four drawers and several lockers. The galley sink is located just off centerline, almost under the companionway. While this location is good for ensuring that the sink will drain on either tack, care must be taken going below when well heeled on the port tack to avoid stepping into the sink.

The galley stove is a recessed two-burner Kenyon alcohol stove. Stoves of this type, which have integral fuel tanks with the fuel fill located between the burners, present a potential fire hazard if the fuel tank is refilled before the burners have cooled adequately.

On pre-1982 boats, the icebox is well insulated with the exception of the top. Given the fact that Sabre has gone so far as to install an icebox pump to keep ice melt from smelling up the bilge, we were pleased to see them complete the otherwise well designed icebox in 1982 by insulating the top and lids.

Wiring, plumbing—in general, all finishing details—are well designed and neatly finished. The location of the main electrical panel next to the companionway, where it is vulnerable to spray, is an exception to the generally well thought out installations.

Four opening ports are standard; an additional hatch over the main cabin is optional. We recommend this additional ventilation if the boat is to be used in a warm climate. The dorade box over the head is the only provision for foul-weather ventilation.

Conclusions

The Sabre 28 is an attractive, well-built, well-finished boat. Although her price is above average, construction and finish details are also well above average for a stock boat. Despite her modern underbody, she is a conservative design, conservatively built.

The Sabre 28 is neither an all-out racer, nor an all-out cruiser. She is a good compromise boat, strong enough to cruise with confidence and fast enough not to embarrass.

She is good-looking in a modern way, without being so modern as to be trendy. She will probably not appeal to the hard-core traditionalist, nor to the flat-out modernist. She appeals mostly as a well turned out coastal cruiser for the couple or a small family. The Sabre 25 may be no Swan, but she's a long way from an ugly duckling. **• PS**

Pearson Triton

Possibly the world's cheapest long-range cruiser; where else could you get a boat like this for $10,000?

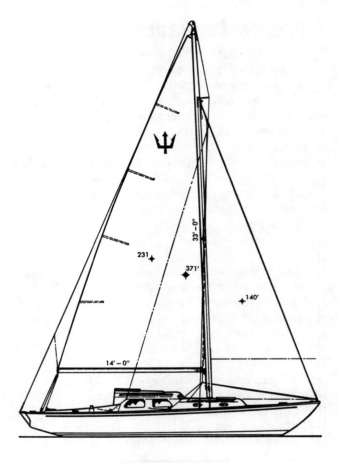

When cousins Clint and Everett Pearson took the first Pearson Triton to the 1959 New York Boat Show, they had no idea that ultimately they would build more than 700 hulls, the boat would establish Pearson Yachts as a premier builder of fiberglass boats, and that more myths would surround the Triton than practically any other boat of its time.

Returning to their Bristol, Rhode Island yard with 16 orders in hand, the success of the young company was assured.

We owned a Triton for a number of years, cruising it from the Great Lakes to the East Coast. Our affection has not blinded us, however, as ownership also exposed the boat's several problem areas. In any case, this is a landmark boat that many good sailors cut their teeth on.

History

Myth: The Triton was the first production fiberglass sailboat auxiliary. Not true. The Rhodes-designed Bounty, built by Fred Coleman, owns that distinction.

The story of Pearson Yachts is well documented, so we'll repeat here just the essentials. The company was founded in 1956 and built rowboats, dinghies and runabouts until the Triton arrived in 1959. A few were built in Sausilito, California, but the venture wasn't to last long. During the next few years, Carl Alberg and Philip Rhodes accounted for more than half a dozen other designs, including the Vanguard, Alberg 35, Bounty II and Rhodes 41. The last Triton was launched in 1967.

In 1964 the company was bought by Grumman Allied Industries. Clint Pearson later left to start Bristol Yachts and later yet Everett departed to form a partnership known as Tillotson-Pearson. Bill Shaw

Specifications

LOA	28' 6"
LWL	20' 6"
Beam	8' 3"
Draft	4' 0"
Displacement	8,000 lbs. (approx.)
Ballast	3,019 lbs.
Sail area	362 sq. ft.

emerged as the principal designer and later served as president. In 1990 Pearson went bankrupt and its assets were auctioned off. Aqua Buoy bought the molds but despite promises to resume production on a limited basis, no new boats have been built since. Blame the recession in part.

It's a sad ending to what was once a very fine boatbuilding company. To this day, many of the early Pearsons are still sailing, and, to our mind, represent some of the best buys on the market.

Design

The Triton is vintage Alberg—skinny, long overhangs, low freeboard, large mainsail and small foretriangle. Typical of boats designed to the CCA (Cruising Club of America) rule. Alberg was born in

Owners' Comments

"I feel that the boat can handle more than the crew. Initial stability is poor, but she stiffens up as the wind increases. Wooden rudder is a weak link. Otherwise, construction is well above anything made today. Small interior but has 6' 2" headroom and seats six below. Also has six opening portlights."

—1960 model in Levittown, NY

"Have been knocked flat with tip of mast in the water. She floats on her side fine. No water enters the cockpit."

—1960 model in Brookfield Center, CT

"The Triton was built by both Pearson in Rhode Island and Aeromarine Plastics in Sausalito, California. Very early Pearsons had some problems with balsa core and other minor items. 'West Coast Tritons' were built like battleships."

—1963 model in Seattle, WA

"Outstanding seaworthiness. Rides all waves comfortably. Tacks through eye of wind beautifully. The galley requires lots of imagination. I love my Triton!"

—1964 model in Berwyn, PA

"Hit a channel buoy about eight feet from the bow. Had to patch a little internal damage to a shelf (inside). Only had to scrub off the black smudge on the topsides. Rig had been oversized to 1/4-inch shrouds and stays by previous owner."

—1965 model in Ridgecrest, CA

"It is very difficult to permanently damage the hull of a Triton. Check deck for softness of core. I'll be surprised if core has not absorbed water somewhere."

—1961 model in Berlin, MD

"My only complaint is the slot between the rudder and keel. Lobster gear loves it. I have put a stainless steel strap on the keel bottom. Also, I wish I could find a sheet material to glue to the inside of the hull to combat condensation."

—1964 model in Rockland, ME

"Large main should be reefed early. Cockpit plenty big for comfort underway or at anchor. Takes some spray in six-foot seas. Atomic 4 not totally accessible but enough so that oil changes, tune-ups, etc., can be done without too much trouble."

—1965 model in Wahiana, HI

Sweden where people love skinny keelboats with long overhangs, such as the Folkboat. It is easy to trace the Triton's lineage to such designs. Credit is also due to Tom Potter, of Jamestown, Rhode Island, who brought the project idea to the Pearsons, and had a hand in its development.

Many folks refer to the underbody as a full keel, but as a glance at the profile drawing shows, the forefoot is well pared away, and the rudder is located below the helmsman. The keel is long enough to provide excellent directional stability and minimize leeway. Still, there's a lot of wetted surface by today's standard.

There were so many changes made to the Triton over its nine-year production run, one could fill a book trying to mention every one. Displacement, for example, is listed at 6,930 pounds until the last year or so, when it was changed to 8,400 pounds. Like most boats, if you actually weighed them they'd probably come in all over the place. The ballast-to-displacement ratio of the lighter models is 44 percent, which coupled with the Triton's fairly firm bilges, gives her plenty of stability.

An aesthetic problem of Alberg's smaller designs is caused by the low freeboard; the cabin trunk, to provide headroom, is tall and rather ungainly looking. There's six-foot-plus headroom in the main cabin, but the step in the coachroof reduces headroom forward to well below six feet.

The cockpit is long enough to lie down in, yet even when pooped (it happened to us), won't hold enough water to threaten the boat. The bridge deck, which adds a measure of safety for offshore work, certainly helps. Some of the earliest boats had side-opening seat lockers, which are dangerous unless modified to seal tightly.

The original rig was a three-quarter fractional rig, however, a somewhat shorter masthead rig was later available, though it didn't perform quite as well. A number of boats were built with yawl rigs (the main mast was shortened two feet and the boom one foot). The jumper struts on the fractional spars make the Triton easy to identify at a distance. The early Tritons were rigged with single lower shrouds, which proved inadequate. Richard Henderson, in his book, *Choice Yacht Designs*, reports that after about hull #120, double lower shrouds were standard and rigging kits supplied to owners of existing boats. We have several reports of rigging tangs failing; as with any old boat, we'd check the rigging carefully before subjecting the boat to much wind.

Despite the Triton's tall cabin, she is an attractive

boat, especially if viewed from the classic photographer's position at the quarters or off the bows.

Construction

Myth: The hull of the Triton is an inch thick. Not true. Despite the fish stories of owners, the hull thickness varies from about 3/8-inch at the rail to perhaps 3/4-inch in the keel area. When you drill holes for transducers, you'll be cutting through about 5/8-inch. Nevertheless, this is a good solid hull, though we have noticed, when examining hull plugs that some fibers were not completely wetted out.

Recently we heard from a former Triton owner in the Caribbean who lost his boat to Hurricane Hugo. Larger boats dragged down on it and carried it onto the beach at the St. Croix Yacht Club. "It finished up outside one boat," he wrote, "inside two others and with another two on top. That magnificently built hull was completely intact, albeit with a few gouges. The deck had always been weak and it was penetrated by the intruders; in places it had parted from the hull, another soft area. We pumped it out, water-blasted it, and sold it to someone who patched it up, sorted out and resurrected the mast, and now lives on board."

The Triton was built of conventional mat, cloth and woven roving, and polyester resin. Balsa core was used in the decks. Ballast, in boats after about hull #385, is cast lead lowered into the keel cavity and glassed over (which widened the keel two inches and deepened the draft about one inch). Voids in this area are commonplace. Water entering the cavity from a grounding theoretically should not enter the cabin, but repair is messy if straightforward. The earlier boats had external ballast. Which is better is the subject of constant debate. Internal ballast obviates the need for keel bolts, which are a source of concern and maintenance. On the other hand, grounding of an internally ballasted boat results in damage to the fiberglass hull, the repair of which is quite labor intensive.

Besides deck delamination, which is common to many old boats, a weakness of the Triton is insufficient load-carrying ability of the beams that support the deck-stepped mast. Because the walkway is on centerline, the main bulkhead and the one separating the head from the forward cabin cannot take all of the loads. A square beam was fastened to the forward bulkhead and run underneath the deck; it is

The most conspicuous shortcoming of the Triton's interior is the small galley. Most owners use a portable stove.

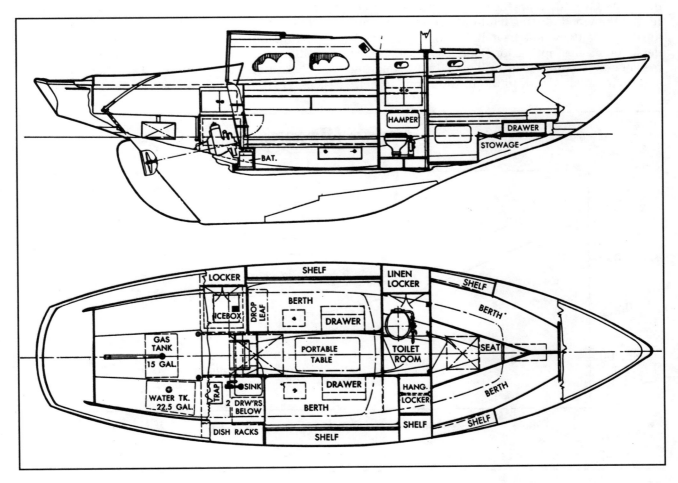

supported at either end by beams that run down the bulkhead to the hull. Nevertheless, numerous owners report caving of the deck underneath the mast. Repair means unstepping the spar, removing the beams and replacing them with new, stouter materials. Not an easy job, but not too tricky either.

Any boat as old as the Triton (more than a couple of decades) cannot hope to retain its original gel coat. Most Tritons have been painted, a few may have been sprayed with new gel coat.

In looking at Tritons for sale, the quality of the paint job may be a decisive factor. A professional or well-done home job is probably worth paying a little extra for. Be wary of the amateur paint job in which the owner has prepped with a sander run amok: telltale little half-moons visible when the light is right.

Our late model Triton was delivered standard with a lightning ground system, bronze Wilcox-Crittenden seacocks and generally good quality hardware. The South Coast winches are out-of-date now, but still serviceable. A nice set of self-tailers would be a great upgrade, but they're expensive. The spreader sockets are aluminum sand castings and can break without warning. Also check for electrolysis of the bronze rudder shoe.

The rudder was built of mahogany with bronze drift pins. Over the years the expansion and contraction of the wood (during haul-out) causes cracks to develop. Many owners have had to build new rudders, sometimes opting for fiberglass. A few have redesigned the rudders as well, usually by squaring and giving more depth to the trailing edge to help fight weather helm. This is the shape Alberg specified in a later redrawing of the Triton for Henderson's book.

Interior

The Triton's interior plan is simple. The 6' 3" settees in the main cabin double as sleeping berths. They are wider than normal, so it is often necessary to place a pillow behind your back for comfort. The head is private but small.

Furniture components are plywood covered with plastic veneer intended to look like teak. This makes for a dark cabin. You can paint the veneer, but it needs a good scuffing to hold paint, and will still chip. People have tried just about everything to get rid of it, including gluing mildew-resistant designer fabrics to the surfaces.

The sole is teak, supported by wooden, athwartship beams ("floors"). A wet bilge can cause these to rot, so inspect beneath the sole carefully.

The icebox also is built up out of plywood, with just an inch or two of styrofoam in the middle. Equally bad is its side-loading door. This method of construction and design won't keep ice for long, and again, many owners have rebuilt theirs. Unfortunately, the original location doesn't allow for much expansion, so you may need to relocate the box to the head of a settee. Any owner or prospective owner of a Triton should read *Spurr's Boatbook: Upgrading the Cruising Sailboat*, which details many of the modifications necessary.

Regarding the ice box, you'll also note that there's access to its upper shelf from the cockpit, which was

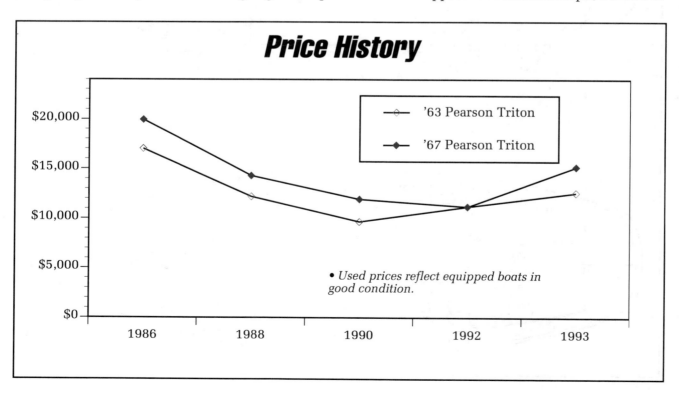

a clever way of grabbing beers, but does nothing to help retain ice.

The early Tritons did not have a headliner anywhere inside. Later, a gel-coated fiberglass liner was added to the main cabin, which improves its looks enormously. The forward cabin, in all but the last Tritons, was unfortunately left bare. You may see the original, dreaded, speckled spray paint jobs there, but most owners will have painted it over.

The best feature of the Triton's interior is the pair of forward-facing, opening portholes in the main cabin. These are situated at the step in the coachroof, and provide excellent ventilation down below as well as allowing you to see forward, a feature seldom found on other boats.

Engine

The 30-hp Atomic 4 was the standard powerplant, which provides more than enough power and easily drives the boat at hull speed—a little more than six knots. Access is not any better than any other boat of this size, but by removing the companionway ladder the front end can be worked on fairly easily. You'll need your kid to tighten the stuffing box.

So many of these engines were built, and so many are still in service, we won't bother to detail all the problems, solutions and repowering considerations attendant to the Atomic 4. Suffice to say that if you like tinkering with engines, the Atomic 4 is simple and can be successfully goaded to perform adequately. Some Tritons have been repowered, most often, we suspect, with Universal's four-cylinder diesel, which was billed as a drop-in replacement. To the best of our knowledge, some modification of the engine beds still is required. A major problem, of course, is corrosion due to sea water cooling.

Performance in reverse, as with nearly all boats of this type with long keels and propellers in apertures, is unpredictable. But that has nothing to do with the engine.

Performance

The Triton is surprisingly quick for her short waterline, which when the boat is heeled, lengthens nicely.

The boat heels rapidly to about 15 degrees, then stiffens satisfyingly. It's tough to push the rail under, though it can and has been done often. Water still won't enter the cockpit.

The nice thing about this type of boat is that you can carry on overcanvased without stalling the rudder. Just luff the mainsail a bit and even the gusts won't send you reeling out of control, as often happens with spade rudders. And it tracks well. Conse-

quently, the Triton is a very forgiving boat, especially for the beginner.

Because of its large mainsail and small foretriangle, the boat has weather helm when carrying working sails. Better to carry a #2 genoa and reef the main. That way you'll balance the sail plan better and find the helm easier to manage.

The PHRF rating of the Triton averages about 246. There aren't many boats slower in the U.S.S.A. listings. For comparison, how about a Tanzer 22 or Venture 25? The Tartan 27, a S&S design of similar vintage, rates 228. These figures can be misleading, however. We recall sailing away from an entire fleet of Pearson boats during one of the builder's rendezvous on Narragansett Bay. Whipping a Sabre 28 (PHRF—192) another day. Perhaps we were borne by some favorable and undetected current, which no doubt gives rise to those familar comments of "shows her heels to a lot of larger boats."

In any case, the rating does allow for competitive sailing. We placed first and second in our only two PHRF races. And for cruising, which is her forte, speed is just fine for such a short waterline.

Conclusion

Prices of Pearson Tritons peaked in the early 1980s at about $18,000. Since then, their value has dropped along with practically every other boat. And, of course, they're getting older, requiring more time and money to keep in shape or upgrade. Today you can buy a Triton for less than $10,000, which makes her a real bargain. (You'll pay in the low teens for a good one.) We feel fairly confident in saying that it is the smallest, most affordable offshore boat you can buy. At least one has circumnavigated, Jim Baldwin in *Atom*. And we know of many others that have made safe trans-oceanic passages. You should consider fitting storm shutters to the main cabin windows, as they are on the border of being too large.

It's too bad that Pearson is out of business, as they always had a good customer service department. Over the years we've obtained old parts from them, or referrals to the original suppliers, even foundries for bronze and aluminum castings.

If you're on a budget and willing to do your own upgrading, the Triton at least gives you a solid structure as a starting point. Given the strength of the hull, devotion of owners, and active owner's association (National Triton Association, 300 Spencer Ave., East Greenwich, RI 02818; (401) 884-1094) with active racing and rendezvous in most parts of the country, we fully expect to see the Triton well into the next century. **• PS**

Columbia 8.7

A good entry-level coastal cruiser that offers a large interior volume and long waterline for her length.

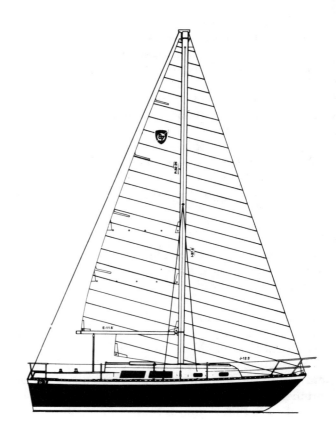

The Columbia 8.7 was one of the first of a series of modern small cruisers built by Columbia in the late 1970s. All were given metric length designations to distinguish them from Columbia's older boats, most of which were designed by Bill Tripp. The metric Columbias—the 7.6, 8.7, 9.6, 10.7 and 11.8—were drawn by Alan Payne, the Australian who designed the America's Cup challengers *Gretel* and *Gretel II,* two of the more competitive boats to participate in the Cup races prior to 1983.

Columbia labeled the entire Payne line as "widebody supercruisers," the implication being that the boats were designed exclusively for cruising, and that you were getting more boat per foot of length. In fact, the metric Columbias are a few inches beamier than most other "modern" cruisers of the late 1970s, and quite a bit wider than slightly older-style cruising boats of the same period. By way of comparison, the Cape Dory 28 has a beam of 8' 11"; the Ranger 28, 9' 7"; the Newport 28, 9' 7"; and the Cal 2-29, 9' 3".

The Columbia 8.7 had a checkered production history, spanning more than a decade. After her introduction in 1976, the 8.7 was built by a variety of companies, including Columbia as a division of Whittaker Corporation, Hughes Columbia, and Aura.

As with any boat that has been built by several different companies, opinions vary about who built the best Columbia 8.7. Our owners' surveys do not reveal any definite pattern of superiority among any of the three builders that were involved with the boat: owners of boats from all three companies tend to believe that their boats are better than earlier or later incarnations.

For better or worse, the Columbia 8.7 is modern in appearance, with a very straight sheer, pronounced

Specifications

LOA	28' 7"
LWL	23' 2"
Beam	10' 0"
Draft	4' 8"
Displacement	8,500 lbs.
Ballast	3,500 lbs.
Sail area	424 sq. ft.

forward overhang, and no overhang aft. The stern is decidedly unusual, with an exaggerated wineglass-section transom. This reduces the apparent size of the back end of the boat, which would otherwise look very ungainly since beam is carried well aft. From an aesthetic point of view, you either like the stern or you don't.

This is a plain vanilla boat. It has an off-white hull, off-white decks, and off-white non-skid. The only contrast is the aluminum toerail and a very few pieces of exterior teak trim. On the plus side, this means minimum maintenance: on the minus side, it means undistinguished appearance.

As is true of many small cruisers that strive to get more headroom without increasing freeboard to an ungainly height, the Columbia 8.7 has a fairly high,

Owners' Comments

"The Aura Columbia is very well built. I was quite surprised by her speed in anything but the lightest airs. Better livability than any boat her size."
— 1984 model in Pennsylvania

"Fittings are OK. Rigging wire size seems light to me. All-teak interior suits me. The bow isn't very high, but fine entry and topside flare keep her dry on deck. The stuffing box is difficult to reach. The boat is a good all-around cruiising boat. I know of one that has been singlehanded from Los Angeles to Hawaii. She steers easily, is fast off the wind, and maneuvers well under power."
— 1981 model in Ontario, Canada

"Exceptional space below for a 29-footer. Easy to sail, tracks well."
— 1979 model in Minnesota

"The boat is a dog in light air, but does well when the wind is up. She's so stiff that it's tough to bury the rail. A common problem prior to 1978 is profusely leaking ports. Be wary of cracks where the deck and cabin house join: cracks probably mean wet core material."
— 1978 model in Virginia

"The interior looks beautiful, but all fasteners are undersized on interior woodwork—they stripped and pulled out. The deck drains to the cockpit can't work—bad design, easily replumbed to through hulls above the waterline. Short berths might be a concern to taller people. Boat contains a lot of sloppy workmanship, most of which is easily corrected."
— 1978 model in New York

"The boat is actually faster than I thought it would be. It is not as fast as many other boats of the same length, but this is an acceptable trade-off for comfort in a cruising boat. It has incredible interior space for a boat 28' 7" long. It has turned out to be a very satisfactory boat. Yes. I'd buy it again, and no, I'm not ready to trade up."
— 1978 model in New Hampshire

"Poor window design is a notorious Columbia shortcoming. I have yet to find a boat in the same size range that provides as many amenities and as good an accommodation plan in a sound hull. She is well-designed and well-suited for coastal family cruising. She would not be my choice for racing or offshore."
— 1977 model in Minnesota

boxy deckhouse. The underwater form of the boat is unusual. It features a double-stepped skeg and bustle, which was a fairly radical way of thinking at the time. The lower skeg eliminates a prop strut, and provides protection for the prop.

Sailing Performance

You might think that a cruising boat designed by one of the more successful 12-meter designers would be a real screamer under sail. But the 8.7 is about 500 to 1,000 pounds heavier than other boats of her size and type, while the rig is about average in size. In winds of below about 10 knots, owners report that the boat is no faster than other boats of her type.

This mediocre light-air performance is borne out by the boat's PHRF ratings. In areas of light air, the boat rates as high as 222; in breezier sailing areas such as San Francisco, the rating drops as low as 192.

One big performance plus is the boat's balance under sail. A large number of owners say the boat is perfectly balanced on all points of sail, and in all wind velocities. Part of this probably stems from the shape of the stern. The pronounced tuck in the stern that creates the wineglass transom also creates a fairly symmetrical waterplane, which stays symmetrical as the boat heels.

The 8.7 is quite stiff. The hull is slab-sided amidships, with a hard bilge turn that is practically a chine. This form provides a lot of initial stability as well as increasing interior volume.

Since the shrouds are set well inboard, headsail sheeting angles can be quite narrow. The genoa track is tucked close alongside the cabin trunk, keeping it out of the way. For reaching, snatch blocks can be attached to the slotted aluminum toerail.

The mainsheet traveler is recessed in the aft end of the bridgedeck at the forward end of the cockpit. This puts the three mainsheet blocks fairly close to the end of the boom, reducing the amount of effort needed to trim the main. The mainsheet is trimmed directly on the traveler using a block and cam cleat. This is a good arrangement for a boat this size. The helmsman can actually reach all the sheets, so the boat can easily be sailed by one person.

Originally, the boat was fitted with a tiller, which comes up through the deck at the aft end of the cockpit. This keeps the cockpit uncluttered. Some later boats were equipped with pedestal wheel steering, which eats up a lot of cockpit space.

There is simply no reason to have wheel steering on a well-balanced boat this size, other than some ego satisfaction that comes from thinking you're sailing a bigger boat. If you want to sit outboard to see the sails better, get a tiller extension. It's simpler and cheaper to install than a wheel.

You will find different rigs in the boat depending on when and where that particular boat was built, even though all have the same sail plan.

Aura-built 8.7s use a Cinkel rig, the extrusions and fittings of which are almost identical to those of Isomat. Cinkel spars are painted rather than anodized.

The original rig was neither anodized nor painted, so you may find corrosion in an older mast. Very early in the production run, there was a free factory retrofit which modified the masthead shroud tangs. It will be next to impossible to determine if this has been done on any particular mast, so you should carefully examine the masthead for any signs of metal fatigue or unusual wear.

All in all, the 8.7 is well-balanced and well-mannered under sail, though under-powered in light air. The deck layout is fairly performance-oriented, but this works just as well for cruising as it does for racing. The 8.7 was never touted as a racer, and it isn't. But it has very adequate performance for family cruising and daysailing.

Engine

A wide variety of engines have been fitted in the Columbia 8.7. The original engine was the gas Atomic Two, with a Volvo MD6B diesel as an option. Very few boats probably have the Atomic Two. By 1978, the larger Atomic Four gas engine was standard, with the Volvo diesel still an option.

When Hughes Columbia took over production from Columbia, they retained the Atomic Four, but changed the optional diesels to the Volvo MD-7A, with 13 hp, or the Yanmar 2QM15, with 15 hp. A few boats were also fitted with the Yanmar 3GMD, a three-cylinder engine rated at 22.5 hp.

With the Atomic Two, we think the boat would be underpowered by modern standards. Likewise, some owners of the smaller Volvo diesel consider that engine to be a little small.

Engine choice is always a problem, and seems even more so in a small boat like the 8.7. The weight

The interior of the 8.7 is large for a 28 1/2' boat, with plenty of headroom. Ventilation is not very good in older boats, though later 8.7s had opening ports as an option.

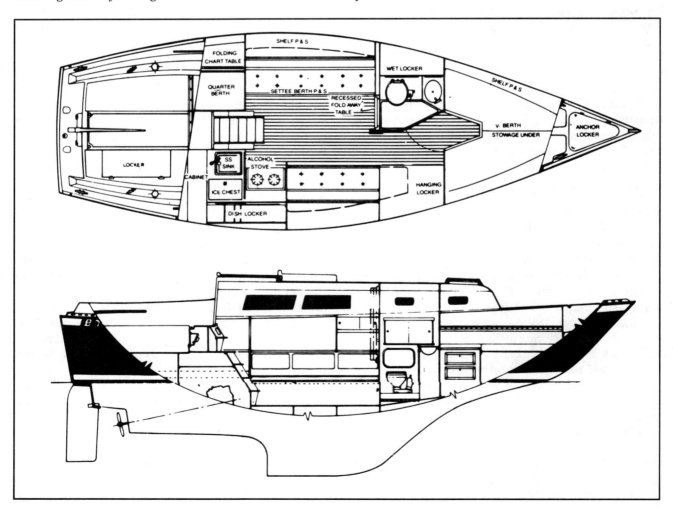

of a larger engine can have a negative effect on sailing performance and trim in a small boat, and the greater fuel requirements of a bigger engine reduce cruising range for a given fuel capacity. At the same time, small boats seem really sensitive to being underpowered, particularly when trying to make way into a head sea. The small boat pitches more, losing forward momentum, and always seems to be the wrong size for the wave pattern.

Engine cost is a factor, too. Larger engines cost more than smaller engines. Adding $500 or $1,000 to the price of a 29' boat by putting in a larger engine undoubtedly cost some sales, particularly to first-time buyers who may not have understood the change in performance that may come from an extra 3-5 hp.

In a boat, the difference between 13 hp and 15 hp may mean a difference of a half knot in cruising speed, which can be significant if you're in a hurry to get somewhere. It can mean even more difference in power and speed when bucking a 3' chop and 25-knot headwind.

The Yanmar 2QM15 is probably the best engine choice for the boat. One owner reported breaking two prop shafts when the shaft separated from the coupling in reverse. We have heard of similar problems with some Yanmar engines in other boats from this same period. We suspect the problem is related to early Yanmar engine mounts. Another part of the problem is probably the shaft itself, which is only 3/4" in diameter, and has an unsupported run of about 4' from the transmission to the stuffing box.

Engine instruments are mounted in a recess in the cockpit under the bridgedeck, while controls are mounted on the side of the cockpit well. This is a pretty good location for the instruments on a coastal cruiser, but it would be too close to the cockpit sole for an offshore cruiser that might take a lot of water into the cockpit in severe weather.

Engine access for service is excellent, although it requires disassembling the engine box behind the companionway ladder.

Construction

Boats from Columbia are known as middle-of-the-road production sailboats. The metric-series boats are different in many construction details from earlier Columbias, but owners' responses to our survey suggest that these later boats were not significantly better or worse than their predecessors.

The Columbia 8.7 hull is an uncored laminate with integral longitudinal stringers. The interior is built up of plywood, rather than based on a fiberglass molding or body pan with wood trim. A plywood interior properly glassed to the hull can add significant stiffness.

Because the plywood interior is a structural component, you must make a careful survey of every secondary bond in the boat. A secondary bond is any bond made after the original hull lamination. In order to achieve strength comparable to the rest of the hull, careful surface preparation and workmanship are required for secondary bonds. Poor secondary bonds are unfortunately not rare in production sailboats, even though there is nothing in our owners' surveys of the 8.7 to suggest that it is either better or worse than any other boat in this respect.

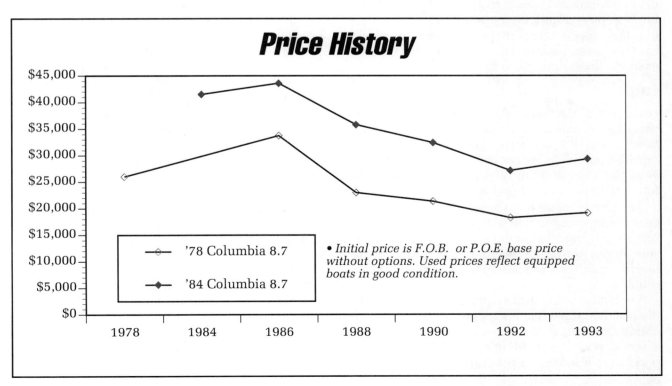

Price History

Legend:
- '78 Columbia 8.7
- '84 Columbia 8.7

• *Initial price is F.O.B. or P.O.E. base price without options. Used prices reflect equipped boats in good condition.*

Several owners of early model 8.7s report leaking around non-opening, recessed cabin windows. Leaking ports should show up as water stains on the inside of the teak-veneered cabin trunk. A long-term cure for leaking ports requires complete removal and rebedding: recaulking is at best a temporary fix.

According to our reader surveys, the 8.7 has suffered from a common ailment in the production boatbuilding industry: inconsistency of detailing. Some owners rave about finishing detail such as interior joinerwork and systems installation, some complain about its mediocre quality. Some of these differences are in the eye of the beholder, while others are likely to be real. No production boat, no matter how carefully construction is supervised, will have absolutely consistent quality from one hull to another.

Companionway dropboards and hatch are teak-veneered plywood. While dimensionally stable, teak plywood has to be kept varnished when exposed to the weather, or the veneer will very quickly erode away after a few cleanings.

Owners report that cockpit and deck drainage is a problem. An aluminum toerail can trap water on deck, and improperly-designed cockpit seats can pocket water on the leeward side.

Gelcoat is of typical production boat quality. Some owners report inconsistent gelcoat quality, crazing, and blistering, but the reports are average in frequency.

Another problem mentioned by several owners is rudder delamination. This is fairly common in two-piece rudders, and repair involves cleaning and drying the cracked area, then glassing over it. Merely forcing epoxy or polyester putty into the joint is not a suitable repair. Check for play between the rudder blade and rudder stock at the same time that you examine the rudder blade for flaws.

Interior

A big part of the "widebody supercruiser" concept was to get maximum interior volume in minimum length. The 8.7 achieves this by her slab-sided topsides and wide beam carried well aft. In fact, in both plan view and profile the boat looks like a 31-footer with the stern chopped off.

The interior of the 8.7 is big for a 28 1/2' boat. Main cabin headroom is about 6' 1", and the headroom is carried out almost to the sides of the cabin. The cabin sole slopes upward forward of the mast, so that headroom falls off quickly in the head and forward cabin.

Ventilation belowdecks is poor. As originally built, the boat had three fixed ports per side, and a single aluminum-framed hatch over the forward cabin. There were no cowl vents or opening ports. Opening ports were optional on pre-Aura Hughes Columbia boats, and four opening ports— one each in head and main cabin, two in forward cabin—were standard on Aura boats. Dorade vents over the head and passageway opposite were options on pre-Aura Columbia boats.

Because the original fixed ports were large, odd-shaped, and recessed in the cabin trunk, installing opening ports in older boats is a problem. There is room, however, for a double-opening aluminum-framed hatch over the main cabin between the main hatch and the mast, which would help ventilation in good weather. Cowl vents in dorade boxes can also be installed on either side of the sliding companionway hatch over the aft part of the main cabin.

Because the forward V-berths come almost to a point, they will not be comfortable for two people over 6' tall. With the V-berth insert in place, the entire forward cabin becomes a reasonably large double berth, although you must remove the insert to get to the stowage areas below.

On a boat this size, it makes more sense to make the head the full width of the boat than to try to maintain the big-boat layout of the head off to one side. On the 8.7, the head is still further reduced in size to make it easier to get into the forward cabin. This is not a head compartment for large people.

Opposite the head is a hanging locker and a three-drawer bureau. While drawers waste a lot of space, they are the best way to stow folded clothes. You don't see too many drawers on boats this size. The foot of the starboard settee berth extends forward under the bureau. The backs of both settees swing up and out of the way to make wider berths for sleeping—a good design feature.

Aft of the port settee, there is a quarterberth tucked under the cockpit. Unlike the quarterberths on many small boats, the head of the berth on the 8.7 is not under the cockpit itself, so you won't get claustrophobic. The rudimentary fold-down chart table over the head of the quarterberth is nothing to write home about, but few 28 1/2-footers have anything better. A real nav station ain't usually in the cards on a boat this size.

Pushing the starboard settee forward leaves the starboard aft end of the main cabin free for the galley, and it's really a pretty good galley for a boat this size. A deep single Polar sink is standard—much better than the toy sinks frequently seen on small boats. There is also room for a two-burner gimballed stove with oven, which is a genuine luxury, although you won't find anything but an alcohol stove unless an owner has changed it. Owners comment that the insulation in the icebox leaves something to be desired.

Aft of the sink and icebox is a long locker with sliding doors, plus smaller lockers. All in all, this is a very serviceable galley for a 28' boat.

Despite the lack of ventilation and the relatively dark teak joinerwork, this is a good interior—definitely a major selling point when the boat was introduced. It still looks modern today.

Conclusions

When the Columbia 8.7 was introduced, one of its big selling points was the large interior volume and long waterline for the boat's overall length. In the last decade, the proportions of the 8.7 have become the norm, not the exception, for boats just under 30'.

Frequently, interior volume is one of the things you give up when buying an older boat. The aesthetic of the older small cruiser called for fairly short waterline, long ends, and relatively narrow beam. The Columbia 8.7 and her sisters were not the first boats to feature more volume in less length, but they did it with fewer compromises than a lot of more "modern" cruising boats.

The Columbia 8.7 does not look particularly dated, either inside or out. She is certainly not classic, either, despite what anyone may claim about her unusual stern shape.

Performance is about what you would expect from a small modern cruiser: only fair in light air, lively in breezes over 10 knots. Because of her excellent balance under sail and relative stability, the boat would make a good entry-level coastal cruiser, even for relatively inexperienced sailors. The boat is not handicapped by poor hull shape or bad deck layout, which run rampant in small boats touted as cruisers rather than racers. Unfortunately, the term "cruising sailboat" has become equated with "slow." That is true for a lot of small boats, but it need not be if designer and builder have done their homework.

Columbia has high name recognition, even though its boats were only middle-of-the-road in quality. When you want to sell a Columbia 8.7, you won't get blank stares. If we were shopping for a used 8.7, we'd choose the latest model we could afford.   • **PS**

Jeanneau Arcadia

A sleek, modern European-style cruiser from one of the world's largest boat builders.

A mixture of old and new, of reality and hype, seems to characterize the Jeanneau company and its boats. A bit of old-fashioned attention to detail; a bit of high-tech stamp-em-out production. A bit of old-fashioned engineering; a bit of "to hell with tradition, let's make this boat different."

To most Americans, the Jeanneau boats seem to have appeared suddenly, but the company has been around since l956. Aggressive entry into the American market resulted when Lear Siegler bought Jeanneau and the other Bangor Punta boat companies (Cal, O'Day, Ranger) in 1983.

Like most of the Jeanneaus, the Arcadia (pronounced "Are-caw-dee-yah") is rare in America— only a few were imported—but, also like most of the Jeanneaus, the total production run is incredible— the factory popped out 600 completed boats in the Arcadia's first two years. The only American company that could even aspire to such numbers in a 30-footer is Catalina, and they produce a miniscule number of models compared to Jeanneau.

A notable thing about Jeanneau is the diversity of designers—almost all "big names," at least in Europe, and almost all with grand-prix racing credentials: Guy Dumas, Doug Peterson, Philippe Briand, Jacques Fauroux, the Joubert/Nivelt team.

The designer of the Arcadia is Tony Castro, new to Americans but an established designer in Europe. Of Portuguese descent, Castro began his work with Ron Holland in Ireland, then set up his own shop in 1981 and achieved success designing successful IOR racing machines. Now a British citizen, he has two other designs in production at Jeanneau, and a third—an IOR half-tonner—scheduled for production soon.

The design of the Arcadia is not IOR. We would call it "moderate modern," of relatively light displacement and shallow hull, with a high aspect ratio keel, separated spade rudder, and beamy hull.

Her appearance is, well, "European." The flat sheer, a doghouse that slopes forward into the foredeck, long black windows (you can't call them "ports"), and blunt ends make up that "European" look which is decidedly—almost blatantly—non-traditional. "Thoroughly modern" is a term that appears several times in Jeanneau's advertising blurbs.

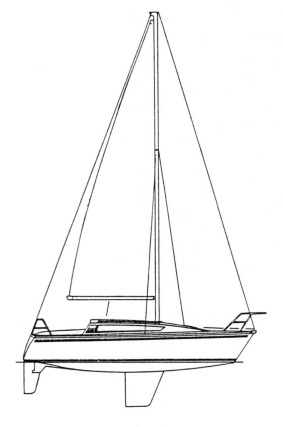

Specifications

LOA	29' 6"
LWL	24' 5"
Beam	10' 4"
Draft	4' 3"/5' 4" (cb/keel)
Displacement	6,175 lbs.
Ballast	2,360 lbs.
Sail area	332 sq. ft.

Construction

In contrast to the boat's image, the construction of the Arcadia is anything but high-tech.

The hull is standard hand laid fiberglass mat and roving; the deck is standard hand laid fiberglass with balsa core in spots. The balsa-core "spots" seemed to be less extensive than normal (we couldn't examine much of the deck molding because of the interior ceiling liner), but the deck was stiff enough underfoot. The deck hardware we could examine was through-bolted with big washers, but there were no backing plates on anything.

The hull-to-deck joint typifies the construction of the boat. The joint appears to be a standard inward-turning flange on the hull, on which the deck molding rests. Then 1/4" stainless bolts are set through an aluminum toerail as well as the deck and the hull flange.

Pretty normal so far, but Jeanneau finishes off the joint on the inside by laying a thick layer of fiberglass over everything—from the hull, over the seam, covering the bolts, onto the deck. It looks strong—a good way to build a decent hull-to-deck joint on a fast-moving production line. The reservation we have about it is in repairs—if the joint is damaged, it will be tough to examine thoroughly and tough to fix. Similarly, the joint should never leak, but if it does, tracking down the source will be nearly impossible. Generally, the glasswork and gelcoat look good; the two hulls we examined were smooth and fair.

The boat's strength and stiffness probably come from Jeanneau's practice of bonding everything to everything else. Not only are the athwartship bulkheads bonded to the hull and deck with fiberglass tape, but cabinet fronts are bonded to hull and bulkheads, cabinet sides are bonded to fronts and bulkheads, the head door frame is bonded to the engine box frame which is bonded to the hull and to the cockpit, and so on. The whole interior is obviously prefabricated in typical production line fashion, but we've never seen another production boat in which the interior parts were so much fiberglassed to each other and to the hull. It seems like a good low-tech method of acquiring stiffness without skeleton framing or coring the hull.

Like many of the Jeanneaus, the Arcadia comes with either a centerboard or an external keel—about 70% having been keel models. The keel is unusual in two respects. First, rather than lead, it's iron, coated with fiberglass to prevent corrosion. Second, the keelbolts are not vertical and on centerline in the normal fashion. Instead, they are set in pairs, angled from the sides of the keel inward so that, inside the hull, the bolts, were they long enough, would converge and touch. Further, once the keel is bolted on, a heavy layer of fiberglass is laid in the bilge to fully cover the bolts. As with the hull-to-deck joint, this looks strong and leak proof, but again we would be concerned about the difficulty of repairs and finding leaks following a hard grounding. The keel that we examined was fair and well finished. We did not inspect a centerboard model.

The spade rudder is supported by a small skeg; the one we saw was well finished except for a rough trailing edge. Tiller steering is standard on the Arcadia, but both boats we examined had the optional Plastimo wheel steering, with a "European size" wheel, about 24" diameter. Most Americans like a much bigger wheel; unfortunately a larger one could not be fitted without major modifications to the cockpit seats.

The rig generally looks to be pretty standard issue—masthead rigged sloop, with upper and aft-lower shrouds and a "baby stay" forward. The boat we examined had double spreaders, whereas the company literature and photos show a single-spreader mast. The company does advertise an optional tall "lake" rig, but this is designed only for European inland lakes and would be unsuitable for coastal, Great Lakes, or offshore sailing. None were imported into the U.S.

The upper shroud chainplates are anchored on a transverse overhead frame which begins at a settee bulkhead on the hull and then extends up over the cabin and down to the hull on the opposite side, with a compression post in the middle of the cabin under the mast. The frame is bonded to the hull and deck and should provide adequate strength and mast support. The lower shroud chainplates are anchored to a similar frame, bonded only to the hull and side decks.

A final note on the Jeanneau's construction. We asked the dealer who was showing us one of the Arcadias to pick out one thing that made the Jeanneau different from the three American brands he also handles. "They are dry," he said. "I don't know how they do it, but they just don't leak, either from the top of the deck downward or from the bottom of the hull upward." From a dealer who has sponged out a lot of bilges before bringing customers on board, those are words of praise.

Handling Under Power

The two Arcadias that we looked at had two-banger diesels—one a Yanmar, the other a Volvo (production line changes, again). Sales literature lists an outboard version—thankfully no such monster is likely to be imported—and a version with either a one or a two cylinder Yanmar. For a 6000+ pound boat, we would consider the one cylinder very marginal and recommend the two cylinder, along with the optional folding prop.

The engine installation is well done (stringers and beds bonded to everything in sight) with sound-proofing on the compartment walls, a waterlift muffler, and a seven gallon fuel tank. There is good accessibility to the engine through the aft cabin and through the removable companionway, except that the dipstick on the Yanmar is hard to get at.

Two details impressed us. The engine compartment has a small electric bilge pump as standard equipment in the sump below the prop shaft's packing gland—one place that is likely to have water. And, in the front of the companionway steps that open onto the engine, there's a 2" hole with a plastic cover, the function of which baffled not only us but also the first person who showed us the boat. Finally, the dealer explained its purpose: in the event of an engine room fire, pull the plastic cover, insert the working end of a fire extinguisher, and discharge it. Eminently more practical than pulling off the companionway steps and feeding more oxygen to the flames.

Under power with the folding prop, the boat handled satisfactorily, backing where we wanted to back it, with adequate power in forward and reverse. Visibility from behind the wheel is decent, but there is no comfortable place to sit aft and the wheel is too small to reach from the sidedeck. The engine had no more vibration than you'd expect from a two-cylinder diesel and was a bit quieter than other boats, probably because of the insulation in the engine compartment.

Handling Under Sail

We were able to sail the Arcadia for only about an hour; unfortunately, we have too few reader responses to make many valid judgements about the Arcadia's performance under a variety of conditions (most of our owner's responses are based on a single season's sailing, or less).

In our limited experience, we found that she went to weather, reached, and ran very much like other contemporary racer-cruisers. She pounded a bit in a short chop, as you might expect from her shallow hull design, but we saw no other bad habits. (Her sails are from a small French loft, "Ton," and are adequate. Racers will want to get better.)

Her PHRF rating of 150 suggests that overall performance under sail is about midway between older racer-cruisers like the Pearson 30 or Tartan 30 and the newer racer-cruisers like the Santana 30/30 or the S2 9.1. We were hoping that—as a Tony Castro design—she might be a rocketship, but she's not. She will be a fast cruiser, and an owner will be able to race her under PHRF.

Deck Layout

With inboard shrouds, wide sidedecks, and the sloping cabin top, the Arcadia is easy to move around on and to work under sail. We only noted two problems: first, the foredeck becomes very narrow—an impediment to easy foresail and anchor handling that is all too common in modern designs. Second, the cockpit was uncomfortable—the seats a little too narrow, the backs too vertical, and the footwell maybe a little too deep. We also had trouble reaching the small wheel from either the windward or leeward sidedecks where you would normally sit while racing.

Deck fittings are generally good quality and adequately sized, with everything necessary to race the boat except spinnaker gear coming as standard equipment. We did feel that the designer had not quite thought through crew positions for working the boat—what should be done at the mast, what from the cockpit—surprising for a contemporary IOR designer who must attend to those details. Most owners will probably rearrange things after a season's experience.

The non-skid is average, but there are some nice details on deck such as the twin bow rollers for anchor handling, the sturdy latch on the anchor

The interior layout of the Arcadia is decidedly non-traditional. It has its drawbacks: the sloping deck house makes for poor headroom, the V-berth is too small, and there's little headroom over the settees.

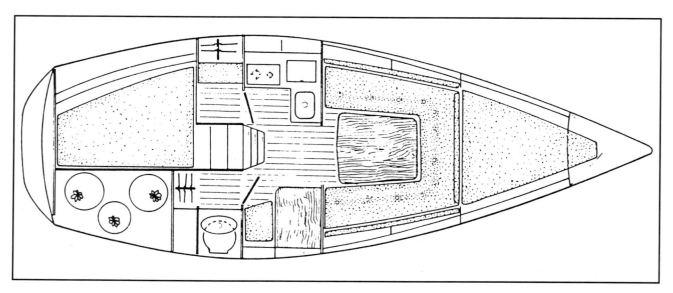

locker, and the large mooring cleats. There's a space at the back of the cockpit for life raft stowage and for propane bottles, and a stowage bracket for a horse-shoe buoy built into the stern pulpit. The stern pulpit opens up to a folding stainless ladder.

Belowdecks

It is "downstairs" that Jeanneau really spits in the eye of tradition—not just in the Arcadia but in most of their models. Most obvious is the layout, with the Arcadia's head and the owner's double-berth cabin packed into the rear third of the boat, partly under the cockpit. Both head and owner's cabin are a little cramped, but for a smallish 30-footer, it's surprising they are possible at all.

The rest of the cabin is wide open, with a small galley and navigation table opposite each other, then settee berths on either side of a fold-up centerline table, then a crawl-in forward berth.

We noted three drawbacks. First, the forward V-berth is too short for adults. Second, anyone over 5' 8" or so cannot sit upright on the settee berths without banging the overhead. Third, the standing headroom at the aft end of the cabin disappears as you walk forward under the sloping deckhouse.

This last item we really find hard to understand, since headroom is something most people are looking for, and the only apparent reason not to have it in a 30-footer is to satisfy the "style" of the sloping deck house. (There is a bit of a weight saving that might be important in a racer but hardly valuable in the Arcadia.) Oddly, the same headroom problem exists even in the 34' Jeanneau Sunrise that we looked at.

The interior of the Arcadia is all woody and undoubtedly one of the strong selling points at boat shows. Teak-faced plywood is all over the place. We thought the veneer work was good for production line work, especially where the veneer covered the plywood edges—for example in the window cut-outs. The wood has a light coating of varnish, even inside lockers and drawers. The overhead has a soft vinyl covering that looks a little better than bare fiberglass. Inside hardware—like hinges and latches—is noticeably better than on the usual American production boat.

A strange detail is the manual bilge pump whose handle sticks out of the side of the chart table into the middle of the cabin.

Oddly, the boats we inspected were not "Americanized." Most owners would likely want shore power, but this is not a company option—it will have to be installed by the owner or dealer. The galley stove comes with hook-ups for butane which will have to be converted to propane. And many Americans looking at a 30-footer might expect a shower, which will be difficult to install on this boat.

Conclusions

Overall the Jeanneau Arcadia surprised us. We were expecting a boat comparable in quality to mid-line American production boats; we found the Jeanneau to be somewhat better in construction and in many details. Being fond of tradition, we have a problem with the style of most of the Jeanneaus, including the Arcadia, but ultimately style is a tenuous criticism of a boat, unless it is truly ugly.

• PS

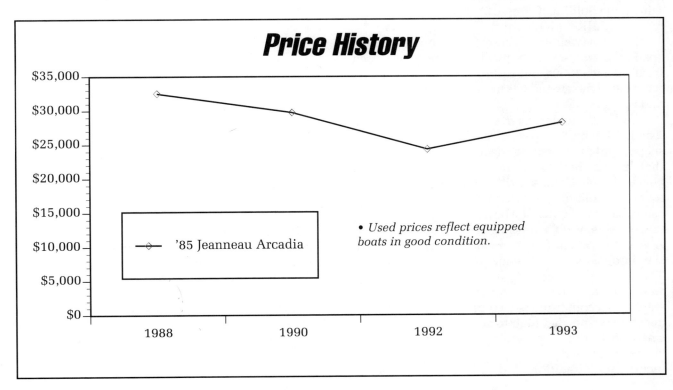

Price History

• *Used prices reflect equipped boats in good condition.*

Legend: ◇ '85 Jeanneau Arcadia

Pearson 30

A successful design that's good for both club racing and short-term cruising, the 30 is a good investment.

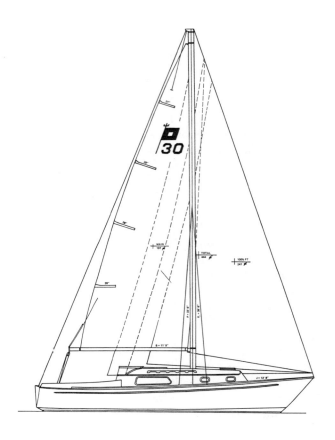

The Bill Shaw-designed Pearson 30 entered production in late 1971. By January 1, 1980, 1,185 of the fin-keel, spade-rudder sloops had been built in the company's Portsmouth, Rhode Island plant. Peak production years were 1973 and 1974, with about 200 boats produced in each of those years. Production tapered off to about 70 boats per year in the last three years of production, and the P30 was discontinued with the 1981 models, later replaced in the Pearson line by the Pearson 303.

The Pearson 30 was designed as a family cruiser and daysailer with a good turn of speed. The boat is actively raced throughout the country, however, with some holding IOR certificates, and many more racing in PHRF, MORC, and one-design fleets.

The P30's swept-back fin keel and scimitar-shaped spade rudder are fairly typical of racing boat design from the late 1960s and early 1970s but look somewhat dated next to today's high aspect ratio fin keels and rudders.

The boat's underwater shape is somewhat unusual, The hull is basically dinghy-shaped. The sections aft of the keel are deeply veed, however, so that deadrise in the forward and after sections of the boat is similar. Coupled with a fairly narrow beam by today's standards, this provides a hull form which is easily balanced when the boat is heeled—an important consideration in this relatively tender 30-footer. Above the water the Pearson 30 carries out the standard Pearson credo—moderation in all matters. The hull has a moderate amount of conventional sheer curvature with modest overhangs at bow and stern. The cabin trunk is well proportioned but is of necessity somewhat high to achieve headroom in a small boat without excessive freeboard. Styling is clean and modern with—thankfully—no attempt to incorporate "traditional" detailing. The boat's ap-

Specifications

LOA	29' 9"
LWL	25' 0"
Beam	9' 6"
Draft	5' 0"
Displacement	8,320 lbs.
Ballast	3,560 lbs.
Sail area	444 sq. ft.

pearance may not stir the soul, but neither will it offend the eye.

The Pearson 30 has a well-proportioned masthead rig. The mainsail comprises 44% of the working sail area, more than is found on many modern "racer-cruisers," but a reasonable proportion for a true multi-purpose boat.

Base price in 1971 was $11,750. By November 1979, base price had jumped to $28,300. The builder's option list included about $8,000 worth of goodies for the gadget addict, including wheel steering, a LectraSan toilet system, and a $500 stereo system. Average 1979 sailaway price was about $35,000. The average 1992 price for that 1979 model is $20-$21,000.

After years of using the Palmer 22 horsepower and 30 horsepower Atomic Four gasoline engines, the late model Pearson 30s came with a two-cylinder Universal diesel, which weighs about the same as the Atomic Four.

Construction

Pearson is one of the oldest fiberglass boatbuilders in the country. Their Triton and Alberg 35 are two of the classic "modern" boats. With over 20 years of fiberglass boatbuilding experience, Pearson has solved most of the construction problems that seem to plague some builders.

The layup schedule of the Pearson 30 did not change during the production life of the boat. The hull structure is a hand layup in a one-piece mold of alternating plies of 1 1/2-ounce mat and 18-ounce woven roving. Two layers of omnidirectional mat are used beneath the gelcoat to prevent "printthrough" of the first roving layer, an unsightly and unfortunately common problem with some builders.

Below the waterline, the Pearson 30 hull is a solid seven-ply layup, yielding an average bottom thickness of .29". Along the keel, the plies from each side are overlapped, doubling the thickness in this critical area. The topside skin is five plies of mat and roving, with an average thickness of .21". The deck is a fiberglass/balsa sandwich.

The hull-to-deck joint is made by glassing together the external flanges of the hull and deck. This chemical bond is backed up by stainless steel self-tapping screws at intervals of approximately 4". The flanges are covered by an extruded plastic rubrail holder, covered by the familiar Pearson soft vinyl rubrail.

One Pearson 30 owner who races his boat reported that the hull-to-deck joint had opened slightly at the bow from excessive headstay tension. No other owner reported this problem, and examination of a large number of Pearson 30s failed to reveal another hull with this problem. Excessive headstay and backstay loading is often found in racing boats and can damage any boat not designed for this type of loading.

The Pearson 30's spade rudder has provided the only recurrent problem with the boat. The rudder stock consists of a thick-walled stainless steel pipe. The stock enters the hull through a slightly larger diameter fiberglass rudder tube, which projects above the waterline to the cockpit sole, eliminating the need for a stuffing box. The rudder stock rides in two Delrin bushings, one at the top and one at the bottom of the fiberglass rudder tube. Wear in these Delrin bushings causes play to develop in the rudder stock. This wear can be accelerated by failing to tie off the tiller when the boat is at rest, thus letting the stock turn from the natural motion of the boat.

The bushings are owner-replaceable when the boat is hauled out, requiring removal of the tiller fitting and dropping the rudder through the bottom of the boat. The bushings can then be pried out and replaced.

The frequency with which rudder bushings must be replaced varies with the amount of use the boat receives. Pearson considers the bushings an item of routine maintenance. We would recommend that they be replaced whenever any slop develops. About 30% of the boats we examined showed significant bushing wear.

We also found annoying and excessive play in the tiller fitting which might sometimes be confused with bushing wear. Correcting this requires shimming or bushing the cast aluminum tiller socket.

The first Pearson 30s had an aluminum pipe rudder stock rather than stainless. Several rudders broke off as a result of corrosion at the narrow gap between rudder and hull. To Pearson's credit, the firm recalled and replaced the rudders on the approximately 200 boats built with aluminum stocks. The error in using aluminum stocks was far outweighed by the company's willingness to correct a potentially serious problem.

The Pearson 30's 3,560 lbs of lead ballast is encapsulated in the fiberglass keel molding, This avoids the necessity of keel bolts but makes the keel more vulnerable to grounding damage.

The deck-stepped, polyurethane-painted aluminum mast is supported by the main cabin bulkhead and an oak compression column. This column is glassed into the top of the keel.

If coaming-mounted genoa turning blocks are installed—and they are necessary for genoas larger than 150%—it is essential that large backing plates be used. Some of these blocks which were improperly installed by owners have pulled through the coamings, which are a relatively thin solid fiberglass molding.

Through hull fittings appear to be bedded with silicone, a less than ideal choice for underwater fittings. Proper seacocks or gate valves are installed in all underwater openings, although none are installed with backing blocks, which is highly recommended. Chainplates, where visible, are properly bolted to primary structural bulkheads.

Much of the interior construction is bonded to the hull, including the molded fiberglass floor pan and molded headliner. Molded hull liners are relatively expensive, and are seen less and less frequently in modern stock boat construction. Interior surfaces are teak- or Formica-covered plywood. Exposed plywood edges are covered by glued-on plastic trim, which, we noted, has often pulled off, even on new boats.

Seat back lockers have friction catches, which unless properly aligned can let the seat back/locker doors come open when the boat is heeled. The cabin sole is non-skid fiberglass. Exposed interior fiberglass surfaces are now covered by foam-backed tan basket weave vinyl which enhances appearance.

Pearson hull strength has never been questioned. Their boats tend to have slightly heavier scantlings than average, which is hardly a shortcoming. The construction of all their boats, including the Pearson 30, is of above average stock boat quality.

Handling Under Sail

The Pearson 30 is an active sailor's boat. We find it responsive, and a pleasure to sail. It is also tender, and very sensitive to the proper sail combination. All owners responding consider the boat to be somewhat "tippy." The P30 does, in fact, put the rail under quite easily.

In 15 knots apparent wind, we find that the boat is almost overpowered with the full main and 150% genoa. Gusts of 12-14 knots bury the rail, slowing the boat. The P30 does not, however, carry any substantial weather helm even when overpowered. Any tendency to round up or spin out can usually be controlled by a strong hand on the tiller and easing the mainsail.

As you would expect in a dinghy-hulled, spade-rudder fin-keeler, the boat is quick in tacks. It is so quick, in fact, that the jib sheet winch grinder is likely to be growled at by the skipper for being too slow. The winch grinder is also handicapped by the difficulty of his bracing himself properly to exert full power on the winches, a common problem on production boats of almost any size. We strongly recommend the optional Lewmar #40 jib sheet winches, whether the boat is used for racing or cruising. The standard halyard winches are perfectly adequate. The optional roller-bearing mainsheet traveler is practically a must for effective trim of the mainsail although it does reduce cockpit room.

Although the Pearson 30 was not specifically designed for racing, some of the boats have had very successful racing careers. Pete Lawson's *Syrinx* won the Three-quarter Ton North American Championship in 1972. Under IOR Mk IIIA, the boat's average rating has dropped nearly two feet, making the boat rate just over Half Ton. The boat is still a successful club racer and is hotly raced as a one-design class in some areas, including Chesapeake Bay. Pearson 30s also race in MORC classes, and the boat has been

The interior layout of the Pearson 30 is about average for a 30-footer, with too many berths. However, the cabin is light and airy, with good storage and headroom.

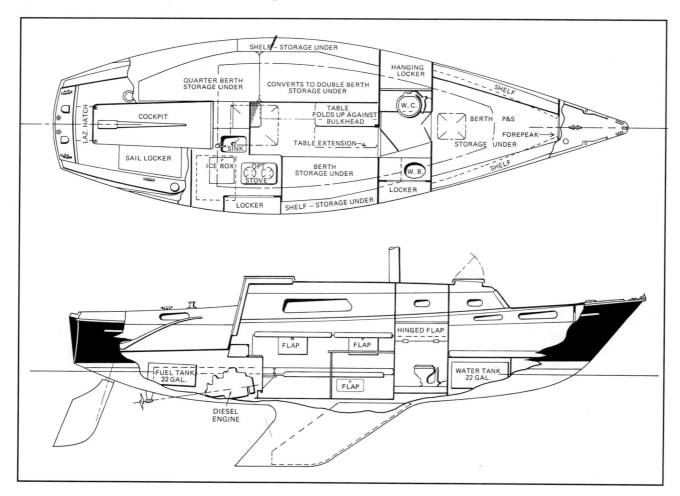

measured for USYRU Measurement Handicap System (MHS) for hull standardization.

Owners report that typically only about 10% of their sailing time is devoted to racing. Another 10% is spent cruising, while fully 80% of sailing time is spent daysailing.

The boat will be sailed quite differently by racers and cruisers. Experienced Pearson 30 racers keep the boat moving by reefing the main and carrying on with larger headsails as the breeze pipes up.

Cruisers will find it more comfortable to sail with smaller headsails and more mainsail even though there will be some sacrifice in performance on the wind. A good selection of headsails—at least a 150% genoa, a #3 genoa, and a working jib—is necessary. A small heavy-weather jib would be a good idea for boats that cruise in exposed waters.

Handling Under Power

The Pearson 30's underwater configuration creates a boat that maneuvers remarkably well under power. The P30 easily turns in a circle its own length in diameter. The standard two-cylinder Universal diesel pushes the boat well, albeit with some vibration, although it lacks the power of the old Atomic Four when punching through a chop.

A strong arm on the tiller is required when backing down under power. "It's a tough boat to handle in reverse. It can tear your arm off," said one experienced Pearson 30 sailor. The aft-raking unbalanced rudder will easily go hard over if too much helm is applied while backing down, and an unprepared or off-balance helmsman could be thrown off his feet by

the sweeping tiller under these conditions. Applying minimum rudder corrections reduces this tendency, but a rudder of this type, which is free to rotate through 360 degrees, can pose a real threat to the unwary.

Deck Layout

Certain compromises in deck layout are inherent in almost any 30-footer; the Pearson 30 is no exception. The shrouds hamper access to the foredeck, so that it is easier to walk on the cabin top to go forward than along the sidedecks. This is almost a universal shortcoming in boats of this size, as the requirements of interior living space necessitate a large cabin trunk and relatively narrow sidedecks.

The bow cleat is located well forward and is adequate for the size of lines likely to be used on the boat. However, we would prefer two bow cleats, nearly side by side, in the same location. This is particularly useful in boats which spend a major amount of their lives tied to a dock, as the rule of thumb is that the dockline which needs adjusting is always the bottom line on any cleat.

The vinyl rubrail around the hull-to-deck joint presents a problem when anchoring the Pearson 30. It will undoubtedly be chafed by the anchor line. Redesign or relocation of the bow chocks would be necessary to correct this potential chafe problem.

The large starboard cockpit locker is designated as the boat's sail locker. We recommend that the locker be put to its intended use. The locker is so deep that small items would end up in a heap in the bottom almost out of reach if they were stored here. Space in

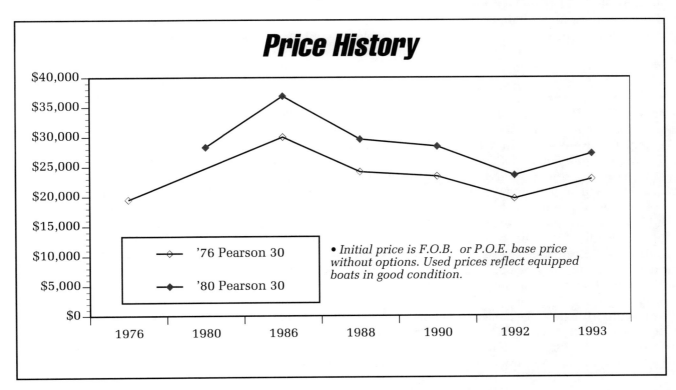

Price History

'76 Pearson 30
'80 Pearson 30

• Initial price is F.O.B. or P.O.E. base price without options. Used prices reflect equipped boats in good condition.

the lazarette locker—a natural place for fenders, docklines, and sheets—is limited by the engine exhaust hose. Rerouting this hose would increase the usefulness of this space.

The large cockpit seats four adults comfortably for daysailing and six if they are active enough to stay out of the way of the tiller and the mainsheet. The 4' long tiller definitely encroaches on the cockpit living space. We would normally be reluctant to recommend wheel steering for a high-performance 30-footer: it would, however, increase cockpit space and might reduce the idiosyncrasies created by the spade rudder when handling the boat under power.

Interior

The Pearson 30 has a light, roomy interior for a boat of its size. In the 1980 model, all four ports in the head and forward cabin are of the opening type, greatly improving ventilation, particularly when coupled with the optional, but recommended foredeck-mounted cowl ventilator.

The overhead hatch in the forward cabin is basically a ventilation hatch and is too small for either sails or emergency exit. Anchor storage is awkward without a foredeck anchor well, a welcome addition to many more recently designed boats the size of the Pearson 30.

The 22-gallon water tank and the standard holding tank occupy much of the space under the forward double berth. This double berth is actually the entire forward cabin, and can be closed off from the full-width head by double doors. The standard marine toilet is equipped with a proper vented loop. The head wash basin is tucked under the deck and is difficult to use for anyone with less agility than a contortionist. The location of this wash basin is the only serious flaw in the otherwise functional head compartment.

The P30's main cabin is large and comfortable, with capacious storage above, behind, and below the settees. Owners may find these storage spaces more useful if they are subdivided by partitions to prevent gear stored in one locker from ending up in another. The under-settee and under-galley lockers cannot be considered dry storage unless the bilge is kept bone dry. Although the lockers are sealed to the bilge at the bottom, owners report that, with their boat heeled, bilge water finds its way into the lockers by running up the inside of the hull behind locker partitions, then down into storage spaces. Most dinghy-hulled boats lack real bilge space or a sump, and as little as a gallon of water in a boat of this type can be annoying.

It is unfortunate that a large number of berths has become a criterion for livability in modern boats. In the past, a 40-footer was likely to have four or five berths. Now six berths are standard on a 30-footer,

Contrasting deck colors go a long way towards relieving glare. Note the long tiller, which obstructs the cockpit: here, the helmsman is actually sitting at the front edge of the cockpit.

including the Pearson 30, seven on a 35-footer, and eight on a 40-footer.

Cruising longer than overnight with six on a boat the size of the Pearson 30 is a sure way to terminate friendships and wreck marriages. No responding Pearson 30 owner reported cruising with more than four people on a regular basis.

The standard fold-down cabin table is a practical solution on a boat of this size. The optional slide-out chart table limits room over the quarterberth and lacks the fiddles which are necessary because of its slanted surface.

The Pearson 30 galley is typical of 30-footers. As much as possible is jammed into a necessarily small space. The deep lockers behind the stove and icebox will probably be partitioned into several smaller compartments by the moderately handy owner. Annoyingly, a short person has a hard time reaching the depths of the icebox, particularly if the stove is in use.

We cannot recommend the self-contained alcohol stoves almost always installed on the Pearson 30 and other boats of this size. There is a very real and well-documented risk of explosion if the stove must be refueled while hot. It is the fault of the marine stove industry—and an uninformed consuming public—that these potentially dangerous stoves are still used on many boats.

The galley sink and spigot partially block the companionway. The top companionway step is actually the lid of a nifty storage box, handy for winch handles, spare blocks, and tools.

Engine access is via the companionway steps, which lift out to expose the front of the engine. Two slatted doors in the quarterberth provide additional if awkward access to the engine and fuel tank under the cockpit. There is no soundproofing in the engine compartment.

The new, smaller diesel engine is more accessible for service than the old Atomic Four. It has molded fiberglass engine beds and drip pan, an excellent idea, although some engine vibration is transferred to the hull despite the flexible engine mounts and shaft coupling.

It is rare for a 30-footer to have good engine access. The Pearson 30 is no better than average in this respect.

Despite the above shortcomings, the P30 is highly livable. The advertised 6' 1" headroom is really an honest 5 11" in the main cabin. Achieving good headroom in a 30-footer without serious compromises in appearance is nearly impossible. The Pearson 30 comes as close to achieving this as any boat we have seen in its class.

Conclusions

The Pearson 30 was an industry success story. The boat is fast and responsive. Finish quality is above average. The interior is comfortable and reasonably roomy within the limitations inherent in a 30-footer. Many of the minor design problems can be corrected by the imaginative and handy owner who enjoys tinkering.

Pearson has a reputation for building solid, middle-of-the-road boats: a deserved reputation well in evidence in the P30. The Pearson 30 would be an excellent choice of boat for the aggressive and self-confident beginning sailor who desires high performance for daysailing or club-level racing as well as for reasonably comfortable short-term cruising. It is not the boat for the timid sailor, male or female. The family with two children will find it a comfortable cruiser. Sailors with friends who enjoy spirited sailing and who don't mind frequent sail changes will also find it a good choice for daysailing and local racing.

The long production run and continued popularity have created a boat with few inherent major problems and high resale value. The Pearson 30 is a good investment. **• PS**

The J/30

If possible, be sure to compare the redesigned version of this racer-cruiser to an earlier model.

A year after its introduction, *The Practical Sailor* evaluated the J/30, reaching the conclusion then that "The J/30 is a high performance racer with surprisingly good accommodations...intelligently laid out, strongly built, and well finished...(that provides) 'big boat' style racing and high performance at a reasonable cost."

Since the 1979 introduction of the J/30 as the second model in the J-Boat line (after the J/24) a lot of water has passed by J-Boat keels. By the mid-'80s, with the debut of its 40' cruising boat, J-Boats had put eight more models into its line and continued to build the 30 until 1988. There's now no 30' J-Boat: the extensive line currently includes the 22, 24, 27, 33, 35, 37, 39, 40 and 44.

Not all the J-Boats have been successful as racers and none has been as popular as the original J/24. However, with several hundred hulls built in the ten years of production, the J/30 would be regarded by industry standards as a popular and profitable boat.

The 30 was intended to be a combination of racing boat and family cruising boat, a lively sailing craft. It was introduced with the promise that it could provide competitive racing for half the price of 30' one-off racing machines and would afford cruising amenities to boot. If owner comments are any indication, the 30 has managed to deliver as promised, albeit with conditions. As a racing boat the 30 is best at one-design and round-the-buoys PHRF racing as opposed to anything resembling Grand Prix competition. As a cruising boat the 30 offers interior accommodations for a couple or small family which at least equal those of a lot of 30-footers more heralded for their livability and offering less performance. However, she is short on cockpit comfort and stability.

In 1984 J-Boats modified the interior and cockpit

Specifications

LOA	29' 10"
LWL	26' 0"
Beam	11' 2"
Draft	5' 5"
Displacement	7,000 lbs.
Ballast	2,100 lbs.
Sail area	461 sq. ft.

of the J/30. Below, one quarterberth was eliminated and the galley enlarged and improved. Better still, the cockpit seats were lowered and the bridgedeck eliminated with the intention of making the cockpit drier, more spacious, and more comfortable, as well as to provide a seat locker.

Construction

The J/30 was built by Tillotson-Pearson in Fall River, Massachusetts. The Pearson in Tillotson-Pearson is Everett Pearson, one of the pioneers in fiberglass boat construction. The hull of the J/30 is cored with Baltek Contourkore end-grain balsa. After the balsa core was glassed to the outer hull skin, the two-part mold was bolted together, and the centerline joint heavily glassed over. The layup was then finished

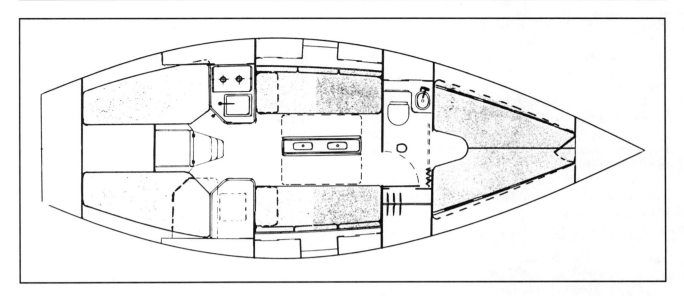

the same as any one piece molded hull.

Exterior finish quality of the molding is good, with little evidence of gelcoat blistering or roving print-through. The hull-to-deck joint is made by laying the deck molding over the internal flange of the hull molding, This joint is heavily bedded in 3M 5200 and through-bolted on 8" centers with 1/4" stainless steel bolts. The joint is covered on the outside by the teak toerail, which is cut away around the lifeline stanchion bases to provide deck scuppers. The toe rail is through-bolted, further backing up the hull-to-deck joint. The deck molding and the hull flange are not always a perfect fit on the inside, and in some areas there is no evidence of the bedding compound squeezing out on the inside. This joint can be visually inspected on the inside of the boat throughout most of its length.

If the hull and deck flanges matched better, this would increase the strength of the bond.

All deck hardware is through-bolted, with either washers or backing plates. Stanchion bases and chainplates utilize what appear to be acrylic plastic backing pads. Aluminum backing plates might allow higher torque on the fastenings without the risk of cracking the plates. There is no backing plate behind the stem fitting.

Through-bolts which intrude into the cabin overhead space utilize acorn nuts, which yields a finished appearance. Unfortunately, acorn nuts are notorious headcrackers. In Bob Johnstone's J/30, they have been replaced in high-traffic areas with a new type of recessed tubular nut which yields an even more finished appearance without encroaching on headroom. *The Practical Sailor* would like to see these nearly flush nuts used not only on the J/30, but in all boats. Acorn nuts or exposed bolts can be a serious hazard in rough conditions.

The outboard high-aspect ratio rudder is very strongly attached to the boat with stainless steel

The older interior shows remarkable roominess for a racing boat. The chart table to starboard is unusual, in that it slides aft to give access to the ice box. It's necessary to reach over the sink to get at the stove.

pintles and gudgeons. The bolts which attach these to the rudder should be periodically tightened.

The tiller head is also a strong stainless steel fabrication. A stainless steel tiller extension on the ash tiller allows the helmsman to sit on the weather rail with the rest of the crew. The steering system is simple, strong, and cheap. It should give little or no trouble if the fastenings are checked periodically.

Many J/24s had a disconcerting structural shortcoming: the main bulkhead tended to come adrift. Since the main bulkhead provides almost all of the transverse rigidity of the J/30, quite a bit more thought has gone into it. The main bulkhead of the J/30 is a fairly sophisticated combination of cored and solid construction—solid where the chainplates attach, cored elsewhere,

This bulkhead is glassed to the hull along its outer perimeter, and butt-joined with 3M 5200 to the deck molding. A recess in the deck molding to receive the bulkhead would be better than a simple butt joint. There is no evidence of this bulkhead's moving—panting or creaking, for example—as the boat works to windward. In fact, the inside of the boat is remarkably quiet going to weather.

Two large fiberglass moldings form the floor pans and the basic furniture structure. In our test boat, the forward floor pan was cracked in the area of the mast step, and had separated from the main bulkhead. It had obviously buckled upward when glassed into the boat, and had been cracked by the compression load of the mast.

Water tanks are cast polyethylene. Although these have glassed-in retainers, we would want to reinforce them before going offshore for any period of time. Large storage bins under the berths and settees have polyethylene liners, a practical solution to keeping anything dry in these areas. The boat also has a good-sized bilge sump, an absolute necessity in a boat with flat bilges.

The J/30 has a bendy, fractional Kenyon Spars rig with swept-back spreaders and single swept-back lowers. Both uppers and lowers share a single stainless steel chainplate. Playing with the rig adjustments is an integral part of making the J/30 go fast. Despite the apparent fragility of the rig, it has shown little tendency to crumple. It is obviously stronger than it at first appears.

A Close Look at the Boat

The original idea behind the J/30 was to provide a racing-cruising boat capable of sailing competitively against more sophisticated and more expensive boats. The 30, despite her then light displacement and innovative fractional rig, did not succeed. Her IOR rating (about 25.8) proved more than she could handle and even PHRF tended to give her a rating (130-145) she could sail to only in a breeze. The best J/30 racing became one-design fleets. Recognizing the limitations on the 30 for racing, J-Boats in 1983 introduced its J/29, a boat with minimal accommodations, 1,000 pounds lighter and $10,000 cheaper than the J/30, and then upgraded the 30 for cruising.

As a handicap racing boat, the J/30 has distinct liabilities. She is sluggish in light winds, especially in a chop. At the same time, for optimum performance in her most favored conditions, a breeze, she needs weight on the windward rail—four or five lumps of live ballast.

For club or family racing this is a demanding requirement, yet she does not sail to her rating without it. Her fractional rig makes depowering the mainsail easy and the headsail is small, but the boat is initially tender and a heel angle in excess of 15°

hurts windward performance.

This same tenderness is her most critical liability for family cruising. Few sailors find rail sitting the way to cruise. Thus, while the liveliness and basic weatherliness of the 30 is a virtue, it does carry a price.

With performance in mind, the original cockpit is more of a sit-on than a sit-in affair, without backrest or protection. Water running aft on the weather side runs over the vestigal coaming. The cockpit and outboard rudder virtually preclude wheel steering, now almost de rigeur for cruising 30-footers (despite its arguable practicality). Visibility forward is excellent and the convenience for sheet handling exemplary, but there again, is a price to pay.

Belowdecks the J/30 is comfortable, roomy and attractive. The port quarterberth, highly desirable for overnight racing, raised hob with galley space and layout, one reason for the 1984 modification as more and more 30s were bought as cruisers.

Engine accessibility is good; performance under power, excellent. What isn't excellent is the noise and vibration of the 15 hp Yanmar diesel auxiliary cement mixer, a complaint voiced almost unanimously by J/30 owners.

Handling Under Sail

"Performance under sail" is the hallmark of the J/30, just as it is for the J/24. The J/30 was not designed to rate well under any rating rule, and she doesn't. What she does is sail fast with a minimum of hard work.

The J/30 is a delight for the sailor who loves to tweak rig and sails for maximum performance with-

The 1984 redesign of the interior gave owners a larger galley in exchange for one of the quarterberths. All in all, it's a fair tradeoff. Note the easier access to the stove in the new interior.

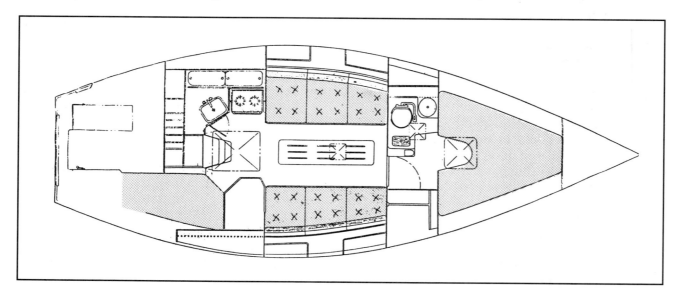

out spending a fortune. The boat is the ideal choice for the racing sailor with two-ton aspirations and a mini-ton pocketbook. The J/30 one-design class specifications limit sails to mainsail, three jibs, and one spinnaker when racing. There are minimum specified cloth weights for all sails.

Wisely, the Johnstones have not insisted on a single sailmaker for one-design racing. Sailmakers have become the gurus of the modern racing sailor, and like charismatic religious or political leaders, each racing sailmaker has his own band of faithful followers. Specifying a single sailmaker, as C&C originally did with the Mega, is the sure kiss of death for a boat which is intended to be mass-marketed in all parts of the country.

Despite a maximum beam of just over 11', the J/30 has a relatively narrow waterline beam. This produces a boat which has fairly low initial stability—good for light air—but which rapidly acquires form stability when heeled. The J/30 has a ballast/displacement ratio of only .30, less than that of the CSY 37.

With 18-22 knots of wind over the deck, the J/30 will do about 5.5 to 6 knots to windward in a slight chop using the genoa and a single-reefed mainsail. In puffy conditions, the mainsheet traveler should be played constantly to keep the boat on her feet. This is typical of fractionally-rigged boats with their relatively large mainsails.

As with all modern, low-wetted-surface boats, the J/30 goes fastest when sailed almost upright, and a great deal of sailing effort should be directed to keeping her in that upright trim.

With light displacement for her waterline, the J/30 should be sailed around waves rather than into them. It is important to keep the boat from hobbling in a chop, which can stop her dead in her tracks.

Spinnaker reaching, the boat is far more stable than the typical IOR boat, which has a pronounced rounding-up tendency when overpowered by the spinnaker. This lack of broaching tendency is the characteristic that makes the J/30 sail well above her rating off the wind in heavy air. Under these conditions, the typical IOR boat spends a substantial part of her sailing time dragging her rudder through the water sideways in an attempt to keep the boat on her feet and pointed in the right direction. The J/30 has a straight, relatively flat run aft, with the rudder well aft of the normal waterline. This produces a boat which surfs easily and quickly while maintaining fairly straightforward steering characteristics.

There are no hydraulics on the J/30, but there are still plenty of ways to play with the rig. The powerful block and tackle backstay adjuster is easily capable of putting all the bend in the rig that you could ever want without loading the backstay heavily. Since both upper and lower shrouds lead aft of the mast, backstay tension increases forestay tension without the need for either jumpers or running backstays.

For offshore work, however, it would be a good idea to equip the boat with running backstays to minimize pumping. Because the shrouds lead aft and to some extent double as backstays, shroud tension should be much tighter than you would normally expect to use in a boat of this size, If there is any slack in the leeward shrouds when going to

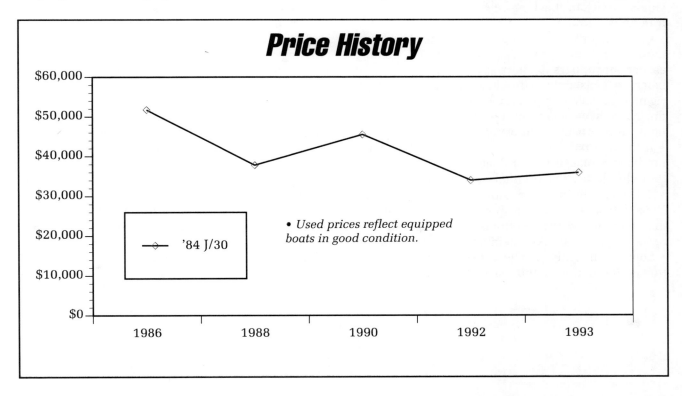

windward even in heavy air, there is not enough tension on the shrouds.

Sailing any fractional rig is substantially different from sailing the masthead rig. The mainsail is far more important in the fractional rig, both because of its size and the fact that the leading edge of the main is the highest sail on the boat.

For this reason, J-Boats recommends that the full main be carried whenever possible, to keep the upper part of the sail in clear air.

Fortunately, the J/30 class newsletter is full of suggestions on how to sail the fractional rig. Given the fact that the boat is a 30-footer that rates the same under the IOR as many 34- to 36-footers, many sailors will have to learn a new set of sail trim rules to be competitive.

The J/30 was one of the first boats to receive a standard MHS rating. This allows owners to participate in high-level open racing while minimizing measurement costs.

The J/30 is treated quite fairly under MHS. Average speed predictions are 4.24 knots in eight knots of wind, 5.35 knots in 12 knots of wind, and 5.92 knots in 16 knots of breeze.

What to Look For

The J/30 has proven as durable as *PS* originally assessed her to be. What eventually fail are fittings, not structural components. The balsa-cored hull has been essentially trouble free. This durability does not mean that there is nothing to check prior to making a committment to buy an older boat, nor should one be purchased without a thorough professional survey. In checking out a prospect, look for the following:

• Cracking in the floor supports around the engine mounts and mast step. A number of 30s, notably earlier ones apparently have suffered from structural cracking caused by vibration and over-tightened rigging. This cracking is repairable but awkward to do. There have also been reports of bulkhead problems, in part because of water penetration.

• If the original rudder pintles and gudgeons have not been replaced (and J-Boats supplied retrofits), they should be. The original ones proved too light.

• Bottom blistering seems more commonplace in the J/30s than average, in part perhaps because owners may have faired their bottoms for racing and thus reduced gelcoat thickness, increasing permeability.

• Some of the fittings have not stood up. Deterioration of the coating on the spars, corroded aluminum

cleats, cracked plastic hatch covers, failed mainsheet travelers, and non-skid worn smooth on decks are common although not serious complaints.

• For successful racing a well faired keel is a must. So too are good sails, although the number and construction of sails is limited by J/30 class rules (and a number of PHRF fleets assume for rating purposes that only class sails will be used). Owners strongly suggest checking both sails and keel carefully before buying a 30 for racing.

Price—The Bottom Line

At its introduction the J/30 carried a price tag of close to $35,000 plus an inventory of class sails and electronics, almost $10,000 less than an Ericson 30+. A 1985 J/30 ran a bit over $50,000 equipped, almost $10,000 less than a Sabre 30, about that amount more than a Hunter 31. In the intervening years a reasonably well cared for J/30 seems to have held its value especially in areas where there is an active one-design fleet and/or competitive PHRF base ratings (140+).

The going price for such boats has been approximately their original base price with notably lower prices available in areas where their competitiveness is less. In general, J-Boats has a favorable reputation for quality vis a vis price in the marketplace, and though it is also known somewhat for racing success, this reputation is perhaps a tad less justified.

Conclusions

Given its drawbacks for cruising, notably the cockpit, the original J/30 looks like a good bet as a used boat mainly for buyers who want a relatively lively boat to do some racing as well as cruising. For cruising alone it is a boat for a small, active family who won't demand much in the way of galley fare and won't object to a sit-on cockpit.

If performance is not an all-but-exclusive priority, we think there are better boats on the brokerage market for comparable prices. An older Tartan 30, Ericson 30, or Sabre 30 should carry about the same price as a J/30 but with more amenities. Moreover, these are boats that have tended to maintain their value.

We would be concerned that the J/30, with its functional styling and dual purpose, may not continue to represent good equity as different styling becomes fashionable and/or as their popularity for racing diminishes.   • **PS**

Catalina 30

One of the most popular, and least expensive, 30-foot cruiser-racers ever built, but there are some trade-offs.

The Catalina 30 may well be the most successful 30' cruiser-racer ever made. Since the Catalina 30 went into production in 1974, output has been steady, and thousands have been built.

The success of Catalina is even more remarkable when you consider that the company does no advertising. You will not find a single ad for Catalina in any national magazine. The company depends on its extensive dealer network and on word of mouth promotion from satisfied owners.

The average boat manufacturer spends between 5% and 10% of gross revenues on advertising. By eliminating that cost, Catalina may well be saving as much as $1,000 to $2,000 per Catalina 30. Any way you look at it, that translates into a lower price in the marketplace.

The entire Catalina line is extremely popular with new boat dealers, who are required by Catalina to represent other lines as well. Usually, the Catalina line is priced about 5% lower than a comparably equipped boat of the same size and type from other manufacturers.

Catalina owners frequently trade up through the line. Some dealers make a policy of offering the customer full trade-in value for a smaller Catalina traded up for a larger one within the first two years after purchase. A remarkable number of owners do.

The line has grown over the years, and Catalina now makes a 22, 28, 30, 34, 36, 42 and 50, all available with either a fin or wing keel.

The Catalina 30 is a typical, fairly light displacement modern design. The boat has a swept-back fairly high aspect ratio keel of the type made popular by IOR racing boats in the early 1970s. The high aspect ratio spade rudder is faired into the underbody with a small skeg.

Specifications

LOA	29' 11"
LWL	25' 0"
Beam	10' 10"
Draft	5' 3" (std.), 4' 4" (shoal)
Displacement	10,200 lbs.
Ballast	4,200 lbs.
Sail area	444 sq. ft.

On a waterline length of 25', the Catalina 30's displacement of 10,200 lbs is slightly above average for modern cruiser-racers. By way of comparison, the Newport 30 displaces 8,000 lbs, the Cal 31 9,200 lbs, the O'Day 30 11,000 lbs.

The boat is conventionally modern in appearance. She is moderately high-sided, with a fairly straight sheer and short ends. The cabin trunk tapers slightly in profile, and is slightly sheered to complement the sheer of the hull. When coupled with the tapered cabin windows—a Catalina trademark—this yields a reasonably attractive appearance compared to many modern boats.

Construction

The hull of the Catalina 30 is hand layed up of solid

fiberglass. In areas of high stress, such as the tops of the cockpit coamings, where winches are mounted, the laminate has been reinforced with plywood.

The external lead keel is bolted to the hull with stainless steel bolts. On most Catalina 30s we examined, there was slight cracking at the joint between the hull and ballast, which is typical of boats with narrow external ballast keels. The surface of the keel is roughly faired with polyester putty at the factory. This must be sanded properly fair by the owner or commissioning yard before the boat is launched, or light air performance will suffer. The hull must also be heavily sanded before paint is applied, or there is likely to be paint adhesion failure.

The hull-to-deck joint is simple. The deck molding is wider than the hull molding. At the outboard edge of the deck, the molding forms a downward-facing right-angle flange. This is slipped over the hull molding, and the joint filled with what appears to be fiberglass slurry. The joint is finished with a soft plastic rubrail held by an aluminum extrusion. The aluminum extrusion is held in place by stainless steel self-tapping screws, which reinforce the chemical bond. An integral solid wood sheerstrake, laminated into the hull, further strengthens the joint. This joint is suitable for use in a boat which is used for daysailing and coastal cruising. We would not choose it for an offshore boat. Any projection beyond the side of a boat's hull can be subject to tremendous strains from bashing into a head sea, Despite the fact that the joint and rubrail project only about 1/2" beyond the hull, there is some inherent weakness in this mode of hull-to-deck attachment.

There was some play in the rudder stocks of every Catalina 30 we examined. This is similar to the problem found in the Pearson 30. It is more likely to be a minor annoyance than a serious problem.

Lifeline stanchions are more closely placed than on almost any production boat we have seen. Double lifelines are standard, as are double bow and stern rails. Stanchions are through bolted, but with washers rather than the backing plates we prefer. Some owners report problems with leaking stanchions. This is easily corrected, as the stanchion fastenings are readily accessible from inside the boat.

The rig is a simple masthead sloop, with a straight section aluminum spar, double lower shrouds, and, at least on older models, wooden spreaders. The mast is stepped on deck, supported by a wooden compression column belowdecks. All the boats we examined showed local deflection of the top of the cabin trunk in the way of the mast step. This varied from as little as 1/16" to over 1/4". There was no evidence of stress in the form of cracks around any of the steps, however.

It is difficult to assess the method of attachment of the chainplates and bulkheads to the hull. The interior of the hull is completely lined, showing no raw fiberglass, nice to look at but preventing examination of the internal structure of the hull. Lower shroud chainplate attachments have been beefed up since the first hulls were produced. Owners warn that when considering the purchase of a used Catalina 30, be sure that the chainplates have the new reinforcements installed.

A shoal draft model, drawing 11" less than the standard model, is popular in some areas where the water is spread thin, such as Florida and the Chesapeake. A taller rig is also offered, and might be recommended in traditionally light air areas, such as Long Island Sound.

Handling Under Sail

With the standard rig, the Catalina 30 will be slightly undercanvassed in areas with predominantly light weather conditions. In areas with normally heavier conditions, such as San Francisco, the standard rig should yield good performance. The working sail area with the standard rig is 446 square feet. For comparison, the Pearson 30, with the same sail area, weighs 1,900 lbs less than the Catalina 30. To get good performance in light air, the boat will either have to be ordered with the taller rig, or very large headsails must be carried. If headsails larger than a 150% genoa are carried with the normal rig, turning blocks will have to be added aft in order to get a proper lead to the headsail sheet winches.

The Catalina 30 is a very stiff boat. The combination of a high ballast/displacement ratio, extraordinary beam, a deep fin keel, and a fairly small sail plan produce a boat that stands on her feet very well. Owners consider the boat to be just about as fast as other boats of the same size and type. PHRF ratings suggest that the tall rig boat is substantially faster than the boat with normal rig. With the tall rig, and well-cut racing sails, the boat should be competitive with other cruiser-racers that are actively raced, such as the Pearson 30, the O'Day 30, and the Ericson 30-2.

Sails are available from the factory, and are cheaper than one is likely to find either from a local racing sailmaker or one of the big national names. If the boat is to be used only for daysailing and cruising, the factory-supplied sails are likely to be adequate. If, however, you are concerned with performance, it is always advisable to have sails made either by a national sailmaker with a local loft, or by a local racing sailmaker. The sailmaker who is familiar with local weather conditions, and who probably races himself, is most likely to provide a faster suit of sails for any boat than those provided as a factory option.

The Catalina 30 does not have any particularly disturbing or exciting characteristics under sail. Like many wide modern boats, she rapidly develops weather helm when heeled. The boat should be sailed on her feet. Because she is quite stiff, headsail changes will not be as frequent as with a boat such as the Pearson 30.

Handling Under Power

The standard engine for the early Catalina 30 was the workhorse, 65 cubic inch Atomic-4 gasoline engine. For an additional $785, the boat could be delivered with a 31 cubic inch, 11 horsepower Atomic-Diesel. The small diesel is barely adequate power for a 10,200 lb boat. The 16 horsepower Atomic-Diesel might have been a better choice.

In a flat calm, the small diesel will push the boat at about 5 knots. With the old Atomic-4, the boat should easily reach hull speed under power.

Although the engine has flexible mountings and a flexible shaft coupling, there is substantial vibration under power with the small engine. This is felt most acutely in the cabin, because of the midships location of the engine. The engine box has no sound-proofing. The main cabin is very noisy under power. Long periods of powering would be uncomfortable for the people belowdecks.

With a fin keel and spade rudder, the boat is quite maneuverable under power, both ahead and astern. With the wheel steerer—one of the most popular options—very little steering effort is required.

Deck Layout

The deck layout of the Catalina 30 is typical of small cruiser-racers. There is a small foredeck anchor well. Access to the hull-mounted running lights is via this well. The running lights are protected from damage inside the well by molded fiberglass covers. We are not fond of running lights mounted in the topsides, which often short out. Other manufacturers who mount the lights in the hull could take a lesson from Catalina, however. Neither C&C nor Cal protects their running lights on the inside of the anchor well.

There are double bow cleats, but no bow chocks. There are also double stern cleats, but no stern chocks.

Despite the wide cabin trunk, it is reasonably easy to maneuver on deck. The shrouds are placed far enough inboard to allow going outside them on the way to the foredeck. There are well-mounted teak grabrails on the cabin top.

The cockpit is large and comfortable. With wheel steering, it easily accommodates the helmsman and four companions. There is a large sail locker under the port cockpit seat, and a smaller locker under the starboard seat. There is also a fair-sized lazarette locker. The sail locker is properly separated from the under-cockpit area.

The cockpit is too large for offshore use. There are only two fairly small cockpit drains, whose size is greatly reduced by strainers. Despite the fact that the companionway has a fairly high raised sill, at least two of the three companionway drop boards would have to be in place to raise the sill to the level of the main deck.

The strong taper of the companionway allows the drop boards to be removed by lifting them only about 1.5". In a bad knockdown in really severe weather, the boards could fly out or float out much easier than if the companionway were more parallel-sided.

The sliding companionway hatch is unnecessarily large. This is useful when sitting in a marina in a hot climate, such as southern California, but it is a disadvantage at sea.

Because the main cabin bulkhead slopes forward, the drop boards cannot be left out of the companionway for ventilation when it rains. For this reason, boats used in rainy climates frequently have cockpit

---

The Catalina 30 has, on the whole, a well-designed interior, boasting a large, comfortable cabin, spacious head, and an unusually good galley design for a boat of this size.

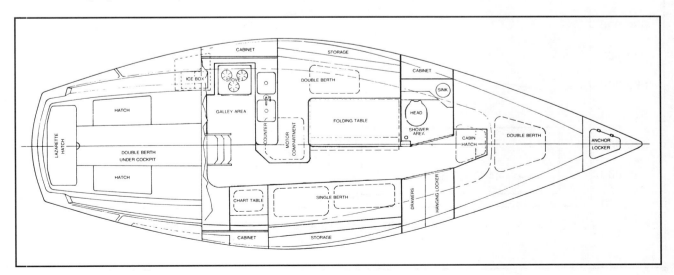

dodgers. Otherwise, they become stifling below in wet weather. There is no provision for ventilation below in rain or heavy weather.

There is a permanently mounted manual bilge pump operable from the cockpit. Other manufacturers would do well to include such a pump as standard equipment. Not many do.

Interior

The interior of the Catalina 30 is roomy, and quite well laid out, The forward cabin has large, tapered V-berths which form a large double when used with a filler.

A molded hatch which forms part of the front of the cabin trunk, will provide good ventilation in port, but is likely to be a leaker in heavy weather.

The head is quite comfortable. The optional shower drains directly to the bilge. Toilet installations are all optional. There is good storage space for clothes in a hanging locker and drawers opposite the head.

Interior bulkheads are teak-faced plywood. The hull is completely lined with fiberglass hull liners, yielding a very finished appearance.

The main cabin is large and comfortable for a 30' boat. There is an L-shaped settee to port, and a straight settee to starboard. The cabin table folds up against the forward bulkhead when not in use.

The engine is mounted under the settee and part of the galley counter. It's a tight fit. Access for service is excellent through traps in the settee. The location of the engine in the lowest part of the bilge does make it vulnerable to bilgewater, however.

Under the cockpit to starboard, there is a large double quarterberth. Unfortunately, the occupant of the inboard half of the berth had better be pretty thin and non-claustrophobic, for headroom over that portion is only a little over one foot.

A large, U-shaped galley is to port. A gimballed alcohol stove with oven is standard, as are double sinks. The icebox is uninsulated except for the side facing the stove, and it drains directly to the bilge. Storage space in the galley is plentiful, although not as much as it might first appear, for the lockers under the sinks are filled by hoses for the engine and water tanks. Batteries are well-mounted under the small chart table opposite the galley.

The appearance of the interior is one of spaciousness and good design, This initial impression breaks down somewhat on careful examination of details. Interior finish is of average stock boat quality.

Conclusions

According to Frank Butler, president and chief designer of Catalina, the company's goal is to provide "as much boat for the money as we can." The Catalina 30 is definitely among the lowest-priced of the 30' cruiser-racers. This boat is similar in price to the Hunter 30. For their displacements, these are two of the least expensive 30' cruiser-racers on the market. It is not reasonable to compare these boats with more expensive 30-footers such as the Ericson 30+ or the Cal 31.

There are tradeoffs to be made when one purchases a cheaper boat. In boats, as in most other things, you may not always get what you pay for, but you always pay at least for what you get.　• **PS**

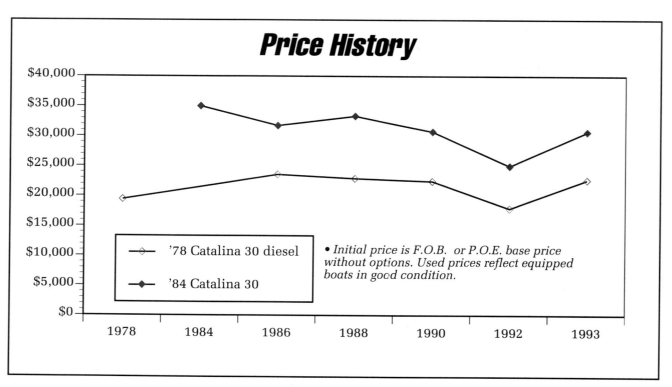

Price History

Legend:
- ◇ '78 Catalina 30 diesel
- ◆ '84 Catalina 30

• *Initial price is F.O.B. or P.O.E. base price without options. Used prices reflect equipped boats in good condition.*

Hunter 30

This coastal cruiser is aimed squarely at the bottom end of the market—a lot of boat for little money.

Hunter began building auxiliary sailboats in 1974, largely as the result of the first oil embargo and the new energy consciousness that followed in this country. Hunter began as a division of Silverton, one of the country's large manufacturers of small powerboats, which was interested in expanding its offerings and taking advantage of the new interest in saving fuel.

The new company's aim was high-volume production, keeping prices low by standardizing design, making as few tooling changes as possible, and offering its boats "fully equipped," this in the days when other companies were selling such things as bow pulpits and lifelines as options on a 30-foot boat.

The original boats came with sails, dock lines, fenders, lifejackets, and fire extinguishers, in what Hunter came to call the "Cruise Pak" of standard features. About the only option available on the early Hunters was a choice of shoal or deep draft keels.

The company's corporate goals seem little different today, a remarkable consistency in marketing sailboats through the ups and downs of the last 18 years. The company continues the Cruise Pak on its boats to this day, now offering even electronic equipment and a copy of *Chapman's Piloting, Seamanship, and Small-Boat Handling.* The one notable change in Hunter over the years has been in the number of models offered. Hunter began—like its chief competitor, Catalina Yachts—with a small group of standardized models. From 1974 through 1977 they offered only the Hunter 25, 27, and 30 models, and from 1977 through 1979 they added only the 33 and 37.

Nowadays, unlike Catalina, Hunter is offering an almost bewildering variety of models, with frequent updates and design changes. Model lines called

Specifications

LOA	29' 11"
LWL	25' 9"
Beam	10' 1"
Draft	4' 0"/5' 3" (shoal/deep keel)
Displacement	9,700 lbs.
Ballast	4,100 lbs.
Sail area	444 sq. ft.

"Hunter," or "Vision," or "Legend," have little in the way of family resemblance.

The Hunter 30 is a John Cherubini design, as was the companion Hunter 27. The third of the original Hunters—the 25—was designed by Cherubini and Robert Seidelmann.

The company has been remarkably reticent about giving out information—more so than any other boat builder *Practical Sailor* has ever dealt with. We called for information on how many 30s had been built, for example, and were told simply, "We don't release that information."

We asked also for design information, both for the original 30 and the current Hunters, which are advertised as the product of CEO "Warren Luhrs and the Hunter Design Team." Again, the company declined,

Owners' Comments

"The Hunter 30 offers a lot of boat for the investment, but by no means is she a blue-water passagemaker. An excellent, sheltered water or limited coastal cruiser, she's a good buy for the novice-to-intermediate sailor."

—1980 model in New York

"In spite of the low prestige, it is a good boat and a good value. I wanted a 30-footer for headroom and the capacity for family cruising. I have had much pleasure and am satisfied."

—1976 model in Virginia

"Both before and after I bought the boat new, I heard people 'knock' the Hunter line. The criticism is totally unjustified in my opinion. I am convinced that my boat is well designed and reasonably well built. There is not a lot of 'hand-finishing' in a Hunter, but things are not too rough either."

—1979 model in Michigan

"If a close friend were looking for a similar boat, I'd advise him/her to get a later model with the bigger engine and roomier cockpit."

—1978 model in Green Bay

and we can only guess as to who is responsible for this policy.

The latest 30 we examined was a 1980 model, hull #934. The 30 we sailed was a 1978, hull #568. The boats were built from 1974 until 1983, and we presume that more than 1,000 were built.

Some number of them were sold as "Quest 30s," which was essentially a sail-away bare-hull kit boat, with the purchaser completing the interior and the fitting out.

The Hunter 30 owners who responded to our reader surveys generally felt they were decently treated by the company. Most said the company had responded to warranty problems and to inquiries and complaints, though a number of owners did remark on the long time it sometimes took to get a response.

One example of good customer relations was in the owner's manual that we found on each Hunter 30—a good, clear, simple manual. It has always amazed us how many other makers of low-priced, and even expensive, boats provide the buyer with little or no printed information.

The Boat

In contrast to today's Hunters, the early Cherubini-designed models were conservative and conventional in design.

The longer sister models—the 33 and 37—were in our opinion good-looking boats, moderately styled, with an attractive bow line and sheer and a pleasing coach roof. The smaller boats, the 25 and 27, were not ugly; however, packing a lot of room into a short waterline caused them to be higher-sided with boxier cabin houses than would be ideal for appearance's sake.

The 30 lies somewhere between—handsome from some angles but just a little bit too flat in the sheer and high in the cabin top to be considered beautiful. Still, most traditionalists will consider it a much more attractive boat than the modern Euro-style Hunters.

The hull is very full to give a lot of interior room, but otherwise quite typical of the racer-cruisers of the 1970s. Overall, the boat is 29' 11"—the maximum allowable length under the then popular Midget Ocean Racing Club (MORC) rule. The short overhangs result in a long waterline, fundamental for sailing speed. The beam, at just a hair over 10 feet, is moderate by 1970s standards, but narrow in comparison to the "big" 30-footers that have appeared since. The Catalina 30, for example, is nine inches wider, and many current boats carry a foot more beam (and generally carry it further aft) than the Hunter 30.

A conventional fin keel, drawing 5' 3", was standard, with a 4' 0" shoal keel as an option. We sailed only on the deep keel version, and suspect it is much to be preferred unless you absolutely need the shallower draft. Company literature lists the displacement and ballast as identical on both models. If true, the shallow keel version will be more tender, calling for a reef early as the wind pipes up. There's a full skeg ahead of the rudder. If you have to remove the propeller shaft for some reason, you'll have to remove the engine first, or tear the skeg off.

In construction, the boat is very conventional—an economical solid-glass layup in the hull and a balsa-cored deck with plywood for backing under cleats. A conventional flange, with a through-bolted aluminum toerail, joins the hull and deck together. Our opinion of the fiberglass work was that it was good but a little light—marginal for offshore sailing but strong enough for typical coastal cruising. On one of the boats we looked at there was extensive delamination of the cockpit sole and the bench seats.

The conventional construction is quite in contrast to the present-day Hunters. CEO Warren Luhrs has heavily advertised his participation in long-distance singlehanded races, featuring boats with high-tech construction and exotic materials. And the new Hunters can generally be described as highly engineered, at the opposite end of the spectrum from the early Hunters, like the 30.

Finally, on the two 30s that we examined thoroughly, there was a good bit of sloppy glass work—ragged edges, un-resinated glass—in compartments and otherwise out of sight. And among responses from Hunter 30 owners, there's a surprisingly high number of complaints about what we would collectively call quality control problems: fuel-return lines improperly hooked up, chafed hoses, leaking ports, plumbing kinked, untightened screws and nuts, poorly fitted hatch boards and lazarette covers, improperly installed exhaust systems, and so on.

On Deck

The foredeck is a bit small for anchor work and sail handling because the cabin house extends quite far forward. The 1978 and later models have an anchor well built into the foredeck.

A significant shortcoming of the boat's design is the narrow walkway on each side of the cabin. The wide cabin house makes it clear that the top priority was interior room, with deck work being a distant consideration. It's hard to get past the chainplates, especially on the leeward side when under a press of canvas. The boat we sailed had a furling jib, a desirable option in view of the small foredeck.

The boat has a good cockpit, a bit smaller than many other 30s (again, a result of extending the cabin house for maximum interior room). A wheel was standard on the boat; it's small, which is good for moving around the cockpit, but less than ideal for sailing. We're not big fans of steering wheels on boats under 40 feet or so, but Hunter is obviously successful in appealing to the entry level sailor or the small boat sailor moving up to a first cruising boat.

A "T" cockpit became standard following 1980, and some people prefer that arrangement; however, you can lie down on the older bench seats and you can't with the T. The bench seats would benefit from some sort of drain arrangement since they trap water. In addition, cushions, especially back cushions, would make the cockpit seats more comfortable.

A peculiarity of the decks on the early Hunters is that the non-skid pattern was not molded in as is customary on fiberglass decks. Instead, non-skid material was painted on. In almost all older Hunters we've seen, that material is coming off in spots or even large patches. Fortunately, repair is straightforward (though time-consuming), requiring the filling and fairing of any holes and then the application of a new non-skid paint.

On the boats we examined, there was minimal sail handling equipment on deck—one pair of jib sheet winches, a small halyard winch for the jib, no winch at all for the main halyard, no Cunningham or vang, no control lines on the traveler, no flattening reef, a single jiffy reef block, two jib lead blocks out on the toerail, no backstay adjuster.

Interior

The interior was originally a strong selling point for the boat. Almost every owner commented on the size of the interior—often relative to low price—when talking about their reasons for buying the 30.

Layout is conventional, with a good V-berth forward, then a head with small hanging locker opposite, settee berths on each side with a drop-leaf table in the middle, an L-shaped galley, with the sink underneath the companionway, and a quarter berth, with a tiny chart table at its head. The berths are of decent size, though a tall person will wish they were all a few inches longer.

The interior is well laid out, but plain. Some of the details could use changing, like the alcohol stove, lack of vents and small water tank. There's a lot here for the money, however.

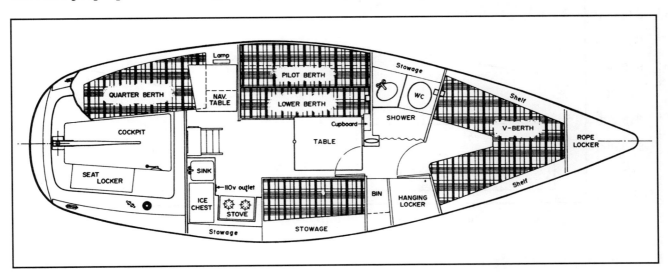

Many of the boats have alcohol stoves ("Cooks about like a solar oven," said one owner) that will be due for upgrading. The icebox on the boat we looked at had minimal insulation and would benefit from several more inches all around.

The deck house is high and wide, and this gives a look of spaciousness below. The white hull liner overhead helps to offset the extensive teak veneer on the bulkheads, ceilings, sole, and furniture.

There are adequate windows and hatches for adequate light inside, and opening portlights (Hunter was one of the first production boats to offer numerous opening ports as standard) to give good ventilation. If the boat has not been upgraded by the time of purchase, the new owner will probably want to add some Dorade or solar vents to keep the air moving when the opening ports must be closed.

Finish below is average—typical of the low-cost production boats which depend on pre-fab components, rapidly installed in the hull. In our owner surveys, there were a great many complaints about sloppy detailing in the joinerwork, door hinges, hardware, and loose trim. Storage space is minimal, and water tankage of 35 gallons is marginally adequate for cruising.

Engine

For the first four years, a 12-hp Yanmar diesel was standard. After 1978, a 15-hp Yanmar and finally an 18-hp Yanmar.

The 12 was a particularly noisy engine, the later models less so. Most of the owners who completed our survey thought the engines were minimal for powering the boat, especially in any kind of head seas; however, by traditional standards even the 12-hp model should be adequate for the weight and length of the boat. Although the 12 is highly praised for its reliability, many people may find later models to be more desirable because of their larger and smoother running engines.

Engine accessibility is criticized by almost all the owners who completed our survey. "Access is awful," said one. "You must be a left-handed midget to work on this engine."

We thought accessibility was far from ideal, but it really isn't too unusual for this size boat. With a big interior and a small cockpit, it's hard to stuff an engine under the cockpit sole without cramping.

The boat we sailed (with the Yanmar 12) was well behaved under power, backing nicely, turning crisply, driving through strong winds (though in protected water) with no problem. Our impression was that the vibration and noise were more of a concern than the power of the engine. Anyone buying the boat with the Yanmar 12 will probably want to spend the time to get perfect alignment. We'd also look closely at the engine mounts and the shaft strut mounting.

A two-blade solid prop was standard, but a number of owners refitted the boat with a three-blade solid prop, apparently to improve powering. We doubt if the gain would offset the loss in sailing ability.

Sailing

We were pleasantly surprised by the sailing performance of the Hunter 30. We sailed one in a long

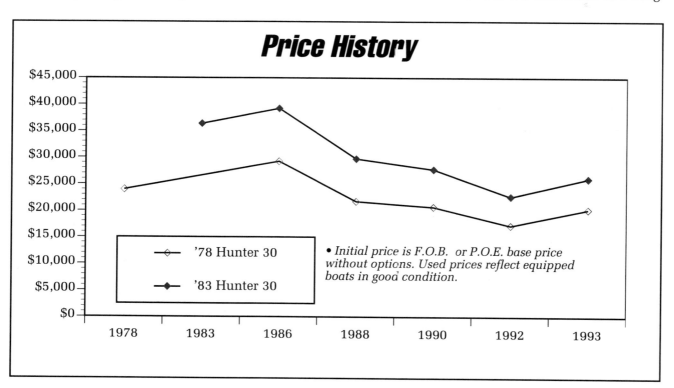

triangular race—two triangles, then windward-leeward-windward legs—in heavy air, a little over 20 knots at the start.

Considering that the boat had almost no sail controls and old sails, and that the underbody was rough and a bit weedy, the boat moved very well, going to weather respectably in a serious racing fleet, and reaching and running competitively.

The jib we used was the 130-percent genoa on roller-furling, and this was about right for the boat in those conditions. When the wind faded near the end of race, the boat was clearly under-canvassed.

The boat is slightly under-rigged with its short mast. To sail well in light air, especially with the solid prop that almost all the 30s have, a huge jib is required, with all the consequent hassle of tacking and winch cranking.

Nonetheless, the 30 is a good sailing boat, responsive and easy to steer. Its PHRF rating of 186 would probably be very favorable if the boat were rigged with a full complement of sail controls and modern sails. It should be able to stay with other 30-footers of the same era, such as the Pearson 30, Catalina 30 (not the tall rig), and O'Day 30. Since sailing is what sailing is all about, our opinion of the Hunter 30 was improved dramatically when we took a first in our main-and-jib class.

Conclusions

The Hunter 30 was a boat built to a price—to sell at the bottom end of the market and appeal to the sailor who wanted a lot of room for the least amount of money.

As long as the buyer understands that, not expecting custom quality at barnyard prices, the Hunter 30 can be a good value in a used boat. It's easy to pay too much for a used boat these days, but for a roomy coastal cruiser in good condition, the Hunter 30 can be had at a decent price—a lot of cruisability at a very minimal investment. **• PS**

O'Day 30

With good performance, low maintenance, and a big interior, the 30 is a good coastal cruiser.

The first O'Day 30 we saw back in 1977 was named *Moby Dick*. Compared to most of the boats in our boatyard, she did look a lot like a great white whale: beamy white hull with high topsides, white deck, white cabin trunk, and not much exterior wood trim. But what really struck us about the boat was the amount of interior volume. The boat had as much interior space as most 34-footers built at that time.

With her straight sheerline and short overhangs, the O'Day 30 was not as handsome to our eyes then as more traditional-looking boats, but the design has held up surprisingly well. Today it still looks quite modern, yet more conservative than many newer Eurostyled boats.

Over 350 O'Day 30s were built between 1977 and 1984. During 1984, the 30 was modified by changing the keel and rudder, and the stern was lengthened to accommodate a European-style boarding platform. This "new boat" was called the O'Day 31, and it stayed in production until 1986.

O'Day 31 hulls are numbered, quite correctly, as a continuation of the O'Day 30 series. About 150 "stretched" O'Day 31 models were built.

Sailing Performance

With a typical PHRF rating of 177, the O'Day 30 is very close in speed to other modern cruiser/racers of the same length. The boat was never marketed as a racing boat: performance cruising has always been an O'Day concept.

The boat was originally built in two underwater configurations: a keel/centerboarder, and a fin keel of moderate depth. The centerboard version of the boat is about 500 pounds heavier than the keel version. The extra weight is mostly in ballast to give the two boats similar stability. Where PHRF commit-

Specifications

LOA	29' 11"
LWL	25' 5"
Beam	10' 9"
Draft	4' 11" (keel)
Displacement	10,500 lbs.
Ballast	4,200 lbs.
Sail area	441 sq. ft.

tees distinguish between the two underwater configurations, the centerboard boat is rated about three seconds per mile slower—about what you would expect for the difference in displacement.

Upwind performance is good. Shrouds and genoa track are inboard, and the hull and keel shape from C. Raymond Hunt Associates is clean and modern without being extreme. Downwind, the boat is slow without a spinnaker.

The mainsail is very high aspect ratio, almost 4:1. Off the wind, this is ineffective sail area, and a poled-out headsail will not provide enough area in light air to really keep the boat moving. At the very least, an asymmetrical cruising spinnaker is called for.

Because the mainsail is small, the boat needs large headsails, and they will need to be changed fre-

Owners' Comments

"The vintage year for this boat is 1979. the engine is bigger, rigging is better, interior fittings are better. Newer models with the dinette interior are great for daysailing and overnighting, but the original interior is better for cruising."

—1978 model in Port Washington, NY

"This is not a racer. It is a good, stiff, easily-sailed boat which well suits us for family cruising. It has an airy, light interior. It needs adequate headsails for good performance."

—1980 model in Chicago, IL

"I would suggest a 1979 or earlier boat with the double-settee interior. I think a dinette is a waste of space. The boat is strong and heavy for a 30-footer. It goes well in medium to heavy air but is not particularly swift in light air. I have the keel/centerboard model, but rarely use the centerboard. I strongly recommend this boat for family cruising."

—1979 model in Annapolis, MD

"Belowdecks, the boat has met with unqualified approval from a judge even more demanding than myself, namely my wife. One feature that stands out as affecting positively the livability if the boat is the dinette. We have had as many as eight people aboard without suffering the claustrophobia that is often standard equipment in a sailboat."

—1983 model in Boston, MA

quently for optimum performance. With a small main, reefing is a relatively ineffective way to reduce sail area.

Standard sails with new boats were a main and 110% jib. In addition, the boat really needs a 150% genoa and a 130% genoa for good performance in a wide range of wind velocities. With a wide waterline beam and 40% ballast/displacement ratio, the boat can carry a fair amount of sail.

Unless the original owner specified the optional larger headsail sheet winches, you'll have to consider upgrading if you go to big genoas: the stock winches are too small for headsails larger than 110%.

Most owners report the boat to be well-balanced under sail, but some early boats suffered from a lot of weather helm due to an excessively-raked mast. The solution is to shorten the headstay and eliminate almost all mast rake. This may require shifting the mast step aft 1/2" for the mast to clear the forward edge of the mast partners.

Although the rig size did not change over the course of production, spars from three different manufacturers were used in the boat. The original rigs are by Schaefer. Kenyon spars were used in the middle of the production run, Isomat rigs in later boats. All the rigs are stepped through to the keel, and are properly stayed.

The standard location for the mainsheet traveler is on the bridgedeck at the forward end of the cockpit. From a purely functional point of view, this is a good location. Several owners in our survey, however, complain that the traveler limits the installation of a cockpit dodger. As an option, the mainsheet traveler was available mounted on a girder atop the deckhouse.

This is a tough call. The bridgedeck location is very handy for shorthanded cruising, since the person steering can reach the mainsheet from the helm, particularly on tiller-steered boats. At the same time, a good dodger is almost a must for cruising, and the midboom sheeting arrangement simplifies dodger design.

Although wheel steering was an option, you'll find it on a large percentage of boats. Owners report no problems with the wheel installation.

Early boats have a conventional, centerline backstay. On later models, a split backstay was standard, permitting a stern boarding ladder to be mounted on centerline.

All things considered, the O'Day 30 is a boat that performs well under sail. She's not really a racer, but she will stay up with almost any boat of her size and type, and is easy to handle, to boot.

Engine

O'Day was one of the first big builders to take the all-diesel route, even though the Atomic 4 was still a popular engine when this boat went into production. Not all of the engine installations in the O'Day 30, however, have been equally successful.

Originally, the boat was equipped with a single-cylinder, salt water cooled, 12 hp Yanmar diesel. This was one of the first Japanese diesels on the market, and one O'Day 30 owner reports that Yanmar replaced his engine—three years after the boat was built—due to a series of problems that simply could not be solved.

During 1978, the engine was upsized to a Yanmar 2QM15, since the boat was really underpowered with the smaller engine. Owners report that Yanmar installations are noisy, which is partially due to the fact that there is no sound insulation in the engine compartment.

As first built, the engine beds were attached to the walls of the engine box. According to one owner, this was such a bad arrangement that the vibration from the engine loosened the beds. Later boats have a molded fiberglass engine bed/drip pan combination, which is far better than the original installation.

With 1980 models, the Yanmar engine was dropped in favor of a two-cylinder, 16 hp Universal diesel. Owners report no problems with this engine.

Engine access is very good, particularly on later models. In early models, a panel behind the companionway ladder must be unscrewed to get to the front of the engine. On later models, a sloping panel in front of the engine can be removed, and the galley counter over the top of the engine can be lifted out of the way for complete access.

Lack of sound insulation is the weak point of the engine installation. It probably would have cost about $100 to provide halfway-decent sound insulation in the engine compartment when the boat was on the assembly line. You can do it after the fact, but not as simply or cheaply. We'd highly recommend this project, since without insulation the engine compartment resonates like a drum.

With the exception of the original, single-cylinder Yanmar, all of the engines are big enough to push the boat to hull speed in most conditions.

The standard, exposed, two-bladed solid prop causes a fair amount of drag under sail, but you should probably keep it unless you race. We feel a folding prop is not the way to go on a cruising boat, and a feathering prop would be disproportionately expensive on this boat.

Early boats have an 18-gallon aluminum fuel tank. Later models—after 1980—are usually equipped with a 26-gallon aluminum tank. The larger tank gives better range under power, despite the fact that the more powerful engines used late in the production run also use more fuel.

Construction

The hull of the O'Day 30 is an uncored fiberglass laminate. Hull stiffness is increased through the use of a full-length molded body pan, glassed to the hull.

Construction is basically solid, but is certainly not

Shown here is the revised, post-1980 interior. The dinette table drops down to form a double berth. Though O'Day claimed space for five at the table, even four is a tight fit.

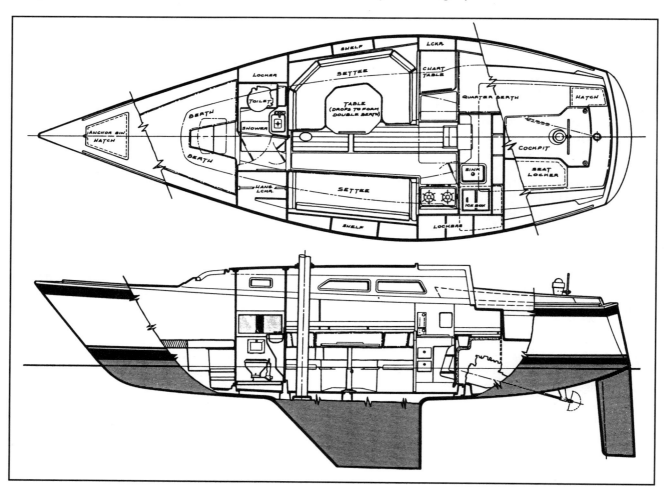

fancy. Owners in our survey report a fairly standard number of minor production-boat complaints: surface crazing in gelcoat, leaks around mast, leaks around deck hardware and ports, poor interior finish quality. Gelcoat blistering is neither more nor less common than on other boats.

The O'Day 30 was one of the first small cruising boats to use Navtec rod-type chainplates, which are anchored to the body pan. This is a good, strong arrangement.

In our experience, O'Day's approach to building was to use good-quality fittings, combined with reasonably sturdy construction. The boats generally have pretty mediocre finishing detail, and costs were kept down by keeping the standard boat fairly simple.

For example, there is no sea hood over the main companionway. This may seem like a minor shortcoming, but it means that this hatch is going to leak if you take solid water over the deck. Instead of a labor-intensive full-length teak toerail, there are short, thin teak strips screwed to a raised, molded fiberglass toerail. The strips do not have to be curved or tapered, since they can be easily bent to shape.

Likewise, most of the interior furniture is part of the molded body pan, trimmed out with teak. The cabin sole is fiberglass, with teak ply inserts. You do not buy these boats for their high-quality joinerwork, nor do you buy them for sophisticated systems or creature comforts.

A single battery was standard, as was a two-burner alcohol stove without oven. Propane cooking was not an option. Double lifelines were optional. Even a spare winch handle was an extra-cost option: only one winch handle was supplied, although four winches were standard!

Because the O'Day 30 is a relatively heavy boat, its basic construction is fairly expensive. To keep the price comparable to other boats in its size range, costs had to be cut somewhere, and they were cut in finish, detailing, and systems. You simply can't build a boat that weighs 500 to 1000 pounds more than the competition, provide the same systems and detailing, and keep the price the same.

All in all, this is a reasonable tradeoff. You could, if you wanted, add a propane stove, bigger batteries, engine compartment insulation, bigger winches, and many of the other things that you might expect to find on a well-equipped 30-footer. But you won't get your money back when you sell the boat. The price of your used O'Day 30 will be controlled by the price of other O'Day 30's on the market, even if they are less well equipped than your own.

The standard water tank varies in capacity from 25 to 30 gallons, depending on the model year. On late models, which have the smaller tank, you could also get an extra 25-gallon water tank, which is mounted under the port settee. With this tank full, the boat has a noticeable port list. Without the optional tank, water capacity is inadequate for cruises extending beyond a long weekend.

Deck layout is reasonably good. There is an anchor locker forward, although its so large that it's tough to straddle while hauling in the anchor rode. You can walk forward on deck outboard of the shrouds on either tack.

The cockpit is fairly small, thanks to the big

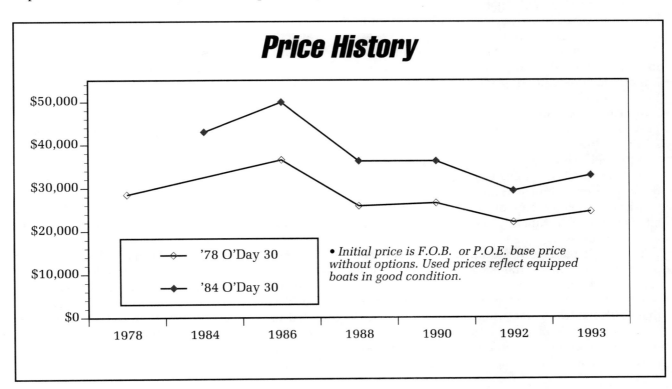

Price History

• Initial price is F.O.B. or P.O.E. base price without options. Used prices reflect equipped boats in good condition.

◇ '78 O'Day 30
◆ '84 O'Day 30

interior. There is a large locker to port that can be used to store sails, and a small locker to starboard at the aft end of the cockpit.

With 1980 models, ballast was reduced by 350 pounds in the keel version, 400 pounds in the center-board boats, according to factory specifications. Still later, ballast in the keel version was increased by 150 pounds. Although these are significant changes, owners of later boats do not report that the boat is noticeably more tender, nor do the PHRF ratings reflect any change in performance.

Interior

With her wide beam and long waterline, the O'Day 30 has a big interior. In fact, we have little doubt that if the boat were still in production, O'Day would have figured out how to modify the interior to get three in separate cabins, which has become fairly common on contemporary 30-footers.

For the first three years of production, the boat had a very standard interior, with settees on either side of the main cabin. In 1980, the interior was retooled. The starboard settee was replaced with a U-shaped dinette with permanent table, and the head compartment was shifted to the starboard side of the boat.

The forward cabin in the old layout is bigger due to the placement of partitions and doors, which gave more cabin sole area. With the V-berth insert in place to give a double berth, you could still stand up in the forward cabin to dress. In the newer interior, there is no place to stand in the forward cabin if the door is shut.

Headroom is 6' on centerline in the forward cabin.

There is a molded fiberglass hatch in the forward end of the cabin trunk. In our experience, molded glass hatches are a compromise. They are easy to distort by overtightening hatch dogs to compensate for old gaskets. If dogged unevenly, they tend to leak. It is also next to impossible to fit a dodger on a hatch like that on the O'Day 30, so it must be kept shut in rain or bad weather. Since the boat lacks any real provision for foul-weather ventilation, it can be stifling below.

Although the head compartment in both interior layouts is small, it's a fairly good arrangement. To use the optional shower, doors to both the main and forward cabins can be closed off, giving plenty of elbow room. Unfortunately, the shower drains to the bilge, a nasty arrangement.

In the original layout, a dropleaf centerline table divides the middle of the main cabin. Four people can sit comfortably at the table using the two settees.

Four diners are far more cramped in the dinette than with the two-settee arrangement, even though O'Day's literature claims space for five. There's no way that anyone seated on the port settee opposite the dinette can reach the table. On the plus side, fore and aft movement through the boat is not restricted by the dinette, as it is in the two-settee interior when the table is in use. You pays your money and takes your choice on this one.

Storage space behind the settees shrank in the new interior, a significant loss on a boat this size.

The dinette table drops down to form a good-sized double berth, but because the mattress is made up of five (count 'em) separate cushions, this is not a very comfortable berth to sleep on. Its shape is so complex that making sheets fit well is just about an impossibility. In the old layout, the port settee can be extended to form a more normally-shaped double.

Even with opening ports, ventilation in the main cabin is pretty mediocre. There is room atop the cabin aft of the mast for a small aluminum-framed ventilation hatch, and this was an option on later boats. If you don't have the hatch, you should add it. Cowl vents—other than one on the foredeck—weren't even options, but could be added.

Headroom in the main cabin is 6' 3" on centerline aft, slightly less at the forward end of the cabin.

The galley and nav station are the same in both interiors, but some detailing varies depending on the year. Aft to port there is a stove well, with storage outboard.

The icebox is in the aft port corner of the galley. It is not particularly well insulated, and drains into the bilge. There is a deep single sink next to the icebox.

Originally, there was a long step from the companionway to the top of the galley counter, to which a teak board was fastened to form a step. Stepping on galley counters offends our sensiblities, since we prefer to delete the sand from our sandwiches.

Later boats have a more conventional companionway ladder, eliminating the giant first step and the possibility of a foot in the middle of your lasagna, but making it difficult to use the galley counter, now hidden behind the ladder. There is a compact nav station opposite the galley. It has a small chart table, and some storage and space for electronics outboard. The chart table must be kept small to give access to the quarterberth.

You'll find the electrical panel in one of two places: under the bridgedeck in the galley, or outboard of the chart table. The nav station location offers more protection from water coming down the companionway—which it will—but space for electronics is sacrificed.

Sales literature refers to the quarterberth, which is 41" wide at its head, as a "cozy double." Cozy isn't really the word for a "double" berth that tapers to less than 2' wide at the foot. Forget it. Many owners have added an opening port from the quarterberth into the cockpit, and this helps ventilation a lot.

The interior of any 30' boat is a compromise. For the coastal cruising for which she was designed, the interior of the O'Day 30 is spacious and functional, and is probably the boat's best selling point.

Conclusions

With her good performance and big interior, the O'Day 30 makes a reasonable coastal cruising boat. This is a low-maintenance boat, with little exterior wood. Along with low maintenance, you get pretty plain-Jane appearance.

The boat still looks modern. If she appeared in a boat show today, she wouldn't look dated.

Unless you need shoal draft, we'd opt for the deep-keel boat, for its simplicity, if nothing else.

The extended stern of the O'Day 31 makes that boat much better looking in our opinion, since the big, fat stern of the 30 is probably her least attractive feature. The 31' boat is far more expensive on the used boat market, however, so you have to decide how much you're willing to pay for improved looks and a boarding platform.

Compared to a lot of newer 30-footers, the O'Day is quite heavy, but we consider that a plus for a boat that may sail in fairly exposed waters. For the type of use most boats this size will get, the boat looks like a good value on the used boat market. You could spend a lot more money for a lot less boat. • **PS**

S2 9.2

A roomy, well-built middle-of-the-road cruiser with both aft and center cockpit versions.

The history of S2 Yachts is in many ways a parable for the modern fiberglass sailboat industry. Begun in 1974 by an experienced fiberglass builder, the company grew rapidly, building first some unattractive "two-story" cruisers, followed by a series of conventional cruiser-racers in the late '70s and early '80s, then a successful fleet of race-oriented cruisers in the mid '80s. Finally, as sailboat sales took a nosedive in the late '80s, the company converted its entire production to powerboats.

In late 1989, the company was approached by the class association of its popular 26' racer, the S2 7.9. Would the company be willing to do a small run of 7.9s for those serious racers who wanted to replace their seven-to nine-year-old boats? The company thought it over and said, yes—provided they could be guaranteed 10 orders.

As we write this, the class association and S2 dealers around the country have been unable to come up with the 10 orders, and the company has cancelled the offering, perhaps the end of sailboat building by this prosperous company, and perhaps also an unfortunate commentary on the sailboat industry.

During its heyday, S2 developed a strong reputation for good quality boats. The company was founded by Leon Slikkers after he had sold his powerboat company, Slickcraft. As part of the sales agreement, he was not to make powerboats for a period of time, but there was no restraint on sailboat building. So he built a new plant which was, at the time, a model for production-line efficiency. Among other things, the hulls were laid up in an enclosed, climate-controlled room, and they remained in molds until most of the interior was installed to ensure that there was as little deformation of the basic molding as possible.

Specifications

LOA	29' 11"
LWL	25' 0"
Beam	10' 3"
Draft	3' 11"/4' 11" (shoal/deep)
Displacement	9,800 lbs.
Ballast	4,000 lbs.
Sail area	468 sq. ft.

In the late 1970s, S2 did start building powerboats again, and soon established its Tiara line at the top end of the market. As evidence of Slikkers' insight into the business (as well as a bit of luck, perhaps), when the conglomerate that owned Slickcraft began to see declining sales in the early '80s, S2 was able to buy Slickcraft back at a fraction of its original sale price. And of course, S2 enjoyed the boom in powerboat buying which accompanied the decline in sailboat sales during the mid and late '80s.

From the start, Slikkers also assembled an experienced crew of builders and sellers from the local area. At the time, Holland, Michigan, was the home of Chris Craft as well as Slickcraft and several other smaller powerboat builders.

The company continues today with a strong crew,

managed primarily by Slikkers' son, David, and other family members. The company personnel helped establish a reputation for good relationships with S2 owners, a reputation which continues, even though the company is no longer in the sailboat business.

In preparing this story, we talked with a number of S2 9.2 owners who reported that they are still able to get information, advice, and some parts and equipment from the company.

The Boat and Builder

As its nomenclature suggests, S2 Yachts was one of those few American companies willing to commit to the metric system when the government said it would be a good thing to do. The 9.2 stands for 9.2 meters, as with the company's other boats (7.3, 7.9, 10.3, etc.). S2 stuck with the classification for a long time, only advertising the 9.2 as the S2 30 after it had been in production for years (not to be confused with the later S2 30 designed by Graham & Schlageter). The boat overall is 29' 11", the most common length of 30-footers in those days when one of the popular racing rules—the Midget Ocean Racing Club (MORC)—required boats to be "under 30 feet."

The boat was built in two configurations, from 1977 to 1987. The 9.2C was a center-cockpit version, and the last one built was hull number 427. The 9.2A was the aft-cockpit version, and the last one built was hull number 520.

From talking to the company, it is unclear whether the hull numbers represent the actual number of boats built. In the 70s, it was not unusual for compa-

nies, as part of their marketing strategy, to start a production run with hull number 10, or even hull number 100, so that a model would appear to be more popular or successful than it actually was. The people currently at S2 simply didn't know if that had been done, but we suspect the total of 947 hull numbers is more than the actual number of S2 9.2s built. Nonetheless, the 9.2 had a successful run.

The 9.2 was designed by Arthur Edmunds, who was S2's "in-house" designer. Beginning in 1981, S2 built a number of racing-oriented cruisers designed by the Chicago naval architects Scott Graham and Eric Schlageter, but all of the earlier cruising boats were done by Edmunds. Edmunds also contributed engineering and design detail to Graham & Schlageter's hull designs.

We would describe the 9.2 design—and all of Edmunds' S2s—as moderate and conventionally modern. The hull has short overhangs, a relatively flat sheer, a long fin keel, and spade rudder. The boats are reasonably attractive, and the aft-cockpit model has pleasing proportions. The center-cockpit model has a high, boxy superstructure whose profile is relieved by good contour moldings of the deckhouse, cockpit, and aft cabin.

One advantage of the conventional looks of the 9.2 is that it is not likely to go out of fashion—a plus for the boat holding its value. Though the rigs were identical on all versions, shallow-draft keels were a popular option; these reduced the draft from 4' 11" to 3' 11". The deeper keel doesn't seem excessive for most waters and is our choice. The lead ballast is internal. S2 did a good job of embedding and sealing

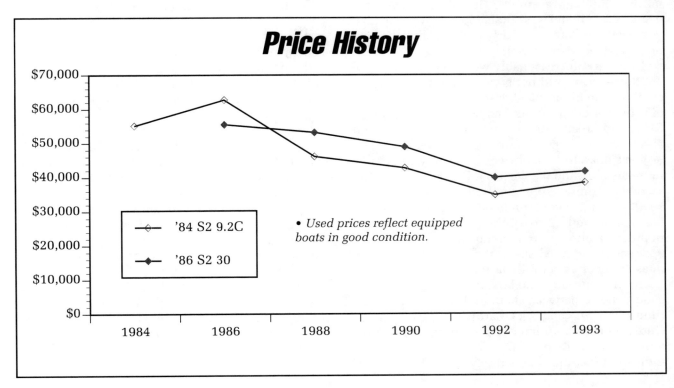

Price History

● Used prices reflect equipped boats in good condition.

Legend: —◇— '84 S2 9.2C   —◆— '86 S2 30

the lead in the keel cavity, so leaking should be minimal even in a hard grounding.

The hull is a conservative hand-laid laminate, and the deck is balsa-cored. S2 used a conventional inward-turning flange to attach the deck, with an aluminum toerail for protecting the joint. S2 is known for good glass work, particularly gelcoats, and almost all the used 9.2s that we have seen still are cosmetically good or recoverable with a good rubbing out.

Sailing Performance

'Adequate' would be a good way to describe the sailing performance of the 9.2. The boat came with a deck-stepped Kenyon spar and North sails as standard, later with Hall or Offshore spars. The rigging and other sailing hardware was good enough in quality that little re-rigging or upgrading is likely to be needed.

The used 9.2 we examined thoroughly, for example, had internal halyards, reef lines and outhaul, a good Harken mainsheet traveler, Lewmar #8 halyard winches, and two-speed Lewmar #30s for the jib sheets. On the down-side, every equipment list of used S2s we looked at listed the original North sails, with an occasional newer furling genoa. One disadvantage of a late model boat with good gear is that the owner is less likely to upgrade before he sells it, so the second owner probably will be facing the purchase of new sails.

When we sailed a shoal-draft 9.2, our initial reaction was surprise at its tenderness. Other owners in our survey agree that the shoal-draft model heels fairly easily, and a number thought that even the deeper draft model was tender. Several reported that you need to reduce sail fairly early to keep the boat on its feet and sailing well.

The boat sails reasonably well. The one we were on, however, would not go to weather decently—a combination of the shoal draft and a well-worn suit of sails. On other points, the boat was respectable. Close and broad reaching, it moved very well and was just a bit sluggish running.

She's not a fast boat by contemporary standards. In most areas, the 9.2 carries a PHRF rating of 180 seconds per mile (six seconds slower for the shoal-keel), which is six seconds per mile slower than a Pearson 30 and 12 to 15 seconds slower than the popular Catalina 30 with a tall rig. In contrast, the 9.2's racing-oriented sister, the S2 9.1, a 30-footer, rates 50 seconds per mile faster.

On the plus side, the boat is easy to sail, with a good balance between main and jib sail area. The running rigging and deck hardware is well set up. Oddly, not one equipment list for used 9.2s that we looked at had a spinnaker or spinnaker gear, an indication that the boat is rarely raced. However, if someone is interested in an occasional club race, the boat should sail up to its rating, assuming the sails are good and the boat well handled.

The deck is well laid out, though the walkways are a bit narrow for getting forward, and there's a considerable step up into the center cockpit. Details of the deck—anchor well, bow fittings, cleats, halyard runs, and so forth—are well executed.

Performance Under Power

A few of the 1977/1978 boats were sold with an Atomic 4 gas engine. After 1979, diesels were installed. Through 1984, the engines were 12-hp or 15-hp Yanmars, or 12-hp Volvos. In 1985, a Yanmar 23 was optional.

The Atomic 4 was a good engine for the boat, as was the Yanmar 23. However, a number of owners report that the boat is underpowered with the Yanmar 12 and 15, and the Volvo 12. For a 10,000 pound boat, 12 to 15 hp would be adequate by traditional standards, but many sailors seem to want a little more these days. The Yanmar 15 in the boat we sailed had no trouble pushing the boat in calm waters, but the owner did say that the boat couldn't buck any kind of head sea. For some, the optional Yanmar 23 will make the later models more desirable.

In the center-cockpit model, many owners complained about the inaccessibility of one side of the engine and the difficulty of getting at the dipstick, but otherwise the engine was serviceable. A few boats were apparently sold with raw-water cooling rather than a heat exchanger. We'd be cautious about one of the older boats with raw-water cooling unless it had been kept exclusively in fresh water.

Interior

The interior was undoubtedly the strong selling point of the boat. For the most part, the belowdecks finish is well done, and there's about as much usable room below as you could get without making the hull significantly larger.

S2 was one of the first sailboat builders to use fabric as a hull liner, and it became almost a trademark of S2 interiors. The fabric is a neutral-colored polypropylene, treated to be mildew resistant. When we first saw the fabric, we were skeptical, wondering how it would hold up to saltwater soakings. But having owned a smaller S2 for five years, we finally became converts; in fact, in refitting our current boat, we used the fabric extensively, rather than replacing aged vinyl and wood veneer ceilings. The fabric is contact-cemented to the hull, and it holds up amazingly well, absorbing virtually no water. It is quite resistant to mildew and stains. The new owner of an S2 will want to find a good, compact wet/dry vacuum cleaner, which is the required maintenance equipment for the fabric.

The rest of the interior has teak veneer plywood, Formica, and solid teak trim, and the workmanship is good. Layouts changed little throughout the production of the boats. The aft-cockpit model is conventional, with a V-berth that is a bit short, a large head and hanging locker, a large dinette/settee with a settee opposite, and an L-shaped galley with a chart area/quarter berth opposite. There's adequate stowage under the berths and decent outside stowage in the lazarettes.

The center-cockpit model moves the main cabin forward and the head aft, near to and partially underneath the center cockpit. The galley is opposite the head, running lengthwise down the port side of the cabin and partially under the cockpit. The aft-cabin is roomy, with an athwartship double berth and good locker space. The shortcoming of the center cockpit is that there is virtually no outside storage.

Choosing between the center and aft cockpit is largely a matter of personal preference. With children, or two couples cruising, the aft cabin is hard to beat for livability.

Overall, the interiors are well enough designed and executed that little major work or upgrading should be necessary on most used boats. Many people will want to replace the alcohol stoves on earlier models, perhaps add refrigeration (or replace the original Unifridge), and perform the normal long-term maintenance of re-upholstering, but otherwise the interiors should need little major attention.

Conclusions

The S2s were well-built. Whereas other production companies frequently cheapened or upgraded models from year to year to find marketing niches, S2 made boats to sell near the high end of the production boat market, and kept the quality at a consistent level.

The 9.2s have maintained their value about as well as any 30-footer in the current market. Because the only significant advantage of the 1986 model is the larger Yanmar engine and newer equipment, we would gladly take one of the older 9.2s at a lower price, since the necessary upgrades could easily be done (sails, cushions, electronics) and the final cost would still be much lower than the newer boat.

It's easy to pay too much money for a used boat these days, but S2 owners generally think they have a good product, and they'll probably be harder to dicker with than many sellers. **• PS**

Tartan 30

A boat that exemplifies the fast, comfortable and solidly built 30-footer of the 1970s.

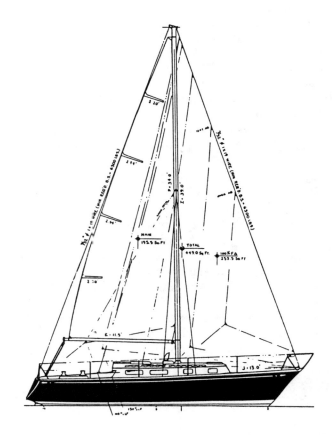

The early 1970s was the heyday of the 30' racer/cruiser. The phenomenon was not a coincidence. The Midget Ocean Racing Class (MORC) with a maximum boat length of 30' had become highly popular. The IOR Three-Quarter Ton Class (a "poor man's One Ton Class") had just been formed. And most persuasive of all, a 30' boat could offer eager boat buyers what they thought they wanted: five or six berths, full headroom, fully enclosed head, complete galley, and big boat heft. Better still, the rapidly maturing fiberglass boatbuilding industry was ready to produce such boats.

These elements combined to produce a whole generation of boats with moderate displacement, beam and draft; rudders well separated from shortened modified fin keels; and masthead rigs with a fairly high aspect ratio, none of which were particularly distorted by the dictates of a rating rule. Much about their design was traditional, yet there were significant departures: long waterlines relative to overall length, high topsides, and reverse transoms that gave them a contemporary look.

The result was such production boats as the Pearson 30, the Yankee 30, the Newport 30, the Cal 2-30, the Morgan 30/2, and the Scampi, to name but a few of the more familiar ones. In all, no less than two dozen boats of a similar size and type were introduced in just three years, many of them to become highly successful among sailors eager for the performance and amenities of big boats at a modest price.

Among the most noteworthy and enduring of the 30-footers from this era has been the Tartan 30. Designed by Sparkman & Stephens when that name was far and away the most prestigious in yacht design, the Tartan 30 exemplified the solidly built, comfortably appointed, fast production boat which

Specifications

LOA	29' 11"
LWL	24' 3"
Beam	10' 0"
Draft	4' 11"
Displacement	8,750 lbs.
Sail area	449 sq. ft.

typified not just the early 1970s, but, as it turned out, almost the whole decade (the Tartan 30 was discontinued in 1980). In her first year, 1971, the Tartan 30 was the most successful 30-footer on a wide variety of race courses; in 1976 it won the MORC of Long Island Sound, just as another had five years before.

On modern race courses the Tartan 30 gives away a lot to newer racer-cruisers with more efficient sailplans, keel configurations and use of live ballast. And, of course, they give away even more to the present breed of lighter, faster boats which are less compromised by full accommodations, interior room, and heavy rigs.

Yet these are boats whose heritage is the Tartan 30, many of which may no longer be around, let alone competitive, when the Tartan will still be winning some races.

A Close Look at the Boat

The dilemma for a designer in 1970 was to put livable accommodations in a boat with a waterline length that, a decade or so earlier, would have been a daysailer—and still have the boat perform like a racer and not a houseboat. Many of the 30-footers, indeed even larger boats, were only moderately successful with their interior layouts. The Tartan 30 is one of them. In fact, two layouts were available in the 30, one with the galley aft and the other with the galley amidships, stretched out along the starboard side. The midship galley permitted a pair of quarterberths in addition to the "convertible" cabin table/double berth available in both models. The aft galley eliminated a quarterberth but left room for a settee berth to starboard. Owners are clearly divided in their opinions of the two plans. Cooking is avowedly enhanced with the midship galley (although there is no room for a stove with oven); sleeping accommodations benefit from the settee berth arrangement.

The accommodation plan is further complicated by the placement of the engine in the forward end of the main saloon. The engine box is in the way of living space; yet, for accessibility to the engine, the location and openness are unparallelled even in boats twice the size of this one.

As with many boats of the era, the head of the 30 is cramped; so too are the V-berths in the forward cabin, the quarterberth(s), and the aft galley—all the result of the 1970 mandate by boatbuilders' marketing honchos that as many berths a possible be crammed into all available spaces—not so the boats could sleep that many, but so the advertising could say they could.

The Tartan 30 sails well. In a breeze to windward—perhaps the best test of any boat—she is at her best: comfortable, stable, reasonably handy, and modestly dry. Off the wind she is more steerable than a host of successors with free-standing spade rudders and dagger-thin keels. Only on a broad reach with biggish following seas can her weather helm be tough to handle. Under such conditions, good sail control hardware—vang, traveler, reefing, adjustable backstay, etc—is important.

Under PHRF the Tartan 30 typically has a base rating of 170 to 180, rating faster in areas with heavier winds. In fact, in some quarters the Tartan 30 is regarded as the archetypal PHRF competitor. Her narrow inboard shroud base helps keep her competitive upwind against newer boats, and her directional stability off the wind is better. She does well against such basically similar boats with comparable ratings as the Catalina 30, the C&C 29 and 30, and, except perhaps in the lightest of air, the Pearson 30. She can stay with the likes of a J/30 (PHRF 135 or so) unless the J has a mob on her rail.

For performance in heavier winds, she needs merely a good hand on the helm and some constructive crew work. In lighter winds the Tartan 30 wants all the help she can get: a folding prop, a large, well shaped mainsail, and a genoa of at least 150%. In sailing regions with lots of really light air, her tall rig (optional at one time) is a plus.

The original engine in the 30 was the Atomic 4; by

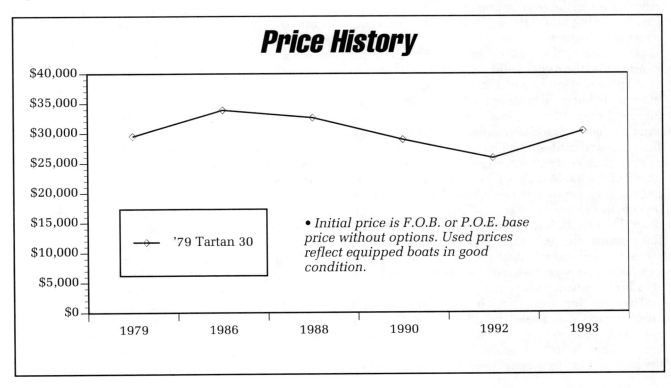

Price History

• Initial price is F.O.B. or P.O.E. base price without options. Used prices reflect equipped boats in good condition.

Legend: ◇ '79 Tartan 30

1975 the Farymann two-cylinder diesel was an option. Located amidships, the engine turns a shaft that exits the after edge of the keel, putting the prop in perhaps its most nearly ideal location: well forward where it is protected and, offset a few degrees, efficient. In reverse, though, it is even less efficient than boats with fully exposed props on shafts.

The cockpit is of average size for boats of the Tartan 30's vintage. Her low wood coamings are uncomfortable to either sit on or against, but the tiller is far enough aft so that there is good seating forward. The mainsheet and engine controls are awkward to handle, though. And the 30 should have a higher sill in the companionway; the original is too low to keep a flooded cockpit from emptying belowdecks.

Storage aboard the 30 is less than on many comparable boats. With either the two quarterberths or the aft galley and its cockpit-opening icebox there is little cockpit locker space. Sails are thus commonly in the way and a number of owners who sail as a couple have turned the forward berths into a sail locker. Others use the quarterberth. The area under the cockpit sole is also available but less accessible.

A word of warning. The Tartan 30 is a wetter boat belowdecks than most. Not only are the quarterberths highly vulnerable to spray and rain through the companionway, but the sink is prone to filling and letting water slosh onto the sole.

What To Look For

As with so many boats as old as the 30, the potential problems fall conspicuously into two categories: cosmetic and structural. Most owners report notable degradation of the gelcoat: crazing, voids, and chalking. Blistering and deck delamination seem about average in frequency.

Belowdecks, the teak cabin sole gets the most complaints; the rather solid (if aesthetically pedestrian) plywood joinerwork gets the fewest. Like such other plain but solid boats as the Pearson 35 and C&C 35, the Tartan 30 lends itself to dressing up of the interior decor. The chainplates are prone to leaks; the ports and hull-to-deck joint seem not to be.

Any prospective owner can do his own quick check of the likeliest structural problems. Since the mast is keel-stepped, the under-deck support is not a problem. However, the mast step and mast butt should be checked, since corrosion from water leaking around the partner is common. The tabbing around the main bulkhead should also be checked carefully. Likewise the tierod between the deck and step in the way of the mast.

The most important check is in the bilge fore and aft of the external keel. Groundings and improper hauling or storage can result in loosened floor timbers and keel bolts and flexibility or even tearing of the hull. A misaligned engine and/or a gap between

deadwood and ballast are clues to such problems. Some owners, either for prevention or during repair, have reinforced the bilge area and parts of the hull where poppets bear weight during dry storage. Note: the Tartan 30 seems to be one of those boats that is more comfortable being stored in a good cradle rather than on jackstands.

The rig, like most of those specified by Sparkman & Stephens, was designed to be practically indestructible. Given its inherent strength, look primarily for the effects of corrosion at the spreaders and the butt. Many 30s have been fitted with babystays in lieu of forward lower shrouds. For typical cruising we think the babystay is a pain and probably unnecessary, so we'd make it detachable.

Given its accessibility that should have encouraged better than average TLC, the old Atomic 4 should still be in reasonable shape. But have it mechanically checked. There have been reports of engines needing rebuilding after water backed through the exhaust. The fuel tank also tends to rust. The alternative to the Atomic 4, the Farymann diesel, is not necessarily a better bet as an engine since parts are difficult to obtain and expensive.

Conclusions

Having raced alternately on and against a well-sailed Tartan 30, we think there are few boats that have a better blend of performance, strength, and enduring styling from its era. Sure, the 30, like almost all of her contemporaries, sails, feeds, socializes, and nurtures a lot fewer crew members than she can comfortably sleep. Yet, she is a boat well suited for weekend and vacation cruising for a couple, perhaps with a child or two or an occasional guest. With a crew of four or five and a modest outlay for equipment and sails, she can be raced hard in semi-serious PHRF competition. The Tartan 30 does a lot of things of which a good 30-footer, even an old one, should be capable, while remaining a good investment.

Serendipitously, she offers rare dividends: a choice of two quite different accommodation plans, plus both an interior and an exterior that offer a superb opportunity for dressing up and customizing. The 30 is thus remarkably versatile, something that in used boats is a true—and rare—virtue.

At the risk of offending opponents of editorializing, we'd opt for the aft galley arrangement largely because we're not big fans of quarterberths, gourmet shipboard meals, or boats that have no leeward settee berth on one tack. We would then if necessary upgrade our 30 with a good dodger, added ventilation, additional exterior wood trim, big self-tending winches (inadequate winches seem a chronic deficiency). Then, finally, for racing we'd outfit her with whatever it took to stuff it to those newer designs that think the 30 is an outdated relic.   • **PS**

Olson 30

This speedster is as specialized as it gets; mind-blowing performance, but almost no living space.

The Olson 30 is of a breed of sailboats born in Santa Cruz, California called the *ULDB*, an acronym for *ultra light displacement boat.* ULDBs are big dinghies—long on the waterline, short on the interior, narrow on the beam, and very light on both the displacement and the price tag. ULDBs attract a different kind of sailor—the type for whom performance means everything.

For some yachting traditionalists, the arrival of ULDB has been a hard pill to swallow. Part of this is simple resentment of a ULDB's ability to sail boat-for-boat with a racer-cruiser up to 15' longer (and a whole lot more expensive). Part of it is the realization that, to sail a ULDB might mean having to learn a whole new set of sailing skills. Part of it is a reaction to the near-manic enthusiasts of Santa Cruz, where nearly 100 ULDBs race for pure fun—without the help of race committees, protest committees, or handicaps (in Santa Cruz, IOR is a dirty word). And part of the traditionalists' resentment is their gut feeling that ULDBs aren't real yachts.

In 1970, Californian George Olson tried an experiment and created the first ULDB. He thought if he took a boat with the same displacement and sail area as a Cal 20, but made it longer and narrower, it might go faster. The boat he built was called *Grendel* and it did go faster than a Cal 20, much faster than anyone had expected. The plug for *Grendel* was later widened by Santa Cruz boatbuilder Ran Moors, and used to make the mold for the Moore 24, a now-popular ULDB one-design.

In the meantime, George Olson had joined up with another Santa Cruz builder by the name of Bill Lee, and together they designed and built the Santa Cruz 27. Olson also helped Lee build his 1977 Transpac winner *Merlin*, a 67', 20,000 pound monster of a ULDB (she was subsequently legislated out of the

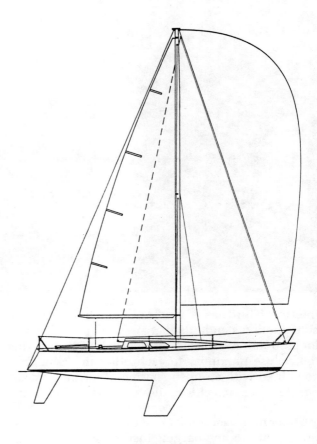

Specifications

LOA	30' 0"
LWL	27' 6"
Beam	9' 4"
Draft	5' 1"
Displacement	3,600 lbs.
Ballast	1,800 lbs.
Sail area	380 sq. ft.

Transpac race). Then Olson and several other of Lee's employees started their own boatbuilding firm (in Santa Cruz, of course) called Pacific Boats.

The first project for Pacific Boats was the Olson 30, which was put into production in 1978. Pacific Boats later became Olson/Ericson, and produced a 25 and a 40. The latest incarnation of the 30 is called the 911.

Construction

Some people wonder how ULDBs can be built so light, yet still be seaworthy offshore. The answer is three-fold: first, a light boat is subjected to lighter loads, when pounding through a heavy sea, than a boat of greater displacement. Second, there is a tremendous saving in weight with a stripped-out

interior. Third, as a whole, ULDB builders have construction standards that are well above average for production sailboats. The ULDB builders say that their close proximity to each other in Santa Cruz combined with an open sharing of technology has enabled them to achieve these standards.

The Olson 30 is no exception. The hull and deck are fiberglass vacuum-bagged over a balsa core. The process of vacuum-bagging insures maximum saturation of the laminate and core with a minimum of resin, making the hull light and stiff. The builder claims that they have so refined the construction of the Olson 30 that each finished hull weighs within 10 pounds of the standard. The deck of the Olson does not have plywood inserts in place of the balsa where winches are mounted, instead relying on external backing plates for strength.

The hull-to-deck joint is an inward turned overlapping flange, glued with a rigid compound called Reid's adhesive, and mechanically fastened with closely spaced bolts through a slotted aluminum toerail. This provides a strong, protected joint, seaworthy enough for sailing offshore. We would prefer a semi-rigid adhesive, however, because it is less likely to fracture and cause a leak in the event of a hard collision. The aluminum toerail provides a convenient location for outboard sheet leads, but is painful to those sitting on the rail.

The Olson 30's 1,800 pound keel is deep (5.1' draft) and less than 5" thick. Narrow, bolted-on keels need extra athwartships support. The Olson 30 accomplishes this with nine 5/8" bolts and one 1" bolt (to which the lifting eye is attached). The lead keel is faired with auto body putty and then completely wrapped with fiberglass to seal the putty from the marine environment. Too many builders neglect

The deck layout of the Olson 30 is quite good for her designed purpose: flat-out racing.

sealing auto body putty-faired keels, and too many boat owners then find the putty peeling off at a later date. The Olson's finished keel is painted, and, on the boats we have seen, remarkably fair.

The keel-stepped, single-spreader, tapered mast is cleanly rigged with 5/32" Navtec rod rigging and internal tangs. The mast section is big enough for peace of mind in heavy air. The halyards exit the mast at well-spaced intervals, so as not to create a weak spot. The shroud chainplates are securely attached to half-bulkheads of 1" plywood. In addition, a tie rod attaches the deck to the mast, tensioned by a turnbuckle. While this arrangement should provide adequate strength, we would prefer both a tie rod and a full bulkhead that spans the width of the cabin so as to absorb the compressive loads that the tension of the rig puts on the deck.

The rudder's construction is labor intensive, but strong. Urethane foam is hand shaped to templates, then glued to a 4" thick solid fiberglass rudder post. The builder prefers fiberglass because it has more "memory" than aluminum or steel. Stainless steel straps are wrapped around the rudder and mechanically fastened to the post. Then the whole assembly is faired, fiberglassed, and painted.

Handling Under Sail

For those of you who agonize over whether your PHRF rating is fair, consider the ratings of ULDBs. The Santa Cruz 50 rates 0; that's right—*zero*. The 67' Merlin has rated as low as minus 60. The Olson 30 rates anywhere from 90 to 114, depending on the local handicapper. Olson 30 owners tell us that the boat will sail to a PHRF rating of 96, but she will almost never sail to her astronomical IOR rating of 32' (the IOR heavily penalizes ULDBs).

ULDBs are fast. They are apt to be on the tender side, and sail with a quick, "jerky" motion through waves. Instead of punching through a wave, they ride over it. You may get to where you are going fast, but with the motion of the boat and the Spartan interior you won't get there in comfort. Olson 30 owners tell us that they do far less cruising and far more racing that they had expected to do when they bought the boat. They say it's more fun to race because the boat is so lively.

Like most ULDBs the Olson 30 races best at the extremes of wind conditions—under 10 knots and over 20 knots. Although her masthead rig may appear short, it is more than powerful enough for her displacement. Owners tell us that she accelerates so quickly you can almost tack at will—a real tactical advantage in light air. In winds under 10 knots they say she sails above her PHRF rating both upwind and downwind.

In moderate breezes it's a different story. Once the wind gets much above 10 knots, it's time to change down to the #2 genoa. In 15 knots, especially if the seas are choppy, it's very difficult for the Olson 30 to save her time on boats of conventional displacement, according to three-time national champ Kevin Connally. The Olson 30 is always faster downwind, but even with a crew of 5 or 6, she just cannot hang in there upwind.

In winds above 20 knots, the Olson 30 still has her problems upwind, but when she turns the weather mark the magic begins. As soon as she has enough wind to either surf or plane, the Olson 30 can make up for all she loses upwind, and more. The builder claims that she has pegged speedometers at 25 knots in the big swells and strong westerlies off the coast of California. That is, if the crew can keep her 1800 pound keel under her 761 sq. ft. spinnaker.

The key to competitiveness in a strong breeze is the ability of the crew. Top crews say that, because she is so quick to respond, they have fewer problems handling her in heavy air than a heavier, conventional boat. However, an inexperienced crew which cannot react fast enough can have big problems. "The handicappers say she can fly downwind, so they give us a low rating (PHRF), but they don't understand that we have to sail slow just to stay in control," complained the crew of one new owner.

Like any higher performance class of sailboat, the Olson 30 attracts competent sailors. Hence, the boat is pushed to a higher level of overall performance, and the PHRF rating reflects this. An inexperienced sailor must realize that he may have a tougher time making her sail to this inflated rating than a boat that is less "hot." The two most common mistakes that new Olson 30 owners make are pinching upwind and allowing the boat to heel excessively. ULDBs cannot be sailed at the 30 degrees of heel to which many sailors of conventional boats are accustomed. To keep her flat you must be quick to shorten sail, move the sheet leads outboard, and get more crew weight on the rail. You can't afford to have a person sitting to leeward trimming the genoa in a 12-knot breeze. To keep her thin keel from stalling upwind, owners tell us it's important to keep the sheets eased and the boat footing.

Being masthead-rigged, the Olson 30 needs a larger sail inventory than a fractionally rigged boat. Class rules allow one mainsail, six headsails (jibs and spinnakers) and a 75% storm jib. Owners who do mostly handicap racing tell us they often carry more than six headsails.

Handling Under Power

Only a few of the Olson 30s sold to date have been equipped with inboard power. This is because the extra weight of the inboard and the drag of the

The interior is barely habitable, as befits a pure racing machine. Headroom is only 4' 5". The head is a portable, the sink has no drain, and it's necessary to kneel on the cabin sole to use the stove.

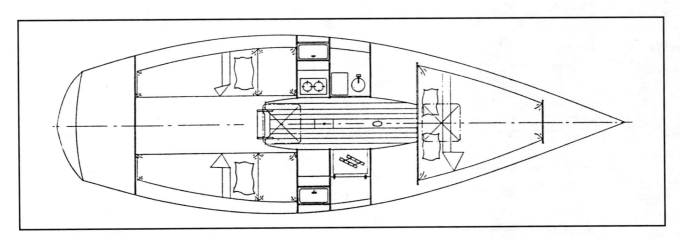

propeller, strut and shaft are a real disadvantage when racing against the majority of Olson 30s, which are equipped with outboard engines.

The Olson 30 is just barely light enough to be pushed by a 4-5 hp outboard, which is the largest outboard that even the most healthy sailor should be hefting over a transom. It takes a 7.5 hp. outboard to push the Olson 30 at 6.5 knots in a flat calm. The Olson's raked transom requires an extra long outboard bracket, which puts the engine throttle and shift out of reach for anyone much less than 6' tall: "A real pain in the ass," said one owner. Storage is a problem, too. Even if you could get the outboard through the stern lazarette's small hatch, you wouldn't want to race with the extra weight so far aft. So most owners end up storing the outboard on the cabin sole.

The inboard, a 154 pound, 7 hp BMW diesel, was a $4,500 option. Unlike most boats, the Olson 30 will probably not return the investment in an inboard when you sell the boat, because it detracts from the boat's primary purpose—racing.

Without an inboard there's a problem charging the battery. Owners who race with extensive electronics have to take the battery ashore after every race for recharging. If the Olson 30 weren't such a joy to sail in light air, and so maneuverable in tight places, the lack of inboard power would be a serious enough drawback to turn away more sailors than it does.

Deck Layout

In most respects, the Olson 30 is a good sea boat. Although the cockpit is 6 1/2' long, the wide seats and narrow floor result in a relatively small cockpit volume, so that little sea water can collect in the cockpit if the boat is pooped or knocked down. However, foot room is restricted, while the width of the seats makes it awkward to brace your legs on the leeward seat. The seats themselves are comfortable because they are angled up and the seatbacks are angled back. There are gutters to drain water off the leeward seat. The long mainsheet traveler is mounted across the cockpit—good for racing but not so good for cruising.

The Olson 30's single companionway drop board is latchable from inside the cabin, a real necessity in a storm offshore. A man overboard pole tube in the stern is standard equipment. Teak toerails on the cockpit coaming and on the forward part of the cabin house provide good footing, and there are handholds on the aft part of the cabin house.

The tapered aluminum stanchions are set into sockets molded into the deck and glassed to the inside of the hull, a strong, clean, leak-proof system. However, the stanchions are not glued or mechanically fastened into the sockets. If pulled upwards with great force they can be pulled out. We feel this is a safety hazard. Tight lifelines would help prevent this from happening, but most racing crews tend to leave them slightly loose so as to be able to lean farther outboard when hanging over the rail upwind. If the stanchions were fastened into the sockets with bolts or screws they would undoubtedly leak. A leakproof solution to this problem should be devised and made available to Olson 30 owners.

The cockpit has two drains of adequate diameter.

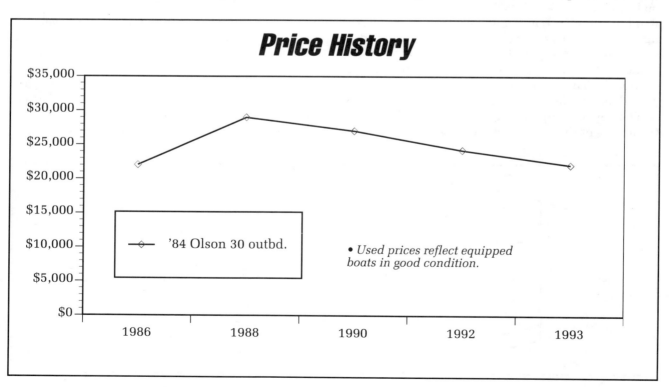

Price History

Legend: ◇— '84 Olson 30 outbd.

• *Used prices reflect equipped boats in good condition.*

The Olson 30 has several good features for offshore racing: note the man-overboard pole tube, high companionway sill and small cockpit volume.

The bilge pump, a Guzzler 500, is mounted in the cockpit. The Guzzler is an easily operated, high capacity pump. However, its seeming fragility worries us. As is common on most boats, the stern lazarette is not sealed off from the rest of the interior. If the boat were pooped or knocked down with the lazarette open, water could rush below through the lazarette relatively unrestricted. As the Olson 30 has a shallow sump, there is little place for water to go except above the cabin sole.

A "paint-roller" type non-skid is molded into the Olson 30's deck. It provides excellent traction, but it is more difficult to keep clean than conventional patterned non-skid.

The Olson 30 is well laid out with hardware of reasonable, but not exceptional, quality. All halyards and pole controls lead to the cockpit though Easylock I clutch stoppers. The Easylocks are barely big enough to hold the halyards; they slip an inch under heavy loads. Older Olsons were equipped with Howard Rope Clutches.

The primary winches, Barient 22s, are also barely adequate. Some owners we talked to had replaced them with more powerful models. Schaefer headsail track cars are standard equipment. One owner complained that he had to replace them with Merrimans because the Schaefers kept slipping. Leading the vang to either rail and leading the reefs aft is also recommended. The mast partner is snug, leaving no space for mast blocks. The mast step is movable to adjust the prebend of the spar. The partner has a lip, over which a neoprene collar fits. The collar is hose-clamped to the mast. This should make a watertight mast boot. However, on the boat we sailed, the bail to which the boom vang attached obstructed the collar, causing water to collect and pour into the cabin.

The yoked backstay is adjustable from either quarter of the stern, one side being a 2-to-1 gross adjustment and the other side being an 8-to-1 fine tune. A Headfoil II is standard equipment. There is a babystay led to a ball-bearing track with a 4-to-1 purchase for easy adjustment. The track is tied to the thin plywood of the forward V-berth with a wire and turn-buckle. On the boat we sailed, the pad eye to which the babystay tie rod is attached was tearing out of the V-berth.

There is a port in the deck directly over the lifting eye in the bilge. This makes for quick and easy drysailing. The Olson 30, however, is not easily trailered; her 3600 pounds is too much for all but the largest cars, and her 9.3' beam requires a special trailering permit.

Belowdecks

The Olson 30 is cramped belowdecks. Her low free-board, short cabin house and substantial sheer may make her the sexiest-looking production boat on the water, but the price is headroom of only 4' 5". There is not even enough headroom for comfortable stoop-ing; moving about below is a real chore.

To offset the confinement of the interior, the builder has done all that is possible to make it light and airy. In addition to the lexan forward hatch and cabin house windows, the companionway hatch also has a lexan insert. The inside of the hull is smoothly sanded and finished with white gelcoat. There are no full height bulkheads dividing up the cabin. All of the furniture is built of lightweight, light-colored, 3/8" thick Scandinavian plywood of seven veneers.

The joinerwork is above average and all of the bulkhead and furniture tabbing is extremely neat. There isn't much to the Olson 30's interior, but what there is has been done with commendable crafts-manship. The interior wood is fragile, though. There are several unsupported panels of the 3/8" plywood; if someone were to fall against them with much force it's likely they would fracture. The cabin sole is narrow, and with the lack of headroom the wood-work is especially susceptible to being dinged and scratched from equipment like outboard engines. Once the finish on the wood is broken, it quickly absorbs water, which collects in the shallow bilge.

The Olson 30 is not a comfortable cruiser. Even after you've taken all the racing sails ashore, the belowdecks is barely habitable. To save weight the quarterberths are made of thin cushions sewn to vinyl and hung from pipes. These pipe berths are comfortable, but the cushions are not easily re-moved. Should they get wet it's likely they would stay wet for quite a while. Two seabags are hung on sail tracks above the quarter berths, which should help to insure that some clothes always stay dry.

Just forward of each quarterberth is a small uncushioned seat locker. Behind each seat is a small portable ice cooler. In one seat locker is the stove, an Origo 3000 which slides up and out of the locker on tracks. The Origo is a top-of-the-line unpressurized alcohol stove, but to operate it the cook must kneel on the cabin sole. To work at the navigation station, which is in front of the starboard seat, you must sit sideways. In front of the port seat is the lavette, with a hand water pump and a removable, shallow drainless sink. Drainless sinks eliminate the need for a through-hull fitting, a good idea; but they should be deep, not shallow.

The portable head is mounted under the forward V-berth, which we think is totally unsuitable for a sailboat. Who wants a smelly toilet under his pillow? Although there are curtains which can be drawn across the V-berth, we think human dignity deserves an enclosed head, especially on a 30' boat. The V-berth is large and easy to climb into, but there are no shelves above it nor a storage locker in the empty bow. In short, if you plan to cruise for more than a weekend you had better like roughing it.

Conclusions

For 30-footers, the price of an Olson 30 is cheap; but for boats of similar displacement, it's damned ex-pensive.

What do you get for the money? You get a boat that is well-built, seaworthy, and reasonably well laid out. You get a boat that, in light air, will sail as fast as boats costing nearly twice as much. Downwind in heavy air, you have a creature that will blow your mind and leave everything shy of a bigger ULDB in your wake. If you spend all of your sailing time racing in a PHRF fleet in an area where light or heavy air dominates, the Olson 30 will probably give you more pleasure for your dollar than almost anything afloat.

However if you race often in moderate air or enjoy more than a very occasional short cruise, you are likely to be very disappointed. Before you consider the Olson 30, you must realistically evaluate your abilities as a sailor. There's nothing worse than, after finding out that you can't race a boat to her potential, knowing that she is of little use for the other aspects of our sport.
• PS

Cape Dory 30

Our pick of these boats is a cutter-rigged late model with full-width galley and pedestal steering.

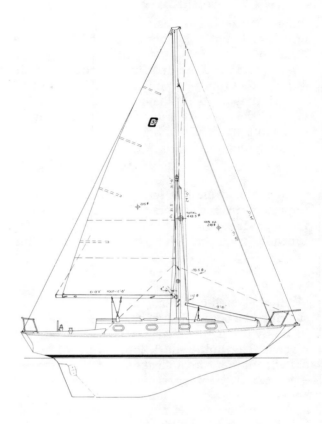

When the Cape Dory 30 entered production in 1976, it was the largest boat in the expanding line of the Taunton, Massachusetts boatbuilder. In 1986, when production ceased, over 350 Cape Dory 30s had been built, and what had been the largest boat in the company's fleet was one of the smallest.

In 1986, Cape Dory introduced the Cape Dory 30 Mk II, an entirely different boat, designed in-house (rather than by Carl Alberg), longer on the waterline, 1 1/2' wider, and with a far roomier and more modern interior.

The old Cape Dory 30 was designed as a ketch, with cutter or sloop rigs optional. In the middle of the production run, the more efficient cutter rig replaced the ketch as standard. The ketch remained an option.

The Cape Dory line always consisted of traditional-looking, long-keel cruising boats, and their appeal has been strongest on the East Coast, particularly in New England, a well-known hotbed of sailing reactionaries.

Specifications

LOA	30' 2"
LWL	22' 10"
Beam	9' 0"
Draft	4' 2"
Displacement	10,000 lbs.
Ballast	4,000 lbs.
Sail area	437 sq. ft.

Sailing Performance

No one buys a Cape Dory looking for a flashy speedster. The original ketch rig has a lot of windage, and relatively small, inefficient sails. The rig does, however, give the boat a distinctly "shippy" traditional appearance.

A PHRF rating of about 220 shows the ketch to be a slow boat. By way of contrast, the old original C&C 25 carries about the same rating. The cutter-rigged Cape Dory 30 is about 15 seconds per mile faster.

The Cape Dory 30 was originally equipped with worm gear steering. This type of gear is powerful, foolproof, and requires no steering pedestal in the cockpit. The wheel will also hold the rudder in position without a brake. The disadvantage is that there is almost no rudder feedback, so that it's hard to tell when the boat is properly balanced. Worm gear steering will not make you a better sailor.

The worm gear steerer is especially compatible with the original ketch rig. Since the mizzen is stepped in the middle of the cockpit, it's nice to get the steering wheel back aft where it won't take up any usable space. The top of the steering gear box also serves as a good helmsman's seat.

With the cutter rig, it became feasible to put a more conventional pedestal steerer in the boat. However, moving the steerer further forward meant that the old steering box—now a storage locker—was too far away from the wheel to be used as a seat.

In practice, you usually sit to the side of the wheel with a pedestal steerer, not behind it. But this re-

Owners' Comments

"Figure this boat is really the equivalent of a cruising 28-footer. It's not a big family boat just because it's 30' long. It's a nice singlehanding boat. Faults include a deck not bolted to the hull. The molded inner pan makes it difficult to find leaks if they happen. The location of the alcohol tank behind the stove is dangerous in case of a fire or a ruptured hose. No boat should ever have a single-cylinder diesel."

—1976 model in Maine

"The engine cannot be reached for repair and is impossible to crank by hand. The boat is too small for an offshore cruiser, too big for a daysailer. It's probably best for rough New England daysailing only."

—1977 model in Maryland

"With the ketch rig balanced and the worm gear steering, the boat sails herself. The boat will turn in its own length under power, but is poor in reverse. The hull-to-deck joint is not through-bolted, but there are no leaks so far. Exterior trim is good throughout the boat. Interior trim could be better. The cockpit could be a bit larger the seats are too narrow and lack back support. The cockpit is too crowded if you're sailing with more than four people. We've made a lot of minor modifications: altered the fresh water plumbing, added instruments, a dodger, a boarding ladder and drop-end tables. Parts for the Volvo diesel are expensive."

—1978 model in New York

"The boat is very stiff and seaworthy, but not especially dry. It is unresponsive under power, especially in a crosswind. It is very difficult to back down to port. I've had no trouble with the engine, but anything major would be tough to work on. Changing belts is a chore. The boat is classic-looking and well put together."

—1980 model in Florida

"The boat is well built: extremely seaworthy. With the Volvo engine it is a bit underpowered. The interior is restricted by the 9' beam. The only problem we've had since new is that the non-skid areas of the deck developed orange spots. My boat is down in the stern because the engine location is too far aft. I've put additional weight in the bow by filling the holding tank with water."

—1981 model in Virginia

"The boat is a bear in reverse due to the deep keel. It is supposed to sleep five, but is very comfortable for the two of us and an occasional overnight cruise with another couple. It's a well-made boat that has a solid feel."

—1984 model in New York

quires a wheel that is big enough to let you get far enough outboard to see sail trim. Most helmsmen will only sit directly behind the wheel when the boat is under power and they can see straight ahead, with no sails in the way.

The big steering wheel that's the easiest to use with pedestal steering almost requires a T-shaped cockpit for easy maneuverability. The Cape Dory 30 stuck with the straight bench cockpit seats, and used a fairly small destroyer wheel. Although you don't need the leverage of a big wheel on this boat, it will make steering less tiring, and there is room between the seats to fit a larger-diameter wheel. It would make it necessary to climb over the seats to go forward, however.

Most owners report that the boat—with either rig—is easy to balance under sail. The percentage reporting difficulty in balancing the boat complain of excessive weather helm on a close reach.

Hard steering when reaching is a common complaint on boats with attached rudders and a lot of rake to the rudderpost. The Cape Dory 30 does have a relatively efficient Constellation-type rudder, even if it is located about 2' further forward than it would be with a comparable fin keel and spade rudder underbody.

Weather helm when reaching is frequently caused by overtrimming the main. On a boat without a vang, the boom tends to lift quickly as the sheet is eased, and the top of the sail twists off and begins to luff. Thinking they've eased the sheet too much, many sailors will at that point overtrim the main, shifting the draft of the sail aft and creating weather helm. Under those conditions, the proper thing to do with the Cape Dory 30 is use mainsheet tension to create a fair leech, then ease the traveler down to keep the whole sail working.

On both rigs, the mainsail is controlled by a traveler over the main companionway.

With the ketch rig, the mast is stepped further forward than the cutter, and the mainsheet attaches to the boom about two-thirds of the way aft, giving reasonable leverage. With the cutter, the mast location means that the mainsheet attaches almost exactly at the boom midpoint, reducing leverage and making the sail somewhat harder to trim.

In either case the traveler location at the forward end of the companionway is out of the way, but it makes installing a cockpit dodger more difficult.

The cutter's main boom is at a reasonable height, but the taller helmsman should still watch his head when tacking.

With the advent of modern headsail reefing systems, the cutter rig is really superfluous on this boat. The small gap between the forestay and headstay makes it difficult to tack a big genoa, yet you really need a big genoa if this fairly heavy boat is to be properly powered in light air. The double head rig is fine in breezes over 15 knots, but in lighter air it's much slower than a good number one genoa.

According to owners, the boat's only sailing weakness is light air. With a lot of wetted surface and an inefficient foretriangle, the boat is simply not going to be fast in very light air. All in all, though, owners say the boat is faster than they expected it to be in all conditions.

With a 40% ballast/displacement ratio, the Cape Dory 30 is reasonably stiff despite the very narrow beam. You can get stability with a lot of ballast down low, or with a lot of beam. The Cape Dory 30 gets it from a lot of ballast, placed low in the hull.

With less weight aloft, the cutter should be slightly stiffer than the ketch.

Both the ketch and cutter rig use simple, untapered aluminum masts, stepped on deck. With a stiff section and double lower shrouds, these rigs are fairly foolproof.

Engine

Unlike many builders, Cape Dory put diesel engines in every inboard-powered sailboat they built after 1975. You won't find an Atomic 4 here.

What you will find, unfortunately, is an engine installation and selection that is somewhat less than ideal.

Because this is a narrow boat with slack bilges, it wasn't possible to get the engine far enough down in the bilge to be out of the way in a normal installation. Instead, the engine is mounted under the cockpit, using a V-drive. The engine is kept out of the way, but out of sight in this case means poor access for servicing. Getting to the alternator belts for adjustment, for example, requires crawling under the cockpit through a locker.

The original engine was a single-cylinder Yanmar diesel rated at 12 hp. This engine is too small for the boat, and single-cylinder engines are notorious for their vibration.

Starting with 1977 models, the Yanmar diesel was replaced with a Volvo MD7A, rated at 13 hp. The Volvo engine has more displacement, and has two cylinders. Nevertheless, some owners still complain that the boat is underpowered with the Volvo diesel.

Despite the long keel, the Cape Dory is reasonably maneuverable under power. The exception is handling in reverse, which according to many owners varies from unpredictable to impossible. This is not a characteristic unique to this boat; it is a fault of most long-keel boats with attached rudders. You learn to act as if reverse were nothing more than a set of brakes—not very good ones, at that.

Other than its location, the engine installation itself is pretty good, with dual fuel filters, 1" bronze shaft, and oil drip pan under the engine. The fuel tank capacity of 20 gallons should give well over 200 miles range under power with any of the engines.

During the 1983 model year, a switch was made to a two-cylinder Universal diesel. We would definitely prefer a boat with either the Volvo or Universal engine over the original small Yanmar.

Construction

The Cape Dory 30 is solidly built, although there is

The Cape Dory 30 is rather cramped compared to newer designs. Still, the layout is good. Later boats have a quarterberth and chart table on one side; we'd rather have a boat with the full-width galley.

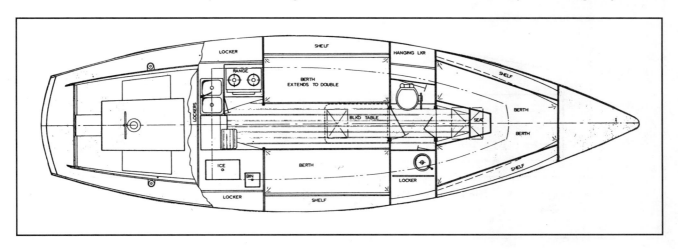

nothing particularly innovative or unusual about the construction. The hull is a solid fiberglass laminate, the deck is balsa cored. No owners in our survey mention problems with either hull or deck construction.

A number of owners have reservations about the hull-to-deck joint, which is not through-bolted. Other owners mention that there are washers but no backing plates on deck hardware such as lifeline stanchions. Although none report problems either with deck hardware or the hull-to-deck joint, their concerns are valid. Backing plates on deck hardware help distribute loads, and reduce the chance of stress cracks around fittings. Likewise, a through-bolted hull-to-deck connection offers a foolproof mechanical backup should the polyester putty bond between the hull and deck fail. Bolts won't stop leaks, but a through-bolted joint won't come apart until the surrounding glass fails.

As in most boats this size, the lifeline stanchions are only 24" high. This is too low for any real security—the lifelines strike most people just about at knee height, the right height for tripping.

There are some bolts through the hull-to-deck joint, since both the lifeline stanchions and chainplates fasten through the inward-turning hull flange. We would, however, prefer to see closely-spaced bolts throughout the length of the joint.

Chainplates are cast bronze lugs bolted through the hull and deck flange. As long as the hull and deck are adequately reinforced—and they are, in this case—this type of installation is fine.

We've seen the same general type of chainplates on 40' boats with Lloyds certificates, so they can't be all bad.

All Cape Dory boats came with deck hardware—cleats, winch islands, bow fittings, seacocks and chainplates—by Spartan, a sister company to Cape Dory. This is good stuff that will last the life of the boat and then some. The only disadvantages are that it is heavy, being bronze, and is not very well finished. Going from burnished to polished finish just about doubles the price of a piece of hardware—polishing is very labor intensive—and on most Cape Dory 30s you'll find burnished hardware. It's rugged, though.

There's a fair amount of exterior teak on these boats, including cockpit coamings, toerails, hatch trim, and eyebrow trim around the cabin on later models. This gives the boat a yachty appearance, but it does increase maintenance.

You could get the Cape Dory 30 in any color you wanted, as long as it was Cape Dory white with a nicely-contrasting tan deck. Several owners report discoloration of the colored portion of the non-skid decks. The non-skid itself is quite functional.

Early boats in this series have an unusual water tankage arrangement. One tank is plumbed to the head sink, the other to the galley.

Since you use a lot more water in the galley than in the head, that tank runs out first. Many owners have replumbed these tanks so that you can use the entire water supply.

Some early boats also have the water tank fills located below, which may be fine for keeping salt water out of the tanks, but can make for a fire drill

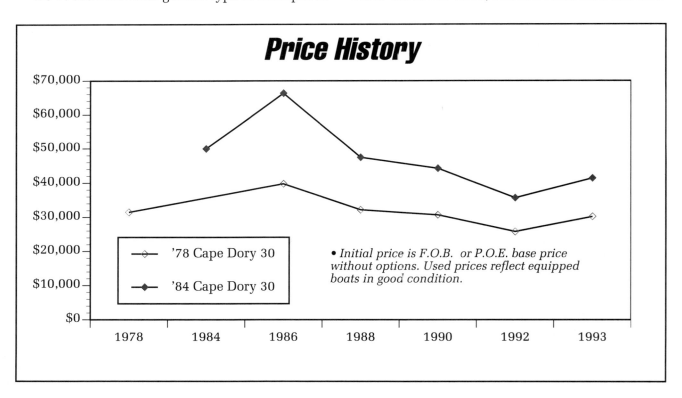

when trying to fill them without making a mess. On later boats there is a 30-gallon water tank under each main cabin settee, and the system is correctly plumbed.

There are proper seacocks on all fittings below the waterline.

The deck-stepped rigs in both the cutter and ketch are well engineered, as no owners in our survey report any deck deflection or stress cracking in that area.

Unlike a lot of 30-footers, the Cape Dory 30 was designed as a small seagoing boat. For example, it has a reasonable bridge deck, although it is lower than the main cockpit seats and the cockpit coamings. There is also a sea hood over the main companionway hatch.

The main companionway is an unusual design. The vertical part of the companionway is fairly narrow and straight sided—good features in terms of seaworthiness. The sliding hatch and its opening are wider, letting more light and air below.

Relatively few owners in our survey report gelcoat blistering. The only glasswork complaints were gelcoat crazing in an early model, and discoloration of the gelcoat in the hull liner, cabin overhead, and non-skid areas in the deck.

Interior

Compared to newer 30-footers, the Cape Dory 30 is cramped below. The boat is more than a foot narrower than the typical cruiser/racer built today, and about 2' shorter on the waterline. There's no way around it: this is a small boat.

Within these limitations, the interior layout is pretty good. There are V-berths forward, with a drop-in insert to form a double. The forward berths are narrow at the foot.

Ventilation in the forward cabin is provided by two opening ports plus an overhead Bomar aluminum-framed hatch. There are drawers and lockers beneath the berths.

The head compartment utilizes the full width of the boat, the way it should on a boat this narrow. Outboard of the toilet is a hanging locker. Opposite the toilet there is a dresser with sink.

A grate in the head sole for a shower was standard equipment, but the pressure water necessary to use it was an option. If you're going to spend more than a weekend on a boat, a shower is almost mandatory.

Inexplicably, the head sink and shower drain into the bilge. This is unacceptable. Because of the boat's low freeboard, the head sink is too low to be plumbed directly overboard if you expect it to drain on port tack. The best solution, although it is somewhat awkward, would be to install a closed sump tank in the bilge. It could be emptied overboard by either a manual or an electric pump. You wouldn't want

your bathroom sink and shower to drain into your basement, would you?

Two opening ports plus a cowl vent in a Dorade box provide ventilation in the head. If it were our boat, we'd also install a small venting hatch or another Dorade box over the head, even though the standard arrangement is better than you find on many larger boats.

The main cabin has settees which double as berths along either side. There are narrow shelves above and outboard of each settee.

Since the water tanks take up most of the volume below the main cabin settees, there is little storage space available in the main cabin.

As in most boats this size, the main cabin table folds down from the forward main bulkhead. It will seat four, although in a somewhat cramped fashion.

In the original layout, the galley aft runs the full width of the boat. On the port side there is a pressurized, two-burner gimbaled alcohol stove with oven. If you want to stay with alcohol cooking fuel, we recommend switching to a non-pressurized stove such as the Origo. Despite the fact that alcohol fires can be extinguished with water, pressurized alcohol stoves can be dangerous because most people underestimate the volatility of the fuel.

The sinks are aft of the stove, and are somewhat difficult to reach because the slope of the bilge intrudes into the space where you would normally stand.

Opposite the stove there is a good galley dresser containing an icebox, storage bin, and drawers. The icebox drains into the bilge. This is a poor arrangement, since organic matter from the icebox will inevitably contaminate the bilge, even if it is pumped daily. The icebox could either be pumped into the galley sink, or into the sump you install for the head sink and shower.

With this layout, you use the top of the icebox as a navigation table. The lack of a good place to do chart work is a common failing in older designs of this size.

Late in the production run, the interior layout was "modernized" by adding a quarterberth and small chart table. The arrangement takes up a lot of the space that was formerly used for the galley. You get another berth—which you don't need—at the cook's expense. We don't think this layout is an improvement, despite the fact that the navigator gets his or her own workspace.

Headroom on centerline in the main cabin is just over 6', with slightly less further forward.

Main cabin ventilation is good, with four opening ports—excellent bronze Spartan ports—and an overhead Bomar hatch. We'd add a pair of cowl vents in Dorade boxes on either side of the ventilation hatch. The space is there, and the job is pretty simple.

Although the galley has reasonable storage, there is little storage space in the rest of the boat. This makes the boat unsuitable as a long-term cruising boat, unless you want to do a fair amount of modification to the interior.

Joinerwork and finishing detail throughout are of good production boat quality. Since a lot of teak is used for interior woodwork, the boat is quite dark below.

You could brighten this up a lot by finishing the interior with gloss varnish, rather than the standard satin oil finish.

Conclusions

With her narrow beam and short waterline, the Cape Dory 30 is a lot smaller than newer boats of this length and displacement. The boat will have a strong appeal to the traditionalist who places a high value on appearance.

The boats are well constructed, suited for serious coastal cruising, and perhaps for limited offshore sailing.

Cape Dory boats were quite expensive, but they hold their value well. When production began in 1976, the Cape Dory 30 had a base price of about $29,000. By the time production ceased a decade later, the price had almost doubled—but so had the price of just about everything.

Although some might prefer the "shippiness" of the ketch rig, the cutter is both faster and more practical. Some boats were built as sloops, and this would be the best rig of all.

Inevitably, the Cape Dory 30 will be compared to the Alberg 30. The Cape Dory 30 is longer on the waterline, wider, heavier, and has a roomier interior. The Cape Dory 30 cutter is slightly faster than the sloop-rigged Alberg 30.

Our choice in a Cape Dory 30 would be a late-model cutter with full-width galley, Edson pedestal, and the Volvo or Universal diesel.

For the money, you get a well-designed traditional boat that is a good coastal cruiser for a couple or a small family. We don't think the boat is big enough for four adults for anything more than weekend sailing.

If you want the looks of an older boat but the construction details and diesel engine found in newer boats, the Cape Dory 30 is a good choice.   • **PS**

Alberg 30

One of Carl Alberg's most successful boats, the Alberg 30 enjoyed a production run of a quarter-century.

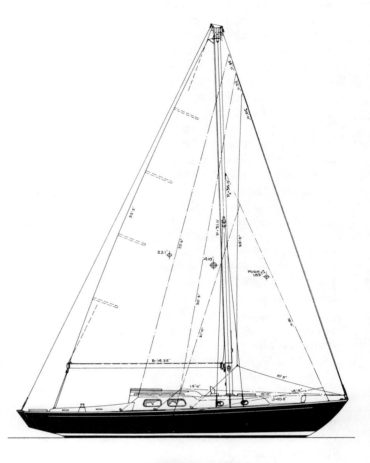

The Alberg 30 was in continous production from 1962 until 1987, an impressive run of 25 years. Made the entire time by the original builder, Whitby Boat Works, production was down to a trickle towards the end of the run: only three Alberg 30s were delivered in 1984, for example.

No other sailing auxiliary that we know of has a production record of that duration, the previous record belonging to the old Tartan 27 that was introduced in 1961 but discontinued in 1979.

During those 25 years, over 700 Alberg 30s were built with virtually no substantive changes: boats built 30 years ago can race one-design with 30s built at the tail end of the run.

The designer of the 30, Carl Alberg, most successfully made the early transition from wood to fiberglass boat design. His 28' Triton for Pearson Yachts is credited with starting the boom in fiberglass auxiliaries (1958).

A series of Alberg designs have been the mainstay of the successful line of Cape Dory Yachts since the early 1970s.

The Alberg 30 is an adaption of a 30-footer Alberg designed for San Francisco Bay and was first built in response to a request by some Toronto sailors for a cruising auxiliary that could be fleet raced.

By the time the first boat was built, a large group of Chesapeake Bay sailors had also commissioned a fleet. Today those two areas are still the hotbeds of Alberg 30 ownership with more than 100 boats represented in the Toronto association, almost 200 in the highly active and enthusiastic Chesapeake Bay association.

Price of the first 30s was $10,000 delivered and reasonably well equipped; 25 years later the "base price" of a 30 was about $45,000 Canadian, or $34,000 US at the time.

Specifications

LOA	30' 3"
LWL	21' 8"
Beam	8' 9"
Draft	4' 3"
Displacement	9,000 lbs.
Sail Area	410 sq. ft.

A Close Look at the Boat

Clearly the Alberg 30 is anachronistic. Her low freeboard, long overhangs, narrow beam, low aspect rig with long boom and short foretriangle base, broken cabin profile are clearly vintage, harking not just from the time of early fiberglass, but of the previous era of wood. So too is her accommodation layout: settee berths, ice box top doubling as a chart table, jammed head, and split galley.

Yet a demonstrable demand has endured for such "old fashioned" boats on both the new and used boat markets.

Owners of boats of this heritage accurately perceive that they are ruggedly built and seaworthy. At the same time, with their moderately heavy displacement and large wetted surface, they are relatively sluggish performers and, because of their short waterline lengths and narrow beam, cramped for space compared to more modern boats of comparable overall length and/or displacement. Similarly, with their relatively slack hull sections and narrow beam, they seem quicker to heel than the more initially stable modern hull forms, although at about 20 degrees they firm up reassuringly. Ballast is encapsulated cast iron.

The Alberg 30 is well built, modestly finished, and so-so performing. Owners report a remarkable absence of structural problems that cannot be attributed to normal wear in a vintage boat. The finish and decor of the boats has undergone routine upgrading during the long production run, reflecting the changing marketplace and styles, although the 30 has never been considered to have an elegant or even especially "yachty" decor. Plain oiled teak has been commonly used topside and below, though earlier boats (pre-1970) had the more fashionable, at that time, mahogany .

Performance of the Alberg 30 has systematically suffered by comparison with newer boats introduced over the years. At an average PHRF base rating of 220, the 30 may be equated with such full-keel kin as the 28' Triton (245), the Seawind 30 (240), the Bristol 29 (225), the 32' Vanguard (230), and the redoubtable Tartan 27 (235). At the same time, the maintenance of the one-design standard of construction and absence of major changes permits excellent fleet racing as a class.

Although changes during the production run have been minimal, they are important to the prospective buyer. These include a variety of engines and, in 1969-70, the adoption of a fiberglass interior liner as well as some changes to the cockpit.

The original engine in the 30 was the Graymarine 22 hp, followed by the Atomic Four, the 10 hp single cylinder Bukh diesel, the more powerful Volvo Penta MD7A and finally the Volvo 2002.

The Gray and the Bukh reportedly are shy of adequate power for the 30 as well as not being easy

(or cheap) to get parts for. The Atomic Four, as dependable as it is, should be getting close to the end of its expected life span; repowering with the Universal diesel should be feasible, though not inexpensive.

The changes in 1970, as much the result of tired tooling as of inherent drawbacks, did away with a cockpit access to the icebox (a "beer box" that melted ice at an unconscionable rate), improved the non-skid deck pattern, replaced teak plywood hatch covers, changed the hull-to-deck joint, added a seahood for the companionway, and provided the winch bases with a molded recess for handles. The wood coamings remained.

Below, per the fashion of the era and production economy, the interior became a molded component, although the most recently built boats have more teak trim.

What to Look For

With a boat as fundamentally solid, built for as many years, as the Alberg 30, prospective buyers should feel a warm confidence in her structural soundness. The major areas of concern are the condition of her engine, rig, and cosmetics. On the basis of owner input, we'd especially check the following:

• Some rudders on earlier boats failed, the strapping pulling away from the glass laminate. It should be checked regardless of the age of the boat. Rudder bearings have also become worn on older boats, resulting in a discomforting amount of play. The gudgeon and/or the heel fitting may need bushing. On tiller-equipped 30s the tiller head fitting is subject to wear as well as cracking.

• Perhaps the weakest part of the 30 may be the forward lower shroud chainplate fillet: a number of owners report having them enlarged and reglassed. This seems to have occurred as a gradual failure that can be anticipated; creaking and signs of separation from the hull give prior warning.

• Any engine, but particularly those in older 30s,

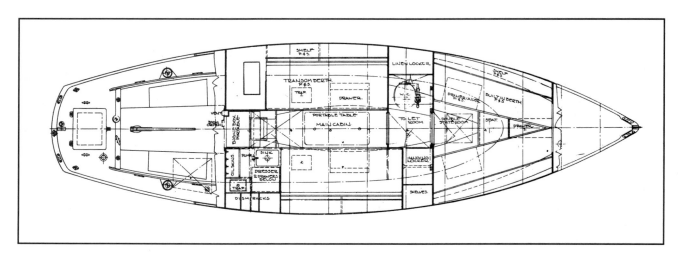

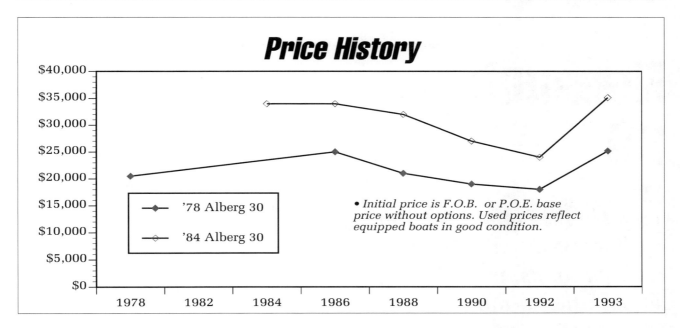

Price History

• *Initial price is F.O.B. or P.O.E. base price without options. Used prices reflect equipped boats in good condition.*

should be carefully examined prior to purchase of a boat, not an easy task since engine accessibility is not good. The original galvanized steel gas tanks have a history of eventually rusting through; optimally they should be replaced with ones of greater capacity (original gas, 22 gal; present for diesel, 12 gal) but this is not easy in the existing space.

• All the equipment should be checked. This includes the stove and head, but it particularly applies to the rig and deck hardware. The same mast and boom have been used on the 30 since its inception. However, earlier boats had wooden spreaders that, if original, will undoubtedly need replacement. Similarly, roller mainsail furling was standard and should have been replaced with slab or jiffy reefing (important given the 30's large mainsail and initial tenderness). Rigging swages should be meticulously examined as should tangs and spreader bases. In cases of doubt, attachments should be removed to check the condition of the spar underneath.

Given the age of many of the Alberg 30s as well as the active racing life many have undergone, owner replacements of original equipment and upgrading seem commonplace. If done to quality standards, such work has much to recommend itself to buyers.

Price—The Bottom Line

Getting a handle on how much a buyer should expect to pay (or a seller to ask) for an Alberg 30 is difficult. About half the boats are concentrated in areas where there are strong, active owner associations. Indeed, most of the boats bought and sold in those areas are to some degree transactions involving the associations. This is decidedly to the advantage of buyers in those areas in that there is a readily available list of boats on the market, absence of broker involvement (and brokerage commissions), and a promise of continual efforts to maintain the value of the boats. For buyers outside of those areas, we find that 30s can be bought for lower prices.

Clearly the upgrading that took place about 1970 (hull #410) has increased the value of those boats, even though the changes were perhaps more textural than substantive.

At the same time, buyers must consider the relative differences in auxiliary engines as well as the question of whether a lined hull is preferable to an interior of joinerwork.

Given the lack of real difference between the various model years, we'd look for an older boat in above average condition and save a few thousand dollars.

Conclusions

Clearly and simply, the Alberg 30 is not a boat for everyone. A buyer has to be willing to compromise on the 20% to 25% less interior space in this boat, compared with more modern 30-footers that are just as readily available at a comparable price.

At the same time, not many 30-footers old or new seem as basically seaworthy and rugged as the Alberg. Add to these decided appeals the 30's traditional (pleasing) appearance plus the benefits of highly active, albeit localized owner associations, and the result is a boat that should appeal to a moderately large number of prospective buyers.

In buying an older boat we'd budget some refurbishing and upgrading on top of the purchase price. The boat lends itself to being retrofitted with wheel steering, good sails, polyurethane restoration of the gelcoat, some improvement to the interior decor, etc. If not done already, replacing an original old engine, improvement of the galley, and adding some amenties would make an older 30 a better boat.   • **PS**

Nonsuch 30

This slightly odd 30-footer, with its wishbone rig and catboat looks, is easily sailed and comfortable.

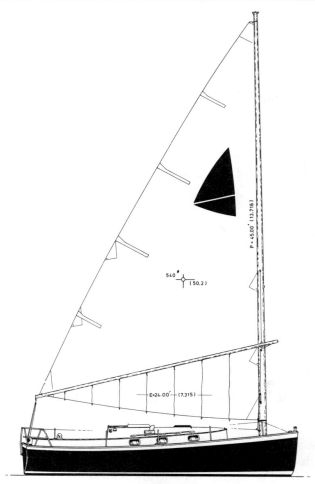

The Nonsuch 30 is an oddity. She is a fin keeled, spade ruddered boat with an unstayed wishbone cat rig. Weird.

She was built in Canada, whose main boatbuilding export has been C&C sailboats. Come to think of it, all her construction details look very much like those of C&C boats. This isn't unusual, since George Hinterhoeller, the builder, was formerly the president of C&C, and one of the founders of the three-company merger that created C&C Yachts.

When Hinterhoeller left C&C to recreate Hinterhoeller Yachts Ltd., he took with him those characteristics that have given C&C a reputation for quality: good attention to finish detail and high-quality balsa-cored hull construction.

The Nonsuch 30 is the concept of retired ocean racer Gordon Fisher, the design of Mark Ellis, and the created child of Hinterhoeller, who is one of the few production boatbuilders with the legitimate title Master Boatbuilder, earned the hard way through apprenticeship in Europe.

The Nonsuch 30 was originally a Great Lakes phenomenon, which is to be expected considering her origins. She proved quite popular elsewhere, however. This is not surprising considering the amount of boat that has somehow been slipped into an LOA of less than 31'.

Production of the Nonsuch line ceased in 1989.

Construction

George Hinterhoeller's reputation as a builder is not unearned. His balsa-cored hulls are known for being light and strong. It is probably not an exaggeration to say that he knows as much about cored construction as any boatbuilder around.

Both hull and deck of the Nonsuch 30 are balsa cored. The hull and deck are joined by a through-

Specifications

LOA	30' 4"
LWL	28' 9"
Beam	11' 10"
Draft	5' 0"
Displacement	10,500 lbs.
Ballast	4,500 lbs.
Sail area	540 sq. ft.

bolted, butyl-bedded joint capped with an aluminum toerail. The butyl tape used for this purpose has no real structural properties, but does create a good watertight seal. A sealant such as 3M 5200 provides equivalent sealant properties with greater structural properties, and we prefer its use in hull-to-deck joints. It is hard to quibble with the Nonsuch's strongly through-bolted joint, however.

The external lead keel is bolted on with stainless steel bolts. These pass through floor timbers of unidirectional roving, transferring keel loading from the garboard section to a greater area of the hull.

The cockpit seats and coamings contain a surprisingly large number of sharply-radiused turns. Gelcoat cracks are likely to develop here earlier than anywhere else in the hull.

The forward end of the wishbone, showing the "choker," a line that controls the fore-and-aft movement of the wishbone. This, in turn, controls sail shape.

The freestanding mast requires modification of normal construction methods. While no chainplates are required, substantial bulkheading is required in the area of the mast to absorb the considerable forces generated by the unstayed mast. The forward six feet of the hull is strongly bulkheaded for this purpose, and no sign of undue strain could be detected.

Because there is no rigging to hold the mast in the boat should she capsize, alternative means must be found. This is accomplished by lagging a cast aluminum, hexagonally-shaped female mast step to the hull. The butt of the mast is fitted with a hexagonal male counterpart which is strongly joined to the mast step by stainless steel hex-head set screws. The mast is further connected to the hull by a deck-level pin which passes through the mast and the cast aluminum deck collar. Deck hardware is properly backed for load distribution.

There are a few surprising shortcomings. The aluminum rudder quadrant stops have sharp edges which could easily cut into the exhaust line inside the cockpit lockers. This could happen—it had happened on the boat we sailed—if the upper rudder retaining nut is loose, allowing the rudder to drop down slightly. Gate valves are used on most through hull fittings below the waterline, rather than seacocks or ball valves, and no valves at all are fitted on drains and exhaust lines at the bottom of the transom, despite the fact that they could be submerged in a heavily loaded boat.

Despite these deficiencies, construction is generally to very high standards, well above average for the industry.

Handling Under Sail

The Nonsuch 30 is one of the most boring boats we have ever sailed. Tacking requires no yelling, releasing of sheets, cranking, tailing, or trimming. The helmsman simply says "I think we'll tack" and gives the wheel a quarter turn, being careful not to upset his Mt. Gay and tonic. Nonsuch quietly slides through about 85 degrees and settles on the other tack with a minimum of fuss. Beating up a narrow channel simply requires repeating the above process.

The person who learns to sail on a Nonsuch 30 will receive a rude awakening when switching to a more athletic boat—which means almost any other 30 foot sailboat. The Nonsuch 30 is simply one of the easiest boats to sail we've seen.

This doesn't mean that it's necessarily easy to sail well. Getting the most out of the boat upwind definitely requires some practice. The aluminum mast is quite flexible, allowing the top of the mast to fall off as the wind increases. The sail's draft will shift, changing its efficiency. In about 10 knots of breeze, the top of the mast falls to leeward about a foot. This can be a little disconcerting to those used to a fairly rigid stayed mast.

Sail shape is controlled by the "choker," a line which controls the fore and aft trim of the wishbone and functions as a clew outhaul. Tensioning the choker pulls the wishbone aft, flattening the sail. The sail is slab reefed pretty much the same as a conventional mainsail.

The Nonsuch mainsail is 540 square feet, with a hoist of 45 feet and a foot of 24 feet. By way of comparison the mainsail of the Irwin 52 is 525 square feet, and that of the Cal 31 210 square feet. The sail does not handle like a sail of 540 square feet, fortunately. The wishbone is rigged with permanent lazy jacks which hold the sail as it is dropped. Furling merely involves putting ties around the neatly cradled sail for the sake of aesthetics. Dousing the main or reefing is easily accomplished by one person, as all of the sail controls lead back to the cockpit.

The Nonsuch does not suffer from "catboat disease"—the tendency to develop monstrous weather helm as the breeze pipes up. She is, rather, remarkably well mannered, with a surprisingly light helm in the light to moderate winds in which we sailed her. Downwind she held course with the wheel brake off and hands off the wheel. Her performance was almost as good upwind at moderate angles of heel.

She is a stiff boat. The flexible mast allows a substantial amount of air to be spilled from the main as the wind pipes up, removing much heeling force. We found that the boat went better upwind with a reef in the main even at moderate angles of heel once the upper mast began to fall off. Getting sail off the more flexible upper part of the mast allows better draft control as the wind increases.

Having only one sail can be a real nail-chewer to the uncured racer. Whether it blows five knots or 25, the maximum amount of sail you can have is already up. Some unreconstructed racers have equipped the Nonsuch 30 with a blooper for light air downwind performance.

The Nonsuch 30 is no Cape Cod catboat under the water. She has a moderate aspect ratio fin keel, low wetted surface, and a freestanding semi-balanced spade rudder. These characteristics greatly add to her performance.

With all sail controls led back to the cockpit, she is a natural candidate for singlehanding. We strongly recommend the optional self-tailing winches for all functions if shorthanded sailing is contemplated.

The Nonsuch 30 is not the boat for the hard-core grand prix racer. Her entire sail inventory consists of that one big sail, with perhaps, but not necessarily, a single downwind sail. You will not become the bosom buddy of any racing sailmaker by owning a Nonsuch. Then again, no sailmaker will ever have a second mortgage on your boat, either.

Handling Under Power

The Nonsuch 30 was originally equipped with a 23 horsepower Volvo MD 11C diesel with saildrive. This basically eliminated engine installation and alignment problems for the builder, saving both time and money.

These units have an integral cast zinc to protect the vulnerable aluminum lower unit from galvanic corrosion. A special Volvo-supplied zinc is required—not an item that you can pick up in any boatyard. About hull number 125, this installation was changed to a more conventional engine and shaft arrangement, utilizing a new 27 horsepower Westerbeke diesel.

Either engine will drive the boat to hull speed. We greatly prefer the conventional engine installation, which is understood and can be worked on by most boatyards. It is less vulnerable to corrosion, and runs quietly and smoothly.

Because of her high freeboard the Nonsuch 30 will be susceptible to crosswinds when docking. With most of her windage forward she will have a tendency to blow bow downwind. A good hand on the throttle and gearshift will be a real plus in tight docking situations. Without the complication of wind we found her easy to back down into a slip once a sharp burst of throttle was given to activate the folding prop with which our test boat was equipped.

Deck Layout

Because the Nonsuch 30 has no standing rigging, her side decks are devoid of obstacles. Because she has no headsails there are no sheeting angles to be concerned with.

For cruising the optional bowsprit/anchor roller with hawsepipe to the otherwise unusable forepeak is highly desirable. Otherwise, anchor and rode must be stored in one of the cockpit lockers and dragged forward every time you wish to anchor. We also recommend the installation of a bow pulpit. With no shrouds to hold when forward there is a great feeling

The cabin layout is somewhat unusual, though sensible, placing the main salon forward and the galley and head amidships, in the center of activity. A later version of the boat, called the "Ultra," offered a more conventional forward stateroom with settees and table aft of the galley and head.

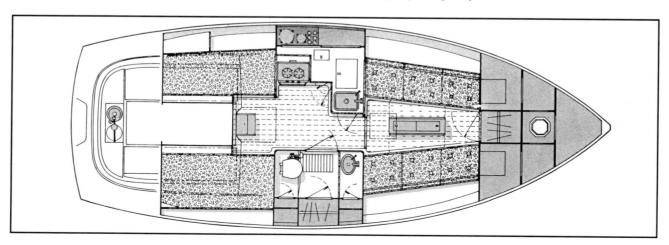

of vulnerability on the bow. These things may make the Nonsuch 30 un-catboatlike in appearance, but they will greatly add to the safety and convenience of both sailing and anchoring.

The cockpit of the Nonsuch 30 is large and deep. It is not particularly comfortable, and without four inch or thicker cockpit cushions it is impossible for a person of average height to see forward over the cabin. The helmsman's position is elevated above that of the other seats, but visibility even from that position is only fair.

With the standard white-on-white gelcoat scheme the cockpit of the Nonsuch 30 is sterile and generates a lot of glare on sunny days. The optional contrasting nonskid and teak cockpit grate alleviates part of this problem.

The large cockpit creates other problems. First, you should never raft up with other boats at anchor. A friendly crowd of eight could easily fit in the cockpit.

There are more serious problems associated with the cockpit design. The Nonsuch 30 is promoted as a "new offshore concept." We think this is an unfortunate choice of words, because the standard cockpit is not suited to offshore use. There is no bridgedeck. The companionway goes almost to the level of the cockpit sole—about three feet below the level of the lowest point in the cockpit coamings. Coupled with the huge cockpit volume, this creates a situation that cannot in any good conscience be called an offshore configuration. If this boat is to be called an offshore sailboat, we think there should be an optional cockpit arrangement—a large bridgedeck which could incorporate life raft storage, two more large cockpit drains, and perhaps a raised cockpit sole to further reduce the cockpit's volume.

There are three cockpit lockers; deep port and starboard lockers, and a lazarette propane locker set up to hold two ten-pound gas bottles. The large side locker should incorporate some form of easily-removed retainer system to prevent items there from rolling under the cockpit.

On the boat we sailed the drain line from the propane locker overboard was too long. At the low point in the loop water had collected in the hose, which exits through the transom and is underwater in many sailing conditions. This water prevents any propane leakage from draining overboard as designed. The hose should be shortened to remedy a potentially hazardous situation.

When tacking or jibing it is easy for the helmsman to get caught by the mainsheet as the boom comes over. A better lead would be welcome here, perhaps having the mainsheet system incorporated into the stern rail.

Interior

The interior volume of the Nonsuch 30 is an eye opener, even to those used to the modern trend toward maximum interior volume on minimum overall length. To anyone used only to the interior space of an older boat, the interior of the Nonsuch 30 is absolutely stunning.

The waterline and beam of the Nonsuch 30 are about the same as that of a modern 36 foot cruiser-racer, and that beam is carried quite a bit further

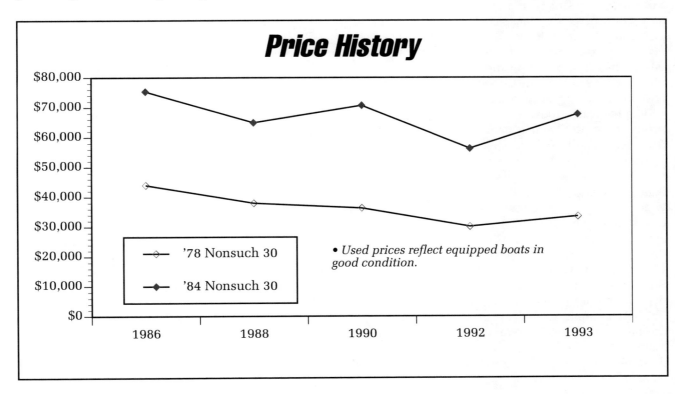

Price History

- ◇ '78 Nonsuch 30
- ◆ '84 Nonsuch 30

• *Used prices reflect equipped boats in good condition.*

forward. Coupled with high topsides and a highly-crowned deck house, this yields a boat with tremendous interior volume for her overall length.

The interior layout is unusual but practical. There is no forward cabin in the conventional sense. This isn't a real drawback. The forward cabin on the typical 30 footer is only useful for sleeping or sail stowage, and frequently has berths which narrow so much forward that an all-night game of footsie for the occupants is a necessity rather than a pleasure.

The forwardmost six feet of the boat is given over to two huge hanging lockers and a great deal of storage space which has been created by the three transverse and two fore and aft bulkheads that stiffen the hull in the way of the mast. This storage space is not readily accessible, and will probably end up as the boat's attic, collecting little-used piles of gear until the day when it must be all removed to get at the mast step to remove the mast.

The rest of the boat is basically one large cabin. What would be considered the main cabin occupies the forward third of the interior. At the forward end are the aforementioned hanging lockers and a bureau. There are shelves and bins outboard of the two long settees that face each other at a comfortable distance across the cabin, with a dropleaf table on centerline. Varnished pine ceiling behind the settees is a welcome note in an otherwise dark teak interior.

The galley is to port midships. The cook is out of the traffic flow yet located in the center of activity if there are people both below and topsides. The galley has a gimballed propane stove with oven, a well-insulated icebox with (hurrah!) an insulated, gasketed lid, and a deep sink nearly on centerline which will easily drain on either tack. The icebox melt water is pumped into the galley sink. For the sake of aesthetics the icebox drain should tee into the sink drain below the sink, relieving the cook of the dubious pleasure of watching the things which dribble to the bottom of the icebox flow through the sink.

The head is opposite the galley. Because of the pronounced deckhouse camber, headroom there decreases rapidly as you move outboard.

An unusual option was a demand propane-fired hot water heater. This compact unit mounts on a head bulkhead, and has electric ignition. When a hot water faucet is turned on the heater fires, and will heat steaming hot water as fast as the water pressure system will deliver it. This is much less complicated than the normal engine water heat exchanger/110 volt powered water heaters found on most boats. Since the boat is already plumbed for propane, installation of this heater is straightforward.

There are quarterberths port and starboard aft of the galley and head. The standard berth starboard is a double, with a single to port. An option provides doubles on both sides, although filling all the berths

on the boat requires an open mind and no highly-developed sense of privacy.

Despite the open interior of the boat, privacy can be attained through another unusual interior option. A hidden slide-up partition can be installed between the galley and the forward/main cabin, and a bifold louvered teak door which folds up against the head bulkhead. When closed, the door and partition divide the boat into two large compartments for sleeping, with reasonable separation between them. The occupants of the thus-created forward cabin must enter the aft cabin either to go on deck or to use the head, an inconvenience.

Like the cockpit, the huge interior invites company. In the event of a sudden rainstorm, the eight people who previously occupied your cockpit could easily move below to continue their revelry. If there were already eight below—a not unlikely circumstance—you may be in trouble. Sixteen people is too many belowdecks even in the Nonsuch 30.

Ventilation of the interior is excellent, with seven opening ports, two hatches, and two dorade boxes. The propane heater vents overboard through its own exhaust stack.

Conclusions

The Nonsuch 30 is an unusual boat by any standards. The unstayed wishbone cat rig is becoming increasingly popular. It does greatly reduce the cost of sails, spars, and rigging.

The general appearance of the boat is similar to a traditional catboat, although she will never be taken to be a product of the Crosby yard. Her generally catboatlike hull dimensions produce the maximum hull volume on a minimum overall length.

Despite her billing we do not consider her an offshore cruiser with her standard cockpit arrangement. She will make an excellent coastal cruiser for a couple or family with up to three small children or two older children.

Because she is easy to sail and rig, has a big cockpit and a roomy, well-ventilated interior, she should make a good Caribbean charter boat for two couples, although head access is a minor problem from the forward cabin. Surprisingly, none have entered the southern charter business.

The Nonsuch 30 is not a traditionalist's catboat. She lacks the sweeping sheer, low freeboard, gaff rig, and barndoor rudder of the Cape Cod catboat. She also lacks that boat's infamous sailing characteristics—ferocious weather helm, inability to go to windward, and a man-killing mainsail.

She is a relatively simple, easily sailed boat for the convivial sailor who doesn't mind being seen in what many might consider an oddball boat with an oddball interior and an oddball rig, The more you look at it, the less oddball it seems. • **PS**

Gemini 31/3000

Long America's only production cruising multihull, this boat has many fans.

Tony Smith sure knows how to make the most of a good thing. The British multihull lover has gotten more mileage out of one design than any boatbuilder we know. And why not? With more than 200 Geminis built to date, and interest building, why switch?

History

In 1972 Smith designed and developed the 26-foot folding trimaran Telstar in England. He brought the molds to the U.S. and built 350 of them before a devestating fire destroyed the molds in 1981. Desperate to resurrect his business, he grabbed some old catamaran molds he had—the Aristocat—changed the name and that same year launched the first Gemini 31.

Three years and 27 boats later, he retooled to produce the Gemini 3000, which is essentially the same boat, but longer. Today, yet another incarnation of that first design—the Gemini 3200—continues to sell well.

Several years ago, Smith planned to introduce a larger 37-foot version, but the cost was much higher and despite building one boat, he changed his mind. The multihull business in this country has been slow to take off. And as even the established monohull builders like Pearson and C & C have found out, there ain't much room for error. Instead, Smith has refined the Gemini much like the Volkswagen Beetle. By listening to owners' comments, and by incorporating his own evolving ideas, the boat has changed a good deal, though one would be hard pressed to distinguish, at a glance, between a 1984 Gemini and a 1992 model.

Design

The funny thing about the Gemini is that it's an old

Specifications

LOA	30' 6"
LWL	27' 7"
Beam	14' 0"
Draft	1' 6"/4' 9" (boards up/down)
Displacement	7,000 lbs.
Ballast	N/A
Sail area	425 sq. ft.

design. Ken Shaw drew the lines in 1969. There's nothing particularly contemporary about it. However, by painting the cabin sides black (Euro styling), adding a swept-back fiberglass "pilothouse" and gradually adding length to the full-bodied hulls, the Gemini has always looked like she belonged with her contemporaries, whether that was the 1980s or 1990s.

The most important thing to remember when evaluating this design is that the Gemini is essentially used as a 30-foot live-aboard, cruising catamaran. While faster than most monohulls of equal length, it has no pretense of being a racer. How could it be with such a spacious interior? Further, many of Smith's customers are older folks who are tired of heeling, don't have $200,000 to spend, and don't plan to circumnavigate. In fact, most Geminis we've

Owners' Comments

"Kids play table games under way. Beer stays upright. Cats pose a unique power problem; there's nowhere to put a single engine and the water between the hulls is aereated. The Gemini has a unique lowering motor platform—a reasonable solution."

—1983 model in MA

"Like a lot of monohulls, she doesn't sail under main only. I went to the Gemini from an Allied Princess 36 ketch. The Gemini is much better suited to coastal cruising, especially Chesapeake Bay, the Bahamas, and the Florida Keys. The Gemini is also a much better sailer in light air than the Princess."

—1984 model in Annapolis, MD

"Check finish before accepting, especially on deck. Can be a beast to handle under power in tight spaces if breezy. A wonderful boat. Sails like a dream. Tacks and points and foots well. No heeling. My wife loves it. Lots of space. Would buy another without hesitation."

—1986 model in Bremerton, WA

"Deck and hatch edges should be better. Windows leak badly. Outboard motor is noisy. Boat needs about 40-45-hp. with extra long shaft."

—1984 model on Chesapeake Bay

"Interior perfect. Cockpit perfect."

—1987 model in Long Boat Key, FL

"Wheel steering has light helm. Autopilot works well. Stability and 'pilothouse' protection help in heavy weather."

—1985 in Newton, NJ

"Great cruising boat. Many small defects have been corrected in later models. There is an esprit de corps among Gemini owners."

—1988 model in McLean, VA

"This is a lightly built boat that I consider basically a 'bay boat,' although I know that some would disagree. Great combination of space, livability and a fast, good-handling sailer. I'm planning to order a new one a year from now. Great price!"

—1985 model in Alexandria, VA

"Centerboards help upwind. Only boat of this type that has them. Very safe. Big waves slow it down. Interior and exterior comfort are superb. Cockpit is so big we put a kid's pool in it on hot days. On the sailing side, it's always fun to get into a little impromptu competition with a 30'-40' monohull. They quickly find some reason to disengage."

—1985 model on Chesapeake Bay

seen are happily puttering up and down the Intracoastal Waterway along the Eastern Seaboard and Gulf Coast. It's perfect for that.

Summing up the design gets a little dicey when offshore work is discussed. The Gemini's liabilities here are several. Because of the substantial accomodations built on the bridge, which necessitates lowering it for headroom, and the solid bridge forward (as opposed to netting), it's a bit heavy. Smith says that if loaded for extended cruising, there is not a lot of clearance between the bottom of the bridge and the surface of the water, and it will pound going to weather in choppy seas. Sailed light, the Gemini will do quite nicely and be much more comfortable.

The performance of full bridgedeck cats, such as the Gemini, also suffer a bit from the extra weight and windage. Smith, a racer at heart, admits that if he had his druthers he'd build an open bridge forward, but for his cruising clientele, the full bridge makes more sense.

Nevertheless, Geminis have, according to Smith, crossed the Atlantic, cruised the South Pacific and Caribbean.

Having spent a week cruising the Chesapeake Bay aboard a Gemini 31, we found the boat extremely comfortable and fun to sail. With a large queen-size stateroom forward and double staterooms aft in each hull, there's room for Mom and Dad, Junior and Sis, each in their own private cabins.

Speed reaching and sailing upwind was about 50 percent faster than what we could do in our 33-foot Pearson Vanguard. We hit double digits just once. But sailing in moderate winds we'd make eight and nine knots when our Pearson would do five and six. Three or four knots may not seem like a lot, but for sailboats on an all-day passage, the difference cuts hours off sailing time.

Best of all, it's *level* sailing. This makes for very restful cruising.

Punching to windward in a chop, we did buck a bit, and the quicker motion of a multi takes some getting used to. All in all, we came away impressed with its space and performance.

Construction

The key to high-performance multihull construction is lightness and strength. The rapid evolution of composite building techniques now makes possible the use of lightweight core materials, specialized fibers such as Kevlar, and strong resins that in combination yield a panel that is much lighter and stiffer than solid fiberglass or fiberglass with just "traditional" core materials such as end-grain balsa and PVC foam. Vacuum bagging helps assure uniform bonding of all the "parts." Naturally, such construction is costly.

Construction of the Gemini, which is marketed as a comfortable, low-priced cruising catamaran rather than a spartan high-tech racing machine, is quite conventional. The hull is built of solid fiberglass—mat and woven roving. The deck is cored with balsa for stiffness. The new Gemini 3200 incorporates a layer of vinylester resin as a blister barrier. Twenty percent of the owners of older models responding to our survey reported "some" blistering—a below average incidence.

The centerboard trunks were laid up separately in the early boats, but Smith said it was difficult getting good tolerances for the centerboards to fit right. Now the trunks are part of the hull mold and the slot is a guaranteed two inches and the polyurethane-coated plywood centerboards 1-7/8".

Obviously, to keep weight light, a multihull builder isn't going to use any unnecessary laminations. Consequently, many multihulls feel flimsy compared to monohulls. One Gemini owner said, "The strength is a little lower than I would have liked, but it helps hold the cost down." And, we might, add, the weight that is so important to multihull performance. The rock steady feel of thick decks is somewhat at odds with the requirements of multihull design and construction.

A frequent complaint of Gemini owners is gelcoat flaws. "Gelcoat has many voids," wrote one owner. "Some gelcoat yellowing and crazing," said another.

The interior woodwork is acceptable to some owners, and not to others. "Woodwork finish is inept," said one owner. "Finish work is my biggest complaint," said the owner of a 1985 model.

Smith admits that leaky windows were a problem in early boats. The design has since been changed, including the use of Lexan in place of Plexiglas, and a new system to bed the large panels allows for thicker beads of sealant to absorb the expansion and contraction of the windows.

Most owners, however, seemed to feel that these are minor problems they're willing to live with. They rate construction lower than other attributes of the boat, but overall still are satisfied with their choice of the Gemini. We'd like to see a bit more glass in the Gemini, or the use of a core for stiffness and strength, though we acknowledge it would increase the price.

Performance

Besides accomodation space and low heel angles, speed is a major factor in choosing a multihull. Only one owner expressed disappointment in his Gemini's maximum speed attainable. True, it won't hit those

The standard layout has a queen-size berth forward and two smaller staterooms aft. There is standing headroom in the two hulls and underneath the so-called pilothouse.

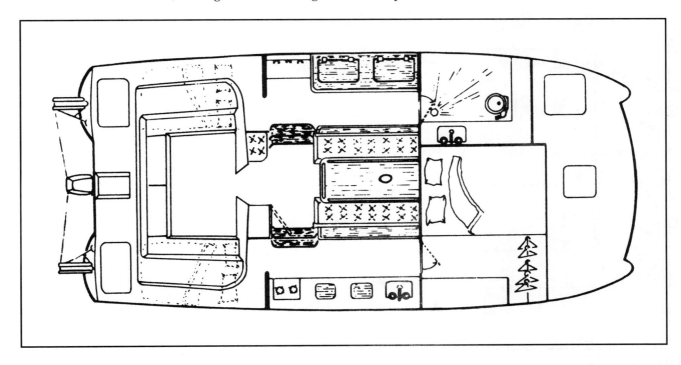

15- to 20-knot speeds possible in more performance-oriented cats and tris. Nearly all owners, however, remarked on the Gemini's good light-air performance. And, as we found during our week's cruise of the Chesapeake Bay, the boat is definitely faster than a cruising monohull of equivalent size.

A key to performance in any multihull is keeping weight down. Unfortunately, many owners overload their boats and this has a direct effect on speed and pointing ability. It's a problem with no easy answers for live-aboards and long-term cruisers: Either buy a boat with longer hulls and hence greater payload capacity, or live with sub-par performance.

A significant feature of the Gemini is its centerboards, which improve pointing and tacking considerably. Many production catamarans today have fin keels on each hull. The thought here is that the problems inherent with centerboards (broken pennants, jammed boards in the trunk) are eliminated, while acceptable upwind sailing characteristics are retained. This may be true, but there seems no denying that centerboards improve overall performance. Further, the fins add to wetted surface, which increases drag and adversely affect maneuverability.

It is interesting that author Bernard Perret wrote in the October 1990 issue of *Cruising World* regarding his search for a cruising cat: "We focused in on exactly what we wanted: two sideboards to help us tack more efficiently against the wind and to maintain a shallow draft…"

Having ourselves sailed on production cats without centerboards that were dogs to windward (close reaching was virtually impossible, leaving motorsailing the only option), we consider daggerboards or centerboards an important criteria in selecting a catamaran. Perret said he tacks his French-built 36-foot Naviplane through 115 degrees true, but that's nothing to write home about. We're sure he could do better if he wasn't loaded down with cruising gear for five. Under optimal conditions, Smith says the Gemini can tack through 80 degrees. Burdened with bicycles, computers, three anchors, a library, and food for six months, that number is sure to increase.

A number of owners noted the boat's lack of directional stability (because there's not a lot of boat underwater). But they also acknowledged that it is very easy to steer, and that with the lee board down, it balances nicely.

The wide sheeting angle of the early boats made the genoa inefficient upwind. Smith says this has been improved, by means of lengthening the track, in the Gemini 3200.

Under power, the Gemini performs well. The outboard turns with the rudders for assistance in close quarters—most multihulls need it. And it retracts for sailing. The arrangement has been modified several times over the years.

The current Gemini 3200 comes equipped with a 40-hp. Tohatsu. Some 31 owners felt more power was needed. The results of our recent Reader Survey didn't rate Tohatsus very highly, but Smith says a 25-inch shaft is very important for maximum performance. The Mercury 35, standard on Gemini 31s and 3000s, is no longer made. The Tohatsu, he said, is the only engine in that power range available with a 25-

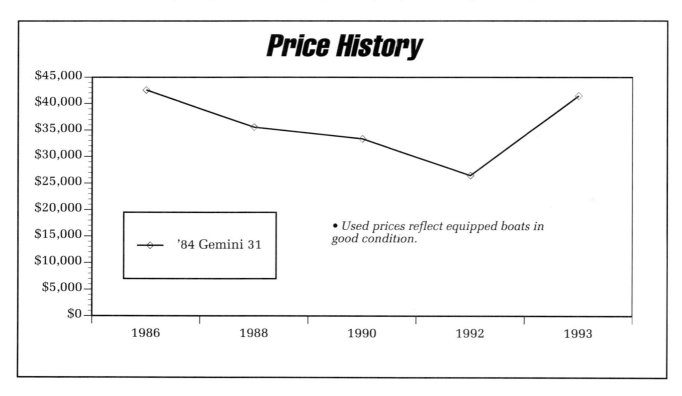

Price History

• *Used prices reflect equipped boats in good condition.*

Legend: —◇— '84 Gemini 31

(Chart values, $ vs. year)
- 1986: ~$42,000
- 1988: ~$35,500
- 1990: ~$33,500
- 1992: ~$26,000
- 1993: ~$41,000

inch shaft. In any case, motoring the Gemini at decent speeds, and in comfort, is certainly possible, though punching into head seas isn't its cup of tea—multis are too light and their motors often too weak to grind out the miles like a heavy, diesel-powered monohull.

Twin Yanmar and Volvo diesels were available, but at such an increase in cost, few buyers would consider them. We'd take the outboard for cost savings, clean interiors, and ease of repair and maintenance. So what if it's a little noisier? You'll motor less with a catamaran than your old monohull anyway.

Accomodations

There are numerous appeals to the cruising cat—the large foredeck, large cockpit and the possibility of three or more private sleeping cabins. The Gemini has all three.

The full bridge means there is no netting between the hulls as seen on many cats. This adds weight, but does help deflect waves. From a particularly hedonistic point of view, the netting is best for lying on face down, watching the water fly by. On the other hand, footing is precarious. The full bridge makes anchor handling easier and provides for possibly a little extra stowage space.

The Gemini's cockpit is large enough to walk around in, with good footing and stowage. Bulkhead wheel steering is convenient whether standing under the so-called pilothouse (added after hull #10), or sitting either on the bench seat or coaming top.

There is not standing headroom in the saloon forward of the 6' 2" pilothouse, but this isn't a major item. Several interior plans have been offered over the years. The one we chartered had a 64" x 75" double berth forward in the starboard sector. The view from the bunk looking through the forward windows is stunning! The head with shower was in the port bow and aft, in each hull, was a quarter cabin. The 48" x 75" bunks in these weren't quite as wide as a couple might like, but tolerable, and

certainly more than big enough for kids. The nav station was amidships to port and the galley in the starboard hull, with 6' 3" headroom. Headroom forward is 6' 0".

An interesting dilemma of outboard-powered boats is the question of generating power for live-aboard conveniences. Outboard engines aren't able to generate the amps necessary to run a lot of hungry electrical appliances. To combat the problem, Smith has elected to use RV-type propane/12-volt/110-volt refrigerators. These are well suited to multihulls because they work most efficiently when level. LPG, of course, will be the usual energy source for these units, though at the dock shorepower works well. We sailed with a Dometic three-way refrigerator for several years and found them too poorly insulated for 12-volt service.

An instantaneous gas-fired water heater services the Gemini's shower, which again eliminates the need for electricity.

About the only appliances that must then be accounted for are cabin lights, fans, stereo and pumps. This can be handled by several good quality batteries, though some owners note the need for alternate energy sources. Solar panels, in our experience, can help a great deal, but several fairly large ones will be needed. They are difficult to place where shadows won't limit performance, and where they aren't likely to be stepped on. Plus, their life expectancy is depressingly brief—several years in our experience. A better bet, for many cruisers, will be a pole-mounted wind generator capable of producing, say, six to seven amps in 15 to 18 knots of wind.

Conclusion

The Gemini 31 is a comfortable coastal cruiser that benefits from its builder's undying devotion. The quality of workmanship isn't what you'll find in more expensive monohulls or multihulls, but this is also one of the few cruising multihulls that's affordable to buyers in the $50,000 to $80,000 range—used or new.   **• PS**

Island Packet 31

A beamy, shoal-draft cruiser whose fanatical followers find little wrong except upwind sluggishness.

In the 13 years since naval architect Bob Johnson founded Island Packet Yachts, he's developed quite a following. We've had many requests to review one of his boats, mostly from satisfied owners. The others have come from couples considering the boat for living aboard and cruising. In a period when most boatbuilders are foundering, Island Packet has found a niche and is servicing it admirably.

History

Bob Johnson is a graduate of the Massachusetts Institute of Technology. Before founding Island Packet Yachts he worked as a designer for Endeavour Yachts and Irwin Yachts. In 1979 he launched his own company, Traditional Watercraft, with the 21-foot Lightfoot. A year later he followed with the beamy 26-foot Island Packet (originally called the Bombay Express). Its catboat lines, complete with barn door rudder, caught everyone's attention. But it was the completely redesigned Mark II version that really catapulted the company to success.

In 1983 Johnson followed with the Island Packet 31. Orders for 14 were taken at that year's U.S. Sailboat Show in Annapolis. It remained in production until 1989, after 262 boats had been built. The 31 was replaced with the Island Packet 32. In case you hadn't noticed, successful builders must at some point introduce new models, even if only a foot shorter or longer, so as not to compete with their own used boats. At present, the company builds a 27, 29, 32 and 35, though, like most owners of boats with bowsprits, you'll find owners referring to the same models as 30, 32, 35 and 38, generously adding the three-foot length of their bowsprits for LOA (length overall). This is where you need to add LOD (length on deck) to the specifications.

In 1990, the company enjoyed its best year, build-

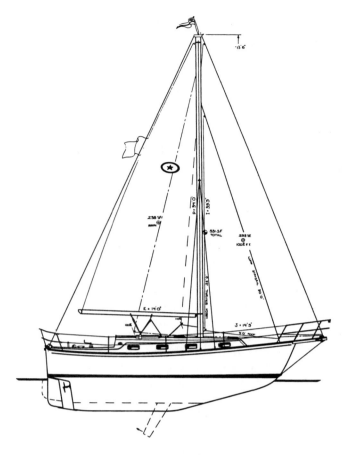

Specifications

LOD	30' 7"
LWL	27' 9"
Beam	11' 6"
Draft	3' 0"/4' 0" (cb/deep keel)
Displacement	11,000 lbs.
Ballast	4,500 lbs.
Sail area	531 sq. ft.

ing 163 boats. At a time when most are losing ground, Traditional Watercraft continues to prosper.

The Design

The entire Island Packet line springs from that first catboat-like 26. You'll rarely see other boats with the beam of an Island Packet. The overhangs are very short, and the bottom is what the company calls "U-shaped." The bow is almost plumb and the stern is vertical, in line with the trailing edge of the keel-attached rudder. Add a coachroof parallel with the waterline and a cutter rig and you have all the makings of a traditional looking yacht. There is no doubt that this look has found favor with the boatbuying public, and to a large degree is responsible for the company's success.

Owners' Comments

"She's beamy but about the smallest vessel that two folks can comfortably live aboard for an extended period of time. An excellent value on the used boat market."

—1985 model in Ohio

"Sloop rig needs more sail—well trimmed it is hands off sailing and walk around the deck. Overall, Mr. Johnson has done a good job. Highly recommended."

—1987 model in Illinois

"Almost impossible to bury the rail. Tracks well without much helm unless overpowered with jib. Great cockpit. Cockpit shower a plus. It's hard to find a slower boat to wind. However, all other chracterics are great. The boat is built with care to detail. The builder does not skimp on quality workmanship or materials. It is a very safe, stable cruising boat that the entire family will enjoy and tolerate in all conditions."

—1984 model in Florida

"Good speed. Requires considerable momentum to maneuver. This gets tricky docking. In reverse there is poor control at very slow speeds."

—1985 model in Michigan

"Quality of construction, equipment, fittings, etc., are best money can buy. The boat is outstanding in all respects for my taste. Builder has focused upon quality, thus the boat is not cheap. It is designed and built for cruising, not racing. She is an extremely comfortable and roomy boat."

—1985 model in Virginia

"Upwind performance improved with backstay adjuster. Been through several severe storms. Cutter rig is an asset. Sailed 65 nautical miles across Lake Ontario close hauled in 25-knot winds with little attention to helm."

—1987 model in New York

"Have cutter rig with self-tending club-footed staysail. Have never been very satisfied with set of sail. Am presently converting to loose-footed staysail and roller furling. Boat is a blast when wind is above 15 knots. Can handle full main and 130-percent genoa to 20 knots."

—1987 model in Maryland

"Its major irritants have been the shower and icebox draining into the bilge. It has a deep, full bilge, but must be cleaned more often when showering. That's the worst. We are pleased."

—1986 model cruising the Gulf of Mexico

Let's discuss, for a moment, the wide beam of the 31. At 11' 6", it exceeds many other boats of this length. The reasons for it are several. First, a boat derives its stability from two sources—ballast and beam. Both help resist heeling. Johnson obviously started his design with the premise that the boat would be a shoal-draft cruiser. The centerboard version draws just 3' 0" board up, and the fixed keel draws just 4' 0". With either configuration (about half built were centerboards), it isn't possible to concentrate ballast very low in the boat, especially since iron ingots set in concrete are used (in the deep keel model only) instead of the customary lead, which has a much higher specific gravity.

Given the shallow draft, additional stability is achieved by adding to the beam. This brings us to the second reason for the wide beam—greater volume, which is always desirable in a live-aboard boat.

There is nothing inherently wrong with shallow draft and wide beam, assuming you know what you're trading off. In this case, it's upwind sailing performance and the increased possibility of achieving inverse stability, that is, the tendency of a hull form to remain upside down and not right itself. Beamy, shallow boats have a greater potential to achieve inverse stability than narrow hulls with deep, heavy keels.

On the face of it, all this suggests that the Island Packet 31 is a fine coastal cruiser, but is less suited to severe offshore work than a narrower hull with a deep, heavy keel.

Few remarks seem to vex readers more than our stating a boat design is best suited to *coastal* sailing. "What do you mean I can't take this boat offshore?" they say, incredulous.

We didn't say you couldn't. The operative phrase is "best suited." People have crossed oceans in rowboats, sailboards and mini-boats that were hardly more than bathtubs with decks and spars. Sure you can take this boat offshore (the definition of which is yet another semantical quagmire. For the purposes of this argument, let's say offshore is anywhere away from the coast from which one cannot make harbor at the approach of severe conditions). And probably do so quite happily.

All the talk of capsize screening formulas and righting moment and the like are essentially responses to yachting disasters, such as the famous 1979 Fastnet Race, in which racing boats were damaged by heavy storm conditions, sometimes with the loss of life. Often poor engineering and construction (in the pursuit of light weight) is to blame. In some instances it's design. Good seamanship probably is more important than either engineering or design.

That said, the Island Packet 31 is a handsome, rugged boat that is, according to readers, a delight to sail, well built, and emminently suited to the cruising life.

Construction

The Island Packet hull is solid fiberglass, using triaxial cloth and polyester resin. The deck is "cored" with a mixture of polyester resin and microballoons (called by the company PolyCore) that the company says weighs about the same as a deck with 1/2-inch balsa core. The intent of this innovative method is to avoid using the more common end-grain balsa. This makes for a chemically coupled deck structure without possibility of delamination, common in older boats with balsa cores. No readers have reported problems with their decks. Similarly, we do not have any reported cases of blisters.

The interior is developed by means of a PolyCore liner tabbed to the hull. We are not fond of such liners, because they do not absorb sound as well as wooden soles, make modification of the layout much more difficult, and, if the builder hasn't carefully planned his tooling, they can obstruct access to some parts of the hull (always imagine that if you struck an object in such and such location, could you reach the hole to plug it). However, Johnson has done a nice job tooling his liners. We like especially the fact that the liner isn't brought up to window level, but terminates at the backrest of settees so that wood and fabrics hold the eye at mid-heights rather than large, austere panels of fiberglass. The liner also incorporates structural stringers that are bonded to the hull. The sand color of all Island Packet interior and exterior moldings is a trademark, and if you had to commit to one color, this one is easy on the eyes.

The ballast, as mentioned, is encapsulated in the keel cavity. The rudderstock is 1 1/2-inch stainless steel. The semi-balanced rudder has a high-density foam core and is covered with fiberglass. A stainless steel box functions as a "lobster strap." This connects the keel to the rudder and prevents lines from riding up into the propeller. The centerboard is built essentially the same way, with some lead at the tip.

A 22-hp Yanmar diesel was standard in the 1984 boats, which one owner said was inadequate power. The next year a 27-hp Yanmar was installed, which provided better power. Island Packet owners cited few problems with their Yanmars.

Hardware is for the most part of good quality—Edson rack and pinion steering, Ronstan blocks, Isomat spar, etc. One owner complained of his Par toilet. Few builders can justify installing expensive models—no one buys a boat for its toilet, despite the fact that malfunctions with the toilet are one of the most onerous repair jobs imaginable. We think the investment in a top quality toilet is repaid many times over.

Readers report overall construction as excellent. Many said that the company pays close attention to detail. Nearly all report good response from Bob Johnson and his staff in resolving problems.

Performance

The Island Packet 31 was offered as a cutter or sloop. Most owners seemed to have chosen the cutter.

One reader wrote: "The boat is not a true cutter, but a double-headsail sloop with a 110-percent lapper and a free-set staysail. I recommend either a staysail stay and a hanked-on staysail or disposing with the staysail and sailing her as a proper sloop with roller reefing 150-percent genoa."

The quarterberth doubles as a navigation station. The area can be enclosed by a "folding pocket door," which gives it a nice versatility.

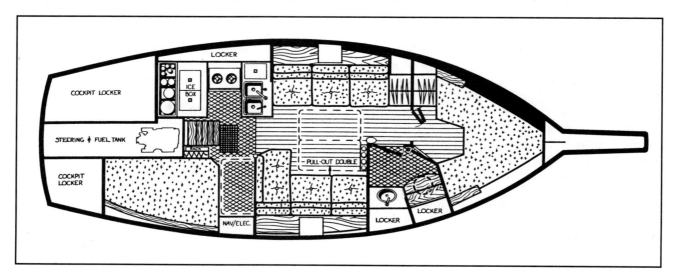

This is technically correct, though the line between cutter and double-headsail sloop is not always clear. On a cutter, the mast is usually stepped near the center of the boat.

On a double-headsail sloop, the mast is stepped farther forward, which is the case with the Island Packet 31. There are no running backstays, but the company says the Isomat spar was engineered to withstand the loads of the inner forestay without additional support.

Owners report being very happy with the cutter rig. Some admit to having to learn the nuances of proper trim of the staysail and jib.

While not necessarily as efficient as a large genoa on a sloop, the advantage of two sails occupying essentially the same area is that trimming is easier, and when the wind pipes up, the jib can be dropped altogether.

Not surprisingly, the Island Packet 31's best point of sail is a reach. Owners say she's quite fast. Upwind is a different story. One reader said, "Forward wide beam slows boat in seas." Another said she's slow in light air, fast in heavy air." Several reported difficulty tacking through the wind, finding it easy to end up in irons. Full-keel boats don't tack as readily as fin keel boats, but on the Island Packet this tendency seems to be exacerbated by the wide beam forward.

The boat balances well. Readers say she will steer herself for miles with little attention to the helm. One wrote: "Sometimes we thought the autopilot was on and then discovered she was just tracking on her own." And she is stiff. "I can't intentionally wet the rail," said one reader.

Performance under power is rated as good, as is engine accessibility and reliability.

The only complaint is control in reverse, which is to be expected of a full keel design with the propeller in an aperture. But for a serious cruising boat, that's exactly where you want the prop—backing down be damned.

Interior

Besides looks and quality, many readers chose the Island Packet for its voluminous interior.

There's nothing particularly unusual about the layout, which is fine. It works. There are 6' 6" V-berths forward, a generous head compartment with shower, settees in the main cabin, a doubled quarter berth aft to starboard, and a U-shaped galley in the port quarter.

The quarter berth doubles as a nav station, and can be enclosed by a folding door. Headroom in the cabin is 6' 3".

"The icebox is huge and exceptionally well insulated (we have Adler-Barbour refrigeration)," wrote one owner. "Used as an icebox it is also great. The interior design is user friendly."

Conclusion

We have reviewed few boats whose owners are more uniformly enthusiastic. This applies to the company as well as the boat itself.

"Ask any owner how they feel about their boat," wrote one owner. "All Island Packet owners are the sales force of the company. Sit aboard one for an hour, sail one and it's yours." **• PS**

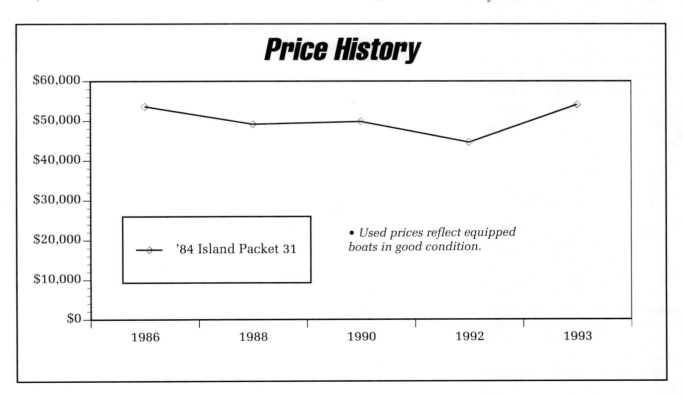

Price History

$60,000

$50,000

$40,000

$30,000

$20,000

$10,000

$0

◇— '84 Island Packet 31

• *Used prices reflect equipped boats in good condition.*

1986   1988   1990   1992   1993

Nicholson 31

This is certainly not a hot racer-cruiser: rather it's a true blue-water cruiser good for going offshore.

Few British sailboats have been a success in the US market. The traditional strength of the British pound against the dollar has meant that British boats have in the past been inordinately expensive compared to American boats of similar quality. Coupled with the design eccentricity of some imports—e.g., the smaller Westerly boats with their bilge keels and bulbous deckhouses—the high price was always a formidable obstacle to a successful invasion.

Nicholson yachts are well known for quality construction. The firm was a pioneer in British fiberglass boatbuilding. If experience counts, then Nicholson must be somewhere near the top of the list: the firm of Camper & Nicholsons, Ltd., was building yachts in the days of Lord Nelson.

The Nicholson 32 was an archetypal boat of the British boatbuilding industry, much like the Triton in this country. Despite a long and successful production run, the Nicholson 32 was starting to look dated: narrow, low freeboard, with longish ends. In 1976, the venerable 32 was replaced by the Nicholson 31, maintaining the concept of a real cruising boat on a small scale, with more modern styling, more volume, and more displacement. Relatively few Nicholson 31s were built; only a few dozen were imported into the US.

In appearance, the Nicholson 31 is not unlike many of the current generation of production cruiser-racers. She has a straightish sheer, moderate forward overhang, and a low profile cabin trunk.

Below the waterline, however, there are substantial differences. She has a deep, powerful hull, and a moderately long keel with attached outboard rudder. Her displacement of almost 15,000 pounds is fully 50% more than that of the typical cruiser-racer, and equal to the heaviest of the pure cruisers.

Specifications

LOA	30' 7"
LWL	24' 2"
Beam	10' 3"
Draft	5' 0"
Displacement	14,750 lbs,.
Ballast	5,300 lbs.
Sail area	497 sq. ft.

Even with the pound at its early-'80s level of $1.70, the Nicholson 31 cost a heavyweight $67,000, duty-paid and delivered in the US. A big chunk of that cost was tied up in shipping and import duty.

The 1992 price of a 1985 Nicholson 31 (the last model for which information is available) averages some $54,000, still pretty staggering for a 31' boat.

Before the price scares you away, you must recognize that the boat was delivered unusually well equipped, including such items as sails, dodger, anchor, chain, docklines and fenders, pressure water, even the dishes in the galley. Oh yes, and the name and hailing port painted on the stern.

This is a go-anywhere boat. She is not a teak veneered Colin Archer copy, and she is not a fast coastal cruiser or racer.

She is austere to the point of plainness. External wood consists of a teak toerail, teak grab rails, a cockpit grate, the companionway drop boards, and the tiller. On the positive side, this austerity means low maintenance for the cruiser.

At the same time, she is no Clorox bottle. Detailing and workmanship are excellent. The boat looks functional and businesslike, and she is.

Construction

Like many European boatbuilders, Camper & Nicholsons did not mold their own hulls. Rather, the hulls were subcontracted to another firm which specialized in hull molding.

The hull of the Nicholson 31 is a solid glass layup, reinforced with foam-filled longitudinal stringers. Isopthalic resin is used in the gelcoat layer to reduce porosity and the subsequent possibility of osmotic deterioration. Deck and cabin trunk are balsa cored. Molding and gelcoat quality are very good.

When through hull fittings were installed in the boat, the cut out hull pieces were burned to determine the resin to glass ratio.

The Nicholson 31 was available in a wide range of hull and deck colors at no extra cost. Because the deck molding is a large, unrelieved area of fiberglass, we would recommend looking for a boat that has the deck nonskid in a color contrasting to the base deck color. Teak decks were available as an option.

Hulls were molded to Lloyd's specifications, and Lloyd's hull certificates were available. Full Lloyd's classification of the finished boat required slight modification to the standard boat, notably the addition of more ground tackle, some alterations to the electrical system, and more ventilation for the battery box. The Lloyd's modifications, additional equipment, and surveys added about $1,500 to the price of the boat when new.

Hull and deck are joined with a wide internal flange, bedded with polysulfide and through-bolted at close intervals with stainless steel bolts. Fit of the hull and deck flanges is excellent, with no gaps or irregularities. A through-bolted teak toerail covers the hull-to-deck joint.

All deck hardware is properly through-bolted. Removable panels in the interior give access to every part of the underside of the deck.

Ballast is an internal lead casting weighing 5,300 pounds, giving a ballast/displacement ratio of 36%. It is ironic that the Nicholson 31, a true cruising boat, has internal ballast rather than an external lead keel. An external keel is far less vulnerable to damage in either an intentional or inadvertent grounding.

Nicholson chainplates deserve comment. They consist of stainless steel rod formed into an inverted V-bolt. The top of the V is properly radiused for the appropriate size clevis pin. The legs of the V-bolt pass through the deck and hull flanges and a heavy backup plate. The hull flange is about 1/2" thick, Two major structural bulkheads and a hanging knee reinforce the hull and deck immediately adjacent to the chainplates.

The same chainplate arrangement is used on larger boats in the Nicholson line. The obvious advantage is that the chainplates are just about leakproof.

A few years ago we would have been skeptical of the strength of this installation. However, we have examined a Nicholson 40—equipped with the same chainplates—which was rolled over and dismasted during a winter passage south. The chainplate had bent about 45 degrees, but there were neither deck leaks nor stress cracks in the deck or hull. They work, and you can't argue with that.

The reasons that the chainplates work are an exceptionally thick hull flange and local reinforcement with knees and structural bulkheads.

The outboard rudder is attached to the transom by massive nylon-bushed stainless steel pintle and gudgeon castings. Polished stainless castings are infinitely preferable to weldments in a fitting exposed to salt water, since they are less vulnerable to corrosion.

A large molded fiberglass water tank fills most of the bilge space. The tank is gelcoated inside, and is equipped with two large manholes for easy cleaning. The manholes are also used to fill the tank, as there is no deck fill pipe. While this is a slight nuisance, it pretty much insures that salt water will not get in the tank. The water tank is properly vented inside the boat, rather than outside. Again, the risk of contamination by salt water is eliminated.

Unlike many modern boats, there is a deep bilge sump aft of the water tank. The bilge slopes sharply aft to the sump, so that any water getting into the bilge will quickly drain to the sump. Bilge water lapping about the cabin sole should not be a problem.

Construction of the Nicholson 31 is strong and heavy, perhaps too heavy for coastal cruising in light air. The boat's displacement of almost 15,000 pounds yields a staggering displacement/length ratio of 468, one of the highest we've ever seen. That heavy construction and Lloyd's hull certificate will be comforting, however, hove to in a 60 knot nor'easter in the Gulf Stream or a typhoon in the South Pacific.

Handling Under Sail

With her displacement/length ratio of 468, the Nicholson 31 is no racer-cruiser. She's not even a cruiser-racer. Just a pure cruiser, and one close to being underpowered at that.

Fully loaded for cruising, she will displace 18,000 pounds or more. At that point the boat will need all the sail that can be piled on in light air.

Shrouds mounted at the outboard edge of the deck will limit the boat's ability to point. She is most definitely at her best off the wind.

There is a great deal of inherent stability in the hull form of the Nicholson 31. With her relatively hard bilges, wide beam, and reasonable ballast/displacement ratio, the boat is quite stiff, particularly when these hull characteristics are coupled with a fairly short rig.

Spars are by Proctor. The mast is a heavy, untapered section with airfoil spreaders. The boom is equipped for slab reefing. A short mainsheet traveler mounted on top of the transom will help mainsail control. A boom vang is supplied as standard equipment.

Lewmar winches are used for sheets and halyards. They are of adequate size for the job, although we would consider slightly larger self-tailing winches than the standard single-speed Lewmar 34 STs. All sheets are within easy reach of the helmsman.

The boat came with mainsail and #1 jib. These were made by Horizon, and are of mediocre quality.

A Hydrovane VDA2 self-steering gear was a factory option. Since we'd plan to do a lot of off-wind sailing on our cruise, we'd like to have an autopilot such as the Autohelm 2000 in addition to or in place of the vane steerer. Modern autopilots draw very little power and will steer the boat in a light following breeze or under power in a flat calm—something that no vane can do.

The characteristics of the Nicholson 31 that make her such a good offshore cruiser—stability, heavy displacement, and good motion in a seaway—will make her a poor choice for daysailing or even coastal cruising in areas of light air, On a long offshore passage, however, the boat should shine—provided you've got big headsails, including a spinnaker, for light air.

Handling Under Power

Standard engine is a three cylinder, 22.5 horsepower, raw water cooled Yanmar. If you want pressure hot water on the boat, it is necessary to find a boat equipped with the fresh water cooled version of the engine. Independent of the hot water system, we'd prefer the fresh water cooling.

The engine is just about the right size for the boat. She should putt along at about five knots using less

Good features in the cabin include a full-width head, excellent nav station, and gas-fired stove with oven. If we had our druthers, however, we'd do without the pilot berth on the port side.

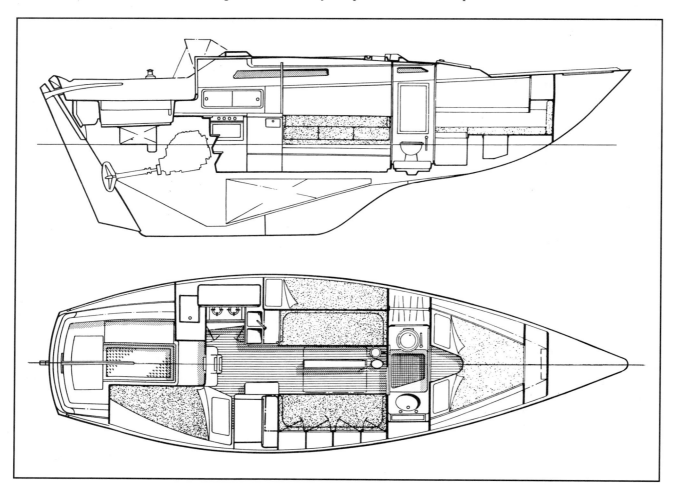

than a half gallon of fuel per hour. That's when the autopilot comes in handy. Steering under power is the most boring job on any sailboat.

The fuel tank is of molded fiberglass mounted under the cockpit sole. The top of the tank, in fact, forms part of the cockpit sole. This means that the teak cockpit grate must be kept in place to keep from walking on top of the tank.

We have always been leery of fiberglass diesel fuel tanks. Unless the proper type of resin is used, the tank may be slightly permeable to diesel oil.

Fortunately, the fuel tank of the Nicholson 31 is a separate molding and is not integral to the hull. Even if trouble were to develop over time, removal and replacement of the tank would be a relatively easy task.

The fuel tank is equipped with a small sump on the bottom which is fitted with a drain to remove accumulated water. While this is a good idea, ABYC standards specifically preclude a drain on the bottom of the fuel tank. Lloyd's is not quite so finicky in that respect.

Capacity of the tank is 25 gallons. This should give the boat a range of 250 to 300 miles under power, perfectly adequate for a 31' cruising boat. The location of the fuel fill on the cockpit sole makes it easy to check the fuel level, but a fuel spill could turn the cockpit into a skating rink if the grate were not in place.

For long passages, it is desirable to be able to line up the prop in the aperture behind the deadwood. Unfortunately, access to the stuffing box and shaft requires climbing into the port cockpit locker after removing the access hatch, an exercise most people will find not worth the effort.

The engine installation is a good one. There is a deep molded drip pan under the engine. The shaft is fitted with a flexible shaft log and a flexible shaft coupling, as well as flexible engine mounts. This combination of flexible components is essential with a vibration-prone diesel engine.

Access to the engine for service is excellent. The companionway steps remove for access to the front of the engine, and a side panel in the quarterberth removes for access to the rest of the engine. The engine is easily removed through the companionway with no disassembly of joinerwork. However, there is no easy access to the oil dipstick.

The entire engine compartment is equipped with excellent soundproofing. All wiring and plumbing in the engine compartment is neat and workmanlike. Hidden carpentry inside the engine box is as well executed as any finish work in the boat.

Deck Layout

Deck layout of the Nicholson 31 is that of a pure cruiser. The recessed stemhead fitting is a massive stainless steel weldment equipped with two heavy cast bronze rollers. If the rollers are used with rope anchor rode they will have to be polished out, as the roller castings are rough enough to damage line. The rollers are designed to stow CQR anchors. Standard equipment includes a 35-pound CQR and a 15-fathom shot of 5/16" chain.

The anchor well is unusual. The lid has a strong, positive latch, and the well contains a large mooring

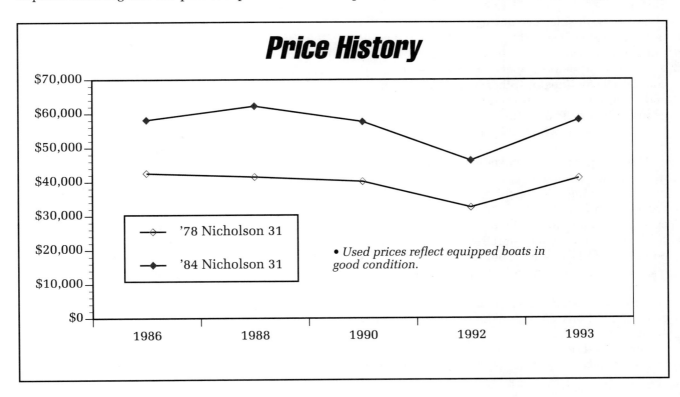

Price History

- ◇— '78 Nicholson 31
- ◆— '84 Nicholson 31

• *Used prices reflect equipped boats in good condition.*

bitt, lashing eyes for anchors and the bitter end of the anchor rode, and a pipe to the chain locker. The chain locker pipe should have been extended higher above the bottom of the anchor well to keep water out of the boat's interior when she takes solid water over the bow.

Because the stemhead fitting and anchor rollers are recessed below deck level, the 35-pound CQR actually stows inside the anchor well, so that sheets and sails cannot snag on it. There is also enough space inside the well to install a windlass, and two different models were listed as factory options. This is perhaps the best anchor well and anchor stowage arrangement we've seen on a small cruising boat.

There are full length hand rails on either side of the deckhouse. Bow and stern rails, double lifelines, and tapered stainless steel stanchions are standard, and are properly mounted.

The cockpit is a good compromise for a cruising boat. Seats are narrow, but are over six feet long for comfortable lounging. A high bridgedeck protects the companionway.

The companionway is fairly narrow and almost parallel-sided, with two drop boards. Because the companionway sill is well below coaming level, the lower drop board should be left in place for offshore sailing. In accordance with ORC requirements for offshore racing, the drop boards and companionway slide have permanent positive inside latches to prevent accidental opening in a rollover.

Cockpit scuppers consist of two large holes through the transom, fitted with external flaps to keep following seas from crawling through the scuppers into the cockpit.

The cockpit sole, a removable teak grate, lacks a positive means of securing in place, so that it could fall out in a severe knockdown or rollover.

There is a shallow locker under the starboard cockpit seat for lines and other small items. At the aft end of this locker is a molded recess for a single propane bottle. The bottle locker is designed for a European bottle, which may prove difficult to replace if it rusts out.

The scupper for this locker drains into the cockpit. Inevitably, the steel gas bottle will turn into a pile of rust, staining the cockpit where the drain discharges. An aluminum gas bottle or a thoroughly epoxied steel bottle is called for here.

No provision is made for the storage of a spare gas bottle. We'd like to see the bottle locker modified to take two aluminum cylinders of at least 10 pounds capacity.

Under the port cockpit seat is a deep locker which can rightfully be called a sail locker. The lid is large enough for the largest headsail on the boat. The locker should accommodate most if not all of the boat's inventory. It is sealed off from the bilge and the underside of the cockpit, and the lid is deeply scuppered.

A full width cockpit dodger came standard. It fits neatly into a plastic extrusion attached to a wraparound breakwater. The forward end of the cockpit will be dry, dry, dry, even in heavy weather, allowing the upper drop board to be left out until it gets really nasty. The only disadvantage of the molded breakwater and low dodger is that the halyards cannot be led aft without fairly complex modifications to the breakwater.

The cockpit is deep and well protected. It is so deep that a short person will have a hard time seeing over the deckhouse. Also, we'd like to see a molded-in transom tube for a man overboard pole, since this is a serious cruising boat.

All in all, the deck layout and cockpit are well suited for serious cruising: simple, clean, and devoid of toe bashers. It is a layout designed not for high performance, but rather for a long haul.

Belowdecks

The interior layout of the Nicholson 31 approaches the ideal for a minimum long distance cruiser for two, but falls short in a few important details. There is a total of six berths, equally divided between the port and starboard sides. Each berth is equipped with a lee cloth.

The forward cabin contains the standard V-berths with an insert to form a double. Shelves along the side of the hull and a small linen locker over the foot of the berth are standard.

There are large bin-type lockers under the V-berths with molded drop-in liners. These should provide good dry storage in any conditions.

A Camper & Nicholsons (Canpa) aluminum framed hatch over the berth provides ventilation and can be used as an exit. Teak steps mounted on the bulkhead serve as a ladder for climbing out the hatch.

Aft of the forward cabin is a full width head. A full width head makes a lot of sense on a small boat. In the attempt to avoid a full width head in a small boat, builders invariably end up with a cramped compartment barely big enough to turn around in, much less shower or dress in comfort.

The water closet is the unique Lavac design, which uses a separate diaphragm pump in place of a built-in pump. This is an incredibly efficient toilet which absolutely will not splash when pumped.

Outboard of the toilet is a good-sized hanging locker. It is, unfortunately, the only hanging space on the boat. The lack of a wet hanging locker will be sorely felt by the serious cruiser.

A pressure cold water shower is standard. The shower sump is fitted with a separate electric pump, and does not drain to the bilge.

Opposite the toilet is a huge sink, the largest we've

seen in the head of any boat. The sink is fitted with both manual and pressure water taps. The head sink has the only manual fresh water pump on the boat. We would also install one in the galley. A heavy stainless steel grab rail is mounted horizontally in front of the sink. Above the sink, tucked under the side deck, is a mirror-fronted medicine chest. The mirrors are angled upward so that it isn't necessary to duck to see your face in the mirror when shaving—a small touch, but typical of the thought which has gone into the interior.

The head compartment has solid, heavy sliding doors which have positive latches to hold them open. They are held shut only by magnets, which could prove inadequate offshore. Ventilation is provided by a small cowl vent in a molded dorade box. We would replace the cowl with a larger one.

The main cabin has a number of excellent features, not the least of which is a strongly mounted dropleaf cabin table. Bolted to an aluminum plate under the cabin sole, the table is as sturdy as any we've ever encountered. The folding leaves should be fitted with fiddles, however, for use in a rolly anchorage. (At sea, a lap is more often used than a table. We can recall very few sit-down dinners at sea.)

Settees port and starboard are fitted with lee cloths, as are the pilot berth and quarterberth. There is good dry, compartmented storage below, behind, and above the settees. Footwells under the chart table and galley counter make the settees long enough for sleeping. Both settees pull out to increase width for sleeping.

While the pilot berth and quarterberth afford permanent sea berths on both sides of the main cabin without using the settees, this configuration wastes storage space that the cruising couple would find handy. We doubt if four berths in the main cabin are really necessary. Instead, we'd like to have seen the pilot berth replaced by lockers and bookshelves similar to those above the settee on the starboard side. The port settee could then have been shifted outboard almost a foot, allowing two or three more galley drawers to be added under the existing single drawer. Galley counter space would have been increased by eliminating the pilot berth extension into the galley, and the main cabin table could have been shifted slightly to port to give a wider passageway to the head and forward cabin.

The galley is the weakest part of the interior, as it is on most small boats. The single small oval sink has a flush lid which reverses to act as a cutting board. Unfortunately, on the boat we examined the sink lid is asymmetrical, and doesn't quite fit into the sink when reversed.

There is one small drawer in the galley. It's the only drawer in the whole boat. Admittedly, drawers are expensive and waste a certain amount of space, but the one place they do make sense is the galley, and one is barely adequate.

A two burner, gimballed, strongly mounted propane stove with oven and broiler is standard. The stove is a simple enameled steel model, and will probably last for only a few years of hard service before it rusts out. At the same time, it probably only cost a couple of hundred dollars rather than the $600 or more you would pay for a good stainless steel model.

The gas system lacks a shutoff valve belowdecks, a violation of ABYC standards for propane installations. We suggest you fit a Marinetics or Bass electromagnetic propane solenoid, or a good manual valve somewhere in the galley.

As is typical in many European boats, the icebox is a bit of an afterthought. In much of the world, ice isn't the readily available commodity that it is here, and people simply learn to do without. When cruising offshore, ice only lasts a few days anyway, so unless you have a refrigeration system, why bother with an icebox? So the logic goes, anyway. In this country, most cruising is well within range of sources of ice, and we'd damned well want a good box to keep it in.

While the icebox of the Nicholson 31 is well insulated, including the lid, the lid lacks a sealing gasket. The lid is so small that a 25 pound block of ice must be broken in half to pass through, and a gallon jug of wine would be a close fit. In addition, the rounded cabin trunk liner protrudes so much into the space over the icebox that access is difficult. This inconvenience is totally unnecessary, as there is plenty of dead space behind the liner that could be eliminated to make the galley more workable. The icebox also lacks shelves to keep food off the ice, and it drains into the bilge sump.

There is fairly good storage outboard of the stove in well-fiddled shelves behind plexiglass sliding doors. Crockery and glasses are provided as standard items.

Treadmaster is used on the cabin sole in the galley and at the aft end of the main cabin. This is an excellent nonskid surface which is, unfortunately, very difficult to clean. The rest of the main cabin sole is varnished teak and holly plywood.

On the starboard side opposite the galley is an excellent nav station, with a huge chart table and plenty of bulkhead space for radios, instruments, book cases, and other goodies. The electrical panel—again typical of European boats—lacks adequate circuits for the addition of many extras. The electrical system does have a built-in ground system utilizing an external ground plate, which greatly improves the functioning of SSB radios, shortwave receivers, and Loran.

The navigator sits at the head of a large, comfortable quarterberth. Batteries mount under the quarterberth in the best battery box we've seen, with a positively latched lid. Two heavy-duty 96 amp-hour batteries are standard, and should be adequate for the electrical needs of a 31' cruising boat. The battery box does lack adequate ventilation to disperse charging gases, a fairly easily remedied problem.

Ventilation of the main cabin is provided by a large aluminum framed hatch in the middle of the cabin, and two small cowl vents in molded dorade boxes at the aft end of the cabin. These tiny, low, 3" diameter cowls should be replaced by taller 4" vents, which have almost twice the cross-sectional area—hence twice the air flow—of 3" vents.

The ventilation hatches in both the main and forward cabins open aft. When fitted with side curtains, they can be left open at sea for additional ventilation. Forward facing hatches are fine in port, but cannot normally be left open at sea.

The interior of the Nicholson 31 is clearly that of a seagoing boat. There are full length hand rails along each cabin side, and vertical posts in the galley and nav station.

With the changes mentioned above, this interior would be just about ideal for a cruising couple. Interior workmanship is excellent, with a good blend of very light teak and off-white molded components. The interior is cheery and homelike. It's easy to imagine a long cruise aboard.

Conclusions

The Nicholson 31 is a well designed, well built serious cruising boat. Her somewhat modern appearance above the water may confuse those who connect serious cruising boats with lots of teak, bowsprits, sweeping sheers, and "traditional" appearance.

The Nicholson 31 is not a copy of any "ideal" cruising hull form. She is, rather, a well thought out answer to the problem of putting a lot of carrying capacity, volume, and comfort in a minimum size boat for extended cruising.   • **PS**

Southern Cross 31

The Southern Cross 31 is an ocean-going dream machine designed for offshore cruising.

The Southern Cross 31 might best be described as a double-ended ocean cruising cutter of moderate beam, moderate draft, moderate-to-heavy displacement, and moderate sail area. She has a pronounced concave sheer, moderately cut away forefoot, and outboard rudder. To many she would embody the ideal ocean cruising hull form.

The Southern Cross 31 might also be termed a dream machine. She is a boat pitched to those sailors whose idea of sailing—whether they achieve it or not—is palm-fringed islands, the aquamarine of the sea off soundings, and long tradewind passages. She is the type of boat to make accountants from Iowa run away to the South Seas.

In the early 1970s an effective promotional campaign by Westsail rekindled a relatively dormant interest in the wide, heavy, double-ended hull form of the Norwegian rescue boat for long-distance cruising. Since then that hull form has proliferated to the point of faddish absurdity. Arguing whether the double ended hull form—whether the stern be of the "cruiser," "canoe," or "Baltic" variety—was better than all others for seakeeping ability dominated conversation among would-be long distance cruisers in much the way that the cutter cranks and the sloop supporters duked it out in the late 19th century. A generation of cruising boats, many over-heavy, under-canvassed, poorly designed, poorly built, and with all the windward ability of a sand barge flooded the market. If it wasn't pointed at both ends, or at least rounded, it wasn't a world cruiser.

In 1976, in the midst of the double-ended doubletalk, Clarke Ryder, who had set up a fiberglass molding company for industrial parts, began building the Southern Cross 31. In the next five years over 130 hulls were built, many finished off by their owners. The boat went out of production in 1987.

Specifications

LOA	31' 0"
LWL	25' 0"
Beam	9' 6"
Draft	4' 7"
Displacement	13,600 lbs.
Ballast	4,400 lbs.
Sail area	447 sq. ft.

At first glance the Southern Cross 31 might appear to be another boat designed to leap upon the Colin Archer bandwagon, because of the double-ended hull, long keel, and outboard rudder. With those characteristics the resemblance of the Southern Cross 31 to most of the "modern" offshore cruising double-enders ceases.

The Tom Gillmer designed Southern Cross 31 is very similar to another of his designs, the Allied Seawind—later reincarnated, modified, and called the Seawind II. The original Seawind was the first fiberglass sailboat to circle the world. The Southern Cross 31 is basically the same hull as the original Seawind with the stern redrawn from transom-type to a canoe-type stern, the beam increased by 3", and the displacement increased by 1,500 lbs.

For the single-handed or double-handed world cruiser who tends toward the conservative the Southern Cross 31 may appear to be the ideal combination: a proven cruising hull design combined with a pointed stern.

Construction

The Southern Cross 31 is one of the few Airex-cored production boats ever built. The hull is molded in one piece, with solid laminate along the centerline, Airex-cored from the turn of the bilge nearly to the sheer line. The glass laminate is solid abreast the mast where the main chainplates are attached.

The deck is a one-piece molding, balsa cored for rigidity. The cabin top is also balsa cored, although the area around the mast step is cored with plywood rather than balsa for greater strength in compression.

Airex and balsa coring relieve the Southern Cross 31 of some of the least desirable characteristics of fiberglass construction. Coring greatly reduces the pronounced tendency of fiberglass to sweat in cold weather, deadens the notorious sound transmission of glass construction, and provides strength and rigidity without either a heavy solid layup or a complicated system of internal framing. Coring also functions as an insulator, making a glass hull cooler in the summer and easier to heat in the winter.

We have some reservations about the Southern Cross hull-to-deck joint. There is no doubt that it is simple and strong. At the sheer the hull molding turns outward 90 degrees. The deck molding drops down into the hull, with an external flange overlapping the hull flange. The hull and deck are bolted together, the joint filled with a polyester compound. Our reservation is that the flange sticks outboard of the hull more than an inch, almost at right angles to the hull. Not only is this hard to finish off neatly, but it is somewhat vulnerable.

Consider the boat tied alongside the government dock in St. John, US Virgin Islands. The ferry from St. Thomas comes in, dragging a large wake. If your boat rolls this flange into the dock from the wake of the ferry, it could easily be damaged, and repair would not necessarily be simple. An inward-turning flange might be more complicated to engineer or lay up, but it would be far less vulnerable to damage of this kind. We also suspect that the exposed stainless steel nuts on the underside of the flange will discolor and begin to bleed on long passages.

Ballast of the Southern Cross 31 is an internal lead casting, glassed into the keel cavity. This obviates the need for keelbolts, and the attendant possibility for leaking. It has the disadvantage that should the vessel run aground—a not infrequent event for the long distance cruiser, who frequently enters unfamiliar ports, the hull rather than the lead keel takes the brunt. We have seen other internally-ballasted fiberglass hulls so abraded by a few hours on rocks or coral that the ballast literally fell out of the hull. For our world cruiser, we'd prefer an externally bolted-on lead keel, which should be capable of surviving a severe grounding without damaging the fiberglass hull.

The rudder of the Southern Cross 31 is set well up from the bottom of the rudder post, protected from grounding damage. Rudder design has been changed from a traditionally-shaped rudder to a more modern design with greater area near the bottom of the rudder blade.

Pintles and gudgeons are heavy stainless steel weldments. We prefer castings to weldments for use under water, particularly if the metal chosen is stainless steel. Bronze is usually considered superior for underwater fittings due to the greater susceptibility of stainless steel to some types of corrosion.

Bulkheads are glassed directly to the hull using Airex fillets. Tanks are of molded fiberglass, set deep into the bilge. There are bronze seacocks on all through-hull fittings.

In 1981, for another $1,275 above the base price of $62,500 for the finished boat, the standard anodized aluminum or epoxy-coated deck hardware could be replaced with all bronze hardware. For the person simply seeking a boat to get away in this may have been an extravagance. For the person seeking to keep a very traditional looking boat completely in character, the bronze option was worthwhile.

The Southern Cross 31 is neither a cheaply constructed, nor cheaply priced, imitation of an ocean-going sailboat. In general, her construction characteristics are up to her billing as a real offshore cruiser.

Handling Under Sail

A boat designed for offshore passagemaking is not likely to have the windward performance of a modern fin keel racing boat. At the same time, she should be able to claw off a lee shore in a gale—something that many of the so-called "world cruisers" would be hard pressed to do.

In many ways the all around performance of the long-distance cruiser must be better than that of the coastal cruiser or daysailer. She must be able to sail in light winds, for few small offshore cruisers can carry enough fuel to motor to distant ports. She must have a motion that doesn't tire her crew. Her rig must be easy to handle, and must offer sailing versatility without the huge sail inventory of the racing boat.

The boat can be expected to meet most of these requirements. A huge masthead genoa can be carried in light air, but a staysail and double reefed main should carry her to windward in heavy going. The hard turn of her bilge implies good initial stability.

There is nothing in the hull form of the Southern Cross 31 that implies poor sailing characteristics.

This is borne out by the record of the prototype, which finished third in class in the 1977 Marion-Bermuda Race. Owners report that the boat sails well, and there is nothing to indicate otherwise. Her displacement of 13,600 lbs on a 25' waterline is a little heavy by modern standards, but is certainly not excessive by any traditional standard.

Standard rig of the Southern Cross 31 is modern masthead cutter. The anodized aluminum mast is stepped on the cabin top. Compression is transferred to the keel via a wood compression column securely glassed to the hull structure. At least one owner who had a taller than standard rig reported a depressed cabin top in the area of the mast step. Ryder repaired that with an oversize load-distributing steel plate attached to the cabin top. If the boat is to be owner-finished, care must be taken to be sure that the wood compression column adequately bears the load of the mast.

The standard boat shows intermediate shrouds led slightly aft of the after lower shroud. Both the main boom and the mainsail will bear on this intermediate shroud when running before the wind. Care must be taken to protect the main from chafe. We would prefer running backstays, which would lead further aft, giving a better angle for tensioning the forestay. With the runners set up, mast pumping in a seaway—a problem not uncommon with deck-stepped rigs—could probably be eliminated.

Originally, the boat was drawn with a short boomkin to accommodate the standing backstay. This complicated the mounting of a vane steerer. The backstay is now split, carried to chainplates at either side of the back of the cockpit. The mainsail should be cut with little or no roach to avoid fouling on the backstay with this arrangement.

While a cutter rig may seem unnecessarily complicated on a boat this small, it does allow strength and versatility. These are definitely desirable characteristics in the shorthanded cruiser.

Handling Under Power

With a 22 horsepower diesel to push just short of seven tons, the Southern Cross 31 is very adequately powered. The fuel capacity of 34 gallons will probably give about 65 hours of powering at five knots, for a range of about 325 miles under power. This provides very adequate cruising range under power without the need to carry extra fuel in cans in the cockpit, which is always a nuisance, and can be dangerous.

Deck Layout

Deck layout of the boat is clean and functional. Side decks are fairly wide and unobstructed. The low bulwarks provide a feeling of security when working on deck. We would prefer all halyards led aft to the cockpit for shorthanded sailing, and we would make all winches self-tailing.

A molded seahood is standard, and is an absolute must for any offshore cruiser. A molded-in spray rail will accommodate a cockpit dodger, another very useful piece of gear for the offshore sailor.

The cockpit is small and fairly deep, with a good bridgedeck. The deck mold was retooled beginning with hull 85. The crown of the deck was changed slightly, provision was made for a hatch over the main cabin, and the cockpit was lengthened about 6" aft. Cockpit scuppers were moved from the aft end of the cockpit to the forward end, and the pitch of the cockpit sole changed slightly to facilitate draining.

Deck layout is clean and functional. A life raft can be carried on top of the main cabin—a little high for such a substantial weight, but perhaps the best solution on a boat this small. We would prefer that the winch islands be big enough for a set of secondary headsail sheet winches.

The small cockpit gives a great feeling of security. This is a very important characteristic in a boat designed to carry her crew to distant places. Big cockpits may be nice in port, but at sea all you can

The Southern Cross 31 has minimal interior room for a couple undertaking a long cruise. Since the boat was available in kit form, the actual interior may bear no resemblance whatever to the standard layout.

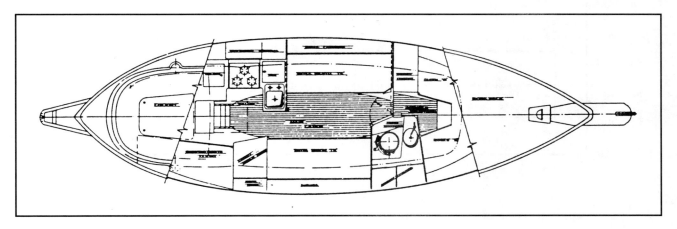

think of is the amount of water they could hold if the boat were to be pooped. We'll take a small cockpit for offshore use.

Belowdecks

The Southern Cross 31 has what is really the minimal amount of interior volume for one or two people for long distance cruising. There are two standard layouts—one with fixed chart table over storage space, the other with a folding chart table over a quarterberth. Although as a rule we are partial to quarterberths, the space in this case is best given over to storage space, and the larger fixed chart table is more useful.

With this arrangement, the main cabin settees must be used as berths at sea. This is not really an inconvenience for the shorthanded sailor. The windward settee, fitted with a lee cloth, would keep the sleeper's weight high and on the proper side of the boat for going upwind, while the leeward settee will provide secure sleeping if upwind performance is not a consideration. The forward cabin would be used for sails and other storage when passagemaking.

The galley is small, as it pretty much must be on a boat of this size. Double sinks are now standard, rather than the single sink of early models. The standard stove is a two-burner Shipmate with oven, alcohol fueled. We feel that only a masochist will cook for long periods of time on an alcohol stove (or perhaps a hermit trying to learn the ultimate lessons of patience).

With eight opening ports and two hatches plus the main companionway, ventilation is not a problem.

At sea the main cabin overhead hatch could be left open if fitted with a small dodger.

Those who finish off kit boats frequently have weird ideas of what the interior of a boat should look like. One should think long and hard before making major alterations to any standard layout. The standard interior of the Southern Cross 31 is a good, if prosaic interior. We think this may well be better than a highly-personalized but perhaps offbeat interior when the time comes to sell the boat.

Conclusion

Is she a good boat for offshore cruising? Most definitely so. We would, however, change some of the details of her construction, as outlined above.

About half of the Southern Cross 31s sold were "stage" boats, rather than factory completed. No one really knows how many of those were completed, and how many rest in driveways and backyards. We suspect that a fair number are still in the unfinished stage. We looked at one such boat that the owner had been "working" on for years. We're sure it looked worse than when he started. For this reason, there is no real established market value for owner finished boats. With the base price of an early-'80s factory-completed boat at $62,500, she was a very expensive 31' boat when finished off by the factory. In cruising trim, you could easily have $75,000 invested without being extravagant.

1992 prices for early-'80s boats run in the high 30s and low 40s, a not inconsiderable sum. The bottom-line question should be: How much is your dream worth to you, really? • **PS**

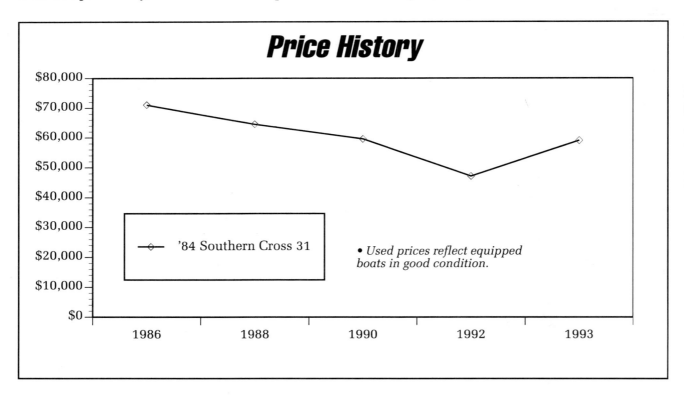

Tartan 31

The newest version of the 31 has been "Piperized," and is a well-equipped mid-range cruiser.

The Tartan 31 is one of the new line of performance cruising yachts from the venerable—and durable—Grand River, Ohio boatbuilder. In the last few years, Tartan Marine has come out with a range of new models, including the T-28, the 3500 and the 4600. A 41-footer is in the works. Both the 28 and the latest version of the 31 are part of the new Piper series, which are marketed in sailaway condition.

The Boat and the Builder

Tartan, now a division of NavStar, has come along way since its early days as one of the pioneer manufacturers of fiberglass auxiliary sailboats. In 1980, Tartan was Douglass and McLeod Plastics, formed by Charlie Britton, among others, to build the now-classic Tartan 27 centerboarder from Sparkman & Stephens. The first hull was produced in 1961, the last in 1980 for a total of 712—approximately 700 more than Britton's initial expectation.

During that run, Tartan took its place as one of the major auxiliary builders in America, competing almost on a model-by-model basis with Cal, Pearson and, later, Catalina in producing mid-range cruisable sailing yachts. Tartan also has seen its share of troubles, from a serious plant fire in 1971, through ownership upheavals in the 1980s, and even a brush with voluntary bankruptcy in 1990 when the company shut down for three months. Under NavStar, which also markets the Thomas line of sailboats, Tartan has bounced back and retains unusually strong loyalty among its customers.

By 1991, company sales were outstripping production once again, an enviable position in these down-market times (so bad that even the National Marine Manufacturers Association has stopped tracking sailboat sales). Tartan has been looking for new

Specifications

LOA	31' 4"
LWL	26' 0"
Beam	10' 11"
Draft (deep/shoal)	6' 6"/4' 4"
Displacement	9,030 lbs.
Ballast	3,600 lbs.
Sail area	506 sq. ft.

markets abroad, following up with dealerships in Holland, Great Britain and Japan. In 1992, 25 percent of its business was exports.

There are two versions of the Tartan 31, both the work of Tim Jackett, Tartan's in-house designer since the 1980s. The first 31s were built in 1987, and 118 were made before Jackett "Piperized" the model for 1992. Aside from adding a sailaway package, which includes North sails, Harken furling gear and lazy jacks, and Autohelm ST 50 instruments, the Piper offers a revised interior layout and a new shoal draft keel. The Piper also carries slightly less ballast with the same hull and rig; otherwise, the two versions are the same.

The 31 is classic Tartan—a medium-displacement cruiser with lots of power for performance and

Owners' Comments

"On her first trip from Plymouth to Westport (Massachusetts), she held course for 20 minutes without me touching the wheel. I can't imagine a better boat."

1988 model in Massachusetts

"This is the best boat I've ever seen—the way it's put together, and the sail plan. The only negative thing is a (persistent) leak at the bottom of the mast."

1991 model in New York

"I race mine avidly. I am in my 80s, the youngest guy in the crew is 55. It's very easy to move about on."

1988 model in Vermont

"I love this boat and am pleased with my choice after looking at about 40 new and used boats. I have full racing and cruising sails and have enjoyed the racing as much as the weekend cruising."

1988 model in New York

as many amenities as can be worked into 26 feet of waterline. The double-spreader masthead rig carries 507 square feet of sail, 266 in the foretriangle, 241 in the fully-battened main, for a sail area/displacement ratio of 18—enough to provide good speed without being overpowering. Tartan elected to use swept-back spreaders on the Piper, eliminating the babystay, which also clears the way for a (no-cost) optional self-tacking jib. (The standard jib is 135 percent.)

The original 31 displaces 9,030 pounds and carries 3,900 pounds of lead in its external keel, for a 43 percent ballast-to-displacement ratio; ballast in the Piper is reduced to 3,600 pounds for a still-respectable ratio of almost 40 percent. Both versions come with a six-foot deep fin, which most owners eschew for the shoal-draft version. The first 31s carry a Scheel keel, which draws 4' 4". For the Piper, Jackett designed (and named) the Beaver Tail, which draws the same but differs in shape, with NACA foil sections for greater lift and a somewhat flattened bulb intended to create an endplate effect and reduce drag. By concentrating the weight lower, the Beaver Tail provides the same righting moment with 300 pounds less ballast. "We feel it's more performance oriented, that it gives more lift," said Doug Zurn, a Tartan design engineer.

The hull itself, with an 11-foot beam (one foot more than the old Tartan 30), is full, with a distinct turn at the bilge for less wetted surface in light air, and stability, when the wind rises and the boat digs in. All in all, the 31 offers a stable platform and a blend of good looks and blue-water function. Since Tartans are semi-custom, you have the option of a traditional counter transom or a sportier scoop-style stern, with a somewhat wider swim ladder. Most customers choose the scoop.

Construction

Tartan has a reputation for solid construction and

good workmanship and that's what the 31 is: solid and well put together. The hull is hand-laminated with alternating layers of chopped strand mat and unidirectional E glass. Behind the NPG/ISO gelcoat there's a layer of vinylester resin, which so far appears to provide the best osmotic blister protection available. Tartan, also a pioneer in cored hulls, has limited its balsa end-grain coring to the deck, because of the 31's small size.

At a time when such reputable builders as Tillotson-Pearson (now TPI) are moving toward glued-together hull and deck joints, with bolts only at the cleats and stanchions, Tartan is still through-bolting the length of the hull, with stainless steel bolts driven every six or seven inches through the solid teak toerail into a molded-in 1/4" aluminum backing strip. The connection is further solidified by 3M's 5200 adhesive. Down below, a partial liner to support the flooring is bonded to the hull. The keel is secured to the hull by seven 3/4" stainless steel bolts and a thick bedding. Gear throughout is quality—Harken roller furling, Harken winches and a white Awlgrip-finished mast from Offshore Spars, which rises 48' 6" above the water. Deck hatches and opening ports are Lewmar. The engine is an 18-hp. Yanmar diesel.

The 31 has a comfortably deep T-shaped cockpit, a roomy foredeck and sufficiently wide sidedecks to facilitate moving around. Teak handrails and molded nonskid (plus the inboard shrouds) make the fore and aft trip safer. Even so, Tartan has made things easier by leading all sail control lines aft to housetop-mounted winches. Traveler controls also are mounted on the cabin top, although some serious racers have moved the traveler aft of the helm. The helm consists of a large Destroyer-type wheel by Edson "or equivalent" and the helm seat is raised slightly for a better view; owners have commented favorably on its comfort, even after long hours at the wheel. Tartan supplies an emergency backup tiller.

Several 31 owners complain about mast leaks. One found the solution in liberal application of silicone sealer. Another has been frustrated by a persistent leak, possibly from the head of the mast, which requires constant pumping out of the bilge. One owner spoke of her tie rod not being secured, but attributed the oversight to her dealer. Other Piper owners bemoaned the absence of handy stern chocks.

Performance

Although its design teams have changed, Tartan over the years has shown a knack for getting performance out of its cruising boats. That's because Tartan emphasizes performance first in its cruisers, Zurn said. "You get a nice teak interior, but they do go fast," he said. Racers we've talked to seem as happy with the 31's performance as the weekend cruisers are with its accommodations. The 31, like other Tartans present and past, avoids the extremes of some other manufacturers.

One reason for Tartan's successful blending of elements would appear to be careful attention to rig and sail plan. The double-spreader masthead rig permits extra sail area, resulting in a nicely balanced boat that's "very forgiving," in the words of several owners. With 241 square feet in the main, there's enough sail area for good offwind speed; the big 135-percent jib, with 359 square feet, provides plenty of power to windward, the 31's best point of sail. Upwind sail trim angles are further enhanced by the inboard shrouds. The boat moves nicely to windward, especially in a breeze, and also handles well dead downwind. Like other Tartans, it is least effective on a broad reach, especially when seas build up, but the good-sized "subtly" elliptical rudder provides adequate control. However, the 31 we sailed last spring on Long Island Sound managed a respectable 5-plus knots on a beam reach in about 10 knots of wind.

The 31 can carry sufficient sail partly because of its keel, particularly the deep fin version preferred by racers (and apparently Tartan's overseas customers in Holland and Japan). With the shoal keel, the boat naturally loses some windward performance, but does not appear noticeably more tender. According to Zurn, the boat heels 10-12 degrees then "holds its own." There's no talk of reefing on this boat until the winds are well over 20 knots; owners report comfortable sailing in 35-40 knots, with a double reef. Adjusting the bendy mast and experimenting with sail trim may be necessary to increase performance in lighter airs. Those to whom performance is a priority should consider installing an optional hydraulic or mechanical backstay adjuster.

Under PHRF, the Tartan rates between 141 and 153, with 150 as an average, and compares favorably to most cruisers of its size and vintage, many of which were trumpeted as "performance" cruisers when introduced. The British-made Moody 31, for example, which displaces about 100 pounds less, carries slightly less ballast and has almost identical sail area, rates between 174-180; the Freedom 32, considerably lighter at 7,610 pounds (with ballast of 3,100) carries 50 square feet less total sail area and rates about 15 seconds slower per mile; the Pearson 31, marginally heavier with about 10 square feet less sail area, has an average PHRF in the 170s.

Interior

Down below, the most obvious differences between the original 31 and the Piper are apparent. Both have

The Piper interior shows many interesting angles, especially in the bulkheads forward, the nav station and the galley. Note the position of the ice box, which is not buried near a bulkhead.

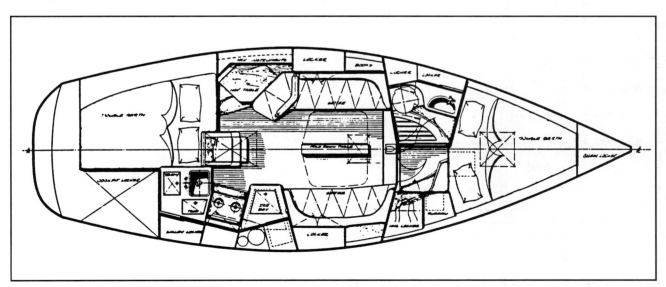

a definite seaworthy look—angled bulkheads, a businesslike nav station and a U-shaped galley for cooking in offshore conditions. Bulkheads, furniture and cabinets are all teak, offset by an off-white partial liner. The sole is varnished teak and holly. Settee cushions are a plush six inches thick.

In an effort to increase stowage space on the Piper, Tartan removed the port pilot berth and added cabinets and shelves. Settee berths were shifted outboard slightly and the bulkhead-mounted table moved to the centerline. Switching the table permitted the designers to add a second door from the main cabin into the head, through the port bulkhead. This increases access, although some observers feel it decreased privacy.

Also changed was the navigation station, to port as you come down the companionway. The original has a fold-down station (with instruments optional), separated from the main cabin by a full bulkhead. The new, permanent station faces aft behind a partial bulkhead and offers more room for instruments. The change "opened up the cabin tremendously," Zurn said. Also under the old arrangement, access to the port quarterberth was partially blocked when the chart table was in use; that's no longer the case.

Interestingly, owners of the original version prefer the old layout, although for different reasons. One was glad to see the "coffin" pilot berth go, but disliked the nav area changes; another preferred the new nav station, but felt the centerline table intruded on cabin space. Yet another preferred the old CNG stove to the new propane burners.

The forward cabin has the usual double V-berth, with bureau and hanging locker to starboard. Several owners we talked to find the forward berths (about 6' 9" long, 6' 6" wide at the head, but narrowing considerably) somewhat cramped and stifling and prefer to sleep elsewhere, in the double quarterberth to port or amidships. The quarter berth, 7' x 5', is the most comfortable sleeping spot on the boat. The main settees are bunk-sized; the port berth, 6' 6" x 2', will fit an adult, but the starboard bunk, 5' 6" x 2', is more suitable for a child. Overall, Tartan has done a decent job of packing reasonable accommodations into a 31-footer, while retaining some sense of space in a pleasantly nautical environment. Standing headroom is 6' 2" in the main cabin, an even 6' in the forecabin.

Just about everyone praises the easy access to the engine, which is gained by swinging aside the companionway stairs. This allows access to all sides of the engine, including the rear; even the stuffing box is readily accessible.

Light and ventilation are provided by a total of eight opening ports on the house sides, mid-cabin and foredeck hatches, and an extra opening port to the cockpit. Storage below, especially on the Piper, is adequate, if not expansive; topsides, there's a cockpit locker opening to the starboard quarter, and lockers port and starboard of the helm.

Conclusions

The Tartan 31 strikes a nice balance between performance and cruising comfort. There's enough power

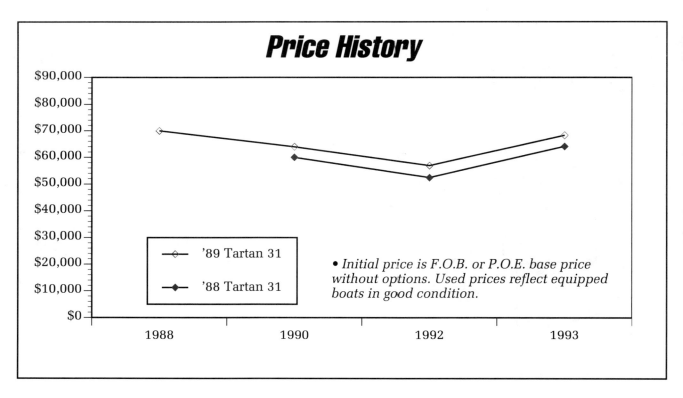

Price History

Legend:
- '89 Tartan 31
- '88 Tartan 31

• Initial price is F.O.B. or P.O.E. base price without options. Used prices reflect equipped boats in good condition.

to keep the casual racer feeling competitive, and enough stability to keep the relative newcomer out of trouble. The Piper, fully equipped, retailed in 1993 for $88,580. Tartans traditionally retain their value, and the manufacturer and many of its dealers receive excellent notices for their post-sale service. The BUC *Used Boat Price Guide* is listing the 1988 pre-Piper 31 at between $61,200-$67,200, but current asking prices from dealers and individuals in classified acts are higher. (BUC, which, in our opinion, used to have slightly inflated values for used boats, seems to have reacted to the soft market by significantly underestimating true value, in the opinion of many dealers we've talked to recently.)

There may not be anything earth-shatteringly innovative about the Tartan 31, but it can lay solid claim to being an All-American mid-range cruiser, suitable for inland lake or coastal sailing. • **PS**

Cal 31

A well-designed and well-executed 31-footer with an excellent interior and good racing performance.

The Cal 31 is the thirteenth Bill Lapworth-designed Cal boat between 27' and 34' built by the Costa Mesa, California firm. Cal, a pioneer in fiberglass sailboat construction, later became a division of Bangor Punta Marine, whose boatbuilding group also included O'Day and Ranger. Cal boats went out of production in 1989. Cal and Bill Lapworth are best known for the breakthrough Cal 40, which many years ago began the trend toward moderately light displacement, fin-keel spade-rudder ocean racers.

The hull configuration of the Cal 31 is typical of Lapworth designs: shallow-bodied and round-bilged, with a fairly short fin keel, a shallow skeg, and a well faired high aspect ratio spade rudder. Production of Cal 31 began in the fall of 1978; 130 boats were built in the first three years.

The entire Cal line was heavily promoted as dual-purpose boats, the ubiquitous "cruiser-racer" which now seems to dominate the sailboat market. The company's colorful, catchy ads were prominent in sailing magazines and were geared toward the affluent 30- to 40-year old consumer with a lot of experience. Surprisingly, many new Cal 31 purchasers were buying their first sailboat larger than small one-design daysailers. One Cal 31 owner reported that the 31 was his fourth Cal boat. Cal 31 owners typically spend 70% of their sailing time daysailing, 20% short-term cruising, and 10% club racing.

Owners report relatively few defects, but the ones they do report are recurrent, and almost exclusively associated with water getting where it's not supposed to be—inside the boat. The most common problems with the Cal 31 are leaking stanchion bases, leaking chainplates, and leaking hatches. These are probably the most common warranty claims throughout the industry and are generally the result

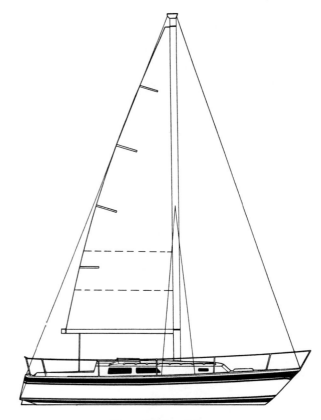

Specifications

LOA	31' 6"
LWL	25' 8"
Beam	10' 0"
Draft	5' 0"
Displacement	9,170 lbs.
Ballast	3,600 lbs.
Sail area	490 sq. ft.

of the fact that adequate bedding to prevent leaks requires fairly careful work, can be messy, and takes time to clean up.

Construction

The hull of the Cal 31 is a solid hand layup. Cal hull weight, less ballast, is about average for performance cruisers of comparable length and beam, although total displacement tends to be lighter than average.

Exterior cosmetic finish is good. There is slight printthrough of the first layer of roving, and some pinholes appear in the gelcoat where surface blemishes have been patched.

The deck molding is plywood-cored in areas where heavy hardware is mounted. The cabin top is sandwich construction: Klegecell foam, cored with plywood inserts in the mast partner area. The cabin top under the deck-stepped mast is solid 3/4" fiberglass.

The companionway of the Cal 31 is about its weakest design point. It is too wide and has a strong taper which allows drop boards to be removed by lifting a little more than an inch. The mating surface between the two solid teak drop boards is a simple square butt. In every Cal 31 we examined, daylight was visible between the two boards—in one case, almost 1/4". Simple reverse bevels, or preferably, a stepped joint, would take about two minutes more to make and would be infinitely better in terms of water-tightness.

The companionway slide design is not water-proof. The optional sea hood is essential on any boat going offshore or sailing in areas with boisterous conditions.

The split backstay arrangement allows use of an integral centerline swimming ladder incorporated in the stern rail. Backstay chainplates are through-bolted, but fiberglass backing plates are used where we would prefer aluminum or stainless steel. The welded combination bow fitting and chainplate is through-bolted but lacks a backup plate. In fact, the only deck fittings, including winches and cleats, which utilize backup plates are the lifeline stanchions and bow pulpit.

As a rule, *The Practical Sailor* prefers to see metal backup plates on through-bolted fittings, even cleats and winches which are normally only subjected to shear loads. Overkill in the mounting of hardware is cheap insurance.

The hull-to-deck joint is made by chemically bonding the two moldings together. An extruded rigid plastic rubrail holder and soft vinyl rubrail insert cover the hull-to-deck joint on the outside of the hull.

The ballast keel is an encapsulated lead casting. The fiberglass-covered, high-density foam-cored rudder utilizes a stainless steel rudder stock.

The main structural bulkhead is teak-faced plywood, bonded to the hull with fiberglass fillets. To avoid hard spots, the bulkhead itself does not touch the hull. The mast is supported by a teak compression column which rests on a deep molded fiberglass floor timber, part of the molded floor pan, which is bonded to the hull.

Chainplates for the inboard shrouds are heavy stainless steel flat bar, properly bolted to the main bulkhead and other plywood webs. Inside the head locker, the chainplates are bolted through a web which is covered with the carpet-like hull liner before installation of the chainplates. We would prefer to have the chainplate and backup pads bear directly on the wood or fiberglass web, rather than on the hull liner.

The rig is a basic masthead sloop with single airfoil spreaders and double lower shrouds. Lower shroud terminations are inboard and about a foot from the molded fiberglass toerail. The Cal 31 utilizes a polyurethane coated Kenyon aluminum mast and boom. Although rope-to-wire tailspliced halyards are listed as standard, the boat we sailed had eye-spliced halyards.

The wire portion of the main halyard was too short to allow an adequate number of wire wraps around the winch. Other boats we examined had properly spliced halyards.

Water tanks are cast polyethylene, with flexible plastic hose piping. A definite plastic taste is imparted to the water by this system. The fuel tank is welded aluminum. Tanks and batteries are mounted under the cabin settees, below the waterline with the weight concentrated in the middle of the boat. This location utilizes a space often given over to lockers which in many boats tend to be wet from bilge water. The battery boxes are well secured, but it is difficult to remove the box covers to inspect the battery electrolyte level.

The Cal 31 is one of the few current production boats with a real bilge sump. Unfortunately, both the icebox and the shower drain through the bilge to this sump. Organic matter and food particles in icebox water quickly lead to smelly bilges. Soap residue from showers can gradually clog impeller-type bilge pumps, which could be a problem in the event of a serious hull leak.

Through-hull fittings below the waterline are bronze, recessed flush with the hull surface and well bedded but without backing blocks. Shutoff valves are glass-filled nylon ball valves originally developed for the chemical industry. Above-water through-hulls are nylon, with no provision for emergency shutoff. One owner we contacted had bronze seacocks installed on underwater openings, as he was leery of the standard nylon valves.

Handling Under Sail

Sailing performance of the Cal 31 is consistent with her performance-cruiser image. Most owners consider the boat somewhat tender. The boat does tend to bury the rail quickly in gusts about five knots above mean wind speed. On the wind, with 14 knots of breeze over the deck, the boat is on the verge of needing a short reef when sailed with a 145% genoa and full main.

The Cal 31 is not particularly wide, but her beam is carried well forward and aft. She therefore develops less weather helm when overpowered than a comparably-sized racing boat and will be a bit more forgiving of improper sail combination than a wider boat whose ends are more pinched.

The Cal 31 is a comfortable boat for a couple to handle. The boat we sailed had Barient 23 self-tailers instead of the standard Barient 21s. We would recommend the larger self-tailers instead of the standard winches on a boat that will be used for short-handed cruising.

The Cal 31 will hold her own with other performance cruisers of comparable size. She is closer-winded and faster than the Cal 29 in light air.

The Cal 31 has generally good handling characteristics under sail. She balances well and can be made to sail herself on the wind with judicious use of sail trim. The boat has a good, solid feel under sail, more like a 35-footer than a 31-footer.

Handling Under Power

The standard engine in the Cal 31 is a two-cylinder 16 horsepower Universal diesel. Earlier models were equipped with two-cylinder Volvo diesels. Owners consider the engine adequate power for the boat.

The instrument panel is mounted on the forward end of the cockpit, and includes gauges for alternator output, water temperature, and fuel level. There is an oil pressure warning light. An oil pressure gauge and a tachometer would be welcome.

The boat handles well under power, but the engine transmits substantial vibration to the hull. This vibration could be tiring if long periods of motoring are required.

Handling in forward gear is uncomplicated. Like most fin-keel boats, the Cal 31 turns in a very tight circle. Handling in reverse is more complicated. With the Volvo engine, owners report that the stern of the boat pulls sharply to starboard. Some owners of Universal-powered boats also report uncertain steering behavior in reverse. We find the steering reasonably predictable, but she does require a firm hand on the tiller or wheel to keep the rudder from going hard over once sternway is made. Gradual application of rudder in reverse prevents rudder stall, which could cause unpredictable steering.

Deck Layout

The initial reaction of most owners to the cockpit of the Cal 31 is that it is too small. Their response after living with it is that it is just about the right size. With either the wheel or the tiller, it is comfortable for a maximum of four when sailing.

There is a wide bridgedeck at the forward end of the cockpit. The roller-bearing mainsheet traveler, with its essential athwartships control lines, is located on the bridgedeck on older Cal 31s, but it was later moved up above the companionway.

There are two huge cockpit lockers. These would be more useful if divided into smaller spaces and if partitions were inserted to prevent gear from slipping under the cockpit, where it might fetch up against the engine.

The cockpit lockers have an excellent molded-in

Owners consider the Cal 31 to be somewhat tender initially, and she tends to bury the rail in gusty conditions. She does have good handling characteristics under sail, and is fairly fast.

scupper arrangement which allows the leeward seats to drain at all angles of heel. Unfortunately, the boat has an inexplicable method of securing the locker lids. A line is attached to the underside of the starboard lid. This leads under the cockpit to a jam cleat which is reached through the port cockpit locker. The port locker has a similar arrangement which can only be released from belowdecks, in the galley. If the lockers are secured, one must go below, release the port locker hold-down, go back on deck, open the port cockpit locker, and release the starboard hold-down to get into the starboard cockpit locker.

The logic of this system escapes us.

Access to the rudder stock head in wheel-steered boats is via a deckplate in the cockpit sole. If this were removed to rig emergency steering, a substantial amount of water could find its way below in rain or heavy weather.

The inboard shrouds provide a narrow sheeting base for jib leads but make it almost mandatory to go over the cabin top to go forward of the mast.

There is an anchor well at the forward end of the deck. This well contains a strong eyebolt for securing the bitter end of the anchor rode, an excellent idea. Connections for the pulpit-mounted running lights are under the deck immediately forward of the lid to the anchor well and will be subject to rapid corrosion from water finding its way below as well as to mechanical damage when stowing the anchor rode.

The stemhead fitting incorporates a roller, handy for stowing an anchor. There are no bow chocks. The anchor roller can be used as a starboard chock, although the lack of a fair lead to a bow cleat is a serious shortcoming. Anchoring with two anchors would be problematic without good bow chocks.

The long inboard track for jib lead blocks provides for flexible sheet leads but should be augmented by a toerail-mounted track for greater variety. If genoas larger than 150% are used, the stock track will prove too short for optimal leads.

Interior

The Cal 31 has perhaps the most spacious and attractive interior in its class. It is the boat's most outstanding feature. Belowdecks, it is hard to believe you are aboard a boat only 31' long. "The interior sold us on the boat" was the most common owner response.

The forward cabin has large V-berths with an insert to form a huge double. There is a good sail bin under the port berth, and shelves at the foot of the berth. Most owners find the short hanging locker in the forward cabin useless. Most would prefer more drawers instead.

The foredeck-mounted hatch provides good ventilation and is big enough for sail bags, but its location requires that it be tightly secured when sailing to prevent water from getting below. Close attention will have to be paid to the water-tightness of the hatch if the berth below is to be kept dry.

The large head is comfortable and incorporates a shower. An overhead deadlight augments the light provided by the opening port. The door to the head also serves as the door to the forward cabin. When this door is used to shut off the forward cabin, the

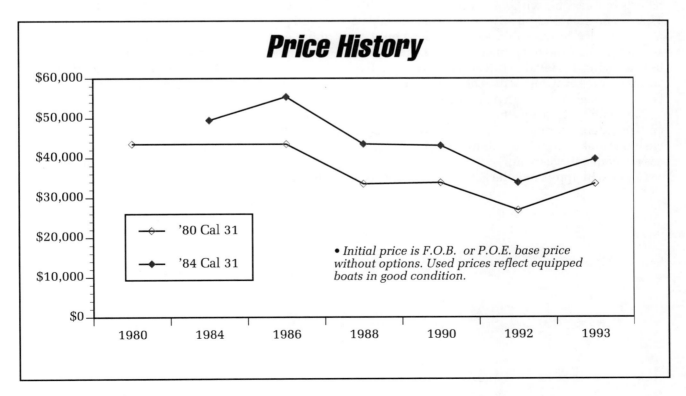

Price History

Legend:
- ◇ '80 Cal 31
- ◆ '84 Cal 31

• *Initial price is F.O.B. or P.O.E. base price without options. Used prices reflect equipped boats in good condition.*

The mainsheet traveler was moved from the bridgedeck to the cabinhouse roof forward of the companionway on later models of the Cal 31. The companionway itself has rather sharply angled sides, meaning that the drop boards can be removed easily—too easily for offshore use, we feel.

door to the large starboard hanging locker can be used to separate the head from the main cabin.

The main cabin interior is rather dark due to the abundance of teak. This can be offset by a bright carpet.

The main cabin is huge. There is good storage in bins and alcoves behind the settees. A large magazine/book rack on the bulkhead behind the fold-up table is inaccessible without folding down the table. There is no means of positively securing the table's fold-down leg to the cabin sole. The leg could be accidentally kicked out of place when the table is in use, allowing it to fall down. The table is too small to accommodate even four with real comfort. The cabin is wide enough to utilize a permanently fitted table.

The main cabin sleeps three in a large single berth and an extension double. The deeply-tufted settee cushions look rich and are comfortable for sitting but are miserable to sleep on.

Cooks will appreciate the galley, which is excel-

lent for a boat of this size. There is a large gimballed stove with oven, well secured and capable of being latched in place in port. It is available in both alcohol and gas models.

The icebox top is one of the few we have seen which can reasonably double as a chart table. The icebox lids are insulated, but are poorly fitted, allowing a large gap—over 3/8"—between the two trap-type lids. The lids are also usually not flush with the icebox top, a complication for doing smooth chart work.

There is a large-diameter tube for rolled charts which extends under the cockpit. With a good surface available for chart work, folded charts make much more sense.

The engine is reached for service by lifting out the companionway steps. The steps should have a positive latch to prevent their bouncing out of place in rough conditions. Engine access for maintenance is excellent.

Selection valves for the water tanks are located under the deep galley sink. This is typical of the well-thought out plumbing and wiring systems, which are generally well-bundled and usually protected from chafe when passing through bulkhead cutouts.

Basically, the interior of the Cal 31 is one of the most livable and attractive we have seen in a boat of this size. Interior finish work is of very good stock boat quality.

Conclusions

The Cal 31 is one of the best designed and better executed 31-footers we have seen. Her interior is remarkable. She has a wide range of buyer appeal, selling to first-time sailboat buyers as well as to the more experienced. She is a reasonably good club-level racer, yet a comfortable cruiser for up to four adults. Realistically, the boat will be used more for cruising and daysailing than for racing.

The Cal 31 was produced until 1985, and was very expensive when new. The 1980 base price was around $43,000, and delivered prices ran close to $50,000. The 1992 average price for that 1980 model is about $25-$26,000, making it considerably more expensive than other boats in this size range. • **PS**

Allied Seawind II

A true world cruiser with a choice of rigs. Our advice: Take the sloop, and gain upwind performance.

When Allied Yachts went out of business for the fifth—and last—time at the end of 1981, they did so in a rather messy fashion. At least two potential owners were left holding the bag, having made down payments of about $20,000 each for boats that were never built. Brax Freeman, who managed Allied, seemed to disappear, along with the dreams of the would-be owners of the unbuilt Seawind IIs.

Sailboat dealer Freeman took over management of Allied Yachts in the spring of 1980, when the venerable boatbuilding firm in the unlikely town of Catskill, New York, was on the verge of financial disaster for the fourth time in less than 20 years. Over the years Allied had suffered from mediocre management, severe underexposure, and the vagaries of the boat-buying public—a not unusual story in the boatbuilding industry.

Allied had the reputation of fashioning solidly built (if uninspiringly finished) boats, unabashedly oriented toward cruising, with the exception of a single foray into the world of racing yachts with a Britton Chance 30-footer.

Allied had already secured its place in the boatbuilding pantheon with the original Seawind ketch, which became the first fiberglass boat to circumnavigate, and the Luders 33, recognized as a classic design of the era preceding the introduction of the fin keel racer-cruiser.

Unfortunately, while its products were heading for glory on the high seas, the company was repeatedly headed for the boneyard.

In 1975, Allied began building the foot-longer, foot-wider Gillmer-designed Seawind II as a replacement for the original 30' 6" Seawind.

The extra foot of length and beam, 1 1/2 feet of waterline length, and 2,700 lbs of displacement add

Specifications

LOA	31' 7"
LWL	25'6"
Beam	10'5"
Draft	4'6"
Displacement	14,900 lbs.
Ballast	5,800 lbs.
Sail area	555 (ketch)/512 (cutter)

up to make the Allied Seawind II a significantly larger boat than her predecessor.

Like its cousin the Southern Cross 31, the Seawind II is a dream machine, Walter Mitty's escape hatch. The dream comes with a hefty price tag. Delivered price for a new Seawind II fully loaded with an extensive cruising inventory was in the $70,000 range. For this you got a well-equipped, well-built, proven world cruiser with standard features such as hot and cold pressure water, shower in the cockpit and below, shore power, and wheel steering.

Freeman tried hard to overcome Allied's dowdy image. Older Allied boats were heavy on woodgrain Formica, bland expanses of fiberglass, and mediocre woodwork. He actively sought to overcome that hard-to-shake reputation by using large quantities of interior wood (which hide most of the interior glass), good hardware, and the imagination of a builder who has spent a good deal of time living on boats.

Construction

The hull of the Seawind II is a solid hand layup. Deck and cabin trunk are balsa cored. The top of the cabin trunk in the way of the deck-stepped mast is cored with solid filled epoxy for greater compression strength.

The hull-to-deck joint is complex, expensive, time-consuming to make, and extremely strong. In this day of simple through-bolted inside flanges it is an anachronism. Both hull and deck have outward-turning flanges at the sheer line. These flanges are coated with 3M 5200 and a teak batten is placed between them, laid on the flat. Hull, deck, and batten are through-bolted vertically with stainless steel bolts. After the sealant cures, which takes several days, the joint is ground off on the inside of the boat and heavily glassed over.

On the outside a heavy aluminum extrusion is filled with bedding, slipped over the flange, and fastened horizontally with screws into the teak batten. (Now you know what the teak batten is for.)

This is an incredibly labor intensive joint, substantially improved over the old Seawind joint which was the same basic design but had a reputation for developing small leaks. The aluminum extrusion makes an excellent rubbing strake, but damage to it would require getting a replacement piece from the builder, rather than a patch job with resin, putty, and a little teak. The rubbing strake may look a little massive for a boat of this size, but it is an excellent idea for a serious cruising boat.

Though rather primitive, this hull-to-deck joint has been retained because it was cheaper to beef up and modify the old design than to modify the Seawind tooling, given Allied's low production volume.

The ballast keel is lead, molded to shape and glassed into the keel. While this technique eliminates keel bolts, it also makes the fiberglass hull more vulnerable to grounding damage.

The mast is stepped on deck, and uses a massive oak compression frame under the cabin trunk for support. This frame forms the head door framing, and is solidly, though a little crudely, attached to the top of the ballast.

Seacocks are used on all through hull fittings. These are through-bolted to the hull and have double clamped hoses—cheap insurance for any boat.

All deck hardware is through-bolted and reinforced with fiberglass backing plates. We prefer aluminum backing plates to fiberglass for their greater strength and rigidity for a given thickness and area.

There is very little exterior wood on the Seawind

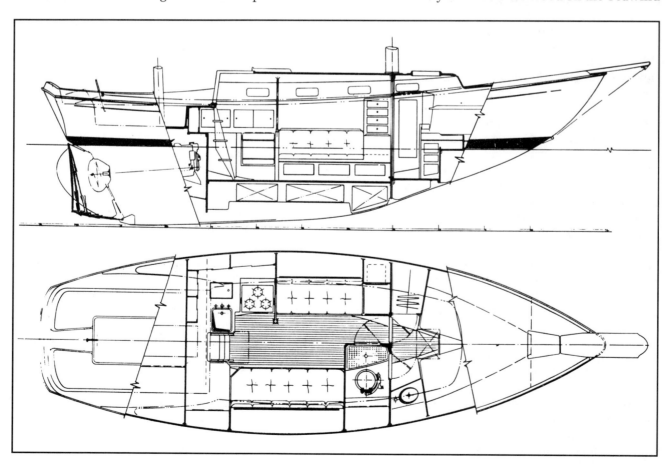

II. The molded toe rail is capped with teak; there are teak hand rails on the cabin top, and teak trim around the edge of the cabin. That's all. Even the dorade boxes are molded in. This results in low maintenance, a highly desirable characteristic on a serious cruising boat, but one that leads to an appearance of austerity that can border on plainness. The austere appearance of the Seawind II is greatly relieved by contrasting cockpit, deck, and deckhouse molded-in non-skid surfaces. The Seawind II will never look as flashy as a Taiwan-built teak plantation, but neither will her owners have to make the decision between endless wood maintenance or the drabness of unfinished "natural" teak—i.e., mildewed gray.

Handling Under Sail

The standard rig of the Seawind II is a masthead ketch. The ketch rig is not particularly desirable for a boat of this size. The mizzen adds considerable weight and windage and almost no drive upwind, since the mizzen sail acts almost completely in the backwind of the mainsail. The real purpose of a mizzen upwind is to balance the boat, and for this purpose the smaller, more out-of-the-way mizzen of the yawl is equally useful.

Off the wind, the area of the mizzen plus the added bonus of a mizzen staysail do provide considerable drive.

The mizzenmast clutters up the cockpit, although it does provide a good handhold. Its position five feet forward of the helmsman is guaranteed to make him crosseyed if he has the habit of sitting directly behind the wheel.

Sail area of the Seawind II is small enough that the oft-cited advantage of the ketch rig—smaller individual sails—is rather unimportant. A mizzen is useful for heaving to, for anchoring and weighing anchor, and to enable the boat to weathercock in a rolly anchorage. It is, however, a most inefficient rig upwind.

An optional cutter rig is available. It uses the same mainmast as the ketch rig, but shifts it aft about a foot. The mainsail is longer on the foot and the base of the foretriangle is a little longer than that of the ketch rig. The total sail area of the cutter rig works out to slightly less than that of the ketch rig, but the reduced windage and slightly increased stability probably make up for the loss of sail area, For tradewind passages, the double headstays on either rig allow the use of twin downwind jibs. With a working sail area of just over 500 square feet for a displacement of 14,900 pounds, the Seawind II is not underrigged as are many cruising boats.

The Seawind II's rudder is a rather large, old fashioned design of the barn door variety. It would be interesting and not at all difficult to change it to a more modern Constellation style rudder, which could

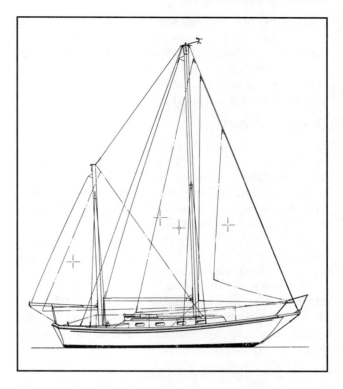

The standard ketch rig has some good features, such as a boost downwind, but it suffers from poor upwind performance.

slightly reduce wetted surface and perhaps give a little better performance with no loss of control.

With the cutter rig that we prefer, twin running headsails, and sails built for speed as well as durability, the Seawind II should have good performance for a pure cruising boat. Without a large genoa she will not be at her best in light air, although owners report that she is surprisingly spritely in those conditions. Unfortunately, she will not be able to use a genoa to its full efficiency upwind due to the wide shroud base and wide spreaders.

Handling Under Power

The Seawind II is powered by a lightweight four-cylinder Westerbeke 27 horsepower diesel. This is plenty of power for the Seawind II's displacement. A welded aluminum fuel tank is located in the bilge.

The standard propeller is a three-bladed fixed bronze in-aperture installation. Rather than be burdened by the considerable drag of such a propeller, we would install a two-bladed model that could be lined up behind the deadwood to reduce drag when under sail, Alternatively, a two- or three-bladed feathering propeller could be installed. On a boat with the considerable wetted surface of the Seawind II, reducing drag becomes critical to performance in light air, and no matter what the builders of ocean-going dreadnoughts may tell you, much of the sailing in the world—even on the ocean—is in light air.

Do not expect the Seawind II to maneuver like a modern fin keeler under power. Despite her cutaway forefoot, there is enough lateral plane here to require a little planning ahead in a tight situation under power; but then you should plan ahead no matter how well your boat handles.

Deck Layout

An unusual feature of the Seawind II is lifeline stanchions and pulpits that stand 30" off the deck rather than the more usual 24". Coupled with a fairly high toerail, they give the foredeck hand a real feeling of security. Unfortunately, they also require that a long tack pennant be installed if you want to get the foot of the jib above the lifelines. The cutter rig is an advantage here, for a high-cut yankee jibtopsail will easily clear the lifelines.

The bowsprit is a massive teak platform with attached rail. There are double bow rollers at the end of the bowsprit, but these are so far outboard that the anchor chain or warp chafes against the forward pulpit stanchion when the rollers are used. This defect also prevents secure storage of an anchor in the roller, as the stock would bear against the pulpit. The pulpit is a comfortable and secure place to handle sails or ground tackle.

The Seawind II is one of the few boats we've seen with properly sized bow cleats. There are two 12" foredeck cleats, with hawsepipes to the divided anchor rode locker outside of each cleat. An anchor windlass is optional, and will fit nicely between the cleats.

Because of the width of the cabin trunk, it is easier to get to the foredeck by walking over the cabin top than by squeezing inside the shrouds. Good nonskid on the cabin top makes this fairly easy.

Unfortunately, it's not particularly easy to hoist the sails on the cutter rig, because the two dorade boxes fall exactly abreast the mast, making it necessary to straddle them awkwardly. This is less a problem with the ketch rig, whose mast is stepped further forward. For shorthanded cruising, it makes more sense anyway to lead the halyards aft on the cabin top to the forward end of the cockpit.

A variety of mainsheet leads have been used on the Seawind II. One version uses a Fico traveler mounted over the companionway sea hood. In this version, the blocks are located far apart on the boom, giving poor mechanical advantage. The best of the Seawind II mainsheet arrangements consists of a traveler mounted on the bridgedeck, which reduces seating but gives much better sail control. This should be used on either the ketch or the cutter, as the old end-of-boom arrangement was only necessary with a roller-furling mainsail, which should appropriately be considered a thing of the past.

The standard steerer on the boat is an Edson rack and pinion model, mounted directly on the head of the rudder stock. This is the only steering placement possible with the ketch rig.

There are more possibilities with the cutter rig. The most appealing would be to mount an Edson pedestal steerer at the forward end of the cockpit. Then the helmsman could reach the mainsheet on the bridge-deck, the headsail sheets, and even the halyards if they were led aft. If a cockpit dodger were

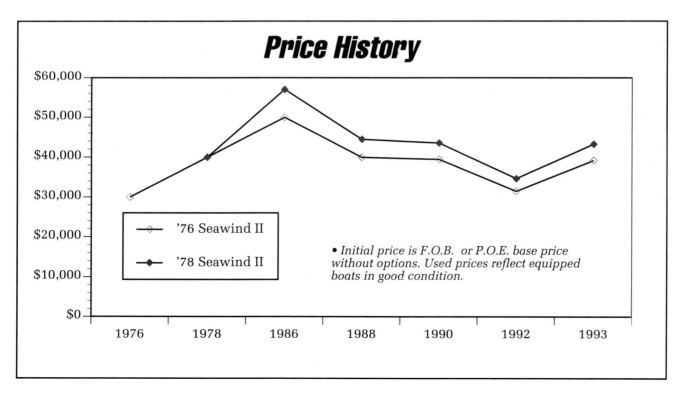

Price History

Legend:
- '76 Seawind II
- '78 Seawind II

• Initial price is F.O.B. or P.O.E. base price without options. Used prices reflect equipped boats in good condition.

also installed, the helmsman would be protected from all that nasty spray when going upwind.

The cockpit is large and reasonably comfortable. It was probably made so large to accommodate the mizzen mast, which also serves as a handy foot brace. Without the mizzen, the cockpit looks rather large and empty. It is too wide, in fact, to adequately brace your feet on the opposite cockpit seat when the boat is heeled over.

There is a deep gutter at the back of the cockpit seats on either side. This is a good feature, for it means that water will not collect in a puddle against the leeward coaming on a long, wet beat to weather.

Be sure to check the fit of the emergency tiller. The rudder stock of the boat we examined had been improperly machined, and the emergency tiller was overly sloppy in its fit.

A large underseat locker on either side of the cockpit will hold a lot of gear, and is equipped with drop-in dividers to keep items from the depths of the bilge. Another unique feature of the cockpit is a fresh water shower, whose spray head and hose are recessed into the side of the footwell. This means that it isn't necessary to track either sand or salt water belowdecks after a swim.

The companionway is narrow with almost parallel sides. While this may make it a bit less convenient to get below, it is far more seamanlike than most companionways, which seem to be more concerned with letting overweight sailors get below than with keeping water out of the interior. Coupled with a molded seahood and a good bridgedeck, it provides well-designed access for people, but not water.

Belowdecks

The days when it was necessary to ignore the mediocre detailing on the inside of Allied boats happily appear to be behind us. The late-model Seawind II we examined had the best finished interior of any Allied boat we've seen.

The layout was conventional. As befits a cruising boat, there is tremendous storage throughout. There are also a number of storage options, such as a bureau, extra drawers, and extra cabinets, which allow the owner to tailor the boat to his or her individual needs.

A forward cabin contains vee berths, a hanging locker, and a wash basin. There are drawers and bins under the berths, and a large stainless steel holding tank. We might replumb the holding tank as a fresh water tank—before it's used, of course—to greatly increase the standard water capacity.

A door from the forward cabin gives access to the head without entering the main cabin. The primary door between the main cabin and the forward cabin does double duty as a door which shuts the head off from the main cabin.

The head is small, containing only the water closet and the shower. Having the head wash basin in the forward cabin is unusual, but does make the head much less cramped.

Despite the spacious interior, the Seawind II is not a fat person's boat. The head doors are extremely narrow, since their heavy framing also carries the compression load of the rig.

Because the settees in the main cabin are asymmetrical, it is not possible to accommodate more than four people at the fold-down dining table. Since, quite rationally, there are only four berths in the boat, this should rarely be a problem. The space behind the settees is given over to storage, rather than attempting to cram more berths into the boat.

A number of galley stove options were available, including surface burner kerosene and alcohol stoves, gimballed kerosene or alcohol stoves with oven— which sacrifices galley storage space—or a three burner, gimballed LPG stove with oven. Alcohol should not be considered as a cooking fuel for a serious cruising boat, and kerosene, while hot, soon turns the galley overhead to a dingy greyish-brown.

The icebox is insulated with four inches of urethane foam, and has a tight-fitting, well-gasketed top. It is among the best we've seen.

Although there is no navigation station—which would be a little much to expect on a boat of this size—there is a large dresser surface on the starboard side aft of the settee. Like most boats, there really isn't enough room at the table for navigation electronics, a sextant, and the navigator's pile of books.

The large, deep sink is equipped with both pressure fresh water taps and a manual pump—absolutely essential as a backup or to save electrical power at sea.

Engine access is poor. The engine is tucked away under the cockpit, and it is necessary to remove both the companionway ladder and the bulkhead panel behind in order to check the oil. Needless to say, this is not conducive to good engine maintenance. There is an oil pan under the engine, so that spilled oil will not drain into the bilge sump. Neither the shower nor the icebox drain to the bilge, a good feature.

With a wide cabin, good headroom, and no attempt to sleep an army in tiny, uncomfortable berths, the Allied Seawind II offers excellent accommodations for a couple either living aboard or for extended cruising. That is what this boat is all about.

Conclusions

The Seawind II is truly a boat that can call herself a world cruiser without apology or explanation. Her construction is strong without being inordinately heavy. She makes no attempt to be all things to all people. It would be a shame to see her tied up to the dock in a marina, for she deserves better. **• PS**

Westsail 32

The 32 bears a serious look for those who want to go offshore on a budget: a good buy in a rugged boat.

When approaching the Westsail 32, whether to buy, sell, or just write about it, one ventures into a realm of myth, prejudice, and perceptions of a very subjective nature. Few boats evoke as broad a spectrum of opinions—favorable and unfavorable—as the 32.

To some extent this reaction is justified. The Westsail has a multi-faceted reputation, much of it unfair, as a boat that is slow, quasi-traditional, and uncomfortable at sea, as well as seaworthy, rugged, and roomy. These dichotomies make the 32 an obvious choice for a *PS* survey to which must be added its appeal for those dreaming of The Passage.

Westsail International, builders of not only the 32 but a 42/43-footer and a 28-footer, did much to revolutionize the boat market in the early 1970s. By some of the most effective marketing ever done in the marine industry it promoted a out-and-out cruising boat, a production replica of a Colin Archer North Sea pilot boat, that sold a lot of buyers and dreamers on its suitability for offshore sailing. That boat and its promotion polarized the market into racers and cruisers.

After several years with sold-out production, Westsail fell upon hard financial times in 1978, partly the result of that success. The boats were being built on both coasts, the expanded building facilities were too costly, too many older boats began appearing on the used boat market to compete with the new ones being built, the pricing of new Westsails could not keep pace with the then-high inflation rate, and there was a steady growth of directly competing boats, many of them less expensive and better performing imports from the Far east. Added to these causes was the loose system developed by Westsail called "cruising centers" whereby Westsail owners acted as dealers who then had to compete against the

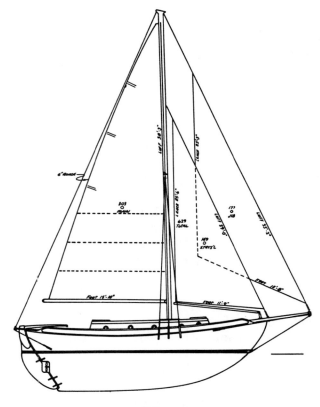

Specifications

LOA	32' 0"
LWL	27' 6"
Beam	11' 0"
Draft	5' 0"
Displacement	19,500 lbs.
Sail area	629 sq. ft.

more organized and efficient dealer networks of competing products.

In 1981 Westsail International, following a brief revival, folded completely, although 32s continued to be available for a couple of years, from P&M Worldwide, mostly in kit form.

A Close Look at the Boat

In all, nearly 800 Westsail 32s were built between 1970 and 1981. Originally the William Crealock adaption had a flush deck. Then, in 1971 Lynn and Snyder Vick (she a marketing whiz; he, production) acquired the tooling, added a trunk cabin and, with hull #37, produced the first 32 in the configuration that has become so familiar. By the mid-1970s the backlog of orders for new boats actually reached 18 months.

The cockpit of a Westsail 32, such as it is, is very exposed. While seaworthy, it's bound to be very wet.

After the financial problems from 1978 to 1980, the tooling was acquired by P&M Worldwide, who sold about 15 32s in kit form. During its production run about half of the 32s molded were sold in various stages of completion as kits, some for professional finishing but most to amateurs for homebuilding. This makes the Westsail 32 the most popular amateur-built boat ever marketed and complicates the task of a prospective buyer in evaluating used 32s.

When 32s were molded, each hull and deck was earmarked for either builder or owner completion. Hull plates with the code letters WSSK were sold as kits, WSSF as factory-finished boats. Although half were not finished by Westsail, the vast majority were built to almost identical specifications and with similar layouts, since the kits as sold left little flexibility in redesigning the accommodations, rig, or structural components. What did—and of course still does—differ is the quality of the finish work and the choice of engines (mostly the Volvo Penta MD2, MD3, and Perkins 4-107, all about equally popular).

Some aspects of the 32 were built essentially the same throughout its production run. The hull laminate schedule, bulkhead attachment, hull-to-deck joint, etc, remained constant. What differed significantly was the makeup of the ballast. Original specs on the 32 called for about 2000 pounds of lead pigs and about 5000 pounds of small steel punchings held in place in the bilge with polyester resin. In some boats by special order the punchings were replaced with lead shot. Then, in 1975 the lead pigs were replaced by cast lead and a few 32s had as much as 500 pounds more ballast. However, optimum ballast seems to be about 7000 pounds.

One apparently bad rap under which the Westsail 32 seems to have labored is that in the event of a keel holing, the punchings can "pour out," a scenario for which we can find no verification, except perhaps in a home-built boat where the binding resin might have been done away with. Most 32 kits were sold with the ballast factory installed, hence resin-bound. Besides, the hull laminate in way of the 32 ballast is among the thickest ever used in fiberglass hulls.

The general finish and quality of the factory-completed 32s seems to have been at its best in boats built from 1973 through 1975. Until 1975, boats were individually assembled and finished, both in the East and West Coast facilities. Then, with a move to

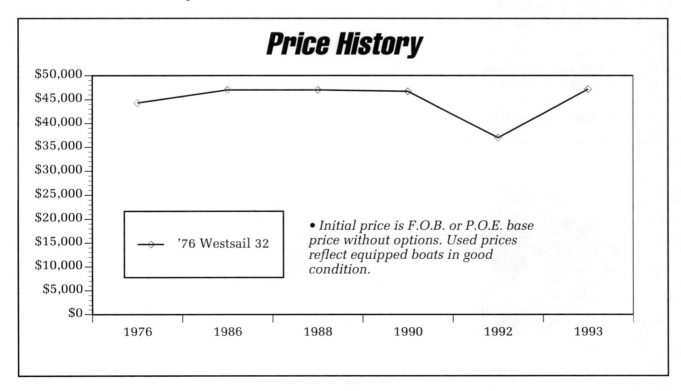

Price History

Legend: —◇— '76 Westsail 32

• Initial price is F.O.B. or P.O.E. base price without options. Used prices reflect equipped boats in good condition.

Year	Price
1976	~$44,000
1986	~$47,000
1988	~$47,000
1990	~$47,000
1992	~$37,000
1993	~$47,000

a large new site, production lines replaced boat-by-boat construction and the general impression is that the detailing slipped, the decline accelerating as Westsail fell upon hard times. The later boats were not built badly, just not finished as well or with the attention to detail.

More significant to the used boat buyer is the question of owner-completed boats. Obviously the quality of such boats varies widely. Much is readily apparent in the joinerwork, fittings, engine installation, etc. Less evident is the bonding of joinerwork to hull, attachment of fittings, etc. where only a professional survey can assess the quality.

There is no reason an amateur-completed boat should be inherently inferior to a factory equivalent, given the potential for very close amateur replication of the professionally finished 32. Moreover, by the time the boat has reached middle-age, 10 years or so old, maintenance has become far more important than original construction in most aspects, and flaws in that original construction are likely to have already become evident.

What to Look For

Many owners of used Westsail 32s report exhaustive searches among available 32s before deciding to buy the boat they own. Given the differences among owner-completed boats, the variation in quality produced by Westsail in its 10-year life, the widely varying uses to which 32s have been put by their owners, and the often ambitious plans of prospective owners, such dilligence seems to make sense. These factors also make it extremely difficult to list specific points buyers should look for. On the basis of our research we would make two strong recommendations:

• First we suggest buyers look for 32s with the Perkins 4-108 diesel engines. Owners report the Volvo Penta MD2 is not sufficiently powerful for the boat in all but calm water. The MD3 gives more power but is not as good an engine for the 32 as the

Perkins. Since the 32 with its long keel, aperture-mounted prop, and heavy displacement has barely adequate maneuverability under power, better to have more than enough engine, not too little.

• Compare interior joinerwork (and perhaps to a lesser extent, exterior trim) for evidence of ruggedness and skill in installation. The best measure of a 32 that will retain its equity is to judge whether its details will appeal to future buyers just as they do you. Replacing sloppy joinerwork is expensive, time consuming work, so start with a well finished boat, whether factory or owner completed. The best looking 32 decor we ever saw had a combination of light Formica and woods trimmed out with mahogany belowdecks, an amateur-completed interior that was well fitted and finished.

• A few additional details we would look for: a hull-to-deck joint free of signs of leaking (despite its basic strength, leaky toerails are the most common complaint voiced by owners), signs of wear and corrosion cracking on rudder fittings, chainplates, etc, and evidence of water damage to the engine (the original exhaust system seemed prone to letting water reach the engine).

Conclusions

In its 10th anniversary edition in 1980, *SAIL* magazine named the Valiant 40 as the winner of a reader poll for the most important cruising boat of the previous 10 years. The Westsail 32 finished second for reasons that are hard to fathom. The 32 certainly has to be considered the boat that set cruisers apart from racers (thus insuring the popularity of such boats as the Valiant 40), that instilled the dream of world cruising and then made it possible, and that set a standard for amateur boat building. It has even

The fact that some Westsail 32s were owner-built means that there may be significant differences belowdecks. Interior livability benefits from the boat's beaminess.

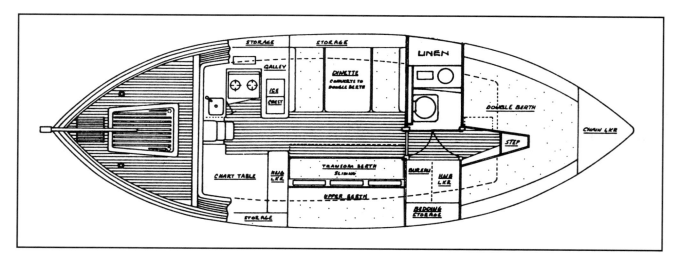

proved to have been a comfortable liveaboard boat. These are heady credentials.

At the same time the Westsail 32 has not been a complete success. Its performance is mediocre even offshore.

It can be wet to sail and clumsy under power. The quality of construction and especially finish, both factory and owner done, is inconsistent.

The weaknesses of the 32 show up most conspicuously in coastal sailing; its strengths, offshore. For those who have progressed beyond the dreaming to become intent on realizing a desire for offshore cruising on a moderate budget, a Westsail 32 bears a serious look. It is among a very few boats on the market—new or used—that can put you in Bora Bora for $50,000 even with the needed ugrading for such passagemaking.

For such buyers we recommend a hefty diesel, some improvements to the rig and deck fittings for sail handling and performance, and a careful choice of amenities (the 32 is, after all, 32' LOA). We also would not let the number of owner-finished boats scare us; they might make us look a bit closer at the quality of workmanship but not assume it is incompetent.

At the going prices on the brokerage market, Westsails represent good buys in a rugged boat. If you like the type, they should do the job, then retain better than average equity than has been typical of boats of its era. 　　　　　• **PS**

Endeavour 32

Though now a bit dated, the Endeavour 32 is a comfortable, capable cruising boat.

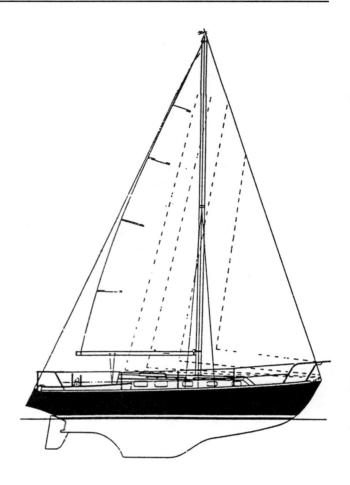

The Endeavour 32 began life back in 1970 as the Irwin 32. Ted Irwin designed her as a dual-purpose cruiser-racer before the development of the IOR. By 1975, the IOR was in full swing, and boats such as the Irwin 32 were obsolete as racers, since PHRF had not yet emerged to help handicap non-competitive boats raced at the club level.

Although the Irwin 32 had been out-designed for racing, the hull was still a comfortable design for cruising. The molds for the Irwin 32 formed the basis for Endeavour Yacht Corporation, which continued to build the boat as the Endeavour 32 until 1982.

Although the Irwin 32 and the Endeavour 32 look identical and have the same displacement, the Endeavour 32 is listed by the builder as being 4" wider, 4" longer overall, and 6" longer on the waterline.

The Irwin 32 was originally available as a keel/centerboard boat drawing 3' 6", or with a long fin keel drawing 5'. The Endeavour 32 was originally a keel/centerboarder with the same configuration as the Irwin 32, or with a fixed shoal keel with 4' 2" draft. The original Irwin deeper keel was discontinued. Beginning in 1979, the keel/centerboard model was discontinued in favor of the shoal keel version.

Sailing Performance

Although the rig of the Endeavor 32 is fairly large, her relatively heavy displacement compared to dual-purpose 32-footers built today makes her somewhat slower than a more modern boat of the same overall length. The Endeavour 32's ballast/displacement ratio of 40% implies a fairly stiff boat, but because of the boat's shoal draft and narrow beam she is not as stiff as newer, lighter boats of the same length. While the Endeavour 32 is not a tender boat, her narrow

Specifications

LOA	32' 4"
LWL	25' 6"
Beam	10' 0"
Draft	4' 2" (keel), 3' 6" (cb)
Displacement	11,700 lbs.
Ballast	5,000 lbs.
Sail area	470 sq. ft.

beam and relatively high center of gravity mean she will heel fairly quickly.

Unless you buy a boat equipped with fairly new sails, there's a good chance that the sails that come with a used Endeavour 32 will be approaching the end of their useful lives. Cruising sailors are notorious for making their sails last forever. After all, they're cruisers, not racers. But cruising boats usually need all the power they can get to drive them due to relatively inefficient hulls and rigs.

The Endeavour 32's PHRF rating of about 186 to 192 suggests a boat that is significantly slower than modern 32-footers, but comparable in speed to other boats of her vintage. The original Ericson 32, for example, has about the same rating, while the original Pearson 33 is about 10 seconds per mile faster.

Owners report the Endeavour 32 to be underpowered in winds of under 10 knots. Owners in our survey have mixed opinions about the boat's balance under sail, with some reporting excessive weather helm while others feel the boat to be well balanced. One advantage of the centerboard version is that the center of lateral resistance can be shifted by moving the board, reducing weather helm on a reach.

With the keel version, you don't have the luxury of shifting the center of lateral resistance. We doubt that the keel version will go to weather as well as the centerboard boat. At the same time, the keel version does have a slightly lower vertical center of gravity, and should be somewhat stiffer when it breezes up. The specifications for the original Irwin 32 claim an extra 200 pounds of ballast for the centerboard boat, but the Endeavour brochure does not specify any difference in ballasting between keel and centerboard versions.

The rig is a simple single-spreader masthead rig with double lower shrouds, stepped on deck. No owners in our survey reported any problems with the deck-stepped spar, and one owner had sailed his boat to Bermuda and back. Tuning of the rig is straightforward, even for beginning sailors. Rigs don't get much simpler than this.

We would be tempted to replace at least one of the mast-mounted halyard winches with as big a two-speed winch as we could fit. You don't necessarily need it to hoist sails, but you're also going to take crewmembers to the masthead on the winch. People on 32-footers weigh just as much as people on 40-footers, yet the standard halyard winches on the Endeavour 32 and most other boats in this size range make it impossible for a smaller crewmember to hoist a larger one to the masthead. It is one of the perversities of two-person sailing that the larger of the two—usually a man—insists on going up the mast, while the smaller—usually a woman—cranks the winch. You will also see the same logic prevail in anchoring: the man steers while the woman muscles the anchor up and down. It's sort of like having the jockey carry the horse around the racecourse.

Shrouds are mounted at the edge of the deck, but since the boat is relatively narrow, this position does not dramatically reduce windward ability. For reaching, it is possible to sheet the genoa to the slotted aluminum toerail.

One change we would make to improve sail handling for cruising would be to add self-tailing winches. The original winches for the boat are too small for easy trimming of a big genoa, and self-tailers are simply a must on any cruising boat. The coamings are wide enough to go up one or two winch sizes.

We also recommend a modern roller-reefing headsail system for cruising. To use it effectively, it will be necessary to install a genoa track inboard of the lifelines on both sides of the boat. As a roller-reefing headsail is reduced in size, the sheet lead must move forward to accommodate the change in clew position. To do this by shifting the position of a snatch block on the toerail is grossly inefficient, and means you will probably never have the lead in the proper position. Even without roller-reefing headsails, the genoa track is a must for decent windward performance.

Engine

All Endeavour 32s came with diesel engines, but there is a lot of difference in the engines that were used. In 1975, 1976, and 1977 models, a 12 hp Yanmar diesel was standard equipment. In our opinion, that engine is simply too small for a boat this size. It will be fine in a flat calm, but there's not enough power to push the boat into any wind or sea. Some boats in the same period were equipped with the Westerbeke L-25 engine, and others with the Yanmar 2QM20. The bigger Yanmar became standard in 1978, but a three-cylinder Universal diesel of about 24 hp was also an option in late-model boats.

With every engine except the single-cylinder Yanmar, performance under power is more than adequate. Our own engine preference would be either the larger Yanmar or the Universal diesel.

The most serious complaint voiced about the engine installation is noise. The engine compartment has no sound insulation. Access for service is reasonable.

A surprising number of owners responding to our survey report that the boat is impossible to back down in a straight line under power. Part of the problem may stem from the hull shape, but there is little doubt that much of it comes from the extreme downward angle of the prop shaft. In reverse, the water is thrown against the bottom of the boat, which we suspect does little to help steering.

A two-bladed fixed prop is standard. A three-bladed prop was optional. We wouldn't want to drag around a three-bladed fixed prop due to the boat's exposed prop installation. The best choice by far would be a three-bladed feathering prop, which we suspect would also improve the boat's handling in reverse.

Construction

No owners responding to our survey report major structural problems. There are, however, reports of hairline gelcoat crazing on both the hull and deck. One owner also reported extensive deck delamination. Still another comments that a surveyor found loose tabbing around a bulkhead in the forward cabin. In general, there were a higher than average number of owner complaints about gelcoat.

The frequency of bottom blistering reports is about

average for boats generally sailed in warmer waters.

Another odd complaint from one owner concerns flaking gelcoat inside the integral fiberglass water tank under the forward berths. The tank was all but unusable until he cut openings in the top and resurfaced the inside. In addition, once inside the tank he discovered that the internal baffles had come loose. A water tank this far forward in the boat can significantly affect trim as water is consumed. Several owners report that the boat normally sits down by the stern. A full water tank forward will offset this problem, at the expense of increased pitching moment. As a rule, heavy consumables such as water and fuel should be carried near the middle of the boat, where the effect on trim will be minimized.

Several owners mention that their boats are equipped with gate valves rather than proper seacocks. This should show up on any survey. We feel that gate valves are inappropriate for use below the waterline, and should be replaced.

The lead ballast is carried inside the molded fiberglass keel. While this eliminates keelbolts and their associated problems, it means that you should pay prompt attention to any grounding damage to the keel, which could allow water inside the laminate.

On older boats, there is no deck fill for the water tank forward. Later boats do have deck fills, and some owners of older boats also installed them. They're a good idea, since dragging a water hose below can be a real nuisance, and filling the tank from jerry jugs would almost be guaranteed to cause a mess below.

There are no deck scuppers, so water tends to pool at the low point in the sheer inboard of the aluminum toerail. Likewise, the cockpit scuppers are not flush, so the cockpit does not drain entirely.

Several owners of centerboard versions complain about the exposed centerboard pennant. With the board fully extended, about 3' of wire is exposed and vulnerable below the boat. This is an unusual arrangement required by the very high aspect ratio board.

In general, owners of the Endeavour 32 feel that the boat is sturdily built, and reasonably finished, with the exception of the large number of reports of gelcoat defects.

Interior

For a relatively narrow boat, the Endeavour 32 is roomy. Headroom on centerline is about 6' 4". The original stepped cabin trunk—an Irwin design trademark—was replaced in the middle of the boat's production history with a more modern-looking cabin trunk which is slightly tapered in profile. Cabin headroom was not significantly altered. Headroom is carried well forward over the forward cabin.

There is no door between the main cabin and the forward cabin, which limits privacy when cruising with more than two people. A privacy curtain was an option.

Storage space is used very effectively on the Endeavour 32. Since the water and fuel tanks are located in the ends of the boat, there is a lot of space available under the settees in the main cabin.

The galley is fairly small, which is typical of boats of this period. The icebox, however, is huge—about 10 cubic feet. We'd be tempted to reduce its size by adding more insulation on the inside of the box. Six cubic feet of icebox is more than adequate for a boat this size.

There are three legitimate sea berths on the Endeavour 32: the port and starboard main cabin settees, and the port quarterberth. These berths are all parallel to the boat's centerline, so your head is neither above nor below your feet when the boat heels. Berths at odd angles to the centerline may be interesting visually, but they're only functional when the boat is at rest.

Adding overhead handrails in the main cabin

Given the relatively narrow beam, the Endeavour 32 is quite roomy below. Headroom is 6' 4", and there's plenty of storage space. The layout suffers from the lack of a proper nav station, however.

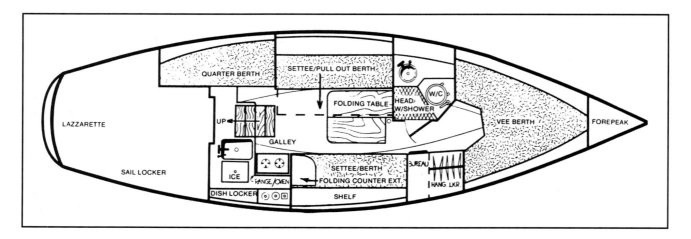

would be useful; there are very few things to grab onto in a seaway.

There are 10 opening ports in the cabin trunk of the Endeavour 32. This makes for very good ventilation when the boat is docked or anchored, but does nothing when the boat is underway and the ports are closed. If you leave ports open underway, you're asking for a drenched interior from a stray wave or powerboat wake.

Ventilation would be greatly improved by installing cowl vents in dorade boxes. We would put two at the aft end of the main cabin, just forward of the dodger breakwater on later models, one over the head, and one over the passageway between the main cabin and the forward cabin. Be careful not to place the forward vents where they will interfere with working at the mast.

The biggest single complaint about the interior of the Endeavour 32 is the lack of a navigation station or chart table. When this boat was designed, navigators of even 40-footers frequently had to work on the cabin table or icebox lid. Today, almost every boat over 30' has some sort of nav station—a must in the days of electronic gizmos.

All in all, the interior of the Endeavour 32 is comfortable and workable. Joinerwork is of good production boat quality. In later boats, the interior teak is varnished. There's no reason you couldn't do this to an older boat if that finish appeals to you.

Conclusions

The Endeavour 32 is a comfortable, reasonably capable cruising boat. It would make a good coastal cruiser or island hopper. The basic design and construction are sound enough to justify the numerous additions and modifications necessary to make the boat suitable as a limited offshore cruiser for areas such as the Bahamas or the Caribbean.

The most troublesome aspect of the boat is the large number of owners in our survey reporting gelcoat flaws. While in most cases these are cosmetic, they are expensive to repair, and unsightly if not repaired.

Later boats with the more modern deck molding—recognizable by the lack of step in the profile of the cabin trunk—are in our opinion more desirable than the earlier boats. Likewise, look for a boat with a bigger engine than the original 12 hp Yanmar diesel.

To make it easier to handle, you'll have to spend a fair amount of money on upgrading things such as winches and sail handling equipment. This is only worthwhile if you plan to keep the boat for a while.

The Endeavour 32 is quite a bit narrower than a modern boat of the same length, which makes the interior look a little smaller. At the same time, the beam is carried well aft, which tends to increase space in the cockpit.

Because of the lack of privacy below, this is not really a good family cruising boat for long periods of time. A privacy curtain forward would help, but a door for the forward cabin would be even better.

In appearance, the Endeavour 32 is somewhat dated, yet we would hesitate to call her appearance "classic." Still, her styling may be a little easier on the eye long after today's Euroboats have gone the way of tailfins and chrome bumpers.　**• PS**

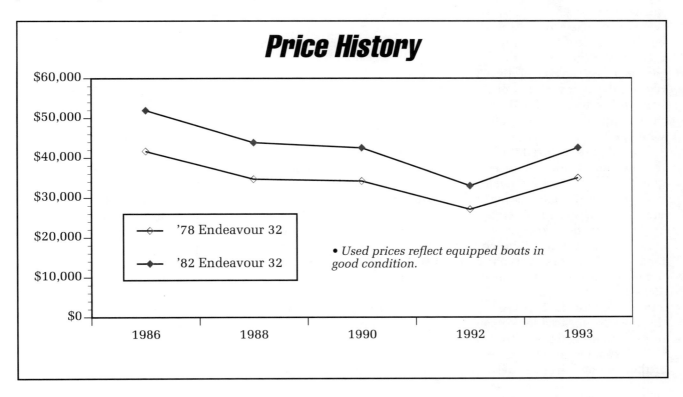

Price History

'78 Endeavour 32
'82 Endeavour 32

• *Used prices reflect equipped boats in good condition.*

C&C 33

While not the best pure racer or pure cruiser, the C&C 33 is a good choice as an all-around boat.

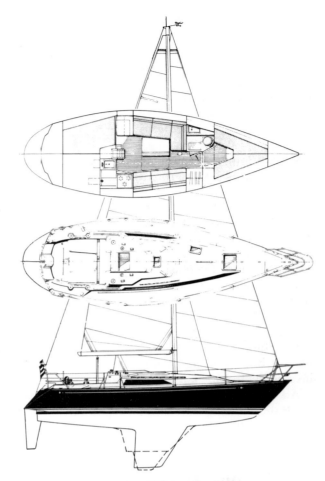

When the C&C company shut down operations in 1986, it was big news in the North American boating community. Since the company's formation in 1969, it had been a stalwart of the industry—the leading Canadian builder, by far, and one of the major brands wherever fiberglass sailboats raced or cruised.

The company had gone through numerous changes, of course. The original two Cs, George Cuthbertson and George Cassian, have not been involved with the company in over a decade. And during the 1970s, the design and building shops were known for their "revolving doors," as personnel worked for the company for a few years and then went out on their own. Almost all Canadian designers and builders practicing today have worked for C&C at one time or another, and we would wager that, at any given boat show in North America, 25% of the salesmen with ten or more years experience have either worked for the company or for a C&C dealership. The company always employed people who like to sail.

C&C always featured the combination sailboat—the dual purpose racer-cruiser—and always aimed at quality construction and detail, fitting a niche in the market below the outstanding luxury yacht but above the standard, midline fiberglass auxiliary.

C&Cs have been known for good-looking moderate designs, a tradition started by the original partners and the company's chief designer Rob Ball. Some models—like the early Corvettes and C&C 35s—have become classics of production sailboats, and (except for the Mega, a one-design 30-footer of the late 70s) it's hard to think of any C&C which has been extreme or unattractive to the eye.

Performance always was a hallmark of C&C. Most of their models were heavily marketed as serious

Specifications

LOA	32' 7"
LWL	26' 2"
Beam	10' 6"
Draft	6' 4"/5' 9" (fin/shallow keel)
Displacement	9,450 lbs.
Ballast	3,975 lbs.
Sail area	511 sq. ft.

racers, and old C&Cs continue to be actively raced in PHRF fleets throughout the country. Even their out-and-out cruising line—the Landfall series—is based on their racer-cruiser hulls. The old Landfall 38, for example, used the hull of the highly competitive C&C 38, with modified keel, deckhouse, rig, and accommodations.

The company always was known for building on the high-tech side of the spectrum. They were the first major company to commit to cored construction of hulls, and only Tillotson-Pearson can compare to C&C in terms of experience with balsa-cored laminates. They were also the first major company to commit to solid rod rigging, and they have a tradition of rigging and equipping their boats with first-class spars and fittings.

The C&C 33 is often referred to as the "new" C&C 33, to distinguish it from the totally different C&C 33 produced between 1974 and l977. While some of the specs are similar, the later 33 is an entirely new boat, not sharing any of the tooling of the old 33. The old 33 was widely regarded as one of the prettiest racers around, and 209 of them were built. They continue to be highly salable on the used boat market.

In design, the C&C 33 is distinctly modern, though it has conservative lines. C&C did not go after the "Euro" look in any of their models. Like the other new C&C models, the boat has a flat sheer, sharply reversed transom and sharply angled bow. Though most people will probably consider the older models prettier—with their saucy sheer and low deckhouses—the later 33 is good looking and recognizable as a C&C even from a distance.

The hull is modern but not radical, with a fine entry and cutaway forefoot. There's a hard turn to the bilge about a foot below the waterline, and the very center of the hull is flat. The standard fin keel is conventionally modern, but there was both an optional shorter fin and a keel/centerboard combination available for the boat. A small skeg is fitted ahead of the spade rudder. The static waterline is somewhat shorter and the beam somewhat narrower than most other boats in her size. "Moderate" is a good term to summarize the whole concept of the boat.

The new 33 was introduced in 1984, and over 200 of them were built in the four years the boat was in production—impressive considering the company's business problems in the middle of the run, and the heavy competition in this size from American and European companies. The success of this model indicates that there is still a hard-core clientele out there who are not interested in style fads but instead want a good moderate design that is well engineered and well built, a boat that can be both raced and cruised.

Construction

Hull construction represents a departure from traditional C&C practices, in that only the forward panels of the hull are balsa cored. The rest of the hull is a conventional hand lay-up of mat and roving, with an isophthalic gelcoat and skinning resin. The 33's larger sisters (35, 38, 41, and 44) have balsa coring throughout their hulls, while the smaller sisters (30 and 27) have no coring at all in the hull.

The cored laminate offered stiffness and strength combined with light weight, and was one of C&C's keys to building tough race boats that wouldn't flex too much, yet which still kept the total weight down. To achieve stiffness and strength without the coring, C&C used what they call a "spider" system: basically a structural framing bonded to the hull and integrated with the attachment points for the rig and keel. The hull laminate itself becomes relatively less important structurally, as the frame becomes the primary load-bearing structure of the boat.

Undoubtedly the decision to move from balsa coring to "skin and frame" construction was based partly on the economics of building and partly on the strength calculations for the engineering, and we really cannot say what proportion of each affected the decision.

The deck is one-piece molding with balsa core in the horizontal surfaces, and hardware is backed up with both aluminum and Coremat for strength in the attachment points. The textured non-skid is adequate.

The gelcoat is generally of good quality and the hull is generally fair. We examined a two-year-old boat and found that the finish had held up and that there were no signs of stress cracking anywhere, even though the boat had been raced seriously and used hard.

The hull-to-deck joint is standard practice, with an inward-turning hull flange on which the deck is set. Stainless bolts run through the joint and through an aluminum toerail which covers the joint. The whole stem fitting as well as the corner pieces for the toerail are the heavy aluminum castings that are traditional on C&C boats, but it is interesting that C&C used plastic moldings for the stanchion bases on the 33.

The rudder is fiberglass over a webbing of stainless welded to the stainless steel rudder post. The standard fin keel (6' 4" draft) is external lead, bolted to a stub on the hull. The centerboard option is unusual in that it is a fiberglass molding with some lead inside, and the board is fitted entirely inside a shallow keel (4' 4" draft) fitted to the hull.

The fiberglass board is lighter (for lifting) and quieter than a more common steel board which will tend to bang around in the centerboard trunk. The fiberglass molding also makes for a better-shaped and fairer fin for upwind work. The lifting cable is housed inside the keel, so it presents no drag and makes no noise at speed. The cable passes through the cabin, housed in a stainless steel tube which also supports the cabin table, and is led to a stopper and winch on the aft end of the cabin house.

The fin keel weighs 3,975 pounds (42% of total displacement); the keel/centerboard, at 5,258 pounds, is much heavier. Nominal displacement for the fin-keel version is 9,450 pounds; for the centerboard version 10,733 pounds.

Rig

The early model that we sailed had a rig from the C&C spar shop, known in its time as a builder of sturdy high-performance rigs. The spars on the later models came not from C&C but from Offshore Spars in Detroit. Though well known in the Midwest (they made the spars for the S2 7.9 and 9.1, as well as custom race rigs), the company's rigs are not often seen on the East or West Coasts except on grand prix racers.

We examined just one spar from Offshore, and it appears that little was lost in the change. The mast and boom are fairly heavy extrusions, painted white, with integral grooves for taking bolt rope or slugs. The mast comes standard with internal halyards and lifts, as well as an internal wiring conduit and VHF cable. The boom has built-in slab reefing gear. The mast is stepped on the keel.

The standing rigging is made up of Navtec stainless rod, tangs, and turnbuckles, with 1 x 19 stainless for the adjustable babystay and for the split part of the lower backstay. Main and jib halyards are stainless with rope tails, and we were surprised to discover that the wing halyard is galvanized steel with a rope tail. The shroud chainplates, set inboard for close sheeting, are attached to the hull by stainless rods between the deck and hull anchorpoints.

The boat came standard with good quality hardware for rig control. Spinnaker winches and gear, boom vang, and backstay adjuster were options.

Engine/Mechanical Systems

The Yanmar 2GM engine is a bit tight in the engine compartment, but otherwise the installation is first rate. The engine beds are actually part of the structural "spider" beams. The engine box is insulated with sound deadener, and the engine is about as quiet as you can expect a two-cylinder diesel to be. The standard solid prop should be replaced with a folder.

The electrical system and plumbing are well done. Electricity includes a good 12-volt system with ample interior lighting. A 120-volt shore power system, with a 50' shore cord, was standard equipment. A three-burner propane stove with oven and safety solenoid was standard, as was hot-and-cold pressurized water. The 30-gallon water tank is adequate for typical cruising, though ocean sailors may want to convert the standard 24-gallon head holding tank to fresh water storage. Installation of all the equipment—like the electrical hot water heater, and the valving for the water system—is secure and seamanlike.

Handling Under Power

The 20 hp Yanmar is big enough to handle the boat. We were under power only in fairly flat water, with an optional Martek folding prop, and had no problems backing or turning. The engine pushed the boat to hull speed easily. We suspect a big head sea will challenge the peak output of the engine, probably slowing the boat to four knots or so, but the amount of power is ample for all reasonable sailors in almost all conditions.

Steering is with the standard 36" destroyer wheel. Throttle and shift controls are integral to the pedestal, and visibility over the deck house is good when you are sitting on the "bubble hump" behind the wheel.

The aluminum fuel tank holds 20 US gallons which should be good for about 180 miles of powering under normal conditions. The engine control panel is in one "bay" of the T-shaped cockpit. You can't see it easily from the steering position, but that's a very minor inconvenience.

Access to the engine is adequate, through the removable companionway steps, through opening panels on both the port and starboard side of the engine, and through the cockpit seat locker.

Handling Under Sail

We probably wouldn't have considered writing up the C&C 33 if we hadn't sailed it first. The boat does look like it should be an all-around wholesome boat, but we initially thought of it as not particularly a standout in its size and price range.

Our sail convinced us otherwise, and we eventually chartered one for three races in a four-race series. We found the 33 to be a fine sailer, just about everything we would want in its size.

What did we find so appealing? Basically, it is a boat that combines good performance with comfortable sailing. To put it another way, it performs well without demanding the incessant tweaking and crew movement of so many high-performance boats. We found that a group of five (nearly) middle-aged racers could push the boat hard and make it sail well, without reverting to being collegian hot-shot Laser sailors. In short, unlike so many performance boats, the C&C 33 is not an oversized dinghy.

We sailed the centerboard version and found no particular shortcomings. With a good set of sails, the boat was at least as weatherly as any boat in her PHRF division. We tried sailing the reaches and the runs with the board up and with the board down and could not discern any difference in speed, though as charterer we deferred to the owner's conviction that the boat was faster off the wind with the board up. (It did give the crew something to do.) The boat seemed to steer as well with the board up as with it down.

With the extra weight, we presume that the centerboard model is a little harder to push around a race course in light air, but in 15-knot winds, she had to ask no favors, and in the 22-knot wind we saw for one race, she was a pleasure to sail compared to the other boats on the race course.

Very noticeable about her behavior was that her motion was not at all the quick hobble so characteristic of contemporary lightweight racers. She has a heavyweight feel but still is responsive and lively.

In heavy air, she seemed to easily sail to her PHRF rating of 135, making her roughly comparable in speed to a J/30, Pearson 39, and many of the early 1970s one-tonners. For racing, the fin-keel model is supposedly three to six seconds per mile faster than the centerboard model.

Interestingly, for the fourth race of the series, we left the C&C docked and sailed on one of the boats in her class, an S2 9.1, known as a speedy boat with good accommodations. It was a striking contrast, like a big dinghy which has to be tamed and brought to submission in order to go fast. The C&C 33—with approximately equal speed through the water—seemed like a sweet kitten in contrast.

Our handicap let us win the series of races with two firsts and a second. In absolute terms, we know that there are faster boats around. Most of them, unfortunately, are a pain to handle as the wind pipes up, and we wouldn't want to sail them on some of the long, rainy slogs that we often encounter in cruising. Shorthanded, most of the faster boats are miserable.

The C&C 33, in contrast, is an easy sailer, respectable in light winds, and a pleasure in heavy.

On Deck

The deck layout on the C&C 33 is conventional. The double lifelines with port and starboard lifeline gates, pulpit, and pushpit are sturdy, well made, and come as standard equipment. The pushpit has a gate which can be fitted with stern ladder—a good idea for both the racer and cruiser.

Like most modern boats, the foredeck is quite narrow, so anchoring and sail handling can be difficult. The walkways leading aft are wide because of the inboard shrouds and easy to move along either heeled or upright because of the moderate deck camber.

Because of the sculpting and window shape, the cabin house looks low, but it is actually quite high— a difficult step up from the walkways or cockpit. Fortunately, because all the lines lead aft to the back edge of the cabin, there's not much occasion to walk on the cabin top abaft the mast. Forward of the mast, the cabin slopes gradually into the deck, and movement is easy. However, the skylight over the head and the forward hatch are slippery stumble-makers and need to have non-skid tape put on them.

We haven't seen a dodger for the 33 yet, and the sculpting of the cabin house may make it difficult to design a wide one. A narrow dodger, fitting just over the companionway, would work well.

The cockpit is a conventional T-shape with a bridgedeck on which the traveler is mounted. An optional cabin-top traveler is available, but there seems to be little to recommend it. The cockpit seats are comfortable for sitting but too short to lie down on. The forward part of the coaming is okay for sitting, but you'll be inclined only to stand on the cockpit sole, aft of the bench seats. The cockpit is definitely skewed a little toward the racing side of this boat's dual purposes, and it will be a much better cockpit underway than dockside.

Hardware is good quality and well arranged. The standard winches are of adequate size, though the

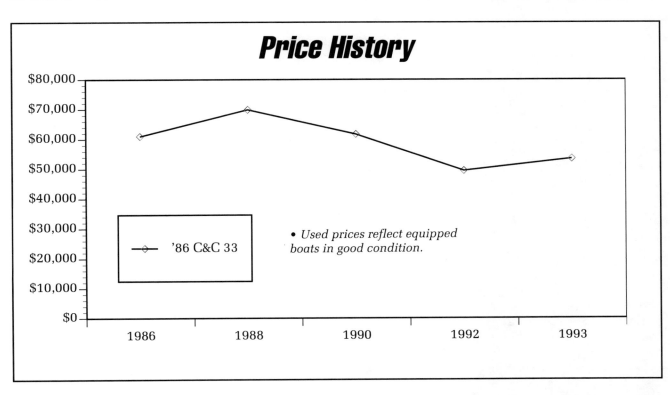

Price History

• *Used prices reflect equipped boats in good condition.*

Legend: —◇— '86 C&C 33

(Y-axis: $0 to $80,000 in $10,000 increments. X-axis years: 1986, 1988, 1990, 1992, 1993)

boat is stiff enough to carry a heavy 150% genoa in 20 knots of wind, and that's a handful for the #24 primaries unless the racing crew is on board.

As is the case in most modern boats, there's not too much abovedecks storage room. An anchor well forward will stow a Danforth, but everything else will have to go into the one aft locker under the starboard cockpit seat. It's a cavernous locker, but the serious cruiser will have to devise a way to subdivide it to make it more usable. Behind the helmsman are a small locker for propane bottles and a small stowage spot for winch handles or beer cans.

Belowdecks

The arrangements belowdecks are conventional: a V-berth forward, head with shower opposite a hanging locker; port and starboard settees outboard of a saloon table; L-shaped galley; nav station at the head of a double quarterberth (well, maybe one-and-three-quarter quarterberth). From the center bulkhead aft, the boat is wide open, which seems to us like a more sensible arrangement than the "Euro" compartmentalizing of the aft cabin and aft head, at least in a boat this size.

Here's a couple of good details. A decent built-in bureau in the forward cabin is a nice touch. The head compartment is a single fiberglass molding, including even the wash basin—all compact and well designed. The galley is quite serviceable, with a good stove and a stainless bash bar to keep you from crashing into it.

The teak ceiling and bulkhead veneer contrast with the off-white hull liner. The liner is well done, with removable panels for servicing hardware fittings, wiring, and so on.

For some reason, the covers for the instrument "pods" on the aft bulkhead were a chintzy teak plywood, poorly cut. But otherwise, all the detail below was plain but well thought out—pretty characteristic of C&C cabins.

Overall, the cabin is comfortable. We've often heard older C&C's rapped as "leaky" boats, with drips around windows and under heavily-loaded deck hardware, but the boat we sailed had several seasons of serious racing and cruising and was completely dry.

Conclusions

If we were entirely devoted to racing, we'd probably look at something different—maybe a Frers 33 or perhaps the J/33 or possibly even a J/35. If we were entirely into cruising, we'd also look at different boats—maybe something more like a Nonsuch or a Mason 33.

But if we wanted to continue the kind of sailing we enjoy most—with a good share of racing contrasted with some serious weekending and at least one long cruise a season, sailed shorthanded—the C&C 33 would be among the boats we'd buy. Though in some ways she seems plain and undistinctive, she is admirably suited to be both a racer and a cruiser—a tough combination to find in the modern market. It's a boat for sailors who truly want a racer-cruiser and know what they're looking for.   • **PS**

Pearson Vanguard

The ravages of time notwithstanding, the Vanguard can represent a lot of boat for the money.

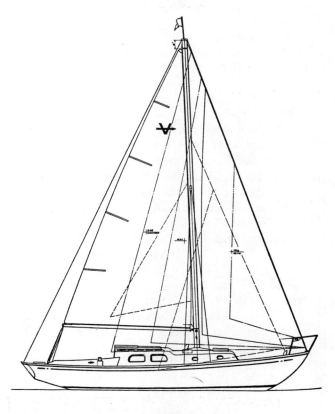

Pearson Yachts, of Portsmouth, Rhode Island, was founded in 1956 by cousins Clinton and Everett Pearson, and fellow Brown University graduate Fred Heald. For the first few years it produced dinghies and runabouts in fiberglass, a boatbuilding material pioneered in the early days of post-war America by Ray Greene, Taylor Winner and a handful of other erstwhile inventors. Then in 1959 Pearson exhibited its prototype Carl Alberg-designed Triton at the New York Boat Show, wrote enough orders to pay its hotel bill, and sold public stock to raise the necessary capital to expand facilities. The Triton, while not the first auxiliary sailboat built of fiberglass, was the first boat to enjoy a long production run (over 700), and keep its builders in the black.

The Vanguard, designed by Philip Rhodes, followed in 1962 and remained in production until 1967, totalling 404 hulls. It was preceded by the Invicta, Alberg 35, Bounty II, Ariel, Rhodes 41, and of course the Triton. This line of fiberglass cruisers and sometime racers gave Pearson a strong position in the market. The pedigree of the designers was odorless, and construction quality was good for that particular moment in the timetable of plastic boatbuilding technology.

Sailing Performance

The early Pearsons were club raced with moderate success under the now-defunct CCA Rule, and in some offshore events. Indeed, the 37' Invicta yawl *Burgoo* won the 1964 Bermuda Race. It was the first time a fiberglass boat had won the event and prompted a lot of advertising ballyhoo from the company. While the Vanguard never acquired as memorable a victory as the Invicta, it performed decently.

One does not, however, buy a vintage Pearson for scintillating performance. A PHRF rating of 216

Specifications

LOA	32' 7"
LWL	22' 4"
Beam	9' 3"
Draft	4' 6"
Displacement	10,300 lbs.
Ballast	4,250 lbs.
Sail area	437 sq. ft.

indicates the Vanguard will spend a lot of time watching the transom of even a Pearson 32, a 1979 design with a divided keel and rudder underbody whose rating is 174. The reasons include greater displacement and shorter waterline. The theoretical hull speed of the Vanguard's 22' 4" waterline is just 6.3 knots. As the boat heels, however, the waterline's sailing length quickly increases, as will speed. Therefore, the Vanguard was intended to sail at about 15° of heel for maximum efficiency. Once its "shoulder" is immersed, the boat is fairly stiff.

Maneuverability is good. Comments from our reader surveys say, "Turns on a dime." Despite bearing the "full keel" appellation, the Vanguard's generous overhangs, cutaway forefoot and raked rudderpost mean there's not as much lateral surface

Owners' Comments

"This is a rugged, Plain Jane type of boat. The Philip Rhodes hull with long overhangs and low freeboard is very good looking as well as being a boat that can sail. It is an outstanding bargain in today's market."

—1963 model in Norwell, MA

"I'm 6' 2", 240 pounds, and the bunks are a little short. The doorway to the head and forward cabin are a little small and I bump my head frequently.

"My Vanguard survived a severe beating from Hurricane Alicia. I called Pearson to ask about a replacement rudder and pulpits. They still have the pattern for the old mahogany rudder and made a new one. Marine Fashion still had the pattern for the pulpits and they made them for me also."

—1964 model in Houston, TX

"Handles 5' to 6' chop going to windward in 25 mph. winds very well. We carry a 150% genoa up to 18 knots, working sails with no reef to 25 knots.

"The exhaust system allows salt water into the engine with heavy following seas.

"Hull-to-deck joint is poorly sealed but correctible."

—1965 model in Wickford, RI

"I can leave the wheel unattended on several points of sail by proper sail trim. The full keel and large rudder allow good maneuverability at low speeds and in winds while docking, etc.

"The cockpit is just right for sleeping but not too large. Very dry in foul weather. Wide decks make going forward easy.

"The hull cavity for lead ballast should be filled with filler mixed with resin. Mine had sawdust that absorbs water through the fiberglass. I drained it and packed it full of epoxy.

"If you are willing to be a test case for how long fiberglass boats are going to last, you can't go wrong with a Vanguard."

—1964 model on Chesapeake Bay

"The Vanguard is very forgiving. It'll go anywhere in any weather. We get comments in every port on its style and beauty. Lots of headroom.

"Check for rot at the base of spreaders and at base of tiller—a common problem easily rectified.

"This boat was built before they figured out how strong fiberglass was. Consequently, it is overbuilt."

—1964 model in Milwaukee, WI

area as one might suppose. Backing down is dreadful, but that's to be expected with a keel-hung rudder and propeller in the aperture. One learns to aim in the direction of the prop; to attempt otherwise is to thumb your nose at physics and invite the maledictions of watchful owners on nearby boats.

Like many CCA-inspired designs with large mainsails and small foretriangles, the Vanguard likes to carry a large headsail longer than is customary on more contemporary designs. Instead of switching down from, say, a 150% or 165% genoa when the wind approaches 18 knots, the wiser practice is to reef the main. The consequence of any other strategy is a wicked weather helm that makes tiller steering seem like a two-handed wrassle with an alligator.

Owners have dealt with the weather helm problem in various ways. Because raking the mast forward (to move the center of effort forward) is an insufficient measure, some have installed double-duty bow platforms to relocate the headstay farther forward, and as a permanent home for their main anchor. Others have tried roachless mainsails. The easiest solution is simply to adjust your thinking about sail combinations. As one reader wrote, "It took me three years to learn to shorten the main (before reducing headsail size)."

A small number of Vanguards were delivered with yawl rigs, and though none of the readers in our survey were owners of split rigs, they presumably would be easier to balance than the sloop.

Despite these idiosyncracies, the Vanguard is well behaved in deteriorating weather. It is never skittish while tacking or during sail-changing maneuvers, and in fact, by luffing the mainsail it is possible to carry sail longer than is prudent. Switching down, of course, is inevitable. "In 50 knots with a storm jib and trysail," said one reader, "she can make three knots to windward."

Engine

The ubiquitous Atomic 4 gasoline engine was the standard auxiliary for the Vanguard. Many are still in operation though it is more and more common to find thrifty replacement diesels, a certain improvement in resale value. If the Atomic 4 hasn't been replaced yet, one should factor in the cost of repowering in the not-so-distant future.

Accessibility varies dramatically between the standard aft galley layout and the dinette arrangement with quarter berths aft. In the first, the engine is located under the sink; access is from the front via a cupboard door and from the side by removing the offset companionway counter steps. Needless to say, this is not a convenient setup for even routine oil changing, let alone major repair work. In the second, the engine is covered by a box directly under the bridgedeck; removable panels, fastened by knurled thumbscrews, expose the engine on all sides except the aft transmission end, which is under the bridge deck. While ease of engine maintenance is certainly an important factor in choosing a boat, in the case of the Vanguard the two general arrangement plans also have significant impact on livability at anchor and at sea, giving prospective buyers pause to contemplate the many implications of the two different layouts. More on this later.

Construction

Owners' faith in the integrity of older Pearsons borders on the religious. "They don't make 'em like they used to!" is a frequent call in the hallelujah chorus of these proselytes, usually followed by some refrain of boatyard wisdom such as, "Back then they didn't know how thick fiberglass had to be." Or they say, "My hull is...*this* thick!" as the space between their thumb and finger grows like Pinocchio's nose. There is probably some truth to these beliefs—that scantlings for fiberglass boats were for a time loosely derived from the builder's knowledge of wooden boats—but a thick skin doesn't necessarily result in a well made boat, nor does the hull layup tell the whole construction story. Amen.

The Vanguard's single skin hull was indeed the beneficiary of generous laminations of 1 1/2-ounce mat and 24-ounce woven roving, but probably not as many as some owners would like to believe. One indication of panel stiffness is whether the hull changes shape in its cradle; a door that suddenly won't open is a telling clue, and with the Vanguard, this is seldom the case. It is also true that most Vanguards weigh about 1,500 pounds more than the designed displacement.

Perhaps the most dramatic difference between old and new Pearsons (and most older boats for that matter) is the use today of many more fiberglass molds: furniture foundations, iceboxes, shower stalls, etc. In some instances this practice may represent an improvement, in others not. The Vanguard's interior was constructed of plywood taped to the hull. Correct building procedures were generally followed, such as peeling the plastic laminate where bulkheads are taped to the hull for better adhesion. Neatness, however, sometimes was lacking; examples might include wrinkles in the cloth and frayed, untrimmed edges.

The all-wood interior, properly taped to the hull, nevertheless creates a strong internal support struc-

---

There were two interior arrangements: the standard one shown here, and a dinette with drop-down table. Both had their problems. Headroom is unusually generous, at 6' 5" in the main cabin.

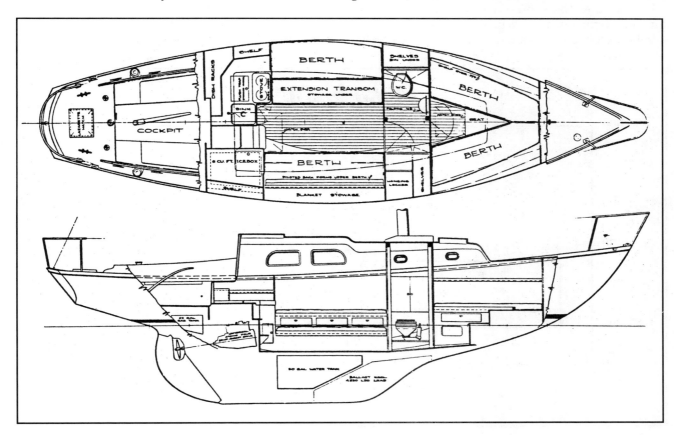

ture and is amenable to do-it-yourself modification. Where it becomes unsatisfactory is in some structures such as the icebox, which in the Vanguard was built in situ from plywood and sheets of Styrofoam; the result is too many thermal leaks, not enough insulation, and more weight than necessary. Owners wishing to upgrade the icebox have the dubious choice of adding insulation on the inside (resulting in an unacceptably small box) or ripping out the entire box and building a new one from scratch, which is a devil of a job.

The deck is balsa cored and the hull-to-deck joint is a simple flange that is sealed and through-bolted. The balsa is terminated several inches from the rail so that deck hardware such as lifeline stanchions and cleats are mounted on solid glass. As with most older boats, bedding compound tends to deteriorate over time, and severe gelcoat cracking allows the ingress of water. This is of particular concern where coring is involved. Extreme remedies for punky decks—grinding away one skin of the deck sandwich, removing watersoaked wood and reglassing—is a major and costly project.

The one real problem with the Vanguard's basic structure is the keel (it's not a problem as long as you don't hit anything, but groundings, for the curious cruiser, are as predictable as the tide). The lead ballast castings were set in a bed of resin inside the hollow keel, which is part of the hull mold, then glassed over so that water entering the keel cavity will not enter the cabin. Without fiberglass reinforcement, the resin bed is brittle and provides little added protection from a grounding. Voids between the ballast and keel sides were filled with various types of material over the years, including sheets of balsa, which can soak up water like sponges if the keel is holed.

The Vanguard's mast step is a welded steel box bolted to the deck. Twenty years seems to be about the maximum useful life of these steps, eventually succumbing to rust and requiring the custom fabrication of a new one. Entrance to the forward cabin is offset to starboard so that a solid teak compression post could be fitted to the head side of the bulkhead.

Fuel (21 gals) and water (45 gals) tanks are Monel, the former mounted under the cockpit footwell and the latter under the main cabin sole on centerline. The fuel tank should be removable, but replacing the water tank would require dismantling the sole, which unfortunately is not an unusual situation in many boats. On the plus side, Monel is an excellent tank material and will probably survive the boat itself. Plumbing is straightforward with bronze, barrel-type seacocks on through-hull fittings.

Interior

Most owners have strong opinions about the two arrangement plans—standard and dinette. Neither is without problems. The forward cabin is the same in both plans, as is the head. In the main cabin, the standard arrangement features a settee/berth to starboard with a pipe berth over; to port is an extension settee that pulls out to form a full-width single berth and a pilot berth outboard, totaling four decent sea berths. The aft galley is divided by the offset companionway with icebox to starboard and sink and

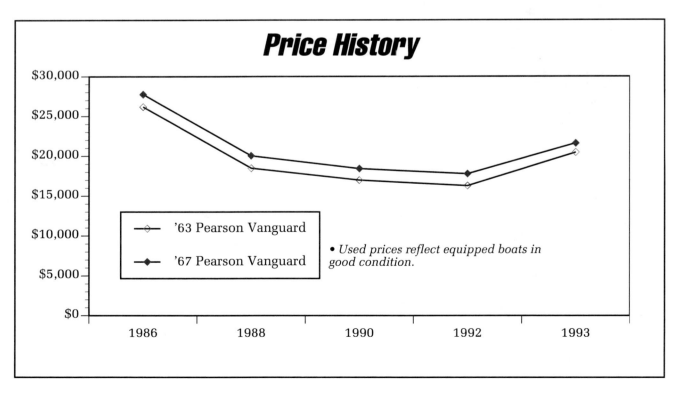

Price History

Legend:
- ◇ '63 Pearson Vanguard
- ◆ '67 Pearson Vanguard

• *Used prices reflect equipped boats in good condition.*

(Y-axis: $0, $5,000, $10,000, $15,000, $20,000, $25,000, $30,000)
(X-axis: 1986, 1988, 1990, 1992, 1993)

stove to port. There is no provision for an oven in this plan, which may be a drawback for live-aboards and some cruisers. The fold-down bulkhead-mounted table makes for more open space but is something of a contraption.

The dinette plan has a more useful table, which is handy for chartwork and lowers to form a double berth. But because of the Vanguard's comparatively narrow beam, the dinette is small. The galley is a sideboard affair with adequate plate and food stowage. Its chief advantage is a three-burner stove/oven, and its greatest liability is a sink that won't drain with the rail down on port tack. In fact, in such conditions the sink overflows into the stowage bins behind and ultimately into the bilge. This requires closing the sink drain seacock in blustery weather. Two quarter-berths are secure at sea though adults might find them a bit claustrophobic on a regular basis. But at least they won't have to be stripped of bedding each morning, as do settee berths in the main cabin.

The stepped coachroof provides unusual headroom in the main cabin (about 6' 5"), and marginal headroom in the head and forward cabin (6' 0" plus). Berth lengths are all just over 6'. The head is small, though there is adequate stowage space, and an aluminum fold-down sink at least makes shaving a semi-civilized possibility.

The Vanguard's interior is virtually all plywood, with bulkheads and furniture foundations taped to the hull. The imitation teak-grain plastic laminate is hardly the fashion today, and contributes to a drab, dark feeling inside. The cabins could be given a real breath of life by painting over the laminate (good sanding required for adhesion, though results may still be marginal) or applying a new veneer on top.

A molded fiberglass inner liner was used for the overhead, and the hull sides are covered with vinyl, the latter being a popular target of home renovation projects. The installation of a wood ceiling or cementing some durable fabric or other foam-backed material is a relatively easy and quick way to spruce up the interior. Fiddles, moldings, handholds and other trim are teak. The cabin sole is teak over plywood, and the floors are wood fiberglassed to the hull.

Conclusions

A reasonable shoal draft of 4' 6" makes the Vanguard suitable for cruising the Bahamas and Florida Keys, yet also gives it enough stability for offshore sailing. Perhaps the boat's major drawback for living aboard or extended cruising is its size; a short waterline and narrow beam condemn owners to stowing on deck surplus drinking water and fuels, sail bags, ground tackle and the like.

Prospective buyers cannot ignore age either; at more than 25 years old, wiring, bedding compound, wood, plastic and metal parts experience a steady rate of failure when a boat gets this old. If the boat hasn't been the beneficiary of a major upgrading effort, it soon will.

The Pearson Vanguard is a traditionally styled boat, and therein lies her appeal. Rhodes could draw a mean sheerline and this boat is no exception. Like most of the early Pearsons, the Vanguard offers a lot of boat for the money. Its value peaked in the early 1980s between the high $20s and low $30s, more than twice it's original cost. In recent years, age and the glut of used boats on the market has brought prices down well below $30,000, often into the teens. Much depends on the amount of upgrading performed by past owners, the most important being engine, topside reconditioning, interior customization, condition of teak and non-skid, and sail inventory.   • **PS**

Freedom 33

Funny-looking to some, innovative to others, the Fredom 33 is certainly an unusual boat.

When a restless 40-year-old advertising executive with a background in one-design sailing (1970 World's Sunfish Champion) went shopping for a cruising boat some years ago, he could not find one that made him happy. Conventional cruisers he found poor performers, needlessly difficult to sail shorthanded with their big headsails and complicated rigs, and with hull forms that demand auxiliary power any time the wind is forward of abeam.

It was in 1972 that this sailor, Garry Hoyt, set about developing an alternative. His alternative was the original Freedom 40. Discarding conventions one by one, he came up with a long-waterline, quasi-traditional hull form and a wishbone cat-ketch rig. Then, to prove he had something, he took his prototype to Antigua Race Week and decisively out-performed the cruising boats with which he had been so unhappy. Granted, his talents as a sailor were considerably better than those of his competition and granted, his prototype without an engine had no propeller or aperture drag; nevertheless his concept gained a qualified validity.

In the intervening years Hoyt refined his rig and developed a whole line of boats: a 21, 25, 28, 39 (express and pilothouse models), and the 44. The Freedom 33 is no longer in production, having been replaced in the line by the 32, which is a single masted "cat sloop" with a self tacking jib and gun mount spinnaker. More rig innovation.

Hoyt's natural ingenuity produced the innovative boats, basic good luck led him to Ev Pearson of Tillotson-Pearson when he went looking for a builder, and his background in advertising let him create attention-getting explanations of his concept. His one notable weakness has been in marketing; until recently he tried with little success to bring potential

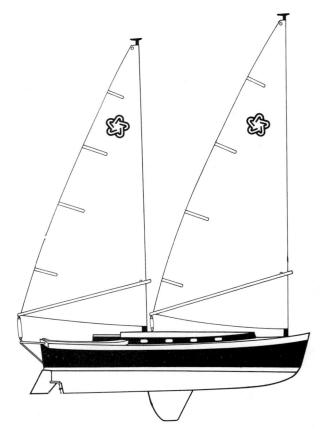

Specifications

LOA	33' 0"
LWL	30' 0"
Beam	11' 0"
Draft	3' 6"/6' 0" (board up/down)
Displacement	12,000 lbs.
Ballast	3,800 lbs.
Sail area	516 sq. ft.

buyers to the boat rather than putting together a dealer network that takes the boat to the public.

The US builder, Tillotson-Pearson, has been one of the most successful low-profile boatbuilders, putting together such popular boats as the J-Boat line and the Etchells 22 one-design. The firm has been a leader in the development of balsa coring for hull structure and carbon fiber for light, stiff laminates.

Unlike the situation with more conventional craft, selling the sailing public on the concept behind the Freedoms is a stiff challenge. The rig in particular is unfamiliar to most cruising sailors and for the concept to gain acceptance they need to be educated. Not only must they be convinced that the stayless masts, wishbone booms, and wrap-around sails are durable, they must be literally taught how to use them advantageously, For this reason reception to the idea has been mixed, and the appeal of the Freedom has been to sailors outside of the mainstream.

Construction

Basic construction of the Freedom 33 hull and deck is, in our opinion, among the best in the production boat building industry. From our observation as a result of examining boats both finished and under construction, we can detect no serious cost cutting or scrimping in the way of materials or techniques.

The Freedom 33 (as with other boats in the Freedom line) has a balsa-cored hull and deck. There are advantages to this type of construction—hull rigidity, thermal and acoustical insulation, reduction in hull weight—that we believe recommends it for hull structure provided it is properly engineered. In the case of the Freedom 33, we believe it is.

Lead ballast, 3,800 lbs, is cast in wedge-shaped pieces and fiberglassed into the bilge. The aluminum fuel tank (25 gallons) is also deep in the bilge. The centerboard, a combination of lead and fiberglass, is a hefty 1,200 lbs, also contributing to stability. The centerboard is the product of perhaps the most thoughtful design and engineering on the boat. It is pivoted in a channel, eliminating the need for a pin that breaches the hull.

Hoyt, with his eye firmly on performance, adopted an idea of designer Jay Parris for a centerboard configuration having a triangular profile and a constant chord. The design permits a centerboard with a shape that gives lift at any angle and, more importantly in reducing drag, a centerboard that fits its slot closely.

If the centerboard is not the most extensively engineered feature of the Freedom 33, then the spars are. Initially the Freedom 33 had two-part aluminum tubular masts that were heavy, reducing stability and increasing pitching moment. To help cure this weakness, Tillotson-Pearson undertook a research program into building one-piece spars using a carbon-fiber laminate.

The result is an approximately 30% saving in weight and considerably stiffer spars. The saving translated itself into markedly better performance, so much so that we suggest any buyer considering one of the increasing number of boats available with stayless spars should look into spar weight and stiffness.

Additional construction details of note on the Freedom 33 include a hull-to-deck joint through-fastened with 5/16" stainless steel bolts and bonded with 3M 5200 adhesive sealant, a technique we recommend. Bulkheads are tabbed to the inside fiberglass skin, leaving the core intact to prevent hard spots from showing up on the topsides. The interior joinerwork, fetchingly of oak, ash, and spruce,

is done to a high quality; our only serious reservation is discussed below.

Performance

Our evaluation of the performance of the Freedom 33 is in part the product of having spent a week sailing aboard the boat during Antigua Race Week. For comparison with that experience on the prototype, we recently sailed a production version, as well.

For those sailors used to masthead headsails and conventional mainsails with their sheeting, reefing, and halyard systems, the rig of the Freedom 33 does require some re-education. Initially one has the impression that the boat is under-rigged and that the sailplan is inefficient. That impression is, however, deceptive. The boat does have speed and liveliness that exceeds that of most out-and-out cruising boats of her size and in many conditions can rival the performance of the many so-called racer-cruisers or "performance cruisers."

The mainsail and mizzen are efficient in that almost all their area forms an effective airfoil. The wishbone boom permits a longer luff than a conventional boom and does not interfere with the draft at the foot. The wishbone does create windage, though. Draft control is easier with a wishbone boom through either outhaul tension (the Freedom 33 mizzen) or adjustment of the effective length of the wishbone (the mainsail). Similarly the wrap-around sails are more efficient aerodynamically than sails set on a mast track or groove which are in part blanketed by the spar section. Given the greater diameter of stayless spars versus conventional spars, the wrap-around system is important in this type of rig.

For performance, proper sail shape, adjustment, and trim are as vital for this rig as for more conventional rigs. There are still some aspects of the Freedom rig about which we have reservations but from our experience we believe the Freedom line has come closer to perfecting the system than any of its rivals boasting similar rigs. Incidentally, Ulmer Sails (in particular Ulmer sailmaker Bob Adams), has worked hard to develop Freedom sail shape plus reefing and trimming systems and we therefore urge buyers to order the sails offered as "factory installed options" rather than trying to find another sailmaker who will have to go through the extensive design exercise needed to provide suitable sails.

The Freedom 33 is stiffer (and, we think, foot-for-foot, faster) than her sisters in the Freedom line. Her sailplan gives optimum performance in a mid-range of wind strengths, say 10 to 15 knots. In winds below 10 knots, especially to windward in any chop, the stubby hull, with a centerboard and plenty of wetted surface, is sluggish. In fact, no Freedom is as lively as we would wish in lighter winds, a factor to consider in such areas as Chesapeake Bay and Puget Sound.

For such conditions we strongly recommend at least one mizzen staysail. Moreover, although we are not sold on poleless spinnakers (i.e., Flashers) for conventionally rigged cruising boats, we think they are superb as a mizzen spinnaker on a boat like a Freedom 33.

The wishbone booms and stayless masts combine to make the Freedom a delightful boat to sail with the wind from astern. The absence of shrouds lets the mainsail (and boom) swing forward of thwartships, encouraging her to sail wing and wing with the wind as much as 25 degrees or so off the quarter. Moreover, the sail stays out to windward in light winds without a preventer. Nor does it need a vang; the angle of the wishbone boom off the mast eliminates any tendency for the boom to lift. On a run almost any sailor accustomed to wrestling with blanketed or poled out headsails, cringing as his mainsail chafes on shrouds, and paranoid over the threat of accidentally jibing, will have to appreciate the Freedom rig.

Closewindedness is a relative term but a major attraction of the better modern designs. The Freedom 33 is not closewinded, as much as a result of her hull shape as her rig. However, she does not give away anything upwind to boats with shallow hull forms and long keels. Boat for boat she will sail by

Morgan 41s, Irwin 44s, CSY 44s, Westsails, and their ilk.

The Freedom rig uses a slab or jiffy reefing system. Moreover, instead of the reefed portion gathering above the boom as with conventional sailplans the excess material gathers at the wishbone in aerodynamically messy folds. It is just not a rig that lends itself to simple, uncluttered reefing and we think finding combinations of reduced sail using staysails would be a better solution than trying to reef main and mizzen. Yet the present rig seems to have proven itself in offshore sailing. Several boats have made long passages without difficulty and weathered severe storms at sea with no breakdowns or crises. In fact, we sailed a Freedom 33 that a few days before had beat her way up Long Island sound in an easterly gale with gusts as high as 60 knots.

The sails are two-ply loosely connected at the leech. Furling is easy; the sail gathers into a basket formed of shock cord stretched across the wishbone. More shock cord across the top keeps the sail se-

The interior is obstructed by a 5' long centerboard trunk running down its center. On deck, the Freedom 33 is well suited for singlehanding—all lines lead aft to the cockpit, and can be handled by one person.

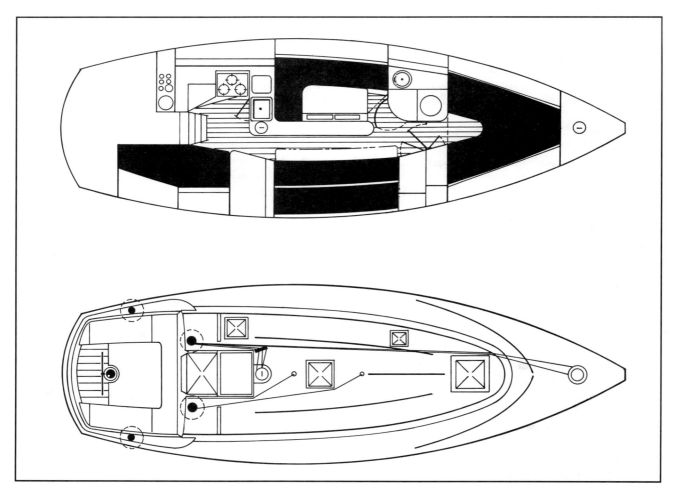

cured. The convenience of this system, obvious as it may be, is one of the major recommendations of the rig, doing away with the onerous chores of conventional mainsail furling or headsail folding and bagging.

In all, we have been favorably impressed with the performance of a boat that experience and instinct tells us should be poor. The wrap-around sails take getting used to, but the more we played with them, the more effective they seemed to be.

Deck Layout

Other than to handle ground tackle or docking lines, there is no reason why anyone has to leave the cockpit of a Freedom 33 under sail. All halyards, sheets, outhauls, reefing pennants, and the centerboard pennant lead aft to the cockpit where they are handled by a pair of self-tailing winches (Barient 23s) and an array of sheet stoppers. Moreover, the cockpit is short enough so that anyone handling these lines can also keep one hand close to the steering wheel, a boon for shorthanded or singlehanded sailing.

The cockpit seating is deep and the coamings are unobstructed perches on the Freedom 33. Best of all, the cockpit space is entirely usable. In fact, because the mizzen traveler is mounted aft, the Freedom 33 is a distinct rarity among production boats—a boat in which the traveler does not threaten to squash one's legs or the mainsheet garrote the crew. The feature alone makes the cockpit of the Freedom noteworthy.

The steering wheel on a pedestal is mounted well aft, the helmsman standing (or sitting on a fold-up seat) on a teak grate under which, uncommonly accessible, is the steering cable and quadrant for the outboard rudder. The grate also serves as the cockpit drain with scuppers through the transom, a most effective arrangement for quickly draining a flooded cockpit. A sliding door at the after end of the cockpit houses propane fuel bottles.

The decks and house top are uncluttered sundecks and lounging platforms. Sailors used to gingerly stepping around a conventional deck may feel disoriented—missing are chainplates and shrouds, headsail sheets and blocks, and a spinnaker pole. The anchor sits in an optional fiberglass bowsprit. Man-sized chocks on either side of the bow and amidships are integrally fitted into the teak toerail.

Interior

Garry Hoyt's forte as a designer is clearly in his ability to develop performance. It has not been in his ability to design an interior. The Freedom 40 originally appeared with a midships cockpit and an interior so broken into segments as to be a disaster. The public understandably could not accept an accommodation plan in a 40-footer that was best suited for a chummy young couple (that to go with a rig that already took a vivid imagination to comprehend). Marketplace pressure dictated an alternative version with an aft cockpit and more versatile layout and the present Freedom 40 is a more successful product.

Similarly the Freedom 33 was first designed with an aft cabin that reduced cockpit space and a main cabin that succumbed to, rather than accommodated itself to, the centerboard trunk dividing it. The present

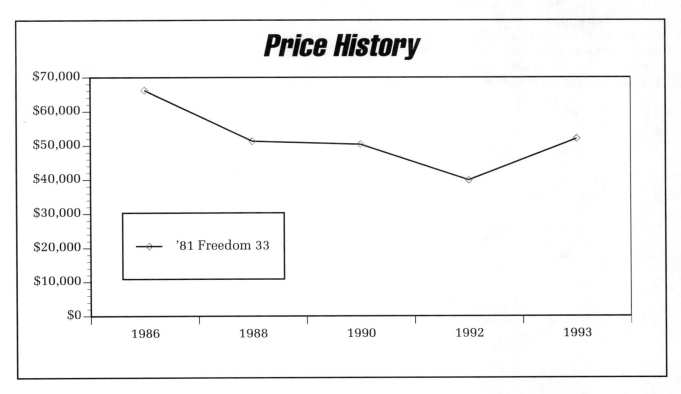

production version does away with the aft cabin, locates the galley conventionally at the base of the companionway, tucks a dinette (convertible to a double berth) to port of the trunk, and has a settee berth to starboard. The result is a main cabin laid out much like other production boats of comparable proportions.

By having her waterline stretched out to virtually the overall length of the boat, the 33 has exceptional roominess for her modest length on deck. Moreover, with her mast stepped close to the stem, her hull fullness has to be carried well forward to support the weight. The forward cabin with its V-berth is the beneficiary. Farther aft the roominess is deceptive, however, because the main cabin is broken up by a 5' long, waist high centerboard trunk running down the middle and the mizzen mast rising at the after end of it.

Had Hoyt not had his eye so fixed on performance, he might have opted for a longer, narrower centerboard permitting a lower trunk that could be located where it would intrude little if at all into the main cabin. As it is, the centerboard does offer minimum drag, does not "thunk" annoyingly in the trunk, and is rugged. It also needs a trunk that makes casual conversation awkward and it makes the dinette a cul-de-sac, leaving the person on the inside no convenient way to get out.

The aesthetic impression created by the interior joinerwork is among the best we have had about any production boat. All the wood below—and there is plenty—is a combination of oak, ash, and spruce (plus the teak and holly cabin sole). We have long been critical of interior decor relying on dark woods such as teak and mahogany. The warmth and illusion of spaciousness imparted by these light colored woods will appeal to many sailors. It certainly does to us.

There is a place for teak below. Grab rails, companionway treads, the framing around hatches, and the trim in the head—all areas liable to wear and getting wet—would be better in teak than in woods like ash and oak which are subject to staining. Moreover, oak is less dimensionally stable than teak, so moisture may eventually affect the structure as well as the finish.

We have some further observations about the interior. The comfortably wide quarterberth to starboard has little overhead foot room. The pilot berth to starboard is accessible only to a person shorter than 4' and weighing less than 40 lbs; it is either a luxuriously cushioned shelf or a berth for an agile ship's cat. Both the chart table and the clever dinette table need removable fiddles, and the hinges on the chart table lid would be better recessed.

And we have some incidental compliments. The stowage capacity of the Freedom 33 is by far the best we have seen in a boat of this size. In particular, the huge galley drywell, incorporating a sliding section for seldom used items, is nonpareil. The engine (Yanmar 3GM diesel) under the companionway is well above average in accessibility. The forward cabin can be completely closed off from the rest of the boat, including the head, by its own door.

The Freedom 33 thus offers an intriguing dichotomy—impressive and innovative decor and layout offset to a disturbing extent by drawbacks that may justifiably turn off many buyers and give owners things they will "have to live with."

Conclusions

The Freedom 33 is an interesting boat. She is, however, not a conventional boat and the concept behind her rig takes getting used to, especially for someone born and raised in the tradition of headsails, standing rigging, mainsails that ride on tracks, hulls with overhangs and aesthetic proportions, and other quaint qualities.   **• PS**

Luders 33

Though a dated design with short waterline and full keel, this boat sails better than her contemporaries.

The 1960s produced a whole passel of smaller production yachts of a similar style designed by the likes of Phil Rhodes, Carl Alberg, Olin Stephens, and Ted Hood. These are quite traditional boats with moderate overhang fore and aft, modest topside height, full keel, heavier displacement, low aspect rig, and perky sheerline.

One of the most popular and typical of this style of boat is the Luders 33 designed by Bill Luders and built by Allied Yachts of Catskill, NY, from 1966 to 1974. Luders, a former boatbuilder as well as designer, designed the 1964 America's Cup contender *American Eagle*, a fleet of 44' yawls for the US Naval Academy, and the Sea Sprite 34.

It is unfortunate that the builder of the Luders 33, Allied Yachts, had such a troubled existence, struggling for survival from the early 1970s until the firm finally succumbed for good in 1981. In its heyday in the late 1960s, Allied built some popular boats including the 35' Seabreeze, the 39' Mistress, and the semi-classic Seawind 30 (later the 32' Seawind II) as well as the Luders 33.

The problem for the used boat buyer in considering a boat from a defunct builder is compounded in the case of Allied. In its struggle in its latter years the quality of the boats Allied built became inconsistent. This is more notable in the detailing and finish work than in basic construction, but it is a factor to consider. However, this should not be as much a problem for buyers of the 33 as for later Allied products.

A Close Look at the Boat

Throughout its nine year production run, a bit more than 100 Luders 33s were built. Still, like such similar boats as the Alberg 30, the relative scarcity and traditional styling have made it a bit of a cult object.

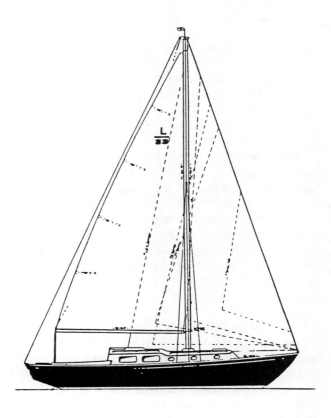

Specifications

LOA	33' 1"
LWL	24' 0"
Beam	10' 0"
Draft	5' 0"
Displacement	12,800 lbs.
Sail area	574 sq. ft.

With her short waterline, heavy weight, short rig, large amount of wetted surface, and small prop in aperture, the 33 can hardly be termed a spritely performer under either sail or power. For instance, against the more modern (designed in 1968) but otherwise comparable Tartan 34, the 33 gives away more than 20 seconds per mile under PHRF.

At the same time the 33 is no slouch when sailing among heavier boats of her type. At her introduction, much was made of her hull design having been tank tested; indeed in the later 1960s, 33s compiled a creditable racing record. At their best in winds of 10 to 15 knots and smoother seas, a number are still successfully raced in PHRF events in the Northeast where winds are typically moderate. Although short, the rig with its big mainsail and masthead foretriangle provides plenty of sail power; however, a good reefing system is needed to prevent overpowering in a breeze. One advantage of the large mainsail is the ease with which the boat can be handled under mainsail alone, in contrast to the difficulty of sailing a modern tall, skinny mainsail design without a headsail.

For power the 33 will have either the original Gray 25 hp gas engine, the 27 hp gas Palmer (after 1967), or a small retrofitted diesel. All can provide enough push ahead, but the prop location and size hurts backing down.

Belowdecks the 33, like so many of boats of her size and type, is decidedly cramped compared to more recent 33-footers, although it's spacious for a boat with a waterline length of merely 24'.

The forward berths are comfortable; the upper or pilot berth in the main saloon is handier as a catchall than it is for sleeping; the pull-out transom berth is not bad as either a seat or a berth; and the "convertible dinette" is just fine for those who want to have a double berth and who don't object to the compromise.

Other than the dinette, the layout of the 33 is definitely "traditional" with an athwartships galley aft, a small head, and an icebox lid that doubles as a chart table. The raised cabin trunk with large windows was a popular feature in production boats of this era, providing headroom, light, and cockpit protection.

The interior decor of the 33 was intended to be plain and functional, although a number of owners report dressing it up with wood, replacing Formica surfaces. The quality of the joinerwork and finish varied somewhat during the production run but in general can be deemed about average.

The cockpit is short by modern standards but has more abundant stowage space in seat lockers and lazarette than in later boats fitted with quarterberths and cockpits extending to the transom. The original design was for tiller steering, but many 33s have been subsequently fitted with wheel steering. Owners report wheel steering preferable for ease at the helm but are divided on whether it should be located forward or aft in the cockpit.

The decor might be plain, but there seems no question that the basic construction of the 33 is rugged. The weight of the boat apart from ballast amounts to a whopping 8,000 pounds, a weight that today is closer to the all-up displacement of boats with waterlines 2' to 4' longer.

What to Look For

As with so many boats built more than, say, 10 years ago, weaknesses such as inadequate hull-to-deck joints, poor bulkhead tabbing and the like have long since become apparent and should be found in any professional survey. What may be less apparent in the 33 is deck and cabintop delamination—separation of the laminate from the balsa core.

Similarly there are reports of gelcoat problems (crazing, voids, etc). And, as with any deck-stepped mast the step and under-deck support system should be carefully checked. So too should the rudder and its hangings.

In the era in which the 33 was built, strength was often obtained by using heavy fiberglass scantlings

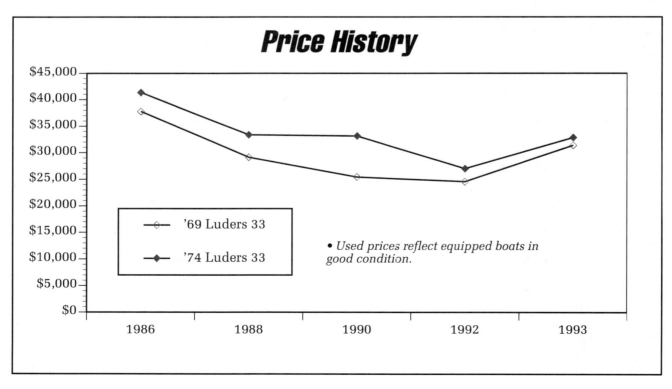

in place of good construction engineering, one result of which is sloppy glasswork although not necessarily a weaker hull structure.

With a boat of the type of the 33, upgrading and refurbishing seems a worthwhile investment. Performance can be markedly improved with slab reefing, a roller traveler, good sails, etc. The looks of the boat can be dramatically enhanced with well finished exterior wood trim and refinished gelcoat surfaces. Thus, in considering used 33s, look for those in which past owners have worked—and spent—to make their boats better. The alternative is to look for a sound but unimproved model at the right price and plan to invest in bettering her. Finding the right one may take time and effort, but they do come on the market. As one owner put it, "Look for three years and close the deal in three minutes if you find her."

Conclusions

Given the price on the used boat market of similar "traditional" boats such as Cape Dories, Sea Sprites, and Albergs, the Luders 33 strikes us as a most promising alternative. The 33 sails better than most of her full keel/short waterline kin, is built to last as long, and should represent good equity. In return, the 33 may need some refurbishing, perhaps a new diesel engine if not already retrofitted, but the result is a superb boat at a price that should be well below that of other production boats of her type.   • **PS**

Tartan Ten

While not as well-built or comfortable as some other boats, the Ten does her thing—racing—very well.

The Tartan Ten was born out of a popular rebellion against the international Offshore Rule (IOR) in the mid 1970s. This was the worst period in the IOR's history, when production sailboats were outdesigned even before their molds were finished. Although the IOR has since then gotten its act together, a great many of its early proponents had been lost for good by 1979. The disenchanted went in two directions—PHRF and offshore one-design.

The Tartan Ten is the child of Charlie Britton of Tartan Marine. Britton was one of the first to recognize the market for offshore one-designs. While he was conceptualizing the Tartan Ten, the J/24—soon to become the most successful offshore one-design—was being tooled up for production, although Britton didn't know it was on the horizon. He was impressed by the Danish-built Aphrodite 101. It's no coincidence that the Tartan Ten bears a resemblance to some of her features. Sparkman and Stevens designed the boat for Tartan in 1977; production began in early 1978, and ran through 1989.

Most of the boats built went to sailors on the Great Lakes, and most of them spend most of their time racing one-design. There are several hundred boats in the national class association, and the majority of those members race in one-design fleets on Lake Erie and Lake Michigan. According to class officials, there is one-design racing every weekend on Lake Erie, and small fleets in Long Island Sound, Chesapeake Bay, Houston and Jacksonville. Unlike a great many boats that tout themselves as offshore one-designs, the Tartan Ten is one of the few boats that has accumulated enough numbers to actually race as a one-design.

When the Tartan Ten was introduced in 1978 at a base price of $21,500, she sold easily. Several boats

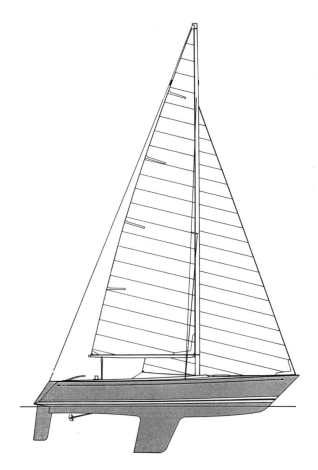

Specifications

LOA	33' 1"
LWL	27' 0"
Beam	9' 3"
Draft	5' 10"
Displacement	6,700 lbs.
Ballast	3,340 lbs.
Sail area	486 sq. ft.

a week were produced in the years immediately following. Then a steady series of price increases, the recession of 1981 and the first signs of a saturated market began to take their toll on sales. For Charlie Britton, a boatbuilder first and a businessman second, the problems of running so large a business was more than he wished to handle. So in the spring of 1982, production of the Tartan Ten ceased and Britton put his company up for sale. By the spring of 1983 he found a buyer in John Richards and production began again at the rate of two Tartan Tens a month.

Construction

While we wouldn't consider the Tartan Ten to be one of the better-built racers, she doesn't have to be. Since she is primarily intended to race against her

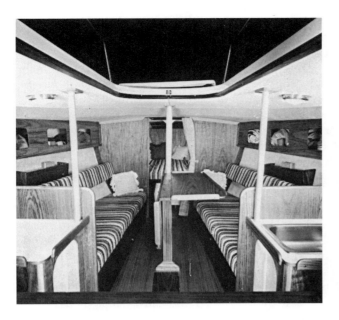

Interior accommodations are Spartan. The head is a portable, there's no stove, and precious little headroom. The large removable companionway hatch helps to alleviate the claustrophobia, however.

sisters, consistency between boats is perhaps more important than superior (and hence, more expensive) construction. The major construction criterion she must meet is to be sufficiently seaworthy to endure an occasional short offshore race. She meets this criterion, although, like too many production boats, she barely makes it.

There have been a number of problems with the Tartan Ten over the years. Tartan Marine generally acted responsibly in correcting them. The worst problems occurred in the first 100 boats. For example, the original hollow stainless steel rudder posts were too light and bent too easily. According to Tartan, every boat with that type of rudder post was located and repaired by inserting a second post inside the original one.

A second problem was with the reinforcement of the hull around the keel sump and under the mast step. From 5' forward of the transom, the Tartan Ten's hull is cored with 1/2" balsa, except in the bilge area, which is stiffened by a grid of hollow, hat-shaped fiberglass floors and stringers. Because the Tartan Ten has a relatively flat underbody and fin keel, she is more susceptible to flexing of the bilges than a boat with deeper, more rounded bilges.

In the first 90 boats, the grid was neither stiff enough nor attached to the hull securely enough to prevent flexing. As a result the fiberglass tabbing which holds the grid to the hull began peeling off. On a few boats, small cracks developed in the grid and in the bilges. Tartan claimed that it sent repairmen all around this country to track down and fix every

boat earlier than hull #84. In most cases the repair consisted of removing the old tabbing and re-tabbing with a heavier laminate. In cases where the grid or hull actually showed damage, more substantial repairs were made. According to Britton, "We got every one of them."

The mast step has been strengthened several times during the Tartan Ten's history. The Tartan Ten has a deck-stepped mast, rare in non-trailerable racers, because they offer less control of mast bend. They are no less seaworthy than a keel-stepped mast, provided there is adequate support underneath the mast, such as a compression post or bulkhead in the cabin.

The Tartan Ten's compression post sits on top of the floor grid. After the initial problems with the first 83 boats, a 5"x4"x1/4" aluminum plate was used under the compression post to distribute the load. The thickness of the aluminum plate was later increased to 1/2". Mast step problems still existed to some degree after the first 83 boats. On a hull numbered in the 150s, we observed that the compression post had been moved off the floor grid (presumably because it was crushing it) and lengthened with a threaded extension so it rested directly on the hull.

Unlike most boats, which have shroud chainplates which extend above deck, the Tartan Ten's shrouds pass through the deck to chainplates in the cabin. Although this may reduce windage and genoa chafe, the hole in the deck is difficult to seal. Many owners report chronic deck leaks around the shrouds.

The chainplates are anchored on a heavy fiberglass "tab" which extends up from the topsides inside the main cabin. According to the manufacturer, there were two chainplate tab delaminations in the first 100 boats. Tartan attributes this to the hull being cored under the tab. Tartan didn't take steps to correct the potential problem until nearly 100 boats later. One owner of a 150-series boat reported that he had reglassed one chainplate tab after he noticed the telltale signs of delamination—the color of the tab changing from dark green to white where it is anchored to the hull.

By hull #200 Tartan had eliminated the core under the tab and began anchoring it directly to the outer skin of the hull. This didn't completely solve the problem, according to Britton. Because the section of the topsides around the chainplates was uncored, that section could dimple inward slightly under heavy rig loads, causing isolated incidences of gelcoat blistering and delamination. Tartan corrected this problem shortly afterward—"about hull #270," according to Britton, by widening the chainplate tab from 12" to 18".

Although the Tartan Ten is cored through 80% of her hull, she exhibits a fair amount of structural flexing. As one successful Tartan dealer pointed out, "she's not overbuilt like the rest of the Tartan line." We had several reports of the cockpit flexing noticeably while sailing in rough weather. Part of the reason is that the bulkheads under each side of the cockpit are glassed firmly to the hull, but very poorly attached to the cockpit seats. Also the main bulkhead is well forward of the mast and divided by the forward berth. A bulkhead in two halves located away from the chainplates is not very effective in absorbing rig loads. Instead the hull will flex.

The Tartan Ten's hull-to-deck joint consists of an inward turned hull flange overlapped by the deck and topped by an aluminum toerail. The hull-to-deck joint is bedded with butyl tape, which stays soft and rubber-like for the life of the boat. It has no adhesive properties, but is a good watertight sealant. We have seen it melt and "bleed" out of hull-to-deck joints on occasion.

A strip of aluminum is glassed under the hull flange. This allows Tartan to fasten the hull and deck with bolts, but without nuts, by tapping the bolts through the aluminum insert—a real time saver. The bolts must be bedded, though, or corrosion would compromise the integrity of the joint, especially important since there is no chemical bond to fall back on. Tartan beds the bolts with silicone, which is probably adequate, but a chromate paste would be a better (although more expensive) bedding material.

The hull laminate was strengthened when production was into hulls numbered in the early 100s. A heavier mat was added to improve the bond between the balsa core and the laminate. An extra layer of fiberglass was added to the hull laminate as well.

Rig

The mast of the Tartan Ten is a "safe" section. It bends easily with the backstay, but is sufficiently strong to sail without running backstays in a strong breeze. The shrouds are swept back.

The mast is not anodized. On early boats, it was finished with clear lacquer; later it was painted black. According to Frank Colaneri of Bay Sailing Equipment, who rigged all Tartan Ten masts until the mid-'80s, finishing with lacquer or paint is cheaper than anodizing.

On the first 150 or so boats the jib and spinnaker halyards are both wire and exit the mast above the hounds. They then lead through "bullseye" fairleads which have a tendency to chew the wire. (Colaneri called them "wireeaters.") This system was redesigned so that now the wire jib halyard exits below the mast without a fairlead, and the spinnaker halyard, still exiting above the hounds, was changed to rope.

Schaefer booms were used on the first 70 boats, and bent reefing hooks were a problem. Since then Tartan has used Kenyon booms. The Kenyon booms have no outhaul car, instead relying on clew slugs to support leech tension. According to Colaneri, many booms had to be retrofitted with stainless plates over the sail slot because the clew slugs had pulled through the slot.

Handling Under Power

After hull #309 the Tartan Ten was equipped with an 11 hp Universal diesel. Before then a Farymann 7.5 hp diesel was standard. On boats prior to hull #200, excessive vibration and shaft coupling failures were a problem. According to Britton, the cause was poor shaft alignment. Britton says flexible shaft couplings were used on the first 200 boats, because Tartan was afraid the boat would bend under rig tension. The use of flexible couplings meant less attention was paid to alignment—hence occasional coupling failure and excessive vibration. Solid couplings were used on subsequent boats. "We thought we were bending the boat (by tensioning the rig), but we were wrong. Now we know it's better to concentrate on alignment and use solid shaft couplings," says Britton.

Because vibration could be a problem, when con-

The deck is clean, with all lines leading aft to the cockpit. The cockpit itself is huge—9' long—making life easier for the crew. The deck is nearly flush, limiting interior headroom to only 5'2".

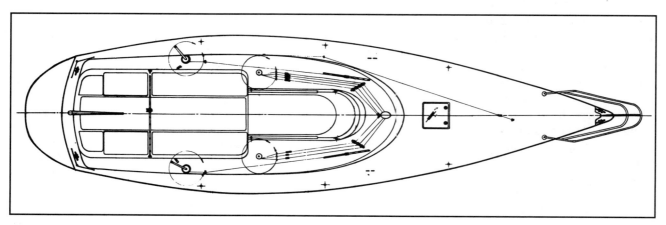

sidering a used Tartan Ten you should check both the engine mounts and the electrical harness on the back of the engine. The covering of any wires attached to the engine should be checked for wear.

Tartan Ten owners report that the Farymann is relatively trouble free, runs well and is easy to hand start should the battery run down. Owners also say it tends to be underpowered. "Doesn't do well into the wind," reported one owner. A folding prop is standard equipment.

Access to the engine is excellent. The fiberglass engine box is light and lifts off easily and, because it also doubles as the companionway step, slides forward without obstruction. The box is easy to refit and latch in place. With the box off, all engine parts are accessible.

Handling Under Sail

Tartan Ten owners rave about performance. She may not be a ULDB, but she's fast for a 33-footer. Typical comments are "Offwind we pass 36' masthead rigs," "rides waves well; good control downwind," and "recorded 15.2 knots, sustained 10.5 knots."

However, owners do not rave about her handicap ratings. The Tartan Ten was not designed to fit any handicapping rule. She carries an astronomical IOR rating of about 28.5. Under PHRF she rates from 123 to 132, depending on the handicapper. Most PHRF fleets assume that you have a 155% genoa, and the most common rating is 126. Some fleets, such as Detroit, allow the Tartan Ten to sail with its one-design inventory (100% jib) at a rating several seconds slower.

Owners report that she will sail to a rating of 126 in light air with a 155% genoa. However, with her narrow beam, she is tender and becomes overpowered quickly. In winds over 12 knots, she has difficulty winning with a rating of 126. Using a one-design inventory, the Tartan Ten will sail to a rating of 132 in medium winds. Although she is always fast downwind, owners say she has a difficult time making up what she loses upwind in a strong breeze.

Those who want to race both one-design and PHRF have several problems. Until 1982 headfoils were illegal for class racing. The class has dropped this rule to encourage Tartan Ten owners to race PHRF. Running backstays are still illegal for class racing. Although they're not necessary to keep the spar in the boat, backstays nonetheless will improve performance slightly without rating penalty. Another, more subtle problem, is that a sailmaker will design the working sails of a class inventory differently than he would for a larger inventory. For example, a 100% jib that must be used for both light and heavy air in one-design racing will be a lot more powerful than a 100% jib for a larger PHRF inventory.

Despite its drawbacks the Tartan Ten still makes for enjoyable PHRF racing because its sailplan is so manageable, the boat is so maneuverable, and its cockpit is so easy to work in. It's hard to believe you're on a 33' when you're racing one; the boat feels much smaller.

As good as PHRF racing can be, one-design racing is even better. Owners report that all boats are extremely well-matched. In this year's 40' national

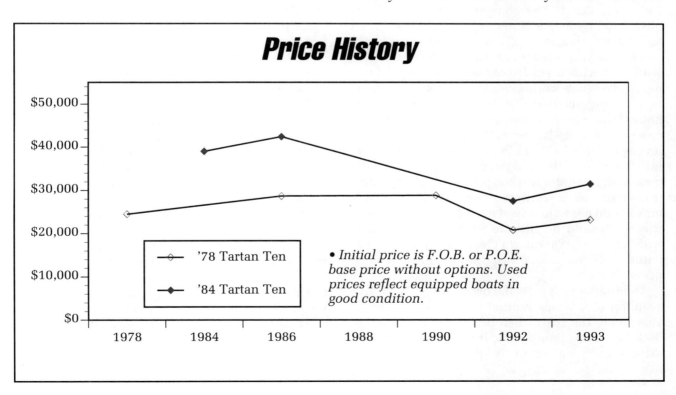

Price History

- ○ '78 Tartan Ten
- ◆ '84 Tartan Ten

• Initial price is F.O.B. or P.O.E. base price without options. Used prices reflect equipped boats in good condition.

championship, the second and third place teams sailed borrowed boats—boats that had not done well in previous regattas. Tartan Ten sailors may push their boats hard, but as a whole they don't push them hard enough to cause major gear failures. We have no doubt that a hot SORC team could rip a Tartan Ten apart, but for its purpose the boat is well suited.

Before each boat leaves the factory, it is placed in an outdoor pool, and 50-100 lbs of lead is glassed to the hull 5' forward of the mast to make her float on her lines. Flotation marks are molded into the hull to insure that the lead is not subsequently moved to change the boat's trim. This helps make the boats equal in performance.

The keels are relatively fair from the factory, although most racers will want to spend a weekend making them smoother.

Most Tartan Tens race with a crew of 5-8. Although she is a light boat, her narrow beam limits the effectiveness of crew weight. Unlike beamier counterparts, such as the J/30, packing on more crew in a strong breeze is not essential. For best performance, the backstay and traveler must be constantly adjusted. Some of the more successful racers routinely barber-haul the jib outboard in strong puffs. As with any light displacement boat, you must be quick on sail trim to keep her level and driving.

Deck Layout

The Tartan Ten is equipped with a tiller, as any boat this small and light should be. With a tiller, though, you need a larger cockpit. The cockpit of the Tartan Ten is 9 1/2' long, which gives the crew plenty of room for racing. The companionway, though, is obstructed by long stainless steel handrails. When tacking, the crew must all pass through the cockpit.

The cockpit seats have short, outward-angled seatbacks with a small coaming. This provides a modicum of day sailing comfort without sacrificing much racing efficiency. The slotted aluminum toerail does, however, compromise racing comfort. The crew could slide farther outboard for more hiking leverage if it weren't for the toerail painfully biting into the backs of their thighs. Owners report that the cockpit drains quickly when pooped by a large wave. It nevertheless is worrisome, because its large volume would hold a lot of water, and its 6" companionway sill would do little to keep that water from rushing below. We wouldn't race it in rough weather without all companionway drop boards locked in place.

The rudder post exits the deck through a cockpit coaming that wraps around the stern. A tiller is attached to the post; when lifted and lashed to the backstay it leaves the cockpit unobstructed for an extraordinary amount of cockpit space at the mooring.

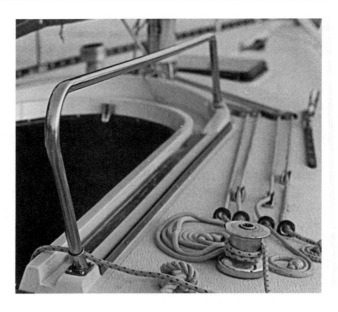

A pair of handrails guard the 5' long companionway opening. Aside from the lifelines, they're the only handholds on deck.

The mast is stepped into a cast aluminum collar on deck. The collar is not hinged. The running rigging exits through the bottom of the mast, then runs through sheaves built into the collar and aft through sheet stoppers to Lewmar 16 winches on each side of the cabin house. Several owners said they had moved or replaced the stoppers made by Delta.

The primary winches are Lewmar 30s. Secondary winches are permitted under class rules, but are not offered as a factory option. Some owners report that larger primary winches are helpful to trim the genoas used for handicap racing. On the boat we sailed, the sheet tracks were backed with strips of aluminum, but the backing plates for the winches were 1/8" plywood.

The deck gelcoat provides good traction, but this also makes it more difficult to clean. Stanchion bases, made for Tartan by High Seas, bolt through the deck and through the toerail. On the boat we examined there were no backing plates on the through-deck stanchion bolts, but bolting through the toerail gives the installation adequate rigidity. Several owners reported that the welded sockets for the stanchions have failed.

The boom vang runs in a single part up from the mast step to the boom, then forward to the gooseneck, down to the deck via a 6:1 purchase, and aft to a winch. At the gooseneck, it attaches to a small welded eye, which could be of heavier gauge.

The backstay is split with a 4:1 purchase deadended on the stem. A crewmember would have to sit aft of the helmsman to play the backstay. The ball bearing traveler spans the cockpit and is easily adjusted with its 3:1 purchase. The 5:1 mainsheet deadends on the traveler car.

Belowdecks

For a 33-footer, there isn't much to the Tartan Ten's interior. Headroom is only 5' 2". However, the companionway hatch is in three pieces and lifts off for stowage below, opening a 5' long "skylight" in the cabin. This feature provides some amount of standing headroom below, without having to sacrifice the clean lines of the deck to a high cabin trunk. Erecting a dodger over the companionway encloses the standing headroom. The hatch cover could be stronger: we nearly cracked it by stepping on it.

There is no icebox in the cabin. A portable cooler stores in one of the two cockpit lazarettes. The standard head is a portable, stowed under the forward V-berth. Nearly every owner we talked to complained of its smell and said that it is difficult to empty. Most had either discarded it for a cedar bucket or installed a full marine head. There is no built-in stove and the chart table is small.

There is a small sink with a hand pump on the port side. On boats prior to hull #200, the water tank was installed under the starboard quarterberth, with the fuel tank under the port quarterberth. With the water tank and sink on opposite sides, all the water in the tank would drain out through the sink on port tack. Tartan's retrofit was a rubber plug for the sink nozzle. By hulls numbered in the early 200s, they had switched the position of the fuel and water tanks, solving the problem.

The interior of the Tartan Ten is dark. The bulkheads, cabinetry and cabin sole are teak-veneered plywood. We would paint the settees white. The forward V-berth is a comfortable 6' long. The "filler," or section of the berth that covers the Porta Potti is removable for access to the head. However, the filler sits on very narrow cleats, so when you climb over it to get out of the berth, the filler frequently falls off its cleats and you tumble onto the head (Ugh!).

Vertical posts from the overhead to both the sink and the nav station make good handrails for moving about below in a seaway. Under both the sink and nav station are small lockers with zippered cloth coverings instead of doors. There is further stowage under the main berths and quarter berths. These stowage bins are not insulated from the hull, but because the boat is cored, condensation should be minimal. The bins are sealed from the shallow sump;

if they weren't sealed, any water in the bilge would predictably soak their contents. One owner commented, "There should have been no attempt to create six berths at the expense of adequate storage."

On the boat we sailed the joinerwork and furniture tabbing were mediocre. The overhead panels were sloppily fitted. The ceiling is covered with a padded vinyl liner. A strip of wood covers the hull-to-deck joint.

There were several major changes to the interior after hull #160. In earlier boats, both the main berths and quarterberths were "root" berths. Root berths are somewhat like pipe berths. They consist of cloth anchored to the side of the hull and slung to a pipe running the length of the berth. The pipe fits into notches so that the angle of the berth can be adjusted to suit the boat's angle of heel. Another piece of cloth attaches with Velcro to the pipe to form a seat back. While the root berth makes for comfortable sleeping underway, it is far less comfortable than a fixed berth to sit in while the boat is anchored.

After hull #160, the root berths in the main cabin were abandoned for fixed berths, with a dual purpose design backrest/leeboard. Additional stowage bins were added over the main berths. A drop leaf table was also added between the main berths. It is doubtful whether it would survive the rough and tumble of hard racing. We suspect most owners remove it for racing.

Conclusions

Like any boat, the Tartan Ten is built to a price for a particular purpose. She is not built as well, nor laid out as lavishly as, say a J/30; but she is also much less expensive. People don't buy Tartan Tens to make long offshore passages, nor do they buy them for extended cruising. People buy them to day race, either as a one-design or under a handicap rule. Maybe they throw in an occasional weekend cruise.

The Tartan Ten is a joy to day race. It is easy to maneuver and crew on, offers lively performance, and is affordable. We think that one-design racing would be far more fun than handicap racing. At least under one-design you are competitive in all wind velocities.

The Tartan Ten class association appears to be well organized, which should help keep the resale value of the boat high. If you live near a Tartan Ten fleet, you should give offshore one-design racing a try. But beware; you might get hooked. **• PS**

Ranger 33

This boat would be a pretty good choice for either an entry-level club racer or a coastal cruiser.

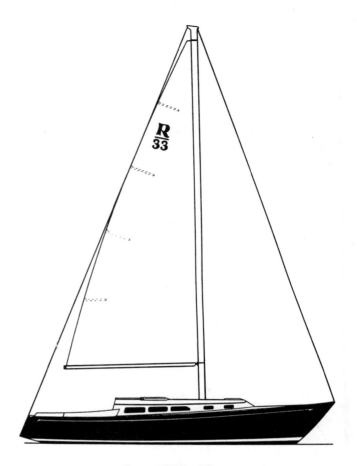

The Ranger Yacht division of Jensen Marine was created in 1969 to build performance-oriented boats designed by Gary Mull. Jensen's Cal division had been successful with both racer/cruisers (Cal 34 and Cal 40) and pure cruisers (Cal 46), but the Ranger line was racier, with consistent styling and appearance throughout the series.

Ranger stopped building the 33 in 1978, after 464 boats had been turned out. Many minor changes were made over the years of production, and boats built after 1974 are generally more desirable, with restyled interiors and a diesel engine option.

Bangor Punta was an early boatbuilding conglomerate, and included Cal, O'Day, and Ranger sailboats, plus several powerboat building companies. Several changes of ownership later, the three sailboat companies gradually sank in a sea of red ink, with O'Day and Cal finally succumbing in the spring of 1989, several years after Ranger bit the dust.

With a subtle but attractive sheerline, low cabin trunk, and reverse transom, the Ranger 33 was very modern in appearance in 1969. The styling looks very traditional compared to late-1980s Eurostyling, however.

Underwater, the boat has a moderate aspect ratio fin keel, flattish run without the distorted buttock lines typical of IOR boats, and a semi-balanced spade rudder. The keel would look perfectly at home on a modern racer/cruiser, since it has a vertical trailing edge and a sloping leading edge. Radical keel shapes were as common around 1970 as they are today. The Ranger 33's fin keel, on the other hand, is conservative and reasonably efficient.

Sailing Performance

The original sales brochure produced for the Ranger 33 defines the boat as a "high performance racing

Specifications

LOA	33' 2"
LWL	26' 3"
Beam	9' 7"
Draft	5' 0"
Displacement	10,500 lbs.
Ballast	4,500 lbs.
Sail area	529 sq. ft.

design by Gary Mull," and that's a reasonable summary of the boat's performance compared to her contemporaries. The 33's PHRF (Performance Handicap Racing Fleet) rating of about 153 looks pretty sporty when you put the boat up against other boats that were in production in the early to mid 1970s: the Cal 34 rates 174; the Pearson 33, 174; the Columbia 34-2, 170.

Since the Ranger 33's production spanned such a long period, however, there were a lot of other boats of about the same size with similar ratings by the late years of her manufacture. Mid-70s IOR-derived racer/cruisers were beamier, roomier, stiffer, and frequently faster than the Ranger 33, which was designed in the last years of the CCA (Cruising Club of America) rule. The Ranger 33 had a poor IOR (International Off-

Owners' Comments

"The boat is excellent in light air, which is an important quality in Long Island Sound. Typical of light-displacement fin-keel boats, she needs to have sail shortened intelligently. Any light boat needs a small jib for heavy weather.

"She is well-balanced—one of the finest fin-keel spade-rudder boats I've ever sailed.

"The boat is well built for a regular production boat: decidedly above average. The surveyor was surprised to find floors under the cabin sole. There are no deck leaks.

"Look for a boat with a diesel larger than 15 hp. Wheel steering is also nice. Some boats have stoves with ovens. I prefer a cook top only, to get some extra storage space."

—1976 model in Long Island Sound

"Watch for leaks in the toerail, and loose bulkheads. Gary Mull, the designer, was very helpful in solving the bulkhead problem.

"This is a good, fast cruising boat which has the space of a modern 30' boat. It has better construction than many new boats, and I would recommend it."

—1969 model in New England

"There are a lot of Ranger 33s in really bad shape out there now.

"Watch out for bulkheads coming apart, leaky hull-to-deck joint, loose steering. I've taken every inch of my boat apart, and rebuilt it. It now has a beautiful custom interior. The original gelcoat is still going strong.

"The boat has too much weather helm in a blow. Mine has a rudder with a modified skeg, so it doesn't turn as well as it used to."

—1970 model in CA

"The Ranger 33 is a delightful boat for our use: cruising the Chesapeake with two of us.

"It performs well enough to win most of our informal races, and the speed gives us a wider cruising range.

"The boat moves well, and points higher than similar-sized boats.

"The interior living space is comfortable. Small fuel and water tanks make us conservative with water and engine use. This is only a problem on long cruises.

"Looseness in the rudder tube was corrected with Teflon shims and lubricant. The only other problem has been poor water drainage under the floor pan."

—1973 model in the Chesapeake

"I bought the boat for its seaworthiness and sailing qualities. She is very fast, and is structurally very sound. She is stiff, with a good solid feel. I like the sandwich construction for hull and deck, and the through-bolted aluminum toerail.

"The only structural defect has been the stern rail, which had to be re-welded.

"The Ranger 33 is not radical in its design, materials, or construction. It is very seaworthy. Its ability to sail close to the wind is an excellent quality, particularly to get off a lee shore. I feel very safe sailing the boat, and it is very reasonable for two or three people to handle."

—1976 model in the Chesapeake

"The boat is strong, but bendy. Headstay sag seems excessive, and I can't take it out with backstay adjustment.

"The rudder rattles due to excessive wear in the fiberglass rudder tube. I fixed it by wrapping pieces of plastic milk bottle around the rudder shaft.

"I bought the boat because it was the most boat for the money, it was of generally good quality, and is a very good sailer. It was in rather tatty condition when I got it, but I've made a number of improvements.

"The boat's a bit tender; you learn to reef early. Then, it's no problem. The boat moves well if not overpowered.

"Maneuverability under power is excellent, but prop wash against the rudder can take the tiller out of your hands if you put it over more than 10° at high speed."

—1971 model in NY

shore Rule) rating, particularly compared to more modern fully-developed IOR-based production boats.

Owners report that the boat has one negative sailing characteristic: a tendency to rapidly develop weather helm as she heels. The normal, rational remedy is to reduce sail.

As a rule, relatively flat-bottom boats such as the Ranger 33 like to be sailed on their feet. Narrow beam gives the boat somewhat lower initial stability than many dual-purpose boats built today, despite the 40% ballast/displacement ratio. A modern mainsail reefing system would make it possible to reduce sail area quickly, but you'll find old-fashioned roller reefing on most Ranger 33s.

Like most boats of this size built in the early '70s, the Ranger 33 was originally fitted with a tiller. The tiller certainly provides adequate power to steer the boat, particularly since the rudder area is semi-balanced. In fact, the rudder may be a little too balanced. Owners report that if you put the rudder hard over, the tiller can just about knock you down as the water flow begins to act on the forward section of the rudder.

Many later boats are equipped with wheel steering, and a lot of earlier boats have no doubt been retrofitted with wheels. In any retrofit installation, you should carefully survey the workmanship. Look particularly for signs of strain, such as gelcoat crazing around the pedestal base or tabbing failure around sheave mounting blocks. Examining for cable wear and proper tensioning would be a normal part of a survey on any boat with this type of steering gear.

Check the condition of the tiller itself. One owner reported having to replace two tillers, which delaminated.

In tiller-steered boats, the helmsman's position is somewhat awkward for shorthanded sailing, particularly on boats with end-of-boom sheeting. The helmsman sits at the forward end of the cockpit, ahead of both the jib sheet winches and the mainsheet.

One criticism several owners voiced about the rig is that the main boom is not strong enough. With end-of-boom sheeting, a good vang is required to flatten the sail, but you could fold the boom in the middle with a lot of vang tension in heavy air.

The Ranger 33 is definitely a performance boat. This certainly does not preclude its use as a coastal cruiser, nor does it mean the boat is hard to sail. It's a good, fast boat, which, if updated with modern sails and sailhandling equipment, could still be a formidable PHRF club racer.

Construction

By today's standards, the Ranger 33 is not an extremely light-displacement boat. She was fairly light for her day—remember that most boats still had long keels and attached rudders in 1970—but not exceptionally so. Her Cal 34 stablemate, for example, was 1,000 pounds lighter on the same waterline length.

The Ranger 33 makes extensive use of modular fiberglass moldings, including a deck liner and extensive interior furniture moldings. The original interior was almost completely molded fiberglass with teak trim. Late in the production run, the interior was restyled somewhat to provide a more woody look, which was the rage by the mid 1970s.

Extensive hull and deck liners can make alterations or repairs to wiring and plumbing difficult, as these systems are frequently installed behind molded components. Some of the wiring in the Ranger 33 is inaccessible.

Several owners report that the support system for the deck-stepped mast is not strong enough. Mast compression is borne by a wood column which is attached to the main bulkhead. The main bulkhead also carries the upper shroud loads via strap-type chainplates.

This bulkhead was designed to be glassed to both hull and deck, but one owner told us that the bulkhead in his boat was only glassed to the hull—the overhead glassing had been omitted. The bulkhead had come partially adrift, allowing the boat to wrack in this heavily-loaded area.

Another owner reported measurable deck deflection around the mast step on top of the cabin. This could be the result of inadequate filling between the deck and the overhead liner in the way of the mast support column, or may mean a partially detached main bulkhead.

A deck-stepped mast requires not only good engineering, but careful quality control in construction to make sure the designer's intentions are fulfilled. Since several owners report problems in this area on the Ranger 33, a very careful survey of the mast support structure is called for. Stress cracks around the mast step, joinerwork around the bulkhead that doesn't quite line up properly, and inability to keep proper headstay tension are symptoms that may indicate a problem.

You should also pay attention to the aft lower chainplate anchorages, which simply bolt through the deck.

Originally, the Ranger 33 had teak toerails. Later models use a perforated aluminum toerail, which is certainly less maintenance. Some owners report small leaks along the hull-to-deck joint, as well as around the chainplates.

There are no bearings supporting the rudder stock on early boats, and this can eventually result in slop in the rudder as the rudder tube wears. One owner installed Teflon shims between the stock and rudder tube, which both eliminates play and reduces friction. Excessive wear will show up in the form of a rudder stock that clunks around in the rudder tube. You can check this with the boat out of the water by grasping the rudder and trying to move it from side to side. In the water, the wear shows up as a spongy feel in the steering, or in extreme cases as a clunk when the boat is tacked.

Tankage for both fuel and water is minimal: 20 gallons of each. For more than weekend cruising, you'll need to increase at least the water capacity.

A gasoline Atomic 4 was the standard engine. A 16 hp Universal diesel was optional from 1975 onward. Either engine is adequate power for the boat. Engine access for either engine is only fair, despite the fact that the engine box sticks well into the main cabin.

Be careful handling a tiller-steered Ranger 33 under power. Prop wash past the rudder can cause the tiller to crash over if you try to apply a lot of helm.

Most complaints about the Ranger 33's construction are age-related. Serious concerns are the main bulkhead/mast support system, and rudder tube wear. Both of these problems should show up on any reasonably careful survey, and may not be cause for rejecting the boat if you feel confident in your ability to analyze the problem and make repairs. Obviously, the price of the boat should reflect the amount of work necessary to correct serious flaws.

Interior

With only 9' 7" of beam, there's not a lot of hull volume in the Ranger 33. By comparison, the current Pearson 33—a typical more modern cruiser/racer—is 11' wide. Somehow, that extra foot and a half of beam translates into a lot more interior space.

The Ranger 33 has a decent interior layout, but the proportions seem slightly miniaturized to fit in all the pieces, particularly in the galley and nav station. At the same time, at least there is a nav station; in 1970, the navigator usually used the icebox top.

The forward cabin has the usual V-berths, wide at the head and narrow at the foot. A fiberglass hatch overhead provides fair-weather ventilation, but that's about it for fresh air. Headroom is just over 6' in the forward cabin.

A small head compartment is just aft of the forward cabin, offset to port. A dogleg in the bulkhead between the head and cabin renders the toilet a fairly tight fit. There is some storage space under the head sink, with a shelf above. Headroom is 6'.

On the port side of the main cabin is a U-shaped dinette, which can be converted to a double berth. Ranger's advertising optimistically lists the dinette and settee opposite as seating eight people. That means squeezing five people into the dinette. We wouldn't want to be one of them.

Realistically, three would be perfectly comfortable eating dinner, four would fit but would have little room for their plates. For more than four, you'll need to limit your entertaining to cocktails and conversation, as the table is not expandable. If you'd like to feed more, you could devise a drop leaf for the passageway side of the table.

There's 6' 2" of headroom on centerline in the main cabin. Headroom is fairly constant throughout the boat, as the top of the cabin is parallel to the cabin sole. In profile, the cabin top appears to slope downward further forward, but this illusion is the result of the rising sheerline forward. Gary Mull draws some very nice boats, and the 33 is one of them.

As designed, there is no ventilation in the main cabin, except for the main companionway. A large flat space atop the deckhouse just abaft the mast cries out for a modern, aluminum-framed deck hatch. Since there's no molded boss for a hatch, you should build up a teak hatch coaming for mounting the hatch, rather than just bolting it to the deck. This raises the hatch slightly, perhaps keeping the interior drier, and it stiffens the deck in the way of the hatch cutout.

Main cabin storage is somewhat limited, with

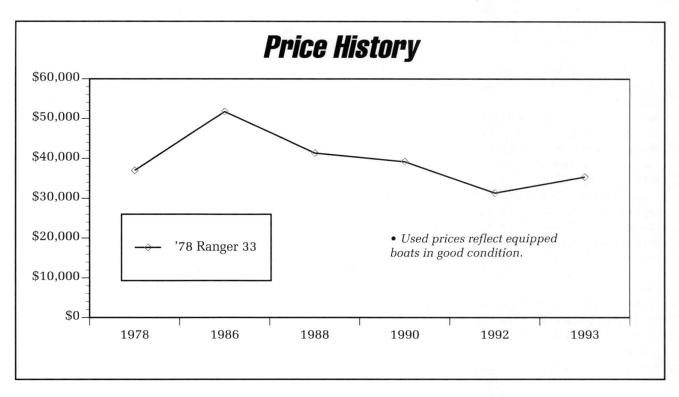

Used prices reflect equipped boats in good condition.

shelves outboard of the settee and dinette, bulk storage beneath.

The galley and nav station are at the aft end of the main cabin. The port-side galley has room for a two- or three-burner stove with oven. Unless an owner has retrofitted with propane, it will be an alcohol stove. In our opinion, pressurized alcohol stoves should be consigned to the nearest dumpster at the first opportunity.

An icebox is built in under the counter just aft of the stove. It's a long reach to the bottom of the box for a short person, and a potentially hazardous one if the stove is fired up while you're trying to get things out of the box. A single sink is mounted in the galley counter at its inboard end.

Aside from a locker under the sink and a shelf behind the stove, there is virtually no storage space in the galley. Instead, racks for plates and utensils are built into the shelf outboard of the dinette, forward of the partial bulkhead separating the galley from the rest of the main cabin.

If you're only going to store plates, glassware, and flatware in these main cabin racks, they will be fairly convenient to use. If you have to get access to them while you're cooking, it will be a nuisance, particularly if there are guests seated in the dinette. With a long stretch, you can reach over the stove to the main cabin racks, but we wouldn't recommend it when the stove is in use.

A hand-operated fresh water pump supplies water to the sink. If you don't want to add pressure water, replace the hand pump with a foot-operated Whale pump. You'll be surprised at how much easier it is to rinse dishes when you can use both hands.

Opposite the galley is a nav station, which uses the head of the quarterberth as a seat. The chart table is small, but is large enough to take a chart book such as the Chart Kit. You'll have to use your imagination to figure out how to mount navigation instruments, since there are no suitable shelves. It would be possible to attach bracket-mounted items such as a VHF radio to the underside of the deck, using stainless steel self-tappers into the plywood core. Obviously, these screws must not penetrate to the upper skin of the deck.

Sitting at the chart table is awkward. The flat of the cabin sole ends at the inboard edge of the nav station, and the side of the hull rises sharply in the footwell, making it difficult to sit facing the chart table. Instead, you'll probably sit at an angle, with your legs canted toward the center of the boat. It's somewhat awkward, but it could be a lot worse. The quarterberth itself is roomy and comfortable. If it hasn't already been done, you can install an opening port in the side of the cockpit well next to the quarterberth.

The interior of the Ranger 33 is quite livable for two people, and even for four for short cruises. The primary drawbacks are mediocre ventilation and lack of usable storage space, both of which can be improved by the owner.

While the layout is good, it is somewhat cramped due to the narrow beam of the boat. The same arrangement in a boat a foot wider would seem remarkably more roomy.

Conclusions

The boats in the Ranger line were designed to be more powerful and faster than their Cal sisters. Many of these boats have been raced, and raced hard. A careful survey will be required to see if the boat is in reasonable condition.

According to our owners' reports, the Ranger 33 has an average history of hull blistering. There are no indications of particular model years to avoid.

In November, 1969, the base price of the Ranger 33 was about $18,000. This did not include some pretty basic items: lifelines and pulpits, bilge pump, stove, anodized spars. You even had to pay extra if you wanted fabric-covered cushions rather than vinyl!

You're likely to find big variations in sailhandling equipment on Ranger 33s. On boats that are still actively raced, you may well find state-of-the-art gear: ball-bearing travelers, self-tailing winches, the whole nine yards. On a boat that was never raced, or has not been raced in years, you may well find the type of gear that was on boats 20 years ago—dreadfully old-fashioned and inefficient.

Some Ranger 33s have been cruised extensively. We know of one which made a Pacific circumnavigation. Boats that have been used for cruising may well have added amenities such as hot and cold water, shower, and gas cooking—all of which are near-necessities to move cruising beyond the camping-out stage.

The rather paltry standard equipment list means that boats will be equipped very differently. This complicates a purchase decision, because you have to factor in the quality and age of retrofitted equipment, as well as competence of the installation itself. Even if you have a lot of experience in systems maintenance, you should specifically request that your surveyor pay particular attention to creature comforts that have been added over the years.

The Ranger 33 would still be a pretty good choice for an entry-level club racer. A boat that has been raced is probably not encumbered with a lot of fancy, heavy goodies, yet it is likely to have the same rating as a "cruiser" version.

This would also be a pretty good coastal cruiser for a couple, although tankage, storage, and other amenities would need augmentation. You'll have to do some comparison shopping, particularly in today's market, when late-model used boats may sell for little more than tired, much older designs. • **PS**

Cal 34

An older Cal 34 can be a good entry-level cruiser for the handyman, but we like the later interior.

Bill Lapworth didn't invent light-displacement cruiser-racers, but his name is indelibly linked with the type. At 15,000 pounds of displacement on a 30' waterline, the Cal 40 is still a fairly light boat, especially considering the low-tech materials and techniques available when she was introduced. Lapworth designed a number of smaller sisters to the Cal 40 in the late 1960's, all looking as alike as peas in a pod.

If imitation is the sincerest form of flattery, then Lapworth should have been very flattered at the interest his Cal designs generated, for Frank Butler, now owner of Catalina, designed several successful boats for Coronado that were remarkably similar to Lapworth's Cals.

Perhaps the most successful of the little sisters to the Cal 40 was the Cal 34. The Cal 34 was in production off and on, and in various configurations, from 1966 until 1979.

Although the hull form of the Cal 34 remained basically unchanged during its production life, enough changes were made in the rig, deck molding, and interior for the boat to have three model designations: Cal 34, Cal 2-34, and Cal 3-34.

Specifications

LOA	33' 3"
LWL	26' 0"
Beam	10' 0"
Draft	5' 10"
Displacement	9,500 lbs.
Ballast	3,750 lbs.
Sail area	515 sq. ft.

Sailing Performance

The Cal 34 was conceived as a true racer-cruiser, and early promotional literature stressed her racing performance. The original rig was a low aspect ratio masthead sloop. With a foot length of 14' and a hoist of 33.5', the mainsail was of typical late CCA (Cruising Club of America) Rule proportions. The long boom of the original short rig overhangs the cockpit awkwardly, with the mainsheet traveler just forward of the aft end of the cockpit. According to owners, this makes access to the cockpit lockers a nuisance, as well as squandering cockpit space. The tiller occupies the entire forward half of the cockpit, so that the helmsman sits just aft of the deckhouse, while the sail trimmers sit further aft.

The rig on the 2-34 and the 3-34 is just over 2' taller and the boom 3' shorter than the original. These dimensions give the rig much more modern proportions, reducing the size of the mainsail by 40 square feet and increasing the aspect ratio of the main from about 2.5:1 to 3.25:1. With the taller rig, the typical PHRF rating of the boat is six seconds per mile faster.

Most Cal 34 owners we surveyed consider the boat to be about the same speed as similar boats upwind, and somewhat faster downwind. This assessment jibes with the performance of most Lapworth designs, which are at their best off the wind. The boat's PHRF rating, however, suggests that, on the whole,

Owners' Comments

"Each boat show we find it's hard to equal her main cabin, foc's'le, and cockpit layout."
—1968 boat in New York

"As a 'production boat' it needed some customizing to be of maximum use."
—1977 boat in Washington

"Was in aproximately 30' seas of Cape Hatteras last year; performed extremely well."
—1969 boat in Connecticut

"Good all around value as a roomy, comfortable coastal cruiser which is still capable of winning races in some conditions."
—1968 boat in New York

"Competitive when new but now outclassed. Cut 2' off foot of main, and the boat balances much better."
—1968 boat in Texas

"Gelcoat is chipping on deck and trim is beginning to come unglued. Regluing fabric hull liner is becoming necessary."
—1977 boat in Tennessee

"We were dismasted when a backstay turnbuckle broke. Wooden trim below was poorly done in certain areas, such as around the hatches."
—1970 boat in Wahington

"Rig is very out of date but can be modernized at high cost. Deep bilge is impossible to get at."
—1966 boat in New Jersey

---

the boat is actually slower than more modern designs of the same size. The C&C 34, for example, is rated about 25 seconds per mile faster than the Cal 3-34.

According to owners, it takes a good breeze to get the Cal 34 moving. With her large, trapezoidal fin keel, the Cal 34 simply has a lot more wetted surface than more modern fin keel boats, although substantially less wetted surface than a full keel design.

Many owners of the original Cal 34 have shortened the foot of the mainsail to improve the boat's balance. The taller-rigged boats have inherently better balance, since the center of effort of the entire sail plan is further forward. Boats with the short rig and a shortened mainsail foot are likely to be underpowered in light air.

One advantage of the shorter boom is to get rid of the traveler at the aft end of the cockpit. Instead, the traveler is mounted on the bridgedeck, or over the main companionway. While this location would be awkward for racing a tiller-steered boat, it's good for cruising, since the helmsman could handle the mainsheet as well as the tiller.

One of the most commonly-seen modifications to earlier boats is the installation of wheel steering. This requires relocating the mainsheet on the longer-boom boats, but it frees up the space in the cockpit dramatically. The Cal 34 really has a large cockpit, but the tiller and original mainsheet arrangement wasted a huge amount of space. Wheel steering is standard in the 3-34 version of the boat, built in 1976 and later.

Construction

The Cal 34 has a relatively unsophisticated, hand laid-up hull. Owners consider the boat to be above average in strength of hull, deck, and rig. A number of owners report that the main bulkhead tends to delaminate due to leaking chainplates. Since this is potentially a serious structural problem, any Cal 34 should be carefully surveyed for signs of leakage in this area. Be particularly cautious about any boat in which the main bulkhead has been painted out, rather than left varnished: look carefully for water stains around the chainplates.

Other areas to check are the deck around the mast step, and the fiberglass keel molding. Internally-ballasted boats such as the Cal 34 frequently suffer damage on the toe of the keel when running aground. The keel molding should not ring hollow when tapped with a mallet, which would indicate a loose ballast casting—a sign that the boat has been run aground hard.

Older Cal boats are not heavily built: their light displacement precludes excess material. Furniture and bulkhead tabbing are relatively light, notoriously so in the old Cal 40. The saying about the Cal 40 is that when the berths pop loose in the forward cabin, it's time to reduce sail.

Despite fairly light construction, we know of several Cal 34s that have done impressive ocean voyaging. We wouldn't consider a boat of this age and construction suitable for ocean cruising without a careful survey of all structural components. Light-displacement hulls such as that of the Cal 34 get a lot of stiffness from the bonding of furniture to the hull. Keeping it in place is important.

One problem area is the chainplates. Several owners report chainplate failure due to metal fatigue, and one owner found several other partially broken chainplates when he replaced on that had broken.

On the whole, however, the Cal 34 is relatively free of structural defects that would be the result of poor workmanship or choice of materials. The faults you find are more commonly a function of the age of the individual boat. For example, some owners report sloppy rudders due to wear of the fiberglass tube which serves as stuffing box and bearing for the rudder stock—a common aging problem with this type of rudder installation.

Pay particular attention to the condition of the gelcoat, particularly the deck gelcoat. Crazing is very common. Unless it has been painted, the distinctive blue Cal sheerstrake is likely to be badly faded in older boats.

In the late 60's and early 70's, many West Coast boats, including Cals, were notorious for mediocre systems installations, particularly wiring and plumbing. If an older Cal 34 has had a lot of electronics added, there's a good chance that the wiring has been pigtailed onto existing circuits, a poor practice. Older Cal 34s also had gate valves rather than seacocks on through hull fittings. These should be replaced.

Other minor weak points include the lack of backing plates on stanchions, which can cause localized crazing of the deck, and leaking aluminum-framed main cabin ports.

Owners recommend putting in larger cockpit scuppers. The big cockpit can hold a lot of water, and the two small stock scuppers are inadequate.

Interior

There have been two interior layouts in the boat. The original Cal 34 and the 2-34 have two quarterberths aft, with the galley to starboard and a dinette to port in the main cabin. The later Cal 3-34s have a more modern conventional layout, with galley aft to port, quarterberth and chart table to starboard. The saloon of the last version has a settee to starboard, dinette to port. Both layouts have V-berths in the forward cabin with the head between the main cabin and forward cabin. Head layout is different in the two models.

On the whole, we think the later layout is superior, although the galley is actually larger in the original version. On older boats, most owners use the dining table for chart work, although it would be quite easy to design a slide-away chart table to fit over the head of one of the quarterberths.

The interior finish of the boats changed a lot over the years. The original Cal 34 had a varnished mahogany plywood interior with varnished mahogany trim. Later boats went to the oiled teak cave look of the 1970s.

There is no doubt that the original interior is lighter and brighter than the later teak interior. However, a varnished mahogany interior requires more upkeep than an oiled teak interior, and is harder to restore to good condition if it has been allowed to deteriorate. Mahogany blackens when exposed to salt water, while teak merely bleaches out and can be reclaimed with a little sanding.

There's a lot more in the way of creature comforts in the 3-34, in keeping with the growing view that cruising should be more than an expensive form of camping out. Water capacity was increased from the marginal 26 gallons of the early boats to a more serviceable 60 gallons, hot and cold pressure water were standard, and a shower was installed.

The interior is a good selling point in any of the three models. For its length overall, the Cal 34—which is really just over 33' long—has a lot of interior volume. Headroom on centerline in the main cabin is 6' 2". The boat easily has as much interior space as older boats 3' or more longer.

Engine

Like most boats built in the late '60s, the Cal 34 was originally powered by the Atomic Four gas engine. The engine is located under the cockpit, but is reasonably accessible from either of the quarterberths.

The original interior was somewhat unusual in that it gave over space usually reserved for a settee to the galley, which occupies the starboard side of the main cabin. Later arrangements were more conventional.

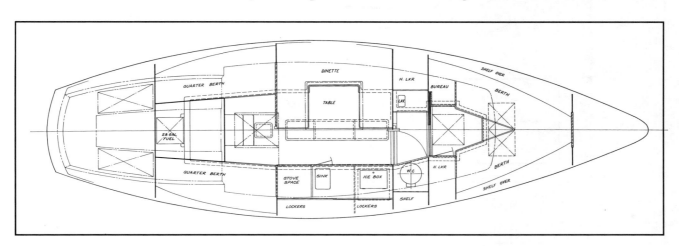

The propeller is driven through a V-drive, and some owners report problems with this unit. A thorough mechanical survey is a must when buying a Cal 34.

In the mid-'70s, diesel engines made their appearance in the boat. A variety of diesels have been installed, including Farymann, 25 and 30 horsepower Westerbekes, and the Perkins 4-91. We would not buy a boat with a Farymann diesel, since parts are difficult or impossible to find. Oddly enough, the most desirable engine for the boat may be the old Atomic 4, which many owners report to be still running strong at 15 years of age or more. Parts are readily available, and are likely to be for some time to come. You could also consider replacing the Atomic Four with one of the Universal diesels designed as a drop-in replacement for the engine.

One disadvantage of the new version of the interior is that engine accessibility has been sacrificed. Owners consider access fair to poor in the aft galley interior, fair to good in the double quarterberth version

One oddity is that many owners report that the boat pulls strongly to starboard under power, requiring a lot of helm for correction, while another owner reports that the boat pulls strongly to port with the same engine!

Buying a Used Boat

Early models of the Cal 34 are well over two decades old today. A lot of changes have occurred in the industry in those 25 years, as well as in the expectations we have for medium-sized cruising boats. Certainly a lot of features of the later Cal 34s—the more efficient rig, better sail handling layout, wheel steering, anchor locker, diesel engine, bigger water capacity and other creature comforts, and more useful interior layout—make them more desirable for most uses. Of course, the price of newer boats reflects the improvements.

An older Cal 34 would be a good choice as an entry-level, medium-sized family cruising boat. A lot of the gear on older models will be painfully obsolete. The rigging, sails, and electronics are likely to be old. Unless the boat has been unusually well maintained, the wood cockpit coamings may need replacing, the hull is likely to need painting, and the deck gelcoat will be crazed.

Blistering has been a relatively minor problem with older Cals, but the hull should obviously be carefully surveyed for high moisture content.

The base price of the Cal 34 in 1969 was $16,800. This was for a stripped boat—the base price didn't even include lifelines and stanchions.

The next year the base price climbed to $19,277, and it continued to escalate throughout the boat's production history.

There's a good chance that an older Cal 34 will give you all the oportunities your heart could ever desire to learn to tinker with fiberglass repairs and the upgrading of systems.

If you're willing to do this type of stuff yourself, a 20-year-old performance cruiser that you can buy in today's market for $20,000 or so may be a lot of boat for the money. If you want a lower-maintenance boat, stick to a late model Cal 34—but be prepared to pay significantly more.   **• PS**

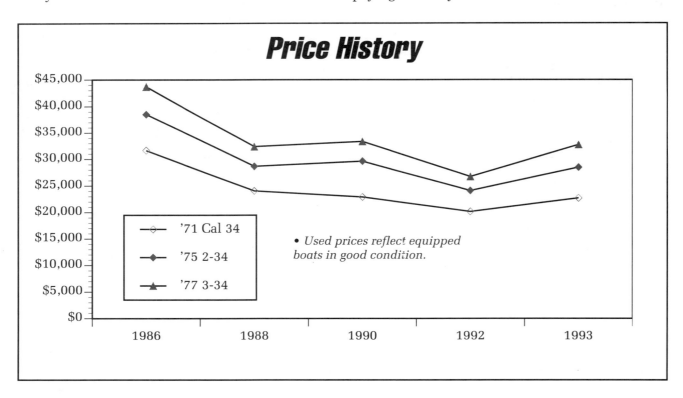

Price History

'71 Cal 34
'75 2-34
'77 3-34

• *Used prices reflect equipped boats in good condition.*

Tartan 33

The Tartan 33 is a good choice in a fairly fast, high quality, late model cruiser-racer.

By the late 1970s, the old Tartan 34 had become very dated. The boat had been in production for a decade, and hundreds of families had cut their racing and cruising teeth on the S&S keel/centerboarder. But the market was changing. Boats were faster and lighter, keels and rigs more efficient, interiors roomier and more functional.

In 1978, Tartan brought out the Tartan Ten, a 33', fairly light, fractionally-rigged "offshore one design." The boat was a huge success: fast, easy to sail, and unencumbered by the design limitations of a rating rule.

But the Tartan Ten had one big problem: limited accommodations with stooping headroom, an interior most kindly described as spartan. A hardy crew could take the Tartan Ten on a multi-day race such as the Mackinac, and you might even coax your family aboard for a weekend of camping out. But cruising or extended racing in comfort? Forget it!

If, however, you could combine the size and performance of the Tartan Ten with a boat having decent accommodations, you had a good shot at a winning combination, particularly in a time when interest in sailing was growing at an astounding rate. As a bonus, the venerable Tartan 34 could be retired with the dignity she deserved.

The answer to all these prayers was the Tartan 33.

Introduced as a 1979 model, the Tartan 33 bore a strong resemblance to the Tartan Ten, with a big fractional rig, flattish sheer, and wide stern. But unlike the Tartan Ten, the new 33 had good accommodations.

The Tartan 33 was a moderate success, with about 220 boats built over a five-year period. The fractional rig, touted as being easier to handle due to smaller headsails, may have turned off some customers who associated that type of rig with high performance

Specifications

LOA	33' 8"
LWL	28' 10"
Beam	10' 11"
Draft	4' 5"
Displacement	10,000 lbs.
Ballast	4,400 lbs.
Sail area	531 sq. ft.

boats such as J/24s and 12 meters. The slotted aluminum toerail of the 33 was more reminiscent of Tartan's racing boats, such as the 41 and the Ten, than it was of a high-quality cruiser/racer.

In 1984, the Tartan 33 went out of production. In its place came the "new" Tartan 34, a boat that could directly cash in on the reputation of the famous old Tartan 34. Interestingly, the new Tartan 34 is the Tartan 33, with the stern drawn out 9" to a more pleasing termination, the interior redesigned to the demands of today's market, and the 33's fractional rig replaced by the masthead rig of the Tartan 33R.

Compared to the Tartan 33, the new 34 is more finely finished, with teak toerails and nicer interior detailing.

When first introduced, the Tartan 33 had a base

Owners' Comments

"The boat is tender, lively, solid, and fun to sail. We got oversize self-tailing winches, and the longer we own the boat, the more convinced we are of this choice. The fractional rig and good cockpit layout allow my wife and me to handle the boat in safety and comfort in high winds and heavy seas.

"The Scheel keel offers shallow draft with good stability, but performance is a little poor close hauled in slop and light air."

—1980 model in Columbus, OH

"I added a propane stove, larger winches, electric refrigeration, an electric anchor windlass, and larger batteries. I also led the halyards back to the cockpit. I bought the boat for ease of singlehanding (I'm a 5' tall, lightweight female).

"I live aboard for much of the summer. The interior is a palace for one, fine for two, a bit tight for three, but in a pinch, okay for four.

"Tartans are not for tightwads. Be prepared to write fat checks. But the boats maintain their value. I got an excellent deal on insurance because I have a Tartan."

—1980 model in Lexington, MA

"The boat is strong and extremely seaworthy. Poor upwind performance is my greatest frustration. The huge main means that I must reef early. The boat is perfectly balanced with a working jib and a full main, but this isn't exactly optimum for racing."

"Warranty claims included minor flaws in the gelcoat, which Tartan repaired shortly after delivery. My major claim was for fire damage in the engine starter, solenoid, and ignition system, which was eventually honored by the engine manufacturer.

"Once the dealer got my money, he forgot about me, and I started dealing directly with Tartan. It was the only way I could get any satisfaction. A great designer (S&S) and a good builder equal strength and quality."

—1981 model in Stamford, CT

"With a fractional rig and Scheel keel, she cannot point as well as comparable masthead boats, but the large main gives an off-wind advantage. Since Tartan came out with the 33R with masthead rig and fin keel, I assume that the upwind performance of my boat did not appeal to some racers.

"The lower lifelines interfered with the winch handles on the original Lewmar 40s. I eventually put on Lewmar 44 self-tailers, which are taller and allow the handles to swing between the lifelines.

"Construction is excellent for a production boat. The interior is not as plush as some cruising boats, but it is very utilitarian. For a cruising boat with good racing potential, my boat is fine. It's my aim to make the boat I have more competitive, not to look for greener pastures with another boat."

—1980 model in W. Bloomfield, MI

price of just over $46,000. By the time production ceased, the base price had increased to $66,000. Remember, those were the years of double-digit inflation.

Sailing Performance

As originally configured—Scheel keel and fractional rig—performance of the Tartan 33 might be a little disappointing for someone coming from a Tartan Ten, but is certainly on a par with most other boats of the same size, type, and vintage. In absolute terms the Tartan 33 is spritely, but not stunning, with a PHRF rating of about 160. By comparison, the old C&C 34—a good all-around cruiser/racer from the same period—rates 144, 16 seconds per mile faster. The C&C 34 and Tartan 33 are almost identical in length, sail area, and displacement.

In lighter winds, the fractionally-rigged Tartan 33 is at its biggest disadvantage, particularly off the wind. The big mainsail allows you to sail fairly low, but you go pretty slow. By comparison, a boat with a big masthead spinnaker will be sailing a little higher and quite a bit faster for optimum off-wind VMG in the same conditions.

IMS (International Measurement System) velocity predictions show that the Scheel keel Tartan 33 must in general be sailed a little lower and flatter than a comparable fin keel boat, although the 33's righting moment is very similar to that of a fin keel boat of the same size and type, as is her range of positive stability.

The Tartan 33 was not designed to any rating rule, but a number have been rated under the IMS. In some areas, there are enough of the boats to allow them to sail together as a one-design class, but the boat is not fast enough in absolute terms to stir the blood of most sailors interested in one-design racing. In addition, Tartan 33 sailors disagree on the proper amount of headsail overlap for the boat, making level racing more difficult.

To offset the rather average performance of the Tartan 33, the 33R was introduced in 1982. The 33—"R" for "Racing"—has a deep fin keel and a double-spreader masthead rig. The difference in performance between the 33 and the 33R is pretty amazing: the 33R is almost 30 seconds per mile faster than the stock 33, even though the sail area is almost identical.

Righting moment of the fin keel and Scheel keel boats is virtually the same, so the extra performance isn't the result of increased stability. The combination of the fin keel and the masthead rig is simply faster in most conditions.

It's interesting to compare the performance with the new 34, which combines the Scheel keel of the 33 with the masthead rig of the 33R. Although the specifications for the 33 say the boat is a thousand pounds lighter than the 34, the 33 was never as light as that. The typical 33, in IMS measurement trim, weighs pretty much the same as the new 34—11,000 pounds.

Typically, the 34 has a PHRF rating of about 141 with the optional deep keel, 147 with the standard Scheel keel. This places the 34 pretty squarely between the 33 and the 33R in the performance spectrum, suggesting that the masthead rig accounts for about half the performance difference betweeen the 33 and the 33R.

In order to keep the rig simple, the 33 was designed without running backstays. Instead, forestay tension is maintained by carrying a lot of load on the swept-back upper shrouds. Some 33s that have been actively raced have added running backstays, but they are not necessary if the boat is used strictly for cruising. Our experience with fractional rigs on larger boats is that it is very difficult to maintain adequate headstay tension without runners or jumpers, even though runners are a pain for shorthanded sailing.

If you want the best performance in a Tartan 33, there's no question that you should look for a 33R. It may be a long look, as relatively few of the higher-performance boats were built. The 33R's draft of over 6' 3" could be a disadvantage in areas of shoal water.

One advantage of the fractionally-rigged boat's large mainsail—it's just over 300 square feet, about what you'd find on most masthead-rigged 37-footers—is that the boat balances and sails reasonably well under mainsail alone. This is a useful feature for shorthanded cruising, when you may find yourself circling a harbor under sail looking for a place to anchor. With the Tartan 33, you can drop the jib and clear the foredeck for anchoring while still maintaining good sailing ability under mainsail.

Shrouds are set well inboard, and you'll almost always find inboard genoa tracks just outboard of the cabin trunk, even though it was an option.

Wheel steering was standard on the boat, and the 32" wheel provides plenty of power as well as good feedback. The rudder is partially protected by a vestigial skeg, and is a deep, high-aspect-ratio appendage—practically parallel-sided in profile—rather than the more efficient elliptical shape seen in more modern racing boats and performance cruisers.

Cockpit layout is efficient for sailing, but is somewhat better for cruising than for racing. A mainsheet traveler spans the cockpit well, just forward of the wheel, and genoa sheet winches are outboard of the main coamings, just forward of the traveler. For racing, it would be better to have the genoa winches further forward, so that trimmers would be well clear of the helmsman, and their weight would be further forward. For shorthanded cruising, however, the location is good.

Unfortunately, self-tailing winches were not standard equipment. The stock Lewmar 40s are about the right size for the fractional foretriangle, but would be a little small on a masthead rig with a 150% genoa.

Sparkman & Stephens is one firm that can always

The interior of the 33 is something you either love or hate. Dealers have told us that there is some resistance to it, but those who have lived with it for a while find it workable.

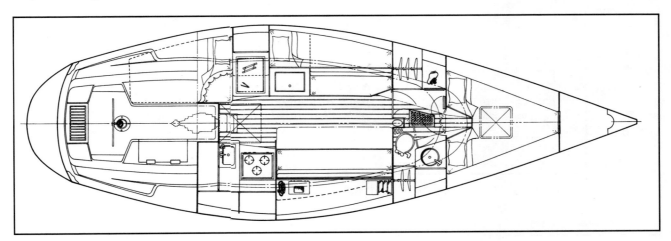

be counted on to design in a molded dodger breakwater, and Tartan has faithfully put them on their cruiser/racers over the years. Other builders should take note of the simple, functional breakwater on the Tartan 33, which has openings molded in to allow halyards to be led aft if you want to set the boat up for singlehanding.

Construction

Tartan has always had the reputation of being one of the country's higher-quality production builders, and they deserve it. In general, owners report very few construction shortcomings, and very few warranty claims.

Four owners in our survey had gelcoat blistering problems. That does not constitute an unusually large percentage, but interestingly, the boats reporting blistering were two pairs that were sequential in the production series. That may be a coincidence, but it's an unusual one.

Balsa coring is used in both the hull and deck of the Tartan 33. If you replace or move any deck or hull fittings, be sure to seal any exposed balsa with epoxy resin before installing new hardware.

The hull-to-deck joint is made with a standard inward-turning hull flange, overlapped by the deck molding, which is bolted to the hull through an anodized aluminum toerail. The joint is bedded with both butyl and polysulfide. Builders like to use butyl as a bedding compound, since it's cleaner to use than most gunned compounds such as polysulfide or polyurethane. Butyl has no adhesive properties, however, and in our experience it can be squeezed

out of a joint over time if you continue to tighten down bolts to cure a leak. Since only one owner in our survey reported any deck leaks, Tartan's combination seems to work well.

Several owners complain about the lack of a foredeck anchor well. Wells can be a nuisance when racing, since they frequently hold a fair amount of water. For cruising, however, an anchor well lets you clear the foredeck without making a soaking mess of a cockpit locker.

There is an absolute minimum of exterior wood on the Tartan 33: handrails atop the cabin, trim around the companionway. The boat is much more austere than you think of when Tartan comes to mind, but the racing Tartans have always been pretty basic.

Two-tone decks were an option, although the standard monotone deck was available either in white or a light buff. With the two-tone deck package, non-skid areas on the deck, coaming tops, cockpit seats and deckhouse were a nice buff color, contrasting with the stark white of the rest of the deck molding. If you buy a monotone boat, the areas could be painted a contrasting color. A white Tartan 33 with white monotone decks is a plain vanilla boat, indeed.

You'll find a three-cylinder, 24-hp Universal diesel in every Tartan 33. Owners report that the engine has been smooth-running and reliable, and that it's adequate power for the boat. An aluminum fuel tank holds 26 gallons, giving a range of about 200 miles under power.

All in all, there's little to quibble with in the

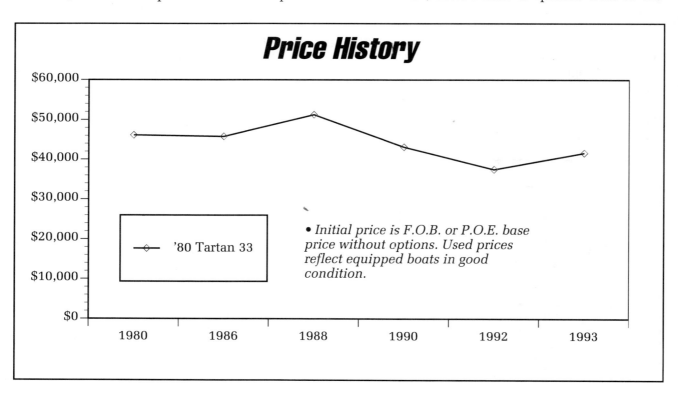

Price History

- ● Initial price is F.O.B. or P.O.E. base price without options. Used prices reflect equipped boats in good condition.

'80 Tartan 33

design and construction of the Tartan 33: it's simple, straightforward, and well executed.

Interior

The interior layout of the Tartan 33 has both fans and detractors. The head configuration, for example, is something you either love or hate. To give more room, particularly for showering, the head compartment runs the full width of the boat. A bi-fold door shuts off the head from the forward cabin, and another bi-fold door closes the head to the main cabin. Two opening ports provide ventilation in fair weather.

The difficulty with this arrangement is that you cannot get either into or out of the forward cabin if someone is using the head. This wouldn't be a problem for cruising with a couple, but it could be a nuisance with a lot of people aboard. Closing the door to the forward cabin also cuts off ventilation forward, unless the weather is good enough to have the foredeck hatch open.

The problem is made even worse when the insert is used in the V-berth to form a double. This completely eliminates any standing room in the cabin, so that you climb into the berth directly from the head compartment.

It works, but there's a fair amount of psychological resistence to the arrangement, since it is one usually seen on smaller boats.

Ironically, the full-width head is a really good one, with plenty of elbow room for showering and dressing. Even without the berth insert in place, standing room in the forward cabin is marginal, and headroom is very limited.

While the forward berths are quite long, they are extremely narrow at the foot, so that two tall people will be tangling feet if they use the berths as two singles. As a double, sleeping parallel to the centerline, this is less of a problem.

The main cabin layout is also unusual. To starboard, there is a fairly standard settee that extends to form a reasonably-sized double, with a shelf outboard. A dining table folds up against the starboard forward bulkhead.

On the port side, the arrangement is less standard. Instead of a normal settee berth, there is a short settee—less than 5' long—with the icebox occupying a high counter at what would normally be the head of the berth. This short settee could function as a berth for a child, but obviously not for an adult. Outboard of the settee, there is a narrow pilot berth, which is comfortable and secure, and fortunately isn't jammed as high under the side decks as they frequently are.

Main cabin ventilation is provided by six opening ports, two cowl vents in dorade boxes, and an aluminum-framed centerline hatch, which was an option, but a common one.

The galley—aft on the starboard side—is not the most efficient in the world, since you have to turn around and step across the main cabin to reach the icebox. In addition, the icebox top is the only usable food preparation counter space, which puts the cook in the middle of the main cabin, smack in the traffic flow.

A two-burner alcohol stove was standard equipment, but a large percentage of boats have the optional three-burner gimbaled alcohol stove with oven. A deep single sink is just aft of the stove, but it's a bit of a reach to use, since the flat of the cabin sole doesn't extend very far outboard in this part of the hull.

Aft of the icebox is a sit-down chart table. The working surface is a reasonable size, and the outboard locker could be sacrificed for the installation of electronics.

While there is a contoured, upholstered seat for the nav station, it does not exactly face the chart table, and it is offset from the center of the table. The navigator has to twist at an awkward angle to reach the outboard part of the table, or to use any electronics mounted outboard.

Aft of the nav station is a big double quarterberth. A drop-in insert which covers the nav station seat forms the head of the inboard portion of the quarterberth, although the berth can be used as a single without disturbing the navigator. This is basically the same quarterberth layout used in the Tartan 37. We thought it a bit awkward on the bigger boat, but it's a bit more acceptable on a smaller boat where space is at even more of a premium.

Most owners who have lived with the interior for some time find it quite workable. A top Tartan dealer told us, however, that he has definitely seen buyer resistance to it. Certainly the redesigned interior of the Tartan 34 is substantially better.

Conclusions

If you're looking for a fairly fast, high-quality, late model cruiser/racer, the Tartan 33 is a good choice. In general, prices will be very comparable to those of other quality boats of the same size and vintage, such as the C&C 34 and Sabre 34. Performance of these three boats is also similar.   • **PS**

Mason 33

Though expensive, the Mason 33 is of high quality; we can find little about her we don't like.

The 33 was built in the mid and late '80s by the Ta Shing yard in Taiwan, and imported by Pacific Asian Enterprises in California. She is a moderate traditional design that harks back to the CCA handicapping rule of the 1960s. It might best be described as a modern full-keel hull, with a cut away forefoot and sharply turned bilges to reduce wetted surface. Though narrow and short on the waterline compared to modern lightweight fin-keelers, she is beamier, with shorter overhangs, than you would find on a typical 1960s design. If the CCA racing rule had survived into the 1980s, we suspect the Mason 33 would be a typical, if conservative, specimen.

PAE's requirements to the designer were for a seakindly hull with the capability for carrying ample stores and an ability to take a couple or small crew anywhere. The company makes no bones about their distaste for the standard issue contemporary fin-keelers which they condemn as limited-purpose boats, suitable only for minimal coastal cruising, with too many berths and totally inadequate storage space. They believe the moderate traditional design of their 33 makes for not only comfortable coastal cruising and daysailing, but also blue-water passagemaking and living aboard. And it's conceivable you could even race one in PHRF.

Construction

The hull is a standard solid fiberglass hand-laid laminate. It's different from others in a couple of respects. The company specified a somewhat heavier than normal laminate, and the hull also has four full length longitudinal stringers to give additional support to the bulkheads and floors.

Isophthalic resin is used in the laminate—the current theory is that iso resins are less water permeable and hence less likely to allow hull blistering to

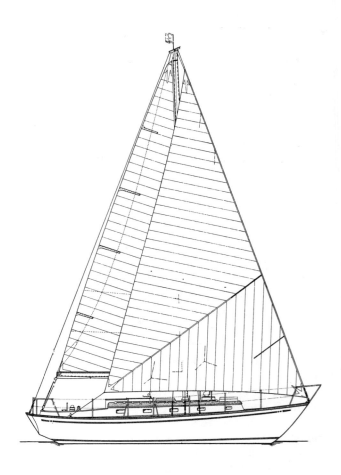

Specifications

LOA	33' 9"
LWL	25' 5"
Beam	10' 10"
Draft	5' 0"
Displacement	14,020 lbs.
Ballast	5,320 lbs.
Sail area	602 sq. ft.

develop. PAE also recommended that buyers have an epoxy coating put on at the factory.

The ballast keel is iron, placed inside the hull molding in two pieces, taped into place, and sealed to minimize rust or leakage problems in case of a hard grounding. Americans are more accustomed to lead keels, which are unquestionably preferable for exterior ballast, but iron interior keels are fairly common in the Oriental boats, and we don't hear of many problems. (The external iron keels common on European boats are more rust prone and a higher maintenance item.)

The full keel gives a roomy bilge, and there's a 20 gallon sump tank as well as a good, deep bilge sump. The interior of the hull itself is generally hidden by joinerwork, but where it shows it is sealed with resin

The nav station is compact, but workable. Note the superb electrical panel, protection from spray coming through the companionway, and wet locker next to the companionway steps.

and painted. The hull is reinforced in the way of seacocks. A neat touch is that each of the through-hulls has an identifying nameplate so visitors and guests can follow your instructions without you having to go through elaborate descriptions of what they should be turning off, turning on, or plugging up in case of emergency.

The deck molding is a standard glass layup with balsa core, with plywood in the cabin trunk and other spots to provide additional backing strength and attachment points for the interior joinerwork. The non-skid on deck is satisfactory, but the optional teak overlay is generally preferable. While it did cost $2,280, the price was reasonable (probably about a third of what it would cost in the US), especially considering the quality of it and the finished appearance it gives the boat.

Further, the hull has the displacement, ballast, and form stability so that the added weight of the teak deck won't be the problem it could be on a lighter design.

The hull-to-deck joint is a standard inward turning hull flange, on top of which the deck rests. It's somewhat unusual in that the teak toerail sits on top of (and hides) a stainless steel flat bar on top of the deck. Inside the hull there's a matching stainless flat bar. The flat bars act as extended washers for the through bolts which fasten the joint together, with every other bolt going through the toerail as well as through the joint. About the only complaint we have heard about the older Masons was some leaking in the hull-to-deck joint, but it's hard to see how the joint could leak on the 33.

The exterior finish of the hull and deck is generally good, with no evident hardspots to mar the fairness of the hull in any of the three boats we examined. The gelcoat work also appeared good. Although we went over the topsides and cabin house

of one of the three boats carefully, we found no flaws—a rarity in fiberglass boatbuilding.

The boat has fairly extensive teak trim on the exterior, most notably the heavy-duty toerail, cockpit grates, and cabin trim. The standard hatches are teak, with lexan tops. If you're not into the high maintenance of wood hatches, you could get optional Goiot or Taiwan brand ("Manship") hatches. (The Taiwan hatches look like knock-offs, as well made but cheaper than the Goiot.) Having the exterior teak varnished was a $625 option. The result is the look of real quality, but requires the owner to get involved with the continuous maintenance required of varnished teak.

One of the things that marks the construction as good quality is the exterior detail. The custom made cleats and chocks, for example, are well done and well fitted to the teak trim, and the little stainless steel chafing strips to protect the teak around the stern chocks are just one of the many nice touches.

Although we might have preferred some things to be different (like using lead ballast rather than iron), it is clear that the developers and builder have given thought to all details of the boat's construction. Overall, it is hard to find fault with any aspect of it.

Handling Under Power

Early models of the boat came with a 21 hp Westerbeke, normal for an offshore cruiser but probably near the minimum size for the American market. Later boats have a Yanmar three-cylinder diesel, at 27 hp adequate for the boat and more in line with what most Americans like in a coastal cruiser. The fuel tanks holds 35 gallons for a good powering range.

Standard is a three-blade propeller. A two-blade would be much preferable for performance under sail, since it could be positioned upright in the

The galley is good overall, with a well-insulated icebox, deep sinks and hot and cold pressure water. About the only thing wrong is the awkward upturn of the cabin sole to follow the hull.

aperature between the aft end of the keel and the forward edge of the rudder. However, under power, the two-blade "hammers"—that is, it creates a sharp vibration because the two blades are alternately in the water flow but then hidden behind the keel and not pushing any water when vertical.

The hammering is a minor irritant, but we can imagine it becoming major during long motoring sessions. Unfortunately, it is inherent in the hull design.

The company recommended buying both a three-blade and a two-blade, using the three-blade most of the time but putting on the two-blade prior to long passages under sail. We would be inclined to go with a two-blade and put up with the vibration, but that's a choice each person will have to make.

The boat we sailed had a two-blade prop and the Westerbeke diesel, and we found that the boat generally behaved well under power, being just a mite disinclined to back up in a straight line. Otherwise, she tracks and turns well, though long keel/attached rudder boats always have a longer turning radius than the fin keel/separate rudder models most people are accustomed to these days.

The engine installation is well done—there's a good drip pan under the engine and everthing is neat and tidy. Full access to the engine, however, requires not only removing the companionway steps but also taking out a drawer assembly. It's not a complicated job—you have only to remove two wing nuts, but it takes some time.

Handling Under Sail

The Mason 33 is heavy by comparison to most boats its size, and it definitely has a different "feel" to it. We sailed it on a fairly calm day on the Pacific, but it was easy to sense that it would handle rough conditions in a more sedate fashion than typical modern lightweights.

Given that it is a long keeled boat with lots of wetted surface, it probably will not be a sprightly performer in light airs, but it has a powerful enough sail plan that the boat moved well in the 8-10 knots of air that we sailed in. Our sense was that the hull must be quite efficient for its type, since the boat sailed better than we expected in the conditions. Though we did not try it in heavy air, we suspect that the boat will be at its best sailing in a good blow.

The Mason 33 points well enough considering her outboard shrouds and her hull design, but windward work will not be her forte. She will do her best with the wind slightly ahead of the beam and next best from a beam reach to a broad reach. She rolls a lot dead downwind in heavy air.

Compared to modern racer/cruisers like the Pearson 33 or Beneteau 345, she will be quite slow for typical coastal cruising, especially in light air and to windward, but for sailing she was obviously designed for long distance passages, at which she should be respectable.

The boat comes with a mainsail and 100% working jib as standard equipment, so most people will want to add a genoa and spinnaker. The boat we sailed had a roller furling jib of about 130% which would be right for moderate- to heavier-air locales. For light-wind areas, a 140% would probably be better. The boat should handle a reefable 150% if you decided not to get furling gear.

The standard sails are made by Sobstad Watts. The main on the boat we sailed was good, the jib average. If we had a sailmaker whom we knew and trusted, our inclination would be to try to negotiate a purchase so we could have the sails made by our own sailmaker. However the standard sails are good enough that we wouldn't feel "stuck" if we got them. That's not common when stock sails come with a boat these days.

Though the interior seems small, that's really an illusion. There's plenty of usable space, and excellent storage. Forward is the owner's cabin, with a port side berth instead of the more ususal V-berth.

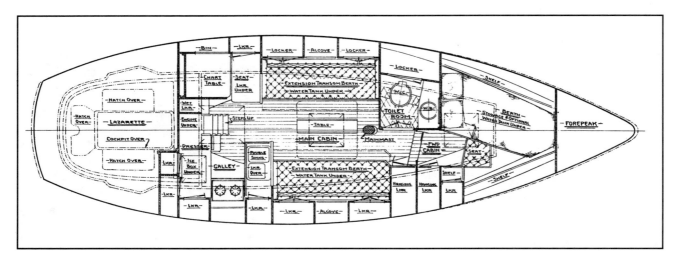

On Deck

The teak decks, high toerail, and grabrails on the cabin top make movement around the deck easy. The walkways are plenty wide, and even the outboard shrouds require only a small duck and dodge when going forward.

We liked the deep cockpit of the boat, with its high coaming and comfortable seats, but it is somewhat smaller (more suited for seagoing) than is common nowadays. It's definitely a cruising cockpit, and a racing crew of four or five would rapidly get in each other's way, but it works well for a couple. Tiller steering is standard, but most everyone opts for the wheel which does provide more room. The cockpit lockers are enormous. They're actually too big in the new boat configuration, and most owners will want to subdivide them with partitions, canvas, or netting so things can be got at.

The Lewmar #40 self-tailers are adequate, with easy access, but 43s are optional for weaker or harder-driving owners. A set of secondary winches is available; however, there's scarcely enough room on the coaming top—we'd probably try to get by without them, even when flying a staysail or spinnaker.

The standard mainsheet winch is a Lewmar 16—we'd spring for the self-tailing Lewmar 30, since the traveler is ahead of the companionway and the sheet is not only loaded up but also prone to plenty of friction as it leads forward to the mast before turning down to the deck and back underneath the dodger coaming. Sail controls are minimal—you have to go to the mast to adjust the Cunningham, outhaul, or vang, so you won't be doing much tweaking of sail trim.

The foredeck is small, adequate for sail handling and anchor work, but with not much room for sunbathing or lounging. The bow anchor roller is set up for a CQR. The forepeak is called a chainlocker. We would consider stowing nylon anchor rode there, but chain would put way too much weight forward. One problem to solve is where to put the anchors and rodes necessary for serious cruising. In this, the 33 is typical of most boats her size.

One shortcoming on deck—again inherent in the design of the boat—is that there is no good way to permanently install a swim ladder. The conventional transom mount does not work well because of the traditional slope of the transom, and a permanent mount has not been devised for the port or starboard side gates. The company sells a handsome teak ladder as an option, but it has to be removed and stowed when you're underway.

Belowdecks

The interior of the Mason 33 does not look spacious. That's partly because it is quite teaky and fairly dark, but mostly because everything inside the boat is good sized, especially the storage spaces. In fact, there is considerably more storage on the Mason 33 than there is on many larger boats, like the O'Day 40. We particularly liked the roomy forepeak (which has all but disappeared on many current boats), the double hanging lockers, the small hanging locker next to the companionway for wet gear, and the adequate space for food stowage in the galley.

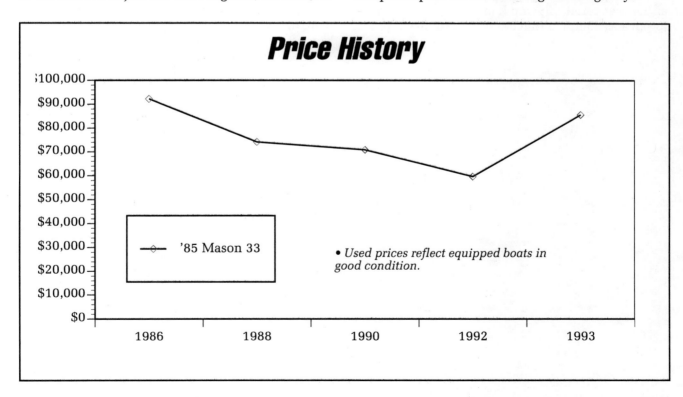

Price History

• *Used prices reflect equipped boats in good condition.*

Legend: ◇ '85 Mason 33

Layout below is fairly conventional, but the spacing and all the details have been attended to—we found few nits to pick and many details that were pleasantly surprising.

The galley has ample fiddled counters and good deep sinks and should work well under sail. At anchor, it's awkward in that the floor rises to follow the hull contour. The icebox is big enough and apparently well insulated, hot and cold pressure water are standard, and there are two water tanks for a total of 65 gallons.

Opposite the galley is the navigation station, with an adequately sized chart table and a sort of "screen" bulkhead to protect charts and electronics from sea or rain water entering through the companionway. The electrical panel is beautiful.

Settees are port and starboard of a centerline table, and a pilot berth is available portside, though most owners will likely use the space for storage.

The head has a shower which drains into the sump tank, good storage space, and a decent wash basin.

The forward cabin is the owner's cabin, and the portside double berth is big and roomy. It should be comfortable at anchor or in mild conditions, but during heavy air passagemaking, the settees will have to be used for sleeping.

The berthing arrangement makes it clear that the boat is primarily designed for a couple, with perhaps at most one child or two young children and only occasional guests.

Notable below is the joinerwork which is uniformly of good quality. Teak is most everywhere—either veneered plywood or solid—with white formica as contrast. Hatches and portholes provide good light, augmented by deck prisms. Ventilation is adequate, with a big dorade and cowl forward, exhausting the forward cabin and head, and ten opening ports as standard equipment. For passagemaking, a couple more deck vents would be desirable.

Conclusions

We hate to sound mush headed, but there is simply little to criticize in the Mason 33.

It is true that some people may not like the full keel design of the boat, preferring a lighter, high performance hull. But given the design, there is hardly anything wrong.

Her construction is solid, her deck is well laid out with good equipment, her spars and sail handling equipment are good quality, her interior is well laid out and well finished, the machinery and mechanical systems are made well and installed properly, and she's a pretty good looking boat, though on the plain side.

We can't even object to the price. She is expensive, but there are almost no boats of comparable quality in her size range, and the few you could buy are so much more expensive that they are not realistic alternatives.

For someone wanting a serious blue water cruiser or a livaboard boat in her size range, she is the logical choice. For others, wanting a coastal cruiser or a weekender/daysailer, she is probably less practical—more boat than would be needed. But of course many people buy not just a boat, but the dream of being able to take off at any moment and leave the boss and the rat race behind. The Mason is one of the few boats we've seen recently that is capable of actualizing the dream.   • **PS**

Morgan 34

A handsome shoal-draft keel/centerboarder well-suited to cruising the Keys or the Chesapeake.

In the late 1960s and early 1970s, the names Charley Morgan and Ted Irwin were practically synonymous with Florida boatbuilding. Charley Morgan was definitely one of the designers and builders that shaped the early and middle years of fiberglass sailboat building.

Morgan designs from that period run the gamut from cruising houseboats—the Out Island series—to the 12 meter sloop *Heritage,* the 1970 America's Cup defense candidate that Morgan designed, built, and skippered.

But before *Heritage,* before the Out Island series, Charley Morgan designed cruiser/racers to the CCA rule. His successful one-off boats were typified by *Paper Tiger, Sabre,* and *Maredea.* Early Morgan-designed production boats included the Columbia 40 and the Columbia 31.

In 1962, Morgan Yacht went into business to build the 28' Tiger Cub. In 1965, the company really got rolling, building the Morgan 26, the 36, and the 42. In 1966 the Morgan 34 was added to the line. It stayed in production until the 1972 model year, when it was phased out in preference to the Morgan 35, a slightly larger, faster boat which fit a little better into the new IOR racing rule.

The Morgan 34 is a typical late CCA-rule centerboarder. Charley Morgan specialized in this type of boat, which was favored under the rating rule and well-adapted to life in the shoal waters of the Florida coast and the Bahamas.

By today's standards, the Morgan 34 is a small boat, comparable in accommodations to a lot of 30-footers. When the boat was designed, she was as big as most other boats of her overall length.

In profile, the boat has a sweeping, moderately concave sheer. The ends of the boat are beautifully balanced: the bow profile is a slight convex curve,

Specifications

LOA	34' 0"
LWL	24' 9"
Beam	10' 0"
Draft	3' 3"/7' 9" (board up/down)
Displacement	12,500 lbs.
Ballast	5,000 lbs.

the overhanging counter aft is slightly concave. Esthetically, hull shapes of this period from the best designers are still hard to beat.

Sailing Performance

With a typical PHRF rating of 189, the Morgan 34 is not as fast as some of the more competitive cruiser/racers of the same vintage, such as the Tartan 34. With just a little more sail area than the Tartan 34, the Morgan 34 is about 1,300 pounds heavier.

Most owners rate the boat as about the same speed both upwind and downwind as boats of similar size and type. At the same time, the boat's performance is at least as good as a lot of more modern "pure" cruisers of the same length.

The rig is a simple, fairly low aspect ratio masthead sloop, using a slightly-tapered aluminum spar,

Owners' Comments

"The boat has been safe and stable in some miserable dusters in Vineyard Sound. We replaced the Atomic 4 with a Universal diesel, and now the boat is a bit underpowered.

"It's built like a brick outhouse: solid. The mast sits on a steel plate which is slowly rusting away.

"I'd suggest the following: replace the wooden spreaders; replace the vermiculite icebox insulation, which packs down and is inefficient; install a seacock on the side galley drain line, since the sink goes below the water when heeled over."

—1969 model in New York

"The boat is faster than a Swiftsure 33 or Seabreeeze 35, slower than a Pearson 33 or Pearson 35. It has a large turning radius under power, and poor controllability in reverse.

"Failures have been a rotten wooden spreader (replaced before it failed), several centerboard pennants, a crack along the rudderpost, and the straps on the tiller fitting. The centerboard lifting arrangement is a Charley Morgan "go-fast" design, and is very prone to failure. It is the weakest link in this lovely boat."

—1968 model in North Carolina

"I would look for a pre-1970 model. Later boats have a great deal of molded-in furniture. Earlier boats have built-up interiors. Prior to hull #250, centerboards were bronze, which is a plus.

"The only second-class areas of construction are in the interior. The Formica looks bleak but it was a big advertising feature in 1967. The head doors are particle board, which swells up and comes apart when it gets wet.

"The hatches are not as watertight as modern ones. Ours drip when heavy spray comes over the cabintop. The lazarette and cockpit locker lids leak, too.

"The boat is sound and well-constructed. The shoal draft is a very attractive feature."

—1967 model in Ohio

"The boat has a classic exterior, a below-average interior. There's too much plastic and fake wood. The side galley layout is not the greatest. I'd look for a boat with the aft galley, which is much more practical.

"Overall, it's a well-built and well-balanced boat that endured over a year of cruising full time with four living aboard. At no time did we question the boat's integrity."

—1969 model in New York

stepped through to the keel.

Although there are double lower shrouds, the forward lowers are almost in line with the center of the mast, with the after lowers well behind the mast. On a lighter, more modern rig, this shroud arrangement would just about require a babystay, but on the stiff masts of the late 1960s, it would be essentially superfluous.

Early boats in the series have wooden spreaders. Unless well cared for, they can rot. For some reason, wooden spreaders on aluminum masts tend to get ignored more than the same spreaders on wooden masts.

The boom is a round aluminum extrusion equipped with roller reefing. Roller reefing is tedious, inefficient, and usually results in a poorly-shaped sail. If we were to buy a Morgan 34 for cruising, the first thing we'd do would be to buy a modern boom equipped with internal slab reefing.

Shroud chainplates are located right at the edge of the deck, so inboard genoa tracks would just about be a waste of time. The spreaders are short enough that you can sheet the genoa just inside the lifelines when hard on the wind.

Just about every piece of sailhandling equipment you'd normally expect on a cruiser/racer was an option on this boat. You may find extremely long genoa tracks—some boats originally carried 170% genoas, which were lightly penalized under the CCA rule—or you may find very short genoa tracks. Likewise, turning blocks, spinnaker gear, and internal halyards were all options.

The original jib sheet winches were Merriman or South Coast #5s. Compared to modern winches, they are slow and lack power. For anything other than casual daysailing, you'll want to upgrade to modern two-speed self-tailing winches for the genoa.

At the aft end of the cockpit, there is an old-fashioned flat mainsheet traveler track. Although this isn't a bad arrangement for a cruising boat, it would be tempting, while replacing the boom, to install a modern recirculating ball traveler. You could then keep the boat on her feet a little better close reaching in a breeze by simply easing the traveler car to leeward without slacking the mainsheet.

With the standard tiller, the mainsheet location is a bit of a problem, since the helmsman sits almost at the forward end of the cockpit. This is fine for racing, when the helmsman does nothing but steer, but it is awkward for shorthanded cruising.

Like a lot of boats with low aspect mainsails, the

Morgan 34 tends to develop weather helm quite quickly as the breeze builds. Despite a 40% ballast/ displacement ratio, the boat is not particularly stiff. She is narrow, and the shoal draft keeps the vertical center of gravity quite high.

The boat is quite easy to balance under sail in moderate conditions, thanks to a narrow undistorted hull, a long keel with the rudder well aft, and a centerboard. Owners report that on wheel-steered boats, you can tighten down the brake and the boat will sail itself indefinitely upwind.

Engine

Standard engine in the Morgan 34 was the Atomic 4 or the Palmer M-60, both gasoline engines. Perkins 4-107 and Westerbeke 4-107 engines were $2,000 options.

If you can buy a used boat cheaply enough and plan to keep it for a few years, it would be a natural candidate for installation of one of Universal's new drop-in Atomic 4 diesel replacements. However, since a new diesel would cost about 25% of the total value of the boat, such an upgrade is not something to be taken lightly.

With the side-galley interior with quarterberths aft, engine access for minor service is reasonable through panels in the quarterberths.

Engine access is less straightforward with the aft galley arrangement, requiring removing the companionway steps just to get to the front end of the engine.

Almost unanimously, owners in our survey state that the boat is next to impossible to back down under power in any predictable direction. With a solid two-bladed prop in an aperture, reverse efficiency is minimal with no prop wash over the rudder.

A 26-gallon Monel fuel tank was standard. Monel, an alloy of copper and nickel, is one of the few tank materials that serves equally well for gasoline, diesel oil, or water. It is prohibitively expensive, and is therefore rarely used for tanks in modern production boats. You may also find a Morgan 34 with another, optional, 15-gallon fuel tank.

Construction

In the late 60s and early 70s, Morgans were of pretty average stock boat quality. Glasswork is heavy, solid, and unsophisticated.

The construction is a combination of good features, coupled with corners cut to keep the price down.

Through hull fittings are recessed flush to the hull—good for light air performance—yet gate valve shutoffs were standard. Believe it or not, you could buy bronze seacocks as options for about $5 to $25 each! That's what we call cutting corners.

Lead ballast is installed inside the hull shell. The

There were a few different interior arrangements offered. This one is our least favorite: we prefer a more conventional aft galley layout.

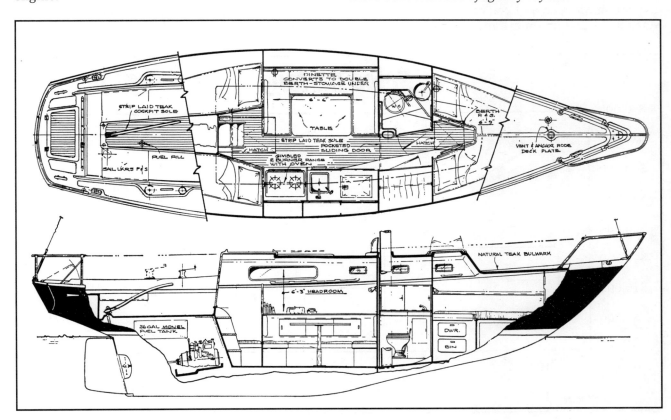

classic drawback to inside ballast is the vulnerability of the hull shell to damage in a grounding.

The cockpit is very large, larger than desirable for offshore sailing. In addition, there is a low sill between the cockpit and the main cabin, rather than a bridgedeck. You can block off the bottom of the companionway by leaving the lower dropboard in place, but this is not as safe an arrangement as a bridgedeck. Cockpit scuppers are smaller than we would want for offshore sailing.

Molded fiberglass hatches are in most cases more watertight than badly designed or maintained wooden hatches, but they are almost never as good as a modern metal-framed hatch. They're simply too flexible. When the seals get old, you tend to dog the hatch tighter and tighter, further compressing the seals and putting uneven pressure on the hatch cover. The result is almost always leaking. Leaking hatches may seem like a small problem, but they are like a splinter in your finger: the pain and nuisance are all out of proportion to the item inflicting the injury.

Like many centerboards, the Morgan 34's can be a problem. The original board was a bronze plate weighing about 250 pounds. When fully extended, the bronze board is heavy enough to add slightly to the boat's stability. Later boats have an airfoil fiberglass board of almost neutral bouyancy. There's a lot less wear and tear on the wire pennant with the glass board.

You may find a Morgan 34 that has been owner-finished from a hull or kit. Sailing Kit Kraft was a division of Morgan, and you could buy most of the Morgan designs in almost any stage of completion from the bare hull on up.

A kit-built boat can be a mixed blessing. If you find a boat that was finished by a skilled craftsman, it could be a better boat than a factory-assembled version. On the other hand, it could also be a disaster. Since the quality control of a kit boat is monitored only by the person building it, an extremely careful survey is required.

No matter how well executed it may be, an owner-completed kit boat rarely sells for more than a factory-finished version of the same boat. Most buyers would rather have a boat with a known pedigree, even if the pedigree is pretty average.

There's a decent amount of exterior teak on this boat, including the cockpit coamings, toerail, grabrails on the cabin, drop boards, hatch trim, and cockpit sole. Check the bedding and fastening of the cockpit coamings carefully. If you want to varnish coamings that have been either oiled or neglected, it may be necessary to remove and rebed them.

Exterior appearance of older boats such as the Morgan 34 is greatly improved by varnishing the teak trim. It particularly spiffs up boats with the faded gelcoat that is almost inevitable after 20 years of use.

The standard Morgan 34 was a pretty basic boat. There were single lifelines, a single battery. There was no sea hood over the main hatch, and no electric bilge pump. Most boats left the factory with a fair number of options, but you may not find a lot of things that would be standard today.

In general, the construction and design of the Morgan 34 are suited to fairly serious coastal cruising. We would not consider the boat for offshore

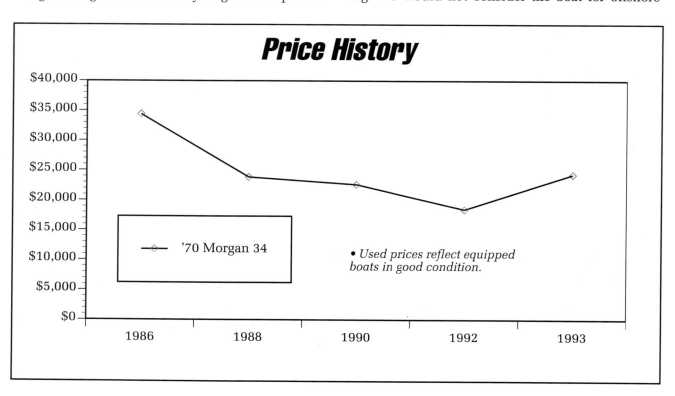

Price History

• *Used prices reflect equipped boats in good condition.*

Legend: ◇ '70 Morgan 34

passagemaking without improving cockpit scuppers, companionway and hatch sealing, cockpit locker sealing, and bilge pumps.

Interior

The Morgan 34 dates from the heyday of woodgrained Formica interiors. Woodgrained mica bulkheads are even more lifeless than oiled teak bulkheads. However, mica makes a pretty decent painting base if it is thoroughly sanded so that all traces of gloss are removed. Freshly-painted white bulkheads with varnished trim would make a world of difference in the interior appearance of this boat.

The interior trim on a lot of Morgan 34s is walnut, which is a pretty drab wood, even when varnished. For an extra $400 or so you could get teak trim. Unvarnished teak and walnut are very similar in appearance, although walnut is usually a bit darker.

The forward cabin contains the normal V-berths, with a drawer and bin below on each side. A stainless steel water tank fills most of the space under the forward berths. The standard tank holds 30 gallons, but many boats have the optional 60-gallon tank.

A fiberglass hatch provides fair-weather ventilation for the forward cabin. A double-opening hatch was optional, as were opening ports in place of the standard fixed ports. Below the hatch, headroom is just over 6'.

The head compartment on the port side is quite cramped when the door is closed. However, it almost doubles in size if you close off the forward cabin with the dual-purpose head door, then close the sliding pocket door that separates the forward passageway from the main cabin.

Unfortunately, this pocket door is particle board, and it is likely to be a mushy mess, since any leaks around the mast drip right onto the door. "Waterproof" particle board found its way into a lot of boats in the 1960s and early 1970s. It shouldn't have.

A shower installation was optional, and added about $800 to the base price of the boat for a pressure system, sump, pump and water heater. It is a desirable option if you plan on cruising.

You will find three different main cabin layouts. All were available as no-extra-cost options.

In the most common layout, the galley occupies the starboard side of the main cabin, with a dinette opposite. This arrangment was fairly common in the late 1960s and early 1970s. You either love this galley/dinette arrangement or you hate it. Having spent a fair amount of time sailing offshore with a similar layout, we can say unequivocally that we hate it.

With the modern U-shaped galley, the cook can stand in one place and reach everything by simply turning around. With a linear galley, the cook has to take several steps to move from the icebox to the stove. This is fine when the boat is tied to the dock, but offshore it means that there's no way the cook can wedge himself or herself in a single secure location while preparing meals.

A dinette also presents problems under way. Offshore, the most secure way to eat is to sit on the leeward settee, holding your plate in your lap. Unless there is a settee opposite the dinette, half the time you'll be sitting on the uphill side of the boat while you're trying to eat. This may be good for weight distribution while racing, but it's not very secure. We've seen more than a few bowls of beef stew go flying from the windward to the leeward side of the main cabin when the boat took a knockdown.

Two different aft galley arrangements were options. In one, the dinette is retained, with a settee opposite. In the other, the dinette is replaced by a settee and pilot berth.

Choosing between these two is purely a matter of taste. The pilot berth layout gives three sea berths in the main cabin. On the other hand, the dinette table can be lowered to form a double berth.

The aft galley is larger than the side galley. To port, there is a gimballed stove, a large dry well, and outboard lockers. A sink, icebox, and other lockers are located on the starboard side.

Reduced access to the engine is the only disadvantage we see to the aft galley layout.

In common with a lot of boats of this period, the electrical panel is inadequate for the amount of goodies that are likely to have been installed in the boat over its life. The panel is also located in the worst possible place—directly under the companionway hatch.

With the aft galley, a good location for the electrical panel would be outboard of the sink tucked under the side deck. In all likelihood, you're going to sacrifice that galley storage space to install navigation electronics anyway, since the top of the icebox is the only reasonable space to use as the chart table. That's right, there's no nav station in this boat: we're talking the late 1960s, when a boat with a radio, a depthsounder, and a knotmeter was heavily equipped with electronics.

There is reasonable storage space throughout the boat. Space under the settees is not taken up by tankage.

Headroom is 6' 3" on centerline throughout the main cabin, falling off to about 6' at the outboard edge of the cabin trunk. All the berths are at least 6' 6" long, and they are proportioned for normal-sized human beings.

Decor in the main cabin is decidedly drab, between woodgrain laminate bulkheads and a sterile white fiberglass overhead liner. The original upholstery was vinyl, completing the low-maintenance theme. Paint, varnish, and nice fabric cushions would make a Cinderella of an interior that is reasonably roomy, laid out well, and uncluttered.

Ventilation in the main cabin isn't great. There's no overhead ventilation hatch, although there's room to install one. Once again, the stock two small fixed ports may have been replaced with optional opening ports—a plus, but a small one.

A single long oval fixed port on either side of the main cabin gives the boat a very dated look. It would be tempting to remove the aluminum-framed port and replace it with a differently-shaped smoked polycarbonate window mounted on the outside of the cabin trunk and bolted through. We'd make a number of different patterns out of black construction paper and overlay them on the outside until we found a pleasing shape. You'd be surprised at how this would dress up appearance.

Conclusions

The Morgan 34 is similar in design and concept to the more-popular Tartan 34, which dates from the same period. By comparison, the Tartan 34 is lighter, faster, and has less wetted surface, since it lacks the Morgan's full keel. As a rule, we prefer the Tartan 34's construction details, although Morgan owners report somewhat less gelcoat crazing and deck delamination.

In 1970, the Morgan 34 and the Tartan 34 were almost identical in price. Today, however, the same Tartan 34 will cost about 20% more than the Morgan 34. Part of that difference in price stems from the fact that the Tartan 34 is less dated in appearance, design, and finishing detail.

If you want a keel/centerboarder for cruising in shoal waters such as the Bahamas, the Gulf of Mexico, or the Chesapeake, but don't want to spend the money for the Tartan 34, a Morgan 34 is a good alternative. With effort and money, you can upgrade the Morgan 34 quite a bit. As always, however, you should compare the dollars and amount of time invested before getting involved with a boat that dates from a period when the aesthetics of hull design were light years ahead of the nitty gritty of detailing and interior design.　　• **PS**

O'Day 34

An all-around family boat with a highly livable interior, but mediocre workmanship.

For many years O'Day was the builder of small boats. Founded by former Olympic champion, George O'Day, the company made its name with boats such as the International Tempest, International 505, Flying Dutchman, Madner, Rhodes 19, and the 16' 9" Daysailer. During the trailer-sailer revolution of the 1970s, O'Day added a series of retractable keel boats, most notably the O'Day 22 and 23. The O'Day 27, with a fixed keel, was queen of the nest. In 1975 a 32-footer was added, a 39-footer in 1982, and the largest boat the company was to build, the O'Day 40, in 1985.

One of the first American builders to pick up on Euro-styling, O'Day almost saved itself from ruin with the introduction in 1986 of the 272, and in the years immediately following, the 302 and 322. Unfortunately, these popular boats weren't enough, and O'Day went on the auction block. Pearson Yachts picked up some of the molds from Lear Siegler, the conglomerate that had bought it in turn from Bangor Punta, but Pearson, too, fell to the auctioneer's gavel not long after.

The Design

The O'Day 34 was built between 1981 and 1984. It was the 11th design the company commissioned from C. Raymond Hunt Associates. At the time, the principal designer at Hunt was John Deknatel.

It's always interesting to read the magazine ads and sales brochures hyping older boats. For example, the O'Day 34 brochure uses such phrases as, "Traditional lines. Contemporary style." "A luxuriously comfortable and practical offshore cruiser. " And, "The high performance sailing machine."

We'd agree most with the first quotation. The proportions of the boat are nicely balanced between topsides and cabin, and the raked bow and reverse

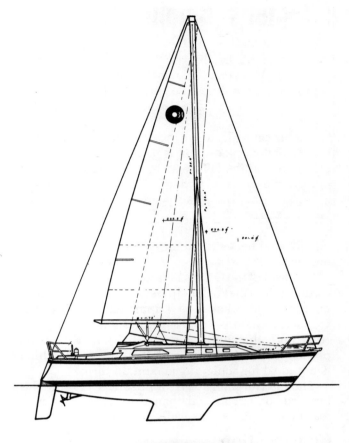

Specifications

LOA	34' 0"
LWL	28' 9"
Beam	11' 3"
Draft (shoal/deep)	4' 5"/5' 7"
Displacement	11,500 lbs.
Ballast (shoal/deep)	4,650/4,600 lbs.
Sail area	524 sq. ft.

transom work pretty well together. Calling the O'Day 34 an "offshore cmiser" and "high perfonnance sailing machine" is stretching it a bit, however. We have always felt that O'Day's strong suit was the building of wholesome, all-around family boats.

The O'Day 34 is no exception. There is nothing radical about it: 40 percent ballast-to-displacement ratio, displacement-to-length ratio of 216, and a sensible sloop rig in terms of both design and sail area.

There is a not-so-old saying that it's much less expensive to build a boat that sits *on top* of the water than one that sits *in* the water. Boats that sit on the water have so-called flat bottoms with bolt-on keels. There isn't much beneath the cabin sole but space to collect condensation. Tanks and machinery are usu-

Owners' Comments

"Floor could be thicker; will flex under heavy weight. Make sure the cast iron keel has been properly maintained (i.e., primed, painted, etc.)."
1982 model in Massachusetts

"Significantly faster on port tack than on starboard tack; weight placement is uneven. My wife and I have found the O'Day 34 to be an ideal cruising boat. We previously had a Tartan 30 and quite frankly find the quality and amenities of the

O'Day to be every bit as good. Rig needs careful tuning to achieve optimum performance. Motoring at anything over six knots is somewhat noisy and probably taxing the engine a bit. Boat becomes tender in a blow (over 30 knots)."
1973 model in Rhode Island

"Not a light air boat. Must be *something* she can't handle, but I have not found it yet. Very stiff."
1971 model in Virginia

ally located beneath the furniture or aft around the engine.

The keel of the O'Day 34 is modest, with a flat run on the bottom that will help it sit on a cradle. The hull fairs into a small skeg as it approaches the rudder, which is located as far aft as the designer could get it. Also note that with this type of underbody the propeller shaft is angled sharply downward, which is not ideal for achieving maximum thrust.

The interior plan speaks for itself as it is straightforward, practical, and thanks to 11' 3" of beam, reasonably spacious as well.

Construction

The hull of the O'Day 34 is constructed of solid fiberglass, while the deck is cored with balsa. The rudder is foam-cored fiberglass. A flange on the deck mold turns down over the hull, where it is mechanically fastened, glassed over inside and covered on the outside by a vinyl gunwale guard.

Company literature says the keel is lead, though several readers told us theirs are cast iron, a discrepancy we can't explain.

A distinguishing feature of production fiberglass boats in what might he called the modem era has been the increasing sophistication of the molds. Nowhere is this more evident than in the design and execution of interior pans (you can't really call them "liners"). These pans are carefully engineered to not only form the foundations of nearly all furniture, but also to take the place of stringers and some bulkheads by supporting the hull structure in key areas. The "unified grid pan" of the O'Day 34 is well done, with cutouts to provide decent access to most parts of the hull. Fiberglass floors support the keel. The inboard shrouds are anchored to the pan by means of Navtec chainplate rods. This method of building works well, but the pan must be strongly bonded to

The drop-leaf table on centerline seems to work well, despite the odd complaint. It features a storage well in its center, a handy feature. We like the U-shaped galley and separate nav station. The headroom is six-foot plus, and there's separate access to the head from the forward cabin.

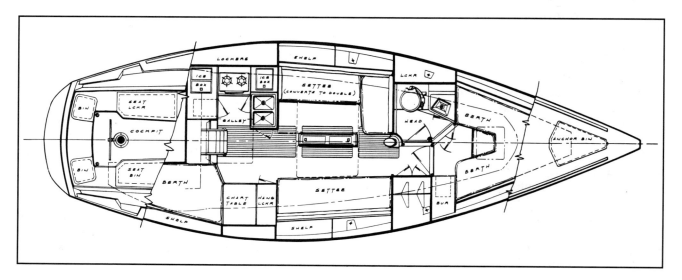

the hull, without causing hard spots, and this can can be difficult to ascertain, even by a professional surveyor.

According to the brochure, major bulkheads are bonded to the hull, bolted to the pan and screwed to the headliner. All wooden components are solid teak or teak-faced plywood.

The O'Day 34 was mass produced and built to a price. Owners' comments range from, "She's survived groundings, rocks and hurricanes, " to "Worst finish I have seen. Entire surface of boat has pinholes in gelcoat." Most disturbing are the several remarks referring to fastenings and supports, such as, "Reinforcement is missing in key areas."

We have received numerous complaints about the gelcoat, including porosity, voids, and stress cracking.

One reader said his rudder delaminated due to leakage, and that the replacement rudder blistered after three days.

Owners give at best fair ratings to the woodwork and cosmetics.

The Isomat spar and rig received generally high ratings with no failures reported.

Like most production boats built in large quantities, the O'Day 34 was never intended as a long-distance cruising boat, nor an offshore racer—the beef simply isn't there. It is, however, a good coastal cruiser that may be raced in local club regattas under the PHRF.

Performance

Owners rate speed upwind and off the wind between good and above average, with numerous caveats. The PHRF rating of the O'Day 34 with standard keel is about 147, with the shoal draft model rating a few seconds per mile slower. Some owners indicate ratings as much as 12 seconds faster, but these do not appear in our master listing.

The boat tracks fairly well upwind, but owners are not as fond of its handling off the wind, which is a little surprising given the extreme aft location of the rudder. However, compared to a full keel boat, most fin keelers will seem a bit skittish.

The vast majority of owners say the boat is very stable, even the shoal keel models. A large number also say the boat has a bothersome weather helm. One said he raked the mast forward and eliminated the problem. Another said it takes 18 knots of wind with full mainsail and 150-percent genoa to put the rail in the water. As would be expected of this design, it doesn't balance well at extreme angles of heel. Flat bottom boats like to sail on their bottoms, not on their sides, at which attitude their water planes become asymmetrical and their spade rudders tend to stall.

Under power, the O'Day 34 performs reasonably well with its three-cylinder, 21-hp. Universal diesel (30-gallon aluminum fuel tank). Power is cited as adequate only. Most owners say it backs down well. "First sailboat I've owned that (almost) backs in a straight line! " wrote a Wisconsin reader.

Interior

As suggested earlier, we don't have a lot to say about the interior, as the plan is quite conventional. We do note that it does have a nice, snug, U-shaped galley, which gives the cook his or her own private space to work. And there is a separate navigation area, as well as a wet locker.

Headroom is 6' 2" in the main cabin, lowering to 6' 1/2" forward. The V-berth measures 6' 7" by 6' 6". The settees are 6' 6" long and the quarter berth is 6' 5".

The galley is all twos, with twin sinks, twin iceboxes, and space for a two-burner stove. A propane stove with oven was optional. The water supply is contained in two tanks totaling 50 gallons.

The head has a 15-gallon holding tank standard, and an optional shower with hot and cold pressure-water system.

Owners give the interior generally high marks for livability and comfort. As seems the trend with this boat, however, such ratings are not without qualifications. One owner said, "Layout of settees and table is poor for any sitting position." More commonly, a Port Jefferson, New York owner called it "Superbly designed, inside and out. It feels like a much bigger boat."

Conclusion

The O'Day 34 does have its fans. Most owners like their boats, though most also have a few gripes, typically minor stuff that can be fixed or upgraded without a great deal of expense. We worry more about reports of deck and rudder delamination, and the absence of reinforcements in such areas as the bow. An owner in Tierre Verde, FIorida, sums it up well, saying, "Do not buy this boat if you want an offshore cruiser. Do buy this boat if you want a with-everything daysailer, a lake or bay or coastal cruiser. For the right purpose it's a great buy!"

This is a great boat for some people—fairly fast, most of the amenities for comfortable cruising, and nice looking. For those looking for a more solid, long-range cruiser, the O'Day 34 comes up short on several counts. The spade rudder, especially on the shoal keel version where it is essentially the same depth, is vulnerable. Complaints about delamination and inadequate reinforcements worry us, too. We don't know if our conclusions are justified, but we've always felt that O'Day was best at building smaller boats, and that their boats over 30 feet were just too "all-around" to excel at anything. Unless we found one at a price we couldn't refuse, we'd look for a 34 with more quality, like the Sabre 34. **• PS**

Irwin Citation 34

A mainstream coastal cruiser from an economy builder still managing to survive.

Irwin Yachts has been in operation for 27 years, one of the true old-timers in the fiberglass sail boat business. When we talked to them regarding the Irwin 34, they had just weathered the roughest storm of their history, having settled with their creditors and recovered from Chapter 11, when many other companies in similar situations were folding.

Irwin's recovery was marked by the start of a new production 50-foot cruiser. The new boat, like all the boats throughout the company's history, was designed by Ted Irwin, who has served continuously as CEO of the company as well as chief designer. In this respect, Irwin is like Catalina Yachts, whose CEO and chief designer Frank Butler is second only to Irwin in business longevity.

Like Catalina, Irwin has generally aimed at the economy end of the sailboat spectrum. However, unlike Catalina, Irwin Yachts has built a great variety of sailboats, 47 different models before their latest 50-footer—all sailboats, all larger than 20', from all-out race machines to full-tilt cruisers. Among American companies, only Pearson comes close to Irwin in the variety of cruising sailboats produced over the last quarter of a century.

The Irwin 34 is in many respects a typical Irwin boat. It was originally called the "Citation 34," which was meant to indicate that it was more of a plush cruiser than the race-oriented Irwins at the time, but more of a racer than the larger cruisers.

According to the company, 305 Irwin 34s were built in the production run, from 1978 to 1985, a moderate but successful model for the era. Near the end of its production, the boat was advertised as the Irwin 34 rather than the Citation 34. There were no major changes in the boat from beginning to end, just the details and equipment that are typical of any long production run.

Specifications

LOA	34' 3"
LWL	27' 4"
Beam	11' 3"
Draft	4' 0"/5' 4" (cb/keel)
Displacement	11,500 lbs.
Ballast	4,100 lbs.
Sail area	538 sq. ft.

Owners report mixed feelings in dealing with the company. Irwin dealers got good marks, though there are a few complaints about "incompetents and crooks." The main objection over the years has been about slow response from the company, especially regarding warranty claims on new boats and getting basic information on older models. However, long-term owners report that the company seems to have ups and downs in customer service.

Design and Construction

In design, the 34 looks like a cross between the old 1960s beamy CCA centerboarder and the mid-70s IOR racer, a combination that results in a moderate design and hence a healthy coastal cruiser. The bow has a distinctive concave curve, typical of many

Owners' Comments

"The hull is good, but the fittings seem to be borderline. It has the best layout I have seen in a 34, but I would not buy another one because the exterior finish is so poor."

—1980 model in the Chesapeake

"For a liveaboard, the boat offers the best price/size factor. A lot of little problems, though: gate valves are sealed with 3M-5200, making installation of seacocks very difficult. Tanks utilize excessive under-bunk space, Irwin's own wheel pedestal creates problems in mounting instruments, and the wheel is too large for the cockpit. It needs a self-tailing mainsheet winch and the sheet winches should be mounted further aft. Head lighting is terrible."

—1984 model in Galveston Bay

"There is little I can complain about, but I don't have the confidence I should in a boat this size. The fiberglass work is not, or doesn't seem to be of high quality. The mast also seems light, but I've had no problems."

—1980 model on Long Island Sound

"Don't hesitate—buy it. It's a great boat. I think it is built a little light for distance cruising. For the way I use it, it fits my needs."

—1982 model in Massachusetts

"This is a good boat for the money—fine for coastal cruising in fair weather. Irwin could spend more time on details."

—1981 model in Massachusetts

"The Irwin 34 is a 'price' boat, but after looking at the Sabre 34, Aloha 10.4, Baba 30, Pearson 34, O'Day 34, Cal 35, Catalina 36, and others, I feel that this is a better boat, and it was $10,000-$15,000 cheaper than any of the above."

—1983 model in Texas

"The boat needs to come with an owner's manual, including wiring and plumbing diagrams."

—1983 model on Lake of the Ozarks

"I had many problems, especially leaks which I had to fix, but I would buy another as it is a very good value and sails well for shoal draft."

—1982 model in Louisiana

"The Citation 34 is a well-designed and fast sailboat. More attention to details would make it watertight below decks and afford some badly needed privacy (a must in a boat designed to sleep six!). There is an obvious shortage of locker space, particularly a wet locker."

—1979 model in Lake Erie

"I had nine pages of warranty claims. Water and fuel tanks leaked; all ports leaked; all hatches leaked, the sump pump didn't work, the starboard chainplate wasn't installed properly, the shaft strut failed, all stanchions leaked, the teak finish-work below was not completed, gelcoat voids everywhere, traveller leaked, etc. etc. The words 'quality control' cannot be used with the word Irwin when describing production."

—1978 model in Florida

Irwin designs, and a flattish sheer, with a molded-in cove stripe to make the sheerline appear a bit higher in the bow. The stern sections have the peculiar tuck-up typical of IOR boats of the era. The trunk cabin is traditional looking and fairly low. Overall, we think the boat is an attractive example of the modern racer-cruiser.

Underwater, the hull is beamy and saucer shaped. The centerline of the hull aft of the keel forms a shallow fence which runs back to form a skeg in front of the spade rudder. Though the boat was available with a deep fin keel, drawing 5' 4", the centerboard model was far more popular. Company literature advertises a shoal draft keel as standard, with the fin and centerboard as options, but we have never seen a shoal-draft model and none of the owners in our surveys had the shoal-draft version. Brochures show the shallow-draft keel as identical in outline to the

centerboard model but with no board installed.

The centerboard lifts into a shallow stub keel, and the pennant is a Dacron rope; it runs to the deck through a tube which forms a grab rail at the front edge of the galley. We examined three used 34s, and the two centerboard models each had badly chafed centerboard pennants needing replacement.

Other than the chafe problem, the centerboard version of the boat is probably to be preferred if you have a choice. Unlike some boats which are designed for a fin and compromised with a centerboard, the hull shape looks well matched to the board, and few designers have as much experience with centerboards as Ted Irwin.

The hull is a conventional lay-up of mat and woven roving. The deck is a conventional balsa core sandwich.

The three boats we examined all had decent gelcoat

and exterior finish, but owners in our surveys report an inordinate incidence of gelcoat problems, including patches coming off, large voids, and excessive crazing. One boat we looked at had quite a few repaired spots in the deck molding, and we suspect most of the gelcoat problems were new boat problems. Once fixed, they should not be a major concern for the used boat buyer.

With regard to other elements of construction, quality is on the poor side. In fact, the three boats we examined were serious contenders in our own used-boat search but were finally rejected because we didn't like many details of the way the boats were built. For example, two of the boats we looked at clearly had a history of deck leaks at the portlights and a variety of fittings. The interior is generally well finished with teak-faced plywood and an interior liner, but the ceiling and liner made it very difficult to get at the inside of the hull and deck to trace or fix the leaks. It was clear that the previous owners had little luck in stopping the leaks. Further, the hull-to-deck joint is fastened with sheet metal screws rather than bolts. The screws are installed both vertically, from the top of the aluminum toe rail, and horizontally, from the side of the toe rail. Through-bolting is preferable.

More importantly, on the boat we were most interested in, it was evident that the hull-to-deck joint was leaking, at best a nuisance, at worst a major repair job. Though we couldn't examine most of the joint because of the interior joinerwork, we did find one spot where the deck molding actually did not overlap the hull flange. You could see the underside of the toerail from inside the boat.

On one boat, the deck cleats were fastened only with sheet metal screws, and on all the boats, the bow and stern pulpits were only screwed down rather than through-bolted.

There were several details—cheap through-hull valves, no washers on chainplate bolts—which were relatively easy to correct, but they put us off the boat.

Obviously, Irwin believes these construction details are adequate, but we consider them very minimal or problematic—something we would feel compelled to correct.

In contrast to the details, the basic fiberglass work seemed solid and good on all the boats we examined.

Interior

The interior of the 34 is generally well done, good production-line work with teak veneer and plastic. Some of the details of the cabinetry were a little sloppy on the boats we examined, but all in all the interior of the boat, when new, was undoubtedly a strong selling point.

There are three good berths—a V-berth double and a quarter berth. The quarter berth will be just a little tight, especially at the foot, for a large, tall man. The settee is usable as a single berth (it's a very comfortable settee), and the dinette opposite is convertible to a small double. The head is of good size, and the galley is well arranged in a sort of wrap-around U. There's a good electrical panel at the aft side of the galley. The nav station is set at an angle, with the table a bit small though adequate.

The Irwin 34 came with seven opening ports as well as forward and midship hatches, so ventilation should be good.

Stowage below is minimal, since tankage occupies space below the berths—a shortcoming of the modern hull shape. Tankage is adequate on the boat—30 gallons fuel, 80 gallons water, and a big holding tank for the head—a rarity on production boats of this size.

There's little bilge in the boat, which can cause problems when you take water inside the hull. This showed up in the discolored and delaminated teak/

The Irwin 34's interior has a fairly straightforward layout, but with a number of angled bulkheads to add interest. The sink is near the centerline to facilitate draining on either tack.

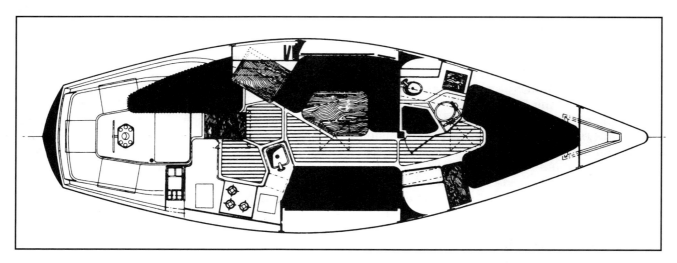

holly plywood on the cabin sole of two of the boats at which we looked.

Original standard equipment is quite complete and modern—hot/cold pressure water, shower, propane stove, 4" cushions, AC and DC electrical systems, and so on, meaning that little upgrading should be necessary, assuming the boat has been well kept.

Overall, the interior seems very desirable for a couple cruising or a couple with one or two children. There are no privacy doors for the forward cabin, so two couples will have to be (or become) intimate while cruising.

On Deck

The deck is conventional but well done for working the boat. There's a deck-opening anchor locker forward, wide side decks, and a good big cockpit with a small ice/beer locker, two lazarettes, and a propane tank locker.

A wheel was standard on the boat. A nice feature is that a portion of the cockpit sole is removable for superior engine access, the best we have seen on a boat this size. Cockpit drains are also large, another rarity on production boats.

The companionway opening is large, with just a small lip/step above the cockpit sole. While not desirable in an offshore boat, this is okay in a coastal cruiser and makes for easy access to the interior. Most owners will want to arrange a way to secure the lowest companionway drop board, so it can be left in place during rough conditions.

The mainsheet traveler is on the cabin top, just ahead of the companionway. While this is a conve-nient location, the boats we looked at had exceptionally unsightly dodgers because the multi-part mainsheet was somewhat in the way.

Performance

The boat came with a Yanmar 15, which generally gets good reports from owners, though some think the boat is a bit underpowered. A 20-hp Yanmar was available as an option, and this would be desirable if a buyer were choosing between otherwise similar boats; the 20-hp model would be smoother running as well as more powerful.

The boat we sailed handled adequately under power, though some owners report it difficult to back up straight. Most of the 34s had solid props, and the performance-oriented sailor will want to upgrade to a folding or feathering prop so the boat's sailing ability isn't hurt.

The boat has a big rig, well balanced between mainsail and jib, and as you can expect from Ted Irwin's design board, it is a good sailing boat. With a PHRF rating around 160, it is slightly slower than other cruiser/racers of that era, like the C & C 34, but it will make good passages, especially off the wind.

Many owners report that they consider the boat quite tender, especially the centerboard model, but we found the boat to be reasonably stiff, with lots of initial stability from the beamy hull. We didn't sail the boat in heavy air, but we suspect an early reef would be desirable. Cruisers will find that it works well to sail the boat under roller-furling jib alone.

Early boats may have the DynaFurl roller which came as an option from Irwin, and buyers may want

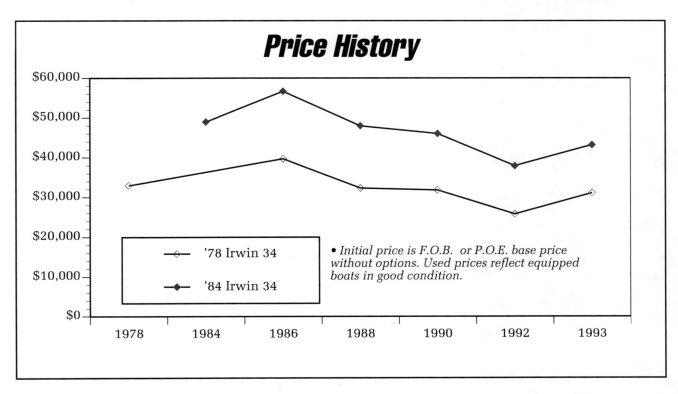

to factor in a replacement in their price figuring. The boats are generally of an age where the original sails are still aboard and, for all practical purposes, best used as drop cloths. Though the boat was advertised as a "club racer," we saw no used 34s with spinnakers or any spinnaker gear, so a chute and related gear may also have to be purchased to complete a sail inventory.

Standard winches on the boat were minimal, and an upgrade will be desirable if the original owner didn't buy the optional package when the boat was new.

The rig is adequate, the only problem reported by owners being paint problems on the mast, perhaps from a poor priming job on the aluminum. The mast of one boat we looked at had been re-painted.

Conclusions

It is an excellent design, a wholesome all-around racer/cruiser with shallow draft that would serve a family's needs as a coastal cruiser, at a reasonable cost.

Unfortunately, the Irwin 34 suffers from some corner-cutting: details of construction which are cheap or shoddy, such as using only screws to secure the hull-to-deck joint.

Realistically, those details should not hamper the boat's use in normal conditions as a coastal cruiser, but are substandard compared to many other boats available. We generally would not recommend the boat to anyone contemplating ocean passages, unless considerable basic upgrading had been completed.

But for a coastal cruiser, for an owner who likes to do some upgrading, the boat is a handsome, well-thought-out design, with a good interior, well-equipped. In today's market, it offers a lot of basic boat, especially if bought at the right price. • **PS**

Hunter 34

Like other Hunters, the 34 bears the stamp of a mass-produced boat—but she's better than older Hunters.

When the Hunter 34 was introduced in late 1982, it was the second of the "modern" generation of Hunters, the first being the rather remarkable Hunter 54. The Hunter company has been strongly identified with the long-distance singlehanded racing of its president, Warren Luhrs. Although Luhrs has not been particularly successful in his racing, his own boats have been innovative, and the concepts of innovation and high-tech have to some degree rubbed off on Hunter's production boats.

Hunter has always gone after the entry-level cruising boat owner, and has traditionally pushed its "Cruise Pac" concept—a boat delivered equipped down to the life jackets, and ready to go. This certainly reduces the amount of decision making required by inexperienced boat owners, and has been a successful marketing strategy. For more experienced sailors who would rather choose their own gear, the Cruise Pac idea is not necessarily a plus.

In just over three years, over 800 Hunter 34s were built. For the 1986 model year, the 34 was phased out in favor of the even more Eurostyled Legend 35.

A number of Hunter 34 owners responding to our survey moved up from smaller boats in the Hunter line—exactly what every builder would like to see happen. All reported that the Hunter 34 was light-years ahead in both design and workmanship compared to earlier models.

Because the Hunter 34 was only in production for a few years, few changes were made between model years. You are therefore less likely to find major upgrades on older boats than you would find on a boat that has been in production for a long time.

Sailing Performance

The Hunter 34 is a fast boat, particularly in light air. This is due almost entirely to her huge rig, which

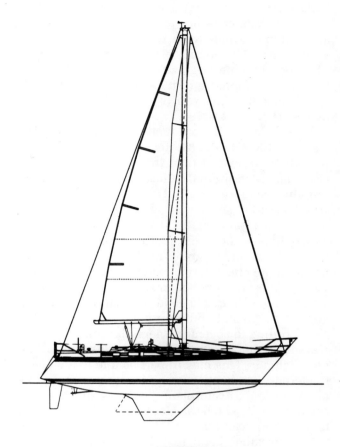

Specifications

LOA	34' 5"
LWL	28' 3"
Beam	11' 7"
Draft	4' 3"/5' 6" (shoal/std)
Displacement	11,820 lbs.
Ballast	5,000 lbs.
Sail area	577 sq. ft.

towers over 51' above the waterline. Owners report that in winds of from seven to 12 knots, the boat is practically unbeatable in club racing. The typical PHRF rating of 135 for the deep keel boat is faster than most other cruiser/racers of her size.

There is a price to be paid for that speed, however. A number of owners responding to our survey report that the original Hunter 34 is a very tippy boat, in either the deep keel or shoal draft version. In winds of 15 knots true or more, it's time to reef the main when going upwind. In fact, the boat's lack of stability is the single most commonly criticized aspect of the Hunter 34's performance in our survey. One owner was considering cutting several feet off his mast. Others have stepped down from 150% headsails to 135% or smaller overlaps.

Normally, you would expect a boat with a 42% ballast/displacement ratio to be stiff. The keel of the deep-draft Hunter 34, however, has most of its weight and volume up high, while the shoal draft keel, even with its extra 220 pounds of ballast, still has a fairly high vertical center of gravity. This just goes to show that you can't judge a boat's stability by its ballast/displacement ratio—you've got to know how far down that weight is, too.

Models late in the production run had more ballast. The 1985 Hunter 34 brochure shows about 450 pounds more ballast than in the 1983 model. For cruising, the additional ballast would be a real plus. For club racing with a full crew, the lighter boats could be sailed faster.

Using headsails smaller than 150% on the Hunter 34 would be a good idea, particularly if you couple them with a modern roller furling system. A 135% jib can more effectively be reduced to 110% than a 150% genoa can be reefed to 120%. Since the boat is sensitive to sail area, a good headsail roller furling system is a must, in our opinion.

According to several owners, the Hunter 34 carries substantial weather helm in anything more than very light air. This may in part be due to the boat's tenderness. As boats with wide sterns and narrow bows heel, the waterplane becomes substantially asymmetrical, which can give the boat a pronounced tendency to head up.

This weather helm may be exacerbated by an original rudder design that some owners report was both too small and too weak for the boat. Several owners reported cracking of the original rudders, which Hunter replaced with a larger, stronger, "high performance" rudder. Unfortunately, in some cases Hunter only paid part of the replacement costs; owners were stuck with the rest. We wouldn't want a Hunter 34 without the high performance rudder. The better rudder was standard equipment on 1984 and 1985 models.

The complex B&R rig, with its swept-back spreaders and diamond shrouds, is also a headache for some owners. There's a lot of rigging for a novice to adjust, and according to our survey, the dealers who commissioned the boats were not necessarily more capable of adjusting the rig than the owners.

One problem with the B&R rig is that, on any point of sail freer than a broad reach, the mainsail will fetch up on the spreaders and shrouds. You can apply patches to keep the spreaders from poking holes in the mainsail, but we think the shrouds are likely to chafe on the sail almost from head to foot when running, no matter what you do.

In addition, the lack of either forward lower shrouds, baby stay, or inner forestay means that if the headstay goes, the rig may follow before you can do anything to prevent it. One owner in our survey reported losing his rig when the roller furling headstay failed. Most new sailors have enough trouble tuning a simple, single-spreader rig with double lower shrouds. The multi-spreader, multi-shroud B&R rig may seem incomprehensible to them, and they may never be able to tune the rig for good performance.

The boat is very fast upwind, but only average in speed off the wind. With a spinnaker, downwind performance would be greatly improved. The high aspect ratio mainsail simply doesn't project enough area for efficient downwind sailing, particularly since you can't square the boom to the mast due to the swept-back spreaders.

Engine

Most Hunter 34s are equipped with the Yanmar 3GMF, a three-cylinder, fresh water cooled diesel that puts out about 22.5 hp. This is an excellent engine, although early versions, according to some owners in our survey, were plagued by vibration.

Some of the first Hunter 34s were equipped with the Westerbeke 21 diesel. In our opinion, the Yanmar is a much more desirable engine. For boats to be used in salt water, check to make sure that the engine is fresh water cooled, rather than raw water cooled. Some early versions of this engine lacked fresh water cooling, and they will not last as long when used in salt water.

Access to the engine for service is good. The Yanmar is more than adequate power for the boat, and she should cruise under power at 5 1/2 knots or more without any trouble. The fuel capacity of 25 gallons should give a range of about 275 miles.

Construction

Hunters are mass-produced boats at the low end of the price scale. The Hunter 34 was the first "small" Hunter to be built with a molded hull liner. A molded liner can add considerable strength to a single-skin boat, and the use of integral molded furniture components can greatly speed assembly. Assembly is the right word, too: these boats are assembled, rather than built.

The original tooling for a hull liner is quite expensive. It is therefore only practical on a boat that is expected to have a fairly large production run.

Not everything about the Hunter 34's hull liner is a plus, however. According to several owners, any leakage from the stuffing box can be trapped between the liner and the hull, never draining to the bilge. This could not only smell bad after a while, but could possibly cause problems in a cold climate if trapped water freezes without room to expand. The pre-assembly technique common with liners also means that many systems are installed in ways that can make them difficult to service after the hull, deck, and liner are put together.

Hunter quality control is criticized by some owners in our survey. Complaints include chafed hoses, raw edges, systems hooked up improperly, and leaking ports and hatches. In our opinion, that's a quality control problem, pure and simple, and it can be a maintenance headache for owners. One owner reported a leaking hull-to-deck joint. When he checked it, he found that many of the bolts had apparently never been torqued down when the hull and deck were joined. We don't think the boat should have left the factory in that condition.

On the positive side, owners of Hunter 34s who had owned older Hunters report that in general the construction details of the 34 are superior to those of older boats.

Do not expect to find a lot of fancy teak joinerwork on the Hunter 34. Some owners complain that both the interior and exterior teak trim is poorly fitted and poorly finished. Obviously, you could do a lot to improve this if you wanted to—as some owners have—but don't expect a dramatic increase in the value of the boat for your efforts.

The iron keels of the Hunter 34s can also be a maintenance headache. Some owners say the keels did not come from the factory with adequate protection to avoid rusting—which is almost impossible to prevent with an iron keel. Other owners report that the keel-to-hull seam cracks open, allowing salt water into the joint—which results in more rust. This is a cosmetic problem now, but we think it could over time become a structural problem.

The deck molding has been a source of trouble on some boats. The molded non-skid isn't very non-skid when it gets wet. There are also a number of reports of gelcoat flaws in the deck, including voids and blistering. At least one owner reports that the outer deck laminate in his cockpit has separated from the wood core.

Several owners complain that some molded deck components—cockpit locker covers, anchor well covers—are simply too light, and tend to crack.

Interior

The Hunter 34 was one of the first boats under 35' to offer a tri-cabin layout, and this interior design is frequently cited as a primary reason for buying the boat. Now, of course, it is common for boats this size to have three cabins.

The only real complaint voiced about the interior of the Hunter 34 is the narrowness of the foot of the forward V-berth. Despite being pushed far forward in the hull, the forward cabin feels big due to the long cabin trunk, which extends clear to the anchor well, giving extra headroom over the berth. Standing headroom in the forward cabin drops off to less than 6' due to the sloping cabin trunk.

Just aft of the forward cabin is a full-width head. This makes a lot of sense in a boat this size, since the combination of head and passageway would make for both a cramped head and a narrow passageway.

According to some owner surveys, the plumbing for the toilet leaves a lot to be desired. They report that the holding tank system smells, apparently due to porous hoses and a poor vent design.

Instead of the more common U-shaped dinette, the Hunter 34 has a rather old-fashioned dinette with athwartships seating. This certainly makes it easier to convert the dinette to a double berth, but it means that you can seat a maximum of four at the table for dinner. On the port side, the head of the settee berth is used as the seat for the chart table—a design compromise, since that settee is one of only two potential sea berths on the boat.

This was one of the first boats in its size range to offer a three-cabin interior, and overall it works well. Owners cite the interior as one of the boat's major selling points.

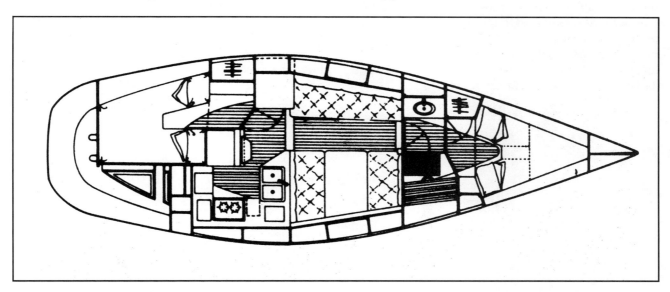

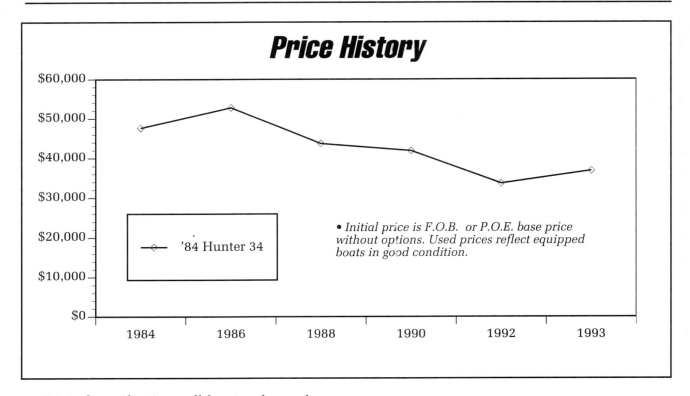

Price History

'84 Hunter 34

• Initial price is F.O.B. or P.O.E. base price without options. Used prices reflect equipped boats in good condition.

Original specifications call for a two-burner kerosene stove. Kerosene never caught on as a cooking fuel in this country, partly because it is so difficult to get high-grade kerosene here. Propane or CNG would be far better choices for cooking fuel, since low-grade kerosene is a dirty fuel, and alcohol is expensive, inefficient, and in our opinion, dangerous.

As you would expect on a boat this size, the aft cabin is pretty small, with limited standing area. Despite the fact that the double berth is mostly under the cockpit, there is adequate headroom over it due to the fact that the cockpit is quite shallow.

The privacy of the tri-cabin layout is very important for a family with children, or owners that like to cruise with another couple. The single fixed berth in the main cabin means that the boat will sleep only five without making up the dinette. "Only" five is a pretty good number in a boat this size, and the most important thing is that it sleeps five in a reasonable level of comfort. All in all, the interior of the Hunter 34 is well thought out and livable.

Conclusions

The general design and finish of the Hunter 34 are far ahead of older boats by the company. The Eurostyling of the deck and interior were pretty unusual when the boat first came out, but fairly typical of boats built five years after the Hunter 34 was introduced.

Nevertheless, this is still a mass-produced boat with what some owners consider mediocre quality control and finishing details. It is a fast sailer, but may be so tippy that it discourages some novices. You should definitely sail the boat before you buy it. The B&R rig may also scare off some new sailors.

Because of the problems with the deck molding, a used Hunter 34 should be carefully and professionally surveyed before purchase.

If you want a fast, modern small coastal cruiser with maximum room at minimum cost, a Hunter 34 would be a good choice. But remember that you're buying a mass-produced boat, and it's not realisitic to expect custom quality at this price.   • **PS**

Tartan 34

There are a lot of shortcomings to the 34. But she's well designed and well built, and the price is right.

It may be hard to believe, but it's been about 25 years since Olin Stephens designed the break-through 12 meter sloop *Intrepid*. Just a year later, he designed the Tartan 34, a keel/centerboard, CCA racer/cruiser, for Douglass & McLeod Plastics, the company that became Tartan Marine.

The CCA was a true racer/cruiser rule. Heavy displacement was encouraged, and keel/centerboarders were treated more than fairly, as the success of designs such as S&S's *Finisterre* shows. Even top racing boats had real interiors—enclosed heads, permanent berths, usable galleys. You could buy a boat like the Tartan 34, and given good sails and sailing skills, you could actually be reasonably competitive on the race course. And then a couple could take their racing boat cruising, without a crew.

This was no "golden age" of yacht design, however. Interiors were unimaginative and fairly cramped. Galleys were small, and few boats had such amenities as hot water, gas cooking, refrigeration, and showers—things that are taken for granted today. Navigation stations were rudimentary. Sailhandling gear, by modern standards, was almost a joke. There were no self-tailing winches, few hydraulic rig controls, and roller-reefing headsail systems were primitive. Mylar and Kevlar were off in the future, loran was expensive and hard to use.

Yet some boats from this period, for all their "shortcomings" by modern standards, are classics in the truest sense: the Bermuda 40, the Luders 33, the Bristol 40, the Cal 40. And the Tartan 34.

More than 500 Tartan 34s were built between 1968 and 1978. By 1978 the CCA rule was long gone, PHRF racing was beginning to surge, and the MHS (now IMS) was in its infancy. The Tartan 34 had passed from a racer/cruiser to a cruiser, not because the boat had changed, but because sailboat racing

Specifications

LOA	34' 5"
LWL	25' 0"
Beam	10' 2"
Draft	3' 11"/8' 4" (board up/down)
Displacement	11,200 lbs.
Ballast	5,000 lbs.
Sail area	483 sq. ft.

had changed. The Tartan 34 was succeeded by the larger, more modern Tartan 37, a boat of exactly the same concept.

The boats are widely distributed in this country, but there are large concentrations along the North Atlantic coast, the Chesapeake, and in the Great Lakes. You'll find them wherever the water is shallow.

Read this and weep: in 1970, a Tartan 34, complete with sails, cost about $22,000. By 1975, the price had gone all the way up to $29,000. Today, equipped with more modern equipment, the boat would cost $100,000 to build.

Sailing Performance

The Tartan 34's PHRF rating of about 168 to 174 is

Owners' Comments

"Gelcoat on deck and cabin trunk is a bit thin and shows air pockets. Check for stress cracks in deck and forward cabin trunk corners, also wear between centerboard and centerboard axle.

"Check through hull fittings. Ours has brass pipe nipples and gate valves which have failed, but all in all we have a good vessel which sails very well."

—1971 model in Vermont

"I've really come to appreciate the traditional lines and the teak, although it's a pain to keep the teak looking good. Storage space is awkward and not all usable without difficulty.

"The large cockpit is great for daysailing with guests. We'd like a shower in the head. We added a wheel. Watch the placement: it should be between the icebox hatch and the cockpit locker, well forward.

"I wasn't in love with the boat when I bought her, but I've come to appreciate her quality, performance, and livability while adjusting to her few shortcomings."

—1972 model in Maryland

"The stainless steel water tank and icebox liner were poorly soldered, with cold joints. This is a great-sailing, forgiving boat for those who like a relatively fast traditional boat. You need to like teak and enjoy caring for it to keep the boat looking its best."

—1972 model in Pennsylvania

"The centerboard operating mechanism has broken twice, and the boom was shortened excessively in response to the IOR rule.

"Never crank the centerboard when there is any pressure or resistance on the board. This is a solid, attractive cruising boat."

—1975 model in Pennsylvania

"We've had problems with the deck gelcoat since day one, otherwise she has been a trouble-free boat. Other Tartans have had similar gelcoat problems.

"I would recommend the boat. She is a good sailing boat and an excellent value compared to new boats of her size."

—1976 model in New Jersey

"The icebox should be insulated better. The centerboard mechanism is unusually susceptible to damage. I've probably been further in a Tartan 34 than anyone: the Virgins, the Dominican Republic, Haiti, Puerto Rico, the Bahamas."

—1974 model in Florida

"The head is too small. The chart table is awful. Electrical switches are in a bad location. We shifted the traveler to the cabin top—much better.

"Overall it's a great boat, all boats being compromises of sorts. Engine location cannot be praised enough. Keep the tiller."

—1972 model in Rhode Island

comparable to more modern fast cruisers of similar displacement, such as the Nonsuch 30 and Pearson 31. The boat is significantly slower, however, than newer cruiser/racers of similar length but lighter displacement, like the C&C 33.

Like most centerboarders, the Tartan 34 is quite a bit faster downwind than upwind, and the boat can be run downwind more effectively than a fin-keeler. For example, in only 16 knots of true wind, optimum jibe angle is 173°—about 5° lower than the typical modern fin-keel boat.

Because of her shoal draft, the boat's center of gravity is fairly high. Righting moment at 1° is about 630 ft/lbs—some 20% less than a modern fin-keel cruiser/racer of the same displacement. This means that the Tartan 34 is initially more tender than a more modern deep-keel boat.

As first built, specifications called for 4,600 pounds of ballast. That was increased to 5,000 pounds on later models, although the boat's displacement is not listed by the builder as having increased with the addition of the ballast. We're not sure where the 400 pounds of displacement went.

The boat originally had a mainsail aspect ratio of about 2 1/2:1, with a mainsail foot measurement of 13'. The mainsheet on this model leads awkwardly to a cockpit-spanning traveler just above the tiller, well aft of the helmsman. An end-of-boom lead was essential because of the old-fashioned roller-reefing boom. This traveler location really breaks up the cockpit.

Although a tiller was standard, you will find wheel steering on many boats. Owners report no particular problems with either tiller or wheel. In both cases, the helmsman sits at the forward end of the cockpit.

With the introduction of the IOR, mainsail area was penalized relative to headsail area, and the main boom of the Tartan 34 was shortened by about 2 1/2'. This allowed placement of the traveler at the aft end of the bridgedeck, a far better location for trimming the main, which was still equipped with a roller-reefing boom.

Neither the base of the foretriangle nor the height of the rig was increased to offset the loss of mainsail area. According to some owners, the loss of about 35 square feet of sail area can be felt in light-air conditions. At the same time, shortening the foot of the mainsail did a lot to reduce the weather helm the boat carries when reaching in heavy air. Some boats with the shorter boom have made up the missing sail area by increasing jib overlap from 150% to 170%, but this lowers the aspect ratio of the sail, costing some efficiency.

We would recommend a compromise on boats with the roller-reefing boom. When the time comes to buy a new mainsail, get a new boom equipped with internal slab reefing, internal outhaul, and stoppers at the inboard end of the boom. If it's not already there, install a modern traveler on the bridgedeck. Instead of going with either the short or long mainsail foot, compromise on one of about 12'. A modern, deep-section boom would not require that the mainsheet load be spread out over the boom. You could sheet to a single point over the traveler, about 2' inboard of the end of the boom.

A major advantage of a centerboard is that the lead (the difference in fore-and-aft location between the center of lateral resistance of the hull and the center of effort of the sailplan) can be shifted as the balance of the boat changes. Tartan 34 owners report using the board to ease the helm when reaching in heavy conditions.

Like almost all S&S designs, the Tartan 34 is a good all-around sailing boat without significant bad habits. Owners who race the boat say that she should be sailed on her feet: at an angle of heel of over 20°, the boat starts to slow down and make leeway. USYRU's velocity prediction program disagrees, saying that the boat should be sailed at higher angles of heel upwind and reaching in wind velocities of 14 knots or more.

Since the boat is relatively narrow, the position of the chainplates at the deck edge is not a serious handicap for upwind performance. With single spreaders and double lower shrouds, the rig is about as simple and sturdy as you get. A yawl rig was optional, but most boats are sloops.

Engine

Like other auxiliaries of its era, most Tartan 34s are powered by the Atomic 4 gasoline engine. Beginning in 1975, the Farymann R-30-M diesel was an option. Either engine is adequate power for the boat, but it is not overpowered by any stretch of the imagination. The Atomic 4 is a smoother and quieter engine.

Those Atomic 4s are starting to get old. On a boat you plan to keep for more than a few years, the expense of switching over to a diesel can be justified. The Universal Model 25 is a drop-in replacement for the Atomic 4 in many cases, but check carefully to make sure there is enough room, since the Atomic 4 is one of the world's smallest four-cylinder engines.

The engine location under the port main cabin settee is a big plus, with one exception: since it's in the bilge, it is vulnerable in the case of hull flooding. Almost everything else about the installation is good. The engine weight is just aft of the longitudinal center of bouyancy, where its effect on trim and pitching moment is negligible. By disassembling the settee, you have complete access to the engine for servicing and repairs, and you'll be sitting in the middle of the main cabin, rather than crunched up under the cockpit. The shaft is short, minimizing vibration. There is no external prop strut to cause alignment problems, create drag, and possibly come loose from the hull.

The interior is utterly traditional, with all the bad features that go along with such a layout. One unusual feature is the cork cabin sole, which may be good for traction and insulation, but it gets dirty.

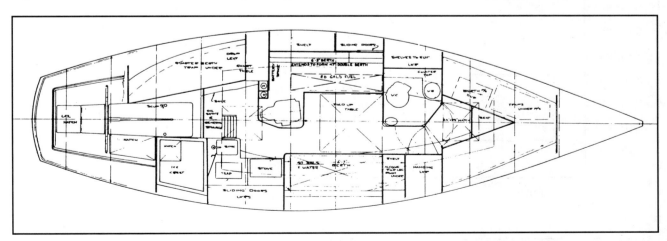

At the same time, clearance between the prop and the hull is minimal, so you can't go to a much bigger engine and prop. Because the prop is located far forward, the boat is difficult to back down in a straight line, and prop efficiency is reduced because the prop is partially hidden behind the trailing edge of the keel to reduce drag.

Some boats that race have replaced the orginal solid prop with a folding one, but if you mark the shaft so that you know when the prop is lined up with the back of the keel, the drag of the solid prop should be virtually indistinguishable from that of a folding prop. For best performance under both sail and power, we would choose a feathering prop if we had money to burn.

Original drawings show a 21-gallon gas tank located under the cockpit. Later boats have a 26-gallon fuel tank under the port settee in the main cabin, where the weight of fuel will have minimal effect on trim and pitching.

Construction

Tartan is a good builder, and the basic construction of the Tartan 34 is sound. There are, however, some age-related problems that show up repeatedly on our owners' surveys. The most common of these is gelcoat cracking and crazing of the deck molding, particularly in the area of the foredeck and forward end of the cabin trunk.

A related problem that some owners mention is delamination of the balsa-cored deck. Modern end-grain balsa coring is pre-sealed with resin by the manufacturer to prevent resin starvation when the core is actually glassed to the deck. A cored deck depends on its solid sandwich construction for rigidity. If there are spots where the core and deck are not completely bonded, the deck will yield in this area. This is what is referred to as a "soft" deck. As the deck flexes, the relatively brittle bond between the core and its fiberglass skin can fail, so that the "soft" areas grow. This is very common in older glass boats.

A very careful survey of the deck should be conducted when purchasing a Tartan 34. This will include tapping every square inch of the deck with a plastic mallet to locate voids or areas of delamination. Minor areas of delamination can be repaired by injecting epoxy resin through holes in the upper deck skin. Large areas of delamination may be cause for rejection of the boat, or a major price reduction.

Another frequently-mentioned problem with the Tartan 34 is the centerboard and its operating mechanism. Unlike many centerboards, this one secures positively in whatever position you set it—it won't freely pivot upward if you hit a rock. Centerboard groundings are extremely common, as it's very easy to forget that the board is down.

One construction detail on a boat of the general quality of the Tartan 34 is disturbing. On early boats, through hull fittings consist of brass pipe nipples glassed into the hull, with gate valves on the inside. This is acceptable on a boat used only in fresh water, since there won't be any galvanic corrosion. In salt water, however, this is an unacceptable installation. Brass pipe contains a lot of zinc, and it will disappear from the pipe nipples and gate valves just like your

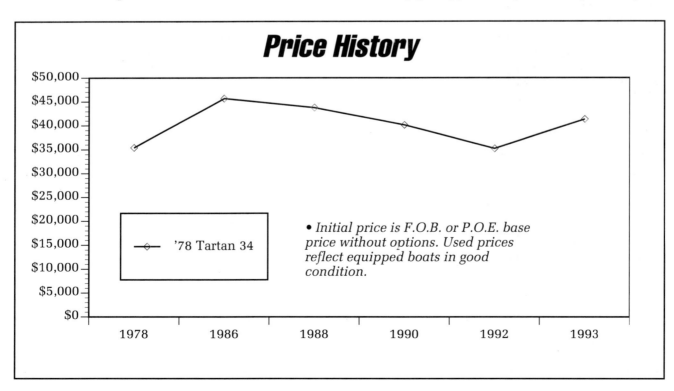

shaft zincs corrode away. Due to the age of the boats, these fittings should be immediately replaced with proper through hull fittings and seacocks, either of bronze or reinforced plastic.

Many deck fittings are chrome-plated bronze, and particularly on boats used in salt water, the chrome is likely to be pitted and peeling. Fortunately, this is a cosmetic problem, and you can get the stuff replated if you really want it to look good.

According to owner reports, the Tartan 34 has had an average number of cases of bottom blistering. That's pretty good for boats of this vintage.

There's a lot of exterior teak on the boat, including teak cockpit coamings, forward hatch frame, handrails, and a high teak toerail. On some boats we have looked at the toerail is kept varnished, but it isn't easy to keep varnish on a piece of teak that periodically gets dipped underwater.

The electrical system is pretty primitive, with a 30-amp alternator, fuses instead of circuit breakers, minimal lighting.

Over the years, most of these boats have added gear such as navigation electronics, more lights, pumps, and probably a second battery. We would carefully examine the electrical system, since pigtailing additional equipment onto a basic system can result in horrible installations.

Interior

If you want three-cabin interiors and condo-like space, you're not going to like the interior of the Tartan 34. This is not a floating motor home. It is a sailboat, and it has an interior layout that is as traditional as they get.

There is no pleasure-dome owner's cabin, shower stall, or gourmet galley. Even the nav station is rudimentary—a drop-leaf table at the head of the quarterberth.

There are fixed berths for five in the original arrangement, and the port settee extends to form a double. In later boats, lockers outboard of the port settee were replaced with a pilot berth. This may be a better arrangement for racing, but you don't need that many berths for cruising.

We wouldn't want to spend more than a weekend on the boat with more than four adults, and we wouldn't cruise for a week or more with more than two adults and two well-behaved children. But then we wouldn't do that on many boats less than 40'.

On the plus side, all the berths are long, including a 7' quarterberth. Even the forward V-berths are wide enough at the foot for big people.

Good headroom is carried all the way forward: 6' 2" in the forward cabin, a little more aft.

The cabin sole is pretty much level throughout the boat, except in front of the galley dresser and quarterberth.

The cabin sole is cork, an unusual feature. Cork is a good natural insulator, and provides great traction underfoot. It does, however, absorb dirt and grease, and it's difficult to keep clean.

Interior finish is typical of boats of this period: pretty drab, pretty basic. There are no fancy curved moldings and rounded laminated door frames. The original finish in early boats is painted plywood bulkheads with oiled teak trim. You can dress this up a lot by varnishing the wood trim. On later boats, the main bulkheads are teak-faced plywood, while the rest of the flat surfaces are white laminate.

There is a drop-leaf main cabin table, covered with wood-grained plastic laminate. Whoever invented wood-grained plastic laminate should be consigned to an eternity of varnishing splintery fir plywood with a foam brush on a foggy day. We'd rather see an acre of white Formica than a square foot of wood-grained plastic laminate, no matter how "real" it looks.

Because the fuel tank, water tanks, and engine are located under the main cabin settees, there's no storage space in these areas. Storage space in the rest of the boat is good, although hanging space for clothes is limited.

Water capacity is 36 gallons. This is inadequate for a boat that will cruise for more than a week with two people.

Like most boats from this period, the galley is small, consisting of a two-burner alcohol stove, an icebox with mediocre insulation, and a single sink. Original specifications called for a stove with no oven. Many boats by now have been upgraded to more modern cooking facilities—a must if you plan any real cruising.

The icebox is large, tucked under the starboard cockpit seat, and accessible from both the galley and the cockpit. It is difficult to reach into the box from the galley, since you have to stretch over the sink, and it has a vertical door rather than a horizontal hatch.

Conclusions

Given the shortcomings of boats such as the Tartan 34, why would you want one? There are lots of reasons. The boat is well-designed and well-built. With modern sailhandling equipment, two people can easily manage the sailing, and the boat will be reasonably fast.

The boat is seaworthy, the type of boat we'd choose for cruising someplace like the Bahamas. With minor upgrading, she is suited to reasonable offshore cruising.

Oh, yes, don't forget. This is a good-looking boat, a real classic. With freshly-painted topsides and varnished teak, she'll still turn heads anywhere. And that means a lot to a real sailor. **• PS**

Beneteau First 345

The marks of mass production on this flashy sloop, though masked, are still evident.

Can a boat be all things to all people? Last year in Rhode Island, two sailors who had differing ideas about what a sailboat should be went shopping for one to go partners on. One was mainly interested in performance and wanted a speedy club racer with sufficient amenities for one or two couples.

The second, with a wife and small child, was looking for more of a cruising boat, one that was stiff and stable but with excellent accommodations below. They settled on a Beneteau First 345, and at the end of their first sailing season both were satisfied with their choice.

History

Beneteau is far and away the most successful sailboat builder in the world right now. Its closest rival is another French company, Jeanneau, and in the United States only Catalina and Hunter match the kind of mass market appeal that Beneteau has enjoyed during the last half-decade. With 30 models available and annual sales last year of more than $70 million, Beneteau clearly is doing something right. Prior to the slowdown of recent years, Beneteau was cranking out 5,000 boats annually, about 400 of which were built in the U.S.

The company was founded by Andre Benjamin Beneteau in 1884 in the Atlantic coast town of Croix-de-Vie as a builder of wooden fishing boats. In the mid-60s at the instigation of Andre's granddaughter, Annette Roux, the firm took its first tentative dip into recreational boating waters with a small yacht called, appropriately, the Halibut.

By 1974, Beneteau had captured 11 percent of the French sailboat market, but it wasn't until the mid-1980s, when the strong U.S. dollar sent Americans searching overseas for bargains, that the company,

Specifications

LOA	34' 6"
LWL	28' 8"
Beam	11' 6"
Draft	6' 4"
Displacement	12,600 lbs.
Ballast	4,651 lbs.
Sail area	690 sq. ft. (with genoa)

along with other European builders, began making serious inroads into the U.S. sailboat market. Today, with Roux as chief executive officer, Beneteau exports 60 percent of its boats, primarily to the United States and Australia.

A favorable currency exchange may have initially attracted American buyers to French boats, but a blend of high style and performance gave them an increasing share of the market. Both Beneteau and Jeanneau had to overcome what Michael Lecholop, Beneteau's U.S. vice president for sales, called a misperception about their quality created by the strong dollar.

The exchange, he said, made the boats appear to be much cheaper than they actually were. Eventually, Beneteau gained a reputation for producing a

Owners' Comments

"Best sailing boat I've ever been on. Maneuverability excellent. Speed under power marginal."
—1987 model in Georgia

"We lose pointing ability due to shoal draft keel. Out in rough stuff, the boat holds up well. Heels rather easily. Cockpit is wet. No real place to put a dodger."
—1985 model in Vermont

"Our boat sails so beautifully. It's a stiff boat and it points high. It's heavy-duty."
—1984 model in Massachusetts

"Put two coats of varnish on the teak down below, don't buy the French sails."
—1985 model in Illinois

"Would prefer that the traveler not be across the companionway."
—1984 model in Virginia

boat of reasonable quality at a reasonable price—with the added plus of performance. In 1987, Beneteau felt confident enough of its U.S. sales to build its own plant in Marion, South Carolina. The firm, which had sales of $22 million last year in this country, is third in the American market behind Catalina and Hunter. In terms of quality, Lecholop said Beneteau considers its competition to be Tartan and the now-defunct Pearson.

Design

The Beneteau First 345 was designed as a moderate displacement racer/cruiser, and much of its popularity has been because of its success in blending the two functions. In fact, it could be said that the First is a racing boat that contains a cruising interior. The architect is Jean Berret, a Frenchman noted for his cruising and racing designs (he designed the 1985 Admiral's Cup winner, *Phoenix*, a Beneteau one-tonner).

At 12,600 pounds displacement the 345 is not overbuilt by any means but still substantially heavier than, for example, the Farr 34 (8,176 lbs.) or the J/35 (10,000 lbs.). On the other hand, it's significantly lighter than a full-keel 34-footer like the Mason 34 (14,020 lbs.) yet carries 690 square feet of sail compared to 602 square feet on the Mason.

The First has a PHRF rating of 120 in four of the largest national fleets (slightly higher in several other fleets), making it reasonably quick—faster by 20 seconds per mile than both the Tartan and Pearson 34, and faster than the Cal 34 and Catalina 34.

Within the Beneteau model line, the First series represents the performance-oriented designs, while the Evasion and the newer Oceanis are geared more for cruising. The fin keel and spade rudder of the 345, coupled with a shallow bottom, have minimal wetted surface. The keel comes in either a deep (6' 4") or shoal draft (4' 10") version. The boat is masthead-rigged and equipped with running backstays in addition to a permanent backstay, and carries as a norm a mainsail of 258 square feet (roughly) and a genoa of about 431 square feet. The running backstays apparently are necessary to help stabilize the tall stick when going to windward in heavy weather, but they will be a nuisance to the leisurely cruising couple.

The deck is clean and easy to move about, including the side decks leading forward. The cockpit is deep, roomy and protected by its coamings and wide side decks.

The First came with either a cruising or a racing package. In the racing version, the mast is a foot taller, a tiller replaces the wheel and the mainsheet traveler is positioned across the rear of the bridgedeck rather than across the cabin top. Unless you are adamant about having a wheel, the racing version seems to make the most sense because of easier access to the traveler. The 345 was in production from 1984 until 1988. More than 500 were sold—all but about 20 built in France.

Construction

French-built boats once bore the reputation of good design-poor quality. The French, their American counterparts would say, lacked modern, temperature-controlled facilities and often turned out suspect laminates. We're not sure what the old Beneteau facilities were like, but visitors to their newer plants tell a different story. Jono Billings of Jamestown Boat Yard in Rhode Island, an authorized Beneteau repair yard, called the South Carolina plant "the most modern I've seen. It's clean, there's very little smell and it's really well organized."

Jono Billings' repair work raises another issue about Beneteaus—their reputation for hull blistering. He said that one series of boats was made with a defective catalyst that resulted in a high rate of blistering. The company won a lawsuit against the resin maker and offers free repairs on all affected boats. According to Benetau, the catalyst problem affected several models between 1983 and 1985.

According to our own survey, Beneteau's overall

blistering record is high-average, about on a par with Pearson Yachts and C & C. The newer Beneteaus, that feature a blister barrier in the gelcoat, come with a limited 10-year warranty.

With six manufacturing plants, there's no mistaking that a Beneteau is a mass-produced boat with all the signs—interior liners, molded-in berths, lots of veneer, etc. But the result is a surprisingly well-constructed boat. Hulls are made of uncored reinforced fiberglass, laid up in alternating layers of chopped strand, omnidirectional mat and woven roving saturated with polyester resin. The hull is reinforced by interior stringers, structural bulkheads and by the interior fiberglass liner and pan.

Deck, cabin top and cockpit are a single glass molding, with built-in nonskid surfaces where appropriate. The deck is balsa-cored, and the 1985 model we looked at exhibited some exposed core material visible from within the chain locker that had been saturated with water, according to a recent marine survey. That trouble spot could herald further deck delamination, the surveyor concluded.

The hull-deck joint is a standard inward flange arrangement fastened with 3M 5200 sealant and further strengthened by the aluminum toe rail, which is riveted to the hull. The boats, according to Lecholop, are rated for offshore work under Bureau Veritas standards, the French equivalent of Lloyd's of London. Still, we prefer through-bolts to rivets; even if strength isn't the issue, bolts greatly facilitate future repairs.

The Isomat spar is keel-stepped. The keel, which is cast iron rather than lead, is secured to the hull by means of a laminated plate integral with the hull. The keel bolts, visible in the shallow bilge, appeared to be rusty despite a coating of some flexible compound. The rudder is fiberglass with a stainless steel stock (here again, the surveyor found excessive moisture, indicating potential future problems).

One problem with foreign-made boats is that all components may not meet U.S. standards. On the 1985 boat, the surveyor, A.D. Robbins and Co. of Dover, New Hampshire, found that the gate valve shutoff fixtures for the galley sink drain and engine seawater intake apparently were not of marine-grade copper alloys and thus corrosion prone and subject to failure. All other fixtures were bronze or stainless steel and satisfactory.

Performance

On an early October Saturday, with a moderately strong southeasterly wind blowing, *Godzilla* (nee *Witch of the Waves*) moved smartly out of Narragansett Bay on a close reach toward Brenton Reef tower. Sail consisted of an unreefed main of undetermined French make and a 140-percent roller furling jib from Ulmer-Kolius. The 345 is powerful and fast, and easily cut through the waves and over a cross swell coming in from the Atlantic. According to on-board instruments, the boat was moving along at close to its 7.1-knot hull speed on the reach—about normal for the conditions, the owners said. Switching to a beat, in 18 knots apparent, the boat naturally slowed (here, the crew attached the running backstays). On a run back toward the bay, *Godzilla* sped along at close to seven knots.

With its fin keel and fairly light ballast, the 345 reacted to gusts but was easily controlled. The regular crew felt the helm was nicely balanced, but we detected a tendency to round up in gusts. Some owners responding to our questionnaire also cited annoying weather helm.

The spade rudder, while requiring some working, made for fast tacking and quick response to the tiller. The owner of a 1987 model with a cutter rig reported excellent heavy-weather performance under staysail and reefed main. With a sloop rig, the boat flattens out when reefed before 20 knots. We've heard con-

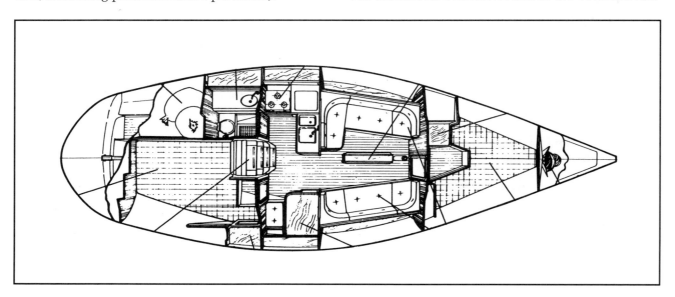

flicting opinions about the shoal draft version's pointing ability; based on our sail, the deep keel is close-winded.

The most common complaint in our questionnaires was the boat's poor speed and maneuverability under power. "Strong helm to fight when under power," wrote one, whose boat was powered by the standard Volvo 2002. "My only complaint is that under power the boat's performance is marginal," another said. The owners of *Godzilla,* which was powered by a 28-h.p. three-stroke Volvo 2003, had no such complaints. (Engine access from three sides, via the aft cabin and behind the companionway steps, is excellent.)

The cockpit is roomy and comfortable with sufficient freeboard and beam to keep things dry from whatever spray was sent up by the bow. The outboard sides of the coamings, over which the crew can hike out, are patterned with nonskid—a nice touch and "something you won't find on a cruising boat," said a racer in the crew.

Shrouds and lead blocks are inboard, allowing narrower sheeting angles. It is difficult, however, for the helmsman to reach the bridgedeck-mounted mainsheet traveler. Raise the jib, and you have a boat that's best sailed by two.

Clearly the boat is better set up for racing than short-handed cruising. Jibs are trimmed on #43 Lewmar winches retrofitted with cheap rubber collars that serve as a form of self-tailing. In reality, the setup was cumbersome and difficult to release under load; replacing them with genuine self-tailing gear is a priority of the owners.

Interior

The interior of the 345 is neat, functional and roomy. The layout, in typical Euro-style, has an aft cabin, dual settees in the saloon and a surprisingly roomy double V-berth forward. The aft cabin, to starboard, is a little cramped vertically, especially the berth under the cockpit—okay for sleeping but not much else. (One couple mitigates this by sleeping athwartships.) Another owner found it the perfect enclosed playpen for his toddler. The 345 comes in a second configuration, with two tiny quarter cabins and the head forward of the main cabin. This version is favored by the charter trade, but the single aft cabin seems preferable for ordinary cruising.

Aft and to port is the head. Both owners liked the location for its privacy and convenience. Like most enclosed heads on a boat this size, the compartment is a little small and could use a grabrail. The head is equipped with a Brydon marine toilet, fitted with a Y-valve leading to a holding tank.

Gray water from the shower is led forward to a bilge sump behind the mast step. Fresh water was contained in two tanks under the settees, totaling about 100 gallons. Some boats have rigid tanks; *Godzilla* has a flexible, bladder-type tank that seemed in good condition. Its light weight is another concession to performance, and it won't last as long as a quality rigid tank.

The L-shaped galley is forward of the head and equipped with a three-burner propane Electrolux stove. Refrigeration is an icebox. To starboard, there is a good-sized chart table, a bit cramped for head-

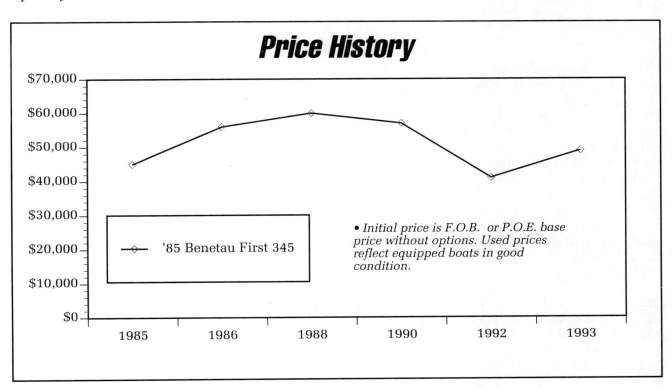

Price History

• *Initial price is F.O.B. or P.O.E. base price without options. Used prices reflect equipped boats in good condition.*

—◇— '85 Benetau First 345

room on the outboard side for anyone over 5' 10". The main saloon is spacious, the double settees comfortable (one reader praised the quality of French foam). The amidships table contains Beneteau's trademark wine rack plus additional storage space in the legs; beneath it is another trademark—the small bilge cover that converts to a dustpan. Headroom is more than six feet. Storage is ample and inconspicuous throughout.

It's almost impossible to find the inside of the hull because of the liner, the liberal use of teak veneer, and padding on the upper bulkheads and ceiling. The overall appearance is pleasant, not gaudy, and the padding is functional as well as aesthetic. Nevertheless, we'd hate to search for the source of a serious leak beneath all the interior decoration.

In the original Benetau First series, the settees and bunks were covered in subdued fabrics—green in this instance; the newer First S-series have the unusual Philippe Starck interiors with dark wood bulkheads and lots of silver and stainless steel, which Lecholop said "you either hate or love, but you won't forget."

The forward V-berth cabin, apparently the sleeping spot of choice for most 345 owners, is spacious, comfortable and private. There's a hanging closet to port, drawers to starboard and lots of natural light from a translucent hatch.

Natural lighting in the main cabin is supplied by side ports covered outside with a sporty, one-piece smoked Plexiglas panel. This is an inexpensive way to manufacture portlights, and it is stylish, but of course they cannot be made to open and the absence of frames often makes for an unfinished look. There is a double overhead sliding hatch that also serves as a spinnaker launching area. Several owners complained that the overhead fluorescent lighting is too dim.

Conclusions

Satisfied Beneteau 345 owners list style and performance as their motivation for selecting this model. They also refer to good value for the money. We'd have to agree on all points. You can get a Beneteau for under $50,000—in the low forties for an older model, which is somewhat more than a Hunter 34 but slightly less than a comparable Tartan. The boat sails exceptionally well, and the interior is pleasant and accommodating. It's not a Swan or a Sabre, but it is a reasonably well-put-together production boat that sells for a fair price.

The boat's strong point is definitely its performance. The deep narrow fin keel and spade rudder, plus shallow bilges, running backstays and flexible water tank make it unsuitable for long-term cruising. We worry too about the riveted toerail, maintenance on the iron keel and gate valves—all indicators of less than top quality construction. **• PS**

Catalina 34

From America's largest sailboat builder, this all-around design represents a good value.

It doesn't take a lot of brains to see that Catalina is doing something right that a lot of other sailboat makers aren't. They're the largest sailboat builder in the country, and a terrible year for them would be Valhalla for almost every other manufacturer. With more than 1,000 built in seven years, the Catalina 34 has to be in the running as the most successful production boat of the 1980s.

Equipment

When we went aboard the Catalina 34 at the 1990 Chicago Boat Show, we were first impressed by the equipment. Whereas many of the 1970s Catalinas came with what we considered second-rate hardware and gear that mandated owner upgrading, the 34, like the other contemporary Catalinas, is well equipped.

Self-tailing primary winches are standard and adequately sized; sail-handling hardware is all good; brand-names abound everywhere—stove, opening ports, pressure-water pump, head. It's all the same or similar to what you'd find on 34' boats costing $30,000 more.

The list of standard equipment is complete enough that you could conceivably sail the boat away with no options, a far cry from the old-fashioned method of selling a base boat with no lifelines, bilge pumps, or cushions aboard.

The 1990 boat we looked at carried a base price of $58,895, which included a main and 110% jib, mainsail cover, two-burner stove with oven, hot & cold pressure-water system, two batteries, 110-volt shore power system, boarding ladder, and lots of other equipment.

With electronics and other factory options (including a Hood furler and a microwave oven), the boat had a price of $75,999, and the dealer was talking "special show price" to a serious customer on board. The only really essential pieces of equipment not on the boat were a couple of anchors, life jackets, flares, and a bell.

Specifications

LOA	34' 6"
LWL	29' 10"
Beam	11' 9"
Draft	5' 7"/3' 10" (fin/wing keel)
Displacement	11,950 lbs.
Ballast	5,000 lbs.
Sail area	528 sq. ft.

Design

Except for the old Catalina 38 (which was not a Frank Butler design), all the Catalinas have a similar conservatively modern look—fin keel and spade rudder, short overhangs, and a flattish sheerline. The distinctive cabin house and diamond-shaped sail emblem help identify a Catalina.

The hull of the 34 is modern, with full sections to provide lots of room below. It seems more refined than the Catalina 27, 30, and 36, which is probably why we prefer the 34. Like the other Catalinas, the 34

Owners' Comments

"Overall, the boat is good. It does what it was designed for well and with good value for the money. It needs some upgrading for any offshore work."

—New Hampshire owner

"I have been extremely pleased with the performance and quality of my 34. Have used it for three seasons with only minor problems—all of them easily corrected by myself."

—Michigan owner

"This is an excellent coastal cruiser built to a low sales price. I feel that basic safety is not compromised, but you do notice some quality problems in the teak and a few gelcoat cracks at corners where the mold was not completely filled. The interior space is excellent, but it does reduce storage space somewhat."

—Connecticut owner

"Blocks used on the mainsheet traveller suck. The ports leak (but have been changed to another manufacturer on newer boats)."

—Southern California owner

"Overall, a pretty good boat for the area we sail in and for the money. It's only average quality. There are much better quality boats out there, but you will pay 10% to 20% more for the same size. My wife says the galley is only fair."

—Detroit owner

"This boat far exceeds other boats of the same size in livability, especially since it costs substantially less than the Pearson, Tartan, and Island Packet. We looked at the Hunter, and it does not compare to the Catalina in quality of material and workmanship."

—New Jersey owner

"I'm not happy with the wing keel. I ordered the boom vang—it does not include the shackle. There were other small nickel and dime things."

—Rhode Island owner

---

combines a long waterline, a moderate to light displacement, and a large sail area to ensure good sailing performance.

The interior design is in the European mode, the first of the Catalinas to have the head aft by the companionway. Unlike European boats such as the Beneteau or Jeanneau in the same size range, however, the Catalina is very full forward, with a big V-berth cabin and a big dinette and settee ahead of the L-shaped galley and the nav station.

The aft cabin will be the principal cabin for most owners. It has a sizable athwartship berth. There's a seating area between the berth and the galley, though we're not sure how usable it would be.

According to our owner survey, the interior is the most praised aspect of the 34, with comments like "most room for the money" appearing in a majority of reports. It's always been a strong selling point with all the Catalinas—they're hard to beat for sheer interior volume.

There are several aspects of the Catalina design we don't like, such as the huge companionway hatches and molded furniture "pans" that limit stowage and access to the hull. But overall we cannot take serious objection to any important aspect of the design. They are wholesome but plain boats.

Performance Under Sail and Power

We sailed the 34 for only one afternoon, on Lake Michigan, and found the boat to be a good performer.

It was a puffy day, so the boat was occasionally overcanvased and developed a strong weather helm (due in part to a poorly shaped mainsail). Even with a good main, we suspect that cruisers will want to take an early reef as the wind builds; in fact, if we owned the boat we'd experiment with sailing it extensively under roller jib alone.

The 34 sailed well on all points of sail, but it seemed a bit sluggish off the wind without a downwind sail.

With a PHRF rating around 144, she is about in the middle of the speed range for contemporary boats her size, considerably slower than the J/35 but significantly faster than the Crealock 34.

We'd call her sailing ability respectable, good enough to make smart cruising passages and quick enough to sail to her handicap rating on the race course.

The 34 we sailed had the standard 5' 7" draft fin keel, but the boat also is available with a wing keel option, drawing 3' 10". Owner reports in our boat surveys give decidedly mixed reviews to the wing, some condemning it as only a "flopper-stopper" and not an efficient foil at all, and others praising its seaworthiness and the good ride it gives in waves. Unless we were desperate for the shallow draft, we'd be inclined to go with the standard fin rather than the wing.

Standard power is a three-cylinder Universal 25 diesel which we found adequate. However, owners again report mixed feelings about the engine. A few thought the boat was underpowered, a few said they wished they'd bought the three-bladed "cruising" prop, which is a popular option.

The boat does come with a four-cylinder Universal 35 diesel as an option, and this may be desirable for the cruiser as it gives more power.

To get better performance under power, we'd opt for the bigger diesel rather than the three-bladed solid prop, which would hurt sailing performance. In fact, we wouldn't consider even a two-bladed fixed prop on this boat, since it would degrade one of the Catalina 34's best qualities—her sailing performance.

Construction

Layup, laminates, balsa core and other construction details are conventional. The boat is generally well-engineered and well-executed. It is certainly adequate for typical coastal cruising, weekending, and daysailing.

If good engineering means doing a good job of adapting means to ends, or materials to functions, then the Catalina 34 is well-engineered.

True, we don't like the feel of the foredeck, which seems a little spongy compared to the teak-over-glass decks of our old Cheoy Lee. But we know a 1972 Catalina 27 well, and its foredeck has the same feel now that it had when new. It has served well and, we must conclude, was engineered and built as planned. We suspect the foredeck of the Catalina 34 will hold up for 20 years as well.

We don't like the way the interior liner flexes either, or the way it hides most of the inside of the hull, but it holds up and it performs the cosmetic function for which it was intended.

The chainplates seem small when we compare them to the half-inch stainless plates on our Carter 36. But we've never heard of a Catalina's chainplates failing, and they're undoubtedly up to the job. Good engineering.

Some boats are overbuilt, which can be expensive—a waste of money for an American coastal sailor who has no plans to sail in the Southern Ocean. Worse is to build a boat no better than the Catalina 34 and charge $30,000 more.

Conclusion

The Catalina 34 is a successful, all-around design from a hugely successful company. Because Catalina sells so many boats and runs an efficient manufacturing facility, its boats typically sell for less than other brands of comparable size.

This fact, plus the great number of used Catalinas on the market, mean that a buyer can be quite selective.

We do not recommend the Catalina 34 for extended offshore cruising, at least not without making some modifications to the companionway, upgrading the rigging, and possibly stiffening areas of the hull.

But the boat was neither designed, constructed, nor intended for such use. Indeed, most owners do not need such a boat. For the majority of American family sailors, the Catalina 34 will satisfy their needs just fine.   • **PS**

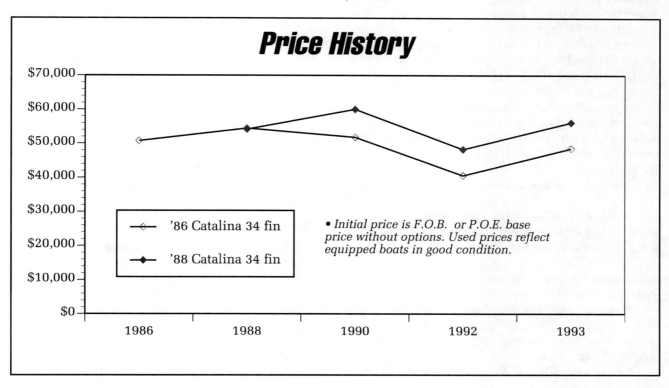

Price History

$70,000
$60,000
$50,000
$40,000
$30,000
$20,000
$10,000
$0

1986   1988   1990   1992   1993

—◇— '86 Catalina 34 fin
—◆— '88 Catalina 34 fin

• *Initial price is F.O.B. or P.O.E. base price without options. Used prices reflect equipped boats in good condition.*

The J/34c

An expensive coastal cruiser that has a single strong suit—sailing performance.

In 1985, J Boats first tested the cruising market with the J/40. They followed up in 1986 with the J/28. In 1987, they introduced yet another cruiser, the J/34c. Twenty-five were sold in the first production year. The last was built in 1990. The designation "c" was added to distinguish the boat from the J/34, an IOR design that failed both on the race course and in the sales room.

Like all the J/cruisers, the J/34c is an example of what happens when a group of "gung-ho" racers designs a cruising boat. Racers are obsessed with how a boat sails, how it feels. They know that ease of handling is essential for enjoyable sailing, and they know that this is as dependent on hardware choice and layout as it is on design.

For a racer, going below is something you do when you're too tired to sail anymore. This isn't to say that the J/34c is poorly laid out belowdecks. It's just that her strong points are abovedecks.

In appearance, the J/34c looks much like her sister J/cruisers. She has a fixed shoal draft keel, a straight sheer, and a slotted Goiot aluminum toerail. Her waterline, at 30', is long. It leaves her little overhang for appearance.

Although she has modest freeboard and cabin house profile (headroom below is barely 6'), she will still seem a little "squarish" for traditionalists. To enhance her appearance, a boat can be ordered with a 4" high teak toerail that tapers as it runs aft.

As a rule, the J Boat line is expensive. The 34c was no exception. Base price in 1989 was almost $100,000. With basic sails and electronics, and options like propane, shore power, vinyl overhead panels, varnished interior, swim ladder, dodger, roller furling, refrigeration, and spinnaker gear, the price could approach $130,000.

This puts the J/34c at the upper end of the price

Specifications

LOA	34' 6"
LWL	30' 0"
Beam	11' 1"
Draft	4' 11"
Displacement	10,000 lbs.
Ballast	4,500 lbs.
Sail area	712 sq. ft.

range for boats of her size. By comparison, the Hunter 33.5, while admittedly of lesser quality, had a 1989 base price of only $55,000. The Crealock 34, of similar quality to the J/34c, also had a similar $100,000 base price.

Hull and Deck

To support their claims of superior construction, Tillotson-Pearson had all of their larger boats, including the J/34c, ABS (American Bureau of Shipping) certified. Similar to a Lloyds certification, this proves that each boat has been built to certain standards and inspected by an independent surveyor at various stages of construction.

ABS has three levels of certification: hull plan approval, hull certification, and A-1 classification

which includes hull, power, electrical and plumbing systems. An ABS-certified boat is fitted with a bronze plaque. Any builder can claim he builds to ABS standards; without the plaque it is only a claim. ABS inspection and A-1 classification added about $2,000 to the cost of the J/34c.

Like all J Boats, the 34c is constructed of fiberglass and polyester resin, and cored with balsa. Standard, uncoated Baltek balsa is used, but the balsa sheets are sprayed with quick-catalyzed polyester before being laid in the mold. This helps seal the balsa end grain and avoid dry spots in the layup. This is an important step, because the laminate is not vacuum-bagged, as would be done on a custom boat.

A barrier layer of vinylester resin between the gelcoat and the first lamination prevents blistering, says the builder. The hull is warranted against blistering for 10 years.

Much of the laminate is of unidirectional cloth. Unlike typical fiberglass cloth, which is woven, unidirectional cloth is constructed by stitching sheets of unidirectional fibers together, typically at 90° or 45° angles. Without the "crimp" caused by having to weave the fibers around each other, the finished laminate is stronger.

The hull-to-deck joint is Tillotson-Pearson's standard, seaworthy, inward-turned hull flange with the deck and toerail through-bolted and bonded with 3M 5200 polyurethane adhesive.

All of the deck fittings are also bedded with 5200.

Superb hardware and good deck layout have resulted in a boat that is very easy to handle. On top of that, she is faster than most coastal cruisers her size.

The holes drilled for deck fastenings are countersunk to further improve the bond and reduce gelcoat crazing. This should ensure a watertight deck. The only drawback is that 5200 is such a powerful adhesive that later removal of hardware for repair or replacement is difficult.

The only molded interior components are the hull stringers, the icebox and the head. The rest of the interior is constructed of lauan teak-faced marine plywood and installed piece by piece.

When an interior is installed this way, you can use more fiberglass tabbing to attach it to the hull. This gives you the potential for a hull which will remain stiffer longer. With a one-piece molded interior, you must set the interior on putty and rely on spot tabbing.

All of the structural interior components in the J/34c are tabbed on both sides, for most of their length, with fiberglass cloth. The small, non-structural components are tabbed on one side with fiberglass mat. Except for the fact that no fillet is used to spread the loads on the tabbing, this is a good method.

Rig

Unlike many builders who have gone to less expensive spars from mass-production manufacturers like

Isomat, J Boats still equips its boats with more expensive rigs from Hall Spars.

The J/34c has a masthead double spreader rig, with speaders swept back 10°. Sweeping the spreaders aft gives the mast fore and aft stability, at the sacrifice of being able to adjust the bend easily. Running backstays are not needed to stabilize the mast.

Sweepback also requires the spreader bases to accept more of the shroud load. It should be no problem, as Hall uses a patented through-mast spreader bar, which incorporates tangs for the lower and intermediate shrouds. The spreaders fit over the bar, resulting in a clean, strong low-windage attachment.

Sweepback does hinder dead downwind performance slightly, because you cannot let the mainsail out as far. And it increases chafe on a fully-battened mainsail. We think the advantages outweigh these small drawbacks.

The mast is tapered and painted with Awlgrip. It is not anodized. The only mechanically fastened hardware items are the halyard exit plates and the spinnaker track. That's good, because like most production masts, the fittings are not bedded when installed. The gooseneck, vang fittings, cranes and halyard boxes are all welded on before the spar is painted.

Rod rigging is used, and the tangs are flush-mounted. Halyards are internal, but the spinnaker halyard turning blocks are hung from a masthead crane—a more seaworthy, traditional approach than the internal sheaves found on racing boats.

The boom has a powerful 6:1 outhaul with a recessed Teflon-lined track. A Hall Quik Vang is standard, and is a very convenient way to adjust boom vang tension. A Navtec hydraulic backstay adjuster is optional. The mast also has a single folding step to enable shorter crewmembers to climb up and attach the main halyard shackle. There are two reef lines, led internally. They cleat on deck-mounted clutch stoppers, a far more convenient system than gooseneck-mounted stoppers. A continuous system, made up of one line through the leech and the luff, would make reefing even simpler.

Engine and Mechanical Systems

The J/34c is powered by a 28 hp Volvo 2003 diesel engine. Being three-cylinder, it is relatively quiet. Engine access is good, but you have to get at it through a number of hatches because the engine is tucked well under the cockpit floor. There are two hatches next to the quarterberth and a single hatch in the cockpit sail locker, as well as the removable companionway ladder.

An aluminum fuel tank holds 26 gallons, which is adequate for coastal cruising.

Wiring and plumbing are done to ABS specifications. However, there is an exposed junction box in the head, where it is likely to get wet whenever someone takes a shower.

The head is equipped with a Raritan PH-2 toilet, and an 18-gallon holding tank with a Y-valve for overboard discharge. The toilet has a ceramic bowl and pumps with a lever handle, which is convenient, but the shut-off valve is operated with a knob instead of a lever. It's hard to dog down because it's often wet from overspray from the pump.

The boat we looked at had optional vinyl cabin overhead panels, held in place by strips of teak. The panels hide the wiring and deck fastenings, yet drop easily for access because they are held in place with un-bunged screws.

Standard water tank is 45 gallons, plenty for coastal cruising; an additional 35-gallon tank was optional. Hot and cold pressure water are standard. On the boat we sailed there was no overflow vent for

The interior is optimized for a couple or small family. Good features include a pair of doors in the main bulkhead, one of which leads to the head, the other to the forward cabin.

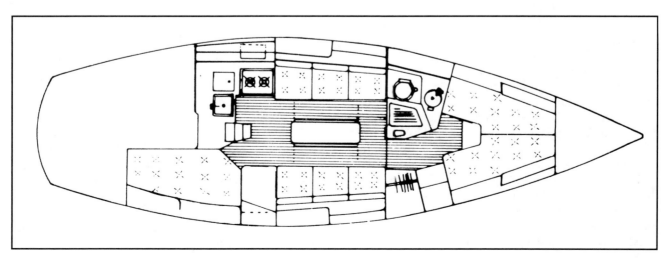

the water tank. Because the tank is plastic, when it is overfilled it expands and can damage the settee in which it is housed.

Propane cooking was an expensive option, but we recommend it over the alcohol alternative. A compartment aft of the cockpit holds two propane bottles, enough to last a summer of weekend sailing. The propane stove is a Force 10, two-burner gimbaled stove with oven.

Handling Under Power

The Volvo engine provides more than enough power. In flat water, the engine we used easily pushed the boat to hull speed, which was nearly 7 knots. A Martec folding prop is standard.

Edson wheel steering is standard, and includes a 40" diameter destroyer wheel. Combined with a balanced rudder and Harken roller rudder bearings, the J/34c is effortless to steer.

The boat is also equipped with an emergency tiller that can be quickly snapped onto the rudder post through a small hatch under the helmsman's seat. This is a good safety measure.

A 5" Ritchie compass is pedestal-mounted in a binnacle. It can only be read from behind the wheel. While this is fine for powering, it is difficult to use when the helmsman will be sitting to weather while sailing. Throttle and shift controls are also mounted on the steering pedestal.

Handling Under Sail

This is the J/34c's strong point, what sets her apart from the run-of-the-mill coastal cruiser. Her ease of handling is probably more a result of her deck layout and hardware than her design.

She is advertised as fast and smooth riding because of her long waterline. True, long waterlines have a higher potential hull speed. They can also make for a smoother ride when combined with short overhangs such as those on the J/34c. Short overhangs cut down on pitching by eliminating parasitic weight in the ends of the boat.

However, if not accompanied by a proportional increase in sail area, lengthening the waterline can detract from light air speed. The boat we sailed did seem to bog down in winds under 5 knots. It only had a 135% genoa. We'd recommend a 150% genoa, but the boat also seemed to be a bit on the tender side when the breeze increased to 12 knots. Remember that this is a shoal draft cruiser.

The J/34c's 30' waterline is long—perhaps too long. The leeward stern quarter was almost 5" under water when close reaching in a 6-8 knot breeze. Short overhangs may make it easier to climb up a stern ladder if thrown overboard, but if the bustle is insufficient to keep the stern from "digging" a hole in the water, speed can suffer.

This isn't to say that the J/34c is slow. In fact, she should be considered a performance cruiser, faster than a majority of cruisers her size. But like most boats, she isn't as perfect as the advertising suggests.

Her advertising also touts her large steering wheel and Harken rudder bearings. True, her steering is tight, quick to respond and frictionless. But like many modern designs, we'd have to say her rudder is overbalanced. A "balanced" rudder has the rudder

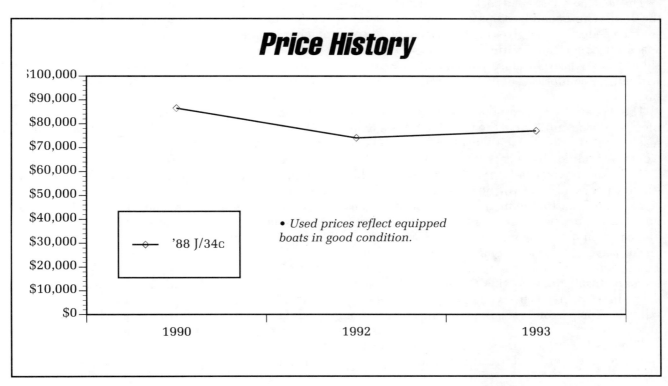

Price History

$100,000

$90,000

$80,000

$70,000

$60,000

$50,000

$40,000

$30,000

$20,000

$10,000

$0

◇ '88 J/34c

• *Used prices reflect equipped boats in good condition.*

1990   1992   1993

post placed somewhere near the center of the rudder blade. The more "balanced," the less helm, or "feel" a boat has.

With the J/34c, there is no helm at all—if you leave the helm, while sailing upwind or reaching, she goes straight. If you start a turn while powering, the wheel won't return to center unless you bring it back. Some sailors like this type of effortless steering, but we think that with roller rudder bearings and a large steering wheel, you are not going to tire your arm with a little bit of weather helm.

The J/34c is equipped with what the Johnstones call a "UFO" keel. It is a shoal draft keel with a conventional leading edge sweepback, the bottom ending in a flattened bulb. Unlike a winged keel, it shouldn't snag lobster pots and weeds.

When run aground, however, the UFO keel will still be more difficult to free than a conventional keel. The Johnstones report that the UFO keel is about seven to nine seconds per mile slower than a conventional keel upwind, but neither slower nor faster when reaching or running—a reasonable trade-off for those who need shoal draft. But for those who sail in deep water, it would be better if there were a deep draft option.

On Deck

The deck layout of the J/34c is what makes her a joy to sail, especially if you're at the wheel. The boat is laid out for shorthanded cruising—singlehanded or doublehanded. The cockpit is designed for sailing, not for sitting at anchor. There is a disproportionate amount of space given to the helmsman.

The boat has a T-shaped cockpit, similar to that on the J/40. The coaming stops just forward of the steering pedestal. This gives the helmsman plenty of space for comfortable sitting on the deck on both sides of the wheel. Because you can sit to weather without discomfort, visibility is improved when sailing.

There is a raised seat, incorporating a horseshoe life ring as a cushion, aft of the wheel. But it's a long reach from the seat to the wheel. A short person would be inclined to steer with his or her toes.

A Harken traveler is located just in front of the steering pedestal. True, you do have to step over it to go forward from the helm, and the mainsheet can hook on the pedestal during a jibe, but the convenience when trimming sails makes it worth it.

The J/34c has a proportionally large mainsail and small genoa. This makes tacking easier, and sailing under mainsail alone possible. However, the size of the mainsail demands that you pay more attention to sail trim. The person best suited to judge that is the helmsman.

The traveler car has a 4:1 purchase, led to cam cleats at each end facing the helmsman. The mainsheet is double-ended, led to two Barient 22 self-tailing winchs, one on each side of the traveler, in easy reach of the helmsman.

Genoa winches, Barient 27 self-tailers, are also in reach of the helmsman, so he can adjust trim or cast off the sheet during a tack. There is a small price for the convenient proximity of these winches—on some points of sail the winch handles cannot be turned through 360°. All winches are adequately sized for the job.

The coaming forms nicely angled seatbacks in the foward half of the cockpit. The aft face of the wide molded coaming faces the helmsman, and is a good location for instrument readouts.

There is a huge cockpit locker to port. The single entry hatch is comprised of the seat and coaming. Because it is so big and heavy, it must be secured to the lifelines before you enter the locker. If the lid fell on you, you'd know it. The locker is large enough to hold a deflated dinghy, outboard, sails, plus other gear.

Stanchion bases are aluminum castings, which we never completely trust. These lock securely onto the aluminum toerail. Stainless steel stanchion bases are provided with the teak toerail option. On the standard boat there is no teak to maintain, save the cabin house handrails.

Reefs and halyards are led through quality Lewmar Spinlock clutch stoppers to Barient 21 self-tailers on the cabin house.

The anchor roller chock is not designed for any particular size or brand of ground tackle. Therefore, the anchor we used had to be secured with extra line to hold it in place while sailing. It would be better to design the chock for one anchor and make that anchor standard equipment.

A hawsepipe leads to a shallow, level compartment, so the anchor rode tends to pile up directly below it, obstructing the deck opening. With this system you should dry the rode on deck before stowing to prevent mildew.

Later boats are equipped with a conventional molded anchor locker.

A locker for a backup, Danforth-type anchor is an option. It holds the anchor vertically in a well just foward of the chainplates. While it saves the hassle of stowing the backup anchor belowdecks, it also constricts the space in the already small hanging locker in the forward cabin.

Belowdecks

This is a simple, old-fashioned interior with a few innovative twists. It is optimized for one couple or small family cruising. It isn't jammed full of under-sized berths, nor is the 43"-wide quarterberth intended as a double berth.

There are two doors in the main bulkhead, one on

each side of the mast. One door opens into a large forward stateroom, the other into the head. You can also get access to the head from the forward stateroom. This is preferable to walking through the head to get to the forward stateroom, which is a more typical layout on a boat this size.

The V-berth in the forward stateroom is over 6' wide at the head and almost 3' wide at the foot, with enough headroom to sit up and read at night. The cushions are 4" foam, comfortable enough to sleep on your side without bruising your shoulders.

The stateroom also has bookshelves, a small dresser with drawers, and good ventilation through two hatches and one port. There are no cowl vents, however, so you may suffer during a rainy night when everything must be closed.

Lockers under the V-berth extend to the bottom of the boat. Although there are limber holes between lockers to drain water from the anchor compartment into the bilge, the holes are not flush with the hull, so water will not drain completely.

The holding tank is also under the V-berth. It would have to be flushed clean and stored without deodorant to make its smell unnoticeable. Access to the seacocks is through a door under the V-berth.

All of the interior is teak-faced plywood trimmed in teak. Hull ceiling is teak battens. On the standard boat the interior teak is oiled; varnish is an option. Joinerwork is of average quality. The cabin sole is varnished teak and holly. J Boats stopped using light-colored ash belowdecks after the J/36, because that wood turns black when it gets wet.

The head has less than 6' of headroom. Ventilation is good—one hatch and one port. The molded shower sump drains into the bilge. Most surfaces in the head drain well, but spilled water collects on the sink countertop. Full-length mirrors on the inside of both head doors give the user the illusion of spaciousness.

There are handrails on the cabin overhead. Unlike many boats, glued-in marine carpet or vinyl are not used on the overhead or the ceiling. Instead, gelcoat or vinyl drop panels are used. This is a good feature, as it gives you access to deck fastenings without major disassembly.

The cabin house and cockpit ports all open, giving good ventilation in fair weather. Some are so large you can stick your head through them. The first 25 boats had Bomar ports with only three dogs per port. The ports could distort and leak and the dogs could shear off if overtightened. In later boats a Bomar port with six dogs is used.

A Lewmar forward hatch is articulated so it can be opened to preset positions. It can be operated from above or belowdecks, but locked only from below.

Galley and icebox are a bit small. Stowage for dishes and silverware is under the companionway, in a compartment which allows them to drain and dry. As with most of the cabin stowage, galley stowage is behind sliding doors.

The sink is deep—so deep that we suspect it might gather a little water when heeled severely on starboard tack. The stove is covered by a counter which slides back for access to the burners.

The cabin table is large, if a bit wobbly on its tube-in-socket legs. It has utensil stowage in the center and fiddles on the edges.

There is a small nav station, using a cabin berth for a seat. It is adequate for weekend cruising, but not long-distance sailing.

Conclusions

The J/34c is a sailor's boat, and a well-to-do sailor, we might add, if he is to afford her hefty price tag. She's a weekend and coastal cruiser, not a blue water cruiser. She is comfortable for one couple with a kid or two, but not two couples. Because she handles so easily she should make an enjoyable beer can racer.

There are few boats that are better built. But there are a number of boats with equal or superior interiors for equal or less money.

You won't find many cruisers with the quality of hardware that is found on the J/34c. And you probably won't find any that are as easy to sail short-handed.

The boat is fast compared to cruisers of her size, but not as fast as the manufacturers would have you believe. That's typically the case with manufacturer hype.

No new boat is ever a good investment. They all depreciate with alarming speed. However, if the boat is well-promoted, and the builder is respected, as is the case with the J/34c, you can be assured of a reasonable resale value.

Is she worth it? If you plan to leave the boat at the dock and use it as a second home, certainly not. If you plan to sail her with regularity, maybe. It depends on how important the little details that make sailing fun are to you.   • **PS**

Contest 35S

This well-executed Dutch cruiser offers performance suitable for coastal and offshore sailing.

Conyplex, builder of the Contest 35S, is an established company that was a pioneer in fiberglass boat construction. In 1958, it began work on fiberglass Flying Dutchmans, and two years later introduced the Contest 25, its first cruiser. More than 5,000 boats have been built since, with about 600 of these being exported to the U.S. through Van Breems Holland Yachts of Westport, Connecticut.

The Contest 35S is a new design, introduced in 1988 to replace the earlier Contest 35.

Martinus Van Breems, who also invented and markets the Dutchman mainsail containment system, brought hull #22 of the Contest 35S to Newport, Rhode Island for *Practical Sailor* to test. This gave us a good opportunity to crawl through the boat and sail it in a variety of wind conditions.

Design

All Contest sailboats are designed by Dick Zaal, who for years was Conyplex's in-house designer. Each displays certain trademarks: high freeboard, wooden rubrails, and low cabin profiles.

The Contest 35S conforms to the traditional Zaal style. The molded cockpit coaming that continues the line of the cabin all the way aft is certainly distinctive. It provides very comfortable back support, though the affect on appearance is not all that attractive, creating as it does a feeling of greater mass high and aft than one is accustomed to seeing on aft cockpit boats.

The hull form is powerful, with relatively full sections compared to many modern racer/cruisers. The moderate displacement-to-length ratio of 249 gives it reasonable speed for a cruising boat while retaining the ability to carry the amount of stores that are necessary for living aboard and short-term cruising.

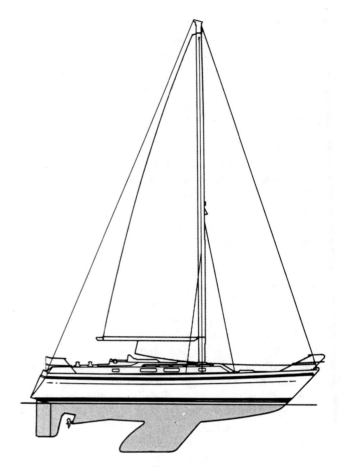

Specifications

LOA	34' 7"
LWL	28' 7"
Beam	11' 2"
Draft	5' 9"/4' 5" (std/wing keel)
Displacement	13,040 lbs.
Ballast	5,513 lbs.
Sail area	586 sq. ft.

Two keels are available. The standard keel is a cruising fin in which the foot is longer than the root (the section that attaches to the hull); the wing keel, which we tested, was developed in tank tests at the Marin Institute in the Netherlands and saves 1' 4" in draft.

The propeller shaft exits through a solid log rather than a strut, and though this increases wetted surface area somewhat, it is strong and also marginally improves directional stability. The rudder is hung on a full skeg—a smart feature on a cruising boat, providing that the skeg is well attached to the hull.

The rig is a conventional masthead sloop with double spreaders, high-aspect mainsail and the ability to carry large genoas. The boat we sailed had a fully battened main equipped with the Dutchman

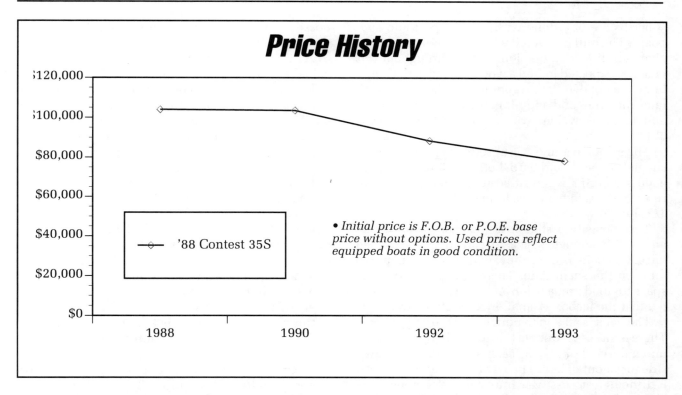

Price History

• *Initial price is F.O.B. or P.O.E. base price without options. Used prices reflect equipped boats in good condition.*

'88 Contest 35S

system, and Profurl furling gear on the headsail. These two devices make a boat of this size about as easy to sail as is possible.

Construction

Because Contest boats are cruisers, built without too much concern for weight, there is nothing exotic about their construction. The hull and deck structure of the 35S is built of chopped strand mat, cloth and woven roving, cored with end-grain balsa.

The pros and cons of balsa coring are debated endlessly. It is an excellent material for using in sandwich with fiberglass, creating a strong, lightweight structure. The likelihood of it absorbing water is problematical and not of immediate concern in a new boat. However, whereas the racing boat must, by necessity, incorporate weight-saving materials and construction techniques, there is no reason the slower cruising boat should compromise itself for weight. We like a single skin fiberglass hull for cruising, if for no other reason than it's easier to repair than a cored hull. If you're trying to patch a hole on the beach of some Third World country, or even in a Caribbean boatyard, you'll appreciate working with solid fiberglass.

Conyplex assembles the hull and deck before building the interior; the opposite is the usual practice. The joint is glassed over with at least seven layers of cloth and also through-bolted. This is an extremely strong hull-to-deck joint that should never leak. By raising the deck a few inches above the joint, the joint, covered by a teak rubrail and stainless steel strip, is less vulnerable to damage from collision with pilings and other boats. This is a superb configuration, though again the raised deck increases apparent freeboard.

Another feature of the Contest that we like is the all-wood, built-up interior. All furniture is marine grade plywood fiberglassed to the hull—no molded fiberglass pans that are cold, noisy and may prohibit access to some parts of the hull. A further advantage of wood is the ability to customize it later; fiberglass simply doesn't allow as much flexibility to change interior plans. Then again, for the price of a Contest, you expect an all-wood interior.

Hardwood stringers and floors are fiberglassed to the hull to increase the rigidity of the structure; in a mass production boat these might be incorporated into the fiberglass pan or liner, along with furniture foundations.

Each Contest is delivered with a Lloyd's certificate, which means it has been constructed under the specific rules of that agency, and under the watchful eye of its inspectors. This costs the builder extra money—about $800—which is passed along to the buyer, but if you're looking for a quality boat to own a long time, it's probably worth it.

Interior

The layout of the Contest 35S is straightforward, with a few unexpected wrinkles.

The companionway hatch slides into a nice seahood, and though a small opening offers safety offshore, the shallow depth of the hatch and the orientation of the ladder make the trip below a little tight—one is careful not to hit his head. The forward

V-berths are 6' 7" long with shelves port and star-board. The hull is covered with an upholstery fabric; given the finely crafted joinerwork throughout this boat, we expected to find a wood ceiling in the bows, but were not overly disappointed as the fabric insulates moisture and sound, is pleasant to the touch, and does save weight over wood. Headroom here is 5' 11".

The saloon features a 6' 6" settee to port and an L-shaped settee to starboard, both of which will make good sea berths when fitted with lee cloths. Headroom in the saloon ranges from 6' 3" aft down to 6' 1-1/2" forward.

The navigation station is the right size for this boat, with enough space to spread charts folded once. Opposite is the galley, which we thought was a bit on the small side. There isn't much counter space for food preparation and even Martinus admitted that the icebox is small by U.S. standards.

The head is aft and to port, under the bridge deck. There is an access door to the double berth stateroom under the cockpit, giving each person his or her own side to get out of bed. The wet locker aft of the head is difficult to access; Martinus said the company was looking at other uses of this space, possibly a freezer.

The matte finish varnishing of the teak is nicely done. Dutch tiles around the galley are a Van Breems trademark. There are numerous stowage compartments, which are always appreciated. We were again surprised that the hull inside many of these compartments was merely spray painted—we expected wood or at least fabric, and we can only speculate that even top-end builders must sometimes find places to save costs. Overall, however, the Contest 35S is beautifully finished with much attention to detail.

Performance

We sailed the 35S in a variety of wind conditions ranging from light to moderate. The first thing we noticed was how well balanced it was under mainsail and #2 furling genoa. Hard on the wind, it was possible to take our hands off the Whitlock wheel; there was little tendency to round up.

A little weather helm, of course, is actually desirable, as it functions not only as a safety feature (allowing the boat to round up and spill wind in a strong gust), but also helps the helmsman develop feel for the optimum angle off the wind.

This observation was corroborated by tests of the boat reported in the British magazine *Yachting Monthly*, in which the author wrote, "If there is a criticism, it is that she was a little reticent about telling the helmsman when she was precisely in the groove."

Other than this, the boat tracked nicely and easily, remaining under control at all times. We found it a pleasure to steer, tacking through about 85 degrees and making about seven knots on a reach in 12 to 15 knots of wind, and about six knots beating in relatively calm bay waters.

Diesel auxiliary power is a 28-hp. Volvo diesel, which is well-insulated and equipped with a flexible drive coupling to minimize vibration. While running, it was quiet and smooth, a real pleasure for motoring and/or motor sailing. Our boat had a three-bladed prop, which didn't help sailing performance, but made backing out of slips a thoroughly manageable process.

Conclusions

To our mind, the Contest 35S is not an exciting boat in terms of looks or performance. Rather it is a solid, well-built, conservative cruiser that is tastefully appointed for comfortable living aboard. It is an able sailer that should carry a crew safely to most any place they wish to go. The Dutch are known for quality workmanship, and the Contest 35S is no exception.
• **PS**

The only real criticisms we have of the interior layout are a too-small icebox and an inaccessible hanging locker.

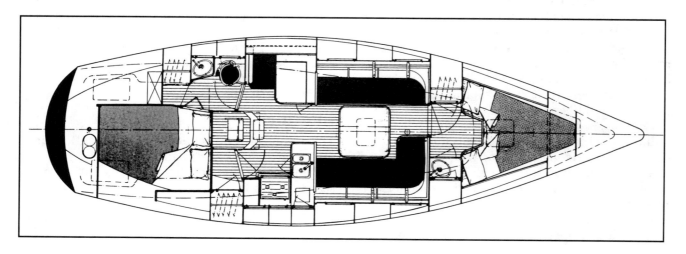

Ericson 35

A good step-up boat for a family on a tight budget; she may not be lavishly equipped, but she sails well.

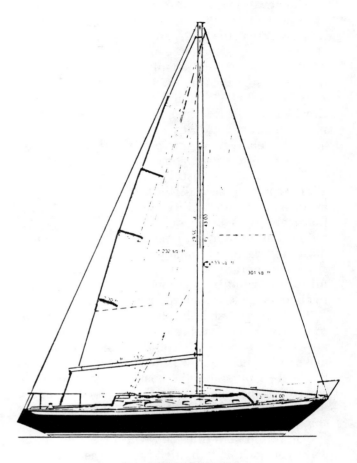

Ericson Yachts has gotten a lot of mileage out of 35-footers over the years. Way back when in 1965, the first Ericson 35 was a typical CCA cruising boat, with a long keel and attached rudder. In 1969, the Ericson 35-2 was introduced. A Bruce King design—as was the original 35—the 35-2 was an up-to-date racer/cruiser, with swept-back moderate fin keel, pronounced bustle, and semi-balanced shallow spade rudder.

The 35-2 stayed in production until 1982, when it was replaced by the 35-3, a larger, more modern boat. The 35-2 was a very successful design—about 600 were built over 13 years. She was not an IOR (International Offshore Rule) design, but the boat rated reasonably well under the new rule, and raced competitively at the local level.

Early IOR boats were little different from their late-CCA predecessors. It took designers several years to develop the types of ill-tempered boats that we now think of as IOR designs. This allowed wholesome production boats such as the Ericson 35 to be reasonably competitive at the local level.

The 35-2 is a good-looking boat. She has a very strong sheerline, powerful forward but not overly springy aft. The stern is hollow in profile, and the stem profile is just convex enough to look like a straight line.

The deckhouse is low in profile, despite the relatively low freeboard of the boat. Aesthetically, the only thing you can quibble with is the overly wide transom, which is fortunately not very high. A lot of current boats, of course, have transoms as wide as the Ericson 35's, and they practically drag the bottom of the transom in the water. The temptation to use these ugly modern rear ends as billboards has proven overwhelming, resulting in a whole new industry in the last decade: transom art. In comparison to many

Specifications

LOA	34' 8"
LWL	25' 10"
Beam	10' 0"
Draft	4' 11"
Displacement	11,600 lbs.
Ballast	5,000 lbs.

of today's production boats, the 35-2's transom looks positively dainty.

Sailing Performance

With a typical PHRF rating of 150 to 156, the Ericson 35-2's performance is respectable, but the boat is no hot rod. She's about the same speed as a Ranger 33.

You need to put the concept of speed into perspective. Despite a lot of "harumpfing" about the poor sailing qualities of modern boats, the fact is that the average fin-keel production cruiser/racer built today is faster—a lot faster—than good boats designed 20 years ago, such as the Ericson 35-2. Appendages and rigs are more efficient, wider beam gives greater sail-carrying ability in a breeze, and hull shapes are frequently more refined, as long as they're not overly influenced by the rating rules.

The newer Ericson 35-3, a slightly larger boat—she's closer to 36' than 35'—is about 30 seconds per mile faster than the 35-2. Same designer and builder, same concept; faster, more modern boat.

At the same time, an older production racer/cruiser such as the Ericson 35-2 is likely to be a lot faster than today's straight "cruising" boat. The Crealock 37, for example, is about 20 seconds per mile slower than the Ericson 35-2. "Fast" and "slow" are pretty relative concepts, particularly when you're moving at a slow jogging pace.

Despite a 43% ballast/displacement ratio, the 35-2 is not a particularly stiff boat. Owners give the boat average marks for stability, frequently commenting that stability is not a problem as long as sail is reduced appropriately. Frankly, this is true on almost any reasonably high-performance boat. We'd shy away from any boat that claims to be able to carry full sail upwind in 20 knots of breeze: the boat is likely to be grossly underpowered in light air.

The "average" stability stems from relatively narrow beam and relatively shoal draft, and is certainly not a major concern. We would recommend that you make a real effort to stow heavy equipment as low in the boat as possible—the boat's vertical center of gravity is somewhere around the height of the tops of the settees. You should also set up the boat so that she can be reefed as easily as possible.

You'll find both tiller and wheel steering on the 35-2. The cockpit is divided into two sections by a full-depth fiberglass bridgedeck which carries the mainsheet traveler. On wheel-steered models, the helmsman steers from the aft cockpit, and the sail handlers work from the forward cockpit. In tiller-steered boats, the helmsman sits toward the forward end of the main cockpit.

For best weight distribution, the forward helmsman's position is better, but it's tough to keep sheet tenders and the helmsman out of each other's way if they're both in that forward cockpit. When racing tiller-steered boats, the mainsheet tender will sit in the aft cockpit.

The aft-mounted wheel does clean up the forward cockpit nicely, giving you very good lounging space.

Several owners have added 400 pounds or so of additional ballast, and report that it makes the boat slightly stiffer without noticeably slowing her down in light air. There is plenty of room in the keel shell to add some extra ballast if you want, but we'd live with the boat for awhile before increasing the ballasting. At the same time, we certainly wouldn't remove ballast that had been added, as long as the boat trims to her lines fore and aft.

As designed, the main boom is very high off the deck, and has a pronounced droop at its after end. This is purely a device to reduce rated sail area for racing. Most boats never had droopy-clewed mains

built, and we wouldn't recommend one. Unfortunately, the high boom can make it really awkward for a very short crew member to furl the sail or hook up the main halyard.

Some 35-2s we have seen have no main boom topping lift. Instead, a short length of wire is seized to the backstay, and hooked into the end of the main boom. This is totally unseamanlike, and potentially very dangerous. This system should be removed immediately from any boat, and replaced either with a permanently-attached topping lift, or a fixed vang such as the Hall Quik Vang.

The double spreader rig—unusual on a boat this small when the 35-2 was introduced—allows for fair tight sheeting angles, particularly when you add in the narrow beam of the boat. The spar section itself is quite rugged—not something you can bend very easily. You wouldn't want to bend the rig much in any case, since the mast is deck-stepped.

This is a good all-around sailing boat, with no particular quirks either upwind or downwind. The boat is not as fast on any point of sail as a newer, more racing-oriented design, but she's a good, solid sailer.

Several owners mention substantial weather helm when reaching in heavy air, but there are few boats that don't suffer from this. Ease the traveler down, flatten the main, and the helm should be reduced.

Construction

The Ericson 35-2 has an uncored hull built in a split mold. The two halves of the hull are glassed together with 11 laminations of mat and roving. There's nothing wrong with building a hull in two halves as long as the joint is adequately reinforced, and this is the proper way to do it. Nevertheless, you should carefully examine the hull centerline on the outside of any boat you are considering, checking for cracks.

Several owners in our survey report that leaking shroud chainplates have caused significant rot in the main bulkhead. Keeping chainplates watertight is a constant battle, particularly on a boat that is sailed hard. Problems should show up in the form of discoloration or delamination of the main bulkhead where the chainplates pierce the deck.

Because this is one of those problems that can cause hidden damage, we would think twice about buying a boat that showed a significant amount of chainplate leakage. Unfortunately, the damage may be hidden under covering fascia at the edge of the bulkhead in the main cabin, so some disassembly and probing may be required.

The chainplates are stainless steel straps, with integral welded caps designed to be bedded to the deck. If the bolts holding the chainplates to the bulkheads are snugged up tight, and if the caps are thoroughly bedded in either polyurethane or polysulfide, you should be able to keep the chainplates dry. However, it may require a one-time disassembly and removal of the chainplates to properly bed and install them. Running a bead of compound around the edge of the chainplate caps won't do the job.

The ballast is a lead casting dropped into the molded fiberglass keel. Examine the leading edge and bottom of the keel carefully for signs of hard grounding which may have damaged the keel shell.

Early 35-2s are equipped with gate valves on through hull fittings, rather than seacocks. Gate valves should immediately be replaced with more conventional tapered plug seacocks or ball valve seacocks, which can be firmly attached to the hull. Depending on the strength of the stem of the through hull fitting to support the shutoff valve—as you do with gate valves—is a risky proposition. We've seen plenty of through hull stems break off when you're trying to open a stuck valve. You can end up with the valve in your hand and a big hole in the hull, which is a bit of a problem if your boat happens to be in the water at the time.

Headsail sheet winches are mounted on fiberglass islands that are part of the deck molding. One owner reports that the plywood reinforcement in the top of the winch islands has rotted, the result of an improperly bedded winch. Plywood is frequently used by builders to add compression strength to laminates under hardware. No builder we know of takes the time to seal the core that is exposed when you drill for through-fastenings, so bedding is required.

Ericson 35-2 owners report an average incidence of hull blistering: about 30% have at least some hull blisters. Owners of two boats in our survey said their hulls were badly blistered.

Engine

Up until 1973, you could get any engine you wanted in the Ericson 35-2 as long as it was the Atomic 4 gasoline engine. After that a variety of diesels were offered as options until 1978, when a switch to diesels was made throughout the sailboat industry.

The most common diesel used in the boat in the mid-70s was the Westerbeke 4-91, a heavy 25-horse engine. But you'll also see Volvo, Yanmar, and Universal diesels, as well as the Westerbeke Pilot 20.

There are two different engine placements. In early models, the Atomic 4 is tucked under the aft end of the dinette, in the main cabin. Owners give this installation high marks for engine accessibility, and it keeps the weight in the middle of the boat.

Boats with the two-settee main cabin have the engine mounted aft, under the companionway. The engine is far less accessible in this location.

Watch out for terneplate steel fuel tanks on older boats. These are a potential fire hazard, as they are very susceptible to rust-out. The fuel capacity of 22.5 gallons is adequate for any of the standard engines.

Several owners report having incorrectly-propped engines, although it is not clear whether these are original engines or replacements. With either the Atomic 4 or any of the optional diesels, the boat should do at least 5 1/2 knots under power in calm seas at normal cruising revs. Don't count on using the stock 12 x 6 prop with anything but the Atomic 4. Likewise, the standard 3/4" shaft is a little small in diameter for any engine bigger than the Atomic 4.

The original engine exhaust is a water jacket system, fabricated of steel. Pinholes eventually develop between the walls of jacketed systems. These can allow water back into the engine. We'd recommend replacing water jacket systems with a simple, modern waterlift.

Interior

Despite the narrow beam, the Ericson 35-2 has a reasonably roomy, well thought out interior. Actually, it has two somewhat different interiors.

While not innovative, the interior arrangement is roomy and well thought out. In an unusual practice for sailboats, there was no attempt to cram too many berths into the boat.

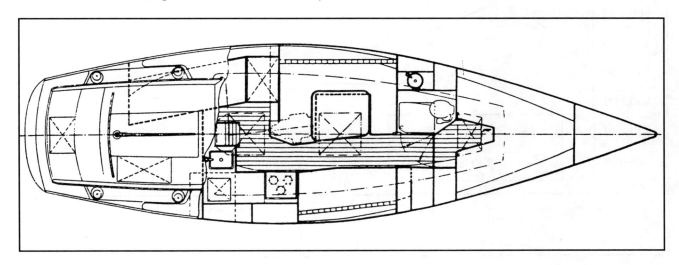

Interior decor changed significantly over the years. Early boats have mahogany interiors: varnished mahogany bulkheads, mahogany trim, mahogany hull ceiling. Very late boats have the all-teak interiors that became the fashion by the late 70s.

The all-teak interior is very dark, although rich-looking. The best thing to do with the teak interior is to varnish it. Use matte-finish varnish for veneered surfaces such as bulkheads, and high-gloss varnish on all solid wood. Of course, this is a lot of work.

The main reason that builders went to teak interiors is that they save a fortune in finishing time and money. The higher cost of teak is more than offset by the time savings. To properly varnish the interior of this boat would take about 200 hours, while a coat of oil could be applied in two working days.

The mahogany interior of older 35-2s is substantially lighter in color then the teak interior. There is also more contrast between the face veneer of the plywood bulkheads and the darker color of the solid mahogany trim. The mahogany must be kept well-varnished; an oil finish will not provide adequate protection for the mahogany surface.

If you're tired of dark wood interiors, it would be fairly easy to paint out the varnished mahogany ply interior. Simply sand the surface to remove all trace of gloss, then paint with a low-luster finish such as Interlux #221 Cabin Enamel. Leave the solid wood trim varnished for a nice contrast.

Painting out teak veneer surfaces is more of a problem, since the teak is likely to be oiled. Paint adheres poorly to teak in the best conditions, and very poorly to oiled teak.

All models have a conventional forward cabin: V-berths, storage shelves over, drawers and bins below. The 25-gallon stainless steel water tank is also mounted under the berth. This is an inadequate water supply for a boat with five berths that is to be used for anything more than weekend cruising. Several owners report adding additional tanks. Don't add them up forward, as it would change the trim of the boat.

Thanks to fine forward sections, the foot of the V-berth is extremely narrow. Several owners have built inserts to turn these berths into a double, but the job is complicated by a cutout at the head of the starboard berth, a feature designed to add elbow room.

In port in good weather, ventilation in the forward cabin is good, thanks to an opening overhead hatch. In rain, it's not so good: no cowl vents.

Older boats have padded vinyl hull liners forward; newer boats have teak ceiling strips.

The head compartment is reasonably roomy, and has good storage. There's a cabinet under the sink, and a locker outboard. There's also a large, tall locker next to the toilet, to which the forward lower shroud chainplate is bolted. Check for signs of leaking around this chainplate.

Ventilation in the head leaves a lot to be desired, but could be improved by a larger cowl vent and a small overhead hatch.

A shower sump was standard, but not all boats were equipped with pressure water. If you install a shower, don't forget to provide a sump pump. You don't want your shower to drain directly into the bilge.

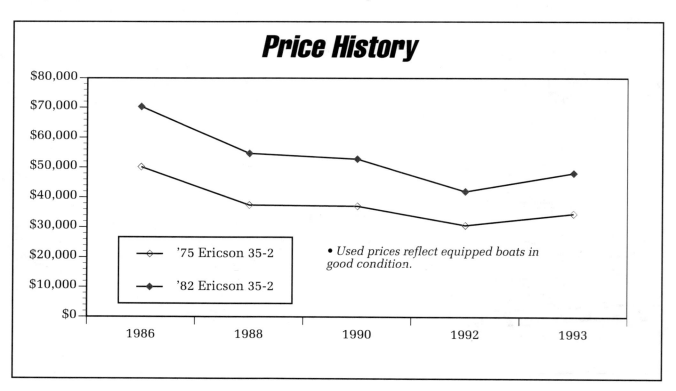

Price History

Legend:
- ◇ '75 Ericson 35-2
- ◆ '82 Ericson 35-2

• *Used prices reflect equipped boats in good condition.*

Both main cabin layouts are roomy and comfortable. Bruce King and Ericson wisely decided not to try to get a pilot berth into a relatively narrow boat, opting for more elbow room and a little storage outboard of the settees.

A settee stretches along the starboard side of the main cabin. The settee is pushed fairly far forward to get more room in the aft galley. A cutout in the starboard forward bulkhead provides a footwell, making the settee long enough to use as a berth. There is a narrow shelf behind the settee—a good place to store books.

In the two-settee layout, there's a drop-leaf table just off centerline, allowing comfortable dinner seating for four on the two settees.

The dinette layout has both plusses and minuses. The fixed table can be lowered to form a big double berth, but in our experience, this type of arrangement is a nuisance. You need a big cushion to fit over the table, and that cushion has to be stowed somewhere when it's not in use. The multiple cushions required to create the dinette double never seem to fit together quite right, resulting in a berth that is big enough, but rarely comfortable.

In addition, the offset dinette table is too far away to allow use of the starboard settee for dining, so the dinette is it as far as company for dinner goes. It seats four in reasonable comfort, but as in most dinettes, you end up playing footsie with your dinner partners a lot of the time, which may or may not be a bad idea.

In the dinette layout, the engine is shoe-horned under the aft seat. This was fine with the Atomic 4, but it's hard to fit a diesel in the same space.

It's also pretty hard to effectively sound isolate an engine mounted in the middle of the main cabin, but modern insulation materials can help a lot.

Ericson owners are divided on the merits of the two main cabin arrangements. The midships engine is easier to service, but you sacrfice a lot of walking-around room in the main cabin. Look at both layouts before making a decision.

The aft half of the main cabin is virtually identical in both interiors. To port, there is a good-sized chart table, with enough space outboard to mount a reasonable array of goodies. The huge quarterberth forms the seat for the nav station.

To starboard is an L-shaped galley. Considering the vintage of the boat, the galley is quite good. There's room for a three-burner gimbaled stove with oven (though you'll find only alcohol stoves unless someone's done a retrofit). Aft of the stove is a decent working surface, with big drawers below. A single deep sink is mounted in the counter just below the companionway, with a big locker beneath.

The icebox is tucked back into a corner, but it's reasonably accessible, if a little small for extended cruising.

Both the battery selector switch and the electrical panel are mounted on the bulkhead aft of the galley. That puts them close to the battery, but the nav station would be a more logical location for electrical system management.

Main cabin ventilation is provided by a big overhead hatch, but there's no provision for ventilation in bad weather.

Surprisingly, the cabin sole throughout the boat is the molded fiberglass floor pan, with teak ply inserts. Compared to the finish in the rest of the boat, this is an unattractive detail, smacking of cost-cutting.

Finish in general is of good production boat quality. Detailing is only average.

The interior of the 35-2 is not in any way innovative, but it is roomy, decently finished, and well thought out. There has been no attempt to cram in a superfluous number of berths—if you ignore the dinette double—and there is reasonable privacy for a family.

Conclusions

The Ericson 35-2 is a wholesome family cruising boat. She sails well, and has enough exterior teak trim to look nice if you want to go to the trouble to keep it up. The Ericson molded fiberglass toerail is not particularly attractive, but it's a lot less maintenance than a teak toerail.

These were not lavishly-equipped boats. A lot of things that we take for granted today—multiple batteries, hot and cold water, a shower, self-tailing winches, double lifelines—were either optional or not available, particularly on early models. Some production shortcuts on older boats—steel fuel tanks, gate valves, small water tank—should be corrected at once, if they haven't already been replaced.

Since a lot of these boats have been raced, you may find a 35-2 with up-to-date sailhandling equipment, bigger winches, and good sails. Because of big differences in age, engine, equipment, and condition, prices range from bargain-basement to close to new-boat prices for entry-level boats of the same size.

This would be a good boat to move up to for a family with two children and a tight budget. The boat sails well enough to do a little club racing if you're so inclined, and it's the type of boat that serves as a reasonable teaching platform for older kids interesting in racing bigger boats. Unlike many modern cruisers, she's not a clunky sailing houseboat.

The relatively shoal draft will allow you to get into places inaccesssible to boats with a deep fin keel, making the boat suitable for areas such as Florida, the Chesapeake, and the Gulf of Mexico. With a little thoughtful upgrading and after a careful survey, you could do some limited offshore sailing—trips like Florida to the Bahamas—while you develop confidence in the boat, and in yourself. **• PS**

Alberg 35

This classic dates from the early days of fiberglass boatbuilding. Though aged, she has her good points.

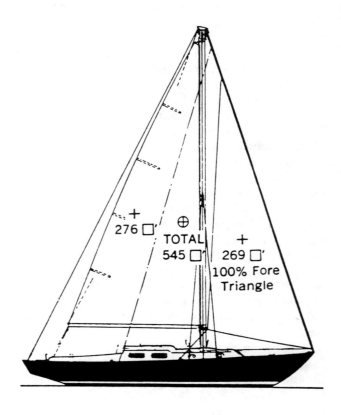

The year 1961 may not seem so long ago to those of us over 40, but believe it or not, it was pretty close to the dawn of big-time fiberglass sailboat building. Only a year before that, Hinckley stopped building production wooden sailboats. Two years earlier, in 1959, Pearson built the first Triton, the boat that was the prototype of the inexpensive small family fiberglass cruising sailboat. The Triton's big selling point was a low-maintenance hull that meant that Mom and Pop and the kids didn't have to spend all spring in the boatyard getting the boat ready for the summer.

These days, when getting the family sailboat ready in the spring may mean little more than a weekend spent washing and waxing the topsides, plus a quick coat of paint on the bottom, it's hard to remember that owning a boat some thirty years ago usually meant work—and a lot of it—or money, and a lot of that, too.

In 1961, Pearson added the 34' 9" Alberg 35 to its expanding sailboat line. The Alberg 35 was a fixture in the Pearson line until 1967. In 1968, the boat was replaced by the Shaw-designed Pearson 35, a slightly larger, more modern boat in keeping with the increasing demands of the market. During six years of production, over 250 Alberg 35s were built.

It's very tempting to call every good-looking, successful boat from the 1960s a classic. Well, the Alberg 35 is good-looking and was successful; we think it deserves to be called a classic. The boat has a handsome sheer, flattish for her day but old-fashioned and springy compared to current boats. She has a low, rounded cabin trunk with slightly raised doghouse, and just about perfectly balanced long overhangs both forward and aft.

Compared to more modern 35-footers, the Alberg 35 is narrow, short on the waterline and cramped.

Specifications

LOA	34' 9"
LWL	24' 0"
Beam	9' 8"
Draft	5' 2"
Displacement	12,600 lbs.
Ballast	5,300 lbs.
Sail area	545/583 (sloop/yawl)

The typical 35' cruiser/racer of the '90s is 4' longer on the waterline and more than a foot wider.

Sailing Performance

The term cruiser/racer was just entering the jargon in 1961. The Pearson sales brochure from 1967 calls the Alberg 35 a "proven ocean racer, cruiser." Note the term "ocean." The Alberg 35 was the smallest boat in the Pearson line to which that word was attached, unlike many builders who push anything with lifelines and a self-bailing cockpit as a "blue-water cruiser."

While the Alberg 35 had moderate success as a racer, the boat was—and still is—a cruising boat.

By current standards, the Alberg 35 is a slow boat for her length overall, with a typical PHRF rating of

Owners' Comments

"New, lighter hulls are clearly faster, but this is an excellent sea boat. Delamination has required considerable re-coring of deck. Gelcoat was seriously pitted when I bought her. Be prepared, until the wind gets up to 15 knots, to see all newer designs leave you far behind."

—1962 model in ME

"Leaks at stanchions can rot balsa core. Solid fiberglass hull looks good, cabin trunk shows small craze lines at curves. Because of the age of this boat, which I've owned for over 20 years, I've replaced items subject to wear or failure such as sails, halyards, sheaves, spreaders, turnbuckles, engine, lights, pumps and electronics. The boat has performed well in the Atlantic and has been incredibly dependable."

—1962 model in MD

"The boat has poor initial stability due to narrow beam, good ultimate stability. Original joinery and trim are primitive, but solid. Glass work is simple, fair, solid. Forward cabin is roomier than needed. My water and fuel tanks failed, causing major surgery. Wooden rudder was rebuilt and sheathed in polypropylene. An Alberg 35 is a pretty, solid, inexpensive, able sailer. The deficiencies are manageable."

—1962 model in MA

"Did Honolulu to Tahiti nonstop in 23 days. Boat is very seakindly. I took this boat on an 8,000-mile cruise through the Pacific. It is an excellent vessel for cruising. I added a pilothouse and heavier rigging, converted to diesel, added radar, an Aires steering vane and a galley freezer."

—1962 model in HI

"Spartan interior, inconvenient galley, cockpit too big for offshore. Berth size adequate, very plain interior, uncomfortable sitting, inconvenient table, no good navigation area. Good storage. Forefoot of keel easily damaged during dry storage. I bought this boat for beautiful lines, full keel, stability and price."

—1962 model in CT

"Reverse under power is a disaster—control is always in question. The boat is 25 years old and needs a lot of cosmetic work. It is solid, a good sailer, has handled our stupidities, and in general is a joy to own. It's not the fastest boat on the block. It's easy to sail, a little old-fashioned, but I'd recommend it without qualification."

—1963 model in MA

"New rig with bowsprit allows me to balance helm and walk away from the wheel for 30 minutes at a time. Deck gelcoat is in poor condition with small craze lines and very dull finish. Boat seems almost indestructible."

—1965 model in NJ

"Interiors nowadays are better designed, but in all other respects the Alberg 35 is an excellent compromise of essential qualities: speed, seaworthiness, looks, comfort, and cost."

—1967 model in IN

---

198. By way of comparison, her replacement, the Pearson 35, rates about 174, and the Ericson 35-2 about 150.

But Alberg 35s take to sea pretty well. The narrow, deep hull form makes for a very good range of positive stability—about 135°—and an easy motion in a seaway. Owners consider the boat slightly slower to slightly faster than other boats of similar size and type.

Unlike modern boats with wide beam and firm bilges, the narrow, slack Alberg 35 heels very quickly, despite a 42% ballast/displacement ratio. But narrow boats sail fairly efficiently at fairly steep heel angles. A modern boat such as the J/35 sails best upwind in 15 knots of true breeze at a 23° angle of heel, while a boat like the Alberg 35 will be sailing at close to a 30° angle in the same conditions.

With a rudder set well forward, it can take a lot of helm to keep the boat on course when reaching in a breeze. This isn't helped at all by the large, relatively low aspect ratio mainsail. At the same time, owners report that the boat tracks well, a quality missing in many newer boats.

The Alberg 35 was built both as a sloop and a yawl. Yawls were popular under the CCA (Cruising Club of America) Rule because mizzen and mizzen staysail area was lightly taxed. The yawl is not a bad rig for shorthanded cruising, since the mizzen can be used to help balance the boat, and is particularly useful in anchoring and weighing anchor under sail. From a performance and handling point of view on a boat this size, however, the yawl rig has few if any advantages. We would look for the sloop rig if we were shopping for an Alberg 35.

The mast is stepped on deck, over the doorway to the forward cabin. This requires substantial reinforcement of the bulkhead. Several owners in our survey report that the coring in the deck under the mast has crushed, allowing the top of the cabin to compress.

Both the sloop and yawl rigs have simple, fairly heavy aluminum masts. A varnished spruce roller-reefing main boom was standard. If we were buying an Alberg 35, we'd forget the roller reefing and set the boat up for slab reefing. In our experience, a roller-reefed mainsail is usually so baggy as to be useless for upwind sailing.

Several owners in our survey have added bowsprits to their boats, converting them to cutter rigs with yankee and staysail. This improves the boat's balance, as well as making sail combinations more flexible for cruising.

The cockpit is long and quite large, with plenty of room for daysailing hordes. Cockpit coamings are teak, and really look nice when varnished. The standard tiller takes up a lot of cockpit space, but most boats we've looked at have the optional pedestal wheel steering.

Big port and starboard cockpit lockers have poor locking arrangements, and drain straight to the bilge. Give a lot of thought to what will happen if the boat is pooped by a following sea, then go to work at improving hatch sealing and fastening.

Sail handling equipment on these boats is likely to be primitive. The old Merriman #5 genoa winches and #2 mainsheet and jib halyard winches date from the time when trimming and setting sails was expected to be a lot of work. We'd replace them all with modern, powerful self-tailing winches if anything other than daysailing is contemplated.

Likewise, there was originally no mainsheet traveler. On a narrow boat like this with the mainsheet led aft, there really isn't that much advantage to a traveler—it simply operates over too small a range of the boom's arc to offer much benefit.

If the mainsheet were re-led so that you could put a traveler on the bridgedeck, just in front of the steering pedestal, a traveler would be worthwhile. This, of course, would mean getting rid of the roller-reefing main, but in our opinion that's a good idea, anyway.

Wheel steering was an option, but you'll find it on a lot of Alberg 35s. We'd consider it a plus.

Engine

All Alberg 35s were powered by the ubiquitous Atomic 4 gasoline engine. If you're thinking about keeping an Alberg 35 for five or more years, the time has come to think about replacing the engine—preferably with a diesel.

Of course, a lot of owners have already retrofitted their boats with diesels, but the installations will obviously vary dramatically in quality.

Fortunately, Universal Motors has a diesel engine that is literally a bolt-in replacement for the Atomic 4. It's the Mini 4, and it will fit the same engine beds, has the same shaft alignment and same length as the Atomic 4, is slightly lighter, and is only 1" higher. There is room to squeeze new diesel into the engine box under the companionway.

Like most boats with the rudder mounted well forward and the prop fitted in an aperture, the Alberg 35 backs down poorly. This is simply a fact of life, so you have to get used to it. Steering ahead, the boat handles fine. The Atomic 4 is perfectly adequate power, giving a cruising speed of about 6 knots in calm water.

Construction

A lot of Alberg 35s are used for offshore cruising. Plain, rugged construction is one reason why. The hull is a heavy, uncored layup, not particularly stiff or strong for its weight, but easy to repair and relatively foolproof.

Rudder construction is a holdover from the days of wooden boats. It consists of a wooden rudder blade bolted to a heavy bronze rod, formed to the shape of the aft edge of the prop aperture. The rudder of any Alberg 35 should be examined carefully, not because this type of construction is poor, but simply because the rudders are getting old. The rudders may have been damaged in groundings, or the stock bolts may be corroded.

One advantage of rudder construction is that it is very easy to change the rudder design. If we had an Alberg 35, we would get rid of the original barn-door rudder blade and replace it with a more modern design with a straight trailing edge and more area near the bottom of the rudder.

This *Constellation*-type profile became pretty much standard with the last long-keel CCA boats designed before the *Intrepid*-type skeg and rudder of the late 1960s. The bottom of the new rudder could be angled up slightly to reduce the chance of damage in groundings.

Two aspects of the boat's construction have caused some problems for owners. The ballast casting is a single chunk of lead which is dropped into the hollow fiberglass keel molding.

Along the bottom of the keel, some boats have a void between the lead casting and the fiberglass shell, making the shell vulnerable to damage in groundings or even when hauling and launching the boat.

A surveyor should carefully evaluate this area for voids by sounding with a mallet. Voids can be fairly easily filled by injecting epoxy resin into the cavity.

The other problem could be more difficult to

solve. Decks of early boats like the Alberg 35 were frequently built using edge-grain rather than end-grain balsa. Edge-grain lacks the stiffness or compression strength of a modern end-grain balsa sandwich. Flexing of decks cored this way can break the bond between the fiberglass skins and balsa core. If the deck feels mushy, it is probably at least partially delaminated.

Repair—assuming the core is dry—involves drilling an extensive network of holes through the deck skin and core, being careful to reach but not penetrate the inner skin. Epoxy resin is then injected in each hole until it runs out of adjacent holes. The deck should be braced upward from below and weighted down from above until the resin cures.

This method works well with small areas of delamination, but is a tedious job in larger areas. At best, you end up with a deck sandwich that is somewhat stronger than the original that failed.

Major refinishing of the deck will then be required. Extensive deck "softness" is cause for rejecting any boat, regardless of age.

You will find a variety of tankage arrangements in boats of different vintages. According to one owner, early boats have galvanized fuel and water tanks, which will eventually rust through. Another owner had a huge built-in fiberglass fuel tank forward, which developed a leak and was replaced by a monel tank in the same location. Design specifications for late boats in the production run call for an integral fiberglass water tank of 48 gallons capacity located in the bilge under the main cabin sole, plus a 23-gallon monel fuel tank under the cockpit sole.

The advantage of the monel fuel tank is that it will not have to be replaced if a diesel engine is installed: simply flush it thoroughly with diesel fuel to remove any traces of gasoline, and you're in business. Monel is absolutely the best material for either fuel or water tanks, but it is prohibitively expensive.

Like most sailboats this old, you may find extensive gelcoat crazing and fading on both the hull and deck. This is a cosmetic problem up to the point where crazing allows water to migrate into the laminate, at which time it can become a structural problem. If the gelcoat has begun to buckle and peel, it's best to avoid the boat unless you're looking for a boat at a rock-bottom price for offshore sailing. Cosmetic repair of superficial crazing is labor-intensive, involving sanding, multiple coats of high-build epoxy primer, and complete refinishing, preferably with polyurethane. To have this done professionally would be prohibitively expensive.

The deck gear, standing rigging, and spars on these boats are getting old. Many of the boats have high mileage, since a large percentage are used for long-distance offshore cruising. Be prepared to do relatively simple jobs like removing and rebedding stanchions and deck fittings, installing backing plates, and replacing a lot of rigging. Sails more than five years old—other than storm sails that have seen little or no use—are candidates for replacement.

Interior

Because the Alberg 35 is narrow, it will seem cramped to those used to the condo-like interiors of modern 35-footers. The arrangement, though, is pretty good.

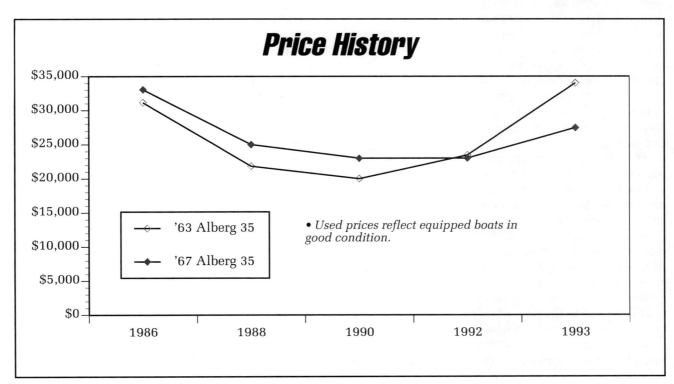

Price History

• Used prices reflect equipped boats in good condition.

Legend:
— ◇ — '63 Alberg 35
— ◆ — '67 Alberg 35

Two interiors were built: one is the "traditional interior #1" of practically every boat built in the last 50 years, the other is "dinette arrangement #1," which became popular when people started looking for more workable galleys about 20 years ago.

Both boats have large forward cabins, with V-berths, a hanging locker, a bureau and drawers under the berths. This is one reason the boat appeals to a lot of minimum-budget livaboards. The forward cabin can be a real owners' stateroom, even though it lacks a double berth. If you were handy, you could rip out the V-berths and build a good-sized diagonal double along either side of the cabin, building in additional storage opposite. The cabin is large enough that this wouldn't totally destroy standing space.

There are two bronze-framed opening ports and a hatch for ventilation in the forward cabin.

The head is aft of the forward cabin, and runs the full width of the boat—a good arrangement on a boat this narrow. With the doors to the main cabin and forward cabin shut, this gives a head compartment with a lot of elbow room. For daysailing, you only need to shut the door to the main cabin to get privacy—no worse than shutting the head door on any boat.

Ventilation is provided in the head via two opening ports plus a pair of cowl vents in Dorade boxes.

The Alberg 35 was one of the first boats of this size to be built with standard hot and cold pressure water, plus a shower. It was a big selling point back then; now it is taken for granted on a 35' boat.

The main cabin will have either the conventional arrangement of settee berths on each side with a fold-down table between, or the galley along one side with a U-shaped dinette opposite.

The dinette arrangement is a decidedly mixed blessing. By lowering the dining table, the dinette converts to a double berth. The original stove well in the dinette arrangement was big enough for a three-burner gimballed stove with oven, while the conventional aft galley has the rinky-dink two-burner alcohol stove that was standard equipment on most boats for many years.

With the dinette, there are two quarterberths aft which extend under the cockpit, and they are reasonable sea berths. In the conventional arrangement you would use the main cabin settees as sea berths, which is also fine.

Quarterberths can be stuffy in tropical climates, and they tend to end up as inefficient catch-all spaces for anything that is too big or awkward to stow in lockers or drawers.

But the aft galley is no prize. Galley counters are quite low due to the boat's low freeboard. There is a small single sink, plus the aforementioned instrument of torture in place of a stove, and an icebox whose top must perform double duty as galley work space and a rudimentary chart table. With the dinette arrangement, the dining table will probably double as the nav station, although we'd be tempted to sacrifice one of the quarterberths to build in storage space plus a usable stand-up nav station.

It's no wonder that at least one owner reports tearing out the entire aft galley and starting from scratch.

Ventilation in the main cabin is non-existent, except for the main companionway hatch. Because of the step in cabin profile, fitting a ventilation hatch over this cabin is tricky, but it can be done.

Interior decor is very "period," and the early 1960s were perhaps the nadir of interior design in sailboats. "Low maintenance" fever was at its peak, and wood-grain plastic laminate ran rampant.

Fortunately, this is nothing that a little painting can't cure, or if you're really handy, you can laminate nice, clean, solid-color Formica over the old stuff on the counters and bulkheads, then varnish the wood trim. The improvement in interior appearance and apparent space would be amazing.

Conclusions

We've presented a pretty intimidating list of drawbacks to the Alberg 35. Now let's look at the positive side. This is a sturdy, ruggedly-built boat whose design and construction are suited for serious offshore sailing, with the caveat that you go through the boat from one end to the other, replacing every piece of gear that's tired, reinforcing and repairing as necessary.

There are not too many boats that you can buy for this kind of money and then head off to Tahiti in reasonable security.

It's a tinkerer's dream. You may not be ready to build a boat from scratch, but you can do modifications on the Alberg 35 to your heart's content without going broke or destroying your investment.

The boat is really good-looking, especially compared to a lot of modern high-sided tubs. If you're a fanatic, you can clean up, paint and refinish the boat to look almost as good as a Hinckley Pilot—almost.

Some Alberg 35s have been meticulously maintained, and are in beautiful condition. Some of them have been beat to pieces by other owners going cruising on the cheap. We'd look for a nice one, or one that had only cosmetic problems. The trick is figuring out which problems are only cosmetic.

A livaboard couple can be comfortable on this boat, having much more elbow room than on a smaller modern "live aboard" cruiser for which you'd pay more money.

You want a decent-sized boat for serious cruising, while spending about the same money as you would for a new 27-footer? Consider the Alberg 35. Buy it, and be off for warmer places. **• PS**

Pearson 35

Rugged, versatile and handsome, the Pearson 35 has held her value well over the years.

Even to those of us who had begun serious sailing in that era, 25 years ago seems like history. *Finisterre,* a beamy centerboarder by the standards of the time, with a yawl rig, had won a remarkable three straight biennial Bermuda Races at the end of the 1950s. In 1964 another relatively beamy centerboard yawl, a Pearson Invicta, won again. It was the beginnings of an era of shallow wide boats that not only sailed through a gaping loophole in the popular rating rule of their day but also offered interior space unavailable in the typically narrower, deeper boats that preceeded them.

Thus, in the mid-1960s when Pearson Yachts sought to replace in its line the venerable but "old fashioned" Alberg 35, it chose to do so with a centerboard 35-footer. Retaining the traditional long overhangs, modest freeboard, curved sheer and moderate displacement, Pearson's in-house designer Bill Shaw put together the Pearson 35.

The 35 was introduced in 1968 and remained in production for the next 14 years. In all, 514 P35s were built, almost all for East Coast and Great Lakes owners attracted by the 35's shoal draft (3' 9" with centerboard up) and "classic" proportions. Even the popular Pearson 30, usually heralded as the enduring boat from a builder otherwise noted for its frequent introductions of new boats and short production runs, remained in production only 10 years, albeit with almost 1,200 boats built.

Equally remarkable during an era when builders were quick to make regular changes to existing boats in concert with their marketing departments (and afix a "Mk" whatever to to designate changes), the 35 remained essentially unchanged. A yawl rig continued to be an option and the original dinette layout was replaced by a traditional settee layout, but otherwise the most significant changes were the variety

Specifications

LOA	35' 0"
LWL	25' 0"
Beam	10' 0"
Draft	3' 9"/7' 6" (board up/down)
Displacement	13,000 lbs.
Ballast	5,400 lbs.
Sail area	550 sq. ft.

of auxiliary engines used over the years. Thus in talking about the Pearson 35 we can talk about 14 years of production all at once.

A Close Look at the Boat

The success of the Pearson 35 was no accident. Like the Tartan 27, the Alberg 30, and its Pearson predecessors the Alberg 35, Vanguard and Triton, the P35 gave a broad spectrum of sailors the type of boat they were looking for: traditional design, contemporary styling, solid construction, and eminently livable space both in the cockpit and belowdecks. And those same qualities continue to make the Pearson 35 a highly sought after boat on the used boat market almost 25 years later.

Introduced in the midst of the how-many-does-she-sleep era and, with that, the convertible dinette fad, the 35 boasted six berths, only three or four of which promised comfort. It took a number of years but the discomfort of the dinette/double berth combination became evident and the small upper berth became shelf space. Remaining have been the good sized forward V-berths and a reasonable transom (pull-out) berth in the main cabin. In the mid-1970s a pull-out double berth replaced the dinette although it remained better as a single berth with the boat capable of sleeping a total of four without crowding.

Excessive berths notwithstanding, the 35 has a livable interior. However, note that it does not have a navigation table, the galley tends to interfere with the companionway, and the head is small by modern standards. We do not consider any of these shortcomings serious.

Although the interior is more spacious than the average boat of her era (but less so than 35-footers nowadays), perhaps the strongest appeal of the 35 is her cockpit. By any standard old or new it is big (over 9' long), comfortable, and efficient, equally suitable for sailing or dockside entertaining, especially with wheel steering and a sloop rig to leave it uncluttered by tiller or mizzenmast. The lack of a quarterberth results in sail lockers port and starboard as well as a usable lazerette.

Below, the decor is strictly functional with a fiberglass head and hull liner and lots of Formica, a plastic enactment of the typical decor of the 1970s.

The performance of the Pearson 35 is moderately good (average PHRF base rating, about 180). Like many moderately beamy boats with full keel and low aspect sailplan, she quickly picks up a weather helm as she heels. However, the combination of adjustable centerboard and judiciously shortened sail makes that helm only inconvenient, not annoying, especially if the 35 is equipped with wheel steering. She tends to be at her worse in lighter winds, particularly when seas are sloppy, at her best on a close reach in at least moderate winds, then she feels fast, solid and seaworthy.

Owners report no lack of confidence in the 35, either in her strength or performance, in storm conditions. However, the size of the cockpit is a serious drawback in heavy seas offshore.

The original engine in the 35 was the Universal Atomic 4, about the largest (and heaviest) boat for which that engine is suitable, with the prop in an aperture. By 1975 the Farymann diesel became an option, followed by a variety of Westerbeke and Universal diesel engines. Accessibility to the Atomic 4 was marginal; for the diesels it became next to impossible, prompting the most common owner complaint about the boat: retrofitting a diesel to replace the Atomic 4 is difficult.

The 35 would never be mistaken for a motorsailer, given her succession of modestly powered engines. It would be a shame to further saddle her mediocre light air performance with the drag of a three bladed prop to improve performance under power; backing down will always be "an adventure," as one owner deems it, regardless of engine or prop.

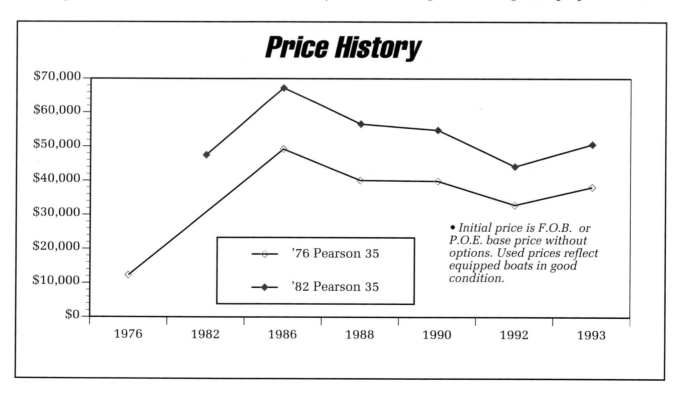

Price History

- '76 Pearson 35
- '82 Pearson 35

• Initial price is F.O.B. or P.O.E. base price without options. Used prices reflect equipped boats in good condition.

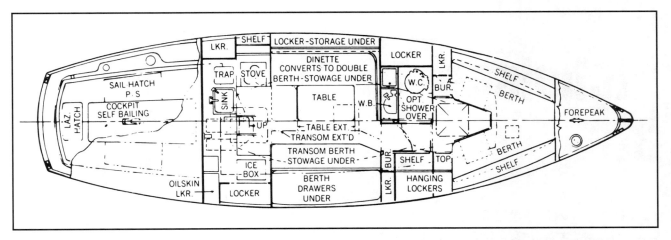

The spars and rig of the 35 are workmanlike. Owners of yawls extol the opportunity to "get anywhere in anything" with jib and jigger. However, with slab reefing we'd opt for the sloop rig. Sail area is not so large that it cannot be worked even with a shorthanded crew, and "modern" conveniences such as roller jib furling and roller travelers make the task even more feasible.

As a further aid, several owners report having fitted their 35s with an inboard staysail, in effect a double head rig, but the short foretriangle base ("J") of the 35 would seem to militate against much effectivess from that rig except in extreme conditions.

What to Look For

With the few changes in the Pearson 35 during her long production run, any basic faults with the boat were soon cured in the earliest models. There seems to have been few even of these. Indeed, the 35 is structurally a rugged vessel. As a result, buyers in the market for a 35 should concentrate on the effects of age on particular boats. Following is a sampling of the problems owners report:

• The aluminum ports, fiberglass hatches, and through deck fittings such as stanchions and chainplates are prone to leaking. So too on occasion does the hull-to-deck joint. These are largely annoying rather than serious and no more so than any boat of the vintage of the 35.

• The centerboard boat definitely has appeal, but with that appeal goes difficulties of maintenance including that of the pennant and pivot. Any survey of a prospective purchase should include a thorough inspection of the board, trunk, pivot and pennant. Incidentally, some owners report having permanently pinned the board up (and wedging them to prevent thunking), but we'd think twice before both compromising windward performance and control of balancing the helm by such a move.

• Gelcoat crazing is a common complaint, although most owners have learned to endure the disfigure-

Originally, the Pearson 35 had six berths. Eventually someone must have listened to reason and altered the layout, adding some welcome storage space instead.

ment while enjoying the rest of the 35's aesthetic qualities. Bottom blistering seems about average for 10+ year old production boats.

• The rig is the typically rugged one that Pearson is noted for, and its problems are apt to be largely corrosion and age.

• Check the condition of the auxiliary engine with the help of a professional. The same goes for the fuel tank. Major repairs or replacement are not easy.

Conclusions

If we were looking for a Pearson 35 we would spend our time checking out those built from the mid-1970s and later but not, if price were an object, one of the last ones built. We would want one with the "standard" (not dinette) accommodation plan, a sloop rig, and a diesel engine, preferably a Westerbeke. Cosmetic abuse would not bother us particularly; the basic quality of the boat lends itself to refinishing with polyurethane outside and even extensive refurbishing inside. A number of owners report upgrading of the interior with woods, fabrics and fittings, reducing or eliminating the formidibly antiseptic fiberglass liner and "teak" faced laminate on the bulkheads.

The degree that the Pearson 35s have retained their value—and seem destined to continue to do so—has to impress any potential buyer faced with the prospect of paying a high price for an older boat. And on this score, make no mistake; a vintage Pearson 35 in good condition has become one of the more expensive used boats of her type and original price on the market. For the kinds of use she is best suited for—coastal cruising for up to four—she is a rugged, versatile, and handsome craft for which there should continue to be a healthy market for many years to come. • **PS**

Nicholson 35

A real-live, serious ocean cruiser. The hard part will be finding one on the used market in the U.S.

Today's new boat market has fragmented about as far as it can: cruiser/racers, racer/cruisers, cruiser/cruisers, racer/racers. But not so long ago, there were a few boats built as plain-old cruisers, with decent performance (but no racing aspirations), seaworthy construction (without overkill), and design that allowed you to take an out-of-the-box sailboat on a cruise for a week, or a year.

Maybe you have to go to a real old-time boatbuilder to get that kind of quality. How old-time? Will 200 years of yacht building experience do?

If not the oldest yacht builder around, Camper & Nicholsons has to be in the running. Over the years, Nicholsons built every kind of boat imaginable, including pure racers and boats that came precariously close to being sailing houseboats. Nicholsons have never had the type of exquisite joinerwork you find in Far Eastern boats, nor have the looks of most of their boats fallen into the category of classic. But the boats have always been built with a high level of integrity, and a few of the designs are classic not in looks or detailing, but in overall quality.

Just over 200 Nicholson 35s were built over more than a 10-year period, with production tailing off in the early 1980s. Most boats were sold in England, but a number were built for American owners, and still more found their way to the U.S. during the rampage of the dollar against foreign currencies in the mid 1980s.

The Nicholson 35 is a cruising boat, plain and simple. Its proportions are about as common-sense and moderate as you can get. The boat is clean, almost austere in appearance, with very little exterior wood trim. You'll find a teak caprail, teak grab rails, teak ply cockpit seats, and that's about it.

It is a true medium-displacement boat: heavy by contemporary racer/cruiser standards, but very rea-

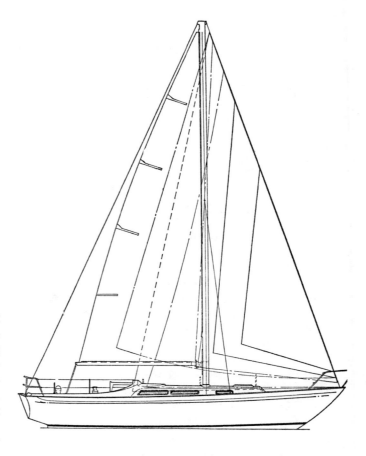

Specifications

LOA	35' 3"
LWL	26' 9"
Beam	10' 5"
Draft	5' 6"
Displacement	15,650 lbs.
Ballast	7,300 lbs.
Sail area	736 sq. ft.

sonable for an offshore cruiser with a waterline almost 27' long.

Sailing Performance

The Nic 35 is no racing boat, but she's no slug, either. Her PHRF (Performance Handicap Racing Fleet) rating of about 156 is some six seconds per mile slower than the Ericson 35-2, but some 20 seconds per mile faster than a "pure" cruiser such as the Tayana 37 or Crealock 37.

A moderate fin keel and skeg-mounted rudder underbody allows reasonable performance in light air, despite a smallish sailplan. The working sail area is just about evenly divided between the foretriangle and mainsail.

The rig is a simple masthead sloop, with double

lower shrouds and single, airfoil spreaders. The mast is a tapered, anodized Proctor spar, which is filled with foam to deaden sound. Halyard winches are mounted on the mast.

While the sailplan never changed, there were many minor revisions to the rig over the years. Early boats have roller-reefing booms, while late boats have slab reefing. Winch specifications and options changed over the years.

Most early boats have halyard winches that are large enough for hoisting sail, but too small to allow you to easily get a person to the masthead. We wouldn't want to hoist a 90-pounder up the mast with the standard Lewmar 8C winches. Larger halyard winches were optional—Lewmar 16 or 25. The 25 is as small a winch as we'd want to use to hoist anyone aloft, and even that would be work for most people.

The mainsheet traveler bisects the cockpit just forward of the wheel, so that you have to step over the traveler and onto the cockpit seats to go forward from the steering position.

While the mainsheet's position just forward of the helmsman is reasonable, the driver cannot easily trim the mainsheet, which secures to a cleat on the front of the teak traveler support. It would be a simple matter to replace this awkward arrangement with a modern traveler, with the sheet ending at a cam cleat on top of the traveler car.

The cockpit seats themselves are short and not very comfortable, with a high, nearly vertical fiberglass cockpit coaming. The deep cockpit does give excellent protection from seas and spray.

One of the best features of the cockpit is a molded-in dodger coaming, much like you find in this country on S&S-designed boats such as the Tartan 37. When fitted with a good dodger, the entire forward half of the cockpit will be bone-dry in almost any conditions.

Despite the fact that the aft side of the deckhouse slopes forward, the companionway is built out slightly, making it vertical. This allows you to remove the top dropboard in light rain, even with the dodger down. The companionway hatch slides have Tufnol runners, allowing the hatch to move easily. This is typical of the good structural detailing in boats from C&N.

Cockpit volume is huge. A bridgedeck protects the companionway, but the high coamings could allow the cockpit to fill almost to the top of the hatch in a major pooping. Later boats have large flapper-protected pipe scuppers through the transom in addition to big cockpit scuppers. We'd suggest retrofitting these to any older boat to be used for offshore voyaging.

Shroud chainplates are just inboard of the low bulwarks. They consist of heavy stainless steel "hair-pins," and are bolted through what would be the beam shelf on a wooden boat. We had some reservations about this construction when we first looked at it more than a decade ago, but after finding no chainplate damage on a similarly-fitted Nicholson 40 that had been rolled over and dismasted, we can't argue with the strength of the installation. Lloyds approves it, and they're notoriously conservative.

Like most boats of the 1970s, Nicholson 35s tend to be under-winched. Standard jib sheet winches are Lewmar 40s or 43s. Larger Lewmars were optional. We'd go for the biggest self-tailing genoa sheet winches that could fit on the coamings, and we'd make it a high priority for shorthanded cruising.

The low bulwarks give an enormous feeling of security under sail. The side decks are wide, and there is a grab rail atop the cabin trunk on each side, although the rail's flattened shape takes a little getting used to. The molded-in fiberglass non-skid is so-so. Teak decks were an option, but not a commonly chosen one.

In general, sailing performance is what you would look for in a serious cruising boat. The hull shape is uncompromised by any rating rule. The ballast/displacement ratio of 42%, with the lead concentrated quite low in the molded keel, results in a reasonably stiff boat by any standard.

Sailing performance can be improved on any boat by replacing a main and genoa more than a few years old. You'll never get racing boat performance out of the Nic 35, but you also won't have to work yourself to death to get acceptable speed, either. That's not a bad trade-off.

Engine

A variety of engines have been used in the Nic 35, all diesels. Early boats have the ubiquitous Perkins or Westerbeke 4-107. Later boats have a smaller Westerbeke L-25 or a marinized Volkswagen Rabbit diesel. Given our druthers, we'd take the Perkins engine. But there's a complication here. Early boats, recognizable by a prop shaft that emerges from the aft end of the keel, utilize a hydraulic drive rather than a conventional transmission. The engine faces aft under the cockpit bridgedeck, with the hydraulic pump mounted on its back end. The hydraulic motor is in the bilge at the aft end of the main cabin.

Hydraulic drives are a mixed blessing. They allow the engine to be mounted anywhere, but most marine mechanics don't know how to work on them. However, heavy equipment mechanics anywhere in the world can solve most hydraulic problems. On the downside, a major problem requiring replacement of the hydraulic motor or pump in a non-industrial area could be a real headache.

Later boats have a more conventional exposed shaft and strut. The engine is mounted further aft, under the cockpit, and the shaft is driven through a V-drive. Access to the engine in either installation is poor. On V-drive boats with a quarterberth, you can get to the front of the engine through the quarterberth. With no quarterberth, it's a crawl through a cockpit locker. The back of the engine is accessed through removable hatches behind the companionway ladder.

Control when backing is better with the V-drive installation, since the prop is much further aft. Likewise, tight maneuvering ahead is better with the same prop configuration, since you get good prop wash over the rudder.

In all boats, the fuel tank is a fiberglass molding. It is not integral to the hull, but is glassed in after the hull is laid up. We have heard no reports of failures of the tank.

Fuel capacity varies from 33 to 40 gallons—adequate for a cruising boat, but a little on the skimpy side for true long-term independence.

Construction

There's nothing to fault in the construction of these boats. Some hulls—but not all—were built under Lloyds survey. A Lloyds Hull Moulding Note—which covers the basic layup of the hull, installation of bulkheads, and the deck molding—is fairly common, as it added nothing to the cost of the boat other than a survey. A full-blown Lloyds 100 A-1 certifi-

cate is rarer, since it added substantially to the price of the boat.

Nicholsons was an early user of isophthalic polyester resin, although it was only used for gelcoat. This made Nicholson 35s more blister-resistant when new, but it probably doesn't substantially reduce a boat's tendency to blister if it is left in the water constantly for years. Structural work in these boats is first-class. We've never understood why good-quality European boats in the late 70s and early 80s seemed to have much neater glass work than most production American boats of the same period, but they do.

The lead ballast casting is dropped into a molded keel cavity, then heavily glassed over. The outside of the keel molding of any boat with internal ballasting should be carefully examined for grounding damage.

There is a deep bilge sump under the cabin sole just aft of the fiberglass water tank. This will keep bilge water where it belongs until it can be pumped overboard.

Two 90 amp-hour batteries were standard on early boats. They were increased to 128 amp-hours each on later boats, and the alternator size was increased

Many changes were made to the interior layout over the years; most were improvements. Pictured here is a standard interior from a mid-'70s model. Many of the boats have custom interiors.

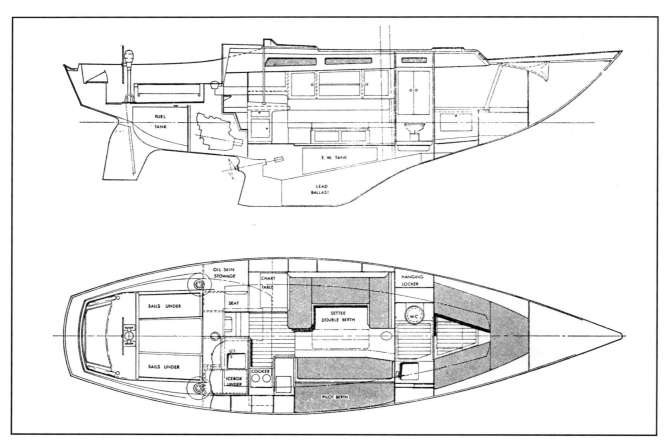

to 60 amps. If you want to go to bigger batteries on an older boat—a must for serious cruising—you'll need to install a bigger alternator if you don't want to run your engine all the time.

Interior

Many small changes were made to the interior design and decor over the years. In addition, the Nicholson 35 was built to order—you didn't buy one off some dealer's lot—so there is a lot of minor interior customizing. This was encouraged by the builder, and the prices for modifications were reasonable. It makes buying a used boat more complicated, however, because the combination of features you're looking for may be hard to find.

The forward cabin on all boats is pretty much the same. There are the usual V-berths, but unlike a lot of boats, they don't come to a point at the bow; there's plenty of foot room. The berths could be converted to a big double, but you won't find that on most boats.

A chain pipe runs vertically between the berths to the chain locker on many boats, rendering moot any modification to a double berth. The chain locker under the berths does keep the weight of chain low and fairly far aft, if you're willing to make the trade-off.

Padded vinyl liners are used on the hull sides, rather than wood ceiling. This looks good when new, but gets tired after a few years. We'd prefer wood. Wood ceilings can be refinished; vinyl can only be cleaned.

The earliest boats have white melamine-finished bulkheads, which lend to the general austerity of older models. Later boats have teak-veneered bulkheads, but the teak used is generally fairly light, so it doesn't dramatically darken the interior.

Ventilation in the forward cabin is poor. A low-profile Tannoy ventilator installed in the aluminum-framed deck hatch was standard, but these don't move nearly as much air as big cowl vents. Original specs called for cowl vents over the forward cabin, but we've never seen them.

Aft of the forward cabin is a full-width head. Camper & Nicholsons used this same basic design on several boats, and it works well. You may not like the idea of walking through the head to get to the forward cabin, but it allows a much larger head than you'll find on the typical boat of this length built in the 1970s.

There are good touches in the head, such as a stainless steel grab rail in front of the sink, and a mirror that angles upward so you don't have to bend over to shave. Using the full width of the boat for the head allows its use as a dressing room without undue contortions.

Early boats do not have pressure water, nor do they have hot water for a shower. These creature comforts came later in the production run, but they can be added to older boats without much trouble.

There is very little wood in the head—just trim around locker doors—which makes it easy to keep clean and dry. A single Tannoy vent provides limited ventilation, but there's plenty of room on deck over the head to add two cowl vents in Dorade boxes. This would help ventilate the entire boat, and would be high on our priority list.

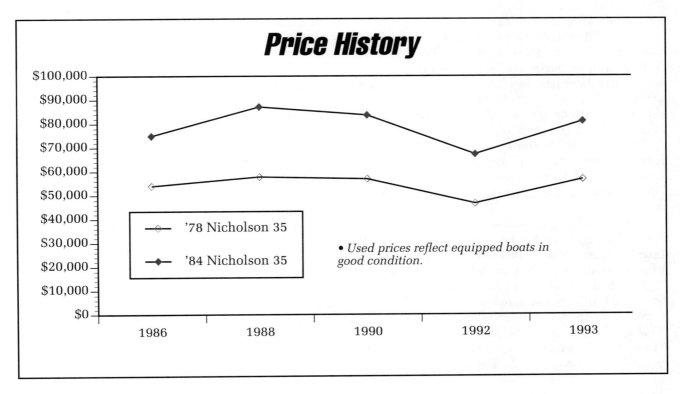

Used prices reflect equipped boats in good condition.

You'll find a lot of variations in the main cabin, and which ones are most desirable is really a matter of choice.

All boats have a U-shaped dinette to starboard, with a permanently mounted dropleaf table. On the later boats we've looked at, the table is mounted on a heavy tubular aluminum base, securely bolted to the cabin sole. It is one of the sturdiest tables we've ever seen. The design allows the table to be reached from both the dinette and the starboard settee, giving lots of elbow room for five for dinner, with elbow-to-elbow seating for seven close friends if a lot of passing of food isn't required.

There is storage space under the dinette, with lockers and bookshelves behind the seat back.

Starboard side layout varies. As originally designed, there is a straight extension settee, with a pilot berth outboard. The pilot berth was deleted on many boats, increasing storage space but visually narrowing the cabin. On a serious cruising boat, the extra storage would be a plus, since both the dinette and settee can serve as good sea berths. All berths, incidentally, are fitted with lee cloths—something you don't find as standard on most American boats, even boats sold as serious cruisers.

Ventilation is provided by an aluminum-framed hatch over the middle of the cabin, plus two small water-trap cowl vents at the aft end of the main cabin. For use in the tropics, you really need to add more cowl vents, at the very least.

Minor changes were made in the galley over the years, but they were not earth-shaking. The earliest boats have good locker space, but no cutlery drawer. This was added under the counter on later boats. It would be a simple retrofit.

Nice molded teak counter fiddles on early boats were replaced by functional but tacky aluminum fiddles on later boats. Galley counters are covered with plastic laminate, and some of it is hideous: God-awful speckly-tweedy stuff, sort of in keeping with the interior decor we've experienced in unnamed cheap bed and breakfast joints in the UK.

There's good storage space in the galley, with lockers outboard, a big pantry locker under one counter, a pot locker under the stove well, and another locker under the sink. The sink itself is quite small.

The icebox is outboard of the sink, next to the stove. It's a good-sixed box—five cubic feet—and insulation is adequate for northern climates. In the tropics, we don't think it would make the grade.

A gimbaled two-burner Flavel propane stove with oven and broiler is standard equipment. It is painted steel—as are most European galley stoves—and will be a ripe candidate for replacement on older boats. The stove well is narrow, so it may take some searching to find a stove that fits. Force 10 makes a stove that is narrow enough to fit most European stove wells, but you'll probably have to special-order it, as most American boats take a wider model.

The propane supply is a paltry 10 pounds, so you may well end up looking for ways to expand that. A Marine Energy Systems two-tank molded gas locker should fit in the starboard cockpit locker if you don't mind giving up some storage space.

All in all, the galley is very good for a 35' cruising boat; exceptional when you compare it to most American boats of the early 1970s.

Although all boats have a nav station at the port after quarter, the layout varies tremendously.

There are two basic configurations: an aft-facing nav station, which uses the dinette for a seat; and a forward-facing station, using the quarterberth head as a seat.

With the aft-facing station, there is no quarterberth; you get an extra cockpit locker. You also get a real curiosity: a belowdecks watch seat next to the companionway, elevated high enough so you can see out both the companionway and the cabin trunk windows.

This is a real seagoing feature, but will be wasted space on boats that are only used for coastal cruising. Offshore, with the boat running under autopilot or steering vane, the watch seat allows you to sit below, out of the weather, while still keeping a reasonable watch unless you're in crowded shipping lanes.

On some boats, the watch seat was deleted, and replaced with a big hanging locker. This would be a feasible and desirable modification on boats not used for serious cruising.

Both nav station layouts have a big chart table, good bulkhead space for mounting electronics, and space for navigation books and tools. It's a tough call as to which arrangement is better.

The quarterberth would make an excellent sea berth. We'd rather sleep in a quarterberth than a pilot berth, particularly in a warm climate. At the same time, a wave down the companionway can douse you in big-time fashion in the quarterberth. We'd take our chances, opting for the quarterberth and forward-facing nav station.

Headroom is over 6' throughout. The long windows of the main cabin make for a well-lighted interior.

A molded fiberglass water tank holding about 70 gallons fits under the sole in the main cabin, smack on top of the boat's longitudinal center of flotation, where it belongs. This is marginal water capacity for long-distance cruising—we'd like to see at least 100 gallons, even for a couple—but it would be simple enough to install auxiliary tanks under both the dinette and settee. A second tank is a good idea on any boat, in case of a leaky tank or a contaminated water supply.

On early boats, the tank is filled from inside the boat—no deck fill. This avoids any chance of salt water contamination from a leaking filler cap, but it complicates tanking up: you have to drag hoses or jerry cans belowdecks.

The tank vents properly, inside the boat rather than outside. Most American boats have water tank vents on deck, many of them in the side of the hull. To put it bluntly, this is really dumb. If a boat spends a lot of time on one tack with the vent submerged, salt water will siphon back into the tank. Heavy water on deck can even get into vents mounted on the side of the cabin.

With the exception of the aluminum galley fiddles, most of the interior changes over the years are a distinct improvement. Storage is excellent for long-term cruising.

Conclusions

This is a real-live, serious ocean cruiser. It's not pointy at both ends, doesn't have a full-length keel, isn't shippy looking, and doesn't have oodles of nicely-fitted exterior teak to drive you wild with pleasure at the boat show, delirious from endless maintenance when you have to live with it.

The cockpit is uncomfortable, but can be improved with seat cushions and back cushions. It's a shame the cockpit seats aren't long enough to lie down on.

The interior is roomy and comfortable for cruising, lacking only a permanent double berth—a shortcoming that can be remedied, albeit with some work. The interior lacks the space and privacy of current 35-footers best suited for marina living or coastal cruising, but is functional for offshore sailing, particularly for a couple.

We wouldn't hesitate to sail this boat anywhere, with virtually no changes. It demonstrates common-sense design and high-grade construction, even though it's not fancy, and there's not a gimmick to be found: no microwave, no stall shower, no recessed lights, none of the things that some people think they need for comfortable cruising.

The hard part, of course, is finding one. English boating magazines have a lot of Nicholson 35s for sale, but there are not too many on this side of the pond. Actually, that might be an advantage.

Buying a boat overseas is relatively painless, and you save yourself the trouble of sailing across the ocean before you can cruise Europe. Buy a boat in England, cruise there for a couple of summers, laying the boat up over the winters. Then, when you retire or get that long-awaited sabbatical, you can do some "real" cruising. You could do a lot worse.   • **PS**

The J/35

She's fast and she's fun—sailing is what this boat is all about. We like the J/35 a lot.

The "J" stands for Johnstone and the "35" stands for 35 feet. Straightforward—a characteristic of both the boat and the company that sells them.

The Johnstones were originally two: Rod Johnstone started things in 1976 when he designed a 24-footer and built it in his garage. He convinced his brother, Bob Johnstone, that the boat could be a success, and Bob became chief salesman, in charge of the business.

The relationship continues to this day, but the family owned company is now run by children of both Johnstones, all serious sailors like their parents. Rod's sons Jeff, Alan, and Phil are president, vice-president, and legal counsel respectively. Bob's son Stuart is chairman of the board and marketing manager, while second son Drake oversees the dealer network and is sales manager of the company.

The original J/24 was sold as a "fast" boat that ignored the existing racing rules. At the time, there was a large group of serious racers who felt that the handicap rules, particularly the International Offshore Rule (IOR) and the Midget Ocean Racing Club (MORC), were encouraging unhealthy extremes in design—not necessarily good, fast sailboats, but rather boats that would sail marginally faster than their low handicap ratings said they should sail, boats that required huge crews to go fast.

At the time, the word on the J/24 was that it spit in the eye of the rules; Rod Johnstone had designed a boat that went fast and was fun to sail, and if it didn't do well in the handicap rating game, then it was the game that was at fault. Except for a couple of aberrations—a 34 and a 41 designed to beat the IOR rule—the J/Boats have remained faithful to that idea. And it is significant that the rating rules have come around to the J/Boats, rather than vice versa. There

Specifications

LOA	35' 5"
LWL	30' 0"
Beam	11' 8"
Draft	6' 11"
Displacement	10,000 lbs.
Ballast	4,400 lbs.
Sail area	633 sq. ft.

are more J/Boats than any other brand, by far, racing under the current PHRF and IMS handicap rules.

Unlike most sailboat companies, J/Boats decided from the beginning to stay out of the boatbuilding end of the business. Rather than a J/Boat factory, the completed boats come from Tillotson-Pearson, an independent company whose president, Everett Pearson, was one of the pioneers of fiberglass boatbuilding.

The arrangement has been mutually satisfactory over the years, with J/Boats having relatively little invested in manufacturing overhead, concentrating on the design and marketing; and Tillotson-Pearson has another steady and successful customer to complement the other lines of boats that they build—Alden and Garry Hoyt's new Manta 32—along with

Owners' Comments

"This is a wonderful sailing boat with the ability to be very, very fast and yet not difficult to handle. The interior is minimal but okay for weekends."
—1985 model on Long Island Sound

"There is almost no interior storage, even though we bought all the interior options. But at least we can't accumulate too much stuff. This is an easy boat to sail—my wife and I cruise it each year and have little trouble."
—1984 model in Lake Erie

"I've been very pleased with the construction. Took a hit broadside by a Beneteau 44 on a reach with minimal damage."
—1983 model in Florida

"Buy the boat; you'll love it. It is very fast, very powerful and easy to sail—always seems to be in balance and easy to steer. My wife and I cruise ours alone. There is nothing like a J/35 going upwind in a breeze and waves."
—1986 model in New York

"I am 6' 5". Otherwise the boat is perfect."
—1987 model in Massachusetts

"The boat is a high-performance rocket. It rocks and rolls upwind in big seas, and I downgrade it for wet sailing—low freeboard and no coamings. But I have never had any problems with the hull, deck, rudder, rig, rigging, etc. The fixed ports need to be resealed every two years."
—1984 model on Lake Michigan

---

some high-tech endeavors, such as fabricating giant carbon-fiber propellers for wind generators.

Over the years, Tillotson-Pearson has established a reputation for high-quality production work, often at the leading edge of fiberglass technology, that has helped J/Boats maintain an image of quality near the top-end of the production spectrum.

The J/35 was a successful racer from its introduction in 1983, and with more than 300 built so far, it has had a successful production run for the company. The 35 is still available as a new boat and will continue to be. A new design, the 35C, is unrelated to the 35, a different design, slower, aimed more at cruising than the original 35.

In design, the 35 looks like a typical Rod Johnstone boat, with short overhangs for a long waterline, relatively low and flat sheerline, a low cabin house, and a moderate well-balanced rig. Obviously, Johnstone knows something about the harmony between a boat's underbody and the water, but a large part of the boat's speed is also dependent on the light weight—10,500 pounds on a 30-foot waterline—as well as a good distribution of that weight.

Traditionalists may think the J/35 is a little plain, but its proportions are pleasing, and many people consider it the most attractive grand prix racer around. If you didn't know the boat's record, you probably wouldn't pick it out of a crowd as a speedster, or know that it's one of the most successful racing boats its size of the 1980s.

The boat has primarily been known as a racer, but the company touts it as a shorthanded cruiser as well. The boat's big cockpit, while principally designed for a racing crew, does make the boat good for day sailing, ideal for taking out guests and for dock partying. The boat has frequently been involved in singlehanded racing (both Tony Lush and Francis Stokes raced J/35s across the Atlantic), and we would agree with the company that it is easily handled by a couple, and could make for good cruising for two people or a family with small children.

Though the hull is a bit more beamy and saucer shaped than would be ideal in an offshore boat, it is one of the few modern racers under 40 feet in which we would consider doing an ocean crossing. In storm or hurricane conditions, it has a greater chance of achieving inverse stability than a narrower, heavier boat, but its speed makes it more likely that the prudent sailor will be able to sail away from such extreme conditions.

Construction

As is necessary to make a strong but lightweight boat, the J/35 uses some sophisticated construction techniques. Both the hull and deck are balsa-cored, with the end-grain balsa inside layers of biaxial and unidirectional fiberglass. As with any cloth, there is less stretch and more strength parallel to the glass fibers than across them, and the biaxial and unidirectional cloth used by Tillotson-Pearson lets the builder arrange the cloth throughout the hull so its strength is in line with the forces that occur under sail.

Unlike most boats, the main structural bulkhead which takes the forces of the rig is a molded fiberglass piece, and the floors are made up of glass beams to which both the mast step and the external lead keel are fastened.

The hull and deck are strong and, perhaps more importantly, stiff, so that there is a minimum of flexing when the boat is being pushed. The quality of the construction is evident in the six- and seven-year-old boats that are still able to handle the rig forces of a pumped-up backstay on a hard beat.

We have a lingering concern about the longevity of balsa-cored boats, since we have seen many 10- to 20-year-old boats with deck delaminations and a few with substantial delamination in the hull. Tillotson-Pearson obviously disagrees with us and continues to be committed to balsa cores.

With other builders, a major part of our concern is that balsa cored laminates seem to be more demanding of good engineering and high-quality workmanship than solid fiberglass laminates. Tillotson-Pearson is one of the few companies that we would trust to consistently do a good job in laying up a balsa-cored hull.

An unusual feature of hulls built after 1988 is that the company provides a 10-year warranty against blistering. In molding the boat, they use a vinylester resin on the first layer inside the gelcoat, and—along with a clean shop and careful workmen—they think this is enough to warrant the guarantee. The guarantee is transferable to later owners.

New J/35s can also be purchased with an American Bureau of Shipping (ABS) certificate. ABS is similar to the better known English Lloyd's certification, in that an independent surveyor periodically checks the shop and the boat during construction to make sure it meets minimum standards. While relatively new to cruising sailors, ABS certification is important to racers in the top echelons. International offshore regattas require it. It seems worthwhile because it is about the only way buyers can get an independent evaluation of the boat without overseeing the entire construction process themselves.

The boat comes with a thorough list of standard equipment. The company lists only 18 options for a new boat, and most of these are aesthetic preferences or cruising options, such as a dark-colored hull, two-tone deck, V-berth, swim ladder, and propane locker.

The rig is excellent, with a Hall Spars mast, rod rigging, and complete state-of-the-art running rigging. All winches are adequate, but if we were planning shorthanded cruising in addition to racing, we would consider larger, self-tailing primaries.

Tiller steering is standard on the boat. In its latest brochures, the company doesn't even list wheel steering as an option, but many earlier models had wheels, and some owners may still want it installed. We sailed both a tiller model and a wheel and believe the tiller is far superior, especially for racing. However, wheels seem to be sufficiently in vogue that there are a preponderance of them on the used 35s for sale.

Interior

The J/35 is primarily a racing boat, and its interior is spartan compared to similarly sized cruising boats. But the interior is decent, and well-finished given the plainness of the boat. The company advertises the high-quality of the interior woodwork, but we would describe it as so-so—better than the cheapest production boats on the market but definitely not "yacht" quality.

The arrangement is conventional. Forward you will find either sail bins or an optional V-berth, decently sized, with a head just aft of that, and a hanging locker and bureau opposite. Two comfortable settee berths are aft of the main bulkhead in the saloon, with an optional fold-up table between them.

The galley is minimal, with a two-burner alcohol stove and sink on the port side and an ice-box with chart-table top opposite. There are two big quarter berths underneath the bridgedeck and cockpit.

Ventilation is good, with eight opening ports and two hatches in addition to the companionway, but there is no provision at all for pushing air through the cabin when underway.

Except for the poor headroom and storage space, the J/35's interior is workable for short-term cruising. Still, racing is the boat's forte.

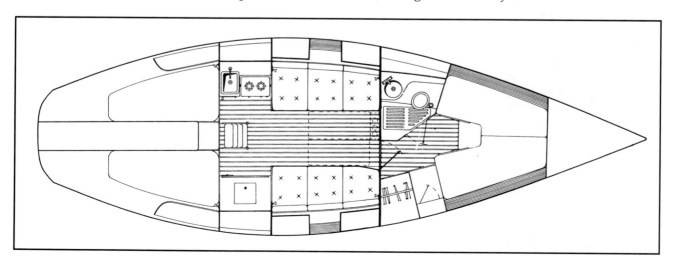

Storage is minimal, adequate for a racing crew or for a couple on a short cruise, but every 35 we looked at had sails and crew gear spread all over the settees and berths.

We would be quite comfortable weekending or cruising on this boat, but it does lack the amenities which most people demand nowadays, like hot-and-cold pressure water, propane stove and oven, and refrigeration. All these things could be added, of course, but they rarely are because they represent weight which is anathema to the high-performance sailor.

For us, the main shortcoming of the interior is the lack of headroom forward, in the head and V-berth, and a tall person will be uncomfortable even in the main cabin.

While this interior may not sound like much to the cruising sailor who looks at other boats with VCR stations and queen-size after berths, it is far superior to the one-off custom racers and almost all other racing boats that are in the same speed class as the J/35. Though the "cruiser" part is minimal, this boat is a true racer-cruiser. Where compromises are made, the racer is clearly favored, but the owner won't feel compelled to check into a motel at the end of a long passage as is the case with most racing machines.

Under Power

The Yanmar 3GM engine has become almost a standard in this size boat. It is a good engine, dependable, relatively quiet, and its 28 horsepower is plenty big for the J/35. A 20-gallon fuel tank gives about 150 miles of range, adequate since this boat will still be sailing in light airs when most others have cranked up the diesel. The boat comes standard with a Martec folding prop, and the boat powers easily to hull speed. The J/35 turns sharply and handles well under power, and it will back up more or less where you want it. Access to the engine is decent, behind the companionway steps underneath the cockpit. Installation of the engine and the other mechanical systems is workmanlike—good but nothing spectacular.

Under Sail

Sailing is what this boat is all about.

We sailed twice on a 35 during their first two years of production, and again last fall, in two heavy-air triangular races.

The boat is obviously quick. With a PHRF rating around 70, it is significantly faster than almost all boats its size. It is 50 seconds-per-mile faster than our own 16-year-old Carter 36 and most other IOR racers between 34 and 37 feet. In the class we raced in last fall, only a Schock 35, and a C&C 37 were comparable in speed. Like most good sailing boats, the J/35 has an "effortless" quality about its motion through the water. To us, it seems that most boats make quite a fuss as you push them up toward hull speed, especially on a beat. Often, you can "hear" how fast you're going by the amount of noise the boat makes. But a J/35 moves easily up to speed, and you have to look at the knotmeter to know whether you're moving five knots or seven.

It's a well-balanced boat, with excellent feel (if you have a tiller model) on all points of sail.

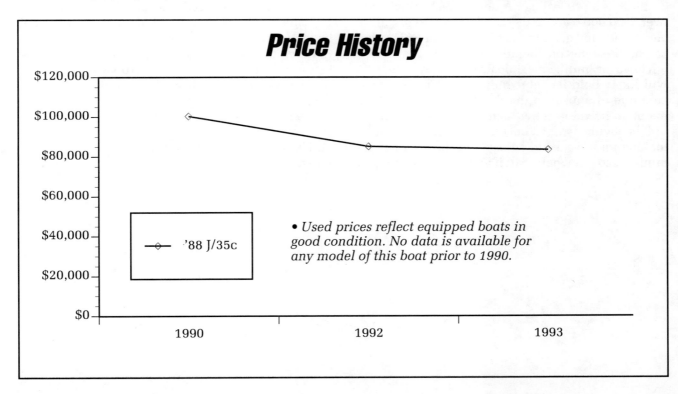

Price History

• Used prices reflect equipped boats in good condition. No data is available for any model of this boat prior to 1990.

◇ '88 J/35c

The boat can be wet working to weather in waves, especially given the lack of cockpit coamings, but otherwise it has few faults in sailing. Unlike many high-performance boats, it's also quite forgiving, so an inexperienced helmsman and crew can achieve good speed and at least finish a race or a passage ahead of other boats, even if losing on handicap.

Conclusions

The J/35 is a pricey boat. A new basic boat will run over $100,000 ready to race, and if you add premium electronics and get into the high-tech sail game, you can up the ante considerably.

However, unlike most boats these days, the J/35 will likely hold its value quite well. The boat will continue to appeal to the die-hard racer and thus maintain its value better than most other boats.

It is obviously not a boat for everybody. If you're looking for a weekend cottage or a floating condominium, go elsewhere. But if you are in the group of sailors who want a boat between 30 and 40 feet, whose time afloat is spent more than 50 percent in racing, you might want to consider the J/35. And if we were rolling in dough, we'd have to have one to park out in front of our condo, just for the fun of sailing it.

For the used boat shopper, the main consideration after price will be the quality of equipment, especially sails. Unlike some boats, it is quite probable that a J/35 has been raced, and usually raced hard, so in many instances a total refit of the basic boat may be in order.

Given that the latest models have several advantages—an ABS certificate and a 10-year anti-blister warranty—most used boat shoppers will probably want to also go the extra distance to get a new boat.

We like the J/35.

It gets down to basics—if sailing is what sailing is all about, you won't find a much better boat anywhere.
• PS

Bristol 35.5C

Ted Hood knows all there is to know about centerboard cruisers; he applied it well to this boat.

Around Bristol, Rhode Island—made famous by Nathanael G. Herreshoff—they tell this story: In the beginning, Bristol Yachts made rather ordinary boats. Along the way to success, Bristol's boss, Clint Pearson, collected some of the most skilled workmen in the business. Somewhere in the 1970s, in order to support about 130 craftsmen, Bristol upgraded sharply and took aim at the big boat, high buck market. It made good sense.

And that's when the centerboard sloop called the Bristol 35.5C was born. She debuted in 1977 and disappeared with the rest of the line a few years ago.

The inestimable Ted Hood designed her. He probably knows more than anyone alive about centerboard cruising boats. He's done a lot of them.

"This one just turned out great," he said. "She's about as small as you can get and still have really big boat appearance and performance. The interior just worked out very well." Hood owned one himself.

"She goes right along, doesn't she?" he said.

The Bristol 35.5C, which also came in a full-keel version (without the "C"), is an extraordinarily orthodox boat. There simply are no extremes in design, construction or performance, unless it is in her ability to flaunt her stern downwind and burn a lot of boats when beating in light to moderate air.

She's what is called medium displacement. Look at her dimensions. Nothing jumps out, except perhaps for slightly less beam than is seen in 35-footers of that era and certainly far less than is seen in more recent designs.

The Interior

Despite the 10' 10" beam, the interior reflects Ted Hood's attention to comfortable detail. There simply are no tight spots, no clumsy corners and no head or hip knockers.

Specifications

LOA	35' 6"
LWL	27' 6"
Beam	10' 10"
Draft	3' 9"/9'6" (board up/down)
Displacement	15,000 lbs.
Ballast	7,000 lbs.
Sail area	589 sq. ft.

You can walk into the head, turn around and even take a shower standing erect, if you're no more than 6' 2" in height.

The forward berths are more than adequate. Especially comfortable for one (but tight for two) are the pull-out extension berths in the main cabin. The big quarter berth is for that nose tackle in your racing crew. Luckily, only a few boats were built with pilot berths, because not having them means that the storage space is that much greater. With pilot berths, the boat theoretically sleeps no less than nine, but you'd feel like a 49er on a crowded clipper ship headed for the California Gold Rush.

The galley is a joy, with more counter space than many larger boats. Unobstructed, durable flat surfaces are always at a premium when preparing meals

Owners' Comments

"Three Bermuda races, three prizes, once second overall. Good sea boat. Broke a centerboard after four years while racing upwind in very heavy going. Builder has treated me well. I'd choose the same type of boat if I were starting over again."
—1978 model in Westwood, MA

"Could use more interior lights in better places. Next to impossible to change oil filter without major spillage into bilge. She's fast and rugged."
—1982 model in Shelton, CT

"Only good V-berth I've ever seen. Completely satisfied, except that you can't even see much less get to shaft stuffing box. Engine access worries me, too."
—1980 model in Norfolk, VA

"Good looking, fast and interior is very livable."
—1979 model in McAllen, TX

"Everywhere you can put a foot is solid as a rock. Passing sailors comment on her good looks."
—1981 model in Long Island City, NY

or washing dishes. The truly huge ice chest obviously has superior insulation. Even with the engine running the ice lasts well.

The spacious cabin interior is enhanced by a well-engineered fold-down table, which, unlike many, can be rigged in five seconds.

If one were to be picky, the lack of a wet locker aft in a boat of this size might be noted.

Engine access is, at best, mediocre. It's in a narrow compartment, with access in the front only by removing some drawers and the heavy step panel and on the port side through a panel in the quarterberth.

All joinery, laminates and solid wood, reflect the individual skills of Bristol's work force. The main and forward cabins are wood-sheathed. The sole is teak with a handsome ash inlay, all hand-layed, screwed, glued and bunged.

Many Bristol 35.5s were customized to some degree. Interior wood, for instance, could be mahogany, cherry or teak, with the latter two carrying a considerable premium. Double sinks in the galley were another fairly expensive option.

However, most equipment is standard. Bristol used topflight components, like Racor filters, Brunzeel bulkheads, Nicro vents, Schaefer hardware, Almag 35 ports, Bomar hatches, Edson steering and Lewmar winches.

The boat's deck is a first-rate work platform and,

for comfort, the cockpit is the equal of any 35-footer. However, because the seats run the full length of the cockpit, one must climb up and over to reach the steering station behind the big wheel. It's annoying. You can't even slide aft.

Construction

The Bristol 35.5s are solid fiberglass. The hull is built in halves and joined down the middle, which makes possible Bristol's fine hull-to-deck joint. The hull is flanged inward and the deck is bolted on top of the flange with a teak toerail also through-bolted. It makes for both a watertight joint and a very rigid structural beam at the rail.

Centerboards frequently are a source of major headaches. However, the Bristol 35.5C's board, which does not protrude into the cabin sole, must be well designed and executed.

The board is controlled by a low-geared horizontal winch on the coachroof. A stainless steel wire runs forward to a stainless vertical pipe at the corner of the chart table, down and across to the centerline under the floorboards. It makes three turns. The cable is entirely enclosed. If it were to cause trouble, it would be difficult to fix. However, only two of the *Practical Sailor* readers who own Bristol 35.5Cs report problems. Only a few boats were built before Bristol made modifications to the centerboard.

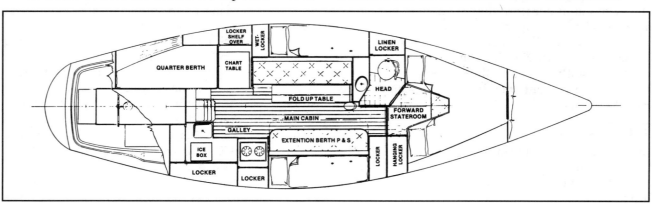

Sailing Characteristics

Make no mistake: The Bristol 35.5C is tender, as are most centerboarders. In return you get a very lively boat that is quick in any air, like many more modern fin keelers except that with her moderate keel and centerboard, the Bristol 35.5 doesn't require slavish attention to the helm.

The centerboard version has an IOR rating of 25.38, which means she should move out on a C & C 35, an Olson 38, a Hughes 38, a Pearson 35, a Tartan 37, a Morgan 38 and a J/34. That's pretty good company for a design of this vintage.

The IMS numbers show the centerboard version to be faster than the keel version. The heavier centerboarder (with 500 pounds more ballast) gives the keel model 6.8 seconds a mile in light air and 9 seconds a mile in 20 knots.

Despite being a centerboarder, the Bristol 35.5C, because of her ballast, has a very respectable calculated static stability of 115°.

The boat's phenomenal light-air performance is delineated in the Performance Package supplied by the United States Yacht Racing Union. In a true wind of 6 knots, close-hauled (44.5 degrees), the Bristol 35.5C, with a 120% jib, should do 3.9 knots. The velocity made good will be 2.8 knots. She'd be heeled only 5°. Beam reaching in the same conditions, the boat should do 5.4 knots.

In 20 knots true, the boat would do 6.1 knots, but would be heeling 31°. Broad reaching in 20 knots, she'd turn up slightly more than eight knots.

We've spent many happy hours sailing out of Newport, Rhode Island, aboard a 35.5C owned by Dwight Webb, who never has been known to overuse the engine. He's a sailorman. Beautifully maintained (with all exterior teak varnished) and with excellent sails, including Hood furling on the headstay and a Doyle Stackpack on the main, Webb's boat always moves well in any air.

In the past, Webb has owned quite a few boats: a Meridian, Triton, Morgan 30, Pearson 33, Pearson 35, Bristol 39, C & C 33, Sea Sprite 34, C & C 34 and a C & C 38.

He's passed on 10 years with the Bristol 35.5C, which he deems simply, "Best boat I've ever owned."

Conclusion

If a Bristol 35.5C takes your fancy, try for one with either a Westerbeke diesel or the equally satisfactory three-cylinder, 24-hp diesel made for a time by Universal. Avoid the Yanmar 2QM 20H, a two-cylinder diesel that struggles unsuccessfully to get up to hull speed.

Beware of a 1978 model without the modified centerboard.

Also, don't pay extra for a boat with a half dozen headsails. The Bristol 35.5C achieves her polar diagram optimums with a single 120% or 130% jib, which ideally will be on furling gear. Jibs bigger than that simply overpower the boat.

You'll pay heavily for a newer one, and because so few were built, the older used ones also are somewhat dear. 1981 is about where the ideal prices seem to occur. Those built later than 1981 seem to carry premium prices.

• **PS**

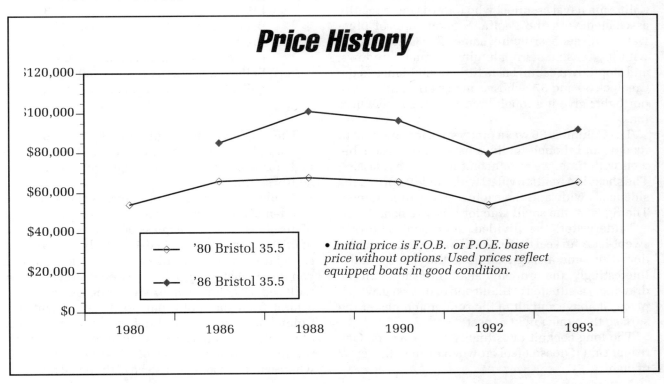

Price History

Legend:
- '80 Bristol 35.5
- '86 Bristol 35.5

• Initial price is F.O.B. or P.O.E. base price without options. Used prices reflect equipped boats in good condition.

(Y-axis: $0, $20,000, $40,000, $60,000, $80,000, $100,000, $120,000; X-axis: 1980, 1986, 1988, 1990, 1992, 1993)

Columbia 36

A bargain-basement racer/ cruiser from a grand-daddy of American production boatbuilders.

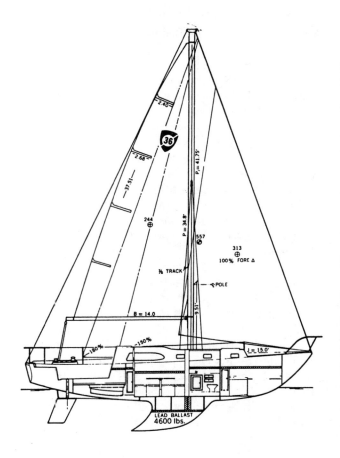

It's hard to believe, especially for those of us who learned to sail in the 1960s, that fiberglass sail boats built back then are now a part of history. The "fiberglass revolution" that seems like just yesterday, is now 30 years in the past. A lot has happened in the world of boatbuilding since then, but many of those old boats are still sailing.

The Design

The Columbia 36 was in production between 1967 and 1972. One reader estimates that more than 600 were built, making it a very successful model.

The boat was designed by William Crealock, the California naval architect who today is more readily associated with the Pacific Seacraft line of blue-water cruisers bearing his name. The Columbia 36, with its transom stern, aluminum frame windows, and step-down cabin, bears little resemblance to the Crealock 34 and 37, whose canoe sterns and bronze portlights give it a tough, traditional, go-anywhere look.

The Columbia 36 was a pretty slick looking boat in its day, and though its lines have worn reasonably well with time, we're reluctant to call it a "classic." The sheer is essentially flat, with modest spring, the sidedecks wide and the cabin nicely proportioned. The rig is on the small side for this size boat.

Underwater, the divided underbody shows a swept-back fin keel that looks like an inverted shark's dorsal fin, and a skeg leading to the spade rudder. Interestingly, the propeller shaft (not shown in the drawings) is situated at the aft end of this skeg, which places it above and aft of the rudder and nearer the surface than one might expect.

The long cockpit rates highly with owners. One reader said it doesn't feel crowded even with a crew of eight.

Specifications

LOA	35' 9"
LWL	28' 3"
Beam	10' 6"
Draft	5' 5"
Displacement	12,000 lbs.
Ballast	5,000 lbs.
Sail area	557 sq. ft.

The displacement/length ratio is 261, which is a nice number for good all around performance—too high for a hot rod, but just right for comfortable family sailing.

A subtle point about Columbias is the tooling. A wooden boatbuilder in Maine once told us that one of his objections to fiberglass boats was the absence of crisp, sharp lines and edges. Study a glass boat, especially an old one like the Columbia 36, and you'll see what he means. Every edge is generously radiused. Of course, some of this is necessary to pull a form from the mold, but not to the extent that Columbia rounded everything. In our opinion, many of the old Columbia's lose a few points in looks for this reason. An exception would be the Columbia 50, where wooden toerails (instead of the usual rounded,

Owners' Comments

"Plan to reinsulate the icebox. Bulkheads are a deep brown Formica veneer. Check wiring, stanchions and lifelines. Tremendous storage access. Very simple systems. Truly sleeps six six-foot adults."

1969 model in Texas

"Replace the rubber rubrail. Add ventilation with Dorades and opening ports. Rubrail constantly falls off. Hull-to-deck joint needs regular caulking. Boat flexes in heavy air."

1969 model in California

"Have the deck area adjacent to the portlights surveyed for water damage. Check fairing between hull and external ballast."

1969 model in New Jersey

molded fiberglass toerails) go a long way toward alleviating the impression of an amorphous, egg-shaped structure.

Construction

Like nearly all production builders in the 1960s, Columbia used standard hull laminates of polyester gelcoat, chopped strand mat and 24-ounce woven roving. Columbia was a pioneer in developing what it called the "unitized interior," or fiberglass pan, in which the engine beds, stringers and furniture foundations are all molded. This pan is then "tabbed" to the hull with wet fiberglass and is presumed to provide the necessary stiffening.

Finish work goes quickly after such a pan is in place. Teak trim, cut and milled in the woodshop, is simply screwed into place. The cabinet doors, juxtaposed against the gleaming white pan, and ubiquitous pinrails are as telltale of the late 60s and early 70s as shag carpeting.

The hull-to-deck joint is unusual in that it incorporates a double-channel length of aluminum into which the hull and deck flanges are fitted top and bottom. It probably made good engineering sense, but given the complaints about leaking, and the fact that this method, to our knowledge, has not been used by other builders, suggest it had its problems. Because aluminum has little or no springback, we imagine that bumping a piling could permanently "dent" this channel, causing leaks that would be very difficult to repair properly.

The deck was cored, and to finish the interior a molded headliner was glassed in. The old Columbia brochures are rather funny to read, showing as they do plant workers dressed in lab coats, installing winches, cleats and windows as if building a boat was no more difficult than assembling pieces from a kit. In fact, Columbia fomented this idea, marketing its boats in kit form and calling them Sailcrafter Kits.

The basic structure of the early Columbias was reasonably sound, and sold with a two-year warranty. That many of those boats are still around says something positive about general construction quality.

On the other hand, the boats were pretty much bare bones. No frills. But then, they were more affordable than a comparable boat today. We don't mind the opportunity to do our own customizing, but the interior pan limits what you can do.

Most readers responding to our Owner's Questionnaire rate the construction quality of the Columbia 36 as above average. No major problems were reported, though we do have some complaints of deck delamination. In all fairness, separation of the fiberglass skins from the coring is common in many older boats and should not be judged as a weakness peculiar to Columbia. But you should have your surveyor check the deck for soundness before buying.

Miscellaneous complaints include inadequate ventilation, need for a sea hood ("The companionway hatch is a joke"); various leaks at windows and hull-deck joint; and mainsheet and wheel poorly located. The brochure says the keels are lead, but at least one reader said his was iron.

Performance

The Columbia 36 was intended to be something of a hot boat when it was introduced. In fact, it was offered with a trim tab on the trailing edge of the keel for better control off the wind. A brochure credits the inspiration to the Twelve-Meter *Intrepid*'s "lopsided defense of the America's Cup."

We don't know how successfully the boat was raced, but do know that its PHRF rating is about 162, making it just a hair faster than a Catalina 30 (168) and a Cal 34 (168). None of our readers indicate that they race. One said, "Built for comfort, not speed." Typical reader ratings for speed are "average" upwind and "above average" off the wind. Several note the importance of sail trim (true of any boat!); annoying weather helm (excessive weather helm is unforgivable, but we suspect there's always a few whiners in this department who must not understand that a boat without any weather helm is a bear to steer); and one reader noted that the spar doesn't bend much to optimize sail shape (bendy rigs weren't in vogue at that time).

The standard sloop rig doesn't carry a lot of sail. One reader said he had a "tall boy" mast, which presumably was available as an option, as was—surprisingly—a yawl rig.

Overall, readers have positive remarks about seaworthiness, stability and balance. "The boat is a very good sailer," wrote one reader, adding that his boat "...has taken all Lake Michigan has to offer and never broken."

Most Columbia 36s were equipped with Atomic 4 gasoline engines. Several readers complain that the 30-hp. doesn't move the boat fast enough—about five knots. One reader had an Albin 20-hp. diesel. Another said engine access was very poor: "No room even to check oil."

Fuel tankage is 29 gallons; water is 44 gallons.

Interior

The layout of the Columbia 36 is standard, with a V-berth forward, U-shaped dinette amidships, and quarter berths aft. The sideboard galley puts the cook in the way of traffic, and the sink may have difficulty draining on port tack.

The most unusual feature of the plan is placement of the chart table opposite the head. This certainly isn't convenient to the cockpit for navigator-helmsman communications, but it does allow two quarter berths instead of just one. Readers note that the boat sleeps an honest six people, and tall ones at that. Headroom is listed at 6' 3".

Fiberglass interior pans tend to make for a rather sterilized appearance—the proverbial inside look of a refrigerator or Clorox bottle. We're not fond of them for several reasons: Pans restrict access to parts of the hull, tend to make the interior noisier and damper, and make it difficult to customize. But, that's the way it is with most production boats.

Conclusion

The Columiba 36 was a popular boat in the late 60s and early 70s, and still has its fans today. The basic structure is good. The interior is plain. We suspect that prospective buyers will find a wide range of customizing by previous owners. The quality of this workmanship will have a lot to do with your decision to buy or look elsewhere.

The *BUC Used Boat Guide* lists average prices for Columbia 36s ranging from about $25,000 to $33,000, depending on year and condition. Our original research showed those prices to be reasonably accurate. In today's market, you should be able to pick up a Columbia 36 in decent shape at a great price. One reader wrote, "The boat can be bought at bargain rates as it is the most underrated boat on the market."

Prices for all boats tend to be higher on the West Coast than the East Coast. Freshwater boats from Canada and the Great Lakes are most expensive (BUC Research says 25-30 percent more), and those in Florida and nearby states are the least expensive (about 10 percent less).

We think the boat represents an outstanding value for the person who wants the most boat for the least money. On the other hand, it suffers from the usual economies and slap-together techniques of large production builders. And the design is beginning to look a bit dated. We doubt that you'll make any money on the boat.   • **PS**

The only unusual element of the Columbia 36's interior layout is the placement of the chart table forward, opposite the head, rather than in its more common location near the companionway. Since radios and instruments are usually mounted near the nav station, we prefer it aft.

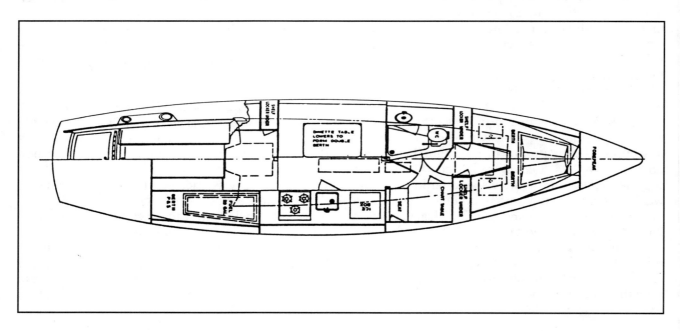

Morris 36 Justine

This semi-custom gem is exceedingly rare on the used market, but worth looking for.

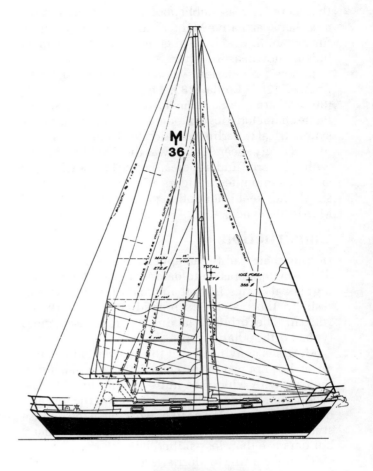

A few decades ago, when you wanted a new boat, you chose a designer, commissioned a design, selected a builder, and nursed your dream through to completion. Not many people could afford boats in those days, and not too many people today could afford to have a boat built in this fashion. Now, you're more likely to go to a boat show, look at a lot of boats, and pick one off a dealer's "lot," just like buying a new car. Until you get into large, very expensive boats, most of the options you can get are add-ons like bigger winches, perhaps a different rig, and more electronics.

You want a bigger nav station? Find another boat. A bigger icebox? Ditto. A non-teak interior? Just keep looking.

Few things are more frustrating than finding a boat that has 90% of the characteristics you're looking for, and 10% that you really can't stand. You can grit your teeth and grin and bear it, or you can keep looking.

Most of today's sailboats are marvels of production line efficiency, but with production lines comes standardization, and with standardization comes a numbing sameness that can remove a lot of the pleasure of owning a boat.

Morris Yachts can hardly be accused of running a production line operation. In his 20 years in the boatbuilding business, Tom Morris has built only about 100 boats. Catalina probably turns out more boats than that every month.

But Morris's boats fall into that intriguing category called the "semi-custom yacht," boats based on a standard hull and interior that can be modified to the desires of individual owners.

This isn't a cheap way to build a boat. Imagine going into the Chevrolet plant—or to Mercedes-Benz, for that matter—and asking to have the dash-

Specifications

LOA	36' 3"
LWL	29' 6"
Beam	11' 7"
Draft	4' 4"/5' 6" (std/Scheel)
Displacement	15,602 lbs.
Ballast	6,500 lbs.
Sail area	627 sq. ft.

board rearranged, or the interior layout changed to suit you.

For most people, the semi-custom boat doesn't make sense. If you're satisfied with what you can find in a production boat, you should by all means buy it. If you're looking for the most amount of boat for the least amount of money, the semi-custom boat isn't for you. If you're an experienced boat owner, have definite ideas about what you want, and are willing to pay significantly more to get it, the semi-custom boat may be the answer.

The Morris 36 Justine is built by Tom Morris and his crew of 16 in Southwest Harbor, Maine. Southwest Harbor is a tiny village that supports an astonishing number of boatbuilders, including the prestigious Hinckley company. Fortunately, this means that there is a reasonable pool of skilled labor in the area, between native Mainers and boatbuilders from further south who have migrated north for the more bucolic downeast lifestyle.

Morris's reputation was built on smaller boats: Frances (26'), Linda (28'), Leigh (30'), and Annie (30'). All are Chuck Paine designs, and all share the Paine characteristics of moderately long keels, nearly symmetrical waterlines, moderate displacement, and lovely, lively sheer. Justine was the first Morris boats with "modern" underbodies, having longish fin keels and skeg-mounted rudders. The patented Scheel shoal draft keel is an option chosen by about 3/4 of Morris 36 owners.

Construction

Despite their traditional appearance, Morris yachts utilize materials as up-to-date as any builder, including biaxial fabrics, isophthalic gelcoat, and vinylester resin in the mat layers immediately beneath the gelcoat. The primary laminating resin is a more typical orthopthalic resin.

Morris is convinced that the answer to hull blistering lies not just in the choice of materials, but in the care with which the hulls are laid up. At most production builders, the glass shop is at the low end of the totem pole. No one likes working in the intense styrene atmosphere of a molding room, and many builders use their less-skilled labor there.

This, according to Morris, is a serious mistake. He believes that the more care that is taken in the molding process, the less likely problems are to develop with the laminate. He is fanatical about the removal of air and excess resin from the laminate. Excess resin adds weight while reducing structural properties, and Morris believes that air in the laminate is a breeding ground for blisters.

A core sample we examined, removed for installation of a through hull fitting, had been burn-tested. It showed a 56/44 resin/glass ratio—nearly perfect.

The hull of a Morris 36 takes two to three men about a week to lay up. The hull stays in the mold at least an additional week while interior structural components such as bulkheads, floor timbers, and supports for hull ceiling are installed.

Leaving the boat in the mold at this stage prevents any distortion of the hull, making sure that the interior furniture modules and deck fit without complication.

For an extra $1,750, Morris will core the hull with Airex foam. If you're going to live aboard the boat in a cold climate, the extra insulation of the Airex hull would both make the boat warmer and reduce condensation. From a pure hull performance and strength point of view, it is unnecessary.

There are no interior molded fiberglass body pans in Morris boats. The interiors are built up of ply-wood, which is glassed to the hull. This method of construction allows substantial latitude in interior design.

Between the major and minor bulkheads, each area of furniture is self-contained, and can be changed to suit the owner's desires. In Justine #14, for example, the standard arrangement of nav station and quarterberth on the port side aft was replaced with lockers, drawers, a huge refrigerator-deepfreeze, and a big standup chart table, while the layout of the forward section of the main cabin remained unchanged.

The hull-to-deck joint is made with an inward-turning flange at the sheer, which is actually raised well above the deck level to form a bulwark. The edge of the deck molding turns upward, then outward, overlapping the hull flange, creating the inner surface of the bulwark.

Hull and deck are bolted together, the joint bedded in 3M 5200 polyurethane.

The keel is an external lead casting, bolted to the hull. Just aft of the ballast there is a deep, molded fiberglass bilge sump, which should do a good job of keeping water out of the bilges and lockers low in the hull.

Glasswork and gelcoat are done to very high standards, although the two-tone deck gelcoat on the new boat we sailed had some variations in color which gave a slightly splotchy appearance.

A year-old boat we examined had several minor gelcoat cracks in various locations on deck. These were not stress-related: they had probably been in the deck since it was removed from the mold, but showed up over time as dirt worked into the tiny cracks. We do not consider them significant. All glass surfaces exposed inside the hull are finished with grey gelcoat.

Chainplates and through hull fittings are electrically tied to a copper strap grounding system, which is glassed over to prevent oxidation and the resultant reduction in conductivity. The strapping is then tied to a keelbolt.

While there are substantial backing plates on deck hardware such as stanchions, there are no backing plates under the foredeck cleats—potentially some of the most heavily-loaded hardware on the boat. Hoses on hull fittings below the waterline are not double-clamped. In some cases this is because Spartan seacocks—which do not require double clamps—are used, but in other areas it simply appears to be an oversight.

Handling Under Power

The hull of the Morris 36 is easily driven. The engine is the three-cylinder Volvo 2003, rated at 28 hp at 3,000 rpm. At a more normal cruising rpm of 2,000 this will give a speed of about 5 1/2 knots.

The boat handles well under power. There is little vibration or noise, although only the forward portion of the engine box is insulated for sound reduction. The boat we sailed was equipped with a feathering Max-Prop, which is probably the single best investment that any cruising sailor could make to improve performance under both sail and power. Max-Props aren't cheap, but they're worth every penny if you're concerned about performance and have an extra $1,000 or so to spend.

Access to the front of the engine for service of filters and belts is good, although it does require removing the companionway ladder and engine box. Access for checking the oil is more difficult— you have to remove the lid to the engine box, which is a tight fit with the ladder in place. This could be easily solved with a small access hatch on the side of the engine box. Oil checks should be a routine part of engine operation.

There is no oil drip pan under the engine. Having rarely succeeded in changing or adding oil without spilling some, and having never seen an engine that didn't eventually leak a little lubrication and fuel oil, we think a drip pan is a must, despite Justine's deep bilge sump.

Handling Under Sail

Chuck Paine likes fast boats. Although the standard rig is a sloop with a fairly conservative single-spreader rig by Metalmast, there is an optional taller, lighter double-spreader rig with the chainplates set well inboard.

No one has yet ordered this rig, but both Paine and Morris would like to talk an owner into the hotter rig, flush through-hulls, and other little goodies that would make the boat faster. The double-spreader rig adds $950 to the base price of the boat. With the standard deep keel, a Justine set up this way should be a formidable IMS racer for an event such as the Marion-Bermuda Race.

Thus far, however, all the owners are cruisers.

Most have opted for the shoal draft Scheel keel rather than the more conventional long fin, which adds 1' of draft.

The Scheel keel is by all reports very slightly less efficient upwind, but about the same speed on other points of sail. The Scheel keel adds $1,200 to the price of the boat. Unless shoal draft is critical for you, we'd stick with the normal keel.

With a half-load displacement of only 15,600 pounds on a 29' 6" waterline, the Morris 36 has a lot of speed potential, particularly when you consider her 42% ballast/displacement ratio. She is no slouch. The boat we sailed was equipped with a rig 2' taller than standard, a Doyle fully-battened main, and a roller-furling Doyle Quicksilver genoa. Despite a slight hook in the leech of the genoa, the boat pointed and accelerated as well as any fast cruiser of her size, and a lot better than most of them.

On Deck

The deck layout of the Morris 36 is simple and clean. Shrouds are set a few inches inboard of the bulwarks—just far enough to be in the way when going forward along the deck, so that it's easier to go forward over the deckhouse.

The helmsman's seat is a little low for looking over the cabin house, but the cockpit coamings are wide enough to sit on in reasonable comfort in order to see the jib telltales.

Sail handling hardware is excellent, with Harken traveler and mainsheet blocks. The other deck hardware comes from a variety of sources: stainless steel genoa track from Hinckley, Lewmar winches, Bomar hatches, and other suppliers for bits and pieces.

The combination of bulwarks and lifelines that are 27" tall give a great feeling of security on deck. Yet the bulwarks are not high enough to be visually

Though there is a "standard" interior, many owners choose to take advantage of Morris' customized layouts.

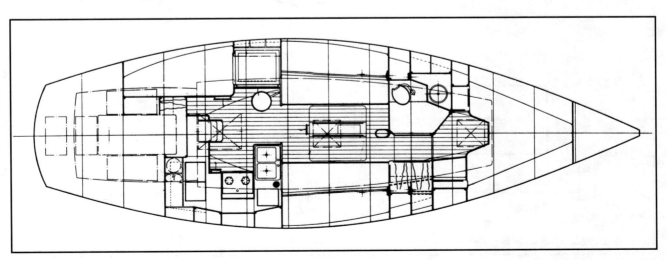

obtrusive—you don't even notice they're there, you just feel more secure.

The stemhead fitting includes a substantial roller for a CQR anchor. A chafe pad should be fitted on the deck at the inboard end of the anchor shank, or a hole will quickly be worn in the deck from the anchor shackle. There is no anchor well on deck, and the forepeak locker for anchor rode storage is so far forward in the hull that we would not suggest storing large amounts of chain there.

We can't imagine a much more secure cockpit for offshore sailing. There are four large cockpit drains, although the actual low point in the cockpit sole requires a quirky little fifth drain to get the last bit of water out with the boat sitting at anchor. The upper parts of the cockpit coamings are angled comfortably outward.

With the optional cutter rig, two staysail sheet winches are fitted to the aft end of the coachroof. With the dodger in place, you can't swing the starboard winch handle in a full circle without fetching up on the dodger frame, an inconvenience. The mainsail sheet winch is also mounted on the coachroof, but there are no obstacles in the way of its operation.

Access to the rudder head for installing the emergency steering requires opening a bronze deckplate and inserting the welded stainless steel tiller. With the tiller in position, you will have a good-sized opening in the cockpit sole, which can allow water below in heavy weather. Some sort of boot over the opening would be a plus. Large cockpit lockers port and starboard will hold all the extra sails, anchors, and other assorted junk you care to load in them. Merriman pedestal wheel steering with Ritchie compass are standard.

Belowdecks

If you're looking for acres of varnished teak and complex joinerwork, the interior of the Morris 36 won't be your cup of tea. If you appreciate honest, solid workmanship to a high grade, and interior finish that is traditional in the best sense of the word, you're going to like this boat.

There are two standard, no-extra-cost interior finishes: oiled teak, or white Formica trimmed in oiled teak. We don't like oiled teak interiors—they're drab. An oiled teak interior is not in any sense traditional. Builders like them because they're cheap to finish. Teak plywood costs just a little more than regular marine plywood. One worker can completely oil the interior joinerwork of a boat the size of the Morris 36 in a couple of days. Varnishing or painting, on the other hand, would take weeks.

If you find that hard to believe, consider the fact that you can get all that interior teak varnished if you want, but it is an option that costs $6,250. At the Morris standard labor rate of $26 per hour, that means that they spend 240 hours—six man-weeks—varnishing the interior.

The interior of white Formica with oiled teak trim is a practical combination that is airy, light, and attractive. It is so superior to the drab varnished or oiled teak interiors of most boats as to defy comparison, although it will appear stark to those with little grounding in traditional yacht interiors. If it were our

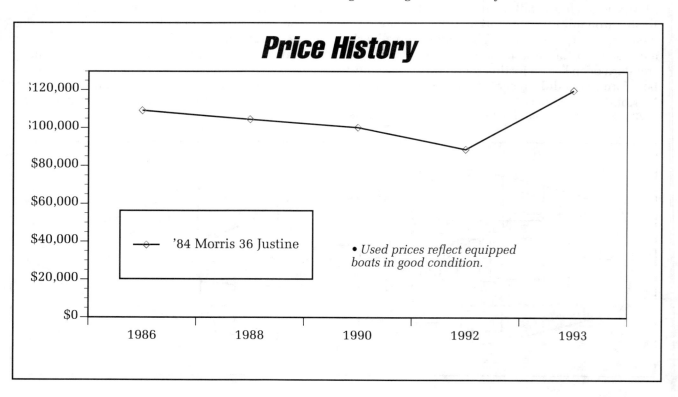

boat, we would get the Formica interior with teak trim, but we would not have the teak trim oiled. We would either have Morris varnish it, or do it ourselves at our leisure. Varnishing just the trim should cut the extra finishing cost by about half, and give you a truly elegant interior. You cannot put varnish over an oil finish, so you have to make a conscious decision about what you're going to have before you start.

Given the cost of domestic labor, there's no way that a US builder can turn out a boat with the exquisite, labor-intensive interior details of the best Taiwan-built boats, such as the Little Harbors, and still deliver a boat at a price much less than that of the space shuttle. You won't find every locker of the Morris 36 lined with varnished wood ceiling, and you can see the hull structure in places that even a lot of cheaper Oriental builders cover up with wood sheathing.

At the same time, Morris refuses to line the overheads, hull, and inside of lockers with the ubiquitous foam-backed vinyl that you find glued into almost every American-built boat from Hunter to Hinckley. For insulation, Morris will line lockers with cork if you want—a practical, if not particularly elegant solution. As another option, you can get the hull above the waterline lined with non-structural foam to reduce condensation and noise.

There's nothing wrong with opening a locker and being able to see what holds a boat together, even if fiberglass construction details lack the hard-edged beauty of traditional wood structural components. But for those not used to seeing fiberglass surfaces, parts of the Morris 36 will have an unfinished appearance.

The forward cabin has V-berths port and starboard, with an insert to form a double. The forward cabin is pushed far into the bow, and the boat's fine entry angle results in a berth which narrows sharply at the foot. Because the berths are quite long, we doubt if the narrowness will be a problem unless the berths are occupied by two giants. Headroom in the forward cabin is an honest 6'.

Aft of the forward cabin, there is a large hanging locker to port, with the head to starboard. The passage between the main and forward cabins is quite narrow, as is the door to the head. There is adequate locker space and elbow room in the head, and a six-footer can stand up without bending. The only interior fiberglass molding in the boat is the head floor pan, which makes sense on a boat with a shower. However, this white, non-skid molding will be tough to keep clean. There is a small teak grate over the shower sump, but the drain is not actually at the lowest point in the head sole, so that you may end up with a small puddle in the aft corner of the head after showering. This is a problem on a lot of boats, and

could be remedied in this case by changing the pan molding so that it angled upwards slightly just aft of the drain grate.

One of the big advantages of a semi-custom boat without a molded hull liner is the ability to alter the interior arrangements without breaking the bank. While the standard main cabin arrangement has settees and pilot berths both port and starboard, there are several other accommodation plans offered as reasonably-priced options. Hull #14, which had just been completed when we visited Morris, has a U-shaped dinette to starboard, and storage lockers in place of the pilot berth to port. This is fine on a boat that will not be sailed offshore, but it means that the only sea berth in the boat is the quarterberth. A more practical arrangement for occasional offshore work would be to retain either the port or starboard pilot berth. With a pilot berth to starboard and the standard port quarterberth, there would be at least one comfortable offshore berth on each side of the boat— a necessity for two-person passagemaking, when an adequate place to sleep can spell the difference between being rested and getting fatigued.

Headroom in the main cabin varies from 6' 3" on centerline at the forward end to 6' 5" on centerline just forward of the companionway.

Aft of the settees, partial bulkheads on both sides of the boat separate the galley and nav station from the main part of the cabin. In the standard arrangement, there is a good wet locker just to port of the companionway ladder, and a large quarterberth outboard of the locker. Forward of the quarterberth is the nav station, which faces athwartships rather than the more common fore and aft. The chart table is big enough to accept almost any chart folded in half, and has adequate space for electronics, navigation paraphernalia, and books. The navigator's bench is a bit narrow for maximum comfort, and we would miss having a backrest when trying to navigate with the boat heeled a lot on port tack.

The electrical panels are fitted behind the companionway ladder, sheltered under the bridgedeck. While this is a good location, it is somewhat vulnerable to spray, and the panels should be protected behind an opening clear acrylic splash shield.

To starboard is a well laid out galley, which includes a three-burner Force 10 propane stove with oven. This is one of the best galley stoves made, and is typical of the quality components which go into the Morris 36. It is also one of the reasons the boat costs so much. Propane is stored in a cockpit locker holding three six-pound aluminum bottles.

The icebox and lid are well insulated, and the box itself has 4" of foam insulation. Sea Frost engine-driven refrigeration is an option costing $2,350. If you're going cruising in warm climates, a good refrigeration system is a must.

On one boat we examined, the owner wanted a larger refrigerator and freezer than would fit in the allocated space, so the nav station was replaced with a huge refrigerator/freezer, retaining the top for chart work. While this wouldn't be everyone's cup of tea, it shows the design flexibility that is the primary advantage of the semi-custom boat.

Deep double sinks manufactured by Polar are pretty much the norm on larger boats, but here, Morris uses a double sink, one large and deep, one small and shallower than usually seen. We like the idea of unequal size sinks—there always seems to be one pot on board that won't fit into the relatively small Polar sinks. At the same time, we'd like the sinks to be at least 9" deep. We wish some sink manufacturer would put out deep double sinks of these proportions, but we haven't seen them yet.

Hot and cold pressure water are standard.

Designer Paine has also drawn a tri-cabin interior for those who want an aft stateroom, although none of the first 14 owners selected this extra-cost option.

Conclusions

The Morris 36 is an expensive boat. It is also a well-built, very attractive boat. The builder is flexible enough to alter the interior in almost any way you want, as long as the main structural bulkheads stay in the same place.

This all comes at a price, of course.

There's no written warranty on the boat. Morris shrugs, and says if something is wrong, he'll fix it. We believe him.

If you take full advantage of Morris's ability to customize your boat, the final price will be a lot higher than the base price. Hull #14, for example, has a custom interior plus such niceties as radar, central heat, and Alpha Marine autopilot. If you want to go all out, you can increase the price of the boat by 40% without batting an eye.

Besides price, the only disadvantage of a semi-custom boat is that you may in creating the boat of your dreams be building a boat that's a nightmare for anyone else, a boat that no one else is willing to buy when the inevitable time comes to sell. Thus far, that hasn't been a problem with the Morris 36. Only one of the boats has come on the resale market, and it was sold before the broker even received the listing. The buyer had only been interested in one other boat: a new Morris 36.

Obviously, the primary advantage of a semi-custom boat is to create a boat you'll keep for years. Many Morris 36 owners do just that. • **PS**

Freedom 36

Though expensive, the Freedom 36 is a boat that sails well and is very easy to handle.

Freedom Yachts were the invention of Garry Hoyt back in the early 1970s. An advertising executive and champion one-design sailor, Hoyt reached a stage in his life when he wanted a cruising boat, but he found the existing fleet ordinary and unsatisfactory. So—the story goes—he set about designing himself a boat. The result was the Freedom 40, an unusual-looking cruiser with a long waterline, conventional hull, and a peculiar wishbone cat-ketch rig.

Hoyt marketed the Freedom 40 with the diligence and success you'd expect of an accomplished advertiser—claiming speed, quality, and simplicity of handling for his innovative-looking boats. In time he designed (often with the aid of professional naval architects like Halsey Herreshoff) and sold a whole line of Freedoms—a 21, 25, 28, 32, 33, and 44, as well as the original 40.

At the time, Hoyt's company was unusual—because Freedom Yachts was a "boatbuilder" that didn't build the boats. Instead, Hoyt went to Everett Pearson, pioneer in the fiberglass boatbuilding industry and one of the founders of Pearson Yachts.

Tillotson-Pearson took on the Freedom line, establishing a reputation for Freedom yachts as top-end, high-quality production boats. Ultimately, Hoyt sold the company to Tillotson-Pearson.

One of the first moves of the new owners was to revamp the Freedom line. The company commissioned new designs from California-based naval architect Gary Mull, well known for his race boats and his wholesome racer/cruiser designs like the Ranger 29 and Ranger 33 in the early 1970s. The Freedom 36 was the first of the Mull designs, and it was followed by a 30, a 28, and a 42. The 36 went out of production in 1989.

The Mull-designed Freedoms share a profile that

Specifications - Sloop

LOA	36' 5"
LWL	30' 7"
Beam	12' 6"
Draft	4' 6"/ 6' 0" (shoal/deep keel)
Displacement	14,370 lbs.
Ballast	6,500 lbs.
Sail area	685 sq. ft.

is rather different from the older Freedoms—with fewer curves and more sharp turns, most noticeable in the square, boxy cabinhouse that is remarkably reminiscent of a Ranger 26. The boats are generally plain and simple looking, with virtually no exterior wood trim.

The most noticeable characteristic of the line continues to be the unstayed carbon fiber mast that had become a hallmark of all the Freedom boats. Most traditional sailors would describe the new designs as big catboats, with the enormous-diameter mast set well forward, but they do carry a vestigial jib and are technically sloops. All the new Freedoms are rigged with the aim of simple handling that has always been associated with the line.

The Mull boats have also maintained the general

Some Freedom 36s were built with the unusual Freedom cat ketch rig.

concept of enormous beam and long waterline with almost no overhangs, and the boats have more interior volume for their length than almost anything else on the market. The major difference from the older boats is that the hull underbodies are thoroughly modern in the Mull designs, with flat bottoms, fin keels, and spade rudders.

Hoyt originally tried to market the Freedoms directly to customers, but the company has since developed a widespread network of dealers which generally have a good reputation for servicing the boats they sell. The company has also developed a good reputation for responding to warranty problems and other customer complaints.

For example, the Freedom 36 that we sailed for this evaluation had originally been sold to an owner on the west coast, and had developed some gelcoat problems on the deck. The company eventually replaced the boat with a new one—an incredibly rare occurrence among boatbuilders—had redone the deck completely, and then re-sold the boat to the current owner at a reduced cost.

Similarly, while we were evaluating the 36, the owner received a package from the company with a kit to modify the lightning protection system in the boat. The new boats were being set up differently, and the builder thought the change was advisable for all boats. They provided retrofit kits—at no charge.

On its latest boats, the company is also offering a 10-year warranty on the hull—even against gelcoat blisters—and a lifetime warranty on the spar to the first owner.

While there has never been a boat line with no problems, buyers of Freedoms should have better expectations than most of successful dealings with the company.

Hull and Deck

Both the hull and deck of the Freedom 36 are fiberglass with a Contourkore balsa core throughout. There are potential problems with water absorption in both hull and deck of balsa cored laminates, with little way for the owner to guard against it except by depending on the integrity of the manufacturer. Tillotson-Pearson is one of the few companies that we would count on to produce a good, long-lasting hull in boat after boat. Basic construction is solid.

The fiberglass itself is a laminate of E-glass mat and stitched unidirectional fiberglass, with vinylester barrier resins in the exterior layer of the hull below the waterline. The outside layer is an isophthalic gelcoat. Both the vinylester and the isophtalic resins are believed to provide the best protection against water absorption and blistering. This is a high-cost fabrication, but Freedom obviously has faith in it.

One of the big advantages of balsa coring is the thermal and acoustic insulation it provides. Condensation problems inside the hull are greatly reduced, and the hull has a solid, quiet feel to it going through waves.

The drawback of balsa coring is that one must exercise more care than normal when installing through-hull and through-deck fittings, for example being careful not to compress the whole laminate and allow for penetration of water. Cracks or other damage to the hull must be attended to promptly.

The hull and deck are laid up separately and joined with an inward-turning flange on the hull on which the deck molding sets. An adhesive caulk, 3M-5200, is laid in the seam, and the joint is through-bolted with 1/4" stainless bolts through an external aluminum toerail.

We examined a number of hulls and found them generally fair, with no obvious problems. Exterior gelcoat work is generally good.

Two keels are available—either a deep fin or a shoal draft fin. The 36 we sailed had the deep fin, which is an external lead casting, bolted to the hull. The shoal keel is encapsulated in a keel cavity and fiberglassed to the hull. If you can stand the draft, the deeper keel will be preferable in terms of performance as well as construction.

Overall, the construction of the Freedom 36 is high-quality, with everything being done pretty much the way industry standards say they should be done. The single exception we found was not in the 36 but in a Freedom 28 we examined. The 28 had a chintzy plastic through hull fitting for a sink drain, with no seacock—an odd oversight in an otherwise well-built boat.

Rig

The unstayed carbon fiber masts were quite radical when Freedom first used them, but they are well-established and proven by now. They are laid up somewhat like fiberglass, with carbon fibers wound around a form and impregnated with resin. For equivalent strength, they are much lighter and stiffer than an aluminum mast.

Under sail, it's a bit shocking at first to see the mast bend in puffs, especially since it's so tall (55' 6" above the waterline). But once you're accustomed to that peculiarity, there should be little to worry about in terms of strength or longevity. We were unable to find any statistics or insurance figures on carbon fiber mast failures compared to aluminum mast failures, but we suspect the odds of a dismasting or other significant failure are no more likely—perhaps even less likely—with the carbon fiber than with aluminum. We are aware of at least one mast that was damaged in a lightning strike.

The Freedom 36 was available with both a sloop rig and Freedom's trademark cat ketch rig.

Handling Under Power

A three-cylinder 27 hp Yanmar diesel is standard. The engine is adequate, though certainly not oversized.

Engine installation is well done, in a small compartment lined with a lead/foam sound deadener. Access to the engine is possible from the front by removing the companionway steps, and from the port cockpit locker by removing a panel. It's hard to get at the Yanmar's dipstick on the engine's starboard side. There is a small screw-out port for access from the aft cabin, but the port is about a foot ahead of the dipstick.

The boat comes with a solid two-bladed prop which most owners will want to trash immediately, replacing it with a folding or feathering prop. The

With her broad beam, the Freedom 36 has lots of room belowdecks. The layout is fairly conventional, but quite comfortable.

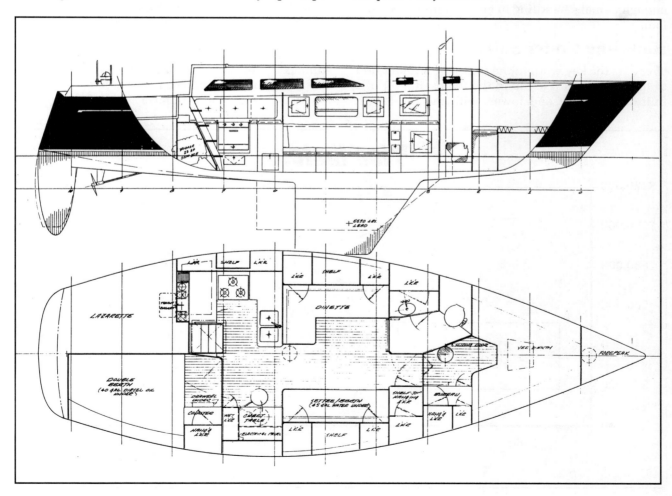

boat we sailed had a three-bladed feathering prop, which not only lets the boat live up to its sailing potential, but also seems to improve backing power. A folding prop would be much cheaper, though motoring performance would not be as good as with the three-bladed feathering prop.

It surprises us that companies which tout the sailing performance of their boats continue to fit them out with solid propellers. There's almost nothing you can do that will degrade sailing performance more than carry an exposed, solid prop, especially when the wind turns light.

With the three-bladed feathering prop, the Freedom 36 performs well. The boat backs out of a slip, goes where you want it to go in reverse, and powers easily to hull speed without overloading the engine. The engine is mounted slightly off-center so the shaft is at an angle to the centerline of the boat, and some people will tell you that this helps the boat track in a straight line under power. The 36 did track straight, but then most boats with centerline installations track straight, too.

With the deep fin to pivot on and the spade rudder located way aft, the boat turns sharply. The large mast and the high topsides provide plenty of windage, but generally the Freedom 36 should be nimble enough to make handling in close quarters no problem.

Handling Under Sail

"Easy" is the key word in the company's promotion of their sailboats. We found the mainsail a bit of a nuisance to hoist and lower, with the full-length battens fouling the lazy jacks, but other than that the boat is truly easy to sail.

All the gear is of good quality. Halyards are led aft to the cockpit, through stoppers to self-tailing winches. The jib can actually be hoisted by hand, but the main requires the winch to raise it the last 10' or so. Other controls (outhaul, reef lines, boom vang, cunningham) also lead to sheet stoppers in the cockpit. A neat feature is the "panel" for hanging the coiled lines, just behind the winches at the front of the cockpit.

The mainsheet is a four-part tackle at mid-boom, running to a Harken traveler ahead of the companionway. Frequently, the mechanical advantage of a mid-boom sheeting arrangement is so low that mainsail trimming is hard, but we found we could handle the mainsheet by hand easily in winds up to about 12 knots. Thereafter, we used the winch. All winches are adequately sized, though self-tailers are an option that almost everyone will want.

The non-overlapping jib uses a sprit that fits in a sleeve on the sail. The jib is self-tacking, with a single sheet that is easily controlled by hand. It is amazing how much speed the dinky little jib adds to the boat. Though the company's literature talks about sailing under main alone, for performance you need the jib. Though we haven't sailed a Nonsuch 36 and a Freedom 36 side by side, we suspect the Freedom will be noticeably faster, largely because of the jib.

The pulpit-mounted spinnaker pole and the other spinnaker handling gear (all optional) are remarkable in making the spinnaker easy to hoist, jibe, and lower. Of course, the spinnaker is tiny for a boat of

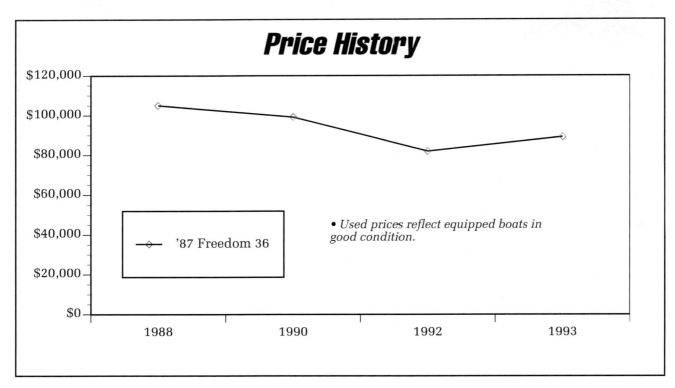

Price History

- *Used prices reflect equipped boats in good condition.*

◇ '87 Freedom 36

this size—closer to what you'd get on a J-24 than on a conventional 36' sloop. Using the pole—which is pinned at the center so that it pivots on top of the pulpit—takes some getting used to, but once you figure things out it's a lot easier than jibing a J-24.

We raced the 36 in two PHRF triangle races to try her performance against more conventional boats. In most respects, we found the boat admirable.

Full crew for the racing was two people, and in terms of performance per amount of energy expended, the boat was a clear winner. It is amazing how getting rid of a big jib lowers the activity required on a sailboat.

We did find that the fully-battened main on the bendy mast required new skills, particularly going to windward. The sail has a very wide "slot" in terms of trim, and does not seem to stall out. We messed with the mainsail almost constantly, first trimming it as we would a conventional main, then dropping or raising the traveler, adjusting sheet tension, cunningham, and so on.

The conventional wisdom concerning the rig is that it will not go to weather: you should foot off for maximum performance. But we found that we could point with most of the fleet, and the boat had a B&G Hornet system which kept telling us that our VMG was highest when we were pinching.

Reaching is the boat's strong suit—as you would want in a good cruiser—and the boat is a surprising combination of effortlessness and power. Handling, including sail trim, is a piece of cake, even with the spinnaker up.

Running, the boat is a little sluggish, even with the spinnaker. We didn't test the boat fully, but we suspect that jibing downwind on broad reaches may be faster than running dead down, at least in lighter air.

Whatever the point of sail, the sailor used to conventional rigs will have to do quite a bit of experimenting and relearning to get the most out of the Freedom 36.

In terms of absolute speed, the boat was a bit disappointing to us. We expected a little more than we got out of her long waterline.

Her PHRF rating is 150, comparable to the speed of racer/cruisers of 10 years ago like the C&C 33 and 34, or the Pearson 10M. Our impression is that the boat will sail much faster than those boats on a reach, but quite a bit slower on a beat or a run. Her strongest performance will be in stronger winds rather than light air.

There is not a lot that you can do about the fundamentals of yacht design, but we sort of expected that the boat would outsail a 15-year-old Mull design like the Ranger 33. In fact, it won't. Of course, any passage on the Freedom will be much easier than on the Ranger, much less demanding, and much less tiring. But it won't be faster, unless you can always make arrangements for a reach.

Nonetheless, after our experience on the boat, we strongly recommend the Freedom 36 as a sailing machine, with the ease of sailing far outweighing any drawbacks. She is a pleasure under sail.

On Deck

You sail the Freedom 36 almost entirely from the cockpit, and it is big and roomy, with plenty of space to do the minimal chores of sail handling.

The benches are wide and comfortable, long enough to use as outdoor berths. It's not a T-shaped cockpit—one of the few straight cockpits we've seen recently, and we decided we sort of like that. There's ample room for lounging about, and with a dodger and bimini it would be an excellent cruising cockpit. There's a propane tank locker, and a cavernous portside locker that will be hard to use well unless you can figure out a way to subdivide it.

Wheel steering is standard. The boat we sailed had an optional oversized wheel that simplified steering from the side decks, but made passage around the wheel difficult.

From the cockpit forward to the mast, the Freedom is wide open. It would be an ideal working platform, though of course there's little working of the boat to be done except from the cockpit. The nonskid of the decks and cabin top seemed generally mediocre.

From the mast forward, the rig gets in the way of things. With the turret-mounted spinnaker pole, the spinnaker in its storage sock, and the wishbone in the jib, the foredeck is crowded. Anchor handling and docking are complicated by having to step over and around the gear, and we suppose many cruisers will think about not having the spinnaker equipment at all. To us, this congestion on the foredeck seems the one major shortcoming of the Freedom rig. Otherwise, the Freedom has a spacious, comfortable deck.

Belowdecks

As you might expect with the long waterline, short overhangs and wide beam, the area belowdecks is huge. We thought the size, especially the beam, might even be a problem under way, but found that that the boat is stiff enough that you should rarely be tossed about.

The interior arrangement is fairly ordinary. A big forward cabin has a good V-berth which can be made into a comfortable double by using an insert in the V. There's a bureau and hanging locker to starboard and a door to the head to port. Headroom is 6' 1" near the entry door.

There is good stowage under the V-berth and in a small forepeak—in fact, this boat generally has more storage than is common in more conventional modern designs.

The head is roomy, mostly a fiberglass molding, and has a second door to the main cabin. Opposite the head is another bureau and storage space.

The main cabin is large, with an L-shaped settee around a table which folds up against the forward bulkhead. The table can be folded out so that the starboard settee becomes the outboard seat for an enormous dining table. There is good storage space behind both settees and beneath the port settee. Headroom is a true 6' 4".

The galley is U-shaped, with deep sinks, a good dry-storage locker, a gimbaled stove with oven, an adequate icebox, and lots of storage space. A garbage trap in the aft bulkhead lets you drop stuff into a wastebasket stored in the cockpit locker. Now if someone would just come up with some similar way to store your returnable cans and bottles.

Opposite the galley is a navigation table with a swing-out seat. Above the table is the electrical panel, and mounting space for most of the electronics.

The aft cabin, mostly under the starboard cockpit seat, is also good-sized, with a bureau, hanging locker, and decent headroom just inside the door.

Finish below is generally good—lots of teak veneer with a nice contrast in the ash battens used as hull ceiling. The cabin overhead is vinyl panels—OK, but a nuisance if you need to mess with the deck hardware fastenings.

Ventilation is adequate, but would be minimal for offshore passages. You might want to look for the optional dorades to improve air movement below.

Conclusions

In general, we came away from the Freedom 36 with renewed respect for the work of Tillotson-Pearson. For us there's no question of the quality of construction or general workmanship.

Though high-quality, the Freedoms are plain. If you're into hand craftsmanship or the sort of excessive teakwork that you find in the best Oriental imports, you probably won't like the Freedoms, though their belowdecks joinery and finish is very good.

In general, we also like the roominess and livability of the boat. In a 36-footer, it's hard to imagine more space, or think of a way the space could be better used.

In sailing, the strong point of the boat is ease of handling, and after our trials on the water, we have no reservations about the unusual rig—it works, and it works pretty well. In a 36' cruiser, we might hope for a little more absolute speed, but the Freedom is no slouch. She will make smart passages, and make them easily.

The sloop rig is somewhat out of the ordinary, with its fully-battened mainsail and vestigial jib.

The major drawback, of course, is price, since the Freedom is on the high end of the price spectrum. With sails and a few "necessary" options like the spinnaker package, self-tailing winches, electronics, and refrigeration, the price of a new boat could easily have topped $110,000.

And if you fully outfitted the boat, including things like customized interior fabrics, you could have quickly gotten the bottom line up to $125,000 or so—a lot of money, even for one of the biggest 36-footers around.

For the price you got a good boat, with assurance of quality construction and a company that will stand behind its products. For many who've owned cheap boats, those characteristics will be worth paying for.

Probably the most distinctive thing you'll be getting in the Freedom 36 is the ease of handling. We can't imagine how you could get a 36-footer that sails well and make it any easier to handle. A lot of the joy of sailing is making the wind work for you, and the Freedom 36 gives you more return for your labor than any other boat we've sailed. **• PS**

Tayana 37 Cutter

This product of the Far East would make a good choice for the retired couple who want to travel.

With several hundred boats sailing the seas of the world, the Tayana 37 has been one of the most successful products of the Taiwan-built boat invasion of the US that began in the early 1970s. Her shapely Baltic stern, scribed plank seams molded into the glass hull, and lavish use of teak above and below decks have come to epitomize the image that immediately comes to mind when Oriental boats are mentioned.

Not all thoughts of Far Eastern boats are pleasant, however. To some, Taiwan-built boats mean poor workmanship, overly heavy hulls, unbedded hardware of dubious heritage, wooden spars that delaminate, and builder-modified boats light years removed from the plans provided by the designer. Add to that a serious language barrier and the inevitable logistical problems of dealing with a boatyard halfway round the world, and you have a situation ready-made to generate potential nightmares for the boat buyer. To the credit of the builder, the designer, the primary importer, and a powerful owners' association, the Tayana 37 weathered an astounding sixteen years of production—a lifetime in the world of boatbuilding—while making steady improvements and maintaining a steady output of over 50 boats per year.

Washington-based designer Bob Perry had just hung out his own shingle when the Tayana 37 was designed in the early 70s. The Sherman tank Westsail 32 had just come lumbering onto the scene, bringing with it a resurgence of interest in the double ended hull form, and more people than ever before were beginning to have the dream of chucking it all and sailing away to a tropical paradise.

Bob Perry has become an enormously successful designer of cruising boats, from traditional full keel designs such as the Tayana 37, to modern fin keel

Specifications

LOA	36' 8"
LWL	31' 10"
Beam	11' 6"
Draft	5' 8"
Displacement	24,000 lbs.
Ballast	7,340 lbs.
Sail area	864 sq. ft.

cruisers such as the Nordic 40, Golden Wave 42, and the Valiant 40. A remarkable number of his designs have been built in the Orient, in both Hong Kong and Taiwan.

Perry conceived the Tayana 37 as a cruising boat of traditional appearance above the water, with moderately heavy displacement, a long waterline, and a reasonably efficient cutter rig of modern proportions. (A ketch rig is also available). Below the water, the forefoot of the long keel has been cut away, and a Constellation-type rudder utilized rather than a more traditional barn door. Perry sought to cash in on the popularity of the double ended hull while keeping displacement moderate and performance reasonable, avoiding the plight of boats such as the Westsail 32—the inability to go to windward, and sluggish performance in anything short of a moderate gale. The stern design of the Tayana 37 borrows heavily from the well known Aage Neilsen designed ketch Holger Danske, winner of the 1980 Bermuda Race. It is one of the more handsome Baltic-type sterns on any production sailboat.

The Tayana 37 began life as the CT 37. In 1979 the boat became known as the Tayana 37, named for Ta Yang Yacht Building Company. While some snobbishness exists among some owners who own the CT version, Perry insists that this is illusory. According to the designer, the CT 37 and the Tayana 37 are the same boat, built by the same men in the same yard. In much the same way that the early Swans imported by Palmer Johnson were known by the name of the importer—the names Nautor and Swan were unknown here in the late 1960s—early Tayanas were known as CTs because the name CT had already become known in this country.

Perry, who has worked with many yards in the Far East, considers Ta Yang one of the best. The yard has been very responsive to input from both dealers and owners. Over the years the Tayana 37 has been in production, this has resulted in steady improvement in the quality of the boat.

The vast majority of Tayanas now imported into this country are brought in by Southern Offshore Yachts, which has offices in eastern Canada, Rhode Island, Maryland, and both coasts of Florida. By working closely with the builder and maintaining good contact with the owners' association, Southern Offshore has had significant input into improving the quality of the boats.

Owners report that Southern Offshore has been very responsive to handling warranty problems. The same cannot be said for all Tayana dealers. One west coast Tayana 37 owner responding to our owner survey reported that "basically, the dealer treated us like second-rate citizens." A similar comment was voiced by a midwestern owner.

Construction

The hull of the Tayana 37 is a fairly heavy solid glass layup. Some roving printthrough is evident in the topsides. The hull-to-deck joint has in the past occasionally been a problem with the boat. There is no doubt it is strong, but there have been numerous reports of leaking.

Part of the problem with the hull-to-deck joint is the fact that the hull and deck moldings form a hollow bulwark extending well above the main deck level. This bulwark is pierced by hawsepipes and several large scuppers at deck level. Careful bedding of all fittings that penetrate the bulwarks is essential to avoid leaks. On new boats, the entire hollow bulwark is glassed over from inside the hull, greatly reducing the possibility of leaks. This results in an incredibly labor intensive joint, but labor intensive is the name of the game in Taiwanese boatbuilding.

None of the numerous through hull fittings is recessed flush with the exterior of the hull. The argument is frequently made that this is unnecessary on cruising boats. Nothing could be further from the truth. The cruising boat is frequently undercanvassed for her displacement and wetted surface. Add to this the low speed drag associated with projections from the hull, and you have a boat that spends a lot of time motoring in light air, when she should be sailing. While the Tayana 37 is far from undercanvassed, she could benefit from a little more bottom fairing as much as the next boat. An option to recessing the through hull fittings would be to fair them in with large microballoon blisters—not as effective as recessing, but perhaps easier to do after the fact.

The rudder stock is a substantial stainless steel rod, with the rudder held on by welded arms riveted through the rudder blade. The heel fitting is a bronze casting. This is fastened to the hull with stainless steel bolts. Inevitably, there will be galvanic action between the bronze and the stainless, with the fastenings coming out on the short end. There is provision for protection of the rudder straps with zincs.

All hardware, including cleats and stanchions, is through-bolted and backed with stainless steel pads. Most hardware is fairly accessible from belowdecks.

The ballast keel is an iron casting dropped into the hollow fiberglass keel shell. The casting is glassed over on the inside of the boat. We prefer an external lead keel for its shock absorbing qualities in case of grounding.

The glasswork of the Tayana 37 is of good quality. There are no rough edges, the fillet bonding is neat, and there is no glass or resin slopped about. Tayana warrants the hull against defects for ten years.

Until recently, the standard steering system was a Taiwanese worm gear system copied from the Edson worm gear. Recurrent problems with this system, notably extremely sloppy and mushy steering, have resulted in significant changes. The standard system is now a pedestal system Taiwanese-built but remarkably similar to the Edson pedestal steerer.

Seacocks are used on all through hull fittings. The seacocks appear to be copies of US-made Groco valves. Hoses to seacocks are all double clamped.

Handling Under Power

Three different engines have been used in the Tayana 37: the Yanmar 3QM30, the Perkins 4-108, and the Volvo MD17C. The standard engine is now the Yanmar. This makes good economic sense, as Japan is rather closer to Taiwan than either England or Sweden. Both the Volvo and Perkins are still available as options. We see no reason to choose either engine over the Yanmar.

While the engine box removes completely to provide good access for service, there is no provision for easy access to the oil dipstick. This means that this vital task is likely to be ignored. A simple door in the side of the engine box would solve the problem.

The placement of the fuel tank has caused substantial discussion on the part of owners. The standard 90 gallon black iron tank is located under the V-berth in the forward cabin. When full, this tank holds almost 650 pounds of fuel. This is about the same weight as 375 feet of 3/8" chain—a substantial amount to carry around in the bow of a 37-footer. A Tayana 37 with the bow tank full and a heavy load of ground tackle will show noticeable bow down trim. The design was originally drawn with the fuel tanks under the settees, but the builder put the tank forward to create additional storage in the main cabin.

This is a good example of one of the basic recurring problems with Far East built boats. Frequently the builders have good glass men and good inside joiners, but their inexperience in sailing results in inconsistencies which compromise their boats.

Fortunately, thanks to the pressure from owners, the builder offers optional tankage amidships, where it belongs. By all means select this tankage option so that the fore and aft trim of the boat will remain unchanged as fuel is consumed.

Although any of the engines is adequate power for the boat, don't expect the Tayana 37 to win any drag races. With her substantial wetted surface and fairly heavy displacement, performance under power is sedate rather than spritely. Owners report handling under power fair to good, although one reported that his boat "backs up like a drunken elephant."

Handling Under Sail

The Tayana 37 comes as a ketch or cutter, with wood spars or aluminum, with mast stepped on deck or on the keel. Few builders offer you so many options.

The standard rig is a masthead cutter with wooden spars, the mast stepped on deck and supported by a substantial compression column. The designer strongly recommends the aluminum cutter rig, and we heartily concur. The wooden mast is poorly proportioned, with a massive section and extremely thick side walls. One new mast we looked at had a large knot on the forward side of the mast just at spreader level. Despite the huge mast section, we feel the knot could weaken the mast significantly.

In contrast to the large section of the mast, the boom is an extremely small spruce box section. With mid-boom sheeting, this spar will probably be about as stiff as a rubber band, complicating mainsail shape. The clew outhaul slide is far too flimsy for a boat of this size, and owners report that the outhaul slide frequently distorts or explodes. Once again, these problems are not atypical in Taiwan boats, where you frequently find excellent craftsmanship but a poor understanding of engineering or the forces involved in ocean sailing.

In contrast, the aluminum rigs, which may come from a variety of sources including France, New Zealand, and the US, are well proportioned and suited to the task.

We see no reason to select the ketch rig. Both performance and balance with the cutter rig will be better. The cutter's mainsail is 342 square feet. Any couple healthy enough to go world cruising should be able to cope with a sail of this size.

The cutter rig is tall and well proportioned. Perry has drawn an unusually high aspect rig for a cruising boat, and the result is a boat with good performance on all points of sail. With the aluminum rig, the optional Nicro Fico ball bearing mainsheet traveler, and a well cut suit of sails, the Tayana 37 will be surprisingly fast. Her working sail area of 864 square feet is generous.

This "standard" interior arrangement is unlikely to reflect any given Tayana 37. The builder offers custom interiors at no extra charge, and nearly all owners have taken advantage of the opportunity.

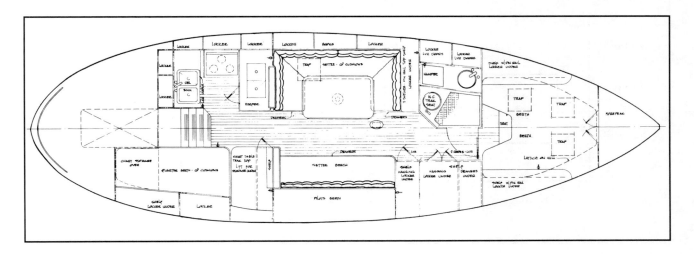

Despite a ballast/displacement ratio of 33 percent, the Tayana 37 is not a stiff boat. This is due in part to the tall, heavy rig and the substantial amount of other weight above the boat's vertical center of gravity. Much of the boat's heavy joinerwork and glass work is well above the waterline, raising the center of gravity and reducing initial stability. Perry believes the initial tenderness to be an asset, reducing the snappiness of the boat's roll and making her a more comfortable sea boat. We agree.

Many owners report that the boat carries substantial weather helm. The sail plan is drawn with significant rake to the mast. This creates just enough shift in the center of effort of the sail plan to create a lot of weather helm. Bringing the mast back toward the vertical by tightening the headstay and forestay while loosening the backstay should cure much of the problem, according to reports from other owners. It may be necessary to shorten the headstay to do this.

The weather helm and initial tenderness may also be due in part to the poor cut of the standard sails provided with the boat. For years, the standard sails have been made by Lam of Hong Kong. The sails have the reputation of being stretchy and having very poor shape. Mainsail draft with this fabric is almost uncontrollable, with the sail becoming baggy and the draft moving aft as the wind increases. This will create weather helm and increase the angle of heel.

Deck Layout

With her bulwarks, high double lifelines, and substantial bow and stern pulpits, the Tayana 37 gives the sailor a good sense of security on those cold, windy nights when he's called out for sail changes. A teak platform grating atop the bowsprit coupled with the strong pulpit relieves that appendage of its widowmaker reputation.

The bowsprit platform incorporates double anchor rollers which will house CQR anchors. Unfortunately, there is no good lead from the rollers to any place to secure the anchor rode. Line or chain led to the heavy bowsprit bitts would chafe on the platform, An anchor windlass mounted to port or starboard of the bowsprit would provide a good lead, and is an available option.

There are hawsepipes through the bulwarks port and starboard well aft of the stem. These will be fine for dock lines, but are too far aft to serve as good leads for anchoring. There is room at deck level outboard of the bowsprit to install a set of heavy chocks for anchoring, although anchor rode led to this point will chafe on the bobstay as the boat swings to her anchor.

This is a classic problem of the boat with bowsprit. The anchor rode must really lead well out the bowsprit to avoid the bobstay, yet the long lead complicates securing the inboard end of the rode.

The long staysail boom makes it difficult to cross from one side of the boat to the other forward. The standard staysail traveler is merely a stainless steel rod on which a block can slide on its shackle. Under load, this can bind when tacking, so that it may be necessary to go forward and kick the block over after every tack. By all means look for the optional Nicro Fico travelers with their roller bearing cars. Complaints about the standard travelers are rife. Stan-

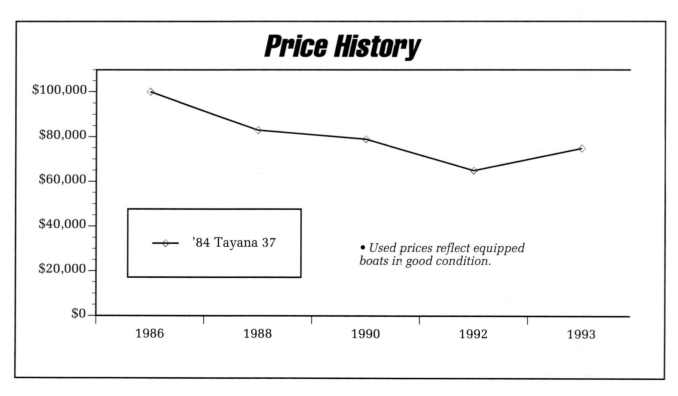

Price History

- *Used prices reflect equipped boats in good condition.*

◇ '84 Tayana 37

dard winches on the boat are Barlow. We suggest that you try to find self-tailing winches for all sheets.

Although the side decks are relatively narrow due to the wide cabin trunk, there is reasonable access fore and aft. A full length hand rail on either side of the cabin trunk provides a good handhold.

The cockpit of the Tayana 37 is small, as befits an oceangoing sailboat. There are cockpit scuppers at each of the four corners of the cockpit well, with seacocks on the through hull outlets.

With the now-standard pedestal steering, the cockpit seems to have shrunk. Only three can be seated in real comfort, although this is no real problem for the cruising couple. It is not a cockpit for heavy entertaining in port. The elimination of the coaming around the stern of the boat has made the cockpit seats long enough for sleeping on deck, but at the expense of exposing the helmsman to a wet seat in a following sea. The coaming can optionally be continued around the rear of the cockpit. Cockpit locker configuration varies with the interior options chosen, but the lockers are large enough to provide reasonable storage, although you should resist the temptation to load them heavily so far aft.

Belowdecks

The interior of the Tayana 37 probably sells more boats than any other feature of the boat. There is not really a standard interior. Every boat that comes through is custom built, and almost every owner takes advantage of the opportunity to create an interior suited to his or her own needs.

The cost of producing these interiors is not prohibitive. Interior joinerwork is labor intensive, but labor in the Orient is still far cheaper than it is here.

Like other Taiwanese boats, the interior of the Tayana 37 is all teak. This results in an interior that can be oppressively dark to some people, exquisitely cool to others. To keep it looking good, someone is going to have to do a lot of oiling or varnishing.

The interior joinerwork is some of the best we have seen on any boat, whether it is built in the US, Taiwan, or Finland. Joints were just about flawless, paneled doors beautifully joined, drawers dovetailed from solid stock. There were no fillers making up for poorly fitted joints, no trim fitted with grinders, no slop anywhere. The men who put the interior in the new boat we examined were real craftsmen. Older boats we have looked at did not boast quite this caliber of workmanship, but their joinerwork was certainly of good quality.

With such an array of interior options it is difficult to really evaluate the boat's interior. Naturally, if you're considering a used Tayana, you're stuck with whatever the original buyer had installed. However, if you're thinking of ordering a new boat, the choices are wide open.

This may be a mixed blessing to the buyer. For the couple who have owned other boats, have kept copious notes about what they want and don't want in their next boat, and who are experienced, well read, and knowledgeable, the ability to plan their own interior offers an opportunity that is probably unequaled in a boat in this price range.

If you have only vague ideas of what you want in the interior of a cruising boat, one of the real advantages of owning the Tayana 37 may be lost. Do you want a pilot berth or storage? Drawers or bins? Propane or kerosene for cooking? Quarterberth or wet locker? Fold up or drop leaf table? To the inexperienced, the choices may be bewildering. To those who know what they want, the opportunity is a gold mine.

In all fairness, there is a "standard" interior. It is prosaic but good, with V-berth forward, followed by head and lockers just aft. The main cabin has a U-shaped settee to port, straight settee and pilot berth to starboard. Aft is a good U-shaped galley to port, nav station and quarterberth to starboard. For not much more money, you can have pretty much what you want, from a "standard" array of interior options to a fully custom interior. You're missing a good bet if you don't spend some time creating your own dream interior.

Conclusions

The Tayana 37 is both typical and atypical of Taiwanese boats, She is typical in the problems that existed due to the builder's inexperience with seagoing yachts, typical with communication and language problems.

She is atypical in that many of these problems have been solved over many years of production, in that a good owners' association has resulted in real improvements in the boat. Anyone considering a Tayana 37 should join the owners' association and read all the back newsletters before buying the boat.

Because of the myriad options, we don't really suggest a new Tayana 37 as a first boat. Between pilot house and trunk cabin versions, ketch and cutter, and the incredible array of interior options, the first time boatowner would have a great deal of difficulty coming up with just the right boat.

The total cost of a well-equipped Tayana 37 with most of the desirable options compares very favorably with other boats of her size, type, and displacement.

The Tayana 37 would make an excellent retirement cruiser for the experienced sailing couple. Properly handled and equipped, she could take you anywhere with confidence and reasonable dispatch. If you want to design your own interior and are willing to wait for your boat to be built, she just may be the right boat for you. • **PS**

Jeanneau Lagoon 37

Built by TPI for the giant French builder Jeanneau, this cat is fast, roomy and pricey.

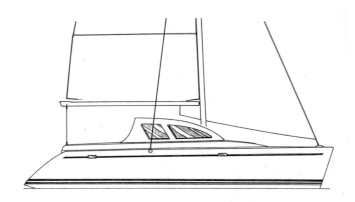

J eanneau's Lagoon 37 catamaran, launched last December, is the second cruising catamaran pro duced as part of a joint venture between the French firm and TPI of Warren, Rhode Island. (As a side note, TPI is the new name of Tillotson-Pearson Industries, following Tillotson's sale of his share to John Walton, owner of Corsair Marine. Walton, who builds the F-24 and F-27 trailerable trimarans, is a member of the family that owns WalMart department stores). The venture was intended to give Jeanneau a foothold in the American market without building its own plant, as arch rival Beneteau did several years back. The first fruit of the collaboration was the Lagoon 42, introduced two years ago and named "Boat of the Year" at the next Annapolis Boat Show. However, the 42 proved too big and too expensive to interest individual buyers, and those built to date have either been acquired by charter fleets or shipped back to France for sale. Not so with the 37. Of the 16 sold in the first two months, more than half are going to individuals.

The Boat

As designed by Marc Van Peteghem and Vincent Lauriot-Prevost, best known for their Route du Rhum-style racing multihulls, the Lagoon 37 is a refined, down-sized version of the 42. This is a fairly light but stable cat aimed at the cruising sailor rather than the adventurer.

In appearance, the 37 like its bigger cousin, is sleeker and sportier than many of the lumbering cruising "cats" that have come onto the market in recent years. At 36' 9" length overall, the boat carries a generous beam of 20 feet. Because the height from the waterline to the top of the coach roof is only 8' 9", the squat look is avoided. The scoop-shaped cabintop adds to the dynamic look. In short, the 37 looks like

Specifications

LOA	36' 9"
LWL	34' 1"
Beam	20' 0"
Draft	4' 0"
Displacement	11,833 lbs.
Sail area	835 sq. ft.

a boat instead of a boat-shaped condominium.

The deck-stepped mast from Sparcraft is white-painted aluminum supported by a forestay, two cap shrouds and tri-diamond innerstays to hold it in column. The backstay was eliminated to permit use of a big-roach main of 473 square feet. The overlapping jib (120 percent) is tacked manually, unlike on the 42. Shore Sails has been making most of the sails for the Lagoon, which are optional. Engine power comes from twin Perkins 20-hp. freshwater-cooled diesels.

Construction

Hull construction is typical TPI, consisting of hand-laid fiberglass over a balsa core, the core ranging from 3/4 inches to as much as 1-inch thick in the mast area. The skin coat is vinylester resin for protection against osmotic blistering, and the Lagoon, like most TPI products (J Boats, Alerion Express, Sundeer, etc.), comes with a 10-year blister guarantee. The twin keels, which have 4 feet of draft, measure about 8 feet fore and aft (with a rake on the leading edge) and are molded in as part of the hull. Also molded in are the stern boarding steps.

The hull-deck joint, as is becoming the norm on other TPI boats, is connected by urethane glue, with additional stainless steel bolts fastened at the stanchions and cleats. We heard of one instance in which the hull-deck joint on one of the 42s opened under enough heavy pounding to create "a pretty good leak" in one of the amas. When we asked TPI's Phil Mosher about it, he said there was no glue in that area and that it was quickly fixed. Mosher further believes that his patented glue joint is superior to caulked and through-bolted joints, and simpler for the builder than fiberglassing over the joint.

Hardware, as expected on a Tillotson-Pearson, is of high quality: Harken traveler, five Lewmar self-tailing winches (30s for the jib lines, 40 for the main), Schaefer fair leads, Spinlock clutches. Hatches and ports are Lewmar; there are 12 opening hatches for ventilation, six opening ports. The large smoked windows that light the saloon are made at the Warren plant of 1/2-inch acrylic.

Performance

We sailed hull #1 on a brisk December day shortly after its launching. On the docks, the wind was just a whisper—not enough to consider taking the average monohull cruiser out for a spin. Once on the open waters of Narragansett Bay, however, the cat seemed to create, as mulithull enthusiasts like to say, its own wind. There were no speed indicators to refer to, but the 37 seemed to be doing 6 or 7 knots, fast enough to catch a tug and its tow (okay, it was slowing for a turn).

According to Chris Bjerregaard, a TPI engineer, the boat should do 8-9 knots in 15 knots of wind, 10 or 11 when the water is flat. Our water was flat and the cat skimmed along as though on a pond, gliding easily over the mild wake kicked up by the tug. Ted Genard of Hellier Yacht Sales of New London, Connecticut, had been out two weeks earlier in snow squalls and winds gusting to more than 25 knots, and reported a smooth ride at 10 knots with less than five degrees of heel.

The 37's steering mechanism incorporates two tillers connected to a crossbar that passes inside the bridgedeck and is hooked by cables to the wheel. All cables run at 90-degree angles for purely linear motion. The system is designed to minimize friction, and the helm in fact is light, almost like power steering. On calm waters, the boat tacked neatly, recovering easily.

No matter what the multihull people say, few cats can sail as close to the wind as a hotshot monohull, although the speed they gain by cracking off a few degrees will often as not negate the difference. The problem usually is in the shallow stub keels, common to many production cats. The 4-foot draft of the keels on the 37 give a measure of lift but not as much as a deeper centerboard would provide. Bjerregaard put it this way: "The 37 will sail upwind with any monohull of 4-foot draft, but there aren't any (of that size)." Deepen the draft, and you'll get better windward performance, he said.

For comparison, the PDQ 36 cat draws just 2' 10", and the 37-foot Antigua by Fountaine Pajot draws 3' 6". Few production catamaran builders use centerboards, presumably due to higher costs and the usual maintenance difficulties. An exception is the Gemini 3200, which, in our experience, profits greatly from its centerboards.

The shallow underbody and comparatively light displacement of the Lagoon 37, or any cat, also make it difficult to slow in heavy air, or heave to. Multihull sailors often deploy parachute anchors tied to a bridle off the bows. One of two Lagoon 42s caught in heavy winds en route to the Caribbean last winter, reportedly tried an alternative measure, trailing its bimini as a drogue to reduce speed (see sidebar).

We can't testify to the 37's heavy-air capabilities, but we can make some educated guesses. It was hull #1 that was abandoned by its delivery crew less than two weeks after our test sail. Although the cockpit is high and dry under light to moderate conditions, one (French) delivery skipper we talked to said cat sailors get used to sailing underwater when the seas rise up and the bows dig in.

We also talked to a passenger on one of the 42s that got caught in 30-plus knots of wind and 8-foot seas during an offshore passage. Beating under a single reef, the boat began hobbyhorsing as the seas grew to more than 5 feet, the leeward bow plunging into the waves and the windward lifting out on occasion. Although he never felt the boat was out of control, the motion was uncomfortable and all on board were seasick. The ride was wet as well, with periodic waves washing the deck. At one point, he said, "there were fish in the cockpit." The bows also tended to labor underwater, possibly because of a tight weave on the forward 6' x 10' trampoline. Bjerregaard said that shouldn't be a problem, but in any event the builder has switched to a looser, 1-1/2-inch weave.

There's nothing like a rough passage to point out shortcomings that escape notice on a calm day. The 37 offers wide sidedecks and comes equipped with double lifelines, but there is a lack of handholds—no problem on light-air days but a worry when you must go forward under adverse conditions.

Minor points: The main halyard, which is led internally and has 2:1 purchase, according to the manufacturer, still took much hauling even with the #40 winch. Presumably, this will become somewhat easier as the sail slides wear.

Jib sheets also tended to hang up during tacking on the earliest 37s, primarily because the winches were angled forward on pads. On new models, the winches have been squared away to the mast.

Under engine power, the 37, like all non-displacement boats, moved smoothly with none of the laboring familiar to monohulls. Cynics might say you need the engines just to tack one of these cats, but that was not the case on our sail. Of course, the drawback of two hulls is the need for two engines—double the trouble. The Lagoon has 52 gallons of fuel capacity.

Accommodations

One of the attractions of a true cruising catamaran is the incredible amount of interior space you get for the length. The 37 has a large, open saloon whose ports offer a 360-degree view as well as lots of light. A semi-circular bench behind a good-sized convertible table looks aft to the cockpit through a folding smoked-acrylic door. The bench, which seats eight according to promotional material, is cushioned with a backrest and can be converted to an extra bunk. The saloon interior is finished with light-colored laminates with teak trim.

The standard interior offers three double sleeping cabins, two with queen-size berths at the forward end of each hull or ama, and a double-size berth aft. The separate hulls, which offer a sense of privacy

rarely found on monohulls this size, are three steps down from the saloon and offer 6' 3" headroom wherever a person is likely to stand. Cabins are well lit from a variety of portlights, including low-level ports in the bows. Ventilation via the ports and opening hatches seems adequate. There's plenty of stowage space, including hanging lockers in each cabin.

The starboard passageway contains a pilot berth/storage area across from a fold-down nav table and station, including electrical panels. The standard setup on the 37 has four 12-volt batteries and includes two electric bilge pumps in addition to two manual pumps operated from on deck. The prototype boat we looked at was equipped with an optional walk-through head between the nav area and the forward cabin.

To port, you step down into a sizable galley area that offers lots of counter space and stowage, double sink, freezer/refrigerator, which can be either electri-

Smaller catamarans are rather cramped inside, but given the size of the Lagoon 37 there's space to spare, much more than in a monohull of similar size. The separate hulls lend a high degree of privacy, as well.

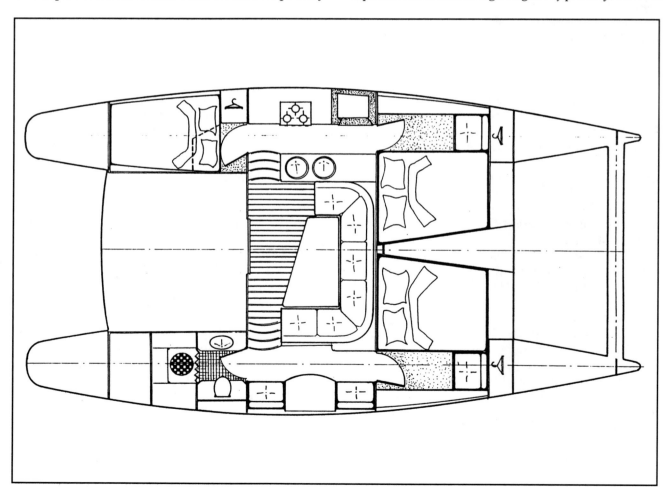

cal or mechanical, and a three-burner Force 10 stove. Aft to starboard is a roomy main head with shower stall. This compartment, like the portside sleeping cabin, provides access to the engines. The color scheme throughout is white or near-white, offset by green bands around the ports and green cushions (and countertops in the galley). A padded headliner is standard; where we saw the bare hull it was well-finished.

The cockpit, intended to serve as an extension of the saloon in temperate weather, is commodious and features two tables that fold to make one larger table. The two-person helm has a padded bench. There's a big anchor locker and seven storage lockers, accessible from the deck. The transom also sports a folding swim ladder. Overall, given the size of the platform and the cockpit, there's plenty of room for five or six people without any need for shifting or scrambling to get out of each other's way.

Conclusions

With the Lagoon 37, Jeanneau has brought its catamaran line within useful range for the individual owner. This is a good-looking boat with seemingly excellent performance capability in light to moderate wind speeds. For those who like to cruise with company or do a lot of entertaining, underway or at the dock, the Lagoon provides plenty of space to socialize or make yourself scarce. Lots of initial stability and lack of heeling under most conditions also make it an attractive option for those who prefer to stay comfortable and dry, rather than experience the traditional sailing experience complete with salt spray in the face.

At a 1993 price of $199,500 plus sails, the 37 isn't cheap (The Fountaine Pajot Antigua 37, for example, has been selling for about $177,000; the PDQ 36 is in the same ballpark.) Still, we'd recommend that those seeking similar accommodations on a monohull, and who do most of their cruising in milder weather and waters, at least check it out. For those who intend to spend a lot of time sailing to windward in coastal or offshore waters, where the winds and waves tend to kick up, a monohull probably remains the better choice. Obviously there's a market out there for the 37; with just four in the water by early 1993, Jeanneau North America and TPI had received orders for 12 more. • **PS**

Crealock 37

A conservative boat that is sold as a "go-anywhere" yacht—and it is, in both design and construction.

The Crealock 37 is the largest boat built by Pacific Seacraft, a California company that has carved a comfortable and ever-growing niche in the boat market by specializing in smaller, high-quality cruising boats. Pacific Seacraft boats could be termed "modern traditional," with pronounced sheerlines, traditional bronze hardware, moderate displacement, and conservative modern underbodies.

This boat was first built by Cruising Consultants, a short-lived California company that built 16 Crealock 37s in 1978 and 1979. In 1980, Pacific Seacraft acquired the tooling.

There's no way around it. To someone who appreciates a traditional-looking boat, the Crealock 37 is about as pretty as they get. The canoe stern isn't for everyone, but Bill Crealock draws it perfectly, in a way that both Will Fife, Jr, and L. Francis Herreshoff would have appreciated.

Because freeboard is fairly low, the cabin trunk must be quite tall to give good headroom below. Its height is somewhat disguised by low bulwarks and teak eyebrow trim dropped down below the actual top of the cabin trunk.

The Crealock 37 was conceived and marketed as a go-anywhere boat, and in both design and construction it fits the bill. That's not to say it's perfect— no boat is.

Hull and Deck

This is a conservative boat, devoid of construction razzmatazz. The hull is an uncored, solid laminate. For those living in colder climates and wanting more insulation, the boat can be built with either foam or balsa core, but these are added to the normal hull layup, resulting in a somewhat heavier boat with slightly reduced interior volume.

Specifications

LOA	36' 11"
LWL	27' 9"
Beam	10' 10"
Draft	4' 5"/5' 6" (Scheel/std)
Displacement	16,000 lbs.
Ballast	6,200 lbs.
Sail area	619 sq. ft.

Longitudinal and transverse stiffness are provided by a full-length molded liner which contains recesses for bulkheads, floors, major furniture components, engine beds, and water tanks. A liner like this can be a mixed blessing. If properly designed and installed, it adds considerable rigidity to the hull structure, and greatly speeds assembly of the boat's interior. Poorly designed or improperly installed, liners can inadequately support the thin outer skin of the boat.

In the Crealock 37, numerous openings in the liner allow it to be securely glassed to the hull, using resin and fiberglass fabric. This is the way it should be done.

Hull liners are not without disadvantages. They constrain the interior layout to that defined by the liner, and they can make later installation of additions to the wiring and plumbing systems difficult.

One unusual feature of the Crealock 37's construction is that the water tanks are an integral part of the hull liner. The sides, ends, and bottom of the tanks are molded. The tops of the tanks are Formica-faced plywood. This is a reasonable way to do the job. We would not recommend using the inside of the hull itself as part of the tank, since this could aggravate a hull's tendency to blister.

The main structural bulkhead at the forward end of the main cabin is both glassed and bolted in place. Since the bulkhead and compression post must absorb the load of the deck-stepped mast, this belt-and-braces attachment is a good idea. Below the hull liner, mast compression is transferred to the hull via a glass-filled PVC pipe. This is a reasonable installation, and we have never seen signs of excess compression loading on a Crealock 37's deck.

Chainplates are stainless steel straps bolted through the topsides. This is a simple, strong, leak-proof installation. But aesthetically, it breaks up the clean flow of the sheerline, and we have seen chainplates like this bleed brown oxidation down the topsides after lengthy ocean passages. Functionally it means the shroud base is a bit wider than necessary, slightly constraining upwind performance.

Hardware and its installation are first-rate. Most of the deck hardware is bronze, and it is both well designed and well finished. Since Pacific Seacraft recently changed porthole suppliers, the familiar trademark oval ports have been replaced with more rectangular models. We think the oval ones look better, but according to the builder, the new ones seal better and have an improved spigot design.

Hull and deck are joined together at the bulwarks. At the top of the bulwarks, there is an inward-turning hull flange. On the deck, the edge of the molding turns upward to form the inner bulwark face, then outward at the top to overlap the hull flange. The joint is bedded in polyurethane sealant and through-bolted. The top of the bulwark is covered with a teak cap. You can't fault this type of joint.

All through hull openings are equipped with either ball valves or tapered-plug seacocks, with the fittings bolted through the hull. This is the right way to do it, but it makes it difficult to use flush skin fittings.

Fiberglass work is excellent. Even on dark-colored hulls, there is no roving print-through, and there are no visible hard spots in the topsides. We have found minor gelcoat cracks around the mainsheet traveler supports, but these may well result from pulling the deck from the mold, rather than from stress on the traveler itself.

Decks are cored with plywood, rather than the more commonly used end-grain balsa. A balsa cored deck is both stiffer and lighter than a plywood cored deck, but you have to put plywood or glass inserts in the balsa deck under heavily-loaded hardware.

The keel is an external lead casting, bolted to the hull with stainless steel bolts. A conventional low-aspect fin keel is standard, but many owners choose the shoal draft Scheel keel.

Rig

The mast is built by LeFiell. It is untapered, and is normally supplied with external halyards. Internal halyards are optional, and while unnecessary on a cruising boat, they do reduce windage and neaten things up around the mast.

Halyard winches are Lewmar 16 self-tailers. At least one of the winches should be upgraded in size so that the smallest member of the crew can hoist the largest member to the masthead if necessary.

The mast and boom are painted. Painted spars look great when they're new, but they tend to get a little bedraggled after a few years of cruising. Anodized spars aren't as pretty, but they usually hold up better over time.

The rig is simple and straightforward, rugged and functional. It's not what you'd put on a racing boat, but it won't fall down in heavy weather, either.

Engine and Mechanical Systems

Over the years, Pacific Seacraft has used both Universal and Yanmar diesels in the Crealock 37. The engine currently used is a four cylinder, 100 cubic inch Yanmar 4JHE, normally aspirated. This is about the ideal size engine for the boat, and it's a very good installation.

A hinged panel lets you lift up the top of the engine box for quick access. You must remove the companionway ladder to get at the front of the engine, which you'd need to do to change the water pump impeller or alternator belt. A removable panel in the quarterberth gives access to the left side of the engine, as well as to the stuffing box. The engine compartment itself is properly sound insulated.

Two 120 amp-hour batteries are standard. The 55-amp alternator supplied is just barely adequate for the standard batteries. If you want more electrical storage capacity, you'll also need to upgrade the alternator.

Wiring and plumbing are neat and workmanlike. Surprisingly, however, some components of the electrical and plumbing systems that should be standard on a boat of this quality, like lightning grounding, hot and cold pressure water, and an electric bilge pump, are options.

Handling Under Sail

You can have the Crealock 37 rigged as a sloop, cutter, or yawl. A divided rig offers no advantages on a boat this size. A double headsail rig is highly desirable, particularly if you use a headsail roller reefing system, since it allows you to hank on a heavy weather staysail without having to remove the genoa from the furling headstay.

The optional cutter rig adds to the price of the boat, but it's worth it.

Another popular option is the singlehander's package, which shifts halyards, reefing lines, jib downhaul, and halyard winches from the mast to the top of the cabin trunk at the front of the cockpit. Unfortunately, this puts the halyard winches directly in the way of a cockpit dodger, preventing you from swinging the winch handle in a complete circle.

Genoa sheet winches are mounted on the molded cockpit coamings. Winches are adequately sized.

The lead from the genoa track through the turning blocks to the winches needs to be altered slightly to reduce friction. An angled shim under the turning blocks would do the job. We'd also go up one size on the turning blocks. Turning blocks are very heavily loaded—roughly twice the sheet load—and are frequently undersized.

Since the boat is fairly narrow by modern standards, the outboard chainplates are only a slight compromise in windward performance. The typical cruiser/racer of this length is almost a foot wider, meaning that sheeting angles on the Crealock 37 are roughly the same as they would be on the cruiser/racer whose chainplates were 6" inboard.

The Crealock 37's rig is very well proportioned. The mainsail's aspect ratio of about 2.7:1 is about ideal, and the main itself is only 272 square feet—no sweat for one person to handle. With a divided foretriangle and headsail roller furling, sailing this boat is a piece of cake.

Compared to a cruiser/racer, the Crealock's waterline is short by contemporary standards. This pushes her displacement/length ratio to 334, decidedly toward the heavy end of the spectrum. But with a sail area/displacement (SA/D) ratio of about 15.6:1, the boat offers pretty good performance in anything other than drifting conditions.

The displacement/length ratio is a tricky number to use. It is meaningless for evaluating performance without considering the SA/D ratio at the same time. For a 37' boat, the Crealock 37's displacement is moderate. For a serious 37' cruising boat her displacement is actually fairly light.

All in all, the Crealock 37 will perform perfectly satisfactorily under sail, particularly on long passages.

Handling Under Power

The Yanmar engine is plenty of power for a boat of this displacement and type.

The boat was designed with a strut-mounted exposed prop. However, this was modifed to provide a prop aperture in the skeg supporting the rudder. The aperture is nicely faired, and the position of the prop immediately in front of the rudder gives good flow over the rudder for steering.

A two-bladed prop is standard, and you can reduce drag under sail by painting a mark on the shaft to help in aligning the blades with the deadwood for long passages. Alternatively, fit the boat with a two-bladed or three-bladed feathering prop. At the risk of sounding like a broken record, we can only reiterate that nothing will improve the typical sailboat's handling in reverse more quickly than adding a feathering prop.

A 40-gallon aluminum fuel tank is located in the bilge under the main cabin sole. It is completely removable without disassembling joinerwork. Although it's unlikely you'll ever have to take it out, this installation is a big plus. You can expect about a 250 mile range under power, which is reasonable for a boat this size. Somewhat greater fuel capacity

The standard layout is a good one for comfortable long-term cruising. That's fortunate, since the molded hull liner makes altering it difficult.

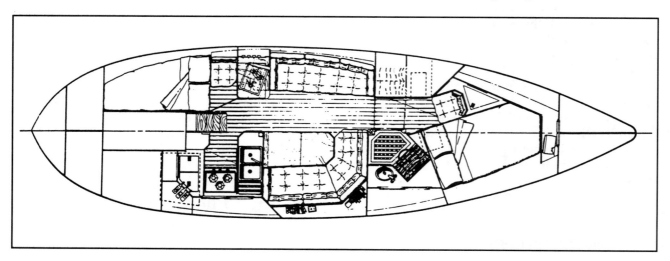

would be desirable for a serious cruiser, but the boat doesn't really have the displacement to carry a lot more fuel and water.

On Deck

The deck is quite well laid out for cruising, but where the heck do you put the dinghy? There's not quite enough room between the mast and the mainsheet traveler for a decent-sized rigid dinghy.

There are dual anchor rollers at the bow, but they don't project far enough forward to get a CQR or Bruce anchor safely away from the topsides. One Crealock 37 we looked at has a custom drop-nose extension on the rollers, an excellent idea that should be incorporated by the builder.

The foredeck is a clear, unobstructed work area. There are four foredeck cleats: two 10" cleats mounted on the inside of the bulwarks next to the hawseholes, and two 12" cleats near the centerline for anchor rodes. Thanks, Pacific Seacraft, for an arrangement that acknowledges the reality of anchoring.

A raised fiberglass boss in the deck forward of the anchor cleats will accommodate an optional anchor windlass. Raising the windlass slightly above deck level greatly reduces the amount of water that gets below through the chainpipe. You'll definitely want a windlass on this boat if you do any serious cruising.

Since the stanchions are bolted to the inside of the bulwarks rather than to the decks, decks are remarkably clear of clutter. Stanchions are 30" high, a good height for a cruising boat. On the downside, the face of the bulwarks can be deflected by leaning against the stanchions.

Despite the wide cabin trunk, the side decks are plenty wide enough for unobstructed passage, and there are teak grabrails along each side of the cabin trunk.

The cockpit is deep and comfortable, with coamings angled slightly outboard. Cockpit seats are just long enough to lie down on.

There are three cockpit lockers: a deep one on the starboard side that can serve as a sail locker, and two smaller lockers under the helmsman's seat. A lazarette on deck aft of the cockpit serves as a propane storage locker. It is properly sealed and scuppered, but it also functions as storage for the stern anchor rode. The lazarette is also big enough that it is tempting to use it for other storage as well.

According to ABYC (American Boat and Yacht Council) standard A-1.11.b(4), lockers used for LPG tank storage "shall not be used for storage of any other equipment." Even storing the anchor rode in the lazarette would violate that section of the standards.

One excellent feature of Pacific Seacraft boats is the removable cockpit sole, which is bolted down on heavy gaskets. On this boat, the entire sole was originally removable, but with the now-standard steering pedestal in place (the boat was designed for tiller steering) you had to remove the entire steering gear and pedestal before the cockpit sole could be taken out. The deck molding has been retooled so that only the forward half of the sole is removable—a substantially more practical arrangement.

A narrow bridgedeck protects the companionway. The sliding companionway hatch itself is an

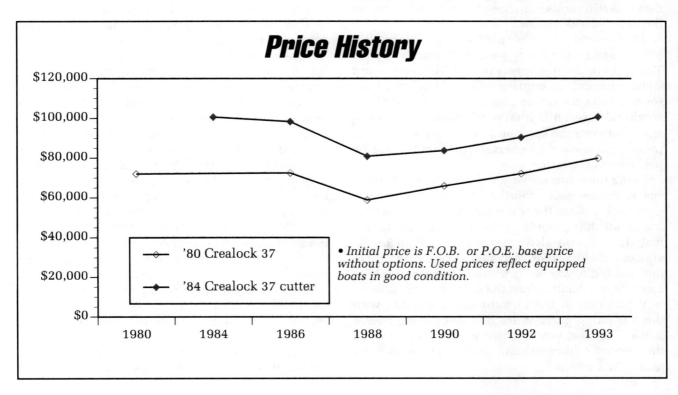

Price History

* Initial price is F.O.B. or P.O.E. base price without options. Used prices reflect equipped boats in good condition.

'80 Crealock 37

'84 Crealock 37 cutter

excellent design, one of the most carefully thought-out and watertight we have seen.

Surprisingly, there is no molded breakwater for a cockpit dodger. The dodger must be fitted around the mainsheet traveler supports and handrails. This makes it almost impossible to get a watertight seal around the bottom of the dodger—a serious drawback on a cruising boat. In general, however, the deck layout is clean, simple, and functional.

Belowdecks

Everyone has a different idea of what the interior of a serious cruising boat should be. The trend today is toward multiple cabins, queen-sized berths, and heads with stall showers. Instead, the Crealock 37 uses a very basic layout devoid of gimmicks and visual tricks, but one that is nearly ideal for a cruising couple.

The Crealock 37 has enough headroom even for tall folks. In the main cabin, there is an honest 6' 4" throughout. In the head and forward cabin, headroom is over 6'.

Despite an interior that is heavy on teak, the boat doesn't look dark inside. The feeling of lightness is helped by multiple ports and hatches, an off-white padded vinyl headliner, and the exposed white fiberglass settee and galley dresser risers that are part of the molded hull liner.

Although an oil finish on the interior teak bulkheads and trim is standard, we highly recommend that you ask the builder not to oil the teak at all. Instead, varnish it. If you really want the interior to look good, use gloss varnish on the teak trim and fiddles, satin varnish on the bulkheads and any other flat areas of teak veneer.

The forward cabin has a nice-sized double berth—50" wide and about 7' long—along the starboard side. The space below it is largely taken up by the forward water tank and the holding tank, although there are several drawers under the head of the berth. A comfortable seat fills what would otherwise be dead space between the berth and the hanging lockers to port. There are cubby lockers above the seat along the port side of the hull.

Using the space under the double berth for tankage is a reasonable solution, but not one free of drawbacks. When the water tank is full, you're adding about 300 pounds at the forward end of the waterline. If you also carry a lot of chain in the anchor rode locker forward, this is enough weight to noticeably alter the boat's trim and increase pitching moment, especially since the entry is fairly fine.

Ventilation in the forward cabin is good, with three opening ports and a double-opening Bomar hatch. The cowl vent over the passageway between the forward cabin and main cabin will help ventilation in bad weather.

The head compartment is on the starboard side, immediately aft of the forward cabin. Ventilation is provided by an opening port and a cowl vent.

A slatted teak seat folds down over the toilet if you want to sit down while showering, which is a good idea if you're doing it while underway. Since the entire lower half of the head compartment is a fiberglass molding, cleanup is quite simple. The shower sump pumps directly overboard with its own pump—a good solution to the problem.

Main cabin seating consists of an L-shaped dinette to starboard, and a straight settee along the port side. A drop-leaf table folds up against the forward face of the galley dresser, and can be folded out in two sections to use for dining. Since you can't reach the table from the settee, you're really limited to four for dinner at the table.

We find the folding table a little awkward. It isn't really sturdy enough to brace against at sea, so you'll tend to leave it folded up. The halfway open position will be useful in port, although that doesn't give you a table that two people can sit at comfortably.

A folding table is used for two reasons. First, the cabin sole in front of the dinette is removable so you can get at the fuel tank. Second, someone somewhere along the line decided that with a drop-in insert, the dinette would make a nice big double berth. Unfortunately, there's no good place to stow the big piece of plywood you need to create that double berth, and you need another double berth on a 37' cruising boat about like you need a hole in the head.

Using the dinette as a single berth is a little awkward, since the corner of the L is a gradual curve rather than a right angle, limiting foot room.

There is good storage space under both the port settee and the dinette, and there are various lockers and shelves outboard of the settees. Surprisingly, the locker doors do not have positive catches. Instead, they rely on friction latches—a mistake on a cruising boat, as you'll discover the first time the lockers empty onto the cabin sole.

The nav station is aft of the port settee, and it has its own seat rather than using the head of the quarterberth. The chart table itself is a reasonable size, but the piano hinge that joins the opening lid to the fixed portion of the table top is not recessed flush, limiting the space you can actually use for plotting. In addition, the fixed part of the table is flat, making it a good place to put your coffee cup, but the rest of the table is angled. If the whole table were in one plane, it would make for a more usable work surface.

A well-designed electrical panel is mounted on the bulkhead next to the navigator. The forward section of this bulkhead is meant to be used for flush-mounting electronics, but the space behind the bulkhead is really too shallow for a lot of equipment, and the location places the instruments at an awkward angle for the navigator. Pacific Seacraft will build an instrument-mounting rack over the forward end of the chart table, and we recommend it.

Cruising boats really need a big, easy-to-use nav station, with plenty of shelf space for electronic goodies, sextant, and navigation books. A couple of drawers to hold small nav tools would also be useful.

Aft of the nav station is a large quarterberth. The boat's accommodation plan shows this as a double, but it's really too small for that, being 42" wide at the head, tapering to about 2' wide at the foot.

Batteries are mounted under the head of the quarterberth, and the second water tank occupies most of the rest of the space below it.

The U-shaped galley is opposite the nav station. With one exception, it is a very workable galley. The exception is that the bottom of the deep double sinks is right at the load waterline, so water sloshes back through the drains, particularly when the boat is on port tack. Since the galley counter is only 34" high—36" is standard household height—a simple alteration would solve that problem.

The icebox is large and well insulated, with 4" of pour-in-place foam. The icebox lid, while insulated, needs to be gasketed to reduce heat transfer.

There is reasonable storage throughout the galley for food and utensils, although a cutlery drawer would be helpful. As a $440 option, you can get a good-sized locker suspended over the sinks. We'd go for it on a boat used for extended cruising.

Access to the bilge is somewhat limited, except for the large hatches over the fuel tank. Opening the small hatch over the aft end of the bilge sump requires removing the companionway ladder, a nuisance.

Light and ventilation in the main cabin are excellent, with four large and two small opening ports, plus a second large Bomar deck hatch. We'd add a second pair of Dorade boxes over the main cabin to improve heavy weather ventilation.

The interior of this boat is very livable for long-term offshore cruising. The three berths in the main cabin are all pretty much parallel to the centerline of the boat, an important consideration for sleeping under sail.

Our quibbles with the interior are small, and none of the faults we find is in any way fatal. The molded hull liner makes for an inflexible layout, but the standard one is good enough that this won't be a problem for most people.

Conclusions

For an off-the-shelf serious cruiser for two people or a small family, you couldn't do much better than this boat. The hull shape and design are pretty ideal, and the looks are classic without being dated or cute.

The Crealock 37 has held its value extremely well in a time when most boats are depreciating rapidly in a glutted market. This is largely due to the reputation of the boat and the builder, and due to the relatively small number of boats produced by the builder.

Pacific Seacraft's ads have stressed the ruggedness and seaworthiness of the boat. One ad shows a Crealock 37 lying on her side on a reef, basically undamaged. Another ad promotes the Circumnavigator package, ready to go anywhere and complete down to the steering vane.

It's pretty clear what the targeted market is: people who want to go places in small boats, who want good boats to carry them there, and have the money to spend. In today's market, that's a pretty good type of boat to build. **• PS**

Irwin 37

A lot of boat for the money, as long as minor points like sailing performance aren't important to you.

An evaluation of the Irwin 37 threatens to expose all our prejudices about boatbuilders and cruising boats. In general we like sturdily built, finely finished, well performing boats that reflect traditional standards (if not design) and lasting value.

Irwin Yachts built boats of mediocre quality and finish and marketed them to buyers looking for as much boat as possible for the price. In every sense of the word, Irwin boats, of which the Irwin 37 is archetypal, are production boats. They were mass produced, carefully priced, simply advertised, and widely sold to a broad spectrum of customers.

More than 600 Irwin 37s were sold between the time the boat went into production in 1971 and its demise in 1982.

The last version was designated the Mark V, representing the popular strategy of numbering the steps in the evolution of a design even though the changes may be minor.

From the outset the Irwin 37 was a roomy, appealing cruising boat that was once described as the Chevrolet Belair of the boat market. Her greatest appeal was to the sailor/owner who is not into tradition, sailing performance, elegance, construction details, or investment.

Irwin Yachts was considered to have the most notoriously slipshod quality control among the larger boat builders. No other boats have as poor a reputation for warranty claims, delays in commissioning, missing or incorrect parts, and mislocated hardware as Irwin. Similarly an examination of virtually any Irwin-built boat reveals details that reflect cost savings but are problems; some, in our opinion, serious (gate valves on all through hull fittings) and some trivial (through hull fittings not installed flush with the hull).

Specifications

LOA	37' 0"
LWL	30' 0"
Beam	11' 6"
Draft	4' 0"/5' 6" (shoal/full keel)
Displacement	20,000 lbs.
Ballast	7,800 lbs.
Sail area	625 sq. ft.

Construction

There are no basic industry standards for fiberglass construction; the primary criterion for adequate hull laminate strength seems largely a matter of in-use durability. Some builders, in the absence of such standards, overbuild their products (CSY, for example). Irwin Yachts, on the other hand, have hulls and decks molded to specifications that are, by industry comparison, light. By our standards the Irwin fiberglass layup is minimal; that is one reason the boats have a low price. Yet basic laminate is not where cost savings are most apparent.

More conspicuous are cosmetic flaws. In two of the later 37s we looked at, there were obvious deep hollows in the bottom. These are evidently the result of pulling a still "green" hull from the mold and setting it in a four-point building cradle. The supports dished the laminate, probably permanently.

For years Irwin Yachts suffered from printthrough whereby the pattern of the underlying roving in the laminate was visible in the topside gelcoat. This later was considerably reduced with the use of Cormat between the roving and the gelcoat; in the later 37s we examined, printthrough was negligible. This printthrough remains an unsightly feature of older 37s, especially in the dark paint of the sheerstrake.

In our examination of the 37s we also noted sloppy underwater fairing around the rudder gudgeon and where the "Adapt-A-Draft" keel is attached. These types of flaws, coupled as they are with such details as protruding through hull fittings and squared off trailing edges, produces needless drag for a boat whose performance under sail is already suspect.

The earliest Irwin 37s did not have bowsprits. The result was a hazy gracelessness that was accentuated by obvious unevenness in the sheerline, unrelieved topside expanse, and Clorox-bottle styling, not to mention dimples and gelcoat blemishes. To improve performance with more sail area Irwin added a molded fiberglass bowsprit. Serendipitously the extension did wonders for the aesthetics. Less fortuitously the glass sprit also became a source of warranty claims when, if tightening the rigging caused it to flex, the gelcoat crazed.

The final version of the bowsprit is of welded aluminum. In a mid-production boat we examined, the bobstay is a threaded stainless steel rod with jaw terminals at each end. The newer boats have the rod welded between two plates on each end, a less costly fitting. As the lower end will be continually awash and thus vulnerable to corrosion, we think the welded construction is a mistake. Similarly we are concerned about the stainless steel rudder gudgeon, which has shown evidence of stress corrosion.

The Irwin 37 has a history of warranty claims against defective gelcoat—too thin (or missing), too thick, discolored, crazed, or covering voids. Where this happened in the diamond pattern non-skid deck surfaces that Irwin produced into the early '80s, inconspicuous repair was well nigh impossible.

The problem drove Irwin dealers and new owners to distraction and fueled much of the scuttlebutt about Irwin's poor handling of warranty claims. In the last boats Irwin put on a random non-skid pattern, easier to repair. Irwin also went to a better quality gelcoat.

Another common question about Irwin Yachts has been its hull-to-deck joint. Contrary to common industry practice, the joint in the Irwin 37 consists of overlapping flanges joined with a polyester slurry and fastened on about 6" centers with stainless steel self-tapping screws. Most builders now use a semi-rigid adhesive and bolts, a technique we favor. We believe this more positive attachment is called for on boats going to sea.

The chainplates of the 37 are stainless steel webs laminated into the topsides during the hull layup. This technique was developed by Irwin and is imitated by a number of builders whose chainplates are at the outer edge of the deck. It seems to be a satisfactory installation and indeed preferable to early Irwin 37s which had the chainplates through-bolted to the topsides.

Handling Under Sail

Virtually everyone from whom we elicited information on the Irwin 37 either dismissed as unimportant or derided her performance under sail. She seems a classic example of the all-too-common cruising boat that does everything better than handle as a sailboat. A number of owners we talked to do not seem bothered by this shortcoming. We, again with our prejudice, would be.

The Irwin 37 comes standard with a sloop rig; the roller furling genoa was an almost unanimously specified option. A cutter rig (with a club jib) and a ketch rig were two other options. In any configuration she is a boat that seems ideally suited for a couple to sail. The sail area is modest with the ketch carrying about 60 square feet more sail than the sloop, just about enough to compensate for the windage of the mizzen mast. Personally we think the cutter rig is the best answer of the three, the staysail providing a handy headsail in hefty conditions and doing away with the clutter, expense and windage of the mizzen.

Plainly the standard shoal draft keel without a centerboard is inadequate for sailing to windward. If a buyer wants shoal draft, he should consider the centerboard version. The board does thunk in its trunk when down, a harmless if annoying distraction. Fully raised it remains quiet; what a relief in the middle of the night at anchor.

For optimum performance we recommend the deep keel. Still, do not hope too earnestly for scintillating windward work; for such joy you should consider a host of boats other than the Irwin 37.

Owners have indicated to us their willingness to accept indifferent performance under sail. However, we have heard complaints about the amount of attention the helm needs and some difficulty in steering the boat both under sail and under power ("Steering is stiff and my wife (98 lbs) has difficulty at times."). We suspect some of this chore is the result of an unbalanced semi-spade rudder being driven by a relatively small diameter steering wheel through an aft-cabin layout that requires considerable routing of the steering linkage.

Handling Under Power

The Irwin 37 has a 40 hp Perkins 4-108 diesel engine driving a three-bladed propeller with 2:1 reduction through the after edge of the keel. That is a combination that bespeaks of performance under auxiliary power. In fact, with the standard shoal keel and that combination for power, the Irwin 37 might reasonably be labeled a motorsailer if that term had not fallen into such disfavor in recent years.

The combination also suggests that the Irwin 37 should appeal to the powerboat owner looking to sail as a way to reduce his fuel consumption without sacrificing the room and amenities of the moderate sized powerboat. Certainly we think it is a worthwhile alternative to the ad hoc conversions of sailboat hulls and rigs to sailing powerboats with their high deckhouses, awkward sail handling systems, and sundry other hermaphroditic compromises.

Interior

If performance is not a priority in the design of the Irwin 37, livability is. The Irwin 37 is a coastal cruiser for two couples or a family of four. She has the most practical aft cabin layout we have seen on a stock boat under 40 feet. The layout has remained essentially unchanged since the 37 was introduced and features a spacious aft cabin, a step-down galley, a more-than-adequate walk-through passageway, and a forward cabin that should not make its occupants feel like they are in steerage.

Fundamental to the Irwin Yachts design and marketing philosophy is that the interior should instantly appeal to women. The decor is Production Boat Contemporary: tufted velour cushions, plenty of teak, and "color coordinated" carpeting. We are not impressed with the so-so craftsmanship and unsanded finish of the joinerwork nor with the antiseptic molded hull liner, but these are details that do not immediately affect the illusion of quality, comfort, and spaciousness.

Thus the interior of the 37 minimizes seagoing machismo: there are no handrails, sea berths, navigation sanctum, or sailbag stowage. Below, with the possible exception of the gimballed stove, one can easily forget that under certain circumstances a sailboat may not always be upright or free from motion.

It would be hard to imagine being aboard an Irwin 37 at sea. There is no berth one could sleep in comfortably. The settee berth to port is too narrow and the settee to starboard is too short. One owner remarked that even when the settee berth is to leeward, a nap-taker is rolled out of it during a gentle afternoon sail.

But what the 37 may lack at sea she more than makes up for at bedtime at anchor. Both the athwartships after berth and the forward V-berth are queen-sized with 4" mattresses. The two cabins are separated by 30 feet of boat and closed doors. Each has a private head.

There are good hanging lockers, lots of drawers, a few scuttles and assorted nooks and crannies. Yet someone forgot to build in places to store dry, warm food. For cold food there are, now get this, one front opening Norcold refrigerator (standard) and two, yes two, large top-opening iceboxes. In fact, both iceboxes are so sizable that their bottoms are difficult to reach. One of them (under the rudimentary chart table) might be better used for dry food storage except that getting at its contents would be at best inconvenient. The alternative is to use the galley icebox as a dry well and rely on the Norcold despite our longtime prejudice against using front opening boxes which depend on electrical power away from a dock. Perhaps this refrigerator is the best giveaway as to what type of cruising the 37 is best suited for.

Two other points about the interior deserve comment, one favorably and one not so. Engine access

---

We may not like the way she sails or her construction quality, but the interior layout is very good. Still, there are some problems when it comes to storage.

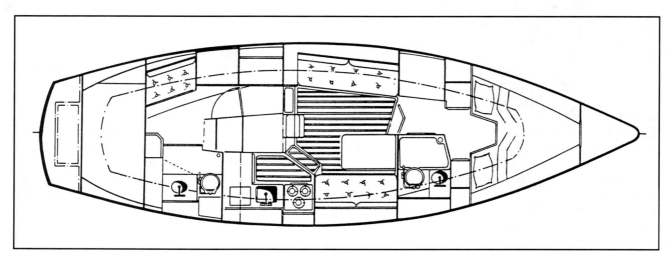

and sound insulation are among the best we have seen in a production boat, helped by removable panels on the sides of the walk-through. To check the dipstick and heat exchanger water there is no need to move the companionway ladder. In short, if the engine of the 37 seizes from lack of oil or overheats for lack of water, the owner has only himself to blame.

On the other side, the bulkhead-mounted fold-up, drop-leaf cabin table will not survive the first fall against it when a powerboat leaves a wake. It might not even withstand the weight of a rib roast. The first thing we would do after buying an Irwin 37 that still had the stock table is find ourselves a rugged, attractive fixed cabin table. (The next thing we would do is to make the seats comfortable.)

Deck Layout

The Irwin 37 is a handy boat to sail. The sidedecks are wide, the rail rises to a low bulwark forward to give a sense of security and the cockpit coaming has an opening to starboard but is low enough to climb out of anywhere. The bowsprit is designed to carry a 30 lb plow anchor housed in a roller chock. Hawseholes (of polished aluminum, replacing the line-chafing fiberglass on older boats) are mounted in the bulwark for docklines. Oddly enough neither the hawseholes nor the roller chock give a fair lead to the pair of deck cleats.

The stanchions are mounted through the deck into blocks drilled to fit, a system that we think gives a rugged support. In early 37s the stanchions went into fiberglass tubes glassed under the deck; in later boats they go into wood blocks (saving cost and complexity). In contrast to this sturdy structure, the bow and stern pulpits are screwed on the teak rail cap. We hardly recommend that attachment.

The cockpit is small, accommodating at the most four adults at a time. Yet the seats are long enough to stretch out on and access below is easy. We are not bothered by the absence of a bridgedeck or companionway sill for safety because the cockpit is high and amidships, hence dry. Besides, Irwin's advertising notwithstanding, we doubt if many owners would consider offshore passages, given all the limitations the 37 would have at sea.

We like the number, design, and placement of the "smoked glass" opening hatches/skylights. Like many designs that have tropical cruising and chartering as part of their destiny, the Irwin 37 has a well ventilated interior.

On deck stowage is limited to one gigantic locker, the lazarette. The trouble is that for storing fenders, docklines, sheets, snorkeling gear, etc. as well as an odd sail or two, it would leave everything hard to get at. You cannot reach the bottom from the deck and without some owner-installed shelves, hooks, and bins the contents would be in chaos.

Conclusions

Having exposed our prejudices we hasten to add that the more than 600 Irwin 37s sold conclusively prove that many sailors do not share those prejudices.

When new in the early '80s, the Irwin 37 was about $15,000 less expensive than, say, the Tartan 37 or the Pearson 365. A Hunter 37, by contrast, could

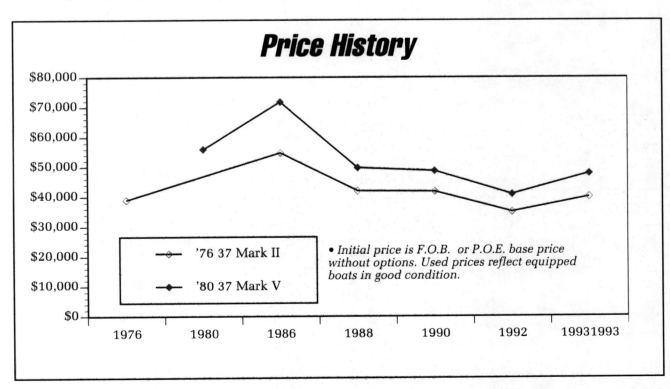

Price History

• Initial price is F.O.B. or P.O.E. base price without options. Used prices reflect equipped boats in good condition.

Legend:
- ◇ '76 37 Mark II
- ◆ '80 37 Mark V

be sailed away for about $10,000 less than the Irwin 37.

Ironically, considering the persistent badmouthing of the Irwin 37 around the waterfront, older models have retained their value reasonably well. The reason seems simple: the Irwin 37 offers many buyers what they are looking for in a boat.

And for the dollars the Irwin 37 is a lot of boat. Many owners report looking seriously at smaller boats and settling on the 37 when they (and their wives) see the spacious 37 for the same price as the smaller boat. For that price they get what they see as a summer home afloat. Deep water cruising may be a distant dream but the immediate desire is a comfortable and impressive boat for weekending and two weeks in the Bahamas, the Eastern Shore, or out of Long Island Sound.

For any boat that retains its stock features, we'd plan systematic and regular upgrading. Expect to replace the standard through-hull gate valves with seacocks or ball valves. Divide the humongous lazarette. Run the halyards aft to the cockpit when they need replacing. Build some pitch into the seats of the settees. Rebuild the "navigation station" into handy food storage. Mount a larger diameter steering wheel so you will no longer have to steer standing up or perched on the edge of your seat.

Finally, take a sail on a boat meant to sail effectively to windward, just so you'll see what you are missing. **• PS**

CSY 37

A strongly built cutter designed with a particular purpose in mind—bareboat chartering.

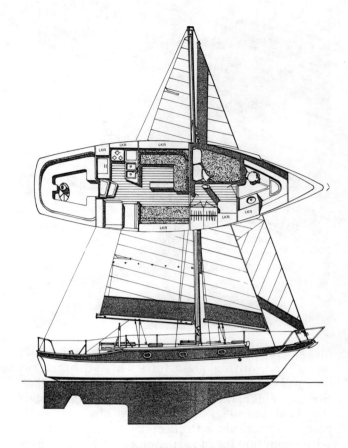

The CSY 37, designed by Peter Schmitt, is the mid-sized boat In the CSY line. Primarily designed for the Caribbean bareboat charter trade, 87 of the raised-deck cutters were built.

Schmitt has combined some features most often found in "traditional" boats—the oval stem, raised deck, and semi-clipper bow—with a relatively modern underbody featuring a fairly long fin keel and a skeg-mounted rudder. On paper, the boat looks pretty good. In person, she is rather tubby and high-sided.

The CSY 37 most closely resembles the Ericson Cruising 36. The styling of both these boats can best be termed "ersatz traditional."

With the short standard rig and shoal keel, she is no performance cruiser. With her huge cockpit she is not really a sea boat. Rather, she is a boat designed for a specific purpose, bareboat chartering, a purpose which she serves admirably. To expand her appeal to the general sailing public would be difficult, as CSY discovered. The company went under in 1981.

Most CSY 37s went into charter service, usually on lease-back arrangements. The boats have to be strong and reliable, for a week out of service for repairs means lost revenue to the charter operator. That the boats can stand up to this constant use and abuse is a credit to both designer and builder. Few other boats could, as CSY's charter experience has shown.

Construction

There are really only two words to describe the construction of the CSY 37: massive overkill. This is a mixed blessing. It means you have a strong, heavy hull. It often also means that you end up with a boat that is undercanvassed in light air. Very often it means a boat that has a fairly low ballast-to-displacement ratio.

Specifications

LOA	37' 3"
LWL	29' 2"
Beam	12' 0"
Draft	4' 8" (shoal), 6' 2" (deep)
Displacement	19,689 lbs.
Ballast	8,000 lbs.
Sail area	610 sq. ft.

Forty percent of the CSY 37's advertised displacement is in the ballast keel. With a 29' waterline, the displacement of about 20,000 lbs is about average by traditional standards, heavy by modern standards.

The hull is an extraordinarily heavy solid glass layup as is the deck. No core materials are used anywhere. Without coring such as balsa or Airex, a glass hull can sweat in a cold climate and can be excessively warm in a hot, humid climate.

The hull-to-deck joint is simple and effective. The hull and deck flanges, which overlap to form a molded rail, are bedded in 3M 5200 and through-bolted with stainless steel machine screws on 4" centers. 3M 5200 is about the most effective and tenacious adhesive sealant on the market.

Keel construction is unusual. The cast lead keel is

glassed into the hollow keel molding, any voids being filled with fiberglass slurry. This is then glassed over to form a double bottom and to keep the ballast in place. This ballast arrangement is identical in both the shoal and deep draft versions. The deep draft boat, however, has a 16" deep keel extension filled with about 600 lbs of cast concrete. If a shoal draft boat is desired, this extension can simply be cut off. The shoal draft boat with less lateral plane will, of course, make more leeway.

The hull is molded in two pieces, then joined in the middle with heavy overlapping layers of mat and roving. This allows some flexibility in hull design allowing such features as a molded-in rubbing strake and a stern with substantial tumblehome.

Installation of hardware is excellent. This is one of the few boats we have ever seen with through-bolted bronze seacocks. Backing plates are used on deck hardware such as cleats and winches.

The rudder stock is a solid 2" round bronze bar. The cast bronze rudder heel fitting would look more at home on a 60' boat than on a 37-footer.

The bow fitting is a massive stainless steel weldment, incorporating an anchor roller, a welded chock, and the headstay chainplate. The edges of the bow chock are not rounded, and could easily chafe an unprotected anchor rode. This bow fitting could double as an effective battering ram. We suspect that the dock boys in the West Indies are pretty wary every time an inexperienced charterer brings one of the CSY charter boats into the slip.

The chainplates are heavy stainless steel flat bars with load-distributing welded webs through-bolted to the hull. The hull layup is further reinforced in the

There are six large opening hatches on deck, making ventilation excellent. There's also plenty of room for lounging about, crucial to the charter trade. There's even enough space to carry along a dinghy.

way of the chainplates, an almost extraneous precaution, given the extreme heaviness of the regular hull layup.

Interior bulkheads are heavy waterproof plywood, attached to the hull with solid and neatly made fillets. Airex pads along the outboard edges of the bulkheads distribute the bulkhead stresses on the inside of the hull, preventing hard spots.

Cabin sole supports are clear fir. The teak-faced cabin sole is screwed to these bearers, with only limited access openings to the bilge. *The Practical Sailor* would prefer that most of the cabin sole be removable, providing access to the bilge spaces in an emergency. CSY appeared to be counting on the massiveness of the hull construction to prevent holing. This conceit could backfire. Remember the *Titanic*?

Hatches are molded fiberglass with translucent panels. They have good gasketing and good holddowns, but a short person will have trouble reaching overhead to open the hatches due to the tremendous headroom.

Exterior finish is of good stock boat quality. Joinerwork is clean with the exception of an awkward transition from the railcap on top of the raised deck to the sheer-level railcap in the foredeck well.

The molded fiberglass trailboards are shielded below the bow by a somewhat awkward molded glass panel. This became standard after a number of

CSY boats blew off their trailboards in heavy seas. We would have preferred it if they had just left the trailboards off entirely.

Handling Under Sail

The CSY 37 was available in two keel configurations, and with two rigs. The four possible combinations offer very different performance characteristics.

Most boats were delivered with the standard short rig. In areas of normally heavy air, such as the West Indies in winter, the normal rig is adequate. In light air with the short rig, the boat is a slug. The engine will come in handy under these circumstances.

Performance is greatly enhanced by the tall rig, which is about 8' taller than the standard rig and incoroporates two sets of spreaders.

With the chainplates set at the outboard edge of the hull, the sheeting base is excessively wide. Sheeting a genoa in tight enough to go to windward effectively is difficult.

To avoid the necessity for running backstays, the intermediate and after lower shrouds are attached to the deck several feet aft of the mast and the upper shrouds. Unfortunately, when broad reaching, the

Anchor handling is made easy by the bow roller arrangement. This boat was fitted with the optional stainless-steel anchor chain. We recommend using galvanized chain instead.

boom and main fetch up on these shrouds far too soon. This is ironic in a boat whose best point of sail is off the wind.

Our test boat had the tall rig and the shoal-draft keel. This is not the combination we would choose to own. Performance with the tall rig is greatly enhanced. However, the higher sail plan does make the boat more tender, and with the cut-down keel combines to produce a boat that makes excessive leeway when heeled more than about 20 degrees. We would prefer to combine the tall rig with the deep keel.

Our test boat was overpowered with full main, staysail and large jib topsail by gusts of a little over 15 knots over the deck, sailing hard on the wind. She also made substantial leeway. With a reef in, the helm eased, the boat stood up, and leeway was less.

Off the wind, the CSY 37 comes into her own. She is stable as a church and visions of long tradewind passages instantly come to mind. Under those conditions she would shine if you had plenty of chafe protection on those aft-leading shrouds.

Halyard winches are mounted on the keel-stepped painted aluminum mast. The boom does not overhang the cockpit, and has a well-made boom gallows which provides a good handhold on deck as well as being an excellent place to store the boom when at rest, or when sailing under the storm jib alone in heavy weather.

Handling Under Power

With such high topsides, the Perkins 4-108 is the smallest engine we would want in the boat. As it is, handling at slow speeds in a crosswind can be tricky. A great deal of practice is required to handle such a high-sided boat under power in a breeze.

The turning radius of the CSY 37 is substantially larger than with a shorter-keeled boat. With her heavy displacement, acceleration is not exactly neck-snapping. She should have enough power to get her out of tight spots, however.

Handling in reverse is tricky. The boat does not go where you aim it until you learn to use a combination of rudder and bursts of throttle.

Engine access through the large cockpit hatch is good, but the heavy hatch should have a more positive means of holding it in the upright position. If it fell on your head, you'd remember it, if you were lucky enough to then remember anything.

To those who have been spoiled by the handling under power of some modern boats, the CSY 37 may be a disappointment. It handles like a boat, rather than a compact car, requiring some patience and planning ahead.

Deck Layout

With her raised deck amidships, the CSY 37 has an amazing amount of deck space, giving the on-deck impression of a small ship. There is plenty of space on deck to carry a rigid dinghy. Designer Peter Schmitt's own CSY 37 carried a beautiful little dory with a varnished transom as a tender; she fit quite neatly on the starboard side and served as a catchall for fenders and lines.

Deck space is important in boats used extensively in the charter trade. Lounging on deck is the primary charter boat activity. In this category, the CSY 37 gets five stars.

Anchor handling is fairly easy with the stub bowsprit. There is, however, only a single bow cleat. This is a pet peeve of *The Practical Sailor,* for it greatly complicates anchoring with two anchors, a common practice for cruising boats. The optional "anchoring package" included a good length of stainless steel chain, which is miserable stuff to handle by hand. Use galvanized instead.

We do not recommend the electric anchor windlass. If you plan on using a windlass, get a boat with the manual unit.

Heavy travelers for both the main and the staysail are located on the main deck. Thwartships control lines should really be used with these to get optimum performance from the sails—essential on a boat which must be tweaked to get a reasonable level of performance on the wind.

The cockpit of the CSY 37 is huge—too big for an offshore boat but good for the charter trade. The large cockpit lockers are well divided and are partitioned from the engine space under the cockpit.

The starboard cockpit locker contains the best battery box installation we have seen on a stock boat.

The port locker contains the optional 110-VAC refrigeration compressor. Unfortunately, its wiring is exposed to the weather when the locker lid is opened. The sound-insulated engine room hatch occupies much of the cockpit sole.

There are four large cockpit scuppers, which are imperative to have with the huge cockpit. The companionway sill should be higher if the boat is to be used offshore. A fiberglass seahood, protecting the forward end of the companionway slide, is standard equipment.

Interior

Two interior arrangements are available, a two-stateroom, two-head plan, and a single-stateroom, single-head plan. The two-stateroom plan is used primarily in the charter trade. It is really too much interior to try to cram in a 29' waterline and designer Schmitt was not particularly proud of it.

The single-stateroom layout is also unconventional. It gives over the forward 40% of the interior space to a large cabin with built-in double berth and a huge head compartment in the forepeak. The problem with this arrangement is that should you have guests aboard, they must troop through the owner's cabin in order to use the head—a major inconvenience.

The space given over to the head in the single-stateroom model is almost exactly the same space occupied by the forward cabin in the two-stateroom model. With a single-stateroom layout, interior space might have been better utilized with a "conventional" layout of sleeping quarters forward with the

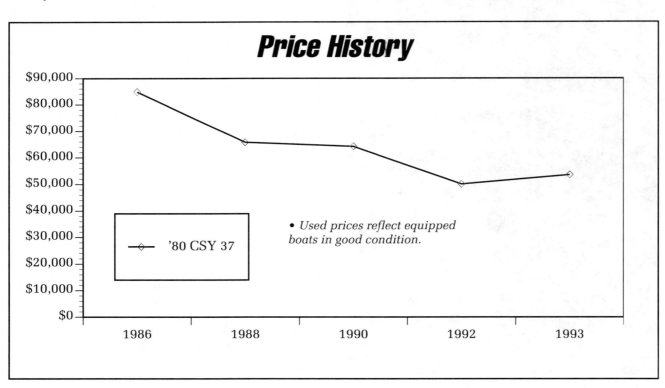

Price History

• *Used prices reflect equipped boats in good condition.*

—◇— '80 CSY 37

head and hanging lockers dividing the forward cabin from the main cabin. Unfortunately, the "conventional" layout was not an option.

The interior volume of the CSY 37 is huge, thanks to the raised deck. There are many well-thought-out interior details, too many, unfortunately, to catalog here. The ice box, for example, is divided into two compartments with separate opening traps. The icebox has a minimum of 4" of urethane foam insulation, probably more than any other stock boat on the market.

There are, however, lapses in this good design. Galley counter tops in our test boat were covered with a slatelike laminate, difficult to clean and too bumpy for a good work surface. Head counters and some shelves were covered with marble-grained plastic, looking more like a slice out of a multi-colored bowling ball than real marble.

The mixture of excellent design details, strange lapses in taste, and execution which ranges from fair to excellent is difficult to evaluate reasonably. It was pleasing to see, that after years of using teak-grained mica-covered bulkheads, CSY switched to real oak-faced bulkheads in newer production boats.

Ventilation of the interior can only be described as excellent. There are six opening hatches or skylights in addition to the companionway. Some dorade boxes, however, might be welcome in steamy climates with frequent rain. One could spend a great deal of time analyzing the interior details, primarily because a lot of thought has gone into them. Both of the interior layouts are unusual, and each will have adherents and detractors.

Conclusions

CSY was an unusual company, and the CSY 37 is certainly an unconventional boat. The boat is strongly built—overly built, in fact, The 1980 base price of $91,670 seems high until you consider that this is a 20,000-lb boat, and very well equipped. Hot and cold pressure water, Edson pedestal steering, and gimballed propane stove were all standard, for example.

CSY boats were probably the strongest production boats ever marketed. They may be ungainly, and not the hottest performers under sail, but they are tough. That's an important consideration if you're trying to get the most for your money. • **PS**

Tartan 37

Good manners and attention to detail set this well-bred Sparkman & Stephens design apart.

The Tartan 37 is a moderately high performance, shoal-draft keel-centerboarder that went out of production in 1989, to be replaced by the Tartan 372.

Over the years, Tartan specialized in the production of well-finished boats geared toward the upper income cruising sailor. Most of these boats were Sparkman and Stephens designs, and many were keel-centerboarders. Tartans were also geared toward "civilized" racing, with boats such as the Tartan 41 and Tartan 46. With their Sparkman and Stephens designs and high quality joinerwork, Tartans provided a somewhat lower priced alternative to lines of boats such as the very expensive Nautor Swans.

Several hundred Tartan 37s were built. Most of these were the keel-centerboard version. An optional deep-keel version was also available. A racing version of the 37, called the Tartan 38, was built in limited numbers.

The Tartan 37 is attractively modern in appearance. She has a gentle sheer and a straight raked stern profile, with moderate overhangs at both bow and stern. Underwater, the boat has a fairly long, low aspect ratio fin keel, and a high aspect ratio rudder faired into the hull with a substantial skeg. Freeboard is moderate. The boat is balanced and pleasant in appearance. She is not a character boat, but is attractive, fairly racy, and functional—a typical modern Sparkman and Stephens design.

Construction

The Tartan 37 is a well-built boat. Tartan made use of both unidirectional roving and balsa coring in stress areas. This yields a stiff, fairly light hull that is less likely to oilcan than the relatively thin solid layup used in many production boats.

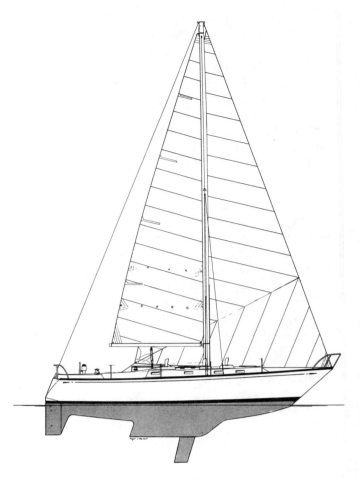

Specifications

LOA	37' 3"
LWL	28' 6"
Beam	11' 9"
Draft	4' 2" (cb), 6' 7" (deep keel)
Displacement	15,500 lbs.
Ballast	7,500/7,200 (std/deep keel)
Sail area	625 sq. ft.

Some roving printthrough is evident. There are also some visible hard spots on the outside of the hull. These may be the result of the heat of secondary bonding of bulkheads and partitions. Gelcoat quality is very good.

The rudder is faired into the skeg with fiberglass flaps to minimize turbulence. All through-hull fittings are recessed flush to the hull skin. For a cruising boat, remarkable attention was given to reducing skin friction and improving water flow.

Tartan's hull-to-deck joint is simple and strong. The wide internal hull flange is bedded with butyl and polysulfide, the deck dropped on, and the two bolted together via the stainless steel bolts which hold on the teak toerail. This toerail is not always properly bedded. We were able to easily insert a

thick knife blade under the toerail in several areas near the bow, where the rail is subject to the most twist. Water will lie in this joint if it is at all open, making it impossible to keep varnish on the toerail.

Most deck hardware, such as cleats, is backed with thick aluminum plates. Pulpits are through-bolted but lack backing plates. The hull-to-deck joint is through-bolted across the transom—one of few boats so built. Running lights are mounted in the topsides, about a foot below the sheerline. The wiring for these lights is located in the forepeak locker, where it could be damaged by anchors or rodes stored there. We generally dislike running lights mounted in the hull. They look neat, but they are nearly invisible at sea, often leak, and frequently stain the topsides with long tears of oxidation after periods at sea.

Interior glasswork is some of the best we have seen. Fillet bonding is absolutely neat and clean. There are no raw fiberglass edges visible anywhere in the hull.

One of the reasons that the Tartan 37 cost so much is that there was a lot of expensive engineering and construction in the boat. The starboard main chainplate assembly, for example, is a complex construction of stainless steel weldments and tie rods that probably added hundreds of dollars to the cost of the boat.

To keep the interior of the boat neat, the centerboard pennant comes up on deck through the center of the mast. This necessitates a complex mast step with transverse floors and a massive hat beam under the mast step to absorb compression. Add another few hundred dollars of engineering and construction.

If price was not a concern, perhaps this is little ground for complaint. However, the more complex a piece of construction is, the more subject it may be to failure, and the more expensive to repair or replace.

Tartan uses bronze ball valves on through hull fittings below the waterline. Exhaust line, cockpit scuppers, and bilge pump outlets are above the waterline, and have no shutoffs. The cockpit scuppers, which would be submerged while the boat is underway, should have provision for shutoff.

Handling Under Sail

Owners report that the Tartan 37 is a well-mannered boat under sail. The boat will not perform at the Grand Prix level, but she is no sluggard, either.

A large percentage of the boats were purchased for family cruising. On these boats, headsail roller furling systems are usually installed. Almost inevitably, there will be some sacrifice in windward performance with roller-furling headsails.

The optional inboard genoa track should be considered essential to those concerned with optimum windward performance. Coupled with the standard outboard track, this allows versatility in sheeting angles.

Headsail sheets and winches are within reach of the helmsman. This feature is vital for short-handed cruising, and can help make the difference between a boat that is easy for two people to handle, and one that is a pain. However, no real provision was made for the installation of secondary headsail winches, should you wish to carry staysails. Small winches could be mounted on the cockpit coamings forward, but they could well interfere with the installation of a dodger.

With good sails, performance of the Tartan 37 is not disappointing on any point of sail. Tartan brochures showed the 37 happily romping along on abeam reach in a 15 knot breeze. We suspect that under those conditions her owner is likely to be as happy as any sailor afloat.

Handling Under Power

The standard 41 horsepower Westerbeke 50 diesel is more than adequate power for the Tartan 37. The tendency in many production boats today is toward smaller, lighter, lower-powered diesels—the opposite of the past American boatbuilding practice, which, like our automobiles, tended toward excessive horsepower.

For a cruising boat, the mechanical power represented by a 40 horsepower engine in a 15,000 lb boat makes sense. The cruising boat needs the ability to punch into a head sea when necessary. Frankly, we prefer a boat to be slightly overpowered, rather than underpowered. We'll take the greater weight and the higher fuel consumption without complaint.

The engine box of the Tartan 37 is only partially sound insulated.

Access to the front end of the engine is good, by removing the companionway ladder. Access to the oil dipstick is another matter. To reach the oil dipstick, one must climb into the starboard cockpit locker. This necessitates removing much of what could be stored in that locker every time the oil is checked. If one is conscientious enough to check the oil every time the engine is run, a lot of loading and unloading will be required. In practice, it means that the oil level is unlikely to be checked regularly. Most sailboat owners rather shockingly neglect their engines. Making the oil dipstick inaccessible can only exacerbate that tendency toward neglect.

Deck Layout

With wide decks, inboard chainplates, and a relatively narrow cabin trunk, fore and aft movement on the deck of the Tartan 37 is relatively easy. It would be easier if the lifeline stanchions had been positioned further outboard, rather than about 3" inboard of the toerail.

There are proper bow chocks, and two well mounted cleats forward. However, a line led through the chocks to the cleats bears against the bow pulpit. Shifting the cleats further inboard would provide a better lead.

Surprisingly, there is no foredeck anchor well. This means that an anchor must be stowed in chocks on deck, if one is to be readily available. Then, you must face the problem of anchor rode storage. Molded foredeck anchor wells are becoming almost universal in modern boats. While the weight of anchor and rode—about 65 lbs in a boat this size—might be objectionable stowed all the way forward, the convenience of such a system generally outweighs the increase in pitching moment that might result. Removing the ground tackle from the deck also reduces clutter and toe stubbers, and simplifies foredeck work.

There are strong, well-mounted teak grabrails on top of the cabin trunk, although the reasoning for using two short rails on each side rather than a single long rail escapes us. The molded breakwater/cockpit coaming is a common Sparkman and Stephens feature, and greatly facilitates the mounting of a dodger—almost standard equipment on a cruising boat.

The T-shaped cockpit of the Tartan 37 is very comfortable for five while sailing. It has several unusual features. Rather than the usual unyielding fiberglass, there are teak duckboards on all cockpit seats. This means that you won't sit in a puddle when it rains, or when heavy spray comes aboard. These duckboards are comfortable, but they are held in

---

The forward cabin is very comfortable, with its own door to the head and plenty of room. In the main cabin, the fold-down table is a poor feature—hard to set up, and flimsy to boot.

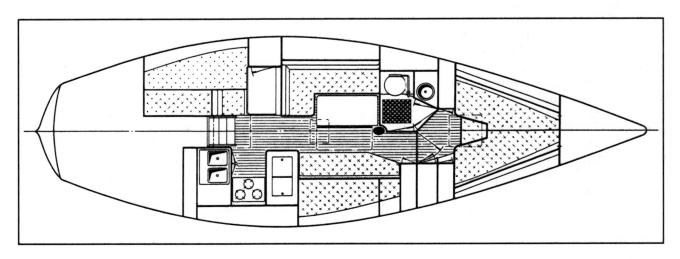

place only by wooden cleats, with the exception of the starboard seat. A more secure arrangement should have been provided for offshore sailing.

There is a teak-grated cockpit sump under the helmsman's feet. This shifts the cockpit drains inboard from the edge of the cockpit. The result is that a puddle can collect in the leeward corner of the cockpit when the boat is well-heeled in a blow, with heavy spray coming aboard.

Access to the steering gear is via the lazarette hatch. There is good provision for an emergency tiller, but the lazarette hatch must be held open in some way to use the emergency steering. There is a drop-in shelf in the lazarette which allows using the locker with less risk of damage to the steering system, but we would be reluctant to store anything small there that might possibly jam in the steering gear.

With a low cabin trunk, visibility from the helm is excellent. We suspect that many helmsmen would prefer a contoured seat to the flat bench provided, however. The relatively wide flat top of the cockpit coaming provides reasonably comfortable seating for the helmsman who prefers to sit well to leeward or well to windward.

The main companionway is narrow and almost parallel-sided—features we like—but the sill is much lower than we prefer for offshore sailing. The low sill facilitates passage of the crew below. Unfortunately, it also greatly facilitates passage of water below should the cockpit fill. Coupled with the thin plywood dropboards, we feel this is a potential weakness in watertight integrity, compromising the boat as an offshore cruiser. For offshore racing, for example, the Special Regulations require that the companionway be permanently closed up to the main deck level or the height of the lowest cockpit coaming.

Belowdecks

Due to an abundance of teak and teak plywood, the interior of the Tartan 37 is dark and cavelike. This is much the same criticism we have made of other well-finished boats. Mind you, it's a rather elegant cave, with excellent joinerwork throughout. Somehow, boat designers and builders have convinced most of the consuming public that teak is the only wood to use belowdecks. The fact is that there are many wonderful woods—ash and butternut, for example—that yield interiors that are lighter in both weight and color than teak.

The forward cabin of the Tartan 37 is truly comfortable for a boat of this size, with drawers, hanging lockers, separate access to the head, and enough room to dress in relative comfort. The completely louvered door separating the forward cabin from the main cabin looks nice, and does assist in ventilating the forward cabin. It limits privacy, however, and one good blow from a crew member caught off balance in a seaway would probably reduce it to a pile of teak toothpicks.

The head is quite comfortable, and it is possible to brace adequately for use offshore. The shower drains into a separate sump—not into the bilge.

Layout of the main cabin is conventional, with settee and pilot berth to starboard, dinette to port. Including a pilot berth on the starboard side necessi-

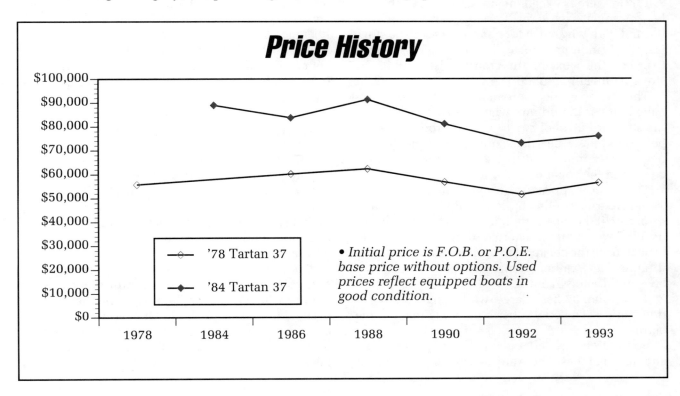

Price History

• Initial price is F.O.B. or P.O.E. base price without options. Used prices reflect equipped boats in good condition.

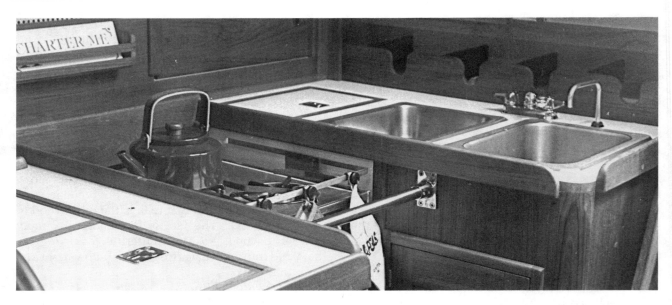

tates the complex chainplate arrangement mentioned earlier, for the berth prevents a simpler and cheaper bulkhead-mounted chainplate.

In what is a rather remarkable lapse in good design for such a boat, there is a bulkhead-mounted, fold-down cabin table. Pins in the bottom of the two legs must be inserted in corresponding holes in the cabin sole—no mean feat at anchor, and a ridiculous expectation offshore. The new Tartan 37 we examined already had a pockmarked cabin sole from setting up the cabin table for potential buyers. Metal plates recessed in the cabin sole would at least minimize the potential for damage here. Once set up, the table is disappointingly flimsy.

While there is excellent storage space in the galley, one must reach across the stove to reach much of it—and it's a long reach for a short person. The stove is securely mounted and has a grab bar across its well to protect the cook, but this grab bar also inhibits the stove's gimballing function.

There is no on-deck provision for storage of propane bottles, should you wish propane rather than the standard alcohol stove. There is room for CNG bottles in the starboard cockpit locker, but CNG has never really impressed us because of its bulkiness compared to propane.

The icebox appears to be well insulated. Why Tartan, like many other builders, fails to insulate and carefully fit the tops of their iceboxes totally escapes us. We have found this shortcoming on every variety of boat, from the cheapest to the most expensive, and it represents a rather strange disregard of the basic laws of thermodynamics.

The Tartan 37 has a large, well-designed navigation station. The quarterberth converts to a double berth.

Ventilation is excellent, with eight opening ports and three hatches. There are also four ventilators for the accommodations areas—two exhaust type and two low plastic cowls in dorade boxes. We think four taller cowls in the dorades would be more effective, or better still, the five tall cowls shown in the original plans for the boat. The vertical aft deckhouse bulkhead also allows a drop board to be left out when it rains, further improving ventilation.

Despite our complaints about the darkness of the interior, joinerwork is of excellent stock boat quality throughout.

The degree of enclosure of the interior of the hull can complicate access to deck hardware, and certainly does not facilitate survey of the vessel. In traditional wooden yacht construction, structural members are often left exposed for their intrinsic beauty, as well as for ventilation and preservation. In fiberglass boats, it is rather difficult to find intrinsic beauty in the structural material. Perhaps we are better off with it all hidden—as long as we know what holds the boat together. We certainly have confidence in what holds the Tartan together, even if we do pay a premium for that confidence.

Conclusions

The Tartan 37 is a well-built, well-mannered fast cruising sailboat. Like many S&S designs, there is a lot of complex engineering in the boat, which helped to boost the price. The boat also shows a generally high degree of finish, and a fair amount of attention to detail—perhaps more than most consumers are willing to pay for.

The Tartan 37 is a gray flannel Buick of a boat, the perfect banker's, lawyer's or stockbroker's boat. She's neither ostentatious nor plain. She is neither cheaply designed, nor cheaply built. One pays a lot for good breeding. Whether it is too much to pay is something only you, and the loan officer at your bank, can decide. • **PS**

Endeavour 37

She's comfortable and heavily built, but her performance leaves a lot to be desired.

Tampa Bay, in some respects, is the new Taiwan of American boatbuilding. Lost in the miles of nondescript tin warehouses, surrounded by chain link fences, where hundreds of virtually anonymous businesses come and go like the rain, it is easy to become disillusioned: My yacht was built *here*?

Relic molds lie about the dirty industrial zones like whitewashed bones. Riggers become salesmen. Salesmen become builders. Builders *never* become businessmen, which is about the only difference between Taiwan and Tampa. An eager, low-paid workforce (read Cuban), favorable business climate (low taxes), and sunny weather (considered 50% of an employee's compensation here) combine to make the environs of Florida's largest west coast city a logical place to rent a shed, buy some used tooling, hire a couple of glass men and a carpenter (there's a sort of floating labor pool in the Tampa area), and hang your shingle—I.M. Starstruck Yacht Co.

In the 1970s, Southern California—Costa Mesa more than any other city—was a major boatbuilding center. It was much the same as South Florida is today, until Orange County got tough on environmental emissions, and for the sake of a few parts per million of styrene fumes, essentially drove the boatbuilders out. Two early giants, Columbia Yachts and Jensen Marine (Cal boats) fled. Islander stuck it out until succumbing to bankruptcy just a few years ago.

Endeavour Yacht Corporation traces its lineage to those good ol' days in Costa Mesa. Co-founder Rob Valdez began his career at Columbia, managed, incidentally, by brother Dick Valdez, who later founded Lancer Yachts. Rob followed Vince Lazzara to Florida to work for Gulfstar. The other co-founder, John Brooks, had worked for Charley Morgan and then

Specifications

LOA	37' 5"
LWL	30' 0"
Beam	11' 7"
Draft	4' 6"
Displacement	21,000 lbs.
Ballast	8,000 lbs.
Sail area	580/640 (sloop/ketch)

Gulfstar and Irwin. "It's so incestuous," he once said, "it's pathetic."

In any case, Rob Valdez and John Brooks founded Endeavour in 1974 using the molds from Ted Irwin's 32-footer to launch the business. The company built about 600 32s in all. Spurred by this success, Valdez and Brooks began looking around for a larger sistership to expand the line. Just how they "developed" the 37 is a tale best left untold until the principals pass away or become too senile to read the yachting periodicals. Brooks calls the 37 a "house design," and that is generous. The total number of Endeavour 37s built is 476—a lot for a boat that size.

In 1986 Brooks sold the company to Coastal Financial Corporation of Denver, Colorado. Despite upgrading the pedigree of its model line with designs

Owners' Comments

"For what the boat is, it is a good value. Lots of room for the length. Well built, solid feel. Would like a better pointing boat, and larger, fewer berths. Otherwise very happy."

—1985 model in Manitowoc, WI

"Boat is a little slow, but otherwise sails well. We took out the electric refrigerator and put in an icebox—great move. Also eliminated the pilot berth for more storage."

—1981 model in Braintree, MA

"I live aboard and love the "A" plan layout. I like not having a V-berth. Very good, seakindly boat, put together very well. I spent four years looking for a Plan "A." Added an electric windlass, Cruisair heat pump, roller main and jib, 4KW generator and am very happy."

—1981 model in Norfolk, VA

"There's lots of weather helm in strong (20-knot) winds. Seems to be a design flaw. Nice use of teak inside and out. Very spacious belowdeck. Spacious cockpit, well suited for entertaining and coastal cruising. Not laid out for offshore, but I don't do that."

—1979 model in Lompoc, CA

"Not a pretty boat due to high freeboard and higher still cockpit coaming. Well built and luxurious if you care nothing for performance. Use your engine when going to windward. Can be bought cheaply."

—1981 model in Huntington, NY

by Johan Valentijn, Endeavour's position was plagued by declining sales and competition with its own products on the used boat market.

Brooks said, "When boats started to blister, I said, 'God's on our side! Maybe they'll disappear and go away. Everything else becomes obsolete—your car, your clothes. We're the only ones building a product that won't go away!' "

The Endeavour 37 represents a decent value for the cruising family more interested in comfort and safety than breathtaking performance. Let's take a closer look.

Sailing Performance

Most Endeavour 37s are sloop rigged, though the company did offer the ketch as an option—an extra $1,800 in 1977. The sloop is somewhat underpowered, so the ketch would appear to give the boat some much needed sail area. With either rig, it is not a fast boat, nor was it intended to be.

A bowsprit was added at one point to increase the foretriangle area and to facilitate handling ground tackle, though some photographs show the forestay still located at the stem despite the presence of an anchor platform, which was an earlier option. Also, a tall mast option was offered. Many readers complain of heavy weather helm in higher wind velocities, and moving the center of effort forward by means of enlarging the foretriangle would be one solution.

PHRF ratings range from a high of 198 for the standard rig in the Gulf of Mexico area, to 177 for a tall rig with bowsprit racing in Florida. PHRF ratings, of course, are adjusted according to local fleet performance, so variances between regions are to be expected. Most 37' club racers rate 10 to 40 seconds per mile faster, and a high-performance boat such as the Elite 37 or J/37 will clean its clock by 80 seconds per mile and more. Make no mistake, the Endeavour is a cruising boat.

Some of the boat's other troubles are presumably attributable to hull design, something most of us can do little about. The boat points no better, despite a fairly fine entry. One reader says he tacks through 115°, a number competitive only with schooners. Another notes excessive leeway.

Such performance may be expected from a boat with a long, shoal-draft keel, though it is cut away at the forefoot and terminates well forward of the spade rudder. Many owners report satisfactory balance as long as they pay attention to trim, reefing, and sail combinations. And it deserves mentioning that the Endeavour 37 has been happily employed as a charter boat by several companies, including Bahamas Yachting Services, which moves its fleet between the Bahamas and the Virgin Islands each season. It has and can make safe ocean passages.

Engine

The standard engine was the freshwater-cooled, 50-hp Perkins 4-108 with 2.5 to 1 reduction gear, a real workhorse that is something of a stick against which all others are measured. It rated tops among mechanics in *Practical Sailor*'s 1989 diesel engine survey. The company began phasing it out that year in favor of a new line. The Perkins 4-108 is a good engine for this boat, adequately sized for the waterline and displacement.

Access to the engine compartment is reasonable; the companionway steps are removable and there are sound insulating materials glued to the inside of the box.

Fuel capacity is about 65 gallons in a baffled tank.

A two-blade, bronze propeller was standard, though many respondents in our owner's survey stated they had switched to a three-blade to improve control backing down. This, of course, is a problem with many boats. A three-blade, automatically feathering prop would improve performance under power and minimize drag under sail. It seems a shame to further destroy the performance of this boat by turning a three-blade, fixed prop, just for control in reverse; at that point one must ask himself just how much time he intends to spend going backwards.

Construction

The Endeavour 37 is a good example of low-tech construction—nothing fancy—no exotic fibers, core materials or unusual tooling. The hull is a single-skin, solid fiberglass laminate. No owners reported structural problems with oilcanning panels or moving bulkheads. Numerous owners, however, complained of gelcoat crazing, a condition also cited of the Endeavour 32. Gelcoat repair kits seldom match old and faded gelcoat colors, so owners are faced with an expensive re-gelcoat job or painting with an epoxy or polyurethane paint system. Since most older fiberglass boats inevitably suffer gelcoat crazing in areas of stress or impact (a dropped winch handle will do it), we'd be more concerned with the condition of gelcoat below the waterline. The results of *Practical Sailor*'s 1989 Boat Owner's Questionnaire showed 8 of 19 Endeavours had blistered; 42% is high.

The interior is built up of plywood with teak trim. Workmanship is generally good. In fact, one owner who said his hobby is woodworking, said, "The trim joints are excellent." In general, owners liked the boat because it feels solid, "built like a tank."

Problem areas included gate valves on through-hulls, which some owners have correctly replaced with sea cocks; side-loading refrigerators on some boats that were replaced with top-loading ice boxes; pumping of the Isomat spar; inaccessible electrical wiring; V-berths too short for people over 6'; listing due to water and holding tank placement; and plastic Vetus hatches crazing and dripping. Ventilation seems to be a concern of many owners, though with 10 opening portlights and three hatches, there's not

The "A" interior plan (top) is popular with those who live aboard their boats; the "B" plan (bottom) was designed more with the charter trade in mind. Both arrangements have pros and cons.

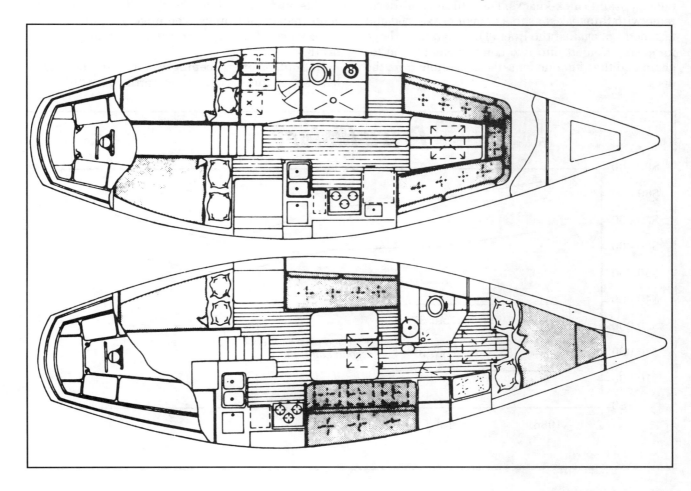

much more to be done except add cabin fans and rig wind scoops.

An Endeavour trademark is the teak parquet cabin sole, which makes you feel like you're dribbling down center court at the Boston Garden. Some like it, some don't, but at least it's different.

The keel is part of the hull mold, with internal lead ballast dropped in and glassed over. There are no keel bolts to worry about, but in the event of a grounding one should look to see if the skin has been punctured and water entered the cavity. The laminate must be thoroughly dried before repairs are made, and this can mean a fairly long waiting period. The shape of the keel is what is sometimes called a "cruising fin," shallow and long with a straight run. The boat should take the bottom well, whether it is an accidental grounding or intentional careening for bottom work on some distant island.

Interior

Two arrangement plans were offered—"A" and "B." The first is a bit unusual in that the forward V-berths are dispensed with in favor of an enormous U-shaped dinette; owners of this plan like it. In its lowered position, the table converts to a huge, sumptuous double berth.

And there is a handy shelf forward for books, television and knick-knacks. The hull sides are decorated with thin teak slats that are widely spaced and fastened flat against the liner. This plan has a large forepeak, divided into two compartments, one for chain and the after one for sails, accessible from the deck.

The galley is a sideboard affair located to starboard and the head is opposite to port, just about midships. Hot and cold pressure water and a shower are standard equipment. The sink is porcelain and there is a full-length mirror. Plumbing has copper tubing and there is an automatic shower sump pump. Aft in Plan "A" are two large double quarter berths.

Plan "B" is the more conventional, with V-berths forward (no sail stowage in the forepeak), the toilet compartment just abaft the head of the bunk, settees in the saloon with an offset dropleaf table, pilot berth outboard above the starboard settee, aft galley and a port quarter cabin.

There is a privacy door to this stateroom (not shown in the layout illustration), which is no doubt what the public demands; however, some owners complain that it is stuffy and cramped. That, of course, is what you get with a small, enclosed cabin aft in the boat; despite overhead hatches, vents, and portlight opening into the cockpit footwell, ventilation is bound to suffer.

There seem to be pros and cons to both plans. "A" is certainly more open, which will suit a couple with few overnight guests. Ventilation is better as air coming in through the forward deck hatch freely circulates in the main cabin; the main bulkhead in "B," as in most boats with this type of layout, obstructs air flow, and nowhere is this problem more acute than in the tropics, where every breath of ocean breeze feels like the difference between life and death.

Both plans offer sleeping accommodations for at least six, including decent sea berths. Plan "B" has a

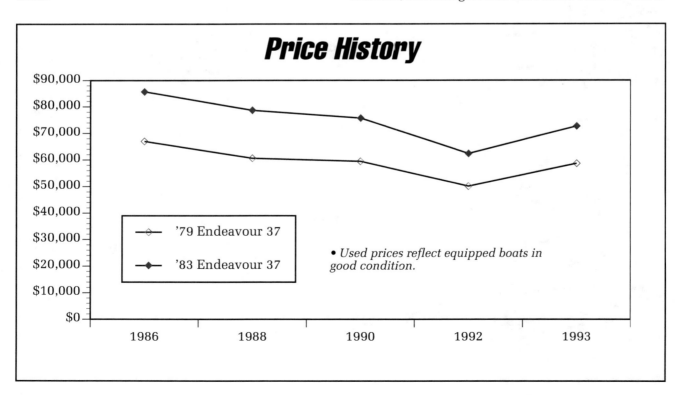

Used prices reflect equipped boats in good condition.

pilot berth that ups the count to seven, but most owners of this layout had converted it to stowage space.

The deep, double sinks in both "A" and "B" are reasonably close to the centerline of the boat, and should drain on either tack.

In the late 70s, a three-burner alcohol stove and oven was standard. On the boat we chartered for a week in the Bahama Islands, the stove was LPG and there was a nifty tank locker in the cockpit coaming, well hidden yet easily accessed. The garbage container and insulated beverage container in the cockpit are nice features.

Both plans also have chart tables, which of course is appreciated. The longer you study the arrangement plans, the more you realize just how much has been fitted into the available space. If any corners have been cut to make this happen it's probably the length of some berths, which a few owners criticized (presumably the endomorphs and Ichabod Cranes among us).

A high percentage of the owners surveyed are live-aboards and almost without exception they consider the boat ideal for their purposes. And it's not difficult to see why. During our week of chartering, there was plenty of space for two couples to move about without knocking elbows at every turn.

The aft cabin is, however, cramped, and getting into the high berth would be easier with a step; one is leery of jumping in, especially given the low overheads of boats. Also, one has to get his bottom on the berth first, then swivel around to get the feet aimed in the right direction. If your mate is already in bed, this can be a maneuver almost impossible to perform politely! The V-berths are preferred for ventilation and ease of getting in and out.

On Deck

The Endeavour 37 is easily appreciated on deck. The side decks are wide and uncluttered. The foredeck, though narrow at the bow, is adequate for sail handling, and the high cockpit coaming makes for a good backrest and a sense of protection. The toerail rises forward so that there is a sort of mini-bulwark for security when changing sails or handling ground tackle.

In profile, the coaming seems too high, especially on top of the high freeboard; one owner said he'd have liked to see an Endeavour 37 without this great, wraparound coaming.

From the helm it's a different story. The varnished cap board on the coaming defines the attractive curve, and does impart a feeling of safety and well being.

Coamings such as this, which extend over the sea hood (a good safety feature), make installation of a waterproof dodger much easier, though the dodger will be large and extend athwartship nearly the full beam of the boat at that station.

The large size of the cockpit is worth noting. In fact, it probably borders on being too large for offshore sailing. A pooping may temporarily affect handling, but given the considerable volume of the hull, the presence of a good bridgedeck, and assuming that weather boards are in place, water shouldn't get below or unduly sink the stern. Still, it is a boat we'd like to see with large diameter scuppers for safety's sake. One owner said he thought it was possible to run two large scupper hoses aft through the transom, which is a sensible idea. Another said the cockpit was too wide and that it was difficult to brace his feet when heeled.

Conclusion

The Endeavour 37 is a Florida boat. Windward sailing performance was purposely sacrificed for shoal draft, which is a requirement of cruising the Florida Keys and Bahama Islands. The cockpit is large and the deck area spacious.

Either you like the Endeavour 37's distinctive cockpit coaming or you don't; we found the cabintop area just abaft the coaming useful for stowing suntan lotion, hats and the usual cockpit clutter; in calm conditions, it even makes a fairly decent, elevated seat when you want to pontificate to the rest of the crew.

Sailing performance is marginal, especially upwind. The rig, however, is very simple and will seldom get the beginner in trouble, which explains the boat's appeal to charter companies. A light, nylon multi-purpose sail will be essential to light air performance, but it is probable that many owners turn on the engine when the wind drops below about 10 knots, and when going to windward to get that extra few degrees.

Our most serious concerns with the boat are, unfortunately, those that are uncorrectable. You can replace the gate valves with sea cocks, rewire the electrical system, even install flexible water and holding tanks to correct minor listing tendencies, but there's nothing practical that can be done about poor hull design.

One reader suggested fitting a hollow keel shoe to improve the boat's windward performance...hollow, he said, because the boat is heavy enough as it is. The boat also appears not to balance well, and though this tendency can be mitigated to some extent by mast rake and sail trim, it may well extend to the shape of the ends of the hull's waterline plane when heeled.

In all fairness, however, the Endeavour 37 is heavily built, reasonably well finished, comfortable to cruise and live aboard, and it sells for an attractive price. **• PS**

C & C Landfall 38

We've yet to find the perfect cruiser, but much of what we'd want can be found right here.

The C&C Landfall 38 was the midsize boat in the Canadian company's three-boat Landfall range, which also included a 35- and a 43-footer. This series was produced as a distinct line until 1987, when the Landfall name was dropped.

Unlike other C&Cs, whose interior and deck layouts are designed for racing as well as cruising, the Landfalls are geared toward cruising, with more comfort, a slightly higher degree of finish detail, and deck layout concessions to the cruising couple.

These are performance cruisers, however. Despite more wetted surface, more displacement, and a slightly smaller rig than the original C&C 38, the Landfall 38 is a fast boat, designed for cruisers who want to get there quickly, as well as in style.

The Landfall 38 is a direct descendant of the old C&C 38, the older hull design having been modified with slightly fuller sections forward, a slightly raked transom rather than an IOR reversed transom, a longer, shoaler keel, and a longer deckhouse for increased interior volume.

Nevertheless, the hull is more that of a sleek racer rather than a fat cruiser. For the additional performance that makes the boat a true performance cruiser, you trade off a hull volume that is slightly smaller than you would expect in a pure cruiser of the same waterline length. This is most notable in the ends of the boat, where the V-berth forward narrows sharply, and the hull rises so quickly aft that C&C's normal gas bottle stowage at the end of the cockpit is eliminated.

C&C was a pioneer in composite fiberglass construction. Balsa coring became synonymous with the company name over the years.

Construction

Construction of the Landfall 38 is typical of the C&C line. Hulls are a one-piece, balsa cored molding. The

Specifications

LOA	37' 7"
LWL	30' 2"
Beam	12' 0"
Draft	4' 11"
Displacement	16,700 lbs.
Ballast	6,500 lbs.
Sail area	648.5 sq. ft. (100% jib)

deck and the top of the cabin trunk are also balsa cored. Hull and deck are through-bolted with stainless steel bolts on 6" centers. The hull-to-deck bolts also serve as fasteners for the teak toerail, which replaces the familiar and businesslike slotted aluminum toerail used on other boats in the C&C line.

C&C used butyl tape as a compound in the hull-to-deck joint. Although this is a good, resilient bedding compound, it has no real structural properties. We would rather see an adhesive rubber compound such as 3M 5200 used in the joint to provide a chemical backup to the strong mechanical fastening.

The keel is an external lead casting, bolted to an integral keel sump. The keel is a fairly low aspect ratio fin, keeping the draft of the Landfall 38 to 5'. The keel is flat on the bottom, and the boat will stand on its keel, something that can't be said for a lot of fin keel boats.

All deck hardware is through-bolted, and is equipped with either backup plates or oversize washers. The relatively narrow hull-to-deck flange, however, means that some of the backup plates do not lie flat on the underside of the deck, as they bridge the narrow flange. This can result in uneven local stresses which can lead to gelcoat cracks in the vicinity of hardware such as lifeline stanchion bases.

The Landfall 38 uses bronze seacocks on all underwater through hull fittings. These are properly bolted to the hull, and their hoses are double clamped. The skin fittings are neither recessed flush to the hull nor faired in, however. This would be a fairly easy task for the owner.

In contrast to many boats, the mast step does not sit in the depths of the bilge where it can slowly turn to mush, taking the bottom of the mast with it. Rather, the mast step spans two deep floor timbers in the bilge sump, keeping the heel of the mast out of the water and providing stiffness in an area which is frequently too weak in fin keel boats.

Although most construction details are excellent, there are some shortcomings surprising on a boat of this quality. The engine compartment has no soundproofing, despite the fact that the engine sits a few feet from the owner's berth.

C&C construction is light but strong. The Landfall 38 is heavier than the old C&C 38 because of extra ballast, more interior joinerwork and molding, and a longer deck.

Handling Under Sail

Although the Landfall 38 is a cruising boat, her performance approaches or exceeds that of many production racer-cruisers. Her hull is basically an undistorted IOR shape, and the rig is a slightly shorter version of the old C&C 38 rig.

The Landfall is a full 2,000 lbs heavier than the original C&C 38. Nevertheless, there is relatively little difference in the performance of the two boats.

In typical C&C fashion, the rig is aerodynamically clean, with airfoil spreaders and Navtec rod rigging. Shroud chainplates—also Navtec—are set inboard for good upwind performance.

The large rig and big headsails of the Landfall may be intimidating to some cruising couples. The 100% foretriangle area of 385 square feet is pretty intimidating, since it means that the 150% genoa has an area of almost 580 square feet.

Because of the large foretriangle, the boat is a natural candidate for a good roller furling headsail system if it is to be cruised by a couple.

Main halyard, reefing, and cunningham lines are all led aft to the cockpit. Headsail halyards, however, lead to winches atop the cabin trunk just aft of the mast. This prevents the helmsman from assisting with headsails when the boat is sailed by a couple. This may or may not be a problem, depending on how agile the foredeck crew is. Since you can get two headsail halyards and two headsail halyard winches, a better solution might be to relocate one of the headsail winches aft, leaving the other near the mast. Then, headsail hoisting and dropping can be tailored to the particular crew's needs.

Surprisingly, self-tailing winches were not standard on the boat, except for the mainsheet winch. On an expensive boat which has hot and cold water as standard items, we'd certainly expect to see self-tailing genoa sheet winches, particularly if the boat is to be used for shorthanded sailing. Self-tailers make sail handling so much easier when cruising that they are just about the first thing we'd add to any cruising boat. And they'd be the biggest self-tailers we could fit on the winch islands.

The Landfall 38 is stiff and well-balanced under sail. Owners report that she is as fast or faster than similar boats of the same size. The Landfall 38's PHRF rating, for example, is 120, squarely between the 114 of the Cal 39 and the 126 of the Tartan 37— two boats to which the Landfall 38 will inevitably be compared in size, type, and price.

To our way of thinking, performance cruising is what it's all about. It's all well and good to have a heavy, underrigged boat if you're cruising around the world. Most people's cruising, however, is limited to a few weeks a year, with moderate distances between ports, and schedules that have to be met. A boat that will get you there fast, safely, and in comfort is a highly desirable type of boat for this kind of cruising. From a performance viewpoint, the Landfall 38 meets those requirements.

Handling Under Power

C&C was one of the first boatbuilding firms to introduce Yanmar diesels into the US market, and they stuck with Yanmar through thick and thin. Yanmar engines have been a paragon of reliability, but they have had the reputation for vibration and noise. Vibration has at times been so bad that engine mounts have broken and shafts have refused to stay in their couplings. It is always difficult to say in an engine installation whether the engine, the design of the installation, or the person doing the installation is at fault when there are problems. One Landfall 38 owner has had three prop shafts in his boat. Now, after careful matching of the shaft flanges and careful alignment of the engine, he reports satisfaction with the installation. C&C picked up a hefty bill on that one, but they did it without hesitation.

Careful engine and shaft alignment is a key to good engine performance, particularly in a modern boat with a short shaft and a flex-mounted diesel engine.

The 30 hp Yanmar 3HM, which replaced the 3QM in the Landfall 38, is perfectly adequate power for the boat, easily achieving hull speed. The boat handles well under power in either forward or reverse.

Engine access for service is a mixed bag. The engine is tucked well aft, under the cockpit, and drives the prop through a V-drive. The oil is checked by removing a panel in the quarterberth in the owner's cabin. The companionway ladder and a bureau next to it remove fairly easily for access to the back of the engine, although it will probably be necessary to empty the drawers before the bureau can be lifted out. The oil filter is reached by climbing down into the starboard cockpit locker. Once again, emptying the locker may be necessary.

Since there is no engine drip pan, you must exercise great care when changing oil and oil filters to keep the bilge clean. The engine is wedged so tightly under the cockpit sole that a funnel is required—with along hose—to add either oil or engine coolant. A partial plywood bulkhead that hangs over the engine complicates this, and could easily be cut away to give slightly better access.

Battery access is poor. A mirror is required to check electrolyte levels, and filling the batteries just about requires removing them from the battery boxes.

The standard prop is a solid two bladed wheel. To reduce the considerable drag of this installation, we'd change to either a folding two bladed prop such as a Martec, or a feathering prop such as the Maxprop.

Deck Layout

Although the deck layout of the Landfall 38 is similar to that of other boats in the C&C line—performance oriented—some changes have been made to make the boat more suited to cruising. The stern rail incorporates a fold down swimming ladder, and the bow pulpit is the walk-through type, suited to tying up bow-to at the dock. The bow pulpit also incorporates international style running lights, rather than the running lights mounted in the topsides that were a C&C trademark for years. Thank God for progress.

Unfortunately, the wiring for the running lights is relatively unprotected inside the anchor locker, and the electrical connections there are simple butt splices with no weathersealing.

The anchor locker has strong hinges, but lacks a positive latch. There is also no means of securing the bitter end of the anchor rode. Prudent owners will install an eyebolt or through-bolted padeye.

A new stainless steel stemhead fitting incorporates bow rollers for both chain and rope. There is no provision for a keeper pin in the bow roller, however, and the cheeks of the fitting do not extend high enough to guarantee that the rode will not jump out of the roller when the boat pitches at anchor.

With the shrouds set well inboard, fore and aft access is excellent. There are handrails along the cabintop, and a stainless steel guardrail over the forward dorade boxes to keep headsail sheets from fouling.

C & C managed to cram three cabins into the Landfall 38 with fair success, and was even able to include an enclosed head with separate shower stall. The nav station and owner's cabin aft of the head need some protection from the weather, however: if the companionway is left open under sail, spray could get below and ruin everything from charts to instruments to bedding.

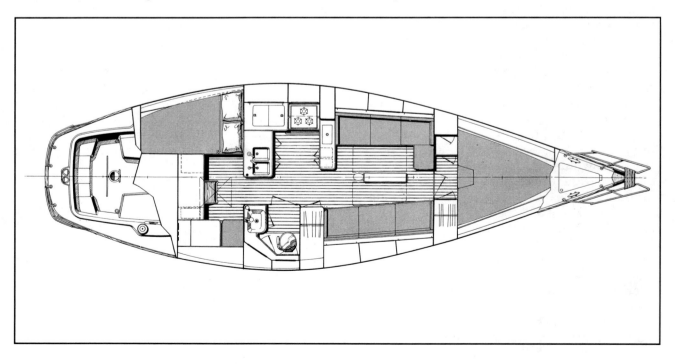

A few Landfall 38s were built with teak decks. This $10,000 option really makes the boat elegant, and is practical underfoot.

Although this is a cruising boat, there is no molded coaming for the attachment of a cockpit dodger, except a small lip around the companionway hatch. Admittedly, leading all sail controls aft along the cabin top complicates the installation of a dodger, but it can be done. Of course, the dodger can be installed even without a breakwater, but it won't be as effective in keeping water out of the cockpit.

The cockpit is a fairly typical T-shaped C&C design. A large-diameter Edson wheel makes it possible for the helmsman to sit to weather or to leeward, but requires making the cockpit seats too short to lie on. On some C&C models, molded seats in the aft corners of the cockpit serve both to support the helmsman's seat and as storage for propane bottles. On the Landfall 38, the cockpit has been pushed so far aft—because of the longer deckhouse—that the hull is too shallow under the aft end of the cockpit for the traditional gas lockers. A separate molded bottle locker that fits under the helmsman's seat is installed when a gas stove is used. Unfortunately, this eliminates the normal life raft storage position. Owners who want both propane and a life raft are going to have to figure out another place to stow the life raft.

A shallow locker under the port cockpit seat is handy for small items, and there is a deep locker under the starboard seat. Changing oil filters requires climbing down into this locker, as does adjusting the stuffing box.

The forward end of the cockpit is protected by a good bridgedeck. Although the companionway is slightly off center, it is not enough to be concerned about in heavy weather. The companionway has other problems, however. Since the bulkhead slopes forward, the drop board must be left in place when it rains. Also, since the bottom of the companionway is below the top of the cockpit coamings, ORC requirements demand that it be left in place when racing offshore. Although this isn't a racing boat, the ORC requirements make good guidelines for offshore cruising practices. Because the drop board is a single teak-faced plywood board, in either situation the companionway must be all the way closed—or left all the way open.

The companionway sill has no lip, so that water can enter the cabin under the drop board. This is a simple fix for owner or factory. The prudent owner will also install a barrel bolt to secure the drop board in place when sailing offshore.

Belowdecks

C&C's interior designs are among the best in the business, and the interior of the Landfall 38 is no exception. The preponderance of teak is a little overwhelming, but it is varnished, rather than oiled, making it slightly lighter than you might expect.

It takes quite a bit of ingenuity to cram a three-cabin interior and huge head with separate shower stall into a 38' boat. In the Landfall 38, this has been accomplished with a reasonable amount of success.

The forward cabin has the usual V-berth, drawers, several lockers, and a cedar-lined hanging locker. This hanging locker is the only really usable hanging

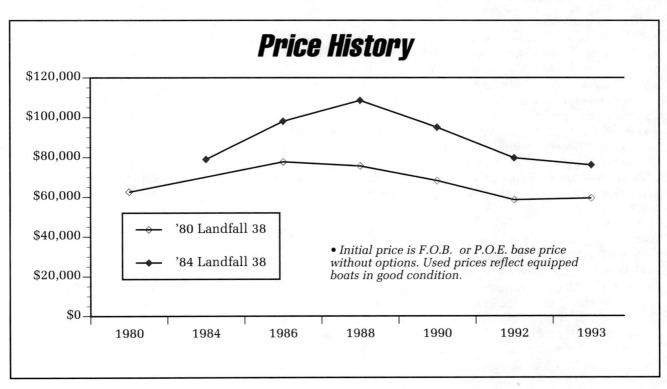

Initial price is F.O.B. or P.O.E. base price without options. Used prices reflect equipped boats in good condition.

space on the entire boat, despite the existence of a rudimentary hanging locker in the aft cabin.

A large hatch over the forward cabin can be used as an escape hatch; a single step is mounted on the bulkhead to make it possible to climb out the hatch. There is solid 6' headroom in the forward cabin, and enough standing room for comfortable dressing. The V-berth, however, is too pointed at the foot for reasonable comfort for two tall people. There are reading lights over each side of the berth, and a light in the hanging locker—a welcome feature.

The main saloon begins aft of the forward cabin, with no intervening head compartment.

Lighting and ventilation of the Landfall 38 is about the best we've seen in a production boat. Both fluorescent and incandescent fixtures are located throughout the main cabin. Remember that you should not use fluorescent lights when you are operating the Loran, as the RF noise of fluorescent lights may interfere with signal acquisition.

The main cabin, galley, and head are ventilated by four large cowl vents in dorade boxes, plus small opening hatches in head and galley. C&C gets an A+ for ventilation in this boat.

Water tanks are located under the main cabin settees, where they belong. Unfortunately, these tanks vent to the outside of the hull, risking contamination of the water supply. This is a common fault in American production boats, and one with no real justification. We'd rather risk spilling a little water in the inside of the boat by overfilling the tanks than risk salt water in our fresh water supply from water siphoning into the tanks in heavy weather through vents mounted in the topsides.

The Landfall 38 uses molded polyethylene water tanks. Occasionally, these tanks are "overcooked" during manufacture, imparting an unpleasant taste to the water that cannot be removed. We've seen it on more than one boat, including C&Cs.

Fresh water plumbing is butyl tubing rather than the more commonly seen clear PVC. Butyl is far less likely to impart any taste to your water, and is highly desirable. It is easily recognized by its battleship gray color and relative rigidity. A manifold under the sink allows switching between the three water tanks, which have a total capacity of 99 gallons. In addition, the 30 gallon holding tank could easily be replumbed as a fresh water tank, giving a very respectable water capacity properly distributed throughout the boat.

In typical C&C fashion, the galley is well laid out and well executed, with deep centerline sinks, kickspace under the counters, and a large icebox. The icebox lid is insulated (hurray!) but ungasketed (boo!), and the icebox melt water is pumped overboard (hurray!) rather than draining into the bilge.

Counter space is excellent. In an attempt to get more, a fold-down counter is fitted over the stove.

Unfortunately, it must be folded up when the stove is in use, making the locker behind the stove inaccessible. Since the boat already has good counter space, we'd eliminate the folding nuisance.

The standard stove is a large gimballed alcohol affair. Don't even consider it. Get either the optional propane installation, or the optional CNG stove. Alcohol has no business as a cooking fuel on any boat to be used as a serious cruising boat.

The stove recess is protected by a stainless steel grabrail which gives the cook a handhold and prevents him from being thrown against the stove in a seaway. A counter with built-in bottle storage separates the galley from the main cabin.

Generally, the galley is usable at sea or at anchor, with excellent storage, usable spaces, and functional appliances. Hot and cold pressure water is standard, and a backup fresh water foot pump is provided at the galley sink.

The main cabin table is strongly mounted to both cabin sole and mast, and easily—and honestly—serves six at dinnertime. Port and starboard settees can be used for sleeping, although the backrests at the head and foot of each settee will have to be removed and stored somewhere for anyone over about 5'8" tall.

Storage is provided outboard of each settee. The handy owner will install shelves in these lockers to better utilize the space.

Opposite the galley is a huge head complete with separate shower stall. The sink and counter are a single fiberglass molding with a large sink and a high protective lip, making this part of the head infinitely more usable than the usual tiny oval sink.

Although at first glance there appears to be a great deal of storage in the head, much of the locker space is occupied by plumbing. The only locker really suited for linens is located in the shower stall, and is equipped with a latch which must be reached through a finger hole in the locker door. Water will inevitably find its way into this locker. The locker could easily be fitted with another type of catch, and ventilation holes could be bored through to the head compartment to help prevent mildew. The separate shower stall will make those unused to boat living far more comfortable, although some might prefer the additional storage space the boat had before the separate stall appeared.

Oddly, the water closet is tucked so far under the side deck that it's impossible to sit upright on it. While you may argue that few people sit upright on the toilet, there will be plenty of cracked crania before you get used to the required position.

Another oddity is that the head door is louvered. Admittedly, there is little privacy in the head on any boat. Since the Landfall's head is already well-vented by a cowl vent and an opening hatch, we'd eliminate the louvered head door to restore at least a bit of privacy.

The aft cabin makes a good owner's stateroom, with large double quarterberth to port and chart table to starboard. Unfortunately, the chart table makes a better dressing table than chart table. There is no provision for the installation of instruments such as radio or Loran in the nav area. A shallow hanging locker occupies the space outboard of the chart table where these instruments would normally be mounted. It's a poor hanging locker, since the garments face thwartships rather than fore and aft. The only thing you can see is the last item you put in. It is unusable as a wet locker, since you'd have to drag your foul weather gear over the chart table.

For serious cruising, we'd eliminate this hanging locker, using the space to mount radios, Loran, repeaters, and provide a bookcase for our navigation books. This has the serendipitous byproduct of allowing the shallow chart table to be made deeper, which it sorely needs.

What about hanging space? Well, here goes. Make the linen locker in the shower a hanging locker by eliminating or reducing the size of the holding tank under it. Or (we can see marketing people putting guns to their heads), eliminate the separate shower stall and create more storage. So much for redesign.

In the way of modifications, however, the nice double quarterberth is going to get soaking wet the first time a big one comes over the weather rail and water pours through the companionway when the boat is on starboard tack. In the same situation on port tack, the chart table will get soaked. A set of plexiglass screens on either side of the companionway should solve that one, and should be considered if the boat is to be used offshore. For shorthanded cruising, that quarterberth is the ideal place for the off watch, provided it can be kept dry. The necessity for keeping the sacrosanct nav station and its fragile electronics—and equally fragile navigator—out of the weather should be obvious.

The basic interior layout of the Landfall 38 is excellent for the cruising couple that likes a private cabin aft, and will sometimes entertain others for extended periods of time. As with most boats, a certain amount of fine tuning of interior spaces will be necessary to get the most out of them. The boat has a fair number of complex systems: hot and cold water, electric pumps, multiple tanks. In fact, the 16 circuits provided for in the electrical panel are almost all used up before you get to things like navigation and performance electronics. Fortunately, there is space for an additional electrical panel. You're probably going to need it.

Conclusions

With an average used price for a 1984 model at around $70,000, the Landfall 38 is not a cheap way to go cruising. The price is typical of luxury performance cruisers in its class.

General design and construction are excellent. The hull is a proven design, the rig is efficient and strong. There are a number of design details that should be improved for serious cruising, notably the companionway, cockpit protection, life raft storage, and provision for shorthanded handling under sail.

A serious cruising boat must function as well bashing to windward for days on end as it does at the dock. Above all, it must keep its crew dry and comfortable. We have yet to find the perfect cruising boat, but many of the things we'd look for are found in the Landfall 38. We wish they were all there, but the fact that they aren't is what keeps designers and builders in business.   • **PS**

Morgan 38 and 382

Charlie Morgan's hurrah becomes Ted Brewer's success story becomes today's pseudo-classic.

We receive many requests from readers to review certain boats. Almost without exception, the requests come from owners of the boat suggested. Few boats have been the object of more requests than the venerable Morgan 38. At first blush, it is difficult to determine which Morgan 38 we ought to address, as two distinct designs were built since the first one appeared 22 years ago. After some thought, we decided to trace the history of both as best we could, including also the Morgan 382, 383 and 384.

History

The Morgan 38 was designed in 1969 by Charlie Morgan. He had founded Morgan Yacht Company in St. Petersburg, Florida, in 1965. The Morgan 34 was his first production model. A hometown boy, he had made a name for himself in the 1960 and 1961 Southern Ocean Racing Conference (SORC), winning with a boat of his own design called *Paper Tiger*. While not a formally trained naval architect, Morgan demonstrated his skill with a variety of designs. Many of these were keel/centerboard models, owing to the shoalness of Florida waters. Seventy-nine were built before production halted in 1971.

In 1977, the Morgan 382 was introduced, designed by Ted Brewer, Jack Corey and the Morgan Design Team. According to Brewer, the boat was loosely based on the Nelson/Marek-designed Morgan 36 IOR One Ton. The most obvious difference between the 38 and 382 was the elimination of the centerboard and the addition of a cruising fin keel (NACA 64 012 foil) with skeg-mounted rudder. They are two completely different designs from two different eras in yacht design.

In 1980, the 382 was given a taller rig and called the 383. About 1983 the boat underwent other subtle

Specifications - 38

LOA	37' 8"
LWL	28' 0"
Beam	11' 0"
Draft	3' 9"/8' 4" (board up/down)
Displacement	16,000 lbs.
Ballast	7,500 lbs.
Sail area	640/681 (sloop/yawl)

changes, now called the Morgan 384. The rudder was enlarged and the interior modified. In its three versions, the Brewer model registered about 500 sales.

The company changed ownership several times during this period. It went public in 1968, was later bought by Beatrice Foods and then Thor Industries. Presently it is owned by Catalina Yachts, who built just 24 38s (three were kits) before discontinuing production in 1986.

Design

The first Morgan 38 was a development of the highly successful 34, which Morgan called a "beamy, keel-centerboard, CCA (Cruising Club of America)-style of yacht. We had a good thing going and didn't want to deviate; we found little interest in those days in

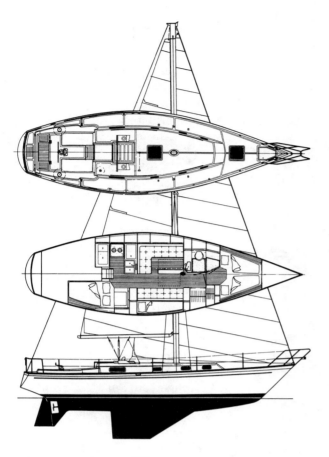

Specifications - 382

LOA	38' 4"
LWL	30' 6"
Beam	12' 0"
Draft	5' 0"/6' 0" (std/deep keel)
Displacement	18,000 lbs.
Ballast	6,800 lbs.
Sail area	668 sq. ft.

keel boats. Centerboards have their own sorts of problems, but there's an awful lot of thin water in the world, and safe refuge and quiet anchorages are mostly in shoal water."

The boat has a long, shoal keel drawing just 3' 9" with the board up. The rudder is attached and there is an aperture for the propeller. "Beamy," in 1969, meant 11 feet. The waterline was fairly short at 28 feet, but the overhangs give the hull a very balanced and pleasing profile. The stern is pure Charlie Morgan—a finely proportioned shape that is neither too big nor too small. In profile, the angle between the stern (which interestingly is a continuation of the line of the backstay) and the counter is nearly 90 degrees. It's a trademark look.

Sloop and yawl rigs were offered, which was typical of CCA designs. The rig has a lower aspect ratio (the proportion of the hoist to the foot of the mainsail) than later designs, including the Brewer-designed 382. Yet this is a very wholesome rig for cruising. Owners responding to our questionnaire said the boat balances very well.

Owners of the 382 and subsequent permutations seemed less pleased. They didn't rate balance as highly, noting most frequently the difficulty in tracking (keeping the boat on a straight course) when sailing off the wind (not uncommon with beamy fin keel designs; it's a trade-off with speed, pointing ability and maneuverability). Others said that they raked their masts forward to improve balance. One thought the problem was caused because the rudder was slightly undersized. Still, these owners liked the way their boats sail.

The rig, of course, isn't the only difference between the Morgan and Brewer designs. The latter has a foot wider beam—12 feet—and a longer waterline. Two keels were offered, the standard five-foot draft and an optional deep keel of six feet. Displacement jumped a thousand pounds to 17,000 despite a reduction in ballast from 7,500 pounds to 6,600 pounds. Centerboard boats, naturally, require more ballast because it isn't placed as low as it is in a deep fin keel boat.

The look of the 382 is much more contemporary. The rake of the bow is straighter, as is the counter, which is shorter than the original 38 as well. Freeboard is higher and the windows in the main cabin are squared off for a crisper appearance.

Construction

The hulls of the early 38s were built of solid fiberglass and the decks of sandwich construction. Some 382 hulls were cored, others not. A variety of core materials were used, mostly Airex foam. The lamination schedule was your basic mat and woven roving, with Coremat added as a veil cloth to prevent print-through.

Both designs have internal lead ballast, sealed on top with fiberglass.

The early 382s did not have the aft bulkhead in the head fiberglassed to the hull, which resulted in the mast pushing the keel down. All boats "work" under load, and bulkheads bonded to the hull are essential to a stiff structure. Anyone who has a boat in which major load-bearing bulkheads are not attached to the hull should do so before going offshore. To its credit, the company launched a major recall program.

The owners of all Morgan 38s, as a group, note the strength of the boat. One said he hit a rock at 6 1/2 knots and suffered only minor damage. Very few problems were mentioned. The owner of a 1981 model, however, said he "drilled through hull at

Owners' Comments

"One of the best combinations of design, workmanship, strength, sailing characteristics available. I live aboard. I know of no other sailboat new or used that offers the knowledgable sailor as much for the money."

—1972 model in Florida

"To my knowledge, the only problem areas have been centerboard cables and the mast foot where it sets on the keel. They don't build hulls and decks that thick anymore."

—1970 model with two Transatlantic crossings

"It is among the finest of the vessels our family has owned. I am a construction engineer and can appreciate the quality."

—1983 model in Connecticut

"She is a great boat to cross the Gulf Stream. A little too much draft for cruising in the Abacos—but you can't have both. She is holding up well in the charter business."

—1980 model in Florida

"The accessibility to the engine leaves a lot to be desired."

—1970 model in Florida

---

waterline and was surprised at thinness of glass on either side of the Airex: 1/8" inside, 1/16" outside." With the stiffness that sandwich construction provides, not as much glass is required; still, protection from collision and abrasion would recommend greater thickness outside. Brewer, incidentally, discounted the report.

Interestingly, Hetron-brand fire-retardant resin was used for a time, prior to 1984; if you recall, this was blamed for the many cases of reported blistering on the early Valiant 40s. About half of the 382 owners responding to our surveys reported some blistering, none serious.

The attached rudder of the early 38 is stronger than the skeg-mounted rudder of later models. But we do prefer the skeg configuration to a spade rudder, at least for cruising. A problem with skegs, however, is the difficulty in attaching them strongly to the hull. One owner said his was damaged in a collision with a humpback whale, but that is hardly normal usage!

Several owners of later models commented that the mast was a "utility pole," recommending a custom tapered spar for those inclined to bear the expense.

Other problems reported in our survey were only minor and were corrected by the company. In fact, owners were nearly unanimous in their praise for Morgan Yachts' customer service.

Interior

The layout of the Morgan 38 is quite conventional and workable. In both incarnations there are V-berths forward, private head with shower (separate enclosure in the 382), dinette in main cabin with settee, galley aft in the port quarter area and nav station with quarter berth opposite to starboard.

Specifications for the first 38s included "attractive wood-grained mica bulkhead paneling, with oiled American walnut trim." This was a popular treatment in the 1960s, and practical, but often done to excess. By the 1980s, fake teak didn't play so well. Owners wanted real wood, and that's what they got in the 382.

Owners of early 38s complained of poor ventilation ("I added six opening ports, and would like an additional center cabin hatch," wrote one), short V-berths ("Could be 4" longer, but I'm 6' 2.""), and more closet space (from a live-aboard).

Owners of later models mentioned the need for a larger forward hatch to get sails through, a hatch over the galley, larger cockpit scuppers, and Dorade vents. (Teak Dorade boxes were added on the 384.) They complained of not enough footroom in the V-berths and poor location of the main traveler in the cockpit. (The traveler was moved to the cabinhouse top on the 384.)

Despite these minuses, most owners cite the volume of the interior and many stowage compartments as major reasons for their satisfaction with the boat.

Performance Under Sail

As implied in our comments on balance in the "Design" section of this review, the centerboard 38 sailed beautifully. She is dry and seakindly, stable and relatively fast for her generation. Its PHRF rating ranges from 145 to about 150. The yawl rig is probably not as fast as the sloop, but for the cruising couple, the mizzen sail gives the skipper another means of balancing the boat, as well as a means to fly more sail when reaching if he's prepared to fuss with a staysail.

The 382 rates between 128 and 150, about 137 on average. The Morgan 383 and 384, which are grouped together, rate a mite lower at 135, on average.

It is not surprising that Brewer's redesign is faster, even though it's 1,000-2,000 pounds heavier. This is due to it's deeper fin and higher aspect rig with the ability to carry larger headsails. There is also less wetted surface.

Performance Under Power

The centerboard 38 was powered by the seemingly ageless Atomic Four gasoline engine, though a Perkins 4-107 or Westerbeke 4-107 was available at extra cost ($1,940 in 1969). The early 38s cruise at about 6 1/2 knots.

A first-generation Yanmar—the 3QM30—was used on some 382s, and as owners of those engines know, they tend to be noisy and vibrate a great deal. Yanmar engines improved a great deal after the manufacturer redesigned and retooled the entire line. But the most common powerplant was the magnificent 50-horsepower Perkins 4-108. If we were looking for a Morgan 38 to purchase, we'd certainly lean toward one with this engine.

Both designs handle reasonably well under power, as well as most sailboats do, meaning that backing down with a two-blade prop is a necessarily cautious procedure.

A number of owners recommend changing to a three-blade prop, but that will affect sailing performance. One should examine his sailing style closely before making the move.

Conclusion

The Morgan 38, in any incarnation, is a handsome boat that sails well and is built strong enough for most people's purposes. Some may pause before taking a centerboard boat far offshore, but it has certainly been done—recall, if you will, Carleton Mitchell's hugely successful racer *Finnisterre*.

Both centerboard and fin keel versions seem to us to have advantages and disadvantages that are essentially tradeoffs.

On the one hand, we like an attached rudder for cruising, as it provides the best protection from collision with logs and other hard objects. On the other, we recognize the importance of placing ballast low, as in the fin keel version, and we appreciate Brewer for giving a nice slope to its leading edge so that damage from hitting logs will be minimized. Brewer said that a 382 that passes survey is capable of cruising just about anywhere. "They've crossed oceans," he said.

To our eye, we admit to being fond of the CCA designs with low freeboard and graceful sheer lines. The yawl is a versatile rig that is especially attractive, though it does require more in the way of tuning and maintenance.

An early Morgan 38, in good condition, should sell in the high 20s. Expect to pay a thousand or so more for the yawl. For sellers, considering that in 1969 the base price of the boat was $22,995, that's not a bad return on investment.

Fifteen years later the price had jumped to $84,995 (1984 model). Those boats today are advertised in the mid to high 60s, and occasionally the low 70s. (What anyone is actually getting for these days is another matter entirely).

Considering the changes in the economy, that's still not bad performance. What it means most to the prospective buyer is that the Morgan 38 and 382 are popular, much admired boats that should, we expect, hold their value as well as or better than most others. • **PS**

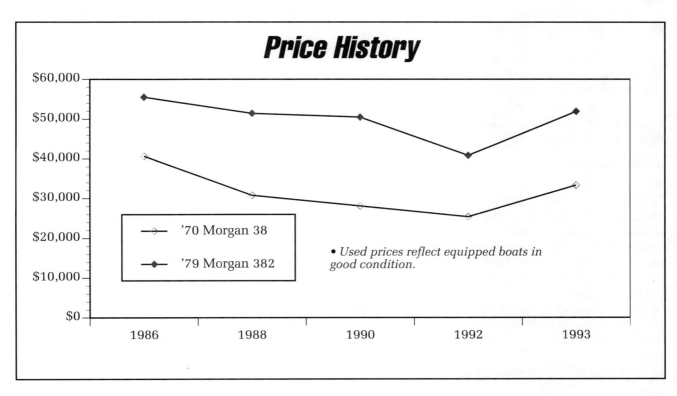

Price History

• *Used prices reflect equipped boats in good condition.*

Legend: —◇— '70 Morgan 38   —◆— '79 Morgan 382

Sabre 38

This stylish sloop with an all-wood interior is a premium fin-keel, spade-rudder club racer.

Sabre Yachts of South Casco, Maine, was founded by Roger Hewson in 1970. Its first boat was the Sabre 28, whose quick acceptance by the public was a portent of good things to come for the fledgling company. In the following years, Sabre built boats up to 42 feet in length. Hewson's formula was to design and build to a curious blend of contemporary hull shapes and traditional interior styling. At one point in time, during the mid-1980s, Sabre was probably the largest builder of production fiberglass boats with built-up wooden interiors. Others, such as Pearson, C & C, O'Day, Hunter, Catalina, et. al., used molded fiberglass pans for furniture foundations. Many custom builders use all-wood, but at about 125 boats per year during its heyday, Sabre built the most. In 21 years, the company built about 1,800 boats.

Unfortunately, Sabre recently joined the growing list of defunct American builders. The company ceased production in January after its major creditor withdrew its line of credit, forcing Sabre to close its doors. A number of boats were claimed by the bank.

The Design

The Sabre 38, like all Sabres, was designed by Roger Hewson and his in-house team. It was introduced in 1982, with an aft-cabin (still with an aft cockpit) version available the next.

In 1986 the boat was redesigned, informally referred to as the Mark II. While this report focuses primarily on the early design, we will touch on some of the changes found in the 1986 redo.

Any builder wishing to produce lots of boats must offer its customers a design that does many things well. It cannot be a flat-out racer, or a lumbering cruiser.

This generally translates to moderate displace-

Specifications - Mk I

LOA	37' 10"
LWL	31' 2"
Beam	11' 6"
Draft	6' 6"
Displacement	15,200 lbs.
Ballast	6,400 lbs.
Sail area	688 sq. ft.

ment, long waterline, fin keel and spade rudder. And so it is with the Sabre 38.

The Sabre 38 has a waterline length of 31' 2" and the choice of a deep, fixed keel or keel/centerboard configuration. A partial shallow skeg provides some support for the rudder to swing on. Sabre called the skeg a Tracker™, saying it improves directional stability.

The coachroof has a fairly low profile with 12 windows and portlights. The 38 has a curious little step-down in the coachroof, which disappeared in the Mark II. Steps were not uncommon in older designs, but today, cleaner lines are favored.

Beam of the early 38 was a relatively modest 11' 6", widened to 12' 4" in the Mark II. Neither is so extreme as to produce unusual handling characteristics.

Owners' Comments

"Best ventilated boat I have seen. Self-bleeding feature of the Westerbeke 33 is a real boon! Refrigerator is too close to the engine for good efficiency. Standard head not up to overall quality of boat. We had a Wilcox Imperial substituted. Varnished interior we now have is far superior to the oiled teak. With offset shaft, boat needs a folding prop for top performance under sail."

—1983 model in Connecticut

"The 150-percent genoa needs to be furled early. If you're not racing, use 135-percent genoa instead."

—1982 model in New York

"Trim affected by amount of water in port and starboard tanks. Even though this is rigged as a racing boat, it is easy for two people to sail and even use the spinnaker in up to 12 to 16 knots of wind."

—1983 model in Michigan

"A true delight to sail in strong winds and seas, or light winds. I would prefer an annodized spar as Awlgrip chips easily. Would prefer a varnished interior. Earliest production models have a much poorer icebox design and do not have a molded fiberglass head compartment. When buying, be sure to have weight balanced due to installation of extra equipment (my boat has starboard list)."

—1989 model on Chesapeake Bay

"I recommend the boat highly. Design, construction and attention to small detail are outstanding. Design and tall rig produce good boat speed in the lighter airs. I wish the boat was not quite so tender, but that's the price for speed and high pointing ability."

—1984 model in Florida

"The crew at Sabre cared about their owners, whether their boats were purchased new or used."

—1982 model in Maine

The hull is fairly shallow, with firm bilges, as is typical of this type. The displacement/length (D/L) ratio is 224. For the sake of comparison, the performance-oriented J/40 has a D/L ratio of 199 and the Hunter Legend 40 226. The Cabo Rico 38 cruiser, with much slacker bilges, has a D/L ratio of 375 and the Caliber 38 293. So you can see that the Sabre 38 is intended to sail fairly fast.

One consequence of moderate to light D/L ratios is the necessity of locating the water tanks under settees rather than on centerline, deep in the keel. This robs precious stowage space and makes trim calculations important.

In fact, several owners said their boats had pronounced lists, especially if they didn't carefully monitor tank levels. This is regrettable and somewhat difficult to understand in a boat of this size, quality and price.

The bow, viewed in profile, is a straight line with an aggressive rake. The reverse stern on the early 38 is conservative; on the Mark II it was given additional rake and convexity for a more modern look.

Beauty lies in the eye of the beholder, but we will say we prefer the lines of the Mark II, largely due to the improved stern shape, the absence of the step in the coachroof, and the ever-so-slight slope to the forward end of it.

Construction

Before about the mid-1980s, all Sabres were built of solid fiberglass, with balsa-coring only in the deck. All of the later designs incorporate balsa coring in all or parts of the hull.

Hence, the early 38 was built without a core and the Mark II has a balsa core. We have in the past had some misgivings about the use of balsa coring below the waterline, not because water entering through a crack might migrate across the grain (it doesn't), but because moisture does enter most laminates and may wet the endgrains, potentially contributing, along with fatigue, to delamination.

Fiberglass skins in sandwich construction (on either side of the core) are by design much thinner than a single-skin hull, and while the sandwich is very stiff, the outer skin won't endure abrasion (say, grinding on a beach or rock) as long. Also, balsa-cored boats, especially for the long-distance cruiser, are more difficult to repair.

We think the newer balsa-cored boats are quite good. We'd consider one for coastal cruising, and think balsa or foam core is mandatory for a competitive race boat. For serious cruising, however, we'd stick with a single-skin, solid glass hull.

In a survey of readers' boats several years ago, we reported that Sabre had a below-average incidence of blistering—about 19 percent.

Still, a few readers completing our Boat Owner's Questionnaire stated their boats had blistered, none seriously. Not surprisingly, Hewson elected in the Mark II edition to use Blisterguard gelcoat and immediately inside it a layer of chopped strand glass fibers and vinylester resin.

Vinylester resins, as we reported in our June 15, 1991 report on barrier coatings, are superior in preventing the ingress of moisture through the laminate. The reason for using chopped strand fiber is that it may be sprayed from a gun, eliminating the sizing used to hold the random fibers together in chopped strand mat (CSM); the sizing is highly suspected in the formation of some forms of blistering.

Sabre called the system DuraLam™, though it is, to the best of our knowledge, the same method originally developed by Tillotson-Pearson and used in a variety of yachts, including J/Boat, Freedom, and Alden boats.

Interior construction is where, to our minds, Sabre has really distinguished itself. The all-wood interiors are strong and warm feeling. Bulkheads, stringers and furniture are bonded directly to the hull, with more contact points than many fiberglass pans.

Wood is a better accoustic and thermal insulator than glass, so the interior is warmer and quieter. And, chances are, an all-wood interior provides better access to all parts of the hull, not to mention greater ease of modification should you desire to make changes at some future time.

Oiled teak is the wood of choice at Sabre. Too bad other woods weren't offered. At the least, we'd prefer a nice varnish job to brighten up the interior. Sabre's interiors have always seemed a bit dull to us.

On deck, there are numerous instances of special attention, from the teak coaming caps to the companionway hatch sea hood to the double lifelines and twin gates.

Readers rate the construction of their Sabres from above average to excellent. None cited any complaints. "Interior joinery is as fine as I have seen on any boat," wrote one owner.

Performance

Owners seem pleased with the performance of the early 38, rating its speed upwind and downwind as above average. It has an average PHRF rating of about 114. The Mark II rates about three seconds per mile faster.

This isn't as fast as the J/40, which rates about 75, the Baltic 38 at about 96, or the C & C 37 at about 105. But then the Sabre's all-wood interior suggests that owners are after more than ultra-light weight and all-out speed. For what it is, the Sabre 38 performs and handles well.

Seaworthiness is another category in which the 38 is well regarded. One owner said he'd sailed his to the Virgin Islands three times. Another said his performed well in "30-knot winds and 10-foot seas off the Jersey coast."

On the down side, most owners cited tenderness as troublesome. We don't know what percentage of the owners responding had centerboard models, but suspect the lack of initial stability is true, to some degree, of both centerboard and deep keel models. This is probably a function of the large, double-spreader rig and modest beam.

Perhaps it explains why the Mark II version was given 10 additional inches of beam; that, of course, would help increase form stability.

Remember, however, that in order for a boat to perform well, it must be able to carry a lot of sail area. And when the wind pipes up, reducing sail is necessary and expected.

A heavier boat with less sail area naturally will be able to carry full sail longer, but then it won't be nearly as fast in lighter airs.

None of the owners who cited tenderness said it would stop them from buying the same boat again. We don't think it should either.

One owner recommended using the 135-percent genoa, instead of a 150, when not racing. That sounds like good advice.

The main sheet traveler is located on the cabin top, out of the way of crew in the cockpit. Mid-boom sheeting, however, requires greater purchase to trim the sail.

A Westerbeke 33 diesel engine was standard in most Sabre 38s. This is a good engine, which owners rate as above average to excellent in terms of reliability and performance.

One owner said the boat "backs straight due to offset prop shaft and strut." Accessibility was rated as pretty good, with no more than the usual difficulties reaching some components.

Several owners said reaching the oil filter is not easy. The fuel capacity of the early 38 is 30 gallons in a single aluminum tank; this was increased to 45 gallons in the Mark II.

Interior

The original layout incorporates the usual V-berths forward. Just aft is the head with separate shower stall and opposite are two hanging lockers.

The saloon has opposing settees with a drop-leaf table on centerline. The galley is aft to port and, with the addition of a safety belt, would be secure in a seaway. To starboard is a navigation table with quarter berth.

The aft-cockpit version is a bit unusual for a boat of this length, but shows several clever features. The galley is about amidship, but instead of locating the sink outboard where it would not drain well, it is placed in an island on centerline.

The head is to starboard of this island, but lacks the separate shower stall of the standard plan. The aft cabin has a double berth to starboard and a single

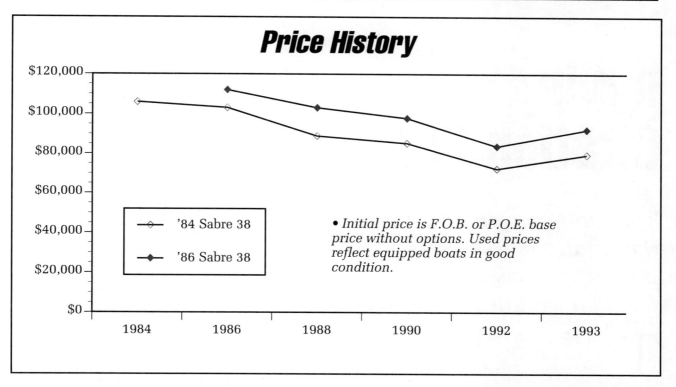

Price History

Legend:
- ◇ '84 Sabre 38
- ◆ '86 Sabre 38

• Initial price is F.O.B. or P.O.E. base price without options. Used prices reflect equipped boats in good condition.

with nav table to port. Berth lengths in both versions are 6' 6" and have five-inch foam cushions. Headroom is 6' 3".

The interior of the Mark II is somewhat more open. The V-berths do not require an insert cushion to make up a double, and there is a changing seat plus wash basin in the forward cabin.

The galley has plenty of space, and just aft of it, in the port quarter, is a double berth under the cockpit. To starboard is the large head, and a separate nav station.

All three plans provide decent sea berths in the settees and quarter berths. Interestingly, no dinette model was offered; while sometimes considered less seaworthy, offsetting the dinette to one side or the other permits meals without obstructing access fore and aft from the forward cabins, as is the case with centerline drop-leaf tables.

Fresh water capacity of the early 38 was 94 gallons and the holding tank held 24 gallons; in the Mark II

these numbers were increased to 106 and 30 respectively.

Conclusion

The Sabre 38 is a well constructed boat with few deficiencies. It is a cut above the plethora of typical fin keel-spade rudder production boats. We like especially the all-wood interior. The only complaints we've read are its initial tenderness (in the early models) and sensitivity to trim.

If you are a serious racer or have dreams of long-distance cruising, you can do better with, say, a J/37 or Crealock 37. With a design such as the Sabre 38, versatility is the operative word. The design and construction of the Sabre 38 will suit the average American sailor just fine.

Hewson earned a reputation for good customer service, and his annual owner rendezvous helped spark a certain esprit de corps. It'll be a shame if he can't find the resources to resume business. • **PS**

Irwin Citation 38

The main reason to choose the Citation 38 is sailing performance: she has the feel of a well-designed boat.

The "Irwin" in Irwin Yachts is Ted Irwin, a boat designer and builder who has been around nearly as long as production fiberglass boats have.

Over the years, Ted Irwin has designed, and Irwin Yachts has built, a variety of sailing boats—from flat-out cruising condos to full-bore racing machines. Starting with the combination racer/cruisers that were then fashionable, Irwin began producing in the 1970s not only cruiser/racers like the Irwin 28, 30, and 37 one-ton, but also roomy center cockpit cruisers like the 37, 38 and 43.

The company has been consistent in the niche they occupy in the sailboat market. Their line has been known as middle of the spectrum, better in quality than the cheapest boats on the market, yet with low enough prices to make the economy shopper think twice before jumping for the cheaper alternatives.

In style, the Citations continue the moderate tradition of Irwin designs. The Citation models are all similar, fairly high-sided with very short overhangs and a low cabin top. The distinctive profile is usually accentuated by a dark sheer stripe that makes a sharp downturn to follow the reverse transom.

In all modern boats with flat bottoms, it's hard getting good headroom without making the boat look ugly. The choice is to keep the sheer line low and attractive and use a high cabin house, or use high sheer and a low cabin top. The Citations use the second method and depend on the sheer stripe to keep the high freeboard from looking ugly. The sculpted cabin top keeps the entire profile low, with a high coaming flowing from the back edge of the cabin to the back of the cockpit.

A distinctive characteristic of the Citations is a complex swim ladder at the aft end of the cockpit.

Specifications

LOA	38' 0"
LWL	30' 8"
Beam	12' 6"
Draft	4' 11"/6' 11" (wing/fin)
Displacement	15,000 lbs.
Ballast	5,800 lbs.
Sail area	675 sq. ft.

The ladder is molded into a section of the transom which opens up and swings down for boarding. With the rear end of the cockpit open, it is an effective ladder, but owners report that it is somewhat awkward and difficult to prepare for use. The owner of the boat we sailed described the deployment of the ladder as a "nuisance."

As the largest of the Citations, the 38 is probably the best looking, handling the high-sidedness better than her smaller sisters. The boat has three windows set in the sheer stripe on each side, so they are not very noticeable. Like the other Citations it is distinctly modern-looking—not pretty, but not ugly either.

The company touts the 38 and the two smaller Citations as developments of Irwin's custom racer,

Owners' Comments

"The boat is built to a price for livability and coastal cruising. She's fine for that—extremely roomy, and therefore ugly. Finishing details are fair, sometimes sloppy and cheap. (Of course, I wanted cheap.)

"The boat sails better than I expected. For her size, she's one of the best designs for the Caribbean, where I sail.

"The manufacturer has been extremely unco-operative in shipping replacement parts. It took seven months to get parts after a grounding and sinking. However, for chartering in the Caribbean and northeast US, I'd trade up to another Irwin—I'm crazy."

—1983 model in the Caribbean

"With the shoal keel, the boat is tender but well balanced—you can lock the helm and go for a walk. I bought it because the price was right and I got a good deal. I've been treated reasonably enough—but very slowly—by the dealer and builder.

"Warranty claims included refrigeration, head, gelcoat, and stanchions. The deck lifted at the halyard turning blocks at the base of the mast. I changed these to cheek blocks mounted on the mast. The trim on the drawers is coming off—very cheaply finished.

"Upwind performance is average. Downwind speed is excellent."

—1983 model in RI

Razzle Dazzle, which performed very well on the Southern Ocean Racing Circuit. But they seem to us at best distant cousins of that flashy racer.

Though Irwin has never gone for super-light-weight boats, the production Citations are so much heavier that the comparison seems to be primarily a marketing ploy.

Hull and Deck

In general, Irwin uses conventional modern techniques in building the fiberglass hull and deck. The hull is a one-piece hand-laminated molding, using 24-ounce roving and biaxial fiberglass. Forward of the mast, the hull molding has a foam core—a design feature to provide stiffness and save weight. In today's market, such cored construction is economically feasible if you want a stiff hull and can charge a price above the bottom of the market.

The hull is further stiffened and strengthened by the interior fiberglass grid which incorporates fiberglass stringers to support the keel, mast, and major components of the cabin interior.

The deck is also a one-piece molding, with foam core in the cabin top and walkways, plywood core underneath the winches and hardware. Hull and deck are bolted together through an aluminum toerail.

Standard keel on the 38 is a lead wing design drawing 4' 11". A conventional lead fin is available as an option, and the boat we sailed had the conventional fin. Both keels are external, bolted through the hull and the interior grid.

The shoal draft of the wing, saving 2' compared to the fin, is an obvious advantage. We generally remain skeptical of the value of the wing keel, having seen some very poorly performing ones which were about as effective going to windward as a flopper-stopper. But Irwin apparently has enough faith in

their design to make it standard. If we were never going to race the boat, we'd consider trying a wing, but otherwise we'd probably opt for the fin and pay the draft penalty.

The rudder is a conventional modern high-aspect spade driven by a 36" wheel on a pedestal.

Exterior finish of the boat is generally good. The gelcoat does not have a high-gloss finish, but rather more of a matte appearance. This should be easier to maintain, making nicks and scratches less noticeable. The hull molding is fair, with no evident hard spots or ridges, and the deck molding is well done. The non-skid pattern is adequate, but minimal; it should be easy on bare feet.

There is hardly any exterior wood to care for—four teak grab rails and two plywood companionway hatch boards. The hatch boards on our test boat were poorly finished. A meticulous owner will want to finish them properly, or perhaps replace them with some higher-quality plywood, teak or plastic.

Rig

The rig is made in-house by Irwin and would generally be considered overbuilt by modern standards. The mast has two sets of spreaders and is stepped on the keel. The backstay is split to accommodate the fold-out boarding ladder in the transom, and the boat we sailed had single lower shrouds with a babystay forward. Halyards and other running rigging are internal.

Although the top quarter of the mast is tapered, the extrusion is so heavy that we had trouble bending it with the backstay adjuster. The adjustable babystay was also arranged in such a way that there was minimal pull forward, but we re-rigged it and were finally able to get enough mast bend to flatten the mainsail in heavy winds. It is not clear to us why

Irwin uses an adjustable babystay rather than forward lower shrouds, especially when the mast is so stiff. Cruisers would more likely prefer the more conventional rig with double lowers, which would be somewhat stronger.

The boom and fittings are good quality, with jiffy-reefing lines and topping lift led internally from the outboard end to exit at the mast.

Halyards and all other running rigging are Dacron. Standing rigging is conventional stainless steel wire with swaged fittings, plenty heavy, but lighter than you might expect with the super-heavy mast. Shroud chainplates are set well inboard, with stainless tierods belowdecks leading to anchor points on the hull grid.

Handling Under Sail

We raced four triangle races on the Citation 38 to judge her sailing ability. In general, she proved to have good sailing characteristics, well behaved with no obvious flaws or other problems.

Irwin advertises her PHRF (Performance Handicap Racing Fleet) rating as 130 with the wing keel, 120 with the fin keel—roughly about the same speed as a C&C 35 or many of the 1970s one-ton racer/cruisers like the Irwin 37 and Morgan 36. However, the local handicap of the boat we sailed is 108, a rating she could sail to only in light air off the wind.

In light winds the boat sails exceptionally well. In heavy winds, she certainly sails well enough to satisfy any serious sailor other than the dedicated racer, but she will not sail up to her rating relative to other modern lighter boats. She is generally fast enough to make good, satisfying passages for the cruising sailor. But we would generally not recommend her to the serious racer since the boat sails to her rating only in one condition, and it will be a struggle to win with the boat in heavy winds. For the very occasional racer who cruises most of the time, she should be satisfactory.

Specifically, the boat is exceptionally close-winded in light air, and ran very well in all winds. Reaching, she is sometimes a handful in a breeze, but overall she is a good sailer, typical of the best modern production boat designs.

We were surprised at the apparent thoughtlessness in many details of the rigging. While the hardware and fittings such as blocks, winches and shackles were all top quality, the way things were set up made for all sorts of problems.

For instance, the backstay adjuster was arranged with what looked like a clever idea. The split backstay was equipped with a typical double-ended block and tackle arrangement. To cleat the line, a tunnel was cut through the coaming so the line could be led to a cam cleat inside the cockpit. Unfortunately, given the anchor points for the tackle, the line bound on itself and on the block, creating so much friction that the tackle was almost impossible to use—we resorted to one person hanging on the line while a second took the slack through the cam cleat.

Similarly, the mainsheet traveler is well forward—a good place to keep it out of the way of people, but a poor place for getting good leverage on the boom. Unfortunately, the traveler hardware was set up so that it was impossible for a single person to move the traveler car in heavy air. Two people were required: one to pull up the boom by hand and the other to pull in the traveler control lines. Before the third race we replaced the whole traveler with a multi-part Harken system that made it possible, if not easy, to control the traveler.

There are a number of other details in the rigging—such as the fact that none of the exits from the mast or boom are labeled in any way—that indicate corners cut in rigging the boat. Fortunately, all the problems are fairly easily corrected by an owner, but it is surprising to see a boat with good sailing poten-

The interior is cavernous, but is well-divided. For long-distance cruising, the Citation 38 could use some extra storage space.

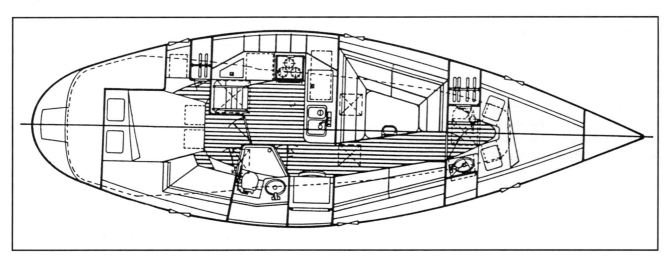

tial handicapped by this rather sloppy attention to detail.

Handling Under Power

The boat is equipped with a 27 hp 3-cylinder Yanmar, which is adequate for the boat's size and weight, although it is certainly not an excess of power. The boat backs well, turns sharply, and is easily driven to hull speed by the engine. The cruiser addicted to powering at a knot over hull speed may want to talk to Irwin about a larger engine, though one is not currently offered as an option. Irwin installs the same engine in the Citation 35, which seems like a better match. The tank on the 38 holds 30 gallons of diesel fuel—ample for good cruising range.

The engine is located in the center of the boat above the keel, underneath part of the settee and the galley cabinet. With an aft-cabin boat, this seems a sensible arrangement to us, giving good access to the engine while keeping the weight centered in the boat.

Like many builders, Irwin continues the practice of shipping the boat with a solid two-bladed prop, a crude way of keeping the price down. Anyone who is likely to order this type of well-performing sailboat will want to get a folding prop immediately. Most similar practices—such as offering the boat without lifelines as standard—have disappeared from the marketplace, but this peculiarity continues with almost all manufacturers.

On Deck

The low cabin house of the 38 makes the decks very usable, both for working the boat under sail and for lounging around. Furthest forward is an anchor roller beside the forestay, just ahead of an ordinary anchor locker to fit a Danforth-type anchor. The foredeck is wide and roomy enough to handle foresails. A big forward hatch in the low cabin top is usable for passing sails up and down.

The walkways are wide, with inboard shrouds, and the cockpit coaming is an easy step. Halyards and other control lines are led aft to the back of the cabin house where two Barient 17s are located. Small Dorade-type air inlets are molded into the cabin top just ahead of the traveler. The companionway hatch is off-center to port.

The cockpit is T-shaped, with comfortable benches and backrests. Barient 24 primaries are just adequate for the boat, but most owners will probably go for self-tailers all around.

There is a shallow cockpit locker on the port side, but the starboard locker is cavernous. We have yet to see a really good way of organizing these huge cockpit lockers, or of handling the oversize locker lid made up of the bench seat and part of the backrest. The helmsman's seat is peculiar in that it is removable as part of the process of folding out the transom ladder. Engine controls are on the steering pedestal.

Double lifelines, pulpit, and stern rail are standard.

Belowdecks

With a 12' 6" beam and a 30' 8" waterline, the interior of the Citation 38 is enormous, but it is broken up enough not to seem like a cavern. Forward is an

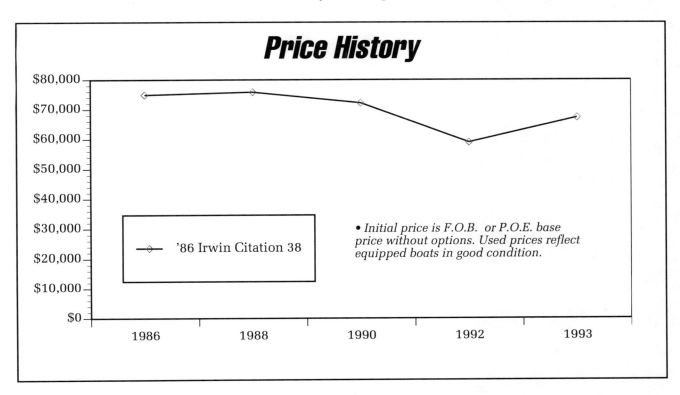

Price History

• Initial price is F.O.B. or P.O.E. base price without options. Used prices reflect equipped boats in good condition.

'86 Irwin Citation 38

ordinary V-berth that should be good for sleeping or sail storage. There's a small bureau and hanging locker opposite, just aft of the berth.

In the main cabin, a U-shaped dinette is opposite a settee which can be used for a berth. The galley is roomy, open, and quite workable.

On the starboard side opposite the galley is a good navigator's station with a swing-out chair and electrical panel above it. Just aft of the nav table is the head, with entrances from both the galley and the aft cabin.

The aft cabin is quite roomy, made possible mostly by the offset companionway hatch and forward engine location. The berth is huge and comfortable, and this cabin will undoubtedly be one of the selling points of the boat.

In general, interior equipment is of good quality, with propane stove, 90-gallon water tank, hot water heater, a dozen opening ports, and good lighting.

Like most modern boats, the interior seems set up for weekending, with very little real storage space. A long-distance cruise will require converting some of the space for basic storage.

The only other shortcoming of the interior is that it looks like a standard, run-of-the-mill production boat, with lots of veneer and plastic, finished a little crudely in spots. But, for a relatively low-priced boat, it's better to compromise here than in the hull construction or mechanical systems.

Conclusions

Overall, the Citation 38 is a good boat that seems a little ordinary, generally representative of mid-line production boats. Though such a statement may sound like faint praise, it really isn't.

The boat is not as well finished as competitive boats like the Pearson 37, but it is generally better done than lower-priced boats such as the Hunter, and the price is appropriately in between.

Why would anyone choose this Irwin rather than one of her competitors? There are, of course, the personal considerations of appearance and aesthetics. Many people will consider the Citation 38 better looking than some of her boxier competitors.

To us, the main reason for choosing this boat would be the sailing performance. She has the feel of a well-designed boat, unlike so many other contemporary models which get their performance merely by combining big sail areas, long waterlines, and light weight. This boat sails very well.

The other consideration, of course, will be price. You can buy cheaper boats and you can easily buy more expensive boats. To us, Irwin has kept the price down in the most sensible way—not by compromising basic construction or eliminating layers of fiberglass, but by going to conventional components and easy construction in the interior.

For the avid racer, the Citation 38 is too much of a cruiser—something like the J/35 would be a better racing boat. And for the pure cruiser more interested in room than in sailing performance, a boat like the center cockpit Irwin 38 might be more suitable.

For a serious cruising sailor who likes a boat that sails well but still wants the size necessary for cruising in comfort, the Citation 38 would be a reasonable choice. **• PS**

O'Day 39 and 40

She started life as a Jeanneau, but wound up as an American boat. She is a good alternative to imports.

The O'Day 40 began life in Europe as a 39-footer, from the drawing board of the French IOR designer Phillipe Briand, and was first built by Jeanneau as the "Sun Fizz." O'Day reached an agreement with their sister company to build the boat in America and began selling her as the O'Day 39 in 1981.

After about 120 boats were built, O'Day had Hunt & Associates do a redesign, leaving the basic hull the same, but lengthening the cabin house, rearranging the interior, moving the mast aft a bit, and adding a platform extension with boarding ladder to the transom. The new version was christened the O'Day 40, and by the end of its first year—in the summer of 1986—50 boats had been built, to make the 39/40 a successful product for the company during a period when most other American builders were not doing too well. The 40 continued as part of the line until O'Day shut down in 1989.

The 39/40 is very typical of modern racer-cruisers in design. She is moderate in displacement by current racing standards, but has a cutaway underbody with fin keel and spade rudder. The widest beam is carried far enough aft to allow for a good sized after cabin and roomy galley, and the shallow bilges are compensated for by rather high topsides, to provide lots of living space below. At a distance of 200 yards, she would be nearly indistinguishable from a dozen Jeanneau and Beneteau models, if she had blacked-out windows and different hull stripes.

Construction

The hull construction is a departure from O'Day's traditional solid fiberglass laminate, since it is balsa cored.

The balsa core makes for a strong and stiff hull and has the advantage of reducing the amount of fiber-

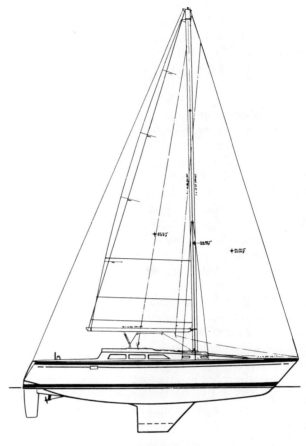

Specifications

LOA	38' 7"/39' 7"
LWL	33' 6"
Beam	12' 8"
Draft	4' 1"/6' 4" (shoal/draft)
Displacement	18,000 lbs.
Ballast	6,600 lbs.
Sail area	701 sq. ft.

glass and resin required for a given strength; consequently it reduces weight and cost. The balsa also provides insulation against heat and sound, and helps to eliminate condensation inside the cabin.

The disadvantage of the balsa cored hull is simply that much greater skill and quality control are required in the laminating process to ensure the potential strength inherent in the fiberglass-balsa-fiberglass sandwich.

There are skeptics with questions about the longevity of the balsa-glass laminate as well as potential problems with water absorption. But the technology has been used in production sailboats for the last 15 years, and a great many hull moldings have been made—particularly by C&C and J-Boats—with little evidence that there has been any more laminate failure or osmotic blistering than with conventional layups.

We extensively examined the hull of one 39 and did a quick examination of a 40, and the glass work looked good. Unfortunately, with balsa coring, there is no way to see the quality of the laminate. Potential owners must depend on the reputation and track record of the builder.

The exteriors of both hulls we examined were fair with no evident hardspots. Gelcoat work seemed to be average production line quality, though the 39 had a bad color flaw in the bootstripe and some peculiar "crinkles" on the transom. Overall, the glass work on the O'Day 40 appeared to be somewhat better than on the O'Day 25, 27, 28, and 32 models that we have examined in the past.

The keels are external lead, bolted to a keel stub on the hull (some early keels were iron). Two versions are available—deep or shoal. The deep keel is a better shape and much to be preferred, unless the extra 17" of draft is a critical consideration. The one keel we examined was poorly faired—anyone thinking of racing the boat in PHRF will have to spend quite a bit of time with fairing compound and a grinder.

The deck layup is a standard balsa core laminate, with plywood inserts under cleats and winches. Non-skid is a molded pattern which is marginally adequate when wet. The 39 we examined had a number of small voids in the cockpit gelcoat, but there was little evidence of stress cracking anywhere outside the cockpit—a sign of decent workmanship.

In the hull-to-deck joint, O'Day adopted the European practice. There's a standard inward-turning flange on the hull, on which the deck molding rests, with polyurethane compound serving as a sealer. Stainless bolts are then inserted through the hull flange, the deck, and an exterior aluminum toerail. A thick layer of fiberglass is laid over the interior of the joint, bonding the hull to the deck. It's a good strong joint, the only concerns being the difficulty of tracing any leaks that develop and the problems of repair resulting from collisions with docks, pilings, or other boats.

Inside, a fiberglass pan forms the foundation for interior cabinetry and is bonded to the hull for additional stiffening. The chainplates are also anchored to this fiberglass pan, with Navtec Rod between the pan and the deck. Early on, O'Day 39 brochures claimed that this construction resulted in "quite possibly the strongest production sailboat of its size built in the United States"—a case of the advertising department conquering both common sense and reason.

Bulkheads are conventional teak-faced plywood, and the overhead is covered with a fiberglass hull liner. For ceiling, cabinetry is used is some spots, carpeting in some spots, and wood strips on a plastic fabric in some spots.

There's nothing very distinctive about the mechanical systems, but the boat comes pretty completely equipped, with shore power, propane stove, pressurized water system and water heater, twin batteries, and 110 gallons of water tankage.

Undoubtedly the best part of the mechanicals is the engine compartment—enormous in the 39 and big and roomy in the 40, to provide plenty of room for add-ons, such as engine-driven refrigeration or multiple alternators. Access is good on the 39—the companionway steps hinge upward—and excellent on the 40, where additional access is provided through the aft cabin.

All the interior woodwork is standard issue production line pre-fab—decent looking from a distance but with a number of sloppy joints, rough interiors, cheap hinges and latches, and loose drawer and door fits when examined close up.

Handling Under Power

The 39 was fitted with a Universal 44 diesel, and the 40 has a Westerbeke 46, both fresh water cooled. The four cylinder engines run smoothly, with minimal vibration. The noise from the engine compartment is muffled by insulation, but if we cruised the boat much, we would want to add a better lead/foam sandwich to quiet things down a bit more.

Both engines provide more than enough power to drive the boat at hull speed in strong head winds and seas; in fact, the horsepower/weight ratio is closer to that of a motorsailer than a typical racer-cruiser. With a 42 gallon aluminum fuel tank, powering range will be well over 200 miles.

We chartered the 39 for a week in the Virgin Islands and found in about 10 hours of powering that the boat handled well with the two-bladed solid prop, backing where it was told to and powering forward in a good straight line. There should be no problem fitting a folding or feathering prop, which would improve sailing performance while retaining ample powering ability.

One bad design detail is that the engine's key and instrument panel is at the front end of the cockpit, well out of reach of the helmsman.

Handling Under Sail

During our week in the Virgin Islands, the boat proved to be a good sailer. The shallow draft keel keeps it from pointing well, but it sailed fast on every point off the wind. With the deep draft keel, she should be a good all around performer. The sail area is divided a bit unevenly—a smaller high-aspect mainsail and a larger jib, on a double spreader mast.

The small main and large foretriangle undoubtedly reflect the designer's racing background and mean that, for high performance off the wind, a spinnaker will be required. However, the mast is tall enough and the sail area great enough that satisfactory performance can be obtained in most conditions with the standard roller furling 150% jib and a main with two reefs. A Hood Stoway mast and mainsail are options, but the main is small enough and easily enough handled that the added expense is probably not a reasonable investment.

The spade rudder far aft makes for quick response to the helm, and the boat demonstrated no serious bad habits in a wide variety of conditions, though it does pound a bit going to windward in a chop. Some might find it a bit tender, and an early reef in the main is necessary to keep the boat upright and sailing well. But, overall it is definitely on the performance end of the cruising boat spectrum, rapid enough to make owners at least think of entering a Wednesday night race. With a PHRF rating of around 114 for the deep draft version, it is the same speed as all out racing boats in that size range were 10 years ago.

Standard equipment on the latest 40 includes a Hood LD furler, but only one pair of Barlow 27 self-tailing winches. The winches are absolutely minimal for easy handling of a 150% genoa; to make for more reasonable jib trimming we would probably want to upgrade to Barlow 32s or their equivalent. The cockpit coaming has built-in recesses for an extra set of winches—only necessary for the racer.

The short boom is sheeted to a traveler ahead of the companionway. With the mainsheet so far forward, hand trimming of the main is impossible, but the standard equipment self-tailing winch is adequate. The traveler has only mechanical stops, so adjustment under load is impossible. With the traveler—as well as most other sail controls—anyone wanting to race the boat will have to add a number of fine-tuning devices to make racing trim feasible.

On Deck

As you might expect on a 40' boat, there is plenty of deck space all around. The side decks are wide enough that the inboard shrouds can be smack in the middle of them and still allow sufficient walk around room. The design of the hull means that the foredeck is relatively pinched, but still there's enough room for sail and anchor handling.

The 39 had a stainless "pulpit" around the mast as standard equipment—a good feature for heavy weather work—but the pulpit was made an option on the 40.

The stanchions—set in aluminum toerail sockets—the bow pulpit, and the stern pulpit are substantial enough, and there are double lifelines all around. The stern pulpit opens up to a transom-mounted ladder on the 39 and to a foot-wide swim platform and off-center ladder on the 40.

The cockpit is long and roomy but has a couple of irritating flaws. The main one is that the wheel is just wide enough that you have to squeeze between it and the cockpit seats. Unfortunately, the hasp for the cockpit lockers is exactly opposite the wheel, and anyone using the boat extensively will have permanent bruises on the shins at hasp level.

The lazarette hatches are outboard of the wheel. The lids are made up of not only the seat but also part of the coaming. This makes for a cavernous opening, but the lid is big and heavy enough to also be an effective guillotine.

The lazarette compartment itself is huge, but in practice too deep for the bottom to be usable. An owner will want to divide up the compartment in some way—with partitions or netting—to provide reasonable access to frequently used gear.

In the 39, a large storage compartment under the cockpit sole offered space for a life raft or other gear, but the compartment was eliminated to provide more aft cabin room in the 40. Propane tanks fit under the helmsman's seat.

The O'Day 40's interior was changed around from that in the 39, the most notable difference being the switch from two small aft cabins to one large one. Overall, the 40's interior is better.

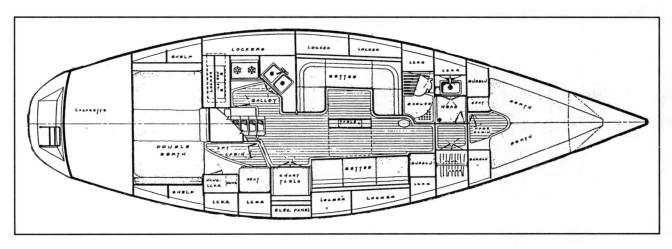

Belowdecks

The principal difference between the 39 and 40 interiors is that the 39 had two aft cabins—one port, one starboard. While this is ideal for charter work, both aft cabins are a squeeze for double occupancy.

On the 40, the port side aft cabin was eliminated, the starboard aft cabin was expanded with a huge athwartship double berth, and the galley was enlarged to occupy what was left of the former port cabin. The 40's arrangements are clearly preferable for an owner or family using the boat.

The galley is good sized and convenient, the only shortcoming being the minimal dry storage areas. The chart table opposite is adequate, with a cute little swing-out seat that looks to be unusable in heavy weather. On the 39, a second icebox frequently replaced the chart table for charter. Unlike many earlier O'Days, the iceboxes are well insulated.

The main salon is comfortable and will seat a crowd, the head is adequate for family use (the 39 had a second toilet and washbasin in the aft cabin), and the forecabin is big enough for an adult couple to use on a two week cruise. Throughout, the dead spaces are used pretty well to provide storage bins and bureaus, as well as two smallish hanging lockers. The bilges are very shallow, so there's no storage there, and any water taken on will make a real mess.

There are hatches and opening ports all over the place and, in fair weather and calm sailing, ventilation is excellent. With hatches and ports closed, however, there are only two dorades on the 40 and there was nothing on the 39. Opening ports into the cockpit footwell alleviate the problem a bit, but additional dorades or other waterproof vents would be mandatory for wet weather cruising.

The opening ports in the topsides are likely to be a concern for some buyers. Sailing, we found it hard to put the ports under water, and when we did leaking was minimal. If we ever went offshore in the boat, we would install storm shutters.

Other than the potential ventilation problems, the interior is well thought out, and the balsa cored hull provides good insulation.

Conclusions

In general, the O'Day 39/40 is a wholesome boat that fits a definite niche in the American cruising boat market. It would be inappropriate to think of her as finished like a high quality yacht—she is definitely mid-line production quality—or to consider her as an offshore or world cruiser.

Rather, she is a contemporary coastal cruiser, the sort of boat to be used mostly for weekends, occasional casual races, and a two or three week cruise each season. For those purposes, we can only conclude that her design and production have been well executed. She will be no one's ideal boat but a moderate and satisfactory compromise for many.

More notably, she is about the only American-made boat her size which is a reasonable alternative to the host of foreign imports that have invaded the American market. There are American-mades in her price and size range—like the Hunter 40 or Morgan 38—but we think she is somewhat better made and an overall better value than those. **• PS**

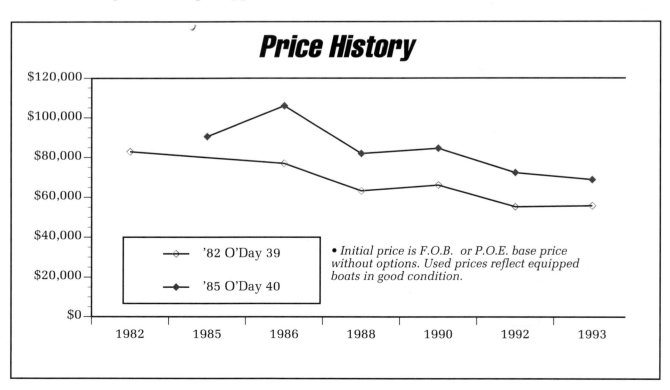

Price History

Legend:
- '82 O'Day 39
- '85 O'Day 40

• Initial price is F.O.B. or P.O.E. base price without options. Used prices reflect equipped boats in good condition.

Cal 40

Though now an old and dated design, the Cal 40 was a hot boat when new, and she carries that legacy.

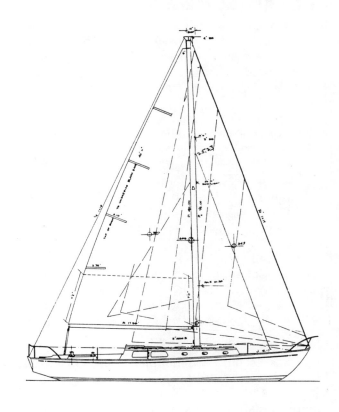

Thunderbird, a Cal 40 owned by IBM president T. Vincent Learson, took first in fleet over 167 boats in the 1966 Bermuda Race. Because this was the first computer-scored Bermuda Race, Learson got a lot of gaff about the IBM computer that had declared him the winner—and about beating out his boss. Thomas J. Watson, IBM's chairman of the board, sailed his 58' cutter, Palawan, second across the line, but ended with second in class, 24th in fleet, on corrected time.

In fact, the computer scoring system was not especially kind to Learson. Both he and Watson would have fared considerably better under the old system that calculated scores from the NAYRU time allowance tables. *Thunderbird*'s victory was a legitimate win, another in a stunning series by Cal 40s that was establishing the boat as a revolutionary design. The first Cal 40 was built for George Griffith in 1963. That winter, hull #2, *Conquistador*, took overall honors in the 1964 Southern Ocean Racing Circuit (SORC). The Transpac races of 1965, '66, and '67 all went to Cal 40s. Ted Turner's Cal 40, *Vamp X*, took first place in the 1966 SORC. In the '66 Bermuda Race, five of *Thunderbird*'s sisterships finished with her in the top 20 in fleet, taking five of the first 15, four of the first nine places. And so on. In their first few years on the water, Cal 40s chalked up an astonishing record.

The 40 was the fifth in a line of Cal designs that C. William Lapworth did for Jensen Marine of Costa Mesa, California. Lapworth had already designed a series of moderately successful racing boats, the L classes, including an L-24, L-36, L-40 and L-50, when he teamed up with Jack Jensen. The Cal designs were built on concepts he had tried in his L-class boats. The first Cal was the 24, Jensen's first boat, launched in 1959. The Lapworth-Jensen team

Specifications

LOA	39' 4"
LWL	30' 4"
Beam	11' 0"
Draft	5' 7"
Displacement	15,500 lbs.
Ballast	6,000 lbs.
Sail area	700 sq. ft.

then produced a 20, 30, and 28 before getting to the Cal 40, which proved to be a successful distillation of Lapworth's thinking up to that time.

Aspects of the boat that departed from the conventional wisdom were her light displacement, long waterline, flat bilges to encourage surfing, fin keel and spade rudder. The masthead rig is stayed by shrouds secured to chainplates set inboard of the toerail, a then unusual innovation that allows a reduced sheeting angle. The success of the design helped legitimize fiberglass as a hull material, establish Jensen Marine as a significant builder of fiberglass boats, and propel Lapworth to the forefront of yacht design.

Three decades have passed since Lapworth drew the Cal 40. In that time, using computers to score

Owners' Comments

"At her best in dirty weather. Has been driven mercilessly; nothing ever seems to fail. Old Westerbeke lost by poor exhaust design. New Perkins and new exhaust expected to outlive me."
—1963 model in Gig Harbor, WA

"Wet, pounds in gales, some waves—green—go over the boat. Good sea boat. Can balance with no one on helm for hours in 15 to 30 knots of wind. Excess sail makes little difference—rail at surface. Classic, large comfortable cockpit, good drainage. Minimum wood, white unpainted gelcoat looks good, plain by today's standards."
—1968 model in Kailua, HI

"Very well built compared to today's stock boats. A used Cal 40, in good condition, should be an excellent buy."
—1964 model in Long Island Sound, NY

"This is a most satisfying boat. She is stable, safe and seakindly. Faster than all but the race machines. Doesn't point as well as high aspect rigs. This only reflects the stage of development when boat was built. Few boats of her size will pass her off the wind. I plan on keeping her forever."
—1969 model in Radnor, PA

"The cockpit is outstanding; the interior is small and not roomy. She sails like a dream and is twice as much boat as I could have afforded new. With another new sail or two, I am convinced she will be a successful club racer again. There is nothing which can touch her performance designed prior to 1974."
—1969 model in Corpus Christi, TX

"Design of mast truck pulleys allows halyards to jump sheaves. Not a roomy cruising or liveaboard boat."
—1965 model in Mitchellville, MD

races has become commonplace—boat measurers and designers would be paralyzed without them. The CCA Rule, the NAYRU tables and the Portsmouth Yardstick have been replaced by IMS, IOR, and PHRF, with the effects of their parameters expressed in the shape, size and weight of new boats. New building materials and techniques have changed the meaning of terms such as "light displacement," "long waterline," "fin keel," and "fast sailboat." Today the Cal 40 is a dated design, having been surpassed in her revolutionary features by her descendents. She remains among the esteemed elite of racing yachts, but she is not especially light, long on the waterline, or fast compared to current designs.

The Cal's builder was transformed by time, as well. Jensen Marine was bought by Bangor Punta Marine, and the Cal production line was moved to Florida about the time that the Cal 40 went out of production in 1972. For the next decade, the company's name and address shifted between combinations of Cal, Bangor Punta and Jensen in California, New Jersey and finally Massachusetts, where it joined O'Day under Bangor Punta's umbrella in the early 1980s. After 1984 the company was called Lear Siegler Marine, Starcraft Sailboat Products, and finally emerged as Cal, a Division of the O'Day Corporation, in Fall River, Mass. Cal and O'Day ceased production in April, 1989.

Construction

The construction of the Cal 40 is typical of Jensen Marine boats of the 1960s. The hull is solid hand laid fiberglass with wooden bulkheads and interior structures. Strips of fiberglass cloth and resin secure the wooden structures to the hull, but this tabbing is rather lightweight and has been reinforced in some Cal 40s where it has failed. If it has not been reinforced, it probably needs it.

Because saving weight was a priority in building the Cal 40, the reinforcement provided by the bulkheads and furniture is critical to hull stiffness. Failure of the bonding can be a significant structural concern.

The hull-to-deck joint is an inward-turning hull flange, upon which the deck molding is bonded, then through-bolted and capped with a through-bolted teak toerail. This is a strong type of joint, but there is some complaint of minor leaking along it in a few boats. The leaks are most likely one result of the relatively light construction of the hull skin, which has a tendency to "oilcan" in heavy weather, creating stresses at the joint.

The deck, also a solid fiberglass layup, has reinforcement designed into it during layup, so no interior metal backing plates are provided under winches, cleats, and other hardware. *PS* generally recommends backing plates behind high-stress hardware as a matter of course. We found little indication of trouble with leaking or working of most of the fittings, but one owner said that his lifeline stanchion bases had to be reinforced. This would be an area to inspect carefully.

Colors and non-skid surfaces are molded in, but due to the age of any Cal 40, the finish will look tired unless it has been renewed. A good Awlgrip job will do it wonders, and is probably warranted for this boat unless it is in general disrepair.

The deck and cockpit of the Cal 40 we inspected have numerous cracks in the gelcoat in corners and other stress areas. Check these areas closely—they are unsightly, but in most cases are not a structural concern.

Ballast is an internal lead casting dropped into the keel before the insides were assembled. If there is evidence that the boat has suffered a hard grounding, invesitgate the ballast cavity to see that it was properly repaired. It should not have a hollow sound when rapped, and there should be no cracks, weeping, or other evidence of moisture inside. Due to the construction sequence, major repairs could be awkward.

Wiring was also installed prior to the interior, which makes it quite inaccessible in some areas. What may be of more concern is that it is low enough in the boat to get wet if the last watch forgot to pump the bilges and the boat heels over to her work. That's what happened to one owner, who lost all the electricity on the boat when approaching Nova Scotia's Bras d'Or Lakes after an all night sail. Fortunately, dawn arrived in time to avert a navigation problem. They anchored in the harbor and found that the electrical system worked fine, once it got dry again. Before the next season rolled around, the boat's entire electrical system had been replaced in elevated, accessible locations. The implication is that you should look carefully at the wiring in a Cal 40 before you make any decisions. If it has been replaced, try to learn who did the work and how well qualified he/she was for the job. If it has not, you may have to work the cost of rewiring into your acquisition expenses. We would suspect the worst until proven otherwise.

You might expect wheel steering on a boat this size, but the stock Cal 40 came with a big tiller. The boat is well enough balanced to be controlled with a tiller, and many helmsmen prefer it to a wheel, which masks feedback from the rudder and makes sensitive steering more difficult.

The cockpit is roomy, but properly designed for offshore work with relatively low volume, a bridgedeck and small companionway. The tiller sweeps the cockpit midsection, allowing the helmsman to sit fairly far forward, a help to visibility.

Winch islands are located aft of the helmsman, where there is room for the crew, but it also makes the sheets accessible to the helmsman for short-handed sailing. The teak cockpit coaming has cutouts giving access to handy storage bins.

The aluminum mast is stepped through the deck to a fitting that meets it at the level of the cabin sole. The shroud chainplates are secured to a transverse bulkhead at the mast station, and then tied into an aluminum weldment in the bilges. This weldment also supports the mast step. While chainplates have been an area of concern in some designs, because they can work under the large loads they carry, our indications from Cal 40 owners are that the chainplate/shroud/mast step attachments have served well.

Sailing Performance

The Cal 40 is in her element in heavy air, especially off the wind. Her long waterline and flat bilges help her get up and go on reaches and runs, surfing in heavy air. On the wind, the flat hull forward pounds in waves and chop, which slows the boat somewhat and is irritating. Owners agree that she sails best with the rail in the water. She is not dry on the wind, so a dodger is a welcome feature.

The masthead sailplan allows relatively easy reduction of headsails to suit heavier conditions, and Cal 40 owners extol the survivability of their boats. "Simple rig, nothing breaks, strong, easy to use," is a typical comment.

Despite her stellar racing record, the Cal 40 is only ordinary in performance by today's standards. She carries a PHRF rating between 108 and 120 seconds

A traditional '60s-style layout with eight berths is found in the Cal 40. Eight people is really too many on this boat, and the spare berths are likely to be used as storage space.

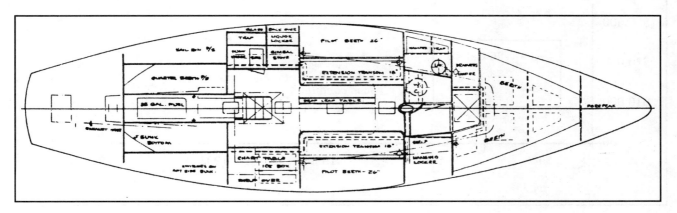

per mile, depending on the region. That's about the same as a C&C 38 or an Ericson 36, both IOR designs of the late 70s. Compared to a mid-1970s design such as the Swan 38, the Cal 40 is a bit slower on the wind and in light air, a bit faster off the wind and in heavier going, about equal in speed overall. It's not surprising that these boats perform alike if you look at the length of their waterlines and their displacements.

In comparing the Cal 40 to boats of her own vintage one sees what all the fuss was about. The Columbia 40, for example, is a 1965 Charles Morgan design, an "all-out racer" with a 27' waterline, displacement of 20,200 pounds, and a PHRF rating of about 170. Or look at the Hinckley 41: 29' on the water, 18,500 pounds, PHRF about 160.

The Cal 40's waterline is almost 31', but she displaces one or two tons less than the Columbia or the Hinckley, and rates nearly one minute per mile faster under PHRF. In that context, she is indeed a fast, light displacement boat with a long waterline. Just look at her "fin keel" and you can see the progression. Compared to a full keel with attached rudder, it is small. Compared to a modern fin keel, it hardly seems small enough to qualify for the name. If Cal 40s win races today, it's because they are well sailed, not because the boat is the fast machine on the race course.

Interior

In the 60s, "accommodations" tended to imply the number of berths in a sailboat, and the more the better. It also included the notion of a basic galley with sink, stove, icebox, and a table of sorts, plus a head with toilet and sink. Space age electronics had not arrived in the galley or the nav station, nor had space arrived in the concept of the main saloon.

Inside, as elsewhere, the Cal 40 is well designed and functional, but she speaks of her own era. The layout is very traditional, with a V-berth forward, separated from the main cabin by a head and hanging locker. Pilot berths and extension settees port and starboard provide sleeping for four. The dropleaf table seats four, six if you squeeze. Next aft is the galley to port and a nav station to starboard, consisting of a chart table over the voluminous icebox. The galley has a usable sink next to the well for a gimbaled stove with oven.

Flanking the companionway steps are the entrances to the quarterberths, known affectionately as "torpedo tubes," which gives you an impression of their dimensions. They extend from the main cabin through to the lazarette, which allows good circulation of air. In fact, on a return trip from Bermuda, one seasick sailor found great solace between tricks at the helm by climbing into one of the cocoon-like torpedo tubes, where he was washed with a fresh breeze from the dorade vent on the lazarette cover. The fact that the quarterberths flank the engine compartment doesn't matter as long as you are under sail, but it's a different story when under power.

So you have sleeping accommodations for eight, which is too many people on a 40-footer, except perhaps when racing. The extension transom berths, however, do not lend themselves to use under way. The interior, not spacious by modern standards, fills up fast with extra bodies aboard. Owners tend to

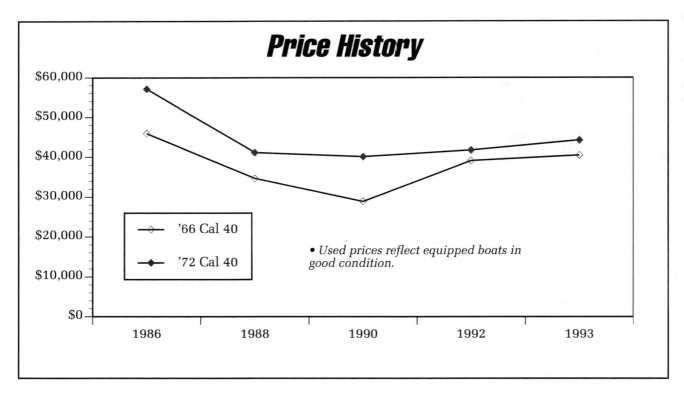

Price History

'66 Cal 40

'72 Cal 40

• *Used prices reflect equipped boats in good condition.*

convert some of the berths to storage space. The pilot berths are especially tempting for that use, but since they are also the most comfortable berths on the boat, the quarterberths are often sacrificed for storage.

One of the best features about the Cal 40's interior is the dining table. Set slightly to port, it is supported by a sturdy sole-to-overhead stainless steel post at each end with a 4' 4" gimbaled mahogany tray between them above the table. The posts make excellent handholds, and the gimbaled tray can serve for everything from salt and pepper holder to bookshelf to diaper-changing table. The table has a drop leaf to port and to starboard, so it can be set up for use from the port settee without blocking fore-and-aft passage through the boat.

Engine

A variety of powerplants will be found in Cal 40s. Some early hulls were equipped with Atomic 4 gasoline engines. Later hulls got Graymarine 4-112 gasoline or Perkins 4-107 diesels. It's likely that the original engine will need to be replaced if it has not already been done. Even the newest Cal 40s are rather old, and the early models have passed the quarter-century mark.

Boats in our files have Volvo MD2B, the Perkins, Pathfinder 50, Westerbeke 4-108, and Pisces 40 from Isuzu listed as replacements for the original engine.

The engine is located under the cockpit, between the torpedo tubes, which allow access to both sides, but are not especially convenient, particularly if the area has been turned into storage space. Better is the companionway ladder, which removes to expose the front of the engine. That can be an inconvenience, too, if the engine needs some attention while under way.

Used for the minimum requirements of a racing yacht, primarily getting in and out of port, you can probably make do with any of the engines. If the boat is to be used for cruising, with greater demands to be made on the engine, the Atomic 4 would likely be inadequate.

Generally the boat will do about six or seven knots under power, depending on the power plant and propeller. We suspect that many Cal 40s will have folding propellers, good for racing but not the best for powering, especially in reverse. The spade rudder set well aft confers good maneuverability under most conditons.

Conclusions

The Cal 40, a hot racing boat when new, carries that legacy with her into maturity. Generally, the boats have been raced hard, some cruised hard as well. Owners have tended to be the type to add gear and modifications to keep the boat comfortable and competitive. The boats are likely to have a large inventory of much-used sails.

Because of her age and dated design, a Cal 40 may be available for much less money than a newer boat offering comparable quality and performance. Prices will vary according to the condition of the boat and gear, but will likely fall in the range of $40,000 to $50,000. If the boat has lots of add-ons in the galley and nav station, modern racing hardware, renewed standing rigging, new finish on the topsides, and the bottom is in good condition, it might fetch something higher. One performance extra to look for is a special (non-factory) fairing job on the keel and rudder that was available when the boats were young.

On the other hand, it should not be a surprise if there are areas that require attention, and you should calculate the cost of the work into the price you are willing to pay. Twenty or 25 years of hard sailing will take its toll. Significant expense could be incurred if the boat needs new wiring, an Awlgrip job on the topsides, extensive reinforcement of the interior furniture tabbing, a new engine, or new rigging. If racing is in your plans, new sails might be scheduled in as well.

This would be a good boat for a handy do-it-yourselfer. Over the years, most of the boat's problems have been solved more than once by other Cal 40 owners, many willing to share their wisdom. You would probably have a choice of solutions, and indications of which worked best.

Although there is not currently an active owners association, there persists a loose fellowship among present and former owners. If you buy a Cal 40, you will acquire a modest boat, with good pedigree and performance, and—should you desire them—a few new friends, as well. • **PS**

Passport 40

Built in Taiwan under American supervision, this handsome sloop can be compared to the Valiant 40.

When Seattle yacht designer Robert Perry designed the Valiant 40 in 1973/4, he broke new ground in the usually conservative world of yacht design. With a fin keel, skeg-mounted rudder and displacement/length ratio of 264, critics said it was unsuitable for serious offshore work. The idea of going trans-oceanic with a divided underbody challenged a lot of old beliefs about what constitutes a safe passagemaker.

Time has certainly proven the critics wrong and Perry right. The Valiant 40 has made numerous circumnavigations, including Dan Byrne's credible showing in the first (1983) BOC Challenge. Ten to 15 years ago, it was considered a fast boat for such an undertaking. Today, alack, it's too slow for competitive long-distance ocean racing. But the fact that all of the circumnavigations of which we are aware were made safely, and with little complaint by the skippers, is strong testimony to the soundness of the design.

The Passport 40, introduced in 1981, represents Perry's evolving ideas about "performance cruising," a phrase originating from his work. "Performance," he once told us, "is a moving target."

The Design

The Passport 40 design was commissioned by several parties, including the Taiwan builder and former furniture maker Wendel Renken, who was to supervise construction and handle distribution in the U.S. According to Perry, he was first given an interior drawing, "an extrapolation of the Islander Freeport 36" with the head in the bow and a Pullman double berth aft of it. "It was," he added, "a classic case of a hull wrapped around an interior." Some readers may be astonished, but this is frequently how the yacht business works.

Specifications

LOA	39' 5"
LWL	33' 5"
Beam	12' 8"
Draft	5' 3"/5' 9" (shoal/std)
Displacement	22,771 lbs.
Ballast	8,500 lbs.
Sail area	771 sq. ft.

In order to place the head so far forward, the cabin trunk had to be extended farther forward than what might be considered normal. Perry said that if he deserves any credit for having done a good job, it was in making a pleasant looking boat with such an extended trunk.

There are numerous differences between the Valiant 40 and Passport 40. Gone is the so-called canoe stern (which Perry calls the "Moses Theory of the stern parting the waves") and the nearly flat coachroof. The Passport 40 has a rather large, conventional transom, which allows beam to be carried well aft and to increase cockpit space. And the coachroof has considerable camber, which, of course, is quite a bit stronger than a flat one.

Perry calls the two boats "totally different." "The

Owners' Comments

"Bob Perry draws beautiful lines. The woodwork is first class all the way. Everything is geared for comfort and livability."
—1985 model in Seattle, WA

"No failures or hints of failures after six years. Interior perfect for two couples. The large galley is important. The cockpit is a bit cramped. Nanni (Mercedes) parts and maintenance support are iffy. Stern ladder is awkward to use. Newer models have been improved."
—1983 model in San Francisco, CA

"The rubrail should be above the wale stripe to be effective. Do not expect the boat to perform well in light air (less than six knots). I'm very impressed with the quality of the rig and its strength. The interior is the best I've seen on any 40-footer. Gelcoat work is not the best but I've been told the yard has been working to improve the problem. I would buy another just like it."
—1983 model in Grand Rapids, MI

"Tracks very well. It's a heavy, spacious boat easily handled by two people. Evokes favorable comments wherever we go. Stable and stiff. Women are very comfortable with this boat."
—1982 model in Brigantine, NJ

"Gelcoat probably not as fine as the other aspects of the boat. Deck drains not at most dependent point. Small amounts of standing water."
—1982 model in Oakland, CA

"My Passport has the Pathfinder diesel and I am very happy with it. It consumes about three-quarters of a gallon per hour.

"Upwind performance is hindered by the roller furling, but I would never give it up. The boat tracks well, stays upright and goes fast.

"I equipped the Passport for comfortable cruising with forced-air heating, microwave oven, roller furling, radar, autopilot, electric windlass, etc."
—1982 model in Seahurst, WA

Passport 40 is a wide-stern boat with assymetrical waterlines, a wedge shape, and flat bottom. The Valiant 40 has symmetrical waterlines and higher deadrise."

Both boats do, however, have large fin keels, often called "cruising fins" due to their comparatively long run and shallow draft. The leading edges are raked for several reasons: to get some ballast further forward, absorb the force of collisions with logs and other objects, and to facilitate removing the ballast casting from its mold. Combined with the skeg-mounted rudder, which is more forgiving than a spade and gives additional lateral plane aft to help tracking, this is a nice underbody configuration for cruising. About all it gives up to the full keel boat is an exposed propeller.

The essential specifications differ somewhat, though not greatly. The Passport 40 is six inches shorter overall, with a waterline seven inches shorter. Beam is four inches wider, and draft is three inches shallower. Displacement and sail area are roughly the same, though Perry says all of the Passport 40s weigh more than listed—"24,000 pounds at least."

In appearance, the sheerlines are also quite similar, as are the bows. Both are very handsome boats and will continue to look good for many years to come. If he had to design the Passport 40 again, Perry said he wouldn't make the stern quite so wide and give it more deadrise for more bilge.

Construction

Passport boats were constructed in Taiwan, first at the King Dragon yard and later at Hi Yang. Renken lived in nearby Taipei with his Chinese wife. His close supervision in the construction of the Passport line, ranging from 37 to 51 feet (the latter designed by Stan Huntingford), represented a changing trend in Far East boatbuilding.

Anyone who has owned one of Taiwan's famous "leaky teakies" knows that Chinese craftsmen are highly capable in some areas, and woefully inept in others. Most of the problems were caused not by lack of skill, but lack of modern boatbuilding knowledge. And, to some extent, by poor facilities and archaic tools. Wiring often wasn't color coded, cockpit seats were plywood thinly covered with layers of fiberglass, and custom metal fittings were cast from inferior alloys.

What Renken and others did in the early 1980s was to move on site and teach the glass men and carpenters how to build to higher standards. The work produced by Passport Yachts International, Ta Shing (builders of the Mason and Tashiba lines), and Ted Hood's Little Harbor yard, are vastly superior to the early clunkers built by Formosa and others. You remember those old pirate ships—the Marine Traders, Sea Wolfs and Yankee Clippers—with the Chinese dragons carved on the doors, and dozens of tiny drawers inside drawers, don't you? In fact, today Taiwan is capable of building boats about as well as any country in the world, *if* they are properly supervised. During our visit to Taiwan in 1987, it appeared to us that nearly all of the good yards had Western supervisors or agents watchdogging construction. The exception was Ta Shing, which builds and markets its own boats.

The hull of the Passport 40 is solid fiberglass (one owner responding to our Boat Owner's Questionnaire said Airex foam core was optional, but Perry said he's never heard of one), hand laminated with 24-ounce woven roving and 1.5-ounce mat. Polyester resin. Very traditional. Wooden transverse stringers are glassed inside the hull to increase stiffness. Hull thicknesses vary, naturally, but one report stated it was about 9/16-inch thick near the keel. According to Perry, the deck is cored with mahogany plywood. The hull/deck joint is through-bolted every eight inches, sealed with polysulfide and the seam filled with resin and filler. Ballast is an iron casting fit into the one-piece hull/keel cavity.

The interior of a Taiwan-built boat is what really grabs people. The Passport 40's doors, frames and trim are solid Burmese teak, amply varnished. Same goes for the chart table and dinette. The cabin sole is teak and holly. Even the cockpit seats have inlaid teak. And the deck is laid 5/8-inch teak bedded in Thiokol. Okay, that's a lot of teak, but Renken used some restraint compared to the earlier Taiwan-built boats. The interior looks great, but you still gotta like teak!

According to one brochure, the diesel auxiliary offered was either a Perkins 4-108 or Nanni diesel (Mercedes Benz). However, owners report also owning Pathfinders (Volkswagen), Isuzu and Yanmar diesel. We'd prefer a boat with the Perkins for reliability and parts availability. The engine is located under the dinette settee, which may seem odd to some, but is in fact a good place for it. Weight is kept close to the center of the boat, it is convenient for maintenance and repair, and there is no need for a V-drive, which would be necessary had Perry put the engine aft under the companionway steps. The only concern with its placement in the saloon would be noise, but generous sound insulation—lead-lined foam—does a good job of muffling even a large diesel.

Fuel tanks (two) were "fiberglassed black iron," according to the brochure. The two water tanks,

Top: The standard layout places the head forward, which required Perry to extend the cabin trunk farther forward than he would have liked. Bottom: The optional interior plan has a double berth forward and a large head, with tub, in the conventional location. Both plans should work well for the liveaboard couple.

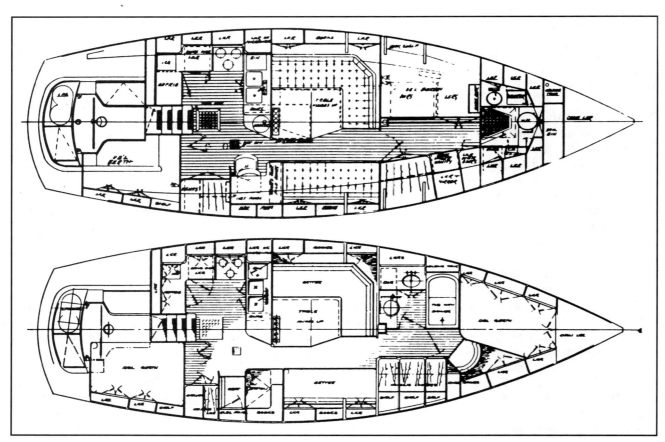

holding about 125 gallons, were either fiberglass or stainless steel. The latter were apparently optional for a time, then later made standard.

A key difference between boats built in Taiwan under people like Renken and the previous generation was the installation of familiar Western hardware and equipment. Stateside distributors realized that to sell successfully to the American public, items such as winches and pumps had to be familiar brands, easily repaired and serviced. The Passport 40, for example, is equipped with products by Lewmar, Barient, Schaefer, Marinetics and Raritan.

There are 10 bronze opening portlights with screens for superior ventilation. The four hatches are by Atkins-Hoyle and are top quality. Like many builders, Passport Yachts apparently often changed suppliers. Some readers report owning Kenyon masts, others Isomat. Owners had the choice of a deck- or keel-stepped mast. All say they are satisfied.

Overall, owners rate construction of their Passport 40s as above average to excellent. "No leaks, no gear failures," wrote one owner. The only complaints involved less than perfect gelcoat. Considering that these boats, like most boats built in the countryside of Taiwan, were built in open-air sheds, it is not surprising. Just 18 percent of owners reported any blistering, none major.

This is a heavily built boat that we consider suitable for serious cruising. We wouldn't expect to find bulkheads working or large, unsupported structural panels that oilcan. The abundance of teak, especially on the decks, will require additional maintenance and probably some repair as the boat ages.

This is not a criticism of the Passport, just a fact of life for owners of boats with laid teak decks.

Performance

Just what is a "performance cruiser"? It certainly isn't a race boat. Nor is it a lumbering, full-keel, heavy-displacement, traditional cruiser. To our mind, a performance cruiser is heavy enough to handle rough, offshore conditions, yet has an easily driven hull form, a nice foil shape to the fin and sufficient sail area to keep moving in lighter air. That would sum up the performance of the Passport 40 with reasonable accuracy.

As is usually the case, owners' ratings of their boats' performance are all over the mark. Some Passport 40 owners rank their boats' upwind performance no better than average, others say it's excellent. Much depends on past experience and the variety of boats sailed for comparative purposes.

"It's amazing how well this heavy boat moves in light air," one owner commented. Another said, "Needs 10 to 15 knots of wind to move it well."

Perry acknowledges that the rig is short and that light air is not its strong suit. "The happiest owners seem to be in San Francisco. This is a full mainsail boat," he said, adding that while a lot of people think they want a high sail area-to-displacement ratio, many owners are more comfortable with a more conservative rig that doesn't need shortening in moderate wind speeds.

The majority of owners rate the boat's offwind performance better than upwind, but not all. One owner, who rated upwind performance as excellent

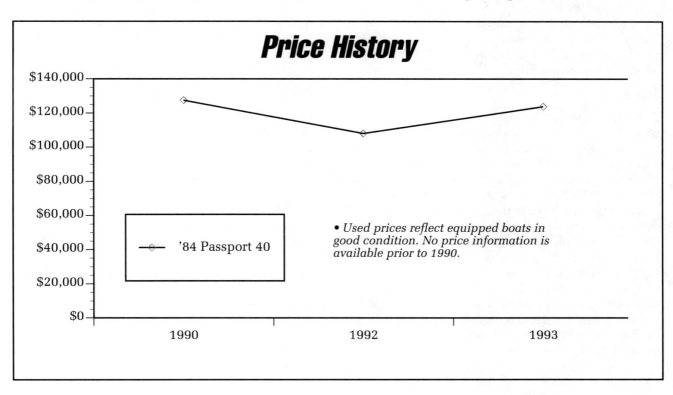

Price History

- Used prices reflect equipped boats in good condition. No price information is available prior to 1990.

◇— '84 Passport 40

and offwind as above average, said, "Points high, a joy to sail upwind."

Seaworthiness, stability, and balance also rate well. "Very dry. No need for dodger," said a San Francisco, California, owner. "Even in 25 knots of wind, the rail does not go under," said another.

Several owners praised the boat's maneuverability, with a few noting that the helm requires constant attention. Well, you can't really have both maneuverability and no-hands steering. The key is good balance, and the Passport appears to have it. "One of the easiest handling boats I've sailed in 20 years," said an Oakland, California owner.

For some perspective on the boat's speed, a check of PHRF handicaps shows the Passport 40 rated anywhere from 114 to 138 seconds per mile. For the sake of comparison, the Valiant 40 and the durable Freya 39 with tall mast also rate about 138. The Crealock 37, which is similar in its designed purpose, though a bit smaller, rates between 168 and 180. A middle-of-the-road Pearson 40 rates about 108 as does the Ericson 39. The more race-happy C&C 40 rates about 90. So it seems safe to say that among offshore cruisers, the Passport 40 has a good turn of speed, not much slower than mainstream fin-keel, spade-rudder sloops of similar length. And, of course, it cannot compete with the hard-core racer.

Perry said that despite its flatter bottom, a Passport 40 can be beaten by a well-sailed Valiant 40. If the boat was built with hull coring and brought down to its designed displacement, he said, it would perform better. It also suffers, he said, from dragging its wide transom when heeled hard over.

In any case, we think the Passport 40 is a very pleasing combination of design tradeoffs that enable her to make safe, reasonably fast passages. And, she can climb away from a lee shore with confidence. That's important.

Interior

Two basic interior layouts were available, though the builder encouraged customization. Consequently, in a used Passport 40 you might find all sorts of adjustments that may or may not suit your taste.

As mentioned, the original layout locates the head virtually in the forepeak, with the forward stateroom just aft of it. The head of the offset double berth is at the main bulkhead, right where the toilet would be in the second plan. The advantage of this layout is locating the seldom-used head away from the principal living area. In the bow it will be well ventilated, but riding the throne in a big sea could be a wild experience! Moving the berth aft increases its utility as a sea berth. The disadvantage is that ventilation of the berth won't be quite as good for sleeping on hot, tropical nights.

The saloon features either an L- or U-shaped dinette to port and a settee to starboard. The galley is aft to port and quite large, too large according to one owner. At eight feet, there's enough room for two people to work together. The stove fuel of choice is propane, which we think is the only way to go. To starboard is an enclosed stateroom with double quarter berth, seat and chart table. Enclosing such a cabin looks appealing at the boat show, and is nearly a prerequisite of the charter trade, where, we are led to believe, every outing is like some scene from the movie "Four Seasons." In reality, such cabins are stuffy and uncomfortable. In fact, in the tropics, even open quarter berths may become untenable, despite overhead hatches (always too small, by necessity) and electric fans.

If we were planning a one-couple cruise, we'd seriously consider removing part of the bulkhead and the door. Communication between the navigation station and the helm would be improved. If, however, we were weekend summer cruisers who liked to cruise with other couples, we'd just install the biggest fan we could afford to run on available battery power.

As implied above, the second basic plan locates the head just forward of the main bulkhead and gives the owner the choice of a V-berth forward or an offset double berth with changing seat. We've tried both types of berths and admit there is no perfect solution. A couple that likes sleeping together must, on a V-berth, install the insert board and cushion. Cushion beading and cracks between cushions may be a bother, but can be at least partially solved by laying down a padded comforter under the bottom sheet. The problem then is climbing into the berth head first from the head compartment. The offset double allows room to stand in the cabin next to the berth. The seat is handy, and entry into the berth is easier. The only drawback is that the person sleeping outboard must climb over the other person to get in and out. We can't remember which was worse: doing the climbing over, or being the one getting trampled.

The joinerwork is, by most standards, very nicely done. Lots of varnished teak. Lots of stowage bins. Many thoughtful details. We like an all-wood interior for its warmth and sound-deadening qualities.

Conclusion

Readers continually ask us to recommend seaworthy cruising boats. The Passport 40 is one. We like Perry's concept of the performance cruiser. If you're planning to venture to remote sections of the world—say, Patagonia or Sri Lanka—we'd probably opt for a full keel design as added protection against the possibility of severe groundings, collision with deadheads, or beaching, but for the Caribbean or the South Pacific, the Passport 40 would be an intelligent choice. **• PS**

C&C 40

Originally built to race under the IOR, this boat remains competitive as a club racer.

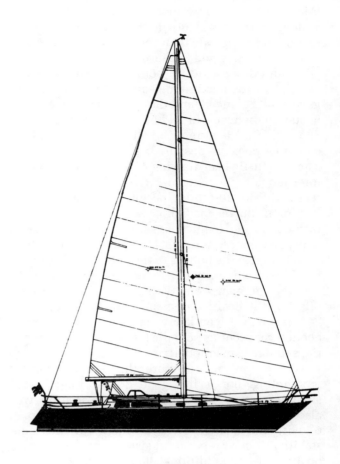

While C&C did not invent the racer/cruiser, the Canadian-based company has remained dedicated for two decades to the concept of the dual-purpose boat.

With the notable exception of a few pure cruisers—the relatively low-performance Landfall 35, 42, 43, and 48—a racer-based cruiser (the Landfall 38), and a real oddball (the Mega 30), most C&Cs have paid at least lip service to contemporary trends in racing boats.

In some cases, C&C's boats have been closely designed to the racing rules. The C&C 38 was a somewhat modified old IOR (International Offshore Rule) one-tonner, the later C&C 41 was a development of several C&C custom IOR boats, and the C&C 37+ was designed to be competitive under the current IMS (International Measurement System) handicapping rule.

The C&C 40 entered production as a 1978 model, and was phased out in 1983, replaced by the higher-performance C&C 41—a bigger, much faster, slightly lighter, more powerful boat, which still managed to be cheaper than the last C&C 40s built.

Specifications

LOA	39' 7"
LWL	31' 6"
Beam	12' 8"
Draft	7' 0" (std keel)
Displacement	17,100 lbs.
Ballast	7,910 lbs.
Sail area	740 sq. ft.

Sailing Performance

The 40 was an IOR design, but she was not heavily optimized to the rule. In the late 1970s, custom IOR designs featured not only somewhat tortured hull shapes to fool the rule into thinking they were slower than they were, but in many cases had grapefruit-sized "bumps" at critical measurement points. By comparison, the hull of the C&C 40 is undistorted, fair, and conservative.

This lack of distortion was reflected in the boat's IOR rating. A reasonably optimized custom 40' IOR design of the late 1970's rated about 10' lower than her overall length. The C&C 40, at 39.58' long, typi-

cally rated from 29.5 to 30.5, depending on the keel and rig configuration of the boat.

With a rating as high or slightly higher than that of custom boats, which most likely were lighter and had better weight distribution, the C&C 40 was reasonably competitive under the IOR in her first year, marginally competitive by the second, and a good club-level racer by 1980. Top-flight IOR boats then had a serious competitive life of two years or less, which was a major factor leading to the near-demise of the rule.

Fortunately for the C&C 40, the MHS (Measurement Handicap System, later renamed the IMS) began to grow in popularity after 1980, giving the boat a new lease on competitive life, at least at second-echelon levels of competition. The boat is no

IMS rule-beater; she's handicapped fairly by IMS, which means she'll do neither better nor worse racing under the rule than the crew sailing her.

This boat has good all-around performance upwind and downwind, in both light and heavy air. Despite a wide maximum beam, the boat's ends are fairly well balanced, and the rudder is deep enough to stay in the water in all but a flat-out broach.

You'll find a number of different keel and rig combinations. As designed, the boat has a high-aspect-ratio fin keel drawing 7', with an "I" (height of foretriangle) dimension of 53'. This configuration is reasonable for all-around performance, but is a little lacking in power for lighter air. A rig 2' taller was introduced, and to increase sail-carrying ability, this is usually coupled with a 4" deep, 300-pound lead shoe bolted to the bottom of the keel. Stability of the two versions is virtually identical: the addition to righting moment from the shoe is almost exactly offset by the heeling moment of the taller rig.

The tall rig, deep keel version is on the average about three seconds per mile faster than the standard rig, standard keel model.

With a draft of 7' or more, this is not a boat for gunkholing, nor is it a good cruiser for areas of shallow water. A keel/centerboard variation was also built, drawing about 4' 9" with the board up, 8' 6" with the board down. To maintain the same stability as her deeper-draft sisters, the centerboard boat carries an additional 885 pounds of ballast, making her noticeably slower in light air. The IMS velocity prediction program shows the standard rig, centerboard model to be about four seconds per mile slower than the standard keel, standard rig version in eight knots of breeze. In 16 knots of wind, all three configurations are virtually identical in speed.

In areas traditionally known for heavy air, a keel shoe coupled to the standard rig has proven to be a powerful and competitive combination.

Like many IOR boats from the mid and late 1970s, the C&C 40 has a very high-aspect-ratio mainsail: about 3.5:1 with the standard rig, almost 3.65:1 with the tall rig. The result is a mainsail of just over 300 sq. ft., but a 100% foretriangle of about 440 sq. ft. This means lots of headsail changes, since reefing the mainsail has relatively little impact on total sail area.

With a racing crew of eight, headsail changes are no big deal. For a cruising couple, wrestling down a #1 genoa of over 650 sq. ft. would be no fun. For shorthanded cruising, a modern headsail reefing system is an absolute must for this boat. We'd also forget the 150% genoa for cruising, using a 130% genoa—about the size of a racing #2—which could be effectively reefed to about 100%.

It's not realistic to expect more reduction from a single sail. In winds of 10 knots or more, the loss in speed from the smaller genoa is virtually meaningless when cruising: it's still faster than 90% of the 40-footers out there.

C&C rigs are generally well designed, with masts of reasonably high-performance characteristics. The 40 has a keel-stepped, double-spreader rig with single lower shrouds, Navtec rod rigging, and a forward babystay. This allows good mast control for racing. Tensioning the babystay pulls the middle of the mast forward, flattening the mainsail in heavy air. With all the shrouds in a single plane, the mast can assume a fair bend from top to bottom.

Most of these boats are equipped with a hydraulic backstay, with the babystay adjusted by a traveler on a track mounted atop the cabin. Boats that have been set up for racing may also have hydraulics for the babystay and vang. Without hydraulic mast controls, it's virtually impossible to take advantage of the spar's sail-shaping capabilities.

The mast is made from a reasonable section for a racer/cruiser. It is bendy enough for sail control when racing, but not nearly as fragile as you would find on a flat-out IOR racer of the same rig size.

If you intend to use the boat only for cruising, and you install a headsail reefing system, it would be almost imperative to add an inner forestay, particularly if you're headed offshore. The existing staysail track in the middle of the foredeck is not really strong enough for the attachment of a true heavy-weather staysail or storm jib.

In addition, we'd add running backstays to counteract the pull of the inner forestay, but you'd only have to set these up in heavy weather when sailing with a staysail or storm jib on the forestay.

The deck layout is definitely designed for racing. Halyard and spinnaker gear winches are mounted atop the deckhouse, aft of the mast. This works fine on a racing boat, keeping the center of gravity low, making it possible for one person to jump the headsail or spinnaker halyard while another tails, out of the way, further aft.

For shorthanded cruising, however, mast-mounted winches are superior. When reefing the mainsail with mast-mounted winches, one person can ease off the halyard, hook in the reefing tack, crank down the clew, and grind up the main halyard, all without moving. With deck-mounted winches, it's back and forth between the mast and the deck if one person has to do the whole job.

Construction

Like most C&Cs, the 40 was built with a balsa-cored hull. The result is a hull that is extremely stiff for its weight, but balsa coring is not without its potential for problems. In the event of delamination or rupture of the hull skin, the balsa coring can absorb moisture. Moisture penetration of the outer laminate could ultimately reach the balsa coring. It is imperative that a balsa-cored hull be carefully examined by a knowledgeable surveyor before purchasing a used boat.

As with most boats, the deck of the C&C 40 is also balsa cored. The deck, too, should be carefully sounded to check for delamination. In our opinion, deck delamination is potentially a very serious problem in almost any boat—not just this one—and the cost and difficulty of repair is frequently grossly underestimated.

C&C uses a basic inward-turning flange for the hull-to-deck joint, with a through-bolted aluminum toerail providing the mechanical fastening. Unlike many builders, C&C uses butyl tape in this joint. Butyl tape has no structural or adhesive properties; it just keeps the water out.

Uniform tensioning of the bolts in the joint is important with this type of bedding compound. Leaks in the joint can frequently be solved by careful re-torquing the bolts, but don't tighten them so much that all the compound's squeezed out.

As is typical of C&Cs, owners give the boat high marks for quality of construction, and in general, their enthusiasm is justifed. The boat does, however, have a potential weak point. Like most late IOR boats, the hull is virtually flat on the bottom, with the shallow bilges having little depth for strong transverse support. The keel has a relatively short root chord, so the keel stresses are very concentrated. In a hard grounding, the trailing edge of the keel can be levered up into the hull, resulting in devastating damage.

We examined one C&C 40 that ran into a rock at about seven knots during a race. The aft edge of the keel punched through the bottom of the boat, and the owner just managed to power the boat 20 miles to a boatyard, which hauled her instantly to keep the boat from sinking.

That boat required massive bottom rebuilding—the boat was actually replaced and the damaged hull repaired and re-sold. Over the years, we have looked at several C&C 40s with similar, though less dramatic, bottom damage as the result of grounding while racing. Remember that with this boat, you need more than 7' of water under you.

Beginning with 1981 models, both the deck and rudder installations were more heavily reinforced.

Most boats were retrofitted with these upgrades, and you should check with previous owners to see that they were done.

Engine

Several different engines were used in the C&C 40. Early models usually have a Yanmar 3QM-30. Later boats typically were fitted with a Westerbeke 30, although some boats were equipped with the more powerful VW-based Pathfinder engine.

All the engines are capable of driving the boat to hull speed in calm water.

The engine is mounted under the bridgedeck, just below the companionway. You must remove the companionway ladder and the front of the engine box to get access to the front of the engine. You can get at the port side through the quarterberth.

The boat handles extremely well under power, thanks to a big rudder well aft, very little wetted surface, and a prop mounted just forward of the rudder. Most boats are equipped with Martec folding props for racing—not the best installation for handling in reverse—but since the prop is so far aft, the boat handles very predictably when moving astern. For cruising, we'd rather see a feathering prop, which is an expensive but worthwhile retrofit.

Interior

C&C never skimped on the interiors of its racer/cruisers, and the 40 is no exception. The interior is built up of teak-faced ply, rather than incorporating a fiberglass liner with molded furniture bases.

The oiled teak ply makes for a darkish interior, which could be lightened considerably by varnishing both the ply and its solid teak edging. A nice combination is to use satin finish varnish on the ply, glossy varnish on the solid teak trim. This is time-consuming, of course, but it can noticeably brighten a drab interior.

The C&C 40's original layout (left) had a conventional racing boat interior with a large galley, a head in the forward section and two pilot berths. The last few boats built had a revamped interior (right). The pilot berths were eliminated, the galley and nav station were flopped, and the head moved aft, all to create a private aft cabin.

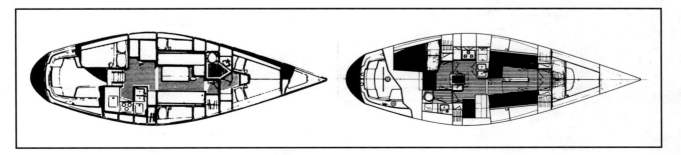

The cabin sole is teak and holly-faced ply, and the teak veneer is so thin that it chips easily, particularly at the edges when you pry up the floor boards.

There are plenty of berths for racing, and too many for cruising. The V-berths forward can be made into a double with an insert, and the quarterberth is wide enough to form a very tight double or a very big single.

Interior layout is fairly prosaic: V-berths forward, settees and pilot berths both port and starboard in the main cabin, quarterberth aft. Some early boats were built with a split quarterberth, with a narrow inboard berth and a narrower pilot berth outboard, tucked under the side deck. This is a particularly useless arrangement for cruising, and we wouldn't be too happy getting stuck in either of those berths when racing, either.

The head compartment is good-sized, and is accessible from either the main cabin or the forward cabin. We're not sure you really need two doors mere inches apart to get into the head, but perhaps the additional privacy for head access from the forward cabin is important to some people. We'd rather have the separation that a solid bulkhead between head and forward cabin would provide.

Main cabin storage is sacrificed to get in the two pilot berths. If you're planning long-distance racing with a big crew—or weekending with lots of friends—the pilot berths are nice. But the lower third of the pilot berths is recessed behind a longitudinal bulkhead which serves as the shroud anchorage. There will be no air circulation around your lower body in this berth.

Space over your feet is further reduced in the pilot berths by a locker tucked into the upper part of this longitudinal bulkhead. The result is a pair of berths that would be okay in cooler climates, miserable in the tropics.

Ventilation below is generally inadequate for anything but cooler climates. While there are good-sized aluminum-framed hatches over both the forward and main cabins, plus a small hatch over the head, the only provision for ventilation in bad weather is a pair of cowl vents in dorade boxes at the aft end of the main cabin.

C&C racer/cruisers have good galleys. The galley—aft on the starboard side—is the classic U-shape, with double sinks and a large bin in the forward counter; a large, well-insulated icebox under the aft counter; and the stove in the middle, at the base of the U.

The builder was a pioneer in the use of propane aboard boats, and that's what you'll find as a cooking fuel in virtually all C&C 40s. It's a good installation, with gas bottles located in small lockers on either side of the helmsman's seat at the aft end of the cockpit.

This is a very usable galley, with good storage outboard, a fair amount of counter space, and a practical layout.

The nav station opposite the galley has its own seat (you don't sit on the quarterberth) and a big chart table.

The bookshelf outboard is usually sacrificed for navigation and communication electronics, leaving you no place for your navigation texts. In fact, that

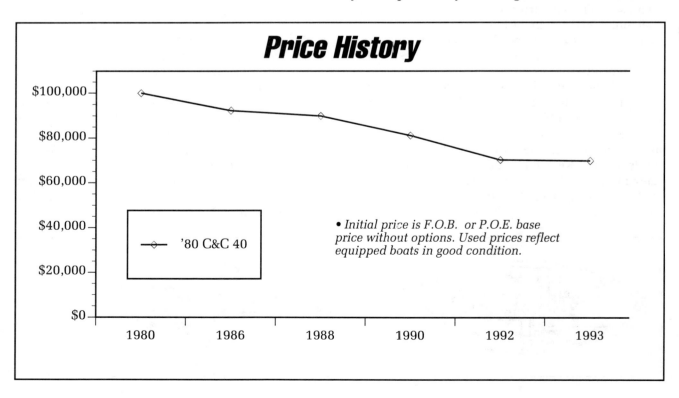

Price History

• Initial price is F.O.B. or P.O.E. base price without options. Used prices reflect equipped boats in good condition.

'80 C&C 40

single 2' shelf is the total amount of book shelving in the entire boat!

If you're thinking of cruising, you may want to sacrifice one or both of the main cabin pilot berths, replacing them with storage lockers and shelves. Otherwise, there's little readily accessible storage space in the boat.

In these days of tri-cabin layouts in 30-footers, it's unusual to find the basic two-cabin layout in a 40' boat. In fact, virtually every 40' cruising boat built since the early 1980s has a three-cabin interior.

With the racing competitiveness of the C&C 40 decreasing, and its desirability as a cruising boat limited by lack of a good owners' cabin with a double berth, a major re-thinking of the boat was required if it was to continue in production. This resulted in the short-lived aft cabin version of the C&C 40. In the last year of production, the deck was re-tooled, and the interior redesigned to create a tri-cabin boat with a stateroom aft.

The new interior was a mixed success. The pilot berths were eliminated, replaced by much-needed storage. The galley lost some space—it became L-shaped, giving up one leg of the old U—and was shifted slightly forward and to the port side. The nav station was flopped to starboard .

Aft, to starboard, is the head. On the port side aft is the owners' cabin, with a double quarterberth, hanging locker, and a seat. A doorway through the starboard bulkhead gives access from the owners' cabin to the head, and there's another doorway to the head from the main cabin.

In order to accommodate this new arrangement aft, the companionway was shifted forward, so that you must climb on top of the deckhouse to get to the companionway, which is a sliding hatch in the deck.

This deck layout is similar to that used on some older Swans, and it's a poor solution for a cruising boat, since it basically eliminates the possibility of a full-width dodger over the front of the cockpit.

You can install a dodger, but it will be so far forward as to offer minimal protection to the cockpit, and it makes climbing down the companionway a gymnastic effort with the dodger in place.

With the aft cabin C&C 40, you still have a high-performance boat, and you still—unless you opt for the centerboard—have a boat that draws at least 7'. The deep-draft, high-aspect-ratio fin keel and small mainsail are not the best combination for most cruising.

On the plus side, the aft cabin boat has significantly more privacy, eliminates unneeded berths, and has much more storage space.

Ventilation and light below are also much better in the aft cabin boat, although the big hatch over the main cabin is lost to the main companionway. In addition to the large hatch over the forward cabin, there are two small hatches over the main cabin, plus small hatches over both the aft cabin and the head. There are also additional fixed ports in the deckhouse, adding light to the main cabin.

Relatively few aft cabin boats were built. It was an expensive layout to construct, and the 40 was already getting pricey due to the built-up interior, which is much more labor-intensive than an interior based on a liner with molded furniture.

Conclusions

Despite her heavy interior, the C&C 40 was a reasonably competitive racing boat when introduced in the late 1970s. On the plus side, the interior was comfortable enough for cruising when the racing was over—as long as deep draft and a big rig don't intimidate you.

Some 200 C&C 40s were built, and many of them did a lot of racing. It's not unusual to find a 40 with very complete electronics, a full hydraulic rig control package, and a big inventory of racing sails.

Since the design's days as a serious racing boat are pretty much over—although you can certainly compete at the local level—many owners interested in racing have unloaded C&C 40s at near fire-sale prices.

In general, the C&C 40 is a well-built boat, in the same class as other boats from the company. The construction is not particularly high-tech, however, and some boats may have suffered under the strains of very heavy racing.

In particular, we'd recommend careful examination of the hull bottom in the way of the keel, and the attachment of structural components in the way of the mast and rudder.

Newer designs from C&C have taken advantage of higher-tech materials such as molded interior and hull support modules, and in general are probably stronger per pound of structural weight than older boats such as the C&C 40. Nevertheless, a C&C 40 which surveys cleanly can be an excellent value for club racing, and—with some re-working of the deck layout—for shorthanded cruising in areas where the deep draft is not a problem. **• PS**

Valiant 40

A semi-custom yacht from Texas that's a true high-performance blue-water cruiser.

The Valiant 40 has a long history. In 1972 Nathan Rothman decided to start a boatbuilding business and approached old friend Bob Perry to design the ultimate cruising yacht. At that time Rothman and Perry were young, poor, relatively inexperienced, and full of ideals. Perry accepted the offer without even asking to be paid right away.

The decision to make the Valiant a double-ender was a marketing one based on the skyrocketing success of the Westsail 32. The Westsail had just been featured on the cover of *Time* magazine; double-enders were "in." Rothman sent Perry a photo of Aage Nielsen's *Holger Danske* and said, "Let's have a stern like that."

"So I took that fanny," said Perry, "and with all my experience on race boats, I designed a high-performance cruising boat." Rothman contracted with Uniflite to build the boats in Bellingham, WA, and the first Valiant was launched in 1973.

In the late '70s Rothman sold Valiant to Sam Dick Industries, who continued to build the boats under contract with Uniflite. Uniflite eventually bought the company from Sam Dick Industries. Finally, in 1984, Rich Worstell, one of Valiant's most successful dealers, bought Valiant Yachts, and began building the boats on Lake Texhoma.

Everyone knows that everything is bigger and better in Texas. Rich Worstell would not disagree with that—at least not if you were discussing the Valiant. Rich is a Valiant zealot.

Since 1984, he has built a relative handful of Valiant 40s. He also manufactures the Valiant 32, 37, Pilothouse 40, and 47. Every boat is semi-custom and each Valiant buyer comes to the factory at least three times—once to decide exactly which options he wants, once to oversee the building, and once to

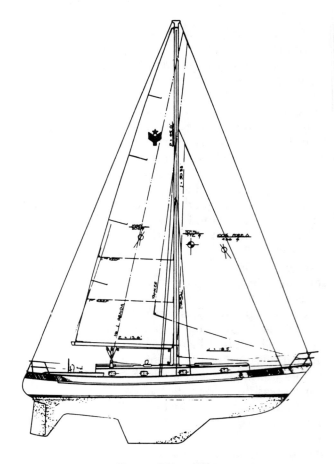

Specifications

LOA	39' 11"
LWL	34' 0"
Beam	12' 4"
Draft	5' 2"/6' 0" (shoal/std)
Displacement	22,500 lbs.
Ballast	7,700 lbs.
Sail area	753 sq. ft.

commission the boat. "We like every customer to shake his boat down at our lake facility so any minor problems can be fixed right here at the factory," says Worstell.

Over the years Valiant has gained a considerable reputation. Veteran singlehander Francis Stokes sailed his Valiant 40 *Mooneshine* to victory (first American monohull) in the 1980 Ostar; in 1983 Mark Schrader sailed a Valiant 40 safely around the world singlehanded, and again, in 1986-87, Schrader's Valiant 47 *Lone Star* completed the BOC.

"But the Valiant is not a boat for everyone," says Perry. "If I were going to hang out in St. Tropez or Portofino, I'd need a different boat—no question—I'd need pointy deck shoes—and a pointy boat. But there's a comfort that comes with being in a slightly less than all-perfect, smarmy environment—and the Valiant seems to suit that."

Hull and Deck

Early in Valiant's boatbuilding history, Uniflite Corporation experienced extensive hull blistering problems both above and below the waterline due to their use of a fire-retardant polyester resin.

To combat the problem, Worstell began using a 100% isophthalic resin used in conjunction with an isophthalic gelcoat. Although tests performed by Comtex Development Corporation in Bridgewater, MA, prove that vinylester blisters less readily than isophthalic resin, Worstell claims he has had no problems with blistering since 1984.

Valiant is convinced that the answer to hull blistering lies not just in the choice of materials, but in the care with which boats are built. Resin is catalyzed a gallon at a time, and hulls are laid up by hand. Valiants also come with 21 mils of epoxy, about eight coats, applied to the bottom of the hull. Topsides are coated with Imron polyurethane paint. While Imron is not as durable as Awlgrip or Sterling, Valiant prefers it because it's easy to repair.

The Valiant hull is an uncored, solid laminate. The deck is balsa-cored fiberglass with molded non-skid surface. Anywhere "stressed" through-bolts enter the deck or cabin house, Valiant puts in high-density foam or hot-coats the end-grain balsa to prevent water from seeping in. All heavily-loaded deck hardware, including grabrails, is installed with backing plates or heavy-duty washers.

Chainplates are stainless steel straps that extend through the deck. Valiant V-cuts their chainplate slots so that extra 3M 5200 sealant can be forced in to form a pressure gasket against the chainplate. Two chainplates through-bolt to 1 1/2" to 2" knees glassed to the inside of the hull. One of the chain plates through-bolts to the main bulkhead. All are very accessible.

The hull-to-deck joint on the Valiant is hard to fault. At the top of the bulwark there is an inward-turning flange. On deck, the edge of the molding turns upward to form the inner bulwark face, then outward at the top to overlap the hull flange. The joint is bedded in 5200 and through-bolted. The bulwark is then capped with a teak or aluminum toerail. We'd be tempted to opt for the aluminum one since it eliminates the upkeep of teak and is more protective against chafe.

The rubbing strake is made of high-density foam glassed to the hull with a sacrificial teak strip on the outside. There is also a stainless rub rail option.

The keel is an external lead casting, bolted to the hull with stainless steel bolts and backing plates. A conventional 6' fin keel is standard, but some owners choose the shoal draft model. Valiant will build the keel anywhere from 5' 2" to 6' in depth, but it can only be cut down in 2" increments.

Rather than molding the skeg as an integral part of the hull, a steel weldment is encased in a two-piece fiberglass shell filled with high-density foam and mish-mash. The skeg is then epoxied to the bottom of the hull and bolted in place with stainless steel bolts, nuts, lock washers, 5200, and a backing plate. Valiant glasses over the skeg again once it is in place to cover the seam. This type of skeg construction is very strong, and should provide adequate protection if you hit a submerged object or run aground.

The skeg heel is through-bolted to the bottom of the skeg. The rudderpost, made of 1 3/4" diameter stainless steel bar, rides on three bearings—one in the gudgeon, one where the rudder post goes through the hull, and a final bearing at the top in the rudder support bracket. Like the skeg, the rudder is filled with high-density foam and mish-mash, and molded in one piece with the rudderpost.

Valiant fabricates over 50% of the components for its boats in-house, including the mast step timber, which is the same for the Valiant 37, 40, 47, and Pilothouse 40. To form the mast step, 1/2" aluminum plate is TIG-welded to form a massive H-beam. The H-beam is then through-bolted to the floor timbers, and the mast sits in an oval-shaped aluminum weldment that is bolted to the custom mast step. This arrangement provides a strong platform, and eliminates corrosion problems that occur if a mast is stepped in the bilge. A tie rod extends from the mast step to the deck to keep the deck from overflexing or "panting."

Wooden bulkheads, which end at the cabin sole, are glassed to the hull with three layers of fiberglass mat and cloth. Valiant also glasses in a series of 12 transverse floor timbers, made of 2 1/2" to 3" high-density Divinycell closed-cell foam, to stiffen the hull.

Many production boats use continuous bulkheads or a molded floor pan for the same purpose. Installing floor timbers, rather than a molded fiberglass body pan, not only provides strength, it also gives Valiant the freedom to customize its interior.

The deep bilge is gelcoated, and all furniture is structurally bonded to the hull. Valiant believes that glassing furniture to hull and bulkheads replaces the need for longitudinal stringers. We question whether this is the best way to reinforce a hull in a semi-custom boat where furniture components are rearranged constantly.

Valiant uses bronze ball-valve seacocks screwed directly onto the threaded tail of the through-hull fitting. We consider this type of seacock potentially unsafe because it can put too much stress on the fitting. Instead, we recommend a flange-type seacock with mechanical fastenings and a doubling plate.

Two water tanks located under the settees port and starboard hold 140 gallons of water. Tanks are built of high-density polyethylene. Each tank has a large inspection plate, and vents to the bilge.

Valiant bonds their boats to protect them from electrolysis. Seacocks, prop shaft, and all underwater hardware are tied to a 6"x6" zinc that is recessed into the hull. Opinion is divided on the efficacy of bonding underwater metal. We've seen bonding solve a boat's galvanic corrosion problems. We've also seen boats suffering from electrolysis solve their problem by eliminating the bonding system. To insure lightning protection Valiant grounds the chainplates and mast base to the keelbolts. A single sideband counterpoise, consisting of copper strapping tied to the keelbolts, is also available as an option.

Engine and Mechanical Systems

The Valiant has a large, well-designed engine room. There's plenty of space to sit down to check the batteries or work on the engine or generator. However, the engine room sole, which follows the curve of the hull, is slippery. We advise coating the sole with non-skid.

Over the years Valiant has used Westerbeke, Perkins and Volvo engines in the 40. Currently, Valiant installs a three-cylinder Volvo 2003 Turbo, rated at 42hp at 3000 rpm with a V-drive transmission and a 3:1 reduction gear.

The front of the engine is accessible from the engine room for servicing filters and belts or changing the oil. The aft ends of the engine and transmission are accessible from the owner's stateroom or head, depending on which interior layout you choose. The engine compartment is properly sound insulated.

Volvo's flexible mounts are bolted to pieces of 4"x4" aluminum angle through-bolted to two high-density foam beds glassed to the hull. The engine has a Volvo water-lift type exhaust system. The exhaust sytem hose is looped high to prevent salt water from back-siphoning into the engine. In general, installation is very good.

However, many mechanics believe that a turbocharged engine is too complicated for a small sailboat, and can present a lot of extra headaches for the cruising sailor. We'd prefer to see the Valiant fitted with a normally aspirated four-cylinder engine of about 100 cubic inches.

The electrical system includes 110-volt AC and 12-volt DC service, and is controlled by a well-designed custom distribution panel mounted next to the navigator. Wiring is to ABYC specification. Wires are color-coded, and neatly run through a PVC pipe to the engine room. There's a handy pennant line supplied for running extra wires. Two 105-amp-hour deep-cycle batteries come standard on the 40, and you can order two extra 105-amp-hour batteries wired in parallel with the original two batteries. (You can also buy four Prevailer gel-cell batteries which Valiant properly installs in wooden battery boxes.) However, we consider wiring batteries in parallel poor practice. As an alternative, we'd recommend you buy two 180-200 amp-hour deep-cycle batteries, or two extra-large Prevailers, and upgrade the size of the alternator.

For those who want all the amenities of home, Valiant neatly installs an auxiliary generator (Northern Lights 5kw) behind a sound-proofed door in the aft end of the engine room. We think installing a generator in a 22,500 lb., 40' sailboat is overkill.

The plumbing system includes hot and cold pressure water. As an option you can also order a Whale foot pump in the galley or head that can be used for fresh or salt water. We consider manual foot pumps mandatory equipment for long-distance cruising. We'd also be tempted to purchase the handy Jabsco deck washdown pump.

There are two standard layouts, but the builder will do anything a buyer wants, within reason (and budget). As a result, a given interior may be very different from the standard one shown here.

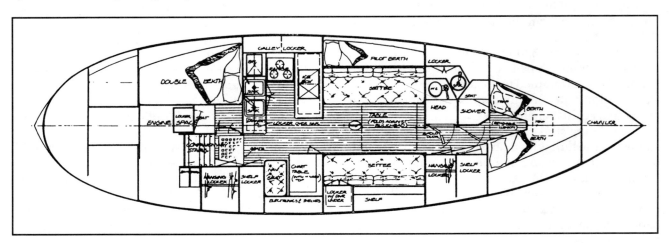

The standard electric bilge pump is a Par 36600 (eight gallons per minute capacity). This pump is inadequate for emergency bilge pumping. We'd recommend adding a second electric pump, even though there is a manual Whale Gusher mounted on the forward end of the cockpit well.

Handling Under Power

The Valiant 40 hull is easily driven; the Volvo 2003 Turbo at a normal cruising rpm of 2400 gives you a speed of 6 knots through the water in flat seas. The boat handles particularly well under power in tight quarters or when docking stern-to.

A two-bladed fixed propeller is standard equipment. You can order a two- or three-bladed feathering Max-Prop, which will improve your performance both under power and sail.

If you order the gen-set option, fuel is stored in two aluminum saddle tanks with a total capacity of 110 gallons. Without a generator, fuel is carried in one 90-gallon aluminum fuel tank. There's a handy fuel gauge mounted at the nav station which eliminates guessing how much diesel you have left.

Handling Under Sail

With a fine entry, a long waterline, a reasonably efficient underbody, and moderate wetted surface, the Valiant sails as well as any fast cruiser of her size.

The Valiant's broad flared bow makes her least efficient in a steep chop to weather. As soon as you bear off, however, the big flared bow becomes all sailing length, and the boat becomes very powerful, especially on a reach or broad reach in heavy air. She

also performs respectably downwind. She's not as fast as a more modern, lighter racer/cruiser, but she's no slouch, either.

The Valiant is cutter-rigged with the mast stepped fairly well aft. This makes for a small, manageable mainsail (306 sq. ft.), and a foretriangle that is substantially larger than it would be on a typical sloop-rigged 40-footer. Still, the boat is unusually well-balanced and easy to handle. You can sail it either as a sloop or cutter (there's a quick release option on the inner forestay), but if you're shorthanded you'll probably prefer the double headsail rig.

Perry broke tradition when he designed a fin keel and skeg rudder for the Valiant. (At that time full keels were considered de rigueur for serious offshore cruising.) Since 1973 Perry has updated the keel twice.

"The initial keel was expensive and difficult to build, so Uniflite asked me to design a stiffer, less expensive one," Perry told us. His second keel design lowered the VCG (vertical center of gravity), deepened the bilge, and generally improved the boat's performance. It was also much easier to build.

The last change was again an effort to make the building effort more efficient, and provide a variety of keels. "With new foil developments we thought we could make it better yet," said Perry, "so I called up Dave Vacanti, who specializes in keels, and we came up with another foil—the same foil shape that was used on *Mongoose* in the Transpac."

The latest keel packs more weight into a shorter chord length and changes the leading edge angle. With increased stability, the newer deep-keeled Val-

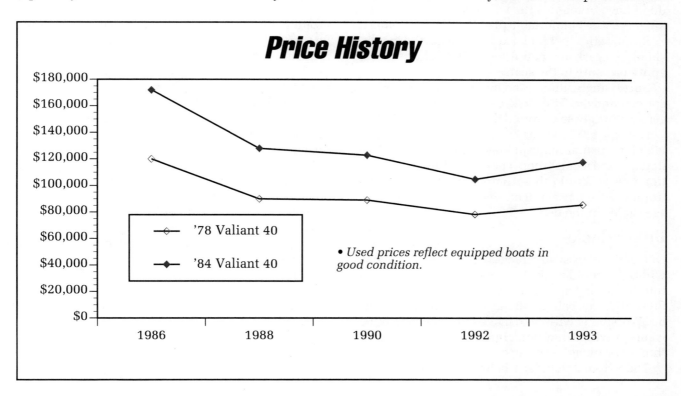

Price History

- ◇— '78 Valiant 40
- ◆— '84 Valiant 40

• *Used prices reflect equipped boats in good condition.*

iants can carry more sail and are faster than older boats. The shoal draft models are a compromise. They don't point as high as the 6' keel, but they do permit the cruising sailor to venture into shallower waters. Still, unless shoal draft is critical for you, we'd stick with the normal keel.

On Deck

The Valiant comes with continuous Navtec rod rigging; the inner forestay and intermediates, however, are wire. Instead of using running backstays to counteract the load of the inner forestay, the standard Valiant rig incorporates fixed intermediate shrouds which lead just behind the aft lower shrouds. The intermediates give minimal fore and aft support to the mast, and could cause unnecessary chafe on the mainsail downwind. We'd opt for running backstays.

A Navtec hydraulic backstay adjuster is optional, but you might want it if you go for roller furling on the headstay. The tapered mast is custom-welded by Spar Tech Inc. in Seattle, and then painted with Imron.

Sail handling hardware is excellent, with Schaefer genoa and staysail tracks. Winches are Lewmar and adequately sized. The halyard winches can be mounted on the mast or on the top of the cabin trunk at the front of the cockpit. Unfortunately, the staysail winches are located directly in the way of the cockpit dodger, preventing you from swinging the winch handle in a complete circle.

Wheel steering is Edson with radial drive. The drive wheel is easily accessible from the cockpit locker. The emergency tiller arm is offset 90° so you don't have to remove the wheel to install the tiller, but there's no comfortable place to sit when using it.

Because the cockpit lockers are huge, the hatches should be gasketed and fitted with latches that can apply pressure to the seal.

Surprisingly, there is no molded breakwater for a cockpit dodger. This makes it almost impossible to get a watertight seal around the bottom of the dodger.

Hatches are Lewmar except for the main hatch, which is custom-made of fiberglass and Lexan. Two dorades and a mushroom vent provide extra ventilation below. While these help beat the heat in the tropics, we are prejudiced against cutting unnecessary holes in the deck.

Belowdecks

One of the biggest advantages of a semi-custom boat without a molded hull liner is the ability to alter interior arrangements to meet an owner's needs. Presently, the Valiant 40 has two standard layouts, but Worstell is willing to make any changes a buyer wants provided they don't interfere with the seaworthiness or integrity of the boat.

The original standard belowdecks arrangement has V-berths forward with an insert to form a double. There's a divided chain locker in the bow, and a 3" PVC pipe can be led to a locker under the forward berth for anchor chain storage. Although we agree with keeping weight out of the bow, we'd worry about the anchor chain jamming in the PVC pipe. Closed cell foam, 1/2" thick, is used throughout the boat above the waterline for insulation.

Aft of the forward berths to starboard are two cedar-lined hanging lockers plus additional storage. The head is to port. The head door has a complicated, levered door handle that, on the boat we inspected, did not catch properly; we prefer very simple closing devices on all doors to avoid this type of problem.

There is ample locker space in the head for towels and sundries. The oval-shaped stainless steel sink is moderately deep, but we'd opt for a manual foot pump as well as the standard hot and cold pressure water. On the boat we inspected the shower and head occupied one space. As an option, you can order a molded fiberglass shower stall with built-in seat and removable teak grates. There's no separate shower sump; shower water is pumped directly overboard. In the main cabin there are settees port and starboard with a choice of shelves or a pilot berth above the settees. You can even opt for a special television shelf. The port berth has a pull-out option that makes a narrow double (6' 8" x 3' 2"). There is a white Formica drop-leaf dinette table which measures 3' 5" x 4' 3" when fully extended. To port, aft of the saloon, is a well-laid-out U-shaped galley. A four-burner Regal propane stove with oven and broiler is standard, but a Force 10 can be installed as an option. We'd buy the Force 10. Propane is stored in a vented lazarette locker holding two 11-lb. tanks. We'd prefer two 20-lb. tanks for long distance cruising, but the propane locker would have to be redesigned.

There are four cedar-lined lock-in type drawers for cutlery, and oodles of storage above the sinks and stove for food stores, spices, and dinnerware. However, we'd like to see the large port side sliding locker divided into smaller cubicles to keep things orderly offshore.

There are adequate double sinks (9" deep) located across from the icebox. Foam insulation in the ice box measures only 2" on the lid, and 3" on the sides. This might keep things cold in northern latitudes, but it won't be effective in the tropics.

A good-sized nav station, facing fore and aft, sits to starboard opposite the galley. The chart table is large enough for any chart folded in half, and has adequate space for electronics, navigation instruments, sextant and books. There is also storage for charts under the nav table, as well as extra storage under the nav seat.

Just starboard of the companionway ladder are three vented storage lockers. One is a wet locker with a canvas door that unzips for ventilation. To port of the companionway is a double stateroom—again with plenty of stowage under bunks and in lockers.

As an alternate arrangement, Valiant has recently designed an interior which we think a couple cruising without children may prefer. As you come down the companionway steps there's a quarterberth to starboard, and a head to port. The layout in the main cabin is the same as the original interior layout. However, forward of the saloon on the port side is a good-sized double berth with hanging lockers and storage opposite. The forepeak then becomes a well-appointed storeroom for sails.

This layout is preferable offshore. First, the head is easily accessible from the cockpit—and aft where the motion is less violent. Second, the off-watch can sleep snugly in the quarterberth, but still be in earshot of the person on deck, or within arm's length of the nav station or galley. The double berth forward can be used for sleeping in harbor.

Headroom everywhere is 6' 2". Lighting is good throughout the boat, especially in the nav station and engine room.

The Valiant comes with two standard interior finishes: oiled teak, or white Formica trimmed in oiled teak. Some people love oiled teak. We don't. If we chose the teak interior, we'd pay the extra money to have it varnished.

An interior of white Formica with teak trim is a practical combination that provides light and a feeling of space, but it may appear stark to those familiar with wood interior spaces. We'd at least opt for the white Formica with teak trim (varnished) in the head and galley.

The cabin sole is not a cheap veneer—it's 1/2" teak with poplar strips mounted on 3/4" ply. Again, we'd choose to have it varnished rather than just sealed, but some people find a varnished cabin sole too slippery.

Conclusions

The Valiant 40 is a true high-performance blue-water cruiser. It's also a well-built boat. You'll be hard pressed to find another builder who is more dedicated to his product than Rich Worstell. Basically, he takes pride in building the Valiant, and, if you buy one, he wants you to be proud of it, too.

For this reason he's willing to pretty much build the boat to an owner's specifications—within reason.

This all comes at a price, of course.

There are a few things we don't like about the Valiant. Most of them, (except for the seacocks) have nothing to do with seaworthiness. They're purely aesthetic. For example, the cabin trunk is too boxy for some people's tastes, and we'd like to see the boat built with oval instead of rectangular ports. The joinerwork is good, but no better than you'll find on other boats in this price range.

Basically, the Valiant is just not as flashy as more expensive semi-custom boats like the Alden 44. But the Valiant is an honest boat. It's strong, it's seakindly, and as Perry so aptly said, it's "been everywhere, and done just about everything."   • **PS**

Bristol 39 and 40

The looks of these twins are strictly traditional, but so is the interior room—modern 33-footers have more.

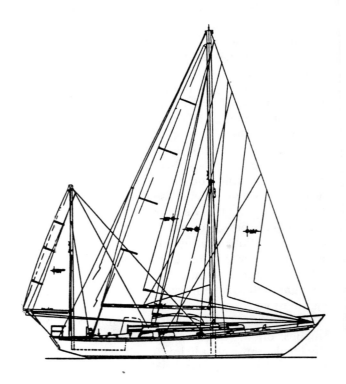

The Bristol 39 and Bristol 40 are basically the same boat, even though the specifications state that the Bristol 40 is nearly a foot longer than the Bristol 39. According to the builder, the hull sections aft were made slightly fuller on the Bristol 40, and the stemhead fitting was altered. After very careful scaling of plans, we can say with reasonable confidence that from one end of the hull to the other, excluding the bow pulpit and the anchor roller, the Bristol 39 and Bristol 40 are about 39' 8" long. Whether you call it a 39-footer or a 40-footer is up to you.

But this is not a 40' boat in the modern sense. Yes, if you take a tape measure to the boat, you'll read almost 40'. But if you go below, you'll swear you stepped onto a 33' boat—at least if you're used to looking at the 33-footers built today.

With a waterline length of 27' 6" and a beam of 10' 9", The Bristol 40's proportions are about as typical as you can get of cruising/racing sailboats built between about 1930, when the CCA (Cruising Club of America) rule was conceived, and 1970, when it was replaced by the International Offshore Rule (IOR). For those 40 years, about 30% of the average boat's length was in overhangs. Today, you find the waterline length and beam of the Bristol 40 on boats less than 35' long.

About 150 Bristol 40s were built. This does not include the relatively small number of boats in the Bristol 39 series.

The 39 was one of the first models built by Bristol Yachts, entering production in 1966. Beginning with 1972 models, the boat was rechristened the Bristol 40. The last Bristol 40 was built in 1986.

If you like traditional yachts, you'll find the Bristol 40 appealing. The boat has the long overhangs, lovely sheerline, low freeboard, narrow cabin trunk,

Specifications - 40

LOA	39' 8"
LWL	27' 6"
Beam	10' 9"
Draft	4' 0"/7' 10" (board up/down)
Displacement	17, 580 lbs.
Ballast	6,500 lbs.
Sail area	707 sq. ft. (yawl)

undistorted hull shape, and narrow beam we associate with the beautiful yachts of the past. If you didn't know she was a Ted Hood design, you might mistake her for a boat by Olin Stephens, John Alden, or Phil Rhodes.

The trade-off for these traditional good looks is a boat with a small interior compared to today's 40-footers.

Sailing Performance

"Fast" is a very relative term when you're talking about sailboats. The Bristol 40 is not fast relative to more modern 40-footers, but her performance is similar to that of other boats of her length built under the CCA rule, when boats were heavier and shorter on the waterline than they are today. The boat is close in speed, for example, to the Hinckley Bermuda 40 yawls with the original low aspect ratio rig. It is about 30 seconds per mile slower, however, than the Cal 40—a boat of the same length on deck, but with a longer waterline, less wetted surface and slightly less displacement.

In both keel and centerboard versions, the Bristol 40 is a fairly tippy boat, as you would expect from her narrow beam, shoal draft, and modest amount of ballast. Like "fast," however, "tippy" is a relative term.

Most narrow boats have relatively low initial stability, even if their ultimate stability is good. For example, the McCurdy and Rhodes 62-footer *Arcadia*, built in 1972, is about 2' narrower than a new IOR 60-footer would be, and has a righting moment about 15% lower than that of the new boat, even though *Arcadia* is significantly heavier.

Yet *Arcadia*'s range of positive stability is about 143°, while the typical "modern" racer/cruiser loses positive stability at 120° or less.

Unfortunately, being narrow and tippy doesn't guarantee a good range of ultimate stability. The keel version of the Bristol 40 loses positive righting moment at about 120°—the absolute minimum we would consider for a serious offshore cruiser. The centerboard version's range of stability is less—about 110° for the only boat rated under the International Measurement System (IMS).

It is not unusual for centerboarders to have very low positive stability. The Hinckley Bermuda 40—the classic keel-centerboarder—typically loses stability at an even lower angle than the centerboard Bristol 40, yet few people would consider the boat unsuitable for passagemaking.

Owners report that the Bristol 40 is very sensitive to the amount of sail carried. We'd suggest a modern headsail reefing/furling system for shorthanded cruising to reduce the number of headsail changes required.

Like most CCA boats, the Bristol 40 is a good reaching boat, lacking the rounding-up tendency of many modern boats with full sterns. The trade-off is that the boat tends to squat when running downwind, digging a hole that's hard to climb out of. A Bristol 40 with a full keel won the 1983 Marion-Bermuda Race, an event that consisted largely of four days of close reaching in light to moderate breezes.

Because the boat is narrow, there is no need to move the genoa track inboard of the toerail. The only real disadvantage of toerail-mounted genoa track is that you may have to relead the sheet to clear stanchions when changing headsails or reducing sail area with a headsail furler, unless there are turning blocks at the aft end of the genoa track. The two most common mainsheet arrangements on the boat are a short traveler spanning the cockpit immediately in

front of the steering wheel, or a longer traveler over the coachroof in front of the companionway. The short traveler in the cockpit doesn't really offer much mainsail control, but it is a convenient location for the sheet.

The rig is a basic masthead sloop or yawl, using an untapered, keel-stepped anodized mast with single spreaders and double lower shrouds: basically foolproof. The lower shroud chainplates do not line up exactly with the pull of the shrouds, which will tend to fatigue the chainplates over time, as well as increasing the likelihood of leaks due to an unfair pulling angle.

Since this is a boat that was in production for the better part of 20 years, it's difficult to generalize about the sailing gear you'll find. On the Bristol 40s we've looked at, the stock winches tend to be one or two sizes smaller than we'd put on the boat today. You're unlikely to find self-tailers on older models.

A lot of Bristol 40s were built as yawls. While the yawl rig is pretty and looks very traditional, the mizzen is generally only useful to help balance the helm, as a convenient place to mount a radar antenna, and to serve as a support for a mizzen staysail on the rare occasion that it pays to carry one. The mizzen makes the boat more tippy and increases windage—disadvantages for upwind sailing.

Engine

Before 1970, Bristol 39s came with either Atomic 4 or Graymarine gas engines. Later model 39s and Bristol 40s were powered either by the Atomic 4 or by a variety of diesels, including the Westerbeke 4-91, Westerbeke 4-107 and 4-108, Perkins 4-108, or Volvo MD2B and MD3B engines. That should be enough variety to satisfy everyone.

The Westerbeke and Perkins 4-108s are essentially the same engine, and in our opinion would be the best engine for the boat, although they're more power than it needs. Diesel engine installations in the Bristol 40 are not without problems. There is little room between the shaft coupling and the stuffing box—so little, in fact, that several owners surveyed reported that it is almost impossible to reach the stuffing box for adjustment or repacking.

In all models, the fuel tank is located under the cockpit sole, above the engine. Fuel capacity is about 30 gallons. Early diesel-powered models have black iron fuel tanks, and at least one owner surveyed reported having to replace a rusted-out tank after a few years. Later models have aluminum fuel tanks, which are less likely to corrode. Range under power with the Perkins 4-108 and 30 gallons of fuel will be about 180 miles.

The gasoline engines used in early models swing a small prop. Unfortunately, when the switch was made to bigger diesels—the Perkins 4-108 displaces

108 cubic inches, the Atomic 4 only 65 cubic inches—the propeller aperture was not enlarged, limiting prop size. We measured the height to be 16 1/2", which means you can really only swing about a 15" prop and still maintain adequate tip clearance. The result is that you end up turning an oversquare prop (more pitch than diameter), which is not the most efficient way to utilize the engine in a sailboat.

Our prop choice would be a three-bladed feathering Maxprop for the best combination of performance under both sail and power. The Maxprop would also slightly improve handling in reverse, which is rated as poor by most owners. A tiny fixed prop tucked in an aperture in the deadwood and rudder is a bad combination for handling in reverse. Powering ahead, the boat handles just fine.

There is no sound insulation in the engine compartment. Access to the front of the engine is fair, requiring removal of the front of the engine box which doubles as the companionway ladder.

Construction

Bristol Yachts has gone through a lot of changes over the years. The prime mover behind Bristol was Clint Pearson, one of the pioneering Pearson brothers—the other, Everett, now runs Tillotson-Pearson.

The boats built by Bristol today are a far cry from those of 15 years ago. Current Bristols are targeted toward the middle to upper end of the production and semi-custom markets, with very good finish detail and systems. Originally, Bristols were aimed at the mass market, and were finished and equipped accordingly.

Since the Bristol 40 was built over a period of 20 years, there were a number of minor changes during the production run, but the last boats are essentially the same as the first ones.

The Bristol 40 is not a particularly lightly built boat, but she is certainly not heavy for her overall length, even by modern standards. The boat is substantially lighter than most long-keel CCA 40-footers. The Hinckley Bermuda 40, for example, displaces about 20,000 pounds in normal trim. The Cal 40, considered a real lightweight in 1966, weighs about 16,000 pounds in IMS measurement trim; the average Bristol 40, right at 17,000 pounds in the same configuration.

By way of comparison, the Little Harbor 38 that won the 1986 Newport-Bermuda Race tips the scales at a hefty 25,000 pounds, and the newer Bristol 38.8 has a designed displacement of just over 19,000 pounds.

None of the Bristol 40 owners we surveyed report any major structural flaws. They do, however, complain of annoyances such as leaking ports, deck

Though there's somewhat less room below than in a more modern 40-footer, the interior is reasonably well laid out. This is one of several different interiors that were offered.

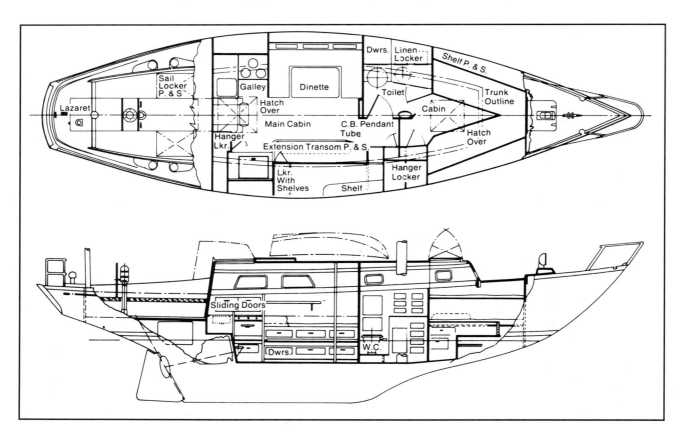

hardware, and hull/deck joints. These are generally assembly and quality control problems, and most can be solved by the owner, albeit with a fair amount of labor. A leaking hull/deck joint may be more of a problem, but this type of leak should show up during a careful examination of the boat. Discoloration and water streaks inside lockers and on bulkheads, rust and drips on through-fastenings, and mysterious puddles of water may indicate leaks in the joint.

From a cruiser's point of view, a nice feature of the Bristol 40 is its water capacity: 130 gallons in two fiberglass water tanks.

Any sailboat hull older that about eight years is getting on toward being a candidate for painting. While the gelcoat in the Bristol 40s we examined still looks reasonable, most of the colored hulls—pastels were popular in the 70s—are badly faded. The colored gelcoat used was not colorfast.

We also noted numerous gelcoat flaws on decks: cracks around stanchion bases, some voids at sharp corner transitions. During the survey, the surveyor should carefully sound the entire deck for voids. If you're going to go to the trouble and expense of painting, you might as well catch all the problems at the same time.

Deck non-skid is a molded-in basket weave pattern, and we have found it to be less effective than more aggressive non-skid designs.

The cockpit is huge, with seats almost 7' long. The well is narrow enough that you can brace your feet against the opposite seat—a good feature on any boat, but especially important on a tippy boat. The big cockpit is a mixed blessing. It gives plenty of space for daysailing or in-port parties, but it is also vulnerable to filling in extremely heavy offshore conditions.

In our opinion, the cockpit scuppers are too small. Each of the two scuppers is about the size of a bathtub drain. Since there is no bridgedeck—just a raised companionway sill—it is particularly important that the cockpit drain quickly. This is a pretty reasonable retrofit job. For offshore sailing, the bottom dropboard should be caulked and permanently secured in place.

There is a reasonable amount of exterior teak trim on the boat, including toerails, cabin eyebrow trim, handrails, and cockpit coamings. A Bristol 40 with a freshly-Awlgripped hull and varnished teak trim would look handsome, indeed.

On the port and starboard quarters, there are large chocks for dock lines. While these look substantial, they are only screwed to the toerails, and can easily tear out. Chocks can be very heavily loaded during panic dockings, and should always be through-bolted, as should all deck hardware.

Through hull fittings are not recessed flush, but can easily be faired in to reduce drag in very light air. The Constellation-style rudder is set slightly above the aft edge of the keel, so that the boat will ground out on the keel rather than the rudder.

Instead of a bolt-on external keel, the Bristol 40 has a molded keel cavity filled with 6,500 pounds of lead. One owner we surveyed had added 1,500 pounds of lead pigs in the bilge to improve stability.

Interior

Bristol has always made extensive use of built-up

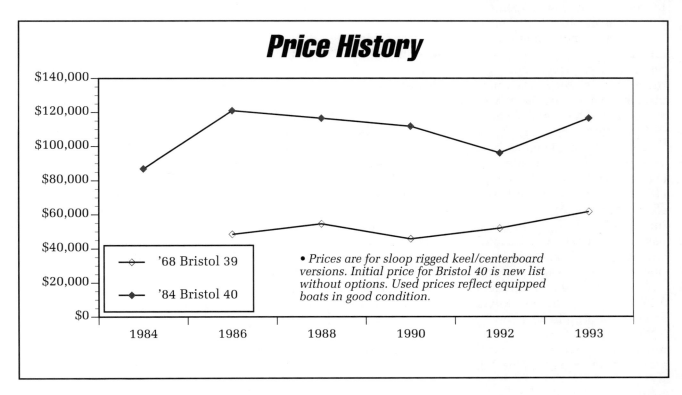

Price History

Legend:
- —◇— '68 Bristol 39
- —◆— '84 Bristol 40

• Prices are for sloop rigged keel/centerboard versions. Initial price for Bristol 40 is new list without options. Used prices reflect equipped boats in good condition.

interiors of plywood and solid wood, rather than fiberglass molded components trimmed out in solid wood. The company has also made extensive use of mahogany rather than teak in interior construction.

If you're used to the dull brown of teak, the brighter reddish-brown of the mahogany interior of the Bristol may or may not appeal to you. Mahogany must be varnished: it is not suited to an oil finish in a marine environment. If you let the varnish wear off, the wood will turn grey, particularly after exposure to water.

At the same time, mahogany is lighter and brighter than teak, and can make an all-wood interior slightly less gloomy. If all else fails, you can always paint out the mahogany bulkheads and leave the mahogany trim varnished. Teak plywood is much harder to paint out, since its waxy surface doesn't hold paint very well.

The built-up interior allowed a number of interior options in the Bristol 39 and 40. As originally drawn, the boat had a wide-open offshore racing interior, with a sail locker forward, the head in the area normally reserved for a forward sleeping cabin, and symmetrical pilot berths, settees, and quarterberths in the main cabin. While it provides six sea berths, this interior has little appeal for a cruising family. Most boats were built with one of several more conventional interior layouts.

One advantage of long-ended boats is that the V-berths don't have to be jammed into the bow. Instead, you get berths that are wide enough at the foot for normal-sized people. The forward cabin of the Bristol 40 is quite roomy, with two berths and various lockers and drawers. An insert turns the V-berths into a reasonable double berth.

The head compartment is aft of the forward cabin, on the port side. It is a big, roomy head, with rather remarkable storage, including 10 small drawers and three lockers. All boats came with hot and cold pressure water, and have a hand-held shower attached to the head sink fixture.

Opposite the head are the usual hanging lockers.

Several different main cabin layouts were offered, with an arrangement to please just about every fairly conventional taste. On the port side, you'll find either a settee berth with storage outboard, a U-shaped dinette, or a narrow pull-out settee with a pilot berth outboard. On the starboard side, you'll usually find a settee with a folding pipe berth above, although some boats were built with a conventional pilot berth outboard of the starboard settee.

On boats without a dinette, the main cabin table folds up against the port forward bulkhead—a reasonable solution in a narrow boat.

Main cabin storage space is quite good, with a number of drawers and lockers. The actual storage arrangement varies with each interior layout.

Ventilation in the main cabin, as well as in the entire boat, is so-so. There is an opening port in the head, and a cowl vent overhead. There is another cowl vent on the other side of the cabin trunk opposite the head, providing some air to the forward cabin and main cabin in foul weather. Over the forward cabin is a large fiberglass hatch.

A fiberglass hatch over the main cabin was optional. The main cabin ports do not open. Ventilation would be greatly improved by adding Dorade boxes just in front of the dodger breakwater at the aft end of the main cabin. If you also put a reversible aluminum-framed hatch directly over the middle of the main cabin, and added a small dodger to it for heavy weather protection, you'd go from lousy ventilation to good airflow in one fell swoop.

We're not keen on the fiberglass hatches used in production boats in the 1970s. They distort easily, and never seem to seal completely.

Headroom is about 6' 4" on centerline aft, decreasing to about 6' in the forward cabin.

In all interior layouts other than the original ocean racing one, the galley is at the aft end of the main cabin. There are two aft galley arrangements. One is spacious but not particularly efficient, the other is tight. On boats equipped with a quarterberth and nav station on the port side, the galley is jammed into the starboard aft corner, and is small for a 40-footer. On boats without a nav station, stove and sink are on the port side, with a large icebox opposite to starboard. The top of the icebox is then used as a navigation table. Neither galley layout is as good as the U-shaped galley used on more modern boats such as the Bristol 38.8.

You'll have to make a choice on the galley layout. A nav station is very desirable if the boat is used for more than daysailing. Yet the starboard galley you get on boats with nav stations is quite small, and doesn't have much storage for foodstuffs or utensils.

Even on boats with the port nav station, the electrical panel is located on the starboard side, above the galley and next to the companionway, in a fiberglass box that's a molded part of the cabin liner. We'd want to give better protection to the panel by building a frame with an opening clear acrylic cover.

Despite the narrowness of the Bristol 40 compared to newer boats, the interior is reasonably laid out and not cramped. Headroom is good, and you can easily make improvements in ventilation. The interior doesn't seem as spacious as a lot of boats due to the fairly narrow, tall cabin trunk. Newer designs have more freeboard, allowing a lower cabin trunk and increasing the feel of interior space.

Conclusions

Like the better-known Bermuda 40, the Bristol 40 is an exceptionally pretty boat, and those good looks are one factor that kept the boat in production for such a long time. But the Bermuda 40 has been carefully refined, and its reputation nurtured by a group of nearly-fanatical owners who are willing to pay rather remarkably high prices for a design that is now 30 years old.

The Bristol 40, on the other hand, lacks that reputation and following. A few Bristol 40s were built for die-hards even after the boat was superseded in 1983 by the faster, roomier, stiffer Bristol 38.8—a design that is a distinctly more modern Hood cruiser/racer.

Because of her large cockpit, small cockpit drains, slightly vulnerable companionway, and fairly low initial stability, this boat wouldn't be a good choice for extended offshore cruising, although Bristol 40s have certainly done their share of it. For cruising in the Chesapeake, Bahamas, or Gulf of Mexico, the keel-centerboard version would be a reasonable choice, and even the deep keel model draws substantially less than most 40-footers.

A late-model, sloop-rigged boat with Perkins or Westerbeke diesel would be our first choice. Since relatively few changes were made in the boat during the years of production, however, you might also find a good older boat on which a lot of attention has been lavished.

If you like traditional looks, and you cruise in shoal coastal waters without extremely heavy winds a lot of the time, the Bristol 40 should appeal to you. You're a natural candidate for the boat if the looks of the Bermuda 40 catch your eye, but you don't have the pocketbook to indulge yourself in Hinckley quality. **• PS**

Hinckley Bermuda 40

With the longest production run of any boat built in the U.S., the 40 is as seaworthy as she is beautiful.

The Henry R. Hinckley & Co. The name is known to every American sailor. Or should be. It connotes different things to different people, mostly depending on their politics: Down East craftsmanship, big bucks, Yankee work ethic, East Coast blue-blooded snobbery. For those familiar with the company's work, it more likely means mirror-like varnish, custom stainless steel castings, the trademark dust bin in the cabin sole and "frameless" portlights. Still, critics are quick to complain that other builders produce boats that are just as good for less money. More often than not, these sentiments are just sour grapes from people who can't afford a Hinckley or even a different brand of comparable quality. While we acknowledge that there probably are a few builders around the world which build boats to the same exacting level, Hinckley is nonetheless unique in North American boatbuilding.

Specifications - Mk III

LOA	40' 9"
LWL	28' 10"
Beam	11' 9"
Draft	4' 3"/8' 9" (board up/down)
Displacement	20,000 lbs.
Ballast	6,500 lbs.
Sail area	776 sq. ft.

History

Henry R. Hinckley started the company that bears his name on graduation from Cornell University. His first boat, launched in 1934, was a 26-foot lobster-type powerboat. Soon moving to sail, he designed and built the Sou'wester 34 and 30-foot Sou'wester Jr. During World War II he built mine yawls, coastal pickets and tugs. While his "production" wooden boats weren't regarded as anything exceptional, his yard did do some first-class work, building the 73-foot *Windigo* (nee *Ventura*) and *Nirvana*.

After the war, Hinckley began experimenting with fiberglass as a potential boatbuilding material, though, true to his conservative Maine heritage, he didn't rush into it. The Hinckley Bermuda 40, introduced in 1959 and still in production today, was a watershed for the company.

According to company notes on the B 40, "The firm had built a wooden 38-foot yawl in 1959 and had called her a Sou'wester Sr. It was Henry's plan to sail the boat hard the coming summer and if she proved her worth, he would use her as a plug from which to build the mold for the first fiberglass Hinckleys. But this was never to occur."

At the 1959 New York Boat Show, Hinckley was approached by a consortium of eight men, who had commissioned Bill Tripp to modify the Block Island 40 for them. The group's front man, Gilbert Cigal, persuaded Hinckley to build the boats. The decision to abandon the Sou'wester Sr. was difficult, but from a business point of view, it made more sense to invest in tooling for boats already sold.

The first B 40 was delivered to consortium mem-

Owners' Comments

"One is hard-pressed to find a critical Hinckley owner. Their boats are solidly built and cabins are beautifully finished. Pride of ownership, and purchase price, lead to well-maintained used offerings, generally."

—1977 model in Pennsylvania

"If buying a new B 40, count on spending an additional 33 to 50 percent on options. The best route might be a used B 40. I've sailed many of these and even 15-year-olds hold up very well. Hinckley has an excellent restoration program for all their boats. It's difficult to imagine another yard providing as much interest and expertise."

—1988 model in New York

"Barn door rudder. Tough to maneuver in close quarters and situations with heavy crosswinds. The Bermuda 40 is one of the classic yawls in CCA design. An absolute pride and pleasure to own and to sail."

—1969 model in Michigan

"Given the traditional layout in this hull, it is not too generous by today's standards, but it does work, especially with four or fewer people. Big lack to us is a really comfortable place to sit below (transoms are not quite the right shape). We also made a mistake in giving up the wet locker for a larger refrigerator. She is a comfortable cruiser, no speed demon, but also easy to sail with limited crew."

—1978 model in Washington, DC

ber Morton Engel in time for that year's Bermuda Race. Though not completely finished, she finished in the top third of the field. In 1964 she won the Northern Ocean Racing Trophy and the next year the Marblehead to Halifax Race.

Many other B 40s achieved notable accomplishments both racing and cruising. One of the more publicized circumnavigations was done by Sy and Vickie Carkhuff, who wrote about their adventures in numerous magazine articles. It is therefore no surprise that the combination of Hinckley quality and Tripp seaworthiness produced a boat that boasts the longest-running production span of any fiberglass boat—32 years.

Hinckley's Rigdon Reese said the company does not sell a lot of B 40s nowadays, in part because their 42 and 43-footers represent many of the major advancements that have been made in yacht design over the past three decades. These are primarily in the areas of increased interior volume and better sailing performance. "But," Reese says, "every now and then someone appears at the door who feels he *must* own a B 40. If we can't sell him a brokered boat (Hinckley sells the vast majority of used—or should we say 'pre-owned'—Hinckleys) or talk him into a newer design, then we'll build him a B 40." The last one launched was during the summer of 1991—hull #203.

The Design

Unlike the Block Island 40, the Bermuda 40 is a centerboarder, and a major reason for its continuing appeal. If shoal draft is a requirement, as it often is in some areas of the U.S., one is forced to consider a centerboard design or, when available, a wing keel. Though not terribly beamy by today's standards, the B 40's 11' 9" beam is substantial. If you can't get stability through ballast located deep (remember, the design parameter was for a shoal draft boat; and, fin keel boats weren't considered suitable in 1960 for offshore work), you must get it from what is called "form stability," that is, the shape and dimensions of the hull. Similarly, the interior would not be considered very spacious by today's standards, but in 1960 it had the room of a wooden 50-footer.

Typical of the CCA (Cruising Club of America) rule, the B 40 has generous overhangs, which contribute greatly to her exceptional looks. The sheer had a nice spring to it, rising just a bit at the stern and considerably more so at the bow. The low point is about two-thirds of the distance aft, helping give the profile its classic lines. Tripp was fond of the concave counter and nearly vertical transom.

The keel draws 4' 1" with a gently cutaway forefoot (no "chin") and straight clean run on the bottom. The rudder, attached to a vertical rudderstock, is hung off the trailing edge of the keel. This is a boat that, should she run aground, won't suffer a lot of damage, and should give the owner a fighting chance to float her, without crippling the rudder, utilizing his own on-board resources.

The down side of this design approach is less than stellar upwind performance. She does not tack as quickly as a boat with a more modern underbody (such as the McCurdy & Rhodes-designed Hinckley 42), and has a tendency to lose speed through the tack until she has a chance to pick up a head of steam. Then again, the B 40 has a heavier displacement than many modern boats of similar length. The Tripp 40 (designed by Bill Tripp's son), an all-out racer, displaces 12,750 pounds. The shoal keel J/40 displaces 18,650. Full-blown cruisers such as the Tashiba 40

(29,000 pounds) and the Lord Nelson 41 (30,500 pounds) are considerably heavier. So the B 40 is actually of moderate displacement, representing a nice comfortable figure for offshore sailing without forsaking light air performance.

Three different versions have been offered over the years—the Bermuda 40 Custom, the Mark II, and the Mark III. The yawl was the rig of choice until the Mark III, which also is available as a sloop. The Mark II was given an airfoil centerboard and a slightly taller mainmast (49' 3" bridge clearance) than the Custom (47' 0"). This increased sail area from 725 sq. ft. to 741 sq. ft.

The Mark III was changed further. According to the company's notes, "In response to the 'new' IOR rule, Peter Cooper of Sound Spar conspired with Bill Tripp and Henry once again to raise the aspect of both mizzen and main. This time the main mast was raised a full four feet three inches and moved aft almost two feet. This enlarged the foretriangle to the point where larger primary sheet winches were needed. The additional sail area raised the center of effort, and it was necessary to add a thousand pounds to the boat's keel. This added weight made her sit lower on her marks and added a foot to her waterline." Obviously, the company was trying to pump up performance to keep up with consumer expectations.

As one would expect, there have been many other refinements made to the original design, though most are minute compared to the changes in rig and ballast.

Construction

The B 40 is built of solid fiberglass—always has been and still is. A "hybrid knit fabric of Kevlar/E-glass" fibers is used in current boats. The deck was originally solid glass. Later it was balsa-cored, and now it is cored with 3/4-inch PVC foam, and vacuum-bagged for good bonding of the skins. The hull-deck joint is unusual in that the fairly standard deck-to-hull flange system is incredibly strong. The flange is 1/2-inch thick and about six inches wide, increasing around the chainplates. There also is a lip on the flange than gives the deck a snug fit. In his book, *The World's Best Sailboats,* Ferenc Mate describes at some length the process of fitting the deck to the hull. The deck is lifted with a chain hoist and lowered onto the hull to determine where the bulkheads should be trimmed. He quotes Bob Hinckley as saying, "We raise it, lower it, raise it, lower it, up and down like whore's drawers until all the tops of the bulkheads fit perfectly." The two mating surfaces are ground and filled until the two match like a piece of joinerwork. Wet fiberglass mat is laid on the flange and then the two pieces are bolted together. The entire process "takes two days for a small crew."

As implied above, the interior is built before the deck is fastened. It is almost a cliche, but true, that Hinckley builds a wooden boat inside a fiberglass hull. No fiberglass is visible. You can probably have any specie of wood you want, including cherry, white ash or the traditional Maine white paint and varnished mahogany trim. Whichever you choose, rest assure it will be gorgeous.

Lead ballast is mounted externally, fastened with one-inch stainless steel bolts. The cast bronze centerboard is not operated by a wire pennant but by a worm gear.

All deck hardware is through-bolted; holes are not oversized for dropping bolts through but tapped so that each machine screw threads not only into the backing plate and lock nut, but also through the deck itself.

Hinckley prides itself on manufacturing as many components as it can, including the stainless steel stem casting, custom tapered mast, steering pedestal, even the stanchions. One could go on and on describing how the through-hulls are countersunk flush with the hull, the number of coats of phenolic tung oil varnish applied to all natural wood surfaces,

---

The Bermuda 40's wide side decks force a tradeoff below—lessened living space. Overall, there is less space than would be found in a more modern design. Detail and finish work are excellent.

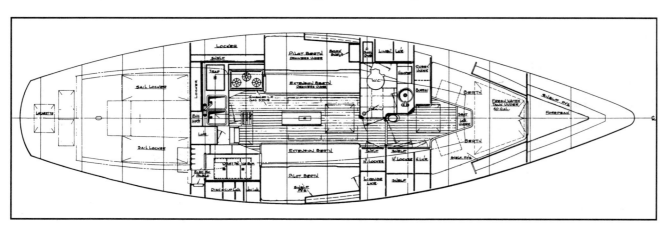

and how sheet copper is used to bond all sea cocks to the boat's lightning and bonding system.

The engines, of course, are not made by Hinckley, but each is test run for several hours and the standard 55-amp alternator replaced with a 105-amp model to charge the house batteries. A 53-amp alternator charges the engine start battery. The Westerbeke 4-107 diesel was standard for many years, though today you can also have the Yanmar 4JH2E. Hinckley makes its own shaft log and muffler. Fuel capacity is 48 gallons in a single Monel tank. Three stainless steel water tanks hold 110 gallons.

The cockpit seat lockers are gasketed and can be locked from below via a latch in the galley. Lockable, watertight seat lockers should be, but seldom are, a requirement of offshore sailing.

Interestingly, Hinckley recommends Marelon ball-valve sea cocks, through-bolted with Monel fasteners (of course, you can have whatever you want). Of equal interest is the one opening portlight. All others are fixed safety glass, which is preferable to Plexiglas or Lexan in terms of scratch resistance and resistance to ultraviolet rays. The frames are mounted inside, so that they are not visible from the outside. One owner said he wished ventilation was better.

Not surprisingly, owners responding to our questionnaire rate construction as excellent—without exception. One reader called his B 40 "bullet proof, over-engineered."

Performance

As mentioned under the "Design" section, the B 40 is an adequate performer. She is not particularly fast upwind, due in part to the fat, shallow keel, but does much better off the wind, according to owners. They rate stability as about average, often citing the relatively low 28 percent ballast-to-displacement ratio. One reader said, "It heels early to about 15 degrees, then stiffens." Another said, "It's hard to keep the rail in after initial 15- to 20-degree heel (with centerboard down)."

On a more positive note, the mizzen sail and centerboard allow the boat to be balanced much better than most designs. One owner said, "On most courses we can almost eliminate weather helm with appropriate sail trim." Another said balance was "especially good from beam reach to a very broad reach." These points of sail, for most other boats, cause the most difficulty in handling.

Owners rated seaworthiness as excellent. One said he'd taken one knockdown and suffered no damage.

Under power there are the usual complaints about losing steering control in reverse, but this is to be expected of a full-keel design with the propeller in an aperature. One reader said, "We sometimes use the centerboard for docking." The 37-hp. Westerbeke auxiliary, while rated as an excellent engine, has barely sufficient power to punch through headseas. (We have no comparative information on the Yanmar.) Access to the engine, incidentally, was rated as fair. One reader wrote, "All service is from the front end. The sides are accessible through cockpit lockers. You can get right down and sit on the reverse gear if you wish." Another noted that the shaft and log are "buried," and difficult to work on.

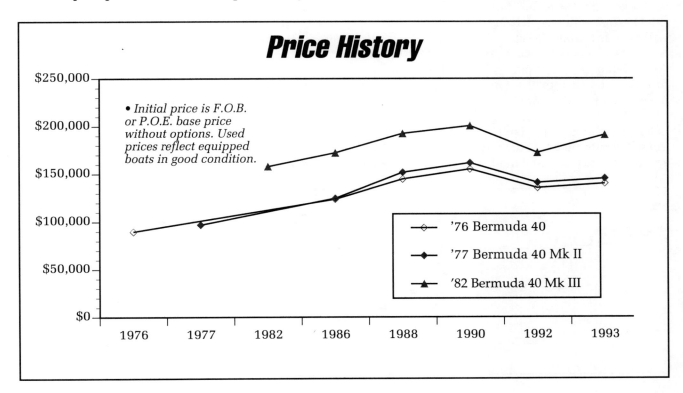

Price History

• Initial price is F.O.B. or P.O.E. base price without options. Used prices reflect equipped boats in good condition.

'76 Bermuda 40
'77 Bermuda 40 Mk II
'82 Bermuda 40 Mk III

Interior

Details of interior layout vary from boat to boat since each B 40 is built to order. The basic plan, however, remains essentially the same.

There are V-berths forward which may be converted to a sumptuous double with the addition of the insert board and cushion. The head has a sink and shower as standard equipment, and opposite are a number of cedar-lined lockers for clothes. Stowage space is generous.

The standard saloon layout has berths for four: two extension settees, and pilot berths port and starboard. These tend to push the furniture in toward the centerline, making the cabin seem less spacious than more contemporary designs. (This also is partly a function of the B 40s very wide sidedecks—a blessing on deck and a trade-off below.)

While a narrow cabin provides better handholds and is therefore safer at sea, the drop leaf dining table restricts access fore and aft when the starboard leaf is up. That can be annoying. The optional U-shaped dinette eliminates the problem.

The galley is aft and is adequate, though compact. There isn't much counter space other than the lid tops of the icebox and stowage bin. Worse, the navigation station is above the icebox on the starboard side. The optional layout features a navigator's seat; in the standard layout one must stand. We'd prefer to see a separate nav area with additional room for electronics.

For extended cruising, the B 40 is best suited to a couple, with occasional guest crew. For a family with children, the kids would have to sleep in the pilot berths, which is okay but means that their junk will rain down on the settees.

Most owners commented on the lack of interior space, but accept it as part of the package, knowing full well that if they'd required more, they could have bought a different boat.

The finish detail of the B 40, indeed, any Hinckley, is legendary, and there isn't space here to describe the many intelligent features that help set this boat apart from the rest of the field. You'll have to see for

yourself, as the interior design and workmanship represent a good part of the total cost.

Conclusion

Hinckley takes enormous pride in its work, and offers to its customers a wide range of services. In effect, you become part of the Hinckley family. Most Hinckleys are serviced by the builder, and most used Hinckleys are sold through Hinckley's own brokerage arm. They also run a charter service, which is a good way to test sail a Hinckley for longer than an afternoon.

Because of the substantial investment owners made in purchasing a Hinckley, and because of the continuing support offered by the company, most used Hinckleys are in excellent condition. And the B 40, because of its 32-year production run, may be found with a wide range of options, and can be purchased at a wide range of prices. Resale value is excellent. For example, the base price of a 1975 B 40 was about $90,000. BUC Research today lists the value of that boat at about $120,000 to $130,000. Assuming the original owner spent, in addition to the base price, another $25,000 equipping his boat, he could still expect to break even 17 years later! If you purchase a good used Hinckley at a fair price, you could conceivably expect to make a small profit on resale, and while that was not uncommon during the 1970s, it is almost unheard of in the late 1980s and early 1990s. BUC lists an average low retail of about $80,000 for a 1960 model and an average high retail of about $350,000 for a 1990 model.

Every B 40 is a bit different than the last, so it would be advisable to check several before making a decision. Looking at used B 40s would also be helpful in selecting features for a new model.

The base price of a 1992 Bermuda 40 yawl is $354,740.

Obviously, Hinckleys aren't for everyone. They are expensive and only you can decide whether the many little quality details are worth the cost. As one owner said, "The B 40 is to be bought on the day that the full significance of 'you only have one life to live' becomes clear."　　**• PS**

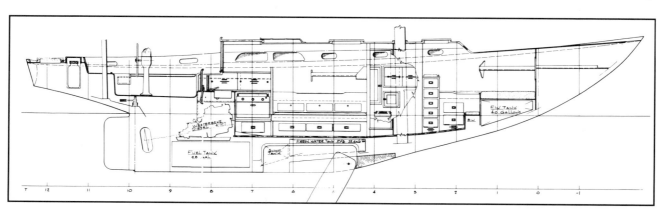

Block Island 40

Bill Tripp's fabled yawl is still being built, almost to the original plans. It has few vices.

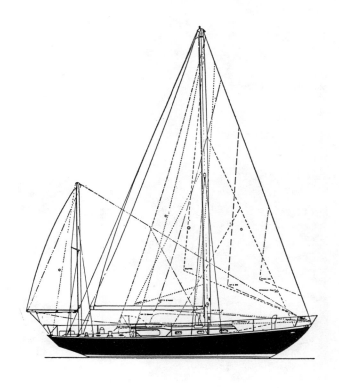

Eric Woods, wearing shorts and sneakers, and a baseball cap with the bill backwards, looks a lot like Johnny Carson as he finishes setting the mizzen staysail and jumps back to the cockpit. He has the same impish grin, the sort of grin a 10-year-old boy has after dropping a frog down a girl's dress.

It's no accident. He's just launched hull #10 of Migrator Yachts' version of the Block Island 40 yawl, we're steaming along at better than seven knots, and he's happy. *Really* happy! And why not? After a lifetime in the boatbuilding business, and a long-time love affair with the BI 40, he's finally his own boss; his two sons Rob and Eric, who work with him, are sailing a sistership abeam of us; sales are picking up; and, hey, this is a perfect day!

History

Richard Henderson, in his book *Choice Yacht Designs*, credits the inspiration of the Block Island 40 to the Sparkman & Stephens-designed *Finnisterre*, a centerboard yawl that won the Bermuda Race three consecutive times. That boat led to the production model Nevins 40, and later to several similar boats by other designers. The Block Island 40 and Hinckley Bermuda 40, both drawn by William H. Tripp, Jr., are the best known.

Tripp's first effort along these lines was the Vitesse class, which he designed in 1957. It was constructed in the Netherlands, and imported to the U.S. for Van Breems International. Not long after that the American Boat Building Corporation of Warwick, Rhode Island, purchased the molds, changed the name, and built 22 boats before in turn selling the molds to Metalmast Marine, Inc. of Putnam, Connecticut. Metalmast, which built 14 of them, at one point commissioned Tripp to modify the underbody by

Specifications

LOA	40' 8"
LWL	29' 2"
Beam	11' 10"
Draft (board up/down)	4' 2"/8' 10"
Displacement	20,000 lbs.
Ballast	7,800 lbs.
Sail area	738 sq. ft.

separating the keel and rudder. They also gave the rig a higher-aspect ratio mainsail.

Numerous accomplished yachtsmen have owned or do own Block Island 40s, among them John Nicholas Brown and *Volta*, Niebold Smith and *Reindeer*, Benjamin DuPont and *Rhubarb*, Van Allen Clark and *Swamp Yankee*. The BI 40 dates to a time when you could own a true dual-purpose boat, equally adept at racing and cruising. Today, unfortunately, it's a rare boat that so qualifies.

In time the molds grew weary and were retired. Until that is, Eric Woods decided to leave his job at C.E. Ryder Corp. (builder of Sea Sprites and Southern Crosses). He and his wife Joan had been interested in having a BI 40 built for their own cruising pleasure. Metalmast declined to build the boat, but

The standard rig on new Block Island 40s is a yawl, though ordering a sloop rig can be done. To date, however, all the new boats have been delivered with yawl rigs.

said they'd sell him the molds so he could do it himself. Accidentally and providentially, Woods found himself in 1985 completely retooling the molds and forming his own company for the dubious purpose of building a 1957-vintage yawl. "The more I sail this boat," he told us, "the more I'm convinced this a better boat for cruising than most of the newer models on the market."

Woods' Migrator Yachts hasn't exactly taken the world by storm, but he's survived some of the toughest years in the sailing industry.

The Design

The BI 40 enjoyed a successful racing career (largely under the CCA rule), which may surprise younger readers whose experience begins with the IOR, IMS or PHRF. The long overhangs quickly immerse when heeled, adding to sailing length, which, of course, relates directly to speed. Freeboard is relatively low, and the keel is long, with a nice flat run. The rudder is attached and the propeller is located in an aperture.

The standard rig is a yawl, though a sloop is possible. Woods, however, says he's delivered only yawls, and isn't sure he'd want to build a sloop, believing as he does in the advantages of a two-stick rig. Because centerboard boats tend to have some initial tenderness in moderate to higher wind velocities, the ability to drop the mainsail and jog along nicely under jib and mizzen is very attractive. This option keeps the center of effort low.

At 11' 10", the BI 40 was quite beamy by 1950 standards, and still provides a nice wide platform by today's standards. A trademark of both the BI 40 and Hinckley B40 are the wide side decks, which enable one to walk forward without ducking or sidestepping the shrouds. This also moves the settees inboard, providing generous stowage outboard as well as minimizing distances between handholds—important features for cruising and rough weather safety.

Woods has made several changes, which aren't immediately obvious, but nevertheless important. He gave his version a more hydrodynamic centerboard (solid fiberglass weighted with lead) for improved windward performance (Woods likes to adjust it to about a 45-degree angle). Off the wind, the board is completely retracted.

Aware that interior volume of the original design was limited, and that so many boats are purchased based on livability, he also lengthened the cabin trunk fore and aft. This has allowed him to install a true U-shaped galley and sit-down chart table, features not found on earlier BI 40s or B40s.

A minor improvement was cleaning up the aperture for a smoother flow of water over the propeller. Ever mindful of performance, Woods is a strong advocate of a three-bladed feathering Max Prop for less drag and better performance backing down.

By nearly any standard, this is a handsome yacht, indeed, what many folks would call a "proper yacht." It's sure to draw praise in any harbor.

Construction

Woods has assiduously followed developments in fiberglass boatbuilding technology. While there is nothing particularly high-tech about the layup, he's doing what he's supposed to for this sort of boat: combination 1-1/2-ounce mat, 18-ounce biaxial, and 24-ounce directional fiberglass set in polyester resin with an isophthalic gelcoat. The first two laminations are vinylester, which as we have reported has proven superior in preventing blistering. Airex core, 5/8-inch thick, is standard. The deck is balsa-cored.

Hull #10 was given a Ferro Copper Clad treatment on the bottom. It's 14 mils thick, adds 126 pounds to the hull, and costs $3,500. Woods, as well as some other builders such as Tom Morris, believe that Copper Clad is very cost effective, even if it doesn't last as many years as the Ferro Corp. claims (15 years-plus). It also looks great.

The interior is all-wood and though perhaps not finished to the same degree of perfection as a Hinckley, it is very nicely done. Bulkheads are tabbed to the hull. Ceilings are ash. Joinery is teak-faced plywood or solid teak. Mahogany is used where concealed. Locker doors are louvered. The headliner is foam-backed vinyl, and is removable. Eleven opening portlights, two hatches and two Dorades provide excellent ventilation. The only fiberglass pan is in the head, where moisture and shower water make this the correct choice.

The hull/deck joint is bonded with 3M 5200 and through-bolted every six inches.

The standard auxiliary is the Yanmar 4JHE 44-hp. diesel with 2.17:1 reduction gear.

Performance

In its heyday, the BI 40 had a good racing record. In the 1960 Bermuda Race six of the first 11 places were won by BI 40s, and in 1978, the BI 40 *Alaris* won her class. Its PHRF rating varies between rig (sloop or yawl) and fleet from a low of 156 to a high of 186. The average seems to be 165. It's difficult to make comparisons, but more contemporary boats with similar ratings include the Hunter 33, Irwin 34 Citation and Island Packet 38. But what's the point? The BI 40 is not a round-the-buoys racer. She's a cruising boat displacing 20,000 pounds.

Upwind is never the forte of a centerboard design,

though the BI 40 delivers decently. In 20- to 25-knot winds with just jib and mizzen, we were able to make good speed with the apparent wind at 30 degrees. The ability to proceed safely and comfortably without the mainsail is an advantage that must be experienced to be appreciated—no excessive heel, no sudden heeling in gusts, no mainsail noise.

On our return to Marion, Massachusetts, with the wind just aft of the beam and the Buzzards Bay chop pushing us, we set the mainsail and mizzen staysail. It was a delightful romp, with speeds of eight knots. The helm was nicely balanced. It was, as the saying goes, one of those days that God will not subtract from our allotted time.

Interior

The drawing shows the essentials of the BI 40 interior. Not so obvious is the large forepeak, separated from the forward cabin by a watertight bulkhead. Access is by means of a hatch in the foredeck. Inside is plenty of room for sails and ground tackle.

Some customization is possible. For example, Woods has built boats with nav stations oriented either fore and aft or athwartship.

When the molds were retooled, Woods extended the cabin trunk a little to make room for a U-shaped galley and sit-down nav station. Note the large forepeak locker.

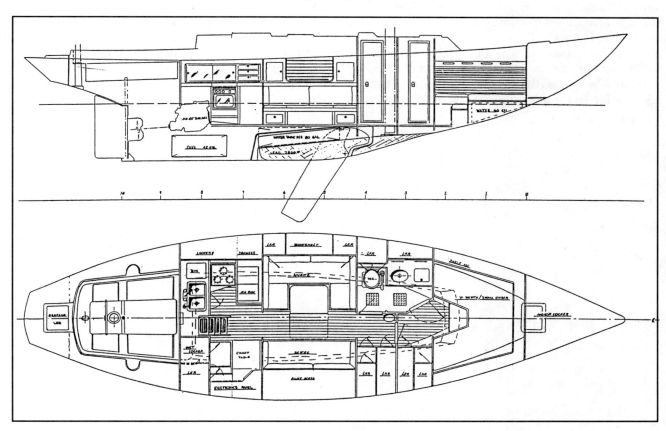

Note also the generous number of stowage areas, including the four hanging lockers opposite the head, bins behind the port-side settee, and the wet locker right where it should be—next to the companionway.

One owner opted for a quarter berth aft of the nav station, but Woods warns about the amount of stowage space lost.

Headroom is 6' 1-1/2" in the main cabin, slightly less forward. Berth lengths range from 6' 4-1/2" to 6' 7". Foam cushions are 6 inches thick.

It is no secret that many boats are purchased on the basis of the interior. Without being chauvinistic, it is often the wife, nearly oblivious to the deck and rig, who either blesses or condemns her husband's choice based on her impression of the interior. This may mean many things, such as overall spaciousness, large galley, adequate stowage. The BI 40 shows well on all counts, though not by some contemporary standards, where the settees are moved outboard to the hull, freeboard is raised as high as possible (often necessitated by bolt-on keels and shallow bilges), and extra berths are shoved in where possible, sometimes even under the cockpit. After viewing, say, a Hunter 40, in which the accommodations have been pushed into the extreme ends of the hull, the BI 40 interior may appear cramped. Such comparisons infuriate Woods, and rightly so. The BI 40 is an honest cruising boat for a couple or small family. Its long overhangs are very traditional. It has adequate tankage (120 gallons water, 45 gallons diesel) and stowage to really go somewhere, a fact that cannot be appreciated until you've gone. The low freeboard helps performance. The wide sidedecks promote safety. All of the berths in the main cabin make comfortable sea berths (you can't sleep in chairs, fashionable in some modern boats). In short, this is an excellent interior arrangement for real cruising.

Conclusion

Over the eight years that Woods has been building BI 40s, he's made numerous small refinements, such as adding a ball-bearing Lewmar traveler to the stern pulpit for trimming the mizzen more efficiently. Breast cleats amidship. A new outhaul and reefing arrangement. Gradually increasing the height of the toerail as it approaches the bow. And he'll work with customers to incorporate their ideas insofar as the basic structure and concept allows.

We can find little to fault in Woods' version of the BI 40. It won't be the right boat for everybody—none is. If you're planning on living aboard at a dock, you can get more space for your buck. If you must have 8-inch teak bulwarks, look at the Lord Nelson or Hans Christian. If you must have more speed, especially upwind, look for a divided underbody.

If it isn't apparent already, we'll admit it here: This is our kind of boat. Moderate displacement. Long keel and attached rudder. Prop in an aperture. Low freeboard. Clean decks. Easy to handle. Strong construction. Good looks. Altogether, a wholesome thoroughbred. But then, ours is a cruising mentality.

The 1992 price was $198,000, fully commissioned including sails. The BUC Research *Used Boat Price Guide* lists those BI 40s built by American Boatbuilding as selling between $31,500 and $48,500. A 1976 or 1977 Metalmast BI 40, the last years that company built the boat, sells between $63,000 and $72,000. Because not that many were built, and because most owners seem to hang onto their BI 40s until death do them part, they are seldom seen on the used market. If you really want one, you'll probably have to have Migrator Yachts build one for you. We should all be so lucky. **• PS**

Tartan 41

This boat offers a good introduction to real-live ocean racing—but watch out for tired equipment.

For a design whose production run totaled only 86 boats over four years, the Tartan 41 has had a rather remarkable impact on the ocean racing world. The newest Tartan 41 is more than 15 years old, yet in long distance races run under the International Measurement System (IMS), the Tartan 41 still shows up regularly near the top of the heap.

In the 1989 Marion/Bermuda Race, for example, two of the top seven boats were Tartan 41s. That's typical of the boat's performance in that race since it began.

The Tartan 41 was an early International Offshore Rule (IOR) design, a boat from back when production racer/cruisers could still do well even in big-time competition. Sparkman & Stephens was still a dominant racing design firm in those days, as they had been for 40 years. The IOR was in its infancy, and unlike recent years of racing under that rule, there were as many series-produced boats as custom boats in big regattas.

1972 was the first year of production of the Tartan 41. The previous year, the company had introduced the 46, a big IOR racer/cruiser that was not particularly successful as a racing boat.

The 41 was conceived as a flat-out racing boat. Late CCA (Cruising Club of America) boats such as the Tartan 34 had been rendered fairly obsolete by the international rating rule. Charlie Britton at Tartan felt he could move a lot of his more competitively-minded customers into a larger racing boat designed to the new rule.

In 1969, just before the advent of the IOR, Palmer Johnson began importing a line of boats from a small builder in Finland by the name of Nautor Ky. One of these PJ boats, an S&S 43-footer, had the general appearance Britton was looking for: flush deck with

Specifications

LOA	40' 8"
LWL	32' 5"
Beam	12' 3"
Draft	6' 4"/7' 2" (std/deep keel)
Displacement	17,850 lbs.
Ballast	9,200 lbs.
Sail area	725 sq. ft.

small deckhouse, good freeboard, and moderate ends. Britton asked S&S for a similar boat, but one that fit more precisely into the new rating rule. The result was the Tartan 41.

When Palmer Johnson began importing their boats from up near the Arctic Circle, they were marketed under the PJ name, since few in this country had ever heard of Nautor Ky. They were graceful boats, well finished and well thought out in typical S&S fashion. The name "Swan" seemed to suit them well. The rest, of course, is history.

1975 was the last model year for the Tartan 41, but the hull design resurfaced from 1980 to 1984 in the form of the Tartan 42. The 42 was a cruiser, with shoal keel, a heavier interior, and a new deck which provided considerably more light and air below than was found in the flush deck Tartan 41. The 42's pinched early IOR stern looked odd in 1980, by which time the rear end of the typical racer/cruiser was about twice as wide as that of the Tartan 41/42.

The slightly reversed transom and flush deck of the 41 make for a much better looking boat than the rather ho-hum deckhouse and more traditional transom of the 42. They're very different boats, but the 42 gave the venerable old design a new lease on life, albeit in a well-disguised form.

Sailing Performance

The Tartan 41 is not as fast as a more modern 41' IOR production racer/cruiser such as the C&C 41. The two designs have similar wetted surface and sail area, but the C&C 41 is faster on every point of sail in every wind condition that you'd want to experience.

Advances in hull and appendage design aside, one big difference is displacement. The designers' specifications called for the Tartan 41 to come in at 17,850 pounds on a waterline length of 32' 5". In fact, the typical Tartan 41 displaces very close to 21,000 pounds before consumables are added. The C&C 41 is about 2,500 pounds lighter.

That doesn't mean that the Tartan 41 is slow in either absolute or relative terms. Her PHRF (Performance Handicap Racing Fleet) rating of 96 to 102 makes her some 15 seconds per mile faster than the Cal 40. Back in 1972, the Tartan 41 was one mean machine.

This is not the world's easiest to handle boat. Just a few years earlier, Sparkman & Stephens had begun separating the rudder from the back of the keel, moving the rudder all the way to the aft end of the waterline.

The increased lever arm of the aft-mounted rudder meant that rudder area could be reduced, cutting down on wetted surface. Likewise, keels were getting smaller, deeper, and more efficient.

But this was a time of experimentation, and not all of the experiments were completely successful. The original rudder and keel of the Tartan 41 were very small. On a close reach, the boat was not extremely stiff, and the rudder was sometimes hard-pressed to generate enough turning moment to bring the boat back on course in puffy conditions. Naval architect Scott Graham, who raced against Tartan 41s on the Great Lakes, remarked that they should have been equipped with turn signals: you weren't sure whether the boat was going to round up or round down in the puffs.

Several solutions to this handling quirk were developed. For several early boats, S&S designed a simple lead shoe weighing several hundred pounds, which bolted directly to the bottom of the keel. This increased draft by about 6" and righting moment by about 8%.

In 1974, S&S designed a new keel for the boat. The new keel fit directly onto the old bolt pattern on the hull, but was about 7" deeper and 700 pounds heavier than the orginal keel, raising the total ballast package to 9,900 pounds. The new keel was offered as an option in 1974 and 1975, and many of the last 20 boats were built with the deeper, heavier keel. In addition, a number of earlier boats were retrofitted by Tartan with the new keel.

It takes a trained eye to determine which keel is on any Tartan 41 you're looking at, since the differences are fairly subtle unless you have both versions standing side-by-side. You can't go by draft or hearsay alone, since almost all of these boats have changed hands several times, and the current owner may not know his or her own boat's history very well. A call to the factory should tell you which keel is on which boat.

The rig, on the other hand, was never altered. The boat has a big, bullet-proof mast, with single spreaders and single lower in-line shrouds. This is no toy rig: lower shrouds are 7/16", other shrouds and stays are 3/8" wire—the same size you'd find on a lot of 50-footers today. The Tartan 41 was meant to be raced, and raced hard.

Many boats have upgraded components of the rig. A more modern boom with internal reefing lines would be a plus. Hydraulic rig controls on vang, backstay, and baby stay have also been fitted to some boats, although they are certainly not essential. It takes a lot of force to bend this telephone pole of a mast, although the single lower shrouds make it somewhat possible.

Sailhandling equipment was state-of-the-art for 1972, but some of it is a little long in the tooth by now. The original Barient 32 primaries are big enough, but the lack of self-tailers is tough for shorthanded cruising or racing. Likewise, the Barient reel main halyard winch should be approached with caution. Safe use of a reel halyard winch on a boat this big requires concentration and a strong arm on the winch handle, particularly when reefing.

For cruising, you'd want to fit a modern headsail reefing system, big self-tailers, and an up-to-date boom—some $10,000 worth of upgrades, but definitely worth it. For your money you'd get a fast, powerful boat that could be handled by two reasonably normal people.

According to IMS calculations, the typical Tartan 41 has a 124° limit of positive stability. This is well above the 120° minimum limit that we consider reasonable for serious offshore cruising and racing.

Despite the tall sail plan and heavy rig, the boat is fairly stiff by contemporary standards, particularly with the modified keel. She is not quite as close-winded as a more modern racing boat. In 12 knots of breeze with flat water, the Tartan 41 tacks through

84°, according to the IMS velocity prediction program. In the same conditions, a C&C 41 tacks through 80°. The C&C 41's computer-predicted VMG (velocity made good to windward) in those conditions is 5.019 knots, while the Tartan 41's is 4.693. Lighter displacement does have its virtues. Interestingly enough, the two boats show about the same velocity prediction differential on all points of sail, in all wind conditions.

Engine

The original engine is probably the Tartan 41's single worst feature. It's not that the engines themselves were bad; they were just too small for a boat of this displacement. Since this was a racing boat, the purpose of the engine was to get the boat to the starting line, and home after the finish. That's about all it was good for.

When first introduced, the boat was fitted with a two-cylinder, 20 horsepower Westerbeke (Bukh) diesel. In mid-production, this was changed to a similarly-sized Farymann. By now, many of these engines have been replaced with bigger, more modern engines. At over 20,000 pounds, this boat needs close to 100 cubic inches of engine displacement for good performance under power.

Fortunately, the engine sits directly under the companionway ladder, and is not jammed under a galley counter. It may be necessary to build new beds and a new engine box to install some larger engines, but there's room to do the job. If you're looking at a boat with an original engine, factor in the cost of a replacement—including the installation—within the next few years.

Unfortunately, the aluminum fuel tank is sized for these small engines. The 26-gallon fuel capacity is marginal for cruising with a bigger, more fuel-hungry engine. It would be a fairly straightforward job to add more tankage, but it does cost money.

Construction

The Tartan 41 is a rugged boat. Fiberglass construction was not terribly sophisticated in 1972, and that's one reason the boat is about 3000 pounds heavier than designed.

Over the production run, a lot of effort went into reducing weight. All of the boats are balsa cored, but the amount of coring varies from boat to boat as changes in the hull layup were made to save weight. According to Charlie Britton, later boats have more extensive coring and a correspondingly lighter fiberglass layup.

The drive to save weight peaked in the seven or so stretched versions of the boat, known as the Tartan 44. The hulls of the 44 were about 20% lighter than those of the first 41s, and some weight was also carved out of the deck. Britton reports that the longer waterline and lighter displacement of the 44 resulted in a boat that was faster both reaching and downwind.

There were actually three hull configurations of the Tartan 41. The hull tooling was for a 43-footer with a conventional transom. An insert in the mold produced the familiar reversed transom of the 41, and an extension on the back of the hull resulted in the 44. The overwhelming majority of the boats were built as the Tartan 41.

Despite the constant weight-saving battle, this is not an underbuilt boat. Owners report no structural problems, even though many Tartan 41s have done thousands of miles of ocean racing. The boat is a racing Sherman tank, if that's not a contradiction in terms.

Cosmetically, however, many of these boats have paid a price for their hard life. Ocean racing is not kind to decks, topsides, or interiors, nor are 15 years of exposure to the elements. Some of the boats look tired.

Several boats we have examined have gone through spectacular cosmetic upgradings, including polyurethane-painted topsides, and decks painted with

Despite a flush deck, there's a remarkable amount of headroom below. Overall, the interior is well suited to the Tartan 41's calling, i.e. ocean racing. Many 41s have owner modifications to improve livability.

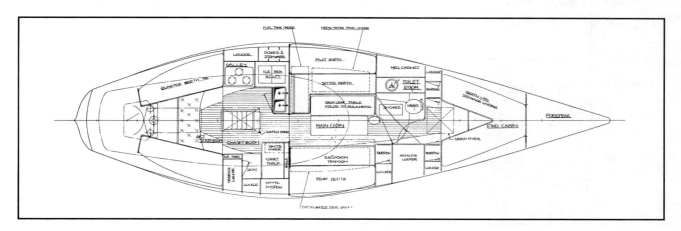

contrasting nonskid areas. The effect is pretty impressive. The boat is particularly good-looking painted dark blue, so that the apparent height of the topsides is camouflaged. A dark hull, however, shows every flaw in the topsides, and would be considerably hotter belowdecks in the tropics.

The Tartan 41 is frequently referred to as a "poor man's Swan," and for good reason. The hull and deck bear a strong family resemblance to Nautor's boats of the mid-1970s, and the Tartans are ruggedly built to similar specifications. But the vast expanses of elegant on-deck and belowdecks joinerwork for which Swans are known are totally absent on the Tartan 41. The boat is pure business.

Typical of S&S designs, structural and hardware specifications for the boat are very complete, down to the round-head screw draft marks on the hull centerline. S&S deck layouts in this period were the most functional you could find, with leads properly positioned, winches and hardware adequately sized, although winches are small by current standards.

The boats were designed and built for ocean racing. You don't have to guess whether a turning block is big enough, whether the deck is adequately reinforced for the hardware—provided it's in the original position—or whether the steering quadrant is going to stay attached to the boat. It ain't elegant or high tech, but it's sturdy.

Interior

Belowdecks, the Tartan 41 continues the fairly Plain Jane theme. There are no fancy touches, no leaded glass liquor cabinets.

On some boats, permanent forward berths were deleted, replaced by sail bins with folding pipe berths over. We'd almost rather have the boat with this configuration. You could tear out the forward cabin and install a big double berth with no compunction whatever.

Headroom in the forward cabin is about 6' 2". An aluminum-framed hatch overhead can provide ventilation in port, and there's a small built-in ventilator in the deck molding, but that's it for fresh air. A big cowl vent in a dorade box is a must addition to the foredeck, despite what it does to that big, clean working area.

The head compartment is just aft to port. It has a pressurized, cold-water shower. Needless to say, many boats have added a water heater. There's a big hanging locker opposite the head.

The main cabin is "offshore racing yacht plan A:" pilot berths both sides, straight settee berth to starboard, L-shaped settee to port. Most boats have water tanks located under the settees.

A drop-leaf table folds up against the port bulkhead: a reasonable arrangement for racing, but a poor substitute for a permanent table on a serious cruising boat. Building a real, live, sturdy main cabin table would be an excellent winter project for a new owner.

You'll find a variety of water tank installations. The original capacity of 60 gallons has in many cases been augmented, particularly in boats used for either cruising or racing in salt water. We've seen fiberglass tanks, polyethylene tanks, and bladder tanks in Tartan 41s. Since many of these are owner retrofits,

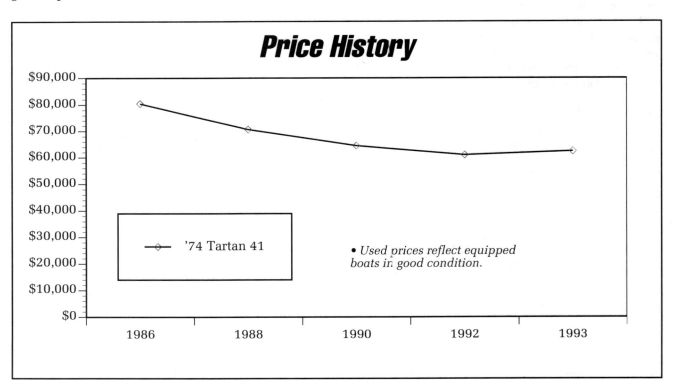

Price History

Legend: ◇ '74 Tartan 41

• Used prices reflect equipped boats in good condition.

examine them carefully for proper installation, including correct venting inside the hull.

The main bulkheads in most boats are teak-faced ply, with furniture risers of plywood faced with plastic laminate and trimmed in teak. In most cases, ivory-colored laminate was used, and it frequently just looks dirty and yellow after 15 years.

The appearance of the interior can be dramatically improved by varnishing the oiled teak trim with high-gloss varnish, and by installing new upholstery.

Despite the flush deck, there's a lot of headroom below. The bubble-type deckhouse extends over more than half the main cabin, giving 6' 7" of headroom, with about 6' 4" in the galley and nav station.

As with many flush-deck boats, both light and ventilation below are pretty mediocre. In fact, you'd want to augment them substantially before taking a Tartan 41 to a warm climate. If it hasn't already been done, a small opening hatch can be fitted at the forward end of the deckhouse, just aft of the mast. With careful work, big dorade boxes could also be fitted into the front of the deckhouse.

Galley and nav station are a small step up from the main cabin. Locker space in the galley is reasonable, but counter space is limited to the top of the icebox.

A gimbaled pressurized alcohol stove was standard equipment. By now, many of these antiquities have been retired, and justifiably so. Some boats we have looked at have installed CNG stoves, with the fuel bottles stored belowdecks. CNG is lighter than air, and will rise if there is a leak in the system. However, CNG should be treated with the same respect as propane, with the bottles kept above decks in a properly-vented enclosure. A lighter-than-air gas is no substitute for caution.

Opposite the galley is the nav station, with a good-sized table and reasonable mounting space for instruments.

Aft of the galley and nav station, tucked under the cockpit, is an area euphemistically labeled "aft stateroom" on the original drawings. It isn't exactly a stateroom, to put it politely. There are two quarterberths, with a narrow area of cabin sole between. On most boats, this area is used for sail storage when racing.

You could, were you so inclined, rebuild the port quarterberth to form a double, but that would mean reducing or eliminating the access from the galley to the quarterberth area, reducing air flow and nurturing a feeling of claustrophobia. You'd be better off converting the forward cabin to a double, saving the Tartan 41's "aft stateroom" for stowage, open-minded overnight guests, and use at sea when passagemaking in temperate climates.

In general, the interior of the Tartan 41 is well-suited for the boat's original purpose: racing. With the exception of the rather coffin-like quarterberth area, there's a lot of volume and headroom in the hull—enough to make you want to start redesigning for a cruising interior.

That, of course, is what the Tartan 42 was all about. On a very similar accommodation plan, the 42 gives you light, ventilation, and a good aft cabin. You lose, however, the flush-deck good looks that are a great part of the Tartan 41's appeal.

Conclusions

For a design that is almost 20 years old, the Tartan 41 still looks strikingly modern and functional, despite her marked tumblehome and pinched stern. The growth of IMS racing has given the boat a new lease on her racing life. With new sails, a smooth bottom, and some upgrading of deck equipment, the Tartan 41 will still be competitive in any IMS event longer than a standard Olympic course.

The boat's moderately heavy displacement and deep sections result in an extremely seakindly motion—a real plus for either racing or cruising.

We would look for a boat with the optional deep keel, particularly if we were interested in racing. The original rig is fine for either racing or cruising, although it's time to consider replacing the standing rigging—including turnbuckles—if it's original. Since the rigging is so big, replacing it is a fairly expensive job: 3/8" wire isn't cheap, and neither are big rigging terminals and turnbuckles.

This is a minimum-cost, entry-level, ocean-going racer. The new-boat price in 1975 was about $65,000.

Watch out, however, for old engines and old sails. A Tartan 41 is likely to come with a huge inventory of sails, many of which are most suitable to use as painting drop cloths. Racing sails more than three years old are probably pretty tired. Tired racing sails do not necessarily make good cruising sails.

Since the foretriangle is so big, a new genoa is a fairly costly item. A fully-battened main would be a good addition for cruising, as would a new headsail reefing system.

Boats that have been used for years of racing are likely to have old luff groove devices on the headstay, and these do get bent, dinged and generally beaten up by the spinnaker pole whacking them—and the afterguy will occasionally get loose, even on the best-sailed boat.

Likewise, an original Bukh or Farymann diesel may also be tired. An old folding prop—most 41s have them—may need to be bushed to get rid of blade slop. Better yet, if you're going cruising, budget in a new three-bladed feathering prop along with the new engine.

At any one time, a number of Tartan 41s are likely to be on the market, so it pays to shop around. You buy this boat by its condition, not its age. It's one thing to get the boat at a bargain price, but if a paint job, a new engine, and new sails are on the list, you're going to spend a good chunk of change before you've got what you want.

If you want a bargain-basement, rugged ocean racer, the engine and cosmetics may be unimportant, but you're likely to want new sails, and you'll almost certainly want to refair the bottom—years of bottom paint make a poor racing finish.

If you want a sturdy, fast long-distance cruiser, tote up the dollars to see what it will cost to bring the creature comfort factor to an acceptable level.

Since there was variation in construction techniques, and since you may find a variety of factory and non-factory keel or rudder molds—at least one boat was built as a centerboarder, and another was converted to a deep, free-standing spade rudder rather than the original small, skeg-mounted rudder—the provenance of the individual boat is important. Many of the boats have changed hands and names several time, so it may take some sleuthing.

Over the years, Tartan has produced a number of boats that deserve reputations as classics: the 27, 30, 34, and 37 come to mind. But the 41 has introduced scads of sailors to real live ocean racing, and will probably continue to do so for another generation, long after many of today's hot boats have disappeared into the ranks of the also-rans.   • **PS**

Whitby 42

Solidly built and easy to maintain, the Whitby 42 is good both at dockside and going places.

The Whitby 42 was one of the small success stories of the boatbuilding industry. Designed by Ted Brewer in 1971, the Whitby 42 went into production in 1972. A few hundred boats were built.

While most boats were built by Whitby in Canada, hulls numbered between 200 and 300 were built under license by Fort Myers Yacht and Shipbuilding in Florida.

When the Whitby 42 was introduced in 1972, cost of the boat, including such features as diesel auxiliary generator, hot and cold pressure water, and refrigeration, was $42,000, including US duty. In the same year the Morgan Out Island 41 had a base price of $33,000, and the Coronado 41 was $30,000.

In 1983, the Coronado 41 was a memory, an Out Island 41 cost about $130,000, and the Whitby 42 would have cost you just shy of $103,000 with the US duty paid. Today, an early-'80s Whitby 42 commands about $3,000 *more* than an Out Island 41 of the same vintage. In other words, the Whitby 42 has good staying power, and, if anything, has improved on its value position in the market.

When we first saw the Whitby 42 in 1973, it seemed an ungainly whale of a boat, with high topsides, white decks, white everything. Over the years, through the subtle use of color—dark sheer strake, two-tone decks—the appearance of the boat was quietly altered. While the Whitby 42 will never have the sleek grace of an ocean racer, she has a sturdy grace of her own, the product of endless refinement and subtle improvement over the many years of her production history.

The Whitby 42 is a fully-powered auxiliary, rather than a motorsailer. Although she won't go to windward like a light fin-keeler, the boat is fully capable of performing well as a sailing vessel.

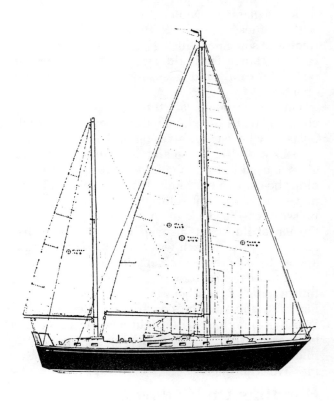

Specifications

LOA	42' 0"
LWL	32' 8"
Beam	13' 0"
Draft	5' 0"
Displacement	23,500 lbs.
Ballast	8,500 lbs.
Sail area	875 sq. ft.

Many owners have put tens of thousands of sea miles on their boats. A fair number of owners are retired couples who purchased the boat as a cruising home. Since the boat has the elbow room, accommodations, storage, and comforts that you would associate with a retirement home, it has proved a remarkable success in that capacity.

The Whitby 42 does not particularly look like an oceangoing boat, with her center cockpit, high topsides, wide beam, and shoal draft. Nevertheless, an astounding percentage of the boats are used for serious passagemaking.

Construction

Construction of the Whitby 42 is sturdy, but without the dramatic overkill frequently seen in cruising boats. The hull is balsa-cored from just below the sheer to just below the waterline.

Hull and deck are joined with an internal flange, which is glassed together and mechanically joined with stainless steel rivets. In the way of the genoa track and some deck fittings, hull and deck are also bolted together. The builder would use bolts through-out to join hull and deck, for a slight additional charge.

On newer boats, all through-hull fittings are equipped with through-bolted bronze seacocks. Older boats may have gate valves on underwater fittings.

Deck and deckhouse are also balsa-cored. Solid glass is used in the way of deck hardware. In some older boats, owners report that the area under the mizzenmast was not solid glass, resulting in com-pression of the deck in the vicinity of the mast. Owners of older boats also report that the under deck support for the mizzen was marginal. Later models appear to have these problems solved.

For those used to looking at the massive construc-tion of some cruising boats, notably those built in the Far East, some of the construction details of the Whitby 42 may look a little light. The success of these boats as cruisers indicates that proper proportioning in design and construction are more important than massive scantlings.

Handling Under Power

With a fuel capacity of 210 gallons, the Whitby 42 has a range under power of about 1,500 miles. The Lehman Ford 4-254 diesel produces about 67 hp, enough to drive the moderate displacement hull in almost any conditions.

Fuel tanks are located amidships. This means that the trim and balance of the boat will not change significantly as fuel is consumed.

Although a three-bladed prop in aperture is stan-dard, light air performance would be significantly improved by replacing the prop with a feathering prop such as the Maxprop or the Luke feathering prop. Using this prop there would be little or no sacrifice in performance under power, but there could easily be an increase in speed of a half knot or more under sail in winds under 10 knots. If you're off cruising in the South Pacific, just carry along the standard prop as a spare.

Amazingly, none of the Whitby 42 owners we talked to had added a feathering prop. It would be one of our first major changes if we owned the boat.

Because of her windage and fairly long keel, the boat does not exactly handle like a sports car under power. One owner says that his boat "turns like the Queen Mary," so give yourself plenty of room and take your time when docking.

Like most center cockpit boats, the Whitby 42's engine is located under the cockpit. The result is a

huge engine room with stooping headroom. The entire cockpit sole is the engine room hatch cover, and it can be unbolted in an hour or so to allow removal of the engine without tearing the interior of the boat apart. For a cruising boat that puts a lot of hours on the engine. this is a real plus.

The engine room has enough space for a small auxiliary generator. A generator was standard when the boat was first built, but later became an option. If you intend to do extensive cruising in the boat, a generator of about 3.5 kw would be worth installing. Unfortunately. the weight of the generator, which is mounted on the port side, may give the boat a slight port list.

Access to the stuffing box is good, through hatches in the cabin sole in the aft cabin. General access to the engine is excellent.

Handling Under Sail

Owners characterize the Whitby 42 as slightly faster than other boats of the same size and type. When equipped with a mizzen staysail and a spinnaker—a very reasonable combination for offwind sailing offshore in this boat—the boat is quite fast. One West Coast owner has raced his boat with remarkable success, but that is certainly not the boat's forte.

In the past, there have been problems with the mizzenmast. Since the main boom ends fairly close to the mizzen, the mizzen forestays do not have a very good angle for forward support. Until relatively recently, it was also absolutely necessary to use the mizzen running backstays when carrying a mizzen staysail. Earlier boats also reported problems with the under deck support system for the mizzen.

All of the mizzen problems are exacerbated if the boat is equipped with a radar antenna mounted on the mizzen mast—the natural location for it on a ketch.

Fortunately, most of these problems have been resolved on later boats. The mizzen spreaders are swept back enough to provide good after support without the use of running backstays, although we would probably still rig them in heavy weather or sloppy seas. Forward support of the mizzen was improved by the addition of a triatic stay between the main and mizzen mastheads.

The use of a triatic probably constitutes a second-best solution, as loss of one mast could well result in the loss of the other, since the masts are tied together. However, there is no simple way to improve the staying of the mizzen.

On later models, the mainsail is equipped with slab reefing, a great improvement over the roller reefing found on older models of the Whitby 42. A separate track on the mainmast for a storm trysail is something we'd go for if the boat is to be used offshore.

Another highly desirable rig option was the doublehead rig, which came in a package with a platform bowsprit and a removable inner forestay. Owners report that the extra sail area forward improves the balance of the boat as well as giving her some extra power.

Despite the great beam of the boat, her midships hull section is almost round. This means that the boat picks up very little form stability as it heels. Coupled with a ballast/displacement ratio of about 35%, this yields a boat that is not particularly stiff under sail, according to owners.

Although the boat comes with hydraulic steering, it is also possible to use an Edson pull-pull system. Since this is a less powerful steering system than the hydraulic steerer, you should go with the maximum size steering wheel that will fit in the cockpit—about a 40" diameter wheel. In addition to providing the extra leverage for the pull-pull system, a larger wheel lets you sit further outboard, an absolute necessity on a center cockpit boat when using a large genoa.

We prefer the pull-pull steerer because it gives the helmsman feedback about the balance of the boat. In the long run, the steering feedback will make you a better sailor. When the boat steers hard, it is out of balance, and is not being sailed to maximum efficiency.

With a high aspect rig and a generous sailplan for her moderate displacement, there is no excuse for the Whitby 42 to be a dog under sail. If you have the boat heavily loaded, you'll just have to add more sail to maintain performance. Fairing in the through hull fittings and adding a feathering prop will also help performance, particularly in light air.

Finally, by all means spring for the bowsprit and the extra sail area it gives you. According to one owner, designer Ted Brewer said the addition of the bowsprit is the single greatest improvement in the boat over the years.

Deck Layout

The deck layout of the Whitby 42 is about as simple as the deck on a boat can be. There are sturdy Skene chocks and large cleats forward, and chocks plus big cleats aft. With the platform bowsprit, anchors can be made self-stowing.

The foredeck has plenty of space for an anchor windlass, an absolute must if the boat is used for extended cruising. The forepeak locker could be used to hold anchor chain, but we'd be reluctant to add another 500 lbs of ground tackle in the front of the boat, since there's already a large water tank under the forward berths.

Despite a wide cabin trunk, access forward along the deck is good. To go from the cockpit aft, however, it is necessary to go over the top of the aft cabin, as the mizzen standing rigging takes up much of the side decks aft. Stanchions, bow, and stern rails are tall and sturdy.

There are two lockers on the afterdeck, one useful for lines and fenders, the other containing the propane bottles. Although the lids of both lockers are equipped with gaskets, surprisingly flimsy turnbutton latches are used to secure the lids. For offshore passagemaking, we'd replace these with sturdier latches.

There is also a large locker on the port side of the cockpit. This locker, too, lacks a good set of hatch

One of the more livable interiors is to be found in the Whitby 42. Engine access from the passage to the owner's cabin is excellent. The two chairs shown here are often replaced by a settee.

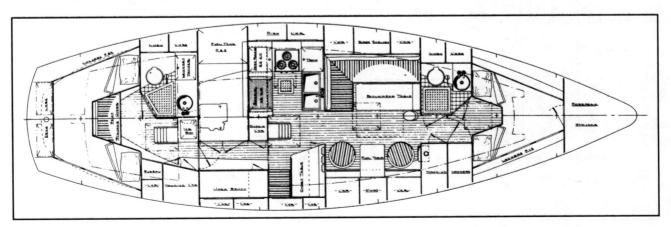

dogs, and since it opens into the engine room, we'd give high priority to making it secure, despite its location well above the water.

The cockpit is huge. However, it is not particularly vulnerable, since it is fairly high. We've seen few cockpits which would be better in port. There's even a big icebox next to the helmsman, making it unnecessary to truck down below for a cold one.

A sturdy molded breakwater protects the front of the cockpit. We'd add a dodger for offshore use. The original drawings of the boat also show a permanent windshield, which would be a good feature on a boat used primarily in northern latitudes.

One Whitby 42 we've seen has a permanent shelter over the front end of the cockpit, which both improved the looks of the boat—the shelter was designed by someone with a good eye—and gave remarkable protection to the front of the cockpit, allowing the companionway hatch to be left open in all but the worst weather offshore.

For offshore use, the louvered companionway drop boards should be replaced with solid boards, since a remarkable amount of water can get below in heavy weather. This is particularly important in the companionway to the aft cabin, which faces forward.

The companionway to the aft cabin makes it impossible to fit a mainsheet traveler. Therefore, a good boom vang is a must.

Belowdecks

Down below, the Whitby 42 really shines. The boat has one of the more livable interiors we've seen.

The owner's cabin aft has two large berths. If they are to be used as sea berths, they must be fitted with lee cloths. Since the berths are not parallel to the centerline of the boat, they do not make particularly good sea berths. The person sleeping in the leeward berth will find his head lower than his feet, while the occupant of the weather berth will be in the opposite situation.

Although there are a fair number of storage bins and a good hanging locker, the aft cabin has few drawers. Although drawers are not a particularly efficient way to use space, they are extremely convenient, particularly for those who have lived their lives in houses.

The aft head is huge. A few handrails would make it more comfortable offshore.

A passageway with stooping headroom joins the aft cabin to the rest of the boat. Getting full headroom in this passage would unnecessarily complicate the cockpit layout.

A workbench which can be converted to a berth is on the starboard side of the passage. The space below the bench is filled by a fuel tank, some storage space, and a big chart storage locker.

Outboard of the workbench is the electrical panel. Despite the stooping headroom, this is just about the ideal location for the electrical panel, since it is completely protected from spray.

On the port side of the passage, just aft of the companionway, there is a large locker for foul weather gear. Little touches like the chart storage area and the wet gear locker make the difference between a floating condominium which is miserable at sea and a true cruising boat.

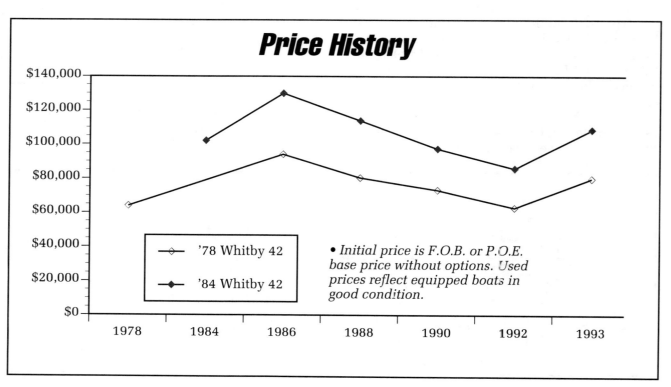

• Initial price is F.O.B. or P.O.E. base price without options. Used prices reflect equipped boats in good condition.

The main cabin is roomy, light, and well-ventilated, The galley to port has a large refrigerator and deep freeze—Grunert holding-plate refrigeration, driven by an engine-mounted compressor—a three burner propane stove, and, on newer boats, deep double sinks.

The only weak point in the galley is the mounting of the stove. On starboard tack, it fetches up against the back of the stove well when the boat heels much over 15 degrees. On port tack, the stove blocks access to the drawers under the sink counter.

There is a ventilation hatch over the galley, a real boon for the cook in hot weather. Except for the stove limitation, the galley gets an A+.

To starboard is the navigation table, with adequate room for the mounting of instruments and a good chart table. The chart table slopes toward the navigator, making it easier to work on from a seated position, but it is equipped with a folding support which allows the table to be leveled for use in port, making a handy desk.

Originally, there was no settee on the starboard side of the boat. Rather, the boat had two swivel chairs, a familiar touch to those used to life ashore. However, if the boat is to be used offshore, it should be ordered with the optional starboard settee, since the main cabin settees are the only good sea berths on the boat.

There is plenty of storage space outboard of the settees on both sides, including a rather excellent liquor locker with a folding cocktail table.

The main cabin table folds up against the port forward bulkhead. On a boat of this size, a fixed cabin table makes more sense. If we owned a Whitby 42, we'd build a narrow dropleaf table with deep fiddles, incorporating a pipe to the cabin overhead for a handhold when sailing offshore.

While this would intrude into the main cabin space, it would reduce the chance of a bad fall in rough conditions, would free up the bulkhead for other uses, and would create a storage space on the cabin sole where bulky objects like spare sails could be stowed offshore.

The forward cabin and head are almost as roomy as the aft cabin. In port, the occupants of the forward cabin are not second class citizens. Except for light

air sailing downwind, the forward cabin will probably not be used for sleeping offshore.

All in all, the interior of the Whitby 42 is an excellent compromise between the needs of the long term live-aboard and the long distance cruiser.

Conclusions

In these days of astronomical prices, the Whitby 42 represents a good value for living aboard or cruising. While finish detail is not particularly fancy, the boat is solidly built, and should be easy to maintain.

The boat came with a rather remarkable list of standard equipment, with such items as hot and cold water, refrigeration, huge tankage, two showers, dual voltage electrical systems, and ground tackle.

The options were practical and born of experience. Many of them are highly desirable, such as the double headsail rig option with bowsprit, contrasting deck, dark sheer indent, autopilot, and windlass.

Fully equipped for cruising — and we mean fully equipped—a new boat in the early '80s cost about $120,000. That boat used in 1992 could bring about $75,000 or thereabouts, depending on condition.

You can expect reasonable sailing performance from the Whitby 42. Obviously, her best point of sail will be reaching in moderate to heavy air.

Most owners are very enthusiastic about their boats. For most of them, this is not a first boat. Although most consider the boat a good boat dockside, they also consider it a boat in which to go places. We agree. **• PS**

Slocum 43

A semi-custom yacht that excells in comfort and livability. Be sure to check out the options, though.

There is no doubt about the Slocum 43's mission in life. This boat is made for blue water cruising. Named for Joshua Slocum, the most famous blue water sailor of all, she has been designed, built and equipped by and for people who spend a considerable amount of time living aboard and sailing offshore. Long and lean she is not. The effort here has gone into making functional and comfortable spaces in a sturdy passagemaker.

The Slocum 43 is a semi-custom double-ender designed by Stan Huntingford of Vancouver, BC, who designed traditional displacement cruising boats for three decades before retiring in 1987. The Slocum 43 is descended from the Passport 42—or perhaps we should say "ascended," because the Slocum is a bit larger than the Passport: 9" longer, 1" wider, and 3,000 pounds heavier. A comparison of the two boats would soon be reduced to a search for the places where they differ. Most of the differences will be in the details of the deck and interior, as both boats are custom designs to one degree or another.

Slocum Yachts also builds a 37' cutter, similar in character to the 43, but even more traditional. She displaces only 1,000 pounds less than the 43, and carries a full keel and attached rudder, in contrast to the 43's long fin keel and skeg rudder. The 37 is also a development by Huntingford of one of his earlier designs, the Rafiki 37.

The Slocum 43 was originally built by Cruising Yachts International, of Houston and Taiwan. Jan Stadman, President of CYI, split Slocum Yachts away from CYI in order to pursue another boatbuilding project. Slocum Yachts was purchased in 1988 by Walter Brown, who is continuing to operate the business out of New York much as Stadman did.

The Slocums are built at Hai-O Yacht Building

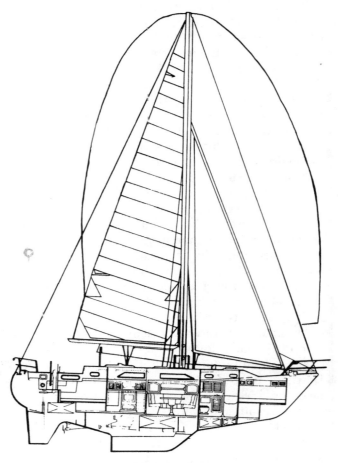

Specifications

LOA	42' 6"
LWL	35' 10"
Beam	12' 11"
Draft	5' 6"/6' 4" (shoal/std)
Displacement	28,104 lbs.
Ballast	9,000 lbs.
Sail area	808 sq. ft.

Corp, Taiwan, and imported into the US for final commissioning. Stadman has been building boats in Taiwan for almost 20 years, and claims to have solved the infamous Taiwan quality control problems by maintaining an on-site British supervisor, who is charged with making the boats come out of the yard according to specifications. In addition, Stadman's hands-on style of management takes him several times a year to Taiwan to implement his design modifications (he has designed most of the interior of the boats himself). As the Slocums' builder, he personally works the boat shows, and maintains a relationship with Slocum owners, garnering feedback on which innovations work and which don't, trading ideas for modifications, and incorporating the owners unofficially into his sales structure by connecting them with prospective buyers eager to admire their yachts.

Slocum owners are a small but devoted cadre of sailors. They are lavish in praising their boat, praise laced with references to Stadman's personal participation in their boat owning experience. Inevitably, the new owner of Slocum Yachts will have a different style of relating to the boats and owners. Brown has adopted much of Stadman's format, and is now making the trips to Taiwan himself. Additionally, Stadman himself continues to work with Brown.

Construction

The Slocum 43 has been designed and built with enormous attention to detail. It boasts many thoughtful and carefully designed features of the sort that can be done when labor costs are at the low end of the scale. Jan Stadman has obviously spent time at sea, and he has incorporated his experience into the Slocum 43. It is surprising, then, to come across the occasional oversights and omissions, a few of which are fairly significant and contradictory.

For example, the hull of the Slocum 43 is a fiberglass sandwich cored with 20 mm of Airex R62-80, a stable and lightweight material that both stiffens and insulates the hull. Full-length box stringers provide further stiffening. The bulkheads are 3/4" marine plywood, set in place with an Airex shock absorbing strip between the edge of the bulkhead and the hull, and taped with fiberglass strips extending 8" from the joints. The deck is also cored, but with balsa instead of Airex.

This is a reasonably sophisticated, modern approach to hull construction, evidencing concern for saving weight, so the cabin sole comes as something of a surprise. It is made of 1/2" plywood faced with 1/2" solid teak and holly—strong, but heavy. The weight of the floorboards soon becomes a matter of personal experience. The entire cabin sole and support system can be removed for full access to the engine, tanks, and bilges. The accessibility is wonderful. Moving all those floorboards around is not.

Another contradiction is in the cockpit. The size, design and layout of the cockpit is generally good and appropriate for a blue water cruising boat. However, the cockpit lockers have three serious problems. First, the massive molded fiberglass lids are heavy and are not equipped to stay up in an open position. Some kind of retainer should be rigged to prevent them from accidentally closing. There's not likely to be a second chance for any fingers in the way of a good slamming from those lids. It might even be worth replacing the lids with something more sensible.

Second, the lockers are cavernous—big enough to enter to repair the steering gear, wiring or plumbing therein. That sounds like a big advantage—it *is* a big advantage when you need to get to those things. The flip side is that anything stowed in those cavernous lockers also has access to the steering gear, the plumbing, and the wiring, and could foul or jam them in rough conditions. The lockers should be subdivided with removable shelving to keep items within reach and away from the works below. Shelving to protect the steering mechanism was added to later hulls (we examined #43).

Third, the lockers are not sealed off from the bilges. That's a common situation, but with lockers this size it becomes more of a concern. If water came aboard when a locker was open, a lot of it could get below very fast. (Maybe when you opened it in those rough conditions to clear the steering gear?) Not likely, perhaps, but it's the sort of unlikely event that can spell the difference between making it or not in survival conditions.

In general, though, the Slocum 43 has the strength and characteristics appropriate to passagemaking. She is quite stable, despite the seemingly low ballast/displacement ratio. The internal iron keel weighs 9,000 pounds, on a displacement of 28,000 pounds. Our rough calculation of her capsize screen value puts her at 1.69, the low end of the scale, comparable to the Bermuda 40, Luders 33, and Fast Passage 39. Her stability can be accounted for in part by the location of the engine in the bilge, below the waterline. Further, the boat is relatively beamy over much of her length. The water tanks are also below the waterline, and will add to stability when they are full.

The hull-to-deck joint is an inward-turning hull flange, overlapped by the bulwark flange at the perimeter of the deck molding. The joint is sealed with 3M 5200 adhesive and through bolted with 3/8" carriage bolts on 5" centers. The assembly is topped with an L-shaped teak caprail. This is a strong joint, and all but the bow is fairly well protected from potential impact by the tumblehome of the hull. A large teak rubbing strake in the area of maximum beam offers some protection to the midsections of the hull.

Below the rubbing strake, the white hull has been scored to simulate planking, which tends to hide irregularities that might show up in smooth gelcoat. Above the strake, a blue stripe fills the area to the caprail. The boat we examined showed some printthrough in the blue gelcoat, which is not scored, but in other areas the gelcoat finish appeared good.

The rubbing strake and sheer stripe reduce the appearance of height of the topsides, making the Slocum 43 seem, from some angles, sleeker than she really is. She is actually rather egg-shaped, and large for her length, a fact that can be appreciated for the roominess it confers below.

Fifteen through hull fittings on the boat exit at or

below the waterline, and are fitted with Taiwan-made bronze seacocks and, as needed, with vented loops to prevent back-siphoning. Although the hull is solid fiberglass laminate in the way of the seacocks, there is no backing plate behind the seacocks—the flange rests directly on the inside of the hull—and there are no additional screws or bolts to secure them. Some of the hoses attached to seacocks at the waterline were not double-clamped. We would prefer to see double hose clamps on all through hull fittings, plus mechanical fastenings, and backing plates to distribute the load. Two nice touches: the seacocks are labeled as to function, and emergency wood plugs are taped to the hull near many of them. There are, however, a lot of openings through the hull, more than we like to see.

The plumbing system includes hot and cold pressure water systems to the head, galley, and cockpit shower, plus manual cold fresh water and salt water systems to the head and galley. Two Rule 2000 electric bilge pumps are backed up by a Henderson manual pump mounted in the cockpit. Most of the domestic plumbing lines are copper tubing. Bilge pumps and drains have 1 1/2" or 2" hoses.

The electrical system includes 110-volt AC and 12-volt DC service, controlled by an American-made Newmar electrical panel. The 12-volt system is supplied by two 120 amp-hour batteries located in a convenient locker in the owner's stateroom at the base of the companionway.

We were unable to see the chainplate attachments because the hull is lined with teak strips glued to plywood sheets, which are in turn screwed to vertical furring strips attached to the hull. According to Stadman, the stainless steel chainplates extend from the deck to near the waterline, and are interconnected below by a welded stainless steel cross-member. They are through-bolted to the hull in the area of the rubbing strake, so the bolts are not visible from outside. Inside, the chainplates are further secured with fiberglass, and, in the area of chainplate attachments, the hull is a solid fiberglass laminate. While this arrangement seems plenty strong, it would be difficult to repair.

The deck reinforcement in the way of hardware is unusual. A stainless steel plate is sandwiched inside the deck molding, in place of the balsa core. Because it is pre-drilled and tapped, deck hardware can be attached without struggling to attach nuts from below while turning bolts from above. Structurally, this system appears to distribute the loads on the hardware only to the upper skin of the deck sandwich. We would be more comfortable with through-bolted attachments, backed up with an interior plate, that would utilize the entire thickness of the deck.

Handling Under Power

A 50 hp Perkins 4-108 diesel, set on flexible mounts near the midpoint of the boat, provides adequate power for the Slocum 43. This engine was rated in our 1989 mechanics' survey as one of the best.

The three-bladed bronze propeller is strut-mounted just forward of the rudder skeg, a good position for balanced maneuvering under power.

Accessibility to the engine is excellent. The engine compartment is provided with a light (great) and soundproofing (could be better). Locating the engine in the bilge is a compromise. It puts 500 pounds where it serves as centrally-located ballast, enhancing stability and reducing pitching moment. It eliminates a large engine box in the cabin, or cramming the engine inaccessibly under the cockpit. The location also allows a nearly horizontal propeller shaft, which is more efficient than an angled shaft. The drawback is the engine's vulnerability to flooding if the boat takes on a lot of water. The Slocum 43 has a large sump which should help avoid

The interior is the best feature of the Slocum 43. Storage, lighting, ventilation and workmanship are all excellent. We could find almost nothing to criticize about it.

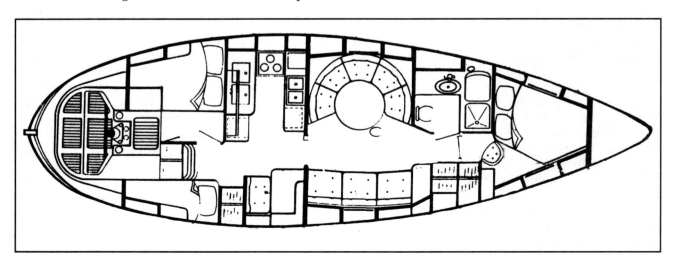

problems, but the owner should be aware of the potential for trouble.

Engine controls are conveniently mounted on the steering pedestal, with the instrument panel recessed into the starboard cockpit coaming and protected with a clear plastic cover. This location might be too vulnerable to spray in some boats, but this cockpit seems to be fairly dry.

Fuel tanks are under the cockpit, with filling ports located at the base of the steering pedestal, a good location because of proximity to the tanks and easy clean-up in case of a fuel spill. The two black iron tanks hold 150 gallons. This capacity gives a powering range of about 700 miles.

We think black iron fuel tanks are a bad idea in sailboats. The Slocum's tanks are painted on the outside with an anti-corrosion coating, but fuel tanks rust from the inside out. Diesel fuel frequently has water in it, and the water settles to the bottom of the tank. The water displaces fuel which would normally coat the sides of the tank. Without a protective coating of diesel fuel, iron tanks can rust out quickly, particularly along welded seams. The additional cost of a fuel tank of high-grade aluminum is minimal compared to the cost of disassembling joinerwork to repair or replace black iron tanks, but iron tanks are still quite common on Taiwanese boats.

Handling Under Sail

The Slocum 43, while not a high performance boat, nevertheless performs adequately for cruising. On the sparkling autumn day that we sailed her, we had optimum conditions: winds of 14 to 16 knots with relatively flat seas. Although the rig was not tuned, the boat was reasonably fast, surpassing our expectations.

Her weakest performance will come when the wind drops below 8 or 10 knots and when working to windward. She will not sail as close to the wind as a narrower boat with finer entry. The genoa sheets to a car on the caprail, which keeps the decks uncluttered, but the rails on a beamy boat present a sheeting platform too wide for good upwind performance. Many new sailboat designs have a wide beam, but the shrouds have been engineered to inboard chainplates, and genoa tracks run inboard instead of along the rail, achieving a closer sheeting angle for the genoa and improving a boat's ability to go to windward.

In general, running rigging is led to the cockpit, so that the boat can be sailed without leaving the cockpit once the sails are up. An exception is the mainsheet traveler, a Nicro 610 X-track and car that require going forward to make adjustments, which proved difficult. The X-track is designed to not bind up when the mainsheet pulls at an oblique angle. In our tests of mainsheet travelers, *PS* concluded that this feature did not offer better performance than other types of travelers tested. In any case, the Slocum's mainsheet lead is perpendicular to the traveler, and so does not demand this special feature. At the very least, we would rig a better athwartships adjustment, perhaps leading the adjustment line to the cockpit. Better, get the Harken traveler system offered as an option.

Standard sail inventory is made by Cheong Lee,

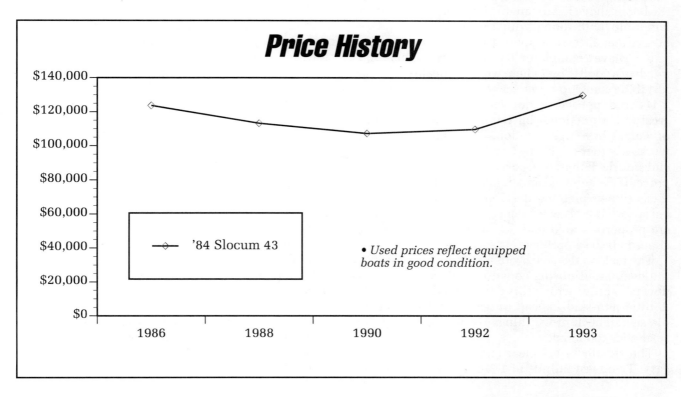

• Used prices reflect equipped boats in good condition.

Taiwan: mainsail rigged with two slab reefs, 150% genoa, #2 working jib, and staysail. The keel-stepped mast, boom, and staysail club are Isomat; internal halyards lead to mast-mounted winches. The double-spreader cutter rig is supported by stainless 1x19 wire and swaged terminals.

On our test boat, all sheet winches were self-tailing Barients, and adequate in size: 32ST as primaries, 22ST on the main, 17ST on the staysail. The halyard winches were generally of adequate size, although none was large enough to winch a person to the masthead, so it might be advisable to upgrade the mainsail halyard winch from a Barient 18 to a 22 or larger. Winch bases are insulated to prevent metal-to-metal contact and resulting corrosion on the mast.

On Deck

The cockpit and decks of the Slocum 43 offer a sense of security and comfort, due to the high freeboard, bulwarks, high lifelines (30" above the deck), heavy stanchions and stanchion bases, beefy pulpit and pushpit, and plenty of handholds and grabrails the length of the boat. Secure footing is provided by the teak underfoot everywhere: in the cockpit, on deck, and on the coachroof.

The T-shaped cockpit is not enormous, but is roomy enough, with comfortable seating on all four sides. The most popular lounging spot is the custom pushpit bench, a crescent-shaped innovation situated above the stern that confers superiority on the occupant.

A massive stainless and laminated wood boom gallows serves multiple functions. Besides holding the boom above head-banging level, it makes a good handhold and, along with the molded fiberglass breakwater, forms a support structure for the dodger.

If we have a complaint, it is that there might be too much of a good thing. There would probably be little lost if the stanchions were made of 1" in place of the 1 1/4" tubing used on our test boat. The teak looks great and is functional, but it represents a fair amount of weight in a high location, and a fair amount of work, whether oiled or varnished. The cockpit sole and side decks have raised teak planking set in black polysulfide, screwed and bunged. The thought of all those screws piercing the fiberglass through to the balsa core is a bit worrisome, but if the screw holes are properly sealed and the bungs stay in place it should not be a problem.

The teak on the coachroof is thinner—inlaid into the deck mold during construction, routed with a dovetail groove which fills with resin during layup. A little non-skid instead of teak in some strategic places might improve things without affecting the aesthetics too much.

The sidedecks are clear and passage forward is easy. Two mast pulpits of 1 3/4" stainless tubing—massive, again—offer good handholds, a place to secure gear and lines, and provide protection for the optional deck boxes.

The foredeck is somewhat obstructed by the staysail boom, but there is ample room to move and work around it. An electropolished stainless steel bow fitting accommodates two anchors. A double rope/chain locker in the bow of the boat can accommodate the anchor rode, but it is not a sensible place to carry the weight of a long anchor chain. There is a hatch on the foredeck which can be useful for sail changes underway.

Despite the fact that much of the deck equipment is overscale, the two 8" bow cleats are grossly undersized for a big, heavy boat. For passage through the Panama Canal, for example, regulations call for docking lines at least 7/8" in diameter. Try bending those around an 8" cleat, and you'll see what we mean.

We recommend the optional Nilsson V-3000 electric anchor windlass, rather than a manual windlass, on this size boat. However, take care that the foot switch is installed out of the way, to avoid losing a finger by accidentally starting up the windlass when you are not prepared.

Belowdecks

Below is where the Slocum 43 is most impressive. The interior is attractive and well thought out in details important to living in confined spaces on a moving platform for extended periods of time. Systems are accessible for maintenance and repair. In spite of extensive use of teak, there is a sense of light and space, and ventilation is good.

The interior joinerwork is quite good, from the circular teak table in the port side settee to the contoured nav station with slant-top opening table, stowage beside and under the seat and table, and hinged electrical panel. The teak and holly cabin sole has recessed dust/drip pans covered by grates at the base of the companionway steps and the base of the mast. A hanging wet locker at the base of the companionway drains directly to the bilge.

In the galley, the double icebox is fitted with a foot pump that delivers ice melt directly overboard, so it won't smell up the bilge. A built-in dish rack also drains overboard. The gimbaled Force 10 propane stove is recessed behind a safety bar. Overhead cupboards have a movable peg system which allows you to custom fit spaces inside to the size and shape of your dishes.

Throughout the interior, ample lighting is provided—brass reading lamps over the berths, broad area illumination by 16 overhead fixtures, and indirect fluorescent lamps above bookshelves.

Stowage is plentiful and well organized: 25 drawers with solid teak front panels slanted to allow ventilation when the drawers are closed; shelves, bins, cabinets and lockers in staterooms and work areas; and good use of potential "dead" spaces around settees and berths.

Two places on the Slocum 43 which would be especially significant to livaboards and passagemakers are the owner's stateroom and the head. The head is a double-compartment, one-piece molding with built-in shower. In the full headroom shower are handholds, alcoves and a seat—better than some shoreside showers. The head compartment is roomy enough for maneuvering, and offers stowage above and below the wash basin as well as in a bulkhead cabinet.

The owner's stateroom has room for two standing adults, a queen size berth, bookshelves, hanging locker, four drawers and three cabinets. Located at the foot of the companionway, it is convenient to most parts of the boat, yet offers good privacy and comfort. Some might object to having the fuel tank and battery access through this cabin, but we are not among them.

The nav station is comfortable, with good working space for chartwork, flat stowage for charts and tools, and ample room for installing electronics. The boat we sailed had an autopilot, Satnav, loran, depthsounder, performance indicators for boat speed, wind speed and direction; log, timer, VHF radio and a stereo receiver/tape player. The pilot berth is aft of the nav station, separated from it by the wet locker. An odd oversight is the lack of a red light for night work at the nav station, although three red floor lights are provided at strategic locations for maneuvering safely from one end of the boat to the other.

Conclusions

The Slocum 43 resides toward the lower end of the price scale for her type of boat, but certainly not in the very lowest position.

The Slocum 43, like all boats, is a mix of compromises. She excells in comfort and livability below. Her shortcomings lie in some of the technical details of construction and equipment, although the boat is generally adequate in those areas as well. A new-boat buyer with a lot of cruising experience could, and should, specify appropriate options to meet those shortcomings. Because the boat has evolved over the years, the earlier models will be different from later hulls, and a prospective buyer might do well to investigate the changes before deciding what to specify for his own boat. Of course, the buyer of a used Slocum 43 will have to live with whatever decisions the first owner made.　　• **PS**

Mason 43/44

Owners say this powerful, Taiwan-built world cruiser carries Hinckley quality at half the price.

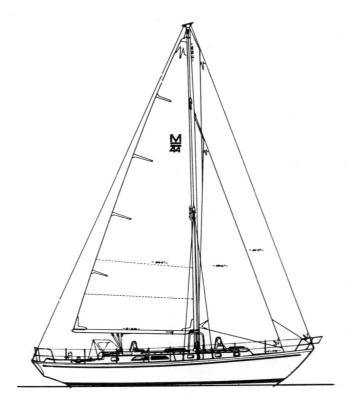

The Mason 43 was introduced in 1978 by Pacific Asian Enterprises (PAE), a California-based "developer" of Taiwan-built yachts. The Mason 44, which uses the same hull but a different deck mold, appeared in 1985, and is still in production today. In all, 180 43s and 44s have been sold. Due to a program of continual refinement, it is probable that no two are exactly the same.

The Masons have earned a reputation for offering quality approaching that of Hinckley, Swan, Alden and Little Harbor at a lower price, largely due to lower labor rates in Taiwan.

The Boat and the Builder

The Mason 43 was designed by Al Mason. During his career Mason worked with Carl Alberg, John Alden, Philip Rhodes and Sparkman & Stephens, as well as independently. His bent is generally traditional, with pleasing proportions and gentle sheer lines.

According to PAE's Joe Meglen, the 43 is an "evolution of a successful CCA ocean racer named *Sitzmark*," which in turn evolved from the Nevins Yawl, *Finisterre*, and farther back, the New York 32.

The 44 was redesigned by PAE's in-house design team. Changes included modifying the rudder, lowering the cabin 2-1/2 inches, increasing fuel tankage, eliminating the single quarter berth, bringing the companionway aft, and making the mainsheet traveler run the full width of the cabin trunk.

PAE was formed by three yacht brokers (including Meglen) who first formed their own brokerage, Lemest Yacht Sales, and later decided to develop their own boats. Besides the Mason line, they've also done the Nordhavn 46 and 62 trawlers and are presently working on a Jim Taylor-designed 52-foot IMS boat.

Ta Shing Yacht Building Co. of Tainan, Taiwan, builds the molds and the boats for PAE. During a tour

Specifications

LOA	43' 11"
LWL	31' 3"
Beam	12' 4"
Draft (shoal/deep)	5' 6"/6' 3"
Displacement	27,400 lbs.
Ballast (43)	8,400 lbs.
Sail area (cutter)	899 sq. ft.

of Taiwan boatbuilders in 1986, we felt that Ta Shing was doing the best work of any Taiwanese-owned and operated yard in the country (the other superior yard at that time was Ted Hood's Little Harbor facility). Ta Shing also builds or has built the Norseman 447, Skye 54, the Babas, Flying Dutchmans and Pandas, and its own Tashiba and Taswell lines, which it markets directly.

The design of the Mason 43, with its long trunk cabin, generous overhangs and full keel, makes no pretenses of modernity. Apt adjectives include traditional, classic, handsome, and, according to the ads, "timeless." With its heavy displacement (d/l ratio = 400) and cutter or ketch rig, cruising is clearly its intention.

Owners' Comments

"She is a seakindly yacht and a joy to sail. According to our B&G we have had her as close as 30 degrees off the wind, although she (and we, too) are happier a little more off the wind."

1991 model in California

"I am absolutely captivated by the boat and am not objective at all in my feelings toward her. The general construction is of the highest standard. Like an Irish hunter, she is a workhorse and a lady—maybe not quite as fast around six furlongs as a racehorse, but for the long pull, through timber, brush and over walls, she is really something."

1986 model in Maryland

"Almost all Masons I have seen list to starboard. This, I think, is because the starboard fuel tank is 100 gallons and the port fuel tank is 70 gallons. In consuming water and fuel, it is important to balance the use of one's tanks.

"I have certain options that I feel are essential: foam insulation, a must for Maine; a freshwater deck pump for washing down the boat; the saltwater deck pump for cleaning the rode and anchor; screens for all ports and hatches; the drain and teak grate at the base of the companionway; bronze edge and channel for companionway drop boards; aft cabin berth four inches longer (I am 6' 1"), which makes the port cockpit locker smaller; fuel skimmer at bottom of fuel tank.

"Boats should be as beautiful and as functional as they are fun. The Mason 44 is all three."

1968 model in Massachusetts

Construction

The Mason boats are heavily built with solid fiberglass hulls, balsa-cored decks, and eight longitudinal foam/ fiberglass stringers for added stiffness. Bulkheads are 3/4-inch mahogany plywood bonded to the hull with foam in between to prevent hard spots (the right way to do it). The hull/deck joint of the 43 was originally through-bolted, caulked with Thiokol and reinforced with stainless steel flat stock. Meglen told us they later felt the stainless steel wasn't doing anything structural and dropped it, in part to save its 600-pound weight. Current boats are through-bolted on 8-inch centers, alternating with self-tapping screws also on 8-inch centers; the entire joint is laminated over with three layers of mat and woven roving. This, plus some other changes, enabled PAE to add 1,000 pounds to the ballast of the 44, without adding to overall displacement.

Fiberglass work is generally very good. One owner responding to our call for reader input said his boat arrived with a slight print through, but that the dealer, Bass Harbor Marine in Maine, painted the hull with Awlgrip at no charge to correct the problem.

A boat yard owner who has worked on a number of Masons said. "Areas the average owner will never see are finished with smooth, clean surfaces. The total absence of fiberglass 'meathooks' in such spots is much appreciated by yard workers."

A number of owners reported minor blistering, none serious.

Teak decks were standard on the 43, but not the 44. Teak is a wonderful non-skid surface, and nothing quite matches its looks. But there are usually attendant problems, especially leaks. One 44 owner said, "I do not have a teak deck, and am not sorry."

The amount of bright work on these boats is considerable. After all, fancy joinerwork is the essential feature Taiwan builders have to offer, and many American buyers lap it up. But savvy owners know it requires a lot of upkeep. The owner of a 1989 model said, "Bright work maintenance has become a nuisance in my life. I could do without the toe rail and have them aluminum. Also, I would eliminate the bright work 'eyelids' around the deck house, as in the Cambria 44, as well as the cockpit coaming and the Dorade boxes."

Speaking of Dorade boxes, the owner of a 1985 Mason 43 said his are mounted on plywood blocks screwed to the deck, which after four years began to delaminate and rot. The inappropriate use of plywood is, or at least was, a common problem on Taiwan-built boats.

Much Taiwan metalwork, such as custom welded stainless steel fittings, has also been suspect. Several owners of earlier Masons mentioned it.

The mast is a Forespar aluminum extrusion, painted with polyurethane. As the cost of anodizing increases (due to the difficulties and expenses of toxic waste disposal), we'll see more and more painted masts. They look great when new, but extra care should he taken to prevent scratches that penetrate to bare metal.

Turnbuckles are by Navtec, which we have rated highly in past evaluations. Blocks are by Schaefer. Running intermediate backstays are provided on the cutter and double headsail ketch rig for added support in heavy air.

Interior

Both the 43 and 44 are aft cockpit, tri-cabin designs. As can he seen in the plan, there is a V-berth or offset double berth forward, U-shaped dinette, galley and nav station amidship, and a private stateroom aft, partially extending under the cockpit.

The companionway is offset to starboard and on the 43 it is positioned several feet forward of the cabin bulkhead. This unusual feature means added distance from the cockpit to the safety of the cabin, a movement that some owners feel is less than ideal when sailing on port tack in a blow (the mainsheet also tends to inhibit access). An additional problem was the difficulty in constructing a full dodger. Of course, a partial dodger over the companionway is possible, but this does little to protect the crew in the cockpit.

In response to these complaints, the companionway of the 44 was moved aft, and the cockpit seating lowered to provide higher backrests; this latter change eliminated the single quarter berth.

As noted above, Taiwan builders are noted for their joinerwork, sometimes performed to ridiculous excess in the form of Chinese dragons, poppy flowers, and as designer Bob Perry is fond of observing, the building of "drawers inside of drawers." Happily the Masons show considerable restraint; their interiors are in fact exquisite.

Owners report very few problems, only a handful of gripes concerning the interior. These include leaky teak hatches (several highly recommend the optional Lewmar hatches), absence of a good sail locker on the 43 (despite voluminous stowage areas). marginal ice box insulation, settee too narrow for maximum comfort, no positive latches for securing cabin sole panels in event of knockdown, and difficulty in accessing tanks for cleaning.

The engine (usually a Perkins 4-108 in the 43, a 55-hp. Yanmar diesel in the 44) is located below the cabin sole. Owners of both engines report high levels of satisfaction with performance, though some feel the Perkins is "one size too small." Sound insulation is excellent ("I can hardly hear it running."). While this location places its weight low and presents no problems building furniture around it, several owners did note that a surprise flooding of the bilge immerses it. An automatic float switch for the bilge pump is now standard: one owner recommends the added measure of an alarm. Another noted that the engine "...is difficult to access, especially at the forward end where there are belts for the alternator and refrigerator compressor." Because of its enormous sump, Meglen says it's not a worry. And the location allows a horizontal propeller shaft for greater efficiency under power.

Fuel tanks are painted steel and water tanks stainless. The owner of a 1988 Mason 44 said, "Her fresh water capacity of 205 gallons is more than enough. The manifold for the five tanks is a work of art." Fuel capacity of the 44 is 160 gallons (a bit less in the 43), giving meaningful ranges under power of 400 miles minimum in worst-case head seas.

Performance

Underway, the Mason 43/44 is a big boat with the displacement to power through choppy seas. Naturally. it does not have a racer's speed or close-windedness (partially due to a fat keel), but owners are generally pleased with their boats' performance. They consistently rate off-the-wind speed superior to upwind speed, and balance as above average.
The one area which nearly every respondent commented on is stability. Due to its comparatively narrow beam, low ballast-to-displacement ratio, and large sail area, the boat heels quickly to 15-20 degrees, to lengthen the waterline, then digs in. This appears more true of the 43 than the 44, which was given additional ballast.

Various layours were offered, including one or two heads, and in the forward cabin, choice of V-berth or offset double. The single quarter berth in the aft cabin was eliminated in the 44.

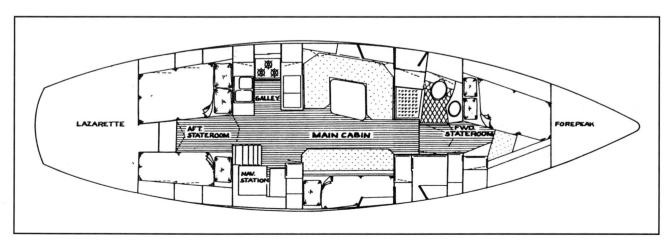

The owner of a 1984 model echoed the sentiments of many when he wrote, "My earliest experiences sailing the boat were frustrating as I found we had to reef beating in 15-16 knots of wind. I thought I'd bought a very tender boat. It took me a while to realize that the enormous mainsail, such a boon to light air breezes, made me crazy when the wind increased. When the first reef is in, the rail comes up and the boat goes like a shot. Once I understood the trade-off between light-air performance and the first reef, I grew to appreciate the design decision leading to the larger main."

In heavy weather, both models are exceptionally seakindly. The owner of a 1985 model recounted spending the night 60 miles offshore in the remnants of a hurricane, with 35-knot sustained winds and much higher gusts. Wave heights averaged 15 feet. "We made progress upwind at 4-5 knots under double-reefed main and staysail, until I was too tired to stay on watch. I hove to for eight hours. The motion was comfortable enough to sleep and not once did I feel unsafe. The boat needed zero attention, staying perfectly balanced."

For powering, owners recommend a feathering prop such as the Max Prop, which one owner said improved handling, and gave him an extra half knot of speed under sail. Several owners noted sluggish response to the helm at slow speeds.

Conclusion

Mason 43 owners have mixed feelings about the changes made in the 44. Some appreciate the 44's additional ballast and conventional companionway, which allows easier fitting of a full dodger. Others feel that the 44 is somewhat less attractive, with a "less sophisticated interior finish."

Mason 44 owners retaliate, saying that their cockpits are "much better" than the 43s, which suffer from a lack of ergonomics, especially backrests that are too low.

Almost all owners emphasized that their complaints are for the most part niggling, and that on the whole they adore their boats. "The Mason 44 is probably the prettiest vessel I have ever seen," wrote one owner. "She has sweet lines, capped by a perfect sheer. Her finish is outstanding and her belowdecks woodwork rivals Hinckley and Little Harbor." Not one regretted his purchase, and many see their Mason as the last boat they'll ever own. With few exceptions, owners feel PAE is a conscientious company that addresses its customers' problems with care and expedition.

The Mason 43/44 is a heavily built cruising boat with complex systems. Most problems are associated with accessories, not with the basic structure and rig. She is seakindly, balances well, and is good in light air, though the large mainsail needs to be reefed early when the wind pipes up.

Prices vary considerably according to age, condition and equipment. Earlier models probably represent better values, as rising labor rates in Taiwan have increased the cost of producing the later models.

It's a good production boat for long-distance cruising. But the large amount of bright work demands constant maintenance. • **PS**

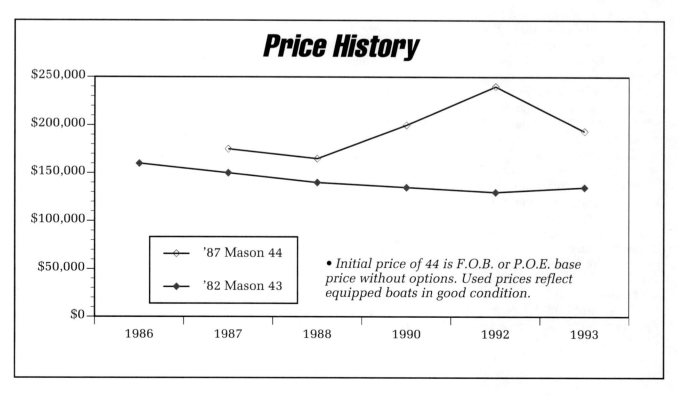

Price History

• Initial price of 44 is F.O.B. or P.O.E. base price without options. Used prices reflect equipped boats in good condition.

Legend:
- ◇ '87 Mason 44
- ◆ '82 Mason 43

Brewer 12.8 Brewer 44

The venerable Whitby 42 has evolved into these two blue-water cruisers, both good, solid values.

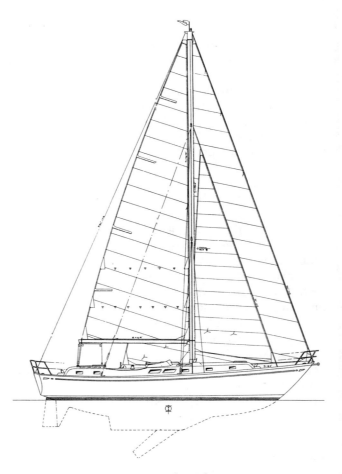

The Brewer 12.8 and the Brewer 44 are developments of the Whitby 42, a cruising boat from the board of Ted Brewer. Brewer is one of the great modern cruising boat designers. His boats are well-mannered, attractive and practical.

According to the designer, the Brewer 12.8 and Brewer 44 use the same basic hull and deck as the Whitby 42, a boat that was designed in 1971. Hull changes to the Whitby 42 were made by cutting out the long keel and attached rudder, replacing them with a more modern short keel and skeg-mounted rudder. This eliminated a lot of wetted surface, improving the light-air performance.

To improve windward performance, a high aspect ratio centerboard extends through the bottom of the 12.8's shallow keel. Since the board is not ballasted, it does not affect stability, but can be used when reaching to shift the center of lateral resistance.

The Brewer 44 is the same boat as the 12.8, with the stern extended slightly, increasing the size of the aft stateroom. This has the fortunate side effect of making the boat slightly narrower aft and reducing the size of the transom.

Both the Brewer 12.8 and the Brewer 44 are semi-custom boats: you don't go down and buy one from a dealer, you have one built. Eliminating a dealer network does away with commissions of approximately 20%—a significant saving to the customer on a boat this size.

Since the Brewer 44 is slightly larger—more boat for the buck—has a better aft cabin, and doesn't cost a lot more to build, it has replaced the Brewer 12.8 as the "standard" model. You can still get a 12.8 on special order if you want a 42' boat. We'd opt for the bigger boat because it's better looking and has a much better aft cabin. Otherwise, the boats are virtually identical.

Specifications

LOA .... 42' (12.8), 44' (44)
LWL .... 33' 9" (12.8), 35' 6" (44)
Beam .... 13' 6"
Draft ....4' 6" (shoal & cb), 5' 2" (deep)
Displ. 23,850 (12.8), 27,500 (44)
Ballast 9,000 (12.8), 12,000 (44)
Sail area .... 867 sq. ft. (cutter)

Absolutely the only advantage the 12.8 has over the 44 is that it is easier to lower a dinghy stowed in davits down the vertical transom of the 12.8. On the reverse transom of the 44, the dinghy tends to hang up as you drop it.

It's easy to get a little confused reading the specifications for the three boats. The beam of the 12.8 and the 44 is listed as 13' 6", while the Whitby 42 is 13' wide. According to the designer, the difference probably comes from including the molded-in guardrails of the Brewer 12.8 and Brewer 44, since no change was made to the hull width.

Both the 12.8 and the 44 have 4' 6" standard draft, yet the 44 has from 2,000 to 3,000 pounds more ballast, from 2,650 to 3,650 pounds more displacement (depending on which ad you read), and a

Owners' Comments

"Exterior cosmetic finish is great. Interior joinerwork—drawers, doors, etc—is only average. For the first time, my wife is ecstatic with the livability of a boat.

"The centerboard version handles well in all winds. She is easily singlehanded even without an autopilot—or a wife—for long passages."

—1984 model 12.8 in New York

"With a 150% genoa, you need turning blocks to lead properly to the sheet winches. The builder is very willing to customize at a reasonable price.

"Delivery time was quoted as four months, but was actually five. Be prepared to spend a month in Fort Myers after the boat goes in the water.

"Excellent electrical and refrigeration systems, but I should have bought a generator. I recommend the cutter rig with a quick-release forestay. I tie it back when using the 150% genoa, then use the staysail when the wind reaches 20 knots.

"There are so many good things about the boat, and so many little problems. So what's new?"

—1985 model 12.8 in Maryland

"The boat sails well, but can't go to windward like my old IOR boat. The base price is low, but by the time you put on the extras, it adds up. It's still much cheaper than a Bristol or an Alden. For the first time, my wife really enjoys spending time on a boat, although she thought we were too old for another boat."

—1987 model 44 in Rhode Island

waterline from 1' 3" to 1' 9" longer. According to the builder, the 44 started out with 11,000 pounds of ballast, but that has gradually increased to almost 12,000 pounds.

Since there is no actual change in the keel depth or position in the two boats, it is reasonable to assume that the increasingly heavier 44 actually draws more than the advertised 4' 6". The extra displacement of the 44 probably translates into a base draft of about 4' 9". In practice, both the 12.8 and the 44 will draw even more in cruising trim, since owners of these boats frequently load them up with heavy items such as generators and bigger-than-standard batteries.

The 12.8 and the Brewer 44 are built by Fort Myers Yacht and Shipbuilding. The yard has built 40 12.8s, and 24 of the 44' version have been sold. The yard also built 33 Whitby 42s under license from the Canadian builder.

The 12.8 and the 44 were conceived as good-performing, long distance liveaboard cruisers. The members of the original syndicate which commissioned the Brewer 12.8 were experienced racing and cruising yachtsmen who wanted the livability and layout of the Whitby 42, coupled with a higher-performance hull and rig configuration.

Hull and Deck

There is nothing fancy about the construction of the Brewer 12.8. The hull is a conventional layup of mat and roving, with balsa core from just below the waterline up to just below the sheer.

The hull-to-deck joint is formed by a glass hull bulwark with an inward-turning flange. The outward-turning bulwark flange of the deck molding overlaps this, and the hull and deck are bolted and bedded together. This is a good, solid joint. It is capped with teak.

A fiberglass rubbing strake is molded into the hull just below the sheer. It's a toss-up between a molded fiberglass rubbing strake and a bolted-on wooden one. Certainly maintenance will be easier with the fiberglass strake, but a wooden strake might absorb a little more impact without damage to the hull, and would probably be easier to repair or replace. In any case, a rubbing strake is a good idea on a boat that may well be laid alongside primitive docks in far-off places to load fuel or water.

Some of the construction details strike us as a little light for a serious cruising boat of this displacement. The shroud chainplates, for example, are 1/4" stainless steel. If this were our own boat, and we were planning serious offshore cruising, we'd want those chainplates to be 3/8" material.

Likewise, rig specifications call for 9/32" wire for shrouds and backstay, plus a 5/16" headstay. We'd rather see at least 5/16" shrouds, plus a 3/8" headstay. The specified wire sizes are adequate, but we prefer a little more margin in an offshore cruiser. The lighter wire saves some weight and windage aloft, and a little money.

Some of the construction details are very good. Lifeline stanchions are 29" tall, spaced closely together, and properly backed with aluminum plates. Some finishing details on the early 12.8 we sailed, on the other hand, were less satisfactory. For example, rather than using solid teak molding in the door frames, the Brewer 12.8 had glued-on veneer edging. Likewise, aft of the settee backs there are access hatches to storage areas. These access hatches are merely cutouts in the plywood, and the edges were not even sanded smooth before painting.

The Brewer 44 we looked at was a totally different animal in finish detail. Doorways have solid teak edge moldings; detailing is much better throughout. Where the early 12.8 rates only "average production boat" in the detailing category, the 44 detailing is "very good production boat" in quality. When we looked at the 12.8, we figured it needed another 200 hours of detailing to match its potential. The 44 is just about there.

Rig

The standard rig of both the 12.8 and the 44 is a well-proportioned, modern, high aspect ratio cutter. The mainsail area of 368 square feet is about the maximum size conventional mainsail that a retired couple would want to handle. If the boat is going to be a long-term retirement home, we'd consider going to a roller-reefing mainsail such as the Hood Stoway or Metalmast Reefaway. This type of decision should be made when the boat is built, since a retrofit is an expensive proposition involving replacement of the spar.

The mast is by Isomat, with Lewmar halyard winches mounted on the spar. The rig is stepped through to the keel.

Engine and Mechanical Systems

Standard engine for the Brewer 44 is a 62 hp Perkins 4-154. A larger 85 hp Perkins is optional. Either engine is more than adequate power for the boat. We prefer the smaller engine for its better fuel economy, but if you want a real motorsailer, the bigger engine is a reasonable choice. The Brewer 12.8 used the 62 hp Lehman Ford engine.

With the standard 135 gallons of fuel and the smaller engine, range under power is about 700 miles. This is just about what you'd want in a big cruising boat that sails well.

Plumbing and wiring systems are good, but the standard batteries are too small for the boat. Although the standard equipment list is reasonably thorough, a lot of equipment you'd want for serious cruising is optional. The basics such as hot and cold pressure water, propane for cooking, fuel tank selection system and fuel filters are standard, and well-executed.

Handling Under Power

The Brewer 12.8 with the Lehman diesel motors comfortably at 6 knots at about 1700 rpm. This is a very economical cruising speed. Both of the Perkins engines are capable of pushing the boat faster, but when you're cruising, fuel economy is more important than how quickly you get there.

The boats have a lot of windage. A major criticism

of the Whitby 42 was that it was difficult to handle at low speeds when docking, particularly in a crosswind. Both the 12.8 and the 44, with their more cutaway underbodies, maneuver substantially better. This is still a big boat, and it will not spin on a dime like a smaller boat.

One change that would dramatically improve both speed under sail and handling under power would be to install a feathering prop such as the Maxprop instead of the standard solid prop. The 44 we looked at had a three-bladed Maxprop, and the owner wouldn't have it any other way. A feathering prop gives full thrust in reverse—unlike either fixed or folding props—yet offers little more resistance under sail than a folding prop.

Midships cockpits with engine rooms below can be noisier both ondecks and belowdecks. These boats have fairly good sound insulation in the engine room: you know the engine is running, but it's not obtrusive.

Handling under Sail

The Brewer 12.8 sails as well as you'd want for a cruising boat. The boat is extremely well balanced. In about 12 knots of true wind—16 knots or so over the deck—we could trim the sails for upwind sailing, then walk away from the helm without even setting the wheel brake. In smooth water, the boat tracks and holds course well.

In puffier conditions, the boat tends to round up sharply when close reaching with the board fully extended. This is not much of a surprise, since most beamy boats do this.

With a large-diameter steering wheel and mechanical pull-pull steering, response and feel are excellent.

The boom on the 12.8 we sailed was very high off the deck. We ended up climbing onto one of the halyard winches to hook up the main halyard. This is a disadvantage, particularly if the crew is older and less agile.

Furling the main is also complicated by the high boom. You can reach the boom for furling at the mast and atop the aft cabin, but it's difficult to do it over the center cockpit. Likewise, with the big dodger up, you can't get to the boom over the main companionway. The boom is probably placed this high to clear a Bimini top, but it sure makes it a chore to set and furl the mainsail.

In contrast, the boom of the new 44 we examined was just enough lower to make hooking up the halyard and furling the mainsail a straightforward proposition.

Most of the standard winches for the boat are marginal in size, particularly if the boat is to be used for retirement sailing. Standard genoa sheet winches, for example, are Lewmar 52 self-tailers. These are approximately equivalent to the Barient self-tailing electric 28s that were on our test boat. Larger Lewmar primaries are optional, and should be chosen. We'd pass up the optional electric primaries at over $6,000, unless it's the only way you can trim the sails.

The main halyard on the boat we sailed—one of the original eight Brewer 12.8s—had a poor lead: from a block at the base of the mast, through a deck-mounted cheek block, through the dodger coaming, to a stopper and winch atop the cabin just forward of the cockpit. The turning block at the base of the mast was too high, allowing the halyard to chafe at several points, particularly on the cheek block. In fact, we could barely crank up the main using the Lewmar 30 halyard winch. This is easily corrected, but it was annoying to see the same poor lead on the brand new 44 we examined. In fact, the owner of the 44 had ordered a larger than standard main halyard winch to overcome the friction in the system.

Our test boat was rigged as a cutter. Staysail sheet winches are self-tailing Lewmar 30s mounted on the forward end of molded winch islands just outboard of the cockpit coamings. With a large cockpit dodger in place, it is difficult to impossible to use these winches: they're actually hidden outside the dodger, and the dodger side curtains have to be unclipped to trim the staysail.

The primary headsail sheet winches are also awkward to use. The winch handle swings through the lifelines. This is a function of the wide, midships cockpit; sailhandling has been compromised to create cockpit room.

There are properly through-bolted aluminum genoa tracks mounted atop the bulwarks. On our test 12.8, there was also a shorter inboard genoa track, which could be used to advantage going to windward, since the main shroud chainplates are set inboard of the rail. In practice, few of these boats will be equipped with a deck-sweeping genoa, so the inboard track is probably superfluous.

The 12.8 we sailed had large Schaefer turning blocks aft for improving genoa sheet leads to winches. However, these blocks were mounted almost flat on their welded winch islands. Since the winch is higher than the turning block, the lead from the block to the winch is not fair, which can cause chafe on the sheet and increased friction in the system. The blocks should be angled upward slightly to correct this, which could be done with shims or with a slight redesign of the mounting weldments.

On the Brewer 44, aft turning blocks are not standard. With a very high-cut genoa whose lead was very far aft, you could end up with an awkward sheet angle at the winch unless turning blocks are installed. This is a disadvantage of sail handling from a cockpit in the middle of the boat.

A full-width mainsheet traveler is mounted atop the aft cabin. Our 12.8 used a Schaefer traveler, while the 44 has a Lewmar unit. Controls for the Lewmar traveler cars are at the back end of the aft cabin. You have to climb out of the cockpit to adjust them. The original Schaefer traveler has car adjusters just aft of the helmsman, with stoppers and a Lewmar 30 winch. We're at a loss to explain why a good setup was traded for a bad one.

The mainsail is trimmed by a Lewmar 30 self-

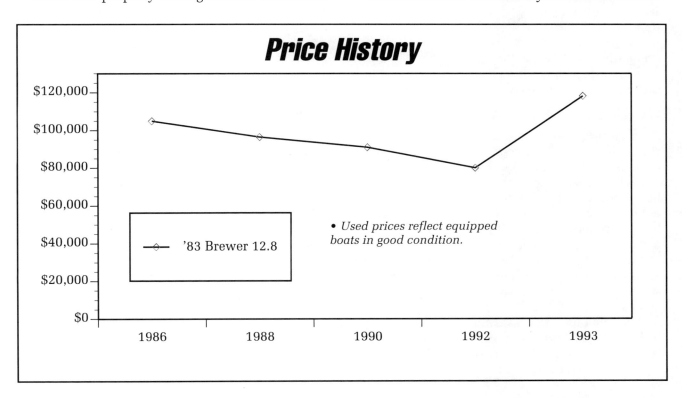

Price History

Legend: ◇ '83 Brewer 12.8

• Used prices reflect equipped boats in good condition.

tailer mounted atop the aft cabin, reasonably accessible to either helmsman or crew. This winch is powerful enough for a mainsail this size.

A double-headsail ketch rig with bowsprit is an option that will set you back about $7,000 by the time you buy the mast, sail and fancy bowsprit. Frankly, if you want a ketch rig because it's easier to handle on a boat this size, you'd be better off spending that seven grand on a Stoway cutter rig, huge self-tailing sheet winches all around, and roller furling on both the genoa and staysail. It would probably be easier to handle than the ketch, and you'd keep the better performance of the single-masted rig.

Despite relatively shoal draft, the Brewer 12.8 is reasonably stiff. With full main and 150% genoa, the boat heels about 20° with 18 knots of breeze over the deck. With the optional deeper keel she would be a little stiffer, but the keel/centerboard combination is probably slightly faster on most points of sail, if a little tippier in heavy air.

We think the extra ballast in the Brewer 44 will make her an even better performer than the Brewer 12.8 in winds of over about 15 knots. Although the extra displacement and wetted surface will slow the boat slightly in very light winds, the standard rig is big enough to keep the boat moving in winds as light as most people care to sail in. When it's too light, you can always turn on the engine. Most cruisers simply aren't interested in squeezing out every ounce of performance in light air.

There are actually three different underwater configurations for the Brewer 44: a shoal fin keel; the same shoal keel with a high aspect ratio centerboard; and a slightly deeper—but still relatively shallow—fin keel.

The centerboard has become optional—it was originally standard on the 12.8—because a lot of people simply never bothered to use it. The boat sails fine without it; it just goes sideways a little more.

On Deck

Sailhandling limitations aside, the cockpit is just about ideal for a cruising sailboat. You can comfortably seat eight in the cockpit for idle hours at anchor.

An Edson wheel steerer dominates the cockpit. It has custom boxes with electrical switches for anchor windlass, autopilot—you can practically run the boat from here. We're a little concerned about the proximity of all this wiring to the steering compass, however. When having the compass swung, be sure to operate every piece of electrical equipment on the steering console to make sure that nothing affects the compass.

A high molded-in breakwater makes installing a full-width dodger fairly easy. A good cockpit dodger is essential on a center cockpit boat. Without a dodger, a center cockpit is a wet place to live sailing or motoring to windward in a blow. Both of the dodgers we looked at, however, blocked access to the staysail sheet winches.

Side decks are very narrow due to the wide cabin trunk. This is a definite compromise. The shroud chainplates come down right in the middle of the side decks, yet there isn't room to walk outboard of the shrouds. Instead, you must step up and over the cabin.

Although it's a $1,500 option, most owners will choose the stainless steel stub bowsprit with twin anchor rollers. The 12.8 we sailed had a CQR plow in the starboard roller, and a Danforth stowed sideways in the port roller. It was not the best arrangement. The 44 we examined had plows in both rollers, and they fit, although it is a tight squeeze.

A lot of these boats are equipped with custom davits for carrying a dinghy off the stern. They're a good idea, since there's little deck space for stowing a dinghy aboard.

At the same time, carrying a dinghy in davits offshore can be a risky proposition, particularly in a following sea. The skipper of one 12.8 had the dinghy fill with water during a rough passage—someone forgot to take the plug out—and was afraid the entire arrangement of davits and dinghy was going to be lost. For passagemaking, we'd probably bring the inflatable aboard and break it down for stowage, as awkward as that may seem.

Fuel fills are located in the waterways at just about the low point in the sheer. Water fills are in the waterways forward. As we found, you have to be careful if you're taking on fuel and water at the same time. We overfilled the water tank, sending water straight toward the open fuel fill. Quick hands—not ours—got the cap back on the fuel fill before water could pour into the tank. It wouldn't be a bad idea to raise the fuel fill about an inch off the deck on a pad to reduce the chances of this happening.

Belowdecks

Some of the compromises in sail handling and deck layout have been made for the sake of the interior. The wide deckhouse that makes for narrow side decks creates a huge interior volume, and the space is used very well.

Because the forward cabin is pushed well into the eyes of the boat, the forepeak anchor locker is small. You can lead the anchor chain aft to the locker under the berths in the forward cabin, which has the advantage of moving a lot of weight further back in the boat, where it has less effect on pitching moment.

The forward cabin has V-berths, with an insert to form a double. The berths are quite narrow at the foot, and are only comfortably long for someone under 6' tall. Outboard of the berths there are storage lockers, and there are drawers below.

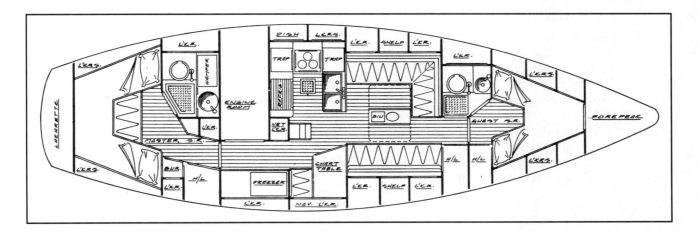

Ventilation in the forward cabin at anchor is provided by a large Lewmar hatch and Beckson opening ports. Offshore ventilation consists of a cowl vent in a Dorade box.

You can enter the forward head from either the main cabin or the forward cabin, since there are two doors. Unfortunately, the door to the forward cabin wipes out the space that would otherwise be used as the head dresser. Instead, you get a little sink with not much space for laying out the essentials of your toilette.

The forward door also means that the head sink is pushed fairly far outboard. With the boat heeled over on starboard tack, seawater backs up through it. One boat we looked at had a big wooden plug to stick in the drain, while the other owner had added a shutoff valve to the drain line just below the sink.

Ironically, the small head dresser is quite low, and could easily have been raised up another 4" or so. This wouldn't eliminate the problem, but the boat could heel over a little more before you'd have to do something about it.

Both the forward and aft heads use inexpensive, bottom-of-the-line waterclosets. Our experience is that cheap heads work fine for daysailing and coastal cruising, but are a curse for the serious livaboard cruiser. We'd rather see a Wilcox-Crittenden Imperial or Skipper on a serious cruising boat.

A solar-powered vent overhead provides exhaust ventilation, but we think in addition that every head should have an opening overhead hatch. A cowl vent in a Dorade box would also be a good idea. It's impossible to have too much ventilation in a head.

The main cabin has a straight settee to starboard, an L-shaped settee to port. You can also have a pair of armchairs on the starboard side instead of the settee, but we see no advantage to this. The L-shaped settee has a drop-in section to convert it to a double, so that you can have three double berths on the boat, if you're masochistic enough to want to cruise with three couples. The good thing is that the boat does contain three separate living spaces, with direct access from each of the spaces both to the deck and to a head compartment. That's a tricky thing to do, and Ted Brewer has pulled it off as well as you can.

Aluminum water tanks holding 200 gallons are located in the bilge under the main cabin.

There is good locker space outboard of the settees in place of the more commonly-seen pilot berths that usually become useless catch-alls. One locker is designed as a large booze locker. When you think about the imbibing habits of a lot of sailors, this makes a lot more sense than stuffing one bottle here, another over there.

Ventilation in the main cabin is good for in port, less good for offshore. There are four opening ports in the main cabin. The standard ports are plastic, which we think is not an acceptable material for an offshore cruiser of this type. Stainless steel opening ports are an option costing $1,890. This buys you very good cast-frame opening ports, which we think should really be standard on a boat of this caliber.

There are also two aluminum-framed hatches over the main cabin. The hatches currently used are single-opening Lewmar hatches with extruded frames. The older 12.8 we sailed had double-opening Atkins & Hoyle cast hatches. A double-opening hatch allows you to open the hatch forward in port for maximum air flow, aft when sailing to keep water from getting below. We wish they had stuck with the more expensive cast hatches.

Two cowl vents in Dorade boxes are provided for sailing ventilation. Like the cowl vents on a lot of boats, the downtake pipes into the cabin of the Brewer boats are improperly proportioned: they should never be smaller than the nominal pipe diameter of the vent itself.

The galley has undergone a lot of minor changes since the first boats in the Brewer 12.8 series were built. The early boat we examined had sinks that were too small, water fixtures that were too low relative to the sinks, drawers that were difficult to operate, and fiddles without corner cleanouts. The 44 we examined had changed all of these things.

One thing has not changed. Between the sinks and the stove, there is a large dry well for storage. This is about the size and shape of a large grocery shopping cart. You wouldn't want to have to dig to the bottom of a grocery cart for the cereal and crackers every time you wanted to use them, but that's pretty much what you have to do with this well. It should at least be divided with sliding shelves to make it easier to use.

At the aft end of the galley, there is a large refrigerator and freezer mounted athwartships. It is well insulated, and has a well-gasketed top.

There's another big opening hatch over the galley, and it is properly placed behind the dodger breakwater, where it can serve as an exhaust vent in any conditions—as long as the dodger is up.

Standard stove is a three-burner propane stove with oven—just what you'd want.

A big chart table is opposite the galley. While it has good storage for navigation books, there is no coherent arrangement for the mounting of the array of electronics that you find on the typical modern cruising boat. Since these boats are built on a semi-custom basis, you could probably have the nav station modified to suit your particular electronics. These boats were designed before the contemporary electronics explosion, and some details have not been upgraded to reflect the state of the art.

Aft of the nav station, there is a passageway with stooping headroom to the aft cabin. On the starboard side of the passage, there is a huge workbench with chart storage and tool storage below. This is a great way to use this space, rather than trying to throw in another berth.

On the older boat we looked at, this same space was filled with a huge freezer and battery storage—an advantage of semi-custom flexibility. The big electrical panel is located over the workbench: out of the way, yet reasonably accessible.

Opposite the work area, under the cockpit, is a real engine room. There's room for the main engine, an optional generator, fuel filtration system, hot water storage tank, and batteries. Although you have to climb over the engine to check the batteries, everything is reasonably accessible. A real engine room is a rarity in a boat this size, and is only practical with the center cockpit configuration.

The aft cabin of the 12.8 has two quarterberths which can be joined by a drop-in section to create a large thwartships double. The extra 2' in the stern of the 44 makes it possible to have a big permanent fore and aft double berth. If you want, you can still get the two berth configuration.

A separate companionway at the forward end of the aft cabin gives access to the cockpit without going through the passageway. This companionway has a slatted dropboard, and since it faces forward, it is vulnerable to spray. For offshore sailing, it should be secured with a tight-fitting canvas cover. In port, it will provide good ventilation at the expense of some privacy. There is also another aluminum-framed hatch over this cabin. It suffers from the same limitations as the hatches over the main cabin.

You can get a sit-down shower stall in the aft head, or have a more conventional arrangement using the entire head as the shower compartment. A sit-down shower may be easier to clean, but you give up a lot of head dresser space to get it.

There is excellent locker space throughout the boat, including three hanging lockers and a foul weather gear locker. Instead of packing in extra berths, the designer and builder have chosen to limit the number of berths and maximize storage. It was a wise choice.

With the exception of the under-cockpit passage, headroom is well over 6' throughout.

Conclusions

Since the Brewer 44 is a lineal descendant of the Whitby 42 and Brewer 12.8, a lot of the shortcomings of those boats have been ironed out over the years. Finishing details have gradually improved, and have generally kept pace with the boatbuilding industry trend toward better detailing.

At first glance, the "sailaway" price of just under $160,000 seems like a misprint. That price includes main and genoa, Hood roller furling on the headsail, propane, refrigeration, basic electronics and pumps. There's also a long options list.

The kicker is that a lot of the things on the options list should be standard on a high-quality cruising boat. For example, the bigger primary sheet winches that we think are required cost an extra $1,800. A teak and holly cabin sole is another thousand; two-tone decks (rather than plain white) add $670. Lightning grounding costs $720, an anchor platform $1,500.

Although the boat was designed as a cutter, staysail rigging, winches, and the sail itself add $2,600.

Standard batteries total only 225 amp hours capacity. For batteries the right size, add $400. For metal ports rather than plastic, shell out almost $1,900. Even the centerboard in a boat that was designed as a keel/centerboarder adds $2,600 to the sailaway price.

With the options that we think are really essentials, the "sailaway" price jumps by about $15,000.

What do you get for $175,000? You get a well-designed, good-sailing, well-built ocean cruising home, a retirement cottage for every romantic port in the world. The boats are not as well detailed or equipped as higher-priced boats such as Aldens, Hinckleys, and Little Harbors. But they're good, solid values, and they'll take you to the same places as more expensive boats. In this day and age, that's not a bad recommendation. **• PS**

PJ/Swan 44

A timeless Sparkman and Stephens design that can boast of construction that's as good as it gets.

The Swan 44, originally imported as the Palmer Johnson (PJ) 44, was designed by Sparkman and Stephens as a production offshore IOR racer, a slightly smaller sister of the Swan 48 which won the 1972 Newport-Bermuda Race. Between 1972 and late 1975, 76 44s were built, and many were imported into the U.S.

While custom IOR boats frequently made off with the big trophies even in the early days of racing under the rule, a well-designed production racer such as the Swan 44 was still competitive, particularly for long-distance racing. Few of these boats are seriously campaigned today on a regular basis, but the Swan 44 is still a competitive boat under the International Measurement System (IMS).

Although the term "classic" is grossly overused, this boat is the real McCoy. The handsome S&S profile still looks good two decades after it was drawn, and it will look just as good in another 20 years. A deep, heavy hull gives full headroom under a nearly flush deck, and the low, teak-decked bubble deckhouse disappears unobtrusively into the foredeck with no fuss.

Construction

The Swan 44's construction is rugged, but unsophisticated by today's standard's. The hull itself is a solid uncored laminate of roving and chopped strand mat, with far more mat than is typical in newer boats.

Mat provides reasonable impact resistance but little stiffness. Hull stiffness is added by three full-length longitudinal stringers. In addition, the furniture is securely bonded to the hull.

Most dark-colored Swan 44 hulls we have examined show significant surface irregularities in the way of stringers, tranverse ceiling supports, bulkheads, and bonded furniture. This is strictly a cos-

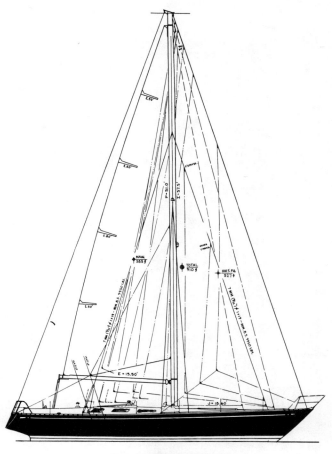

Specifications

LOA	44' 1"
LWL	33' 11"
Beam	12' 7"
Draft	7' 5"
Displacement	28,000 lbs.
Ballast	12,600 lbs.
Sail area	920 sq. ft.

metic concern, but it is a very real one if you wish to paint a light-colored boat a dark color. According to one boatyard owner we talked to, who has considerable experience in repainting older Swans, the typical 44 needs about $1,500 in additional labor and materials for refairing when a dark hull color is chosen over a light color.

Decks are a fiberglass/balsa sandwich, and a teak overlay is standard. Teak decks on a Swan of this vintage are a decidedly mixed blessing. Pride of ownership—and this goes with the territory if you're going to own a Swan—demands that the teak decks be kept looking good. For most owners, this means cleaning the decks at least annually with powerful chemicals.

The chemicals—either acid or a two-step base/

acid combination—are murder on teak decks and their seam compounds. After more than 15 years of religious cleaning, the decks of the typical Swan 44 are pretty tired.

The first signs of trouble are popped bungs, or rusty discolorations around them. Water migrates around the fastenings into the deck core, soaking the balsa and eventually even causing separation of the fiberglass top skin from the core. There usually is little or no leaking belowdecks to tell you of a problem, and by then most of the damage would be done in any case.

If you're buying a Swan 44, an extremely careful survey of the decks is as essential as the hull survey. Replacement of the teak deck covering is an expensive proposition, and could add $30,000 to the price of the boat.

Swan teak decks are not particularly more trouble-prone than teak decks on other boats. The same caveat applies to any teak-decked boat more than about 10 years old. Ironically, the efforts of owners to keep their Swans looking new can cause big problems if enthusiasm is not tempered with a large dose of common sense.

The Sparkman and Stephens-drawn lines of the Swan 44 are a modern classic, especially the flush deck and low-profile deckhouse.

Hull blistering of mid-1970s Swans is about average in frequency. We would be wary of any boat that had spent much of its life in tropical waters, since there is a fairly direct relationship between hull blistering and immersion time.

The hull and deck are bolted together through an anodized aluminum toerail. Inside the boat, the entire hull/deck joint is glassed over—including the fastenings to deck hardware. While this may prevent leakage into the interior, it is a headache when it's time to replace or re-bed deck hardware, and it's time to think about rebedding deck hardware on any boat this age.

Interior

Since the Swan 44 was designed as a racing boat, the interior is not what you would find in a 44-foot cruiser/racer today. The forepeak is given over to sail storage, with two fold-down pipe berths over built-in sail bins. It would be fairly easy to convert this area to a real sleeping cabin. The sail bins are teak-faced ply that could be modified to conventional berths, and there are port and starboard lockers for clothing.

A large sliding hatch over the forepeak provides fair weather ventilation, and serves as a sail hatch. This hatch will leak if solid water comes aboard, so if the forepeak were converted to a stateroom, it would be worth considering replacing the sliding hatch with a modern, watertight aluminum-framed deck hatch. There is no provision for foul-weather ventilation in the forepeak.

The main cabin is positioned immediately aft of the forepeak, rather than being divided from it by the more conventional head and hanging lockers. This pushes the main living area further forward, into a narrower part of the boat. The result is a main cabin that is smaller than you would normally find in a 44-footer.

Pilot berths outboard of the two settee berths make good sea berths, but further restrict the main cabin. At sea, the two extension transom berths, which are parallel to the centerline of the boat, will also be used for sleeping if you cruise or race with a big crew.

Twin 45-gallon stainless steel water tanks are mounted under the settees port and starboard, keeping the weight of consumables in the right location at the expense of under-seat storage.

A large dropleaf table seats four for dining in comfort, six in a pinch. If it's six for dinner, the two persons seated at the aft end of both settees are somewhat cut off from conversation by the mast, which is stepped through the middle of the table to the keel.

The combination of a varnished teak interior and a flush deck make the main cabin somewhat dark, although a fair amount of light is provided by an overhead Goiot hatch and a small deadlight. There are four cowl vents in Dorades over the area for good ventilation.

On at least one boat, the main cabin has been radically altered by removing the port settee and pilot berth, replacing them with a U-shaped dinette.

This would dramatically improve the livability of the main cabin, and is the arrangement most commonly seen on a modern boat of this size and type.

Headroom is 6' 3" on centerline aft, 6' 2" at the forward end of the main cabin.

The galley, navigation area, and head occupy the beamiest section of the boat. The nav station features a large chart table, a comfortable seat, adequate shelf space for books and electronics, and a big bulkhead for mounting instrument repeaters. There's little you could do to improve on it, although for today's offshore cruising and racing you'd tear out the book-shelves to make way for the plethora of electronic goodies most boats carry.

Opposite the nav station is the galley. While it is smaller than you'd find on a boat of this type today, it was huge for 1972, and is more than adequate, with a big, well-insulated icebox, three-burner propane stove, and a fair amount of storage space. Two seven-inch-deep centerline sinks drain directly overboard.

This section of the boat is light and airy, with good light from the two long fixed ports in the low deckhouse, plus the large sliding companionway hatch.

To starboard, immediately aft of the nav station, is the head compartment, with six-foot headroom. It is accessible either from the main living area or from the aft cabin. The lower section of the head compartment is a fiberglass molding, making it easy to clean, while the upper section is the same teak joinerwork that is found in the rest of the boat.

A Baby Blake watercloset was standard issue. This quaint, expensive piece of British marine plumbing is sworn either by or at, depending on your experience with the beast. We can say that replacement parts cost more than a new modern marine toilet.

For offshore sailing, this head location is perfect.

Though the Swan 44 has plenty of good sea berths, she was designed for racing. Adding a double for family cruising would be difficult.

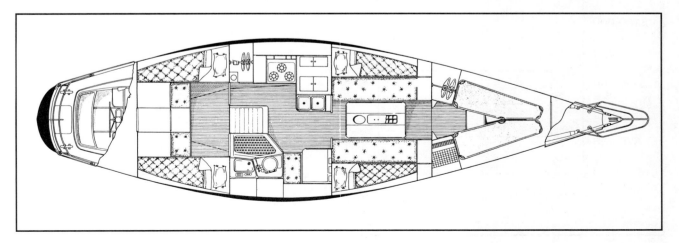

You can come below cold and wet, strip off your foul weather gear, and rinse down without tracking salt water into the living areas of the boat.

The aft cabin was designed more as a sleeping compartment for senior watchkeepers while racing offshore than for long-term living aboard. Twin quarterberths, each 6' 11" long, make good sea berths. For family cruising, many people would prefer a double berth in the aft cabin, but converting this one is a bit of a problem.

The natural location for a double would be the starboard side, but the door to the head makes this impractical without major modifications. Building a larger berth would require sacrificing one hanging locker, a seat, and access from the aft cabin to the head. For long-term cruising for a couple, we'd do it, although a high level of craftsmanship would be required to keep this from looking like an afterthought.

Batteries are located in a fiberglass box on centerline under an unusual locker below the cockpit. A small door at the aft end of this locker, which can best be described as a dog kennel, and is usually used as a catchall, gives access to the steering gear.

There's enough room under the cockpit to mount a belowdecks autopilot, battery charger, and voltage inverter, all of which would be desirable for serious cruising. Since there are no opening hatches in the cockpit giving access to this space, it should remain dry.

Two small hatches overhead, plus a large opening port into the cockpit, provide good light and air to the aft cabin.

In general, interior craftsmanship is excellent, in the Swan tradition. Although the interior tends to be fairly dark and woody, Nautor teak is fairly light in color, which helps avoid the cave-like spaces you often find in a flush-deck boat.

Handling Under Power

All Swan 44s were originally equipped with Perkins 4-108 engines, rated at about 37 horsepower in the normal operating range. The engine is coupled to a Borg-Warner hydraulic reverse-reduction gear, rather than the lightweight mechanical gearbox used today.

This engine is just adequate power for a boat that displaces over 29,000 pounds loaded for sailing. You can expect to cruise at about six knots with good fuel economy—just under one gallon per hour.

Access to the engine for service is reasonable, requiring pivoting up the companionway ladder (it latches to the overhead) and removing the engine box. In the aft cabin, the lower part of the bulkhead removes for servicing the transmission and the back of the engine. You get at the stuffing box by lifting the cabin sole in the aft cabin.

The engine is a tight fit in its well-insulated box. Installing a slightly larger engine when the time comes for replacement might entail rebuilding the box—a minor project.

With the companionway ladder secured to the overhead (it's a head knocker) and the engine box removed, you have sit-down access to the entire engine; there's no excuse for poor maintenance.

A 40-gallon stainless steel fuel tank, giving about a 250-mile range under power, is located below the

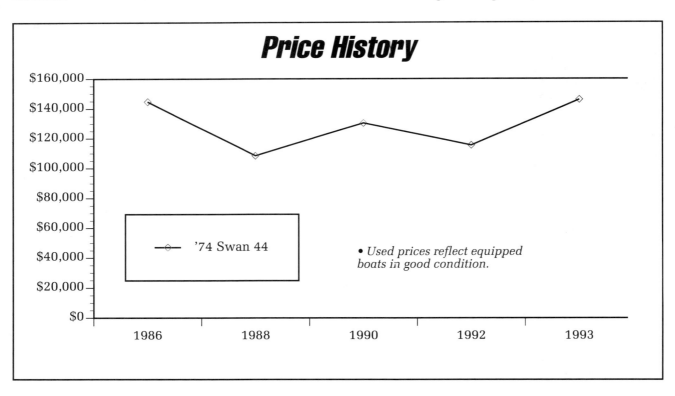

Price History

● *Used prices reflect equipped boats in good condition.*

Legend: —◇— '74 Swan 44

cabin sole just forward of the companionway. This is below the vertical center of gravity, smack dab in the middle of the boat. The location could hardly be better to minimize the effect of fuel consumption on the boat's trim.

Handling Under Sail

Sailing performance is excellent. The boat is reasonably fast both upwind and downwind. The PHRF rating of about 84 is some 30 seconds per mile faster than cruiser/racers such as the F&C 44, Alden 44, or Little Harbor 44, although it is slower than a flat-out modern IMS racer/cruiser. The boat is quite competitive under IMS in anything but very light air, where its heavy displacement is a disadvantage.

Over the years, Swan 44s have won more than their share of races. In the 1990 Swan Atlantic Regatta, the unmodified Swan 44 *Temptress* won her class, beating several newer Frers-designed Swan 46s on both elapsed and corrected time, despite being the oldest boat in the fleet.

With a righting moment of about 1,950 foot pounds, this is a very stiff boat, despite a heavy tree trunk of a mast. The original design called for a keel weighing 10,700 pounds, but boats after hull #64 have additional ballast. Typically, Swan 44s have a range of positive stability of 130°. We recommend a range of 120° or higher for ocean racing or cruising.

Both short rig (mast height about 55 feet above deck) and tall rig (mast height about 57.5 feet) were built. For racing or in areas of lighter winds, the taller rig is more desirable, but this is hardly a make or break choice when buying a used boat.

The boat has a big foretriangle, with a 100-percent area of about 540 square feet for the tall rig. This results in a 150-percent genoa of 800 square feet—a large piece of cloth for a small crew to handle. For shorthanded cruising, we'd recommend a genoa of about 135 percent, set on a roller furler. In winds of 10 knots or more, this smaller sail will give comparable performance, and will obviously be much easier to deal with. For racing, the 150-percent genoa is essential for good light-air performance.

The mainsail on the tall rig is about 380 square feet—a comfortable size for a couple to handle, particularly if the boom is modernized.

By today's standards, the rig is old-fashioned. A conservative modern cruiser this size would have a double spreader rig with a mast section of about 6" x 9.5", weighing some six pounds per foot. A contemporary 44-foot IMS racer would have a triple-spreader rig weighing considerably less.

The Swan 44, on the other hand, has a single spreader rig, with a section that is 7" x 10". The big mast section is the result of having a single set of very short spreaders, which allow a tight headsail sheeting angle.

You would have to work very hard to make this mast fall down. Running backstays are standard on the tall rig, but are usually used only when sailing with a storm staysail in very heavy weather.

There is a removable inner forestay, tensioned by a recessed Highfield lever. For offshore cruising, we'd rig it and leave it. Many racers remove the inner forestay entirely. When released, the forestay stows against the mast, wrapping around a fairlead at the base of the mast, held in place by a small tackle on deck. While it's out of the way, you can still trip over the wire when working at the mast.

The deck layout was close to state of the art for racing in its day, but it is not well suited to short-handed cruising.

Originally, the mainsail was hoisted by a self-stowing reel halyard winch. We lived with one of these for years in a state of cautious mutual tolerance without injury, but we've also had one blow up in our face. This type of winch also has a tendency to break your arm if you're not careful when the brake is released, and more than one person has been brained by a free-wheeling handle which got out of control. All in all, the reel halyard winch should be treated with the same respect you'd give an armed hand grenade. In fact, we'd treat it the same way: throw it as far as we can, then duck.

There are twin mast-mounted headsail halyard winches, and deck-mounted spinnaker halyard winches. This is a satisfactory arrangement, although on a modern cruiser you'll probably want self-tailers with low-stretch non-wire halyards.

Cross-linked Barient 35 primaries are mounted at the forward corners of the low deckhouse. For racing, this keeps the headsail grinders out of the cockpit with their weight amidships, but it is a poor location for primary winches on a cruising boat.

You're more likely to use the cockpit-mounted Barient 32 secondaries for genoa sheets when cruising. They are just big enough for a 130-percent genoa, a little too small for a bigger sail or a smaller grinder.

The cockpit, too, is awkward for cruising. The mainsheet traveler spans the cockpit forward of the wheel, and the main is trimmed to a forward-facing winch mounted just below the traveler. This arrangement works as long as there are two people in the cockpit, but it's not so hot for shorthanded sailing.

The cockpit itself is deep and fairly comfortable. There are no cockpit lockers, but the liferaft and propane bottles store under the lift-up helmsman's seat. A lazarette hatch on the afterdeck gives access to under-cockpit stowage for lines and fenders.

A good cockpit dodger is a must for comfortable cruising, but the Swan 44's midships companionway complicates the issue. The companionway is a sliding hatch with no dropboards in the deck forward of the aft cabin. A molded breakwater allows installation of a big dodger, but it is awkward to crawl under the dodger to get below, and the dodger itself is so far forward that it offers protection only for the very front of the cockpit. The helmsman is left at the mercy of the elements.

The major alterations on deck required for cruising would be the replacement of the sail-trimming winches with modern self-tailers, preferably going to bigger secondaries if you can fit them.

We'd also replace the mainsheet traveler and update the boom (early boats may still have roller-reefing booms).

Steering control is less than perfect. As originally designed, the boat has a small, shallow rudder mounted aft of a big skeg. The rudder was quickly found to be too small, and it went through a series of conservative changes. First, the rudder chord was lengthened by four inches. Next, the rudder was deepened by six inches while retaining the original skeg, resulting in a quirky rudder profile and slightly improved handling. In November 1973, the rudder and skeg were redesigned, adding some eight inches of depth to the original rudder.

The new and old skeg/rudder combinations are very similar in appearance. It is easiest to determine which one you are looking at by getting drawings from Nautor and actually measuring the rudder. Of the factory-built rudders, the last design is by far the best, but it is unclear how many boats were built with this configuration.

A large percentage of Swan 44s—usually those that have extensive racing histories—have had rudder, skeg, or afterbody modifications. These range from slight rudder modifications similar to the factory changes, to major alterations to the stern shape, "padding out" of the quarters to effectively increase the boat's sailing length, and any number of skeg/rudder alterations to the thinking of different appendage designers.

For the buyer of a Swan 44, the major concern is more how well the changes were made, rather than just their effect on performance. As a rule, changes have little positive effect on the value of the boat, and if poorly done, can have significant negative impact.

If you're interested in IMS racing, an unmodified early hull would be a good choice, giving you a blank canvas for underwater alteration.

For the more-than-casual racer, naval architect Jim Taylor recommends complete removal of the skeg and rudder, replacing these appendages with a deeper modern elliptical spade rudder having an area equal to about the total of the original skeg and rudder combined.

The Swan 44 *Diane* was modified in this manner, and performance was dramatically improved on all points of sail, according to Taylor.

Because the IMS is fairly weak in handicapping the efficiency of appendages, the improved performance came at very little rating expense.

Even fairly extensive modifications such as these are not too difficult due to the massive construction of the boat. You simply don't have to worry too much about imposing loads the hull is unable to handle.

With the original rudder, maneuvering in close quarters—such as rounding marks when racing—requires careful planning ahead. In addition, you must carry an undesirable amount of rudder angle in heavier air, particularly when reaching. For cruising, these are fairly minor inconveniences. For racing against modern competition, they are significant drawbacks.

Conclusions

There are few production boats of this vintage that can be considered turnkey operations for offshore sailing. The Swan 44 is one of them. Nautor construction is as good as it gets for a production boat, and the S&S design is truly timeless.

Swan 44s vary dramatically in condition and price. Boats that have been raced hard may be cosmetically beat, and worn teak decks can be more than a cosmetic concern. Condition rather than age is far more important in determining the value of any Swan 44, although later boats would be more desirable due to slight improvements in the design.

We have looked at some boats that are unmodifed in layout and equipment, and others that have undergone spectacular upgrading.

Upgrading, of course, is expensive at typical boatyard labor rates of $40 per hour and more, but you'll probably get back more at resale time on this boat than on almost any other.

There's no denying the appeal of Swans in general, and the 44 in particular. Although as a cruiser/racer it is neither fish nor fowl, the boat is a better compromise than most. With an unmodified deck layout and sail handling equipment, the boat is more than a handful for a couple to sail, and while the basic interior layout is good, there are too many berths in the wrong places for extended shorthanded cruising.

Although this boat may not be anyone's ideal cruiser, it is a boat that you can take offshore with complete peace of mind. You don't have to worry whether the hull is strong enough, the furniture will stay attached, the rudder will stay on, or the rig will stay up. The offshore pedigree is there, and the quality is, too.

In today's depressed market for both new and used sailboats, no boat can be considered a good investment in any real sense. But when you look at the cost of a new boat of this caliber, the Swan 44 starts to look like a real blue chip. • **PS**

Cal 46, 2-46, 3-46

Bill Lapworth's unusual design, with motor sailer accommodations, was ahead of its time.

The early Cal boats were built by Jensen Marine in the old '70s Mecca of fiberglass boatbuilders that was Costa Mesa, California. Columbia and Islander were there, too. For a decade they dominated the burgeoning market for relatively inexpensive, "maintenance-free" boats.

Jack Jensen and designer Bill Lapworth were at the forefront of this revolution, beginning their long association in 1958 with the introduction in 1959 of the Cal 24. The famous Cal 40 sprang from the family tree in 1963, winning the SORC the next. Despite such notoriety as a racer, the Cal 40 and many others in the line were described as good, all-around family boats with modern divided underbodies, relatively light weight, and hence they had an emphasis on performance.

The Cal 46 was introduced in 1967. One reader said he thinks about 10 were built. For several years it was called the Cal Cruising 46. The Cal 2-46, with a redesigned deck, cockpit and interior layout, succeeded it from 1973 until 1976. The Cal 3-46, virtually the same as the 2-46 except for some minor interior changes, was built in 1977 and 1978.

A 1972 profile of Lapworth in *Yachting* magazine said, "A prototype of the Cal Cruising 46, Hale Field's *Fram,* embodying able sailing characteristics with motorsailer cruising comfort, made a circumnavigation of North America (with the help of a train ride from Michigan to the Pacific Northwest)."

David and Beverly Feiges, owners of a Cal 3-46, wrote to us at length about the boat, and in citing the devotion of Cal 46 owners, noted that many have circumnavigated. They added that both Lapworth and Jensen chose the boat as their personal retirement yachts for extended blue-water cruising.

The early Cal boats were built at a time when a handful of big California builders dominated the

Specifications

LOA	45' 6"
LWL	37' 6"
Beam	12' 6"
Draft	5' 0"
Displacement	30,000 lbs.
Ballast	8,000 lbs.
Sail area	784/864 (sloop/ketch)

business. Cal, Columbia (including Coronado), and Islander offered boats from 20 to more than 50 feet. The largest Cal was the 48, modeled more after the highly successful 40. Like some large builders today, such as Beneteau and Hunter, Cal produced two distinct lines—one for racing and short-term cruising, and another for more hard-core cruising. In 1972, Columbia countered the Cal 46 with its Columbia 45 motor sailer, but by most counts it wasn't as successful, nor as pretty.

Today, the Cal 46 stands as a boat that in many ways was ahead of its time, combining as it did a daringly different layout with 270-degree visibility from the deckhouse, a spade rudder and long cruising keel. That they are still revered and sought after comes as no surprise.

Owners' Comments

"We find easygoing days that others think are terrible. Only off the wind in big seas can you work a little. The deckhouse is a bit too high. I have yet to see a boat under 51 feet that can compare to her interior."

—1976 3-46 model in the Caribbean

"Balances well on all points of sail and sea/wind conditions. An outstanding example of a Jensen-built boat."

—1967 Cal 46 model in California

"We have made many minor modifications, including sliding windows, teak sole, roller furling, auxiliary generator, etc."

—1975 Cal 2-46 model in California

"Spade rudder and hull design are excellent. With installation of full roller furling sails, the vessel handles less efficiently, but easily by just me and my wife. We're in our 60s. Most handling at sea can be done from the raised center cockpit, which is dry and comfortable."

—1975 2-46 model in California

The Design

Lapworth certainly knew how to draw a fast hull. Even prior to the fiberglass revolution, he was convinced that light displacement was the way to go. His *Nalu II* won the Transpac in 1959 and his various L-class boats also did well around that time. The Cal 40, as mentioned, won the 1964 SORC.

When it came to designing the ultimate cruising boat, Lapworth wasn't about to settle for a slug. The Cal 46 has a displacement/length ratio of 250, which is considered moderate even today. When in 1973 Robert Perry designed the Valiant 40 with a D/L ratio of 260, many critics said it was too light for offshore work. After numerous, safe circumnavigations, the critics were proven wrong. Of course the Cal 46 is a big boat and when carrying a full load of fuel, water and provisions for cruising, its actual D/L ratio will be higher.

The boat has moderate overhangs by today's standards, though in the 1960s it probably didn't seem so. The spoon bow and carefully proportioned transom balance well. And there is some nice sheer to elevate the bow and keep it drier in bad weather. The deckhouse of the original 46 had large windows and the smallish cockpit was immediately aft of the mast. The coachroof stepped down about midship to the long, windowless cabin trunk, giving it a somewhat awkward appearance.

In the 2-46, the cockpit was pushed aft, the deckhouse windows decreased in size, and windows added to the cabin trunk for a much more handsome and balanced profile.

A sloop rig was the only option until 1973, when a ketch rig was made available. We don't know how many of each were sold, but to our eye, the ketch seems more appropriate to the boat. For cruising, the extra stick enables the crew to sail with "jib and jigger" in high winds, and to fly a mizzen staysail in very light air. Neither rig has a lot of sail area, however. The short rig was mandated by the rela-

tively shoal draft and high center of gravity. It was assumed, correctly, that most owners would find the beefy 85-hp. Perkins diesel the perfect antitdote to doldrums and drifters.

One of the more unusual features of the Cal 46 is its large spade rudder. Lapworth wanted to retain some performance features and apparently a keel-hung rudder was anathema to his creed. The keel is quite long, though cut away significantly in the forefoot. It terminates just behind the cabin trunk, leaving space between it and the spade rudder for the propeller, which in the original 46 exits the deadwood horizontally for top efficiency. The Cal 2-46 relocates the engine closer to midships. Both drive the boat at its hull speed of about 8.5 knots with a cruising range of 1,200 miles.

The spade rudder gives the boat better control in tight maneuvering situations than a keel-hung rudder, especially since the keel is so long. The drawback is the potential to snag lines on both the rudder and propeller. Addressing the question, the Feiges' wrote: "It does have a spade rudder, which many people would call a fault in a cruising boat, but considering the advantages, and considering the damaged rudders of all kinds we have seen in boat yards, we'll take our chances with our big beautiful spade."

Draft is shoal at five feet. Clearly this boat isn't going to climb away from a lee shore like an eight-foot draft fin keel racer, but as cruising is its priority, this was a trade-off Lapworth was willing to make. Even the shallow waters of the Florida Keys and Bahama banks won't pose a problem for the Cal 46. And if you need to get to windward in a hurry? Crank up the iron jenny!

Nevertheless, spade rudders do require extra caution, especially in areas where fish nets and lobster pots are prevalent. Indeed, floating lines and logs are a menace worldwide, and the smart skipper will have some plan in mind for the eventuality of cutting free lines or other obstructions.

Construction

The Cal 46, like most early Cal boats, was hand-laid of solid fiberglass using cloth and woven roving. An early brochure states that the hull was engineered for "maximum impact strength," using "compressive strength materials on the outside" and "tensile strength materials on the inside."

The lead ballast was precast in a mold, then lowered into the fiberglass keel cavity and glassed over. The wood bulkheads and structural furniture were fiberglassed to the hull. According to the company's literature, this occurred before removing the hull from the mold, which is highly desirable. Removing the hull before it is fully supported, as some builders do, encourages the possibility of the hull deforming and making the fitting of the deck sloppy. The joint was "bonded together to form a double-thick seam" and "concealed by a decorative rubber or teak rail on the outside, and rendered invisible on the inside by filling, taping, sanding, and painting." The sealant used was 3M 5200 and the joint was through-bolted with 1/4-inch machine screws.

The deck, according to Feiges, was cored with plywood, which structurally is a good material for this application. It is, however, much heavier than end-grain balsa and much more susceptible to far-reaching rot from water leaking through deck fasten-ers. Interestingly, we have no reports of problems with the plywood. But, if we owned a boat with plywood-cored decks, we'd be certain that all through-deck fasteners were periodically recaulked.

Interior joinerwork is Burmese teak. Overhead panels were covered with vinyl. The sole of some models was plywood supported by 2 x 2s and aluminum angles, with teak and holly over. On other boats, it appears, the soles were fiberglass with carpeting.

The large windows on all models (though their size were progressively reduced after the original 46), are a cause for concern. Most owners mentioned it in completing our Owner's Questionnaire. Not only did they seem weak, but leaked as well. Most owners said they had replaced them with stronger materials or permanently covered them. At the least, some provision for attaching storm shutters should be made.

One owner said the black iron fuel tanks rotted out at 15 years. A 2-46 brochure says the two fuel tanks (totaling 135 gallons) are "10 gauge steel." Water tanks, at least in later models, are stainless steel.

Overall, owners rate the construction of the Cal 46 as excellent. While the smaller Cals may have been

---

The original Cal 46 had large windows in the deckhouse and just two fixed ports in the cove stripe for the saloon. The head was aft of the saloon, which pushed the engine aft, requiring a V-drive.

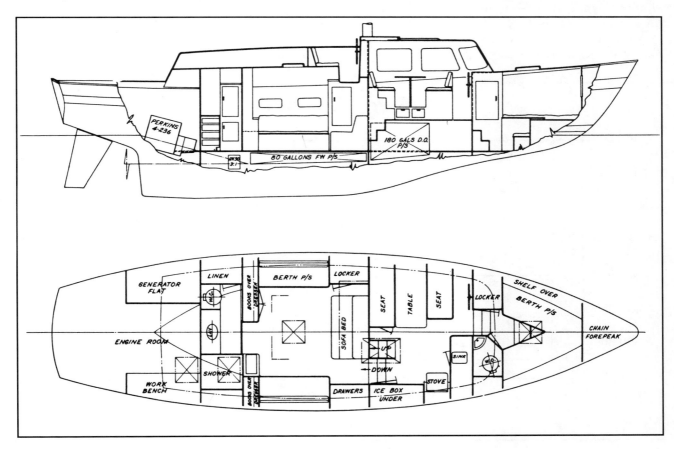

regarded as budget boats, we have repeatedly observed that the larger boats in a company's line are frequently built to higher standards. This appears to be the case with the Cal 46. At the same time, remember that this was a production boat with precut interior components, so don't expect custom quality joinerwork and finish work.

Accommodations

The original Cal 46 featured V-berths forward with its own head compartment, a raised deckhouse with dinette and galley, and a large "living room" aft with settees and a sofa bed. Aft of it is a large head with shower and access to the engine room, which had room for a workbench and generator set. In this configuration, the engine was coupled to a V-drive. Owners of all 46s are unanimous in their praise for the large engine room and its standing headroom. As one owner wrote, when her husband is fixing something on the workbench, "he, and the mess, is not in my hair."

In the 2-46, with its longer deckhouse, two layouts were offered: one with an L-shaped dinette and one with an athwartship dinette with chart table forward of it. Both have sideboard galleys to starboard. The forward and aft cabins were identical, the latter with a double berth and head to port and a settee and hanging locker to starboard. The great appeal of the raised deckhouse is the ability to see through the windows while seated—no need to stand up every time you hear a noise!

An owner of a 3-46 wrote that it doesn't have as roomy an aft cabin, but does have a larger hanging locker and a separate shower stall. It also has a vanity, which she notes contains "a very capacious vegetable bin."

Headroom in the 3-46 is a bit less, and the windows are a bit smaller.

The galley was moved into the passageway aft, making it smaller but more secure. She wrote, "We can hand food directly up into the cockpit through our port located above the sink. The saloon, without the galley, looks huge. There is plenty of storage space, and the largest chart table I've ever seen. At sea, we run a heavy line from the companionway grabrail to the mast to the grabrail on the forward bulkhead, which has always allowed us to move around down below securely." This is an interesting point, as many people don't consider the liability of a large cabin at sea. If one must move from one point to another without benefit of a handhold, there is the danger of being thrown and injured. The safety line is a simple solution, though it won't be as secure a handhold as a solid wood or metal rail through-bolted to a bulkhead.

The center-cockpit layout of the 46 was unusual in the late 1960s and early 1970s. By providing a stateroom at each end of the boat, two couples can cruise in privacy, leaving the dinette "up" all of the time. In a pinch, it could sleep extra crew.

An attraction of the 46 is that neither Lapworth nor Jensen tried to squeeze too much into the hull, leaving plenty of room for stowage and working, which is exactly what a couple or family needs when venturing far from home.

On deck, the cockpit is quite elevated and dry.

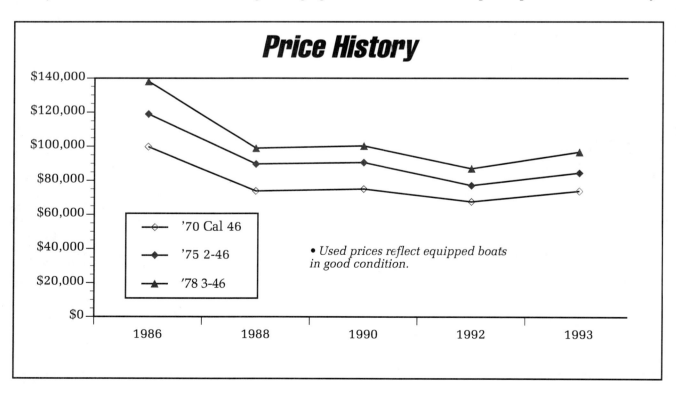

Price History

'70 Cal 46
'75 2-46
'78 3-46

• Used prices reflect equipped boats in good condition.

Consequently, the cabin is tall; some may find it less pleasing to the eye than a lower-profile structure. But that would require higher freeboard, which might impair sailing performance. It may be helpful to install steps somewhere to make it easier to climb from the deck to the coachroof.

The side decks are not as wide as one might expect on a 46-footer, but remember that this design has just 12' 6" beam. And, as is usually the case, the designer wanted to maximize space below. Stepping around the shrouds can be a nuisance, but at least you have a handhold.

The cockpit seats are long enough to sleep on and the backrests are tall.

Performance

As one would expect of a boat with a short rig and shallow keel, sailing performance is not grand prix. The hull, however, is easily driven and the long waterline helps achieve good speeds, especially when the wind is up. Several owners said light-air performance was less than stellar, but then one must remember this boat is part motor sailer, with a large diesel for such exigencies.

On the plus side, the rig fits under the East Coast's Intracoastal Waterway fixed bridges. And, for those venturing to the latitudes of balmy tradewinds, which routinely blow at 20 miles per hour and more, a smaller rig is more easily handled, while still providing sufficient power to reach hull speed. Because it is a bit underrigged, one owner said the boat can carry full sails up to 25 knots of wind.

Most owners rate balance as superb. Several say the boat is a bit tender and that early reefing is a requisite of comfortable passage-making.

Performance under power is good. The Perkins 4-236 diesel is an excellent engine. The reduction gear is 3:1. The standard propeller was a 26-inch, three-blade that gives good power and control. Dragging it around under sail, however, is another matter. A good feathering propeller, such as a Max-Prop, would perceptibly increase sailing speeds as well as improve handling in reverse.

The Feigeses said their 3-46 came with two cutless bearings, counter to Lapworth's drawings. One, they said, was impossible to lubricate or replace. So they removed one and installed instead a pillow block bearing to support the long shaft.

Motor sailers, as critics are wont to say, are neither beast nor fowl, representing either the best of both worlds, or the worst. The Cal 46 represents about a 70/30 split between sail and power. For a blue-water cruising boat, that isn't bad. It sails decently on most points, and has the big diesel necessary not only for long periods of motoring, but also to run all of the convenience items important to long-term comfort at sea, such as refrigeration, inverter, desalinator and electric windlass. Equally important, there's space in the engine room to install all of these goodies.

The original Cal 46 came with a Warner V-drive, which adds expense and complications. We'd prefer the direct drive of the 2-46 and 3-46.

Conclusion

The Cal 46 is a big boat that's sized right for long-distance cruising. It appears that most owners have been devoted to their vessels, and a prospective buyer can only hope that they have maintained them with equal diligence and effort.

Presumably, most of the early bugs have been resolved by now. According to owners, those bugs include large, leaky windows, wooden spreaders, black iron fuel tanks and other items of lesser significance.

The problem, if you're interested, is finding one. Though more than 100 were built, they don't often appear on the market. We'd look for a 2-46 or 3-46, preferring their deck and interior to the original 46. We also like the ketch rig better than the sloop on this design. **• PS**

The FD-12

This German-Dutch designed, Taiwan-built boat is a serious world cruiser with a custom interior.

Sometimes we go to great lengths to look at the boats we evaluate. It might involve a flight across the country to a boatbuilder, or it might be as close as the local boatyard and marina. Evaluating a serious cruising boat, however, often takes a little more effort.

In the case of the Holmann-designed FD-12, we first traveled by air to Belize in Central America, and then by outboard-powered dugout canoe over 20 miles of open ocean to a jungle river in Guatemala. We finally found FD-12 sisterships *Winterhawk* and *Moonshadow* peacefully anchored off the banks of Lake Izabal, 30 miles up the Rio Dulce. We spent a week cruising the FD-12 on this tropical fresh water lake.

Here's what we found out.

The Boat and the Builder

The FD-12 resulted from the collaborative efforts of German designer Eva Holmann and Dutchman Willem Eickholt. In the mid-1970s Eickholt, part owner at the time of Flying Dutchman Yachts, decided to build his dreamboat. A lifelong sailor, he knew he wanted an aft-cockpit, flush-decked cutter of moderate displacement and minimum wetted surface with a fin keel, skeg rudder, canoe stern, and clipper bow. "I also wanted her to be fast. Long passages bore me," says Eickholt. "Last but not least, I wanted her to be pretty in a timeless way."

He chose Holmann, known for her fast, unsinkable cruising designs, to help design the boat.

"Generally speaking, Eva and I got along well," Eickholt told us. "The stormy part of our relationship was Eva's refusal to draw an 'ancient, speed-robbing silly canoe stern,' and my equal determination to have the boat the way I wanted her." But when the German-Dutch war ended, their 'war baby' proved

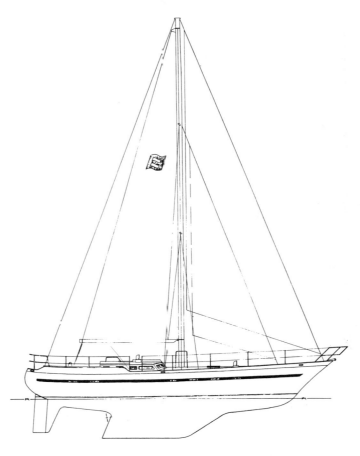

Specifications

LOA	50' 4"
LWL	42' 0"
Beam	14' 3"
Draft	6' 6"/5' 4" (std/Scheel keel)
Displacement	36,000 lbs.
Ballast	14,350 lbs.
Sail area	1,100 sq. ft.

an impressive performer despite, as Eva said, its 'repulsive' stern.

Since the late 1970s, 25 FD-12s have been built at Ta Yang Yacht Building Co. and other yards in Taiwan. In 1980, Eickholt broke away from Flying Dutchman Yachts to form Willem Eickholt and Associates, Inc., and continued to build the FD-12. Each boat is built "on order," and interiors are totally customized.

Construction

The FD-12 hull is a fiberglass sandwich cored with Viny foam, a Japanese product similar chemically to Airex. Viny foam, which is lightweight, and provides both strength and resiliency, also insulates against heat and sound, and helps to eliminate con-

densation within the cabin. A pair of full-length longitudinal stringers and fiberglass and foam floor timbers athwartships provide further stiffening.

Teak plywood bulkheads extend to the base of the hull. A Viny foam wedge insert at the foot of the bulkhead creates a broader bonding angle and distributes transversal stress to prevent bulkhead fractures. The entire bulkhead assembly is fiberglassed to the hull.

The hull-to-deck joint is an inward-turning hull flange, overlapped by the bulwark flange. The joint is through-bolted, filled with Thiokol, coated with fiberglass, and then topped with a teak caprail. This is a strong joint. The owners of the two FD-12s we sailed in Guatemala reported no hull-to-deck joint leaks.

The deck is cored with Philippine fir rather than traditional balsa. Fir is strong, but it's heavy, and puts unnecessary weight high in the boat where you don't want it.

A massive teak rubrail with rectangular-shaped portholes recessed into it offers some protection to the midsections of the hull. However, installing portholes in topsides is always difficult, and both boats in Guatemala had experienced porthole leaks. Leaks in deckhouse ports are simply an annoyance. In a hull they can be dangerous and in extreme cases can lead to loss of the vessel.

The chainplates are stainless steel straps that extend through the deck. Four chainplates (two port and two starboard) bolt to bulkheads, but two chainplates (one port, one starboard) bolt to fiber-glass knees. The knees are hefty, but several owners of FD-12s report their decks have lifted due to a knee-to-hull bond failure. (On the first dozen or so hulls, Ta Yang Yacht Building Co. gelcoated the hull interior before glassing in the knees. In later hulls, knees were properly bonded to the bare hull.)

To form the mast step, an aluminum H-beam through-bolts to a floor timber, and the mast sits in an oval-shaped aluminum weldment that bolts to the mast step. This arrangement provides a strong platform and eliminates corrosion problems that occur if a mast is stepped in the bilge.

The FD-12's underbody has a cruising fin with a long run and a full skeg. The keel is ballasted with cast lead and molded in one piece with the hull. For careening purposes the hull sits squarely on the fin and skeg to avoid damaging the rudder.

The rudder rides on two bearings, the upper one supporting the steering system. To protect the rudder and the steering mechanism, the skeg is designed to break away in case of a collision. This is also a handy feature for those planning to cruise shallow waters where sooner or later even the best sailors usually run hard aground.

There's approximately 200 cubic feet of polyurethane foam wedged into the bow, stern, keel and other nooks and crannies on the FD-12 to provide positive flotation. Positive flotation is rarely built into a cruising boat because it consumes so much space, but we would definitely consider it if we were building the ultimate cruiser.

Holmann comments: "Most composite boats only

need a bit of help to give them positive flotation, but the amount of flotation must be carefully calculated. If you miss it by one cubic foot, you'll have a very expensive sinker, but it *will* sink."

Size of water and fuel tanks varies depending on interior layout, but all FD-12s carry ample water and fuel for long-distance cruising. One FD-12 we sailed carried 250 gallons of water, the other 150. Fuel is stored in two 125- to 150-gallon black iron fuel tanks. Black iron tanks tend to corrode. Aluminum tanks are a better choice for storing diesel. Water tanks are stainless steel, but the metal is an inferior grade, and the tanks we inspected were rusty.

Performance Under Power

The engine is installed underneath the floorboards at the bottom of the companionway in its own separate bilge. This type of installation keeps the engine weight low where you want it. Spilled engine oil is confined to a small area. The separate bilge also protects the engine from water that might enter the other two bilges.

On the downside, the engine is difficult to access. The front of the engine, located under floorboards inside a galley locker, makes it particularly difficult to change or tighten belts, etc. The rear of the engine is more accessible, but overall it's a poor set-up for a big 50-footer.

The FD-12 is so customized that you're liable to find three different engines on three different boats. In Guatemala, one FD-12 was fitted with an 80-hp Ford Lehman diesel with a two-bladed prop, the other a Lehman-Peugeot 4D61 with a three-bladed prop.

The 64-hp Lehman/Peugeot was noisy, vibrated excessively, and overheated if driven over 2,000 rpm. We'd recommend a larger, more reliable engine. The 80-hp Ford Lehman propelled the FD-12 along nicely, but a similar-sized Perkins might be a better choice for marine use. Still, the FD-12 hull is easily driven and both engines gave us a speed of 6 to 6 1/2 knots through the water in flat seas. Like most sailboats, the FD-12 tends to have a mind of its own in reverse, although one *PS* reader reported that it steered well in reverse with a Max Prop. With a 250- to 300-gallon fuel capacity, you can easily expect a 1,000-mile cruising range under power.

Performance Under Sail

With its relatively fine entry, 42' waterline, and efficient underbody, the FD-12 is a high-performance, blue-water cruiser. It's also a hefty boat (36,000 lbs. displacement), and a comfortable passagemaker under most points of sail. However, like many heavy-displacement double-enders, this boat rolls in heavy air downwind.

The FD-12 is powerful on a reach or broad reach in winds over 15 knots, and performs respectably to weather. It loses speed in light air, but in 15- to 20-knot winds, you can count on averaging at least six knots under sail.

The FD-12 is cutter-rigged with the mast stepped fairly well aft. There's a quick release on the inner forestay to accommodate large headsails, but we doubt you'll use it often. Working sails consist of a Yankee, main and staysail, but in winds under 15 knots a roller furling genoa comes in handy. The boat we sailed also carried a cruising spinnaker which the owners reported using on long passages even when shorthanded.

Double spreaders, hefty 7/16" wire rigging, swage fittings, and Ronstan turnbuckles provide a strong rig. The two forward babystays have a quick release lever so they can be led aft when using a spinnaker pole.

Instead of using running backstays to take the load of the inner forestay, the FD-12 rig incorporates intermediates which lead just behind the aft lower shrouds. The intermediate angle is so acute that the intermediate must be large in diameter and strongly tensioned to provide support. This adds a lot of compressive load to the mast. Intermediates can also

There's no such thing as a standard interior in an FD-12. Every one is unique, but all are designed for comfortable, long-distance cruising.

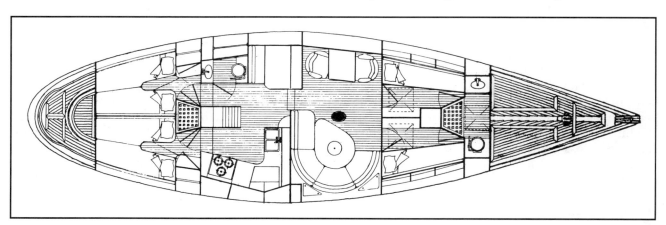

cause unnecessary chafe on the mainsail downwind. Running backstays would be more effective.

The FD-12 is a big 50-footer, but it's well-balanced and easy to handle. Winches on the boats we sailed were self-tailing Barients and Meissners. The Barients were up to par, but the owners complained that the Meissners failed often, and parts were difficult to find and replace.

On Deck

The FD-12's roomy, flush teak deck provides a stable sailing platform. The cockpit is efficient for sailing and safe for passagemaking. It's not too big, has decent cockpit drains, and high coamings that impart a snug, secure feeling, especially offshore.

The steering wheel is hand-laminated teak and spruce. A mainsheet traveler spans the cockpit well just forward of the wheel, and there's an alternative mainsheet arrangement on top of the cabin house. Genoa sheet winches are mounted outboard of the main coamings just forward of the traveler. These winches are well located, but one of the stanchions gets in the way if you are beating to weather and need to ease the sheets to fall off downwind.

Otherwise, the stanchions are strong. They are installed with backing plates and have side braces that bolt to the caprail. To provide a safe way to climb aboard a boat with extremely high freeboard, there are two stainless steel boarding ladders (one port, one starboard) that fold in half over the lifelines.

There were three Bomar hatches forward on one FD-12 we sailed, and one custom teak hatch and Dorade vents on the other. The teak hatch is pretty, but Bomars are easier to maintain, and provide more ventilation.

The aluminum mast is made by Yachtspar of New Zealand and painted with polyurethane. Two stainless steel mast pulpits act as supports when working at the mast, and provide a place to secure gear and lines.

There's a stainless stemhead fitting with double anchor rollers forward. On early hulls this fitting was too flimsy; on later hulls, they strengthened the anchor roller fitting, and also added an extra support strut to the bow pulpit.

The entire forepeak (6' long and 3' to 5' wide) of the FD-12 is designed for storage. You can enter the forepeak cargo hold by opening two huge hatches cut into the deck aft of the anchor chain windlass. These hatches are *extremely* heavy—so heavy they must be tied to the lifelines so you won't lose a finger (or worse) if they slam shut accidentally. They are well-gasketed, but it's disconcerting to see such big holes cut in the foredeck.

The forepeak locker is great for storing sails but it's cavernous and it's sometimes difficult to find things. Also, the anchor chain drops onto a shelf inside this locker, and excess chain can easily get snagged amongst all the rubble.

There are three bronze hawseholes—port and starboard—cut into the bulwarks forward, aft and amidships. They are well-placed but a little under-sized.

Scuppers on the FD-12 do not drain overboard. Instead, hoses are attached to scupper drains and led to through-hull fittings located just above the water-

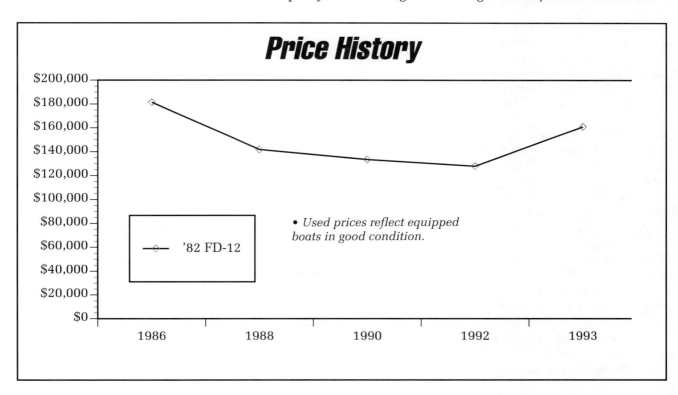

Price History

• *Used prices reflect equipped boats in good condition.*

—◇— '82 FD-12

line. This arrangement prevents water from staining the topsides, but we don't like unnecessary through-hull fittings at the waterline.

Owners report that chainplate covers must be rebedded periodically to prevent deck leaks. Stainless weldments on the FD-12 tend to weep rust, and we question the quality of the stainless used throughout the boat. (Taiwan boatbuilders have a reputation for building with inferior stainless. For some reason, the importance of using superior metals is not a concept they readily understand.)

The two FD-12s in Guatemala both had Fleming Major vane gears which were not sensitive enough in light air. A Monitor would be more effective.

Belowdecks

There is no standard arrangement belowdecks. Every FD-12 has been individually customized to meet the buyer's needs. With such a wide possibility of interiors available, we restrict our comments to *Winterhawk* (hull #19), the boat we sailed in Guatemala.

Belowdecks, *Winterhawk* is incredibly spacious—so spacious that with five crewmembers aboard we never felt cramped or hemmed in. Furniture is built of plywood with a grooved teak veneer. The cabin sole is teak and holly. Bulkheads in staterooms and heads are white Formica, and a number of large round mirrors bolted to bulkheads impart a sense of light and space.

Ten bronze opening deckhouse ports, in addition to hatches, provide adequate ventilation, but you might want to install fans or an extra hatch in the aft cabin.

Indeed, *Winterhawk* has all the creature comforts of home. There are two heads, one forward and one across from the galley, each with hot and cold pressure water and manual fresh and saltwater foot pumps. Both heads have showers with teak grates, and sumps which pump overboard. On our cruise, hot showers flowed freely thanks to a Balmar ASC Aqua Master watermaker. (Driven by a Northern Lights 5kw generator, this AC model desalinates about 19 gallons per hour, and completely eliminates the need to take on water from shore, which is especially helpful in countries where the quality of water is questionable.)

A large L-shaped galley on the starboard side of the doghouse has two deep double sinks, plenty of storage, and enough counter space for two people to cook at the same time. The lockers behind the stove are difficult to reach, but there are plenty of additional galley drawers, as well as cubbyholes for pots and pans.

A huge icebox and freezer with AC and DC refrigeration keeps perishables cold, but insulation could be increased all around to make the box smaller and

more efficient. We had difficulty adjusting the knobs on the Hillerange propane stove, and given our druthers we'd opt for a Force 10. Two 20-lb propane tanks are appropriately stored under the helmsman's seat in a vented locker.

The nav station, across from the galley, is comfortable with good working space for chartwork, ample stowage for charts and tools, a red flourescent light for night work, and ample room for installing electronics. FD-12s come standard with four 200-amp-hour batteries.

Winterhawk has four Prevailer 8Ds, which the owner praises highly. The electrical system includes 110-volt and 12-volt service. Wiring is supposedly to U.S.C.G. regulations, but the electrical connections for the masthead wiring on *Winterhawk* are in the bilge where they are vulnerable to water damage. Two electric bilge pumps backed up by a manual bilge pump are adequate for emergency bilge pumping.

The saloon has a large U-shaped dinette to starboard and a single settee to port. A Dickinson diesel stove sits amidships for heating the cabin in colder climes. Storage for books throughout the saloon is plentiful, and there are big lockers for canned goods underneath the settees.

Forward, port and starboard, are two almost identical cabins. Each has a single berth with teak leeboards, plenty of drawers and two louvered hanging lockers.

The aft cabin is a large owner's stateroom with a double and single berth and a small night table with mirror. Again, there are plenty of drawers and several hanging lockers. Some might object that there is no head in the aft cabin, but for offshore passagemaking a head in the doghouse by the companionway ladder makes more sense.

Some FD-12s, like *Moonshadow* (hull #2) have layouts similar to *Winterhawk* but with a few more berths. Others have completely different interiors. (For example, hull #7, has the saloon in the doghouse, and the galley in the saloon.) However, all are designed to cruise long distances in comfort, and you'd be hard-pressed to find a 50-footer with more room to accommodate your whims and fancies.

Conclusion

The FD-12 is a moderately fast, well-appointed, comfortable world cruiser. In our minds, positive flotation in a cruising boat is a big plus. We'd like to see more boats built with it.

On the negative side, corroding weldments on deck hardware and rusty fuel and water tanks are a source of potential problems. High freeboard and a canoe stern make for a safe, dry boat, but it would be interesting to see drawings of the FD-12 with an Eva Holmann-designed reverse transom. **• PS**

Deerfoot 61

Steve Dashew's and Ulf Rogeberg's world cruiser is fast, efficient, innovative— and very, very expensive.

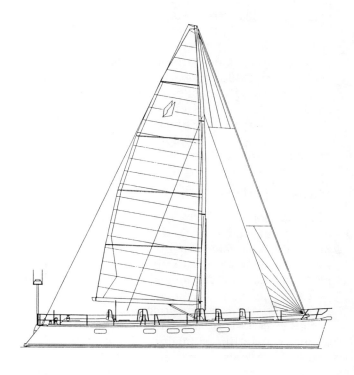

There is no doubt about the Deerfoot 61's purpose in life. This boat is made for long-distance cruising. "We'd sailed thousands of miles on a 50' foot CCA-designed ketch and like most liveaboards we dreamed of the perfect yacht," says Steve Dashew, author of the *Offshore Cruising Encyclopedia.* "We never realized this dream would end in a boatbuilding business."

Dashew built the first Deerfoot, a 68-footer, in New Zealand in 1980. Subsequently, several more Deerfoots, including one for himself, were built in New Zealand and South Africa. "We soon found there was a void in the sailboat market for efficient sailing vessels designed not by the illogical biases of a racing rule, or by concepts thought up by marketing experts," said Dashew.

Since 1980, 16 Deerfoots, ranging in size from 58 to 74 feet have been built. "Four of our fiberglass boats have been built at Scandi Yachts in Finland because they do the best fiberglass work," says naval architect Ulf Rogeberg who worked with the Dashews to create the Deerfoot designs. "The aluminum boats have been built at Walsted's in Denmark."

In 1986, the Dashews, overwhelmed by the size of the Deerfoot project, sold the business to Jim Jackson and Christine Jurzykowski, owners of the 74' aluminum Deerfoot ketch, *Maya.* Jackson, president and executive director of Fossil Rim Wildlife Center, a 2,900-acre wildlife reserve in Glen Rose, Texas, continues to build Deerfoots in the Dashew tradition. Building headquarters have recently moved from New Zealand to Able Marine Inc. in Trenton, Maine.

The Concept

The Deerfoot concept is based on three principles: efficiency, safety, and comfort. "The key is to have a

Specifications

LOA	61' 6"
LWL	57' 6"
Beam	14' 6"
Draft	6' 3"
Displacement	48,200 lbs.
Ballast	16,500 lbs.
Sail area	1,180 sq. ft.

hull which allows you a nice interior while carrying the weight of the boat in the most efficient manner," says Dashew.

Ulf Rogeberg, who previously worked with Paul Elvstrom in Denmark designing 12-meters, explains: "We have tried to create a canoe-shaped hull that is easily driven, a hull with a fine entry angle, narrow waterlines and easy bilges. We have further tried to distribute volume so that the longitudinal center of buoyancy does not move aft when the boat heels. If a boat heels over symmetrically, if its stern doesn't kick up and the bow doesn't bury itself, you'll have better stability, steering control, and performance downwind."

A fine entry angle and a long, narrow hull also reduce drag and provide comfort and efficiency upwind and reaching. With an easily-driven hull, the Deerfoot's rig can be substantially shorter than is needed on a beamy boat with a short waterline. A smaller rig means more stability, less sail changing, less work for a shorthanded crew, and a more comfortable ride.

How does the long, narrow hull affect the interior? While short, fat boats have their beam concentrated amidships, the Deerfoot's relatively narrow beam is carried further forward and aft. This means there's a lot of storage space in the bow and stern. Amidships, the Deerfoot appears spacious because there are few bulkheads, and ceilings are kept void of bookshelves or lockers.

Construction

The Deerfoot's hull, deck and bulkheads are a fiberglass laminate cored with one inch Baltek end-grain balsa. The laminate schedule is unidirectional roving and mat laid up with vinylester resin to resist osmotic blistering. Although balsa is a strong, light core material, a completely water-resistant composite core like Airex seems preferable.

Reinforced with two longitudinal stringers and 13 athwartships stringers made of fiberglass, the hull is strong. There's also extra fiberglass around the mast, and at the turn of the bilge and bow area in case of a collision. The hull-to-deck joint is an inward-turning hull flange overlapped by the bulwark flange. The joint is through-bolted, coated with fiberglass and topped with a teak toerail.

The Deerfoot 61 keel, a NAACA foil fin, is a steel weldment with lead ballast encapsulated at the base. Above the ballast compartment, the keel is divided into three tanks—two for water (140 gallons) and one for fuel (160 gallons). A sump (with bilge pump) divides the water and fuel tanks. Both fuel and water tanks are fitted with Tank Tender pressure gauges for sounding the tanks. The water tanks have an inspection plate on the outside of the keel.

Storing fuel and water in the keel has a number of advantages. First, it gives the Deerfoot 61 a moderately high ballast ratio (about a third of the Deerfoot's weight is in the keel). This lowers the center of gravity and improves stability and windward performance. It also means you have more storage space under seats and bunks. On the down side, there is no way to inspect the tanks from inside the hull, and the water and fuel supply could be jeopardized if your keel is damaged.

Made of aluminum with a six-inch diameter aluminum rudder stock, the Deerfoot's oversized spade rudder improves steering efficiency and windward performance. However, hanging an aluminum rudder behind a steel keel could result in electrolysis. A fiberglass rudder with stainless steel shaft might be a better choice. You also cannot apply copper bottom

paints to aluminum and the proximity of the aluminum rudder and stock to a copper painted bottom could cause corrosion problems.

The mast is stepped on two aluminum plates that are bolted to a fiberglass mount. The steel keel further supports the mast step.

Stainless steel straps form the chainplates, which extend through the deck and bolt to fiberglass knees. In the photos we looked at, the chainplate installation looked strong. However, with the help of two boatbuilders at Able Marine, we unsuccessfully tried to uncover the chainplates by dismantling the interior. Ulf Rogeberg admits getting to the chainplates is "tricky." It might be less so if Deerfoot shortened the valances or bookshelf fiddles running behind the settees.

Seacocks are Marelon. Some people prefer bronze seacocks with bolted flanges (we have had reports of handles breaking off Marelon seacocks), but on a boat with a steel keel and aluminum rudder, Marelon is probably a good idea.

You'll be hard pressed to sink a Deerfoot. The 61 has three watertight bulkheads. One separates the forepeak from the living area, and one separates the living area from the engine room. Each watertight area has its own bilge pump. The bilge pump in the forepeak doubles as a deck wash down pump. There's also a large Edson manual bilge pump mounted in the bilge near the mast.

The 14-foot forepeak, a huge storage area, is a cruising sailor's dream. It has sail bins, anchor bins, and pipes for tying dock lines and sheets. There's also room for fenders and the other paraphenalia that usually collects on deck.

There's a "garage" aft (behind the engine room) for storing propane tanks, outboard motors, and diving tanks. It's also a good place to keep the liferaft where it can be deployed easily if the need arises. The "back porch", a small "sugar scoop" behind the "garage," has a fresh water deck shower, and a stern ladder to make climbing aboard easy. On a boat with such high freeboard, this arrangement could be a real lifesaver if a crewmember were to fall overboard. For everyday use, the fold-up ladder is a bit lethal, however, since the bottom half hinges up but doesn't lock in place. The unwary visitor may reach for a rung and end up in the drink.

Rig

With a 65 foot mast and a working sail area of just 1,150 square feet, the Deerfoot 61 has an efficient, easily-handled cutter rig. Double swept-back spreaders and oversized Navtec 316 stainless steel wire rigging with Norseman terminals provide support for the tapered aluminum spar which has a fair amount of induced bend.

Hydraulics control the permanent double backstays, the boom vang and the inner forestay. The backstays work in tandem to keep the headstay tight for best upwind performance. The hydraulic inner forestay when tightened bends the mast moderately to flatten the mainsail. It can also be removed to facilitate tacking the jib.

Performance Under Sail

The Deerfoot 61, with its narrow, easily-driven canoe shape, fin keel/spade rudder and moderate-sized rig, is a fast passagemaker. Deerfoot claims that one of their 61s averaged 209 miles a day from New Zealand to the Panama Canal. They also claim another averaged 11 knots in 25-knot winds on a broad reach from Marblehead to the Cape Cod Canal. Even if you subtract a few knots (or miles) from these averages, that's still fair sailing.

We sailed the Deerfoot 61 from Newport to the boat show in Annapolis in October, but our story was different. It was a beat to windward the entire way.

In light to moderate winds the boat still averaged seven to eight knots. In 35-knot winds encountered off Delaware Bay, the boat handled well, but pounded in steep, short confused seas.

In most conditions, the 61 is so well balanced that you can steer it with two fingers. There's no weather or lee helm, and you have the feeling you're sailing a racing boat rather than a cruising boat designed for safe, comfortable passagemaking.

In keeping with the philosophy that a cruising boat should be easily handled by two people, the Deerfoot 61's working sails are small. Upwind, the Deerfoot is designed to sail with a jib that just overlaps the shrouds. For light air, there's a reacher that's set on its own stay four feet forward of the headstay and a 1.5 ounce 85% spinnaker for downwind.

Performance Under Power

"Probably 99 percent of maintenance is accessibility," says Steve Dashew. With this in mind, the Deerfoot's large engine room has been designed with attention to detail.

Located aft behind its own watertight bulkhead and entered through either of two cockpit lockers, it houses a four-cylinder 77 hp turbo-charged Yanmar with a 3.2/1 Hurth transmission. There's also an auxiliary two-cylinder, 18 hp Yanmar power plant mounted just starboard of the main engine.

Two 135-amp alternators (one on the larger Yanmar, one on the auxiliary) charge a 600-amp 24-volt Sonnenschein Prevailer Dryfit battery system. A 55-amp alternator (main engine) and a 35-amp alternator (auxiliary engine) charge a second 12-volt system. The 12-volt system is used to start the engines and power some of the navigation equipment. Everything else runs off 24-volt. (The 110-volt AC loads run off an inverter system.)

While 24 volts is good for handling big current draws like an electric windlass or power winches, it's a nuisance when it's necessary to replace equipment in countries where most everything is 12 volt. (For example, 24-volt equipment is quite common in Europe, but usually must be custom ordered in the U.S. or Caribbean.)

The Deerfoot 61 interior shows that a long, narrow hull can be simple and functional, yet spacious and elegant. The 61 is well laid out for long-distance passagemaking or living aboard at anchor.

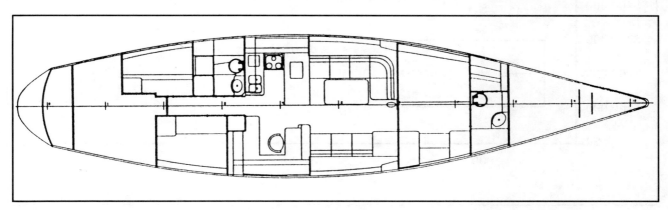

All 24/12 volt DC and AC cabling is laid down in PVC conduits. Wiring is marine grade and tagged with numbers at each end, but the color coding is predominantly red (positive) or black (negative). Color coding the wires to ABYC specifications would be a vast improvement.

Belted onto the engine is a damage control pump (100 gpm) plumbed into the three watertight areas of the boat, and a Sea Recovery watermaker that desalinates 25 gallons of water per hour. The engine room also contains a large hot water heater, two toolboxes, a work bench with sink, and racks for pressure pumps and compressors. There's plenty of work space around the engines, but the watertight bulkhead makes getting to the front of the engine to tighten belts difficult.

At 3,000 RPM the Deerfoot goes eight knots in flat seas. However, the Yanmar runs more efficiently at 2,300 RPM, driving the boat at seven knots in smooth water. Cruising range under power is about 1,100 miles.

Due to hull shape, a 26" three-bladed Max prop, and an extra large rudder, the Deerfoot 61 is extremely handy under power—so handy that it can almost turn (180°) within its own length. The boat handles particularly well in reverse so you're apt to feel smug when docking stern to.

On Deck

The cockpit is in keeping with the Deerfoot philosophy—comfortable for two, a bit cozy for four, but efficient and safe for shorthanded passagemaking. The cockpit drains are huge, four-inch in diameter,

and there are two smaller deck drains all the way aft. The dodger is well made with two opening windows forward for ventilation in warm weather. With forward and side windows closed, it provides a snug, dry place in inclement weather. The trade-off is it hampers visibility for the helmsman.

Two cockpit chairs, one port and one starboard, sit in wells behind the wheel. If you are tall, you can sit comfortably in either with feet planted firmly on the cockpit sole; a shorter person's feet dangle unless you pivot sideways. (In a knockdown the helmsman may go flying since the chairs are not pinned into their sockets.)

The mainsail halyard, main traveler controls and mainsail reefing lines are lead aft to the forward end of the cockpit. However, you must still walk forward to hook the cringle to the reefing hook on the gooseneck. Headsail halyards are located on the main mast along with spinnaker pole controls.

Harken roller furling comes standard on the headstay, although you can opt for jib hanks if you prefer. The cutter stay is left bare for hank-on storm sails.

The Deerfoot 61's long, sleek flush deck provides a stable sailing platform. There are inboard sheeting tracks for the staysail or working jib, and an outboard "T" track bolted to the top of the toe rail from the mast all the way aft for sheeting reachers, spinnakers, and genoas.

Lifeline stanchions, 1 1/4 inch in diameter and 30 inches tall, provide the extra security one needs in an offshore passagemaker. Double lifelines become triple lifelines forward of the mast to help keep crew and

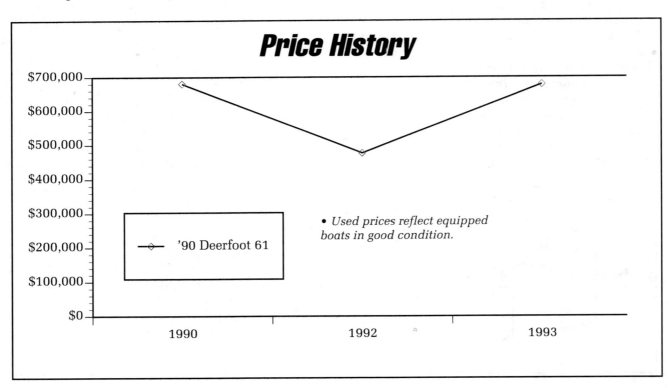

Price History

$700,000
$600,000
$500,000
$400,000
$300,000
$200,000
$100,000
$0

◇ '90 Deerfoot 61

• *Used prices reflect equipped boats in good condition.*

1990   1992   1993

sails on board. The stainless steel pushpit extends around the cockpit as far as the second stanchion for extra safety aft.

The 61 comes standard with a Lewmar windlass, and the anchor chain self stows neatly into a large anchor chain bin located directly beneath the winch. Because the forestay is located four feet aft of the bow, there's a lot of room to handle the anchor.

Seven Bomar hatches and eight dorades provide ventilation below. Stainless steel guards around the dorades prevent jib sheets from fouling and furnish handholds for crewmembers moving forward or aft.

The Deerfoot we sailed was missing some mooring cleats aft and amidships. Also, cleats and winches, though mounted with through bolts and washers into a thick section of fiberglass, have no backing plates to distribute the load.

Interior

Despite its comparatively narrow beam (14 1/2 feet), the Deerfoot's interior is well designed for living aboard in port or offshore. Emphasis is on having an airy, open saloon. Large hull portholes and light-colored, vinyl-covered bulkheads and ceilings create a feeling of light and space. Plush leather settees and a horizontal teak veneer enhance this feeling and give the boat a Scandinavian flair.

Stepping below from the cockpit, there are two guest cabins—one with bunk beds to port and one with a small double to starboard. When cruising, either cabin provides a good place for children or guests. The port cabin, within earshot of the person on deck, is preferable offshore.

The owner's double stateroom forward is designed for sleeping in harbor. You can hear the anchor chain if it drags, and there's good ventilation. This stateroom has oodles of storage and a spacious head forward with sit-down shower, large mirror, and sink.

Aft is another head with shower, stacked washer and dryer, and large linen closet. The shower compartment has big hooks inside for hanging wet towels and foul weather gear. Both heads, sprayed glossy white, are bright and easy to clean.

The long secure passageway between the companionway ladder and saloon is a good place to don your harness or foul weather gear. It also leads you to the galley to port and nav section starboard.

The nav section/office is C-shaped with plenty of room for charts, instruments and electronics. There are two tables and a rotating chair so you can sit forward or aft. (However, there's no space for knees when swiveling the chair outboard.)

Nav lockers along the hull with roll-top lids furnish a nifty way to store books, cassettes, or extra electronics. There's more room for a computer and other equipment on the desk mounted aft.

Across from the nav section, the galley is a typical U-shape with the stove mounted on the aft bulkhead. Counter tops are Corian which can be lightly sanded if scuffed or scraped. There is handsome stowage for dishes and dry goods in lockers above the stove and along the hull.

Two nine-inch deep stainless steel sinks sit outboard and drain via an electric pump to a thru-hull in the aft head. They would drain more efficiently if they were installed near the centerline and plumbed directly overboard.

Hot and cold pressure water are standard, but surprisingly there are no manual salt water pumps, and only one manual fresh water foot pump underneath the galley sink.

There's an eight-cubic-foot fridge and and a five-cubic-foot freezer across from the stove. The fridge stays cold, but its "side opening" door could be better insulated. There's a microwave and more food lockers along the companionway starboard.

The galley and nav section look out over the saloon. There's a large L-shaped dinette to port and a straight settee to starboard. Fiddles for bookshelves mounted behind the settees are inadequately designed for sailing offshore.

To minimize weight above the waterline, the cabin sole and furniture are constructed of teak plywood on a foam core. A good latch-down system secures the sole. However, on the boat we sailed, the cabin sole was divided into five and seven foot lengths which were much too cumbersome.

Lighting on the Deerfoot 61 is excellent. Overhead lights are round recessed halogens and large rectangular flourescents. The saloon has strip lights behind the valances and in the kickspace along the cabin sole. Small reading lights are mounted above bunks and settees.

Large hatches, which provide plenty of light, are fitted with storm cover tracks so they can be left cracked in inclement weather. They also come with an innovative system of bug and sun screens which conveniently slide in and out of the deck.

Conclusion

The Deerfoot 61 is a luxurious boat. It's also a sensible, liveaboard boat that offers outstanding accommodations, superb craftsmanship, and unparalleled performance. It's obvious that Dashew and Rogeberg put a lifetime of ocean voyaging and boatbuilding experience into the Deerfoot design.

All this comes at a price, of course. New, a coastal cruising version of the Deerfoot 61 runs $680,000, add another $120,000 for the offshore package, which comes with sails, two autopilots, watermaker, refrigerator-freezer, ground tackle, and electronics.

This is a lot to pay for any boat, but you'll get top quality for your dollar. **• PS**

Buying Guide
-
Boats

Finding a Cheap Boat

Where to find salvages, repos, and auctions

Finding a bargain boat, if that's what you want, can be a matter of keeping your eyes open for opportunity. Last spring in our yard, we noticed that no one made an appearance at the O'Day 22 next door even as launch day approached. It turned out that the owner had conned the yard into hauling the boat without a deposit and simply disappeared. Could we have bought the boat for yard fees? You bet.

There's one big caveat here. The yard must have followed strict legal procedures in order to make a lawful sale. Since liens travel with a boat, not its owner, "You could be buying into a whole passel of troubles," says Dennis Nixon, a Rhode Island maritime lawyer. Many yards follow the quick route of filing a mechanic's lien, then obtaining a default judgment and holding a sale under the auspices of the state. This is above-board, but it doesn't erase any other liens and you may have difficulty in getting a state title. The safest route, Nixon said, is to buy through a U.S. Marshal's office; in this case, the yard has sued the boat and the marshal has cleared all liens and created a new title. "Never," Nixon said, "buy directly from a boat yard." Notices for both federal and state sales are posted in legal ads in the local newspaper of record.

Storm Bargains

Three summers ago, after Hurricane Bob, Joseph Migliore, an employee of the Rhode Island Department of Environmental Management, began calling insurance companies in hopes of finding a storm-damaged boat at a fraction of market value. Eventually, he was referred to a local salvage yard. After scouring over what he called "a great selection," he settled on a 1985 Hunter 31. The mast was gone, the rudder broken, and there was a six-foot hole on the port side. "It was beat up," Migliore said, "but it didn't sink. And the interior was in pretty good shape."

Migliore then spent close to 400 hours working on the boat. He spent an additional $15,000 for parts before renovations were complete. For Migliore, this was the perfect solution to moving up. "I couldn't have afforded a boat like that otherwise," he said.

Ernie Braatz, technical services director for BOAT/U.S., said BOAT/U.S. sold about 100 boats after Hurricane Hugo, another 75 following Andrew. In one case he handled, a Pennsylvania man got a bargain on a late-model O'Day that had been holed when Hurricane Gloria struck New England. "Three years later, it was a gorgeous boat, better than new," he said.

Braatz suggests going out and looking around after a major storm. "You have to get into the field, literally and figuratively, and poke around." BOAT/U.S. will hold its own regional auctions, usually one to two months after a storm.

But you don't necessarily have to wait for a hurricane. In one day alone last fall, Wentworth said he picked up three boats—two that went on the rocks and one that sank at its mooring. A call to insurance companies, or adjusters, should lead you to a salvage operation in your area.

Auctions

Or, how about those ads that promise to keep you informed of government auctions in your area at which, they promise, you can get "Vehicles Under $200!"—also sports cars, boats, RVs, etc.? We called one advertiser's toll-free number and got the spiel. For just $49.95, "fully refundable" if we weren't satisfied, we'd be on their mailing list for a year. Asked our location (Newport, Rhode Island), we were told, "There's government auctions there about once a week." Already something we didn't know. The annual fee was payable either by credit card or personal check. When we asked where to mail our check, the operator said, "Oh, you just give us your checking account information and we'll make the bank draft." No thanks.

There's no need to hire a middleman to get word of government auctions. Most government agencies in the auction business have their own public auction mailing lists, and an address when you can send a check or money order. U.S. Customs, which also handles boats for the Coast Guard, will send you a list of auctions, two to three weeks in advance of the sale, on a national basis, for $50 a year ($60 if you're out of the country), or, for $25, you can get either the west regional or east regional lists. They can be reached at EG&G Dynatrend, Attn. PAL, 2300 Clarendon Blvd., Suite 705, Arlington, VA 22201; 703/351-7887.

Finally, check the boat ads, especially newspapers and swappers. As with autos, there are a lot of motivated sellers out there. **• PS**

How Much Will $1 Buy?

New boat prices are up, but used prices are stable.

When buying a sailboat, many prospective buyers work from a fixed dollar amount, often a "no-more-than" figure. The question usually is: How much boat can I get for what I want to spend? It matters not whether the amount is $10,000 or $100,000.

Closely coupled with that limitation is the fact that for a given amount of money you can pick up a bigger old boat for far less money than you'll pay for a new one or a used boat only several years old.

For instance: For about $20,000, you can buy a new Precision 23 or J/22. For the same money, you can pick up a Pearson 35 or a Morgan 34—but they'll be about 20 years old.

To illustrate in greater detail, in 1990 *Practical Sailor* compiled (from thousands of advertisements and listings) a chart showing new and used boat prices, with the boats broken into five-year age groups. The chart clearly showed that, considered by the pound or by the foot, new boats carry a heavy premium and that the best buys were boats from 10 to 20 years old and 27 to 40 feet in length. This might be because so many boats in that size range were built in the late '70s and '80s, the halcyon days of sailboat production. In short, most segments of the used boat market still are glutted.

For 1994, we repeated the laborious exercise of scanning ads and listings, from all over the United States, and compiled a second edition of the 1990 chart shown on the following pages. The chart displays about 400 boats, cut down from the working chart because of space limitations. Five new boats, with sails and required equipment, are shown in each price category. We had space for seven boats in each used category. As before, we found too few expensive, old boats to fill some boxes.

It should be emphasized that the used boat prices shown are asking prices, not *selling* prices. Asking prices may be as much as 50 percent greater than the final selling prices.

Further, the asking prices are, with some exceptions, much higher than those listed in the BUC books we use to derive the price charts found in this book. The disparity in the price levels stems largely from the fact that ads and listings are *asking* prices while the BUC books supply *selling* prices based on actual transactions. Wishful sellers sometimes ask twice what a boat is worth. The average difference between "asking" and "selling" appears to be about 20 percent.

BUC's president, Walter J. Sullivan, said the sailboat market, severely battered in the last decade and recently pestered by an economy sweating about war, the banking crisis, a luxury tax and a national election, has shown a bit of a recovery this summer, especially in high-quality boats with good reputations.

"May, June and July were good months," he said. "August was not bad, either. Used boats are moving a bit better. I must emphasize that a boat's condition, equipment and location, which we factor in when compiling the BUC book data, are extremely important. And, the retail 'high' and 'low' must be considered as guides. A high-quality, 25-year-old boat that has been beautifully maintained and upgraded may be worth more than the 'high,' while a shabby, scruffy boat will fall below the 'low.'"

Indeed, it appears that some of the older fiberglass boats (those built in the early '60s) have ceased depreciating; in some instances, they seem to have increased in value.

Sullivan also said that because of the reduced numbers of boats produced in the last few years, it is difficult to find a good "young" used boat. Hence, the prices of some three- to five-year-old boats have increased.

"However," he said, "we're living in a complicated economic environment, and there's not yet a clear signal that anything significant is happening with boat prices."

Our new chart confirms Sullivan's considered judgment that nothing remarkable has happened to boat prices in the last three years.

Comparing our new chart with the prior one indicates clearly that new boat prices have increased 10 percent or more since 1990. Boatbuilders are stuck with increased costs and inflation.

However, the chart provides no trend or even a clue about what has happened to used boat prices in the last three years. For some boats the price appears to have remained the same. For others—usually desirable, high-quality, well-maintained boats like Hinckleys, Shannons and Com-Pacs—the price has gone up a bit. The bulk of them have merely moved down one price category on the chart because they

1993-1994 Sailboat Prices: New & Used

	$5,000		$10,000		$20,000		$30,000		$40,000	
New	Com-Pac 16XL	6,988	MacGregor 26	10,990	Precision 23	15,900	Alerion Express 28	32,900	Nimble Kodiak 26	37,000
	Catalina 16	6,500	Mariner 19	9,795	Hunter 26	18,850	J/24	31,000	Precision 28	39,900
			Beneteau 210	14,500	Nimble 20	18,000	Seaward 25	30,000	Com-Pac 27-2	48,195
			Catalina 22	9,500	J/22	18,750	Classic 26	30,200	F-24 Tri	40,200
			Precision 18	8,560	Com-Pac 23D	23,995	Catalina 270	34,800	Beneteau 265	39,800
1-5 Yrs. Old	'92 West Wight Potter	4,800	'88 Nimble 20	9,900	'88 Bayfield 25	22,000	'88 Com-Pac 27	34,000	'88 Irwin 32	39,950
	'87 Capri 18	5,500	'88 Cal 22	10,500	'88 O'Day 27	18,500	'88 Pearson 27	32,500	'88 Ericson 28	39,500
	'83 Freedom 21	6,000	'88 Beneteau 23	13,900	'88 Olson 25	18,000	'89 Catalina 27	32,900	'89 Hunter 30	39,900
	'84 MacGregor 22	4,450	'89 Hunter 23	9,995	'88 J/24	24,950	'89 O'Day 285	28,500	'91 Nimble 25	36,500
			'89 Precision 23	12,995	'90 Capri 26	23,900	'89 Com-Pac 29	33,000	'91 Catalina 28	39,900
			'90 MacGregor 26	10,000	'89 J/27	21,900	'88 Beneteau 28	34,500		
			'89 Catalina 22	11,500	'89 Marshall 19	19,500				
6-10 Yrs. Old	'79 San Juan 23	5,900	'87 J/22	11,900	'85 C&C 27	21,000	'84 Soverel 33	29,500	83 Beneteau 35	42,000
	'81 Neptune 24	7,800	'84 Hobie 33	13,900	'84 Catalina 27	16,500	'84 J/29	25,700	'85 Bayfield 29	34,500
	'80 J/24	6,500	'84 Watkins 25	9,500	'83 Hunter 30	23,500	'84 Catalina 30	30,500	'84 Endeavour 33	45,000
	'78 Pacific Dolphin 24	9,500	'84 Catalina 25	9,000	'83 Tanzer 27	23,500	'84 Pearson 303	35,000	'85 Hunter 34	42,000
	'81 Balboa 26	6,500	'84 Com-Pac 23	8,400	'85 Gib'Sea 27	24,900	'85 Irwin 34	32,000	'83 Catalina 38	42,500
	'78 Paceship 23	5,000			'84 Cape Dory 25	24,000	'85 Hunter 31	32,500	'84 Tartan 3000	36,000
							'85 Cape Dory 28	30,000	'83 Nonsuch 26	36,000
11-15 Yrs. Old	'74 Tanzer 22	4,500	'83 J/24	12,000	'80 S2 28	21,000	'81 Nicholson 33	31,500	'80 O'Day 37	39,500
	'76 Chrysler 26	5,200	'78 Lancer 30	12,950	'80 Irwin 30	16,500	'78 Ranger 33	31,700	'78 Bristol 35.5	43,500
	'74 Cal 25	5,250	'80 Santa Cruz 27	12,500	'78 Catalina 30	23,950	'82 Morgan 32	34,500	'78 Columbia 35	43,500
	'77 Ranger 23	5,500	'80 Cal 2/25	9,000	'78 Santana 30	17,500	'79 S2 9.2A	27,000	'81 Tartan 33	44,000
	'75 Ericson 23	5,790	'82 Catalina 27	14,500	'82 Islander 28	16,500	'81 C&C 30	29,000	'80 Islander 32	45,000
	'75 Catalina 22	3,500	'82 Albin 28	14,750	'80 Bayfield 29	16,000	'82 Cape Dory 28	28,500	'81 Niagara 31	41,900
	'75 Balboa 23	3,800			'79 Pearson 28	17,500	'78 Sabre 28	26,000	'81 Southern Cross 31	44,950
16-20 Yrs. Old	'68 Sailmaster 26	5,500	'76 Folkboat 26	12,500	'75 Ranger 33	23,500	'75 Fales 32	28,500	'77 Allied Seawind 32	39,900
	'68 Columbia 28	6,500	'74 Tanzer 28	12,900	'76 Bristol 30	20,000	'74 Seafarer 36	33,000	'76 Fuji 32	37,500
	'71 Cal 25	5,900	'74 Chance 30/30	12,000	'79 Seafarer 30	16,900	'76 Kenner Skipjack	32,000	'74 Irwin 37	39,900
	'71 Herreshoff 18	4,000	'76 Catalina 27	8,500	'75 Cal 2-29	17,000	'75 Farr 36	35,000	'77 Sabre 34	39,500
	'69 Yankee Dolphin 24	6,200	'77 Pacific Seacraft 25	15,000	'76 Catalina 30	16,900	'77 Ranger 33	30,000	'77 Downeaster 38	38,000
	'72 O'Day 22	3,995	'74 Pearson 30	15,000	'73 Morgan 30	18,000	'74 C&C 33	24,000	'76 Gulfstar 37	44,000
	'72 MacGregor 22	3,400	'74 Columbia 28	10,000	'76 Irwin 28	15,700	'76 Westerly 36	35,000	'78 Dufour 35	40,000
21-25 Yrs. Old	'67 Shark 24	4,250	'69 C&C 28	9,990	'69 Cal-30	16,900	'71 Contest 33	30,000	'73 Mariner 32	38,500
	'66 East Wind 24	6,400	'68 Tartan 27	12,500	'70 Grampian 30	15,900	'71 Tartan 34	29,000	'72 C&C 39	38,000
	'64 Columbia 26	6,000	'71 Pearson 26	8,000	'72 Tartan 30	18,500	'70 Island Trader 37	30,000	'71 Cheoy Lee 36	43,000
	'67 Pearson Ariel 26	6,000	'69 Seafarer 26	8,000	'68 C&C 31	18,000	'71 Dickerson 36	34,500	'72 Allied Princess 36	42,900
	'68 Coronado 25	6,900	'71 Irwin 23	8,500	'70 Ericson 29	21,500	'72 Bristol 35	30,000	'68 Tartan 34	40,000
	'67 Columbia Sabre 32	7,000	'71 Morgan 27	7,800	'69 Pearson 35	25,000	'69 Cheoy Lee 31	27,950	'79 Downeaster 32	40,000
			'69 Columbia 28	13,000	'70 Morgan 34	16,500	'71 Hughes 38	29,900		
26 Yrs. or Older	'62 Stoutfella 28	6,800	'63 Seafarer 28	13,000	'67 Columbia 34	23,900	'66 Nicholson 32	31,900	'67 Cal 36	35,500
			'66 Pearson Ariel 26	8,000	'66 Pearson 30	17,350	'63 Stonington 42	27,500	'68 Bristol 29	35,500
			'65 Columbia 29	12,000	'65 Galaxy 32	19,900	'64 Bristol 32	28,000	'66 Morgan 34	45,000
			'64 Contest 25	9,500	'65 Pearson Vanguard 32	18,000	'67 Seafarer 35	27,500	'65 Cheoy Lee 35	36,000
			'60 Pearson Triton 28	9,900	'66 Pearson Alberg 35	22,500	'66 Ericson 35	29,900	'65 Allied Seabreeze 35	39,000
							'53 Hinckley 36	29,000	'37 Alden 36	38,500
							'56 Cheoy Lee Lion	32,500		

are three years older.

The chart will not tell you whether a specific used boat you are considering is a good value. The BUC books (based on the old adage that something is worth only what someone is willing to pay) clearly emphasize that much depends on the boat's condition, equipment and location. Boats kept in fresh water in the northern half of the country continue to

$50,000		$75,000		$100,000		$150,000		$200,000+	
Beneteau 310	62,900	Catalina 36	72,000	Morgan 38	118,500	Tartan 372	148,300	J/40	240,000
F-27 Tri	60,600	Nimble 30	84,950	Gozzard 31	116,000	Valiant 37	165,000	Valiant 42	260,000
Tartan 28	62,750	C&C 30	81,000	Com-Pac 35	98,995	Cabo Rico 34	167,200	Endeavour 45	245,000
Hunter 30	52,000	Island Packet 27	73,500	F-31 Tri	95,700	Beneteau 400	139,800	Island Packet 35	199,000
Mariah 27	53,000	Sabre 30	87,500	Island Packet 29	98,950	C&C 40	155,000	Contest 46	360,000
'88 Nonsuch 30	59,000	'91 Hunter 35.5	73,200	'89 Catalina 42	118,500	'88 Sabre 42	169,900	'90 Tartan 412	187,500
'88 Pearson 31	52,000	'88 Irwin 38	61,000	'89 Morgan 41	118,000	'88 Tayana 42	139,500	'90 Nordic 45	297,000
'89 J/33	55,900	'88 J/35	79,900	'88 Beneteau 430	85,000	'88 J/40	175,000	'88 Beneteau First 51	250,000
'88 Frers 30	45,000	'88 Cheoy Lee 40	72,900	'88 CSY 44.5	120,000	'89 Morgan 44	160,000	'89 CS 50	225,000
'90 Hunter 31	46,000	'88 Island Packet 31	72,000	'92 Crealock 34	116,000	'88 Jenneau 47	169,000	'90 Endeavour 52	389,000
'90 Island Packet 27	49,900	'89 Beneteau 35	75,400	'89 Pearson 37	99,000	'89 Hylas 44	174,000	'88 Irwin 54	274,000
'88 Nor'Sea 27	58,000	'89 Nonsuch Ultra	75,000	'92 Pacific Seacraft 34	116,000	'89 Endeavour 42	129,900	'91 Tayana 55	399,000
'85 Bayfield 36	55,000	'86 C&C 41	69,000	'83 Wauquiez 38	95,000	'87 Shannon 37	160,000	'83 Cherubini 48	300,000
'83 Moody 34	53,500	'84 Endeavour 40	75,000	'81 Freedom 44	116,000	'86 C&C 44	149,000	'83 Bristol 45.5	229,000
'84 Islander 36	59,500	'84 Nonsuch Ultra	70,000	'86 Nauticat 33	100,000	'85 Jenneau 45	139,900	'85 Hinckley SW 51	499,000
'85 Ericson 32-3	47,000	'84 Morgan 45	79,500	'85 Gulfstar 45	117,500	'86 Beneteau 51	139,000	'85 Irwin 52	192,500
'85 Tayana 37	60,000	'85 Hunter 40	79,000	'87 J/35	90,000	'85 Moorings 51	174,000	'83 Mason 53	325,000
'84 Catalina 36	47,500	'84 O'Day/ Jenneau 39	71,000	'87 Hans Christian 38T	125,000	'84 Panda 38	149,500	'85 Tayana 55	315,000
'86 Cape Dory 30	49,900	'86 Nauticat 33	79,500	'86 Baltic 35	125,000	'84 Whitby 42	137,500	'83 Swan 57	415,000
'82 Baba 30	55,000	'78 Swan 39R	75,000	'78 Shannon 38	110,000	'82 Hallberg Rassy 42	155,000	'74 Baltic 51	250,000
'82 Beneteau First 43	59,000	'80 Bristol 40	78,000	'82 Tartan 42	109,500	'82 Island Trader 46	145,000	'78 Irwin 52	195,000
'80 Freedom 35	50,000	'79 Morgan 46	80,000	'81 Gale Force 33	95,000	'81 Hans Christian 43	150,000	'79 Bristol 45.5	185,000
'78 Westsail 32	55,000	'79 Pearson 424	85,000	'79 CSY 44PH	119,900	'80 Tayana 42	125,500	'78 Hinckley 49	299,000
'80 Morgan 38	55,000	'78 Cheoy Lee 41	75,000	'80 Cheoy Lee 41	89,900	'81 Pearson 530	185,000	'82 Gulfstar 60	345,000
'81 Pearson 365	50,000	'81 Cabo Rico 38	80,000	'80 Fisher 37	125,000	'80 Valiant 40	165,000		
'81 Sea Sprite 34	60,000	'79 Cal 39	67,500	'79 Gulfstar 43	83,900				
'75 Luders 33	45,000	'77 Valiant 40	65,000	80 Pearson 424	99,995	'76 Hinckley 43	159,000	'74 Alden Dolphin	189,000
'77 C&C 38	46,000	'76 Westsail 42	77,000	'73 Swan 44	116,500	'75 Gulfstar 50	126,500	'76 Nautical 56	395,000
'75 Columbia 45	54,900	'76 Gulfstar 43	75,000	'81 Morgan 46	95,000	'76 Morgan 51 Out Island	135,000	'73 Swan 65	525,000
'73 Irwin 45	58,000	'76 Islander 41	85,000	'76 Cheoy Lee 48	110,000	'77 Irwin 52	149,900	'76 Swan 50 MS	259,000
'75 Gulfstar 41	55,900	'73 Columbia 45	79,000	'76 Apache 41 Catamaran	100,000	'77 Solaris 42 Catamaran	139,000	'77 Hinckley SW 51	255,000
'75 Rasmus 35	45,000	'75 Tartan 41	79,900	'75 Gulfstar 50	97,500	'74 Alden Dolphin 47	145,000	'73 Hinckley 53	325,000
'76 Allied Princess 36	45,000	'72 Whitby 42	85,000	'76 Tartan 42	100,000				
'69 Cheoy Lee 36	48,000	'70 Morgan 42	72,500	'70 Hinckley 38	87,500	'72 Nicholson 48	118,000	'72 Hinckley B40	189,000
'70 Columbia 43	49,000	'72 Chance 44	69,000	'70 Hinckley B40	92,300	'71 Hinckley B40	129,500		
'70 Bristol 40	56,000	'70 Hinckley 35	64,500			'70 Concordia Cutter 45	167,000		
'67 Nicholson 45	55,000	'72 Swan 40	77,000			'71 Ericson 46	135,000		
'70 Banjer 37	62,500								
'72 Alberg 37	47,000								
'72 Allied Seabreeze 35	52,500								
'64 Chinook 34	49,800	'64 Krogen 42	69,500	'66 Hinckley Pilot 35	79,000			'67 Hinckley 48	259,000
'66 Morgan 34	49,500	'67 Morgan 45	74,900	'62 Lapworth 50	100,000				
'63 Hinckley SW 30	59,000	'60 Little Harbor 36	64,500						
'51 Concordia 39	59,000								
'60 Alden Challenger 38	49,000								

carry a premium, if they have been well-maintained and especially if they have been upgraded over the years.

At the least, the chart provides a handy reference for a reader who wants to narrow down the possibilities, to determine generally how much boat, new or used, he can expect to get for a budgeted amount of money.

• **PS**

Shopping for Financing

Banks may be tougher, but they can save you money.

Money for boat loans is relatively cheap as well as plentiful, but that doesn't mean it's easy to get. Banks and other lender, stung by their own loose lending practices of the 1980s and worried about the inherent equity of boats, are thoroughly checking both the would-be borrower's credit and the value and condition of the boats in question.

Some of this is the marine industry's own fault. Boat dealers, brokers and manufacturers for years perpetuated the myth that boats gain rather than lose value. That may have been true once, but no longer. Further, boat buyers, particularly sailboat buyers, were touted as superior credit risks, with an infinitesimal rate of default. That myth fell apart as boat owners, trapped in upside-down mortgages as the market bottomed and boat values plummeted, defaulted in droves in the late 1980s. A contributing factor was the inflation of a boat's true value by unscrupulous dealers (and customers) in order to obtain 100%, or even higher, financing during those anything-goes-days.

The good news is that interest rates are fairly low—about 8% for loans over $25,000 compared to 11%-12% just four years ago. Lenders are stricter about down payments, requiring 15% to 20% on new boats, 25% or more on used boats (BOAT/U.S. wants 30% on multihulls and houseboats).

In these times of low interest, most customers are choosing fixed rates at a slightly higher initial percentage on the premise that rates inevitably will be going up. Low variable rate "products" based on the prime rate are initially attractive, but predicting where your rate will be a few years down the road is a guessing game.

Some lenders won't lend below a minimum of $25,000, while others, such as BOAT/U.S., will make loans between $18,000-$25,000 at a rate of 10%. Lenders like the bigger loans because they prefer to work with boats that are documentable. While few lenders charge points or early payment penalties, many of the marine finance companies levy a hefty $400-$500 fee for a mandatory in-house documentation process. Surveys on used boats can run another $6-$10 a foot, but you often can choose your own surveyor. Some companies also charge a closing fee.

Banks

So what's the best route for obtaining a boat mortgage? One large brokerage house we spoke with suggested making your first trip to the bank. Banks might require a higher down payment, usually 20%, but that can work to your advantage.

"Boats really will depreciate no matter what you do with them," the broker said. "With a low down payment, if you want to sell, the principle isn't down enough—there's all that front-end interest."

In other words, instead of having equity at the time of the sale, you owe the bank.

Banks may limit your loan period to 10 years as opposed to the 15- or even 20-year terms allowed by marine lenders. Again, this can be a blessing.

Buyers often place too much emphasis on monthly payments rather than the overall cost of the loan, said Greg Proteau, executive director of the National Marine Bankers Association. Reducing your term by 40% or 50% can mean big savings, even at higher interest rates. Those who obtained loans at higher rates several years ago might want to refinance if they haven't already done so. Terms are usually the same as for new loans, including rate and minimum balance. Some firms report that about one-third of their current business is refinancing.

Banks also have more flexible ways to finance. Home equity loan rates usually are significantly lower than those offered through marine lenders. Equity loans or equity lines of credit can start as low as 7% (6% on a variable rate), but much of this is tax deductible if your boat doesn't qualify for a second home deduction.

One banker told us the variable rate, at 6% for one year, rising to about 8% after that, makes sense if a customer plans to sell or trade up in five years or so. Marine specialists are unanimous in saying that the average life of a boat loan is four to five years. Another advantage to borrowing on home equity is that there's no need to pay costly documentation fees or for a redundant survey.

Finally, banks may set fairly low maximums on boat loans ($49,999 in one case, or 25' or 5 tons), but they will spring for the smaller loan that the marine lenders won't touch. But, cautioned Proteau, because interest rates in general are so low, and because boats can depreciate rapidly, it doesn't make sense to take a big bite of equity out of your primary home.

Before you can get a loan, the bank (and other lenders) will conduct a fairly thorough credit search. Generally, they will want to see copies of your last two 1040 income tax returns, complete with schedules; self-employed persons will be asked for copies of their company's current balance sheet, income statement and tax returns; some will require a current pay stub.

One problem with banks mentioned to us by several brokers and dealers was their reliance on the BUC Used Boat Price Guide. The problem, they said, was that BUC recently has been undervaluing some boat models, being slow to recognize the upturn in the boat market that began about 12 months ago. As a result, banks were declining to finance the 80% of the boat's value some borrowers needed and deals were being lost.

Walter Sullivan, BUC president, defends the overall accuracy of his price guide, although he did acknowledge that prices had gone up after the publication of his 1992 edition. At any rate, the latest BUC editions are supposed to reflect the return of price stability to the boat market.

Marine Finance Companies

Familiarity with the ins and outs of boats is one reason marine lending specialists say you should seek them out for a loan. In a borderline situation, where a bank is equivocating, a recognized marine lender, such as Essex Credit, can "bring comfort to a deal that might not otherwise be done," said Proteau.

Marine lenders are essentially mortgage brokers, who obtain money from other sources and collect a fee for bringing in the business. A large firm, such as Essex, which does $10 to $15 million a month in boat loans, might use its own money to finance a purchase, make out a check to the seller, then sell off your loan to a third party just before closing. According to Alan Swimmer of Essex' home office in Connecticut, the sheer size of the company and the number of banks it deals with helps keep rates low.

Essex will pre-qualify buyers, checking out their income, debt and net worth.

"This tells us how much boat (a customer) can afford to buy," Swimmer said.

Once a boat is found, a more thorough financial search is conducted, basically to determine whether the customer can afford the down payment as well as the monthly terms. If Essex is satisfied, it will issue a credit commitment, which is basically a promise to close the loan. For new boats, the process can take three days, a week or so for used boats, which must undergo a lien search. Although many insurers don't require a survey until a boat is 10 years old, Essex wants one on all boats older than three years.

"It's cheap insurance," Swimmer says.

Some dealers or manufacturers may offer their own financing, touting quick approval and one-stop shopping; as with auto financing, this convenience is apt to cost you.

At last fall's Newport International Boat Show, we saw one couple get captivated by a 35-footer. Off they rushed to the nearest marine lender's booth to sign up for a loan. Chances are their thoughts were more on the boat than on getting the best financing deal by shopping around.

Conclusion

All the experts, including the lenders themselves, advise the customer to shop around, get all the options, read the fine print and then make a rational decision. Ideally, you'll do this long before you go boat shopping (lenders often will lock in a rate for 60 days).

Check first with your bank to determine the feasibility of a home equity loan as well as standard boat loan rates. Then compare their figures with those of a well-established marine lender, such as Essex and BOAT/U.S.

Like home mortgages, shopping for money deserves the same level of research, care and attention as choosing the boat itself. Fortunately, boat loans are easier to process, plus there are no points or closing costs. **• PS**

The Costs of Ownership

Okay, so you've bought it— now what?

This book is full of information about the going prices for boats of many sizes and types, but the money a boat costs to buy is only the beginning. The old adage about a boat being a hole in the water into which one throws money is as true now as it ever was. Between replacement of old, worn out gear (of particular interest to someone buying a used boat), insurance, slip or mooring fees, surveys, and the like, the actual cost of buying a used boat can add up to considerably more than the asking price.

How much any boat owner spends on his boat is dependent upon a lot of factors: type (and construction) of his boat, who does the work, the owner's degree of involvement, how the boat is used, the age and basic condition of the boat and her size and complexity. Not to mention where she's based—remember, everything costs more in Newport than it does in New London.

Certain generalities apply. Fiberglass boats cost less than boats made of other materials, especially wood. New boats are cheaper to maintain than older boats. Smaller boats are proportionately less expensive than larger boats. It takes more money to race than to cruise. Sailing experience saves money. The better built the boat, the lower the annual costs are relative to value.

To these simple generalities we might add another: compared to other endeavors and forms of equity, there is nothing economical about owning a boat.

A couple of these generalities seem to beg for explanation. First of all, smaller-sized boats owned by those who are experienced and handy mean than maintenance can be of the do-it-yourself variety. Boatyard labor rates are now routinely in excess of $30-$35 per hours and the help working on boats in those yards may be less qualified than the average boat owner. What these workers do have is time, equipment, and their choice of weather to work in. Many owners favor the argument that they can make more money doing their job than they can save by doing their own boat work. But invariably that choice runs up costs.

A second observation about the generalities is that they presuppose a boat owner maintains his boat in order to retain his equity. The more money he has invested in his boat, the more he is likely to be willing to spend to protect that investment. That is why better quality boats can take more money than lower quality craft. Yet quality does beget some savings; stapled drawer slides are apt to need repair before molded plastic drawers, for example.

The variable that is impossible to predict is the intangible personal taste of the boat owner, which is a direct determinant of owner involvement. Some owners are fussier than others.

There are three costs associated with boats: the initial purchase price (with or without financing charges), the annual cost of recurring maintenance that represents the basic cost of owning and using a boat, and, finally, the more or less optional expense of upgrading a boat.

So what items should be included in estimating these costs? Those we include are the following:

• **Insurance:** Premiums normally run about 2% of the value of the boat, and have risen precipitously in recent years; they can be considerably higher. This includes property and personal liability, and damage to the boat. The premium rate will depend on the experience of the owner, the geographical range the policy covers, the amount of time the boat is in commission, the extent of coverage, the amount of the deductible, the underwriters' evaluation of the degree of risk, and the probable cost of repairs. It usually does not pay to under-insure in order to reduce premium costs, but it may pay to increase the amount of the deductible, especially for an owner who does much of his own work or is savvy about contracting for work to be done. Remember, it pays to shop around for insurance. As a start, call one of the underwriters that specialize in boats, like Avemco.

• **Dockage or mooring:** Usually this is a figure related to length, but it may include yacht club dues, launch service or dinghy storage, trailer registration and insurance, and a number of other items apart from the fee for the boat herself. Be prepared, of course, to spend far more for a slip than for a mooring. The difference even for a small boat can be several hundred dollars, often putting a slip out of reach. Still, some marina managers are open to negotiation: we know a person who recently bought his first boat, and was able to negotiate the use of a slip for the first year at the mooring rate—thus saving several hun-

15 Ways to Keep Down the Annual Costs of Boat Ownership

• **Choose a boat with annual costs in mind.** For instance, darker colored topsides may be more attractive on a given boat, but they'll deteriorate faster. Also, remember that simple boats are cheaper to keep than complex ones, and can be just as much fun.

• **Develop a habit of regular routine maintenance.** This will not only make your gear last longer, it can keep you from having a real emergency on the water when a critical gilhickie lets go at the wrong moment.

• **Do the routine boat work yourself.** Why pay a worker of possibly dubious skill and questionable motivation a king's ransom to so simple a job?

• **Protect the boat during off-season storage.** Unstepping the mast and covering the boat will eventually save more than it costs.

• **Shop for price.** Take advantage of discounts, volume purchasing, group or co-op buying, used gear bargains, etc. Consider alternate sources for supplies—don't buy everything at a marine outfitters: a sponge is a sponge, and it costs a lot less at Wal-Mart than at a marine outfitters. Periodically compare boatyard and marina prices and insurance premiums.

• **Consider backyard storage:** There are obvious limits here, but if you can pull it off, you can save a bundle at the cost of considerable inconvenience.

• **Check your engine:** This includes the oil level (and changes!), water intake, exhaust, belts, etc.

• **Give a work order to the boatyard as early as possible:** Many owners wait until the last minute, producing a crunch at the boatyard. Get your instructions in early, and you may not only get better service, but save money as well.

• **Make use of winter evenings:** Many of the jobs that need doing can be done at home.

• **Set limits on the cost of work:** Give the boatyard a price limit and insist that they notify you if they exceed it. It pays here to be as familiar as you can with your equipment to avoid getting ripped off.

• **Insure the boat for its fair market value:** Also, set the deductible as high as you can stand to keep premium costs down.

• **Be on hand for mast stepping and unstepping:** Much of the cost here is for tasks you can perform yourself, like tuning the rig.

• **Protect your sails:** Keep your mainsail covered and your headsails below. Protect them from flogging, salt and abuse.

• **Plan major purchases and yard work in advance:** This can help you prepare your boat (and bank account) accordingly.

• **Know what your recurring costs are:** Set a budget and keep an eye on what you really spend on the boat. It's easy to let things slide, and you'll end up wondering where all the money went.

Finally, remember that using your boat won't lower the costs of her upkeep, but it sure will go a long way towards justifying them.

---

dred dollars. How the boat is kept can make a big difference in how much use it gets: you're far more likely to go for an evening sail after work if you don't have to row a dinghy out to a mooring to get at the boat.

• **Handling, storage and launching:** This is a figure that can vary widely. However, $15-$20 per foot is a fair starting point. If the boat is handled by a boatyard, it can make the owner's job easier by simply checking off those jobs the yard does for decommissioning: winterizing the engine and head, spar storage, battery charging, frame erection, etc. However, while checking them off is easy, writing a check to pay for them is not; you pay a lot for the convenience of having somebody else do the dirty work, and this can up your costs by fifty percent. If you have a boat that's small enough and the trucking distance is reasonable, backyard storage can be cheaper than boatyard storage.

• **Maintenance:** Also a widely varying figure depending on where supplies are purchased, whether routine maintenance work is done by the owner or is contracted for, and other variables. It is also a cost that can be affected by efforts to protect the boat, thereby reducing the amount of maintenance she requires. When estimating the cost of routine maintenance, do not forget the bill from the sailmaker for washing, checking, and repairing sails, travel expenses to and from a boatyard, and the cost of an engine tune-up—items easily overlooked in any flight from fiscal reality. Be sure to check the labor rates at the local boat yards before you decide to make a purchase. It's a good idea to set up a reserve fund to pay for items that you know are going to need replacing or refurbishing in the future: set aside a certain amount each month so that when it comes time to replace the sails or paint the bottom the money will be there. It can help to "rent" the boat from yourself: that is, figure out how much it should cost you to actually use the boat for a day, and put that much into your account every day you sail.

• **Taxes, fees, and the like:** Property taxes, mooring taxes, registration fees, rating certificate renewals, documentation renewal fees, etc. all have to be figured into any total, as does membership in a yacht club. Of course, these fees are different in different areas of the country, and in some areas certain one may not apply. Check with the state DOT and your local boat yard to get a handle on these costs.

• **Depreciation:** Ten years ago owners often saw their boats appreciating in value along with an inflationary economy. You'll note that many of the price charts in this book show a characteristic "hump," and almost all of the boats we've reviewed are steadily falling in value, in keeping with the continuing recession. However, the recession won't last forever (we hope), and historically boats tend to maintain their value over the long term. For those items such as electronics, outboard motors, sails, inflatable tenders and so forth that require periodic replacement, a 10-year or less depreciation schedule can be used. Few owners consider this as a real cost, but it can add up to between 3 and 5 percent of the value of the boat each year.

Obviously many boat owners have found ways—real or imagined—to shave the total annual expense of their boats.

One owner we know quoted us a very low figure for the upkeep of his 40-footer: he left out the cost of dockage because it was included in his condominium maintenance fee, making it a "household" rather than a "boating" expense.

Despite such ploys and self-deceptions, it still seems reasonable to believe that the recurring expenses of any boat over the size of a daysailer are likely to exceed 8-10% of the value of the boat. For owners who depend on boatyards to do their outfitting and use commercial facilities for dockage, the realistic total has to be closer to 15, even 20%, especially if gear depreciation is included.

There are, of course, other costs, such as the addition of gear and modification to the boat to increase her usefulness and, presumably, her value. These are not recurring costs *per se,* and they can be as high as your pockets are deep.　　**• PS**

Buying Guide
-
Gear

Ground Tackle

Overall winners in our tests were the Fortress, Danforth Hi-Tensile, and Delta.

During the last decade, there have been con ducted a number of anchor tests, more than at any time in history. Some have been done by anchor makers and must be scrutinized most carefully, but many others have been managed independently and give more objective information than has been available before.

Unfortunately, none of the tests can be considered the final word on anchors. But taken all together, they do offer the boat owner good information that can be used as the basis for deciding which anchor to buy and what size is appropriate.

Heree take a look at the test information, supplemented by some trials of our own, and present what we think are the best conclusions possible, given the current state of knowledge on anchors.

The Tests:

We gathered together the results of the following tests:

The APAVE French Tests. These were conducted at the request of the makers of Britany anchors, by APAVE (the "Western Association of Steam and Electric Appliances"), an independent organization somewhat like Underwriters' Laboratories in this country. The test results were written up by Alain Connan of the Sailing School, but so far have not been published in an English translation. Don Bamford's book *Anchoring* has an adequate summary.

Tests by Robert A. Smith, NA. These were conducted in Oregon over a long period of time, using a Cascade 27 sailboat in the Columbia River. The test results have been published in Smith's book *Anchors: Selection and Use.* Danforth Standard and High-Tensile (lightweight types), CQR, Bruce, Northill, FOB, Benson, and Forfjord anchors were tested originally, and Smith's testing is on-going. He shared with us preliminary results of tests on the Danforth Plow, Delta, and Fortress anchors.

Navy Tests. The Naval Civil Engineering Laboratory in California has conducted a long series of tests over the years, primarily dealing with large anchors suitable for ships. Many of these tests were the basis for published information on Danforth anchors before the 1980s.

More recently, the Navy conducted tests in Chesapeake Bay (1987) and near Norfolk, Virginia (1989), as part of the Navy's Landing Craft Air Cushion (LCAC) program. The purpose of these tests, in general, was to compare newly available anchors—particularly the Danforth Deepset models and the Fortress aluminum anchors—to existing anchors used by the Navy.

Fortress Anchor Tests. As promotion for their recently introduced aluminum anchors, the Nav-X Corporation sponsored two tests, one in Florida and one in California. The tests, to measure holding power, were observed by a number of anchoring authorities and members of the press.

Bruce, CQR, Danforth Standard and Deepset models, Fortress, Sentinel (U.S. Anchor's Danforth-type anchor), and Delta anchors were tested for comparative holding power, through six pulls. Several other anchors—the Pekny (a Northill-type), Davis Sea Hook, Creative Marine's Max Anchor, Danforth Plow, and Plastimo Plow—also had one or two pull-tests done, but were not included in the regular cycle of tests. The results were published by the makers of Fortress anchors. The California tests were co-sponsored by West Marine Products and looked particularly at anchoring in soft mud. The results of those tests were also written up in a report by Chuck Hawley of West Marine.

Dutch Tests. A series of anchor tests were conducted for the Dutch *Watersport Journal* and published early in 1990. The tests were designed and supervised by Rob van den Haak of Vryhof Anchors, the Dutch manufacturer of anchors.

The tests were conducted in an "anchor box," a huge box filled with sand, with a layer of water on top. The sand was "re-packed" with a "vibrating needle" after each test, and the pull speed and setting procedures were virtually identical, to equalize the test environment for each anchor. These tests generally come closest to rigorous scientific procedure of any tests done.

Strength Tests. A series of tests were conducted by

BOAT/U.S. and *Cruising World* magazine. These tests did not evaluate holding power of the anchors at all but instead concentrated on the physical strength of the anchors. While interesting, the tests indicate that—with a few noteworthy exceptions—available anchors have breaking strengths greatly in excess of their holding power.

Danforth Tests. In 1988, Danforth conducted a series of three tests in San Francisco Bay, measuring the holding power of six anchors: two Danforth light-weight fluke anchors, two Danforth Plows, a Bruce, and a CQR. Weights varied from 13 to 35 pounds, and the anchors were tested in two different locations, one with a sand bottom and one with mud. Anchors were tested on short scope (2.5 to 1) as well as more normal scope (5 to 1). The results were published in *Cruising World*, in May, 1989.

Simpson-Lawrence Tests. Simpson-Lawrence, maker of the CQR plow, conducted tests in June, 1987, comparing their plow to a Danforth Standard, a Danforth Hi-Tensile, and a Bruce, all weighing between 20 and 25 pounds. The tests were conducted, according to the company, because recent tests (in which the CQR did not fare well) were unlike real anchoring situations. In addition to straight-line pull tests, a "veer" test was conducted in which the anchor was set and then the pull direction was changed 90 degrees and then 180 degrees, to evaluate resetting ability. Divers observed and photographed the anchors on the bottom. The results were summarized in the English magazine *Yachting Monthly* in 1988, and a shorter version reprinted a year and a half later in *Cruising World*.

RNLI Tests. In England, the Royal National Lifeboat Institution (RNLI) conducted a series of tests over the last decade, as part of their continuing examination of available anchors for equipping their lifeboats.

The principal tests were two trials, the first at Oban, where five 20-kg. anchors were compared in five "bottoms" over a five-day period, and the second at Weymouth, where five types of anchor—the fisherman, Danforth, Bruce, CQR, and Delta—were trialed in calm weather, and then later the fisherman and Delta were tested in rough weather. These tests followed some experiments done with miniature models of 10 different anchors in a "Model Anchor Tank" at the Hasler Admiralty Research Establishment.

Unlike most anchor tests, the RNLI lowered the anchors using a "running drop" with the boat drifting rapidly as might happen when they were executing a rescue. They also conducted tests using a more typical kind of yachtsman's drop, with the boat standing still or moving very slowly backwards. The results of the tests were printed in a technical paper, presented to a conference on "Surveillance, Pilot, and Rescue Craft for the 21st Century," early in 1990, and summarized last July in an English magazine, *Practical Boatowner*.

Checking The Tests

During the summer and fall of 1990, we performed a series of "checking tests," basically to see if we could replicate the findings of some of the tests, particularly findings that stood out as peculiar. We set and measured the resistance of a Fortress, a Danforth Deepset, a Bruce, an "old" Danforth Hi-Tensile, a "new" Danforth Hi-Tensile, and a Viking aluminum, and tried to evaluate their resetting ability. The tests were in two different bottoms—one sand and one mud—in Muskegon Lake, with a series of three pulls each. Later we repeated the pulls, adding to our tests a new Simpson-Lawrence Delta anchor, a new Max anchor from Creative Marine, an older Northill, and a "no-name" Danforth imitation.

This was all done following an eight-week cruise, in which we anchored 54 times, in a variety of bottoms, observing the characteristics of different types, frequently diving on the anchors to examine how they had set and frequently breaking them out by simulating big wind shifts. In setting the anchors, we observed the anchors' behavior from the dinghy when the water was sufficiently clear and shallow—about half the times. We "lived our tests," dragging anchor three times at night and often setting and resetting repeatedly to get a secure hold.

We also checked most of the available printed comments on anchors and anchoring, including such things as the American Boat and Yacht Council recommendations, and the recommendations of accepted authorities of both power and sail—such as Eric Hiscock, Donald Street, Elbert Maloney, Robert Ogg—and the anchoring books by Don Bamford, Brian Fagan, Alain Gree, Earl Hinz, Alain Peuch, and Robert Smith. We also surveyed all of the literature available from the anchor manufacturers.

The Trouble with Tests

The primary interests of the boat owner are the capability of the anchor 1) to be set easily, 2) to hold onto the bottom, 3) to reset following a wind or tide shift, 4) to be retrieved, and 5) to be stowed.

The primary interest of almost all of the tests has been number 2—the holding ability of the anchor. One test considered as a secondary matter number 3—the reset ability. The other capabilities are considered only in the most incidental way.

Our own trials demonstrated to us very clearly that there are differences in these other capabilities. Though we reached a few subjective conclusions about these other capabilities, it is to be hoped that more extensives studies can be undertaken, particularly with regard to setting and resetting.

However, there are problems even with the most studied capabilities—the holding power. Typically, in all the published tests, an anchor is set in the bottom two or three or six times, the anchor rode is pulled, and the point at which the anchor drags or breaks loose is measured, usually in pounds of force. Then an average figure for the pulls is calculated, and that number is listed as the holding power of the anchor.

If you look at the data rather than these simple conclusions, things are not quite so precise as published figures often appear. In the French tests, for example, the holding power of 26-pound Britany anchors (a lightweight-type) varied from 198 pounds to 2,028 pounds; a 22-pound Bruce varied from 165 pounds to 661 pounds, and a 25-pound CQR plow varied from 226 pounds to 1,102 pounds. All of these were in the same patch of water, with a bottom described as "uniform, good sand."

Similarly, in one of the Fortress tests, a Danforth Deepset's holding power in mud varied from 400 to 1,050 pounds; a Delta varied from 125 pounds to 625 pounds; and a Fortress from 525 to 1,325 pounds.

In our own tests, a new Danforth H-1500 with a nominal holding power of 1,500 pounds tested out all over the scale between 360 and 1,270 pounds, while a new Max anchor showed even greater variation—from 275 to well over 2,500 pounds, beyond our ability to measure.

Such gross variations are not at all unusual in holding-power tests; in fact they are quite typical. The most carefully controlled tests—those by the Dutch—intended at first to do a second pull to verify the first, planning on more only if the second tests varied by more than 10 percent from the first tests. As it developed, all anchors had to be tested on a third pull, and most on a fourth. The testers thought that the anchor rode was messing up the results and repeated some of the tests with a wire cable of small diameter rather than chain. Finally, they used figures for "mean" holding power in order to compare the anchors' abilities.

The science of statistics, of course, involves using lots of bad information to arrive at more accurate information. We spent considerable time plotting and trying to analyze all of the results from all of the different tests available—all to little avail. Below, we include a table which summarizes our findings, but we present the information with a great many cautions and qualifications, believing that accurate and defensible conclusions about usable holding power can be made only by imposing lots of subjective judgments on the available information. Among the qualifications are the following.

• Exactly what "holding" means is not at all clear or uniform in the tests. Many sailors think of anchors as simply sticking into the bottom and then remaining exactly in place until broken out. However, when anchors are actually observed under pull, it is clear that they all "move" through the bottom material. Some move more, some less, some "roll" or "dive" or "overturn" or "rear up," some "spiral" or "rotate," some "hobbyhorse," and so on. There seems to be no agreement on such terminology. An anchor might break one fluke out, for example, and the holding power (perhaps "resistance" would be a better term) will be cut in half. But the fluke begins to catch again, and holding power increases.

• Almost all measurements of tests are made "dead in line," yet holding power will vary significantly with the angle of pull, and an anchor will often show significantly different holding power immediately after resetting. On the other hand, changes in holding power often seem simply to be changes in the bottom consistency—what the texture of the mud or sand is.

Holding Power

Given all of the above qualifiers, we have attempted to rank the holding power of various anchor types, by size. The ranking is intended as a relative representation of holding power in good conditions, with an adequate scope and good bottom. The numbers are a simple arithmetical calculation from all the figures we collected. Comments on the individual anchors will appear in Part 2 of this article, and are intended to qualify the ranking.

The following list is from least holding power to greatest. The base number of 1 refers to the holding power of a traditional fisherman type (sometimes called a kedge or yachtsman's) anchor. A rating of 2 would indicate twice the holding power of a fisherman of the same size, a 3 would be three times the holding power of a fisherman, and so forth.

Anchor	Holding Power
Folding (grapnel)	0.6
Fisherman	1.0
Northill	1.1
CQR plow	2.4
Danforth plow	2.5
Bruce	2.5
Delta	2.7
Max (Creative Marine)	5.1
Danforth Standard	5.2
Danforth Deepset (Std)	5.2
Danforth Deepset (Hi-T)	5.4
Danforth Hi-Tensile	5.5
Fortress	5.6

The table represents anchors of approximately comparable physical size. If weight alone is considered (that is, if fluke size were ignored), the table would be almost exactly identical, except that the Fortress would have a considerably higher ranking—approximately 9.8—due to its aluminum construction.

Now we'll take a detailed look at individual anchor types and models.

Folding

The folding or grapnel-type anchor is useless for general anchoring purposes. If boaters know that they will have to anchor occasionally in rock, a folding grapnel might be worth considering for its compact stowage, but other anchor types are better even for that specialized situation.

Fisherman

The traditional fisherman or yachtsman's anchor is not commonly used as a primary anchor, but is nonetheless still worth considering.

The main problem with the fisherman is its small flukes. In order to achieve adequate holding power in typical sand, mud, or clay bottoms, very large-size anchors have to be carried. For example, a boat that might use a 35-pound CQR plow would have to carry a fisherman's anchor of over 100 pounds to get comparable holding in soft bottoms.

Not only is the weight a problem, but on boats without a long bowsprit the anchors are difficult to drop and bring back onboard without damaging the topsides, and they have to be disassembled to stow. Also, because the stock is perpendicular to the flukes and only one fluke is normally buried in the bottom, the anchor rode can easily be fouled on the stock or the exposed fluke after a wind or tide shift.

On the positive side, the fisherman anchor performs as well or better than a CQR, Bruce, or lightweight-type in pebble or "shingle" bottoms, and it can be used effectively in rock or coral where many other anchors do not work at all. Its weight can also be an advantage in penetrating thick seaweed.

In sizing, the traditional rule of thumb is two-pounds of anchor for every foot of waterline length (eg., a 60-pound anchor for a 30-foot waterline boat).

In this country, the Luke Storm anchor is a good representative of the type. All the other fishermen-type anchors we examined were oriental imports and varied considerably in quality and in fluke shape and size.

Northill

The sailor will have difficulty these days finding a Northill-type anchor to buy, though the Pekny is similar. Since its performance and characteristics are similar to the fisherman type and it offers no advantages, there seems little to recommend this type of anchor.

CQR

This plow-type anchor is made by Simpson-Lawrence, an English company, and the anchor is widely used in this country as well as in Europe. We suspect the ease of stowing it on a small bowsprit or bow roller is partly responsible for its popularity. All tests except those sponsored by the company indicate that its holding power is quite low relative to its weight. For reasons we cannot explain, the CQR does well in tests by the English, even those not sponsored by the manufacturer.

It is interesting to us that most tests of the CQR were done with shorter lengths of chain in the anchor rode than the 18-feet length that the company recommends. In our own cruising experience with a CQR, we were initially very disappointed in the anchor's performance, with only six feet of chain between the nylon rode and the anchor. After adding 12 more feet for a total of 18 feet of chain, it performed much better.

There are a number of claims for the CQR, both from the company and from dedicated users. One is that the pivoting shank of the CQR helps the anchor hold when the pull is not dead on. Another has to do with the structural integrity of the anchor, which also seems true.

Beyond these, it's hard to find any evidence in any of the tests for any other claims of superior performance by the CQR. In fact, the tests tend to make the anchor seem quite ordinary, with some peculiar habits of plowing through softer bottoms rather than burying deep, and twisting out of the bottom under strain or changing pull directions. Generally, the firmer the bottom, the better the anchor performs relative to the lightweight-type anchors; the softer the bottom, the worse the anchor performs relative to the lightweight types. Only in tests in gravelly bottoms does the CQR perform as well, and then not all the time.

It is often said that the CQR will reset better than other anchors after it has broken loose by a tide or wind shift. However, we tried a dozen resets at 90-degrees, comparing it with a Danforth Deepset, and could not conclude superiority for either anchor. Visually, the Danforth would carry a ball of bottom soil between its flukes, which seemed to impede resetting. On the other hand, the CQR often dragged along the bottom for quite a distance before beginning to dig in.

In spite of the mediocre showing of the tests, anecdotal reports from CQR users, including our *Practical Sailor* reader survey, generally indicate satisfaction with the anchor. It may be that the CQR performs adequately over a wide range of bottom conditions. Other anchors are much superior in specific bottoms, but overall the CQR proves satisfactory to these users.

Nonetheless, based on the tests and what we've experienced with the anchor, we would be hesitant to recommend the CQR to a new sailor. For choosing the correct size CQR, the company's recommendations on size are reliable, though a bit on the small side. If your boat is near one of the breakpoints, choose the larger anchor.

Danforth Plow

The Danforth plow is comparable to the CQR, and our thoughts on the CQR apply to it as well. Overall, tests show that the Danforth performs slightly better in terms of holding ability than the CQR. However, our judgment is that its construction is noticeably inferior to the CQR, particularly the pivot pin. For us, that makes it a toss-up with the CQR.

Delta

The Delta is a new plow-type design from Simpson-Lawrence. It bears a resemblance to the CQR but is one-piece with no pivoting hinge, and there are a number of other minor differences in design.

The tests done so far indicate that the Delta is somewhat superior in holding power to the CQR, though the limited testing at this point shows a wide range of results. Our own brief trials found it to be far better in mud but only slightly better in sand. Interestingly, in the reset tests we did, the Delta was noticeably the best at resetting once it had broken loose. In the RNLI tests, its performance was exceptional, showing greater holding power in clay and sand than even the Danforth.

The Delta is also a well-made anchor, and with a weighted plow tip it requires no assistance to drop smoothly from a bow roller. On the bottom, it tends to roll itself over into the dig-in position immediately, even with no pull on the anchor line. It also is easily retrieved over a bow roller, unlike the other plows which almost always require horsing the pivoting joint back on board.

Though there is very little experience with this anchor aboard actual boats thus far, we are impressed enough with it that we would recommend it over the CQR. In soft bottoms, it lacks the high holding power of the lightweight types, but it can be launched and retrieved easily over a bow-roller, and is a good choice for those sailors who demand that convenience.

The company's recommendations with regard to size are reasonable, though on the low side. If your boat is near a break-point, choose the next larger size.

Bruce

The Bruce is peculiar in that test results show its holding power to be low, yet users are almost universally pleased with the anchor's performance. Our own *Practical Sailor* survey showed that users had a more favorable opinion of the Bruce than of any other anchor, though it was also true that the Bruce owners didn't anchor as often as others.

Some tests show the Bruce to have significantly less holding power than a CQR; others show as much or significantly more. Unlike other anchors, it does not seem to be the bottom material that is the cause for the better or worse showing.

We have used the Bruce a number of times while cruising, but two middle-of-the-night fire drills caused by dragging led us to retire the anchor from regular use. Based on holding power tests, we think the company's recommendations on size are somewhat small.

It is often said that the Bruce sets more easily than other anchors and that it is better on shorter scope than other anchors. Tests do not indicate either of these claims to be true. We also found that its ability to reset after being tripped was about average.

On the positive side, the Bruce is physically a well-made anchor. And of course, it stows well on a bow roller and is launched and retrieved quite easily.

Based on tests results alone, we cannot recommend the Bruce strongly. However, owner reports are sufficiently positive that we cannot criticize the Bruce strongly either.

Max

The Max is a new anchor from Creative Marine, a company new on the anchor scene. In design, it is closest to the Bruce, though its flukes are much larger. The shank is also adjustable to three different settings, so that the angle between the shank and the flukes can be adjusted for different bottom conditions. As far as we know, the anchor has been tested only in San Francisco mud and in Michigan mud and sand, and there are no indications how it would perform in clay or less desirable bottoms.

The anchor we tested was one of the first off the production line. The anchor appears well made and should be as strong as the Delta and the Bruce.

When we talked to the company, they recommended a Model 20 as being comparably sized to the other anchors we were testing, such as the Delta 22 and the Danforth 20-H. But the 20 turned out to refer to inches rather than pounds. The anchor weighed 36 pounds, by far the heaviest we tested.

Its greater holding power, compared to the Bruce and the Delta, seems to come mostly from the great increase in fluke size. The flukes look like an enormous scoop shovel. In terms of holding power alone, the anchor seems to be worth considering, and the adjustability of the flukes means that the angle can be increased when you know you are anchoring in very soft mud.

On the negative side, the anchor is very awkward. Because of its big flukes, it would not fit in a bow roller that held a 35-pound CQR, and we are not sure what kind of arrangement would be necessary to make the anchor easy to launch and retrieve, except a long bowsprit.

In setting, we observed that the anchor performed much like the Bruce, normally lying on its side and then turning to dig in. The Max, though, frequently moved longer distances before it started to dig in. It's ability to reset also was similar to the Bruce.

Given the limited experience, we are hesitant to recommend the Max. It does generate much greater holding power in good bottoms, relative to similar anchors such as the Delta and Bruce, but its large flukes make storage, launch, and retrieval problematic. If that problem can be solved, the anchor is worth considering. It should be slightly better than the Bruce or Delta as an all-purpose anchor. At this point, few stores or catalogs carry it.

Danforth

The term "Danforth" is often used generically, but the more proper generic term is "lightweight type," indicating an anchor with long and relatively thin flukes that bury in the bottom, and with a round rod at the base of the flukes in place of a stock. Danforth is a brand name for the lightweight anchors now being manufactured by Rule Industries, Inc. The Danforths have been the most popular of the lightweight types, but a growing list of imitators has appeared.

For a number of years, the most popular Danforth models were the Standard and the Hi-Tensile. Five years ago, the company introduced a new line called the Deepset Standard and the Deepset Hi-Tensile, while maintaining the two original models, and last year it added a VSB (for "very soft bottom") version.

The Danforth became virtually a standard among the lightweights for good reason. Its light weight made it easy to handle and stow relative to other anchors, and its holding power was remarkably high in the right bottom conditions—soft clay, sand, or mud. Such bottoms are very typical of a majority of coastal anchorages where centuries of rain and run off have deposited layers of eroded soil for the anchor to dig into. On the negative side, the Danforth tests out as pretty useless in hard clay, gravel, or rock, and its light weight and broad flukes can actually become handicaps when weeds cover the bottom and the anchor must penetrate them in order to dig in.

The available tests seem to indicate that the old Danforth Hi-Tensile is the best of the lot—only tests sponsored by the manufacturer show that the newer Deepset models are superior.

According to company literature, the superior holding power of the Deepset models comes from the thinner, more-flexible shank. In the older models, a thicker shank, theoretically, keeps the anchor from penetrating the bottom as well. By thinning the shank, penetrating ability was greatly increased. This was demonstrated very well in large anchors, and it is puzzling why tests of the smaller, yacht-size anchors do not bear this out. Our own tests showed that an old (and well-used) 12-H was consistently as good as or better than the new Deepset Hi-Tensile T-3000, though the nominal holding power of the Deepset was triple that of the old 12-H.

Part of it may be that the thin shank of the Deepset could be effective but the thinness is offset by the shackle and chain that everyone carries with a Danforth. The Dutch tests demonstrated that the chain used for the rode decreased holding power, and that, when a thinner cable was substituted for the chain, holding power of the anchors was generally improved.

Impressed by the performance of the 12-H, we bought a new 20-H so that we could compare it with the Deepset T-3000, to which it was closer in size. When the new 20-H arrived we were shocked to discover that the design and construction had been changed significantly from that of the original 20-H. And, in fact, the holding power of the new 20-H proved more erratic in our tests, compared to the old 12-H.

In design, the new 20-H was noticeably different in that the stock is noticeably shorter than on older 20-Hs. Both the French and the Dutch tests suggest that the length of the stock is important to holding power, since one of the most common ways the lightweight-types break loose is by rotating or twisting out of the bottom. The French tests had shown that Britany anchors with rod-extenders held better than those with shorter rods.

We called Rule Industries and basically got a non-answer to our inquiry of why the stock had been shortened, though they did point out that it would make the anchor easier to handle on deck. We have also heard that boat manufacturers wanted it shortened to better fit in-deck anchor wells.

The welds were sloppy, the eyes for the shackle cut roughly and irregularly, and the finish poorer. When we examined them closely, we discovered what we consider a general quality-control problem. It was most significant, we think, in that the fluke angle, which is controlled by the way the head is welded on, varied as much as seven degrees in different anchors. This in itself may be enough to degrade performance.

On examining other tests, we found other comments critical of the newer Danforths. The Navy tests in 1989, for example, tried a Hi-Tensile anchor (H-3600) and "bent the flukes." They found the Deepset anchors they tested "structurally limited in their holding capacity." With the first T-6000 tested, "both the flukes and the stock were broken." The second T-6000 "failed at a weld between the crown and one of the flukes." The Navy found that the anchors "generally did not set quickly or easily."

The Navy also tested a Danforth T-7000. At the end of the first test (in which they got a maximum holding capacity of 2700 pounds) they said "the flukes were spread slightly and the stock was slightly bent." On the second test, "the anchor structurally failed under a 6,100-pound pull. The failure occurred at a weld between the crown and one of the flukes." They tried another T-7000 which held to only 4,300 pounds because "upon retrieval, the anchor's shank was found to be bent about 40 degrees to one side."

Granted, these were big anchors and the Navy doesn't mess around with light pulls. Yet the Fortress anchors in the same test withstood pulls more than double those on the Danforths and only suffered minor bending of the stock and shank.

Of the major-brand anchors in the BOAT/U.S.-*Cruising World* strength tests, only the Danforth S-1600 and the Danforth T-4000 deformed or broke at loads well below their nominal holding power. For the T-4000, for example, with a nominal holding power of 4,000 pounds, the test reported "At a load of 2,600 pounds, the welds holding the crown plate sheared off. Without the crown plate in place, the anchor opened to a full 180 degrees." Only the Danforth H-1500 (formerly the 20-H) exceeded its nominal holding power before breaking. It broke at over triple the holding power—5,250 pounds.

In the same vein, the Dutch tests found that the Danforth "flexed excessively," causing the angle between the shaft and the blades to change by eight degrees, depending on the pressure put on it. Their conclusion was that "the anchor's construction is average since the determining factor of the angle changes with big loads. The construction of the anchor does not match its holding power."

While we were finishing our own tests, we learned that West Marine Products had become sufficiently dissatisfied with the quality control of the Danforths they sell that they have begun production of their own lightweight anchors.

We've also received considerable anecdotal comment from readers on recent Danforth anchors, including numerous broken welds and a shank that had been broken in half during "moderate seas and 15- to 20-knot winds."

We enumerated these concerns to Rule Industries and received this response:

"Since the Deepset's introduction in 1986," general manager Gary Sable wrote to us, "the Deepsets have gone through a myriad of changes, in both design and manufacturing technology. The changes are still continuing. While some changes are visible, others are not. However, all changes represent improvements over previous Deepset anchors and are an integral part of the evolutionary progress that new products must undergo. One recent change was a major design improvement to the T-4000, T-6000, and T-7000 anchors to structurally strengthen them. The anchors currently in production are enormously superior to the ones tested by the Navy."

We hope the quality-control problems will be cleared up as the company claims, but we would recommend that buyers examine the Danforth anchors carefully before purchase. We would not buy one mail-order unless we were sure we could return it.

Given all these concerns, the tests nonetheless indicate that well-made Danforth Standard and Hi-Tensile anchors—both old and Deepset models—are excellent at holding in typical soft clay, sand, and mud, with significantly greater holding ability in those conditions than anchors like the plows or the Bruce.

The tests are also pretty clear that the Hi-Tensile models do consistently better than the Standard versions, enough to justify the higher cost. Probably the best of the lot is the older Hi-tensile model.

On the down side, the Danforths do not perform so well in coarse or hard bottoms. Only the British seem interested in testing in less than ideal conditions, and those tests indicate that anchors like the CQR, Bruce, or Delta are better in some situations.

As far as sizing is concerned, the situation with Danforth is different than with the other types since its holding power is so high. For our 36-foot boat, for example, a five-pound Hi-Tensile might be adequate for anchoring in winds to 30 knots, but we doubt if any 36-foot boat would want a five-pound anchor, for psychological reasons alone.

VSB (very soft bottom) models are similar to the other Danforths except that the angle between the shank and the fluke is much greater. The greater angle dramatically increases holding power in mud, as is shown both by the Fortress San Francisco tests and by the Dutch tests. The Dutch tests found the greatest holding at 50 degrees, a slightly larger angle than on either the VSB or the Fortress with the mud adaptor.

Though it has not been tested, the general feeling is that the large angles of the VSB and Fortress would put too great a strain on the anchors for anchoring in normal sand, clay, or hard mud bottoms. This means that the VSB is a specialty anchor. It definitely works well in these conditions, and one will have to decide whether it's worthwhile to carry an anchor for just this particular condition. Given the high holding power of the normal Danforths, it seems that in most instances they would hold boats adequately even in mud. In the Fortress mud tests in San Francisco, for example, a Danforth H-1800 (35-H) averaged 658 pounds holding, about enough to hold a 40-foot boat in 40 knots of wind. The VSB, by comparison, tested at enough holding power to hold the 40-foot boat to approximately 60 knots of wind.

Other Lightweight Types

The Danforth lookalikes that we have examined—from Crosby, U.S. Anchors, and Davis—appear to be closer in design to the Standard Danforths than the Hi-Tensile. We tried a U.S. Anchor, and the Fortress tests included a U.S. Anchor and a Davis, but we know of no other tests of these imitations. The tests suggest they perform like a Danforth Standard, but not enough has been done to draw definitive conclusions. In general, we believe the Danforth Hi-Tensiles will be a better bet, even though they are priced higher.

Fortress

The Fortress anchors are lightweight types made of aluminum by the Nav-X Corporation. They were introduced several years ago and have been promoted heavily. Old-timers will recognize the Fortress as being very much like the Viking aluminum anchors, similar in design and components, though the Fortress is somewhat better made and much better finished. The Vikings went out of production in the early 1980s.

For a given physical size, the Fortress' holding power is in the same range as the Danforths, some tests indicating slightly higher holding power, some slightly less. In our own tests, it measured well above all the other anchors except the old-style Danforth Hi-Tensile, to which it was just slightly above. We suspect its good performance is dependent in large part on the excellent construction, with the sharp, well-shaped blades and well-shaped shank making it superior to the roughly finished new Danforths.

All the tests indicate that the aluminum construction is sufficiently strong. The Navy bent the shanks, and the Dutch tests bent the cross rod at the bottom of the flukes. Both concluded that the construction was light, but sufficient. "Not adequate relative to the high holding power," said the Dutch report, "although test loads of the kind put on the anchor will seldom occur in actual use."

The company, of course, emphasizes the anchor's holding power relative to weight. In one sense this is fair, since the history of anchor design has involved trying to increase this ratio—the advance from a 500-pound stone to a seven-pound aluminum fabrication. And the aluminum anchors do easily outperform steel anchors of the same weight, so the bar graphs and tables produced by Fortress do look impressive. But in the yacht-size anchors, physical size is probably as important as weight, for stowage and handling purposes. For years we carried around a 33-pound Viking anchor disassembled. Put together, it was six-feet tall and four-feet wide, and the truth of the matter is that it was too big for us to handle, even though we could carry it boxed up under one arm.

We did use a Fortress extensively during a long cruise, and found its performance to be good once it was dug in. The shortcoming of the Fortress is in the difficulty of setting it. This shortcoming doesn't show up in any of the holding power tests, but it definitely showed up in our own tests.

With broad surface area in its flukes and its light weight, the Fortress will "plane" or "fly" when moving through the water. Naval architect Robert Smith found that, deployed off the stern of his boat in the Columbia River, a Fortress FX-7 on 25 feet of 3/8-inch line (no chain) "planed to the surface in 1.5 knots of current. With 20 feet of 3/16" chain," he says, "it planes at about three knots."

In trials, we found that with six feet of 1/4-inch chain we could get an FX-16 to plane to the surface at 2.7 knots. More importantly, at much slower drifting speeds we could easily get the Fortress to do a sort of quasi-plane, lifting off the bottom and then settling back as it twisted and turned in the water.

This characteristic often created problems in trying to set the anchor. First, in lowering the anchor, it would often twist and turn on the way down, settling in just about any direction. Observing the anchor through clear water, we frequently saw it bounce and jerk along the bottom in its quasi-plane, a tip digging in and starting to set. But then a pull at an odd angle would jerk it out and cause it to "fly" a few feet before settling like a nervous sparrow.

We eventually learned that, because of the light weight, a successful set demanded a straight, very slow pull, much more so than is required of the heavier Danforths. The problem occurred most often in windy conditions when the boat would start drifting backwards before the anchor could dig in. Success required that the anchor be put in the correct attitude on the bottom when the boat was dead stopped in the water.

The other problem with the Fortress is that we found the anchor much more problematic when there were weeds. We're not talking only thick weeds, which are a problem for all the lightweight types. With the Fortress we found that even small bits of weeds, which were no problem for a Danforth, presented setting problems. Several times we were able to observe the crown sinking into the weeds more than the flukes, so that the flukes were actually pointing upward rather than downward. In a phone call, the company recommended that we try setting the anchor on short scope—a good theory but erratic in practice.

It appears that the larger Fortresses might be less of a problem setting than the smaller ones, but we were not able to test this.

The Fortress can be assembled and disassembled, which in some instances might be worthwhile for stowage. One other feature is that you can purchase an optional "soft mud" crown for the anchor and substitute it for the regular crown. With the mud crown, the angle between the shank and the flukes is increased. With the mud crown, the Fortress tested well in the Fortress tests, close to the Danforth VSB. The "convertible" aspect of the Fortress may make it a better choice for those who might anchor in super soft bottoms.

The setting problem is a serious drawback to the Fortress anchors, but we nonetheless believe that they are a good anchor for the right bottoms. For sizing, the company's recommendations are good.

Conclusions

All the tests taken together prove the old saying that no single anchor is ideal for all conditions. We conclude that the Fortress and Danforth Hi-Tensile anchors (both the old version and Deepset) are the best bet for anchoring in softer bottoms and that the Delta is the best bet for anchoring in harder bottoms. As indicated, both the Fortress and Danforth have problems, but they are currently the best available of their types. We look forward to examining the West Marine lightweight-type anchors.

You continue to see published recommendations on carrying various sized anchors for a "lunch hook," "kedge," "overnight anchor," "working anchor," and so on—a carryover from the olden days when all anchors were fisherman types and excessively heavy. Given the light weight of modern anchors, those recommendations should be ignored, and all anchors should be sized as "working anchors." Long-distance cruisers will want to carry one larger "ulti-mate" anchor.

The company's recommendations on anchor chain, shackles, and nylon rope size can also be followed. We notice that many sailors choose oversize chain and nylon. This is not really desirable, as the larger diameter chain may hinder the anchor's setting ability and the larger nylon rode will stretch less than it should. Longer lengths of chain (as opposed to larger diameter) can be used, and will be desirable if you anticipate anchoring in coral or rocky areas where nylon can be chafed.

No one recommends that a boat carry a single anchor, but many boats do, particularly smaller sailboats which rarely spend a night at anchor. For those boats, a Danforth or Fortress is probably the best bet.

Larger boats and those that are anchored more frequently should carry at least two anchors, serious cruisers probably three. For anchoring in a variety of conditions, two different types of anchor are desirable. For someone buying new anchors, we think one should be a Delta and the other a Danforth or Fortress.

If we bought a used boat and it had a properly sized CQR or Bruce, we wouldn't go out and buy a Delta to replace it. Similarly, if the boat had an adequately sized Danforth Standard, we probably wouldn't replace it immediately with a Hi-Tensile, Deepset Hi-Tensile, or Fortress.

For a third anchor, we would recommend not duplicating another anchor, since all types work differently. If you carry a Delta and a Danforth Hi-Tensile, it would be better to get a Bruce or Fortress or Fisherman rather than another Delta or Danforth. Because a third anchor will probably be little used, an easily stowed anchor would be desirable—a disassembled Fortress or disassembled fisherman might be good choices.

It would be nice if there were one perfect anchor, but there isn't. And there is no indication that there ever will be.   **• PS**

Which Winch?

A look at four medium-sized winches shows that all are well-made, but Harken has the edge.

Because boat owners are keeping their boats longer or buying older boats, upgrading the equipment has become a paramount consideration. This is clearly indicated in our telephone conversations with readers. Winches are mentioned frequently and, because they are a major expenditure, most boat owners do careful research before buying.

For this report, we'll assume we're dealing with a 30-foot sailboat, give or take a couple of feet, with headsails not exceeding 400 square feet, for which we'd like to have a pair of the latest in two-speed, self-tailing winches.

Although they're costly, we chose two-speed, self-tailing models because they are marvelous modern workhorses.

There's about a five- to 10-percent loss of efficiency when self-tailing is added to a standard winch. However, the loss is more than balanced by the convenience. The only other disadvantage of a self-tailing winch is that when tacking it's difficult to throw off a jib sheet. No longer can you simply, with one vertical motion, free the sheet. It hangs up on the self-tailer arm. You literally must unwind the sheet.

The sizes of winches chosen was dictated by the power ratio needed to handle that 400-square-foot headsail on our hypothetical 30-footer. You need not do any calculations. Winch manufacturers routinely supply such data, and marine books and catalogs contain similar tables. All the recommendations are based on using a 10-inch handle. Those who like the ease and speed of an eight-inch handle must crank in a 20-percent power loss and buy a bigger winch to compensate for the loss.

Generally speaking, those buyers who can afford it are well advised to calculate their needs in primary winches and then move up one size. Especially is this so if one's muscles are not what they once were. We've never heard of anyone saying, "The winches are too *big.*"

Another way of increasing the power of a winch is to use a 12-inch handle (or a two-handed model), but few indeed are the individuals who are comfortable with the two-foot turning circle. But if you're buying several winch handles, it might be wise to have one 12-incher for that unhappy time when you want to bring the anchor rode back to your biggest winch and crank yourself off a sandbank.

You can, of course, get very exotic and go for wide-body winches, three or even four speeds, with electric or hydraulic power or lightweight winches with plastic bearings and rare-metal parts. Winch manufacturers are extraordinarily accommodating, but they can dip into the very deepest reaches of your wallet. Besides, that's big-boat stuff. (The very macho gorillas on racing boats love to use eight-inch, two-handed handles. They get fast line retrieval with the small circle of the short handle, but the short handle subtracts from the very mechanical advantage a winch is designed to provide.)

Traditional sailors, a few of them, go for handsome bottom action winches from Murray. For cruising sailors, bottom action winches make considerable sense.

When taking the conventional approach to upgrading the winches on our theoretical boat, the choice nowadays is between Anderson (from Denmark), Lewmar (from England) and (from the U.S.) Barient and Harken. We'll not digress at this point to discuss who owns these labels. It's a tangled web.

We broke our evaluation into the following segments:

1. A line-pull test to measure the efficiency of each winch

2. A strip-down session to determine serviceability

3. A close examination of construction and appearance

The results of these three categories are shown as rankings on the chart.

The Line-Pull Test

What this test was designed to measure is the simple efficiency of each winch. Because we know that theoretical gear ratios are not the whole story, the question really is: For a given amount of effort exerted on the winch handle, how much pull is applied to the line?

For the line-pull test, we used a half-inch piece of Kevlar-cored braid. No test was made with minimum-sized line. The braid was firmly attached to an electronic load cell. To simulate the action of a jib sheet being trimmed, we used a single (for low loads) or double (for the high loads) length of half-inch, nylon-covered shock cord. This worked also to dampen (and provide increased accuracy of) the readings on the load cell as the line was trimmed.

To measure the force on the winch handle, we used (instead of winch handles) a torque wrench with a special fitting to fit the winch handle sockets. We made dozens of pulls, using torque wrench loads of 10, 15, 40 and 50 pounds. Because the torque wrench is longer than a 10-inch handle, the effort put forth by our trimmer was less than would be required with a handle.

The 10 and 15-pound pulls were, for the trimmer, easy work. The 40- and 50-pound pulls required close to what an average person would regard as maximum effort.

After obtaining a legal-sized sheet full of results, the numbers had to be adjusted for each winch's gear ratios. The four winches have different gear ratios (shown on the chart). This has some importance in a winch's power and line retrieval rate, something not always considered when buying winches.

For instance, the Anderson winch has the highest high gear ratio. At 1.3:1, it retrieves line faster than the other three. The Anderson also has the lowest low gear, 6:1, giving it the greatest theoretical mechanical advantage, but the slowest line retrieval rate. The Barient has gear ratios close to the Anderson. The Harken and Lewmar have more closely coupled gear ratios.

After all the necessary adjustments, our test numbers indicate that, over the entire range of low and heavy loads, Anderson and Harken are the most efficient winches. For the power exerted on the handles, more pull was exerted on the sheet.

The Lewmar was third and the Barient was fourth.

The rankings on the chart, derived from the 10-, 15-, 40- and 50-pound pulls, are shown in fractions to indicate the *amount* of difference between each winch. We regard it as significant.

There were some differences in efficiency between high and low loads. In the 10- and 15-pound loads—what one might experience when trimming a jib sheet in light to moderate air—the Harken ranked first, with Anderson second, Lewmar third and Barient fourth. At high loads, 40 and 50 pounds, as in trimming a sheet in strong winds, the Anderson proved the most powerful, with Barient second, Harken third and Lewmar fourth.

The data makes possible the following observations:

1. If you are *not* inclined to use winches to the absolute maximum of their power, the Harken offers the most efficiency.

2. When maximum power is required, such as sailing in hard air with a full genoa, the Anderson is best, with Barient second and Harken third.

3. With the best line retrieval rate in high gear and the most powerful low gear ratio, the Anderson may, for a cruising sailboat, offer the best combination of the unavoidable compromises.

Serviceability

Because they are such beautiful contrivances, winches thrive on good maintenance. Most of them are left in the open air. They accumulate salt and dirt, especially if they do not have drain holes.

To work properly and deliver the truly awesome power built into them, they deserve frequent cleaning and lubrication.

The ease with which they can be dismantled and reassembled has some importance. It's not nearly as paramount as in the days when stripping a winch sometimes meant a cockpit full of bearings. Good engineering has mercifully moved such a traumatic experience to the not-so-good-old-days category.

While it is true that after becoming familar with the task any modern winch can easily be stripped, cleaned and lubricated, we offer here some subjective views of these four winches. Our opinions are summarized with a numerical ranking on the chart.

To remove the drums, the Anderson and the Harken are the easiest. With an ordinary screw driver, remove three machine screws in the top of the Anderson and the drum lifts off cleanly. On the

Two-Speed, Self-Tailing Winch Comparison

Make	Model	Weight	Gear Ratio			Power Ratio		Drum Dia
			High	Low		High	Low	
Anderson	40ST	10.8	1.3:1	6:1		8.5:1	39.5:1	3.0"
Barient	21-33ST C	13.4	1.7:1	5.4:1		10.6:1	33:1	3-9/32"
Harken	B32.2ST C	11.9	2.4:1	4.7:1		16:1	32:1	2-15/16"
Lewmar	30 C ST	14.4	2:1	4:1		15:1	30:1	2-7/8"

Harken, remove one big machine screw and the cylindrical socket for the handle and off comes the drum. With the Harken, two sets of sleeve bearings may be lifted off inadvertently. Until you get accustomed to looking for the sleeve bearings, it's possible that they could be dropped and lost.

The Barient requires a special tool (don't lose it, or buy an extra one) and an Allen wrench. As with the Harken, there are two sets of sleeve bearings plus a spacer to worry about.

The Lewmar has four Phillips-head machine screws, plus two locking "collets," and two sets of sleeve bearings. When replacing the Lewmar drum, there's a little trick to replacing the collets: The center spindle must be lifted ever so slightly to slide the collets in place. Once the drums are removed, the work has just begun.

If you just going to wash the innards with a proper solvent and regrease the gears, none of the winches are difficult to service.

Complete disassembly, for a more thorough cleaning or replacement of worn parts, is another matter. Lewmar and Harken are easy. At no time will you have more than one pin and three loose parts.

The Anderson requires that you pull the center spindle, at which time you'd better be paying attention. The Barient requires equal caution. The cast base must be dismantled with a hex wrench to get at the gears and pawls. Reassembling the loose parts requires a diagram and some practice.

If only cleaning and greasing is required, we'd rank Harken and Anderson as the easiest. For more serious service, Harken is the easiest, with Lewmar

Do-It-Yourself Calculations

For those who want to get involved in the mathematics, the theoretical power ratio of a winch is derived via this formula:

$$\text{Power Ratio} = \frac{2 \times \text{handle length}}{\text{diameter of drum}} \times \text{gear ratio}$$

For example, using a 10-inch handle (2 x 10 = 20) divided by a three-inch diameter drum (20 ÷ 3 = 6.66) times a 5:1 gear ratio (6.66 x 5 = 33.33), the power ratio would be 33:1.

Once the power ratio is known, you can calculate the pounds of pull on a sheet. For example, if you put 10 pounds of pressure on a winch handle in a winch with a 20:1 power ratio, you'd exert 200 pounds of pull on the sheet. That ignores friction. Because of friction, which can be measured but not calculated, the power ratio of a winch, especially when heavily loaded, must be downgraded. At the very high end of the load curve, friction will eat up nearly half of the power.

That's why winch manufacturers, who rigorously test and measure the actual power of their products, prefer that you follow their recommendations for your boat rather than do your own calculations. They don't want you to buy winches that are too small, and then be unhappy.

To determine the approximate sheet load on your headsails, the formula is:

$$\text{Load (Lbs.)} = SA \times V^2 \times .00431.$$

SA is sail area in square feet and V is apparent wind in knots. For example, a 400-square foot genoa times 15-knot winds would produce a load on the sheet of 388 pounds (400 x 225 x .00431 = 387.9). You'd have to apply about 20 pounds of force to the 20:1 winch to cope with the loads.

second, Barient third and Anderson fourth.

Construction and Appearance

As we learned in our earlier evaluation, materials and features may vary according to model. For example, the smaller Harken winches have two stainless steel pawls, the larger ones four. Therefore, it is important to remember that our observations and conclusions about these four particular models may not be true of other models manufactured by the same company.

We feel that all four winches are well-engineered and should provide years of trouble-free service with minimum maintenance. Drum materials available from the four manufacturers vary according to brand and model. You may be able to choose from aluminum, chrome-plated bronze, polished bronze and stainless steel. Because it is the lightest, aluminum is favored by most racers. Good chrome work is the most resistant to corrosion and will retain its shiny appearance for many years. Polished bronze will turn green where the line does not polish it, and while some may think the color is salty, it isn't very popular these days. Where

Line Size		Efficiency Rank			Servicability Rank		Construction & Appearance Rank
Min.	Max.	Overall	High Load	Low Load	Quick	Thorough	
3/8"	1/2"	2	1	2	2	3	2
5/16"	1/2"	3.33	2	4	3	4	3
3/8"	1/2"	1.66	3	1	1	1	1
3/8"	1/2"	3	4	3	4	2	4

weight isn't a concern, we like chrome-plated bronze. You'll certainly not want aluminum if someday you must use it with wire. Stainless is a nice combination of lighter weight and reasonable durability, though it probably won't weather as well as good chrome.

Inside the four winches we tested, all cages and gears are bronze alloys and appear to be of good quality. There are, however, subtle differences in construction, as well as different approaches to the self-tailing mechanism that are of some interest.

Harken

The Harken B32.2STC is a fine piece of engineering—simple, yet rugged and probably more friction-free than the other three. It is the only one with roller bearings on the center spindle where it revolves inside the metal cage. On the other three, the spindle surface mates directly with the turned cage surface. We're not sure how important this is, but it certainly must cost more and, one assumes, produces less friction.

Roller bearings are stainless steel set in nylon races. There is one drain hole in the bronze base, though it isn't very large. But one is better than none. The stainless steel spindle is of sufficiently large diameter and the general workmanship appears good.

As we have noted in previous evaluations of hardware, we suspect that many purchase decisions are based at least in part on style. And style, like beauty, lies in the eyes of the beholder. Harken, with its distinctive red line, contrasts nicely with the black anodized aluminum base of the drum (the rest of the drum is chrome-plated bronze). It's a minor matter, but we are not impressed with the stick-on name label, which we think will wear off in time. The name "Harken" and model number are, however, cast into the top ring.

The Harken winch is the only one of the four with a roller on the self-tailing arm, and it turns on ball bearings to boot. This is another example of Harken going an extra yard. The self-tailing jaws are of two materials: the grooved, stainless steel drum below and smooth black anodized aluminum above. We were told that Harken plans to add a grooved wave pattern to the top surface in early 1992, and change the narrowly spaced ribbing on the bottom to a crosshatched groove pattern, presumably to improve its grip on the line. The jaws may be adjusted for various size lines by pushing down the spring-loaded top plate and rotating it. Because the two jaw surfaces are essentially parallel (as opposed to V-shaped), the turn of line in the jaws stays in column with the turns on the drum below, which is important for even distribution of loads as well as shedding line at the same rate as it's drawn onto the drum. Spacers are available to adjust to a wider range of line sizes than those handled by the standard self-tailer.

The drum surface is the most abrasive of the four, which means it grips very well, but also will probably abrade line faster. Considering that the job of a winch is to grip line, this is probably a worthwhile trade-off: Would you rather replace line every so many years or have a winch that slips? We thought so.

Andersen

The Andersen 40ST is as handsome as the Harken, though decidedly different in appearance. Andersens are available only with stainless drums, and the quality of materials and workmanship appears to be excellent. The light weight of the cast stainless drum is significant and because stainless work hardens, it should show few signs of wear. A winch with a stainless drum probably won't be quite as light as an aluminum one, but should prove more durable. The Andersen 40ST is equally distinctive though we wish the stamping of the white name and model number on the black top ring seemed more permanent.

For some reason, the Andersen has stainless steel ball bearings on the top of the metal cage and stainless roller bearings on the bottom. These are smaller than the others, and there are fewer sets of races. Less surface area means less friction but higher loads. What is the right compromise? We're not sure. The excellent performance of the Andersen speaks for itself, but whether the bearings would wear faster is unclear to us.

There is a large drain hole in the base of the metal cage, considerably larger than that of the Harken. All castings are aluminum-bronze, which the company says is significantly stronger than the "ordinary bronze used in most other brands."

The self-tailing jaws are V-shaped with widely spaced "Power Ribs" to grip the line. It is the same pattern used on the drum, where the ribs are aligned vertically and spaced about an inch apart. Using braided line, we found the Andersen drum gripped line second best to Harken, though it undoubtedly would not abrade the line as much. It's a nice compromise.

Barient

The Barient 21-33ST C is physically the largest of the four evaluated. It has the smallest diameter spindle of the four, and a composite cage, a carefully-chosen plastic originally used to save weight in Barient's big racing boat models but later added (because it was emminently satisfactory) to all of the company's winches. Its roller bearings are Delrin. (Bigger Barients have bearing made of the more expensive Torlon.)

On this model, there is no drain hole in the base. The name and model are silk-screen etched on the top ring and though it initially looks attractive enough, it will wear off. We like a permanent name and model designation for easy, future ordering of parts.

The drum body has a needle-peened finish, which we found poor in gripping various types of line.

For this test, we bought this Barient 21-33ST C brand new from a discount catalog. In subsequent conversations with Barient, we learned that the top plate (with the black lettering) has been replaced with a thicker embossed version. That's a nice cosmetic improvement. A more important change, Barient said, is that the needle-peened drum has been replaced by 16-grit sandblasting, carefully chosen to permit line slippage at 35 pounds of pull. As Barient's spokesman said, to ease a sheet, the line is supposed to slip. The internal mechanism of this model Barient remains the same.

Barient, noted for meticulous customer service, quickly sent us the new model. Without the black lettering, it is better looking and, more importantly, the new drum surface is similar to that of the Harken.

Perhaps the point learned from our experience is that if you, in the near future, buy a Barient 21-33ST C, check first and make sure it's the new model.

The Barient's strongest feature is its patented self-tailing mechanism. The spring-loaded bottom jaw automatically adjusts to the appropriate line size. And, because the two jaw surfaces are essentially parallel, the turn of line in the self-tailer stays in column with the turns on the drum. Assuming the spring will last a long time, we like this feature a good deal. The Barient does have the advantage of holding the smallest diameter line of the four—5/16 inch. If you're inclined to use your primaries on light-air headsail sheets, this is a distinct advantage.

Lewmar

The Lewmar 30 C ST is the shortest yet heaviest of the four. The cage is bronze, the spindle is large diameter stainless steel, and the roller bearings are stainless. There is no drain hole in the base. It is a simple design and workmanship appears to be good.

Again admitting that style is a matter of personal preference, we like the Lewmar's look even though it isn't quite as distinctive as the Harken or Andersen. The self-tailing jaws are black anodized aluminum and the name and model are cast in—the most permanent and best looking job of the four.

The self-tailing jaws are V-shaped with widely spaced ribs. Like the Andersen, they are not adjustable. The drum has a needle-peened surface that, like the older-style Barients, gripped the line poorly when compared to the Harken and Andersen.

Conclusion

As we have tried to emphasize, we think these all are good quality winches. The average sailor, we believe, won't be disappointed by any of the four we tested. There are, however, differences in performance, design and price.

The Harken B32.2ST is our first choice for its overall power efficiency rating, serviceability and construction. The only reason we would not choose it would be if we felt we needed a higher second gear ratio or lower first gear ratio. The two are fairly close together (2.4:1 and 4.7:1). We think the adjustable self-tailer with essentially parallel jaw surfaces is superior to the V-shape as it develops less friction under load. The ball bearing self-tailer roller and roller bearings on the spindle are features not found on the other three.

It's difficult to choose bertween the Anderson and the Barient, Although quite different, both have very desirable features. We like the Anderson's light-weight stainless steel drum. Although stainless drums are available from other manufacturers, the Anderson drum is a gorgeous piece of metalwork. The ribs on the drum are a nice feature and they work, with less line abrasion than the sand-blasted drums on the Harken and new-model Barient. Another Anderson strong point is the large drain hole. If we wanted a high second gear ratio, Andersen's 6:1 would do the job well. It is by far the most expensive, however. We see the quality, but not enough to rank it above the Harken.

In its favor, the Barient 21-33ST is the lowest priced of the four and has that superb, patented, automatically adjustable self-tailing mechanism. Not only does its parallel jaw surfaces keep the line turns in column, it accommodates the widest range of line diameter. On the down side, the Barient has no drain hole and the poorest low-load efficiency of the four. We, unfortunately, are not able to make a judgment on Barient's claim that its composite spindle will wear better than bronze.

The Lewmar 30 C ST brings up the rear, despite being simply designed and ruggedly constructed. It suffers from its low efficiency ratings, slippery drum and lack of drain hole. And at discount it costs a few dollars more than the Barient.

Depending on how you use them and your own capabilities, the subtle differences in these four winches are important. Choose the one that provides the closest match and you'll not be unhappy with any one of the four.   • **PS**

Winch Handles

An 11-way test we conducted in 1992 found Harken the finest, and Andersen the best value.

When we decided to test winch handles a couple of years ago, as is often true, it seemed doubtful initially that there was enough variety to make the effort worthwhile.

However, as we learned, there are considerable differences in design and in price among the handles offered by the major winch makers, Barient, Harken, Lewmar and Andersen.

In addition, there are handles made by independent companies, including several that because they float offer protection against further littering of the seafloor with winch handles. There must be down there, forever puzzling the creatures of the deep, thousands of Oh-my-God-there-goes-the-winch-handle tragedies.

No matter what size winches you have, there is one standard handle, a 10-inch lever that provides most of the needed mechanical advantage. Eight-inch handles, fast and handy, are favored by those with well-developed muscles to compensate for the 20-percent power loss. There also are 12-inch handles, which increase the leverage about 20 percent, but make for a difficult turning circle.

The basic 10-inch handle comes with a standard socket, which increases the odds of losing the handle overboard, or lock-in models, which have a simple trigger-operated dog to lock the handle in the winch socket. There also are push-button lock-in mechanisms, two-fisted grips, and even ratcheting handles if you like lots of clicking. There'd be a hue and cry if a 10-inch ratcheting handle went overboard. Even at discount, they cost a pair of hundred-dollar bills plus a couple of twenties.

Winch handles come in chromed bronze, which are heavy; stainless steel; plain or anodized aluminum for light weight; and the even lighter "composites." The good metal handles are forgings.

Because they are relatively simple, there's an inclination to view winch handles as unbreakable. We've never done so but we know of quite a few reports of broken handles. In every case, they have been aluminum handles. In some instances, minor injuries (sprains and the occasional nasty gash) have resulted. We can imagine worse injuries. At the very least, a broken winch handle probably would give you a jolt of some kind.

Luckily, because virtually all winches have the same size socket (11/16-inch or 17.5 mm), you can choose any winch handle you like. It's one of the few intelligent bits of international standardization in an industry in which many manufacturers take pride in being different and "better" than the next guy.

After reviewing the catalogs and brochures, we collected quite a few (but not all) of the winch handles, the standard brands from the major winch makers and some from independent manufacturers. We gave them a good work-out, a close examination and considered the widely different prices.

It proved difficult to make direct comparisons and develop rankings. However, some pronounced preferences did develop.

Some general conclusions:

1. It seems to us that on most of the handles the addition of the lock-in feature commands an unusual price premium. The addition of the lock-in mechanism, in most cases, nearly doubles the price of a given handle. For the work involved, the price differential appears extreme. However, for safety and convenience, lock-in handles enjoy a pronounced edge, especially on boats where more than one winch handle has taken a dive.

2. Plated bronze handles are very heavy compared with aluminum and plastic handles. The lightweight handles usually weigh half or a third as much as bronze. The use of stainless steel socket studs in drop-forged aluminum handles with lock-in heads undoubtedly increases the corrosion factor. It's a trade-off that involves personal choice.

3. The new floating handles, made of what the manufacturers call "composite" (because the term plastic still seems to carry a negative connotation), have a mountain to climb before they can be considered to have the strength of good metal handles. One of the composite handles (the Bernard) has a plainly stated load limit. The other, the Titan, is said to be immensely strong.

4. Quality winch handles have ball bearings to reduce friction. Cheap handles with plastic grips bearing on metal shafts bind when loaded. The friction defeats much of the efficiency so carefully designed into a good winch.

The accompanying chart displays the characteristics of the winch handles and our comments extracted from the following fuller observations.

Harken

Harken is a company that seems to give extraordinarily admirable attention to reducing friction. All Harken winch handles have circulating ball bearings. The grips spin freely on the shafts, at least when new. They seem almost friction-free.

In addition, the grips on Harken handles are the only ones with a matte finish, which makes gripping them much easier than the slick smooth grips of other makes. There are no mold marks on the grip.

The Harken grips also are longer than any others, by nearly a half inch, which makes them much more comfortable to use, especially for those with large hands.

The lock-in release trigger is plastic but has the same non-slip matte finish, a small but positive advantage.

The Harken handles, with the company's distinctive red stripe, are beautifully finished, which means that they not only are handsome but, as a practical matter, should resist corrosion better than those less finely finished.

Barient

Barient handles, both the chromed bronze and aluminum models, are nearly equal in finish to the Harkens.

Barient's strong point is a lock-in trigger mechanism that is all metal. The well-designed trigger is the sturdiest of all and has the smoothest, easiest movement. Like most of the others, the lock-in trigger is fastened with a roll pin.

The grip has a good shape but is a bit short. It has a very smooth surface, very slippery compared with the Harken, and the molding marks are very apparent. The Barient handles are the most expensive of the lot.

Andersen

The Andersen handle from Denmark is a stainless steel forging, well designed but, in execution, a bit crude, with grinding marks still visible and the finish definitely second-rate.

The socket stud is welded to the arm, again rather crudely (which may lead to some corrosion), and the grip is a two-cones-joined design that contains no bearings. The grip is, however, very comfortable and effective.

Peculiarly, the lock-in trigger works only in one direction, to the right, which might require a bit of digital orientation, especially for lefthanded individuals.

It is structurally a good, simple design. The lightness of the stainless steel (compared with plated bronze handles) is a definite plus. The handle probably is indestructible.

We don't like the finish work, the lack of bearings in the grip or the single-direction trigger on the lock-in mechanism.

Despite these shortcomings, the Andersen definitely warrants a "best buy" label simply because it is so very inexpensive. Available at discount for only $23, a third of the price of handles made by the other three major winch makers, the Andersen won't cause nearly as much pain if it disappears overboard.

Lewmar

As with its winches, Lewmar makes good, solid handles, but they have shortcomings.

In the grip, the metal bearings, contained in plastic races, are not very free-running. The grip is rather fat and has, in our opinion, a poor shape for good gripping. The lock-in trigger is plastic.

Compared with Harken and Barient, Lewmar's finish work is sub-standard, with many blemishes in the forging work, both in the bronze and the aluminum models we bought.

The plating on the bronze model is crude and the aluminum handle has on the underside of the head an unfinished edge sharp enough to do some damage to tender, wet hands.

The Lewmar handles cost about the same as Harkens, but do not appear, in design and workmanship, to be in the same league.

West Marine Products

From West Marine you can buy a cast stainless steel knock-off of a Barient handle. The little sticker identifies it as made in Taiwan.

The West Marine catalog states, "We're often skeptical of imported knock-offs of name brand products, but this is a truly excellent handle."

We don't think we agree.

The West Marine handle has a plastic grip with rather prominent mold-separation lines. The grip also seems to be off-center and doesn't rotate very freely. And the stainless casting has rather sharp edges and the lock-in trigger is too stiff.

As with too many knock-offs, it's not a very smooth piece of work. It appears to be drastically overbuilt and thus very heavy.

It probably will last forever, but for the money, we don't regard it as outstanding.

Sea-Dog

If you want a true "economy model," here's one that will give you not much pain if you drop it overboard.

Also from Taiwan, this grey-mottled cast aluminum handle looks cheap, feels cheap and is, in fact, only $15. The arm contains not much metal and the stiff, little plastic grip contains no bearings.

Unlike other aluminum handles, this one has an aluminum socket stud that won't take much wear. The square lock-in plate is off center, which makes it bind when being inserted or removed from the winch socket. And, like the Andersen handles, the trigger release works only in one direction, to the right.

To the West Marine catalog statement, "While it's not the same quality as its Barient or Lewmar cousins…," we say, "Amen." We cannot recommend this handle, even as a backup.

Titan

Because it is so very different, this one may be controversial. The material and appearance demands a leap of faith to regard the Titan handle as the equal of high-priced metal handles.

A colorful (available in red or green) floater, the Titan handle, engineered in Holland and manufactured in Australia, is made of glass-filled nylon with a tempered aluminum socket stud.

The U.S. marketer, D.B. Follansbee, said the handle has a breaking strength somewhere around 295 pounds, well beyond what can be exerted by an average human. A company spokesman said that in tests, using a hydraulic ram, the handle bent almost 45 degrees before the extruded 6061 T6 marine-grade aluminum drive shaft let go. The arm of the handle did not break.

Follansbee said it defies any human to break the Titan handle. When placed in the water, the Titan floats, handle up, but barely (see photo).

The grip, which could be a bit longer, contains no bearings and, at least when new, turns rather stiffly. The grip is shaped much like the design used by Barient and Lewmar.

The Titan handles truly deserves the sobriquet of "high tech." And, because of its very modest price, $24 at discount, it is an outstanding product that, as confidence builds in its "newness," may replace metal handles on all boats other than those whose

owners feel that high price is the real badge of proper yachting.

Bernard Engraving

This is the other floating handle and we just don't know what to say.

Said to be made of reinforced Lexan, with a square aluminum socket stud, Bernard Engraving's handle is a shabby-looking thing to which is affixed a paper label that says:

"All warranties of fitness for purpose or merchantability EXPRESS or IMPLIED are EXCLUDED. The Bernard Floating Winch Handle is intended for MARINE USE ONLY under normal sailing conditions and should not be used in severe weather or for abnormal loads."

Defender Industries says in its catalog that the Bernard handle has a "safe workload of 80 pounds radial pull." You'd be at risk to use this handle beyond the stated limits.

At any price, it's not possible to visualize this handle aboard any boat whose owner has a high regard for safety and quality, let alone aesthetics.

The Bottom Line

Of the chromed bronze handles, our choice would be the beautiful 10-inch Harken. It is the closest to friction-free. It's fine finish work is pleasing. The long grip with the nice-feeling matte finish is superior to all the others.

As a best buy in a powerful metal handle, we'll take the Andersen. It has some shortcomings—a one-way trigger and poor finish—but for its very modest price, it cannot be ignored.

If what they say about strength and durability is true, which means that you must be able to accept a "high tech" approach in a very traditional tool, the floating handle from Titan has such immense appeal that it very well could be chosen for typical family sailing, at a very modest price, over all other winch handles. And, because the Titan is light weight, we'd choose it over any of the aluminum handles. • **PS**

Winch Handle Value Guide

Make	Size	Type	Price List/Discount	Material	Weight (Lbs.)	Comment
Barient	10"	Lock-in	$119/$83.50	Chromed bronze	2.5	High quality, but the most expensive
Harken	10"	Lock-in	$83/$70	Chromed bronze	2.4	Our top choice of the traditional handles
Lewmar	10"	Lock-in	$84/$71.50	Chromed bronze	2.75	Lewmar suffers only slightly by comparison
Andersen	10"	Lock-in	$55/$23	Stainless	0.9	Best buy in metal handles
West	10"	Lock-in	$90/$60	Stainless	2.4	An over-engineered, over-priced knockoff
Barient	8"	Std.	$45/$31.50	Aluminum	0.875	Probably the stongest aluminum construction
Harken	8"	Std.	$46.50/$40	Aluminum	0.625	Best of the aluminum 'shorties'
Lewmar	8"	Lock-in	$45/$32.40	Aluminum	0.75	Okay, but needs better-shaped grip
Seadog	8"	Lock-in	$22/$15	Aluminum	0.50	Economy that approaches the dangerous minimum
Titan	10"	Lock-in	NA/$24	Glass-filled nylon	0.50	If you like 'high tech,' this is the top choice
Bernard	10"	Std.	NA/$16.75	Reinforced Lexan	0.625	Don't even think of parking here

Inflatable Tenders

A sailboat might not be the only craft you buy. For many, some form of dinghy is necessary, as well.

While inflatable boats have been around for a long time (the first commercial model was introduced in 1934 to use up leftover dirigible fabric) they didn't become popular in the U.S. until the mid-1970s. Since then, their unique combination of features and characteristics has made inflatables a popular alternative to the hard dinghy.

The most obvious advantage of an inflatable is that it can be deflated when not in use, greatly reducing storage problems. They're also lightweight, which allows lively performance with small outboards; and extremely stable, making them easy and safe to board in a seaway, as well as providing ideal platforms for scuba divers. Inflatables have high-load capacities for their size, and provide a comfortable, if often wet, ride in rough water.

In 1991, we ran a Reader Survey on inflatables. Avon scored the highest "buy again" rating, as well as the lowest amount of trouble reported. At the bottom end were the economical Sea Eagle and Sevylor, which, the manufacturers pointed out, did not deserve to be compared in the same breath with more expensive models. Unresolved was the question of construction material—Hypalon versus PVC. To get a firmer handle on quality, performance and value, last summer we trucked 18 inflatables to the water, assembling, studying and testing each in a variety of conditions. Here's what we learned.

Variations on a Theme

Until the last few years, most inflatable boats sold as tenders or dinghies were designed primarily for rowing. Many of these had motor mounts, but the mount was less-than-rigidly connected to the hull. Hulls on boats of this type, variously described as "dinghies," "soft tails" and "round boats," were relatively flexible, which presented few problems at the low speeds the boats were capable of.

"Sport boats," the other basic alternative, are generally larger, have transom motor mounts integral with the boat, more rigid hulls, and air tubes that extend aft of the motor to provide buoyancy during acceleration. They are faster than dinghies, take larger engines and are alternatives to small runabouts.

The trend today appears to be away from the soft-tail dinghy, and towards the higher performance sport boat, even for owners who envision using them primarily as tenders. The sport boats are more expensive, but they're faster and handle better. When we asked manufacturers to identify their most popular boats in the 8-1/2- to 11-foot range, we found ourselves with only four round boats, as opposed to 14 sport boats.

What We Tested

To restrict this project to boats that would function well as tenders for a small cruising boat, we limited our choice to boats that fold up more or less completely, and, for now, elected not to include RIBs (Rigid Inflatable Boats).

We found ourselves with 18 boats, ranging in length from 8' 2" to 10' 7", and in price from $225 to $3,000, with 15 different brand names representing 10 different manufacturers. We included "house brands" from two major mail-order houses, West Marine Products and Boat/U.S., as well as two boats that double as sailboats, one of which triples as a lifeboat.

The objective was not simply to see which boat was "best." Inflatable boat design, like most marine design, consists of a number of trade-offs and compromises, with price being one of the major factors. We attempted to determine which boats would perform which tasks well, and what are the limitations of each boat.

Floors

We were struck by the variations in design and materials used in the boats tested.

One, the Sevylor Super Caravelle, was a "pure" inflatable, with an unreinforced PVC skin, multiple air chambers and no rigid pieces except for the motor mount and the oars. The Sea Eagle is similarly constructed, but adds a plywood floor, which provides firmer footing, though it doesn't exactly make the boat rigid. The Breeze 9, the only other boat that doesn't use nylon- or polyester-reinforced fabric, has a folding rigid polyethylene floor and a thick EVA inflatable bolster and seats; it provided a much more rigid hull than the other two.

Two boats, the Quicksilver 8' 6" Soft Tail and Boat/U.S.-distributed Seaworthy 8.3, have soft floors stiffened with transverse slats; longitudinal rigidity comes from the side air tubes. The Avon Roll-Up 2.85 and the Tinker Tramp carry this idea a step further. Both use abutting transverse slats to make a solid floor: The Tinker uses wide slats that are locked into place when the side tubes are inflated, while the Avon has narrower slats (something like a large roll-top desk) and uses both the side tubes and an inflatable keel to keep the floor rigid. All four boats are very easy to assemble, since all that's required is to unroll and inflate. The Avon and Tinker designs provide a much more rigid floor, with correspondingly higher performance due to less hull flexing.

The most popular floor-stiffening scheme, used on seven of the boats tested, involves the use of sectional wooden floorboards that fit nose-to-tail into the uninflated boat's bottom. They are pressed into place against the tension provided by the hull, and locked there using grooved aluminum, wood or plastic channels that fit over the edges of the floorboards, securing two sections.

This system provides a reasonably stiff floor, but is more difficult to assemble than the slatted floors, particularly on a small, pitching deck. The necessity for a number of small, easily dropped pieces doesn't help. Boats with sectional floorboards are best left inflated during the season, and towed or stored on davits, rather than deflated and stored between uses.

Two boats, the Calypso and Novurania, also use sectional floorboards, but these are not forced into place to hold them secure. Instead, these boats use a heavy two-section longitudinal beam, or keelson, as a sort of spine to support the floorboards and to provide a rigid structure. The two halves of the keelson are slipped into the ends of the hull, butted together at the center and pressed down to wedge them into the boat. A pair of bolts locks the whole thing into place, and the floorboards simply slip in on top of it.

This arrangement is heavy, but it's very secure and the keelson also gives shape to the boat's bottom. Like the sectional floorboard approach, it's not well suited to frequent assembly aboard.

Two boats, the Bombard A400 and the Zodiac Futura Jr. use an inflatable floor, which unlike those on the Sea Eagle and Sevylor, is extremely rigid. Instead of using a series of air chambers to make up the floor, these two boats use a through-stitched, double-walled design that is inflated to a relatively high pressure. Like the slatted-floor roll-up models, these inflated-floor designs are fairly easy to deflate and store, and simple to set up again. They are lightweight, but have the disadvantage of not providing a solid floor to which you can attach accessories.

Keels

One of the more annoying habits of inflatables is the tendency to steer poorly. This means you have to devote some care to holding a steady course. In a turn, a boat that tracks poorly will skid sideways, rather than carve a smooth, controlled path. Control of tracking is a matter of providing an effective shape to the boat's bottom.

Flat-bottomed inflatables track poorly, but this isn't too serious if you're only dealing with a small engine, pushing the boat at low speeds. Most of the boats that are capable of reaching higher speeds have some sort of keel. The Bombard A400 is an exception.

Most commonly, inflatables have an inflatable keel, consisting of an air chamber between the floorboards and the hull bottom. Inflation of the chamber shapes the bottom. The boats with keelson designs use the keelson to shape the boat's bottom. The Zodiac Futura, Jr. has a flat inflatable floor raised above the water to reduce wetted surface and an inflatable keel on the bottom of each air-tube to improve tracking.

You can have too much of a good thing when it comes to keels, however. A keel that is too deep makes it more difficult for a boat to come up on a plane. We found that some boats with deep-V keels in their forward sections had more difficulty getting up on a plane, sometimes nearly standing on end—an uncomfortable and unstable situation.

Materials—The Great Debate

There was a time when any self-respecting inflatable was made of a nylon fabric laminated to several layers of synthetic rubber, with an outer layer of a Du Pont-developed synthetic called Hypalon®. In the late 1950s, Zodiac, the largest manufacturer of inflatable boats, quit using Hypalon and introduced a PVC-coated fabric. The fight was on.

From a manufacturer's viewpoint, PVC has a very important advantage over Hypalon. Instead of requiring hand-gluing, it's possible to use automatic welding techniques that can transform inflatable boat manufacture from a cottage industry to true mass production.

From a consumer's viewpoint, things aren't quite so clear. Despite occasional reports of poor workmanship, Hypalon has developed a reputation for ruggedness and longevity. PVC fabrics, on the other hand, developed a reputation for premature failure, due largely to a run of problems during the early-to-mid 1980s.

Understanding of the situation is made more difficult by the fact that both PVC and Hypalon fabrics can vary tremendously in quality from fabricator to fabricator, even from batch to batch. To make matters more confusing, the durability of a boat is as much a function of the seams and joints as it is of the hull fabric.

We tried to evaluate the fabrics used in our test

boats by clamping a swatch of fabric in an airtight fixture that left a square of the fabric exposed. We then pressurized the gadget to the working pressure of the boat and dropped a weighted dart onto its surface to evaluate puncture resistance. We inflated another swatch, and dragged a weighted steel rasp across the fabric to see how well it resisted abrasion. And we exposed samples of each fabric to a collection of boat chemicals, fuels, antifreezes and oils to see how well each held up.

What we found was not definitive. There *were* slight differences in puncture and abrasion resistance, but we couldn't find any pattern. All the samples we tested, including unreinforced PVC, showed good abrasion resistance; all the reinforced fabrics showed good puncture resistance. PVC fabrics, however, were severely stiffened and discolored by overnight immersion in gasoline, so we are left with some concerns about spills and leaky hoses. On the other hand, we haven't encountered any reports of failures attributable to contact with gasoline. It seems to us that the way to deal with this problem is to wash off spills immediately, rather than to reject boats made of PVC-coated fabric.

As a side note, silicone compounds should never be used on PVC boats. A reader, Richard Schaefer of Glastonbury, Connecticut, told us he ruined his $2,000 Zodiac by "protecting" it with Armorall. We confirmed with Zodiac that silicone can cause separation of the seams.

The biggest question about PVC is whether it will stand up under severe sunlight for extended periods. We couldn't test for this, because of time constraints, so we contacted 20 inflatable-boat repair shops across the country. To minimize commercial bias, we restricted our survey to shops that either don't sell boats at all, or shops that sell both PVC and Hypalon® boats. We told each shop that replies would be treated confidentially. Each shop was asked the following question: "Making allowance for the fact that there are more PVC boats sold than Hypalon boats, have you encountered a disproportionate number of either type in the boats you repair?"

While responses varied, some patterns of responses did emerge. In the more northerly states, PVC boats and Hypalon boats seem to have comparable service records, at least for boats made since 1986 or so. In the south, most repair shops felt that Hypalon boats have better ultra-violet resistance than PVC boats, particularly in the Caribbean, where boats typically stay inflated all year and ultraviolet attack is strongest.

Our conclusion is that you can make good and bad boats out of PVC or Hypalon. If we were sailing in the tropics, we'd probably opt for Hypalon. If we tended to be careless about spilled fuel, or were cruising to remote areas (Hypalon is easier for do-it-yourself repair) we'd do the same. But, for most people, especially those in more northern climates, we think that the choice of fabric is secondary to the quality of the boat. This opinion is supported by the warranties offered by the manufacturers: Except for Tinker, which offers a spectacular 10-year warranty on material and seams, and Avon, which offers 10 and 5 years on fabric and seams, respectively, all of the other boats made of reinforced fabric offer 5-year warranties on both fabric and seams regardless of construction material.

Load Ratings

Some boats we tested carry load ratings in pounds; some also specify the maximum number of people that can be carried. Inflatables, as a class, have extremely high load capacities (the boats we tested were rated for 700 to 1,140 pounds, and from three to five people), but most boats will perform much better if you keep well below the rated maximum. We found that putting more than three adults in any of these boats almost guarantees an uncomfortable ride and, if the skipper backs off too suddenly on the throttle, a very wet one. None of them have much in the way of freeboard.

Every boat we tested had at least two separate air chambers, and is capable of supporting its rated load with one main chamber deflated; they all have sufficient reserve buoyancy so that sinking one by accident is virtually impossible.

Engine Ratings

A few years ago, inflatables carried maximum horsepower ratings bordering on the suicidal. The industry, through a commendable self-policing policy, has brought engine ratings under much better control.

The boats we tested carry ratings from 3 to 15 horsepower. More to the point, several manufacturers are now issuing suggested engine ratings, which are lower and more reasonable than the maximum ratings. The Calypso we tested, for example, is rated at 15 horsepower, but the company recommends 8.

Speed and Planing

Today's inflatables tend to be a quick lot. The Zodiac Futura Jr., the fastest of the boats we tested, can reportedly approach 30 knots with a 9.9-hp. engine, and several of the other boats are almost as fast. Top speed *per se,* however, isn't really a vital consideration when you're dealing with a boat whose primary function is to ferry you back and forth to your boat. We found that all of the boats capable of planing provide exhilarating rides.

If you don't have any great distances to cover, the ability to plane isn't essential. A non-planing boat, however, is limited to a top speed of less than 5 knots, so if you have some open water to cover, a planing boat is definitely preferable. Unless we were financially strapped, or our needs were extremely modest, we wouldn't consider a non-planing model.

We tested all the boats to see if they'd plane with a minimal engine—3.3 horsepower—and one person aboard. We also checked each with a full load and the maximum rated size engine.

Accommodations

While most of the boats we tested come with seats of some sort, these are primarily for rowing. Most people perch themselves on one of the side tubes when under way. A more important aspect of design for comfort is the provision of handholds. Most boats have a grab line that extends around the outside of the outer tubes, though on some boats these do not extend far enough forward. A few boats are arranged so that oars are stored just where you want to sit, and the Tinker managed to locate a cleat that's part of its sailing package directly under the skipper's rear end.

The carrying handles on a few boats were much appreciated by our testers. Features such as bow dodgers and adequate hoisting and towing eyes are definite pluses. Another handy feature to look for is a tie-down for a fuel can.

Rowing

All of the boats, with two exceptions, were equipped with oarlocks and oars. All the boats could be rowed adequately, with the Breeze and the Tinker excelling in this category, but inflatables, as a class, are too light to be really good rowboats; weight, after all, provides momentum in between strokes. The Zodiac Futura Jr. and the Novurania Whitecap are equipped with paddles instead of oars, probably on the theory that they're essentially powerboats that would only be hand-propelled in an emergency, and too beamy to row well with the short oars that would stow conveniently. Rigid seats, we found, made rowing much more comfortable than did inflatable seats. And, when trying to get up on plane by yourself, with many small boats it's important to sit on the centerline. Some sort of seat is a necessity, even if it has to be purchased as an option.

Ease of Assembly

We noted how easy each boat was to assemble and inflate, as well as how many pump strokes each required. This depends on the design of the boat and the pump supplied, but since most people use the pump that comes with the boat, we think it's a fair comparison. Electric pumps, we found, are easier on the legs than foot pumps, but they aren't faster and don't provide adequate pressure to inflate most boats properly. You'll still need to use the foot pump for the final dozen or so strokes per chamber.

Once deflated, an inflatable has to be stored, which entails carrying it to the storage area. We noted both weight and stored size of each boat; when boats are stored in more than one package, we recorded the size of each.

On-The-Water Performance

We conducted our on-the-water tests at the Old Greenwich Yacht Club in Greenwich, Connecticut. Each boat was fitted with a small 3.3-hp. outboard for its first trials, then with an outboard that approximated its maximum rating, most often a 9.9-hp. We made runs in both calm harbor water as well as runs outside in small to moderate chop. First runs were made with one person, then with one and two passengers. Regardless of load ratings, at high speeds we don't think that any of these boats is really suitable for more than three people. Our "Overall Performance" ratings are based upon planing ability and high-speed handling. If high-performance operation isn't your main interest, you can ignore these ratings in favor of other, more specific characteristics.

While there were many similarities in handling among the 18 boats tested, we did find several noticeable differences: skidding due to absence of keel; boat standing up during acceleration due to short waterline and, possibly, excessive keels; and sluggish performance of "soft-tail" models with clamp-on motor brackets. Rigidity of the hull is an important factor in good high-speed performance; manufacturers achieve this through the use of large-diameter air tubes, higher air pressures made possible by reinforced hull materials, and/or rigid keelsons.

Most of the boats tested are capable of high speeds, especially those rated for 9.9-hp. and 15-hp. motors. In fact, all of the testers remarked that these boats can be dangerous, especially in the hands of an inexperienced person. Because these boats essentially sit on top of the water, at high speed the hull slaps across the water, and if one doesn't hold on tightly, it is easy to see how someone might be thrown into the water.

The situation is exacerbated by the boats' seating positions: You're generally perched on a side tube rather than sitting inside. A friend of ours has gruesome prop scars to prove such accidents are more than flukes. Before turning your teenager loose in such a powerful craft, we strongly recommend on-board instruction and specific rules, including the wearing of life jackets and obeying speed limits. Another surprising and unpleasant, if not actually unsafe, characteristic we noticed, was the tendency of many inflatables to submarine when slowing down too rapidly. What appears to happen is that because the flat bottom has so much drag, the hull is quickly overtaken by its own wake when depowered. Several times we soaked the forward-sitting passengers and on a couple of occasions actually swamped the boat until we learned to gradually depower, waiting for the stern wave to pass beneath before completely stopping. While none of the boats showed any tendency to sink, it made for a cold, wet experience.

Following are our individual remarks, listed in increasing order of discount price.

Sevylor Super Caravelle ($187)

The Super Caravelle is about the least-expensive inflatable you can buy that's usable outside of a swimming pool. It's made of unreinforced PVC, which limits the inflation pressure; as a result the boat is quite bendy. It has seven separate air chambers, which makes it safe, but also makes inflation a nuisance. That, plus the fact that the motor mount requires an undue amount of fiddling to install, makes assembly difficult.

Rowing and motoring were also poor, largely due to excessive hull flexing. When we turned up the throttle on a 3.3-hp. motor, the hull buckled so much we were afraid the motor would be dunked.

If all you need is an inflatable that will get you back and forth from your boat in a small anchorage, the Sevylor will do that job for the least money. If you're looking for higher speeds or exhilarating performance, you'll have to go up considerably in price.

Sea Eagle SE8H ($449)

Much of what we just said about the Sevylor applies to the Sea Eagle. While both are made of unreinforced PVC, the Sea Eagle felt a tad more secure underfoot because it has a two-piece plywood floor. Ease of assembly was poor.

As with the Sevylor, the Sea Eagle's performance problems seem directly attributable to its lack of rigidity, made worse by the donut shape which places the motor considerably outboard of the boat. Rowing performance was poor, and, like the Sevylor, the motor squats as throttle is applied, to the point it is nearly submerged in its own wake. It is more rigid than the Sevylor, but we don't think the difference is worth the extra cost.

Breeze 9 ($748)

The Breeze is very different from the others tested. It's technically an inflatable, but it features a rigid floor that folds in two lengthwise, plus inflatable airtubes and a fixed seat. The Breeze's air tubes are made of a thick non-reinforced EVA plastic. It sets up and deflates extremely easily, but folds to a long, fairly flat bundle that is best stored on-deck or lashed to a rail; it's too large for the lockers on most boats.

The unusual, almost double-ended design of the Breeze allows it to be rowed in both directions, which is convenient. Certainly it rows better than a conventional inflatable, but again it does not carry its way well because of light weight. It did not plane with the small outboard and did take some water over the bow in a chop; it's not rated for more than 4-hp.

The Breeze can be fitted with a sailing kit ($350) that converts it to a single-sail dinghy. Under sail it was reasonably quick and extremely stable, though the small leeboard allows too much leeway. Also, moving the leeboard from port to starboard is a pain and we invariably lost control for half a minute.

If you're not interested in high speed, and the option of sailing your dinghy is appealing, the Breeze is a good, rugged boat at a reasonable price.

Boat/U.S. Seaworthy 8.3 ($799)

The Seaworthy 8.3 is the lowest-price boat we tested with an integral transom. Like the Quicksilver 8.6, it has a slatted floor, which is extremely easy to set up or take down.

On-the-water performance wasn't particularly sporty. We blame the slatted floor for some of its problems. Planing was not possible for one person using either the 3.3-hp. or 6-hp. outboard (max. rating 5-hp.). The 8.3 rated average in most categories. We did notice that it was a bit wetter than other inflatables, perhaps due to its tube diameter and narrow beam.

Quicksilver 8.6 Soft Tail ($800)

Like the Sevylor and Sea Eagle, the Quicksilver 8.6 is a "soft-tail" design. Unlike them, it's made of a polyester-reinforced PVC that permits a higher inflation pressure and greater hull rigidity. It has a slatted floor, which lets you roll it up after deflating, without removing any pieces. The motor mount rolls up with the hull, making storage very easy.

Rowing performance was fair. With a 3.3-hp. outboard, the 8.6 would not plane with one person. With a larger 6-hp (max. rating 4-hp.) it still wouldn't plane, putting up a big wake as it plowed along. It helped convince us that donut-shaped inflatables, with clamp-on motor brackets, have some serious shortcomings compared to conventional transoms. Overall performance was below average. It's a step up from the less-rigid unreinforced PVC boats, but several steps below the integral-transom designs.

Quicksilver 8.9 Sport ($978)

The Quicksilver 8.9 is quicker than any of its less-expensive competitors. It uses a sectional-board floor and features an inflatable keel; ease of assembly was average.

While it will plane with one person and a 3.3-hp motor, it won't with three persons and a 9.9-hp. It's most obvious problem is the tendency to nearly stand straight up on its tail before settling onto a plane, even with crew weight shifted forward. We think this characteristic is potentially dangerous, particularly in high winds. It's certainly unnerving.

OMC Express 305 ($985)

The OMC Express 305 is a sectional-floorboard boat with an inflatable keel. It comes in a bright white fabric, which stays cool, but shows dirt.

Rowing performance was below average and the oars are not captive. With both large and small outboards we noted some skidding in turns. It planed well with one person and a 3.3-hp outboard, but with the 9.9-hp. it would not plane with three testers aboard. The high bow helps keep passengers dry in

Value Guide: Inflatable Boats

Brand	Model	List	Discount	Compact Stowage	Floor	Keel	Material	Warranty (years) Material/ Seams	Max HP	Max Load (Lbs./No. persons)	# Chambers
Sevylor	Super Caravelle XR86GT	$225	$187	Y [3]	Soft	None	PVC	90 days	3.5	700/4	7
Sea Eagle	SE8H	$449	$449	Y [3]	Boards	None	PVC	1/1	3	950/4	5
Breeze	9	$748 [5]	$748	N[6]	Rigid, folding	Hull shape	EVA	5/[4]	4[2]	1000/5	3
Boat/U.S.	Seaworthy 8.3	N.A.	$799	Y	Roll-up slats	Inflatable	Hyp/Polyester	5/5	5	595/N.A.	2
Quicksilver	QSR 8' 6 Soft Tail	$899	$800	N	Roll-up slats	None	PVC/Polyester	5/5	4	770/3	2
Quicksilver	QSR 8'9 Sport	$1,099	$978	N	Boards	Inflatable	PVC/Polyester	5/5	10	1075/N.A.	3+keel
OMC	Express 305	$1,145	$985	N	Boards	Inflatable	PVC/Polyester	5/5	10	882/4	2+keel
West Marine	CS 10.2	$1,350	$995	N	Boards	Inflatable	PVC/Polyester	5/5	10	990/4	2+keel
Boat/U.S.	Seaworthy 9.2	N.A.	$999	N	Boards	Inflatable	Hyp/Polyester	5/5	8	965/N.A.	2+keel
Boat/U.S. Achilles	BA-96	N.A.	$1,195	N	Boards	Inflatable	Hyp/Polyester	5/5	8	970/N.A.	3+keel
Achilles	LS5-BU	$1,850	$1,250	N	Boards	Inflatable	PVC/Polyester	5/5	10	1140/4	3+keel
Bombard	AX400	$1,850	$1,310	Y	Inflatable	None	PVC/Polyester	5/5	8	925/4	2+floor
Calypso	C27	$1,695	$1,445	N	Keelson+Boards	Hard keelson	Hyp/Polyester	5/5	15 [1]	850/4	2
Zodiac	C310XS	N.A	$1,775	N	Boards	Inflatable	PVC/Polyester	5/5	10	1100/4	2+keel
Novurania	Whitecap 285	$2,100	$1,920	N	Keelson+Boards	Hard keelson	Hyp/Polyester	5/5	15	900/4	3
Avon	Roll-Away R285	$2,495	$1,948	Y	Roll-up slats	Inflatable	Hyp/Nylon	10/5	8	720/N.A.	2+keel
Tinker	Tramp	$2,280 [7]	$2,280	Y	Roll-up slats	None	Hyp/Nylon	10/10	4	882/4	4
Zodiac	Futura Jr. 0276	N.A.	$2,900	Y	Inflatable	2 Inflatable	PVC/Polyester	5/5	15	882/4	2+floor+keels

*Planing models only
Ratings: 1 poor, 2 fair, 3 average, 4 very good, 5 superior
[1] 8 HP recommended
[2] 2 HP recommended

[3] Motor mount detaches for storage
[4] Seamless construction
[5] Basic boat., without sailing kit. Sailing kit:$350
[6] Stores on deck or along rail in sailboard bracket

a chop. There are no forward lines for passengers to grab; we think that's a serious omission. Performance otherwise was average.

West Marine CS 10.2 ($995)

The West CS 10.2 is another sectional-floorboard design. The boat we received did not come with a seat, so that ease of rowing was poor; with a seat it would be average.

It planed with one person and a 3.3-hp engine, but planed only marginally with three aboard and a 9.9-hp. The West tended to lift its bow on hard acceleration, though not as much as the Quicksilver 8.9. It was average in dryness and comfort.

Boat/U.S. Seaworthy 9.2 ($999)

Unlike the 8.2, the 9.2 uses a sectional floorboard design, which improves high speed performance, but reduces the ease of assembly to only average. Like all sectional-floorboard designs, the Seaworthy 9.2 breaks down to a fairly large number of separate pieces, which can present problems, especially when working on the deck of a boat.

In general, on-the-water performance was similar to the 8.3. It too was a bit wet. Planing was not possible with the small outboard, but good with the 9.9, even with three people aboard. A minor complaint is that the metal outboard plate on the transom isn't positioned quite right to handle either an OMC or a Mercury 9.9-hp engine.

Performance rating: Fair

Boat/U.S. Achilles BA-96 ($1,195)

This sectional-floorboard model, while carrying the Achilles logo, is distributed only through Boat/U.S. Like all the sectional-floorboard designs, ease of setting up and deflation was average.

The BA-96, with one person aboard, was fairly easy to get up on plane, but with three persons it would not plane, even though we had a 9.9-hp., larger than the recommended 8-hp. Consequently, it created a big wake. And we found it a bit wet. With fewer passengers both Achilles models stayed on plane to very slow speeds, which we liked.

Achilles LS5-BU ($1,250)

The Achilles LS5-BU is another sectional-floorboard design, average in ease of assembly and disassembly.

Rowing performance was average. With a 3.3-hp. outboard, the

Stored Dimensions (inches)	Weight	Plane 3.3 hp (1 person)	Plane max. hp (3 persons)	Total Pump Strokes to Inflate	Ease of Assembly	Rowing	Dryness	Comfort	Handling*	Overall Performance
14-1/2 x 12 x 46	32.5	N	N	388	1	1	4	1	—	1
4 x 30 x 46 + 7 x 19 x 23	46.5	N	N	350	1	1	4	1	—	1
16 x 29 x 108	100.5	N	N	100	5	4	4	5	—	1
9 x 24 x 38	61.5	N	N	280	5	3	2	3	—	1
13 x 22 x 42	57	N	N	251	5	2	5	4	—	1
13 x 22 x 42	81.5	Y	N	575	3	3	4	5	3	1
13 x 20 x 38	69.5	Y	N	421	4	2	5	3	3	2
16 x 24 x 41	71.5	Y	Y (marginal)	547	3	2	2	3	4	3
8 x 24 x 39 + 6 x 22 x 34	96.5	N	Y	492	3	3	3	3	3	2
10 x 18 x 41 + 5 x 23 x 42	78.5	Y	N	407	3	3	2	3	4	2
12 x 21 x 45	88.5	Y	Y	573	3	3	3	3	3	3
14 x 20 x 38	45.5	Y	Y	620	5	2	2	3	2	2
10 x 20 x 40 + 5 x 22 x 35	101.5	Y	Y	260	3	3	5	5	5	5
15 x 22 x 46	90.5	Y	Y (marginal)	358	3	3	3	3	3	3
6 x 8 x 49+ 14 x 26 x 42+ 3 x 27 x 35	109.5	Y	Y	165 (paddles)	2	1	4	5	5	5
20 x 24 x 42	95.5	Y	Y	154	5	3	4	4	4	5
12 x 24 x 50	66.5	Y	Y	162	5	4	4	3	4	4
17 x 27 x 49	68.5	Y	Y	438 (paddles)	5	1	5	5	5	5

[7] Basic boat., without sailing or Lifeboat kit. Sailing kit: $700; Life raft kit: $907 ; Sea Anchor : $97
[8[Estimated. Manufacturer does not supply list prices.

LS5-BU was able to plane with one person, and with the larger 9.9-hp. it planed with three people, distinguishing it from some of the others. We did note that during acceleration the bow tended to rise higher than we liked, though not as badly as the Quicksilver. At high speed, in a chop, the floor-boards buckled and rattled.

Bombard AX 400 ($1,310)

Built by Zodiac, the Bombard A-400 dispenses with floorboards entirely, using a through-stitched double inflatable floor. This makes for light weight, compact storage and easy setup under adverse conditions. Unlike the inflated floor of the Sevylor, the Bombard's floor is inflated to a high pressure, providing a reasonably secure, if slippery, floor. The Bombard was excellent in terms of ease of inflation and deflation.

The Bombard lacks a keel, which severely affects its in-the-water performance. Rowing performance was below average. The oars are not captive. While the Bombard is fast and capable of planing with both small and large outboards, control was poor. In fact, at high speeds we felt it was quite skittish, even scary at times. This problem is exacerbated by the slippery floor. If it weren't for these problems, its "Overall Performance" rating would have been higher.

Calypso C27 ($1,445)

The Calypso, along with the Novurania, uses a two-piece bolt-together rigid keelson, or backbone, to support the floorboards. While this construction helps make for a very rigid boat, it also adds weight and complicates assembly and disassembly. The Calypso's commendable rigidity is enhanced by large-diameter air tubes.

The Calypso's keel gives it excellent control, and the large 17-inch diameter tubes make for a dry ride. It planed easily with all outboards. Rowing was slightly better than average, helped by a rigid, well-placed seat.

Overall, we found the Calypso to be a fine performer and, at a discount price of $1,445, we consider it a Best Buy.

Zodiac C310SX ($1,775)

Similar in appearance to the West CS 10.2, the Zodiac C 310SX was also average in ease of setting up and taking down.

On the water, this model rated average in most categories. It barely got up on a marginal plane with an operator and a 3.3-hp engine. With a 9.9-hp. it had difficulty planing with three persons. We noted some skidding, due to the lack of a keel, but handling was nevertheless satisfactory. The buoyant tube seat allows one to sit in the middle instead of on a tube, which can be important when motoring alone. For

1993, the C310X will be replaced by the YL310; design and performance should be similar to the C310SX.

Novurania White Cap 285 ($1,920)

The Novurania shares the Calypso's keelson-plus-floorboard design and large air tubes. It comes with a bow dodger and solid loops for attaching a hoist. Unlike most of the other inflatables, the Novurania is equipped with paddles instead of oars. This would seem to be an admission that inflatables don't row well and that an alternative approach might be better. Clearly you wouldn't want to paddle an inflatable very far, but for short distances you could make do.

Under power, the Novurania performed very well, though it did tend to skid a little on fast turns. It planed easily and handled well with one person and a 3.3-hp engine as well as three up and a 15-hp.

Overall performance was superior, and construction detailing was excellent.

Avon Roll-Away R285 ($1,948)

The Avon, along with the Breeze, shared the honors for fast and easy setup—we could get it out of its carrying bag and fully inflated in a shade over two minutes. This is due largely to its sectional floorboard design, which works something like a roll-top desk, and in part to a very good foot pump. When unrolled, the floorboard sections are locked into place by the boat's inflatable keel.

Rowing performance was average, but some of our testers didn't like the oar lock system, which does not hold the oars captive. Under power, the Avon tracked nicely and planed easily with one person using a 3.3 hp outboard. With the 9.9-hp operating at part throttle (max. rating 8 hp.) it was very fast, getting up on plane quickly and with the bow staying low. Control was very good except at top speeds, where we encountered some skidding.

Overall, a superior performer, and an excellent choice if you're going to inflate it and deflate it frequently.

Tinker Tramp ($2,280)

The Tinker Tramp is unusual in that it's designed to take a sailing kit ($700); there's a built-in centerboard trunk, built-in cleats and a pointy nose to help sailing performance. It also can be configured as a lifeboat kit with canopy, CO_2 inflation and drogue ($1,004), which we didn't try to evaluate. The Tinker, like the Avon, has a roll-up floor and sets up only a trifle slower than the Avon.

Due to its unconventional design, including a fine bow, the Tinker rowed better than any of the other inflatables. It has wooden oars that are longer than the norm. It rated above average in all categories. It planed with one person and a 3.3-hp. motor; a 6-hp. was too heavy for the transom. Aside from the fact that the Tinker is clearly not a high-speed muscle boat—its maximum rating is for a 4-hp. engine—our only gripes are its narrow beam, which meant that the boat heeled a bit more than most of the others, and the fact that the centerboard trunk and cleats took away some usable space. These represent a trade-off with improved rowing and sailing performance. Performance was very good, given the Tinker's engine size limitation.

It is a surprisingly good sailer, tacking easily, though its light weight sometimes necessitates backwinding the jib to carry through.

Zodiac Futura Jr. O276 ($2,900)

The Futura Jr. uses a drop-stitched inflatable floor, similar to the Bombard, to eliminate floorboards. Unlike the flat-bottomed Bombard, however, the Futura Jr. elevates its flat floor between the air tubes, producing a tunnel effect, and has two inflatable keel tubes at the bottom of the air tubes for tracking and to further raise the floor.

Setup is very easy, although the large tubes require a lot of pumping. Unlike the Bombard, the Futura Jr.'s floor isn't slippery.

Like the Novurania, the Futura Jr. uses paddles instead of oars. Under power, the Futura Jr. has outstanding performance. It planed easily with one tester and a 3.3 hp; it planed easily with three up and a 9.9 or a 15 hp. Skidding was almost non-existent; we attributed the Futura's tracking characteristics to the double-keel. The elevated underbody leaves little wake.

Overall performance under power of the Futura Jr. was the best of the boats tested. This is high praise indeed, in light of the sparkling performances turned in by Calypso, Novurania and Avon.

Conclusions

If high-speed performance is your only requirement, our recommendations are clear: the Calypso C27, the Novurania Whitecap 2.85, the Avon Roll-Away R285 and the Zodiac Futura Jr. 0276 were the cream of the crop. For most people, however, there are other considerations.

While there are other considerations, including stowage size, ease of rowing and towing, the major factor for most people is price. The chart lists the boats in increasing order of average discount price. If your needs are minimal, and all you're looking for is an inflatable that will get you back and forth from your not-too-distant boat, it's hard to beat the Sevylor Super Caravelle at $187. While it doesn't measure up to more-expensive models in terms of performance, it's safe and cheap.

For a generally more versatile boat, the price goes up. The Breeze 9 at $748, is a good, if unusual, boat, assuming planing performance isn't important. It's rugged, rows and motors well with a small outboard. While it doesn't fold up enough for locker storage, it can be set up and taken down quickly and easily for storage along a rail.

For a more conventional inflatable to operate at sub-planing speeds, the Boat/U.S. Seaworthy 8.3, at $799, has a slatted floor so that it rolls up for easy storage.

Until you get up to the $1,900-plus range, you won't find boats with the combination of compact storage and good high-speed planing capability. Of the boats that *don't* lend themselves to being stowed away in a locker, the West Marine CS 10.2 ($995) will plane with one person and a 3.3-hp., and the Achilles LS-5BU ($1,250) had reasonable overall performance. Our favorite in this category, however, is the Calypso C27 at $1,445. It had superior performance under power, was average in rowing capability and was generally well-made. Priced at $475 less than the next lowest-priced boat with comparable performance, we call the Calypso C27 a Best Buy.

The Novurania, a highly respected name among inflatable manufacturers, is similar in design to the Calypso. It discounts for $1,920, and is larger and roomier. Its motoring performance was superior, but it's not designed for rowing.

If you want compact storage *and* sparkling performance, the Avon Rollaway R285 and the Zodiac Futura Jr. 0276 offer both—at a price. The Avon discounts for $1,950; the Zodiac for $2,900. They're very different boats. The Avon is a well-made high-speed tender that rows adequately, motors very well and can be set up and taken down in a minimum of time with a minimum of effort. The Zodiac is essentially a high-performance sports boat that can't be rowed, but can be stored in a small space. The Zodiac is a faster boat than the Avon, but requires almost three times as many pump strokes to inflate.

The Avon is made of Hypalon and the Zodiac of PVC. As discussed in Part 1, if we were planning to cruise the tropics, where ultraviolet attack is more severe, we'd opt for Hypalon. It's also easier to repair in the field. For more casual use in the north, we don't think material is that important a consideration.

The pricey Tinker Tramp ($2,280) is an oddball in this company. What the Tinker does, it does extremely well. It rows better than any of the other boats we tested, planes easily with a 3.3-hp. motor, deflates, inflates and stores easily and is well-made. Its price tag, we feel, is out of line with the other boats if all you want is a tender. If you are interested in the sailing kit and/or the lifeboat kit, the versatile Tinker may well be a less-expensive alternative to buying a tender plus a life raft and/or sailing dinghy. • **PS**

Mainsheet Travelers

In a seven-model comparison, the least expensive traveler turned out to be one of the best.

With a mainsheet traveler, you can sheet to windward in light air to gain pointing ability; you can substitute the mainsheet for the vang upwind; and in heavy and puffy air, you can play the traveler car control rather than the mainsheet to power up or down without altering leech twist. As a consequence, performance-oriented sailors, given the choice, will invariably opt for a traveler rather than the triangular "Crosby" or "Lightning-type" mainsheet rig found on many older boats and a few new ones.

The attractions of the best modern traveler systems are hard to resist: Almost frictionless cars gliding on ball bearings, modular system components that let you lead mainsheet and control lines in virtually any configuration, installation that's so simple even a child can do it, and (at least for two of our test models) almost unbelievably low prices.

Test Procedure

Our test boat for this exercise, a 1968 Morgan 24, is designed to have a traveler located aft in the cockpit, rather than forward on the cabintop, which would call for heavier track because of the greater leverage that goes with midboom sheeting. Because the Morgan's tiller rises from the cockpit sole almost exactly under the boom end, and room is needed to swing the tiller up without interfering with the traveler track, we installed the test tracks 11 inches abaft the boom end, bridged across the cockpit footwell. This location places a sizable side load on the car, which, it turned out, is more easily handled by some car/track designs than others.

To avoid drilling too many holes in the fiberglass cockpit deck to mount our traveler tracks, we bolted a 2" x 4" board to the cockpit seats, and fastened each of the seven test units (and an eighth simple slide-on-

a-T-track) in turn to the board. Only the ends were fastened, simulating a situation where the track would have to bridge across a 4-foot gap, such as an extra-wide cockpit footwell or a companionway.

All tests were conducted with the boat at rest and no mainsail hoisted. We shackled the main halyard to the outboard end of the boom to counteract the downward force of the sheet. Next, using a four-part mainsheet purchase, with the car centered on the track, we trimmed the sheet end to a tension of 50 pounds measured on a spring scale, giving approximately 200 pounds of upward force on the traveler car. Then, by using the spring scale on the car trimming line, we measured frictional car resistance (i.e. force to move the car) for each of the eight designs. It's worth noting that the vertical pull of the mainsheet was considerably more than 200 pounds when we read the trimming force, due to the geometry of the system (straight track, arced boom end path) with the car pulled almost all the way to one side. (It should also be mentioned that since the mainsail wasn't rigged, its side-pull was zero; close-hauled in a blow, a sizable force would be added to the one we measured.)

We also measured the vertical deflection of each track (except the plain T-track) under a 200-pound load with the car centered, cross-sectional dimensions of each track, and total weight of each rig.

Keeping these physical tests in mind, we evaluated each design's relative ease of assembly, installation, operation, and maintenance; its strength and durability; how well it could be adapted to special needs dictated by the configurations of individual boats; and its price.

Evaluations

Plain Slide on T-track

As a check to be sure that ball bearing cars are really necessary to ensure easy movement under load, we tested a 1967-vintage plastic Tuphblox T-track traveler system with a plain no-bearing car. Although it slid fairly well under light loads, it invariably began to bind when heavy pressure was imposed. A force of well over 50 pounds was needed to move the car when our 200-pound standard load was applied—more than triple the force needed for the worst of our modern bearing-equipped units.

Harken

Harken's heads-up product engineering, excellent workmanship, and consumer-oriented packaging all deserve high marks. In fact, we judged the Harken traveler best in every characteristic evaluated except price. And it had more useful features than any of its competitors except Schaefer, with which it was tied.

Installation, with clear printed instructions for assembling every component, was easy and quick. Mounting the track to existing holes in the boat was simple, thanks to the sliding "T-bolts" (actually hex-headed bolts with washers under the heads, riding in a T-shaped slot under the track).

Ease of operation and maintenance was also tops. The Torlon ball system worked superbly; the Harken traveler was the only system we tested in which *all* sheaves, as well as the car and the cam cleats, ride on low-friction balls. On the car, balls are exposed underneath, so hosing with fresh water now and then will keep salt and dirt from gumming up the works. Incidentally, Harken recommends a light lubricant such as LPS-1, WD-40 or dry silicone sprays for travelers (and Schaefer recommends Boeshield T-9); we didn't use any lubricants in our tests, however.

Strength of Harken's track was superior, with the smallest vertical deflection among the units tested. That's not surprising, given the 1-1/2-inch height of the Harken track cross-section—the tallest of the bunch.

Adaptability was also excellent. End sheaves can be stacked either one or two high, and blocks can be added easily to the car, if desired for varying levels of mechanical advantage. Control cams can be turned from approximately 35 degrees inboard to 15 degrees outboard to accommodate different deck layouts. And a unique (but expensive) "windward sheeting traveler car" accessory, which makes it possible to pull the car above the centerline without releasing the leeward control line, can be quickly bolted on.

One interesting sidelight: Consulting the Harken catalog, we discovered that the Harken 038 fiddle block needed for our test wasn't available in a standup model. When we called Harken to express our surprise, they opted to send us a prototype not yet released for production. They plan to have a production part available next fall, although they would supply the same prototype today to other customers if requested. Given this situation, we felt it was fair to give Harken credit for having a standup block available—and kudos for demonstrating quick response to customer needs.

Schaefer

Schaefer prides itself on designing products that are strong, durable, reliable, and easy to use; judging from our test traveler, that pride is justifiable. A case in point is its cam cleats. The color-coded cam bases can be useful as well as decorative. And the stainless steel cams are very strong and extremely corrosion resistant. By comparison, aluminum die castings tend to corrode and wear out faster, especially in a warm, salt-laden environment; plastic cams typi-cally wear even faster than aluminum (though Ronstan's new carbon fiber cams may prove to be the exception). Maintenance-wise, too, the Schaefer cams are well designed: hollow and open at the top so fresh water can be squirted in easily to flush away salt deposits and harbor grime. The open top also permits inspection of the edge of the cam spring, which is a stainless steel ribbon rather than the usual (and less durable) coiled wire.

Every unit tested except Schaefer and Ronstan had cars equipped with recirculating plastic balls in linear races. The Schaefer (and Ronstan) units used stainless steel balls in annular races, e.g. traditional ball bearings. This feature makes it relatively easy to remove the car for servicing (no loose balls to lose), and, judging from our test results, doesn't hurt performance (i.e. force required to move the Schaefer car was equal to or lower than every competitor's except Harken).

The Schaefer design had the best strength-to-weight ratio (tied with one competitor for lowest weight and with another for next-to-lowest deflection under load). The unit also scored well in our "Useful Features" and "Other Judgments" categories. Overall, with a list price 18 percent lower than Harken's, the Schaefer traveler may be the choice of many.

Garhauer I Track

Design of this unit is elegantly simple, with few parts and no worries about how it all goes together. On our test unit, everything worked just as it should, including the Torlon-ball-equipped car with Torlon balls bearing on both bottom and top flanges of the track. This design is especially good for angular loads such as those imposed in our test; the 11 pounds of force needed to move the traveler was well within the reasonable range.

Garhauer Double T

The main objection we had to this unit was its lack of a standup block. We liked the simplicity of design and good low-friction performance. And although we counted fewer useful features than any other traveler tested, to shoppers on a budget the Double T unit's very low price may more than compensate for its lack of frills.

Lewmar

The looks of this British brand's traveler, with its streamlined car, covered end sheaves, and smooth gray anodized finish, appealed to us. So did the T-bolt method of attaching track to the boat (which can help when you want to mount the unit on existing holes). But there were a number of things we didn't like about this rig. It isn't available with a standup fiddle block with integral cam cleat, though we were

Value Guide: Mainsheet Travelers

	Antal	Garhauer I	Garhauer Dbl. T	Harken	Lewmar	Ronstan	Schaefer
List prices							
48" track	$88	$150	$120	$89	$62	$75	$73
Car	$193	inc.	inc.	$114	$172	$103	$114
Block & Cam	$118	$50	$50	$88	$56	$60	$69
Ends & Cleats	$193	inc.	inc.	$200	$94	$114	$147
Total	$592	$200	$170	$489	$383	$352	$403
Tests							
Force to move car (lbs.)	12	11	10	8	9	18	9
Deflection of track (inches)	7/16	1/16	1/8	1/64	3/16	3/16	1/16
Useful Features Included							
Stand-up block w/ cam (5 pts.)	Yes	Yes	No	Yes	No	No	Yes
Mainsheet cam adjustable (3 pts.)	Yes	No	No	Yes	No	Yes	No
Sliding T-bolt on track (2 pts.)	No	No	No	Yes	Yes	No	No
Traveler cams adjustable (2 pts.)	No	No	No	Yes	Yes	Yes	No
Track bumpers (2 pts.)	Yes	Yes	Yes	No	Yes	Yes	No
U.S. threads (2 pts.)	No	Yes	Yes	Yes	No	No	Yes
Stainless cam cleats (2 pts.)	No	No	No	No	No	Yes*	Yes
Color-coded cam cleats (2 pts.)	No	No	No	No	No	No	No
Removable bail block (2 pts.)	Yes	Yes	Yes	Yes	Yes	No	Yes
Lightweight (2 pts.)	Yes	No	No	No	No	Yes	Yes
Total points	14	11	6	16	8	11	15
Other Judgments							
Relative strength (4 pts.)	1	4	3	4	2	2	4
Durability (4 pts.)	4	4	4	4	4	4	4
Workmanship (4 pts.)	3	3	3	4	4	4	4
Ease of maintenance (4 pts.)	4	3	3	4	4	3	4
Ease of assembly (3pts.)	2	3	3	3	2	3	3
Ease of installation (3 pts.)	2	2	2	3	2	2	2
Order/response time (3 pts.)	2	3	3	3	2	2	3
Total points	18	22	21	25	20	20	24
Overall Ratings							
List price	7	21	25	9	11	12	11
Car Friction	17	18	20	25	22	13	22
Useful Features	14	11	6	16	8	11	15
Other Judgments	18	22	21	25	20	20	24
Total Score**	**56**	**72**	**72**	**75**	**61**	**56**	**72**

Track Dimensions (height x width): Antal 25/32 x 1-1/32; Garhauer I 1-3/8 x 1-1/2; Garhauer Dbl. T 29/32 x 1-1/4; Harken 1-3/16 x 1-5/8; Lewmar 1-1/8 x 1-5/32; Ronstan 1-32 x 1-1/32; Schaefer 1-3/32 x 1-3/32.

* Face only

** Total Score represents the sum of individual scores of four attributes, each weighted equally: List Price, Friction and Deflection, Useful Features Included, and Other Judgments, each of which was graded on a scale of 0 (worst) to 25 (best). Thus, a score of 100 would be perfect. List Price scores were derived by assigning a top score (25) to the lowest-price unit, multiplying that score by that unit's price, and dividing the result by each other unit's price. Car Friction and Track Deflection was derived in the same way.

able to get a block with a cam cleat that didn't stand up, and another block without cam cleat that did. (We mounted both on the Lewmar track for our tests).

Then there was the difficulty in feeding the control line around the turning sheaves on both the car and the end fittings. The sheaves are hidden inside tunnels, so to reeve a line around them you must first fish a piece of bent wire through the tunnel and out again—a time-consuming nuisance. And we noted fewer useful features than most of the other units.

Overall we felt that the Lewmar traveler is satisfactory, but overshadowed by the units with more to offer, namely Harken, Schaefer, and Garhauer.

Antal

We had a problem with Antal in getting what we asked for. First the unit came with holes drilled in the wrong places. Then we found the end caps didn't fit properly. Eventually a unit with these problems corrected was air-freighted to us from Italy. Then we had to saw off the track to the 4-foot length we had originally specified, and drill and tap a hole to fit a metric-sized bolt. Altogether, we felt the hassle was more than many sailors would want to endure, especially when the list price was the highest in the group, and results in the friction test were only so-so.

Ronstan

Ronstan generally produces serviceable products; some, like their new turnbuckle with built-in adjustment scale, are quite clever. But we found their traveler's performance rather unimpressive.

In the force test, interference of the inside of the stainless steel bearing race caused the bearing to stop rolling and skid along the track when presented with a substantial angular load. The bearing even left a permanent silvery-white score mark in the aft upper inside corner of the black-anodized track as it skidded along. We're not sure, but we think the problem may have something to do with the sharp-edged shape of Ronstan's outer bearing race (compared to Schaefer's well-radiused edge, which performed near the top of the group). We've alerted Ronstan to the problem, and they are investigating.

The skidding car resulted in a trimming force of 18 pounds in our test—50-percent worse than the next competitor, and 125-percent worse than Harken. That, we think, is a sufficiently serious defect to judge this otherwise reasonably functional rig as unacceptable, at least for use when significant side loads are present.

The Bottom Line

In every category except price, the Harken traveler outshines the competition. There's no question that the Harken design is the target for other manufacturers, though so far no one has succeeded. The Harken engineering is too good, the customer service too responsive and on target, the product options too numerous and enticing.

Garhauer, however, has struck at the one big weakness in the Harken armor: Price. The two Garhauer test units may not have won the prize for beauty or clever design (though in our opinion they are quite adequate), and may have fewer useful features than the majority of the systems we looked at, but both are sturdy, serviceable units, with good enough performance to warrant serious consideration by the average sailor, whether or not he or she is on a tight budget.

Among the other units, the Schaefer rig comes closest to satisfying most typical needs, and (as with most or all of the other units) may be obtainable at prices significantly below list.　　　**• PS**

Genoa Blocks

In this case you get what you pay for. The best brand tested was also the most expensive.

Hardware design and construction has come a long way since many of our boats were built and equipped. And, as many owners of 15- and 20-year-old boats are faced with upgrades, either to increase ease of sailhandling or to replace worn gear, we decided to take a look at two very basic pieces of hardware: genoa lead blocks and fiddle blocks with cam cleats, swivel shackles and beckets. Our report on fiddle blocks appears in the next issue.

We selected blocks from five companies for testing. The Big Three—Harken, Lewmar and Schaffer—dominate the market. Their products are available at discount prices through many mail-order catalogs. To get a look at the low and high end of the hardware market, we also selected blocks from Garhauer and Antal. The California-based Garhauer supplies Catalina Yachts with blocks as well as several semi-custom yacht builders. We were surprised at the company's low prices. The Italian-made Antal blocks are, by comparison, quite expensive, but the difference in quality is evident.

Genoa Lead Blocks

We can remember when many smaller boats built during the 1970s came standard with just working jibs and fixed fairleads. Genoa tracks, blocks and even winches were often optional equipment. The trend over the ensuing years has been to include more gear as standard—not only hardware, but hot pressure water, showers, pumps, etc., which is one reason for the higher relative prices of boats today.

Most of the companies, especially the Big Three, make more than one line of blocks. Lewmar, for example, offers its standard Solent line, for average sailors, with Delrin sheaves running on hollow stainless steel center pins, or needle bearings on larger blocks. Its high-end Frederiksen line has Delrin ball bearings. Schaefer's standard models also use Delrin sheaves turning on stainless steel bolts. But it, too, manufactures Delrin ball bearing blocks in essentially the same styles and models. Harken's Barbarossa line with conventional cars, and Harken's own adjustable ball bearing line of lead blocks—not to mention its titanium line—is similarly distinguished.

Styles differ as much as do materials. Schaefer, for example, manufactures "Twin Sheet Lead Blocks," "Half Moon Lead Blocks," and "Spring Loaded Blocks on Slides." Studying the catalogs of the various makes will help you sort out which blocks are most appropriate for your boat and your kind of sailing. Most of them also contain helpful information on loads, various ways to set up running rigging systems, and recommendations on specific model numbers for various size boats. We think your time will be well served by calling the companies and asking for a catalog.

For this article, we selected five lead blocks for a typical 30- to 32-foot sloop that is used primarily for family cruising. Most of the blocks have rated safe working loads (SWL) of about 3,500 pounds and breaking strengths of twice that—7,000 pounds. We asked Tripp Estabrook of Harken's Newport office to calculate the genoa block loads for a typical 30-footer. A #3 genoa in 35 knots of wind places about 1,200 pounds of load on the lead block, well within the safe working loads of all blocks tested. Shock loads should be absorbed safely by the maximum load rating.

Genoa Lead Block Comparison Guide

Make	Model	List Price/Discount Price	Rated SWL (lbs.)	Cheeks	Sheaves	Bearings
Antal	622.492	$230/N.A.	3,100	SS	Mekton	Composite bushing
Barbarossa	B1872A	$184/N.A.	3,300	AL	AL	Delrin bushing
Garhauer	21-00	$36/N.A.	2,000	SS	Delrin	Delrin
Lewmar	2870	$125/$106	3,500	AL	Polymer	Polymer
Schaefer	32-51	$142/$106	3,500	SS	AL	Nomex/Teflon

All use 1-1/4-inch T-track. Be aware, however, that not all T-track is the same. Schaefer's, for instance, has a lower profile than some others, so that a 1-1/4-inch car from one company may not fit T-track manufactured by another.

We purposely did not include fully adjustable lead blocks, though these merit strong consideration for anyone interested in racing or cruising with a roller furling headsail. Harken, Antal and Lewmar manufacture genoa lead cars that use ball bearings to reduce friction. These, however, generally require installing the company's proprietary track. See sidebar, "Friction Free." Garhauer soon will introduce a ball bearing lead car and block that uses conventional T-track.

Materials

Manufacturers have but a few materials to choose from in engineering genoa lead blocks. Stainless steel or anodized aluminum is used on all five blocks for what the manufacturers variously call the housing cage, stirrup, or sheave carrier. This is the "body" that comprises the block's basic structure. Some larger blocks may be made of chrome-plated bronze, which adds substantially to weight. The sheaves may be aluminum or a plastic such as Delrin treated with an ultraviolet inhibitor and, perhaps, Teflon. The chart lists the materials of each brand.

We're not sure that, for small or mid-size boats, stainless steel is inherently better than anodized aluminum or a plastic, or vice versa. The stronger materials, however, generally carry higher loads, though plastics won't corrode and some are in effect self-lubricating. What seems more important is the grade of alloy or type of polymer, finish, thickness, application and overall engineering.

Barbarossa (Harken)

Barbarossa is an Italian hardware manufacturer owned by Harken. Harken is a strong believer in ball bearing blocks and at this time only makes conventional T-track blocks on special order. They will become standard production hardware in the near future. Harken does at present sell its Barbarossa line of T track blocks, but doesn't push them hard in this country.

Car	Sheave Diameter	Plunger Lock	Weight (oz.)
AL	2-1/4"	Yes	34
AL	1-15/16"	No	60
AL	2"	Yes	26
AL	2-1/4"	Yes	20
SS	2"	No	29

We looked at three Barbarossa blocks: an aluminum-bodied tri-roller, stainless steel tri-roller, and a conventional chrome-plated bronze block with Delrin sheave. The tri-roller design is more popular in Europe than the U.S., but has several advantages. One-piece construction reduces noise and number of working parts. The sheaves are wide for accommodating two sheets during sail changes, and the unusual vertical sheaves lessen the chance of chafe when the sheet leads are unfair. We noted that the listed sheave diameter of 1-15/16 inch is the minimum width of the sheave where the line runs; all of the other companies list sheave diameter as the maximum width of the side lips, which seems to us a bit deceptive. In actuality, the Barbarossa has the widest sheave. The others' minimum diameters are more in the order of 1-1/4 to 1-1/2 inches.

On the downside, these blocks are physically larger and heavier than conventional lead blocks. Racers wouldn't think of adding the extra, unnecessary weight. They do not have integral stops and must be used in conjunction with separate track stops, which adds to cost. A towing bail is provided for adjusting lines. Some people may find separate stops more convenient, others not.

If you're interested in a custom Harken T-track block, you can order by contacting the company. The one we examined had an anodized aluminum car, stainless steel sheave carriers, and a sheave made of anodized aluminum impregnated with Teflon. It turns on Delrin ball bearings. As one would expect, it turns more freely than any of the blocks turning on sleeves. It makes a rather satisfying rattle sound. Again, refer to the sidebar "Friction Free" for a look at Harken's strong suit.

The Barbarossa blocks are distinctively European in design and work well. If you have an unusual lead problem, these could be the answer. They are large and heavy however, and while strong, the sheaves don't turn any easier than lesser priced blocks we examined. We like the one-piece construction; it's difficult to imagine breaking these blocks. Of the five blocks we evaluated, Barbarossa would be our second choice for a cruising boat without roller furling, first if we were totally captivated by the unique tri-roller concept.

Garhauer Two Sheet

The car is anodized, extruded aluminum, the housing cage is 1/8-inch stainless steel and the sheave is Delrin. The sheave rides on a stainless bushing over a stock 3/8-inch bolt with lock nut, which allows for disassembly. There are also round aluminum spacers between the sheave and cage. The cage is welded to the fore and aft pivoting rod. The welds are exposed and appear sloppy. Two rubber grommets are intended to prevent the cage from banging on the top of the aluminum car but loose tolerances in the assembly still cause it to be noisy. There are no plastic inserts in the car to reduce friction with the T-track and help prevent the car from nicking the track when it binds.

The plunger stop is easy to grip and locks in the up position. It works well, but not quite as easily as the Antal's plunger.

The block tilts 45 degrees in either direction, which is about average.

No effort is made to radius the edges of the stainless cage, so lines may chafe when the lead isn't fair.

The low price of the Garhauer makes it a good value for the Mom and Pop cruising team. It will probably function adequately if not too much is asked of it. Still, the welds are unsightly and the finish work is the poorest of the five makes tested.

Schaefer Twin Sheet Lead

The car of the block we examined is stainless steel, the housing cage is 3/16-inch anodized aluminum and the sheave is aluminum. The sheave turns on a "Nomex/Teflon N.T.E." bearing over a stainless steel bolt. The cage is secured to the pivoting pin by a stainless steel roll pin. There are no stops to keep the cage from banging the car and the black finish on ours is showing nicks where it makes contact. Fred Cook of Schaefer said they are constantly refining their products and will probably correct this problem. Schaefer's logo is nothing more than white stick-on letters that slip and can be nicked.

There are no plastic inserts to minimize friction on the T-track.

The plunger is difficult to grip as the lip isn't sufficiently wider than the pedestal upon which it sits. The spring tension feels a bit stiff and we found it difficult to pull and hold the plunger while sliding the car along the track. There is no way to keep the plunger in the up position.

The sheave is wide at two inches and is intended to handle two sheets at once. The idea is that racers can set a new headsail and sheets before lowering the first sail (possible with double-groove headstay foils), thereby maintaining speed. The wide sheave also allows for somewhat wider lead angles to the winch, which may minimize chafe and offer more versatility in deck layout. The edges of the cage, however, don't have much radius.

Cook told us their most popular block in this range is the 32-97, which is very similar to the one we tested, except that the car is machined from an aluminum extrusion and anodized. It has a ring attached to the stop pin, to which one can tie a short piece of line to facilitate raising the pin to move the car. It is available in silver or black anodizing. This model also is less expensive than the stainless car model—$110 list, discounted to $82.50

The Schaefer lead block is sturdily constructed and should last a long time, though the anodizing will nick where the cage hits the car. Workmanship is good, but we can't understand why the plunger on the stainless car model isn't given a wider lip and, on both models, a means of locking in the up position. If you've got Schaefer track already installed on your boat, this may be your best choice as some of the other manufacturer's blocks may not slide freely or at all.

Lewmar

The car and cage are die-cast anodized aluminum with a dull black finish. The sheave is a polymer and rides on a hollow 304 stainless steel tube. This means it can't be disassembled should the sheave need replacement. A red plastic spacer keeps the cage from slamming into the body. It's snug fit also makes it quieter than the Schaefer and Garhauer. Roll pins are used to secure the pin to the car as well as the plunger grip to the stop pin. Our main concern is the thickness of the points where the aluminum cage pivots on the stainless steel pivoting pin; if it were to break, we think it would be here. Its safe working load, as rated by the company, is 3,500 pounds, which is as much as any of the others. The car has plastic inserts to reduce friction and noise.

The anodized aluminum plunger locks in the up position and has knurled sides for easy gripping. The lock feature makes it simple to slide the car along the track without having to maintain a grip on it. On occasion, the plunger did twist sideways when we tried locking it, but for the most part it was the easy to operate. A towing bail is optional.

The sheave width is 1-5/16-inch—not as wide as the Schaefer—but wide enough for two sheets if necessary.

The all-aluminum construction makes it the lightest of the five tested, which may be important to racers but we doubt that four or five ounces will mean much to the average sailor.

The Lewmar lead block is a stylish piece of equipment. We like the lock-up plunger but aren't so fond of the flared sheave tube. It is quiet and light. We also have doubts about cast aluminum and wish we had the means to verify reported breaking strength figures. The Lewmar is a reasonable compromise choice in the medium price range.

Antal

This Italian-made lead block has a car made of anodized, extruded aluminum, a 316 stainless steel cage and a sheave made of Mekton (an HRM resin) turning on a composite fiber sleeve and stainless steel bolt. The sheave tilts 50 degrees to either side and two stainless steel springs return it to the upright position so that it doesn't bang the car. Every component of the block may be disassembled. Antal likes to use stainless Allen screws for many applications, which leave nice flush surfaces. Interestingly, there are no welds.

The sheave cage or carrier is held upright by two stainless springs. They also prevent banging of the cage on the car.

The plunger is an easy-to-grip square shape that locks in the up position when twisted 90 degrees. We liked it the best of those tested.

The stainless cage is flared at the front to prevent chafe; in tests, we found this worked quite well. If the cage sides were narrower, as with some other makes, the flaring probably wouldn't be necessary. But the extra metal makes it that much stronger.

A towing eye is fitted to the front of the car should the owner want to make the car fully adjustable. To do this, the plunger would be left in the up position. Our only criticism is the sharp edge under the bail, which we think would lead to chafe.

The Antal lead block is top quality, but also the most expensive. It has the most features of any conventional T-track block tested, and because of its towing bail and locking plunger, it could be used in a fully adjustable system. If you want the best, buy the Antal. The average owner, however, will probably be just as happy with the Lewmar or Schaefer for less than half the price. • **PS**

Fiddle Blocks

Our look at fiddle blocks turns up Harken as the best buy. Avoid Lewmar and Garhauer.

This chapter is devoted to a look at fiddle blocks with swivel shackles, beckets and cam cleats. The size we selected would be suitable for about a 28-foot production sloop, either as part of a mainsheet system, or as a boom vang.

Because sheave diameter varies so widely among manufacturers, it was difficult to find comparable models. We used maximum line size (all are 1/2-inch, except one), breaking strength, and the manufacturers' recommendations to make our selection. Rated safe working loads (SWL) are typically half the breaking strength.

The safe working loads for these fiddle blocks range from 750 pounds to 2,000, though our bench tests cast doubt on the accuracy of some ratings. We asked Tripp Estabrook of Harken's Newport office to calculate the maximum vertical end boom load of a typical 28-footer. He chose the Tartan 28, and told us that load is 1,393 pounds. Using a four-part tackle, the maximum load per sheave would be one quarter, or about 348 pounds, well within the safe working load of all five blocks.

The five blocks chosen for this article are manufactured by Antal, Garhauer, Harken, Lewmar and Schaefer. These are the same companies represented in our chapter on genoa lead blocks, with the exception of Harken, which does not at present make a conventional T-track lead block. As a substitute, we looked at its Italian-made Barbarossa line.

The Tests

Our criteria for evaluating fiddle blocks focused on three major characteristics: sheave friction, cam operation, and overall construction quality. Friction is difficult to measure without the right equipment and our remarks are based purely on our subjective feelings about the way each product operated. Cam performance, under normal sailing conditions, was much the same. We rigged each block on our test boat and in light air cleated and released the mainsheet to see how easy or difficult it was to pull the line into and out of the cam jaws. We then repeated the test in our shop with the blocks under much heavier loads—270 pounds. Under these heavy loads, the lines released from the cams only with great difficulty.

Also in our shop, we secured each block to a padeye on our test bench. With a load cell and come-a-long, we pulled a 3/8-inch line backwards through the cam, attempting to simulate what would happen in a flying jibe, where a shock load would be applied to the cam. Our objective was to compare the relative effectiveness of the cams to grip the line, and of the overall strength of the blocks' construction. These fiddle blocks all are designed to accomodate 1/2-inch line maximum, except for the Harken, which due to the width of its small sheave, is designed for 3/8-inch line. We tested with 3/8-inch line, which would have seemed to favor Harken, but as the results show, this wasn't necessarily the case.

Antal

Antal hardware is made in Italy and has a definite European look with its dull black anodized finish and clean design. Its gear has faired well in our other evaluations, especially its linestoppers, which were favored highly by BOC Challenge skippers in the

Fiddle Block Comparison Chart

Make	Model	List Price/ Discount Price	Line Size	Load (SWL/Breaking Strength in lbs.)	Cheeks	Sheaves	Straps
Antal	981.652	$106.20/N.A.	1/2"	1,700/3,400	AL	Mekton	AL
Garhauer	30-08-GB	$48/N.A.	1/2"	2,000/4,000	AL	AL	SS
Harken	038	$80.30/$70.65	3/8"	750/2,500	Delrin	AL	SS
Lewmar	9187	$54/$45.90	1/2"	1,350/2,700	Polycarbonate	Delrin	SS
Schaefer	22-55	$67/$56.95	1/2"	1,750/3,500	AL	Delrin	SS

1990-91 race.

Antal fiddle blocks are beautifully made of black anodized 3571 TA16 aluminum, both for the cheeks and straps. Their finish seems harder and more durable than some other anodizing we've seen. Many variations of the Antal blocks are available. We looked at two similar fiddle blocks, one with a composite fiber bearing and one without. Both have Delrin ball bearings to handle side loads. Mekton or aluminum sheaves are available, the latter carrying a higher safe working load rating. While we admired the fancier models, we stuck to the standard Series Two block without composite fiber bearing for purposes of this evaluation because its rated strength and price are more in line with the other four makes. Unfortunately, we were unable to test the cam on our bench as the only block in stock at the distributor's office had been sold.

Even without the composite fiber bearing, the large sheave of model #981.652 moves freely; the small block does not have ball bearings and turned with more difficulty. Tolerances are close, indicating precision machining. This means less noise and less friction. Ball bearings handle the side loads of the large sheave.

Both sheaves turn on stainless steel bolts insulated from the aluminum cheeks by nylon washers. The swivel can be locked in any 90-degree position by aligning a groove in the bottom with a ridge in a Mekton bushing/spacer on the top cheek bolt. A representative of the Antal distributor said this ridge cannot withstand high shock loads. The arms are adjustable to assure the correct lead from the large sheave to the cam.

While Antal makes its own cams, the U.S. distributor also represents the patented Servo Cleat from Germany. Euro Marine Trading told us they generally replace the Antal cams with Servo Cleats.

We are impressed with Antal hardware, but are well aware of the price differential. The fiddle we selected was twice the cost of several others, and the composite fiber model is twice as expensive as the Series Two. If you are equipping your entire boat with Antal hardware, you'll want an Antal fiddle block as well, just for consistency. But at its high price, we didn't feel it represented the best value or even necessarily the best performance.

Garhauer

As noted in the last issue, this California-based hardware manufacturer markets mostly to the OEM (original equipment manufacturer) market, which means it prefers selling to boatbuilders more than over-the-counter, after market sales to consumers. Garhauer supplies Catalina Yachts with hardware, as well as parts for upscale Alden Yachts and others.

The cheeks and sheaves of the 30-08-GB are gray anodized aluminum, the straps, arms and other fittings stainless steel. The arms are not adjustable. The sheaves turn on Delrin ball bearings, which surprised us, since this was the lowest priced block we tested. Ball bearing sheaves usually are found on the more expensive hardware. The sheaves turned freely, though there was noticeably more slop than in Antal's sheaves.

The bearings turn on hollow stainless steel tubes. The model we tested had a swivel snap shackle, unlike the others we tested, but as with all of the makes, different fittings are available.

The aluminum cam jaws didn't close quite properly; one side would hang up on the other because they were too close together. While cleating the line was fairly easy, the absence of a V-shape to the top teeth means you have to pull the line toward you more to get the line into the jaws. A pronounced V-shape, as with some other cams, allows you to simply pull the line down to cleat it.

In our pull test, the line slipped at 1,100 pounds, as much as any other fiddle tested. On inspection, however, the thin stainless steel arms had deformed, leaving the cam cockeyed. We concluded that there simply wasn't enough material in the arms to prevent distortion under high loads.

The Garhauer fiddle looks nice enough, but close inspection revealed several instances of sloppy work, such as loose tolerances and scoring in the cheeks around the rivets. Deformation of the cam arms indicates to us that they are under-engineered. The sizeable price differential we saw with the Garhauer genoa lead blocks doesn't exist with fiddle blocks. Perhaps this is due to the twin ball-bearing sheaves, which certainly add to cost. Though it is the lowest priced fiddle tested, we feel you can buy a better block for a few dollars more.

Harken

The Harken block is physically the largest of the five fiddles tested. Though other blocks tested had ball bearing sheaves, Harken's larger sheave diameters are necessary because the ball bearing movements

Bearings	Sheave Diameter	Weight	Cam Cleat Pull (lbs. at which line slipped)
Mekton/Delrin ball	2-1/2"/1-5/8"	15 oz.	NA
Delrin ball	2-1/4"/1-3/4"	15 oz.	1,100 (bent arms)
Delrin ball	3"/1-3/4"	20 oz.	1,100
Delrin bushing	2"/1-1/4"	13 oz.	600 (bent arms)
Delrin bushing	1-1/2"/1-1/2"	11 oz.	1,000

handle both side and radial loads. The design of the other makes of ball bearing sheaves use ball bearings just for side loads, relying on a hollow sleeve bearing for the radial loads. Because of the ball bearing movements, the Harken's safe working load rating is the lowest of the five; presumably, the Delrin bearings will crush before any other part fails. Despite its lower SWL rating, this is a superior design with noticeably less friction than the other four makes.

The #038 Harken fiddle block has Delrin cheeks or sideplates, solid aluminum sheaves, stainless steel straps and arms, and Cam-Matic cleats. The arms are adjustable. This patented cleat has Teflon-impregnated die-cast aluminum cams and baseplates with three rows of Delrin ball bearings inside. The teeth are rounded to minimize line chafe and there is a deep V-shape at the top to make pulling the line down into the cleat easy. Harken boasts that the Cam-Matic is the easiest cam to uncleat under load, and we agree.

In our pull tests, the Cam-Matic held to 1,100 pounds, then the line popped free. Earlier tests, with the cam slightly out of line with the sheave, caused the line to pop free at 850 pounds, so it is easy to see that adjustable arms are an important feature. Why the line popped free on the Cam-Matic, while on other cams it just started to slip through, is difficult to say. It is probably because of the rounded or "soft" cam teeth. There was no deformation of the arms, straps or cheeks.

Harken told us that the company has developed its strong belief in ball bearing sheaves to facilitate unloading rather than loading. For example, in light air when you want to push the boom out, the line runs more quickly and freely with ball bearing blocks.

The Harken fiddle is a big, almost gaudy block with its large arms and sideplates, both drilled with numerous holes in the name of weight savings. Styling, like beauty, lies in the eye of the beholder. Some people will love Harken's look, others will find the Antal more handsome. And we don't doubt for a minute that many purchases are based on looks. The red base and cam caps are Harken trademarks and make the line highly recognizable. Though priced higher than Lewmar, Schaefer and Garhauer, it costs less than Antal. It has the most features—two ball bearing sheaves, superior design, and the best cam cleat. We think it's the best fiddle block tested, and because the cost differential isn't great, it is therefore also the best value.

Schaefer

Curiously, the Schaefer 22-55 fiddle block was the smallest of the five tested. It's two identical sheaves measure just 1-1/2-inch in diameter, and the body is small. Yet it's safe working load rating of 1,750 pounds is about as high as any of the others tested. It is also available with ball bearing sheaves and a 1,000-pound SWL for just $8 more.

The cheeks are black anodized aluminum, the straps are stainless steel, and the sheaves are Delrin. The arms are very short, almost unnoticeable. The cam appears to sit on a shelf cut out of the cheeks, with the arms hidden inside and riveted. The cams have stainless steel bodies with a softer polymer top. They work well in operation, though we suspect the stainless steel teeth will abrade line faster than rounder or aluminum teeth. In our pull test, the cam held to 1,000 pounds. There was a slight deformation of the baseplate upon which the cams sit, but it was barely noticeable.

The Schaefer fiddle is well designed and well made. It has a very basic look to it; clearly the company has made no real effort to give it the sex appeal of the Antal or Harken, and that's fine with us. It's small size makes it easy to discount, but the truth is it performs well. We think it's a good product, but lacking some of Harken's features. We'd be inclined to buy Schaefer's ball bearing model for a few dollars more, if only to hear the satisfying rattle.

Lewmar

The Lewmar #9187 also is a small block, similar in size to the Schaefer. It does, however, have one large sheave (two inches) and one small sheave (1-1/4-inch). The cheeks are black polycarbonate, the sheaves Delrin, the straps and arms stainless steel, and the cams are patented Servo Cleats from Germany. These have stainless steel teeth molded into the polymer cams.

The Lewmar has a method of locking the pin in 90-degree positions that requires removing the shackle, pushing the pin in, and inserting a roll pin. It works, but we found it a bit tedious. On the other hand, it's not something you'd do very often.

In operation, the cleat works well. We liked the Servo Cleat, but don't rate it any better than Harken's Cam-Matic.

Our pull test showed the Lewmar's biggest weakness. At just 600 pounds, the line slipped and the thin stainless steel arms collapsed inward, pinching the large sheave.

The Lewmar was the biggest disappointment of the group, based on the company's generally good reputation for quality equipment.

This model, however, failed, in our opinion, to live up to its name. Despite being the second lowest priced fiddle tested, we see no reason to recommend it.   **• PS**

Boom Vangs

The Hall Quik Vang is the class act among the seven rigid boom vang systems we tested.

Being the largest moving part on deck, the boom of a sailboat has, as is ruefully known by every knot-headed sailor who ever stepped aboard, the potential to go in harm's way.

A boom can sweep across the horizon and smash a nose or shatter teeth. In its other ugly mood, bouncing wildly up and down when the mainsail is luffing or when the main halyard is released, it can drop squarely on a head or shoulder.

Both ways, people have been killed. It's been going on since the time of square riggers. The commonest exhortation on modern boats is, "Duck!"

The device that can eliminate at least some of the risk is called a rigid boom vang. It tames the boom in one of the two dangerous planes.

A rigid boom vang is, therefore, somewhat of a safety device, although we generally think of it as a way to control undesirable twist in the mainsail when reaching and running, and also to support the boom when parked or while reefing. Mainsail control on many boats is accomplished with a soft vang, an adjustable arrangement of line, shackles and blocks either permanently attached at the base of the mast or rigged at the rail as needed. The rigid vang does that, too, but, in its support function, it also replaces that snapping, whipping, befouling thing called a topping lift, which loves to chew up the ends of batten pockets.

In more exotic forms, the vang can be a hydraulic rod, for those who believe spending money is the key to success in racing, or can be a custom and costly semi-circular track as was seen on Twelve Meter boats during the heyday of the America's Cup.

What's Available

When we looked at rigid vangs in 1987, there were but three available. They were the Hall Quik Vang,

adjudged at that time to be the very best; the Voomwang Vang, an inadequate-for-the-task device which quickly disappeared from the market, and the Selden RodKick, which now in re-engineered and much-improved form is called the RodKicker. We'd also tested an Easykick, then imported by Merriman, but couldn't locate the distributor to retest.

The success of the rigid vang is indicated by the fact that, in addition to the Hall Quik Vang and the Selden RodKicker, we this time were able to gather up for testing five others, from Forespar, Sparcraft, Offshore Spars, Spinlock and LeFiell. And, in a future issue, we will take a look at a quite different device called the Boomkicker, from Seoladair, which is not really a vang but a boom support system.

Because some of these vangs have proper names, plus a manufacturer's name plus a distributor's name, we will, to avoid confusion, refer to them by their proper names as listed in the first column on the chart.

All seven rigid vangs come in at least several sizes. We chose those whose specifications fit *Practical Sailor's* test boat, a C & C 33. The prices on the chart are for those particular vangs. Larger ones would cost somewhat more, smaller ones less. Note also that some are priced with purchase tackle, but the mast and boom fittings always cost extra. If you already have a soft vang, it probably can be used on a rigid vang, if it has enough purchase to compress the spring.

Only of minor interest to you readers is the amount of effort required to figure out how to mount the fittings for seven vangs without riddling the boom and the base of the mast with two to three dozen holes. We solved the problem by using one mast fitting (Forespar's) and a length of track with a car on the boom.

Types of Vangs

There are basically two kinds of rigid boom vangs. There are vangs, generally rectangular in shape, with the purchase tackle or ratchet system rigged internally. There are vangs, usually round, with the purchase tackle mounted externally, although a basic internal purchase sometimes is part of the telescoping tube arrangement.

Because of the leverage exerted by a mainsail in a stiff breeze, selecting a vang for a given boat, and getting it mounted and working, requires some judgment. Taken to extremes, the result can be a broken boom, which on most boats is not a very strong structural beam. In fact, several of these rigid vangs contain in the instructions the warning that if you put a lot of weight on the end of the boom while it is supported by the vang, the boom may break.

We wonder, also, what would happen to a boom if one exercised the option (offered by several vang manufacturers) of taking the purchase up to 32:1.

A further categorization, when considering rigid boom vangs, is whether (to keep the boom from dropping or to cushion it) it has a fixed support, a spring, or a gas cylinder. Those who make vangs with springs say those with gas cylinders, whose cylinders are magnetic steel, corrode, leak gas and wear out. Manufacturers who use gas cylinders claim springs fatigue. To their credit, gas cylinders usually are easy to replace and are available in a wide variety of pressures, which may make it easier to fine tune the vang. However, because the springs used in vangs are hardened stainless steel that are rated for about a million compressions and on good vangs can be adjusted for tension, we'll give the nod to springs for most boats.

One further note: Because of the metal-to-metal connections at the mast and boom, there is virtually no way with a rigid vang to eliminate a certain amount of clicking noise made by the end fittings and clevis pins.

DX Index by Spinlock

Made in England by Spinlock, the DX Index comes in three sizes, with standard and high power options for all. It is the most unusual design, quite different from all the others.

It's a very clean, sleek, aerodynamic design, with a ratchet system and 8:1 purchase, all internal. The purchase can be increased to 32:1 with the attachment of external tackle.

The one we chose to test is a new model that can be switched via a button-operated show-red/show-green lever, from a free running mode to an auto-matic boom support. There's nothing on the DX Index to snag or foul errant lines.

This new model, which is very light, appears to be well-engineered and nicely finished. It can be disassembled via Allen screws. Getting used to its switchable automatic operation would take a bit of practice. It's difficult to estimate how well the internal ratchet system would withstand wear and the forces imposed by any rigid vang.

The DX Index is unique in that it uses no spring or gas cylinder to cushion the boom support function. You simply lift the boom to the desired location, switch from red to green on the switch, release the boom and the next ratchet tooth automatically engages.

With boom and mast fittings and Harken tackle (if you wanted more than the basic 8:1 purchase), the DX Index is very expensive, even at discount.

Bottom Line: In operation, the DX Index, with its "green-switch" free movement and its automatic "red-switch" boom support would be very handy, once the crew learned to use the switch. However, unlike spring or gas cylinder vangs, the DX Index would, if you expected the vang to provide a little support for the boom when running in light airs, require manual adjustment. Changing the switch also requires a bit of tension on the purchase system. It seems unnecessarily complicated. This expensive vang, radically different in principle from the rest, is not in our view preferable to better spring-action vangs.

Sparcraft Pneu Vang

Very ruggedly built, Sparcraft's Pneu Vang is simply two telescoping anodized aluminum tubes with big Delrin collars, sleeves and seals and aluminum end

Specs: Rigid Boom Vangs

Name	Manufacturer	Vang	Fittings	Tackle*	Total	Weight (lbs.)	Boom Support
DX Index	Spinlock (IMTRA)	$790	$237	Included 8:1 Purchase	$1,027	6	Rigid Ratchet
Pneu Vang	Sparcraft (IM)	$475	$205	$250	$930	11.5	Gas Cylinder
Offshore Vang	Offshore Spar	$645	$145	Included	$790	11.5	SS Spring
Quick Vang	Hall Spars	$770	$191	Included	$961	13.5	SS Spring
Rodkicker	Selden (Sailsystems)	$445	$115	$175	$735	9.4	Gas Cylinder
Yacht Rod	Forespar	$501	$187	$250	$938	13.6	SS Spring
Vari-Vang	LeFiell	$500	$185	$250	$935	10	Soft Spring

* For recommended Harken tackle

fittings. The boom-end fitting is riveted; the mast-end fitting is attached with stainless steel screws.

The Pneu Vang has a good, big aluminum sheave to carry the wire strop to attach the tackle, which is all external. The optional 12:1 or 24:1 purchase is applied by an external tackle made by Harken.

The boom support is a gas cylinder, which can be replaced by removing four screws from the big Delrin sleeve.

The mast fitting seems inordinately complicated compared with some of the others but the boom fitting is a simple two-piece welded stainless steel assembly.

Adding up the vang, the fittings and the 12:1 Harken tackle brings the list price to $930.

Bottom Line: We had some trouble with the Pneu Vang in that, despite the big sheave, the six-part Harken block and tackle rubbed against the big collar, binding the action as the tackle tried to get past the collar. Because of that and because this is a gas cylinder vang without a length adjustment (which means it would have to be very precisely mounted), we can't give the Pneu Vang very high marks.

Offshore Vang

The Offshore Vang made in Michigan by Offshore Spars is the same in principle as the Hall Quik Vang. It is two telescoping anodized aluminum tubes with 3:1 internal purchase and additional external purchase applied with the excellent Harken gear.

The Offshore Vang uses a heavy spring as a boom support and it has six (or seven in a larger model) length adjustment holes secured by a big fast pin (which fits in a nicely done stainless steel bushing).

The adjustment holes certainly make less critical the installation of the boom fitting and might be handy to accommodate mainsails with different leech measurements, to retrofit to existing fittings on the mast and boom and, most importantly, make it possible to lift the boom to clear a Bimini top or awning.

The fast pin also fixes one end of the spring within the large tube, which confers the slight advantage that the vang can be installed with either end up. The pin can snag lines, however.

Bottom Line: The Offshore Vang is a well-made, fully assembled piece of equipment that works very well with Harken tackle, which is supplied. Faulted only by the protruding fastpin used in the length adjustment holes, the Offshore Vang comes fairly close in quality and operation to the Hall Quik Vang. If you're looking to save money, this is the choice.

Hall Quik Vang

Designed right in the beginning, the Quik Vang appears to be unchanged from the one we tested five years ago.

It's a precision-made telescoping tube type with a unique feature: The spring tension is adjustable via two Allen head set screws. Adjusting the spring is not something you'd want to do often, but it's not difficult. As the spring fatigues, probably over a few years, the tension can be taken up. The adjustment feature also is handy if the leech of your main stretches a bit or you buy a new mainsail with a slightly different leech length.

The Quik Vang has Delrin slider sleeves and plugs along with closely machined, tapered aluminum end fittings. Hall supplies Harken tackle with a distinctive red take-up line. The telescoping tubes are hard anodized and all parts fit like no other vang in the group.

Hall makes a good scissoring mast fitting, but we liked the one made by Forespar because of its extra holes.

Plainly put, the Quik Vang clearly remains the standard by which all other conventional vangs with telescoping tubes and external tackle must be measured.

The Quik Vang comes in eight different sizes, the most of any vang on the market, with return pressures varying from 400 to 1,000 pounds.

Bottom Line: The Hall Quik Vang is supplied fully assembled and is easy to install. More importantly, the Quik Vang operates very smoothly. Its heavy Delrin plugs provide very friction-free, quiet adjustment. With its tapered, machined end fittings, it is, without doubt, the best quality vang on the

Warranty	Comments
2 Yrs.	Very sleek British design with ratchet mechanism and 8:1 internal purchase. Switchable from free to support mode.
1 Yr.	Rugged, simple gas cylinder design with a big collar that interferes with the purchase tackle. Length is not adjustable.
3 Yrs.	Well made with internal purchase and Harken external gear. Length is adjustable. Fairly close in quality to Quik Vang. Best buy.
3 Yrs.	The best. Comes fully assembled. Top quality. Spring operated with adjustable tension. Works very smoothly.
5 Yrs.	Very simple in concept. Easiest to dismantle, including access to gas cylinder. Light weight and moderately priced.
1 Yr.	A strong heavyweight spring vang. For those who intend to use existing purchase tackle, this is the best buy.
3 Yrs.	An odd design, with a soft spring, that won't support a drooping boom in a level position. Poor welds and magnetic roll pins.

market. Not outlandishly priced, it's the top choice.

Selden Rodkicker

The Rodkicker, imported from Sweden by Sailsystems, is another very simple vang. Rectangular in shape, the Rodkicker comes with a choice of soft or hard gas cylinders.

The gas cylinder is easy to replace because the Rodkicker sections have plastic end caps that remove by simply depressing two locking buttons. The end caps also serve as bushings and shock absorbers. In fact, the Rodkicker is the easiest vang to dismantle and reassemble, but it doesn't seem to us to be an important feature.

The dark gray end fittings are aluminum castings. They are fastened to the rectangular extrusions with rivets, which seems less desirable than machine screws, but at least the rivets are aluminum and avoids mating unlike metals.

The Rodkicker stands out (like the DX Index) because there's nothing to foul errant spinnaker lines or halyard coils. The mast fitting, if you elect to use it, is a trim, gray-anodized aluminum casting with a hefty stainless hinge pin.

We don't care for the "Selden Rodkicker" sticker applied to both sides of the vang, but it's a small point based on our observations that stickers are unsightly when the elements start eating them.

Bottom Line: Although simple in design, the Rodkicker is not very smooth operating. The use of plastic end caps and collar (which is intended also to be a shock absorber) make the fits between the telescoping sections quite sloppy. We like the five-year warranty but don't much admire the cast aluminum end fittings. It's the least expensive but, unless light weight is important, we can't recommend the Rodkicker over the Offshore Vang, which costs just $55 more. If you need or want a return action harder than what's available with coil springs, the Rodkicker with a super hard gas spring would be a viable option.

The Yacht Rod from Forespar

Forespar makes some outstanding sailboat gear but, peculiarly, it doesn't claim to make the best rigid vang. The company very honestly concedes that distinction to Hall Spars.

The Yacht Rod, a very simple design acquired in 1988 from the Canadian company called Yacht Tech, is aimed at cruisers and club racers who elect to refit their existing soft vangs to the rigid vang and save a couple of hundred bucks.

The Yacht Rod is a white anodized aluminum tube into which is inserted a polished stainless steel tube that rides on Nylatron bearings. The end fittings are machined aluminum. It is spring-cushioned.

The cable to which the tackle must be fitted is entirely external and requires attachment below the mast fitting; the purchase tackle is attached to the other end of the strop leading out of the vang. As supplied, it requires some assembly, including fitting and swaging the cable.

To its credit, the length of the Yacht Rod is adjustable. However, the adjustment is a crude affair, just four sets of holes in the tube through which is inserted a clevis pin, which because of its length, can be a line snagger. In that regard, it resembles the Offshore Vang.

Even more to Forespar's credit is its butterfly-shaped mast fitting. (The mast fittings with some vangs are solid affairs that may or may not fit your mast.) The Forespar fitting is scissor-hinged around the pivot pin to make mast fitting easier. A beefy, all-stainless assembly with a hefty price ($103), we elected to use it for all the vangs.

Bottom Line: The Yacht Rod is an honest effort by Forespar to offer a lower-priced vang with the features of the Hall Quik Vang. It works fairly well but lacks the fine workmanship of the Quik Vang. We'd rank it just below the lower-priced Offshore Vang, which it more closely resembles.

Vari-Vang by LeFiell

Here's another vang, on the market but two years, that is rather different from the others. It's a small diameter, thick-walled vang with heavy torpedo-shaped end fittings of machined aluminum, all anodized in a bluish gray shade.

A light spring, fine-tuned (like the Hall Quik Vang) with a sliding block fastened with two Allen screws, is used to lift the boom for light air support. Using a light spring means that when flattening the mainsail, you'll not be working against a 600-pound spring. The instructions state that the Vari-Vang is intended to "bottom out" with the spring fully compressed when the boom is at rest or the mainsail is being reefed.

Besides its light-weight spring action, what also is different about the Vari-Vang is that the pin-to-pin length can be adjusted up to 10 inches by loosening another Allen screw and twisting the large tube on an internal threaded rod. It's a handy feature, both for ease of mounting and for use with mainsails with different leech lengths.

A heavy tang to fasten the purchase tackle is welded on the mast-end fitting. The weld is very crude, as is the welding on the boom fitting.

A magnetic roll pin is used to attach the jaw fitting to the boom end of the vang and the blue-anodized aluminum sheave is held by a big magnetic roll pin, which also must function as a bearing. We don't like roll pins and readers often write about their bad experiences with them.

Bottom Line: If your boat has a boom whose aft

end is lower than the gooseneck while sailing, the Vari-Vang is not for you because with this vang the boom is intended to bottom out (fully compress the spring) while stowed. This means that you would have to stow the mast in the drooping position, with no possibility of lifting the aft end for cockpit convenience or to rig an awning. Because of this, and the poor welding and the use of roll pins, we don't recommend this vang.

Conclusion

A rigid boom vang, with the proper fittings and tackle, is an expensive retrofit item.

Part of the consideration may involve whether you already have an existing boom fitting (that will fit) and a good six-part soft boom vang that can be used to apply the necessary purchase. If so, you need only buy the rigid vang.

If this were the case, the sturdy Yacht Rod (with adjustable length and a spring mechanism) from Forespar, available at discount for about $350, is the best buy.

For a vang equipped with Harken Hexaratchet tackle, you might, if you're interested in saving $150, choose the Offshore Vang over the Hall Quik Vang. Still, the Quik Vang is the best.

Your decision should be based, at least in part, on how you use it. If you're a keen racer, the softer, more responsive coil-spring types allow you to play the vang more easily. In addition to the Quik Vang, you might even like the Vari-Vang, assuming performance is more important than a droopy boom. For cruisers with heavier displacement boats, who probably will hunker down on the boom only when sailing off the wind, the gas spring models will be satisfactory. An advantage of these, including the Rodkicker, is they can be fitted with high load springs to hold up heavy booms. Exchanging springs of different ratings is relatively simple, and the cost quite reasonable. **• PS**

Rope Clutches

Lewmar's new Superlock rope clutch is the class of the field, outperforming Spinlock, Antal and Easylock

In the 15 or so years since rope clutches were first introduced, they've supplanted simple line stoppers as a better means of securing halyards, especially those led aft to the cockpit. But our tests show that some are a lot better than others.

A bank of linestoppers or rope clutches on the cabin top, lined up in front of one or two winches, means you don't need a winch and cleat for every halyard, as might be the case on the mast. After one halyard has been tensioned with the winch, and secured with the clutch, you can then remove the tail from the winch and proceed to raise another sail or a pole. Cleats, of course, don't work because you can't belay the line while it's wound around the winch.

Linestoppers and rope clutches are similar in that both grab the line by means of a toothed cam or compress it between two metal plates. The fundamental difference between stoppers and clutches is that the latter has a clutch mechanism, often employing a spring, to permit winching the line taut with the cam closed, and the gradual releasing of the line if you want to later ease or "bleed off" tension. In practice, we doubt you'd feel real comfortable easing halyard tension without the help of a winch to pay out line. Some clutches allow bleeding, some not at all, but even with the best the chances of letting the line go entirely are pretty good.

In 1987, we tested 11 different models of rope clutches. Our recommendation at the time was the Spinlock Express, made in England. Though some manufacturers have come and gone, we haven't noted much new in the world of rope clutches—until recently. Earlier this year Lewmar introduced its Superlock, proclaiming they had "re-invented the rope clutch." To evaluate their claims, we bench tested the Superlock, and five other models to compare performance.

The Tests

In addition to the Lewmar Superlock, we bought a Spinlock Express, Easylock Midi and Easylock Racing, and an Antal Master 12 Series. We also included a Schaefer EGR Halyard Stopper, only because it gave us a benchmark to compare results with our tests of five years ago; Schaefer no longer makes the EGR, though it may still be found in some discount catalogs, such as Defender Industries. Nor did we

Value Guide: Rope Clutches

Make/Model	Price (List/Discount)	Line Diameter	Ease of Bleeding (Rank)	Slippage (Before-After*)	Abrasion (Rank)
Lewmar Superlock	$57/$42.95 $75/$56	5/16"-3/8" 3/8"-7/16"	1	7/16"-7/16"	1
Antal Master 12	$85/$63.50 $86.80/$65.10	1/2"-9/16" 1/4"-1/2"	2	5/8"-1/2"	4
Spinlock Express	$114.25/$85.65 $54/$37.80	5/16"-5/8" 5/16"-7/16"	3	3/4"-7/16"	2
Easylock Midi	$88.75/$61.75 NA/$42	3/8"-9/16" 1/4"-9/16"	6	5/8"-3-1/4"	3
Schaefer 71-42	$78.54.75 $86.40/$60.50	to 3/8" to 1/2"	5	3/8"-9/16"	5
Easylock Racing	NA/$46	5/16"-1/2"	4	11/16"-13/16"	6

*Slippage was measured two ways, one with the line tensioned before closing the clutch, the other with the line tensioned

elect to include the Antal Junior and Senior, or the Forespar models, all of which produced above average line damage in our tests of five years ago. Our main objective was to see if the Lewmar Superlock is in fact superior to the popular Spinlock Express.

All models tested were singles, except the Superlock, which was a triple. Most clutches are available in single, double or triple configurations.

To test, we mounted the six clutches on a 2" x 6" board, and secured it to our test bench. A length of 3/8-inch braided line was led from our self-tailing winch and through the clutch to heavy shock cord secured to a padeye at the other end of the bench.

We tensioned the line to 600 pounds, five times with the clutch closed before tensioning, and five times with the clutch open (the clutch was then closed, the line released from the winch, and the clutch opened). We measured slippage (the amount the line slipped back through the clutch after the line was released from the winch; slippage of half an inch reduces the load by about 140 pounds), abrasion of the line, and ease of closing and releasing the clutch, particularly the ease of bleeding tension. As noted in the earlier report, slippage is generally greater when the clutch is closed before tensioning. We did, however, find some exceptions, particularly the Easylock Midi. In most instances, the differences in slippage (closing the clutch before or after tensioning) were not great. The results are shown in the accompanying table.

Antal Master 12 Series

Made in Italy, the Antal clutch is the smallest of the five models tested that are currently in production. As with all Antal hardware, materials are top quality, and the design is handsome. Also like most other Antal hardware we've tested (blocks, cams, etc.), performance is at or near the top.

The Antal housing is anodized aluminum, the handle is stainless steel, and the cam mechanism is stainless and bronze. The teeth in the cam compress the line against a series of teeth on the bottom of the rope alley. The unit is easy to install and easy to lead a line through. The flared stainless fittings at each end minimize abrasion, especially with unfair leads. We also found it easy to bleed line tension. While it ranked fourth in abrasion, there wasn't much difference between it and the Spinlock Express and Easylock Midi. In terms of slippage, it had the least, ranking it first.

Antal hardware often costs a premium, but in this instance, the cost of the 1/4"-1/2" model was in the same ballpark as Lewmar and Spinlock.

Bottom Line: We like the Antal for its nicely finished metal parts, small size and minimal slippage. As with most of the toothed cam clutches, abrasion is a concern. Overall, it's our second choice.

Easylock Midi

Made in Denmark, the Easylock Midi is the least expensive of the models tested. Construction is aluminum and stainless steel. The mechanism clamps the line between two corrugated steel plates.

In our tests, the Midi did not perform well. We found it impossible to ease tension; as the handle was released, the line blew out with a bang. No amount of care could control it.

Slippage was unpredictable, ranging from a very acceptable 5/8-inch to an unacceptable 3-1/4 inches. Abrasion was in the middle of the pack.

Bottom Line: While the price of the Easylock Midi is attractive, for $20 more you can have the best. The extra cost is well worth it. We wouldn't put the Midi on our boat.

Easylock Racing

Unlike the Easylock Midi, the Racing version uses a toothed aluminum cam and toothed base plate to grip the line. The housing also is aluminum. Compared to the Antal and Spinlock, the spring seems small. There is a fairlead provided that must be owner installed. We did not use it for our tests.

Operation of the Easylock Racing clutch takes a bit of getting used to. A button on the top engages the cam, indeed justifying the name Easylock. To release, however, you must pull the handle back and then push forward, in effect doubling the operation. It's not hard, just initially confusing. More serious, however, is that when releasing the line with your hand gripping the handle, your fingers may get crimped between it and the housing. Because it doesn't bleed tension easily, we found ourselves slapping the handle down with the palm of our hand to release the line. Under high loads, it gets scary.

The Easylock Racing was the only model tested which broke fibers after 10 repetitions, by far the worst performance. That, plus higher-than-average slippage forced us to rank the Easylock Racing last.

Bottom Line: Being easy to lock isn't as important as abrasion, slippage and release. Though the price is

Comments

Our first choice.

Easy to bleed. Easy to feed line through.

One mount screw difficult.

Cannot be eased.

No longer in production.

Easy to close, but must slap to release.

after closing the clutch.

again low, we can't recommend the Easylock Racing.

Lewmar Superlock

New this year, the British-made Superlock is indeed a better mousetrap. The housing is plastic and the mechanism is stainless steel. It grips by means of a patent pending "wavegrip" device that looks like five rings connected by side plates. As the handle is closed, the rings rotate to close the size of their opening. It can be likened to the domino effect. One obvious advantage is that a much greater surface area of the line is gripped than with a single cam.

Our tests demonstrate the advantages of the wavegrip design. The Lewmar Superlock ranked first in every category except slippage, where it came in just behind Antal, albeit by a mere 1/16 inch. Abrasion was almost non-existent and it was easy to bleed line tension. It is the largest of the models tested, but we don't reckon that's much of a factor.

Bottom Line: Priced in line with the Antal and Spinlock, the Lewmar Superlock is an easy first choice in rope clutches.

Schaefer EGR Halyard Stopper

As noted earlier, Schaefer no longer makes this model, though it does continue to manufacture its Spinnaker Halyard Stopper series.

We have included the data on the table for comparison purposes only. If you currently own Schaefer EGR stoppers, this will let you know how much you might expect to gain by upgrading to a different make.

Spinlock Express

Probably the most popular clutches in the world, we found the Express to be a decent performer. The body is plastic, the handle aluminum, and the clutch mechanism stainless steel. There are flared stainless fittings at both ends of the rope alley. The cam descends onto the line without rotating, by virtue of a well-thought-out design.

In our abrasion tests, the Spinlock Express showed only minute fraying of the cover threads. Slippage was a little more than the Lewmar Superlock and Antal Master. Bleeding tension was satisfactory. One of the mounting screws is difficult to place, but it's a job you'll only do once.

Bottom Line: The Spinlock Express, our top choice five years ago, still is a good piece of hardware. If it was priced lower than the Lewmar Superlock, we'd give it serious consideration.

Conclusion

Five years ago we noted that rope clutches were getting better, but still weren't perfect. The Lewmar Superlock represents the most significant improvement in that time. Based on our tests, especially for abrasion, we think the Superlock is a breakthrough that will save you the cost of replacing line every season or so. Often we expect to see such new products selling for prices much higher than the competition. Fortunately, that's not the case with the Superlock. It is an easy first choice.

Antal and Spinlock are good quality clutches, but toothed cams have certain liabilities that can't be overcome no matter how good the clutch mechanism and materials. The Easylock models were disappointing, especially the Racing model, which literally chewed our line to pieces. Unless Harken or Schaefer decides to put on their thinking caps and do Lewmar one better, the Superlock is, for the time being, the class of the field. • **PS**

Chute Tamers

The addition of one of these devices to your rigging can take the intimidation out of spinnaker flying.

The spinnaker is the sail that makes landlubbers "Uhhh" and "Ahhh" but sailors know it's a devil to handle, hoist and douse. Just getting it up and drawing requires a lot of rigging of the pole, topping lift, downhaul, sheet, guy and halyard. Even a fully trained racing crew often gets something wrong.

For a cruising sailor, a mistake in the preparation can mean a rope burn cut instantaneously by a wayward halyard or sheet. The powerful spinnaker is so fraught with potential trouble that cruising sailors often forego the possibility of the dreaded spinnaker wrap, which can ruin a weekend cruise. Worse, if the sail has to be cut away from the forestay, it can wreck the summer cruise budget.

The spinnaker, by the way, is believed to have acquired its name from "spinxer," which is what the crew called the new-type sail aboard the British yacht *Sphinx* during a race in the Solent in the 1870s.

To check out the "store-bought" devices to manage the billowing beauty, we gathered up everything we could find. It isn't much.

On *PS One,* the magazine's C & C 33, we tried out the Kracor Spinnaker Gun, and two sleeve-type spinnaker tamers, one called a Chutescoop, the other an ATN. All three of these devices also work well on big headsails (whether called cruising spinnakers, MPSs, gennakers or whatever) not attached to the forestay.

Kracor Spinnaker Gun

The Kracor Spinnaker Gun is a molded plastic bucket, with a flared end and no bottom. Its utility is restricted to preparing a spinnaker for hoisting without breaking out prematurely. It's a giant step forward from the old laborious "rotten cotton" method of "stopping" a spinnaker. It also is an improvement on a piece of PVC pipe, which some racing crews have used for years.

To begin, one loads the small end of the Kracor with about 15 or 20 rubber bands. Then, working belowdecks with the loose spinnaker, the head of the sail is handed up through the companionway or a hatch to a crewmember on deck. The head of the sail is inserted in the wide end of the Kracor. While the crewmember below shakes out and aligns the tapes on the edge of the spinnaker, the helper on deck pulls the sail through the gun, stopping every three feet to roll a rubber band off the gun onto the sail. There are nice deep grooves on the gun to permit grabbing the rubber bands one at a time.

It might be done by one person. However, because of the desirability of keeping the tapes parallel, it is a job best done by two.

When finished, the spinnaker is neatly "tubed" in rubber bands, easy to bag or handle and ready for the attachment of the halyard and sheets.

When hoisted, the spinnaker hangs like a sausage until, by yanking the sheets, the sail initially breaks out first at the bottom, snapping rubber bands upward as it fills with wind. In the boat's wake will be a trail of broken rubber bands.

We found the Kracor Spinnaker Gun well-designed for its intended purpose and very easy to use. The spinnaker, hoisted in about 8-10 knots of wind (about the wind velocity in which a cruising sailor might use a chute), hung placidly until the sheet and guy were given a firm tug. Then the sail deployed smoothly, without ado.

The Kracor's liability is that it is somewhat bulky to store (it takes about a cubic foot). In addition, if cruising, one would need a goodly supply of #16 rubber bands. The Kracor comes in eight different sizes. It costs but $27.30, and is a cheap and easy way to preclude the premature deployment of a sail that can be dangerous.

The Chutescoop

Next, we thoroughly tested two sleeve-type devices. More versatile than the Kracor gun, the sleeves permit not only safe hoisting but also quick striking of the spinnaker...if all goes well. They also make storage easier, in that the "sausage" can be either folded into a sail bag or neatly rolled up and secured with a tie or two.

In principle, the two sleeves are exactly alike. Both are simple cloth tubes through which is led a control line to raise and lower the lower end of the tube to deploy the spinnaker. To set the sail, the lower end of the tube is pulled to the masthead (where it remains). To strike the sail, the sleeve is pulled down over the sail, compressing it in the tube as it is lowered. Then the sail can be lowered to the deck.

We first tried the Chutescoop made by the V.F. Shaw Co., Inc., of Bowie, Maryland. It's been on the market a good long time. The Chutescoop is a moderately complicated device that requires careful attention to the directions (which could be better done) and considerable care in executing them. It's best done at home on the living room floor. We rigged it aboard the boat and, to put it plainly, got confused several times. Backtracking and a bit of applied logic put it right.

The Chutescoop contains sewn-in stainless steel rings in the ends of the nylon tube. The bottom ring is, of course, larger than the top ring. Without these rings, the mouth would bind tightly and perhaps even roll and foul the sleeve in the sail cloth.

The Chutescoop requires a few adjustments at the top end. Basically, what must be done is adjust some lines so that the Chutescoop, when pulled in a bundle to the stop of the mast, has sufficient room to park itself without interfering with the full deployment of the spinnaker.

We had no trouble hoisting the Chutescoop, but when running the bottom ring up and down to free and then recapture the sail, it seemed somewhat catchy. Considerable force often was required on the control line. The dousing procedure begins easily when there is little spinnaker to force into the sleeve. But as the sleeve reaches the more voluminous portion of the spinnaker (about a third of the way down), the friction of the sail already in the sleeve plus the force needed to pull more sail into the sleeve makes for a lot of resistance.

We did not have the problem, but the instructions warn that the two small lines within the sleeve may twist and foul on the sail cloth. In fact, the two small lines inside the tube lead down through a few 2 1/2"-wide cloth straps inside the tube. If it happens, the instructions say to try running the sleeve up and down several times. If that doesn't free the jam, the whole thing must be lowered, worked free and repacked.

Further, the instructions say that it's best to have a Chutescoop 2-7 feet shorter than the bundled sail. This not only permits easier attachment of the sheet and guy, but also allows the guy to reach the spinnaker pole end fitting. Dropping the sail can be a problem if the pole is fully aback and the guy is cleated down.

(The company also makes what it calls a TurtleRoo, which is a bag in which to stow the Chutescoop. It has several pockets specifically designed for tying down the spinnaker head and clews. It's another $100 to $125 for the three available sizes.)

The Chutescoop comes in five sizes, ranging from 20 feet long ($95) to 44 feet long ($199). For our C & C 33, we bought from West Marine Products the 37-foot model.

ATN

The ATN, made by A.T.N., Inc., of Fort Lauderdale, Florida, is much better made than the Chutescoop.

To begin, it comes fully rigged. It has a small, tidy top closed by Velcro after simply running the head of the sail up through the tube and attaching it to a shackle on a strop, which is equipped with a swivel. The block for the control line is more substantial than that used on the Chutescoop.

More importantly, the control line, a single piece of high-quality braid, runs through a sleeve sewn to the outside of the tube. This means that the control line cannot foul the spinnaker within the tube, contained as it is in a separate channel. Most important of all, the bottom end of the ATN is a molded fiberglass flared oval securely attached to the sleeve.

We rigged the ATN in a tenth of the time needed for the Chutescoop, attached the halyard, ran it up the mast and set and snuffed the spinnaker a number of times with the greatest of ease. It was readily apparent that the separate channel for the control line, the larger block at the top of the tube and the smooth fiberglass oval at the bottom end all contribute to the very smooth operation of the ATN.

The man behind ATN is French sailor Etienne Griore, who broke a number of records in last summer's Europe 1 single-handed race from Plymouth England to Newport, Rhode Island. The ATN, he says, has been used by a number of BOC skippers. Surfing downwind in the Southern Ocean, with gale winds and huge breaking seas, it's no wonder they demand a strong, well-designed means of controlling their spinnakers.

The ATN costs $7.50 a foot in lengths less than 75 feet long and $9 a foot for lengths greater than 75 feet. That makes an ATN almost twice the cost of the Chutescoop. There is no question in our minds that the difference is worth it.　　• **PS**

Buying Guide

-

Safety

Superb EPIRBs

These gadgets really can save your life. If you can afford it, go for one of the 406-MHz units.

Even with the best life raft, fully stocked with survival equipment, your chances of survival at sea are poor unless someone is looking for you. Marine VHF radios are only reliable to about 20 to 30 miles offshore. The range of portable VHFs is even less, though they can be of great use in hailing passing ships. High frequency (HF) SSB marine radios will carry much farther; however, they require well-engineered antennas and lots of power. Trying to use an SSB radio in a life raft would be a near impossibility. Your only choice for long-range communications after abandoning your boat is an EPIRB (Emergency Position Indicating Radio Beacon). this communication is only one-way. You won't know if anyone has heard your call for help, but the odds are someone will.

EPIRBs aren't only for offshore racing and cruising boats. We recommend that anyone venturing away from the immediate shoreline have one on board. Making a distress call on a VHF radio can often be a one-shot deal, or impossible if your batteries are dead. EPIRBs are automatic, they need only to be turned on. No channel selection or other operations are necessary. Even a young child can activate an EPIRB.

EPIRBs operate by transmitting a beacon signal on one or more predetermined frequencies. They are classified into several categories:

Class A EPIRBs: These are intended for use on commercial vessels, which are required to carry one. A Class A EPIRB is designed to float free of its mounting and activate automatically on contact with seawater.

Class B EPIRBs: These are generally less expensive than their Class A counterparts. Class B units operate on the same frequencies as Class A, but must be manually activated. They are usually supplied with a manually released mounting bracket, similar to those used for fire extinguishers. Class B units are not required to float, but flotation collars are available for most models that don't.

Class A and B EPIRBs continuously transmit a homing signal (a swept AM modulated tone) on boat 121.5 and 243 MHz. The 121.5 MHz frequency is used for international civil aviation emergencies. The 243 MHz frequency is the military aircraft "guard" channel. These two frequencies are routinely monitored by aircraft, especially when traveling on transoceanic routes. Monitoring is not mandatory, however.

Fortunately, the new COSPAS/SARSAT satellite system that monitors the 406 MHz EPIRBs also listens to the 121.5 and 243 MHz frequencies. this system is composed of both former Soviet (COSPAS) and American (SARSAT) satellites. When these satellites receive a signal, they relay to a ground station, an ultimately to the closest available rescue service. All of the models we tested were rated for satellite reception.

The major drawback of Class A and B units is their inability to identify the source of the signal. With a large number of units carried by both boats and aircraft, false alarms are common, and numerous cases have been reported of multiple EPIRB activations in the same geographical area. Rescuers, unfortunately, have no way to differentiate false alarms from actual emergencies. Thus, rescue can often be delayed for a considerable length of time, while authorities attempt to verify that a real emergency exists.

Class C EPIRBs: The Class C EPIRB is completely different from the Class A and B units. the Class C device operates by periodically transmitting a brief signal on VHF channel 16, along with a continuous homing signal on Channel 15. These are intended for use in coastal waters where Channel 16 is routinely monitored. In order to minimize interference, Class C models will turn off automatically after 24 hours of operation. If necessary, they can be manually reactivated.

The principle behind the Class C EPIRB makes sense. Commercial vessels and the U.S. Coast Guard are required to continually monitor channel 16. So theoretically, in coastal waters, someone should always be able to hear your distress beacon. in reality, because of their low output power, the signals from Class C EPIRBs are often masked by the heavy traffic of full-power radios on Channel 16. Unlike Channel 16, the 121.5/243 MHz an 406.025 MHz frequencies are never used for anything but emergency communications.

406 MHz EPIRBs: the 406 MHz EPIRB represents the latest technology for emergency signal transmission. In addition to a 121.5 MHz homing signal, these models also intermittently transmit a digitally coded identification signal on 406-025 MHz. This signal is unique for each individual EPIRB produced. After purchase, the new unit's owner is required to register his ID number with the COSPAS/SARSAT Mission Control Center that covers his intended sailing area.

Oddly, it is reported that only about 70 percent of these EPIRB are registered; some are presumably in the sales pipeline, but it appears that many owners, whether through ignorance or forgetfulness, are not registering them, thereby negating one of the most significant advantages of these more expensive safety devices. A postpaid registration card is provided with each new unit sold. The information supplied on the card is loaded into the worldwide COSPAS/SARSAT computer network, and can be accessed immediately in the event that the EPIRB is activated.

This system solves a major problem with the older, conventional EPIRBs. With those models, no indication is given of the type of vessel or aircraft in distress. The 406-MHz model tells authorities what they are looking for in advance of a search. Additionally, this allows rescue forces to attempt to contact the vessel's owner to determine if the EPIRB was accidentally activated. This can prevent a waste of resources on an unnecessary search-and-rescue mission. More than 90 percent of the signals monitored from Class A and B EPIRBs eventually prove to be false alarms, compared to less than five percent for 406-MHz EPIRBs, in part because a phone call can usually determine quickly if an emergency exists.

The satellites monitoring the 406-MHz frequency can store the particulars of an emergency signal, and postpone relaying it until the satellite is over a receiving station below. This gives the 406 MHz EPIRBs yet another advantage over 121.5 MHz units. the less expensive Class A and B units require "mutual visibility;" that is, the satellite must have both the source of the signal and the ground receiver in sight at the same time.

The 406-MHz EPIRBs are subdivided into Category I units, which include a float-free bracket and are automatically activated when released, and the somewhat less expensive Category II units, which must be manually released and activated. The mounting brackets supplied with the Category I models use a hydrostatic charge to release a cable or clamp that holds the EPIRB securely in its mount. These charges are calibrated to release at 2 to 4 meters under water. To minimize the chances of a false alarm, the Category I units are designed to be unaffected by rain or spray. A Category I EPIRB must be manually turned off if it is necessary to remove it from its bracket.

Test Procedure

Responding in part to complaints from Alaska fishermen, in 1989 the FCC tested all commercially available EPIRBs to determine if they met requirements for signal coherency, watertightness, shock resistance, and transmitter output. With the exception of some ACR models, virtually all failed. This sent manufacturers scrambling to redesign their units to comply with tougher standards, which had to be met before those units could again be sold. All eventually requalified.

Anxious to see if our collection of EPIRBs met those new standards, we tested each of the units in a radio-frequency (RF) shielded screen room (in order to avoid having search and rescue teams dispatched to our test location). Total power output of each unit was measure, along with the actual frequency on which each was transmitting.

Originally, we had planned to run each unit for a full 48 hours to test its rated ability to broadcast for this length of time, while monitoring the total output and actual frequency. However, several problems developed with this approach. First, we found that we were unable to reliably contain the signals during testing. Unfortunately, the shielded room provided to us was designed primarily to keep *out* unwanted interference, not contain signals. At one point, we monitored a signal from one of the EPIRBs over 500 feet away. This was too far, we felt, to insure that the signals would not be detected by the highly sensitive satellites. Therefore, we decided to not risk violating the federal laws that prohibit EPIRB transmissions except in emergencies.

Second, considering that all of our units had brand-new batteries and were being tested at room temperature, we calculated that their battery life should easily exceed 80 hours. Three or four days of continuously monitored testing was simply not practical, or necessary.

We considered removing each unit's battery and testing it on a "dummy load" that would draw the same amount of current. While this sounds simple, it actually is very difficult, especially with the 406-MHz models where current consumption is not constant over time. The 406-MHz units have strobe lights that draw high current during the charge cycle, and little current during the strobe flash. Moreover, the signal is not transmitted continuously. It is composed of periodic data bursts that occur at predetermined intervals. Current consumption is highest during these transmissions. In order to simulate actual operation, each of these functions would have to be simulated for each EPIRB tested.

All of the EPIRBs tested exceeded their rated specifications. And due to the extended life of lithium batteries, we have no doubt that all the units tested will operate for at least 40 hours. This rating takes cold temperatures and adverse conditions into account. In warm weather, all these units would probably operate for nearly a week. With the recommended replacement interval for an EPIRB battery equaling one-half of the battery's rated shelf life, this additional safety factor should ensure that it will operate long enough to effect a rescue. We concluded, therefore, that the difference between the units is primarily in their design and construction details.

406 MHz EPIRBs

The models tested were the Alden Satfind 406, the ACR RLB-23, Raytheon JQE-2A, Litton 948-01, and Litton 952-02.

Generally speaking, the 406-MHz models we tested were of noticeably better quality than the less expensive 121.5 MHz units. The construction of the Raytheon (made by JRC) and Alden units appeared to be especially durable. JRC's high level of experience with radio circuits was especially evident in the Raytheon's internal construction, although we found no fault with the Alden's construction, either. The Raytheon JQE-2A uses a more conventional spring-loaded antenna, while the Alden Satfind 406 uses a printed-circuit antenna that is sealed inside its waterproof housing. The Alden's large strobe light extends above the top of the unit, and its effectiveness is increased by the use of a Fresnel lens. the Raytheon's smaller strobe has a clear lens mounted directly on top of the unit. This could cause it to be more easily obscured in rough weather.

The plastic self-releasing mounts for the Alden Satfind seemed secure and provided adequate protection for the unit. Raytheon's stainless-steel mounting bracket is of an altogether different design, which uses a cable instead of a clamp assembly to retain the EPIRB. We believe it leaves the antenna and top of the unit exposed to potential damage.

The ACR RLB-23 is another well-made unit. Though it is somewhat larger, it closely resembles the company's other models in appearance. ACR's approach to designing a float-free bracket is distinctly different. Instead of a mounting bracket, ACR encloses the EPIRB in a fiberglass capsule, which affords superior protection to the unit. The design's only drawback is that heavy icing may effectively glue the capsule shut, delaying or preventing activation. ACR recommends periodic waxing of the case and frequent inspections if the threat of icing exists.

The fourth 406-MHz unit, the Litton 948-01, was formerly sold by Koden International as the Koden 948-01. Its circuit board was sandwiched between two pieces of styrene foam. The outside of the foam was sprayed with RF-reflective paint, and the foam halves were sealed with copper tape. Due to the fact that the copper tape must be replaced when the unit is refurbished, maintenance costs of this EPIRB necessarily increase. Accordingly, we would have preferred another construction method.

The Litton 952-02 is the only Category II 406 MHz EPIRB we were able to obtain for testing. We expected this model to be similar in design to the Litton 948-01. Fortunately, it was not. The 952-02 is of notably better construction, sturdily built and well designed. Flotation is provided by an external foam collar. The Litton 952-02 is less than half the size of the Category I units we tested, which makes it ideal for use aboard pleasure boats. Its simple design and lack of a complicated and expensive release mechanism make it considerably cheaper than the Category I models—by several hundred dollars. We believe it is a high-quality piece of equipment.

Bottom Line: Our first choices in 406-MHz EPIRBs are the Alden Satfind 406 and the ACR RLB-23. We believe their design gives them a slight edge over the Raytheon/JRC JQE-2A. Nevertheless, the Raytheon is also a top-quality unit, which we do not hesitate to recommend.

The Litton 952-02, the only Category II unit in this test, is recommended for applications where space is at a premium and automatic release is not required. The Litton 948-01's performance was acceptable in our ideal-condition testing. Litton engineers report success with the unit's polystyrene foam construction in terms of component support and thermal insulation. However, we don't prefer this type of construction because it increases maintenance costs.

121.5/243 MHz EPIRBs

ACR RLB-14 and RLB-20: These two models from ACR Electronics are similarly constructed. Each is enclosed in a tightly sealed plastic tube. A bottom plug in this tube unscrews to allow the battery to be replaced. The RLB-20 is a Class B unit, supplied with a fire-extinguisher-type bracket. The RLB-14 is a similar looking but slightly larger Class A transmitter including a float-free bracket.

Both units performed well in our tests, though we have some doubts about the RLB-14's float-free bracket. It does not hold the unit securely in place, and could be problematic on smaller high-performance boats that are subject to a great deal of motion in rough weather.

Bottom Line: Based on their performance, we recommend both the ACR RLB-14 and RLB-20 without reservation. Before purchasing the RLB-14, however, check out the bracket to be sure it is appropriate for use on your boat.

ACR RLB-21 Mini-B: This is a Class B unit intended for use as a man-overboard or life raft EPIRB. Its fully sealed case is about the size of a handheld VHF radio.

A Velcro patch is supplied for attaching it to a life jacket, which we feel is an excellent idea, particularly since it does not float without the optional flotation collar. The Mini-B must be returned to the manufacturer for battery replacement.

Bottom Line: The ACR Mini-B is a good-quality product intended as a back-up or "personal" EPIRB. We recommend it for its intended usage. For a primary EPIRB, however, we'd be inclined to spend an additional few dollars for the RLB-20.

Aquatronics Survivor 1: Like the Mini-B, the Survivor 1 is a smaller EPIRB designed as a backup or personal unit. Its sealed construction precludes repair or battery replacement except by the manufacturer. (We had to virtually destroy it to get a look inside.)

This model performed well and cost less than the ACR Mini-B. Our only complaint is that its BNC-type antenna connector could be prone to corrosion in a salt-water environment.

Bottom Line: The Aquatronics Survivor 1 is well made, but it is not repairable. Like the ACR Mini-B, we can only recommend it for its intended application as a personal EPIRB.

Guest 630A: The Guest is the least expensive model we tested. it is enclosed in a molded-plastic case with a screw-on top. It is the only model tested that has separate antennas for 121.5 and 243.0 MHz. The circuitry is not of the highest quality, in our opinion, but is rated satisfactory. No mounting bracket is supplied.

Bottom Line: We consider the Guest 630A to be acceptable for use on smaller boats for the peace of mind it offers at a reasonable price. We can't recommend it for use in the most severe environments.

ACR RLB-17: This is the only Class C unit we tested. It is similar in construction to ACR's other models, except for its telescoping antenna, which must be manually extended. (Fixed, flexible antennas are used on the other models.) The antenna is very fragile: we doubt it would take much of a beating.

The RLB-17 is the only unit that uses conventional batteries (eight C-cells). A fire-extinguisher-type bracket is included, along with a small strobe light that activates automatically in darkness.

Bottom Line: We are not entirely sold on the concept of the Class C EPIRB, and we are reluctant to recommend the RLB-17 because of its antenna. In any case, we would consider purchasing a Class C device only after having spent roughly the same amount on a good handheld radio.

Recommendations

The 406-MHz EPIRBs have significant advantages over the conventional units, though they are considerably more expensive—five to six times as costly. The additional expense would be justified for fishermen who run to the offshore canyons, and for cruisers exploring the out islands of the Bahamas or the Gulfs of California and Mexico.

Of the 406-MHz Category I units, we're most impressed with the Alden Satfind 406 and the ACR RLB-23. The Raytheon JQE-2A is also a recommended unit. The Category II Litton 952-02 is a good-quality, compact, and relatively inexpensive unit. It brings the power of 406 technology to a new level of affordability for sailor who have ambitions to voyage farther afield.

Of the conventional units, we recommend the RLB-20, though all of their EPIRBs are of excellent quality. If price is a big consideration, the inexpensive Guest 630A is also satisfactory.　• **PS**

Life Rafts

Any raft is better than none, but we'll take the Givens and Swiltik before the others.

Thanks to the wonders of modern technology—EPIRBs, VHF, helicopters and the like—if your boat sinks there's a reasonably good chance that help will be there before too long. The question is: will you? If your boat was equipped with a good life raft, the answer can well be yes.

A life raft isn't a magic charm that guarantees your survival if you have to abandon your boat. It is, rather, a last resort for the crew whose boat can no longer protect them. Or, as Greg Switlik of the Switlik Parachute Company, a major life raft manufacturer, pointed out, "A life raft won't save your life. It just provides a safe place for you to sit while you figure out how to save your own life." The most important thing to remember about life rafts is to get one. A life raft that isn't on board, ready to function, won't help save anybody's life. And, considering the very limited life expectancy of people in the water, even in the best PFDs, we feel that anyone who travels even short distances offshore without a life raft is either foolhardy or suicidal.

The Price of Safety

"You can't put a price on human life" is a statement that's been made so often that people often accept its truth without thinking. Sadly, it ain't so. The major factor that keeps most people from buying a life raft is its cost; as a consequence, raft manufacturers must make tradeoffs between quality and cost.

Unlike commercial and military vessels, recreational sailors are not legally required to carry a life raft. Nor are there generally applicable quality and performance standards for rafts, unless you are participating in racing events controlled by groups like the Offshore Racing Council (ORC), which requires life rafts and has specific design requirements.

As a result, the industry offers a baffling variety of life rafts, ranging from simple inflatable open platforms to highly sophisticated rafts that can help keep their occupants alive for extended periods of very bad weather. The range of capabilities is reflected by an extremely wide range of prices.

Even the most fundamental considerations, such as size, represent tradeoffs between cost and functionality. A six-man raft, for example, will typically have a floor area of 21 to 26 square feet. That's not very spacious. Even the largest of these is the equivalent of a circular-floor camping tent with a diameter slightly under 5' 9". Could manufacturers provide more room? Sure—but at the cost of pricing themselves out of a fiercely competitive market.

The Philosophies of Survival

It would be nice if we—or anybody else, for that matter—could give you an unequivocal answer to the question, "What life raft should I buy?" Or even to, "What's the best life raft?" These questions are much like the questions raised when you select a boat. The answer is: "It depends." Life raft design and construction, like yacht design and construction, is a matter of compromise.

Even if cost considerations could be ignored—and they obviously can't—the different conditions that a life raft may encounter, and the varied factors that add up to survival make it virtually impossible to define a single ideal life raft design.

Obviously, a life raft should be able to withstand tumultuous seas and rotten weather. It should keep you afloat and protected, even in conditions that have sunk your boat—an impressive task for less than a hundred pounds of fabric and synthetic rubber. Jim Givens, of Givens Ocean Survival Systems, Inc., flatly states," A life raft must be more seaworthy than the boat that carries it."

Less obviously, a life raft must provide conditions under which you can stay alive while awaiting rescue. This means providing an environment in which the raft's occupants can remain alive, alert and functional. It includes considerations of ventilation, warmth, adequate physical comfort, and useful activity, as well as water, food and medication.

Livability is a factor whose importance many people tend to minimize. The common feeling is that comfort is something you can do without in life-threatening situations. It's not so. In the words of the Alaska Marine Safety Education Association, "In a survival situation, the decisions you make will be more important than the equipment you carry." And prolonged bouts of thirst, seasickness, hypothermia, cramps and other results of overcrowded, underequipped living don't contribute to making sound decisions.

One of our staffers spent an exciting night in a life raft last September as part of a controlled test; even with Force 7 winds and eight-foot to 10-foot breaking seas, the major problems encountered on the raft were seasickness and overcrowding. A crowded life raft is an exceptionally difficult place in which to maneuver. An urgent need for someone to reach the canopy opening can make for major upheavals, considerable discomfort and feelings of extreme irritation and hostility by the raft's other occupants. On one raft, five of the six occupants were seasick, one sufficiently so that it was necessary to effect a premature "rescue."

Similar experiences are not uncommon. In 1985, Fred Edwards, in *Yachting* magazine, reported that three out of five experienced sailors became seasick within two minutes of entering a test life raft in moderate seas.

One became so dehydrated and electrolyte-depleted that he had to be removed from the raft after 45 minutes. A recent in-the-water test conducted by West Marine Products had to be aborted because of excessive seasickness among the rafts' occupants.

It's difficult enough to make a life raft that can handle worst-case seas adequately. It's just as difficult to make a raft that's livable for long periods of time. Combining the two is a monumental task; combining the two while staying within a tight budget is a virtual impossibility. Something has to give.

Types of Rafts

The two broadest categories of life rafts are coastal and offshore models. There aren't hard and fast definitions, but generally an offshore raft will feature two flotation tubes, stacked one over the other, a closable canopy supported by inflatable arch tubes, and a kit of survival gear that includes food, water and pyrotechnic signaling devices. A coastal raft may use a single flotation tube, a canopy that lacks support arches and a much more limited survival kit, generally not including food or water.

Coastal life rafts represent an attempt on the part of the manufacturers to provide a lower cost raft for people who aren't likely to encounter severe weather conditions and who aren't apt to have a prolonged stay in a raft. They are less expensive and occupy a bit less deck space.

Coastal rafts, with one notable exception, are not approved by the ORC; the single-tube arrangement that is typical with these rafts lacks the redundancy that is felt to be necessary. An exception to the ORC regulations is the Switlik Coastal Raft, which uses a unique "sock" arrangement within its single tube to keep the entire tube inflated if punctured.

The Rafts We Tested

For this test, we rounded up a total of eight life rafts, representing five major manufacturers. Three—from Avon, Plastimo and Switlik— were coastal rafts; the other five—from Avon, Givens, Plastimo, Switlik and Zodiac—were offshore models. We tried to get six-man rafts in each case, but were only able to obtain Avon's offshore raft in its four-man version and Zodiac's in its eight-man size.

The rafts were deployed in a sheltered basin in Rhode Island and key features—flotation tubes, boarding systems, canopies and the like—were carefully inspected and compared. This process actually began with the aforementioned Chesapeake excursion, an experience that gave us a real-world opportunity to assess important features and lifesaving criteria that could be applied to our independent evaluations. In addition to visual inspections, we tried to flip each raft in order to assess capsize resistance, discovering that some rafts turn over easier than others.

Flotation tubes

The Avon Coastline and the Switlik Coastal use a single flotation tube. The Avon's tube is split into two separate chambers. If either is punctured, the other retains its air. Either chamber carries enough air to support the raft's rated load, although a puncture will collapse the canopy support.

The Switlik takes another approach. Inside the large-diameter single tube are a pair of sleeves, with one end sealed, that divide the tube into two sections. If the tube is punctured, air pressure from the intact half forces the sleeves into the punctured section. The result is that the sleeves form an air-tight liner for the damaged tube; the entire tube remains inflated, although at a lower pressure. As with the Avon, the remaining air is sufficient to support the raft's rated load. Unlike the Avon, however, you can then use the hand pump provided to reinflate the tube to its normal buoyancy and pressure. The Switlik's canopy tubes are independent of the flotation tubes, so that a puncture has no effect on the canopy.

The two-tube rafts achieve redundancy by having the two tubes inflate independently, from the same cylinder. Redundancy is an important consideration, not only in case of puncture, but in case of a malfunction in the inflation system. This last is not as rare an occurrence as one might think. In our tests, one raft, the Plastimo Coastal, failed completely to inflate when we pulled the triggering lanyard. About 10 minutes later, its top tube inflated, but the bottom tube never did. We've spoken to several life raft specialists, who told us that a failure rate of 10 percent was not surprising.

Size

Life raft manufacturers rate their rafts in terms of capacity: four-man, six-man, eight-man, etc. We find, however, that a six-man raft will provide usable accommodations for four, at most; an eight-man raft is best suited for no more than five or six. As a general rule, if you load up a raft with more than 60 to 70 percent of its rated capacity, you'll provide an iron-clad guarantee of extreme discomfort. At the same time, too few persons in a large raft with limited stability could become unstable in rough conditions.

The actual design of the raft can affect the usable seating area. The Switlik Coastal Raft, for example, is shaped like a rounded rectangle (or a squared egg.) It's length provides considerably more leg room within its 24 square feet than do pentagonal or round shapes of the same area.

Canopies

The shape of the canopy supports also has a definite effect upon seating comfort in an enclosed life raft. Tent-shaped canopies, where the canopy walls slant in sharply toward a top horizontal tube, tend to force occupants to sit in a tiring, hunched-forward position. The Zodiac 8, with a fairly tall canopy, provided a better seating position than did the lower-profile Avon Coastline. The Plastimo and Avon offshore raft canopies were judged to fall between the other two tent-shaped models in terms of comfort.

The Switlik Coastal Life Raft uses two arched tubes to support the canopy. These tubes are almost vertical at their bases, and the arched canopy that they support provides a good deal more usable room inside the canopy than does a more-conventional tent-type canopy. Unlike the other rafts, the canopy support tubes of the Switlik Coastal do not inflate automatically with the buoyancy tubes; the raft in-flates with the canopy furled, and the arches must be inflated afterward, using a hand pump or an optional separate CO_2 inflator.

The Givens and the Switlik Search and Rescue rafts have self-inflating, curved canopy supports. The Givens inflates with the canopy up and the hatch closed (although easily openable with a push); the Switlik inflates with the canopy furled. The latter arrangement offers both advantages and disadvantages: it simplifies entering the raft, particularly from the water. On the other hand, the raft's occupants get no protection from breaking waves until the canopy is erected. With both of these rafts, the arched canopy tubes provide considerably more seating comfort and usable space than you might expect from their rather limited floor areas—20.9 and 21.6 square feet respectively.

The Plastimo coastal raft has no canopy supports. You crawl under a flat cover if you need weather protection—an uncomfortable arrangement that we don't find all that appealing.

Hatches and Ports

A canopy, when it's closed, can provide needed protection from the elements. When that protection isn't needed, though, a closed canopy presents several serious problems. The lack of a fixed visual reference, in combination with a life raft's inevitable motion, exacerbates the seasickness problem.

It is very desirable for the raft's occupants to able to see outside the raft as much as possible. A collection of survivors in a small volume such as a life raft generates a surprisingly large amount of body heat. While this may be welcome in cold weather, it can rapidly create dangerous overheating conditions in temperate or hot weather. There's not much room

Life Raft Data Sheet

Offshore Models Tested

Make	Persons	Tubes	Material	Ballast	Capsize Resistance	Floor Area (sq. ft.)	Canopy Type
Avon	4	2	Neoprene/nylon	Icelandic	Good	16	Tent
Givens	6	2	Neoprene/nylon	Toroidal/hemispheric	Excellent	20.9	Tripod arch
Plastimo	6	2	Vinyl/polyester	Icelandic	Fair	25.8	Tent
Switlik	6	2	Urethane/nylon	Toroidal	Very good	21.6	T-shaped arch
Zodiac	8	2	Vinyl/PVC	Weighted bags	Poor (2)	32.8	Tent

Coastal Models Tested

Make	Persons	Tubes	Material	Ballast	Capsize Resistance	Floor Area (sq. ft.)	Canopy Type
Avon	6	1	Neoprene/nylon	Icelandic	Good	24	Tent
Plastimo	6	1	Vinyl/polyester	Icelandic	(1)	25.8	Unsupported
Switlik	6	1	Urethane/nylon	Icelandic	Good	24	2 arches

[1] Did not inflate when triggered. 10 minutes later, one tube inflated.

[2] Small, unweighted ballast bags did not open by themselves; plastic stuck together.

for carrying water on a life raft, and excessive perspiration—or seasickness—can lead to fatal dehydration in a short time. The obvious solution is to provide adequate ventilation.

There's also a very real need to provide the raft's occupants with relatively easy access to the outside air, for purposes of elimination and, all too often, vomiting. A small hatch in the canopy of a crowded raft can make such access difficult and slow. Lastly, a closed canopy makes it impossible for a lookout to see if any vessels or aircraft are in the vicinity. A canopy with a small hatch isn't much better, even when that hatch is open.

The design of the hatches on the rafts we tested reflect the manufacturers' differing philosophies of survival. Avon and Givens, for example, opt for a relatively small opening with a sleeved porthole opposite it. This arrangement emphasizes protection against water intrusion in rough seas. Avon uses a triangular opening. Givens has a somewhat larger square one. On both rafts, visibility is limited.

Plastimo's offshore raft and the one Zodiac we tested make provision for opening one full side of their tent-shaped canopies. The Zodiac supplements this with a zippered slit in the opposite wall. Both rafts provided good ventilation and reasonable visibility. On both rafts, however, when the zipper was fully open, we had difficulty reassembling the two sections and starting the zipper.

Switlik has chosen a tack completely opposite to that taken by Avon and Givens. On both Switlik rafts, the canopy can be completely furled, if desired, or adjusted to provide varied degrees of protection. On the offshore Search and Rescue model, the arched canopy supports stay up at all times. A furlable canopy is secured to the raft at one edge; the canopy

can be unrolled over the supports to any degree desired. In the fully closed position, there's a modestly sized conventional hatch that can be closed completely.

The Switlik Coastal Raft offers even greater versatility in terms of canopy configuration. There's a furlable top, two in-dependently furlable sides, and two end sections that are permanently attached to the arched canopy supports that can be "furled" by deflating the support tubes. As a result, it's a fairly simple matter to choose a canopy configuration to suit your needs: ends only, ends and top with one or more open sides, ends and sides with open top and so on. Visibility is excellent.

It's even possible to drop one support and the top and leave what Switlik calls a "sail-away configuration." Considering the hull design of a life raft, we don't think too much of the idea. Even if you were to collapse the ballast pockets, as suggested, by "drawing them tight…," you wouldn't have much of a hull for the 10-square foot "sail" to push. And, in most cases, you'd be best off deploying a sea anchor and not trying to sail; rescuers will be looking for you where the boat was supposed to be. Nevertheless, some survivors, such as Steve Callahan (as recounted in his book *Adrift*), after realizing that help wasn't coming, have successfully accelerated the speed of their rafts toward land.

Boarding

To make any use of your life raft at all, you must first get aboard it. And this can be a bigger problem than most people realize, particularly at night in a rough sea. If you're boarding the raft directly from your boat, the technique is to jump onto the raft's canopy, rather than trying to jump into the small moving target that is presented by the raft's hatch. Canopies are soft, tough, resilient and easier to hit. Once you're on the canopy, it's usually fairly easy to find the entrance hatch in the canopy—the canopy support tubes will pop up again once your weight is removed. The two Switlik rafts deploy without the canopy in place, so you can just jump directly into the raft. We're not convinced this is easier than jumping onto the canopy, but it may make some people feel more comfortable about jumping.

If you can't enter the raft directly from your boat, but must do it from the water, the problem becomes a more serious one. All the rafts have provisions for climbing aboard, but some are distinctly better than others.

All the rafts have webbing or rope lifelines around the perimeter. The Avon Coastline simply lengthens two sections of this lifeline to provide a sort of "boarding ladder." We found that this arrangement, together with a paucity of handholds inside the raft, made for difficult boarding.

Boarding Type	Ease	Visibility	Rain Catchment
Web ladder	Good	Fair	Very good
Web ladder	Very good	Fair	Excellent
2 loops w/rung	Good	Good	None
Platform	Very good	Excellent	Excellent
Web ladder	Good	Very Good	None
Web loops	Poor	Fair	Very good
2 loops w/rung	(1)	Excellent	None
Web ladder	Very good	Excellent	None

The two Plastimo rafts are easier to board. They also use a pair of extended lifeline loops as ladders, but use a short section of garden hose as a rung stiffener. This helps, as does a more-conveniently located grab rope.

The Avon offshore raft and the Zodiac have multi-rung "rope" ladders made of webbing. This works well, but not quite as well the double-width webbing ladders used on the Givens, and the Switlik coastal raft. The ease of boarding either of these rafts is enhanced by well-located grab straps. We particularly liked the Givens arrangement, which consists of a ladder-like network of webbing that extends from the hatchway to the center of the raft, and can be detached and tucked out of the way when not needed.

The Switlik Search and Rescue replaces the boarding ladder with a self-inflating boarding platform. We found this design, which will be found on more rafts in the future due to impending U.S.C.G. regulations, a mixed blessing. While there was no problem in getting aboard the raft from the platform, it wasn't that easy to climb onto the platform itself. It's surface is slippery, and we would have welcomed more handholds. We judged this raft's ease of boarding only "good." On the other hand, the platform provides some welcome extra space if the weather is fair. On the Chesapeake Bay test mentioned above, the only member of one raft's six-person crew that did not become seasick spent the night in a survival suit on the raft's boarding platform.

Stability

This factor is the biggest bone of contention among life raft manufacturers. Life rafts achieve stability through the use of water-filled ballast bags. Until a decade ago, most rafts depended upon a few small bags. Spurred by the tragedy of the Fastnet Race of 1979 , there was a series of tests conducted by agencies of the United States, United Kingdom and Icelandic governments. The findings of these tests were that more effective ballasting was required, a position that Givens pioneered in the middle 1960's, with his patented Toroidal/Hemispheric ballast chamber.

There was a flurry of redesigning among the raft makers, and several different designs emerged. The three basic designs are: the Givens system, a toroidal chamber integral with a hemispherical bag that fills with water and hangs beneath the raft's floor; the Switlik Toroidal Stability Device, a doughnut-shaped water-filled bag that hangs below the bottom inflation tube; and the so-called Icelandic system that has several large bags attached to the underside of the raft around its perimeter containing weights to help open the bags so they can fill with water.

There has been, and will undoubtedly continue to be, a continuing argument about the effectiveness of these different systems. We certainly can't provide the last word in this argument, but we did try to evaluate each raft's stability in the calm water we were dealing with.

The Zodiac we tested was, by far, the easiest of the rafts to capsize. One man was able to accomplish this, with no difficulty, by standing on one inflation tube and pulling on the opposite edge of the raft. When we examined the Zodiac's ballasting system, we were not at all surprised to find that it consisted of several small, unweighted plastic bags. Even after 20 minutes in the water, these did not fill with water.

We judged the capsize resistance of the two Avon rafts to be fair; one man could capsize either raft, but he had to work a bit to do it. Righting was easy. Both Avons use three Icelandic-type ballast bags. The Plastimos' resistance to capsizing and ease of righting were comparable to the Avon models.

The Switlik Coastal was considerably more difficult to capsize than were the other rafts that used an Icelandic-type system. This was undoubtedly due to the large size of the bags.

Righting was also simple, aided by the highly legible instructions printed on the underside of the life raft. We judged the Switlik Coastal's resistance to capsize as good.

The Switlik Search and Rescue, with its toroidal chamber, resisted capsize even better. Two testers, working hard, could not induce a capsize. After some experimentation, we finally were able to turn the raft over by piling three persons against one of the canopy walls, tipping the raft to about 45 degrees, and then simulating the effect of a strong wind by having another person push on the raft's upper edge. When the raft was tilted to about 90 degrees, it finally went over. Righting, since the ballasting toroid was drained when the raft went over, was again easy. We judged the capsize resistance of this raft to be very good.

The Givens raft defied all our efforts to capsize it. We subjected it to the same tests as we did the Switlik, and it resisted capsize even at an estimated angle of 110 degrees. We even tried capsizing it with its lower flotation tube deflated, three persons leaning on the canopy from inside the raft and two others pushing from a dock. The raft did not go over, even at angles in excess of 90 degrees. We judged it's resistance to capsize to be excellent.

What isn't clear is the practical difference between the capsize resistance of these rafts. Our tests were meaningful but hardly realistic. The opportunity to test rafts in an actual hurricane wasn't available, even if we were willing to try it. Elaborate Coast Guard tank tests of the three principal ballasting systems—hemispheric chamber, toroidal doughnut and ballast bag—indicate all three resist capsize in a breaking sea to some extent. Coast Guard slow-motion videotapes reveal, however, that the hemispheric chamber and toroidal doughnut offer greater stability in addition to capsize resistance. Stability of any of the design is enhanced by the use of a substantial drogue.

Miscellaneous Features

Most of the rafts can be supplied in either a valise pack, for stowage belowdecks, or in a hard canister, which is deck mounted. The canister is a safer arrangement, as you may not have the time or opportunity to drag a 50- to 100-pound pack up from below while your boat sinks. The valise is useful if you lack deck space for a canister or must frequently move the raft from one boat to another. Among the hard canisters, only the glass-reinforced ones supplied by Switlik and Givens were judged rugged enough to take the beating that a piece of on-deck equipment must endure. The others are made of unreinforced molded plastic, and can easily crack. The Zodiac and Plastimo rafts are vacuum-packed in a plastic bag within the valise or canister. This seems to be a good idea, because neither the valises nor canisters are absolutely watertight.

With the sole exception of the Zodiac, which comes with a double inflatable floor, all of the other rafts have a single-layer floor design, at least in their plain-vanilla models. A double floor is an option, typically raising the raft's price by several hundred dollars to more than a thousand. It is, we feel, an option that's sufficiently important to be considered essential. Normal skin temperature is in the mid-to-high 80s and even fairly warm water can pull a lot of heat from your body in a very short time. Our testers complained about cold bottoms after only a few minutes in the rafts. The Zodiac's double bottom made a very easily noticed, and much appreciated difference.

Some of the rafts, as noted in the Data Sheet, have provisions for collecting rainwater. This is a helpful feature, but we were surprised to note that only the Givens and the Switlik Search and Rescue rafts come with a container in which this water can be stored.

Survival equipment

No two rafts seem to provide the same level of survival equipment, though all have such items as paddles (of dubious value), a bailer, seasickness pills, a knife, a flashlight and a throwable rescue quoit, attached to some polypropylene line. Offshore rafts often, but not always, include flares (an inadequate number), water (a marginal amount), and food. In any case, it behooves the purchaser of a life raft to obtain and pack a waterproof, floating abandon-ship pack with the items the raft manufacturer omitted for reasons of space and cost.

Probably the four basic additions we'd make to the gear supplied with any life raft are a handheld VHF radio in a waterproof case, a watermaker (preferably a reverse-osmosis water desalinator such as the Survivor 35, as opposed to a solar still), additional pyrotechnic signaling devices and an EPIRB. You'd also want to pack any medication that you or your crew normally take. Less obvious items are warm clothing, a more complete first-aid kit, a decent fishing line (the ones that many provide are awful) a package of plastic garbage bags (useful for all sorts of things) and a deck of waterproof playing cards.

Recommendations

The Plastimo Coastal's failure to inflate, even if it was a fluke, makes us nervous. And we don't trust the skimpy ballasting of the Zodiac. Still, most of the life rafts we looked at are capable of saving your life under the conditions most frequently encountered.

Based on our testing, we deem the Avon Coastline and the Plastimo coastal raft to be clearly less competent rafts than their offshore siblings. They probably shouldn't be considered unless it's a choice between one of them and no raft at all.

Although we think that the Avon and the Plastimo offshore rafts are good, serviceable rafts, we didn't care for the limited ventilation and visibility we encountered on the Avon nor the difficulty we had in working the Plastimo's zipper.

For most people, sailing in waters in which hurricanes and high breaking seas are rare, we like the Switlik Coastal Raft. It's more stable than the Avon or Plastimo coastal models, and is by far the most livable raft we looked at, in terms of seating comfort, ventilation and visibility.

If, on the other hand, we were setting out for an extended ocean cruise, our major concern would be rough seas and foul weather. Our choice under those circumstances would be the Givens, although we recognize we'd be giving up the Switlik Search and Rescue's superior ventilation and comfort. **• PS**

Inflatable PFDs

We tested a dozen models, with and without safety harnesses. Some were impressive.

The lifejackets we tested for this report are all inflatable-only types. Widely used in Europe and England, they are relative newcomers to the U.S. recreational boating scene.

Inflatable lifejackets are less bulky than their inherently buoyant counterparts; inflated, they provide greater flotation. On the downside, inflatables require significantly more maintenance and care in storage than do non-inflatables. Inflatable-only lifejackets are not U.S. Coast Guard approved for recreational boating. If you use one, you'll still have to purchase and carry U.S.C.G.-approved PFDs.

We obtained a dozen different models from seven different manufacturers, and evaluated them for in-the-water performance, as well as comfort, wearability, convenience and details of construction.

We tested Crewfit, Mustang, Sospenders, Techvest, Switlik, Survival Products and Norvik devices. Four models—from Crewfit, Sospenders, Switlik and Norvik—incorporate safety harnesses, while one Mustang product is an inflatable float coat.

What Sets Them Off

All the jackets use one or more CO_2 cartridges to inflate the bladder, with oral inflation as a back-up. CO_2 gas is released from the cartridges(s) either automatically—when a sensor is immersed in water—or manually, when the wearer pulls a tag (or tags) attached to the release mechanism. The jackets that employ automatic inflation also use pull tags as a secondary trigger.

The automatic triggering devices use a piece of water-degradable material to hold back a spring-loaded needle; when the trigger is immersed, the spring releases, allowing the needle to puncture the seal on the CO_2 cylinder. On the manually operated triggers, jerking the release tag pulls a small lever that forces the needle through the seal.

Inflation, with all the automatic triggers we tested, is extremely rapid, requiring three to four seconds after the lifejacket wearer hits the water. This is about the same time required for manual operation. All the jackets we tested are reusable once you replace the CO_2 cartridge and, for automatic models, the water-sensing element.

How We Tested Them

For our in-the-water evaluations, we used a short, bulky male of the type that has little problem in floating and one "sinker"—a tall, slender male who normally requires effort to stay afloat. Each tester put on each PFD (including a conventional Type I and a conventional Type III for comparison purposes.) Each tester then fell into a swimming pool.

We noted how long it took for each jacket to inflate and bring the tester up to the surface, how well each rolled an "unconscious" tester over from a face-down position, and made judgments of the stability of the face-up position. We also noted such factors as ease of manual inflation (if the automatic inflator failed or if the jacket was a non-automatic type) and ease of oral inflation (in case everything else failed.) Each tester commented on comfort, both inflated and uninflated, ease of adjustment and other convenience factors.

After use, each jacket was deflated, dried, and repacked, noting any difficulties encountered. Lastly, we went over each jacket with a critical eye, looking for possible defects in design and making judgments on the overall quality of each model's construction.

To see if a heavy rain or spray will trigger the automatic inflation device, one of our intrepid testers donned each jacket and shivered in a New England breeze while an assistant sprayed him with a garden hose.

We also tested the water-sensing portions of the automatic-inflation models for storage stability under adverse conditions. We stored samples for one week at 150°F and 95-percent-plus relative humidity, and then checked them out to see if they still worked. No automatic inflation device failed either of these tests.

Finally, we asked a number of staffers, associates and friends to try on each jacket, so that we could identify less-obvious problems with instructions, ease of adjustment and fit. Here's what we found.

Sospenders 1-38A (without safety harness) and Sospenders 1-38-AH (with safety harness)

These are the automatic-inflation adult-sized versions of Sporting Lives Inc.'s, inflatable lifejacket, with and without safety harness.

We found both Sospenders to be easy to put on—you slip into one just as you'd put on a suit vest—and easy to adjust for our testers' varying physiques. The harness model's interlocking buckle arrangement is undeniably solid, but some testers complained that it wasn't easy to close.

None of the PFDs tested is really unnoticeable while you're wearing it, but Sospenders comes very close. Both models fit nicely over the chest and feature a curved fitted collar section that doesn't chafe the neck. In our judgment, Sospenders, harness or no, represents the most comfortable—at least before inflation.

When inflated, we found Sospenders a bit less comfortable, due to bunching up of the cover around the neck, but this is a minor complaint. Oral inflation is easy.

Repacking Sospenders is, unfortunately, not easy, despite some new and extensively revised instructions supplied by the manufacturer. The bladder is only tenuously connected to the cover, and it's necessary to completely and thoroughly deflate the bladder (by depressing the check valve and squeezing out the air) before you can start folding the bladder while you are tucking a cover that always seems to be in the wrong orientation.

Crewsaver Crewfit Automatic and Crewfit Automatic with Harness

The British-made Crewfit Automatic Gas model has heavy gauge 1-1/2 inch-wide nylon straps for both the back and chest straps, as well as a double buckle arrangement that avoids the dangling tail of an adjustment strap.

The Crewfit's cover is made of a rugged, closely woven nylon.

It was easy to put on and adjust. Uninflated, it lay flatter against the chest than did any of the other PFDs except for the Techvest.

In the water, it's hard to fault the Crewfit's performance or comfort. The bright-yellow bladder is fastened to the cover along its entire edge, so when the bladder inflates, there is little bunching of cover material.

Manual inflation was easy. The oral inflation tube is equipped with a check valve. We like Crewfit's provision for easy deflation: If you remove the cap from the oral inflation tube and put it back upside down, it holds the check valve in the open position.

Repacking the Crewfit is quick and easy. The Crewfit consists of an inflatable bladder that is firmly attached to its cover for almost its entire length. This construction eliminates any problems in positioning the bladder against the cover when repacking, and makes an otherwise onerous job simple.

A secondary, but useful feature of the Crewfit automatic inflation system is that an automatic model can be converted to a manual one by simply unscrewing the automatic actuator and storing it in a safe (and dry) place. This means that the Crewfit can be used as an emergency flotation device under circumstances that call for you to be in in the water when automatic inflation is undesirable. The Crewfit's automatic actuator, unlike the bobbin used on the other automatic-inflation models, does not require periodic replacement. The most impressive feature of the Crewfit is its quality of construction. The bladder, for example, is made of 30-percent thicker material than that used on most other PFD's we tested. All seams are heat sealed and bound with tape, rather than just sealed. All straps are well stitched and firmly attached.

Techvest

Survival Technologies' Techvest, a new arrival on the market, has obviously been inspired by the Crewfit, so much so that a detailed description of the Techvest would merely echo much of what we said in the previous section.

The Techvest's most interesting design difference from the Crewfit lies in the angle at which a wearer is supported in the water. While most lifejacket manufacturers try to achieve an angle of approximately 45 degrees, Survival Technologies believes that a more-vertical orientation is desirable, since it keeps the head higher out of the water. Exact measurements are difficult, but the Techvest appeared to support a body in the water at an angle of 50-55 degrees, rather than the 45 degrees we encountered with the other products tested.

Survival Technologies has taken a positive step towards encouraging regular maintenance of an automatic PFD—purchasers who send in a registration card will receive a free replacement activator bobbin every nine months for a period of 54 months. CO_2 cartridges are plastic-coated to prevent corrosion.

The Techvest's quality of construction appears to meet the high standards we encountered in the Crewfit, except for its lighter-gauge bladder material.

Norvik 30pu Lifejacket (with and without harness)

Compared to the shawl-type PFDs described above, the Norvik's closed ring design is somewhat more obtrusive when worn uninflated, and a bit more secure-feeling when inflated in the water. The Norvik's cover is a bright-orange, closely woven nylon.

The Norvik Lifejacket with safety harness uses essentially the same flotation gear, but attaches it to a substantial—and totally baffling—tangle of webbing. When we sorted it all out, we found a single 1-inch back strap, a pair of 2-inch-wide shoulder straps and a 2-inch-wide chest strap, with a single D-ring and a stainless steel tongue-and-slot interlocking closure. None of our testers found that sorting out and donning this PFD to be a simple task. Seven of the nine who tried gave up in disgust. The jacket's instructions were of little help—they were printed in Norwegian.

Our testers found that the Norvik's ring design pressed against their necks uncomfortably during long-term wearing evaluations; otherwise, we found the non-harness model easy to wear.

Repacking the Norvik PFDs is easier than the Sospenders, but not as easy as the Crewfit and Techvest. Rearming is similar to that of Sospenders and Techvest.

The Mustang Inflatable Collar

The Mustang Inflatable Collar, while still an inflatable lifejacket with about 35 pounds of flotation, differs noticeably from Sospenders, Crewfit, Techvest and Norvik in design. The Mustang is a zip-front, backless collared vest; there's no safety-harness-equipped model available. We were unable to obtain an automatic-inflation model, but the manufacturer informs us that they achieve automatic inflation with the same Halkey-Roberts valve used by Sospenders and Techvest.

To put on the Mustang, open the zipper, slip the whole thing over your head, close the zipper and fasten the strap. Uninflated, the Mustang is quite comfortable, a feeling that's helped by its light weight.

Our testers preferred the less-confined feel of the Crew-fit and Sospenders in our longer-term tests.

The only problem we encountered with the uninflated Mustang was its propensity to snag on a variety of objects. This was due to gaps in the Mustang's closure: unlike the other models we tested, which use long continuous strips of Velcro to keep the cover in place, the Mustang employs a series of small Velcro patches spaced along the openings.

Our testers noted that if they adjusted the Mustang's strap for a comfortably snug fit when the device was uninflated, it became uncomfortably tight once it inflated. In-the-water adjustment was required. Once adjusted, we found that the Mustang's vest configuration provided an exceptionally secure feeling in the water. Oral inflation wasn't particularly convenient—Mustang's inflation tube doesn't use a check valve, but has a valve that requires you to press in on the tip while you blow into it. Our testers found this inconvenient even in a calm pool.

Repacking the Mustang was little better than repacking Sospenders. Once the bladder is deflated (through the same annoying press-to-open valve at the end of the oral inflation tube), it wasn't difficult to position, but folding it and closing the cover over it was—the little Velcro patches kept popping open.

Switlik Helicopter Crew Vest and Fastnet Crew Vest (with harness)

These vests are serious pieces of life-saving equipment. The Helicopter Crew Vest consists of a nylon mesh vest with a heavy-duty zipper closure.

Inflatable PFD Data Sheet

Rank	Model	Price Vest/Rearm Kit	Type	Inflation Manual/Auto/Oral	Cartridges (# and capacity)	Weight (ounces)
Non-Harness Models						
1 (tie)	Crewfit Automatic	$199.95/$19.95	Shawl	M/A/O	1 x 33 gm.	28
1 (tie)	Survival Technologies Techvest	$159.95/$11.75	Shawl	M/A/O	1 x 33 gm. (1)	24
2	Sospenders 1-38A	$169.95/$14.95	Shawl	M/A/O	1 x 38 gm.	23
3	Norvik 30pu Automatic	$180/$14	Ring	M/A/O	1 x 29 gm.	26
4	Mustang Inflatable Collar	$199.95/$25.99	Vest	M/A/O	1 x 33 gm.	20
5	Switlik Helicopter Crew Vest	$225/$3.80	Vest	M/O	2 x 18 gm.	42
6	Mustang Inflatable Bomber Jacket MIJ145	$239.99/$7.99	Jacket	M//O	1 x 33 gm.	46
7	Survival Products Inflatable Life Vest	39.75	Vest	M/O	2 x 18 gm.	21
Harness Models						
1	Switlik Fastnet Crew Vest	$295/$3.80	Vest	M/O	2 x 18 gm.	54
2 (tie)	Crewfit Automatic	$245/$19.95	Shawl	M/A/O	1 x 33 gm.	34
2 (tie)	Sospenders 1-38AH	$214/$14.95	Shawl	M/A/O	1 x 38 gm.	37
3	Norvik 30pu Automatic	$280/$14	Ring	M/A/O	1 x 29 gm.	53

(1) Rust-resistant coating on cartridge
(2) Distributror says present shipments include patches of reflective tape for user application
(3) Two separate chambers; first tube location is excellent, second is poor, being blocked by bladder
(4) Adjustment may be inadequate for small sizes

The Fastnet Crew Vest is similar in design to the Helicopter Crew Vest except for the presence of a harness of 1-3/4-inch-wide webbing sewn onto the vest and a pair of steel D-rings instead of the plastic buckle.

Switlik's background in aircraft and military safety equipment shows in a number of ways, from the extremely detailed manuals supplied to the extra flaps of cover cloth that help avoid damage to the inflatable bladders. The seams are sealed and bound.

Nowhere does this background show up more clearly than in the use of two independent bladders, providing at least 17.5 pounds of flotation even if one cell fails completely.

Switlik doesn't make an automatic-inflation model; when we asked why, we were told that Switlik doesn't feel that automatic inflators have the degree of reliability that Switlik requires.

One penalty for this commendable degree of care is extra weight (see chart). Another penalty is bulk. While still much less bulky than any non-inflatable, the Switlik vests take up enough space on the wearer's upper chest to make it doubtful if a casual recreational boater would consider wearing one on a regular basis.

In the water, the two Switlik vests were the most secure-feeling. The uppermost bladder pops up around your jaw and cheeks, and holds you well out of the water. This is a feeling that is apt to be appreciated in high seas, but is constraining if the waves are less intimidating.

Oral inflation of a Switlik isn't easy. Since there are two separate bladders, there must be two independent oral inflation tubes. The first one that you can reach is conveniently mounted on the jacket's left side, and is protected by a restraining patch; the valve is an easy-to-use check valve. Once you inflate the first bladder, though, the inflation tube for the second bladder pops up in a position that's very difficult to reach.

The Helicopter Crew Vest has a shoulder-mounted light with a water-activated battery; the Fastnet Crew Vest doesn't.

Survival Products
Inflatable Life Vest

The Survival Products vest has several appealing features. It sells for $39.75. And it's in-the-water performance is as good as any of the jackets we tested. That's the good news. The bad news is the it isn't really suitable for use as a PFD, in our opinion.

This vest looks and behaves like the inflatables that are stowed under the seats in commercial airliners. It consists of two independently inflatable bright yellow bladders with no protective covers. The bladders are fastened together at the bottom to form a ring that goes over your head and is secured with a 1-inch-wide web strap and plastic snap buckle. There is a light, powered by a water-activated battery, attached.

The Survival Products would work in conditions where you always had enough advance disaster warning to put on a PFD immediately before hitting the water. Accidents at sea, unfortunately, don't

Whistle	Light	Pocket	Reflectors	Ease of Oral Inflation Location	Valve	Ease of Adjustment	Comfort (uninflated)	Security in water	Ease of Repacking
Yes	No	No	No (2)	Good	Excellent	Good	Very good	Very good	Excellent
Yes	No	No	Yes	Good	Excellent	Excellent	Very good	Very good	Excellent
Yes	No	Yes	Yes	Excellent	Excellent	Very good	Excellent	Very good	Good
Yes	No	No	No	Good	Fair	Excellent	Good	Excellent	Fair
Yes	No	No	Yes	Good	Fair	Excellent	Very good	Excellent	Fair
Yes	Yes	Yes	Yes	(3)	Excellent	Good	Good	Excellent	Good
Yes	No	Yes	No	Good	Fair	(9)	Excellent (7)	Very good	Excellent
No	Yes	No	No	(3)	Excellent	Excellent	Poor	Excellent	(8)
Yes	No	Yes	Yes	(3)	Excellent	Good	Good (6)	Excellent	Good
Yes	No	No	No (2)	Good	Excellent	Good	Very good (4)	Very good	Excellent
Yes	No	Yes	Yes	Excellent	Excellent	Very good	Excellent	Very good	Good
Yes	No	No	No	Good	Fair	Poor	Good (5)	Excellent	Fair

(5) Very confusing assembly to put on
(6) Some women may object to strap position
(7) Excellent, but restricted to use in cool weather; jacket is quite warm
(8) No repacking required
(9) No size adjustment. Purchase by size

work that way. A life jacket is effective only if worn. If you tried to wear this vest all the time, its unprotected bladders would be continually exposed to abrasion and the risk of puncture. We can't recommend the Survival Products vest at any price.

Mustang Bomber Jacket MIJ145

This is an inflatable float coat. It has a manual valve/cartridge with pull tag and an oral inflation tube concealed under a decorative nylon panel, and a bladder concealed between the outer shell and the lining.

The MIJ145 is a comfortable jacket, and, in the water, an effective lifejacket. We were a bit surprised at how secure it felt, since there are no provisions for adjusting the fit short of purchasing a different-size jacket. But the full jacket configuration kept our testers and the bladders in place quite well, even when the jacket was several sizes too large. A nice feature of this jacket is it's hypothermia protection; our testers noted how much less chilled they became after extended submersion.

The MIJ145, unfortunately, isn't available with automatic operation and suffers from the same awkward press-and-blow oral inflation tube. Otherwise, we had few complaints about its performance or construction.

The Mustang Bomber Jacket isn't a replacement for one of the other inflatable PFDs during the warmer portion of the boating season. In cooler weather, though, it can be a comfortable and effective article of life-saving gear.

Recommendations

In considering the advantages and disadvantages of these 12 PFDs, it's easy to get so wrapped up in comparisons that you forget a basic point: All devices, execept the Survival Products vest with unprotected bladder, are much more comfortable to wear than even the lightest-duty U.S.C.G.-approved PFD, and provide much more protection. What we're discussing here is differences among a group of very good lifejackets.

Non-Harness Inflatable PFDs: The most recent U.S.C.G. figures show that 90 percent of those who drowned were not wearing PFDs. Hopefully, less-bulky and more-comfortable PFDs will encourage more people to wear them. Our major consideration, once we were sure that the PFDs did an adequate job of keeping you afloat, was wearability. And, because there's no guarantee that a person going overboard will be conscious and won't panic enough so that purposeful activity is impossible, we prefer PFDs with automatic inflation.

Of the non-harness models, we like the Crewfit and its virtual clone, the Techvest, best. While lacking some of the niceties of Sospenders, we were

extremely impressed with the well-thought-out design, very high quality of construction and ease of repacking. The Crewfit uses a heavier-gauge bladder material than the Techvest, but otherwise it appears comparable.

The Sospenders was an extremely close third to Crewfit and Techvest in our judgment. We liked the way the uninflated Sospenders felt even after an extended period of time, and we liked the attention to safety details: pocket, whistle, reflective tape. The Sospenders' brilliant orange bladder is likely to be a bit more visible than the yellow used by Crewfit and Mustang. We didn't like Sospenders' more-difficult repacking procedure—it's possible that a lot of practice will make this less of a nuisance, but we think that it's enough trouble to discourage users from conducting necessary periodic checks.

The Norvik, although a bit more secure-feeling in rough water than the first three, was downrated because it was less comfortable than the first three when uninflated. Otherwise, it performed quite well.

The Mustang Inflatable Collar feels great inflated in the water, not so great uninflated out of water. Its awkward repacking procedure helped keep it from a higher rating.

The Switlik Helicopter Vest is extremely well made, and provides the maximum in flotation security of all the non-harness PFDs we tested; it's also the least likely to be worn on a regular basis and can't be bought with an automatic inflation system. Consequently it's at the bottom of our ratings for everyday use.

The Mustang Inflatable Bomber Jacket isn't really for everyday use, but it makes an excellent supplementary device for chilly days and nights.

The Survival Products, we think, is a poor choice for any sailor.

Harness/Inflatable PFD Combinations: Blue-water sailors (we like to think) are more aware of the need for effective lifejackets than are their coastal cousins. As a consequence, our major concerns in rating harness-equipped PFDs were (assuming adequate wearability): flotation security, quality of construction and general ruggedness.

The Switlik Fastnet Crew Vest is our first choice. It's not cheap ($295), it's not light (54 ounces), but it's certainly solid. We liked the double bladder system both in terms of redundancy and support in the water, we found that the mesh vest fit securely without the need for excessive strap-tightening and we liked the heavy-duty cover and the pockets.

The Crewfit Automatic with Harness and the Sospenders 1-38AH were effectively tied for second place: we liked the Crewfit's finish and ease of packing, but we preferred the Sospenders double D-ring/steel buckle arrangement. Neither had the rock-solid feel of the Switlik in the water, but both performed very well and should give satisfactory service under the worst conditions.

The Norvik pu30 with safety harness was an extremely frustrating jacket to use: it's very difficult to put on. Once it's on, it performed quite well, but the agony of trying to sort out the tangle of black webbing was enough for us to rank it dead-last choice among the harness-equipped models.

Conclusions

Putting aside considerations of how well they behave on the high seas (very well, as a matter of fact), we look on these devices as the only PFDs that are comfortable enough to be worn on a regular basis. Regardless of how reliable a non-inflatable may be, the one you're not wearing won't do any good.• **PS**